A Bibliography of Business and Economic Forecasting

A Bibliography of Business and Economic Forecasting

Robert Fildes

with

David Dews and Syd Howell

Facts On File
119 West 57th Street, New York, N.Y. 10019

A Bibliography of Business and Economic Forecasting

Copyright ©, 1981, by Robert Fildes

Published by Facts On File, Inc.,
119 West 57th Street, New York, N.Y. 10019.

ISBN 0-87196-555-0

10 9 8 7 6 5 4 3 2 1

PRINTED IN GREAT BRITAIN

KM
5-23-83

Contents

Acknowledgements

This bibliography has been produced through the collaboration of a large number of people. Institutions have also given their support — the Operational Research Society of Great Britain, the SSRC and in particular the Manchester Business School. Within MBS people have capitulated, giving in to a mixture of cajolery and bribery. A roll-call of helpers would not be appropriate — the death rate of secretarial staff alone would lengthen a volume already too long. However the computer department were particularly generous in helping to resolve the problems presented by our archaic equipment here and in fending off my colleagues who felt their own needs neglected.

My friends and family also felt the burden with Sue Brimelow and Sue Parkyn working hard and long to get this awful job over. It would have required martyrs to do the job uncomplainingly and they certainly aren't that.

Libraries have provided the essential subject matter and their staff have usually given unstinting help: in particular I wish to note that the University of California, Berkeley and the University of British Columbia were especially generous, providing excellent facilities and support. The Manchester Business School library gave me the good base I needed and the staff there could not have been more helpful, with Jim Dickerson offering amiable Welsh insults at my countless requests for books from the British Lending Library.

It only leaves me to thank my two colleagues in this enterprise, David Dews and Syd Howell for their generous help. Without it the task would never have been completed.

Robert Fildes

Manchester Business School,
Summer, 1980.

1 Introduction

Why produce a bibliography? Over the last year or more the three of us associated with the project – a librarian, David Dews, a statistician, Robert Fildes and a researcher, Syd Howell, have increasingly asked that question. The work is laborious and painstaking; and, of course, it has taken much more time on all our parts than we initially envisaged.

I doubt whether when I initiated the project in 1975 I considered the difficulties. During the writing of a book on managerial forecasting[1] I had gathered together a lot of relevant references. It seemed the obvious thing to make them available to a wider audience and save them repeating the work I had done. But a moment's thought raised the obvious question, 'Why had I not used any forecasting bibliographies or abstracting services in writing *Forecasting for Business* although I had been successful in using statistical abstracts for my research in statistics?' The answer was obvious. In the latter case the categories under which the articles were listed were sufficiently refined to allow easy access, while in the economics, statistics and operational research literature, as these applied to forecasting, they were not. A forecasting bibliography that was properly indexed could, however, help at least three kinds of user: the consultant, internal or external, working for an organisation; the academic researcher; and the numerate manager or management student who wanted to improve either his grasp of forecasting in general, or his knowledge of appropriate techniques for a specific project.

From the realisation that a bibliography could prove extremely helpful to a wide range of users, to the publication of this large-scale bibliography, has proved more difficult than expected, despite the support of both the Operational Research Society and the SSRC. We believe that the typical user will find the effort has been worthwhile, for we have tried to do much of his preliminary research work for him. This bibliography contains over 4,000 items, journal articles and books, collected from a search of some thirty journals over the period 1971-1978, together with important references published earlier. The entries are key worded according to a very carefully chosen structure, which allows easy access to some 500 topics of research. Consequently, it is possible to use the bibliography as a 'first resort' for a very wide range of forecasting problems in business and economics.

1

The three different types of user have slightly different needs. The consultant or manager chiefly wants examples of previous forecasting work in a specific sector of the economy, on a specific class of problems, e.g. a declining product in the processed food industry. He will also wish to use certain existing techniques with a high level of sophistication. The academic researcher, like the consultant, will be interested in precedents, but will be far more interested in the theory underlying a forecasting method. Unlike the consultant, he will be familiar with the recent research 'jargon' of a specialised field. The novice user will be unfamiliar with technical terms and with theoretical ideas in most of the fields. In practice, of course, all these three ideal types overlap. Most users of the bibliography will find themselves 'novices' in at least some of the fields from which the bibliography is drawn.

The set of key words we finally selected as of most help was chosen after very careful thought, earlier versions being discarded after lengthy trials. It tries to meet some of the needs of the various users, and we feel confident that it will give efficient, if not always elegant, access to the large range of material included in the bibliography.

For the consultant's use, we have classified examples of forecasting not only by the variable being forecast, and the method used, but also by the use to which the forecast is put, e.g. inventory control, media planning, etc. All the major estimating methods are key worded, as is the evidence on the comparative performance of different forecasting methods. It is now a relatively easy exercise to identify a reasonable method of solving a given problem, and the references also provide a view of the likely effectiveness of the chosen solution.

For the benefit of academic researchers, we have key worded a number of theoretical issues in forecasting, such as the error specification in forecasting models, the stability of the model's coefficients, causality and the effects of bad or incomplete data, etc.

For the sake of the 'novice' we have tried to avoid abbreviations and certain technical terms.

The general level of the bibliography is such that the articles should be accessible to a numerate but non-specialised graduate. We have labelled a minority of articles as either BASIC or ADVANCED*. This is not an evaluation of the article, but an approximate guide to the level of mathematical complexity. A BASIC article is normally non-technical and not usually academically original or rigorous. Nevertheless, a number of the BASIC articles provide valuable introductions to novel ideas. We have used the term ADVANCED on occasion for articles which are heavily quantitative and, for example,

---

*Actual key words are printed in capitals.

make use of complex variable theory or asymptotic multivariate statistical theory. ADVANCED articles are potentially of value to highly specialised researchers, but most are of little general value, because of their inaccessibility.

The range of materials included goes far beyond articles with the words 'forecasting', 'planning' or 'prediction' in their titles. We have included a wide range of topics on applied economics and statistics, time series analysis, estimation, control theory and data characteristics. We also included a number of articles on subjects such as population, social problems like crime, disease and poverty, accidents and natural phenomena such as earthquakes. The primary reason for our eclecticism was that omission of an article that could conceivably seem relevant to a forecaster's problem seemed a more important error than including it unnecessarily.

In summary, the aim of the bibliography is to provide a simple method for identifying those references that touch on the forecasting problem under analysis, whoever the forecaster; manager, consultant, academic, or student.

1.1 The nature of forecasting

'Forecasting' is not simply a collective noun for the activities of a wide range of disciplines. We believe that forecasting is a subject which deserves academic study in its own right, and that it raises questions which are not conventionally raised in the various subject areas. For example, econometricians sometimes suggest that it is their role to explain the 'true' relationship between economic variables from the analysis of past data. As such, the implications of their result, for forecasting the future, are often incompletely analysed. The forecaster in contrast is less concerned with identifying a 'true' model than with finding a robust model that is likely to produce forecasts with a pre-specified accuracy. It may have proved necessary for the forecaster to develop one of the econometrician's 'true' models. However, he must go on to examine its forecasting performance before it can be regarded as usable.

Because of the forecaster's concentration on forecast effectiveness rather than model specification, he will typically consider a number of alternative approaches to building a forecasting model. Time series methods which do nothing more than extrapolate the past data series have met with some success in out-forecasting their econometric rivals. The two methods differ in that the time series approach excludes 'causal' factors, but also uses fewer parameters, with a concomitantly higher ratio of data points to parameters. This not only allows precise estimates to be made of the parameters, but increases the ability of the forecaster to discriminate between alternative model forms.

The question the forecaster wishes to resolve is whether the increased discrimination and precision in the parameter estimates outweighs the omission of the causal factors.

Many areas of research can in fact be criticised from the point of view of what we would consider a rigorous 'forecasting' approach. In the marketing literature, for example, there is a vast range of untested and often 'data free' models for media planning. 'Ad hoc' assumptions abound in univariate forecasting. Even more commonly, in both time series and econometric applications, no attention is paid to the accuracy of the models at forecasting, as opposed to the ex post fit to the same data set as was used in model estimation.

In conclusion, the issues that arise specifically in forecasting include: why one model is better than another and under what circumstances; whether completeness in causal specification is more effective than completeness in statistical specification; and why model performance differs from one situation to another. In a phrase, forecasting is concerned with what stability exists in models and their parameters from period to period, region to region, and product to product, and what determines that stability.

Much more could be said, but we hope that this short discussion has already demonstrated that making a forecast is a subtle applied art, and that it raises questions which are not yet habitually asked in research on Time Series Analysis, Econometrics, or even 'Forecasting' itself. We hope that the bibliography will be a useful aid to research on these issues, as well as to research on the more accepted aspects of the contributing disciplines.

Naturally, our conception of forecasting has not led us to suppress any material which seems to conflict with our own point of view. With some misgivings we have included a number of topics which we suspect the forecaster will find sometimes unhelpful and occasionally even of negative value. We do not at any point give an evaluation of any article, even on the rare occasions where we suspect that an article is seriously at fault.

1.2   Using the bibliography

In order to help the reader to make most effective use of the bibliography we will examine three typical examples where a forecaster would find it helpful to consult the bibliography. The first is chosen to show how a person with some familiarity with regression can extend his knowledge.

The first example described is typical of the questions that concern a corporate planner or marketing manager when planning the firm's medium-term marketing strategy. How effective is the firm's advertising, and at what level should it be set over the planning horizon?

: The effectiveness of consumer durables advertising

Two key words specify this question, **ADVERTISING** − EFFECT OF and **APPLICATION** − **SECTOR (or FIRM)**: CONSUMER DURABLES. The researcher can quickly find those articles which contain both key words. He also notes a review article on advertising effectiveness which helps considerably. From examining the studies cited he realises that something of a problem is posed if he wishes to estimate advertising effectiveness, for many early studies used only simple estimation techniques and found non significant coefficients − but a recent review article in the *Journal of Marketing Research* reassures him. He has the choice of specifying the coefficient (and lag structure), without reference to the data, using another key word, **PRIOR INFORMATION** or he may choose to use a more complicated estimation technique. The subsidiary question of how best to fix the advertising budget is discussed under **ADVERTISING** − OPTIMALITY. How advertising is actually set is considered under **ADVERTISING** − DETERMINANTS.

In this second example we will suppose that the forecaster, new to working an Operational Research department, wishes to check that the inventory control system is functioning well enough.

: The relationship between inventory control and forecasting

Two key words mention inventory control directly: (1) **USE** − INVENTORY CONTROL and (2) **LOSS FUNCTIONS** − FIRM, **Inventory**. Following up the references listed under these two headings he learns that relatively little work has been done in linking forecasting to inventory control problems (1 above), and that the loss likely to be incurred in an inventory situation like his own appears small (2 above). However, a reference on 'materials requirements planning' shows him the potential importance of focussing on (3) **TIMING UNCERTAINTY** with regard to deliveries of partly finished goods. The references already examined suggest that two methods of long standing, exponential smoothing and adaptive smoothing [key words (4) **EXPONENTIAL SMOOTHING** and (5) **EXPONENTIAL SMOOTHING** − ADAPTIVE COEFFICIENTS], still appear relevant to inventory control; which raises the next question. Is any one of the computationally cheap forecasting methods noticeably better than its competitors? The references under key words (6) **COMPARATIVE METHODS** — TIME SERIES MODELS and (7) **COMPARATIVE METHODS** — EXPONENTIAL SMOOTHING, **Adaptive**, suggest only slight differences. The added complexity of adaptive smoothing appears not to be worthwhile. A final check that nothing has been missed (9) **COMPARATIVE METHODS** — THEORY, suggests that if demand patterns are unstable, it is safer to opt for the added complexity of adaptive smoothing.

: Estimating a regression model

After teaching the basic ideas of model building, usually through the use of regression analysis, an elementary book on forecasting, such as Wood and Fildes[1] will go on to warn that although least squares is used to estimate a model's parameters because 'you would expect the pay-off consequences of a major inaccuracy to be totally disproportionate to the consequences of a minor error', failure in any of the model's assumptions can lead to poor parameter estimates. This means, for example, that the frequently occurring problem of autocorrelation in the error term should be eliminated whenever possible because its presence gives a 'spurious impression of the accuracy of the parameter estimates and the fit of the model'. Similarly, it is argued that dependence between the independent variables, multicollinearity, is important in forecasting applications. No alternatives to least squares estimation are considered by Wood and Fildes, although a couple of methods are suggested for solving both the problems of multi-collinearity and autocorrelation.

But are the suggestions made the 'best' or merely the most appropriate for an introductory textbook on forecasting? Is least squares the best method of model estimation and when is it poor? When should we transform a model? Is it worthwhile to go to the extreme of including a complicated error dependence in the model to remove any possible autocorrelation? To solve multicollinearity is ridge regression helpful? Unfortunately, most of the above are not considered by any basic textbook.

The bibliography can help resolve these questions directly. The interest envisaged here is with comparative questions concerning a regression model. The key words with annotations which should be referred to are therefore:

1 **COMPARATIVE METHODS** — ESTIMATION: **Regression**. How should we estimate a regression model?

2 **COMPARATIVE METHODS** — REGRESSION, **Error specification.** Does the autocorrelation matter in a regression model?

3 **COMPARATIVE METHODS** — ESTIMATION: **Regression, Error specification.** If we decide the autocorrelation is important enough to include, we need to know how to estimate the more complicated equation.

4 **MULTICOLLINEARITY** — EFFECT OF. Does multicollinearity matter?

5 **REGRESSION** — RIDGE and **REGRESSION** — RIDGE, **Evaluation.** These key words describe ridge regression and offer an evaluation of its effectiveness. Comparative performance can be considered through **COMPARATIVE METHODS** — ESTIMATION, **Regression, Ridge.**

That may seem a lot of work to do to answer a simple question, but by the time the forecaster has come to grips with these references he is in the fortunate position of knowing as much as he needs about two of the most intractable questions in estimating linear regression models. He at least would not repeat the type of blunder which was very common until recently: a regression model with a highly significant Durbin-Watson statistic and a corresponding discussion of the relative size of the model's coefficients, a totally inappropriate procedure as some of the references given under (2) above show.

The key words

In this section we discuss the basis of our choice of key words. The dimensions that are most useful for describing the bibliography's entries each contain a number of key words (shown in capital letters). These key words are not sufficient to offer a complete key wording of every article and so we have not hesitated to introduce further key words where needed. The total set of key words is therefore able to describe each entry in the bibliography, in effect, offering the user an abstract of the entry.

The major dimensions of the key wording system are introduced below and most of the bibliography's entries are key worded on at least one of them.

These dimensions relate to:

(1) an area of application
(2) a variable to forecast
(3) a model with which to forecast
(4) an aid to model interpretation
(5) a method of model estimation
(6) a set of statistical problems
(7) a use and a user
(8) an analysis of the effectiveness of a forecasting method or a set of forecasts
(9) an aid to monitoring forecasting effectiveness
(10) a theory of how to develop and select a forecasting model
(11) a set of data related problems
(12) a concern with the effect of certain independent variables
(13) a theory underlying the forecasting model
(14) the problems of implementation

The fourteen dimensions are described below in more detail.

: *an area of application*, in the FIRM, an industrial SECTOR, or the economy as a whole, the MACROECONOMIC. In the first two cases the area can be specified more completely by reference to the sector under consideration and the particular product of that sector, e.g. FIRM: Retailing, *Gasoline* or SECTOR: CONSUMER DURABLES, Cars. Typical key words are of the form; APPLICATION – SECTOR: PRODUCTION AND MINING, Machine tools. A limited number of variables have been given their own headings, e.g. HEALTH. Some models have a specific geographical basis (REGIONAL MODELS) or a specific time horizon. The usual division into 'short', 'medium' and 'long' has not seemed helpful so we have only kept the last category, LONG TERM FORECASTING. In a similar vein, certain forecasting methods are more appropriate for different phases of the product LIFE CYCLE, e.g. NEW PRODUCT, LIFE CYCLE – PRODUCT, Declining etc.

: *a variable to forecast*, which is a principle focus in the article, e.g. PRICE. A number of important variables have distinct key words, ADVERTISING, COST, INTEREST RATES, MARKET SHARE, MARKET POSITION, MARKET SEGMENTATION, PRICE, STOCK PRICES, SUPPLY and manpower oriented variables key worded under MANPOWER PLANNING. A large number of the references we list discuss sales, demand or output and because of the frequency of occurrence of these concepts they have not been key worded as such. Thus any article with an area of application but no variable mentioned is concerned with sales etc. Other variables which are less often discussed are listed in the form, e.g. **APPLICATION — SECTOR (or FIRM)**: INVESTMENT, this being a sector level (or firm) study of investment behaviour. In the key word index these are referenced directly following the key words describing firm or sector level areas of application.

: *a model with which to forecast*, and here we have considered four main classes: PROBABILITY MODELS, REGRESSION models being a model with a single dependent variable, SIMULTANEOUS SYSTEM models when there are two-way relationships between the variables leading to a number of equations describing these interactions and TIME SERIES models which rely on only the past history of the variable being forecast to extrapolate ahead. Each one of these headings has a number of sub-headings describing the particular sub-model under consideration, e.g. **REGRESSION — DISCRETE DEPENDENT** catalogues those articles concerned with forecasting a variable which can only take discrete values. Besides these minor headings we thought there were a number of distinct sub-classes, important enough to give separate key words and we list them below as they relate to the four major classes above (1) MARKOV MODELS, (2) DISCRIMINANT ANALYSIS, DISTRIBUTED LAG, and PRODUCTION FUNCTIONS, (3) INDUSTRIAL DYNAMICS, INPUT-OUPUT, DEMAND EQUATIONS, RECURSIVE SYSTEMS, SYSTEMS THEORY, MACROECONOMIC MODELS and SIMULATION, and (4) DIFFUSION MODELS, EXPONENTIAL SMOOTHING and TREND CURVES.

Two approaches to forecasting which do not fit into the scheme we have described are based on the use of BUSINESS INDICATORS and JUDGEMENTAL FORECASTS. Since the former provide quantitative, replicable estimates of turning points they are naturally included.

Judgemental forecasts by their nature are not replicable, so we have only included articles which evaluate their effectiveness in some way or explain how they can be best used.

: *an aid to model interpretation*. The more complicated models, DISTRIBUTED LAG models, the SIMULTANEOUS SYSTEM models, etc. are difficult to understand in that the linkages, lags and feedback make direct inference from the equations difficult. Discussion on this general problem is under **MODEL INTERPRETATION**, while the dynamic effects implicit in a model is referenced under **MULTIPLIERS**, as well as **SIMULTANEOUS SYSTEM — DYNAMIC PROPERTIES**.

SPECTRAL ANALYSIS and SIMULATION, both offer insight into the structure of these complicated models, e.g. SIMULATION — APPLICATION: Policy evaluation, SPECTRAL ANALYSIS — APPLICATION: Business cycle.

SIMULATION is also used to describe a system of equations (definitional or probabilistic) that interact, either simultaneously or sequentially as noted above. Applications of both SIMULATION and SPECTRAL ANALYSIS are listed, e.g. SPECTRAL ANALYSIS — APPLICATION: Policy evaluation, or SIMULATION — APPLICATION: Sector, *Agriculture*. Methodological problems associated with these approaches are also key worded.

: *a method of estimation*. The methods of model estimation typically used depend somewhat on the model, with maximum likelihood estimation (MLE) usually offering the underlying rationale whatever the model. However, we have not concerned ourselves with the fine niceties of estimation methods except as far as we think these results are usable to the forecaster (rather than the statistician). Consequently, articles which concern themselves only with a new method of estimation have been omitted. On the other hand, articles which develop our understanding of how to apply an estimation technique are included, e.g. ESTIMATION — MLE or ESTIMATION — OLS. Bayesian methods are listed separately under BAYESIAN.

: *a set of statistical problems*, such as the form and structure of the error distribution, e.g. ERROR DISTRIBUTION — NON NORMAL, ERROR SPECIFICATION — AUTOCORRELATED, MULTICOLLINEARITY and more generally, SPECIFICATION ERROR. Once these possibilities are admitted, the next stage adopted is often to test for their significance, the tests being described under AUTOCORRELATION — TESTS, MULTICOLLINEARITY — TEST, or SPECIFICATION ERROR — TESTS, etc.

: *a use and user*. Some articles specifically identify an organisational problem, e.g. USE — INVENTORY CONTROL, or USE — PRICING, and show how forecast information can help in its solution. Similarly, some models aim to help a specific user solve his forecasting problem, e.g. USER — FIRM: Production, although this heading is used sparingly.

: *an analysis of the effectiveness of a forecasting method or a set of forecasts*, and these we list under EVALUATION and COMPARATIVE METHODS. Thus an article classified under BUSINESS INDICATORS — EVALUATION examine the strengths and weaknesses of the business indicator approach while under **COMPARATIVE METHODS** — CAUSAL, **Trend curves** the two approaches names are compared. If a model is tested properly, by comparing its forecasts with what occurred after the model had been constructed, we note this additional evidence on effectiveness through the key **EX ANTE**. Articles concerned with whether we can forecast a particular variable are key worded, e.g. **EVALUATION** — INVESTMENT FORECASTS. The question of how models should be compared is described under **LOSS FUNCTIONS** and **EVALUATION** — THEORY OF while the accuracy of models in predicting turning points is described under the heading, **TURNING POINTS** — FORECASTING. Because forecasting is an activity carried out with the intent of influencing action a number of entries discuss the relationship between forecasting and decision-making under the heading **DECISION RULES**. A related heading, entries of which are also concerned with affecting the future through the choice of present actions is **CONTROL THEORY**. In principle the two headings are very similar, but the latter has been developed by control engineers and describes a formal mathematical approach to decision-making. While these headings include general discussion of how a decision is or should be selected, particular policies are also discussed under the headings **POLICY EVALUATION**, and **PUBLIC EXPENDITURE**.

: *an aid to monitoring forecasting effectiveness*, these are described under the general heading, **FORECAST** — MONITORING, as well as three more specific key words, **CONFIDENCE INTERVAL**, **CONTROL CHARTS**, and **TOLERANCE INTERVAL**. The use of forecasts in setting performance targets is described under **USE** — TARGET SETTING. Entries concerned with evaluating the effectiveness of forecasters are key worded **USE** — FORECASTER EVALUATION.

: *a theory of how to develop and select a forecasting model*. These two major questions are key worded: **THEORY** — MODELLING, FORECASTING, MODEL IDENTIFICATION and **MODEL SELECTION**. A related topic in causal modelling is what constitutes a 'cause' and discussion of this epistimological question is listed under **CAUSALITY**.

: *a set of data related problems*. Unfortunately, the data, the building blocks of any forecasting model, are invariably prone to error, both definitional and theoretical. Questions such as whether the data are disaggregated and the differences that result from using aggregated rather than disaggregated data, how to operationalise an economic definition, and how to transform an annual series to comparable quarterly series are listed under **DATA** and its sub-headings. Questions concerning the effects of the different types of error and their estimation are key worded, **DATA ERRORS**. A problem that most often arises with national accounts is that of revisions to the data some time after first publication and the corresponding key word is **DATA REVISIONS**. Data problems arise when using INDEX NUMBERS and SURVEY data, topics discussed under the above. Two data related topics of major interest to economists are the use of **ATTITUDINAL DATA** and **EXPECTATIONS** – DATA.

: *a concern with the effect of certain 'independent' variables*. Economists have long been concerned with the effect of price and income on the demand for consumer goods and services. Similarly, marketing men have tried to identify the effect of advertising or the effect of a sales promotion. Key words such as these are: **ACCOUNTING PRACTICE, ADVERTISING** – **EFFECT OF, CAPACITY, CONCENTRATION, DISTRIBUTION, EDUCATION, EXCHANGE RATE, INCOME, INTEREST RATE, MARKET SHARE, POLLUTION, PRICE, TARIFF, TAX** and **TECHNOLOGY**.

: *a theory*, such as the theory of efficient markets that dominates the financial literature's concern with stock prices. Entries which contain a theoretical discussion are classified by, e.g. **THEORY** – **EFFICIENT MARKETS**: however, this particular set of key words is generally omitted from the index for we think that our headings are too wide to be helpful to the researcher particularly interested in the theory. Also, a large number of theories purport to describe **CONSUMER BEHAVIOUR** and these we list separately.

: *the problem of implementation*. Forecasting models require a set of data (**DATA, DATA ERRORS** etc.) which form a part of a management information system, MIS. The models themselves have to be accurately programmed, discussed under **COMPUTERISATION** and **NUMERICAL METHODS**. A cost-effective forecasting model efficiently linked to an information system is not sufficient to ensure its output is used. Forecasting is in part a political process within an organisation, aimed at convincing the ultimate user of the forecast of a model's worth. These aspects are discussed under **FORECASTER BEHAVIOUR** and **USER REQUIREMENTS**. Particular approaches to forecasting adopted by organisations are described under **FORE-CASTING** – **PRACTICE**, while **FORECASTING** – **USAGE** contains evidence on the frequency of usage of various methods.

There remains a number of key words which do not fall quite so neatly into the categories we have described above. Each article is classified according to its complexity, BASIC and ADVANCED, intermediate articles being unclassified. Often a further mathematical technique is associated with the forecasting model such as mathematical programming (LP), CLUSTER ANALYSIS, FACTOR ANALYSIS, etc. There is also the question of how the forecast variable is specified; the problem might require forecasting cumulative demand (**DEMAND** — CUMULATIVE) rather than the demand within a single period, or perhaps a probability (**PROBABILITIES** — FORECAST OF). The user of the bibliography can perhaps only realise the scope and the limitations of the key wording system by searching for words which seem to him to describe his problem. We hope that our choice, the careful checking that went into it, and the duplication that we consciously included will help him to find the references that he needs quickly.

1.3 Compiling the bibliography

: Problems encountered

Problems were of two kinds: logistical difficulties, which delayed the bibliography but did not change its content; and editorial difficulties, which required an increase in the depth of the coverage, and a corresponding decrease in the range of sources covered. The logistical difficulties do not concern us here except to note that they were extreme, and to recommend caution to any would-be bibliographer.

: Problems of editorial scope

Work on forecasting is done in a wide range of disciplines, from accounting to control engineering. All, of course, use different terminology. The most relevant journals for business and economic forecasting are in the areas of accounting, marketing, operations research, general management, economics, econometrics and pure and applied statistics.

It was originally intended to survey ninety such journals, for a target of at least three thousand references. In the event this proved impossible. This was because our original estimate of the time required to scan a journal allowed for collecting only those articles which were concerned explicitly with forecasting, planning or prediction. It quickly became clear that this scope was too narrow and that in fact most of applied economics was relevant.

The reason for this change can be illustrated by a simple example. A manufacturer confronted with an increase in VAT has to predict his likely level of future sales. Many articles in applied economics attempt to calculate the effect of tax change (**TAX** — EFFECT OF), although they do not concern themselves with forecasting. However, most of these articles would have been omitted if we had stuck to our earlier criteria. A second reason forced us in the same direction. A superficial analysis of a journal's contents might have introduced important omissions which, once recognised, could have led the user to distrust our judgement on which articles were relevant. For this reason we readily decided to improve the quality of our coverage of the journals but to restrict the range of journals to be searched. Our target for the number of entries did not change, and we aimed at the standard of the most rigorous literature search for all the main headings which are key worded.

As the depth of coverage was increased, it became necessary to allow for a wider range of references to other disciplines. This enlarged the scope of the key word system.

: Problems of key word design

As already noted, the various disciplines do not share a common terminology. Our aim was to make this material accessible to a hypothetical 'basic user' of the bibliography, who was assumed to be numerate, but who might at one extreme be completely familiar with the terminology of a given subject area, although needing all its results, or, at the other extreme, be fully familiar with the special subject, and needing access to the prime headings under which recent research has been done.

As a result we have avoided certain technical terms. For example (perhaps idiosyncratically), we do not use the term 'elasticity' preferring the format 'TAX − EFFECT OF' or 'EXCHANGE RATE − EFFECT OF'. We have largely avoided abbreviations.

Other conceptual problems arise. We realised that our selection of categories could either inhibit or assist research on a very wide range of topics. (This is the main reason why so many key words are used.) Whose terminology was appropriate? In simple cases the problem could be solved by cross referencing in the index, e.g. the 'Rational Polynomial Lag' of econometrics is very similar to the 'Multivariate ARIMA' or 'Indicator Model' in time series analysis. If two terms are synonymous this is noted in the index. If the overlap is large the reader is referred to the other sub-category.

As the research progressed, a further problem became apparent. Should a freshly encountered line of research (e.g. a discussion of R^2) be classified on its own, or as a subclass of the 'nearest' existing category? If the latter, should the classification follow verbal logic, or the 'established' (and changing) usage of any of the disciplines, e.g. should a discussion of errors be classified according to whether the errors are empirically observed residuals, or are part of a mathematical specification; if the latter should we distinguish between estimation

15

specifications and specifications of the null hypothesis of a test of error structure; in all cases should we recognise the distributional form, e.g. stable, separately from the autocorrelation structure, and should the 'errors' in prediction variables be treated separately from errors in the predicted variables?

No perfect solution is possible to such problems, particularly if time is rationed. Inevitably we have at times made the opposite mistakes of starting inappropriate new headings, some of which have had to be deleted, and of 'burying' quite separate ideas under more clumsy general headings. We were hindered by not knowing until the end of the exercise what the total 'load' on each key word would be. This was not possible to examine even at the intermediate stages, due to computing problems. As a result some of the key words are 'overloaded' with references, and others are 'underloaded'.

Had time allowed, we would have liked to provide greater discrimination under the 'overloaded' headings, since these leave the user to do a substantial amount of selection. Some of the 'underloaded' headings are included deliberately because they signal areas of research interest which have been defined but remain underexplored, and which are not self evident from more general classifications. Some, however, have been deleted from the index if they were apparently of little direct relevance to forecasting.

: The problem of validation

Some four attempts were made at devising a key wording system before a final choice was made. As we noted in the last section, even this set still necessitated occasional additions throughout the bibliography's preparation. To minimise the effect of these revisions each reference was initially key worded. The reference was subsequently checked during the last year of the project so that only key words compatible with the final key wording system were included and any errors and omissions were then corrected. Most articles were also checked for consistency with other articles in the same area. Ideally, one further independent check of each reference should have been carried out because errors and occasional inconsistencies were still being identified, but resources did not permit this. We should appreciate being told of any important errors by the bibliography's users and will in time, respond with any corrections or additions that have taken place after publication.

1.4 Alternative reference sources

No bibliographies are available that cover similar ground to this one. However, a number of abstracting services offer the user access to a wide range of references with varying degrees of each and relevance. We list below the major sources, the form they take, and their likely usefulness.

1 *Journal of Economic Literature* published by the American Economic Association, with an index compiled annually.

   *Includes an annotated listing of most books published under a broad based definition of economics. The classification system is also broad, e.g. 'Econometric forecasting and econometric models' or 'marketing'. Selected articles are abstracted and selected books are reviewed.

2 *Economic Titles/Abstracts* (abbreviated version: *Key to Economic Science*) published by M. Nijhuff, with an index compiled annually.

   *Essentially an economic abstracting service, references are listed under a broad topic heading, e.g. 'Forecasting Energy'. Only very brief abstracts are supplied.

3 *Current Index to Statistics* published by the American Statistical Association, index compiled annually.

   *As its title implies, its coverage as it relates to forecasting is essentially related to the statistics of forecasting. It is key worded in some depth, by reference to the title, the key words chosen by the author and those given by an editorial panel. However, it appears difficult to use and relies on the user to select the appropriate key word. Redundant key wording protects the reader to a certain extent. No abstracts are provided.

4 *Business Periodicals Index* published by H.W. Wilson, index compiled annually.

   *Broad headings help the reader locate relevant references, e.g. Sales Forecasting. The entries are derived from a wide range of sources. No key words or abstracts are given.

5 *ANBAR* published by the Institute of Management Services, index compiled annually.

*A single key word, 'Forecasting', offers obvious access to the references listed. The references are drawn from a wide range of sources. A brief abstract is included. A list of all titles, key worded under 'Forecasting', is shown in the annual index.

6 *International Abstracts in OR* published by North Holland, index compiled annually.

*A single key word, 'Forecasting', offers the only direct access to relevant references. Only operational research journals are considered. Full abstracts are included.

COMPUTER INFORMATION SERVICES

7 *DIALOG* available through the Lockheed Information Systems, the index continually updated.

DIALOG offers access to a wide range of databases. Databases relevant to forecasting are listed in the 'Subject Guide to Dialog'. Those of particular relevance to forecasting are 'Economic Abstracts International', which is approximately equivalent to the published *Economic Titles/Abstracts* described above; 'Management Contents' which has a wide usage but only very broad key wording, e.g. econometrics and 'ABI/INFORM', again with broad key wording and wide coverage.

Because computer access allows the user to examine articles which are listed by two (or more) of the descriptors, this system can provide much more precise selection than is apparent from the basic key wording. The strength (or weakness) of computer information systems lies in the choice of key words. For many of the databases little attention has been given to this problem, and key wording has been done automatically. The results can often be ridiculous.

1.5 Updating the bibliography

A major problem with bibliographies as compared with abstracting services is they are seldom updated. To meet this criticism the researchers intend to publish two supplements, one in the Autumn of 1981, to include references published in 1979 and 1980; and the second in 1982 to include 1981 references. A small expansion of journal coverage is also intended, in particular IEEE Transactions on Automatic Control. These updates will be available in Manchester Business School 'working paper' format, and priced to cover direct costs only. A pre-printed registration card is enclosed in this volume, and registrees will be notified when the updates are available. It is intended to publish a second volume in the same format in 1983 to include these updates.

Reference

1 Wood, D. and Fildes, R., *Forecasting for Business: methods and application*, Longman, London, 1976.

2 Bibliographical coverage

Journals

Some forty journals have been carefully searched for relevant references. A further four have been scanned for references central to forecasting. Many of the core journals have also been examined for pertinent references in issues between 1965 and 1970.

COMPLETE COVERAGE (Years 1971-78)

Journal	Abbreviation used	Complete coverage Vol. nos.	Scanned Years
Accounting Review	Accntg. Rev.	46-53	–
American Economic Association Proceedings	Am. Econ. Ass. Proc.	61-68	1965-70
American Statistical Association	J. Am. Statist. Ass.	66-73	1965-70
American Statistician	Am. Stat'n.	25-32	1965-70
Annals of Economic & Social Measurement	Anns. Econ. Soc. Meas.	1-8	–
Applied Economics	Appl. Econ.	3-10	1969-70
Applied Statistics	Appl. Stats.	20-27	1965-70
Bell Journal of Economics (& Management Science)	Bell. J. Econ.	2-9	1970
British Journal of Marketing	See Eur. J. Mktg.	–	–
Brookings Papers on Economic Activity	Brookings Pap. Econ. Activity	–	–
Business Economics	Bus. Econ.	6-13	–
Canadian Journal of Economics	Can. J. Econ.	4-11	1965-70
Decision Sciences	Decis. Sci.	2-9	1970
Econometrica	Econometrica	39-46	1965-70
Economic Journal	Econ. J.	81-88	1965-70
Economica	Economica	38-45	–
European Journal of Marketing	Eur. J. Mktg.	5-12	–
Harvard Business Review	HBR	49-56	1965-70
Industrial Marketing Management	Ind. Mktg. Mgmt.	1-8	–
International Economic Review	Int. Econ. Rev.	12-19	–
International Statistical Review	Int. Statist. Rev.	–	–

Journal of Accounting Research	J. Accntg. Res.	9-16	1965-70
Journal of Advertising Research	J. Advtg. Res.	11-18	1965-70
Journal of Business	J. Business	44-51	1965-70
Journal of Econometrics	J. Econometrics	1-8	–
Journal of Finance	J. Finance	26-33	–
Journal of Marketing	J. Mktg.	35-42	1965-70
Journal of Marketing Research	J. Mktg. Res.	8-15	1965-70
Journal of Operational Research Society	J. Opl. Res. Soc.	29	–
Long Range Planning	Long Range Planning	4-11	–
Management Science (A & B)	Mgmt. Sci.	17-25	1965-70
National Institute Economic Review	Nat. Inst. Econ. Rev.	Nos. 55-86	–
Omega	Omega	1-8	–
Operations Research	Ops. Res.	19-26	1965-70
Operational Research Quarterly*	Opl. Res. Q.	22-28	1965-70
Review of Economic Studies	Rev. Econ. Studies	38-45	1965-70
Review of Economics & Statistics	Rev. Econ. & Stats.	53-60	1965-70
Royal Statistical Society Series A	R. Statist. Soc. (A)	134-141	1965-70
Royal Statistical Society Series B	R. Statist. Soc. (B)	33-40	1965-70
Sloan Management Review	Sloan Mgmt. Rev.	12-20	–
The Statistician	Stat'n	20-27	–

*Called the Journal of the Operational Research Society from 1978.

JOURNALS SCANNED

Journal	Abbreviation used	Scanned Years
American Journal of Agriculture Economics	Am. J. Ag. Econ.	1971-78
Journal of Economic Literature	J. Econ. Lit.	1971-78
Journal of Financial & Quantitative Analysis	J. Financial Quant. Anal.	1971-78
Journal of Money, Credit & Banking	J. Money, Credit & Banking	1971-78

Books

Books have been collected from the Journal of Economic Literature, the Journal of American Statistical Association, and Books in Print, together with publishers' lists. Although the coverage is wide, errors of omission are more likely to occur here than with the journals. They are therefore listed separately following the articles.

3 Quick index

The following major category headings are used in the bibliography.

4 Main index

Note: The YA references are articles; YB are books, these being printed separately following the articles.

ADVERTISING
　EXPERIMENTAL DESIGN
　　　YA0937　YA2209　　YA2299　YA2884　　YA3371　YB0000
　EXPOSURE
　　　YA0305　YA1274　　YA1468　YA2044　　YA2167　YA2190
　　　YA2207　YA2947　　YA3136
　OPTIMALITY
　　　YA0234　YA0278　　YA0706　YA0783　　YA1747　YA2070
　　　YA2071　YA2372　　YA2427　YA2441　　YA2442　YA2740
　　　YA2814　YA3231　　YA3402　YA3479　　YA3490　YA3619
　　　YA3620　YA3622　　YA3673　YB0164
　REVIEW
　　　YA0979　YA1035　　YA2386　YA2612
　SCALE ECONOMIES
　　　YA0518　YA3231

AID (AUTOMATIC INTERACTION DETECTOR)
　APPLICATION
　　　YA0127　YA0148　　YA0982　YA1146　　YA1648　YA2183
　　　YA2493
　EVALUATION
　　　YA0815　YA0981
　METHODOLOGY
　　　YA0981　YA1462　　YA2393　YA2437
　REVIEW
　　　YA0067　YA0147　　YA0610　YB0014
　THEORY
　　　YA1360

APPLICATION — FIRM TYPE　The following are studies of particular
types of firm, e.g. a study of conglomerates.
　　　YA0124　YA1789　　YA1852　YA2622　　YA2633　YA2905
　CONGLOMERATES
　　　YA0616　YA3646
　DIVERSIFIED
　　　YA2967
　MULTINATIONALS
　　　YA0040　YA0467　　YA0626　YA0627　　YA0728　YA1749
　　　YA2016　YA2980
　NATIONALISED INDUSTRIES　*see*　**APPLICATION — SECTOR**:
　　　GOVERNMENT, **Nationalised industries.**
　SMALL BUSINESS
　　　YA0251　YA0254　　YA0526　YA2087

APPLICATION — MACRO   The following is a list of macro-economic studies by country, for countries other than the USA. Macroeconomic studies can also be found listed under **MACROECONOMIC MODEL —** (country name) and **INPUT OUTPUT —** (country name). Studies of specific macroeconomic variables, in any country, are separately listed below.

AFRICA
    YA0060 YA3259

AUSTRALIA
    YA0554 YA0623   YA0627 YA0632   YA2279 YA3516
    YA3737 YB0313

BELGIUM
    YA2077

CANADA
    YA0035 YA0113   YA0145 YA0161   YA0163 YA0198
    YA0225 YA0258   YA0324 YA0424   YA0524 YA0558
    YA0578 YA0581   YA0626 YA0627   YA0717 YA0844
    YA0864 YA0909   YA0910 YA0919   YA0925 YA0952
    YA0953 YA0963   YA0964 YA1217   YA1322 YA1365
    YA1465 YA1534   YA1663 YA1724   YA1749 YA1750
    YA2003 YA2004   YA2084 YA2085   YA2101 YA2148
    YA2221 YA2222   YA2260 YA2326   YA2456 YA2670
    YA2694 YA2773   YA2778 YA3000   YA3037 YA3038
    YA3069 YA3167   YA3189 YA3217   YA3281 YA3283
    YA3332 YA3474   YA3481 YA3493   YA3523 YA3579
    YA3726 YA3728   YB0102 YB0147   YB0244 YB0247
    YB0298

EASTERN EUROPE
    YA2875 YA3175

EEC
    YA0059 YA0060   YA0250 YA0856   YA1318 YA1387
    YA3000 YA3094   YA3095

EFTA
    YA0059

FRANCE
    YA2212 YA2348   YA2583

GERMANY
    YA0353 YA0558   YA0987 YA0989   YA1102 YA1264
    YA1624 YA2028   YA2471 YA2702   YA3000 YA3069
    YB0126

ICELAND
    YA1512

APPLICATION — MACRO

INDIA
    YA0345 YA1010   YA2087 YA2093   YA2153 YA2366
    YA3027 YA3221   YA3250 YA3253   YB0167
IRELAND
    YA1008 YA2885
ISRAEL
    YA1325 YA1548   YA3051
ITALY
    YA2482 YA2486   YB0164
JAPAN
    YA0860 YA1866   YA2115 YA3000   YA3204 YA3301
    YA3466 YA3484   YA3500 YA3742   YB0189
LATIN AMERICA
    YA0283 YA0284   YA0334 YA0336   YA0385 YA0455
    YA1178 YA1536   YA1582 YA1821   YA1952 YA2055
    YA2153 YA2401   YA2424 YA2743   YA3142 YA3390
    YA3550 YA3676   YA3705
LDC (Less Developed Countries)
    YA0114 YA0285   YA0287 YA0288   YA0352 YA0468
    YA0728 YA0869   YA1002 YA1263   YA1490 YA1526
    YA1549 YA1647   YA1712 YA1782   YA1814 YA2016
    YA2116 YA2205   YA2506 YA2722   YA3000 YA3079
    YA3232 YA3366   YA3536 YA3727
NETHERLANDS
    YA1008 YA3305   YB0288 YB0302   YB0303
NEW ZEALAND
    YA1352 YB0078   YB0079 YB0080   YB0262
OECD
    YA0027 YA0464   YA0465 YA0925   YA2558 YA2712
    YA3010 YA3366
PAKISTAN
    YA3697
SOUTH EAST ASIA
    YA0037 YA0261   YA1892 YA1894   YA2086 YA2173
    YA2287 YA2964
SWEDEN
    YA0167 YA0215   YA1208 YA2734   YA3677
SWITZERLAND
    YA0071
TURKEY
    YA1291

UK

YA0140	YA0157	YA0186	YA0188	YA0201	YA0248
YA0250	YA0313	YA0353	YA0404	YA0405	YA0442
YA0470	YA0471	YA0486	YA0499	YA0504	YA0558
YA0626	YA0777	YA0819	YA0864	YA0871	YA0891
YA0892	YA0893	YA0894	YA0971	YA0994	YA0998
YA1008	YA1094	YA1095	YA1131	YA1165	YA1195
YA1208	YA1318	YA1512	YA1518	YA1519	YA1536
YA1601	YA1623	YA1679	YA1688	YA1717	YA1795
YA1810	YA2063	YA2199	YA2200	YA2247	YA2278
YA2439	YA2440	YA2461	YA2466	YA2481	YA2508
YA2531	YA2560	YA2565	YA2569	YA2648	YA2657
YA2689	YA2753	YA2759	YA2782	YA2808	YA2945
YA2951	YA3000	YA3035	YA3069	YA3082	YA3083
YA3133	YA3197	YA3332	YA3411	YA3594	YA3657
YA3681	YA3687	YA3698	YB0026	YB0044	YB0054
YB0081	YB0163	YB0234	YB0243	YB0262	YB0276
YB0287	YB0314				

USSR

YA0933	YA1460	YA1759	YA2037	YA2127	YA2817
YA3015	YA3175	YA2358			

WORLD

YA1197	YA1940	YA2417	YA2647	YA2712	YA2990
YB0062	YB0084	YB0092	YB0197	YB0232	

YUGOSLAVIA

YA3497

APPLICATION – MACRO *See also* **MACROECONOMIC MODEL** and **INPUT OUTPUT** – **MACRO**. The following studies consider particular variables at the macroeconomic level.

ADVERTISING *See* **ADVERTISING** – DETERMINANTS.

CAPACITY UTILISATION

YA0740	YA0811	YA0828	YA1983	YA2173	YA2765
YA2907	YA3133	YA3697			

CONSUMER DEMAND

YA0008	YA0113	YA0170	YA0324	YA0334	YA0370
YA0434	YA0486	YA0578	YA0680	YA0687	YA0892
YA0893	YA0945	YA0978	YA1005	YA1307	YA1465
YA1530	YA1544	YA1813	YA1865	YA1886	YA1892
YA1893	YA1894	YA1958	YA2086	YA2115	YA2204
YA2287	YA2477	YA2485	YA2531	YA2583	YA2670
YA2673	YA2735	YA2736	YA2746	YA2811	YA2812

APPLICATION — MACRO
  CONSUMER DEMAND (cont.)

YA2855	YA2856	YA2885	YA3054	YA3250	YA3253
YA3322	YA3417	YA3561	YA3562	YA3579	YA3580
YA3615	YA3742	YB0020	YB0081	YB0159	YB0189
YB0292					

  CONSUMER DEMAND, FINANCIAL ASSETS (AND LIABILITIES)

YA0062	YA0222	YA0256	YA0401	YA0716	YA0768
YA0777	YA0994	YA1005	YA1156	YA1276	YA1668
YA1679	YA1765	YA2475	YA2656	YA2795	YA2897
YA3502	YA3669	YB0097	YB0269	YB0294	

  CONSUMPTION

YA0034	YA0157	YA0158	YA0344	YA0548	YA0674
YA0760	YA0795	YA0827	YA0854	YA0855	YA0871
YA0894	YA0925	YA0958	YA1069	YA1164	YA1309
YA1330	YA1331	YA1549	YA1565	YA1730	YA1759
YA1764	YA1765	YA1794	YA1895	YA2013	YA2094
YA2197	YA2279	YA2289	YA2472	YA2477	YA2485
YA2486	YA2669	YA2670	YA2677	YA2708	YA2785
YA2786	YA2862	YA2937	YA3013	YA3051	YA3083
YA3084	YA3249	YA3251	YA3252	YA3305	YA3323
YA3359	YA3475	YA3591	YA3614	YA3666	YA3679
YA3701	YA3763	YA3765	YA3768	YB0078	YB0111
YB0117	YB0126	YB0154	YB0219	YB0228	YB0292
YB0312					

  COSTS *See* **COST — MACRO**
  DEVELOPMENT

YA1002	YA1076	YA1291	YA1490	YA1549	YA1927
YA2066	YA2399	YA2401	YA2482	YA2504	YA2722
YA3233	YA3631				

  DIVIDENDS

YA1164	YB0154	YB0270

  EARNINGS

YA0035	YA0138	YA0139	YA0140	YA0176	YA0269
YA0368	YA0581	YA0595	YA0666	YA0686	YA0797
YA0888	YA0902	YA0932	YA0957	YA0961	YA0962
YA0964	YA1009	YA1020	YA1026	YA1091	YA1206
YA1208	YA1325	YA1312	YA1417	YA1418	YA1422
YA1423	YA1424	YA1426	YA1438	YA1601	YA1687
YA1688	YA1708	YA1734	YA1810	YA1942	YA1996
YA2013	YA2161	YA2256	YA2257	YA2261	YA2439
YA2479	YA2482	YA2560	YA2646	YA2648	YA2700
YA2707	YA2759	YA2766	YA2767	YA2771	YA2782
YA2827	YA2846	YA2869	YA3017	YA3037	YA3038

APPLICATION – MACRO

EARNINGS (cont.)

YA3123	YA3161	YA3166	YA3197	YA3220	YA3283
YA3428	YA3435	YA3466	YA3493	YA3494	YA3527
YA3556	YA3570	YA3571	YA3594	YB0017	YB0044
YB0139					

EFFICIENCY

YA0948 *See also* PRODUCTIVITY below.

EMPLOYMENT

YA0034	YA0175	YA0313	YA0315	YA0702	YA0888
YA0910	YA1118	YA1478	YA1653	YA1860	YA2504
YA2648	YA2711	YA2753	YA2768	YA2769	YA3018
YA3133	YA3237	YA3241	YA3284	YA3455	YA3566
YA3583	YB0017	YB0106	YB0216		

ENERGY

YA0298	YA0328	YA0498	YA0499	YA0500	YA0853
YA0910	YA1489	YA1628	YA1727	YA1776	YA2559
YA2945	YA2990	YA3267	YA3387	YB0035	YB0108
YB0232	YB0306	YB0320			

ENERGY, SOURCES

YA0298	YA1293	YA1486	YA1628	YA1727	YA3033
YB0142	YB0167	YB0178			

FINISHED GOODS

YA2866

FLOW OF FUNDS

YA0177	YA0361	YA0485	YA0682	YA0718	YA0819
YA0996	YA1669	YA2056	YA2245	YA2366	YA2828
YA2897	YA3060	YA3273	YA3312	YA3553	YA3564
YB0069	YB0079	YB0117	YB0154	YB0161	YB0164

GDP

YA1623	YA2277	YA2820	YA3765

GNP

YA0120	YA0161	YA0225	YA0226	YA0551	YA0669
YA0740	YA1056	YA1251	YA1512	YA1588	YA1589
YA1781	YA1787	YA1831	YA2004	YA2010	YA2215
YA2237	YA2401	YA2411	YA2674	YA2712	YA3167
YA3239	YA3681	YB0076			

GNP, POTENTIAL

YA2559	YA2768	YA2769

GROWTH

YA0201	YA0498	YA0775	YA0895	YA1291	YA1647
YA1777	YA1866	YA1897	YA2725	YA2921	YA3039
YA3306	YA3366	YA3500	YA3551	YB0116	YB0189

APPLICATION – MACRO
INCOME
YA0674 YA1125 YA1178 YA1478 YA1764 YA2014
YA3305 YA3591 YA3764
INTERMEDIATE GOODS
YA2866 YA2917
INTERNATIONAL FINANCE
YA0134 YA0367 YA0463 YA0465 YA0856 YA1490
YA1549 YA1663 YA1698 YA1712 YA1724 YA2042
YA2131 YA2349 YA2350 YA2400 YA2401 YA2443
YA2462 YA2471 YA2722 YA2808 YA2980 YA3067
YA3094 YA3304 YA3329 YA3515
INTERNATIONAL FINANCE, EXCHANGE RATES
YA0249 YA0287 YA0288 YA0353 YA0455 YA0491
YA0558 YA0737 YA0739 YA0774 YA0869 YA1365
YA1534 YA1624 YA1725 YA1782 YA1795 YA1933
YA1947 YA1997 YA2003 YA2055 YA2148 YA2212
YA2260 YA2351 YA2456 YA2657 YA2662 YA2838
YA2993 YA3069 YA3332 YA3551
INTERNATIONAL FINANCE, FOREIGN RESERVES
YA0122 YA0385 YA0690 YA1263 YA1814 YA2352
YA2702 YA3676 YA3686 YA3757
INTERNATIONAL LINKAGE *See also* STOCK PRICES – MODELS, International.
YA0027 YA0039 YA0163 YA0424 YA0464 YA1664
YA1837 YA2326 YA2514 YA2651 YA2837 YA2984
YA3483 YB0019 YB0037 YB0061 YB0197 YB0260
YB0270 YB0311
INTERNATIONAL TRADE
YA0027 YA0056 YA0059 YA0060 YA0086 YA0180
YA0250 YA0464 YA0466 YA0825 YA0970 YA0998
YA1333 YA1403 YA1512 YA1459 YA1756 YA1837
YA1927 YA1934 YA2004 YA2030 YA2239 YA2514
YA2551 YA2565 YA2712 YA3000 YA3010 YA3056
YA3631 YB0019 YB0092 YB0163 YB0182 YB0189
YB0197 YB0201 YB0291
Exports   YA0032 YA0188 YA0248 YA0930 YA1318
YA1548 YA1879 YA2028 YA2029 YA2100 YA2116
YA2713 YA2758 YA2921 YA2976 YA3080 YA3153
YA3205 YA3698
Imports   YA0549 YA0623 YA1010 YA1352 YA1479
YA1741 YA1873 YA1953 YA2105 YA2107 YA2199
YA2200 YA2401 YA2508 YA2550 YA2558 YA2784
YA3203 YA3652 YA3726 YA3728 YB0080 YB0270

APPLICATION – MACRO
MONEY (cont.)

Supply   YA0035   YA0161 YA0163   YA0216 YA0225
YA0441 YA0445   YA0770 YA0994   YA1251 YA1512
YA1563 YA1578   YA1737 YA1787   YA1831 YA2012
YA2014 YA2091   YA2149 YA2215   YA2365 YA2397
YA2802 YA2821   YA2861 YA2965   YA3004 YA3069
YA3167 YA3189   YA3764 YB0022   YB0161

Velocity   YA1171   YA1430 YA1582   YA2013 YA2397
YA3374

ORDERS
YA3552

OUTPUT
YA0581 YA0662   YA0700 YA1016   YA1215 YA1810
YA2481 YA3241   YA3456 YB0155   YB0164 YB0176

PLANT SIZE
YA0738

PRODUCTIVITY
YA0702 YA0950   YA1866 YA1897   YA2264 YA2569
YA2648 YA2717   YA2725 YA2768   YA2769 YA2951
YA3039 YA3657

PROFITS
YA1009 YA1168   YA1187 YA1459   YA2000 YA2233
YA2653 YA3143   YA3395

R & D
YA3133

RAW MATERIALS
YA2866 YA2868   YA3717

SALES
YA1177 YA3237   YB0164 *See also* **APPLICATION –
SECTOR**, DISTRIBUTION AND RETAILING.

SAVINGS
YA0045 YA0256   YA0429 YA0548   YA0796 YA0891
YA1159 YA1164   YA1278 YA1392   YA1490 YA1519
YA1526 YA1758   YA1765 YA1883   YA1884 YA2103
YA2116 YA2205   YA2722 YA2817   YA2875 YA3057
YA3341 YA3407   YA3414 YA3416   YB0097 YB0288

SHIPMENTS
YA3552

STRIKES
See **STRIKE**

UNEMPLOYMENT
YA0167 YA0215   YA0216 YA0442   YA0470 YA0492
YA0546 YA0547   YA0828 YA0963   YA1008 YA1015

34

APPLICATION – MACRO
UNEMPLOYMENT (cont.)

YA1091	YA1094	YA1095	YA1192	YA1208	YA1232
YA1273	YA1422	YA1441	YA1442	YA1509	YA1518
YA1552	YA1554	YA1623	YA1708	YA1732	YA1734
YA1779	YA1900	YA2074	YA2101	YA2179	YA2231
YA2327	YA2440	YA2470	YA2674	YA2689	YA2726
YA2772	YA3070	YA3162	YA3211	YA3284	YA3411
YA3468	YA3517	YA3570	YA3606	YB0226	YB0233
YB0314					

WAGES   *See* EARNINGS above.

APPLICATION – SECTOR (OR FIRM) The following are studies of the output in a number of sectors while those studies which only consider particular sectors or their subdivisions are listed under their appropriate sector heading. Following this list of sectors (and subsectors) is a list of variables with which these sector and firm level studies have been concerned: e.g. APPLICATION – SECTOR: INVESTMENT lists studies of investment behaviour at the sector level. For studies of COST, PRICE or PRODUCTION FUNCTIONS by sector *see* for example, PRICE – SECTOR.

YA0280	YA0604	YA0699	YA1228	YA1384	YA1735
YA2623	YA3179	YA3241	YB0047	YB0126	YB0155
YB0197	YB0234	YB0331			

AGRICULTURAL AND OTHER COMMODITIES

YA0057	YA0144	YA0387	YA0596	YA0597	YA0696
YA0769	YA0816	YA0977	YA1193	YA1364	YA1384
YA1619	YA1972	YA1973	YA2002	YA2049	YA2051
YA2712	YA2868	YA2882	YA3027	YA3232	YA3307
YA3572	YA3749	YB0001	YB0002	YB0089	YB0167
YB0175	YB0186	YB0191	YB0192	YB0280	YB0323

Agriculture

Cereals and feed

		YA0392	YA1451	YA2391	YA2392
YA3040	YA3102	YB0068	YB0191	YB0192	YB0274

Livestock and related products

		YA0043	YA0822	YA1218	
YA1659	YA1660	YA2140	YA2141	YA2271	YA2458
YA2610	YA2941	YA2942	YA3545	YA3591	YA3611
YB0068	YB0191	YB0300			

Other

	YA0241	YA0262	YA0701	YA0703	YA0944
YA0999	YA1012	YA1400	YA1632	YA1642	YA1973
YA2006	YA2255	YA2368	YA2391	YA2392	YA2724
YA2977	YA3293	YA3307	YA3383	YA3419	YA3664
YB0186	YB0191	YB0192	YB0239		

APPLICATION – SECTOR (OR FIRM)
DISTRIBUTION AND RETAILING
    Wholesalers (and other distributors)   YA0205 YA0749
    YA1144
The following consider particular methods of retailing. For applications of forecasting, *see* **USE – DISTRIBUTION, USE – RETAIL,** and **USE – SITE SELECTION.**
    Retailing,

Mail order	YA1461	YA1634	YA2450	
Super markets	YA0833	YA2491	YA3325	YA3655

EDUCATION Here 'firm' is applied to studies of individual institutions. *See also* **APPLICATION – SECTOR (OR FIRM):** GOVERNMENT, **Education** below.
    YA1445 YA1462 YA2232
    Libraries   YA2642 YA3751
    Schools   YA0063   YA0193 YA0810   YA0884 YA3183
    YA3581
    Universities YA0179   YA1415 YA1692   YA1726 YA1744
    YA1833 YA1845   YA1915 YA2005   YA2388 YA2438
    YA2680 YA2764   YA2874 YA2877   YA2895 YA3135
    YA3279 YA3499   YA3537 YB0282
FINANCE   For studies of retail outlets, *see* **APPLICATION – SECTOR (OR FIRM):** DISTRIBUTION AND RETAILING above.
    YA1315 YA1328   YA1457 YA2144   YA2982 YA3230
    YB0262
    Firm: finance, banks   YA0052 YA0068   YA0075 YA0722
    YA0807 YA0852   YA1030 YA1031   YA1106 YA1252
    YA1290 YA1437   YA1614 YA1656   YA1657 YA1658
    YA1898 YA2011   YA2218 YA2248   YA2253 YA2415
    YA2469 YA2529   YA2537 YA2538   YA2545 YA2688
    YA2693 YA2800   YA2854 YA3227   YA3255 YA3320
    YA3374 YA3418   YA3738 YB0194   YB0205 YB0280
    Sector: finance, banks YA0166 YA0255   YA0367 YA0407
    YA0697 YA0778   YA0803 YA0947   YA1003 YA1152
    YA1205 YA1320   YA1345 YA1467   YA1669 YA1698
    YA1706 YA1742   YA1838 YA1878   YA2079 YA2350
    YA2471 YA2503   YA2702 YA2793   YA2796 YA2899
    YA2982 YA3169   YA3170 YA3274   YA3329 YA3374
    YA3451 YA3515   YB0270
    Sector: finance, building societies (and savings and loan associations) YA0716   YA1226 YA1345   YA1819 YA1917
    YA2045 YA2046   YA2079 YA2080   YA2081 YA2666
    YA2899 YA3063   YA3274 YA3351   YA3521 YA3532
    YA3624 YA3769   YB0167

APPLICATION — SECTOR (OR FIRM)
FINANCE
    Insurance companies YA0070 YA0372   YA0735 YA1327
      YA1587 YA1715   YA2775 YA2776   YA2780 YA3130
      YA3280 YB0027   YB0074 YB0280
    Loan companies   YA0306 YA0307   YA0308 YA0407
      YA1472 YA1473   YA2572
    Mutual funds (and Unit Trusts) YA0808 YA1532 YA1533
      YA1986 YA2009   YA2279 YA2346   YA2362 YA3235
      YA3327
    Stock brokers   YA0078 YA0169   YA0874 YA1031
      YA1081 YA1275   YA1314 YA1720   YA2661 YA3151
      YA3158 YA3353   YA3640
GOVERNMENT Here 'firm' is applied to studies of individual institutions. For studies of government policies, *see* **POLICY EVALUATION** — (sub-heading), a major category heading GOVERNMENT.
    YA1100 YA1752   YB0010
    Central   YA3058
     Defence YA0079   YA1080 YA1304   YA1306 YA1444
      YA1605 YA3704   YB0170 YB0196   YB0232
     Expenditure   YA0037 YA3340   YA3423 YB0067
      YB0147 YB0234
     Financing YA0403   YA0417 YA1458   YA3224 YA3400
      YB0161
     Foreign aid   YA2850
     Revenues and tax   YA0037 YA0971   YA2505 YA2750
      YA2890 YA3041   YA3258 YB0147
    Education *See also* **APPLICATION — SECTOR (OR FIRM)**:
    EDUCATION   YA2232 YA2667   YA3105 YB0304
     Schools YA0884   YA2981 YA3183   YA3489
     Universities   YA0755 YA0756   YA0846 YA1851
      YA2818
    Libraries *See* **APPLICATION — SECTOR (OR FIRM)**: EDUCATION, Libraries.
    Local *See also* **REGIONAL MODELS.**   YA1037 YA1315
      YA2667 YA3093   YA3105 YB0096
     Expenditure   YA0316 YA0410   YA1443 YA3093
      YA3294
     Financing YA0286   YA0564 YA0704   YA1439 YA1440
      YA1742 YA3398   YB0161
     Housing YA2637
     Revenues and tax   YA3258

APPLICATION — SECTOR (OR FIRM)
  GOVERNMENT
    Local (cont.)
      Services YA0316   YA0410 YA0426   YA0719 YA0885
        YA1760 YA2667   YA3346 YA3349   YA3600
      Services, emergency YA2008
      Services, leisure   YA0316 YA2943
    Nationalised industries (and postal services)   YA2379 YA2435
      YA2447
    Roads   YA2292   YA2667 YA3397
NATURAL
    Animal populations   YA0096 YA0104   YA0579 YA0580
      YA0642 YA2304   YA3464
    Human physiology   YA1301
    Hydrology YA2097
    Plant populations   YA3712
    Sunspots   YA0061   YA2516 YA2709   YA2803
    Weather   YA2544   *See also*   WEATHER, EFFECT OF.
PRODUCTION AND MINING
      YA0015 YA0057   YA0522 YA0647   YA0878 YA0898
      YA0995 YA1200   YA1384 YA1867   YA2829 YA2980
      YA2987 YA3008   YA3675 YB0191
    Aerospace YA1060   YA1605 YA1922   YA1995 YA2227
      YA3348
    Chemicals and fertilisers YA0018   YA0538   YA1093 YA1253
      YA1485 YA1597   YA1711 YA1761   YA2181 YA2791
      YA2839 YA3352   YB0186
    Coal and mining products   YA0733   YA0853 YA1594
      YA2146 YA3275   YA3771 YB0142
    Computers YA0439   YA2284 YA2793   YA2900 YA2939
      YA3356
    Construction materials and aggregates   YA0358 YA0877
      YA1778 YA2917   YA3593 YA3703
    Diamonds YA2146
    Electrical machinery   YA1761 YA2905   YA2980
    Electronics YA0511   YA0526 YA1836   YA2076 YA2536
      YA3484 YA3522   YA3540 YA3739
    Engineering This broad category includes some of the other pro-
      duction sectors.   YA0447 YA0657   YA1096 YA2303
      YB0310
    Fibres   YA1597
    Gas   YA0327   YA1087 YA1955   YA2615 YA2834
      YA3501 YB0206   *See also* APPLICATION — SECTOR
    (OR FIRM) — UTILITIES, Gas below.

APPLICATION – SECTOR (OR FIRM)
PRODUCTION AND MINING

Glass	YA1812	YA1828		
Instruments, control	YA0025			
Machine tools	YA0435	YA3008	YA1369	YA3009
YB0204	YB0303			
Mined products	*See* **Coal** and mining products above.			
Musical instruments	YA0189			
Packaging	YA0273	YA2946		
Paint	YA0273			
Paper and wood pulp	YA0647	YA0842	YA1642	YA2348
YA2533	YA2946	YA3576		
Waste	YA2196	YA3491		
Petroleum	YA0026	YA0124	YA0788	YA0872	YA1086
YA1357	YA1487	YA1940	YA2110	YA2385	YA2559
YA2640	YA2657	YA2914	YA2968	YA3501	YB0142
YB0178	YB0186	YB0306			
Plant	YA0412	YA0709	YA0790	YA0806	YA0877
YA1068	YA1515	YA1871	YA1916	YA2217	YA2227
YA2751	YA2980	YA3576			
Refractories	YA2917			
Refrigeration	YA2217			
Rubber	YA3386	YB0089	YB0186	
Scrap metal	YA3217			
Ships	YA1357	YA2111		
Steel	YA0164	YA0737	YA0866	YA0898	YA1661
YA2348	YA2515	YA2917	YA2988	YA3476	YA3478
YB0089	YB0186				
Textiles	YA1389	YA2159	YA2464	YA2905	YA2944
YB0238	YB0326				

SERVICES

	YA0034	YA2808		
Computers	YA0439			
Charities	YA0429	YA0430	YA1169	YA1740
Health	*See* **HEALTH**			
Media	YA1468	YA2406		
Magazines and Newspapers		YA0230	YA0305	YA0332
YA0490	YA0959	YA0981	YA1946	YA2285	YA2407
YA2408	YA2659	YA2946	YA2947	YA2953	YA3031
YA3136	YA3651				
TV	YA0303	YA0444	YA0742	YA0804	YA0805
YA0858	YA0955	YA1274	YA1332	YA2299	YA2540
YA2727	YA3049	YA3775			
Other (including Film and Theatre)			YA0587	YA1716
YA2502	YA3623			

APPLICATION – SECTOR (OR FIRM)
    SERVICES (cont.)

Professional expertise	YA1258	YA1692	YA1850
Sport YA0509	YA1785	YA2718	YA3160

    Tourism and leisure facilities   YA0559   YA0695   YA1023
      YA1338 YA1716   YA2041   YA2057   YA2678 YA2679
      YA2943 YA2960   YA3042   YB0060   YB0324

SOCIAL (AND PERSONAL)
    YA1209 YA2361

Accidents	YA1051	YA1198	YA3549	YA3612
Crime	YA0165	YA0508	YA0719	YA1039 YA1507

      YA1849 YA2410   YA2742   YA3257   YA3600 YA3706
      YA3711

    Educational attainment YA1562   YA2512   YA2579
    Inequality and poverty *See also* **MANPOWER PLANNING** –
    DISCRIMINATION. YA0083   YA0254   YA0255 YA0315
      YA0443 YA1030   YA1441   YA2470   YA2487 YA3020
      YA3168 YA3560

    Occupation YA3124   YA3125
    Socio-economic structure   YA0350   YA0443 YA1259
      YA1316

    Strikes   *See* **STRIKE**
    Success   YA0350   YA0633   YA0634   YA1259 YA1360
      YA1497 YA1498   YA1555   YA1911   YA2254 YA3700
      YB0123

TRANSPORT
      YA0260 YA1019   YA1333   YA1356   YA1630 YA1862
      YA2024 YA2227   YA2296   YA2578   YA3642 YA3644
      YB0016 YB0082   YB0087   YB0265   YB0322 YB0328

    Air   YA0129   YA0713   YA0870   YA0935 YA0936
      YA1596 YA1922   YA1949   YA2639   YA3042 YA3138
      YA3140 YA3533   YA3750   YB0083   YB0135

    Rail   YA0076   YA0077   YA0896   YA0918 YA1198
      YA1311 YA1324   YA1395   YA1592   YA1613 YA1923
      YA1924 YA1974   YA2150   YA2592   YB0184

    Road   YA3262   YA3397   YA3643
    Freight YA2150   YA2683   YA2715   YA3310 YA3718
    Passenger YA0383   YA0565   YA3558
    Shipping   YA1822   YA3409   YA3410   YB0176

UTILITIES
      YA0231 YA0462   YA0539   YA0941   YA1388 YA1538
      YA1862 YA1869   YA1870   YA1944   YA2282 YA2925

APPLICATION – SECTOR (OR FIRM)
UTILITIES (cont.)

Electricity	YA0094	YA0210	YA0263	YA0331	YA0363
YA0364	YA0421	YA0523	YA0536	YA0590	YA0613
YA0621	YA0779	YA0781	YA0805	YA0897	YA1068
YA1179	YA1292	YA1404	YA1484	YA1486	YA1488
YA1559	YA1628	YA1672	YA1673	YA1674	YA1702
YA1727	YA1757	YA1778	YA1872	YA2112	YA2142
YA2169	YA2191	YA2447	YA2250	YA2524	YA2549
YA2554	YA2622	YA2751	YA2789	YA2790	YA2801
YA2847	YA2991	YA2994	YA3064	YA3311	YA3415
YA3439	YA3512	YA3522	YA3670	YB0142	

Electricity, nuclear		YA1871			
Gas	YA0181	YA0327	YA0330	YA0573	YA0853
YA1637	YA1832	YA2251	YA2252	YA2999	YA3454
YA3498	YA3633	YB0018	YB0142	YB0206	YB0289
YB0306					

Telephone	YA0148	YA0346	YA0517	YA0611	YA0630
YA0692	YA0713	YA0879	YA0949	YA1006	YA1007
YA1194	YA1413	YA1462	YA1463	YA1529	YA1796
YA2275	YA3065	YA3364	YA3440	YA3540	YA3543
YA3685	YB0258				

Water	YA0286	YA0521			

The following are firm or sector level studies of particular variables such as EMPLOYMENT, or financial variables, listed under, e.g. FINANCE, Profits. The same subheadings, e.g. CAPACITY may be used for macroeconomic studies, and these are referenced under **APPLICATION – MACRO**.

CAPACITY *See also* **APPLICATION – MACRO, CAPACITY.**
YA2533 YA2987

Utilisation YA0335 YA3019 YA3697 YB0186

COMPANY FORMATIONS *See also* NEW VENTURES below.
YA0044 YA1428 YA2692

CONSUMPTION
YA1364

EARNINGS (AND WAGES) *See also* **MANPOWER PLANNING –**
EARNINGS.   YA0176 YA0285 YA0524 YA0552
YA0553 YA1524 YA1551 YA1552 YA1640 YA1672
YA1673 YA1709 YA1891 YA1915 YA2181 YA2421
YA2533 YA2539 YA2654 YA2760 YA2761 YA2770
YA2851 YA2905 YA3027 YA3054 YA3105 YA3160
YA3313 YA3393 YA3497 YA3569 YA3693 YB0096
YB0139 YB0245

APPLICATION — SECTOR (OR FIRM)

FINANCE

APPLICATION — SECTOR (OR FIRM)
  INVESTMENT — SECTOR
       YA0073 YA0363   YA0364 YA0408   YA0576 YA0781
       YA0803 YA1047   YA1099 YA1364   YA1431 YA1861
       YA1862 YA1863   YA1864 YA1867   YA1916 YA2211
       YA2416 YA2839   YA2987 YA3019   YA3064 YA3065
       YA3078 YA3134   YA3156 YA3232   YA3316 YA3576
       YA3645 YA3693   YB0010 YB0127   YB0203 YB0278
       YB0279 YB0305   YB0333
  INVESTMENT, INTERNATIONAL — SECTOR (OR FIRM)
       YA0626 YA0627   YA1749 YA1984
  LOCATION
       YA0068 YA0728   YA1585 YA1661   YA3629 YA3648
       YB0145
  MERGERS   *See also* **USE** — ACQUISITION.
       YA1054 YA1189   YA1249 YA1557   YA1621 YA2040
       YA3247
  NEW VENTURES   *See also* **COMPANY** FORMATIONS above.
       YA1427
  OUTPUT *See* **APPLICATION** — **MACRO** above.
  POLLUTION *See* **POLLUTION.**
  PRODUCTIVITY
       YA0627 YA0728   YA0837 YA0977   YA0995 YA1496
       YA1508 YA2027   YA2379 YA2435   YA2569 YA2645
       YA2951 YA2958   YA3030 YA3657   YA3743 YB0325
  R & D *See also* **USE** — R & D.
       YA0897 YA1432   YA1434 YA1750   YA1761 YA2151
       YA2374 YA2694   YA2938 YA3041   YA3043 YA3061
       YA3670 YA3691   YB0166
  TECHNOLOGY
       YA1369 YA2016   YA3008 YA3009   YA3194 YA3421
  UNEMPLOYMENT
       YA1899 YA2301   YA3411

ATTITUDINAL DATA
       YA0113 YA0166   YA0487 YA0548   YA1225 YA1798
       YA1886 YA2234   YA2815 YA2816   YA3437 YB0101
  EVALUATION
       YA0018 YA0021   YA0024 YA0486   YA2473 YA2954
       YA3186 YB0185   YB0294

BAYESIAN
  ESTIMATION
    Simultaneous system   YA0991   YA1408   YA1990   YA2334
      YB0107   YB0275
    Time series   YA1409   YA1598   YA1770   YA3446
  FORECASTING
      YA0823   YA1461   YA1598   YA1599   YA2524   YB0109
  JUDGEMENTAL FORECASTS   These references comment on how
    judgemental forecasting compares with the Bayesian model
      YA0332   YA1573   YA1939   YA3334
  MODEL SELECTION   *See also* **MODEL SELECTION**
      YA0155   YA0218   YA0324   YA0379   YA0380   YA0382
      YA0446   YA0662   YA0793   YA1323   YA1330   YA1352
      YA1353   YA1599   YA2108   YA3089   YA3666   YA3763
      YB0195   YB0327   YB0333
  PRIOR INFORMATION   *See also* **PRIOR INFORMATION**
      YA1253   YA1352   YA2105   YA2107   YA2109   YA2517
      YA2959   YA3199   YA3200   YA3696   YA3766   YA3768
      YB0107   YB0275

BOOTSTRAPPING   These references describe how judgemental fore-
casts can be improved by modelling the forecaster.
      YA0620   YA1571   YA2450   YA2526   YA3263
  EVALUATION
      YA0142   YA0883   YA1385   YA2527   YA2528   YB0015
  REVIEW
      YA0141   YA0143   YB0015

BRAND CHOICE These articles consider the probability of a consumer selecting a particular brand of product. The probabilities can in
principle be aggregated to produce market share forecasts but usually
are not. If market share forecasts are provided then the article is also
key worded under **MARKET SHARE**. The reader should also
examine **REPEAT BUYING**.
  APPLICATION
      YA0005   YA0017   YA0168   YA0239   YA0516   YA1019
      YA1140   YA1541   YA1637   YA1693   YA2723   YA2745
      YA2947   YA3048   YA3371   YA3651   YA3772   YB0237
  EVALUATION
      YA1366   YA1857   YA3773
  INTRODUCTION
      YA2186
  METHODOLOGY
      YA0001   YA0146   YA0380   YA0382   YA1830   YA1858
      YA2099   YA2129   YA2171   YA2745   YA2932   YA3773

BRAND CHOICE
  REVIEW
    YB0095 YB0218
  THEORY

YA0002	YA0003	YA0242	YA0379	YA0654	YA1694
YA1695	YA1858	YA2098	YA2405	YA2931	YA3509
YA3510					

The following are concerned with specific aspects of brand choice
DETERMINANTS .

YA0147	YA0610	YA0692	YA0754	YA0858	YA0938
YA1145	YA1146	YA1237	YA1362	YA2555	YA3578
YA3775					

INDICATORS

YA0000	YA0423	YA0729	YA1289	YA3213	YA3675

BUSINESS CYCLE
  EVALUATION
    YA3256
  INTRODUCTION
    YA3209
  METHODOLOGY
    YA2369
  REVIEW
    YB0038 YB0045 YB0076 YB0230

The following are more specific references.
DETERMINANTS

YA0424	YA2316	YB0101	YB0150	YB0151	YB0216

EFFECT OF

YA0027	YA0162	YA0769	YA1109	YA1243	YA1308
YA1418	YA1735	YA2079	YA2177	YA2233	YA2648
YA2700	YA3159	YA3570	YB0013		

IDENTIFICATION

YA0162	YA0437	YA0497	YA0999	YA1824	YA2499
YB0045	YB0243	YB0313	YB0331	YB0332	

LONG CYCLE

YA0029	YA0585	YA1220	YA1451	YA1991	YA2762
YA3256	YA3345	YB0093			

PREDICTION

YA0090	YA2348	YA3735	YB0212

  Turning points

YA0603	YA1172	YA2861	YA3334
YB0164			

REGIONAL

YA0371	YA3384	YB0307

BUSINESS INDICATORS
APPLICATION

YA0012	YA0449	YA0546	YA0547	YA0724	YA0898
YA1055	YA1094	YA1172	YA1192	YA1512	YA2000
YA2234	YA2658	YA2664	YA3334	YA3437	YA3503
YB0045	YB0101	YB0209	YB0243	YB0269	

EVALUATION

YA0207	YA0497	YA1016	YA1800	YA2216	YA2499
YA3342	YA3736	YA3737	YB0230		

INTRODUCTION

YA3302	YB0056	YB0063	YB0076

METHODOLOGY

YA0551	YA1021	YA1215	YA2316	YA3735	YA3736

REVIEW

YA2317	YA3207	YB0151	YB0230

For studies of particular business indicators, see under **INDEX NUMBERS**.

CANONICAL CORRELATION

YA0074	YA2067	YB0000

CAPACITY
EFFECT OF

YA0124	YA0188	YA0248	YA0284	YA0632	YA0702
YA1158	YA1168	YA1421	YA1459	YA1479	YA1923
YA2085	YA2765	YA2965	YA3080	YA3411	YA3455
YA3552	YB0204	YB0287			

ESTIMATION

YA0811	YA1983	YA2559	YA2765	YA3408

CAUSALITY
BIBLIOGRAPHY

YA2824	YA3244

REVIEW

YA0785	YA1036	YA1391	YA1447	YA1455	YA2824
YA3709	YB0043	YB0109	YB0123	YB0132	YB0138
YB0167	YB0323				

TEST

YA0161	YA0163	YA0226	YA0571	YA1128	YA1264
YA1341	YA1447	YA1622	YA1623	YA2574	YA2626
YA2821	YA2822	YA3237	YA3239	YA3244	YA3681

THEORY
YA0571

CLUSTER ANALYSIS
INTRODUCTION
YB0000

COMBING FORECASTS
APPLICATION

YA0252	YA0767	YA0807	YA0822	YA1125	YA1253
YA1854	YA1974	YA2499	YA2516	YA2630	YA2943
YA3512	YB0046				

EVALUATION

YA0541 YA0941 YA1125 YA2943

INTRODUCTION
YA0980

METHODOLOGY

YA0252	YA0539	YA0542	YA0544	YA0941	YA2630
YA2681	YB0046	YB0132			

THEORY
YA0940

COMPARATIVE METHODS These references compare methods, e.g. **COMPARATIVE METHODS** − ARIMA, Causal examines the forecasting performance of ARIMA time series models compared with Causal models. Similarly − **Distributed lag** compares the performance of different specifications of the lag structure. The same models can be estimated in a number of different ways and the various estimation methods are compared under the sub-heading ESTIMATION : (estimation methods) or − ESTIMATION : (model), e.g. ESTIMATION : **Regression,** *Error specification* compares various methods of estimating a regression model with autocorrelated errors. This contrasts with the sub-heading REGRESSION, **Error specification** which compares models which have differing error specifications from the standard regression model.

REVIEW
YB0015
THEORY OF
YB0015

The following compare models or estimation methods
ADAPTIVE FILTERING, (Other)

YA0648 YA0656 YA1050 YA2357 YA2497 YA3650

ARIMA, Autoregressive

YA0065	YA0510	YA0918	YA1492	YA1493	YA2630
YA3608	YB0192	YB0241			
Causal	YA2141	YA2549	YA2678	YA2820	YA2943
YA3474	YA3512	YA3765	YB0192		

COMPARATIVE METHODS
ESTIMATION

COMPARATIVE METHODS
RECURSIVE, Simultaneous system
YA1911
REGRESSION, Censored
YA2608

CONSUMER BEHAVIOUR

The references relating to specific approaches to consumer behaviour are given below; *see also* **BRAND CHOICE** and **REPEAT BUYING**.

ECONOMIC MODELS

YA0220	YA0256	YA0401	YA0548	YA0694	YA0768
YA0936	YA1655	YA1696	YA1885	YA1886	YA1893
YA2005	YA2025	YA2115	YA2204	YA2205	YA2531
YA2656	YA3417	YA3615	YB0020	YB0126	YB0159
YB0219	YB0224	YB0288	YB0294		

Evaluation YA0220 YA0324 YA0503 YA0687 YA0688
YA0890 YA1465 YA1615 YA2086

Review YA0503 YA1176 YB0261

Theory YA0208 YA0222 YA0232 YA0310 YA0453
YA0687 YA0802 YA0885 YA0890 YA0892 YA0925
YA0945 YA1014 YA1307 YA1865 YA2287 YA2406
YA2736 YA2811 YA2812 YA2853 YA3250 YA3562
YA3580 YA3583 YA3648 YA3742 YA3768 YB0087
YB0169 YB0265

EXPENDITURE SURVEY

YA1278 YA1813 YA1892 YA1894 YA2855 YA3250
YA3253 YB0159 YB0224

PSYCHOLOGICAL MODELS

YA0003 YA0149 YA0423 YA0531 YA1145 YA1146
YA1239 YA1289 YA1590 YA1689 YA2098 YA2244
YA2488 YA2699 YA3609 YA3675 YA3770 YB0217
YB0224

Evaluation YA0729 YA1147 YA1788 YA2518 YA2883

Review YA0338 YA1912 YA3636 YB0160

PURCHASING

Determinants YA0074 YA0106 YA0147 YA0401
YA0407 YA0423 YA0506 YA0610 YA0712 YA0832
YA0938 YA0946 YA0981 YA1005 YA1143 YA1146
YA1205 YA1237 YA1239 YA1240 YA1289 YA1362
YA1462 YA1463 YA1590 YA1689 YA1716 YA1796
YA1835 YA1916 YA2171 YA2262 YA2393 YA2404
YA2437 YA2490 YA2555 YA2556 YA2557 YA2714
YA2796 YA2816 YA2930 YA3188 YA3219 YA3675
YB0217

Evaluation YA2518

Review YB0160

STOCHASTIC MODELS

YA0000 YA0002 YA0003 YA0004 YA0279 YA0379
YA0655 YA0754 YA1034 YA1108 YA1140 YA1694

CONTROL THEORY
  STOCHASTIC (cont.)

Review	YA0151	YA0671	YA2420	YB0309	
Theory	YA0195	YA0669	YA3402	YA3477	YB0107

COST
  INTRODUCTION
    YA0185
  MACRO
    YA0117 YA0328   YA0908 YA0909   YA1098 YA1293
    YA2007
  SECTOR (OR FIRM)
    YA0272 YA0995   YA2648 YA2980   YA2983 YA3164
    YA3458 YA3459   YA3715

Each subheading covers a separate sector of application.

Agriculture and other commodities				YA1130	
Consumer durables		YA0189	YA3693		
Distribution and retailing			YA1649		
Education	YA0756	YA0884	YA2764	YA2818	YA2981
	YA3183	YA3499	YA3537	YA3581	
Finance	YA0068	YA0070	YA0306	YA0307	YA0372
	YA0722	YA0735	YA0852	YA1031	YA1081	YA1228
	YA1275	YA1327	YA1868	YA1898	YA2011	YA2218
	YA2537	YA2572	YA2661	YA3158	YA3227	YA3418
	YA3640					
Government					
Central	YA2435	YA2642			
Local	YA3346	YA3600			
Health	YA0507	YA0881	YA0882	YA0924	YA1103
	YA1105	YA1154	YA1666	YA2096	YA2373	YB0027
Production and mining	YA0015	YA0026	YA0189	YA0273
	YA0358	YA1605	YA1778	YA1812	YA1940	YA1995
	YA3348	YA3476	YA3501	YA3734	YA3771	
Services	YA0230	YA0804	YA3031		
Transport	YA0260	YA1495	YA1592	YA1822	YA1922
	YA1923	YA1924	YA2639	YA3310	
Utilities	YA0331	YA0462	YA1404	YA1486	YA1778
	YA1872	YA2447	YA2622	YA2789	YA3498

The following relate to costs of particular activities at some given level of aggregation, e.g. firm or sector.

Financing	YA0422	YA1839			
Inventory	YA2706				
Production	YA0015	YA0189	YA1605	YA1778	YA1995
	YA3739				
R & D	YA2468	YA3043			

COST
The following are concerned with general issues relating to costs.
METHODOLOGY
  YA2387 YA2981   YA3092 YA3458
THEORY
  YA0117 YA0550   YA0909 YA3459

The following are more specific.
LEARNING CURVE
  YA0015 YA0189   YA0995 YA1605   YA1707 YA1995
  YA2756 YA3739
  See also **LEARNING CURVE.**
SCALE ECONOMIES
  YA0160 YA0273   YA0306 YA0307   YA0372 YA0628
  YA0722 YA0735   YA0852 YA0884   YA1081 YA1327
  YA1592 YA1778   YA1822 YA2011   YA2435 YA2639
  YA2757 YA2980   YA2983 YA3158   YA3183 YA3310
  YA3346 YA3352   YA3418 YA3581   YA3600 YA3640
  YA3715

CROSS CORRELATIONS
  YA0449 YA1622   YA1623 YA2574   YA2821 YA2822
  YA3244

DATA
AGGREGATION *See also* **COMPARATIVE METHODS** – DATA:
  Aggregate, disaggregate.
  YA0245 YA0493   YA0660 YA0990   YA1033 YA1064
  YA1152 YA1175   YA1285 YA1342   YA1344 YA1452
  YA1524 YA1730   YA1806 YA1894   YA2020 YA2048
  YA2107 YA2228   YA2422 YA2684   YA3012 YA3078
  YA3270 YA3528   YA3722 YA3726   YB0139
  Review   YA1806   YB0139
AGGREGATION OVER TIME
  YA0099 YA0279   YA0481 YA0703   YA0708 YA0906
  YA1340 YA3034   YA3047 YA3147   YA3451 YA3618
  YA3674 YA3764   YB0139 YB0151
ATYPICAL EVENTS *See also* **DATA ERRORS** – OUTLIERS.
  YA2959 YA3616
CATEGORICAL
  YA0052 YA0946   YA1350 YA1462   YA1463 YA2887
  YA2961
CENSORED
  YA1602 YA3616

DATA REVISIONS
EFFECT OF   *See also* **COMPARATIVE METHODS** − DATA :
    Revisions
        YA0023   YA0751   YA0921   YA0922   YA1073   YA1172
        YA1177   YA1544   YA1764   YA2278   YA2279   YA3207
        YA3341   YB0126   YB0230   YB0290
ESTIMATION
        YA2278   YA2632   YB0185

DECISION RULES   The following are used when the decision rules are appropriate for a particular level of aggregation, e.g. firm or sector.
FIRM
        YA1292   YA1571   YA1735   YA1869   YA1872   YA2052
        YA2442   YA2526   YA2528   YA2991   YB0158
MACRO
        YA0818   YA1122   YA1288   YA1663   YA2672
SECTOR
        YA0598   YA0755   YA0756   YA0846   YA0994   YA0999
        YA1297   YA1398   YA1538   YA1642   YA1752   YA1870
        YA2292   YA2850   YA2942   YA2991   YB0302
The following are methodological considerations.
FEEDBACK
        YA0475   YA0818   YA1122   YA1297   YA1397   YA1398
        YA2788   YA3070   YA3599
METHODOLOGY
        YA0142   YA1985   YA2527

DELPHI
        YA0332   YA1357   YA1573   YA1836   YA1850   YA2082
        YA2457   YA2501   YA2962   YB0014   YB0324

DEMAND
CUMULATIVE
        YA0333   YA0645   YA2500   YA3528   YB0229
DEFINITION OF
        YA0750
INTERMITTENT
        YA0817   YA2924   YA3641
REPLACEMENT
        YA0363   YA0364   YA0506   YA0781   YA1047   YA1166
        YA2500   YA3286   YB0013   YB0127
STOCK OUT
        YA3616

DEMAND EQUATIONS
SYSTEMS OF   *See also*   **COMPARATIVE METHODS** – DEMAND
EQUATIONS.

YA0008	YA0051	YA0559	YA0578	YA0685	YA0694
YA0778	YA0860	YA0885	YA0893	YA0936	YA0945
YA1307	YA1484	YA1558	YA1615	YA1865	YA1893
YA2086	YA2204	YA2205	YA2531	YA2734	YA3579
YA3580	YB0235	YB0327			

Review   YA0220   YA0503   YB0263

SYSTEMS OF : Methodology

YA0326	YA0687	YA0688	YA0892	YA2321	YA2735

Methodology, estimation   YA0170   YA0232   YA0326

YA0334	YA0370	YA0453	YA1560	YA1958	YA2583
YA2746	YA2811	YA2855	YA2856	YA3417	YA3742
YB0125					

Theory   YA0324   YA0370   YA0890   YA0892   YA2287

DEPRECIATION

YA0363	YA0364	YA0781	YA0973	YA1166	YA2111
YA2655	YA2733	YA3222	YA3682		

DIFFERENTIAL EQUATIONS
YA2195   YA2809   YA3068   YA3402   YA3765   YB0164

DIFFUSION MODEL
YA0877   YA3009   YB0202

EVALUATION
YA0329

DISCRIMINANT ANALYSIS
See also **COMPARATIVE METHODS** – DISCRIMINATION.

APPLICATION

YA0009	YA0066	YA0076	YA0078	YA0106	YA0193
YA0253	YA0395	YA0418	YA0668	YA0886	YA0982
YA0984	YA1044	YA1106	YA1245	YA1321	YA1385
YA1445	YA1507	YA1587	YA1948	YA2296	YA2301
YA2699	YA2816	YA2830	YA2831	YA2930	YA3148
YA3219	YA3255	YA3702			

EVALUATION

YA0809	YA1043	YA2053	YA2290	YA2519	YA2546

METHODOLOGY

YA0580	YA0641	YA0990	YA1350	YA2304	YA2491
YA2546	YA2793	YA2919	YA2961	YA2970	

DISCRIMINANT ANALYSIS
REVIEW
    YA1043   YA2701   YB0000
THEORY
    YA2918   YA2919

DISTRIBUTED LAG
See also **COMPARATIVE METHODS** — DISTRIBUTED LAG.
BIBLIOGRAPHY
    YA0046   YA1496   YA2619
EVALUATION
    YA0470
REVIEW
    YA0651   YA1496   YA2619   YB0085   YB0143   YB0168
    YB0190   YB0211

The sub-headings are broken down into specific areas of application since distributed lag models have tended to be applied to particular classes of problem, e.g. APPLICATION, Advertising. The second class of headings includes all the methodological subdivisions. The sub-headings refer to the distributed variable.

APPLICATION, Advertising

YA0241	YA0278	YA0518	YA0571	YA0705	YA0708
YA1126	YA1566	YA1665	YA1748	YA1754	YA2068
YA2372	YA2495	YA2814	YA2923	YA3174	YA3232
YA3326	YA3479	YA3602	YA3620	YA3622	YA3628
YB0064	YB0252	YB0253			

Expectations hypotheses

			YA0715	YA0826	YA0954
YA0969	YA1129	YA1685	YA2747	YA2774	YA2776
YA3070	YA3075	YA3281	YA3494	YB0155	

Income	YA0548	YA0795	YA1794	YA3763	YA3768
Interest rate	YA0275	YA0586	YA0588	YA0589	YA0662
YA0715	YA0942	YA0954	YA1272	YA2484	YA2898
YA3181	YA3281				
Investment	YA0404	YA0949	YA1550	YA1723	YA1862
YA1867	YA2416	YA2619	YA3064	YA3237	
Money	YA0071	YA0211	YA1178	YA1426	YA1588
YA1589	YA1781	YA1787	YA1831	YA2821	YA3013
YA3075	YA3126	YA3225	YA3239	YA3282	YA3599
Orders	YA0412	YA0662	YA0700	YA0997	YA1060
YA1304	YA1306	YA1444	YA1568	YA2339	YA2867
YA3110	YA3237	YA3399	YA3456	YA3519	YA3552
YB0331					

DISTRIBUTED LAG
APPLICATION

Output	YA0073	YA0175	YA0604	YA0699	YA0806
	YA1049	YA1099	YA1273	YA1862	YA2751	YA3064
	YA3065	YA3241	YA3481			

The following are methodological key words, although if a reference merely illustrates a method : APPLICATION is added to the description and the reference omitted from the index.

AGGREGATION EFFECT
YA1340 YA3451 YA3618

ALMON
YA0084 YA0593 YA0762 YA1272 YA1286 YA1306
YA1380 YA1568 YA1588 YA1589 YA2221 YA2321
YA2710 YA2867 YA3106 YA3426 YA3602 YB0259
Evaluation YA3126

ARIMA (The references describe the relationship between ARIMA models and DISTRIBUTED LAG models.) YA0046
YA0346 YA0571 YA1623 YA1665 YA2625 YA2629
YA2636 YA2705 YA2823 YA3591 YA3765 YB0034
YB0109

CROSS SECTION DATA
YA2197 YA2605

ERROR SPECIFICATION
YA0046 YA0449 YA0471 YA0662 YA0708 YA0777
YA1353 YA1496 YA1577 YA1623 YA1665 YA1679
YA1681 YA1754 YA1942 YA2241 YA2625 YA2629
YA2636 YA2705 YA2709 YA2784 YA2823 YA2849
YA3071 YA3112 YA3290 YA3315 YA3628 YA3680
YA3765 YB0034 YB0132

ESTIMATION
YA0593 YA0595 YA0732 YA0762 YA0966 YA0967
YA1272 YA1496 YA1568 YA1577 YA2105 YA2339
YA2605 YA2625 YA2710 YA3200 YA3763 YB0085
Evaluation YA3112

EVALUATION (OF MODEL SPECIFICATION)
YA0732 YA1588 YA2221 YA2477 YA3280 YA3426
YB0126 *See also* **SPECIFICATION ERROR** – LAG SPECIFICATION

HYPOTHESIS TESTS
YA1380 YA1681 YA2163 YA3110 YA3115 YA3121

IDENTIFICATION (OF APPROPRIATE LAG SPECIFICATION)
YA0449 YA0593 YA0732 YA1070 YA1071 YA1286
YA1353 YA1380 YA1496 YA1588 YA1589 YA1625

EDUCATION
  EFFECT OF

YA0114	YA0138	YA0350	YA0443	YA0633	YA0746
YA0948	YA1130	YA1207	YA1259	YA1261	YA1478
YA1498	YA1520	YA1583	YA1584	YA1641	YA1736
YA1846	YA1902	YA1989	YA2130	YA2152	YA2180
YA2181	YA2182	YA2183	YA2192	YA2240	YA2378
YA2404	YA2438	YA2444	YA2512	YA2654	YA2761
YA2794	YA2851	YA2952	YA3062	YA3123	YA3124
YA3125	YA3277	YA3560	YA3563	YA3583	YA3634
YA3699	YB0114	YB0123	YB0224		

ERROR DISTRIBUTION
  ASYMMETRICAL

YA0691	YA1183	YA2663	YA3116

  COMPOUND

YA1082	YA1084	YA2120	YA2903	YA3424

  DISCONTINUOUS, ASYMMETRIC

YA0053	YA0057

  EVALUATION
    YA1604
  LOGNORMAL

YA0049	YA0082	YA0701	YA1097	YA1632	YA1633
YA1634	YA1773	YA2367	YA2657	YA2919	YA3422
YA3647	YA3706				

  NONNORMAL

YA0219	YA1704	YA1773	YA1976	YA2368	YA2369
YA3243	YA3758				

Gamma	YA0082	YA2419	YA2978	YA3116	YB0299
Laplace	YA1784	YA3295			
Poisson	YA1051	YA3612			

  OTHER
    YA0985
  POWER LAW

YA3347	YA3647

  STABLE

YA0206	YA0377	YA0378	YA0637	YA0701	YA0774
YA1065	YA1183	YA1457	YA1537	YA1539	YA1710
YA1769	YA1888	YA1908	YA1976	YA2132	YA2367
YA2369	YA2663	YA2880	YA2881	YA2919	YA3026
YA3243	YA3289	YA3424			

T

YA0377	YA0602	YA2880	YA2881

ERROR SPECIFICATION
EVALUATION
    YA1602   YA2551

The following key words specify the assumed structure of the variance-covariance matrix.
ARIMA
    YA0571   YA1204   YA1303   YA1377   YA2625   YA2705
    YA2721   YA2819   YA3293   YA3474   YA3488   YA3546
AUTOCORRELATED
    YA0071   YA0265   YA0266   YA0326   YA0376   YA0383
    YA0591   YA0595   YA0611   YA0662   YA0678   YA0708
    YA0903   YA1049   YA1121   YA1216   YA1323   YA1353
    YA1376   YA1455   YA1534   YA1595   YA1675   YA1678
    YA1680   YA1697   YA1754   YA1756   YA1764   YA1889
    YA1942   YA1947   YA1968   YA2001   YA2084   YA2115
    YA2137   YA2193   YA2221   YA2339   YA2709   YA2784
    YA2849   YA2882   YA2907   YA3037   YA3071   YA3084
    YA3086   YA3109   YA3112   YA3120   YA3280   YA3380
    YA3392   YA3427   YA3437   YA3452   YA3490   YA3590
    YA3593   YA3595   YA3609   YA3628   YA3653   YA3710
    YA3715   YB0106   YB0249   YB0288   YB0331
    Evaluation   YA3290
AUTOCORRELATED, CORRELATED
    YA0327   YA0550   YA0608   YA0706   YA1262   YA1514
    YA1684   YA1790   YA1993   YA2734
CORRELATED
    YA0278   YA1300   YA1323   YA1992   YA2576   YA2618
    YA3379   YB0265
EFFECT OF *See* **AUTOCORRELATION** − EFFECT OF .
HETEROSCEDASTIC
    YA0082   YA0559   YA1367   YA1494   YA1612   YA1746
    YA1825   YA1923   YA2295   YA3122   YA3347   YA3647
MIXED (MULTIPLICATIVE ADDITIVE)
    YB0124
MOVING AVERAGE
    YA0557   YA0623   YA1376   YA1681   YA1942   YA2631
    YA2636   YA2695   YA2711   YA2782   YA2843   YA3516
    YA3682
MULTIPLICATIVE
    YA0049   YA0411   YA1097   YA1378   YA2127   YA2480
    YA3422   YB0125   *See also* LOGNORMAL above.

ERROR SPECIFICATION
The following are used when the reference discusses the appropriate error specification for particular types of model.
DISTRIBUTED LAG   *See* **DISTRIBUTED LAG** — ERROR SPECIFICATION.
PRODUCTION FUNCTIONS
YA0057   YA0411   YA0691   YA2120   YA2127   YA3116
REGRESSION AND SIMULTANEOUS SYSTEM
See **REGRESSION** — ESTIMATION, Error specification.
TIME SERIES *See* **TIME SERIES** — ARIMA, Identification.

ESTIMATION   These key words are used to describe the estimation of a particular type of model. *See also* **COMPARATIVE METHODS** — ESTIMATION.
ARIMA *See* **TIME SERIES** — ARIMA, Estimation.
CROSS SECTION, TIME SERIES
YA0181   YA0245   YA0493   YA0663   YA1636   YA1684
YA1844   YA2262   YA2332   YA2333   YA2513   YA2542
YA3021   YA3023   YA3378   YA3750
DISTRIBUTED LAG *See* **DISTRIBUTED LAG** — ESTIMATION.
ERROR DISTRIBUTION (used when the assumptions concerning the error distribution has implications for the estimation procedure.)
YA3243   YA3758
Stable   YA0378   YA2132
HETEROSCEDASTIC MODEL
YA1746   YA3420
LOGARITHMIC MODEL
YA0049   YA0398   YA1097   YA2940   YA3422   YB0299
REGRESSION *See* **REGRESSION** — ESTIMATION.
SIMULTANEOUS SYSTEM *See* **SIMULTANEOUS SYSTEM** — ESTIMATION.

The following are concerned with particular estimation methods.
2SLS (two stage least squares)
YA0438   YA0595   YA2454   YA2595   YA2725   YA2933
YA2974   YA3090   YA3463   YB0207   YB0235
3PLS (three pass least squares)
YA3590
3SLS (three stage least squares)
YA0328   YA2464   YA2933   YA2974   YA3630

EVALUATION

THEORY OF   This is used when the reference considers how a model, forecasting or estimation method should be evaluated.

YA0125	YA0128	YA0129	YA0131	YA0270	YA0386
YA0470	YA0683	YA0809	YA0905	YA0914	YA0939
YA1041	YA1281	YA1384	YA1408	YA1454	YA1546
YA1591	YA1599	YA1616	YA1618	YA1626	YA1767
YA1774	YA1793	YA1876	YA2286	YA2318	YA2414
YA2591	YA2621	YA2627	YA2628	YA2720	YA2820
YA2842	YA3184	YA3339	YA3354	YA3429	YA3430
YA3446	YA3587	YA3642	YA3685	YB0014	YB0043
YB0047	YB0059	YB0099	YB0108	YB0117	YB0151
YB0185	YB0228	YB0237	YB0303	YB0323	

The following key words offer evaluations of forecasts or of the methods used in forecasting the specified situation.

FORECASTS OR MODELS

of agriculture YA0944

of cash flow YA2691 YA2775

of commodities YA0816 YA2049

of construction YB0273

of consumer behaviour *See* **CONSUMER BEHAVIOUR**.

of consumption YA0795 YA0871 YA0958 YA1330 YA2486 YA2669 YA2785 YB0078 YB0219 YB0278

of earnings YA0902 YA0964 YA2759 YA3038

of electricity YA2142 YA3415

of employment YA1096

of energy YA1628 YB0016

of ex post models This key word is used when an evaluation is made of how well a model performs in forecasting compared to an alternative model, when chosen for its performance over the sample from which it was estimated. YA0871
YA1050 YA1056 YA1101 YA1116 YA1417 YA1713
YA2108 YA2194 YA2414 YA3167 YA3274 YA3526
YA3565 YA3587 YA3764 YB0195 YB0203

of exchange rates YA2662

of flow of funds YA3564

of forecast monitoring schemes YA1383

of gas supply YA2615 YA2834

of government forecasts YA3238 YA3340 YB0067 YB0210 YB0290

of inflation YA0361 YA0601 YA0888 YA1056 YA1370 YA1424 YA1426 YA1688 YA1941 YA2730 YA2871

of interest rates YA0177 YA1056 YA1250 YA2474 YA2773

EVALUATION
FORECASTS OR MODELS
of inventory YA1162　　YA3336
of investment　　　　YA0284　YA0356　YA0357　YA0806
　YA1057　YA1073　YA1431　YA1550　YA1861　YA1863
　YA1864　YA2166　YA2211　YA2570　YA2751　YA2987
　YA3083　YB0168　YB0203　YB0223　YB0277
of learning curve　　　YA0015
of Macro forecasts　　*See also* **JUDGEMENTAL FORECASTS** −
MACRO. YA0504　YA0572　YA0734　YA0862　YA0863
　YA0865　YA2018　YA2318　YA2322　YA2561　YA2562
　YA2563　YA2566　YA2712　YA3056　YA3335　YB0016
　YB0047　YB0108　YB0132　YB0266　YB0330　YB0332
of Macro models　*See* **MACRO MODELS** − EVALUATION.
of manpower　　　　YA0179　YA2388　YA3518　YA3746
of marketing and sales　YA0848　YA1162　YA1366　YA1720
　YA2082　YA2441　YA2741　YA3032　YB0155
of money　YA2149　YA2446　YA2802　YA3425
of new products　　　YA0168　YA0268　　YA2188　YA3406
　YA3486　YA3487
of petroleum　　　　YA2968
of population　　　　YA0734　YA1950　YA2121　YB0016
of portfolio selection procedures　YA0808　YA1065　YA1247
　YA1721　YA3076
of pricing models　　　YA2255　YA3053
of profits　YA2090 *See also* **JUDGEMENTAL FORECASTS** −
PROFITS.
of R & D　YA3127 *See also* **JUDGEMENTAL FORECASTS** −
R & D.
of savings　YA0548　YA0796　YA1758
of technology　*See* **TECHNOLOGICAL FORECASTING** −
EVALUATION.
of transportation　　YB0016

EX ANTE
　YA0009　YA0022　　YA0026　YA0034　　YA0065　YA0078
　YA0089　YA0109　　YA0112　YA0113　　YA0125　YA0127
　YA0129　YA0168　　YA0179　YA0243　　YA0249　YA0278
　YA0280　YA0340　　YA0345　YA0346　　YA0356　YA0357
　YA0361　YA0367　　YA0375　YA0392　　YA0395　YA0407
　YA0419　YA0447　　YA0449　YA0470　　YA0471　YA0473
　YA0501　YA0504　　YA0510　YA0535　　YA0548　YA0556
　YA0583　YA0587　　YA0623　YA0648　　YA0657　YA0674
　YA0683　YA0696　　YA0712　YA0733　　YA0738　YA0758

EX ANTE

YA0760	YA0767	YA0795	YA0796	YA0803	YA0807
YA0822	YA0844	YA0851	YA0862	YA0865	YA0871
YA0878	YA0879	YA0886	YA0918	YA0921	YA0926
YA0939	YA0976	YA0984	YA0988	YA1001	YA1003
YA1006	YA1007	YA1013	YA1028	YA1050	YA1056
YA1059	YA1062	YA1063	YA1066	YA1073	YA1077
YA1078	YA1086	YA1087	YA1096	YA1101	YA1116
YA1119	YA1125	YA1128	YA1129	YA1179	YA1187
YA1197	YA1206	YA1215	YA1218	YA1228	YA1244
YA1282	YA1284	YA1304	YA1306	YA1311	YA1318
YA1330	YA1338	YA1384	YA1395	YA1408	YA1417
YA1419	YA1420	YA1421	YA1430	YA1437	YA1440
YA1461	YA1467	YA1504	YA1507	YA1518	YA1546
YA1596	YA1654	YA1659	YA1660	YA1663	YA1665
YA1669	YA1677	YA1690	YA1697	YA1713	YA1737
YA1745	YA1815	YA1864	YA1943	YA1986	YA1987
YA2018	YA2047	YA2064	YA2091	YA2110	YA2121
YA2138	YA2142	YA2149	YA2159	YA2161	YA2166
YA2171	YA2194	YA2195	YA2223	YA2224	YA2229
YA2247	YA2249	YA2250	YA2273	YA2310	YA2314
YA2318	YA2323	YA2328	YA2357	YA2366	YA2380
YA2388	YA2390	YA2391	YA2414	YA2446	YA2450
YA2458	YA2477	YA2485	YA2503	YA2510	YA2516
YA2532	YA2545	YA2549	YA2560	YA2570	YA2590
YA2595	YA2598	YA2599	YA2604	YA2610	YA2615
YA2629	YA2630	YA2660	YA2666	YA2673	YA2678
YA2679	YA2691	YA2724	YA2732	YA2733	YA2759
YA2766	YA2770	YA2771	YA2781	YA2802	YA2808
YA2820	YA2840	YA2860	YA2862	YA2864	YA2871
YA2874	YA2876	YA2877	YA2887	YA2895	YA2899
YA2943	YA2968	YA2986	YA2988	YA3048	YA3055
YA3056	YA3058	YA3076	YA3133	YA3143	YA3144
YA3167	YA3171	YA3186	YA3202	YA3212	YA3224
YA3226	YA3238	YA3255	YA3264	YA3274	YA3322
YA3332	YA3336	YA3337	YA3338	YA3339	YA3349
YA3354	YA3361	YA3368	YA3397	YA3417	YA3444
YA3456	YA3475	YA3500	YA3503	YA3507	YA3512
YA3514	YA3525	YA3529	YA3564	YA3565	YA3574
YA3608	YA3656	YA3667	YA3668	YA3693	YA3713
YA3746	YA3754	YA3764	YB0013	YB0016	YB0044
YB0047	YB0057	YB0088	YB0089	YB0101	YB0105
YB0109	YB0126	YB0141	YB0152	YB0153	YB0155

EX ANTE
    YB0159   YB0167   YB0186   YB0193   YB0204   YB0219
    YB0223   YB0228   YB0254   YB0270   YB0294   YB0310
EXCHANGE RATE   *See also*   **APPLICATION** — **MACRO**, **INTER-**
NATIONAL FINANCE, EXCHANGE RATES.
  EFFECT OF
    YA0134   YA0145   YA0261   YA0405   YA0464   YA0612
    YA0717   YA0737   YA0739   YA0769   YA0970   YA1548
    YA1663   YA1664   YA1837   YA2003   YA2131   YA2351
    YA2565   YA2713   YA2980   YA3010   YA3551   YB0182
    YB0244
  FORWARD RATE
    YA1264   YA1534   YA1795   YA1947   YA1997   YA2260

EXOGENOUS VARIABLES
  PREDICTION OF
    YA0402   YA0767   YA0797   YA0799   YA0807   YA1078
    YA1116   YA1161   YA1306   YA1713   YA1737   YA1896
    YA2149   YA2820   YA2988   YA3107   YA3238   YB0013
    YB0105   YB0185   YB0207   YB0215

EXPECTATIONS
  DATA
    YA0109   YA0274   YA0291   YA0487   YA0548   YA0602
    YA0605   YA0606   YA0902   YA1047   YA1162   YA1231
    YA1671   YA1723   YA1885   YA1886   YA1904   YA1905
    YA2061   YA2747   YA2816   YA2898   YA2987   YA3006
    YA3429   YA3492   YA3493   YA3494   YB0101

    Evaluation   YA0018   YA0021   YA0130   YA0601   YA0711
    YA1101   YA1372   YA1882   YA2166   YA2363   YA2548
    YA2776   YA2954   YA2988   YA3029   YA3082   YA3186
    YA3322   YA3413   YB0089   YB0155   YB0185   YB0203
    YB0207   YB0228   YB0285   YB0294   YB0303
  DETERMINANTS
    YA0606   YA1024   YA1047   YA1231   YA1916   YB0155
  ESTIMATING
    YA0165   YA0606   YA0770   YA0902   YA1167   YA1229
    YA1264   YA1418   YA1422   YA1564   YA1820   YA2380
    YA2601   YA2747   YA3006   YA3102   YA3494   YA3615
    YB0155   YB0276
  METHODOLOGY
    YA2257

EXPECTATIONS
THEORY *See* **DISTRIBUTED LAG** − APPLICATION, Expectations hypotheses and **THEORY** − EXPECTATIONS.

EXPONENTIAL SMOOTHING
See also **COMPARATIVE METHODS** − EXPONENTIAL SMOOTHING.
EVALUATION
YA0019 YA0183 YA0653 YA1059 YA1062 YA1596
YA2248 YA2249 YA2266 YA2267 YA2876 YA2960
YA3055 YA3574
INTRODUCTION
YB0324
REVIEW
YA0653 YA1596 YA2755 YB0040 YB0041 YB0072
YB0181 YB0198 YB0229
THEORY
YA0431 YA0725 YA0726 YA0727 YA1383 YA1413
YA1596 YA1762 YA2158 YA2267 YA2309 YA2716
YA3495 YB0040

The following are concerned with specific aspects of exponential smoothing.

ADAPTIVE COEFFICIENTS
YA0019 YA0257 YA0535 YA2157 YA2308 YA2908
YA3215 YA3469
Evaluation YA2248 YA3271
COEFFICIENT CHOICE
YA0653 YA0727 YA2075 YA2267 YA2706 YA2716
YB0041
HIGHER ORDER (including HOLT'S, WINTERS' & BROWN'S versions)
YA0030 YA0653 YA0727 YA1383 YA1413 YA1504
YA1596 YA1907 YA2266 YA2500 YB0041
MONITORING
YA0257 YB0229
PROBABILITIES
YA0817 YA2433 YA2924

FACTOR ANALYSIS
YA2404 YB0000 YB0278 *See also* **ESTIMATION** − PRINCIPAL COMPONENTS.

FORECAST
  AGGREGATION
    YA2143 YA3171   YA3324 YA3553
  FEEDBACK
    YA1297 YA1397   YA2859 *See also* **DECISION RULES —**
    FEEDBACK
  MONITORING
    YA1393 YB0198
  REVISION
    YA0010 YA0921   YA1634 YA3361

FORECASTER-BEHAVIOUR *See also* **JUDGEMENTAL FORECASTS**
and **BOOTSTRAPPING**.
    YA0128 YA0603   YA0857 YA1172   YA1573 YA1780
    YA2996 YA3041   YB0242
  INCENTIVES
    YA0859 YA1410   YA1956

FORECASTING
  BIBLIOGRAPHY
    YB0014 YB0075   YB0212 YB0268
  INTRODUCTION
    YA0468 YA0487   YA0723 YA0980   YA1326 YA2202
    YA2226 YA2436   YA2536 YA3302   YA3387
  REVIEW
    YA0128 YA0488   YA0572 YA0635   YA1184 YA2155
    YA2324 YA2330   YA2356 YA2358   YA2359 YB0047
    YB0094 YB0108   YB0185 YB0268
  TEXT
    YB0014 YB0016   YB0021 YB0030   YB0048 YB0050
    YB0051 YB0056   YB0063 YB0071   YB0086 YB0110
    YB0121 YB0132   YB0136 YB0162   YB0177 YB0180
    YB0212 YB0214   YB0227 YB0229   YB0241 YB0255
    YB0258 YB0296   YB0303 YB0316   YB0324
  THEORY
    YA0092 YA1823   YA2600 YA2820

The following are more specific references.

ACCURACY *See also* those articles which consider special aspects of
    forecasting accuracy under, for example, **EVALUATION —**
    FORECASTS OR MODELS, of marketing and sales.
    YA0848 YB0016
COST OF
    YA0635 YA2249   YA2310 YA2353   YA2359 YB0014
    YB0051 YB0214

FORECASTING

MULTISTAGE is used to describe a sequential approach to forecasting.

YA2143 YA2248   YA2459 YA2567   YB0258

PRACTICE is used to describe the organisation of the forecasting
function and its relationship to decision-making.

YA0303 YA1200   YA1506 YA1780   YA2275 YA2826
YA3032 YA3324   YA3649 YA3759   YB0047 YB0063
YB0212 YB0268   YB0305 YB0316   YB0324

USAGE is used to describe the frequency of use of various forecasting techniques.

YA0184 YA0467   YA0848 YA1079   YA1184 YA1200
YA1296 YA1701   YA2358 YA2585   YA2588 YA2589
YA3032 YA3649   YB0212 YB0268   YB0305

VALUE OF

YA0456 YA0457   YA0520 YA0866   YA1184 YA1397
YA1571 YA1815   YA1887 YA2052   YA2425 YA3146
YA3191 YA3619   YB0014 YB0063   YB0158 YB0300
YB0324

HEALTH

SERVICES

YA0924 YA0927   YA1666 YA2804   YA3548 YA3740
YB0027 YB0137   YB0168

The following are more specific references. *See also* **COST** —
SECTOR (OR FIRM) : **Health**, and **PRICE** — **SECTOR (OR FIRM)** :
Health.

ACCIDENTS   *See*   **APPLICATION** — **SECTOR (OR FIRM)**:
SOCIAL (AND PERSONAL), **Accidents**.

BLOOD AVAILABILITY

YA0829 YA1248

DISEASE, INCIDENCE OF

YA0821 YA1265   YA1620 YA2128   YA2845 YA3725

EFFECT OF

YA0746 YA1890   YA2240

FAMILY PLANNING

YA3507

HOSPITAL

YA0927 YA1103   YA1105 YA1154   YA1157 YA1158
YA1221 YA1662   YA1666 YA2096   YA2373 YA2467
YA2793 YA3177   YA3740
Finance   YA0881   YA1061
Manpower YA1791   YA2962 YB0066

HEALTH
HOSPITAL
Patient facilities		YA0668	YA0875	YA0882	YA1907
	YA2467	YA2605	YA3610		
Psychiatric	YA1235	YA2434	YA3470		

INSURANCE
YA0372 YA1158

MANPOWER
YA3740

Earnings	YA0505	YA0507	YA1104	YA2804	YA3333
GPs	YA1590				
Nurses	YA0301	YA0889	YA1791	YB0066	
Physicians	YA0505	YA0507	YA1104	YA2958	YA2962
	YA3177	YA3333			

HETEROSCEDASTICITY   *See* under **SPECIFICATION ERROR**.

INCOME
EFFECT OF
YA0008	YA0032	YA0034	YA0062	YA0125	YA0166
YA0182	YA0208	YA0312	YA0316	YA0327	YA0370
YA0430	YA0499	YA0500	YA0548	YA0600	YA0609
YA0688	YA0746	YA0752	YA0777	YA0795	YA0796
YA0802	YA0835	YA0836	YA0838	YA0854	YA0871
YA0885	YA0899	YA0949	YA0958	YA0973	YA0975
YA0976	YA1156	YA1169	YA1217	YA1223	YA1268
YA1313	YA1356	YA1396	YA1465	YA1520	YA1559
YA1566	YA1659	YA1674	YA1696	YA1729	YA1756
YA1802	YA1813	YA1821	YA1873	YA1892	YA1894
YA1921	YA1953	YA1958	YA1963	YA1966	YA2005
YA2086	YA2159	YA2160	YA2197	YA2204	YA2205
YA2347	YA2404	YA2422	YA2446	YA2502	YA2503
YA2545	YA2549	YA2556	YA2557	YA2643	YA2677
YA2714	YA2736	YA2746	YA2748	YA2750	YA2794
YA2812	YA2852	YA2863	YA2890	YA2911	YA2914
YA2968	YA2986	YA2995	YA3017	YA3042	YA3168
YA3181	YA3270	YA3285	YA3318	YA3358	YA3360
YA3401	YA3415	YA3425	YA3533	YA3548	YA3554
YA3567	YA3641	YA3701	YA3723	YA3726	YB0013
YB0123	YB0126	YB0169	YB0178	YB0288	

EFFECT OF, Determinants
YA2205

Evaluation YA0802 YA3723

INCOME
EFFECT OF, Distribution
YA1223
PERMANENT , Effect of   *See also*   **THEORY** − PERMANENT
INCOME, EVALUATION.

YA0157	YA0158	YA0855	YA1069	YA1364	YA1730
YA1758	YA2055	YA2124	YA2165	YA2477	YA2670
YA2786	YA2795	YA2817	YA3249	YA3251	YA3497
YA3531	YA3561	YA3679	YA3757	YB0219	

INDEX NUMBERS
EVALUATION
YA0496 YA3462   YA3471
METHODOLOGY

YA0294	YA0496	YA0622	YA0782	YA0837	YA0868
YA1536	YA2107	YA3209	YA3471	YA3743	

TEXT
YB0134
THEORY
YA0287 YA0288   YA1293

MACRO
Consumer confidence	YA0024	YA1798	YA1886	YA1914
YA2234 YA2473	YA2815	YA3437	YB0294	
Consumer price	YA0091	YA0868	YA2293	YA3210
YA3471				
Employment vacancies	YA0546	YA0547	YA0828	YA1192
YA1860 YB0269				
Fiscal and monetary policy		YA0226	YA0740	YA2316
Other	YA0496	YA1021	YA1293	YB0279

SECTOR
Construction		YA0343	YA0837	YA1358 YA2293
YA3743				
Consumer goods		YA0782	YA3462	
Finance	YA1247	YA1328	YA1715	YA2957
Health	YA3465			
Social	YA1209	YA2192	YA2361	

INDUSTRIAL DYNAMICS
APPLICATION
Firm	YA1735	YA3703	YA3718	YB0073 YB0242
YB0280				
Macro	YA1220	YB0112	YB0164	YB0216
Sector	YA3409	YA3410		

INDUSTRIAL DYNAMICS
APPLICATION
Urban	YA2606	YA2979		
World	YA2417	YA2647	YB0062	YB0220

REVIEW
    YA0534 YA2647   YA3191 YB0073
    See also **SYSTEMS THEORY**

INFLATION
    YA2871
REVIEW
    YA2065 YA2461   YA2646

The following are more specific references

DETERMINANTS *See also* PHILLIPS CURVE below.

YA0037	YA0186	YA0292	YA0336	YA0385	YA0529
YA0553	YA0632	YA0901	YA0970	YA1026	YA1056
YA1091	YA1102	YA1131	YA1178	YA1340	YA1417
YA1418	YA1421	YA1422	YA1423	YA1426	YA1442
YA1688	YA1941	YA2063	YA2064	YA2327	YA2483
YA2560	YA2641	YA2730	YA2743	YA2770	YA2771
YA2827	YA2866	YA2868	YA2869	YA2871	YA2896
YA2965	YA3014	YA3143	YA3164	YA3197	YA3338
YA3468	YA3550	YA3572	YA3593	YA3687	YB0017
YB0022	YB0061	YB0069	YB0226	YB0256	YB0260
YB0298					

Earnings   YA0035

YA0962	YA1424	YA1551	YA1601	
YA2257	YA2707	YA2759	YA3161	YA3220	YA3457
YA3570	YA3571	YA3594		

EFFECT OF

YA0120	YA0368	YA0459	YA0548	YA0591	YA0592
YA0871	YA0891	YA0903	YA0928	YA0961	YA1021
YA1026	YA1163	YA1271	YA1273	YA1582	YA1671
YA1725	YA1738	YA1758	YA1786	YA1818	YA1884
YA1886	YA1920	YA1948	YA2028	YA2160	YA2185
YA2199	YA2233	YA2237	YA2256	YA2274	YA2482
YA2503	YA2599	YA2662	YA2747	YA2766	YA2778
YA2862	YA2898	YA3072	YA3074	YA3131	YA3181
YA3322	YA3331	YA3466	YA3516	YA3527	YA3569
YA3615	YA3734				

EXPECTATIONS

YA0109	YA0601	YA0602	YA0605	YA0606	YA0826
YA0902	YA0903	YA0928	YA0961	YA1056	YA1102
YA1127	YA1167	YA1231	YA1271	YA1346	YA1396
YA1418	YA1422	YA1671	YA1818	YA1884	YA1886

INTERVENTION
　　　YA0191　YA0452　　YA1907　YA2838
　　　See also　**TIME SERIES** — ARIMA, **Intervention**.

JUDGEMENTAL FORECASTS
　BIBLIOGRAPHY
　　　YA3263　YA3719
　EVALUATION　*See also*　under areas of application below.
　　　YA0014　YA0268　　YA0332　YA0822　　YA0883　YA0944
　　　YA1971　YA2164　　YA2529　YA2544　　YA2657　YA2963
　　　YA3334　YA3555　　YB0015　YB0228　　YB0290
　REVIEW
　　　YA0142　YA2527　　YA3263　YB0136

The following are more specific references.

AGGREGATION
　　　YA2164　YA3324
BIAS
　　　YA3041　YA3350　　YA3486　YA3586
DETERMINANTS
　　　YA0010　YA0064　　YA0387　YA0461　　YA1905　YA2775
　　　YA3041　YA3102　　YA3127　YA3148　　YA3341　YA3719
INCORPORATION (into quantitative models)
　　　See also **COMBINING FORECASTS** and **MACROECONOMIC**
　　　MODEL — METHODOLOGY, Adjustments.
　　　YA0544　YA0657　　YA0822　YA1546　　YA1767　YA1881
　　　YA2068　YA2935　　YA3372　YA3696
LEARNING
　　　YA0014　YA1632　　YA1633　YA1634　　YA1956　YA1957
　　　YA1970　YA1971
　Evaluation　YA1957　YA1970
METHODOLOGY
　　　YA0190　YA0274　　YA0543　YA0545　　YA1253　YA1573
　　　YA1854　YA2217　　YA2517　YA2681　　YA2959　YA3029
　　　YA3496　YA3696　　YB0014
OCCULT
　　　YA2997
PROBABILITIES AND UNCERTAINTY
　　　YA0274　YA0540　　YA0543　YA1468　　YA1573　YA2501
　　　YA2544　YA2657　　YA2681　YA3029　　YA3102
SPECIALIST
　　　YA0129　YA0864　　YA1116　YA1809　　YA1939　YA2457
　　　YA2594　YA2657　　YA2718　YA2963　　YA3324　YA3361
　　　YA3610　YA3754　　YA3755　YB0047

JUDGEMENTAL FORECASTS
SPECIALIST
Evaluation YA0064   YA0212 YA0231   YA0510 YA0794
YA0812   YA1385   YA1491 YA2973   YA3045 YB0015

The following are concerned with different areas of application.

MACRO, Evaluation *See also* TURNING POINTS below.
    YA0862 YA0864   YA0865   YA1116   YA2018 YA2319
    YA3335 YA3361   YA3754   YA3755   YB0047

PROFITS, Evaluation
    YA0010 YA0200   YA0473   YA0510   YA0794 YA0812
    YA1062 YA1720   YA1809   YA2223   YA2973 YA3045
    YA3350

R & D, Evaluation
    YA0190 YA2151   YA3041   YA3127

STOCK PRICES, Evaluation
    YA0212 YA1491   YA1721   YA1956   YA2154 YA2594
    YA3719

TURNING POINTS
    YA0603 YA1172   YA3334

KALMAN FILTER
See **ESTIMATION** − KALMAN FILTER.

LAG − FIXED
    YA0449 YA0724   YA1512   YA1578   YA1705 YA2820
    YA3244

LEAD TIME
EFFECT OF
    YA0129 YA0342   YA0906   YA1007   YA1125 YA1384
    YA1571 YA1618   YA1764   YA1977   YA2062 YA2142
    YA2166 YA2194   YA2323   YA2328   YA2355 YA2526
    YA2629 YA2630   YA2943   YA2987   YA3274 YA3555
    YA3610 YA3713   YA3729   YB0016   YB0041 YB0047
    YB0185 YB0187

LEARNING CURVE
See also **COST** − LEARNING CURVE.
    YA0015 YA0728   YA1995   YA2146   YA3352

LIFE CYCLE
CONSUMER
    YA1159 YA1530   YA2162   YA2937   YB0219

FAMILY
    YA0419 YA0929   YA1236   YA1716

LIFE CYCLE
  FIRM
      YA1433 YA3360
  PRODUCT
      YA0624 YA0976   YA1433 YA2156   YA2409 YA2740
      YA3352 YA3478   YB0030 YB0051   YB0253
   Declining   YA2500
   Evaluation   YA0495   YA0789 YA0938   YA1185 YA2857
   Introduction   YA0635 *See also*   **NEW PRODUCT**

LINEAR PROGRAMMING
(and MATHEMATICAL PROGRAMMING)
      YA0026 YA0105   YA0132 YA0133   YA0331 YA0646
      YA0823 YA0825   YA1485 YA1486   YA1632 YA1633
      YA1940 YA1972   YA2007 YA2263   YA2547 YA2651
      YA2853 YA3433   YA3476 YB0145   YB0282 YB0306

LONG TERM FORECASTING
      YA0129 YA0190   YA0202 YA0246   YA0298 YA0331
      YA0339 YA0502   YA0504 YA0630   YA0734 YA0955
      YA1000 YA1200   YA1315 YA1384   YA1597 YA1682
      YA1699 YA1777   YA1805 YA1823   YA1995 YA1998
      YA2076 YA2184   YA2227 YA2252   YA2398 YA2457
      YA2889 YA2962   YA3060 YA3100   YA3349 YA3397
      YA3500 YB0014   YB0016 YB0024   YB0031 YB0083
      YB0092 YB0099   YB0108 YB0116   YB0128 YB0153
      YB0187 YB0232   YB0263 YB0326
   Evaluation   YA0734   YB0083

LOSS FUNCTIONS
  EVALUATION
      YA0661 YA0905   YA1454 YA2268   YA2621 YB0223
      YB0300
  METHODOLOGY
      YA3446 YA3685   YA3688
  REVIEW
      YA1449 YA1454   YA2842
  THEORY
      YA0664 YA0904   YA0939 YA1408   YA1616 YA1876
      YA1985 YA3431

The following discuss particular statistical criteria.

ABSOLUTE ERROR
      YA1888

LOSS FUNCTIONS
AKAIKE'S INFORMATION CRITERION
YA0061 YA0427 YA0571 YA1626 YA1859 YA2143
YA2268 YA2594 YA2704 YA3089 YA3464 YB0308
ASYMMETRICAL
YA0053 YA0374 YA3688 YA3713 YB0223
CP
YA3441 YA3442
THEIL
YA0386 YA2139 YA2318 YA2720

The following touch on the loss functions appropriate for particular situations.

FIRM
YA0199 YA0866 YA1807 YA2210 YA3433
Inventory control YA0260 YA0362 YA1040 YA1644
YA1227 YA2547 YA2685
Maintenance YA0374
Production control YA0362 YA0661 YB0302
Project planning YA1970
MACRO
YA0445 YA0471 YA0472 YA0799 YA0800 YA1312
YA1714 YA1795 YA2703 YA3220 YB0058 YB0302
SECTOR
Agriculture YA2942
Finance, trading rules YA0366 YA1913 YA2140 YA2392
YA2882
Government, local YA1760

MACROECONOMIC MODEL
The following is a list of macroeconomic models by country or government.
AFRICA
YA3259
AUSTRALIA
YA1540 YB0262
AUSTRIA
YB0311
BELGIUM
YB0311
CANADA
YA0618 YA0865 YA0921 YA1718 YA3096 YA3482
YA3483

MACROECONOMIC MODEL
CANADA

MACROECONOMIC MODEL
UK (cont.)

Cambridge	YA0361	YA0813	YA3287	YB0108	YB0326
Cambridge growth		YA0202	YB0292		
Klein	YA1511				
LBS	YA0187	YA0475	YA2095	YA2561	YA2562
YA2563	YA2564	YA2566	YA2568	YB0108	YB0167
YB0269	YB0311				
NIESR	YA0888	YA2095	YA2561	YA2562	YA2563
YA2564	YA2566	YA2567	YA2568	YB0108	YB0154
YB0167	YB0236	YB0246	YB0247	YB0248	YB0269
YB0297					
Southampton		YB0154	YB0256	YB0269	

US

YA0013	YA0314	YA0673	YA0677	YA0682	YA0751
YA1270	YA1312	YA1341	YA1397	YA1699	YA1777
YA1934	YA1994	YA2259	YA2397	YA2591	YA2673
YA2833	YA3339	YB0112	YB0153	YB0190	YB0251
YB0257	YB0332				

USSR

YA3185   YB0133

WEST INDIES

YA1011   YA1013

The following is a list of particular macroeconomic models of the US by the names of the originator(s) or institutions.

BEA

YA1284	YA1713	YA1714	YA2194	YB0187

BROOKINGS

YA0682	YA0996	YA1100	YA1283	YA1284	YA1285
YA1420	YA1499	YA2478	YA3100	YB0043	YB0090
YB0091	YB0117	YB0150			

CHASE

YA2166   YA2323

DATA RESOURCES

YA0485	YA1028	YA1284	YA1416	YA1714	YA2166
YA2323	YA2485	YB0187			

FAIR

YA0678	YA0758	YA1112	YA1115	YA1116	YA1119
YA1120	YA1284	YA1714	YA2319	YB0104	YB0105
YB0187	YB0273				

FRB, MIT

YA0007	YA0682	YA1078	YA2532	YA2828	YB0290

MACROECONOMIC MODEL

FRB, MIT, PENN

YA0356	YA0548	YA0765	YA0766	YA0767	YA1073
YA1125	YA1408	YA1799	YA1910	YA2598	YA2604
YA2858	YA2860	YA3373	YA3768	YB0069	YB0129
YB0150	YB0241	YB0262	YB0269	YB0273	YB0290

FRIEND et al.

YA1055	YA2840	YA3339	YB0152

KLEIN

YA0325	YA0489	YA0528	YA0569	YA0619	YA1355
YA1627	YA1675	YA1801	YA2328	YA2900	YA3118
YA3339	YA3617	YA3767	YB0152	YB0286	YB0302

KLEIN GOLDBERGER

YA0437	YA0570	YA0670	YA1763	YB0286	YB0301

LIU

YA3339

LIU (MONTHLY)

YA0527	YA1284	YA2193	YA2194	YB0151	YB0187

MICHIGAN

YA0672	YA0681	YA0682	YA1714	YA1731	YA1799
YA1803	YA2018	YA2485	YA2532	YA2673	YA3337
YA3754	YB0138	YB0187			

MIT, PENN, SSRC

YA0107	YA0388	YA0434	YA0484	YA0799	YA0800
YA1077	YA1117	YA1284	YA1442	YA1714	YA1896
YA2472	YA2474	YA2827	YA3202	YB0187	

OBE

YA0682	YA1546	YA1881	YA2673	YA3339	YB0105
YB0141	YB0150	YB0262			

OMB

YA1055	YA1831	YA2058	YA2327

ST. LOUIS

YA0089	YA0095	YA0445	YA0594	YA0681	YA0763
YA0764	YA0765	YA0767	YA1055	YA1284	YA1395
YA1546	YA1588	YA1714	YA2012	YA2259	YA2411
YA2507	YA2672	YA2840	YA2864	YA3202	YA3225
YB0107	YB0187				

WHARTON

YA0022	YA0024	YA0617	YA0682	YA1001	YA1055
YA1100	YA1269	YA1284	YA1546	YA1714	YA1766
YA1799	YA1881	YA2166	YA2194	YA2323	YA2485
YA2590	YA2673	YA2889	YA3201	YA3361	YA3468
YA3480	YA3754	YB0038	YB0101	YB0105	YB0141
YB0151	YB0207	YB0208	YB0263	YB0294	YB0311

MACROECONOMIC MODELS
BIBLIOGRAPHY
    YA3175 YA3185   YA3482
EVALUATION

YA0107	YA0184	YA0361	YA0475	YA0677	YA0682
YA0767	YA0888	YA0922	YA0939	YA1055	YA1100
YA1116	YA1282	YA1283	YA1284	YA1285	YA1420
YA1499	YA1546	YA1713	YA1714	YA1767	YA1881
YA2095	YA2166	YA2194	YA2259	YA2313	YA2318
YA2323	YA2485	YA2564	YA2604	YA2840	YA2860
YA2871	YA3184	YA3202	YA3337	YA3361	YA3480
YA3754	YB0015	YB0105	YB0116	YB0138	YB0141
YB0152	YB0164	YB0167	YB0187	YB0207	YB0210
YB0244	YB0247	YB0248	YB0262	YB0266	YB0290

Review   YB0303
METHODOLOGY

YA0617	YA1398	YA1718	YA1766	YA1896	YA2474
YA2889	YA3468	YB0151	YB0166	YB0185	YB0215
YB0251	YB0266	YB0309			

Adjustments of the forecasts by the modeller YA0617 YA1546
    YA1767 YA1881   YA3372 YB0105   YB0141 YB0207
    See also **JUDGEMENTAL FORECASTS** − INCORPORATION.
Control *See* **CONTROL THEORY**.
Solution describes how the endogenous variables can be found in
    terms of the exogenous.   YA0617   YA1115   YA2614
    Stability   YA2532
MICRO MODELS describes the relationship between microanalytic
    models and macro models.
    YA0025 YA0314   YA1691 YA2018   YB0098 YB0273
REVIEW AND TEXT

YA0339	YA0818	YA0939	YA1281	YA1397	YA1579
YA2194	YA3175	YA3480	YA3615	YB0038	YB0059
YB0146	YB0166	YB0190	YB0258	YB0290	YB0294
YB0303	YB0324				

THEORY
    YA0818 YA1397   YA1579 YA3615

MANPOWER PLANNING The user should also refer to the following
manpower studies: **APPLICATION** − **MACRO (or SECTOR)** :
EMPLOYMENT or UNEMPLOYMENT. References listed here are concerned with more specific aspects of manpower policy and are often
based on cross-sectional survey material. First we list the area of application. In the second set of key words we list major concerns of
manpower policy.
    FIRM
        YA0179 YA0228   YA0563 YA0575   YA0721 YA1368

MANPOWER PLANNING

FIRM (cont.)

YA1744	YA1915	YA1926	YA2172	YA2269	YA2270
YA2271	YA2364	YA2388	YA2390	YA2434	YA2680
YA3135	YA3434	YA3518	YA3529	YA3530	YA3744
YB0282					

MACRO

YA0008	YA0339	YA1038	YA1153	YA1260	YA2766
YA2906	YA3566	YB0005	YB0093	YB0106	YB0226
YB0233					

Demand YA1438 YA3455 YB0282

Supply YA0008 YA0048 YA0429 YA0442 YA0836

YA1325	YA1470	YA1653	YA1734	YA1759	YA1925
YA1996	YA2201	YA3017	YA3020	YA3565	YA3580
YB0017					

REGIONAL

YA0629	YA0835	YA1337	YA1471	YA1583	YA1902
YA2101	YA2152	YA2153	YA2192	YA2541	YA2962
YA3142	YA3384	YA3385			

REVIEW, TEXT AND METHODOLOGY

YA0041	YA1667	YB0024	YB0066	YB0199	YB0282
YB0310	YB0321				

Studies relevant to particular sectors are listed below.

SECTOR

YA0312	YA0699	YA0974	YA1525	YA1586	YA2654
YA2675	YA2737	YA3559	YB0245		

Construction YA1347

Education YB0304

Schools YA0193 YA1445 YA3105 YA3489

Universities YA0179 YA1415 YA1572 YA1692

YA1726	YA1744	YA1833	YA1851	YA1915	YA2388
YA2438	YA2680	YA3135	YA3279	YA3434	YA3485

Government

Central YA0227 YA0752 YA1037 YA1926 YA3058
YB0066

Local and regional YA3105 YA3349

Military YA0079 YA1080 YA2390 YA3704 YB0282
YB0321

Health YA0301 YA0505 YA0507 YA0889 YA1104

YA1590	YA1791	YA2434	YA2804	YA2958	YA2962
YA3177	YA3333	YA3740	YB0066		

Production YA0733 YA2181 YA2303 YA2464 YB0310
YB0321

Services YA1258 YA3160 YA3518

MANPOWER PLANNING
The following discuss particular manpower problems
ABSENCE
   YA2844   YA2845
DISCRIMINATION
   Racial *See also* **MANPOWER PLANNING** — EARNINGS, for
   studies which implicitly touch on discrimination.
   YA0337   YA0741   YA1256   YA1415   YA1441   YA1555
   YA1584   YA1593   YA1641   YA1672   YA1726   YA1846
   YA2130   YA2182   YA2183   YA2654   YA3124   YA3277
   YA3538   YB0168
   Sex   YA0665   YA0773   YA1133   YA1242   YA1833
   YA2179   YA2182   YA2364   YA2760   YA2851   YA3135
   YA3393   YA3489
EARNINGS   These studies purport to explain an individual's earn-
   ings rather than aggregate earnings, referenced earlier under
   APPLICATION — **MACRO** : EARNINGS etc.
   YA0137   YA0313   YA0507   YA0665   YA0773   YA1038
   YA1207   YA1242   YA1259   YA1261   YA1337   YA1415
   YA1572   YA1584   YA1629   YA1631   YA1641   YA1652
   YA1709   YA1736   YA1846   YA1911   YA1915   YA1959
   YA1989   YA2118   YA2180   YA2181   YA2182   YA2183
   YA2201   YA2240   YA2254   YA2364   YA2378   YA2438
   YA2512   YA2654   YA2682   YA2952   YA3027   YA3113
   YA3135   YA3160   YA3277   YA3279   YA3428   YA3485
   YA3489   YA3549   YA3559   YA3560   YA3563   YA3634
   YB0114
   Female   YA0665   YA1133   YA1833
EDUCATION (and TRAINING) PROGRAMS
   YA0137   YA0176   YA1259   YA1369   YA1522   YA1959
   YA2337   YA2607   YA2877   YA2952
EMPLOYMENT VACANCIES *See also* **INDEX NUMBERS** —
   MACRO, Employment vacancies.
   YA0666   YA1732   YA2726   YA3606
INDUSTRIAL COMPOSITION
   YA1846   YA1963   YA2421   YA2675   YA3559
INDUSTRIAL MOBILITY
   YA2176   YA3526
LABOUR FORCE COMPOSITION   This key word is used when
   socio-demographic data is used to explain a manpower variable
   such as ABSENCE.
   YA0963   YA0974   YA1038   YA1118   YA1160   YA1261
   YA1441   YA1584   YA1593   YA1846   YA1890   YA1911

MANPOWER PLANNING
LABOUR FORCE COMPOSITION (cont.)
   YA2035 YA2118 YA2130 YA2201 YA2512 YA2675
   YA2682 YA2766 YA2769 YA2772 YA2906 YA3027
   YA3113 YA3206 YA3284 YA3393 YA3461 YA3560
   YA3565 YA3568 YA3570 YA3634
LABOUR PARTICIPATION
   YA0312 YA0313 YA0919 YA0963 YA1118 YA1210
   YA1412 YA1477 YA1652 YA2035 YA2689 YA2768
   YA2769 YA2906 YA3284 YA3385 YA3460 YA3461
   YA3565 YA3566 YA3568 YB0093
  Female YA0193 YA0301 YA0746 YA0889 YA1445
   YA1470 YA1478 YA1520 YA1650 YA1963 YA1996
   YA2201 YA2444 YA2608 YA3016 YA3017 YA3359
   YB0033
LABOUR TURNOVER
   YA0442 YA0563 YA0721 YA0961 YA0962 YA1160
   YA1181 YA1207 YA1257 YA1521 YA1553 YA2102
   YA2271 YA2319 YA2390 YA2465 YA2737 YA2761
   YA3144 YA3460 YA3461 YA3530 YA3538
MIGRATION
   YA0744 YA0987 YA0989 YA1181 YA3062 YA3272
   YA3573 YA3748
PROMOTION
   YA0563 YA1744 YA1915 YA1926 YA2388 YA2389
   YA3434 YA3700 YA3746 YB0282
QUALIFIED MANPOWER
   YA0079 YA1562 YA2043 YA2172 YA2438 YA2457
   YA2952 YA3135 YA3279 YA3630 YA3699 YB0005
   YB0304 YB0310
  Engineers YA2181 YA2378
  Graduates YA1989 YA2180 YB0114
  Professional YA0744 YA1258 YA1692 YA2962
  Science Degrees YA1260 YA1736 YA1851
SECONDARY LABOUR MARKETS
   YA3206
TECHNOLOGY
   YA3356
UNEMPLOYMENT
   YA0337 YA1038 YA1181 YA1593 YA2130 YA2179
   YA2949 YB0054

MANPOWER PLANNING
  UNEMPLOYMENT (cont.)
    Duration   YA0167   YA0215   YA0337   YA1160   YA1208
    YA1241   YA1243   YA1890   YA2298   YA3344

MARKET POSITION
    YA0707   YA1106   YA2302   YA3509

MARKET POTENTIAL
    YA0119   YA0125   YA0236   YA0506   YA0745   YA0790
    YA0876   YA1690   YA2792   YA3138   YA3219   YA3325
    YA3508
  DISAGGREGATION
    YA0235
  EVALUATION
    YA2829
  TEXT
    YB0160

MARKET SEGMENTATION
    YA0106   YA0147   YA0148   YA0166   YA0279   YA0381
    YA0382   YA0391   YA0506   YA0608   YA0832   YA0959
    YA0984   YA1058   YA1205   YA1236   YA1240   YA1332
    YA1462   YA1689   YA1716   YA2129   YA2135   YA2262
    YA2404   YA2518   YA2557   YA2793   YA2930   YA2936
    YA3171   YA3629   YA3674   YA3695   YA3702   YA3770
    YB0000   YB0160
  EVALUATION
    YA0982   YA2393

MARKET SHARE
  ADVERTISING *See* **ADVERTISING** − DETERMINANTS.
  EFFECT OF
    YA0237   YA0240   YA0393   YA0518   YA0567   YA0624
    YA1185   YA1298   YA1808   YA3097   YA3128   YA3196
    YA3707   YB0109   YB0194
  EVALUATION (OF MARKET SHARE MODELS)
    YA1366   YA2441   YA2741
  INTRODUCTION
    YA3139
  METHODOLOGY
    YA0146   YA0277   YA0290   YA0537   YA0960   YA2189
    YA2576   YA2593   YA3212
  REVIEW
    YB0253

MARKET SHARE
THEORY
      YA2098   YA2300   YA3506

The following give the sector in which the market share is determined.

SECTOR
      YA2749   YB0237

Consumer durables	YA0235	YA0537	YA0783	YA1108
YA1143	YA2069	YA2071	YA2442	YA3199	YA3724
YA3760	YB0186			
Consumer non durables	YA0149	YA0238	YA0242	YA0278
YA0706	YA0707	YA0780	YA0960	YA1747	YA1748
YA1753	YA1978	YA2068	YA2070	YA2314	YA2441
YA2513	YA2723	YA2741	YA2813	YA2814	YA2884
YA2934	YA3097	YA3172	YA3174	YA3212	YA3232
YA3490	YA3506	YA3509	YA3510	YA3627	YA3673
YA3707	YA3708	YA3773	YB0028	YB0279	
Finance	YB0205			
Production	YA2217	YA2939		
Retailing	YA0235	YA2922		
Transport	YA2578	YA3138	YA3140	

MARKOV MODELS
APPLICATION

Brand choice	YA0382	YA1140	YA2186	YA3509
YA3651	YB0218			
Health	YA0821	YA0829	YA0875	
Manpower	YA0227	YA0228	YA0919	YA1368	YA2172
YA2176	YA2254	YA2270	YA2388	YA2434	YA3058
YA3349	YA3434	YA3460	YA3470	YA3518	YA3529
YA3530	YB0066	YB0304		
Stock prices	YA0584	YA1182		
Other	YA0090	YA1003	YA2263	YA3505

ESTIMATION
      YA0738   YA0772   YA0911   YA1108   YA2123   YA2187
      YA2263   YA3651

EVALUATION
      YA2405

METHODOLOGY
      YA0227   YA0652   YA0821   YA2314   YA3651

THEORY
      YA1003   YA3434

MAXIMUM LIKELIHOOD
See **ESTIMATION** — MAXIMUM LIKELIHOOD.

MIS

YA0087	YA0745	YA1184	YA1359	YA1780	YA1969
YA2178	YA2356	YA2492	YA2496	YA2529	YA2587
YA3320	YB0030	YB0110	YB0180	YB0255	

MODEL-BUILDING THEORY *See* **THEORY** — MODELLING.

MODEL IDENTIFICATION
See also **TIME SERIES** — ARIMA, Identification.

YA0152	YA1147	YA2108	YA3589

MODEL INTERPRETATION

YA0105	YA0126	YA1255	YA1788	YA2036	YA2109
YA2215					

MODEL SELECTION *See also* **BAYESIAN** — MODEL SELECTION, **REGRESSION** or **SIMULTANEOUS SYSTEM** — MODEL CHOICE, and **COMPARATIVE METHODS** — MODEL SELECTION.

YA0061	YA0126	YA0152	YA0153	YA0155	YA0218
YA0447	YA0657	YA0939	YA1036	YA1111	YA1599
YA2036	YA2369	YA2480	YA2630	YA2763	YA2785
YA2820	YA2900	YA2960	YA2972	YA3354	YB0110
YB0121	YB0195	YB0222	YB0327		

EVALUATION

YA1608	YA2108	YA2414

MONITORING *See* **FORECAST** — MONITORING.

MULTICOLLINEARITY
EFFECT OF

YA0156	YA0320	YA0791	YA1155	YA1367	YA1466
YA1483	YA1523	YA1741	YA1831	YA2219	YA2236
YA2800	YA3091	YA3376	YA3381	YA3543	YA3609
YA3613					

REMOVAL OF

YA0315	YA0320	YA0521	YA0626	YA0628	YA0658
YA0693	YA1110	YA1543	YA1609	YA1614	YA2105
YA2343	YA2384	YA2405	YA3156	YA3584	YB0278

REVIEW

YA1148	YA2109	YB0240

TESTS

YA1148	YA1543	YA2038	YA2671	YA3229	YA3539
YB0278					

MULTIDIMENSIONAL SCALING
YA0707   YA2129   YA3048   YA3509   YB0000

MULTIPLIERS
INPUT OUTPUT
YB0120
MACRO
YA0024 YA0356   YA0465 YA0489   YA0612 YA0674
YA0683 YA1001   YA1100 YA1282   YA1284 YA1355
YA1436 YA1478   YA1700 YA1713   YA1803 YA1994
YA2397 YA2411   YA2672 YA2889   YA3165 YA3202
YB0101 YB0150   YB0151 YB0153   YB0161 YB0187
YB0263
METHODOLOGY
YA0489 YA1355   YA2168 YA3118   YA3292 YB0185
YB0258
REGIONAL
YA0022 YA2034
SECTOR
YA1467 YA1955

MULTIVARIATE METHODS
TEXT
YB0000 *See also* the names of the various methods, **AID**,
CLUSTER ANALYSIS, etc.

NEW PRODUCTS
APPLICATION is concerned with general procedures for forecasting
the performance of a new product.
YA1463 YA1655   YB0169 YB0218   YB0242

The following have more specific concerns.
ADVERTISING
YA0712 YA2575   YA2739 YA3231
COST AND PRICING
YA3433 YA3739
DIFFUSION MODEL
YA0003 YA0233   YA0329 YA0955   YA0956 YA1369
YA2344 YA2577   YA2623 YA3008
EVALUATION AND TESTING
YA0000 YA0042   YA0150 YA0168   YA0332 YA0375
YA0712 YA0955   YA1090 YA2135   YA2217 YA2491
YA2723 YA2749   YA3211 YA3226   YA3405 YA3413
YA3486 YA3487   YA3510 YA3511   YB0048 YB0051

NEW PRODUCTS
  IDENTIFYING
      YA0983 YA1654   YA2935 YA2936   YA2961 YA3406
      YA3509 YB0000
  NEW BRAND
      YA0000 YA0332   YA0754 YA1034   YA1362 YA1804
      YA2177 YA2186   YA2253 YA2723   YA2739 YA3048
      YA3226 YA3486   YA3509 YA3625

NON LINEAR PROGRAMMING
See **LINEAR (and MATHEMATICAL) PROGRAMMING**.

NON PARAMETRIC (METHODS)
      YA0295 YA1494   YA1595 YA2972   YA3120 YA3453

NUMERICAL METHODS
  CALCULATION ERROR
      YA0270 YA0914   YA1212 YA2345   YA2534 YA3601
  EQUATION SOLUTION
      YA0841 YA0912   YA1269 YA2614
  MATRIX DECOMPOSITION
      YA0365
  OPTIMISATION
      YA0568 YA0678   YA0992 YA1114   YA1120 YA1299
      YA2377 YA2926   YA3396
    Search   YA1088   YA2451 YA2940

PATH ANALYSIS
      YA0350 YA0443   YA1391 YB0123

PATTERN RECOGNITION
      YA1173 YA1215   YB0172

PERMANENT INCOME *See* **THEORY** − PERMANENT INCOME or
INCOME − PERMANENT, EFFECT OF.

POLICY EVALUATION
  MACRO
      YA0471 YA0472   YA0669 YA0672   YA0673 YA1291
      YA1312 YA1460   YA1934 YA2195   YA2651 YA2672
      YA2827 YA2858   YA2860 YA3175   YA3445 YB0026
      YB0069 YB0108   YB0138 YB0187   YB0190 YB0269
      YB0292
  REVIEW
      YA0184

POLICY EVALUATION

The following are concerned with particular target variables for policies at either a macro or sector level.

Advertising	YB0028			
Defence	YA1304	YA1444	YA3704	
Disarmament		YA0986		
Employment		YA1438	YA1522	YA2951 YA3513
YA3632	YA3657	YB0096		
Energy	YA1488	YA1628	YA1727	YA1776 YA1777
YA2253	YB0306			
Fiscal	YA0740	YA0971	YA1078	YA1122 YA1436
YA1686	YA1740	YA2095	YA2677	YA3323 YA3166
YB0020	YB0154	YB0233		
Fiscal, monetary		YA0013	YA0037	YA0292 YA0361
YA0388	YA0484	YA0532	YA0594	YA0612 YA0681
YA0763	YA0800	YA1284	YA1397	YA1580 YA1588
YA1589	YA1714	YA1994	YA2064	YA2131 YA2215
YA2259	YA2411	YA2445	YA2864	YA3013 YA3014
YA3126	YA3225	YA3517	YA3524	YA3609 YB0332
Industrial structure		YA2447		
International finance, foreign exchange				YA0145 YA0187
YA0612	YA1664	YA1795	YA1933	YA2095 YA2679
YB0182				
International trade		YA0059	YA3218	YB0182
Investment	YA0404	YA1416	YA1460	
Monetary	YA0071	YA0107	YA0336	YA0445 YA0682
YA0765	YA0799	YA0947	YA0994	YA0996 YA1078
YA1131	YA1268	YA1270	YA1467	YA1669 YA1910
YA2063	YA2134	YA2474	YA2483	YA2743 YA2826
YA2835	YA2836	YA2865	YA3096	YA3202 YA3282
YA3373	YA3444	YA3457	YB0022	
Population control		YA0369	YA1076	
R & D	YA3133			
Stabilisation	YA0175	YA0484	YA0958	YA1425 YA1550
YA1686	YA2485	YA2833	YA2838	YA3096 YA3301
YB0038	YB0061	YB0115	YB0157	YB0187 YB0257
Unemployment		YA0176	YA0681	YA1038 YA1160
YA1232	YA1442	YA1509	YA1518	YA1631 YA1899
YA1900	YA1925	YA1959	YA2102	YA2303 YA2906
YA2949	YA3411			
Welfare	YA1038	YA1530	YA1899	YA2102 YA2444
YA2487	YA2949	YA3020	YA3145	YA3168

POLICY EVALUATION
METHODOLOGY
YA0451 YA0672 YA0675 YA0677 YA0683 YA0751
YA2474 YA2677 YA2788 YA3240 YA3323 YA3468
YA3524 YA3536 YB0058
REGIONAL
YA0286 YA0986 YA2031 YA2034 YA2305 YA2498
YA2606 YA3648

The following are concerned with policies addressed to particular sectors of the economy.

SECTOR
Advertising YB0028
Agriculture YA0392 YA0696 YA1364 YA1660 YA3027
  YB0068
Commodities YA3275 YB0001 YB0002
Construction YA0873 YA1819 YA2046 YA2525
  YA2979 YA3223 YB0284 YB0293
Consumer durables YA3693
Education YA0063 YA2232 YA2764 YB0239
Finance YA0403 YA0417 YA1226 YA2045 YA2807
  YA3251 YA3624
Health YA1566 YA1666 YA3470
Production YA0788 YA1086 YA3218
Services YA1169
Social YA0253 YA0255 YA1030 YA1039 YA2742
  YA3711
Transport YA2683

POLLUTION
CONTROLS
YA0451 YA1098 YA2007 YA2533 YA3730
EFFECT OF
YA0105 YA0452 YA1213 YA1254 YA1255 YA2853
YB0260

POPULATION
YA0469 YA0895 YA1085 YA1471 YA1530 YA1950
YA2122 YB0093
EFFECT OF
YA0316 YA0924 YA0925 YA1526 YA1647 YA1927
YA2647 YA3233 YA3366
FERTILITY
YA0114 YA0369 YA0746 YA1075 YA1076 YA1477
YA1478 YA1581 YA2121 YA3050 YA3141 YA3366

PROBABILITY MODELS
LINEAR LEARNING
    YA0001 YA0005   YA1366 YA1857   YA2099 YA2171
    YA3665 YA3773   YA3775 YB0218
  Evaluation YA2098
NBD (NEGATIVE BINOMIAL DISTRIBUTION)
    YA0239 YA1034   YA1274 YA1469   YA1634 YA2745
    YA3773 YB0095
POISSON
    YA0563 YA0750   YA1227 YA3501
RENEWAL THEORETIC
    YA2389 YA3349   YB0321
REVIEW
    YB0006
OTHER
    YA0305 YA0541   YA2008 YA2370   YA2390 YA2844

PRODUCTION FUNCTIONS
ESTIMATION
    YA0057 YA0276   YA0411 YA0691   YA1110 YA1310
    YA1515 YA2336   YA2419 YA2709   YA2752 YA2847
    YA2978 YA3116   YA3447 YA3478   YA3484 YA3545
    YA3766 YB0125
  Evaluation YA2039
EVALUATION
    YA0017 YA0321   YA1489 YA1500   YA1608 YA1662
    YA1852 YA1901   YA2161 YA2229   YA2232 YA2916
    YA3152 YA3364   YA3447 YB0168
METHODOLOGY
    YA0053 YA0057   YA0322 YA0326   YA0554 YA0691
    YA0908 YA0950   YA0977 YA1130   YA1487 YA1500
    YA1609 YA2037   YA2120 YA2480   YA2584 YA2684
    YA2983 YA3079   YA3116 YA3152   YA3194 YA3478
    YA3544 YA3630   YA3705 YA3714   YB0259
REVIEW
    YB0176 YB0312
THEORY
    YA0117 YA0118   YA0276 YA0323   YA0328 YA0550
    YA0686 YA0909   YA1157 YA1199   YA1783 YA2117
    YA2635 YA2847   YA3036 YA3081   YA3176 YA3245
    YA3364 YA3540   YA3744
  Joint   YA1485   YA1487 YA1613   YA2379 YA3544
    YA3545

PRODUCTION FUNCTIONS
The areas of application are listed below.
FIRM

YA0210	YA0573	YA0779	YA0949	YA1130	YA1194
YA1852	YA2120	YA3195	YA3221	YA3311	YA3364
YA3484	YA3540	YA3548	YA3744		

MACRO

YA0117	YA0118	YA0321	YA0322	YA0323	YA0328
YA0550	YA0798	YA0908	YA0909	YA0910	YA0933
YA0948	YA0950	YA1489	YA1901	YA2037	YA2084
YA2085	YA2127	YA2161	YA2221	YA2222	YA2228
YA2229	YA2456	YA2570	YA2584	YA2635	YA2717
YA2916	YA3245	YA3484	YA3544	YA3745	YA3766

SECTOR

YA0057	YA0276	YA0283	YA0373	YA0521	YA0554
YA0611	YA0719	YA0950	YA0995	YA1157	YA1193
YA1404	YA1608	YA1661	YA1662	YA1783	YA1861
YA2117	YA2146	YA2379	YA2416	YA2419	YA2424
YA2480	YA2684	YA2734	YA2752	YA2958	YA2978
YA2983	YA3015	YA3019	YA3030	YA3054	YA3079
YA3081	YA3152	YA3375	YA3390	YA3478	YA3545
YA3630	YA3705	YA3753	YB0125	YB0176	YB0189

Two aspects of production functions of particular interest are:
SCALE RETURNS

YA1861	YA2084	YA2085	YA2424	YA2983	YA3245
YA3364	YA3543				

SUBSTITUTION

YA0283	YA0321	YA0323	YA0328	YA0373	YA0550
YA0719	YA0908	YA0909	YA0910	YA1193	YA1489
YA1500	YA1783	YA1861	YA1901	YA2117	YA2221
YA2416	YA2456	YA2584	YA2684	YA2734	YA2752
YA3030	YA3079	YA3195	YA3364	YA3375	YA3630
YA3705	YA3753	YB0168	YB0189		

PROMOTIONS *See* **USE – PROMOTION EVALUATION.**
REVIEW
YA0004

PROXY VARIABLES

YA0050	YA0209	YA0226	YA1002	YA1247	YA1264
YA1536	YA1651	YA2089	YA2258	YA2506	YA3103
YA3188	YA3663	YB0195			

PUBLIC EXPENDITURE
 EFFECT OF
   YA0037 YA0176 YA0669 YA0986 YA1100 YA1444
   YA1550 YA1660 YA2057 YA2366 YA3093 YA3100
   YA3301 YB0170 YB0307 YB0308
  Aid programmes   YA0083 YA1441 YA1490 YA1522
   YA2130 YA2487 YA2722

QUALITY
 ADJUSTMENTS
   YA0091 YA0582 YA0752 YA0783 YA0824 YA3310
 DURABILITY
   YA0973
 EFFECT OF
   YA1337 YA1978 YA2192 YA2285 YA2659 YA3128
   YA3199 YA3325 YA3578 YA3724 YB0108
 MEASURING
   YA1158
 PRICE
   YA0435 YA0782 YA0783 YA0824 YA1294 YA1358
   YA1728 YA2939 YA3356 YA3577 YA3743

RANDOM WALK
 METHODOLOGY
   YA1182 YA1409 YA3403 YB0131 YB0193
 REVIEW
   YB0070 YB0192
 TEST
   YA0183 YA0414 YA0558 YA0774 YA0820 YA0830
   YA1182 YA1211 YA1539 YA1639 YA1804 YA1930
   YA2050 YA2098 YA2104 YA2140 YA2369 YA2391
   YA3001 YA3147 YA3303 YA3752 YB0131 YB0303
  Trading rule YA0596 YA0659 YA0774 YA1402 YA2212
   YA2879 YA2882 YA3638
 THEORY
   YA0159 YA0213 YA0701 YA0703 YA0776 YA2367
   YA2370

RECURSIVE SYSTEMS
   YA2114 YA2203 YA2337 YB0043 YB0235 YB0323
 See also **COMPARATIVE METHODS — RECURSIVE SYSTEMS**

REGIONAL MODELS
    SECTOR
        Government YA1315   YA1439   YA3346   YB0096
            Finances and expenditure   YA0286   YA0410   YA1443
            YA3093   YA3258   YA3401   YB0147
            Services   YA0426   YA2008
        Health   YA2962
        Transport   YA0870   YA1356   YA2296   YA3138   YA3219
            YA3260   YA3261   YA3533   YA3558   YA3643   YB0082
            YB0087
        Utilities   YA1007   YA0286   YA1871

The following key words are concerned with methodological questions.

AGGREGATION (to a macroeconomic model)
        YB0307
BUSINESS CYCLE *See* **BUSINESS CYCLE – REGIONAL.**
DATA
        YA3684   YB0325
INPUT OUTPUT *See* **INPUT OUTPUT – REGIONAL.**
INTER-REGIONAL
        YA0371   YA0986   YA3272   YA3533   YA3573   YB0145
        YB0196   YB0307

REGRESSION *See also* **COMPARATIVE METHODS – REGRESSION**
and **COMPARATIVE METHODS – CAUSAL** (Other). The latter key
word is used when CAUSAL forecasting models are compared to other
models. Estimation methods are given under the main category
ESTIMATION.
    EVALUATION
        YA0128   YA1603   YA1604   YA2729
    INTRODUCTION
        YA2315   YB0000   YB0324
    REVIEW
        YA0785   YA2420   YB0056   YB0249
    TEXT
        YB0053   YB0221   YB0267   *See also* **ECONOMETRICS –**
        TEXT.

The following are concerned with specific aspects of regression
models.

AGGREGATION
        YA0235   YA0244   YA0493   YA1524   YA3034   YA3722
        YB0139

REGRESSION

CENSORED

YA0786 YA1652 YA1919 YA2060 YA2119 YA2608

CONSTRAINED   This is only used when the article stresses the specifications of a constrained model. For discussion of constrained estimation, *see* **ESTIMATION − CONSTRAINED.**

YA0235 YA0646 YA0686 YA1042 YA1666 YB0014
YB3084

CONTROL

YA3412

COVARIANCE MODEL

YA0054 YA0135 YA0425 YA1151 YA1466 YA1666
YA1772 YA1840 YA2714 YA3059 YA3182 YA3375
YA3388 YB0188

DISCRETE (OR ORDINAL) DEPENDENT

YA1654 YA2395 YA2520 YA2621 YA3612

ERROR COMPONENTS

YA0135 YA0137 YA0245 YA0391 YA1585 YA1684
YA1757 YA1808 YA1834 YA1840 YA1909 YA2333
YA2422 YA2513 YA2521 YA2542 YA2618 YA3534
YB0265

ERRORS IN VARIABLES

YA0048 YA0050 YA0052 YA0209 YA0390 YA0621
YA0622 YA0785 YA1069 YA1327 YA1497 YA1544
YA1629 YA1722 YA1730 YA2061 YA2124 YA2147
YA2258 YA2579 YA2795 YA2928 YA2996 YA3071
YA3179 YA3249 YA3251 YA3663 YA3679 YB0327

ESTIMATION

YA0049 YA0052 YA0562 YA0658 YA0758 YA0904
YA1051 YA1097 YA1137 YA1299 YA1348 YA1494
YA1523 YA1636 YA1681 YA1684 YA1704 YA1710
YA1992 YA1993 YA2115 YA2170 YA2175 YA2311
YA2376 YA2404 YA2843 YA2893 YA2940 YA3157
YA3243 YA3300 YA3377 YA3412 YA3422 YA3542
YA3587 YA3653 YA3758 YB0179 YB0200 YB0333
Evaluation   YA1042 YA1876 YA3309 YB0221
Error specification   YA0265 YA1303 YA1680 YA1942
YA2127 YA2849 YA3290 YA3595 YB0154 YB0179
YB0323
Evaluation   YA0449 YA2485

REGRESSION
  ESTIMATION, REVIEW
    YA1602 YA1603   YA1604 YA1636   YA1681 YA3309
    YB0221
  EXPERIMENTAL DESIGN
    YA0787 YA2721
  GROUPED OBSERVATIONS
    YA0054 YA1266   YA1894 YA2797   YB0140
  HYPOTHESIS TESTS (OF COEFFICIENTS)
    YA0108 YA0325   YA0389 YA0684   YA0801 YA1048
    YA1136 YA1299   YA1414 YA2073   YA2163 YA2413
    YA2480 YA2927   YA3034 YA3086   YA3091 YA3156
    YA3317 YA3587   YA3588 YA3613   YA3733
    Evaluation YA0684   YA1302 YA1620   YA2573 YA3546
  LAGGED DEPENDENT
    YA0320 YA0360   YA1373 YA1375   YA1376 YA1377
    YA1935 YA1936   YA1942 YA2062   YA2340 YA3315
    YA3381 YA3590   YA3593
    Evaluation YA1129   YA3357
  LIMITED DEPENDENT
    YA0081 YA0793   YA0838 YA1553   YA1626 YA1652
    YA1845 YA1959   YA2005 YA2119   YA2289 YA2609
    YA2701 YA2850   YA3360 YA3535   YB0149
    Evaluation   YA3642
    Logit   YA0085   YA0335 YA0537   YA0821 YA0919
      YA1257 YA1356   YA1462 YA1463   YA1520 YA1620
      YA1872 YA2024   YA2150 YA2162   YA2254 YA2298
      YA2292 YA2296   YA2682 YA2733   YA2745 YA2895
      YA3125 YA3429   YA3502 YA3644   YA3700 YB0087
      YB0327
    Evaluation   YA2887
    Probit   YA0407   YA0692 YA1869   YA1916 YA2470
      YA2488 YA2936   YA3028 YA3404   YA3643
    Review   YA2291
    Tobit   YA0082   YA1114 YA1522   YA1925 YA3206
  MODEL CHOICE
    YA0075 YA0140   YA0153 YA0171   YA0241 YA0263
    YA0320 YA0427   YA0479 YA0777   YA0785 YA0871
    YA0895 YA0932   YA0939 YA0964   YA1022 YA1036
    YA1130 YA1456   YA1608 YA1626   YA1679 YA1981
    YA2313 YA2413   YA2480 YA2611   YA2738 YA2763
    YA2783 YA2785   YA2885 YA3089   YA3109 YA3111
    YA3232 YA3587   YA3589 YA3628   YA3680 YB0195
    YB0222

REGRESSION
  SCATTERGRAM
      YA0115 YA0214   YA0530
  SEEMINGLY UNRELATED
      YA0373 YA0590   YA0678 YA0694   YA0706 YA1150
      YA1262 YA1517   YA1666 YA1753   YA1993 YA2288
      YA2382 YA2734   YA2814 YA3114   YA3294 YA3379
      YA3673
    Evaluation YA1300   YA2423
  SHIFTING COEFFICIENTS   Used when the regression coefficients
  are themselves modelled. *See also* **DISTRIBUTED LAG** −
  VARIABLE LAG and **REGRESSION** − STATE SPACE.
      YA0034 YA0248   YA0264 YA0296   YA0594 YA2740
      YA2955 YA3009   YA3252 YA3478   YA3552 YB0253
  SPECIFICATION OF VARIABLES
      YA0209 YA0548   YA0715 YA0798   YA0925 YA1014
      YA1946 YA2010   YA2012 YA2165   YA2408 YA2482
      YA2765 YA2934   YA3167 YA3179   YA3407 YA3723
      YB0204
    See also **DATA** − SPECIFICATION OF VARIABLES.
  SPURIOUS CORRELATION
      YA0294 YA0449   YA0755 YA0846   YA2631 YA2920
      YB0132
  STATE SPACE
      YA0158 YA0304   YA0759 YA0760   YA0761 YA1599
      YA1764 YA1842   YA2073 YA2329   YA2420 YA2709
      YA2893 YA3022   YA3092 YA3756   YB0167
    Evaluation YA2092   YA2093
  STEPWISE
      YA0075 YA0127   YA0299 YA0300   YA0317 YA0710
      YA0724 YA1008   YA1222 YA1267   YA1319 YA1848
      YA1849 YA1981   YA3011 YA3441   YA3589
  SUMMARY STATISTICS
      YA0108 YA0171   YA0214 YA0279   YA0560 YA0801
      YA0814 YA0815   YA1022 YA1032   YA1390 YA1408
      YA1455 YA1456   YA1464 YA1547   YA1719 YA1981
      YA2037 YA2074   YA2126 YA2288   YA2395 YA2494
      YA2511 YA2518   YA2520 YA2522   YA2523 YA2621
      YA2793 YA2885   YA2888 YA2927   YA3034 YA3109
      YA3111 YA3156   YA3463 YA3613   YA3674 YB0267
  SWITCHING
      YA1180 YA1399   YA1401 YA2009   YA2901 YA2903
      YA3377 YB0125

The first set of key words designates firms or sector level studies etc; in particular areas of the economy.

SIMULATION
  APPLICATION
    Sector

Education	YA2764			
Finance YA1467	YA1805	YA1878	YB0074	
Government	YA1304			
Health YA0829	YA0924	YA1221	YA1265	YA3507
YA3740				
Production	YA0026	YA1093	YA1594	YA1940
YA2968 YA3476	YB0238			
Social YA1075	YA1076	YA1581		
Utilities YA1486	YA1871			
World models	YA2417	YA2647	YA2990	YB0062
YB0084				

The following references are to activities undertaken either in an organisation or by an individual. If the references are directly concerned with the use of the simulation model they are also key worded **USE** — (subhead).

APPLICATION

Advertising YA1143	YB0028	YB0280		
Consumer behaviour	YA0531	YA1067	YA1145	YA1147
YA1788 YA2244				
Finance YA0879	YA2144	YA2878	YA3604	
Financial modelling	YA1055	YA1501	YA1949	YA2144
YA2878 YA3128	YB0109	YB0258		
Investment appraisal	YA0615			
Marketing YA0006	YA1201	YA1202	YA2068	YA2068
YA2135 YA3623				
Micro YA0314	YA0531	YA0598	YA1033	YA1067
YA1530				
New products	YA0150	YA2135	YA2749	YA3212
Policy evaluation	YA0472	YA0485	YA0765	YA0873
YA0986 YA1078	YA1122	YA1304	YA1436	YA1664
YA1686 YA2095	YA2195	YA2533	YA2827	YA2836
YA3165 YA3275	YB0077	YB0088	YB0166	YB0281

The following are methodological references.

ANALYTIC METHODS
  YA0056 YB0238
DYNAMIC PROPERTIES
  YA0437 YA1766 YA2168 YA3118 YA3293

SPECIFICATION ERROR
TESTS

Transformations	YA1611	YA1733	YA2913	YA3448

Variable inclusion   *See also* **REGRESSION** — VARIABLE INCLUSION, and —HYPOTHESIS TESTS and the corresponding sub-heads for **SIMULTANEOUS SYSTEM**.

					YA0108
YA0363	YA0570	YA0618	YA0781	YA1022	YA1301
YA2913	YA2970	YA2971	YA3085	YA3111	YA3448

SPECTRAL ANALYSIS
EVALUATION

YA0483	YA2212	YA2369

INTRODUCTION

YA0483	YA0638	YA3308

REVIEW

YA0203	YA0229	YA0650	YA1610	YA3298	YB0012
YB0036	YB0058	YB0118	YB0132	YB0143	YB0144
YB0181					

TEXT

YB0029	YB0052	YB0111	YB0174	YB0250

The following key words describe areas of application.

APPLICATION

Macro	YA0770	YA1412	YA1512	YA1860	YA2326
YA2838	YA3161	YA3162			

Sector (or firm)

Agricultural and other commodities   YA0043   YA0597

YA2050	YA2140	YB0192

Finance	YA0111	YA0770	YA1211	YA1388	YA1457
YA2807	YA3308	YB0131			

Other	YA0203	YA0205	YA0585	YA1070	YA1388
YA3345					

The following are studies of particular phenomena.

APPLICATION

Business cycle	YA0162	YA0205	YA0371	YA0424
YA0437	YA0587	YA1450	YA3159	
Business cycle, long cycle	YA0029	YA0104	YA0585
YA1451	YA1991	YA2762	YA3345	YB0111
Business indicators	YA1800	YA2954	YA3437	
Distributed lag	YA0595	YA0966	YA1069	YA1610
YB0085	YB0111			
Futures trading	YA0597	YA2051		
Interest rate YA0414	YA0586	YA2837	YA3297	

SPECTRAL ANALYSIS
  APPLICATION
    Lag identification   YA0203 YA1070   YA1578 YA1625
    YA1705
    Model interpretation   YA0104
    Regression and simultaneous system models YA1576 YA1610
    YA1763
    Seasonality YA0203   YA0555 YA1008   YA1480 YA2616
     YA2845 YA2954   YA3025 YA3210   YA3242 YA3595
    Simulation evaluation   YA0437 YA0939   YA1766 YA2591
    YA2741 YB0238
    Time series YA0229   YA0639 YA0649   YA0726

The remaining key words describe methodological or theoretical references.

CHANGING SPECTRA
    YA1071 YA1569   YA2892 YA2893   YA3362 YA3363
CROSS
    YA0203 YA0650   YA1617 YA1705   YA2893 YA3161
  Review   YA0043   YB0058
METHODOLOGY
    YA0229 YA0348   YA0394 YA1214   YA1617 YA2762
    YB0111
MULTIVARIATE
    YB0274
THEORY
    YB0143

SPECULATION
  MODELS OF
    YA0134 YA0457   YA1534 YA1947   YA2370

SPLINE FUNCTIONS
    YA0221 YA0561   YA1088 YA1556   YA2021 YA2022
    YA2274 YA2846   YA2847 YA2848   YA3367 YB0259

STABILITY OF COEFFICIENTS
  INPUT OUTPUT
    YA0340 YA0536   YA2295 YA3430   YA3514 YB0049
    YB0322
  PROBABILITY AND MARKOV MODELS
    YA0227 YA2805
  REGRESSION
    YA0196 YA0264   YA0296 YA0307   YA0396 YA0420
    YA0480 YA0561   YA0575 YA0594   YA0760 YA0785

STABILITY OF COEFFICIENTS
REGRESSION (cont.)

YA1036	YA1401	YA1424	YA1433	YA1529	YA1724
YA1802	YA2003	YA2022	YA2092	YA2596	YA2740
YA3023	YA3143	YA3225	YA3234	YA3252	YA3265
YA3414	YA3532	YA3672	YA3694	YA3708	YB0188
YB0259					

Application YA0113

		YA0175	YA0478	YA0591	YA0611
YA0717	YA0850	YA0878	YA0932	YA0976	YA1026
YA1095	YA1246	YA1308	YA1371	YA1511	YA1640
YA1688	YA1864	YA1873	YA2014	YA2081	YA2103
YA2179	YA2280	YA2424	YA2447	YA2466	YA2538
YA2617	YA2863	YA3010	YA3037	YA3166	YA3336
YA3364	YA3606	YA3671			

Test YA0517

		YA0759	YA0898	YA1141	YA1142
YA1196	YA1217	YA1313	YA1388	YA1519	YA1607
YA1825	YA2422	YA2801	YA2848	YA2948	YA3122
YA3149	YA3467	YB0325			

Application YA0421 YA0595 YA0927 YA2363
YA2610

Evaluation YA1313 YA3467 YB0188

REVIEW
YA0093 YA3021 YB0108

SIMULTANEOUS SYSTEM

YA0594	YA1404	YA1408	YA1471	YA1677	YB0105
Test	YA0939	YA1527	YA1659	YA1826	YA1827
YA2532					

TIME SERIES

YA1598	YA2310	YA2355	YA2708	YA2892	YA3362
Test	YA0088	YA0173	YA0421	YA1639	

STATIONARITY
TESTING
YA0172 YA0348 YA0575 YA2892 YA3363
TRANSFORMING TO

YA0016	YA0447	YA0640	YA0726	YA0777	YA0871
YA1409	YA1599	YA1679	YA2341	YA2843	YA3680

STOCK PRICES
See also **APPLICATION — SECTOR (OR FIRM)** : STOCK PRICES.
INTRODUCTION
YA1721
REVIEW
YA1829 YA2185 YB0166

STOCK PRICES
TEXT
    YB0070
THEORY
    YA0660 YA2145   YA2370

The following are concerned with the formation of stock prices.

BETA

YA0197	YA0351	YA0399	YA0400	YA0402	YA0422
YA0440	YA0478	YA0757	YA1279	YA1287	YA1411
YA1432	YA1392	YA1538	YA2145	YA2957	YA3047
YA3150	YA3667				

Determinants   YA0009 YA0040   YA0297 YA0477
    YA1561 YA2800   YA2992 YA3438
Evaluation YA1066
Variable   YA0196   YA0396 YA0397   YA0421 YA0480
    YA0830 YA1109   YA1246 YA1986   YA1987 YA2009
    YA2801 YA2992   YA3234

COVARIATION

YA0033	YA0038	YA0039	YA0351	YA0473	YA1063
YA1066	YA1805	YA2088	YA2114	YA2138	YA2198
YA2203	YA2956	YA2984	YA3304	YA3328	YB0131

DATA ERRORS
    YA0281 YA3024
DEBENTURES
    YA1245
DETERMINANTS (AND FORECASTING MODELS)

YA0175	YA0211	YA0291	YA0302	YA0409	YA0449
YA0724	YA0770	YA1089	YA1173	YA1230	YA1287
YA1433	YA1563	YA1574	YA1702	YA1737	YA1738
YA1818	YA1945	YA2023	YA2112	YA2312	YA2365
YA2385	YA2474	YA2599	YA2617	YA2660	YA2781
YA3004	YA3395	YA3503	YA3596	YA3776	YB0131

DISTRIBUTION (OF RESIDUAL ERROR)

YA0206	YA0377	YA0421	YA0776	YA1065	YA1183
YA1537	YA1710	YA1769	YA1908	YA2132	YA2663
YA2880	YA2881	YA3424			

EFFECT OF

YA0073	YA0434	YA0788	YA0894	YA1073	YA1798
YA1831	YA1913	YA2327	YA2472	YA2477	YA2937
YA3046	YB0262				

EFFICIENT MARKET (TEST) *See* MODELS, **Efficient market** below.

SURVEYS
  METHODOLOGY
    Scaling   YA1510
    Validation   YA2553   YA2624
  REVIEW
      YA0487   YB0047   YB0056   YB0136

SYSTEMS THEORY
  REVIEW
      YA3191   YB0073   YB0108

TARIFF
  EFFECT OF
      YA0017   YA1186   YA1224   YA1717   YA2429   YA2508
      YA2558   YA2694   YA2758   YA2977   YA3152   YA3204
      YA3694   YA3727

TAX
  EFFECT OF
      YA0007   YA0429   YA0437   YA0485   YA0524   YA0577
      YA0578   YA0740   YA0753   YA0788   YA0971   YA0978
      YA1009   YA1029   YA1078   YA1086   YA1100   YA1156
      YA1164   YA1165   YA1167   YA1169   YA1325   YA1436
      YA1530   YA1740   YA1777   YA1835   YA1966   YA1967
      YA2015   YA2416   YA2485   YA2487   YA2505   YA2569
      YA2653   YA2673   YA2677   YA2839   YA2951   YA3016
      YA3017   YA3020   YA3100   YA3133   YA3166   YA3168
      YA3222   YA3323   YA3404   YA3556   YA3582   YA3645
      YA3657   YB0178   YB0182   YB0269

TECHNOLOGICAL FORECASTING
      YA0526   YA1405   YA1828   YA1918   YA2076   YA2184
      YA2652   YA3449   YA3496   YB0099   YB0177   YB0202
      YB0212   YB0296   YB0324
  EVALUATION
      YA0972   YA3689   YB0016
  REVIEW
      YA1336

TECHNOLOGY
  EFFECT OF
      YA0044   YA0109   YA0164   YA0276   YA0611   YA0852
      YA0933   YA1157   YA1428   YA1901   YA1938   YA2692
      YA3194   YA3364   YA3478   YA3745

THEORY
EFFICIENT MARKETS
YA0197	YA0399	YA0402	YA0440	YA0477	YA0770
YA0943	YA1127	YA1276	YA1564	YA1829	YA2002
YA2088	YA2113	YA2138	YA2370	YA2474	YA3007
YA3304	YA3646	YB0070	YB0166		

Evaluation YA2718
EXPECTATIONS
YA0557	YA1264	YA1653	YA1905	YA2251	YA2484
YA2600	YA2859	YA3070	YA3072	YA3074	YA3075
YA3466	YA3599	YB0106	YB0155	YB0230	YB0289

Evaluation YA0601   YA0954   YA2260   YA2363   YA2474
YA2776   YA3492   YA3492   YB0187
MODELLING
YA0092	YA0315	YA0470	YA0611	YA0734	YA0777
YA1281	YA2108	YA2367	YA2470	YA2677	YA2853
YA3354	YA3511	YA3589	YA3709	YA3763	YB0015
YB0043	YB0095	YB0108	YB0195	YB0266	

MONETARY
YA0353	YA0361	YA1127	YA1178	YA1305	YA1344
YA1365	YA1941	YA1980	YA2064	YA2446	YA2476
YA2646	YA3743	YA2965	YA3550	YB0069	

Evaluation YA0031   YA0361   YA1057   YA1426   YA1579
YA2058   YA2864
PERMANENT INCOME, EVALUATION
YA0158	YA0855	YA1895	YA2094	YA2786	YA2794
YA2795	YA3249	YA3251	YA3679	YB0219	

STOCK ADJUSTMENT
YA3641   YA3682   YB0159

TIME – VALUE OF
YA0008	YA0936	YA1019	YA2024	YA2150	YA2502
YA2608	YA2998	YA3188	YA3421	YA3557	YA3580
YA3642	YA3643	YA3644	YB0135	YB0265	YB0322

TIME SERIES
EVALUATION
YA1089   YA1383   YA2353
REVIEW
YA0097	YA0579	YA0651	YA1351	YA1448	YA2307
YA2353	YA2355	YA2891			

TEXT
YB0012	YB0036	YB0042	YB0052	YB0118	YB0121
YB0132	YB0143	YB0172	YB0181	YB0212	YB0213
YB0229	YB0250	YB0319			

TIME SERIES

The following are more specific references. *See also* **COMPARATIVE METHODS** — ARIMA, AUTOREGRESSIVE etc. for companions of the two methods named and **SPECIFICATION ERROR** — EFFECT OF, **Model specification.**

TURNING POINTS
See also **JUDGEMENTAL FORECASTS** — TURNING POINTS.
  FORECASTING
YA0515	YA0603	YA1016	YA1182	YA1800	YA2316
YA3201	YA3342	YA3736	YB0051		
Evaluation	YA0024	YA0551	YA0878	YA1016	YA1101
YA1172	YA1431	YA1800	YA2216	YA2218	YA2499
YA2861	YA3202	YA3334	YB0150	YB0155	YB0164
YB0241					

UNIONISATION
  DETERMINANTS
YA0138	YA2118	YA2682	YA3113

  EFFECT OF
YA0138	YA0552	YA0553	YA0741	YA0957	YA1132
YA1206	YA1474	YA1551	YA1891	YA2118	YA2479
YA2539	YA2682	YA2760	YA2896	YA3113	YA3123
YA3435	YA3436	YA3549	YA3571		

USE
These references discuss how a model is used, with a particular agency in mind. For aggregate Government policies, *see under* **POLICY EVALUATION**. If the concerns of the user are also considered it is key worded below under **USER**.
  REVIEW
    YA2359

  ACQUISITION
YA0805	YA1557	YA3247	YB0257

  ANTITRUST
YA0070	YA0240	YA0395	YA0462	YA1054	YA1785

  BANK REGULATION
YA1467	YA1472	YA1698	YA1742	YA1878	YA1898
YA2254	YA2415	YA2469	YA2537	YA2899	YA3255

  BANKRUPTCY PREDICTION
YA0076	YA0077	YA0078	YA0395	YA0886	YA1052
YA1385	YA1587	YA1939	YA1948	YA2164	YA2688
YA3247					

  CAPACITY EXPANSION
YA0331	YA0346	YA1406	YA2764	YA3307	YB0242
YB0280					

  CAPITAL INVESTMENT
YA0440	YA0615	YA0624	YA1185	YA2238	YA3443
YA3496	YB0255				

USE
INVENTORY CONTROL

YA0036	YA0191	YA0359	YA0362	YA0535	YA0698
YA0749	YA0817	YA1040	YA1227	YA1248	YA1606
YA1644	YA1735	YA1762	YA2052	YA2075	YA2425
YA2459	YA2460	YA2500	YA2547	YA2685	YA2706
YA2944	YA3145	YA3347	YA3450	YA3547	YA3575
YA3647	YA3660	YB0040	YB0041	YB0042	YB0048
YB0158	YB0198	YB0285			

INVESTMENT MANAGEMENT *See* PORTFOLIO SELECTION below.

LOAN (AND INTEREST RATE) REGULATION *See also* BANK REGULATION above.   YA0307   YA0525   YA1819 YA2697   YA2995

LOCATION *See* SITE SELECTION below.

MANPOWER PLANNING *See* **MANPOWER PLANNING**.

MARKETING POLICY *See also* MEDIA PLANNING and PRO-MOTION EVALUATION below.   YA0006   YA0087

YA0381	YA0531	YA0692	YA0780	YA0937	YA1200
YA1201	YA1202	YA2082	YA2189	YA2226	YA2358
YA2492	YA2496	YA2923	YA3138	YA3508	YA3511
YA3623	YB0048	YB0109	YB0237	YB0253	YB0255

MEDIA PLANNING

YA0106	YA0305	YA0354	YA0625	YA1332	YA1468
YA2032	YA2044	YA2068	YA2189	YA2190	YA2206
YA2699	YA2947	YA3049	YA3136	YA3231	YA3402
YA3490	YA3770	YA3772	YA3774		

ORGANISATION DESIGN

YA1184	YA1780	YA3649	YB0048	YB0316

PERSONNEL EVALUATION
YA0990   YA1410

PORTFOLIO SELECTION

YA0224	YA0400	YA0409	YA0659	YA0660	YA0808
YA1063	YA1066	YA1246	YA1532	YA1533	YA1720
YA1721	YA1737	YA1815	YA2079	YA2279	YA2310
YA2363	YA2432	YA3076	YA3101	YA3638	

Evaluation, portfolio selection procedures   YA0808   YA1065 YA1247   YA1721   YA3076

PRICING
YA0847   YA1253   YA1869   YA2171   YA2489   YA3433 YA3506

5 The references

YA0000   AAKER D.A.
         "A measure of brand acceptance"   J. Mktg. Res., vol,9, 1972, pp.160-167.
         BRAND CHOICE - INDICATORS * CONSUMER BEHAVIOUR - STOCHASTIC MODELS *
         PROBABILITY MODELS - BETA * APPL - SECTOR : CONSUMER NON DURABLES * NEW
         PRODUCTS - NEW BRAND * NEW PRODUCTS - EVALUATION

YA0001   AAKER D.A.
         "A new method for evaluating stochastic models of brand choice"   J. Mktg.
         Res., vol,7, 1970, pp.300-306.
         PROBABILITY MODELS - LINEAR LEARNING * BRAND CHOICE - METHODOLOGY *
         EVALUATION - CONSUMER BEHAVIOUR , STOCHASTIC MODELS

YA0002   AAKER D.A.
         "The New Trier stochastic model of brand choice"   Mgmt. Sci. (B), vol,17,
         1971, pp.435-450.
         CONSUMER BEHAVIOUR - STOCHASTIC MODELS * BRAND CHOICE - THEORY * EVALUATION
         - CONSUMER BEHAVIOUR , STOCHASTIC MODELS * ESTIMATION - MINIMUM CHI - SQUARE
         : APPL

YA0003   AAKER D.A.
         "The new Trier stochastic model of brand choice"   Mgmt. Sci. (B), vol,17,
         1971, pp.435-450, errata p.831.
         BRAND CHOICE - THEORY * CONSUMER BEHAVIOUR - PSYCHOLOGICAL MODELS * CONSUMER
         BEHAVIOUR - STOCHASTIC MODELS * NEW PRODUCTS - DIFFUSION MODEL * APPL - FIRM
         : CONSUMER NON DURABLES , GROCERIES * EVALUATION - CONSUMER BEHAVIOUR ,
         STOCHASTIC MODELS * ESTIMATION - MINIMUM CHI - SQUARE : APPL

YA0004   AAKER D.A.
         "Towards a normative model of promotional decision making"   Mgmt. Sci.
         (B), vol,19, 1973, pp.593-603.
         PROMOTIONS - REVIEW * CONSUMER BEHAVIOUR - STOCHASTIC MODELS

YA0005   AAKER D.A., JONES J.M.
         "Modeling store choice behaviour"   J. Mktg. Res., vol,8, 1971, pp.38-42.
         APPL - SECTOR : RETAILING * APPL - SECTOR : CONSUMER NON DURABLES *
         EVALUATION - CONSUMER BEHAVIOUR , STOCHASTIC MODELS * BRAND CHOICE - APPL *
         PROBABILITY MODELS - LINEAR LEARNING

YA0006   AAKER D.A., WEINBERG C.B.
         "Interactive marketing models"   J. Mktg., vol,39, no,4, Oct 1975,
         pp.16-23.
         USE - MARKETING POLICY * SIMULATION - APPL : MARKETING * COMPUTERISATION -
         PLANNING MODELS * BASIC

YA0007   AARON H.J., RUSSEK F.S., SINGER N.M.
         "Tax changes and composition of fixed investment: an aggregative simulation"
         Rev. Econ. Stats., vol,54, 1972, pp.343-356.
         MACRO MODEL - FRB , MIT * TAX - EFFECT OF * APPL - MACRO : INVESTMENT * APPL
         - SECTOR : CONSTRUCTION

YA0008   ABBOTT M., ASHENFELTER O.
         "Labor supply, commodity demand and the allocation of time"   Rev. Econ.
         Studies, vol,43, 1976, pp.389-411.
         DEMAND EQUATIONS - SYSTEMS OF * TIME - VALUE OF * APPL - MACRO : CONSUMER
         DEMAND * PRICE - EFFECT OF * INCOME - EFFECT OF * MANPOWER PLANNING - MACRO
         , SUPPLY * SPECIFICATION ERROR - TESTS , CONSTRAINTS

YA0009   ABDEL-KHALIK A.R.
         "Using sensitivity analysis to evaluate materiality"   Decis. Sci., vol,8,
         1977, pp.616-629.
         APPL - FIRM : FINANCE , STOCK PRICES * STOCK PRICES - BETA , DETERMINANTS *
         APPL - FIRM : FINANCE , PROFITS , PER SHARE * EX ANTE * DISCRIMINANT
         ANALYSIS - APPL * ACCOUNTING PRACTICE - EFFECT OF

YA0010   ABDEL-KHALIK A.R., ESPEJO J.
         "Expectations data and the predictive value of interim reporting"   J.
         Acctg. Res., vol,16, 1978, pp.1-13.
         EVALUATION - JUDGEMENTAL FORECASTS , PROFITS * JUDGEMENTAL FORECASTS -
         DETERMINANTS * FORECAST - REVISION

YA0011   ABDEL-KHALIK A.R., McKEOWN J.C.
         "Understanding accounting changes in an efficient market: evidence of
         differential reaction"   Acctg. Rev, vol,53, 1978, pp.851-868.
         ACCOUNTING PRACTICE - EFFECT OF * STOCK PRICES - INFORMATION EFFECT * APPL -
         FIRM : FINANCE , STOCK PRICES

YA0012   ABDEL-KHALIK A.R., O'CONNOR M.C.
         "On the usefulness of financial ratios to investors in common stock:
         comments"   Acctg. Rev, vol,49, 1974, pp.551-556.
         STOCK PRICES - INDICATORS * APPL - FIRM : FINANCE , STOCK PRICES * BUSINESS
         INDICATORS - APPL

YA0013   ABEL A.B.
         "A comparison of three control algorithms as applied to the
         monetarist-fiscalist debate"   Anns. Econ. Soc. Meas., vol,4, 1975,
         pp.239-252.
         MACRO MODEL - US * CONTROL THEORY - STOCHASTIC , APPL * POLICY EVALUATION -
         MACRO : FISCAL , MONETARY * COMPARATIVE METHODS - CONTROL

YA0014   ABERNATHY W.J.
         "Subjective estimates and scheduling decisions"   Mgmt. Sci. (B), vol,18,
         1971, pp.80-88.
         JUDGEMENTAL FORECASTS - LEARNING * USE - PROJECT , PLANNING * EVALUATION -
         JUDGEMENTAL FORECASTS

YA0015   ABERNATHY W.J., WAYNE K.
         "Limits of the learning curve"   H.B.R., vol.52, Sept-Oct, 1974,
         pp.109-119.
         EVALUATION - LEARNING CURVE * APPL - SECTOR : PRODUCTION * COST - SECTOR :
         PRODUCTION * COST - LEARNING CURVE * BASIC

YA0016   ABRAHAM B., BOX G.E.P.
         "Deterministic and forecast-adaptive time-dependent models"   Appl. Stats.,
         vol.27, 1978, pp.120-130.
         TIME SERIES - ARIMA : INTERPRETATION * TIME SERIES - ARIMA : THEORY * TIME
         SERIES - HARMONICS * STATIONARITY - TRANSFORMING TO

YA0017   ACHESON K.
         "Revenue vs. protection: the pricing of wine by the Liquor Control Board of
         Ontario"   Can. J. Econ., vol.10, 1977, pp.246-262.
         APPL - SECTOR : CONSUMER NON DURABLES , LIQUOR * BRAND CHOICE - APPL *
         TARIFF - EFFECT OF

YA0018   ACZEL J.A.
         "The usefulness of the C.B.I. Industrial Trends Surveys for forecasting in
         the chemical industry"   Appl. Econ., vol.1, 1969, p.205-210.
         EVALUATION - EXPECTATIONS , DATA * APPL - SECTOR : PRODUCTION , CHEMICALS *
         EVALUATION - ATTITUDINAL DATA * EVALUATION - SURVEYS , BUSINESS

YA0019   ADAM E.E.
         "Individual item forecasting model evaluation"   Decis. Sci., vol.4, 1973,
         pp.458-470.
         COMPARATIVE METHODS - DECOMPOSITION , EXPONENTIAL SMOOTHING * COMPARATIVE
         METHODS - EXPONENTIAL SMOOTHING , ADAPTIVE * EVALUATION - EXPONENTIAL
         SMOOTHING * EXPONENTIAL SMOOTHING - ADAPTIVE COEFFICIENTS * DATA -
         SIMULATION

YA0020   ADAMS E.W., SPIRO M.H.
         "The timing of the response of employment to construction authorisation"
         Appl. Econ., vol.4, 1972, pp.125-133.
         APPL - SECTOR : CONSTRUCTION * APPL - SECTOR : EMPLOYMENT * COMPARATIVE
         METHODS - DATA : AGGREGATE , DISAGGREGATE * COMPARATIVE METHODS - ESTIMATION
         : OLS , 2SLS

YA0021   ADAMS F.G.
         "Prediction with consumer attitudes: the time series-cross section paradox"
         Rev. Econ. Stats., vol.47, 1965, pp.367-378.
         FACTOR ANALYSIS - APPL * DATA - CROSS SECTION , TIME SERIES * APPL - SECTOR
         : CONSUMER DURABLES , CARS * EVALUATION - SURVEYS , CONSUMER * EVALUATION -
         EXPECTATIONS , DATA * EVALUATION - ATTITUDINAL DATA

YA0022   ADAMS F.G., BROOKING C.G., GLICKMAN N.J.
         "On the specifications and simulation of a regional econometric model: a
         model of Mississipi"   Rev. Econ. Stats., vol.57, 1975, pp.286-298.
         REGIONAL MODELS * SIMULATION - APPL : REGIONAL MODEL * EX ANTE * MACRO MODEL
         - WHARTON * COMPARATIVE METHODS - ESTIMATION : SIMULTANEOUS SYSTEM *
         MULTIPLIERS - REGIONAL

YA0023   ADAMS F.G., DEJANOSI P.E.
         "On the statistical discrepancy in the revised U.S. national accounts"   J.
         Am. Statist. Ass., vol.61, 1966, pp.1219-1229.
         DATA ERRORS - NATIONAL ACCOUNTS , US * DATA REVISIONS - EFFECT OF

YA0024   ADAMS F.G., DUGGAL V.G.
         "Anticipations variables in an econometric model: performance of the
         anticipations version of Wharton Mark III"   Int. Econ. Rev., vol.15, 1974,
         pp.267-284.
         MACRO MODEL - WHARTON * EVALUATION - ATTITUDINAL DATA * INDEX NUMBERS -
         MACRO : CONSUMER SENTIMENT * SURVEYS - CONSUMER , DETERMINANTS * MULTIPLIERS
         - MACRO * EVALUATION - TURNING POINT FORECASTS

YA0025   ADAMS F.G., DUGGAL V.G., THANWALA S.
         "Industrial linking functions for the macro models"   Bus. Econ., vol.11:4,
         1976, pp.87-90.
         INPUT OUTPUT - METHODOLOGY : MODEL LINKAGE * MACRO MODELS - MICRO MODELS *
         APPL - SECTOR : PRODUCTION , INSTRUMENTS , CONTROL

YA0026   ADAMS F.G., GRIFFIN J.M.
         "An econometric-linear programming model of the US petroleum refining
         industry"   J. Am. Statist. Ass., vol.67, 1972, pp.542-551.
         APPL - SECTOR : PRODUCTION , PETROLEUM * COST - SECTOR : PRODUCTION * LP *
         SIMULATION - APPL : SECTOR , PRODUCTION * PRICE - SECTOR : PRODUCTION * EX
         ANTE

YA0027   ADAMS F.G., JUNZ H.B.
         "The effect of the business cycle on trade flows of industrial countries"
         with discussion   J. Finance, vol.26, 1971, pp.251-268 & 303-305.
         APPL - MACRO , OECD * APPL - MACRO : INTERNATIONAL LINKAGE * APPL - MACRO :
         INTERNATIONAL TRADE * BUSINESS CYCLE - EFFECT OF

YA0028   ADAMS W.J.
         "International differences in corporate profitability"   Economica, vol.43,
         1976, pp.367-379.
         APPL - SECTOR : FINANCE , PE RATIO * CONCENTRATION - EFFECT OF * DATA -
         CROSS SECTION

YA0029   ADELMAN I.
           "Long cycles - fact or artifact?"   Am. Econ. Rev., vol.55, 1965,
           pp.444-463.
           BUSINESS CYCLE - LONG CYCLE * SPECTRAL ANALYSIS - APPL : BUSINESS CYCLE ,
           LONG CYCLE
YA0030   ADELSON R.M.
           "The dynamic behaviour of linear forecasting and scheduling rules"   Opl.
           Res. Q., vol.17, 1966, pp.447-462.
           EXPONENTIAL SMOOTHING - HIGHER ORDER * USE - PRODUCTION , CONTROL
YA0031   ADIE D.K.
           "An international comparison of the quantity and income-expenditure
           theories"   J. Am. Statist. Ass., vol.68, 1973, pp.63-65.
           EVALUATION - MONETARIST THEORY * DATA - INTERNATIONAL
YA0032   ADLER F.M.
           "The relationship between the income and price elasticities of demand for US
           exports"   Rev. Econ. Stats., vol.52, 1970, pp.313-319.
           APPL - MACRO : INTERNATIONAL TRADE , EXPORTS * INCOME - EFFECT OF * PRICE -
           EFFECT OF * DATA - INTERNATIONAL
YA0033   ADLER M., HORESH R., AGMON T.
           "The relationship among equity markets: comment"   J. Finance, vol.29,
           1974, pp.1311-1319.
           DATA - INTERNATIONAL * APPL - FIRM : FINANCE , STOCK PRICES * STOCK PRICES -
           COVARIATION * STOCK PRICES - MODELS , INTERNATIONAL
YA0034   AGARWALA R., DRINKWATER J.
           "Consumption functions with shifting parameters due to socio-economic
           factors"   Rev. Econ. Stats., vol.54, 1972, pp.89-96.
           APPL - MACRO : EMPLOYMENT * APPL - SECTOR : CONSUMER NON DURABLES * APPL -
           SECTOR : CONSUMER DURABLES * APPL - SECTOR : SERVICES * REGRESSION -
           SHIFTING COEFFICIENTS * APPL - MACRO : CONSUMPTION * EX ANTE * PRICE -
           EFFECT OF * INCOME - EFFECT OF * REGRESSION - PRIOR INFORMATION
YA0035   AGARWALA R., ET AL.
           "A neo-classical approach to the determination of prices and wages"
           Economica, vol.39, 1972, pp.250-263.
           INFLATION - PHILLIPS CURVE * APPL - MACRO : EARNINGS * APPL - MACRO : MONEY
           , SUPPLY * APPL - MACRO , CANADA * PRICE - EFFECT OF * INFLATION -
           DETERMINANTS , EARNINGS
YA0036   AGGARWAL S.C.
           "A critique of 'the distribution system simulator' by M.M. Connors et al"
           Mgmt. Sci. (B), vol.20, 1973, pp.482-486.
           SIMULATION - METHODOLOGY * USE - INVENTORY CONTROL * USE - DISTRIBUTION ,
           CONTROL
YA0037   AGHEVLI B.B., KHAN M.S.
           "Inflationary finance and the dynamics of inflation: Indonesia, 1951-72"
           Am. Econ. Rev., vol.67, 1977, pp.390-403.
           APPL - MACRO , SOUTH EAST ASIA * APPL - MACRO : MONEY * POLICY EVALUATION -
           MACRO : FISCAL , MONETARY * APPL - SECTOR : GOVERNMENT , EXPENDITURE *
           PUBLIC EXPENDITURE - EFFECT OF * APPL - SECTOR : GOVERNMENT , REVENUES *
           INFLATION - DETERMINANTS
YA0038   AGMON T.
           "Country risk: the significance of the country factor for share-price
           movements in the UK, Germany and Japan"   J. Business, vol.46, 1973,
           pp.24-32.
           APPL - SECTOR : FINANCE , STOCK PRICE INDEX * DATA - INTERNATIONAL * STOCK
           PRICES - COVARIATION * APPL - FIRM : FINANCE , STOCK PRICES * STOCK PRICES -
           MODELS , INTERNATIONAL
YA0039   AGMON T.
           "The relationship among equity markets: a study of share price co-movements
           in the US, UK, Germany and Japan"   J. Finance, vol.27, 1972, pp.839-855.
           APPL - FIRM : FINANCE , STOCK PRICES * APPL - SECTOR : FINANCE , STOCK PRICE
           INDEX * STOCK PRICES - COVARIATION * DATA - INTERNATIONAL * APPL - MACRO :
           INTERNATIONAL LINKAGE
YA0040   AGMON T., LESSARD D.R.
           "Investor recognition of corporate international diversification"   J.
           Finance, vol.32, 1977, pp.1049-1055.
           APPL - FIRM : FINANCE , INVESTMENT , INTERNATIONAL * APPL - FIRM : FINANCE ,
           STOCK PRICES * STOCK PRICES - MODELS , INTERNATIONAL * STOCK PRICES - BETA ,
           DETERMINANTS * APPL - FIRM TYPE : MULTINATIONALS
YA0041   AHAMAD B., SCOTT, K.F.N.
           "A note on sensitivity analysis in manpower forecasting"   R. Statist. Soc.
           (A), vol.135, 1972, pp.385-392.
           MANPOWER PLANNING - METHODOLOGY * CONFIDENCE INTERVAL - PREDICTIONS :
           PROBABILITY MODELS
YA0042   AHL D.H.
           "New product forecasting using consumer panels"   J. Mktg. Res., vol.7,
           1970, pp.160-167.
           NEW PRODUCTS - TESTING * REPEAT BUYING

YA0043   AHLUND M.C., BARKSDALE H.C., HILLIARD J.E.
          "Multivariate spectral analysis- an illustration"   Decis. Sci., vol.8,
          1977, pp.734-752.
          SPECTRAL ANALYSIS - CROSS : REVIEW * SPECTRAL ANALYSIS - APPL : SECTOR ,
          COMMODITIES * APPL - SECTOR : COMMODITIES , LIVESTOCK
YA0044   AHMAD I.V., CONSTABLE G.K., LANFORD H.W.
          "The investigation of innovations and their effect on the number of firms
          entering and leaving an industry"   Ind. Mktg. Mgmt., vol.3, 1974,
          pp.243-255.
          APPL - SECTOR : GROWTH * CONCENTRATION - EFFECT OF * TECHNOLOGY - EFFECT OF
          * APPL - SECTOR : COMPANY FORMATIONS
YA0045   AHMED N.
          "A note on the Haavelmo hypothesis"   Rev. Econ. Stats., vol.53, 1971,
          pp.413-414.
          DATA - INTERNATIONAL * DATA - CROSS SECTION * APPL - MACRO : SAVINGS
YA0046   AIGNER D.J.
          "A compendium on estimation of the autoregressive-moving average model from
          time series data"   Int. Econ. Rev., vol.12, 1971, pp.348-371.
          TIME SERIES - ARIMA : REVIEW * EVALUATION - DISTRIBUTED LAG , SOLOW *
          BIBLIOGRAPHY - TIME SERIES , ARIMA * BIBLIOGRAPHY - DISTRIBUTED LAG *
          DISTRIBUTED LAG - ERROR SPECIFICATION * TIME SERIES - ARIMA : ESTIMATION *
          DISTRIBUTED LAG - ARIMA
YA0047   AIGNER D.J.
          "A note on the verification of computer simulation models"   Mgmt. Sci.
          (A), vol.18, 1972, pp.615-619.
          SIMULATION - EVALUATION OF RESULTS
YA0048   AIGNER D.J.
          "An appropriate econometric framework for estimating a labour supply
          function from the SEO file"   Int. Econ. Rev., vol.15, 1974, pp.59-68.
          ESTIMATION - MAXIMUM LIKELIHOOD * MANPOWER PLANNING - MACRO , SUPPLY *
          REGRESSION - ERRORS IN VARIABLES
YA0049   AIGNER D.J.
          "Asymptotic minimum - MSE prediction in the Cobb-Douglas model with a
          multiplicative disturbance term"   Econometrica, vol.42, 1974, pp.737-748.
          ERROR DISTRIBUTION - LOGNORMAL * ERROR DISTRIBUTION - MULTIPLICATIVE * DATA
          - SIMULATION * REGRESSION - TRANSFORMATIONS , LOGARITHMIC * COMPARATIVE
          METHODS - ESTIMATION : REGRESSION , TRANSFORMATIONS * REGRESSION -
          ESTIMATION * ESTIMATION - LOGARITHMIC MODEL
YA0050   AIGNER D.J.
          "M.S.E. dominance of least squares with errors of observation"   J.
          Econometrics, vol.2, 1974, pp.365-372.
          DATA ERRORS - EFFECT OF * DATA - SPECIFICATION OF VARIABLES * REGRESSION -
          VARIABLE INCLUSION * REGRESSION - ERRORS IN VARIABLES * PROXY VARIABLES
YA0051   AIGNER D.J.
          "On estimation of an econometric model of short run bank behaviour"   J.
          Econometrics, vol.1, 1973, pp.201-228.
          APPL - FIRM : FINANCE , BANKS * INTEREST RATE - EFFECT OF * DEMAND EQUATIONS
          - SYSTEMS OF * ESTIMATION - CONSTRAINED , NON LINEAR * COMPARATIVE METHODS -
          ESTIMATION : REGRESSION , ERROR SPECIFICATION
YA0052   AIGNER D.J.
          "Regression with a binary independent variable subject to errors of
          observation"   J. Econometrics, vol.1, 1973, pp.49-59.
          DATA ERRORS - EFFECT OF * REGRESSION - ERRORS IN VARIABLES * DATA -
          CATEGORICAL * REGRESSION - ESTIMATION * ADVANCED
YA0053   AIGNER D.J., AMEMIYA T., POIRIER D.J.
          "On the estimation of production frontiers: maximum likelihood estimation of
          the parameters of a discontinuous density function"   Int. Econ. Rev.,
          vol.17, 1976, pp.377-396.
          ESTIMATION - MAXIMUM LIKELIHOOD * LOSS FUNCTIONS - ASYMMETRICAL * ERROR
          DISTRIBUTION - DISCONTINUOUS , ASYMMETRIC * PRODUCTION FUNCTIONS -
          METHODOLOGY * DATA - SIMULATION * COMPARATIVE METHODS - ERROR DISTRIBUTIONS
YA0054   AIGNER D.J., GOLDBERGER A.S., KALTON G.
          "On the explanatory power of dummy variable regressions"   Int. Econ. Rev.,
          vol.16, 1975, pp.503-510.
          REGRESSION - GROUPED OBSERVATIONS * REGRESSION - COVARIANCE MODEL *
          SPECIFICATION ERROR - EFFECT OF , CATEGORIZATION
YA0055   AIGNER D.J., GOLDFELD S.M.
          "Simulation and aggregation: a reconsideration"   Rev. Econ. Stats.,
          vol.55, 1973, pp.115-118.
          SIMULATION - METHODOLOGY , MICRO * SIMULATION - ANALYTIC METHODS *
          COMPARATIVE METHODS - DATA : AGGREGATE , DISAGGREGATE
YA0056   AIGNER D.J., JUDGE G.G.
          "Application of pre-test and Stein estimators to economic data"
          Econometrica, vol.45, 1977, pp.1279-1288.
          APPL - MACRO : INTERNATIONAL TRADE * COMPARATIVE METHODS - ESTIMATION :
          REGRESSION * ESTIMATION - PRE TEST * ESTIMATION - STEIN * ADVANCED

YA0057   AIGNER D.J., LOVELL C.A.K., SCHMIDT P.
         "Formulation and estimation of stochastic frontier production function
         models"   J. Econometrics, vol.6, 1977, pp.21-37.
         PRODUCTION FUNCTIONS - ESTIMATION * PRODUCTION FUNCTIONS - METHODOLOGY *
         ERROR DISTRIBUTION - DISCONTINUOUS , ASYMMETRIC * DATA - SIMULATION *
         PRODUCTION FUNCTION - SECTOR * APPL - SECTOR : PRODUCTION * COMPARATIVE
         METHODS - ESTIMATION : PRODUCTION FUNCTIONS * APPL - SECTOR : AGRICULTURE *
         ERROR SPECIFICATION - PRODUCTION FUNCTIONS

YA0058   AIGNER D.J., SAWA T.
         "Identification and normalization: a note"   J. Econometrics, vol.2, 1974,
         pp.389-391.
         SIMULTANEOUS SYSTEM - IDENTIFICATION

YA0059   AITKEN N.D.
         "The effect of the E.E.C. and E.F.T.A. on the European trade: a temporal
         cross section analysis"   Am. Econ. Rev., vol.63, 1973, pp.881-892.
         APPL - MACRO : INTERNATIONAL TRADE * DATA - CROSS SECTION , TIME SERIES *
         APPL - MACRO , EEC * APPL - MACRO , EFTA * POLICY EVALUATION - MACRO :
         INTERNATIONAL TRADE

YA0060   AITKEN N.D., OBUTELEWICZ R.S.
         "A cross-sectional study of EEC trade with the association of African
         countries"   Rev. Econ. Stats., vol.53, 1976, pp.425-433.
         APPL - MACRO , AFRICA * APPL - MACRO , EEC * APPL - MACRO : INTERNATIONAL
         TRADE * DATA - CROSS SECTION

YA0061   AKAIKE H.
         "On the likelihood of a time series model"   Stat'n., vol.27, 1978,
         pp.217-225.
         MODEL SELECTION * TIME SERIES - ARIMA : IDENTIFICATION * LOSS FUNCTIONS -
         AKAIKE'S INFORMATION CRITERION * APPL - SECTOR : NATURAL , SUNSPOTS

YA0062   AKERLOF G.A., MILBOURNE R.D.
         "New calculations of income and interest elasticities in Tobin's model of
         the transactions demand for money"   Rev. Econ. Stats., vol.60, 1978,
         pp.541-546.
         APPL - MACRO : CONSUMER DEMAND , FINANCIAL ASSETS * INCOME - EFFECT OF *
         INTEREST RATE - EFFECT OF

YA0063   AKIN J.S., YOUNGDAY D.J.
         "The efficiency of local school finance"   Rev. Econ. Stats., vol.53, 1976,
         pp.255-258.
         APPL - SECTOR : EDUCATION , SCHOOLS * APPL - SECTOR : EFFICIENCY * POLICY
         EVALUATION - SECTOR : EDUCATION

YA0064   ALBRECHT W.S., ET AL.
         "A comparison of the accuracy of corporate and security analysts' forecasts
         of earnings: comments"   Acctg. Rev., vol.52, 1977, pp.736-745.
         APPL - FIRM : FINANCE , PROFITS * JUDGEMENTAL FORECASTS - DETERMINANTS *
         EVALUATION - JUDGEMENTAL FORECASTS , SPECIALIST

YA0065   ALBRECHT W.S., LOOKABILL L.L., McKEOWN J.C.
         "The time-series properties of annual earnings"   J. Acctg. Res., vol.15,
         1977, pp.226-244.
         COMPARATIVE METHODS - ARIMA , AUTOREGRESSIVE * EX ANTE * DATA -
         SPECIFICATION OF VARIABLES * APPL - FIRM : FINANCE , PROFITS

YA0066   ALEXANDER A.J.
         "Prices and the guideposts: the effects of government persuasion on
         individual prices"   Rev. Econ. Stats., vol.53, 1971, pp.67-75.
         PRICE CONTROLS - EFFECT OF * DISCRIMINANT ANALYSIS - APPL * APPL - FIRM :
         FINANCE , PROFITS * USER - SECTOR : GOVERNMENT * CONCENTRATION - EFFECT OF

YA0067   ALI M.A., HICKMAN P.J., CLEMENTSON A.J.
         "The application of automatic interaction detection (AID) in operational
         research"   Opl. Res. Q., vol.26, 1975, pp.243-252.
         APPL - SECTOR : AGRICULTURE , FISHING * AID - REVIEW

YA0068   ALI M.M, GREENBAUM S.I.
         "A spatial model of the banking industry"   J. Finance, vol.32, 1977,
         pp.1283-1303.
         APPL - FIRM : LOCATION * APPL - FIRM : FINANCE , BANKS * COST - FIRM :
         FINANCE , BANKS * APPL - FIRM : FINANCE , PROFITS * DATA - CROSS SECTION

YA0069   ALLDREDGE J.R., GIBB N.S.
         "Ridge regression: an annotated bibliography"   Int. Statist. Rev., vol.44,
         1976, pp.355-360.
         BIBLIOGRAPHY - REGRESSION , RIDGE * REGRESSION - RIDGE

YA0070   ALLEN R.F.
         "Cross-sectional estimates of cost economies in stock property-liability
         companies   Rev. Econ. Stats., vol.56, 1974, pp.100-103.
         DATA - CROSS SECTION * APPL - FIRM : FINANCE , INSURANCE COMPANIES * COST -
         FIRM : FINANCE * USE - ANTITRUST

YA0071   ALLEN S.D.
         "Rising Swiss inflation"   Bus. Econ., vol.13:2, 1978, pp.5-8.
         APPL - MACRO , SWITZERLAND * INFLATION - INDICATORS * POLICY EVALUATION -
         MACRO : MONETARY * DISTRIBUTED LAG - APPL , MONEY * ERROR SPECIFICATION -
         AUTOCORRELATED

YA0072   ALMON C., ET AL.
           "Programs and methods for input-output analysis"   Anns. Econ. Soc. Meas.,
           vol.2, 1973, pp.307-316.
           COMPUTERISATION - INPUT OUTPUT , PROGRAMS * INPUT OUTPUT - REGIONAL
YA0073   ALMON S.
           "Lags between investment decisions and their causes"   Rev. Econ. Stats.,
           vol.50, 1968, pp.193-206.
           APPL - MACRO : INVESTMENT * APPL - SECTOR : INVESTMENT * DISTRIBUTED LAG -
           ALMON : APPL * DISTRIBUTED LAG - APPL , OUTPUT * INTEREST RATE - EFFECT OF *
           STOCK PRICES - EFFECT OF
YA0074   ALPERT M.I., PETERSON R.A.
           "On the interpretation of canonical analysis"   J. Mktg. Res., vol.9, 1972,
           pp.187-192.
           EVALUATION - MULTIVARIATE METHODS , CANONICAL CORRELATION * CONSUMER
           BEHAVIOUR - PURCHASING , DETERMINANTS
YA0075   ALPERT M.J., BIBB J.F.
           "Fitting branch locations, performance standards and marketing strategies: a
           clarification"   J. Mktg., vol.38, no.2, April 1974, pp.72-74.
           USE - RETAIL , SITE MONITORING * REGRESSION - STEPWISE * REGRESSION - MODEL
           CHOICE * APPL - FIRM : FINANCE , BANKS * BASIC
YA0076   ALTMAN E.I.
           "Predicting railroad bankruptcies"   Bell J. Econ., vol.4, 1973,
           pp.184-211.
           APPL - FIRM : TRANSPORT , RAILWAYS * USE - BANKRUPTCY PREDICTION *
           DISCRIMINANT ANALYSIS - APPL
YA0077   ALTMAN E.I.
           "Railroad bankruptcy propensity"   J. Finance, vol.26, 1971, pp.333-345.
           APPL - SECTOR : TRANSPORT , RAILWAYS * USE - BANKRUPTCY PREDICTION
YA0078   ALTMAN E.I., LORIS B.
           "A financial early warning system for over-the-counter broker-dealers"   J.
           Finance, vol.31, 1976, pp.1201-1217.
           APPL - FIRM : FINANCE , STOCK BROKERS * DISCRIMINANT ANALYSIS - APPL * EX
           ANTE * USE - BANKRUPTCY PREDICTION
YA0079   ALTMAN S.H., BARRO R.J.
           "Officer supply - the impact of pay, the draft and the Vietnam war"   Am.
           Econ. Rev., vol.61, 1971, pp.649-664.
           MANPOWER PLANNING - SECTOR : GOVERNMENT , MILITARY , SUPPLY * DATA - CROSS
           SECTION , TIME SERIES * APPL - SECTOR : GOVERNMENT , DEFENCE * MANPOWER
           PLANNING - QUALIFIED MANPOWER * REGRESSION - QUALITATIVE DEPENDENT
YA0080   AMEMIYA T.
           "A note on a Fair and Jaffee model"   Econometrica, vol.42, 1974,
           pp.759-762.
           SIMULTANEOUS SYSTEM - DISEQUILIBRIUM * SIMULTANEOUS SYSTEM - ESTIMATION *
           ESTIMATION - MAXIMUM LIKELIHOOD
YA0081   AMEMIYA T.
           "Qualitative response models"   Anns. Econ. Soc. Meas., vol.4, 1975,
           pp.363-372.
           REGRESSION - QUALITATIVE DEPENDENT * REGRESSION - LIMITED DEPENDENT
YA0082   AMEMIYA T.
           "Regression analysis when the variance of the dependent variable is
           proportional to the square of its expectation"   J. Am. Statist. Ass.,
           vol.68, 1973, pp.928-934.
           ESTIMATION - MAXIMUM LIKELIHOOD * COMPARATIVE METHODS - REGRESSION , ERROR
           DISTRIBUTION * ERROR SPECIFICATION - HETEROSCEDASTIC * ESTIMATION - GLS *
           ERROR DISTRIBUTION - LOGNORMAL * ERROR DISTRIBUTION - NONNORMAL , GAMMA *
           COMPARATIVE METHODS - ESTIMATION : REGRESSION , ERROR SPECIFICATION *
           COMPARATIVE METHODS - ESTIMATION : OLS , GLS * COMPARATIVE METHODS -
           ESTIMATION : OLS , MLE * SPECIFICATION ERROR - TESTS , ERROR DISTRIBUTION
YA0083   AMEMIYA T., BOSKIN M.
           "Regression analysis when the dependent variable is truncated lognormal,
           with an application to the determinants of the duration of welfare
           dependency"   Int. Econ. Rev., vol.15, 1974, pp.485-496.
           APPL - SECTOR : SOCIAL , POVERTY * PUBLIC EXPENDITURE - EFFECT OF , AID
           PROGRAMS * REGRESSION - LIMITED DEPENDENT , TOBIT * COMPARATIVE METHODS -
           REGRESSION , LIMITED DEPENDENT * ESTIMATION - MAXIMUM LIKELIHOOD , ITERATIVE
YA0084   AMEMIYA T., MORIMUNE K.
           "Selecting the optimum order of the polynomial in the Almon distributed lag"
           Rev. Econ. Stats., vol.56, 1974, pp.378-386.
           DISTRIBUTED LAG - ALMON , IDENTIFICATION
YA0085   AMEMIYA T., NOLD F.
           "A modified logit model"   Rev. Econ. Stats., vol.57, 1975, pp.255-257.
           REGRESSION - LIMITED DEPENDENT , LOGIT * APPL - SECTOR : CONSUMER DURABLES *
           COMPARATIVE METHODS - ESTIMATION : REGRESSION , LIMITED DEPENDENT
YA0086   AMSDEN A.H.
           "Trade in manufactures between developing countries"   Econ. J., vol.86.
           1976, pp.778-790.
           APPL - MACRO : INTERNATIONAL TRADE * DATA - INTERNATIONAL

YA0087   AMSTUTZ A.E.
          "Market-orientated management systems: the current status"   J. Mktg, Res.,
          vol.6, 1969, pp.481-496.
          USER REQUIREMENTS * USE - MARKETING POLICY * MIS * BASIC
YA0088   ANDERSEN A.
          "An application of post-sample stability theory to time-series forecasting"
          Opl. Res. Q., vol.28, 1977, pp.93-98.
          STABILITY OF COEFFICIENTS - TIME SERIES , TEST
YA0089   ANDERSEN L.C., CARLSON K.M.
          "St. Louis model revisited"   Int, Econ, Rev., vol.15, 1974, pp.305-327.
          MACRO MODEL - ST.LOUIS * EX ANTE
YA0090   ANDERSON E.E.
          "A probabilistic forecast of contractionary phase time: 1975-2000"   Bus.
          Econ., vol.12:2, 1977, pp.17-21.
          BUSINESS CYCLE - PREDICTION * DATA - INTERNATIONAL * MARKOV MODELS - APPL :
          MACRO
YA0091   ANDERSON H.
          "Living costs and quality change "   Am, Stat'n., vol,27, 1973, pp,32-37.
          INDEX NUMBERS - MACRO : CONSUMER PRICE INDEX * QUALITY - ADJUSTMENTS
YA0092   ANDERSON H.
          "Population and sample in economic forecasting"   Int, Statist, Rev.,
          vol.41, 1973, pp.149-153.
          FORECASTING - THEORY * THEORY - MODELLING * ERROR SPECIFICATION - EFFECT OF
YA0093   ANDERSON H.
          "The sample period in economic prediction"   Am, Stat'n., vol,25:3, 1971,
          pp,46-49.
          DATA - SAMPLE SIZE * STABILITY OF COEFFICIENTS * BASIC
YA0094   ANDERSON K.P.
          "Residential demand for electricity:econometric estimates for California and
          the US"   J, Business, vol,46, 1973, pp,526-553.
          APPL - SECTOR : UTILITIES , ELECTRICITY * DATA - CROSS SECTION , TIME SERIES
YA0095   ANDERSON L.C.
          "The St. Louis econometric forecasting model"   Bus, Econ., vol,6:4, 1971,
          pp,29-32.
          MACRO MODEL - ST.LOUIS
YA0096   ANDERSON O.D.
          "A Box-Jenkins analysis of the coloured fox data from Nain, Labrador"
          Stat'n., vol,26, 1977, pp,51-75.
          TIME SERIES - ARIMA : INTRODUCTION * APPL - SECTOR : NATURAL , ANIMAL
          POPULATIONS * TIME SERIES - ARIMA : TRANSFORMATIONS
YA0097   ANDERSON O.D.
          "A commentary on 'A survey of time series'"   Int, Statist, Rev., vol,45,
          1977, pp,273-297.
          TIME SERIES - REVIEW * BIBLIOGRAPHY - TIME SERIES
YA0098   ANDERSON O.D.
          "Moving average processes"   Stat'n., vol.24, 1975, pp.283-297.
          TIME SERIES - ARIMA : APPL * TIME SERIES - MOVING AVERAGE
YA0099   ANDERSON O.D.
          "On the collection of time series data"   Opl, Res. Q., vol,26, 1975,
          pp.331-335.
          DATA ERRORS - EFFECT OF * TIME SERIES - ARIMA : INTERPRETATION * DATA -
          AGGREGATION OVER TIME
YA0100   ANDERSON O.D.
          "On the distributional properties of serial correlations for general time
          processes"   Stat'n., vol.26, 1977, pp.221-230.
          AUTOCORRELATION - COEFFICIENTS
YA0101   ANDERSON O.D.
          "The interpretation of Box-Jenkins time series models"   Stat'n., vol,26,
          1975, pp.127-145.
          TIME SERIES - ARIMA : INTERPRETATION
YA0102   ANDERSON O.D.
          "Time series analysis and forecasting: another look at the Box-Jenkins
          approach"   Stat'n., vol.26, 1977, pp.285-303.
          TIME SERIES - ARIMA : REVIEW
YA0103   ANDERSON O.D., ET AL.
          "Box-Jenkins rules OK - provided you know it makes sense" with discussion
          Mgmt. Sci., vol.24, 1978, pp.1199-1205.
          TIME SERIES - ARIMA : INTERPRETATION
YA0104   ANDERSON O.D., WILLIAMSON M.
          "The biological interpretation of time series analysis"   Stat'n., vol,26,
          1977, pp.46-50.
          APPL - SECTOR : NATURAL , ANIMAL POPULATIONS * SPECTRAL ANALYSIS - APPL :
          BUSINESS CYCLE , LONG CYCLE * SPECTRAL ANALYSIS - APPL : MODEL
          INTERPRETATION
YA0105   ANDERSON R.J., CROCKER T.D.
          "Air pollution and property values: a reply"   Rev. Econ. Stats., vol,54,
          1972, pp.470-473.
          APPL - SECTOR : CONSTRUCTION , RESIDENTIAL * POLLUTION - EFFECT OF * LP *
          MODEL INTERPRETATION * PRICE - SECTOR : CONSTRUCTION , RESIDENTIAL

YA0106   ANDERSON W.T., CUNNINGHAM W.H.
         "Gauging foreign product promotion"   J. Advtg. Res., vol.12:1, 1972,
         pp.21-34.
         MARKET SEGMENTATION * DISCRIMINANT ANALYSIS - APPL * CONSUMER BEHAVIOUR -
         PURCHASING , DETERMINANTS * APPL - FIRM : CONSUMER DURABLES , CARS * USE -
         MEDIA PLANNING
YA0107   ANDO A.
         "Some aspects of stabilization policies, the monetarist controversy and the
         MPS model"   Int. Econ. Rev., vol.15, 1974, pp.541-571.
         MACRO MODEL - MIT , PENN , SSRC * CONTROL THEORY - MACRO : STABILISATION *
         POLICY EVALUATION - MACRO : MONETARY * EVALUATION - MACRO MODELS
YA0108   ANDO A., KAUFMAN G.M.
         "Evaluation of an ad hoc procedure for estimating parameters of some linear
         models"   Rev. Econ. Stats., vol.48, 1966, pp.334-340.
         REGRESSION - SUMMARY STATISTICS * REGRESSION - VARIABLE INCLUSION * DATA -
         SIMULATION * REGRESSION - HYPOTHESIS TESTS * SPECIFICATION ERROR - TESTS ,
         VARIABLE INCLUSION * DATA - SAMPLE SIZE
YA0109   ANDO A.K., ET AL.
         "On the role of expectations of price and technological change in an
         investment function"   Int. Econ. Rev., vol.15, 1974, pp.384-414.
         INFLATION - EXPECTATIONS * EXPECTATIONS - DATA * APPL - MACRO : INVESTMENT *
         EX ANTE * THEORY - INVESTOR BEHAVIOUR * TECHNOLOGY - EFFECT OF
YA0110   ANDREWS D.F., PREGIBON D.
         "Finding the outliers that matter"   R. Statist. Soc. (B), vol.40, 1978,
         pp.85-93.
         DATA ERRORS - OUTLIERS * REGRESSION - OUTLIERS * ADVANCED
YA0111   ANG J.S.
         "Dividend policy: informational content or partial adjustment?"   Rev.
         Econ. Stats., vol.57, 1975, pp.65-70.
         SPECTRAL ANALYSIS - APPL : SECTOR , FINANCE * SPECTRAL ANALYSIS - CROSS :
         APPL * APPL - SECTOR : FINANCE , DIVIDENDS
YA0112   ANG J.S., PATEL K.A.
         "Bond rating methods: comparison and validation" with discussion   J.
         Finance, vol.30, 1975, pp.631-640 & 674.
         USE - CREDIT CONTROL , BOND RATING * RISK - ESTIMATION * EX ANTE
YA0113   ANGEVINE G.E.
         "Forecasting consumption with a Canadian consumer sentiment measure"   Can.
         J. Econ., vol.7, 1974, pp.273-289.
         APPL - MACRO : CONSUMER DEMAND * EVALUATION - SURVEYS , CONSUMER * STABILITY
         OF COEFFICIENTS - REGRESSION : APPL * SURVEYS - CONSUMER , DETERMINANTS * EX
         ANTE * APPL - MACRO , CANADA * APPL - SECTOR : CONSUMER DURABLES , CARS *
         ATTITUDINAL DATA
YA0114   ANKER R.
         "An analysis of fertility differentials in developing countries"   Rev.
         Econ. Stats., vol.60, 1978, pp.58-69.
         POPULATION - FERTILITY * DATA - INTERNATIONAL * DATA - CROSS SECTION * DATA
         - LDC * EDUCATION - EFFECT OF
YA0115   ANSCOMBE F.J.
         "Graphs in statistical analysis"   Am. Stat'n., vol.28, 1974, pp.17-21.
         REGRESSION - SCATTERGRAM * BASIC
YA0116   ANSLEY C.F., SPIVEY W.A., WROBESKI W.J.
         "A class of transformations for Box-Jenkins seasonal models"   Appl.
         Stats., vol.26, 1977, pp.173-178.
         TIME SERIES - ARIMA : TRANSFORMATIONS * COMPUTERISATION - ESTIMATION , TIME
         SERIES , PROGRAMS
YA0117   APPELBAUM E.
         "Testing neoclassical production theory"   J. Econometrics, vol.7, 1978,
         pp.87-102.
         COMPARATIVE METHODS - PRICE ELASTICITY , ESTIMATION * PRODUCTION FUNCTIONS -
         THEORY * PRODUCTION FUNCTIONS - MACRO * EVALUATION - PRODUCTION FUNCTIONS *
         COST - THEORY * COST - MACRO * ADVANCED
YA0118   APPELBAUM E., HARRIS R.
         "Estimating technology in an intertemporal framework: a neo-Austrian
         approach"   Rev. Econ Stats., vol.59, 1977, pp.161-170.
         PRODUCTION FUNCTIONS - THEORY * PRODUCTION FUNCTIONS - MACRO
YA0119   APPLEBAUM W.
         "Methods for determining store trade areas, market penetration and potential
         sales"   J. Mktg. Res., vol.3, 1966, pp.127-141.
         APPL - SECTOR : RETAILING * USE - SITE SELECTION , RETAIL * USE - RETAIL ,
         SITE MONITORING * MARKET POTENTIAL
YA0120   ARAK M., LUCAS R.E.
         "Some international evidence on output-inflation tradeoffs: comment"   Am.
         Econ. Rev., vol.67, 1977, pp.720-731.
         SPECIFICATION ERROR - EFFECT OF , SIMULTANEOUS SYSTEM BIAS * APPL - MACRO :
         GNP * INFLATION - EFFECT OF
YA0121   ARAK M., SPIRO A.
         "A theoretical explanation of the interest inelasticity of money demand"
         Rev. Econ. Stats., vol.55, 1973, pp.520-523.
         INTEREST RATE - EFFECT OF * APPL - MACRO : MONEY , DEMAND

YA0122   ARCHIBALD G.C., RICHMOND J.
          "On the theory of foreign exchange reserve requirements"   Rev. Econ.
          Studies, vol.38, 1971, pp.245-263.
          APPL - MACRO : INTERNATIONAL FINANCE , FOREIGN RESERVES * DATA -
          INTERNATIONAL
YA0123   ARCHIBALD T.R.
          "Stock market reaction to the depreciation switch-back"   Acctg. Rev.,
          vol.47, 1972, pp.22-30.
          STOCK PRICES - INFORMATION EFFECT * ACCOUNTING PRACTICE - EFFECT OF * APPL -
          FIRM : FINANCE , STOCK PRICES
YA0124   ARMOUR H.O., TEECE D.J.
          "Organisational structure and economic performance: a test of the
          multidivisional hypothesis"   Bell. J. Econ., vol.9, 1978, pp.106-122.
          APPL - FIRM : FINANCE , PROFITS * APPL - FIRM TYPE * VOLATILITY - EFFECT OF
          * CAPACITY - EFFECT OF * APPL - FIRM : PRODUCTION , PETROLEUM
YA0125   ARMSTRONG J.S.
          "An application of econometric models to international marketing"   J.
          Mktg. Res., vol.7, 1970, pp.190-198.
          EVALUATION - THEORY OF * APPL - SECTOR : CONSUMER DURABLES , CAMERAS *
          MARKET POTENTIAL * PRICE - EFFECT OF * INCOME - EFFECT OF * EX ANTE *
          EVALUATION - PRIOR INFORMATION * REGRESSION - PRIOR INFORMATION * DATA -
          INTERNATIONAL
YA0126   ARMSTRONG J.S.
          "How to avoid exploratory research"   J. Advtg. Res., vol.10:4, 1970,
          pp.27-30.
          MODEL SELECTION * PRIOR INFORMATION * REGRESSION - TRANSFORMATIONS * MODEL
          INTERPRETATION * REGRESSION - VARIABLE INCLUSION * BASIC
YA0127   ARMSTRONG J.S., ANDRESS J.G.
          "Exploratory analysis of marketing data: trees vs. regression"   J. Mktg.
          Res., vol.7, 1970, pp.487-492.
          APPL - FIRM : RETAILING , GASOLINE * REGRESSION - STEPWISE * COMPARATIVE
          METHODS - REGRESSION , MULTIVARIATE METHODS * AID - APPL * EX ANTE
YA0128   ARMSTRONG J.S., ET AL.
          "Forecasting with econometric methods: folklore versus fact" with comments
          J. Business, vol.51, 1978, pp.549-600.
          FORECASTING - REVIEW * ECONOMETRICS - REVIEW * EVALUATION - CAUSAL MODELS *
          COMPARATIVE METHODS - AUTOREGRESSIVE , CAUSAL * COMPARATIVE METHODS - CAUSAL
          , JUDGEMENTAL * FORECASTER BEHAVIOUR * COMPARATIVE METHODS - MACRO MODELS *
          EVALUATION - THEORY OF
YA0129   ARMSTRONG J.S., GROHMAN M.C.
          "A comparative study of methods for long range market forecasting"   Mgmt.
          Sci. (B), vol.19, 1972, pp.211-221.
          LONG TERM FORECASTING * APPL - SECTOR : TRANSPORT , AIR * USER - FIRM :
          TRANSPORT * COMPARATIVE METHODS - JUDGEMENTAL , TREND CURVES * COMPARATIVE
          METHODS - CAUSAL , TREND CURVES * COMPARATIVE METHODS - CAUSAL , JUDGEMENTAL
          * EX ANTE * EVALUATION - THEORY OF * JUDGEMENTAL FORECASTS - SPECIALIST *
          LEAD TIME - EFFECT OF
YA0130   ARMSTRONG J.S., OVERTON T.
          "Brief vs. comprehensive descriptions in measuring intentions to purchase"
          J. Mktg. Res., vol.8, 1971, pp.114-117.
          EVALUATION - SURVEYS , CONSUMER * SURVEYS - METHODOLOGY , DESIGN *
          EVALUATION - EXPECTATIONS , DATA
YA0131   ARMSTRONG J.S., SHAPIRO A.C.
          "Analyzing quantitive models"   J. Mktg., vol.38, no.2, April 1974,
          pp.61-66.
          EVALUATION - THEORY OF * APPL - FIRM : CONSUMER NON DURABLES * BASIC
YA0132   ARMSTRONG R.D., FROME E.L.
          "A comparison of two algorithms for absolute deviation curve fitting"   J.
          Am. Statist. Ass., vol.71, 1976, pp.328-330.
          ESTIMATION - MSAE * LP * COMPUTERISATION - ESTIMATION , REGRESSION MODELS ,
          PROGRAMS
YA0133   ARMSTRONG R.D., KUNG M.T., FROME E.L.
          "Least absolute value estimates for a simple linear regression problem" with
          comment   Appl. Stats., vol.27, 1978, pp.363-366 & 378.
          ESTIMATION - MSAE * LP * COMPUTERISATION - ESTIMATION , REGRESSION MODELS ,
          PROGRAMS
YA0134   ARNDT S.W.
          "International short term capital movements: a distributed lag model of
          speculation in foreign exchange"   Econometrica, vol.36, 1968, pp.59-70.
          APPL - MACRO : INTERNATIONAL FINANCE * EXCHANGE RATE - EFFECT OF *
          COMPARATIVE METHODS - ESTIMATION : OLS , 3PLS * THEORY - SPECULATION
YA0135   ARORA S.S.
          "Error components regression models and their applications"   Anns. Econ.
          Soc. Meas., vol.2, 1973, pp.451-461.
          DATA - SIMULATION * REGRESSION - COVARIANCE MODEL * REGRESSION - ERROR
          COMPONENTS * COMPARATIVE METHODS - DATA : CROSS SECTION , TIME SERIES *
          ADVANCED

YA0136   ASCH P., SENECA J.J.
          "Is collusion profitable"   Rev. Econ. Stats., vol.53, 1976, pp.1-12.
          APPL - FIRM : FINANCE , PROFITS * CONCENTRATION - EFFECT OF * COMPETITION -
          EFFECT OF * ADVERTISING - EFFECT OF
YA0137   ASHENFELTER O.
          "Estimating the effect of training programs on earnings"   Rev. Econ.
          Stats., vol.60, 1978, pp.47-57.
          MANPOWER PLANNING - EARNINGS * MANPOWER PLANNING - EDUCATION PROGRAMS *
          REGRESSION - ERROR COMPONENTS : APPL
YA0138   ASHENFELTER O., JOHNSON G.E.
          "Unionism, relative wages, and labour quality in US manufacturing
          industries"   Int. Econ. Rev., vol.13, 1972, pp.488-508.
          APPL - MACRO : EARNINGS * UNIONISATION - EFFECT OF * UNIONISATION -
          DETERMINANTS * EDUCATION - EFFECT OF
YA0139   ASHENFELTER O., JOHNSON G.E., PENCAVEL J.H.
          "Trade unions and the rate of change of money wages in US manufacturing"
          Rev. Econ. Studies, vol.39, 1972, pp.27-54.
          BIBLIOGRAPHY - EARNINGS * APPL - MACRO : EARNINGS * COMPARATIVE METHODS -
          ESTIMATION : SIMULTANEOUS SYSTEM * COMPARATIVE METHODS - ESTIMATION :
          SIMULTANEOUS SYSTEM , 2SLS , 3SLS
YA0140   ASHENFELTER O., PENCAVEL J.H.
          "Wage changes and the frequency of wage settlements"   Economica, vol.42,
          1975, pp.162-170.
          APPL - MACRO , UK * APPL - MACRO : EARNINGS * REGRESSION - MODEL CHOICE
YA0141   ASHTON R.H.
          "The predictive-ability criterion and user prediction models"   Acctg.
          Rev., vol.49, 1974, pp.719-732.
          BOOTSTRAPPING - REVIEW * ACCOUNTING PRACTICE - EFFECT OF * JUDGEMENTAL
          FORECASTS - APPL
YA0142   ASHTON R.H.
          "The robustness of linear models for decision-making"   Omega, vol.4, 1976,
          pp.609-615.
          JUDGEMENTAL FORECASTS - REVIEW * EVALUATION - BOOTSTRAPPING * DECISION RULES
          - METHODOLOGY
YA0143   ASHTON R.H.
          "User prediction models in accounting: an alternative use"   Acctg. Rev.,
          vol.50, 1975, pp.710-721.
          BOOTSTRAPPING - REVIEW * BIBLIOGRAPHY - BOOTSTRAPPING
YA0144   ASKARI H., CUMMINGS J.T.
          "Estimating agricultural supply response with the Nerlove model: a survey"
          Int. Econ. Rev., vol.18, 1977, pp.257-292.
          SUPPLY - SECTOR : AGRICULTURE * BIBLIOGRAPHY - AGRICULTURE * PRICE - EFFECT
          OF * APPL - SECTOR : AGRICULTURE
YA0145   ASKARI H., RAYMOND A., WEIL G.
          "Long-term capital mobility under alternative exchange systems"   Can. J.
          Econ., vol.10, 1977, pp.69-78.
          APPL - MACRO : INVESTMENT , INTERNATIONAL * EXCHANGE RATE - EFFECT OF * APPL
          - MACRO , CANADA * POLICY EVALUATION - MACRO : INTERNATIONAL FINANCE ,
          FOREIGN EXCHANGE
YA0146   ASSAEL H.
          "Comparison of brand share data by three reporting systems"   J. Mktg.
          Res., vol.4, 1967, pp.400-401.
          MARKET SHARE - METHODOLOGY * BRAND CHOICE - METHODOLOGY * DATA ERRORS -
          ESTIMATION OF * APPL - SECTOR : CONSUMER NON DURABLES * EVALUATION - SURVEYS
          , CONSUMER
YA0147   ASSAEL H.
          "Segmenting markets by group purchasing behaviour: an application of the AID
          technique"   J. Mktg. Res., vol.7, 1970, pp.153-158.
          MARKET SEGMENTATION * AID - REVIEW * CONSUMER BEHAVIOUR - PURCHASING ,
          DETERMINANTS * BRAND CHOICE - DETERMINANTS * APPL - FIRM : CONSUMER NON
          DURABLES , FOOD
YA0148   ASSAEL H.
          "Segmenting markets by response elasticity"   J. Advtg. Res., vol.16:2,
          1976, pp.27-35.
          MARKET SEGMENTATION * AID - APPL * PRICE - EFFECT OF * APPL - SECTOR :
          UTILITIES , TELEPHONE * APPL - FIRM : CONSUMER NON DURABLES
YA0149   ASSAEL H., DAY G.S.
          "Attitudes and awareness as predictors of market share"   J. Advtg. Res.,
          vol.8:4, 1968, pp.3-10.
          CONSUMER BEHAVIOUR - PSYCHOLOGICAL MODELS * MARKET SHARE - SECTOR : CONSUMER
          NON DURABLES * APPL - FIRM : CONSUMER NON DURABLES , GROCERIES * APPL - FIRM
          : CONSUMER NON DURABLES , HEALTH AIDS
YA0150   ASSMUS G.
          "NEWPROD: the design and implementation of a new product model"   J. Mktg.,
          vol.39, no.1, Jan 1975, pp.16-23.
          NEW PRODUCTS - TESTING * REPEAT BUYING * SIMULATION - APPL : NEW PRODUCTS

YA0151   ATHANS M.
         "The discrete time linear-quadratic-Gaussian stochastic control problem"
         Anns. Econ. Soc. Meas., vol.1, 1972, pp.449-492,
         CONTROL THEORY - STOCHASTIC , REVIEW * BIBLIOGRAPHY - CONTROL THEORY ,
         STOCHASTIC
YA0152   ATHANS M.
         "The importance of Kalman filtering methods for economic systems"   Anns.
         Econ. Soc. Meas., vol.3, 1974, pp.49-64,
         MODEL IDENTIFICATION * ESTIMATION - KALMAN FILTER * MODEL SELECTION *
         SIMULTANEOUS SYSTEM - MODEL CHOICE * SIMULTANEOUS SYSTEM - MODEL
         IDENTIFICATION
YA0153   ATKINSON A.C.
         "A method for discriminating between models" with discussion   R. Statist.
         Soc. (B), vol.32, 1970, pp.323-353,
         MODEL SELECTION * REGRESSION - MODEL CHOICE * ADVANCED
YA0154   ATKINSON A.C.
         "Testing transformations to normality"   R. Statist. Soc. (B), vol.35,
         1973, pp.473-479,
         REGRESSION - TRANSFORMATIONS , BOX COX * SPECIFICATION ERROR - TESTS , ERROR
         DISTRIBUTION
YA0155   ATKINSON A.C., COX D.R.
         "Planning experiments for discriminating between models" with discussion,
         R. Statist. Soc. (B), vol.36, 1974, pp.321-348,
         SIMULATION - EXPERIMENTAL DESIGN * MODEL SELECTION * BAYESIAN - MODEL
         SELECTION
YA0156   ATKINSON S.E.
         "Small-sample properties of simultaneous equation estimates with
         multicollinearity" J. Am. Statist. Ass., vol.73, 1978, pp.719-723,
         COMPARATIVE METHODS - ESTIMATION : SIMULTANEOUS SYSTEM * MULTICOLLINEARITY -
         EFFECT OF * DATA - SIMULATION * SIMULATION - METHODOLOGY , MONTE CARLO *
         COMPARATIVE METHODS - ESTIMATION : OLS , 2SLS * COMPARATIVE METHODS -
         ESTIMATION : OLS , 3SLS * COMPARATIVE METHODS - ESTIMATION : SIMULTANEOUS
         SYSTEM , 2SLS , 3SLS
YA0157   ATTFIELD C.L.F.
         "Estimation of a model containing unobservable variables using grouped data:
         an application to the permanent income hypothesis"   J. Econometrics,
         vol.6, 1977, pp.51-63,
         APPL - MACRO , UK * DATA - CROSS SECTION * SIMULTANEOUS SYSTEM - ERRORS IN
         VARIABLES , UNOBSERVABLE * APPL - MACRO : CONSUMPTION * INCOME - EFFECT OF ,
         PERMANENT * DATA - GROUPED * SIMULTANEOUS SYSTEM - GROUPED OBSERVATIONS
YA0158   ATTFIELD C.L.F.
         "Estimation of the structural parameters in a permanent income model"
         Economica, vol.43, 1976, pp.247-254,
         THEORY - PERMANENT INCOME * DATA - CROSS SECTION * APPL - MACRO :
         CONSUMPTION * INCOME - EFFECT OF , PERMANENT * REGRESSION - STATE SPACE
YA0159   AUCAMP D.
         "Comment on 'the random nature of stock-market prices' authored by Barrett
         and Wright"   Ops. Res., vol.23, 1975, pp.587-591,
         RANDOM WALK - THEORY * STOCK PRICES - RUNS * PROBABILITY MODELS - DIFFUSION
YA0160   AUERBACH R.
         "The measurement of scale economies"   J. Business, vol.49, 1976, pp.60-61,
         SCALE ECONOMIES * COST - SCALE ECONOMIES
YA0161   AUERBACH R.D., RUTNER J.L.
         "A causality test of Canadian money and income: a comment on Barth and
         Bennett"   Can. J. Econ., vol.11, 1978, pp.583-594,
         CAUSALITY - TEST * SPECIFICATION ERROR - EFFECT OF , FILTERING * APPL -
         MACRO , CANADA * APPL - MACRO : MONEY , SUPPLY * APPL - MACRO : GNP
YA0162   AUERBACH R.D., RUTNER J.L.
         "The misspecification of a nonseasonal cycle as a seasonal by the X-11
         seasonal adjustment program"   Rev. Econ. Stats., vol.60, 1978, pp.601-603,
         BUSINESS CYCLE - IDENTIFICATION * SEASONALITY - ESTIMATION , CENSUS *
         BUSINESS CYCLE - EFFECT OF * SPECTRAL ANALYSIS - APP : SEASONALITY *
         SPECTRAL ANALYSIS - APPL : BUSINESS CYCLE
YA0163   AUERBACH R.D., RUTNER J.L.
         "Time and frequency domain tests of some US-Canadian relationships under an
         autoregressive filter"   Appl. Econ., vol.8, 1976, pp.165-178,
         APPL - MACRO , CANADA * APPL - MACRO : INTERNATIONAL LINKAGE * CAUSALITY -
         TEST * APPL - MACRO : MONEY , SUPPLY * TIME SERIES - AUTOREGRESSIVE
YA0164   AULT D.
         "The determinants of world steel exports: an empirical study"   Rev. Econ.
         Stats., vol.54, 1972, pp.38-46,
         DATA - CROSS SECTION * APPL - SECTOR : INTERNATIONAL TRADE * APPL - SECTOR :
         PRODUCTION , STEEL * TECHNOLOGY - EFFECT OF
YA0165   AVIO K.L.
         "The supply of property offences in Ontario: evidence on the deterent effect
         of punishment"   Can. J. Econ., vol.11, 1978, pp.1-19,
         APPL - SECTOR : SOCIAL , CRIME * EXPECTATIONS - ESTIMATING

YA0166   AWH R.Y., WATERS D.
         "A discriminant analysis of economic, demographic, and attitudinal
         characteristics of bank charge card holders: a case study"   J. Finance,
         vol.29, 1974, pp.973-980.
         MARKET SEGMENTATION * APPL - SECTOR : FINANCE , BANKS * APPL - SECTOR :
         FINANCE , CONSUMER CREDIT * USE - CREDIT CONTROL , CONSUMER * INCOME -
         EFFECT OF * ATTITUDINAL DATA

YA0167   AXELSSON R., ET AL.
         "On the length of spells of unemployment in sweden: comments"   Am. Econ.
         Rev., vol.67, 1977, pp.218-224.
         MANPOWER PLANNING - UNEMPLOYMENT , DURATION * APPL - MACRO : UNEMPLOYMENT *
         APPL - MACRO , SWEDEN

YA0168   AYAL I.
         "Simple models for monitoring new product performance"   Decis. Sci.,
         vol.6, 1975, pp.220-236.
         BRAND CHOICE - APPL * NEW PRODUCTS - EVALUATION * EVALUATION - NEW PRODUCT
         MODELS * REPEAT BUYING * COMPARATIVE METHODS - DATA : AGGREGATE ,
         DISAGGREGATE * EX ANTE * APPL - SECTOR : CONSUMER NON DURABLES , HEALTH AIDS
         * EVALUATION - CONSUMER BEHAVIOUR , STOCHASTIC MODELS

YA0169   AYAL I., MAIMON Z.
         "Sales demands on securities brokers"   Ind. Mktg. Mgmt., vol.7, 1978,
         pp.161-169.
         APPL - FIRM : FINANCE , STOCK BROKERS * USER - FIRM : FINANCE * USE - SALES
         FORCE MANAGEMENT * CANONICAL CORRELATION - APPL * BASIC

YA0170   AYANIAN R.
         "A comparison of Barten's estimated demand elasticities with those obtained
         using Frisch's method"   Econometrica, vol.37, 1969, pp.79-94.
         APPL - MACRO : CONSUMER DEMAND * SUBSTITUTE PRODUCTS * COMPARATIVE METHODS -
         PRICE ELASTICITY , ESTIMATION * DEMAND EQUATIONS - SYSTEMS OF : METHODOLOGY
         , ESTIMATION

YA0171   BACON R.W.
         "Some evidence on the largest squared correlation coefficient from several
         samples"   Econometrica, vol.45, 1977, pp.1997-2001.
         REGRESSION - MODEL CHOICE * REGRESSION - SUMMARY STATISTICS

YA0172   BAESEL J.B.
         "Two tests of the ergodicity of monthly security return distributions"
         Omega, vol.2, 1974, pp.119-126.
         APPL - FIRM : FINANCE , STOCK PRICES * STOCK PRICES - RUNS * STATIONARITY -
         TESTING

YA0173   BAGSHAW M., JOHNSON R.A.
         "Sequential procedures for detecting parameter changes in a time-series
         model"   J. Am. Statist. Ass., vol.72, 1977, pp.593-597.
         STABILITY OF COEFFICIENTS - TIME SERIES , TEST * TIME SERIES - ARIMA :
         DIAGNOSTICS * CONTROL CHARTS - CUSUM

YA0174   BAILEY D., BOYLE S.E.
         "The optimal measure of concentration"   J. Am. Statist. Ass., vol.66,
         1971, pp.702-706.
         CONCENTRATION - MEASURING

YA0175   BAILY M.N.
         "Stabilisation policy and private economic behaviour" with discussion
         Brookings Paps. Econ. Activity, 1978, pp.11-59.
         APPL - MACRO : EMPLOYMENT * DISTRIBUTED LAG - APPL , OUTPUT * APPL - MACRO :
         INVENTORIES * APPL - MACRO : INVESTMENT * APPL - SECTOR : FINANCE , STOCK
         PRICE INDEX * STOCK PRICES - DETERMINANTS * STABILITY OF COEFFICIENTS -
         REGRESSION : APPL * POLICY EVALUATION - MACRO : STABILISATION

YA0176   BAILY M.N., TOBIN J.
         "Macroeconomic effects of selective public employment and wage subsidies"
         with discussion   Brookings Paps. Econ. Activity, 1977, pp.511-544.
         POLICY EVALUATION - MACRO : UNEMPLOYMENT * APPL - MACRO : EARNINGS *
         MANPOWER PLANNING - TRAINING PROGRAMS * APPL - SECTOR : EARNINGS * PUBLIC
         EXPENDITURE - EFFECT OF

YA0177   BAIN A.D.
         "Flow of funds analysis"   Econ. J., vol.83, 1973, pp.1055-1093.
         BIBLIOGRAPHY - FLOW OF FUNDS * APPL - MACRO : FLOW OF FUNDS * EVALUATION -
         INTEREST RATE FORECASTS

YA0178   BAKER S.H.
         "Risk, leverage and profitability: an industry analysis"   Rev. Econ.
         Stats., vol.55, 1973, pp.503-507.
         APPL - SECTOR : FINANCE , PROFITS * CONCENTRATION - EFFECT OF * DATA - CROSS
         SECTION * APPL - FIRM : FINANCE , FINANCIAL STRUCTURE , LEVERAGE * RISK -
         EFFECT OF * VOLATILITY - EFFECT OF

YA0179   BALACHANDRAN K.R., GERWIN D.
         "Variable work models for predicting course enrolments"   Ops. Res.,
         vol.21, 1973, pp.823-834.
         APPL - FIRM : EDUCATION , UNIVERSITIES * EVALUATION - MANPOWER PLANNING
         MODELS * MANPOWER PLANNING - SECTOR : EDUCATION , UNIVERSITIES * EX ANTE *
         MANPOWER PLANNING - FIRM

YA0180   BALDWIN R.E.
          "Determinants of the commodity structure of US trade"   Am. Econ. Rev.,
          vol.61, 1971, pp.126-146.
          APPL - MACRO : INTERNATIONAL TRADE * DATA - INTERNATIONAL * BIBLIOGRAPHY -
          INTERNATIONAL TRADE
YA0181   BALESTRA P., NERLOVE M.
          "Pooling cross section and time series data in the estimation of a dynamic
          model: the demand for natural gas"   Econometrica, vol.34, 1966,
          pp.585-612.
          APPL - SECTOR : UTILITIES , GAS * ESTIMATION - CROSS SECTION , TIME SERIES
YA0182   BALL M.J., KIRWAN R.M.
          "Urban housing demand: some evidence from cross-sectional data"   Appl.
          Econ., vol.9, 1977, pp.343-366.
          DATA - CROSS SECTION * APPL - SECTOR : CONSTRUCTION , RESIDENTIAL * INCOME -
          EFFECT OF * PRICE - EFFECT OF
YA0183   BALL R., WATTS R.
          "Some time series properties of accounting income"   J. Finance, vol.27,
          1972, pp.663-681.
          APPL - FIRM : FINANCE , PROFITS , PER SHARE * RANDOM WALK - TEST *
          EXPONENTIAL SMOOTHING - APPL * EVALUATION - EXPONENTIAL SMOOTHING
YA0184   BALL R.J.
          "Art and science in economic policy making"   J. Opl. Res. Soc., vol.29,
          1978, pp.397-407.
          FORECASTING - USAGE * POLICY EVALUATION - REVIEW * EVALUATION - MACRO MODELS
          * BASIC
YA0185   BALL R.J., BURNS T.
          "Econometric analysis and mangerial decision making"   Omega, vol.2, 1974,
          pp.295-311.
          ECONOMETRICS - INTRODUCTION * COST - INTRODUCTION * BASIC
YA0186   BALL R.J., BURNS T.,
          "The inflationary mechanism in the UK econdmy"   Am. Econ. Rev., vol.66,
          1976, pp.467-484.
          INFLATION - DETERMINANTS * APPL - MACRO , UK
YA0187   BALL R.J., BURNS T., LAURY J.S.E.
          "The role of exchange rate changes in balance of payments adjustment - the
          UK case"   Econ. J., vol.87, 1977, pp.1-29.
          MACRO MODEL - UK , LBS * POLICY EVALUATION - MACRO : INTERNATIONAL FINANCE ,
          FOREIGN EXCHANGE
YA0188   BALL R.J., EATON J.R., STEUER M.D.
          "The relationship between UK export performance in manufactures and the
          internal pressure of demand"   Econ. J., vol.76, 1966, pp.501-518.
          APPL - MACRO , UK * APPL - MACRO : INTERNATIONAL TRADE , EXPORTS * CAPACITY
          - EFFECT OF
YA0189   BALOFF N.
          "Extension of the learning curve - some empirical results"   Opl. Res. Q.,
          vol.22, 1971, pp.329-340.
          APPL - FIRM : PRODUCTION , MUSICAL INSTRUMENTS * COST - LEARNING CURVE *
          APPL - FIRM : CONSUMER DURABLES , CLOTHING * APPL - FIRM : CONSUMER DURABLES
          , CARS * COST - FIRM : PRODUCTION * COST - FIRM : CONSUMER DURABLES *
          BIBLIOGRAPHY - LEARNING CURVE
YA0190   BALTHASAR H.U., BOSCHI R.A.A., MENKE M.M.
          "Calling the shots in R & D"   H.B.R., vol.56, May-June, 1978, pp.151-160.
          USE - R&D * JUDGEMENTAL FORECASTS - METHODOLOGY * EVALUATION - JUDGEMENTAL
          FORECASTS , R&D * LONG TERM FORECASTING * BASIC
YA0191   BAMBER D.J.
          "A versatile family of forecasting systems"   Opl. Res. Q., vol.20,
          (special issue) 1969, pp.111-121.
          USE - INVENTORY CONTROL * TRACKING SIGNAL - APPL * USE - PROMOTION
          EVALUATION * INTERVENTION * TIME SERIES - BOX JENKINS PREDICTOR
YA0192   BANKS F.E., DESAI M.
          "An econometric model of the world tin ecomomy: a comment"   Econometrica,
          vol.40, 1972, pp.749-755.
          APPL - SECTOR : COMMODITIES , TIN * PRICE - EFFECT OF
YA0193   BAQUEIRO A.J., ET AL.
          "The labor force decision of married female teachers: comments"   Rev.
          Econ. Stats., vol.53, 1976, pp.241-245.
          APPL - SECTOR : EDUCATION , SCHOOLS * MANPOWER PLANNING - SECTOR : EDUCATION
          , SCHOOLS * MANPOWER PLANNING - LABOUR PARTICIPATION , FEMALE * DISCRIMINANT
          ANALYSIS - APPL * DATA - SPECIFICATION OF VARIABLES
YA0194   BAR-SHALOM Y.
          "Effect of uncertainties on the control performance of linear systems with
          unknown trajectory confidence tubes"   Anns. Econ. Soc. Meas., vol.6, 1978,
          pp.599-611.
          CONTROL THEORY - STOCHASTIC , METHODOLOGY * EVALUATION - CONTROL THEORY ,
          STOCHASTIC * SIMULTANEOUS SYSTEM - CONTROL * ADVANCED
YA0195   BAR-SHALOM Y., TSE E.
          "Caution, probing and the value of information in the control of uncertain
          systems"   Anns. Econ. Soc. Meas., vol.5, 1976, pp.323-337.
          COMPARATIVE METHODS - CONTROL * SIMULTANEOUS SYSTEM - CONTROL * CONTROL
          THEORY - STOCHASTIC , THEORY * DATA - SIMULATION * ADVANCED

YA0196   BAR-YOSEF S., BROWN L.D.
"A reexamination of stock splits using moving betas"   J. Finance, vol.32,
1977, pp.1069-1080.
STOCK PRICES - BETA , VARIABLE * STABILITY OF COEFFICIENTS - REGRESSION *
ACCOUNTING PRACTICE - EFFECT OF * APPL - FIRM : FINANCE , STOCK PRICES *
COMPARATIVE METHODS - REGRESSION , SHIFTING COEFFICIENTS

YA0197   BAR-YOSEF S., KOLODNY R.
"Dividend policy and capital market theory"   Rev. Econ. Stats., vol.53,
1976, pp.181-190.
APPL - FIRM : FINANCE , STOCK PRICES * APPL - FIRM : FINANCE , DIVIDENDS *
THEORY - EFFICIENT MARKETS * STOCK PRICES - BETA

YA0198   BARBAR C.L., McCALLUM J.S.
"The term structure of interest rates and the maturity compostion of the
government debt: the Canadian case"   Can. J. Econ., vol.8, 1975,
pp.606-609.
INTEREST RATE - TERM STRUCTURE * INTEREST RATE - DETERMINANTS * APPL - MACRO
, CANADA

YA0199   BAREFIELD R.M.
"Comments on a measure of forecasting performance"   J. Acctg. Res., vol.7,
1969, pp.324-327.
LOSS FUNCTIONS - FIRM * USE - FORECASTER EVALUATION * BASIC

YA0200   BAREFIELD R.M., COMISKEY E.E.
"The accuracy of bank earnings forecasts"   Bus. Econ., vol.11:3, 1976,
pp.59-63
APPL - FIRM : FINANCE , BANKS * EVALUATION - JUDGEMENTAL FORECASTS , PROFITS
* APPL - FIRM : FINANCE , PROFITS * BASIC

YA0201   BARKER T.S.
"A maximum sustainable growth rate for British industrial output"   Rev.
Econ. Studies, vol.38, 1971, pp.369-376.
APPL - MACRO , UK * INPUT OUTPUT - MACRO , UK * APPL - MACRO : GROWTH

YA0202   BARKER T.S., WOODWARD V.H.
"Inflation, growth, and economic policy in the medium term"   Nat. Inst.
Econ. Rev., no.60, 1972, pp.37-55.
MACRO MODEL - UK , CAMBRIDGE GROWTH * LONG TERM FORECASTING

YA0203   BARKSDALE H.C., GUFFEY H.J.
"An illustration of cross-spectral analysis in marketing"   J. Mktg. Res.,
vol.9, 1972, pp.271-278.
SPECTRAL ANALYSIS - APPL : SEASONALITY * SPECTRAL ANALYSIS - CROSS :
METHODOLOGY * SPECTRAL ANALYSIS - REVIEW * SPECTRAL ANALYSIS - APPL : SECTOR
, CONSUMER DURABLES * SPECTRAL ANALYSIS - APPL : LAG IDENTIFICATION * APPL -
SECTOR : CONSUMER DURABLES , CARS

YA0204   BARKSDALE H.C., HILLIARD J.E.
"A cross-spectral analysis of retail inventories and sales"   J. Business,
vol.48, 1975, pp.365-382.
SPECTRAL ANALYSIS - CROSS : APPL * APPL - SECTOR : INVENTORIES * APPL -
SECTOR : RETAILING * CAUSALITY - TEST : APPL

YA0205   BARKSDALE H.C., HILLIARD J.E.
"A spectral analysis of the ineraction between inventories and sales of
merchant wholesalers"   Decis. Sci., vol.6, 1975, pp.307-323.
SPECTRAL ANALYSIS - APPL : BUSINESS CYCLE * SPECTRAL ANALYSIS - APPL :
SECTOR , DISTRIBUTION * APPL - SECTOR : DISTRIBUTION , WHOLESALERS * APPL -
SECTOR : INVENTORIES * SPECTRAL ANALYSIS - CROSS : APPL

YA0206   BARNEA A., DOWNES D.H.
"A reexamination of the empirical distributions of stock price changes"
J. Am. Statist. Ass., vol.68, 1973, pp.348-358.
APPL - FIRM : FINANCE , STOCK PRICES * ERROR DISTRIBUTION - STABLE * STOCK
PRICES - DISTRIBUTION

YA0207   BARNES L.
"Long-lead vs. medium-lead cycle indicators as business and stock market
forecasters"   Bus. Econ., vol.12:2, 1977, pp.1-11.
EVALUATION - BUSINESS INDICATORS * APPL - SECTOR : FINANCE , STOCK PRICE
INDEX * STOCK PRICES - INDICATORS

YA0208   BARNETT W.A.
"Recursive subaggregation and generalised hypocycloidal demand model"
Econometrica, vol.45, 1977, pp.1117-1136.
CONSUMER BEHAVIOUR - ECONOMIC MODELS , THEORY * APPL - SECTOR : CONSUMER NON
DURABLES , FOOD * PRICE - EFFECT OF * INCOME - EFFECT OF * ADVANCED

YA0209   BARNOW B.S.
"The use of proxy variables when one or two independent variables are
measured with error"   Am. Stat'n., vol.30, 1976, pp.119-121.
PROXY VARIABLES * REGRESSION - SPECIFICATION OF VARIABLES * DATA -
SPECIFICATION OF VARIABLES * REGRESSION - ERRORS IN VARIABLES

YA0210   BARON D.P., TAGGART R.A.
"A model of regulation under uncertainty and a test of regulatory bias"
Bell J. Econ., vol.8, 1977, pp.151-167.
PRODUCTION FUNCTIONS - FIRM * APPL - FIRM : UTILITIES , ELECTRICITY * THEORY
- PRICING * USE - FINANCIAL , REGULATION * APPL - FIRM : FINANCE , FINANCIAL
STRUCTURE

YA0211   BARONE R.
          "The use of money in stock price models"   Bus. Econ., vol.7:4, 1972,
          pp.23-25.
          APPL - SECTOR : FINANCE , STOCK PRICE INDEX * STOCK PRICES - DETERMINANTS *
          DISTRIBUTED LAG - APPL , MONEY
YA0212   BARONE R.N., HUNING G.S.
          "Measuring investment analyst performance"   Bus. Econ., vol.10:3, 1975,
          pp.54-59.
          EVALUATION - JUDGEMENTAL FORECASTS , STOCK PRICES * USE - FORECASTER
          EVALUATION * EVALUATION - JUDGEMENTAL FORECASTS , SPECIALIST
YA0213   BARRETT J.F., WRIGHT D.J.
          "The random nature of stock-market prices"   Ops. Res., vol.22, 1974,
          pp.175-177.
          RANDOM WALK - THEORY * STOCK PRICES - RUNS * PROBABILITY MODELS - DIFFUSION
YA0214   BARRETT J.P.
          "The coefficient of determination- some limitations"   Am. Stat'n., vol.28,
          1974, pp.19-20.
          REGRESSION - SUMMARY STATISTICS * REGRESSION - SCATTERGRAMS * BASIC
YA0215   BARRETT N.S., FLANAGAN R.J.
          "The US Phillips curve and international unemployment rate differentials:
          comments"   Am. Econ. Rev., vol.65, 1975, pp.213-225.
          MANPOWER PLANNING - UNEMPLOYMENT , DURATION * APPL - MACRO : UNEMPLOYMENT *
          APPL - MACRO , SWEDEN * DATA - INTERNATIONAL * INFLATION - PHILLIPS CURVE
YA0216   BARRO R.J.
          "Unanticipated money growth and unemployment in the US"   Am. Econ. Rev.,
          vol.67, 1977, pp.101-115.
          APPL - MACRO : MONEY , SUPPLY * APPL - MACRO : UNEMPLOYMENT
YA0217   BARRODALE I.
          "L1 approximations and the analysis of data"   Appl. Stats., vol.17, 1968,
          pp.51-57.
          ESTIMATION - MSAE * DATA - SIMULATION * COMPARATIVE METHODS - ESTIMATION :
          OLS , MSAE
YA0218   BARRY C.B., WILD A.R.
          "Statistical model comparison in marketing research"   Mgmt. Sci., vol.24,
          1977, pp.387-392.
          MODEL SELECTION * BAYESIAN - MODEL SELECTION
YA0219   BARTELS R.
          "On the use of limit theorem arguments in economic statistics"   Am.
          Stat'n., vol.31, 1977, pp.85-87.
          REGRESSION - ROBUST * ERROR DISTRIBUTION - NONNORMAL
YA0220   BARTEN A.P.
          "The systems of consumer demand functions approach: a review"
          Econometrica, vol.45, 1977, pp.23-51.
          DEMAND EQUATIONS - SYSTEMS OF , REVIEW * CONSUMER BEHAVIOUR - ECONOMIC
          MODELS * EVALUATION - CONSUMER BEHAVIOUR , ECONOMIC MODELS * BIBLIOGRAPHY -
          DEMAND EQUATIONS , SYSTEMS OF * ADVANCED
YA0221   BARTH J., KRAFT A., KRAFT J.
          "Estimation of the liquidity trap using spline functions"   Rev. Econ.
          Stats., vol.53, 1976, pp.218-222.
          REGRESSION - PIECEWISE * APPL - MACRO : MONEY , DEMAND * INTEREST RATE -
          EFFECT OF * SPLINE FUNCTIONS
YA0222   BARTH J., KRAFT A., KRAFT J.
          "The 'moneyness' of financial assets"   Appl. Econ., vol.9, 1977, pp.51-61.
          CONSUMER BEHAVIOUR - ECONOMIC MODELS , THEORY * APPL - MACRO : CONSUMER
          DEMAND , FINANCIAL ASSETS
YA0223   BARTH J.R., BENNETT J.T.
          "Deposit variability and commercial bank cash holdings"   Rev. Econ.
          Stats., vol.57, 1975, pp.238-241.
          APPL - FIRM : FINANCE , BANKS * VOLATILITY - EFFECT OF * USE - PORTFOLIO
          SELECTION * APPL - FIRM : FINANCE , FINANCIAL STRUCTURE , LIQUID ASSETS
YA0224   BARTH J.R., BENNETT J.T.
          "Seasonal variation in interest rates"   Rev. Econ. Stats., vol.57, 1975,
          pp.80-83.
          INTEREST RATE - SEASONALITY * SEASONALITY - TESTING : APPL
YA0225   BARTH J.R., BENNETT J.T.
          "The role of money in the Canadian economy: an empirical test"   Can. J.
          Econ., vol.7, 1974, pp.306-311.
          APPL - MACRO : MONEY , SUPPLY * CAUSALITY - TEST : APPL * APPL - MACRO : GNP
          * APPL - MACRO , CANADA
YA0226   BARTH J.R., BENNETT J.T., HENDERSHOTT P.H.
          "Is the 'neutralized money stock' unbiased? comments"   J. Finance, vol.31,
          1976, pp.1509-1515.
          APPL - MACRO : MONEY * PROXY VARIABLES * CAUSALITY - TEST * APPL - MACRO :
          GNP * INDEX NUMBERS - MACRO : MONETARY POLICY
YA0227   BARTHOLOMEW D.J.
          "Errors of prediction for Markov chain models"   R. Statist. Soc. (B),
          vol.37, 1975, pp.444-456.
          MANPOWER PLANNING - SECTOR : GOVERNMENT , CENTRAL * MARKOV MODELS - APPL :
          MANPOWER * BAYESIAN - ESTIMATION : MARKOV MODELS * MARKOV MODELS -
          METHODOLOGY * CONFIDENCE INTERVAL - MARKOV MODELS * STABILITY OF
          COEFFICIENTS - MARKOV MODELS

YA0228   BARTHOLOMEW D.J.
          "The statistical approach to manpower planning"   Stat'n., vol.20, 1971,
          pp.3-36.
          MANPOWER PLANNING - FIRM * MARKOV MODELS - APPL : MANPOWER
YA0229   BARTLETT M.S.
          "Correlation or spectral analysis"   Stat'n., vol.27, 1978, pp.147-158.
          SPECTRAL ANALYSIS - REVIEW * SPECTRAL ANALYSIS - METHODOLOGY * SPECTRAL
          ANALYSIS - APPL : TIME SERIES
YA0230   BARZEL Y.
          "The market for a semipublic good: the case of American Economic Review"
          Am. Econ. Rev., vol.61, 1971, pp.665-674.
          APPL - FIRM : SERVICES , MEDIA , MAGAZINES * COST - FIRM : SERVICES
YA0231   BASI B.A., CAREY K.J., TWARK R.D.
          "A comparison of corporate and security analysts' forecasts of earnings"
          Acctg. Rev., vol.51, 1976, pp.244-254.
          EVALUATION - JUDGEMENTAL FORECASTS , SPECIALIST * APPL - FIRM : FINANCE ,
          PROFITS * APPL - SECTOR : UTILITIES
YA0232   BASMANN R.L., ET AL.
          "Comments on B.P. Byron's 'the restricted Aitken estimation of sets of
          demand relations'"   Econometrica, vol.41, 1973, pp.365-374.
          DEMAND EQUATIONS - SYSTEMS OF : METHODOLOGY , ESTIMATION * CONSUMER
          BEHAVIOUR - ECONOMIC MODELS , THEORY
YA0233   BASS F.M.
          "A new product growth model for consumer durables"   Mgmt. Sci. (A),
          vol.15, 1969, pp.215-227.
          APPL - SECTOR : CONSUMER DURABLES , APPLIANCES , TELEVISION * NEW PRODUCTS -
          DIFFUSION MODELS * APPL - SECTOR : CONSUMER DURABLES , APPLIANCES
YA0234   BASS F.M.
          "A simultaneous equation regression study of advertising and sales of
          cigarette data"   J. Mktg. Res., vol.6, 1969, pp.291-300.
          ADVERTISING - EFFECT OF * APPL - FIRM : CONSUMER NON DURABLES , CIGARETTES *
          ADVERTISING - OPTIMALITY
YA0235   BASS F.M.
          "Decomposable regression models in the analysis of market potentials"
          Mgmt. Sci. (B), vol.17, 1971, pp.485-494.
          MARKET POTENTIAL - DISAGGREGATION * ESTIMATION - CONSTRAINED * REGRESSION -
          CONSTRAINED * APPL - FIRM : RETAILING , FOOD * REGRESSION - AGGREGATION *
          APPL - SECTOR : CONSUMER DURABLES * MARKET SHARE - SECTOR : RETAILING *
          MARKET SHARE - SECTOR : CONSUMER DURABLES
YA0236   BASS F.M.
          "Decomposable regression models in the analysis of market potentials"
          Mgmt. Sci. (B), vol.17, 1971, pp.485-494.
          MARKET POTENTIAL * ESTIMATION - CONSTRAINED * APPL - SECTOR : CONSUMER
          DURABLES , FURNITURE * APPL - SECTOR : CONSUMER NON DURABLES , FOOD * APPL -
          SECTOR : CONSUMER DURABLES , APPLIANCES
YA0237   BASS F.M.
          "Profit and A/S ratio"   J. Advtg. Res., vol.14:6, 1974, pp.9-19.
          APPL - FIRM : FINANCE , PROFITS * ADVERTISING - EFFECT OF * CONCENTRATION -
          EFFECT OF * DATA - CROSS SECTION * MARKET SHARE - EFFECT OF * COMPARATIVE
          METHODS - ESTIMATION : OLS , GLS
YA0238   BASS F.M.
          "Testing vs. estimation of simultaneous equation regression models"   J.
          Mktg. Res., vol.8, 1971, pp.388-389.
          APPL - FIRM : CONSUMER NON DURABLES , CIGARETTES * ADVERTISING - EFFECT OF *
          MARKET SHARE - SECTOR : CONSUMER NON DURABLES * SIMULTANEOUS SYSTEM - MODEL
          INTERPRETATION * SPECIFICATION ERROR - EFFECT OF , IDENTIFICATION
YA0239   BASS F.M.
          "The theory of stochastic preference and brand switching"   J. Mktg. Res.,
          vol.11, 1974, pp.1-20.
          BRAND CHOICE - APPL * PROBABILITY MODELS - ENTROPY * PROBABILITY MODELS -
          NBD * APPL - FIRM : CONSUMER NON DURABLES , FOOD * EVALUATION - CONSUMER
          BEHAVIOUR , STOCHASTIC MODELS
YA0240   BASS F.M., CATTIN P., WITTINK D.R.
          "Firm effects and industry effects in the analysis of market structure and
          profitability"   J. Mktg. Res., vol.15, 1978, pp.3-10.
          MARKET SHARE - EFFECT OF * CONCENTRATION - EFFECT OF * APPL - FIRM : FINANCE
          , PROFITS * ADVERTISING - EFFECT OF * USE - ANTITRUST
YA0241   BASS F.M., CLARKE D.G.
          "Testing distributed lag models of advertising effect"   J. Mktg. Res.,
          vol.9, 1972, pp.298-308.
          REGRESSION - MODEL CHOICE * ADVERTISING - EFFECT OF * DISTRIBUTED LAG - APPL
          , ADVERTISING * COMPARATIVE METHODS - DISTRIBUTED LAG * APPL - SECTOR :
          CONSUMER NON DURABLES , FOOD , SPECIAL * COMPARATIVE METHODS - ESTIMATION :
          DISTRIBUTED LAG
YA0242   BASS F.M., JEULAND A., WRIGHT G.P.
          "Equilibrium stochastic choice and market penetration theories: derivations
          and comparisons"   Mgmt. Sci., vol.22, 1976, pp.1051-1063.
          BRAND CHOICE - THEORY * MARKET SHARE - SECTOR : CONSUMER NON DURABLES * APPL
          - SECTOR : CONSUMER NON DURABLES , LIQUOR * EVALUATION - CONSUMER BEHAVIOUR
          , STOCHASTIC MODELS

YA0243   BASS F.M., PARSONS L.J.
"Simultaneous equation regression analysis of sales and advertising"
Appl. Econ., vol.1, 1969, pp.103-124.
ADVERTISING - EFFECT OF * SIMULTANEOUS SYSTEM - PRIOR INFORMATION * APPL -
FIRM : CONSUMER NON DURABLES , GROCERIES * EX ANTE * ADVERTISING -
DETERMINANTS

YA0244   BASS F.M., WITTINK D.R.
"Pooling issues and methods in regression analysis: some further
reflections"   J. Mktg. Res., vol.15, 1978, pp.277-279.
REGRESSION - RANDOM COEFFICIENTS : APPL * EVALUATION - REGRESSION ,
AGGREGATION

YA0245   BASS F.M., WITTINK D.R.
"Pooling issues and methods in regression analysis with examples in
marketing research"   J. Mktg. Res., vol.12, 1975, pp.414-425.
DATA - AGGREGATION * APPL - SECTOR : CONSUMER DURABLES , FURNISHINGS * APPL
- SECTOR : CONSUMER DURABLES , APPLIANCES , ELECTRICAL * ESTIMATION - CROSS
SECTION , TIME SERIES * APPL - SECTOR : CONSUMER NON DURABLES , FOOD *
REGIONAL MODELS - SECTOR * COMPARATIVE METHODS - REGRESSION , RANDOM
COEFFICIENTS * COMPARATIVE METHODS - DATA : CROSS SECTION , TIME SERIES *
REGRESSION - ERROR COMPONENTS

YA0246   BASSETT P.C.
"Progressive approach to pension funding"   H.B.R., vol.53, Nov-Dec, 1972,
pp.125-135.
LONG TERM FORECASTING * APPL - FIRM : FINANCE , PENSIONS * USER - FIRM

YA0247   BASU S.
"Investment performance of common stocks in relation to their price-earnings
ratios: a test of the efficient market hypothesis"   J. Finance, vol.32,
1977, pp.663-682.
APPL - FIRM : FINANCE , STOCK PRICES * APPL - FIRM : FINANCE , PE RATIO *
STOCK PRICES - INFORMATION EFFECT

YA0248   BATCHELOR R.A.
"A variable-parameter model of exporting behaviour"   Rev. Econ. Studies,
vol.44, 1977, pp.43-57.
REGRESSION - SHIFTING COEFFICIENTS * APPL - MACRO , UK * APPL - MACRO :
INTERNATIONAL TRADE , EXPORTS * CAPACITY - EFFECT OF * APPL - MACRO :
INTERNATIONAL TRADE , PRICE * PRICE - EFFECT OF * REGRESSION - PIECEWISE

YA0249   BATCHELOR R.A.
"Sterling exchange rates 1951-1976: a Casselian analysis"   Nat. Inst.
Econ. Rev., no.81, 1977, pp.45-66.
APPL - MACRO : INTERNATIONAL FINANCE , EXCHANGE RATES * EX ANTE

YA0250   BATCHELOR R.A., BOWE C.
"Forecasting UK international trade: a general equilibrium approach"
Appl. Econ., vol.6, 1974, pp.109-141.
APPL - MACRO : INTERNATIONAL TRADE * PRICE - EFFECT OF * APPL - MACRO , EEC
* APPL - MACRO , UK

YA0251   BATES J., HENDERSON S.J.
"The determinants of corporate saving in small private companies in Britain
1954-1956"   R. Statist. Soc. (A), vol.130, 1967, pp.207-224.
APPL - SECTOR : FINANCE , SAVINGS * APPL - FIRM : FINANCE , SAVINGS * DATA
ERRORS - EFFECT OF * COMPARATIVE METHODS - ESTIMATION : REGRESSION , ERRORS
IN VARIABLES * APPL - FIRM TYPE : SMALL BUSINESSES

YA0252   BATES J.M., GRANGER C.W.J.
"The combination of forecasts"   Opl. Res. Q., vol.20, 1969, pp.451-468.
COMBINING FORECASTS - METHODOLOGY * TIME SERIES - BOX JENKINS PREDICTOR *
COMBINING FORECASTS - TIME SERIES

YA0253   BATES T.M.
"An econometric analysis of lending to black businessmen"   Rev. Econ.
Stats., vol.55, 1973, pp.272-283.
APPL - FIRM : FINANCE , LOANS * USE - CREDIT CONTROL , COMPANY * POLICY
EVALUATION - SECTOR : SOCIAL * DISCRIMINANT ANALYSIS - APPL * USER - FIRM :
FINANCE * POLICY EVALUATION - FIRM : FINANCIAL SUPPORT

YA0254   BATES T.M.
"Financing black enterprise"   J. Finance, vol.29, 1974, pp.747-761.
APPL - FIRM TYPE : SMALL BUSINESS * APPL - FIRM : FINANCE , FINANCIAL
STRUCTURE * APPL - FIRM : FINANCE , LOANS * APPL - FIRM : SOCIAL ,
INEQUALITY

YA0255   BATES T.M., HESTER D.D., EDELSTEIN R.H.
"Analysis of a commercial bank minority lending program: comments"   J.
Finance, vol.32, 1977, pp.1783-1794.
APPL - SECTOR : FINANCE , BANKS * APPL - SECTOR : SOCIAL , INEQUALITY * APPL
- SECTOR : FINANCE , LOANS * USE - CREDIT CONTROL , COMPANY * POLICY
EVALUATION - SECTOR : SOCIAL

YA0256   BATRA H.
"Dynamic interdependence in demand for savings deposits"   J. Finance,
vol.28, 1973, pp.507-514.
APPL - MACRO : SAVINGS * CONSUMER BEHAVIOUR - ECONOMIC MODELS * APPL - MACRO
: CONSUMER DEMAND , FINANCIAL ASSETS

YA0257   BATTY M.
"Monitoring on exponential smoothing forecasting systems"   Opl. Res. Q.,
vol.20, 1969, pp.319-325.
EXPONENTIAL SMOOTHING - ADAPTIVE COEFFICIENTS * EXPONENTIAL SMOOTHING -
MONITORING * TRACKING SIGNAL - THEORY

YA0258　BAUMANN H.
"Structural characteristics of Canada's pattern of trade"　Can. J. Econ.,
vol.9, 1976, pp.408-424.
APPL - SECTOR : INTERNATIONAL TRADE * APPL - MACRO , CANADA

YA0259　BAUMOL W.J., ET AL.
"Earnings retention, new capital and the growth of the firm"　Rev. Econ.
Stats., vol.52, 1970, pp.345-355.
APPL - FIRM : FINANCE , FINANCIAL STRUCTURE * APPL - FIRM : FINANCE ,
PROFITS

YA0260　BAUMOL W.J., VINOD H.D.
"An inventory theoretic model of freight transport demand"　Mgmt. Sci.
(A), vol.16, 1970, pp.413-421.
USER - FIRM : TRANSPORT * APPL - SECTOR : TRANSPORT * COST - SECTOR :
TRANSPORT * USE - TRANSPORT PLANNING * LOSS FUNCTIONS - FIRM , INVENTORY

YA0261　BAUTISTA R.M.
"Effects of major currency realignment on Philippine merchandise trade"
Rev. Econ. Stats., vol.59, 1977, pp.152-160.
APPL - MACRO , SOUTH EAST ASIA * EXCHANGE RATE - EFFECT OF * APPL - SECTOR :
INTERNATIONAL TRADE

YA0262　BAUTISTA R.M.
"Interrelated products and the elasticity of export supply in developing
countries"　Int. Econ. Rev., vol.19, 1978, pp.181-194.
APPL - SECTOR : INTERNATIONAL TRADE , EXPORTS * APPL - SECTOR : AGRICULTURE
, COCONUTS

YA0263　BAXTER R.E., REES R.
"Analysis of the industrial demand for electricity"　Econ. J., vol.78,
1968, pp.277-298.
APPL - SECTOR : UTILITIES , ELECTRICITY * REGRESSION - MODEL CHOICE * APPL
- SECTOR : ENERGY , SOURCES * PRICE - EFFECT OF

YA0264　BEACH C.M.
"An alternative approach to the specification of structural transition
functions"　Can. J. Econ., vol.10, 1977, pp.132-141.
REGRESSION - SHIFTING COEFFICIENTS * APPL - SECTOR : INTERNATIONAL TRADE ,
IMPORTS * APPL - SECTOR : CONSUMER DURABLES , CARS * COMPARATIVE METHODS -
REGRESSION , SHIFTING COEFFICIENTS * STABILITY OF COEFFICIENTS - REGRESSION

YA0265　BEACH C.M., MacKINNON J.G.
"A maximum likelihood procedure for regression with autocorrelated errors"
Econometrica, vol.46, 1978, pp.51-58.
DATA - SIMULATION * REGRESSION - ESTIMATION , ERROR SPECIFICATION *
ESTIMATION - MAXIMUM LIKELIHOOD * ERROR SPECIFICATION - AUTOCORRELATED

YA0266　BEACH C.M., MacKINNON J.G.
"Full maximum likelihood estimation of second-order autoregressive error
models"　J. Econometrics, vol.7, 1978, pp.187-198.
ERROR SPECIFICATION - AUTOCORRELATED * COMPARATIVE METHODS - ESTIMATION :
REGRESSION , ERROR SPECIFICATION * COMPARATIVE METHODS - ESTIMATION : OLS ,
MLE * DATA - SIMULAION

YA0267　BEALE E.M.L., LITTLE R.J.A.
"Missing values in multivariate analysis"　R. Statist. Soc. (B), vol.37,
1975, pp.129-145.
DATA ERRORS - MISSING OBSERVATIONS * COMPARATIVE METHODS - DATA ERRORS :
ESTIMATION

YA0268　BEARDSLEY G., MANSFIELD E.
"A note on the accuracy of industrial forecasts of new products and
processes"　J. Business, vol.51, 1978, pp.127-135.
EVALUATION - NEW PRODUCT FORECASTS * EVALUATION - JUDGEMENTAL FORECASTS

YA0269　BEARE J.B.
"Wage and price change relationships in post-war Canada"　Can. J. Econ.,
vol.6, 1973, pp.260-265.
INFLATION - PHILLIPS CURVE * APPL - MACRO : EARNINGS

YA0270　BEATON A.E., RUBIN D.B., BARONE J.L.
"The acceptability of regression solutions: another look at computational
accuracy"　J. Am. Statist. Ass., vol.71, 1976, pp.158-168.
COMPUTERISATION - CALCULATION ERROR * DATA ERRORS - EFFECT OF * NUMERICAL
METHODS - CALCULATION ERROR * EVALUATION - THEORY OF

YA0271　BEBEE E.L.
"Regional housing markets and population flows in Canada: 1956-67"　Can.
J. Econ., vol.5, 1972, pp.386-397.
APPL - SECTOR : CONSTRUCTION , RESIDENTIAL * REGIONAL MODELS - SECTOR :
CONSTRUCTION * PRICE - SECTOR : CONSTRUCTION

YA0272　BECK F.F.
"An econometric study to evaluate proposal estimates"　Omega, vol.1, 1973,
pp.777-779.
USE - PROJECT , PLANNING * COST - FIRM

YA0273　BECKENSTEIN A.R.
"Scale economies in the multiplant firm: theory and empirical evidence"
Bell J. Econ., vol.6, 1975, pp.644-657.
COST - SCALE ECONOMIES * APPL - SECTOR : PRODUCTION , PACKAGING * APPL -
SECTOR : PRODUCTION , PAINT * COST - SECTOR : PRODUCTIUN

YA0274   BECKER B.W., GREENBERG M.G., ROSHWALB I.
          "Probability estimates by respondents: does weighting improve accuracy?"
          J. Mktg. Res., vol.15, 1978, pp.482-488.
          JUDGEMENTAL FORECASTS - METHODOLOGY * EXPECTATIONS - DATA * SURVEYS -
          CONSUMER , DESIGN * SURVEYS - METHODOLOGY * JUDGEMENTAL FORECASTS -
          UNCERTAINTY

YA0275   BECKER W.E.
          "Determinants of the US currency-demand deposit ratio"   J. Finance,
          vol.30, 1975, pp.57-74.
          APPL - MACRO : MONEY , DEMAND * INTEREST RATE - EFFECT OF * DISTRIBUTED LAG
          - APPL , INTEREST RATE

YA0276   BECKMANN M.J., SATO R., SCHUPACK M.
          "Alternative approaches to the estimation of production functions of
          technical change"   Int. Econ. Rev., vol.13, 1972, pp.33-52.
          PRODUCTION FUNCTIONS - ESTIMATION * PRODUCTION FUNCTIONS - THEORY *
          TECHNOLOGY - EFFECT OF * PRODUCTION FUNCTIONS - SECTOR

YA0277   BECKWITH N.E.
          "Concerning the logical consistency of multivariate market share models"
          J. Mktg. Res., vol.10, 1973, pp.341-344.
          MARKET SHARE - METHODOLOGY * SIMULTANEOUS SYSTEM - CONSTRAINED

YA0278   BECKWITH N.E.
          "Multivariate analysis of sales responses of competing brands to
          advertising"   J. Mktg. Res., vol.9, 1972, pp.168-176.
          APPL - FIRM : CONSUMER NON DURABLES * DISTRIBUTED LAG - APPL , ADVERTISING *
          ADVERTISING - EFFECT OF * MARKET SHARE - SECTOR : CONSUMER NON DURABLES *
          COMPARATIVE METHODS - REGRESSION , SEEMINGLY UNRELATED * ADVERTISING -
          OPTIMALITY * EX ANTE * ERROR SPECIFICATION - CORRELATED

YA0279   BELKWITH N.E., SASIENI M.W.
          "Criteria for market segmentation studies"   Mgmt. Sci., vol.22, 1976,
          pp.892-903.
          MARKET SEGMENTATION * DATA - AGGREGATION OVER TIME * REGRESSION - SUMMARY
          STATISTICS * CONSUMER BEHAVIOUR - STOCHASTIC MODELS

YA0280   BEEDLES W.L.
          "A micro-econometric investigation of multi-objective firms"   J. Finance,
          vol.32, 1977, pp.1217-1233.
          SIMULTANEOUS SYSTEM - APPL : FIRM * APPL - FIRM * EX ANTE * COMPARATIVE
          METHODS - ESTIMATION : OLS , 2SLS * COMPARATIVE METHODS - AUTOREGRESSIVE ,
          CAUSAL(SIMULTANEOUS SYSTEM)

YA0281   BEEDLES W.L., SIMKOWITZ M.A.
          "A note on skewness and data errors"   J. Finance, vol.33, 1978,
          pp.288-292.
          DATA ERRORS - EFFECT OF * APPL - FIRM : FINANCE , STOCK PRICES * STOCK
          PRICES - DATA ERRORS

YA0282   BEHRMAN J.R.
          "Econometric modeling of national income determination in Latin America with
          special reference to the Chilean experience"   Anns. Econ. Soc. Meas.,
          vol.4, 1975, pp.461-488.
          MACRO MODEL - LATIN AMERICA * DATA SOURCES - LATIN AMERICA

YA0283   BEHRMAN J.R.
          "Sectoral elasticities of substitution between capital and labour in a
          developing economy: time series analysis in the case of post-war Chile"
          Econometrica, vol.40, 1972, pp.311-326.
          APPL - MACRO , LATIN AMERICA * PRODUCTION FUNCTIONS - SUBSTITUTION *
          PRODUCTION FUNCTIONS - SECTOR

YA0284   BEHRMAN J.R.
          "Sectoral investment determination in a developing economy"   Am. Econ.
          Rev., vol.62, 1972, pp.825-841.
          APPL - MACRO : INVESTMENT * ESTIMATION - NON LINEAR : APPL * THEORY -
          INVESTMENT BEHAVIOUR * APPL - MACRO , LATIN AMERICA * CAPACITY - EFFECT OF *
          EVALUATION - INVESTMENT MODELS

YA0285   BEHRMAN J.R.
          "The determinants of the annual rates of change of sectoral money wages in a
          developing economy"   Int. Econ. Rev., vol.12, 1971, pp.431-447.
          APPL - SECTOR : EARNINGS * DATA - LDC

YA0286   BEIGHTLER C.S., THURMAN V.R.
          "Management science models fo evluating regional government policies"
          Omega, vol.3, 1975, pp.71-78.
          APPL - SECTOR : UTILITIES , WATER * INPUT OUTPUT - REGIONAL * POLICY
          EVALUATION - REGIONAL * REGIONAL MODELS - SECTOR : GOVERNMENT , LOCAL ,
          FINANCE * REGIONAL MODELS - SECTOR : UTILITIES , WATER * APPL - SECTOR :
          GOVERNMENT , LOCAL , FINANCE * BASIC

YA0287   BELASSA B.
          "The rule of four-ninths: a rejoinder"   Econ. J., vol.84, 1974,
          pp.609-614.
          APPL - MACRO : INTERNATIONAL FINANCE , EXCHANGE RATES * INDEX NUMBERS -
          THEORY * DATA - MACRO , LDC

YA0288　BELASSA B., DAVID P.A.
"Just how misleading are official exchange rate conversions? comments"
Econ. J., vol.83, 1973, pp.1258-1276.
APPL - MACRO : INTERNATIONAL FINANCE , EXCHANGE RATES * INDEX NUMBERS -
THEORY * DATA - LDC

YA0289　BELKAOUI A.
"Canadian evidence of heteroscedasticity in the market model"　J. Finance,
vol.32, 1977, pp.1320-1324.
SPECIFICATION ERROR - TESTS , HETEROSCEDASTICITY * APPL - FIRM : FINANCE ,
STOCK PRICES * STOCK PRICES - MODELS , CAPM

YA0290　BELL D.E., KEENEY R.E., LITTLE J.D.C.
"A market share theorem"　J. Mktg. Res., vol.12, 1975, pp.136-141.
MARKET SHARE - METHODOLOGY

YA0291　BELL F.W.
"The relation of the structure of common stock prices to historical
expectational variables"　J. Finance, vol.29, 1974, pp.187-197.
STOCK PRICES - DETERMINANTS * STOCK PRICES - CROSS SECTION * EXPECTATIONS - DATA *
APPL - FIRM : FINANCE , STOCK PRICES * APPL - FIRM : FINANCE , PE RATIO

YA0292　BELLANTE D.M., ROSE P.S., HUNT L.H.
"The relative importance of monetary and fiscal variables in determining
price level movements: comment"　J. Finance, vol.28, 1973, pp.188-193.
INFLATION - DETERMINANTS * POLICY EVALUATION - MACRO : FISCAL , MONETARY

YA0293　BELSLEY D.A.
"Estimation of systems of simultaneous equations and computational
specifications of GREMLIN"　Anns. Econ. Soc. Meas., vol.3, 1974,
pp.551-614.
SIMULTANEOUS SYSTEM - ESTIMATION * ESTIMATION - REVIEW * COMPUTERISATION -
ESTIMATION , SIMULTANEOUS SYSTEM MODELS , PROGRAMS

YA0294　BELSLEY D.A.
"Specification with deflated variables and specious spurious correlation"
Econometrica, vol.40, 1972, pp.923-927.
DATA - TRANSFORMED , DEFLATED * INDEX NUMBERS - METHODOLOGY * REGRESSION -
TRANSFORMATIONS , RATIO * REGRESSION - SPURIOUS CORRELATION

YA0295　BELSLEY D.A.
"The relative power of the tau test: a furthering comment"　Rev. Econ.
Stats, vol.55, 1973, pp.132-133.
NON PARAMETRIC - TEST * COMPARATIVE METHODS - TESTS , AUTOCORRELATION *
EVALUATION - TEST , AUTOCORRELATION

YA0296　BELSLEY D.A., KUH E.
"Time-varying parameter structures: an overview"　Anns. Econ. Soc. Meas.,
vol.2, 1973, pp.375-381.
STABILITY OF COEFFICIENTS - REGRESSION * REGRESSION - RANDOM COEFFICIENTS *
REGRESSION - SHIFTING COEFFICIENTS * ESTIMATION - KALMAN FILTER

YA0297　BEN-ZION U., SHALIT S.S.
"Size, leverage and dividend record as determinants of equity risk"　J.
Finance, vol.30, 1975, pp.1015-1026.
STOCK PRICES - RISK , DETERMINANTS * STOCK PRICES - BETA , DETERMINANTS *
APPL - FIRM : FINANCE , STOCK PRICES * APPL - FIRM : FINANCE , DIVIDENDS *
APPL - FIRM : FINANCE , FINANCIAL STRUCTURE , LEVERAGE

YA0298　BENDANIEL D.J., ET AL.
"An econometric analysis of energy over the next 75 years"　Ind. Mktg.
Mgmt., vol.6, 1977, pp.197-210.
LONG TERM FORECASTING * APPL - MACRO : ENERGY * APPLICATION - MACROECONOMIC
: ENERGY , SOURCES

YA0299　BENDEL R.B., AFIFI A.A.
"A criterion for stepwise regression "　Am. Stat'n., vol.30, 1976,
pp.85-87.
REGRESSION - STEPWISE

YA0300　BENDEL R.B., AFIFI A.A.
"Comparison of stopping rules in forward 'stepwise' regression"　J. Am.
Statist. Ass., vol.72, 1977, pp.46-53.
REGRESSION - STEPWISE * DATA - SIMULATION * SIMULATION - METHODOLOGY , MODEL
SPECIFICATION

YA0301　BENHAM L.
"The labour market for registered nurses: a three-equation model"　Rev.
Econ. Stats., vol.53, 1971, pp.246-252.
HEALTH - MANPOWER , NURSES * MANPOWER PLANNING - SECTOR : HEALTH * MANPOWER
PLANNING - LABOUR PARTICIPATION , FEMALE

YA0302　BENISHAY H.
"Market preferences for characteristics of common stock"　Econ. J.,
vol.83, 1973, pp.173-191.
APPL - FIRM : FINANCE , STOCK PRICES * STOCK PRICES - DETERMINANTS * STOCK
PRICES - VOLATILITY

YA0303　BENNETT B.C.
"Economic forecasting for a television company"　Long Range Planning,
vol.11:5, 1978, pp.63-71.
FORECASTING - PRACTICE * USER - FIRM : SERVICES * APPL - FIRM : SERVICES ,
MEDIA , TV * BASIC

169

YA0304   BENNETT R.J.
         "Consistent estimation of nonstationary parameters for small sample
         situations-a monte carlo study"   Int. Econ. Rev., vol.18, 1977,
         pp.489-502.
         ESTIMATION - KALMAN FILTER * COMPARATIVE METHODS - ESTIMATION : REGRESSION ,
         RANDOM COEFFICIENTS * REGRESSION - RANDOM COEFFICIENTS * REGRESSION - STATE
         SPACE * DATA - SIMULATION

YA0305   BENSON P.H.
         "Bivariate normal distribution to calculate media exposure"   J. Advts.
         Res., vol.9:3, 1969, pp.41-47.
         ADVERTISING - EXPOSURE * USE - MEDIA PLANNING * APPL - FIRM : SERVICES ,
         MEDIA , MAGAZINES * PROBABILITY MODELS - NORMAL

YA0306   BENSTON G.J.
         "Graduated interest rate ceilings and operating costs by size of small
         consumer cash loans"   J. Finance, vol.32, 1977, pp.695-707.
         APPL - FIRM : FINANCE , CONSUMER FINANCE COMPANIES * COST - FIRM : FINANCE *
         COST - SCALE ECONOMIES

YA0307   BENSTON G.J.
         "Rate ceiling implications of the cost structure of consumer finance
         companies"   J. Finance, vol.32, 1977, pp.1169-1194.
         APPL - FIRM : FINANCE , CONSUMER FINANCE COMPANIES * COST - FIRM : FINANCE *
         DATA - CROSS SECTION , TIME SERIES * STABILITY OF COEFFICIENTS - REGRESSION
         * COST - SCALE ECONOMIES * USE - LOAN , REGULATION

YA0308   BENSTON G.J.
         "Risk on consumer finance company personal loans" with discussion   J.
         Finance, vol.32, 1977, pp.593-607 & 622-625.
         APPL - FIRM : FINANCE , CONSUMER FINANCE COMPANIES * APPL - FIRM : FINANCE ,
         CONSUMER CREDIT * USE - CREDIT CONTROL , CONSUMER

YA0309   BENSTON G.J., BRUCKER E.
         "A microeconomic approach to banking competition: comments"   J. Finance,
         vol.27, 1972, pp.722-726.
         APPL - FIRM : FINANCE , BANKS * APPL - FIRM : FINANCE , BANK , ASSETS * DATA
         - CROSS SECTION

YA0310   BENUS J., KMENTA J., SHAPIRO H.
         "The dynamics of household budget allocation to food expenditures"   Rev.
         Econ. Stats., vol.53, 1976, pp.129-138.
         CONSUMER BEHAVIOUR - ECONOMIC MODELS , THEORY * APPL - SECTOR : CONSUMER NON
         DURABLES , FOOD * PRICE - EFFECT OF

YA0311   BERENBLUT I.I., WEBB G.I.
         "A new test for autocorrelated errors in the linear regression model"   R.
         Statist. Soc. (B), vol.35, 1973, pp.33-50.
         AUTOCORRELATION - TEST * COMPARATIVE METHODS - TESTS , AUTOCORRELATION

YA0312   BERG S.V., DALTON T.R.
         "Labour participation in goods and services: 1958-71"   Rev. Econ. Stats.,
         vol.57, 1975, pp.518-522.
         MANPOWER PLANNING - LABOUR PARTICIPATION * MANPOWER PLANNING - SECTOR ,
         SUPPLY * INCOME - EFFECT OF * APPL - SECTOR : EMPLOYMENT * DATA - CROSS
         SECTION

YA0313   BERG S.V., DALTON T.R.
         "UK labour force activity rates: unemployment and real wages"   Appl.
         Econ., vol.9, 1977, pp.265-270.
         MANPOWER PLANNING - LABOUR PARTICIPATION * APPL - MACRO , UK * APPL - MACRO
         : EMPLOYMENT * MANPOWER PLANNING - EARNINGS

YA0314   BERGMANN B.R.
         "A microsimulation of the macroeconomy with explicitly represented money
         flows"   Anns. Econ. Soc. Meas., vol.3, 1974, pp.475-489.
         SIMULATION - APPL : MICRO * MACRO MODELS - MICRO MODEL * MACRO MODEL - US

YA0315   BERGMANN B.R.
         "Combining microsimulation and regression: a 'prepared' regression of
         poverty incidence on unemployment and growth"   Econometrica, vol.41, 1973,
         pp.955-963.
         APPL - MACRO : EMPLOYMENT * MULTICOLLINEARITY - REMOVAL OF * APPL - SECTOR :
         SOCIAL , POVERTY * SIMULATION - METHODOLOGY , MICRO * THEORY - MODELLING *
         COMPARATIVE METHODS - REGRESSION , SIMULATION

YA0316   BERGSTROM T.C., GOODMAN R.P.
         "Private demand for public goods"   Am. Econ. Rev., vol.63, 1973,
         pp.280-296.
         APPL - SECTOR : GOVERNMENT , LOCAL , EXPENDITURE * APPL - SECTOR :
         GOVERNMENT , LOCAL , SERVICES , LEISURE * APPL - SECTOR : GOVERNMENT , LOCAL
         , SERVICES * INCOME - EFFECT OF * POPULATION - EFFECT OF

YA0317   BERK K.N.
         "Tolerance and condition in regression computations"   J. Am. Statist.
         Ass., vol.72, 1977, pp.863-866.
         COMPUTERISATION - CALCULATION ERROR * COMPUTERISATION - ESTIMATION ,
         REGRESSION MODELS * REGRESSION - STEPWISE

YA0318   BERKOWITZ E.N., GINTER J.L.
         "Time management of sales managers"   Ind. Mktg. Mgmt., vol.7, 1978,
         pp.250-256.
         USE - SALES FORCE MANAGEMENT

YA0319   BERMAN L.S.
"Recent improvements in official economic statistics"   R. Statist. Soc.
(A), vol.134, 1971, pp.630-651.
DATA SOURCES , UK * DATA ERRORS - NATIONAL ACCOUNTS , UK

YA0320   BERMAN R.A., McLAUGHLIN R.L.
"An econometrician's reaction to 'A non-econometrician's guide to
econometrics'"   Bus. Econ., vol.9:1, 1974, pp.81-82, and vol.9:3, 1974,
pp.76-78.
MULTICOLLINEARITY - EFFECT OF * MULTICOLLINEARITY - REMOVAL OF * REGRESSION
- MODEL CHOICE * REGRESSION - VARIABLE INCLUSION * AUTOCORRELATION - EFFECT
OF * REGRESSION - LAGGED DEPENDENT * BASIC

YA0321   BERNDT E.R.
"Reconciling alternative estimates of the elasticity of substitution"
Rev. Econ. Stats., vol.58, 1976, pp.59-68.
BIBLIOGRAPHY - PRODUCTION FUNCTIONS * PRODUCTION FUNCTIONS - MACRO
EVALUATION - PRODUCTION FUNCTIONS * DATA - SPECIFICATION OF VARIABLES *
COMPARATIVE METHODS - ESTIMATION : OLS , 2SLS * COMPARATIVE METHODS -
REGRESSION , TRANSFORMATIONS * PRODUCTION FUNCTIONS - SUBSTITUTION

YA0322   BERNDT E.R., CHRISTENSEN L.R.
"Testing for the existence of a consistent aggregate index of labor inputs"
Am. Econ. Rev., vol 64, 1974, pp.391-404.
PRODUCTION FUNCTIONS - MACRO * PRODUCTION FUNCTIONS - METHODOLOGY *
COMPARATIVE METHODS - DATA : AGGREGATE , DISAGGREGATE * ADVANCED

YA0323   BERNDT E.R., CHRISTENSEN L.R.
"The translog function and the substitution of equipment, structures and
labour in U.S. manufacturing 1928-1968"   J. Econometrics, vol.1, 1973,
pp.81-113.
PRODUCTION FUNCTIONS - MACRO * PRODUCTION FUNCTIONS - THEORY * PRODUCTION
FUNCTIONS - SUBSTITUTION * ESTIMATION - GLS , ITERATIVE * COMPARATIVE
METHODS - ESTIMATION : OLS , 2SLS * COMPARATIVE METHODS - ESTIMATION :
DEMAND EQUATIONS

YA0324   BERNDT E.R., DARROUGH M.N., DIEWERT W.E.
"Flexible functional forms and expenditure distributions: an application to
Canadian consumer demand functions"   Int. Econ. Rev., vol.18, 1977,
pp.651-675.
BAYESIAN - MODEL SELECTION * DEMAND EQUATIONS - SYSTEMS OF , THEORY * APPL -
MACRO , CANADA * APPL - MACRO : CONSUMER DEMAND * COMPARATIVE METHODS -
PRICE ELASTICITY , ESTIMATION * EVALUATION - CONSUMER BEHAVIOUR , ECONOMIC
MODELS

YA0325   BERNDT E.R., SAVIN N.E.
"Conflict among criteria for testing hypotheses in the multivariate linear
regression model"   Econometrica, vol.45, 1977, pp.1263-1277.
REGRESSION - HYPOTHESIS TESTS * COMPARATIVE METHODS - TESTS , REGRESSION
COEFFICIENTS * MACRO MODEL - KLEIN

YA0326   BERNDT E.R., SAVIN N.E.
"Estimation and hypothesis testing in singular equation systems with
autoregressive disturbances"   Econometrica, vol.43, 1975, pp.937-957.
ERROR SPECIFICATION - AUTOCORRELATED * DEMAND EQUATIONS - SYSTEMS OF :
METHODOLOGY , ERROR SPECIFICATION * SPECIFICATION ERROR - TESTS ,
CONSTRAINTS * DEMAND EQUATIONS - SYSTEMS OF : METHODOLOGY , ESTIMATION *
SIMULTANEOUS SYSTEM - CONSTRAINED * PRODUCTION FUNCTIONS - METHODOLOGY *
AUTOCORRELATION - TEST * SPECIFICATION ERROR - EFFECT OF , CONSTRAINTS *
ADVANCED

YA0327   BERNDT E.R., WATKINS G.C.
"Demand for natural gas: residential and commercial markets in Ontario and
British Columbia"   Can. J. Econ., vol.10, 1977, pp.97-111.
APPL - SECTOR : PRODUCTION , GAS * APPL - SECTOR : UTILITIES , GAS * DATA -
CROSS SECTION , TIME SERIES * WEATHER - EFFECT OF * PRICE - EFFECT OF *
INCOME - EFFECT OF * ERROR SPECIFICATION - AUTOCORRELATED , CORRELATED *
REGRESSION - NON LINEAR : APPL

YA0328   BERNDT E.R., WOOD D.O.
"Technology, prices and the derived demand for energy"   Rev. Econ. Stats.,
vol.57, 1975, pp.259-268.
PRODUCTION FUNCTIONS - MACRO * PRODUCTION FUNCTIONS - THEORY * APPL - MACRO
: ENERGY * ESTIMATION - 3SLS , ITERATIVE * COST - MACRO : ENERGY * PRICE -
EFFECT OF * PRODUCTION FUNCTIONS - SUBSTITUTION

YA0329   BERNHARDT I., MACKENZIE K.D.
"Some problems in using diffusion models for new products"   Mgmt. Sci.
(B), vol.19, 1972, pp.187-200.
NEW PRODUCTS - DIFFUSION MODELS * EVALUATION - DIFFUSION MODELS

YA0330   BERRISFORD H.G.
"The relation between gas demand and temperature: a study in statistical
demand forecasting"   Opl. Res. Q., vol.16, 1965, pp.229-246.
APPL - SECTOR : UTILITIES , GAS * DATA - SPECIFICATION OF VARIABLES *
WEATHER - EFFECT OF * BASIC

YA0331   BESSIERE F.
"The "investment '85" model of Electricite de France"   Mgmt. Sci. (B),
vol.17, 1971, pp.192-211.
LONG TERM FORECASTING * APPL - SECTOR : UTILITIES , ELECTRICITY * USER -
FIRM : UTILITY * USE - CAPACITY EXPANSION * COST - SECTOR : UTILITIES * LP

YA0332   BEST R.J.
         "An experiment in Delphi estimation in marketing decision making"   J.
         Mktg. Res., vol.11, 1974, pp.448-452.
         DELPHI * BAYESIAN - JUDGEMENTAL FORECASTS * EVALUATION - JUDGEMENTAL
         FORECASTS * APPL - SECTOR : SERVICES , MEDIA , MAGAZINES * NEW PRODUCTS -
         NEW BRAND * NEW PRODUCTS - EVALUATION
YA0333   BESTWICK P.F.
         "A forecast monitoring and revision system"   Opl. Res. Q., vol.26, 1975,
         pp.419-429.
         TRACKING SIGNAL - APPL * DEMAND - CUMULATIVE * STYLE GOODS * SEASONALITY -
         SINGLE SEASON * BASIC
YA0334   BETANCOURT R.R.
         "The estimation of price elasticities from cross-section data under additive
         preference"   Int. Econ. Rev., vol.12, 1971, pp.283-292.
         APPL - MACRO : CONSUMER DEMAND * DEMAND EQUATIONS - SYSTEMS OF : METHODOLOGY
         , ESTIMATION * APPL - MACRO , LATIN AMERICA
YA0335   BETANCOURT R.R., CLAGUE C.K.
         "An econometric analysis of capital utilisation"   Int. Econ. Rev., vol.19,
         1978, pp.211-227.
         COMPARATIVE METHODS - REGRESSION , LIMITED DEPENDENT * REGRESSION - LIMITED
         DEPENDENT , LOGIT : APPL * DATA - INTERNATIONAL * APPL - SECTOR : CAPACITY
         UTILISATION
YA0336   BETANCOURT R.R., SHEEHEY E.J., VOGEL R.C.
         "The dynamics of inflation in Latin America: comment"   Am. Econ. Rev.,
         vol.66, 1976, pp.688-698.
         INFLATION - RAPID * POLICY EVALUATION - MACRO : MONETARY * APPL - MACRO ,
         LATIN AMERICA * INFLATION - DETERMINANTS
YA0337   BETSEY C.L.
         "Differences in unemployment experience between blacks and whites" with
         discussion   Am. Econ. Ass. Proc., 1978, pp.192-199.
         MANPOWER PLANNING - UNEMPLOYMENT * MANPOWER PLANNING - UNEMPLOYMENT ,
         DURATION * MANPOWER PLANNING - DISCRIMINATION , RACIAL
YA0338   BETTMAN J.R., JONES J.M.
         "Formal models of consumer behaviour: a conceptual overview"   J. Business,
         vol.45, 1972, pp.544-562.
         CONSUMER BEHAVIOUR - STOCHASTIC MODELS , REVIEW * CONSUMER BEHAVIOUR -
         PSYCHOLOGICAL MODELS , REVIEW
YA0339   BEZDEK R.H.
         "The state of the art- long range economic and manpower forecasting"   Long
         Range Planning, vol.8:1, 1975, pp.31-42.
         LONG TERM FORECASTING * INPUT OUTPUT - MACRO * MACRO MODELS - REVIEW *
         MANPOWER PLANNING - MACRO * BASIC
YA0340   BEZDEK R.H., WENDLING R.M.
         "Current-and constant-dollar input-output forecasts for the US economy"
         J. Am. Statist. Ass., vol.71, 1976, pp.543-551.
         EX ANTE * EVALUATION - SPECIFICATION OF VARIABLES * DATA - SPECIFICATION OF
         VARIABLES * INPUT OUTPUT - MACRO , US * EVALUATION - INPUT OUTPUT *
         STABILITY OF COEFFICIENTS - INPUT OUTPUT : APPL * DATA - TRANSFORMED ,
         DEFLATED
YA0341   BHANSALI R.J.
         "A Monte Carlo comparison of the regression method and the spectral methods
         of prediction"   J. Am. Statist. Ass., vol.68, 1973, pp.621-625.
         TIME SERIES - ARIMA : ESTIMATION * DATA - SIMULATION * COMPARATIVE METHODS -
         ESTIMATION : TIME SERIES
YA0342   BHANSALI R.J.
         "Asymptotic mean square error of predicting more than one step ahead using a
         regression method"   Appl. Stats., vol.23, 1974, pp.35-42.
         TIME SERIES - AUTOREGRESSIVE * LEAD TIME - EFFECT OF * CONFIDENCE INTERVAL -
         PREDICTIONS : TIME SERIES
YA0343   BHATIA K.B.
         "A price index for nonfarm one-family houses, 1947-64"   J. Am. Statist.
         Ass., vol.66, 1971, pp.23-32.
         APPL - SECTOR : CONSTRUCTION , RESIDENTIAL * PRICE - SECTOR : CONSTRUCTION ,
         RESIDENTIAL * INDEX NUMBERS - SECTOR : CONSTRUCTION
YA0344   BHATIA K.B.
         "Capital gains and the aggregate consumption function"   Am. Econ. Rev.,
         vol.62, 1972, pp.866-879.
         APPL - MACRO : CONSUMPTION * WEALTH - EFFECT OF * COMPARATIVE METHODS -
         REGRESSION , ERROR SPECIFICATION
YA0345   BHATTACHARYA B.B.
         "Demand and supply of money in a developing economy: a structural analysis
         for India"   Rev. Econ. Stats., vol.56, 1974, pp.502-510.
         APPL - MACRO : MONEY * APPL - MACRO , INDIA * EX ANTE
YA0346   BHATTACHARYYA M.N.
         "Forecasting the demand for telephones in Australia"   Appl. Stats.,
         vol.23, 1974, pp.1-10.
         APPL - SECTOR : UTILITIES , TELEPHONE * USER - FIRM : UTILITIES * USE -
         CAPACITY EXPANSION * TIME SERIES - ARIMA : APPL * DISTRIBUTED LAG - ARIMA *
         EX ANTE * DISTRIBUTED LAG - RATIONAL POLYNOMIAL

YA0347   BIANCHI C., CALZOLARI G., CORSI P.
          "A program for stochastic simulation of econometric models"   Econometrica,
          vol.46, 1978, pp.235-236.
          COMPUTERISATION - SIMULATION , PROGRAMS * COMPUTERISATION - MACRO MODELLING
          , PROGRAMS
YA0348   BIBBENGER J.E., SMITH V.K., MARCIS R.G.
          "A time series analysis of post-accord interest rates: comment"   J.
          Finance, vol.29, 1974, pp.1320-1327.
          INTEREST RATE - INDICATORS * SPECTRAL ANALYSIS - CROSS : APPL * STATIONARITY
          - TESTING * TIME SERIES - DECOMPOSITION , TREND REMOVAL * SPECTRAL ANALYSIS
          - METHODOLOGY * SPECIFICATION ERROR - EFFECT OF , STATIONARITY
YA0349   BICKSLER J.L., HESS P.J., BENISHAY H.
          "Market preferences for characteristics of common stocks: comments"   Econ.
          J., vol.85, 1975, pp.615-627.
          STOCK PRICES - RISK * STOCK PRICES - VOLATILITY * APPL - FIRM : FINANCE ,
          STOCK PRICES
YA0350   BIELBY W.T., HAUSER R.M., FEATHERMAN D.L.
          "Response errors of nonblack males in models of the stratification process"
          J. Am. Statist. Ass., vol.72, 1977, pp.723-735.
          DATA ERRORS - EFFECT OF * DATA ERRORS - ESTIMATION OF * APPL - SECTOR :
          SOCIAL , SOCIOECONOMIC STRUCTURE * APPL - SECTOR : SOCIAL , SUCESS * PATH
          ANALYSIS * SURVEYS - METHODOLOGY , RESPONSE ERROR * EDUCATION - EFFECT OF
YA0351   BILDERSEE J.S.
          "Some aspects of the performance of non-convertible preferred stocks"   J.
          Finance, vol.28, 1973, pp.1187-1201.
          APPL - FIRM : FINANCE , BONDS * STOCK PRICES - BETA * STOCK PRICES -
          COVARIATION
YA0352   BILSBORROW R.E.
          "The determinants of fixed investment by manufacturing firms in a developing
          country"   Int. Econ. Rev., vol.18, 1977, pp.697-717.
          APPL - FIRM : INVESTMENT * DATA - CROSS SECTION , TIME SERIES * DATA - LDC *
          BIBLIOGRAPHY - INVESTMENT
YA0353   BILSON J.F.O.
          "The current experience with floating exchange rates: an appraisal of the
          monetary approach" with discussion   Am. Econ. Ass. Proc., 1978, pp.392-397
          & 412-416.
          THEORY - MONETARY * APPL - MACRO : INTERNATIONAL FINANCE , EXCHANGE RATES *
          APPL - MACRO , UK * APPL - MACRO , GERMANY
YA0354   BIMM E.B., MILLMAN A.D.
          "A model for planning TV in Canada"   J. Advtg. Res., vol.18:4, 1978,
          pp.43-48.
          USE - MEDIA PLANNING * BASIC
YA0355   BIRCH E.M., SIEBERT C.D.
          "Uncertainty, permanent demand, and investment behaviour"   Am. Econ. Rev.,
          vol.66, 1976, pp.15-27.
          APPL - FIRM : INVESTMENT
YA0356   BISCHOFF C.W.
          "Business investment in the 1970's: a comparison of models" with discussion
          Brookings Paps. Econ. Activity, 1971, pp.13-64.
          APPL - MACRO : INVESTMENT * MACRO MODEL - FRB , MIT , PENN * EVALUATION -
          INVESTMENT MODELS * EX ANTE * MULTIPLIERS - MACRO
YA0357   BISCHOFF C.W.
          "The outlook for investment in plant and equipment" with discussion
          Brookings Paps. Econ. Activity, 1971, pp.735-753.
          APPL - MACRO : INVESTMENT , EQUIPMENT * EX ANTE * EVALUATION - INVESTMENT
          MODELS
YA0358   BISHKO D., WALLACE W.A.
          "A planning model for construction minerals"   Mgmt. Sci. (B), vol.18,
          1972, pp.502-518.
          APPL - SECTOR : PRODUCTION , AGGREGATES * USER - FIRM : PRODUCTION * USE -
          PRODUCTION , CONTROL * COST - SECTOR : PRODUCTION
YA0359   BISHOP J.L.
          "Experience with a successful system for forecasting and inventory control"
          Ops. Res., vol.22, 1974, pp.1224-1231.
          USE - INVENTORY CONTROL * EXPONENTIAL SMOOTHING - APPL
YA0360   BISIGNANO J.
          "Cagan's real money demand model with alternative error structures: bayesian
          analysis for four countries"   Int. Econ. Rev., vol.16, 1975, pp.487-502.
          APPL - MACRO : MONEY , DEMAND * BAYESIAN - ESTIMATION : DISTRIBUTED LAG *
          COMPARATIVE METHODS - DISTRIBUTED LAG , ERROR SPECIFICATION * COMPARATIVE
          METHODS - REGRESSION , TRANSFORMATIONS * INFLATION - RAPID * REGRESSION -
          LAGGED DEPENDENT
YA0361   BISPHAM J.A.
          "The new Cambridge and monetarist criticisms of 'conventional' economic
          policy-making"   Nat. Inst. Econ. Rev., no.74, 1975 pp.39-55.
          THEORY - MONETARY * MACRO MODEL - UK , CAMBRIDGE * POLICY EVALUATION - MACRO
          : FISCAL , MONETARY * APPL - MACRO : FLOW OF FUNDS * EX ANTE * EVALUATION -
          MACRO MODELS * EVALUATION - INFLATION MODELS * EVALUATION - MONETARIST
          THEORY

YA0362   BITRAN G.R., HAX A.C.
"On the design of hierarchical production planning systems"   Decis. Sci.,
vol.8, 1977, pp.28-55.
USE - PRODUCTION , CONTROL * LOSS FUNCTIONS - FIRM , PRODUCTION CONTROL *
LOSS FUNCTIONS - FIRM , NVENTORY CONTROL * USE - INVENTORY CONTROL

YA0363   BITROS G.C., KELEJIAN H.H.
"A note on the variability of the replacement investment capital stock
ratio: a reply"   Rev. Econ. Stats., vol.59, 1977, pp.510-513.
APPL - SECTOR : UTILITIES , ELECTRICITY * APPL - SECTOR : INVESTMENT ,
UTILITIES * SPECIFICATION ERROR - TESTS , SIMULTANEOUS SYSTEM BIAS *
SPECIFICATION ERROR - TESTS , VARIABLE INCLUSION * DATA ERRORS - EFFECT OF *
DEMAND - REPLACEMENT * DEPRECIATION - ESTIMATION

YA0364   BITROS G.C., KELEJIAN H.H.
"On the variability of the replacement investment capital stock ratio: some
evidence from capital scrappage"   Rev. Econ. Stats., vol.56, 1974,
pp.270-278.
DEPRECIATION - ESTIMATION * COMPARATIVE METHODS - ESTIMATION : OLS , 2SLS *
APPL - SECTOR : INVESTMENT * APPL - SECTOR : UTILITIES , ELECTRICITY *
BIBLIOGRAPHY - INVESTMENT * DEMAND - REPLACEMENT

YA0365   BJORCK A.
"Comment on the iterative refinement of least-squares solutions"   J. Am.
Statist. Ass., vol.73, 1978, pp.161-166.
NUMERICAL METHODS - MATRIX DECOMPOSITION * COMPUTERISATION - ESTIMATION ,
REGRESSION MODELS * ESTIMATION - OLS

YA0366   BLACK F., SCHOLES M.
"The valuation of option contracts and a test of market efficiency" with
discussion   J. Finance, vol.27, 1972, pp.399-417 & 456-458.
APPL - FIRM : FINANCE , OPTIONS * LOSS FUNCTIONS - SECTOR : FINANCE ,
TRADING RULES

YA0367   BLACK S.W.
"An econometric study of euro-dollar borrowing by New York banks and the
rate of interest on euro-dollars"   J. Finance, vol.26, 1971, pp.83-88.
EX ANTE * APPL - MACRO : INTERNATIONAL FINANCE * INTEREST RATE - EFFECT OF *
APPL - SECTOR : FINANCE , BANKS * APPL - SECTOR : FINANCE , INTERNATIONAL
FINANCE

YA0368   BLACK S.W., KELEJIAN H.H.
"The formulation of the dependent variable in the wage equation"   Rev.
Econ. Studies, vol.39, 1972, pp.55-59.
APPL - MACRO : EARNINGS * INFLATION - EFFECT OF * DATA - SPECIFICATION OF
VARIABLES

YA0369   BLACK T.R.L, FARLEY J.U.
"Responses to advertising contraceptives"   J. Advtg. Res., vol.17:5, 1977,
pp.49-56.
APPL - SECTOR : CONSUMER NON DURABLES , HEALTH AIDS * POPULATION - FERTILITY
* POLICY EVALUATION - MACRO : POPULATION CONTROL * ADVERTISING - EFFECT OF *
PRICE - EFFECT OF * BASIC

YA0370   BLACKORBY C., BOYCE R., RUSSELL R.R.
"Estimation of demand systems generated by the Gorman polar form: a
generalisation of the S-branch utility tree"   Econometrica, vol.46, 1978,
pp.345-363.
PRICE - EFFECT OF * SUBSTITUTE PRODUCTS * DEMAND EQUATIONS - SYSTEMS OF :
THEORY * DEMAND EQUATIONS - SYSTEMS OF : METHODOLOGY , ESTIMATION * APPL -
MACRO : CONSUMER DEMAND * INCOME - EFFECT OF

YA0371   BLAIN L., PATERSON D.G., RAE J.D.
"The regional impact of economic fluctuations during the inter-war period:
the case of British Columbia"   Can. J. Econ., vol.7, 1974, pp.381-401.
BUSINESS CYCLE - REGIONAL * REGIONAL MODELS - INTERREGIONAL * SPECTRAL
ANALYSIS - APPL : BUSINESS CYCLE * SPECTRAL ANALYSIS - CROSS : APPL

YA0372   BLAIR R.D., JACKSON J.R., VOGEL R.J.
"Economies of scale in the administration of health insurance"   Rev. Econ.
Stats., vol.57, 1975, pp.185-189.
COST - FIRM : FINANCE * APPL - FIRM : FINANCE , INSURANCE * HEALTH -
INSURANCE * COST - SCALE ECONOMIES * DATA - CROSS SECTION * APPL - SECTOR :
FINANCE , INSURANCE COMPANIES

YA0373   BLAIR R.D., KRAFT J.
"Estimation of elasticity of substitution in American manufacturing industry
from pooled cross-section and time series observations"   Rev. Econ.
Stats., vol.56, 1974, pp.343-347.
DATA - CROSS SECTION , TIME SERIES * PRODUCTION FUNCTIONS - SECTOR *
PRODUCTION FUNCTIONS - SUBSTITUTION * REGRESSION - SEEMINGLY UNRELATED

YA0374   BLANNING R.W., HAMILTON W.F.
"Regression analysis with asymmetric linear loss"   Decis. Sci., vol.5,
1974, pp.194-204.
LOSS FUNCTIONS - FIRM , MAINTENANCE * COMPARATIVE METHODS - ESTIMATION : OLS
, MSAE * LOSS FUNCTION - ASYMMETRICAL

YA0375   BLATTBERG R., GOLANTY J.
"TRACKER: an early test market forecasting and diagnostic model for new
product planning"   J. Mktg. Res., vol.15, 1978, pp.192-202.
NEW PRODUCTS - TESTING * EX ANTE * ADVERTISING - EFFECT OF * APPL - SECTOR :
CONSUMER NON DURABLES

YA0376   BLATTBERG R.C.
          "Evaluation of the power of the Durbin-Watson statistic for non-first order
          serial correlation alternatives"   Rev, Econ, Stats,, vol,55, 1973,
          pp,508-515,
          EVALUATION - TEST , AUTOCORRELATION * DATA - SIMULATION * ERROR
          SPECIFICATION - AUTOCORRELATED * AUTOCORRELATION - EFFECT OF

YA0377   BLATTBERG R.C., GONEDES N.J.
          "A comparison of the stable and student distributions as statistical models
          for stock prices"   J, Business, vol,47, 1974, pp,244-280,
          APPL - FIRM : FINANCE , STOCK PRICES * STOCK PRICES - DISTRIBUTION * ERROR
          DISTRIBUTION - STABLE * ERROR DISTRIBUTION - T * COMPARATIVE METHODS - ERROR
          DISTRIBUTIONS * DATA - SIMULATION

YA0378   BLATTBERG R.C., SARGENT T.
          "Regression with non-Gaussian stable distributions: some sampling results"
          Econometrica, vol,39, 1971, pp,501-510,
          ERROR DISTRIBUTION - STABLE * ESTIMATION - MSAE * COMPARATIVE METHODS -
          ERROR DISTRIBUTIONS * DATA - SIMULATION * ESTIMATION - ERROR DISTRIBUTION ,
          STABLE

YA0379   BLATTBERG R.C., SEN S.K.
          "A Bayesian technique to discriminate between stochastic models of brand
          choice"   Mgmt, Sci, (B), vol,21, 1975, pp,682-696,
          BAYESIAN - MODEL SELECTION * CONSUMER BEHAVIOUR - STOCHASTIC MODELS * APPL -
          SECTOR : CONSUMER NON DURABLES , GROCERIES * BRAND CHOICE - THEORY

YA0380   BLATTBERG R.C., SEN S.K.
          "Application of mimimum chi-square procedures to stochastic models of brand
          choice"   J, Mktg, Res,, vol,10, 1973, pp,421-427,
          ESTIMATION - MINIMUM CHI - SQUARE * BAYESIAN - MODEL SELECTION * BRAND
          CHOICE - METHODOLOGY * DATA - SIMULATION * EVALUATION - CONSUMER BEHAVIOUR ,
          STOCHASTIC MODELS

YA0381   BLATTBERG R.C., SEN S.K.
          "Market segmentation using models of multidimensional purchasing behaviour"
          J, Mktg,, vol,38, no,4, Oct 1974, pp,17-28,
          MARKET SEGMENTATION * APPL - FIRM : CONSUMER NON DURABLES , GROCERIES * USE
          - MARKETING POLICY * BASIC

YA0382   BLATTBERG R.C., SEN S.K.
          "Market segments and stochastic brand choice models"   J, Mktg, Res,,
          vol,13, 1976, pp,34-45,
          BRAND CHOICE - METHODOLOGY * BAYESIAN - MODEL SELECTION * REPEAT BUYING *
          APPL - FIRM : CONSUMER NON DURABLES * MARKET SEGMENTATION * PROBABILITY
          MODELS - BINOMIAL * MARKOV MODELS - APPL : BRAND CHOICE

YA0383   BLATTBERG R.C., STIVERS S.R.
          "Statistical evaluation of transit promotion"   J, Mktg,, Res,, vol,7,
          1970, pp,293-299,
          APPL - FIRM : TRANSPORT , ROAD , PASSENGER * COMPARATIVE METHODS -
          REGRESSION , ERROR SPECIFICATION * ADVERTISING - EFFECT OF * COMPARATIVE
          METHODS - ESTIMATION : OLS , MSAE * COMPARATIVE METHODS - ESTIMATION : OLS ,
          GLS * COMPARATIVE METHODS - ESTIMATION : REGRESSION * ERROR SPECIFICATION -
          AUTOCORRELATED

YA0384   BLAZEY T.W.
          "Putting forecasts to work in the firms"   Bus, Econ,, vol,11:1, 1976,
          pp,41-44,
          USE - CORPORATE PLANNING * USER REQUIREMENTS * BASIC

YA0385   BLEJER M.I.
          "The short-run dynamics of prices and the balance of payments"   Am, Econ,
          Rev,, vol,67, 1977, pp,419-428,
          INFLATION - DETERMINANTS * APPL - MACRO : INTERNATIONAL FINANCE , FOREIGN
          RESERVES * APPL - MACRO , LATIN AMERICA

YA0386   BLIEMEL F.
          "Theil's forecast accuracy coefficient: a clarification"   J, Mktg, Res,,
          vol,10, 1973, pp,444-446,
          LOSS FUNCTIONS - THEIL * EVALUATION - THEORY OF

YA0387   BLIEMEL F., CATTIN P.
          "Analysis of influence sharing in judgemental forecasting regression models
          and perceptual measures"   Decis, Sci,, vol,7, 1976, pp,319-330,
          JUDGEMENTAL FORECASTS - DETERMINANTS , PSYCHOLOGICAL * APPL - SECTOR :
          COMMODITIES

YA0388   BLINDER A.S., GOLDFELD S.M.
          "New measures of fiscal and monetary policy, 1958-73"   Am, Econ, Rev,,
          vol,66, 1976, pp,780-796,
          POLICY EVALUATION - MACRO : FISCAL , MONETARY * MACRO MODEL - MIT , PENN ,
          SSRC

YA0389   BLOCH F.E.
          "Measurement error and statistical significance of an independent variable"
          Am, Stat'n,, vol,32, 1978, pp,26-27,
          DATA ERRORS - EFFECT OF * REGRESSION - HYPOTHESIS TESTS

YA0390   BLOMQVIST A.G.
          "Approximating the least squares bias in multiple regression with errors in
          variables"   Rev, Econ, Stats,, vol,54, 1972, pp,202-204,
          REGRESSION - ERRORS IN VARIABLES

YA0391   BLOMQVIST A.G., HAESSEL W.
          "Small cars, large cars, and the price of gasoline"   Can. J. Econ.,
          vol.11, 1978, pp.470-489.
          APPL - SECTOR : CONSUMER DURABLES , CARS * MARKET SEGMENTATION * APPL -
          SECTOR : RETAILING , GASOLINE * PRICE - EFFECT OF * REGRESSION - ERROR
          COMPONENTS * COMPARATIVE METHODS - DATA : CROSS SECTION , TIME SERIES *
          COMPARATIVE METHODS - ESTIMATION : OLS , 2SLS

YA0392   BLOND D.L.
          "External effects and US wheat prices"   Bus. Econ., vol.11:4, 1976,
          pp.70-81.
          APPL - SECTOR : AGRICULTURE , GRAIN * POLICY EVALUATION - SECTOR :
          AGRICULTURE * EX ANTE

YA0393   BLOOM P.N., KOTLER P.
          "Strategies for high market-share companies"   H.B.R., vol.53, Nov-Dec,
          1975, pp.63-72.
          MARKET SHARE - EFFECT OF * USE - CORPORATE PLANNING * APPL - FIRM : FINANCE
          , PROFITS

YA0394   BLOOMFIELD P.
          "Spectral analysis with randomly missing observations"   R. Statist. Soc.
          (B), vol.32, 1970, pp.369-380.
          DATA ERRORS - MISSING OBSERVATIONS * SPECTRAL ANALYSIS - METHODOLOGY , DATA
          ERRORS

YA0395   BLUM M.
          "Failing company discriminant analysis"   J. Acctg. Res., vol.12, 1974,
          pp.1-25.
          DISCRIMINANT ANALYSIS - APPL * USE - ANTITRUST * USE - BANKRUPTCY PREDICTION
          * EX ANTE

YA0396   BLUME M.E.
          "Betas and their regression tendencies"   J. Finance, vol.30, 1975,
          pp.785-795.
          STOCK PRICES - BETA , VARIABLE * STABILITY OF COEFFICIENTS - REGRESSION

YA0397   BLUME M.E.
          "On the assessment of risk"   J. Finance, vol.26, 1971, pp.1-10.
          APPL - FIRM : FINANCE , STOCK PRICES * STOCK PRICES - RISK * STOCK PRICES -
          BETA , VARIABLE

YA0398   BLUME M.E.
          "Unbiased estimators of long run expected rates of return"   J. Am.
          Statist. Ass., vol.69, 1974, pp.634-638.
          ESTIMATION - LOGARITHMIC MODELS

YA0399   BLUME M.E., FRIEND I.
          "A new look at the capital asset pricing model"   J. Finance, vol.28, 1973,
          pp.19-33.
          THEORY - EFFICIENT MARKETS * STOCK PRICES - BETA * APPL - FIRM : FINANCE ,
          STOCK PRICES * RISK - EFFECT OF * STOCK PRICES - MODELS , CAPM

YA0400   BLUME M.E., FRIEND I.
          "Risk, investment strategy and the long-run rates of return"   Rev. Econ.
          Stats., vol.56, 1974, pp.259-269.
          APPL - SECTOR : FINANCE , STOCK PRICE INDEX * STOCK PRICES - RISK * USE -
          PORTFOLIO SELECTION * STOCK PRICES - BETA

YA0401   BLUME M.E., FRIEND I.
          "The asset structure of individual portfolios and some implications for
          utility functions" with discussion   J. Finance, vol.30, 1975, pp.585-603 &
          624-629.
          APPL - MACRO : CONSUMER DEMAND , FINANCIAL ASSETS * CONSUMER BEHAVIOUR -
          PURCHASING , DETERMINANTS * CONSUMER BEHAVIOUR - ECONOMIC MODELS

YA0402   BLUME M.E., HUSIC F.
          "Price, beta and exchange listing" with discussion   J. Finance, vol.28,
          1973, pp.283-299 & 317-320.
          STOCK PRICES - BETA * APPL - FIRM : FINANCE , STOCK PRICES * THEORY -
          EFFICIENT MARKETS * RISK - EFFECT OF * EXOGENOUS VARIABLES - PREDICTION OF ,
          EFFECT

YA0403   BOATLER R.W., ET AL.
          "Treasury bill auction procedures: an empirical investigation: comments"
          J. Finance, vol.30, 1975, pp.893-899.
          APPL - SECTOR : FINANCE , BONDS * POLICY EVALUATION - SECTOR : FINANCE * USE
          - COMPETITIVE BIDDING * APPL - SECTOR : GOVERNMENT , FINANCE

YA0404   BOATWRIGHT B.D., EATON J.R.
          "The estimation of investment functions for manufacturing industry in the
          UK"   Economica, vol.39, 1972, pp.403-418.
          APPL - MACRO : INVESTMENT * APPL - MACRO , UK * DISTRIBUTED LAG - APPL ,
          INVESTMENT * COMPARATIVE METHODS - DISTRIBUTED LAG * POLICY EVALUATION -
          MACRO : INVESTMENT * DISTRIBUTED LAG - ALMON : APPL * DISTRIBUTED LAG -
          SOLOW : APPL

YA0405   BOATWRIGHT B.D., RENTON G.A.
          "An analysis of UK inflows and outflows of direct foreign investment"
          Rev. Econ. Stats., vol.57, 1975, pp.478-486.
          EXCHANGE RATE - EFFECT OF * APPL - MACRO : INVESTMENT , INTERNATIONAL * APPL
          - MACRO , UK

YA0406   BOCK M.E., JUDGE G.E., YANCEY T.A.
         "Some comments on estimation in regression after preliminary tests of
         significance"   J. Econometrics, vol, 1, 1973, pp.191-200.
         ESTIMATION - PRE TEST * REGRESSION - PRIOR INFORMATION * REGRESSION -
         VARIABLE INCLUSION * ADVANCED
YA0407   BOCZAR G.E.
         "Competition between banks and finance companies: a cross section study of
         personal loan debtors"   J. Finance, vol,33, 1978, pp.245-258.
         APPL - SECTOR : FINANCE , BANKS * REGRESSION - LIMITED DEPENDENT , PROBIT :
         APPL * CONSUMER BEHAVIOUR - PURCHASING , DETERMINANTS * APPL - SECTOR :
         FINANCE , CONSUMER CREDIT * EX ANTE * USE - CREDIT CONTROL , CONSUMER * APPL
         - SECTOR : FINANCE , CONSUMER FINANCE COMPANIES
YA0408   BODDY R., GORT M.
         "The substitution of capital for capital"   Rev. Econ. Stats., vol,53,
         1971, pp.179-188.
         INPUT OUTPUT - SECTOR : INVESTMENT * APPL - SECTOR : INVESTMENT
YA0409   BODIE Z.
         "Common stocks as a hedge against inflation" with discussion   J. Finance,
         vol,31, 1976, pp.459-470 & 483-487.
         INFLATION - INDICATORS * APPL - SECTOR : FINANCE , STOCK PRICE INDEX * STOCK
         PRICES - DETERMINANTS * USE - PORTFOLIO SELECTION * TIME SERIES - ARIMA :
         APPL
YA0410   BODKIN R.G., CONKLIN D.W.
         "Scale and other determinants of municipal government expenditures in
         Ontario: a quantitative analysis"   Int. Econ. Rev., vol,12, 1971,
         pp.465-481.
         APPL - SECTOR : GOVERNMENT , LOCAL , EXPENDITURE * APPL - SECTOR :
         GOVERNMENT , LOCAL , SERVICES * REGIONAL MODELS - SECTOR : GOVERNMENT ,
         EXPENDITURE * DATA - CROSS SECTION
YA0411   BODKIN R.G., KLEIN L.R.
         "Nonlinear estimation of aggregate production functions"   Rev. Econ.
         Stats., vol,49, 1967, pp.28-44.
         PRODUCTION FUNCTION - ESTIMATION * COMPARATIVE METHODS - ESTIMATION :
         PRODUCTION FUNCTIONS * COMPARATIVE METHODS - REGRESSION , ERROR
         SPECIFICATION * COMPARATIVE METHODS - REGRESSION , SIMULTANEOUS SYSTEM *
         ERROR SPECIFICATION - MULTIPLICATIVE * COMPARATIVE METHODS - SIMULTANEOUS
         SYSTEM , ERROR SPECIFICATION * ERROR SPECIFICATION - PRODUCTION FUNCTIONS
YA0412   BODKIN R.G., MURTHY K.S.R.
         "The orders shipment mechanisms in Canadian producer goods industries"   J.
         Am Statist. Ass., vol,68, 1973, pp.297-305.
         APPL - SECTOR : PRODUCTION , PLANT * DISTRIBUTED LAG - VARIABLE LAG *
         DISTRIBUTED LAG - APPL , ORDERS
YA0413   BOEHM W.T., MENKHAUS D.J., PENN J.B.
         "Accuracy of least squares computer programs: another reminder"   Am. J.
         Ag. Econ., vol,58, 1976, pp.757-760.
         COMPUTERISATION - CALCULATION ERROR * COMPUTERISATION - ESTIMATION ,
         REGRESSION MODELS
YA0414   BOHI D.R.
         "Tobin vs. Keynes on liquidity preference"   Rev. Econ. Stats., vol,54,
         1972, pp.479-481.
         INTEREST RATE - LIQUIDITY PREFERENCE * THEORY - LIQUIDITY PREFERENCE *
         RANDOM WALK - TEST * SPECTRAL ANALYSIS - APPL : INTEREST RATE
YA0415   BOLCH B.W., ET AL.
         "Seasonal variations in interest rates- comments"   Rev. Econ. Stats.,
         vol,59, 1977, pp.118-126.
         INTEREST RATE - SEASONALITY * COMPARATIVE METHODS - SEASONALITY
YA0416   BOLEN W.H.
         "Profitability of speciality advertising"   J. Advtg. Res., vol,12:3, 1972,
         pp.14-16.
         USE - PROMOTION EVALUATION * ADVERTISING - EFFECT OF * APPL - FIRM :
         RETAILING
YA0417   BOLTEN S.
         "Treasury bill auction procedures: an empirical investigation"   J.
         Finance, vol,28, 1973, pp.577-585.
         APPL - SECTOR : FINANCE , BONDS * POLICY EVALUATION - SECTOR : FINANCE * USE
         - COMPETITIVE BIDDING * APPL - SECTOR : GOVERNMENT , FINANCE
YA0418   BOLTEN S.E.
         "Residential mortgage risk characteristics"   Decis. Sci., vol,5, 1974,
         pp.73-90.
         DISCRIMINANT ANALYSIS - APPL * USE - CREDIT CONTROL , CONSUMER * APPL -
         SECTOR : FINANCE , MORTGAGES * USER - FIRM : FINANCE
YA0419   BOMBALL M.R., PRIMEAUX W.J., PURSELL D.E.
         "Forecasting stage 2 of the family life cycle"   J. Business, vol,48, 1975,
         pp.65-73.
         LIFE CYCLE - FAMILY * POPULATION - MARRIAGE * EX ANTE
YA0420   BOND R.E.
         "Deposit composition and commercial bank earnings"   J. Finance, vol,26,
         1971, pp.39-50.
         APPL - FIRM : FINANCE , BANKS * APPL - FIRM : FINANCE , PROFITS * APPL -
         FIRM : FINANCE , LIABILITIES * DATA - CROSS SECTION , TIME SERIES *
         STABILITY OF COEFFICIENTS - REGRESSION

YA0421   BONESS A.J., CHEN A.H., JATUSIPITAK S.
"Investigations of nonstationarity in prices"   J. Business, vol.47, 1974,
pp.518-537.
APPL - FIRM : UTILITIES , ELECTRICITY * APPL - FIRM : FINANCE , STOCK PRICES
* STATIONARITY - TESTING : APPL * STOCK PRICES - BETA , VARIABLE * STOCK
PRICES - INDUSTRIAL STRUCTURE * STOCK PRICES - DISTRIBUTION * STABILITY OF
COEFFICIENTS - REGRESSION , TEST : APPL * STABILITY OF COEFFICIENTS - TIME
SERIES , TEST : APPL

YA0422   BONESS A.J., FRANKFURTER G.M.
"Evidence of non-homogeneity of capital costs within 'risk-classes'"   J.
Finance, vol.32, 1977, pp.775-787.
REGRESSION - RANDOM COEFFICIENTS : APPL * COST - FIRM : FINANCING * RISK -
EFFECT OF * STOCK PRICES - BETA

YA0423   BONFIELD E.H.
"Attitude, social influence, personal norm and intention interactions as
related to brand purchase behaviour"   J. Mktg. Res., vol.11, 1974,
pp.379-389.
BRAND CHOICE - INDICATORS * CONSUMER BEHAVIOUR - PSYCHOLOGICAL MODELS *
CONSUMER BEHAVIOUR - PURCHASING , DETERMINANTS * APPL - SECTOR : CONSUMER
NON DURABLES

YA0424   BONOMO V., TANNER J.E.
"Canadian sensitivity to economic cycles in the U.S."   Rev. Econ. Stats.,
vol.54, 1972, pp.1-8.
BUSINESS CYCLE - DETERMINANTS * SPECTRAL ANALYSIS - APPL : BUSINESS CYCLE *
SPECTRAL ANALYSIS - CROSS : APPL * APPL - MACRO : INTERNATIONAL LINKAGE *
APPL - MACRO , CANADA

YA0425   BOOKSTEIN F.L.
"On a form of piecewise linear regression"   Am. Stat'n., vol.29, 1975,
pp.116-117.
REGRESSION - PIECEWISE * REGRESSION - COVARIANCE MODEL

YA0426   BORCHERDING T.E., DEACON R.T.
"The demand for services of non-federal governments"   Am. Econ. Rev.,
vol.62, 1972, pp.891-901.
DATA - CROSS SECTION * APPL - SECTOR : GOVERNMENT , LOCAL , SERVICES *
REGIONAL MODELS - SECTOR : GOVERNMENT , LOCAL , SERVICES

YA0427   BORTH D.M.
"A total entropy criterion for the dual problem of model discrimination and
parameter estimation"   R. Statist. Soc. (B), vol.37, 1975, pp.77-87.
REGRESSION - MODEL CHOICE * LOSS FUNCTIONS - INFORMATION CRITERION * DATA -
SIMULATION * ADVANCED

YA0428   BOSCHAN C.
"The NBER time series data bank"   Anns. Econ. Soc. Meas., vol.1, 1972,
pp.193-216.
DATA SOURCES - US * COMPUTERISATION - DATA , SOURCES

YA0429   BOSKIN M.J.
"On some recent econometric research in public finance"   Am. Econ. Ass.
Proc., vol.66, 1976, pp.102-109.
APPL - SECTOR : SERVICES , CHARITIES * TAX - EFFECT OF * MANPOWER PLANNING -
MACRO , SUPPLY * APPL - MACRO : SAVINGS

YA0430   BOSKIN M.J., FELDSTEIN M.S.
"Effects of the charitable deduction on contributions by low income
households: evidence from the national survey of philanthropy"   Rev. Econ.
Stats., vol.59, 1977, pp.351-354.
APPL - SECTOR : SERVICES , CHARITIES * PRICE - EFFECT OF * INCOME - EFFECT
OF

YA0431   BOSSONS J.
"The effect of parameter mis-specif and non stationarity on the
applicability of adaptive forecasts"   Mgmt. Sci. (A), vol.12, 1966,
pp.659-669.
EXPONENTIAL SMOOTHING - THEORY * TIME SERIES - NON STATIONARY * TIME SERIES
- STATE PACE * SPECIFICATION ERROR - EFFECT OF , MODEL SPECIFICATION

YA0432   BOSWORTH B.
"Analyzing inventory investment" with discussion   Brookings Paps. Econ.
Activity, 1970, pp.207-234.
APPL - MACRO : INVENTORIES

YA0433   BOSWORTH B.
"Patterns of corporate external financing" with discussion   Brookings
Paps. Econ. Activity, 1971, pp.253-284.
APPL - SECTOR : FINANCE , FINANCIAL STRUCTURE

YA0434   BOSWORTH B.
"The stock market and the economy" with discussion   Brookings Paps. Econ.
Activity, 1975, pp.257-300.
STOCK PRICES - EFFECT OF * APPL - MACRO : CONSUMER DEMAND * MACRO MODEL -
MIT , PENN , SSRC * WEALTH - EFFECT OF * APPL - MACRO : INVESTMENT

YA0435   BOSWORTH D.L.
"Price and quality changes in metal working machine tools"   Appl. Econ.,
vol.8, 1976, pp.283-288.
QUALITY - PRICE * APPL - SECTOR : PRODUCTION , MACHINE TOOLS

YA0436   BOULDEN J.B.
          "Computerised corporate planning"   Long Range Planning, vol.3:4, 1971,
          pp.2-9.
          USE - CORPORATE PLANNING * COMPUTERISATION - PLANNING MODELS
YA0437   BOWDEN R.J.
          "More stochastic properties of the Klein-Goldberger model"   Econometrica,
          vol.40, 1972, pp.87-98.
          MACRO MODEL - KLEIN GOLDBERGER * SIMULATION - DYNAMIC PROPERTIES * BUSINESS
          CYCLE - IDENTIFICATION * SPECTRAL ANALYSIS - APPL : SIMULATION EVALUATION *
          TAX - EFFECT OF * SPECTRAL ANALYSIS - APPL : BUSINESS CYCLE * ADVANCED
YA0438   BOWDEN R.J.
          "Specification, estimation and inference for models of market in
          disequilibrium"   Int. Econ. Rev, vol.19, 1978, pp.711-726.
          SIMULTANEOUS SYSTEM - DISEQUILIBRIUM * ESTIMATION - 2SLS * ESTIMATION -
          INSTRUMENTAL VARIABLES * COMPARATIVE METHODS - ESTIMATION : SIMULTANEOUS
          SYSTEM , DISEQUILIBRIUM
YA0439   BOWER R.S.
          "Market changes in the computer service industry"   Bell J. Econ., vol.4,
          1973, pp.539-590.
          APPL - SECTOR : PRODUCTION , COMPUTERS * APPL - SECTOR : SERVICES ,
          COMPUTERS
YA0440   BOWER R.S., LESSARD D.R.
          "An operational approach to risk screening"   J. Finance, vol.28, 1973,
          pp.321-337.
          USE - CAPITAL INVESTMENT * RISK - EFFECT OF * STOCK PRICES - BETA * APPL -
          FIRM : FINANCE , STOCK PRICES * THEORY - EFFICIENT MARKETS
YA0441   BOWERS D.A., DURO L.E.
          "An alternative estimation of the 'neutralized money stock'"   J. Finance,
          vol.27, 1972, pp.61-64.
          APPL - MACRO : MONEY , SUPPLY * DATA - SPECIFICATION OF VARIABLES
YA0442   BOWERS J.K., ET AL.
          "Some aspects of unemployment and the labour market, 1966-71"   Nat. Inst.
          Econ. Rev., no.62, 1972, pp.75-88.
          APPL - MACRO , UK * APPL - MACRO : UNEMPLOYMENT * MANPOWER PLANNING - LABOUR
          TURNOVER * MANPOWER PLANNING - MACRO , SUPPLY
YA0443   BOWLES S., NELSON V.I.
          "The 'inheritance of IQ' and the intergenerational reproduction of economic
          inequality"   Rev. Econ. Stats., vol.56, 1974, pp.39-51.
          APPL - SECTOR : SOCIAL , SOCIO ECONOMIC STRUCTURE * EDUCATION - EFFECT OF *
          PATH ANALYSIS * APPL - SECTOR : SOCIAL , INEQUALITY
YA0444   BOWMAN G.W.
          "Demand and supply of network television advertising"   Bell J. Econ.,
          vol.7, 1976, pp.258-267.
          APPL - SECTOR : SERVICES , MEDIA , TV * ADVERTISING - DETERMINANTS *
          SIMULTANEOUS SYSTEM - APPL * PRICE - EFFECT OF * SUPPLY - SECTOR : SERVICES
YA0445   BOWMAN H.W., LAPORTE A.M.
          "Stochastic optimisation in recursive equation systems with random
          parameters with an application to control of the money supply"   Ann. Econ.
          Soc. Meas., vol.1, 1972, pp.419-435.
          APPL - MACRO : MONEY , SUPPLY * POLICY EVALUATION - MACRO : MONETARY *
          CONTROL THEORY - STOCHASTIC , APPL * MACRO MODEL - ST.LOUIS * LOSS FUNCTIONS
          - MACRO * BAYESIAN - CONTROL
YA0446   BOX G.E.P., HILL W.J.
          "Discrimination among mechanistic models"   Technometrics, vol.9, 1967,
          pp.57-71.
          BAYESIAN - MODEL SELECTION * DATA - SIMULATION
YA0447   BOX G.E.P., JENKINS G.M.
          "Some comments on a paper by Chatfield and Prothero and on a review by
          Kendall" with a reply   R. Statist. Soc. (A), vol. 136, 1973, pp.337-352.
          EVALUATION - SEASONALITY * APPL - SECTOR : PRODUCTION , ENGINEERING * TIME
          SERIES - ARIMA : IDENTIFICATION * EX ANTE * PRIOR INFORMATION * MODEL
          SELECTION * SEASONALITY - ESTIMATION , ARIMA * STATIONARITY - TRANSFORMING
          TO * EVALUATION - TIME SERIES , ARIMA * TIME SERIES - ARIMA :
          TRANSFORMATIONS
YA0448   BOX G.E.P., JENKINS G.M., MacGREGOR J.F.
          "Some recent advances in forecasting and control"   Appl. Stats., vol.23,
          1974, pp.158-179.
          CONTROL CHARTS * CONTROL THEORY - REVIEW * USE - QUALITY CONTROL * TIME
          SERIES - ARIMA : APPL * DISTRIBUTED LAG - RATIONAL POLYNOMIAL : APPL * USE -
          PRODUCTION , CONTROL
YA0449   BOX G.E.P., NEWBOLD P.
          "Some comments on a paper of Coen, Gomme and Kendal"   R. Statist. Soc.
          (A), vol.134, 1971, pp.229-240.
          APPL - SECTOR : FINANCE , STOCK PRICE INDEX * DISTRIBUTED LAG -
          IDENTIFICATION * LAG , FIXED * DISTRIBUTED LAG - ERROR SPECIFICATION * CROSS
          CORRELATIONS * STOCK PRICES - DETERMINANTS * EVALUATION - REGRESSION , ERROR
          SPECIFICATION * EX ANTE * REGRESSION - SPURIOUS CORRELATION * BUSINESS
          INDICATORS - APPL

YA0450   BOX G.E.P., PIERCE D.A.
         "Distribution of residual autocorrelations in discrete integrated moving
         average models"   J. Am. Statist. Ass., vol.65, 1970, pp.1509-1526.
         RESIDUALS - ANALYSIS OF , AUTOCORRELATION * SPECIFICATION ERROR - TESTS ,
         MODEL SELECTION * TIME SERIES - ARIMA : DIAGNOSTICS * ADVANCED
YA0451   BOX G.E.P., TIAO G.C.
         "Comparison of forecast and actuality"   Appl. Stats., vol.25, 1976,
         pp.195-200.
         POLLUTION - CONTROLS * POLICY EVALUATION - METHODOLOGY * TIME SERIES - ARIMA
         : INTERVENTION
YA0452   BOX G.E.P., TIAO G.C.
         "Intervention analysis with applications to economic and environmental
         problems"   J. Am. Statist. Ass., vol.70, 1975, pp.70-79.
         TIME SERIES - ARIMA : INTERVENTION * POLLUTION - EFFECT OF * INFLATION -
         GOVERNMENT CONTROLS * DISTRIBUTED LAG - RATIONAL POLYNOMIAL * INTERVENTION
YA0453   BOYCE A.
         "Estimation of dynamic Gorman polar form utility functions"   Anns. Econ.
         Soc. Meas., vol.4, 1975, pp.103-116.
         DEMAND EQUATIONS - SYSTEMS OF : METHODOLOGY , ESTIMATION * CONSUMER
         BEHAVIOUR - ECONOMIC MODELS , THEORY * APPL - SECTOR : CONSUMER NON DURABLES
         , FOOD
YA0454   BOYER K.D.
         "Informative and goodwill advertising"   Rev. Econ. Stats., vol.56, 1974,
         pp.541-548.
         ADVERTISING - EFFECT OF * CONCENTRATION - EFFECT OF * APPL - SECTOR :
         FINANCE , PROFITS
YA0455   BOYES W.J., GERKING S.D.
         "A liquidity trap in the foreign exchange market: the case of Mexico"
         Int. Econ. Rev., vol.19, 1978, pp.777-785.
         SPECIFICATION ERROR - TESTS , MODEL SELECTION * APPL - MACRO : INTERNATIONAL
         FINANCE , EXCHANGE RATES * APPL - MACRO , LATIN AMERICA * REGRESSION -
         TRANSFORMATIONS , BOX COX : APPL * COMPARATIVE METHODS - REGRESSION ,
         TRANSFORMATIONS * INTEREST RATE - EFFECT OF
YA0456   BRADFORD D.F., KELEJIAN H.H.
         "The value of information for crop forecasting in a market system: some
         theoretical issues"   Rev. Econ. Studies, vol.44, 1977, pp.519-531.
         FORECASTING - VALUE OF * ADVANCED
YA0457   BRADFORD D.F., KELEJIAN H.H.
         "The value of information for crop forecasting with Bayesian speculators:
         theory and empirical results"   Bell J. Econ., vol.9, 1978, pp.123-144.
         APPL - FIRM : AGRICULTURE , FARMING * FORECASTING - VALUE OF * THEORY -
         SPECULATION * THEORY - PRICING * ADVANCED
YA0458   BRADY E.A.
         "Forecasting housing starts"   Bus. Econ., vol.6:4, 1971, pp.18-22.
         APPL - SECTOR : CONSTRUCTION , RESIDENTIAL
YA0459   BRANCH B.
         "Common stock performance and inflation: an international comparison"   J.
         Business, vol.47, 1974, pp.48-52.
         APPL - SECTOR : FINANCE , STOCK PRICE INDEX * DATA - INTERNATIONAL *
         INFLATION - EFFECT OF
YA0460   BRAND R.J., PINNOCK D.E., JACKSON K.L.
         "Large sample confidence bands for the logistic response curve and its
         increase"   Am. Stat'n., vol.27, 1973, pp.157-160.
         TREND CURVES - LOGISTIC * CONFIDENCE INTERVAL - REGRESSION , MULTIVARIATE *
         REGRESSION - TRANSFORMATION , LOGARITHMIC
YA0461   BRANDON C.H., JARRETT J.E.
         "Experimenting with students' ability to forecast"   Acctg. Rev., vol.52,
         1977, pp.697-704.
         APPL - FIRM : FINANCE , PROFITS , PER SHARE * JUDGEMENTAL FORECASTS -
         DETERMINANTS
YA0462   BRANDON P.S.
         "The electric side of combination gas-electric utilities"   Bell J. Econ.,
         vol.2, 1971, pp.688-703.
         APPL - FIRM : UTILITIES * APPL - FIRM : FINANCE , PROFITS * USE - ANTITRUST
         * COST - FIRM : UTILITIES
YA0463   BRANSON W.H.
         "Monetary policy and the new view of capital movements" with discussion
         Brookings Paps. Econ. Activity, 1970, pp.235-270.
         APPL - MACRO : INTERNATIONAL FINANCE * INTEREST RATE - EFFECT OF
YA0464   BRANSON W.H.
         "The trade effects of the 1971 currency realignments" with discussion
         Brookings Paps. Econ. Activity, 1972, pp.15-69.
         APPL - MACRO : INTERNATIONAL TRADE * EXCHANGE RATE - EFFECT OF * APPL -
         MACRO : INTERNATIONAL LINKAGE * COMPARATIVE METHODS - PRICE ELASTICITY ,
         ESTIMATION * APPL - MACRO , OECD
YA0465   BRANSON W.H., HILL R.D.
         "Capital movements among major OECD countries: some preliminary results"
         with discussion   J. Finance, vol.26, 1971, pp.269-286 & 306-309.
         APPL - MACRO : INTERNATIONAL FINANCE * APPL - MACRO , OECD * INTEREST RATE -
         EFFECT OF * MULTIPLIERS - MACRO

YA0466   BRANSON W.H., JUNZ H.B.
          "Trends in US trade and comparative advantage" with discussion   Brookings
          Paps. Econ. Activity, 1971, pp.285-345 & 754-759.
          APPL - MACRO : INTERNATIONAL TRADE * APPL - SECTOR : INTERNATIONAL TRADE
YA0467   BRASCH J.J.
          "Forecasting in multinational and locally owned Salvadorian companies"
          Ind. Mktg. Mgmt., vol.6, 1977, pp.231-236.
          FORECASTING - USAGE * APPL - FIRM TYPE : MULTINATIONALS * BASIC
YA0468   BRASCH J.J.
          "Sales forecasting in a developing country"   Ind. Mktg. Mgmt., vol.7,
          1978, pp.354-360.
          DATA - LDC * FORECASTING - INTRODUCTION * USER - FIRM * BASIC
YA0469   BRASS W.
          "Perspectves in popuation" with discussion   R. Statist. Soc. (A), vol.137,
          1974, pp.532-583.
          POPULATION * BIBLIOGRAPHY - POPULATION
YA0470   BRAY J.
          "Dynamic equations for forecasting with the GDP-unemployment relation and
          the growth of GDP in the UK as an example" with discussion   R. Statist.
          Soc. (A), vol.134, 1971, pp.167-227.
          DISTRIBUTED LAG - RATIONAL POLYNOMIAL * EVALUATION - DISTRIBUTED LAG *
          THEORY - MODELLING * COMPARATIVE METHODS - CAUSAL , DISTRIBUTED LAG *
          EVALUATION - THEORY OF * CONFIDENCE INTERVAL - EX ANTE * APPL - MACRO , UK *
          EX ANTE * APPL - MACRO : UNEMPLOYMENT
YA0471   BRAY J.
          "Optimal control of a noisy economy, with the UK as an example" with
          discussion   R. Statist. Soc. (A), vol.138, 1975, pp.339-373.
          CONTROL THEORY - STOCHASTIC , APPL * APPL - MACRO , UK * POLICY EVALUATION -
          MACRO * DISTRIBUTED LAG - SIMULTANEOUS SYSTEM * LOSS FUNCTIONS - MACRO * EX
          ANTE * DISTRIBUTED LAG - RATIONAL POLYNOMIAL * DISTRIBUTED LAG - ERROR
          SPECIFICATION
YA0472   BRAY J.
          "Predictive control of a stochastic model of the UK economy simulating
          present policy making practice by the UK government"   Anns. Econ. Soc.
          Meas., vol.3, 1974, pp.239-255.
          POLICY EVALUATION - MACRO * SIMULATION - APPL : POLICY EVALUATION * CONTROL
          THEORY - STOCHASTIC , APPL * LOSS FUNCTIONS - MACRO * MACRO MODEL - UK
YA0473   BREALEY R.A.
          "Some implications of the comovement of American company earnings"   Appl.
          Econ., vol.3, 1971, pp.183-196.
          APPL - FIRM : FINANCE , PROFITS * APPL - FIRM : FINANCE , STOCK PRICES *
          STOCK PRICES - COVARIATION * EX ANTE * EVALUATION - JUDGEMENTAL FORECASTS ,
          PROFITS
YA0474   BREALEY R.A., HODGES S.D., CAPRON D.
          "The return on alternative sources of finance"   Rev. Econ. Stats., vol.53,
          1976, pp.469-477.
          APPL - FIRM : FINANCE , FINANCIAL STRUCTURE * APPLICATION - FIRM : FINANCE ,
          PROFITS
YA0475   BRECH R.
          "Creating confidence about the future: the forecasting business"   Long
          Range Planning, vol.11:5, 1978, pp.89-93.
          MACRO MODEL - UK , LBS * EVALUATION - MACRO MODELS * DECISION RULES -
          FEEDBACK * USER REQUIREMENTS * BASIC
YA0476   BRECHT H.D.
          "Regression methodology with gross observation errors in the explantory
          variables"   Decis. Sci., vol.7, 1976, pp.57-65.
          COMPARATIVE METHODS - ESTIMATION : OLS , MSAE * DATA ERRORS - EFFECT OF *
          REGRESSION - OUTLIERS * DATA ERRORS - OUTLIERS
YA0477   BREEN W.J., LERNER E.M.
          "Corporate financial strategies and market measures of risk and return" with
          discussion   J. Finance, vol.28, 1973, pp.339-351 & 368-372.
          USE - FINANCIAL , PLANNING * APPL - FIRM : FINANCE , STOCK PRICES * STOCK
          PRICES - BETA , DETERMINANTS * THEORY - EFFICIENT MARKETS * RISK -
          ESTIMATION * STOCK PRICES - VOLATILITY * STOCK PRICES - RISK
YA0478   BREEN W.J., LERNER E.M., MYERS S.C.
          "On the use of beta in regulatory proceedings"   Bell J. Econ., vol.3,
          1972, pp.612-627.
          APPL - FIRM : FINANCE , STOCK PRICES * STOCK PRICES - BETA * STABILITY OF
          COEFFICIENTS - REGRESSION : APPL
YA0479   BREIMAN L., MEISEL W.S.
          "General estimates of the intrinsic variability of data in nonlinear
          regression models"   J. Am. Statist. Ass., vol.71, 1976, pp.301-307.
          REGRESSION - NON LINEAR * REGRESSION - MODEL CHOICE * REGRESSION - PIECEWISE
          * DATA - SIMULATION
YA0480   BRENNER M., SMIDT S.
          "A simple model of non-stationarity of systematic risk"   J. Finance,
          vol.32, 1977, pp.1081-1092.
          STOCK PRICES - BETA , VARIABLE * APPL - FIRM : FINANCE , STOCK PRICES *
          STABILITY OF COEFFICIENTS - REGRESSION

YA0481   BREWER K.R.W.
          "Some consequences of temporal aggregation and systematic sampling for ARMA
          and ARMAX models"   J. Econometrics, vol.1, 1973, pp.133=154.
          TIME SERIES - ARMA : INTERPRETATION * DATA - AGGREGATION OVER TIME
YA0482   BRICK J.R., THOMPSON H.E.
          "Time series analysis of interest rates: some additional evidence"   J.
          Finance, vol.33, 1978, pp.93=103.
          INTEREST RATE - TERM STRUCTURE * CROSS CORRELATIONS - APPL
YA0483   BRIGHTMAN H.J.
          "Comments on 'Application of spectral analysis'"   Decis. Sci., vol.2,
          1971, pp.375=376.
          SPECTRAL ANALYSIS - INTRODUCTION * EVALUATION - SPECTRAL ANALYSIS
YA0484   BRIMMER A.F.
          "Alternative monetary=fiscal policies and sectoral credit flows"   Am.
          Econ. Assn. Proc., 1974, pp.112=120.
          MACRO MODEL - MIT , PENN , SSRC * POLICY EVALUATION - MACRO : FISCAL ,
          MONETARY * POLICY EVALUATION - MACRO : STABILISATION
YA0485   BRIMMER A.F., SINAI A.
          "The effect of tax policy on capital formation, corporate liquidity and the
          availability of investment funds: a simulation study" with discussion   J.
          Finance, vol.31, 1976, pp.287=318.
          APPL - MACRO : FLOW OF FUNDS * MACRO MODEL - DATA RESOURES * SIMULATION -
          APPL : POLICY EVALUATION * TAX - EFFECT OF
YA0486   BRISCOE G.
          "The significance of financial expectations in predicting consumer
          expenditures: a quarterly analysis"   Appl. Econ., vol.8, 1976, pp.99=119.
          APPL - MACRO , UK * APPL - MACRO : CONSUMER DEMAND * EVALUATION -
          ATTITUDINAL DATA
YA0487   BRISCOE G., HIRST M.
          "A further appreciation of demand forecasting models: some methods based on
          survey information"   Long Range Planning, vol.8:1, 1975, pp.87=97.
          SURVEYS - REVIEW * ATTITUDINAL DATA * EXPECTATIONS - DATA * DATA - CROSS
          SECTION * INPUT OUTPUT - INTRODUCTION * FORECASTING - INTRODUCTION * BASIC
YA0488   BRISCOE G., HIRST M.
          "An appreciation of alternative sales forecasting models: recent techniques
          based on historical data"   Long Range Planning, vol.6:3, 1973, pp.79=89.
          FORECASTING - REVIEW * BASIC
YA0489   BRISSIMIS S.N., GILL L.
          "On the asymptotic distribution of impact and interim multipliers"
          Econometrica, vol.46, 1978, pp.463=470.
          MULTIPLIERS - METHODOLOGY * MACRO MODEL - KLEIN * MULTIPLIERS - MACRO
YA0490   BRITT S.H., O'LEARY J.C., STURGES R.R.
          "The accuracy of claimed subscribership"   J. Advtg. Res., vol.13:6, 1973,
          pp.29=32.
          DATA ERRORS - ESTIMATION OF * APPL - SECTOR : SERVICES , MEDIA , MAGAZINES
YA0491   BRITTAIN B.
          "Tests of theories of exchange rate determination" with discussion   J.
          Finance, vol.32, 1977, pp.519=529 & 545=551.
          APPL - MACRO : INTERNATIONAL FINANCE , EXCHANGE RATES * INTEREST RATE -
          EFFECT OF
YA0492   BRITTAIN J.E.
          Testing for and removing bias in the seasonally adjusted unemployment
          series" with discussion   Brookings Paps. Econ. Activity, 1976, pp.211=224
          & 239=245.
          APPL - MACRO : UNEMPLOYMENT * SEASONALITY - ESTIMATION * SEASONALITY -
          TESTING
YA0493   BROBST R., GATES R.
          "Comments on pooling issues and methods in regression analysis"   J. Mktg.
          Res., vol.14, 1977, pp.598=600.
          DATA - AGGREGATION * ESTIMATION - CROSS SECTION , TIME SERIES * REGRESSION -
          AGGREGATION * COMPARATIVE METHODS - DATA : CROSS SECTION , TIME SERIES
YA0494   BROBST R., GATES R., GLOUDEMANS R.J.
          "Comments on Gloudemans and Miller's multiple regression analysis applied to
          residential properties: comments"   Decis. Sci., vol.9, 1978, pp.174=182.
          APPL - SECTOR : CONSTRUCTION , RESIDENTIAL * REGRESSION - MODEL
          INTERPRETATION * PRICE - SECTOR : CONSTRUCTION , RESIDENTIAL
YA0495   BROCKHOFF K.
          "A test for the product life cycle"   Econometrica, vol.35, 1967,
          pp.472=484.
          APPL - SECTOR : CONSUMER DURABLES , CARS * ESTIMATION - NON LINEAR *
          EVALUATION - LIFE CYCLE , PRODUCT
YA0496   BRODER I.E.
          "Base year revisions in the FRB index: problems in interpreting historical
          movements"   J. Am. Statist. Ass., vol.71, 1976, pp.62=67.
          INDEX NUMBERS - METHODOLOGY * EVALUATION - INDEX NUMBERS * INDEX NUMBERS -
          MACRO : PRODUCTION

YA0497 BRODER I.E., SCHOEPFLE G.K.
"Classification of economic indicators: an alternative approach" Anns.
Econ. Soc. Meas., vol. 4, 1975, pp.435-446.
BUSINESS CYCLE - IDENTIFICATION * EVALUATION - BUSINESS INDICATORS * CLUSTER
ANALYSIS - APPL

YA0498 BROOKES L.G.
"Energy and economic growth" Ind. Mktg. Mgmt., vol.1, 1971, pp.3-10 &
1972, pp.262-263.
APPL - MACRO : GROWTH * APPL - MACRO : ENERGY * DATA - INTERNATIONAL * BASIC

YA0499 BROOKES L.G.
"Energy and the economy" Long Range Planning, vol.10:1, 1977, pp.54-58.
APPL - MACRO : ENERGY * APPL - MACRO , UK * INCOME - EFFECT OF

YA0500 BROOKES L.G.
"Energy resources and world economic growth" Long Range Planning,
vol.6:3, 1973, pp.39-43.
APPL - MACRO : ENERGY * DATA - INTERNATIONAL * INCOME - EFFECT OF * BASIC

YA0501 BROOKS L.D., BUCKMASTER D.A.
"Further evidence of the time series properties of accounting income" J.
Finance, vol.31, 1976, pp.1359-1373.
APPL - FIRM : FINANCE , PROFITS * EX ANTE * DATA - DISAGGREGATION

YA0502 BROOKS R.J., ET AL.
"A note on forecasting car ownership" R. Statist. Soc. (A), vol.141,
1978, pp.64-68.
APPL - SECTOR : CONSUMER DURABLES , CARS * LONG TERM FORECASTING *
EVALUATION - TREND CURVES

YA0503 BROWN A., DEATON A.
"Models of consumer behaviour" Econ. J., vol.82, 1972, pp.1145-1236.
CONSUMER BEHAVIOUR - ECONOMIC MODELS , REVIEW * DEMAND EQUATIONS - SYSTEMS
OF , REVIEW * BIBLIOGRAPHY - CONSUMER BEHAVIOUR , ECONOMIC MODELS *
EVALUATION - CONSUMER BEHAVIOUR , ECONOMIC MODELS

YA0504 BROWN C.J.F., SHERIFF T.D.
"Approaches to medium-term assessments" Nat. Inst. Econ. Rev., no.86,
1978, pp.55-64.
LONG TERM FORECASTING * APPL - MACRO , UK * EX ANTE * EVALUATION - MACRO
FORECASTS

YA0505 BROWN D., FELDSTEIN M., LAPAN H.
"The rising price of physicians' services: a clarification" Rev. Econ.
Stats., vol.56, 1974, pp.396-398.
HEALTH - MANPOWER , EARNINGS * SUPPLY - SECTOR : SOCIAL , HEALTH * PRICE -
EFFECT OF * HEALTH - MANPOWER , PHYSICIANS

YA0506 BROWN D.A., BUCK S.F., PYATT F.G.
"Improving the sales forecast for consumer durables" J. Mktg. Res.,
vol.2, 1965, pp.229-234.
APPL - SECTOR : CONSUMER DURABLES * MARKET POTENTIAL * TREND CURVES -
RATIONAL POLYNOMIAL * DEMAND - REPLACEMENT * MARKET SEGMENTATION * CONSUMER
BEHAVIOUR - PURCHASING

YA0507 BROWN D.M., LAPAN H.E., FELDSTEIN M.S.
"The rising price of physicians' services: comment" Rev. Econ. Stats.,
vol.54, 1972, pp.101-107.
HEALTH - MANPOWER , EARNINGS * MANPOWER PLANNING - SECTOR : HEALTH *
MANPOWER PLANNING - EARNINGS * PRICE - SECTOR : HEALTH * COST - SECTOR :
HEALTH * HEALTH - MANPOWER , PHYSICIANS

YA0508 BROWN G.F., SILVERMAN L.P.
"The retail price of heroin: estimation and applications" J. Am. Statist.
Ass., vol.69, 1974, pp.595-606.
APPL - SECTOR : CONSUMER NONDURABLES , DRUGS * APPL - SECTOR : SOCIAL ,
CRIME * PRICE - SECTOR : CONSUMER NONDURABLES

YA0509 BROWN G.M., HAMMACK J.
"Dynamic economic management of migratory waterfowl" Rev. Econ. Stats.,
vol.55, 1973, pp.73-82.
APPL - SECTOR : SERVICES , SPORT * CONTROL THEORY - DETERMINISTIC , APPL *
USE - CONSERVATION

YA0510 BROWN L.D., ROZEFF M.S.
"The superiority of analyst forecasts as measures of expectations: evidence
from earnings" J. Finance, vol.33, 1978, pp.1-16.
APPL - FIRM : FINANCE , PROFITS , PER SHARE * EX ANTE * COMPARATIVE METHODS
- ARIMA , JUDGEMENTAL * EVALUATION - JUDGEMENTAL FORECASTS , PROFITS *
COMPARATIVE METHODS - ARIMA , AUTOREGRESSIVE * EVALUATION - JUDGEMENTAL
FORECASTS , SPECIALIST

YA0511 BROWN L.O.
"Forecasting sales trends in the solid state industry" Ind. Mktg. Mgmt.,
vol.7, 1978, pp.243-249.
APPL - FIRM : PRODUCTION , ELECTRONICS * INPUT OUTPUT - FIRM * BASIC

YA0512 BROWN P., KENNELLY J.W.
"The information content of quarterly earnings: an extension and some
further evidence" J. Business, vol.45, 1972, pp.403-415.
APPL - FIRM : FINANCE , PROFITS , PER SHARE * STOCK PRICES - TRADING RULES *
APPL - FIRM : FINANCE , PROFITS * STOCK PRICES - INFORMATION EFFECT

YA0513   BROWN P., PAYNE C.
          "Election night forecasting" with discussion   R. Statist. Soc. (A),
          vol.138, 1975, pp.463-498.
          REGRESSION - RIDGE * VOTING

YA0514   BROWN R.G.
          "A model for measuring the influence of promotion on inventory and consumer
          demand"   J. Mktg. Res., vol.10, 1973, pp.380-389.
          APPL - SECTOR : CONSUMER NON DURABLES * DISTRIBUTION - EFFECT OF * USE -
          PROMOTION EVALUATION

YA0515   BROWN R.G.
          "Detection of turning points in a time series"   Decis. Sci., vol.2, 1971,
          pp.383-403.
          TURNING POINTS - FORECASTING * CONTROL CHARTS - CUSUM * APPL - FIRM :
          FINANCE , STOCK PRICES * STOCK PRICES - RUNS

YA0516   BROWN R.G.
          "Sales response to promotions and advertising"   J. Advtg. Res., vol.14:4,
          1974, pp.33-39.
          USE - PROMOTION EVALUATION * BRAND CHOICE - APPL

YA0517   BROWN R.L., DURBIN J., EVANS J.M.
          "Techniques for testing the constancy of regression relationships over time"
          with discussion   R. Statist. Soc. (B), vol.37, 1975, pp.149-192.
          STABILITY OF COEFFICIENTS - REGRESSION , TEST * CONTROL CHARTS - CUSUM *
          RESIDUALS - ANALYSIS OF , RECURSIVE * RESIDUALS - ANALYSIS OF , MODEL
          SPECIFICATION * APPL - SECTOR : UTILITIES , TELEPHONE * APPL - MACRO : MONEY
          , DEMAND

YA0518   BROWN R.S.
          "Estimating advantages to large-scale advertising"   Rev. Econ. Stats.,
          vol.60, 1978, pp.428-437.
          ADVERTISING - SCALE ECONOMIES * ADVERTISING - EFFECT OF * APPL - FIRM :
          CONSUMER NON DURABLES , CIGARETTES * COMPETITION - EFFECT OF * ADVERTISING -
          DETERMINANTS * COMPARATIVE METHODS - ESTIMATION : SIMULTANEOUS SYSTEM *
          MARKET SHARE - EFFECT OF * DISTRIBUTED LAG - APPL , ADVERTISING

YA0519   BROWN S.J.
          "Heteroscedasticity in the market model: a comment"   J. Business, vol.50,
          1977, pp.80-83.
          SPECIFICATION ERROR - TESTS , HETEROSCEDASTICITY * STOCK PRICES - VOLATILITY
          * APPL - FIRM : FINANCE , STOCK PRICES * * STOCK PRICES - MODELS , CAPM

YA0520   BROWN S.L.
          "Earnings changes, stock prices, and market efficiency"   J. Finance,
          vol.33, 1978, pp.17-28.
          APPL - FIRM : FINANCE , PROFITS , PER SHARE * APPL - FIRM : FINANCE , STOCK
          PRICES * STOCK PRICES - INFORMATION EFFECT * FORECASTING - VALUE OF

YA0521   BROWN W.G., BEATTIE B.R.
          "Improving estimates of economic parameters by use of ridge regression-with
          production function applications"   Am. J. Ag. Econ., vol.57, 1975,
          pp.21-32.
          COMPARATIVE METHODS - ESTIMATION : OLS , RIDGE * DATA - SIMULATION * APPL -
          SECTOR : UTILITIES , WATER * PRODUCTION FUNCTIONS - SECTOR *
          MULTICOLLINEARITY - REMOVAL OF

YA0522   BROWNE S.J., O'BRIEN D.
          "Product line forecasting and planning"   Bus. Econ., vol.9:3, 1974,
          pp.63-71.
          USER - FIRM : PRODUCTION * STRIKE - EFFECT OF * USE - PROMOTION EVALUATION *
          APPL - FIRM : PRODUCTION * BASIC

YA0523   BRUBACHER S.R., WILSON G.T.
          "Interpolating time series with application to the estimation of holiday
          effects on electricity demand"   Appl. Stats., vol.25, 1976, pp.107-116.
          DATA - INTERPOLATION * TIME SERIES - ARIMA : ESTIMATION * APPL - SECTOR :
          UTILITIES , ELECTRICITY * TIME SERIES - ARIMA : INTERVENTION

YA0524   BRUCE C.J.
          "The wage-tax spiral: Canada 1953-1970"   Econ. J., vol.85, 1975,
          pp.372-376.
          APPL - MACRO , CANADA * APPL - SECTOR : EARNINGS * TAX - EFFECT OF

YA0525   BRUCKER E., GREER D.F.
          "Usury legislation and market structure: an alternative approach: comment"
          J. Finance, vol.32, 1977, pp.1339-1347.
          APPL - SECTOR : FINANCE , CONSUMER CREDIT * USE - LOAN REGULATION * SUPPLY -
          SECTOR : FINANCE

YA0526   BRUND A.V., ET.AL.
          "Technological forecasting in small business"   Sloan Mgmt. Rev., vol.15,
          no.1, 1973, pp.49-63 & vol.15, no.3, 1974, pp.89-95.
          TECHNOLOGICAL FORECASTING * APPL - FIRM TYPE : SMALL BUSINESS * APPL - FIRM
          : PRODUCTION , ELECTRONICS * BASIC

YA0527   BRUNDY J.M., JORGENSON D.W.
          "Efficient estimation of simultaneous equations by instrumental variables"
          Rev. Econ. Stats., vol.53, 1971, pp.207-224.
          SIMULTANEOUS SYSTEM - ESTIMATION * MACRO MODEL - LIU(MONTHLY) * COMPARATIVE
          METHODS - ESTIMATION : SIMULTANEOUS SYSTEM * ESTIMATION - INSTRUMENTAL
          VARIABLES

YA0528   BRUNDY J.M., JORGENSON D.W.
         "The relative efficiency of instrumental variables estimators of systems of
         simultaneous equations"   Anns. Econ. Soc. Meas., vol.3, 1974, pp.679-700.
         COMPARATIVE METHODS - ESTIMATION : SIMULTANEOUS SYSTEMS * SIMULTANEOUS
         SYSTEM - ESTIMATION * ESTIMATION - INSTRUMENTAL VARIABLES * MACRO MODEL -
         KLEIN

YA0529   BRUNNER K., MELTZER A.A.
         "The explanation of inflation; some international evidence"   Am. Econ.
         Ass. Proc., 1977, pp.148-154.
         INFLATION - DETERMINANTS * DATA - INTERNATIONAL

YA0530   BRY G., BOSCHAN C.
         "Interpretation and analysis of time series scatters"   Am. Stat'n,
         vol.25:2, 1971, pp.29-33.
         REGRESSION - SCATTERGRAM * BASIC

YA0531   BRYANT J.W.
         "A simulation model of retailer behaviour"   Opl. Res. Q., vol.26, 1975,
         pp.133-149.
         CONSUMER BEHAVIOUR - PSYCHOLOGICAL MODELS * SIMULATION - APPL : MICRO *
         SIMULATION - APPL : FIRM * APPL - FIRM : CONSUMER NON DURABLES * USE -
         MARKETING POLICY * APPL - SECTOR : RETAILING * SIMULATION - APPL : CONSUMER
         BEHAVIOUR

YA0532   BUDD A.P.
         "The debate on fine-tuning; the basic issues"   Nat. Inst. Econ. Rev.,
         no.74, 1975, pp.56-59.
         POLICY EVALUATION - MACRO : FISCAL , MONETARY

YA0533   BUFFA E.S., COSGROVE M.J., LUCE B.J.
         "An integrated work shift scheduling system"   Decis. Sci., vol.7, 1976,
         pp.620-630.
         USE - SCHEDULING , MANPOWER * TIME SERIES - ARIMA : APPL

YA0534   BUFFA E.S., DYER J.S.
         "Managerial use of dynamic structural models"   Decis. Sci., vol.7, 1976,
         pp.73-94.
         INDUSTRIAL DYNAMICS - REVIEW

YA0535   BUFFA F.P.
         "The application of a dynamic forecasting model with inventory control
         properties"   Decis. Sci., vol.6, 1978, pp.298-306.
         USE - INVENTORY CONTROL * TRACKING SIGNAL - METHODOLOGY * COMPARATIVE
         METHODS - EXPONENTIAL SMOOTHING , ADAPTIVE * EXPONENTIAL SMOOTHING -
         ADAPTIVE COEFFICIENTS * EX ANTE

YA0536   BULLARD C.W., SEBALD A.V.
         "Effects of parametric uncertainty and technological change on input-output
         models"   Rev. Econ. Stats., vol.59, 1977, pp.75-81.
         STABILITY OF COEFFICIENTS - INPUT OUTPUT * APPL - SECTOR : UTILITIES ,
         ELECTRICITY * INPUT OUTPUT - SECTOR : UTILITIES * TOLERANCE INTERVAL

YA0537   BULTEZ A.V., NAERT P.A.
         "Consistent sum constrained models"   J. Am. Statist. Ass., vol.70, 1975,
         pp.529-535.
         APPL - SECTOR : CONSUMER DURABLES * ESTIMATION - GLS * MARKET SHARE - SECTOR
         : CONSUMER DURABLES * MARKET SHARE - METHODOLOGY * COMPARATIVE METHODS -
         ESTIMATION : OLS , GLS * REGRESSION - LIMITED DEPENDENT , LOGIT

YA0538   BUNGAARD-NIELSEN M.
         "Forecasting in the chemical industry"   Ind. Mktg. Mgmt., vol.1, 1972,
         pp.205-210.
         APPL - SECTOR : PRODUCTION , CHEMICALS * APPL - SECTOR : PRODUCTION ,
         FERTILIZER * BASIC

YA0539   BUNN D.W.
         "A Bayesian approach to the linear combination of forecasts"   Opl. Res.
         Q., vol.26, 1975, pp.325-329.
         COMBINING FORECASTS - METHODOLOGY * APPL - SECTOR : UTILITIES * BAYESIAN -
         COMBINING FORECASTS

YA0540   BUNN D.W.
         "A Bayesian forecasting model for house account sales"   Omega, vol.6,
         1978, pp.455-457.
         APPL - FIRM : CONSUMER NON DURABLES , HEALTH AIDS * JUDGEMENTAL FORECASTS -
         PROBABILITIES * PROBABILITY MODELS - DIRICHLET : APPL

YA0541   BUNN D.W.
         "A comparative evaluation of the outperformance and minimum variance
         procedure for the linear synthesis of forecasts"   Opl. Res. Q., vol.28,
         1977, pp.653-662.
         EVALUATION - COMBINING FORECASTS * PROBABILITY MODELS - WISHART * BAYESIAN -
         COMBINING FORECASTS * PROBABILITY MODELS - DIRICHLET * DATA - SIMULATION

YA0542   BUNN D.W.
         "A simplification of the matrix beta distribution for combining estimators"
         J. Opl. Res. Soc., vol.29, 1978, pp.1013-1016.
         COMBINING FORECASTS - METHODOLOGY * PROBABILITY MODELS - BETA

YA0543   BUNN D.W.
         "Estimation of a dirichlet prior distribution"   Omega, vol.6, 1978,
         pp.371-373.
         PROBABILITY MODELS - FIRICHLET * JUDGEMENTAL FORECASTS - METHODOLOGY *
         JUDGEMENTAL FORECASTS - PROBABILITIES

YA0544 BUNN D.W.
        "Prior belief on the forecast variable"   Omega, vol.3, 1975, pp.611-612.
        PRIOR INFORMATION * JUDGEMENTAL FORECASTS - INCORPORATION * COMBINING
        FORECASTS - METHODOLOGY
YA0545 BUNN D.W., MUSTAFAOGLU M.M.
        "Forecasting political risk"   Mgmt. Sci., vol.24, 1978, pp.1557-1567.
        SOCIAL FORECASTING * JUDGEMENTAL FORECASTS - METHODOLOGY
YA0546 BURCH S.W., FABRICANT R.A.
        "A further comment on the behaviour of help-wanted advertising"   Rev.
        Econ. Stats., vol.50, 1968, pp.278-281.
        APPL - MACRO : UNEMPLOYMENT * DATA - SPECIFICATION OF VARIABLES * BUSINESS
        INDICATORS - APPL * INDEX NUMBERS - MACRO : EMPLOYMENT VACANCIES
YA0547 BURCH S.W., FABRICANT R.A.
        "Cyclical behaviour of help-wanted index and the unemployment rate: a reply"
        Rev. Econ. Stats., vol.53, 1971, pp.105-106.
        DATA - SPECIFICATION OF VARIABLES * APPL - MACRO : UNEMPLOYMENT * BUSINESS
        INDICATORS - APPL * INDEX NUMBERS - MACRO : EMPLOYMENT VACANCIES
YA0548 BURCH S.W., WERNEKE D.
        "The stock of consumer durables, inflation, and personal saving decisions"
        Rev. Econ. Stats., vol.57, 1975, pp.141-154.
        MACRO MODEL - FRB , MIT , PENN * APPL - MACRO : SAVINGS * APPL - MACRO :
        CONSUMPTION * DISTRIBUTED LAG - APPL , INCOME * EXPECTATIONS - DATA *
        INFLATION - EFFECT OF * EX ANTE * CONSUMER BEHAVIOUR - ECONOMIC MODELS *
        EVALUATION - SAVINGS MODELS * ATTITUDINAL DATA * REGRESSION - SPECIFICATION
        OF VARIABLES * WEALTH - EFFECT OF * INCOME - EFFECT OF
YA0549 BURGESS D.F.
        "A cost minimisation approach to import demand equations"   Rev. Econ.
        Stats., vol.56, 1974, pp.225-234.
        APPL - MACRO : INTERNATIONAL TRADE , IMPORTS * PRICE - EFFECT OF *
        SUBSTITUTE PRODUCTS
YA0550 BURGESS D.F.
        "Duality theory and pitfalls in the specification of technology"   J.
        Econometrics, vol.3, 1975, pp.105-121.
        ERROR SPECIFICATION - AUTOCORRELATED , CORRELATED * PRICE - EFFECT OF * COST
        - THEORY * PRODUCTION FUNCTIONS - SUBSTITUTION * PRODUCTION FUNCTIONS -
        THEORY * PRODUCTION FUNCTIONS - MACRO * ADVANCED
YA0551 BURKHOLDER A.A.
        "A new leading indicator"   Bus. Econ., vol.13:3, 1978, pp.5-10.
        BUSINESS INDICATORS - METHODOLOGY * APPL - MACRO : GNP * EVALUATION -
        TURNING POINT FORECASTS
YA0552 BURKITT B.
        "The relationship between earnings and unionization in the inter-war years"
        Appl. Econ., vol.6, 1974, pp.83-93.
        UNIONISATION - EFFECT OF * APPL - SECTOR : EARNINGS * BASIC
YA0553 BURKITT B., BOWERS D.
        "Wage inflation and union power in the UK: 1949-67"   Appl. Econ., vol.8,
        1976, pp.289-300.
        UNIONISATION - EFFECT OF * INFLATION - DETERMINANTS * APPL - SECTOR :
        EARNINGS
YA0554 BURLEY H.T.
        "Production functions for Australian manufacturing industries"   Rev. Econ.
        Stats., vol.55, 1973, pp.118-122.
        PRODUCTION FUNCTIONS - SECTOR * DATA - SPECIFICATION OF VARIABLES * DATA
        ERRORS - EFFECT OF * APPL - MACRO , AUSTRALIA * PRODUCTION FUNCTIONS -
        METHODOLOGY
YA0555 BURMAN J.P.
        "Moving seasonal adjustment of statistical time series"   R. Statist. Soc.
        (A), vol.128, 1965, pp.534-558 & vol.129, 1966, pp.155,274.
        SEASONALITY - ESTIMATION , CENSUS * TIME SERIES - DECOMPOSITION * TIME
        SERIES - BOX JENKINS PREDICTOR * SPECTRAL ANALYSIS - APPL : SEASONALITY *
        COMPARATIVE METHODS - SEASONALITY * SEASONALITY - CHANGING * DATA ERRORS -
        OUTLIERS
YA0556 BURROWS P.
        "Explanatory and forecasting models of inventory investment in Britain"
        Appl. Econ., vol.3, 1971, pp.275-289.
        APPL - MACRO : INVENTORIES * COMPARATIVE METHODS - AUTOREGRESSIVE , CAUSAL *
        EX ANTE * COMPARATIVE METHODS - CAUSAL , JUDGEMENTAL * COMPARATIVE METHODS -
        AUTOREGRESSIVE , JUDGEMENTAL
YA0557 BURROWS P., GODFREY L.
        "Identifying and estimating the parameters of a symmetrical model of
        inventory investment"   Appl. Econ., vol.5, 1973, pp.193-197.
        APPL - MACRO : INVENTORIES * ESTIMATION - MAXIMUM LIKELIHOOD * THEORY -
        EXPECTATIONS * ERROR SPECIFICATION - MOVING AVERAGE
YA0558 BURT J., KAEN F.R., BOOTH G.G.
        "Foreign exchange market efficiency under flexible exchange rates"   J.
        Finance, vol.32, 1977, pp.1325-1330.
        APPL - MACRO : INTERNATIONAL FINANCE , EXCHANGE RATES * APPL - MACRO , UK *
        APPL - MACRO , CANADA * APPL - MACRO , GERMANY * RANDOM WALK - TEST

YA0559   BURT O.R., BREWER D.
          "Estimation of net social benefits from outdoor recreation"   Econometrica,
          vol.39, 1971, pp.813-827.
          APPL - SECTOR : SERVICES , TOURISM * DEMAND EQUATIONS - SYSTEM OF * ERROR
          SPECIFICATION - HETEROSCEDASTIC * ESTIMATION - GLS * ESTIMATION -
          CONSTRAINED : APPL * USE - TOURISH DEVELOPMENT
YA0560   BUSE A.
          "Goodness of fit in generalised least squares estimation"   Am. Stat'n.,
          vol.27, 1973, pp.106-108.
          ESTIMATION - GLS * REGRESSION - SUMMARY STATISTICS
YA0561   BUSE A., LIM L.
          "Cubic splines as a special case of restricted least squares"   J. Am.
          Statist. Ass., vol.72, 1977, pp.64-68.
          REGRESSION - PIECEWISE * STABILITY OF COEFFICIENTS - REGRESSION * ESTIMATION
          - CONSTRAINED * SPLINE FUNCTIONS * SPECIFICATION ERROR - TESTS , CONSTRAINTS
YA0562   BUTCHART R.L.
          "Conversational non-linear regression"   Opl. Res. Q., vol.24, 1973,
          pp.129-130.
          ESTIMATION - NON LINEAR * REGRESSION - ESTIMATION
YA0563   BUTLER A.D.
          "An analysis of flows in a manpower system"   Stat'n., vol.20, 1971,
          pp.69-84.
          MANPOWER PLANNING - FIRM * PROBABILITY MODELS - POISSON * MANPOWER PLANNING
          - LABOUR TURNOVER * MANPOWER PLANNING - PROMOTION
YA0564   BUTLER A.D., WARREN S.A.
          "An optimal temporary loan model for state borrowers"   J. Finance, vol.32,
          1977, pp.1305-1312.
          APPL - SECTOR : GOVERNMENT , LOCAL , FINANCE * USER - SECTOR : GOVERNMENT ,
          LOCAL * INTEREST RATE - DETERMINANTS
YA0565   BUTTON K.J.
          "A critical review of techniques for forecasting car ownership in discrete
          areas"   Stat'n., vol.23, 1974, pp.117-128.
          APPL - SECTOR : CONSUMER DURABLES , CARS * APPL - SECTOR : TRANSPORT , ROAD
          , PASSENGER * TREND CURVES - LOGISTIC * BIBLIOGRAPHY - CONSUMER DURABLES ,
          CARS
YA0566   BUZZELL R.D., BAKER M.J.
          "Sales effectiveness of automobile advertising"   J. Advtg. Res., vol.12:3,
          1972, pp.3-8.
          ADVERTISING - EFFECT OF * APPL - FIRM : CONSUMER DURABLES , CARS * DATA -
          CROSS SECTION
YA0567   BUZZELL R.D., GALE B.T., SULTAN R.G.M.
          "Market share - a key to profitability"   H.B.R., vol.53, Jan-Feb, 1975,
          pp.97-107.
          APPL - FIRM : FINANCE , PROFITS * MARKET SHARE - EFFECT OF
YA0568   BYRON R.P.
          "Efficient estimation and inference in large econometric systems"
          Econometrica, vol.45, 1977, pp.1499-1515.
          NUMERICAL METHODS - OPTIMISATION * SIMULTANEOUS SYSTEM - ESTIMATION *
          ADVANCED
YA0569   BYRON R.P.
          "Testing for misspecification in econometric systems using full information"
          Int. Econ. Rev., vol.13, 1972, pp.745-756.
          SPECIFICATION ERROR - TESTS , IDENTIFICATION * MACRO MODEL - KLEIN *
          SIMULTANEOUS SYSTEM - IDENTIFICATION
YA0570   BYRON R.P.
          "Testing structural specification using the unrestricted reduced form"
          Econometrica, vol.42, 1974, pp.869-883.
          SPECIFICATION ERROR - TESTS , IDENTIFICATION * DATA - SIMULATION * MACRO
          MODEL - KLEIN GOLDBERGER * COMPARATIVE METHODS - TESTS , VARIABLE INCLUSION
          * SPECIFICATION ERROR - TESTS , VARIABLE INCLUSION
YA0571   CAINES P.E., SETHI S.P., BROTHERTON T.W.
          "Impulse response identification and causality detection for the
          Lydia-Pinkham data"   Anns. Econ. Soc. Meas., vol.6, 1977, pp.147-163.
          LOSS FUNCTIONS - AKAIKE'S FPE * APPL - FIRM : CONSUMER NON DURABLES , HEALTH
          AIDS * DISTRIBUTED LAG - APPL , ADVERTISING * DISTRIBUTED LAG - RATIONAL
          POLYNOMIAL * ERROR SPECIFICATION - ARMA * ADVERTISING - EFFECT OF *
          ADVERTISING - DETERMINANTS * CAUSALITY - TEST * CAUSALITY - THEORY *
          DISTRIBUTED LAG - ARIMA
YA0572   CAIRNCROSS A.
          "Economic forecasting"   Econ. J., vol.79, 1969, pp.797-812.
          FORECASTING - REVIEW * EVALUATION - MACRO FORECASTS * BASIC
YA0573   CALLEN J.L.
          "Production, efficiency, and welfare in the natural gas transmission
          industry"   Am. Econ. Rev., vol.68, 1978, pp.311-323.
          APPL - FIRM : UTILITIES , GAS * PRODUCTION FUNCTIONS - FIRM * USE -
          FINANCIAL , REGULATION

YA0574   CAMBELL T., BRENDSELL L.
          "The impact of compensating balance requirements on the cash balance of
          manufacturing corporations: an empirical study"   J. Finance, vol.32, 1977,
          pp.31-40.
          APPL - SECTOR : FINANCE , FINANCIAL STRUCTURE , LIQUID ASSETS * COMPARATIVE
          METHODS - REGRESSION , ERROR SPECIFICATION
YA0575   CAMERON M.H., NASH J.E.
          "On forecasting the manpower requirements of an organisation with homogenous
          workloads"   R. Statist. Soc. (A), vol.137, 1974, pp.288-218.
          TIME SERIES - ARIMA ; APPL * MANPOWER PLANNING - FIRM : ESTIMATION -
          PRINCIPAL COMPONENTS : APPL * STABILITY OF COEFFICIENTS - REGRESSION *
          STATIONARITY - TESTING
YA0576   CAMPAGNA A.S.
          "Capital appropriations and the investment decision"   Rev. Econ. Stats.,
          vol.50, 1968, pp.207-214.
          APPL - SECTOR : INVESTMENT
YA0577   CAMPBELL H.F.
          "An input output analysis of the commodity structure of indirect taxes in
          Canada"   Can. J. Econ., vol.8, 1975, pp.433-441.
          INPUT OUTPUT - MACRO , CANADA * TAX - EFFECT OF
YA0578   CAMPBELL H.F.
          "Deadweight loss and commodity taxation in Canada"   Can. J. Econ., vol.8,
          1975, pp.441-447.
          TAX - EFFECT OF * APPL - MACRO : CONSUMER DEMAND * DEMAND EQUATIONS -
          SYSTEMS OF * APPL - MACRO , CANADA
YA0579   CAMPBELL M.J., WALKER A.M.
          "A survey of statistical work on the Mackenzie River series of annual
          Canadian lynx trappings for the years 1821-1934 and a new analysis" with
          discussion   R. Statist. Soc. (A), vol.140, 1977, pp.411-431, & 448-468.
          APPL - SECTOR : NATURAL , ANIMAL POPULATIONS * TIME SERIES - REVIEW * TIME
          SERIES - HARMONICS * TIME SERIES - AUTOREGRESSIVE
YA0580   CAMPBELL N.A.
          "The influence function as an aid in outlier detection in discriminant
          analysis"   Appl. Stats., vol.27, 1978, pp.251-258.
          DISCRIMINANT ANALYSIS - METHODOLOGY * DATA ERRORS - OUTLIERS * APPL - SECTOR
          : NATURAL , ANIMAL POPULATIONS
YA0581   CANZONERI M.B.
          "The returns to labour and the cyclical behaviour of real wages: the
          Canadian case"   Rev. Econ. Stats., vol.60, 1978, pp.19-24.
          APPL - MACRO : EARNINGS * APPL - MACRO : OUTPUT * APPL - MACRO , CANADA
YA0582   CARBONE R., LONGINI R.L.
          "A feedback model for automated real estate assessment"   Mgmt. Sci.,
          vol.24, 1977, pp.241-248.
          APPL - SECTOR : CONSTRUCTION , RESIDENTIAL * PRICE - SECTOR : CONSTRUCTION ,
          RESIDENTIAL * USE - REAL ESTATE APPRAISAL * QUALITY - ADJUSTMENTS *
          ESTIMATION - FILTERING , ADAPTIVE
YA0583   CAREY K.J.
          "Nonrandom price changes in association with trading in large blocks:
          evidence of market efficiency in behaviour of investor returns"   J.
          Business, vol.50, 1977, pp.407-414.
          STOCK PRICES - TRADING RULES * STOCK PRICES - TRADING VOLUME * APPL - FIRM :
          FINANCE , STOCK PRICES * EX ANTE
YA0584   CAREY K.J., SHERR L.A.
          "Market and price factors in transaction-to-transaction price change
          behaviour of common stocks"   Appl. Econ., vol.6, 1974, pp.45-58.
          APPL - FIRM : FINANCE , STOCK PRICES * STOCK PRICES - RUNS * MARKOV MODELS -
          APPL : STOCK PRICES
YA0585   CARGILL T.F.
          "Construction activity and secular change in the US"   Appl. Econ., vol.3,
          1971, pp.85-97.
          BUSINESS CYCLE - LONG CYCLE * SPECTRAL ANALYSIS - APPL : SECTOR ,
          CONSTRUCTION * SPECTRAL ANALYSIS - APPL : BUSINESS CYCLE , LONG CYCLE
YA0586   CARGILL T.F.
          "The term structure of interest rates: a test of the expectations
          hypothesis"   J. Finance, vol.30, 1975, pp.761-771.
          INTEREST RATE - TERM STRUCTURE * BIBLIOGRAPHY - INTEREST RATE * SPECTRAL
          ANALYSIS - APPL : INTEREST RATE * DISTRIBUTED LAG - APPL , INTEREST RATE *
          ESTIMATION - HANNAN : APPL
YA0587   CARGILL T.F., EADINGTON W.R.
          "Nevada's gaming revenues: time characteristics and forecasting"   Mgmt.
          Sci., vol.24, 1978, pp.1221-1230.
          SPECTRAL ANALYSIS - APPL : BUSINESS CYCLE * TIME SERIES - ARIMA : APPL *
          APPL - SECTOR : SERVICES , ENTERTAINMENT * EX ANTE
YA0588   CARGILL T.F., MEYER R.A.
          "A spectral approach to estimating the distributed lag relationship between
          long and short term interest rates"   Int. Econ. Rev., vol.13, 1972,
          pp.223-238.
          ESTIMATION - HANNAN * INTEREST RATE - TERM STRUCTURE * DISTRIBUTED LAG -
          APPL , INTEREST RATE

YA0589   CARGILL T.F., MEYER R.A.
"Estimating term structure phenomena from data aggregated over time"   J. Money, Credit, Banking, vol.6, 1974, pp.503-515,
INTEREST RATE - TERM STRUCTURE * DISTRIBUTED LAG - APPL , INTEREST RATE *
ESTIMATION - HANNAN

YA0590   CARGILL T.F., MEYER R.A.
"Estimating the demand for electricity by time of day"   Appl. Econ.,
vol.3, 1971, pp.233-246,
APPL - SECTOR : UTILITIES , ELECTRICITY * USE - PRODUCTION , CONTROL * PRICE
- EFFECT OF * BIBLIOGRAPHY - ELECTRICITY * REGRESSION - SEEMINGLY UNRELATED
: APPL

YA0591   CARGILL T.F., MEYER R.A.
"Interest rates and prices since 1950"   Int. Econ. Rev., vol.15, 1974,
pp.458-471,
INTEREST RATE - DETERMINANTS * INFLATION - EFFECT OF * STABILITY OF
COEFFICIENTS - REGRESSION : APPL * COMPARATIVE METHODS - ESTIMATION :
DISTRIBUTED LAG , ERROR SPECIFICATION * ESTIMATION - HANNAN : APPL * ERROR
SPECIFICATION - AUTOCORRELATED * DISTRIBUTED LAG - APPL , INFLATION *
CAUSALITY - TEST : APPL

YA0592   CARGILL T.F., MEYER R.A.
"Intertemporal stability and the relationship between interest rates and
price changes"   J. Finance, vol.32, 1977, pp.1001-1015,
INTEREST RATE - INDICATORS * INFLATION - EFFECT OF * COMPARATIVE METHODS -
DISTRIBUTED LAG

YA0593   CARGILL T.F., MEYER R.A.
"Some time and frequency domain distributed lag estimators: a comparative
Monte Carlo study"   Econometrica, vol.42, 1974, pp.1031-1044,
COMPARATIVE METHODS - ESTIMATION : DISTRIBUTED LAG * DISTRIBUTED LAG -
IDENTIFICATION * DISTRIBUTED LAG - ALMON , ESTIMATION * DISTRIBUTED LAG -
ESTIMATION * SPECIFICATION ERROR - EFFECT OF , LAG SPECIFICATION * DATA -
SIMULATION * AUTOCORRELATION - EFFECT OF * ESTIMATION - HANNAN

YA0594   CARGILL T.F., MEYER R.A.
"The time varying response of income to changes in monetary and fiscal
policy"   Rev. Econ. Stats., vol.60, 1978, pp.1-7,
MACRO MODEL - ST.LOUIS * POLICY EVALUATION - MACRO : FISCAL , MONETARY *
REGRESSION - SHIFTING COEFFICIENTS * STABILITY OF COEFFICIENTS - REGRESSION
* SIMULTANEOUS SYSTEM - SHIFTING COEFFICIENTS * STABILITY OF COEFFICIENTS -
SIMULTANEOUS SYSTEM

YA0595   CARGILL T.F., MEYER R.A.
"Wages, prices and unemployment: distributed lag estimates"   J. Am.
Statist. Ass., vol.69, 1974, pp.98-107,
SPECIFICATION ERROR - EFFECT OF , FILTERING * DISTRIBUTED LAG - ESTIMATION *
SPECTRAL ANALYSIS - APPL : DISTRIBUTED LAG * ESTIMATION - 2SLS * APPL -
MACRO : EARNINGS * ERROR SPECIFICATION - AUTOCORRELATED * COMPARATIVE
METHODS - ESTIMATION : OLS , 2SLS * COMPARATIVE METHODS - DATA : SMOOTHED *
STABILITY OF COEFFICIENTS - REGRESSION , TEST : APPL * ADVANCED

YA0596   CARGILL T.F., RAUSSER G.C.
"Temporal price behaviour in commodity futures markets"   J. Finance,
vol.30, pp.1043-1053,
APPL - SECTOR : COMMODITIES * RANDOM WALK - TEST , TRADING RULE * EVALUATION
- TEST , AUTOCORRELATION

YA0597   CARGILL T.F., RAUSSER G.C.
"Time and frequency domain representations of futures prices as a stochastic
process"   J. Am. Statist. Ass., vol 67, 1972, pp.23-30,
APPL - SECTOR : COMMODITIES * APPL - SECTOR : FINANCE , FUTURES TRADING *
SPECTRAL ANALYSIS - APPL : FUTURES TRADING * SPECTRAL ANALYSIS - APPL :
SECTOR , COMMODITIES

YA0598   CARLETON W.T., BRYAN W.R.
"Deposit expansion and Federal Reserve-Banking System interaction: a micro
unit simulation"   Am. Econ. Rev., vol.61, 1971, pp.901-915,
DECISION RULES - SECTOR : GOVERNMENT * APPL - FIRM : FINANCE , BANKS *
SIMULATION - APPL : FIRM * SIMULATION - APPL : MICRO

YA0599   CARLETON W.T., SILBERMAN I.H.
"Joint determination of rate of return and capital structure: an econometric
analysis"   J. Finance, vol.32, 1977, pp.811-821,
APPL - SECTOR : FINANCE , PROFITS * APPL - SECTOR : FINANCE , FINANCIAL
STRUCTURE , LEVERAGE * DATA - CROSS SECTION * SIMULTANEOUS SYSTEM - APPL

YA0600   CARLINER G.
"Income elasticity of housing demand"   Rev. Econ. Stats., vol.55, 1973,
pp.528-532,
APPL - SECTOR : CONSTRUCTION , RESIDENTIAL * INCOME - EFFECT OF * DATA -
CROSS SECTION

YA0601   CARLSON J.A.
"A study of price forecasts"   Anns. Econ. Soc. Meas., vol.6, 1977,
pp.27-56,
EVALUATION - EXPECTATIONS , DATA * INFLATION - EXPECTATIONS * EVALUATION -
INFLATION FORECASTS * EVALUATION - EXPECTATIONS , THEORY

YA0602   CARLSON J.A.
          "Are price expectations normally distributed?"   J. Am. Statist. Ass.,
          vol.70, 1975, pp.749-754.
          EXPECTATIONS - DATA * INFLATION - EXPECTATIONS * ERROR DISTRIBUTION - T

YA0603   CARLSON J.A.
          "Forecasting errors and business cycles"   Am. Econ. Rev., vol.57, 1967,
          pp.462-481.
          BUSINESS CYCLE - PREDICTION , TURNING POINTS * TURNING POINT FORECASTS *
          FORECASTER BEHAVIOUR * JUDGEMENTAL FORECASTS - TURNING POINTS

YA0604   CARLSON J.A.
          "The production lag"   Am. Econ. Rev., vol.63, 1973, pp.73-86.
          APPL - SECTOR : OUTPUT * DISTRIBUTED LAG - APPL , OUTPUT * APPL - SECTOR :
          INVENTORIES

YA0605   CARLSON J.A., ET AL.
          "Short-term interest rates as predictors of inflation: comments"   Am.
          Econ. Rev., vol.67, 1977, pp.469-496.
          INTEREST RATE - EXPECTATIONS * INFLATION - INDICATORS * EXPECTATIONS - DATA
          * INFLATION - EXPECTATIONS * TIME SERIES - ARIMA : APPL

YA0606   CARLSON J.A., PARKIN M.
          "Inflation expectations"   Economica, vol.42, 1975, pp.123-138.
          EXPECTATIONS - DETERMINANTS * INFLATION - EXPECTATIONS * EXPECTATIONS - DATA
          * EXPECTATIONS - ESTIMATING

YA0607   CARLSON R.D.
          "Demand analysis for toothpaste"   Bus. Econ., vol.12:4, 1977, pp.61-66.
          APPL - SECTOR : CONSUMER NON DURABLES , HEALTH AIDS

YA0608   CARLSON R.L.
          "Seemingly unrelated regression and the demand for automobiles of different
          sizes, 1965-75: a disaggregate approach"   J. Business, vol.51, 1978,
          pp.243-262.
          APPL - SECTOR : CONSUMER DURABLES , CARS * ERROR SPECIFICATION -
          AUTOCORRELATED , CORRELATED * COMPARATIVE METHODS - REGRESSION , SEEMINGLY
          UNRELATED * PRICE - EFFECT OF * MARKET SEGMENTATION

YA0609   CARMAN H.F.
          "Improving sales forcasts for appliances"   J. Mktg. Res., vol.9, 1972,
          pp.214-218.
          APPL - SECTOR : CONSUMER DURABLES , APPLIANCES * INCOME - EFFECT OF *
          REGRESSION - PRIOR INFORMATION * PRICE - EFFECT OF * DATA - CROSS SECTION ,
          TIME SERIES

YA0610   CARMAN J.M.
          "Correlates of brand loyalty: some positive results"   J. Mktg. Res.,
          vol.7, 1970, pp.67-76.
          CONSUMER BEHAVIOUR - PURCHASING , DETERMINANTS * AID * BRAND CHOICE -
          DETERMINANTS * REPEAT BUYING * APPL - SECTOR : CONSUMER DURABLES , FOOD

YA0611   CARR J.
          "A suggestion for the treatment of serial correlation: a case in point"
          Can. J. Econ., vol.5, 1972, pp.301-306.
          ERROR SPECIFICATION - AUTOCORRELATED * TECHNOLOGY - EFFECT OF * APPL -
          SECTOR : UTILITIES , TELEPHONE * THEORY - MODELLING * STABILITY OF
          COEFFICIENTS - REGRESSION : APPL * PRODUCTION FUNCTIONS - SECTOR *
          EVALUATION - AUTOCORRELATION

YA0612   CARR J.L., JUMP G.V., SAWYER J.A.
          "The operation of the Canadian economy under fixed and flexible exchange
          rates: simulation results from the TRACE model"   Can. J. Econ., vol.9,
          1976, pp.102-120.
          POLICY EVALUATION - MACRO : INTERNATIONAL FINANCE , FOREIGN EXCHANGE *
          POLICY EVALUATION - MACRO : FISCAL , MONETARY * EXCHANGE RATE - EFFECT OF *
          MACRO MODEL - CANADA , TRACE * MULTIPLIERS - MACRO

YA0613   CARTER A.P.
          "Energy, environment, and economic growth"   Bell J. Econ., vol.5, 1974,
          pp.578-592.
          INPUT OUTPUT - MACRO : ENERGY * APPL - SECTOR : UTILITIES , ELECTRICITY

YA0614   CARTER E.E.
          "A performance appraisal of price-earnings filter rules on Dow Jones
          industrial average securities"   Sloan Mgmt. Rev., vol.16, no.3, 1975,
          pp.75-89.
          STOCK PRICES - TRADING RULES * APPL - FIRM : FINANCE , STOCK PRICES * APPL -
          FIRM : FINANCE , STOCK PRICES * BIBLIOGRAPHY - STOCK PRICES

YA0615   CARTER E.E.
          "What are the risks in risk analysis"   H.B.R., vol.50, July-Aug, 1972,
          pp.72-82.
          USER REQUIREMENTS * USE - CAPITAL INVESTMENT * SIMULATION - APPL :
          INVESTMENT APPRAISAL

YA0616   CARTER J.R.
          "In search of synergy: a structure-performance test"   Rev. Econ. Stats.,
          vol.59, 1977, pp.279-289.
          APPL - FIRM TYPE : CONGLOMERATES * APPL - FIRM : FINANCE , PROFITS * DATA -
          CROSS SECTION * CONCENTRATION - EFFECT OF

YA0617　CARTER N.G., SANDBER L.G., KLEIN L.R.
"A note on the solution of the Wharton model" with comment　Rev. Econ.
Stats., vol.49, 1967, pp.642-651.
MACRO MODEL - WHARTON * MACRO MODEL - METHODOLOGY , MODEL SIMPLIFICATION *
MACRO MODELS - METHODOLOGY , SOLUTION

YA0618　CARTER R.A.L.
"Least squares as an exploratory estimator"　Can. J. Econ., vol.6, 1973,
pp.108-114.
MACRO MODEL - CANADA * SPECIFICATION ERROR - TESTS , VARIABLE INCLUSION *
COMPARATIVE METHODS - ESTIMATION : OLS , 2SLS * EVALUATION - ESTIMATION :
OLS * SIMULTANEOUS SYSTEM - HYPOTHESIS TESTS

YA0619　CARTER R.A.L., NAGAR A.L.
"Coefficients of correlation for simultaneous equation systems"　J.
Econometrics, vol.6, 1977, pp.39-50.
SIMULTANEOUS SYSTEM - SUMMARY STATISTICS * MACRO MODEL - KLEIN

YA0620　CASEY C.J., ASHTON R.H.
"The predictive-ability criterion and user prediction models: comments"
Acctg. Rev., vol.51, 1976, pp.677-682.
BOOTSTRAPPING

YA0621　CASSON M.C.
"Generalised errors in variables regression"　Rev. Econ. Studies, vol.41,
1974, pp.347-352.
REGRESSION - ERRORS IN VARIABLES * APPL - SECTOR : UTILITIES , ELECTRICITY *
COMPARATIVE METHODS - ESTIMATION : REGRESSION , ERRORS IN VARIABLES *
COMPARATIVE METHODS - ESTIMATION : OLS , MLE

YA0622　CASSON M.C.
"Linear regression with error in the deflating variable"　Econometrica,
vol.41, 1973, pp.751-759.
DATA - TRANSFORMED , DEFLATED * REGRESSION - ERRORS IN VARIABLES * DATA
ERRORS - EFFECT OF , DEFLATION * INDEX NUMBERS - METHODOLOGY * DATA - CROSS
SECTION * APPL - FIRM : INVESTMENT * REGRESSION - TRANSFORMATIONS , RATIO

YA0623　CATON C.N., HIGGINS C.I.
"Demand-supply imbalance, unexpected imports and unintended inventory
accumulation"　Int. Econ. Rev., vol.15, 1974, pp.75-94.
APPL - MACRO , AUSTRALIA * APPL - MACRO : INVENTORIES * APPL - MACRO :
INTERNATIONAL TRADE , IMPORTS * EX ANTE * ERROR SPECIFICATION - MOVING
AVERAGE

YA0624　CATRY B., CHEVALIER M.
"Market share strategy and the product life cycle"　J. Mktg., vol.38, Oct
1974, pp.29-34 & vol.39, no.4, Oct 1975, pp.59-60.
LIFE CYCLE - PRODUCT * USE - CAPITAL INVESTMENT * MARKET SHARE - EFFECT OF *
APPL - FIRM : FINANCE , PROFITS

YA0625　CATRY B., CHEVALIER M.
"The evolution of French media models"　J. Advtg. Res., vol.13:3, 1973,
pp.19-26.
USE - MEDIA PLANNING * BASIC

YA0626　CAVES R.E.
"Causes of direct investment: foreign firms' shares in Canadian and Uk
manufacturing industries"　Rev. Econ. Stats., vol.56, 1974, pp.279-293.
APPL - SECTOR : INVESTMENT , INTERNATIONAL * DATA - CROSS SECTION *
MULTICOLLINEARITY - REMOVAL OF : APPL * APPL - SECTOR : INTERNATIONAL TRADE
* APPL - MACRO , UK * APPL - MACRO , CANADA * APPL - FIRM TYPE :
MULTINATIONALS

YA0627　CAVES R.E.
"Multinational firms, competition, and productivity in host-country markets"
Economica, vol.41, 1974, pp.176-193.
APPL - FIRM TYPE : MULTINATIONALS * APPL - SECTOR : PRODUCTIVITY * APPL -
SECTOR : FINANCE , PROFITS * APPL - SECTOR : INVESTMENT , INTERNATIONAL *
APPL - MACRO , CANADA * APPL - MACRO , AUSTRALIA

YA0628　CAVES R.E., ET AL.
"Scale economies in statistical analysis of market power"　Rev. Econ.
Stats., vol.57, 1975, pp.133-140.
CONCENTRATION - EFFECT OF * ADVERTISING - EFFECT OF * DATA - CROSS SECTION *
APPL - SECTOR : FINANCE , MARGINS * COST - SCALE ECONOMIES *
MULTICOLLINEARITY - REMOVAL OF * DATA - SPECIFICATION OF VARIABLES

YA0629　CEBULA R.J.
"Interstate migration and the Tiebout hypothesis: an analysis according to
race sex and age"　J. Am. Statist. Ass., vol.69, 1974, pp.876-879.
REGIONAL MODELS - MANPOWER PLANNING , MIGRATION * MANPOWER PLANNING -
REGIONAL

YA0630　CHADDHA R.L., CHITGOPEKAR S.S.
"A 'generalisation' of the logistic curves and long-range forecasts
(1966-1991) of residence telephones"　Bell J. Econ., vol.2, 1971,
pp.542-560.
TREND CURVES - LOGISTIC * APPL - SECTOR : UTILITIES , TELEPHONE * LONG TERM
FORECASTING

YA0631   CHAI J.C.
          "Correlated measurement errors and the least squares estimator of the
          regression coefficient"   J. Am. Statist. Ass., vol.66, 1971, pp.478-483.
          DATA ERRORS - ANALYSIS OF , INDEPENDENCE * APPL - SECTOR : CONSTRUCTION ,
          RESIDENTIAL * DATA ERRORS - EFFECT OF * EVALUATION - ESTIMATION : OLS * DATA
          ERRORS - ESTIMATION OF * DATA - SIMULATION * SURVEYS - METHODOLOGY ,
          RESPONSE ERROR
YA0632   CHALLEN D.W., HAGGER A.J.
          "The role of excess demand in the Australian price equation"   Economica,
          vol.45, 1978, pp.165-177.
          INFLATION - DETERMINANTS * APPL - MACRO , AUSTRALIA * CAPACITY - EFFECT OF
YA0633   CHAMBERLAIN G.
          "Education, income and ability revisited"   J. Econometrics, vol.5, 1977,
          pp.241-257.
          APPL - SECTOR : SOCIAL , SUCCESS * SIMULTANEOUS SYSTEM - ERRORS IN VARIABLES
          , UNOBSERVABLES * EDUCATION - EFFECT OF
YA0634   CHAMBERLAIN G., GRILICHES Z.
          "Unobservables with a variance-components structure: ability, schooling and
          the economic success of brothers"   Int. Econ. Rev., vol.16, 1975,
          pp.422-449.
          SIMULTANEOUS SYSTEM - ERRORS IN VARIABLES , UNOBSERVABLES * SIMULTANEOUS
          SYSTEM - ERROR COMPONENTS * APPL - SECTOR : SOCIAL , SUCCESS * COMPARATIVE
          METHODS - ESTIMATION : SIMULTANEOUS SYSTEM , ERRORS IN VARIABLES *
          ESTIMATION - MAXIMUM LIKELIHOOD * ADVANCED
YA0635   CHAMBERS J.C., MULLICK S.K., SMITH D.D.
          "How to choose the right forecasting technique"   H.B.R., vol.49, July-Aug,
          1971, pp.45-74.
          FORECASTING - REVIEW * LIFE CYCLE - PRODUCT , INTRODUCTION * USER - FIRM :
          PRODUCTION * USER - FIRM : CONSUMER DURABLES * APPL - SECTOR : CONSUMER
          DURABLES , APPLIANCES , TELEVISION * TIME SERIES - DECOMPOSITION *
          SEASONALITY - ESTIMATION , CENSUS * FORECASTING - COST OF * DATA - SAMPLE
          SIZE * BASIC
YA0636   CHAMBERS J.M.
          "Regression updating"   J. Am. Statist. Ass., vol.66, 1971, pp.744-748.
          COMPUTERISATION - ESTIMATION , REGRESSION MODELS , PROGRAMS
YA0637   CHAMBERS J.M., MALLOWS C.L., STUCK B.W.
          "A method for simulating stable random variables"   J. Am. Statist. Ass.,
          vol.71, 1976, pp.340-344.
          ERROR DISTRIBUTION - STABLE * SIMULATION - METHODOLOGY , RANDOM DEVIATES
YA0638   CHAN K.H., HAYYA J.C.
          "Spectral analysis in business forecasting"   Decis. Sci., vol.7, 1976,
          pp.137-151.
          SPECTRAL ANALYSIS - INTRODUCTION * TIME SERIES - HARMONICS
YA0639   CHAN K.H., HAYYA J.C.
          "Spectral analysis in business forecasting: the Wiener-Kolmogorov method"
          Decis. Sci., vol.9, 1978, pp.700-711.
          TIME SERIES - AUTOREGRESSIVE * SPECTRAL ANALYSIS - APPL : TIME SERIES *
          ESTIMATION - HANNAN * COMPARATIVE METHODS - ESTIMATION : TIME SERIES
YA0640   CHAN K.H., HAYYA J.C., ORD J.K.
          "A note on trend removal methods: the case of polynomial regression versus
          variat differencing"   Econometrica, vol.45, 1977, pp.737-744.
          TIME SERIES - DECOMPOSITION , TREND REMOVAL * STATIONARITY - TRANSFORMING TO
YA0641   CHAN L.S., GILMAN J.A., DUNN O.J.
          "Alternative approaches to missing values in discriminant analysis"   J.
          Am. Statist. Ass., vol.71, 1976, pp.842-844.
          DATA ERRORS - MISSING OBSERVATIONS * DISCRIMINANT ANALYSIS - METHODOLOGY
YA0642   CHAN W.T., WALLIS K.F.
          "Multiple time series modelling: another look at the mink-muskrat
          interaction   Appl. Stats., vol.27, 1978, pp.168-175.
          APPL - SECTOR : NATURAL , ANIMAL POPULATIONS * TIME SERIES - MULTIVARIATE *
          TIME SERIES - ARIMA : APPL
YA0643   CHANG H.
          "A computer program for Box-Cox transformation and estimation"
          Econometrica, vol.45, 1977, pp.1741.
          COMPUTERISATION - ESTIMATION , REGRESSION MODELS , PROGRAMS * REGRESSION -
          TRANSFORMATIONS , BOX COX
YA0644   CHANG H.
          "Functional forms and the demand for meat in the US"   Rev. Econ. Stats.,
          vol.59, 1977, pp.355-359.
          APPL - SECTOR : CONSUMER NON DURABLES , MEAT * REGRESSION - TRANSFORMATIONS
          , BOX COX : APPL * COMPARATIVE METHODS - INCOME ELASTICITY , ESTIMATION *
          COMPARATIVE METHODS - REGRESSION , TRANSFORMATIONS
YA0645   CHANG S.H., FYFFE D.E.
          "Estimation of forecast errors for seasonal style goods sales"   Mgmt. Sci.
          (B), vol.18, 1971, pp.89-96.
          STYLE GOODS * SEASONALITY - SINGLE SEASON * CONFIDENCE INTERVAL -
          PREDICTIONS * ESTIMATION - KALMAN FILTER * DEMAND - CUMULATIVE

YA0646   CHARNES A., COOPER W.W.
"Goal programming and constrained regression: a comment"   Omega, vol.3,
1975, pp.403-409.
LP * REGRESSION - CONSTRAINED * ESTIMATION - MSAE * ESTIMATION - CONSTRAINED
* BASIC

YA0647   CHATEAU J.D.
"La politique de distribution de dividendes des societes: une etude
microeconometrique" Can. J. Econ., vol.9, 1976, pp.255-272.
APPL - FIRM : FINANCE , DIVIDENDS * APPL - SECTOR : PRODUCTION , PAPER *
APPL - SECTOR : PRODUCTION

YA0648   CHATFIELD C.
"Adaptive filtering: a critical reassessment"   J. Opl. Res. Soc., vol.29,
1978, pp.891-896.
TIME SERIES - ADAPTIVE FILTERING * COMPARATIVE METHODS - ADAPTIVE FILTERING
, ARIMA * COMPARATIVE METHODS - ADAPTIVE FILTERING , EXPONENTIAL SMOOTHING *
COMPARATIVE METHODS - ARIMA , EXPONENTIAL SMOOTHING * EX ANTE

YA0649   CHATFIELD C.
"On analysing time-series data showing cyclic variation" Stat'n., vol.27,
1978, pp.55-56.
TIME SERIES - MODEL INTERPRETATION * SPECTRAL ANALYSIS - APPL : TIME SERIES
* BASIC

YA0650   CHATFIELD C.
"Some comments on spectral analysis in marketing" J. Mktg. Res., vol.11,
1974, pp.97-101.
SPECTRAL ANALYSIS - REVIEW * SPECTRAL ANALYSIS - CROSS : METHODOLOGY * BASIC

YA0651   CHATFIELD C.
"Some recent developments in time series analysis" R. Statist. Soc. (A),
vol.140, 1972, pp.492-510.
TIME SERIES - REVIEW * BIBLIOGRAPHY - TIME SERIES * DISTRIBUTED LAG - REVIEW

YA0652   CHATFIELD C.
"Statistical inference regarding Markov chain models" Appl. Stats.,
vol.22, 1973, pp.7-20.
MARKOV MODELS - METHODOLOGY * AUTOCORRELATION - TEST

YA0653   CHATFIELD C.
"The Holt-Winters forecasting procedure" Appl. Stats., vol.27, 1978,
pp.264-279.
EXPONENTIAL SMOOTHING - HIGHER ORDER * COMPARATIVE METHODS - ARIMA ,
EXPONENTIAL SMOOTHING * EXPONENTIAL SMOOTHING - COEFFICIENTS CHOICE *
EXPONENTIAL SMOOTHING - REVIEW * EVALUATION - EXPONENTIAL SMOOTHING

YA0654   CHATFIELD C., GOODHART G.
"Results concerning brand choice" J. Mktg. Res., vol.12, 1975,
pp.110-113.
BRAND CHOICE - THEORY * CONSUMER BEHAVIOUR - STOCHASTIC MODELS , THEORY *
PROBABILITY MODELS - BETA

YA0655   CHATFIELD C., GOODHART G.J.
"A consumer purchasing model with Erlang inter purchase times" J. Am.
Statist. Ass., vol.68, 1973, pp.828-835.
CONSUMER BEHAVIOUR - STOCHASTIC MODELS * PROBABILITY MODELS - GAMMA * REPEAT
BUYING * APPL - FIRM : CONSUMER NON DURABLES

YA0656   CHATFIELD C., NEWBOLD P.
"Adaptive filtering: viewpoint" Opl. Res. Q., vol.25, 1974, pp.494-495.
TIME SERIES - ADAPTIVE FILTERING * TIME SERIES - AUTOREGRESSIVE *
COMPARATIVE METHODS - ADAPTIVE FILTERING , AUTOREGRESSIVE

YA0657   CHATFIELD C., PROTHERO D.L.
"Box-Jenkins seasonal forecasting: problems in a case study" with discussion
R. Statist. Soc. (A), vol.136, 1973, pp.295-336.
EVALUATION - SEASONALITY * TIME SERIES - ARIMA : REVIEW * JUDGEMENTAL
FORECASTS - INCORPORATION * EVALUATION - TIME SERIES , ARIMA * EX ANTE *
PRIOR INFORMATION * MODEL SELECTION * APPL - SECTOR : PRODUCTION ,
ENGINEERING * COMPARATIVE METHODS - ARIMA , EXPONENTIAL SMOOTHING

YA0658   CHENG D.C., IGLARSH H.J.
"Principal component estimation in regression analysis" Rev. Econ.
Stats., vol.53, 1976, pp.229-234.
ESTIMATION - PRINCIPAL COMPONENTS * MULTICOLLINEARITY - REMOVAL OF *
COMPARATIVE METHODS - ESTIMATION : REGRESSION * REGRESSION - ESTIMATION

YA0659   CHENG P.L., DEETS M.K.
"Portfolio returns and the random walk theory" J. Finance, vol.26, 1971,
pp.11-30.
RANDOM WALK - TEST , TRADING RULE * APPL - FIRM : FINANCE , STOCK PRICES *
USE - PORTFOLIO SELECTION * STOCK PRICES - MODELS , EFFICIENT MARKET * STOCK
PRICES - TRADING RULES

YA0660   CHENG P.L., ET AL.
"Tests of portfolio building rules: comments" J. Finance, vol.26, 1971,
pp.965-981.
DATA - AGGREGATION 'BIAS' * USE - PORTFOLIO SELECTION * AUTOCORRELATION -
EFFECT OF * STOCK PRICES - THEORY

YA0661   CHENTNIK C.G.
          "The use of forecast error measures as surrogates for an error cost
          criterion in the production smoothing problem"   Decis. Sci., vol.3:2,
          1972, pp.54-75.
          LOSS FUNCTIONS - FIRM , PRODUCTION CONTROL * EVALUATION - LOSS FUNCTIONS
YA0662   CHETTY V.K.
          "Estimation of Solow's distributed lag models"   Econometrica, vol. 39,
          1971, pp.99-117.
          DISTRIBUTED LAG - SOLOW , ESTIMATION * DISTRIBUTED LAG - APPL , ORDERS *
          BAYESIAN - ESTIMATION : DISTRIBUTED LAG * DISTRIBUTED LAG - APPL , INTEREST
          RATE * INTEREST RATE - TERM STRUCTURE * APPL - MACRO : OUTPUT * ERROR
          SPECIFICATION - AUTOCORRELATED * DISTRIBUTED LAG - ERROR SPECIFICATION *
          BAYESIAN - MODEL SELECTION
YA0663   CHETTY V.K.
          "Pooling time series and cross section data"   Econometrica, vol.36, 1968,
          pp.279-290.
          ESTIMATION - CROSS SECTION , TIME SERIES * APPL - SECTOR : CONSUMER NON
          DURABLES , FOOD * BAYESIAN - ESTIMATION : CROSS SECTION , TIME SERIES
YA0664   CHILDRESS R.L.
          "Optimal planning: the use of sales forecasts"   Decis. Sci., vol.4, 1973,
          pp.164-171.
          LOSS FUNCTIONS - THEORY * CONFIDENCE INTERVAL - INTRODUCTION * BASIC
YA0665   CHIPLIN B., SLOANE P.J.
          "Personal characteristics and sex differentials in professional employment"
          Econ. J., vol.86, 1976, pp.729-745.
          MANPOWER PLANNING - EARNINGS , FEMALE * MANPOWER PLANNING - EARNINGS *
          MANPOWER PLANNING - DISCRIMINATION , SEX
YA0666   CHIPLIN B., SLOANE P.J.
          "Real and money wages revisited"   Appl. Econ., vol.5, 1973, pp.289-384.
          APPL - MACRO : EARNINGS * MANPOWER PLANNING - EMPLOYMENT VACANCIES
YA0667   CHO D.W.
          "A spectral measurement of the cyclical patterns of multivariate time
          series"   Decis. Sci., vol.8, 1977, pp.663-676.
          SPECTRAL ANALYSIS - CROSS : APPL * APPL - SECTOR : EMPLOYMENT * REGIONAL
          MODELS - MANPOWER PLANNING , EMPLOYMENT
YA0668   CHORBA R.W.
          "Potential avoidability: a statistic for controlling inpatient utilization
          in acute care hospitals"   Mgmt. Sci., vol.22, 1976, pp.694-700.
          USER - FIRM : HEALTH , HOSPITAL * DISCRIMINANT ANALYSIS - APPL * USE -
          UTILISATION CONTROL * HEALTH - HOSPITAL , PATIENT FACILITIES
YA0669   CHOW G.C.
          "A solution to optional control of linear systems with unknown parameters"
          Rev. Econ. Stats., vol.57, 1975, pp.338-345.
          CONTROL THEORY - STOCHASTIC - COMPARATIVE METHODS - CONTROL * APPL - MACRO :
          GNP * PUBLIC EXPENDITURE - EFFECT OF * POLICY EVALUATION - MACRO * ADVANCED
YA0670   CHOW G.C.
          "An approach to the feedback control of nonlinear econometric systems"
          Anns. Econ. Soc. Meas., vol.5, 1976, pp.297-309.
          SIMULTANEOUS SYSTEM - NON LINEAR * SIMULTANEOUS SYSTEM - CONTROL * MACRO
          MODEL - KLEIN GOLDBERGER * CONTROL THEORY - STOCHASTIC , METHODOLOGY *
          ADVANCED
YA0671   CHOW G.C.
          "Control methods for macro policy analysis" with discussion   Am. Econ.
          Ass. Proc., vol.66, 1976, pp.340-345 & 356-360.
          CONTROL THEORY - STOCHASTIC , REVIEW
YA0672   CHOW G.C.
          "Evaluation of macroeconomic policies by stochastic control techniques"
          Int. Econ. Rev., vol.19, 1978, pp.311-319.
          POLICY EVALUATION - METHODOLOGY * POLICY EVALUATION - MACRO * CONTROL THEORY
          - STOCHASTIC , APPL * MACRO MODEL - MICHIGAN
YA0673   CHOW G.C.
          "How much could be gained by optimal stochastic control policies"   Anns.
          Econ. Soc. Meas., vol.1, 1972, pp.391-406.
          CONTROL THEORY - STOCHASTIC , APPL * EVALUATION - CONTROL THEORY ,
          STOCHASTIC * POLICY EVALUATION - MACRO * MACRO MODEL - US
YA0674   CHOW G.C.
          "Multiplier, accelerator, and liquidity preference in the determination of
          national income in the US"   Rev. Econ. Stats., vol.49, 1967, pp.1-15.
          APPL - MACRO : CONSUMPTION * APPL - MACRO : MONEY * APPL - MACRO :
          INVESTMENT * APPL - MACRO : INCOME * EX ANTE * MULTIPLIERS - MACRO
YA0675   CHOW G.C.
          "Problems of economic policy from the viewpoint of optimal control"   Am.
          Econ. Rev., vol.63, 1973, pp.825-837.
          CONTROL THEORY - STOCHASTIC , APPL * CONTROL THEORY - REVIEW * POLICY
          EVALUATION - METHODOLOGY
YA0676   CHOW G.C.
          "The control of non linear econometric systems with unknown parameters"
          Econometrica, vol.44, 1976, pp.685-695.
          CONTROL THEORY - STOCHASTIC , METHODOLOGY * SIMULTANEOUS SYSTEM - NONLINEAR
          * SIMULTANEOUS SYSTEM - CONTROL

YA0677　CHOW G.C.
　　　　　"Usefulness of imperfect models for the foundation of stabilization
　　　　　policies"　Anns. Econ. Soc. Meas., vol.6, 1977, pp.175-187,
　　　　　POLICY EVALUATION - METHODOLOGY * CONTROL THEORY - STOCHASTIC , APPL * MACRO
　　　　　MODEL - US * EVALUATION - MACRO MODELS

YA0678　CHOW G.C., FAIR R.C.
　　　　　"Maximum likelihood estimation of linear equation systems with
　　　　　auto-regressive residuals"　Anns. Econ. Soc. Meas., vol.2, 1973, pp.17-28,
　　　　　ERROR SPECIFICATION - AUTOCORRELATED * ESTIMATION - NON LINEAR *
　　　　　SIMULTANEOUS SYSTEM - ESTIMATION , ERROR SPECIFICATION * ESTIMATION -
　　　　　CONSTRAINED * ESTIMATION - MAXIMUM LIKELIHOOD * REGRESSION - SEEMINGLY
　　　　　UNRELATED * COMPARATIVE METHODS - ESTIMATION : SIMULTANEOUS SYSTEM * MACRO
　　　　　MODEL - FAIR * NUMERICAL METHODS - OPTIMISATION

YA0679　CHOW G.C., LIN A.
　　　　　"Best linear unbiased estimation of missing observations in an econometric
　　　　　time series"　J. Am. Statist. Ass., vol.71, 1976, pp.719-721,
　　　　　DATA ERRORS - MISSING OBSERVATIONS * DATA - INTERPOLATION

YA0680　CHOW G.C., LIN A.
　　　　　"Best linear unbiased interpolation, distribution, and extrapolation of time
　　　　　series by related series"　Rev. Econ. Stats., vol.53, 1971, pp.372-375,
　　　　　DATA - INTERPOLATION

YA0681　CHOW G.C., MEGDAL S.B.
　　　　　"An econometric definition of the inflation - unemployment tradeoff"　Am.
　　　　　Econ. Rev., vol.68, 1978, pp.446-453,
　　　　　MACRO MODEL - ST.LOUIS * MACRO MODEL - MICHIGAN * INFLATION - PHILLIPS CURVE
　　　　　* POLICY EVALUATION - MACRO : FISCAL , MONETARY * POLICY EVALUATION - MACRO
　　　　　: UNEMPLOYMENT * INFLATION - GOVERNMENT CONTROLS

YA0682　CHRIST C.F.
　　　　　Econometric models of the financial sector" with discussion　J. Money,
　　　　　Credit, Banking, vol.3, 1971, pp.419-468,
　　　　　MACRO MODEL - WHARTON * MACRO MODEL - OBE * MACRO MODEL - MICHIGAN * MACRO
　　　　　MODEL - BROOKINGS * MACRO MODEL - FRB , MIT * MACRO MODEL - US * APPL -
　　　　　MACRO : FLOW OF FUNDS * EVALUATION - MACRO MODELS * POLICY EVALUATION -
　　　　　MACRO : MONETARY

YA0683　CHRIST C.F.
　　　　　"Judging the performance of econometric models of the US economy"　Int.
　　　　　Econ. Rev., vol.16, 1975, pp.54-74,
　　　　　COMPARATIVE METHODS - MACRO MODELS * EX ANTE * COMPARATIVE METHODS - ARIMA ,
　　　　　CAUSAL(SIMULTANEOUS SYSTEM) * MULTIPLIERS - MACRO * EVALUATION - THEORY OF *
　　　　　POLICY EVALUATION - METHODOLOGY

YA0684　CHRISTENSEN L.R.
　　　　　"Simultaneous statistical inference in the normal multiple linear regression
　　　　　model"　J. Am. Statist. Ass., vol.68, 1973, pp.457-461,
　　　　　REGRESSION - HYPOTHESIS TESTS * CONFIDENCE INTERVAL - REGRESSION ,
　　　　　MULTIVARIATE * EVALUATION - REGRESSION , HYPOTHESIS TESTS

YA0685　CHRISTENSEN L.R.
　　　　　"Substitution effects in consumer expenditures"　Bus. Econ., vol.10:1,
　　　　　1975, pp.58-63,
　　　　　SUBSTITUTE PRODUCTS * DEMAND EQUATIONS - SYSTEMS OF * PRICE - EFFECT OF *
　　　　　BASIC

YA0686　CHRISTENSEN L.R., JORGENSON D.W., LAU L.J.
　　　　　"Transcendental logarithmic production frontiers"　Rev. Econ. Stats.,
　　　　　vol.55, 1973, pp.28-45,
　　　　　PRODUCTION FUNCTIONS - THEORY * APPL - MACRO : INVESTMENT * REGRESSION -
　　　　　CONSTRAINED * APPL - MACRO : EARNINGS * ADVANCED

YA0687　CHRISTENSEN L.R., JORGENSON D.W., LAU L.J.
　　　　　"Transcendental logarithmic utility functions"　Am. Econ. Rev., vol.65,
　　　　　1975, pp.367-383,
　　　　　CONSUMER BEHAVIOUR - ECONOMIC MODELS , THEORY * APPL - MACRO : CONSUMER
　　　　　DEMAND * DEMAND EQUATIONS - SYSTEMS OF : METHODOLOGY , HYPOTHESIS TESTING *
　　　　　EVALUATION - CONSUMER BEHAVIOUR , ECONOMIC MODELS * ADVANCED

YA0688　CHRISTENSEN L.R., MANSER M.E.
　　　　　"Estimating US consumer preferences for meat with a flexibility utility
　　　　　function"　J. Econometrics, vol.5, 1977, pp.37-53,
　　　　　DEMAND EQUATIONS - SYSTEMS OF , METHODOLOGY * APPL - SECTOR : CONSUMER NON
　　　　　DURABLES , FOOD , MEAT * PRICE - EFFECT OF * INCOME - EFFECT OF * EVALUATION
　　　　　- CONSUMER BEHAVIOUR , ECONOMIC MODELS

YA0689　CHRISTOFIDES L.N.
　　　　　"Supply variables in term structure equations"　Can. J. Econ., vol.8,
　　　　　1975, pp.276-281,
　　　　　INTEREST RATE - DETERMINANTS * INTEREST RATE - TERM STRUCTURE

YA0690　CHRYSTAL K.A.
　　　　　"Demand for international media of exchange"　Am. Econ. Rev., vol.67,
　　　　　1977, pp.840-856,
　　　　　APPL - MACRO : INTERNATIONAL FINANCE , FOREIGN RESERVES

YA0691　CHU S., SCHMIDT P.
　　　　　"On the statistical estimation of parametric frontier functions: a reply and
　　　　　further comments"　Rev. Econ. Stats., vol.60, 1978, pp.479-482,
　　　　　PRODUCTION FUNCTIONS - ESTIMATION * PRODUCTION FUNCTIONS - METHODOLOGY *
　　　　　ERROR DISTRIBUTION - ASYMMETRICAL * ERROR SPECIFICATION - PRODUCTION
　　　　　FUNCTIONS

YA0692   CHURCH J.G., GORDON I.M.
"Market share model of rural telephone service"   Omega, vol.6, 1978,
pp.59-64.
APPL - FIRM : UTILITIES , TELEPHONES * BRAND CHOICE - DETERMINANTS *
REGRESSION - LIMITED DEPENDENT , PROBIT : APPL * USE - MARKETING POLICY

YA0693   CHURCHILL G.A.
"A regression estimation method for collinear predictors"   Decis. Sci.,
vol.6, 1975, pp.670-687.
REGRESSION - RIDGE * COMPARATIVE METHODS - ESTIMATION : OLS , RIDGE * APPL -
SECTOR : CONSTRUCTION , RESIDENTIAL * MULTICOLLINEARITY - REMOVAL OF

YA0694   CICCHETTI C.J., FISHER A.C., SMITH V.K.
"An econometric evaluation of a generalised consumer surplus measure: the
Mineral King controversy"   Econometrica, vol.44, 1976, pp.1259-1276.
USE - TOURISM DEVELOPMENT * DEMAND EQUATIONS - SYSTEMS OF * REGRESSION -
SEEMINGLY UNRELATED * SIMULTANEOUS SYSTEM - CONSTRAINED * CONSUMER BEHAVIOUR
- ECONOMIC MODELS * ESTIMATION - CONSTRAINED * COMPARATIVE METHODS -
ESTIMATION : SIMULTANEOUS SYSTEM , CONSTRAINED * ESTIMATION - STEIN

YA0695   CICCHETTI C.J., FISHER A.C., SMITH V.K.
"Economic models and planning outdoor recreation"   Ops. Res., vol.21,
1973, pp.1104-1113.
USE - TOURISM DEVELOPMENT * APPL - SECTOR : SERVICES , LEISURE

YA0696   CIGNO A.
"Production and investment response to changing market conditions"   Rev.
Econ. Studies, vol.38, 1971, pp.63-94.
APPL - SECTOR : AGRICULTURE * INPUT OUTPUT - SECTOR : AGRICULTURE * POLICY
EVALUATION - SECTOR : AGRICULTURE * EX ANTE

YA0697   CLARK C., BOND D.E.
"The behaviour of the aggregate reserve rates of Canadian chartered banks
revisited"   Can. J. Econ., vol.5, 1972, pp.435-442.
APPL - SECTOR : FINANCE , BANK , LIABILITIES * APPL - SECTOR : FINANCE ,
BANKS * INTEREST RATE - EFFECT OF

YA0698   CLARK C.J., DAVIES O.L.
"Forecasting 'stock out' date"   Opl. Res. Q., vol.19, 1968, pp.77-85.
EXPONENTIAL SMOOTHING - APPL * USE - INVENTORY , CONTROL * TIMING
UNCERTAINTY

YA0699   CLARK C.S.
"Labour hoarding in durable goods industries"   Am. Econ. Rev., vol.63,
1973, pp.811-824.
APPL - SECTOR : EMPLOYMENT * MANPOWER PLANNING - SECTOR , DEMAND *
DISTRIBUTED LAG - APPL , OUTPUT * APPL - SECTOR

YA0700   CLARK C.S., NGUYEN M.H.
"A variable-length shipments-orders mechanism, with application to industries
in Canada"   Can. J. Econ., vol.9, 1976, pp.121-137.
DISTRIBUTED LAG - VARIABLE LAG * DISTRIBUTED LAG - APPL , ORDERS * APPL -
MACRO : OUTPUT

YA0701   CLARK P.K.
"A subordinated stochastic process model with finite variance for
speculative prices"   Econometrica, vol.41, 1973, pp.135-155.
APPL - SECTOR : FINANCE , VOLATILITY * APPL - SECTOR : COMMODITIES , COTTON
* ERROR DISTRIBUTION - STABLE * ERROR DISTRIBUTION - LOGNORMAL * COMPARATIVE
METHODS - ERROR DISTRIBUTIONS * RANDOM WALK - THEORY * TIME SERIES -
OPERATIONAL TIME * APPL - SECTOR : FINANCE , FUTURES TRADING

YA0702   CLARK P.K.
"Capital formation and the recent productivity slowdown" with discussion
J. Finance, vol.33, 1978, pp.965-975 & 1001-1010.
APPL - MACRO : PRODUCTIVITY * APPL - MACRO : EMPLOYMENT * CAPACITY - EFFECT
OF

YA0703   CLARK P.K.
"The use of operational time to correct for sampling interval
mis-specification"   Rev. Econ. Stats., vol.57, 1975, pp.225-230.
APPL - SECTOR : COMMODITIES , COTTON * APPL - SECTOR : FINANCE , FUTURES
TRADING * RANDOM WALK - THEORY * DATA - AGGREGATION OVER TIME * TIME SERIES
- OPERATIONAL TIME

YA0704   CLARK T.N.
"Fiscal management of American cities" with discussion, (Studies on
measurement and evaluation of the economic efficiency of public and private
nonprofit institutions)"   J. Acctg. Res., vol.15, supplement; 1977,
pp.54-106.
REGIONAL MODELS - CITY * APPL - SECTOR : GOVERNMENT , LOCAL , FINANCE * APPL
- SECTOR : FINANCE , BONDS * USE - CREDIT CONTROL , BOND RATING

YA0705   CLARKE D.G.
"Econometric measurement of the duration of advertising effect on sales"
J. Mktg. Res., vol.13, 1976, pp.345-357.
ADVERTISING - EFFECT OF , REVIEW * DISTRIBUTED LAG - APPL , ADVERTISING *
EVALUATION - ADVERTISING EFFECTIVENESS * BIBLIOGRAPHY - ADVERTISING
EFFECTIVENESS * APPL - FIRM : CONSUMER NON DURABLES , HEALTH AIDS

YA0706　CLARKE D.G.
"Sales-advertising cross elasticities and advertising competition"　J.
Mktg. Res., vol.10, 1973, pp.250-261.
ADVERTISING - EFFECT OF * ADVERTISING - OPTIMALITY * APPL - FIRM : CONSUMER
NON DURABLES , GROCERIES * MARKET SHARE - SECTOR : CONSUMER NON DURABLES *
REGRESSION - SEEMINGLY UNRELATED * ERROR SPECIFICATION - AUTOCORRELATED ,
CORRELATED * SUBSTITUTE PRODUCTS

YA0707　CLARKE D.G.
"Strategic advertising planning: merging multidimensional scaling and
econometric analysis"　Mgmt. Sci., vol.24, 1978, pp.1687-1699.
MULTIDIMENSIONAL SCALING * MARKET POSITION * ADVERTISING - EFFECT OF * APPL
- FIRM : CONSUMER NON DURABLES , FOOD * MARKET SHARE - SECTOR : CONSUMER NON
DURABLES

YA0708　CLARKE D.G., McCANN J.M.
"Cumulative advertising effects: the role of serial correlation: a reply"
Decis. Sci., vol.8, 1977, pp.336-343.
ADVERTISING - EFFECT OF * APPL - SECTOR : CONSUMER NON DURABLES , HEALTH
AIDS * ERROR SPECIFICATION - AUTOCORRELATED * DISTRIBUTED LAG - APPL ,
ADVERTISING * DISTRIBUTED LAG - ERROR SPECIFICATION * DATA - AGGREGATION
OVER TIME * COMPARATIVE METHODS - DATA : AGGREGATE , DISAGGREGATE

YA0709　CLAURETIE T.M.
"Interest rates, the business demand for funds, and the residential mortgage
markets: a sectoral econometric study"　J. Finance, vol.28, 1973,
pp.1313-1326.
APPL - SECTOR : FINANCE , MORTGAGES * INTEREST RATE - EFFECT OF * SUPPLY -
SECTOR : FINANCE

YA0710　CLAWSON C.J.
"Fitting branch locations, performance standards and marketing strategies to
local conditions"　J. Mktg., vol.38, no.1, Jan 1974, pp.8-14.
REGRESSION - STEPWISE : APPL * USE - SITE SELECTION , RETAIL * USE - RETAIL
, SITE MONITORING * USE - TARGET SETTING * APPL - FIRM : FINANCE , BANKS *
APPL - FIRM : RETAILING , BANKS

YA0711　CLAWSON C.J.
"How useful are 90 day purchase probabilities?"　J. Mktg., vol.35, no.4,
Oct 1971, pp.43-47.
EVALUATION - EXPECTATIONS , DATA

YA0712　CLAYCAMP H.J., LIDDY L.E.
"Prediction of new product performance: an analytical approach"　J. Mktg.
Res., vol.6, 1969, pp.414-420.
NEW PRODUCTS - EVALUATION * APPL - FIRM : CONSUMER NON DURABLES *
ADVERTISING - EFFECT OF * EX ANTE * NEW PRODUCTS - ADVERTISING * CONSUMER
BEHAVIOUR - PURCHASING

YA0713　CLEVELAND W.P., TIAO G.C.
"Decomposition of seasonal time series: a model for the Census X-11 program"
J. Am. Statist. Ass., vol.71, 1976, pp.581-587.
SEASONALITY - ESTIMATION , CENSUS * SEASONALITY - ESTIMATION , ARIMA *
COMPARATIVE METHODS - SEASONALITY * APPL - SECTOR : TRANSPORT , AIR * APPL -
SECTOR : UTILITIES , TELEPHONE

YA0714　CLIFF A.D., ORD J.K.
"Model building and the analysis of spatial pattern in human geography" with
discussion.　R. Statist. Soc. (B), vol.37, 1975, pp.297-348.
SPATIAL ANALYSIS - REVIEW * BIBLIOGRAPHY - SPATIAL ANALYSIS

YA0715　CLINTON K.
"Interest rate expectations and the demand for money in Canada: comment"
J. Finance, vol.28, 1973, pp.207-214.
APPL - MACRO : MONEY , DEMAND * DISTRIBUTED LAG - ALMON : APPL * DISTRIBUTED
LAG - EXPECTATIONS HYPOTHESES * INTEREST RATE - EFFECT OF * INTEREST RATE -
EXPECTATIONS * DISTRIBUTED LAG - APPL , INTEREST RATE * REGRESSION -
SPECIFICATION OF VARIABLES

YA0716　CLINTON K.
"The demand for liabilities of trust and mortgage loan companies"　Can. J.
Econ., vol.7, 1974, pp.191-204.
APPL - SECTOR : FINANCE , SAVINGS * APPL - MACRO : CONSUMER DEMAND ,
FINANCIAL ASSETS * APPL - SECTOR : FINANCE , BUILDING SOCIETIES

YA0717　CLINTON K.
"The demand for money in Canada 1955-1970 some single equation estimates and
stability tests"　Can. J. Econ., vol.6, 1973, pp.53-61.
APPL - MACRO : MONEY , DEMAND * EXCHANGE RATE - EFFECT OF * STABILITY OF
COEFFICIENTS - REGRESSION : APPL * APPL - MACRO , CANADA

YA0718　CLINTON K., LADENSON M.L.
"Pitfalls in financial model building: comments"　Am. Econ. Rev., vol.63,
1973, pp.1003-1008.
APPL - MACRO : FLOW OF FUNDS * SIMULTANEOUS SYSTEM - CONSTRAINED

YA0719　CLOTFELTER C.T.
"Public services, private substitutes, and the demand for protection against
crime"　Am. Econ. Rev., vol.67, 1977, pp.867-877.
APPL - SECTOR : SOCIAL , CRIME * PRODUCTION FUNCTIONS - SECTOR * PRODUCTION
FUNCTIONS - SUBSTITUTION * APPL - SECTOR : GOVERNMENT , LOCAL , SERVICES *
DATA - CROSS SECTION * COMPARATIVE METHODS - ESTIMATION : SIMULTANEOUS
SYSTEM

YA0720   CLOTFELTER C.T.
          "The effect of school desegregation on housing prices"   Rev. Econ. Stats.,
          vol.57, 1975, pp.446-451.
          APPL - SECTOR : CONSTRUCTION , RESIDENTIAL * PRICE - SECTOR : CONSTRUCTION ,
          RESIDENTIAL
YA0721   CLOWES G.A.
          "A dynamic model for the analysis of labour turnover"   R. Statist. Soc.
          (A), vol.135, 1972, pp.242-256.
          MANPOWER PLANNING - LABOUR TURNOVER * MANPOWER PLANNING - FIRM
YA0722   COATES R., UPDEGRAFF D.E.
          "The relationship between organisational size and the administrative
          component of banks"   J. Business, vol.46, 1973, pp.576-588.
          APPL - FIRM : FINANCE , BANKS * COST - FIRM : FINANCE , BANKS * COST - SCALE
          ECONOMIES
YA0723   COATES R.G.
          "A partially subjective system for setting sales targets"   Stat'n.,
          vol.20, 1971, pp.19-34
          FORECASTING - INTRODUCTION * BASIC * USE - TARGET SETTING
YA0724   COEN P.J., GOMME E.D., KENDALL M.G.
          "Lagged relationships in economic forecasting" with discussion   R.
          Statist. Soc. (A), vol.132, 1969, pp.133-163.
          APPL - SECTOR : FINANCE , STOCK PRICE INDEX * LAG , FIXED * REGRESSION -
          STEPWISE : APPL * BUSINESS INDICATORS - APPL * STOCK PRICES - DETERMINANTS
YA0725   COGGER K.O.
          "Extensions of the fundamental theorem of exponential smoothing"   Mgmt.
          Sci. (A), vol.19, 1973, pp.547-554.
          EXPONENTIAL SMOOTHING - THEORY * ADVANCED
YA0726   COGGER K.O.
          "Specification analysis"   J. Am. Statist. Ass., vol.68, 1973, pp.899-905.
          TIME SERIES - ARIMA : DIAGNOSTICS * SPECIFICATION ERROR - EFFECT OF , MODEL
          SPECIFICATION * SPECTRAL ANALYSIS - APPL : TIME SERIES * EXPONENTIAL
          SMOOTHING - THEORY * COMPARATIVE METHODS - ARIMA , EXPONENTIAL SMOOTHING *
          BIBLIOGRAPHY - TIME SERIES * STATIONARITY - TRANSFORMING TO * ADVANCED
YA0727   COGGER K.O.
          "The optimality of general-order exponential smoothing"   Ops. Res.,
          vol.22, 1974, pp.858-867.
          EXPONENTIAL SMOOTHING - THEORY * TIME SERIES - MOVING AVERAGE * EXPONENTIAL
          SMOOTHING - HIGHER ORDER * EXPONENTIAL SMOOTHING - COEFFICIENT CHOICE
YA0728   COHEN B.I.
          "Comparative behaviour of foreign and domestic export firms in a developing
          economy"   Rev. Econ. Stats., vol.55, 1973, pp.190-197.
          DATA - LDC * LEARNING CURVE * APPL - FIRM-: PRODUCTIVITY * APPL - FIRM :
          LOCATION * DATA - INTERNATIONAL * APPL - FIRM TYPE : MULTINATIONAL
YA0729   COHEN J.B., ET AL.
          "The nature and uses of expectancy-value models in consumer attitude
          research" with discussion   J. Mktg. Res., vol.9, 1972, pp.456-467.
          EVALUATION - CONSUMER BEHAVIOUR , PSYCHOLOGICAL MODELS * APPL - FIRM :
          CONSUMER NON DURABLES * BRAND CHOICE - INDICATORS
YA0730   COHEN K.J., ET AL.
          "The determinants of common stock returns volatility: an international
          comparison" with discussion   J. Finance, vol.31, 1976, pp.733-740 &
          751-752.
          STOCK PRICES - VOLATILITY * DATA - INTERNATIONAL * STOCK PRICES - TRADING
          VOLUME * APPL - FIRM : FINANCE , STOCK PRICES * VOLATILITY - DETERMINANTS
YA0731   COHEN K.J., MULLER W., PADBERG M.W.
          "Autoregressive approaches to disaggregation of time series data"   Appl.
          Stats., vol.20, 1971, pp.119-129.
          DATA - INTERPOLATION
YA0732   COHEN M., GILLINGHAM R., HEIEN D.
          "A Monte Carlo study of complex finite distributed lag structures"   Anns.
          Econ. Soc. Meas., vol.2, 1973, pp.53-63.
          DISTRIBUTED LAG - IDENTIFICATION * DATA - SIMULATION * DISTRIBUTED LAG -
          ESTIMATION * EVALUATION - DISTRIBUTED LAG , LAG SPECIFICATION
YA0733   COHN E., NELSON J.P., NEUMANN G.R.
          "Forecasting aggregate demand for coal miners"   Appl. Econ., vol.7, 1975,
          pp.81-92.
          MANPOWER PLANNING - SECTOR : PRODUCTION , DEMAND * COMPARATIVE METHODS -
          CAUSAL , TREND CURVES * APPL - SECTOR : PRODUCTION , COAL * COMPARATIVE
          METHODS - CAUSAL , JUDGEMENTAL * COMPARATIVE METHODS - JUDGEMENTAL , TREND
          CURVES * EX ANTE
YA0734   COLE H.S.D.
          "Accuracy in the long run- where are we now?"   Omega, vol.5, 1977,
          pp.529-542.
          EVALUATION - LONG TERM FORECASTING * LONG TERM FORECASTING * EVALUATION -
          POPULATION FORECASTS * EVALUATION - MACRO FORECASTS * THEORY - MODELLING *
          BASIC

YA0735   COLENUTT D.W.
          "Economies of scale in the UK ordinary life assurance industry"   Appl.
          Econ. vol.9, 1977, pp.219-225.
          APPL - FIRM : FINANCE , INSURANCE COMPANIES * COST - SECTOR : FINANCE * COST
          - SCALE ECONOMIES * DATA - CROSS SECTION * COMPARATIVE METHODS - REGRESSION
          , TRANSFORMATIONS
YA0736   COLLETT D., LEWIS T.
          "The subjective nature of outlier rejection procedures"   Appl. Stats.,
          vol.25, 1976, pp.228-237.
          DATA ERRORS - OUTLIERS
YA0737   COLLEY S.
          "International financing"   Opl. Res. Q., vol.26, 1975, pp.827-845.
          APPL - FIRM : PRODUCTION , STEEL * USE - FINANCIAL , CONTROL * APPL - FIRM :
          FINANCE , INTERNATIONAL FINANCE * EXCHANGE RATE - EFFECT OF * APPL - MACRO :
          INTERNATIONAL FINANCE , EXCHANGE RATES * USE - SPECULATION * BASIC
YA0738   COLLINS L.
          "Estimating Markov transition probabilities from micro unit data"   Appl.
          Stats., vol.23, 1974, pp.355-371.
          MARKOV MODELS - ESTIMATION * APPL - MACRO : PLANT SIZE * EX ANTE
YA0739   COLLINS M., MEDCALF T., SCHROLL D.
          "The possible effects of exchange rates upon domestic price levels"   Bus.
          Econ., vol.13:3, 1978, pp.57-62.
          EXCHANGE RATE - EFFECT OF * DATA - CROSS SECTION * DATA - INTERNATIONAL *
          APPL - MACRO : INTERNATIONAL FINANCE , EXCHANGE RATES
YA0740   COLWELL P.F., LASH N.A.
          "Comparing fiscal indicators"   Rev. Econ. Stats., vol.55, 1973,
          pp.321-326.
          APPL - MACRO : GNP * POLICY EVALUATION - MACRO : FISCAL * TAX - EFFECT OF *
          APPL - MACRO : CAPACITY UTILISATION * INDEX NUMBERS - MACRO : FISCAL POLICY
YA0741   COMANOR W.S.
          "Racial discrimination in American industry"   Economica, vol.40, 1973,
          pp.363-378.
          MANPOWER PLANNING - DISCRIMINATION , RACIAL * UNIONIZATION - EFFECT OF *
          DATA - CROSS SECTION
YA0742   COMANOR W.S., MITCHELL B.M.
          "Cable television and the impact of regulation"   Bell J. Econ., vol.2,
          1971, pp.154-212 & 704.
          APPL - SECTOR : SERVICES , MEDIA , TV * USE - FINANCIAL , REGULATION * APPL
          - SECTOR : FINANCE , PROFITS
YA0743   COMANOR W.S., WILSON T.A.
          "Advertising; market structure and performance"   Rev. Econ. Stats. vol.49,
          1967, pp.423-440.
          ADVERTISING - EFFECT OF * CONCENTRATION - EFFECT OF * APPL - SECTOR :
          FINANCE , PROFITS * SPECIFICATION ERROR - EFFECT OF , VARIABLE INCLUSION *
          SPECIFICATION ERROR - EFFECT OF , HETEROSCEDASTICITY
YA0744   COMAY Y.
          "The migration of professionals: an empirical analysis"   Can. J. Econ.,
          vol.5, 1972, pp.419-429.
          MANPOWER PLANNING - QUALIFIED MANPOWER , PROFESSIONAL * MANPOWER PLANNING -
          MIGRATION
YA0745   COMER J.M.
          "ALLOCATE; a computer model for sales territory planning"   Decis. Sci.,
          vol.5, 1974, pp.323-338.
          MARKET POTENTIAL * USE - SALES AREA ALLOCATION * MIS
YA0746   CONGER D.J., CAMPBELL J.M.
          "Simultaeity in the birth rate equation: the effects of education, labour
          force participation, income and health"   Econometrica, vol.46, 1978,
          pp.631-641.
          POPULATION - FERTILITY * MANPOWER PLANNING - LABOUR PARTICIPATION , FEMALE *
          INCOME - EFFECT OF * EDUCATION - EFFECT OF * HEALTH - EFFECT OF
YA0747   CONLISK J.
          "Optimal response surface design in Monte Carlo sampling experiments"
          Anns. Econ. Soc. Meas., vol.3, 1974, pp.463-473.
          SIMULATION - EXPERIMENTAL DESIGN
YA0748   CONNIFFE D., STONE J.
          "A critical view of ridge regression"   Stat'n,, vol.22, 1973, pp.181-187.
          EVALUATION - REGRESSION , RIDGE
YA0749   CONNORS M.M., ET AL.
          "The distribution system simulation"   Mgmt. Sci, (B), vol.18, 1972,
          pp.425-453.
          APPL - SECTOR : DISTRIBUTION * SIMULATION - METHODOLOGY * USE - DISTRIBUTION
          , CONTROL * USE - INVENTORY CONTROL
YA0750   CONRAD S.A.
          "Sales data and the estimation of demand"   Opl. Res. Q., vol.27, 1976,
          pp.123-127.
          DATA - SPECIFICATION OF VARIABLES * DEMAND - DEFINITION OF * PROBABILITY
          MODELS - POISSON

YA0751   CONRAD W.E., WALL K.
          "Imperfect observation and systematic policy error" with discussion   Anns.
          Econ. Soc. Meas., vol.6, 1977, pp.247-260.
          MACRO MODEL - US * DATA ERRORS - EFFECT OF * DATA REVISIONS - EFFECT OF *
          POLICY EVALUATION - METHODOLOGY

YA0752   COOK A.A.
          "Quality adjustment and the excess supply of air force volunteers"   Rev.
          Econ. Stats., vol.54, 1972, pp.166-171.
          MANPOWER PLANNING - SECTOR : GOVERNMENT , SUPPLY * QUALITY - ADJUSTMENTS *
          INCOME - EFFECT OF

YA0753   COOK T.Q., HENDERSHOTT P.H.
          "The impact of taxes, risk and relative security supplies on interest rate
          differentials"   J. Finance, vol.33, 1978, pp.1173-1186.
          INTEREST RATE - DETERMINANTS * TAX - EFFECT OF * RISK - EFFECT OF

YA0754   COOK V.J., HERNITER J.D.
          "NOMMAD, or how consumers behave"   Sloan Mcmt. Rev., vol.12, no.3, 1971,
          pp.77-97.
          REPEAT BUYING * BRAND CHOICE - DETERMINANTS * APPL - FIRM : CONSUMER NON
          DURABLES * CONSUMER BEHAVIOUR - STOCHASTIC MODELS * NEW PRODUCTS - NEW
          BRANDS

YA0755   COOK W.R.
          "Curious correlations - a reply"   R. Statist. Soc. (A), vol.140, 1977,
          pp.511-513.
          DECISION RULES - SECTOR * REGRESSION - MODEL INTERPRETATION * REGRESSION -
          SPURIOUS CORRELATION * APPL - SECTOR : GOVERNMENT , EDUCATION , UNIVERSITIES

YA0756   COOK W.R.
          "How the University Grants Committee determines allocations of recurrent
          grants-a curious correlation"   R. Statist. Soc. (A), vol.139, 1976,
          pp.374-384.
          DECISION RULES - SECTOR * APPL - SECTOR : GOVERNMENT , EDUCATION ,
          UNIVERSITIES * COST - FIRM : EDUCATION * USER - FIRM : EDUCATION ,
          UNIVERSITIES

YA0757   COOLEY P.L., ROENFELDT R.L., MODANI N.K.
          "Interdependence of market risk measures"   J. Business, vol.50, 1977,
          pp.356-363.
          STOCK PRICES - RISK * STOCK PRICES - VOLATILITY * STOCK PRICES - BETA * APPL
          - FIRM : FINANCE , STOCK PRICES.

YA0758   COOLEY T.F.
          "A comparison of robust and varying parameter estimates of a macroeconomic
          model"   Anns. Econ. Soc. Meas., vol.4, 1975, pp.373-388.
          MACRO MODEL - FAIR * REGRESSION - OUTLIERS * ESTIMATION - ROBUST *
          COMPARATIVE METHODS - ESTIMATION - OLS , ROBUST * EX ANTE * REGRESSION -
          ESTIMATION * ESTIMATION - MAXIMUM LIKELIHOOD * COMPARATIVE METHODS -
          ESTIMATION : REGRESSION * COMPARATIVE METHODS - REGRESSION , STATE SPACE

YA0759   COOLEY T.F., PRESCOTT E.C.
          "Systematic (non random) variation models: varying parameter regression: a
          theory and some appllications"   Anns. Econ. Soc. Meas., vol.2, 1973,
          pp.463-474.
          STABILITY OF COEFFICIENTS - REGRESSION , TEST * REGRESSION - STATE SPACE

YA0760   COOLEY T.F., PRESCOTT E.C.
          "Tests of an adaptive regression model"   Rev. Econ. Stats., vol.55, 1973,
          pp.248-256.
          COMPARATIVE METHODS - REGRESSION , STATE SPACE * APPL - MACRO : CONSUMPTION
          * EX ANTE * COMPARATIVE METHODS - REGRESSION , ERROR SPECIFICATION *
          REGRESSION - STATE SPACE * STABILITY OF COEFFICIENTS - REGRESSION * DATA -
          SIMULATION * BAYESIAN - ESTIMATION : REGRESSION , STATE SPACE *
          AUTOCORRELATION - EFFECT OF

YA0761   COOLEY T.F., ROSENBERG B., WALL K.D.
          "A note on optimal smoothing for time varying coefficient problems"   Anns.
          Econ. Soc. Meas., vol.6, 1977, pp.453-456.
          REGRESSION - STATE SPACE * ESTIMATION - KALMAN FILTER * ADVANCED

YA0762   COOPER J.P.
          "Two approaches to polynomial distributed lags estimation: an expository
          note and comment"   Am. Statn., vol.26:3, 1972, pp.32-35.
          DISTRIBUTED LAG - ALMON * DISTRIBUTED LAG - POLYNOMIAL

YA0763   COOPER J.P., FISCHER S.
          "A method for stochastic control of nonlinear econometric models and an
          application"   Econometrica, vol.43, 1975, pp.147-162.
          CONTROL THEORY - STOCHASTIC , MACRO * MACRO MODEL - ST. LOUIS * SIMULATION -
          EVALUATION OF RESULTS * SIMULTANEOUS SYSTEM - NON LINEAR * SIMULTANEOUS
          SYSTEM - CONTROL * POLICY EVALUATION - MACRO : FISCAL , MONETARY

YA0764   COOPER J.P., FISCHER S.
          "A method for stochastic control of nonlinear econometric models and an
          application: abstract"   Anns. Econ. Soc. Meas., vol.3, 1974, pp.205-206.
          CONTROL THEORY - STOCHASTIC , METHODOLOGY * MACRO MODEL - ST.LOUIS *
          SIMULTANEOUS SYSTEM - CONTROL * SIMULTANEOUS SYSTEM - NON LINEAR

YA0765   COOPER J.P., FISCHER S.
          "Stochastic simulation of monetary rules in two macroeconomic models"   J.
          Am. Statist. Ass., vol.67, 1972, pp.750-760.
          MACRO MODEL - FRB , MIT , PENN * MACRO MODEL - ST.LOUIS * SIMULATION - APPL
          : POLICY EVALUATION * SIMULATION - EXPERIMENTAL DESIGN * POLICY EVALUATION -
          MACRO : MONETARY
YA0766   COOPER J.P., FISCHER S.
          "The use of the secant method in econometric models"   J. Business, vol.46,
          1973, pp.274-277.
          CONTROL THEORY - DETERMINISTIC , METHODOLOGY * SIMULTANEOUS SYSTEM - CONTROL
          * MACRO MODEL - FRB , MIT , PENN * SIMULTANEOUS SYSTEM - NON LINEAR
YA0767   COOPER J.P., NELSON C.R.
          "The ex ante prediction performance of the St.Louis and FRB-MIT-PENN
          econometric models and some results on composite predictors"   J. Money,
          Credit, Banking, vol.7, 1975, pp.1-33.
          MACRO MODEL - ST.LOUIS * MACRO MODEL - FRB , MIT , PENN * EXOGENOUS
          VARIABLES - PREDICTION OF , EFFECT * COMPARATIVE METHODS - MACRO MODELS *
          COMPARATIVE METHODS - ARIMA , CAUSAL(SIMULTANEOUS SYSTEM) * COMBINING
          FORECASTS - CAUSAL , TIME SERIES * EVALUATION - MACRO MODELS * EX ANTE
YA0768   COOPER R.L.
          "An econometric forecasting model of the financial sector of U.S.
          households"   Appl. Econ., vol.5, 1973, pp.101-117.
          APPL - MACRO : CONSUMER DEMAND , FINANCIAL ASSETS * CONSUMER BEHAVIOUR -
          ECONOMIC MODELS
YA0769   COOPER R.N., LAWRENCE R.Z.
          "The 1972-75 commodity boom" with discussion   Brookings Paps. Econ.
          Activity, 1975, pp.671-723.
          APPL - SECTOR : COMMODITIES * BUSINESS CYCLE - EFFECT OF * EXCHANGE RATE -
          EFFECT OF
YA0770   COOPER R.V.L.
          "Efficient capital markets and the quantity theory of money"   J. Finance,
          vol.29, 1974, pp.887-908.
          SPECTRAL ANALYSIS - APPL : MACRO , MONEY * APPL - MACRO : MONEY , SUPPLY *
          STOCK PRICES - DETERMINANTS * APPL - SECTOR : FINANCE , STOCK PRICES *
          THEORY - EFFICIENT MARKETS * EXPECTATIONS - ESTIMATING * TIME SERIES -
          AUTOREGRESSIVE * SPECTRAL ANALYSIS - APPL : SECTOR , FINANCE * SPECTRAL
          ANALYSIS - CROSS : APPL
YA0771   COPELAND R.M., MARIONI R.J.
          "Executives forecasts of earnings per share versus forecasts of naive
          models"   J. Business, vol.45, 1972, pp.497-512
          APPL - FIRM : FINANCE , PROFITS PER SHARE * COMPARATIVE METHODS -
          AUTOREGRESSIVE , JUDGEMENTAL
YA0772   CORCORAN A.W.
          "The use of exponentially-smoothed transition matrices to improve
          forecasting of cash flows from accounts receivable"   Mgmt. Sci., vol.24,
          1978, pp.732-739.
          APPL - FIRM : FINANCE , FINANCIAL STRUCTURE , LIQUID ASSETS * EXPONENTIAL
          SMOOTHING - APPL * MARKOV MODELS - ESTIMATION * USE - CASH MANAGEMENT *
          BASIC
YA0773   CORCORAN M.
          "The structure of female wages" with discussion   Am. Econ. Ass. Proc.,
          1978, pp.165-170.
          MANPOWER PLANNING - EARNINGS * MANPOWER PLANNING - DISCRIMINATION , SEXUAL
YA0774   CORNELL W.B., DIETRICH J.K.
          "The efficiency of the market for foreign exchange under floating exchange
          rates"   Rev. Econ. Stats., vol.60, 1978, pp.111-120.
          RANDOM WALK - TEST * APPL - MACRO : INTERNATIONAL FINANCE , EXCHANGE RATES *
          DATA - INTERNATIONAL * RANDOM WALK - TEST , TRADING RULE * ERROR
          DISTRIBUTION - STABLE
YA0775   CORNWALL J.
          "Diffusion, convergence and Kaldor's laws"   Econ. J., vol.86, 1976,
          pp.307-314.
          APPL - MACRO : GROWTH * DATA - INTERNATIONAL
YA0776   COSSOLINO J.M., ZAHNER M.J.
          "The maximum-entropy distribution of the future price of a stock"   Ops.
          Res., vol.21, 1973, pp.1200-1211.
          RANDOM WALK - THEORY * PROBABILITY MODELS - ENTROPY * STOCK PRICES -
          DISTRIBUTION
YA0777   COURAKIS A.S.
          "Serial correlation and a Bank of England study of the demand for money: an
          exercise in measurement without theory"   Econ. J., vol.88, 1978,
          pp.537-548.
          COMPARATIVE METHODS - DISTRIBUTED LAG , ERROR SPECIFICATION * APPL - MACRO :
          MONEY , DEMAND * STATIONARITY - TRANSFORMING TO * AUTOCORRELATION - EFFECT
          OF , EVALUATION * REGRESSION - MODEL CHOICE * DISTRIBUTED LAG - ERROR
          SPECIFICATION * INCOME - EFFECT OF * APPL - MACRO , UK * APPL - MACRO :
          CONSUMER DEMAND , FINANCIAL ASSETS * THEORY - MODELLING * ESTIMATION -
          MAXIMUM LIKELIHOOD : APPL

YA0778   COURAKIS A.S.
    "Testing theories of discount house portfolio selection"   Rev. Econ.
    Studies, vol.42, 1975, pp.643-648.
    APPL - SECTOR : FINANCE , BANKS * DEMAND EQUATIONS - SYSTEMS OF *
    SPECIFICATION ERROR - TESTS , CONSTRAINTS

YA0779   COURVILLE L.
    "Regulation and efficiency in the electric utility industry"   Bell J.
    Econ., vol.5, 1974, pp.53-74.
    APPL - FIRM : UTILITIES , ELECTRICITY * APPL - FIRM : EFFICIENCY * USE -
    FINANCIAL , REGULATION * DATA - CROSS SECTION * PRODUCTION FUNCTIONS - FIRM

YA0780   COWEY A., GREEN D.
    "A marketing model for a price-promoted consumer good: a case study"   Opl.
    Res. Q., vol.26, 1975, pp.3-14.
    APPL - FIRM : CONSUMER NON DURABLES , FOOD * APPL - SECTOR : CONSUMER NON
    DURABLES , FOOD * PRICE - EFFECT OF * USE - MARKETING POLICY * USER - FIRM :
    CONSUMER NON DURABLES * USE - PROMOTION EVALUATION * SIMULATION - APPL :
    SECTOR , CONSUMER NON DURABLES * ADVERTISING - EFFECT OF * MARKET SHARE -
    SECTOR : CONSUMER NON DURABLES * BASIC

YA0781   COWING T.G., SMITH V.K.
    "A note on the variability of the replacement investment capital stock
    ratio"   Rev. Econ. Stats., vol.59, 1977, pp.238-243.
    APPL - SECTOR : UTILITIES , ELECTRICITY * APPL - SECTOR : INVESTMENT ,
    UTILITIES * DATA ERRORS - EFFECT OF * SPECIFICATION ERROR - TESTS ,
    SIMULTANEOUS SYSTEM BIAS * SPECIFICATION ERROR - TESTS , VARIABLE INCLUSION
    * DEMAND - REPLACEMENT * DEPRECIATION - ESTIMATION

YA0782   COWLING K., CUBBIN J.
    "Hedonic price indexes for UK cars"   Econ. J., vol.82, 1972, pp.963-978.
    QUALITY - PRICE * INDEX NUMBERS - METHODOLOGY * INDEX NUMBERS - SECTOR :
    CONSUMER DURABLES * PRICE - SECTOR : CONSUMER DURABLES * APPL - SECTOR :
    CONSUMER DURABLES , CARS

YA0783   COWLING K., CUBBIN J.
    "Price, quality and advertising competition: an econometric investigation of
    the UK car market"   Economica, vol.38, 1971, pp.378-394.
    ADVERTISING - EFFECT OF * ADVERTISING - OPTIMALITY * APPL - FIRM : CONSUMER
    DURABLES , CARS * QUALITY - ADJUSTMENT * QUALITY - PRICE * MARKET SHARE -
    SECTOR : CONSUMER DURABLES * COMPARATIVE METHODS - ESTIMATION : OLS , 2SLS

YA0784   COWLING K., WATERSON M.
    "Price-cost margins and market structure"   Economica, vol.43, 1976,
    pp.267-274.
    APPL - SECTOR : FINANCE , MARGINS * CONCENTRATION - EFFECT OF

YA0785   COX D.R.
    "Notes on some aspects of regression analysis" with discussion   R.
    Statist. Soc. (A), vol.131, 1968, pp.265-279 & 315-329.
    REGRESSION - MODEL CHOICE * CAUSALITY - REVIEW * REGRESSION - OUTLIERS *
    REGRESSION - REVIEW * DATA ERRORS - MISSING OBSERVATIONS * REGRESSION -
    TRANSFORMATIONS * REGRESSION - ERRORS IN VARIABLES * BIBLIOGRAPHY -
    REGRESSION * STABILITY OF COEFFICIENTS - REGRESSION

YA0786   COX D.R.
    "Regression models and life - tables" with discussion   R. Statist. Soc.
    (B), vol.34, 1972, pp.187-220.
    REGRESSION - CENSORED * ADVANCED

YA0787   COX D.R., SNELL E.J.
    "The choice of variables in observational studies"   Appl. Stats., vol.23,
    1974, pp.51-59.
    REGRESSION - EXPERIMENTAL DESIGN * BIBLIOGRAPHY - REGRESSION , EXPERIMENTAL
    DESIGN * REGRESSION - VARIABLE INCLUSION

YA0788   COX J.C., WRIGHT A.W.
    "The determinants of investment in petroleum reserves and their implications
    for public policy"   Am. Econ. Rev., vol.66, 1976, pp.153-167.
    APPL - SECTOR : PRODUCTION , PETROLEUM * INTEREST RATE - EFFECT OF * STOCK
    PRICES - EFFECT OF * POLICY EVALUATION - SECTOR : PRODUCTION * TAX - EFFECT
    OF

YA0789   COX W.E.
    "Product life cycles as marketing models"   J. Business, vol.40, 1967,
    pp.375-384.
    APPL - SECTOR : CONSUMER NON DURABLES , PHARMACEUTICALS * EVALUATION - LIFE
    CYCLE , PRODUCT * BASIC

YA0790   COX W.E., HAVENS G.N.
    "Determination of sales potentials and performance for an industrial goods
    manufacturer"   J. Mktg. Res., vol.14, 1977, pp.574-578.
    MARKET POTENTIAL * APPL - FIRM : PRODUCTION , PLANT , METAL WORKING

YA0791   CRAGG J.G.
    "On the relative small sample properties of several structural equation
    estimators"   Econometrica, vol.35, 1967, pp.89-110.
    COMPARATIVE METHODS - ESTIMATION : SIMULTANEOUS SYSTEM * DATA - SIMULATION *
    COMPARATIVE METHODS - ESTIMATION : OLS , 2SLS * COMPARATIVE METHODS -
    ESTIMATION : OLS , FIML * COMPARATIVE METHODS - ESTIMATION : OLS , 3SLS *
    MULTICOLLINEARITY - EFFECT OF * COMPARATIVE METHODS - ESTIMATION :
    SIMULTANEOUS SYSTEM , 2SLS , 3SLS * COMPARATIVE METHODS - ESTIMATION :
    SIMULTANEOUS SYSTEM : 2SLS , FIML * ESTIMATION - MAXIMUM LIKELIHOOD ,
    LIMITED INFORMATION * ESTIMATION - K CLASS

YA0792   CRAGG J.G.
         "On the sensitivity of simultaneous equations estimators to the stochastic
         assumptions of the models"   J. Am. Statist. Ass., vol.61, 1966,
         pp.136-151.
         SPECIFICATION ERROR - EFFECT OF , RANDOM COEFFICIENTS * COMPARATIVE METHODS
         - ESTIMATION : SIMULTANEOUS SYSTEM * COMPARATIVE METHODS - ESTIMATION : OLS
         , 2SLS * COMPARATIVE METHODS - ESTIMATION : OLS , FIML * AUTOCORRELATION -
         EFFECT OF * SPECIFICATION ERROR - EFFECT OF , HETEROSCEDASTICITY

YA0793   CRAGG J.G.
         "Some statistical models for limited dependent variables with application to
         the demand for durable goods"   Econometrica, vol.39, 1971, pp.829-844.
         BAYESIAN - MODEL SELECTION * REGRESSION - LIMITED DEPENDENT * DATA -
         SIMULATION * APPL - SECTOR : CONSUMER DURABLES * COMPARATIVE METHODS -
         REGRESSION , LIMITED DEPENDENT

YA0794   CRAGG J.G., MALKIEL B.G.
         "The consensus and accuracy of some predictions of the growth of corporate
         earnings"   J. Finance, vol.23, 1968, pp.67-84.
         APPL - FIRM : FINANCE , PROFITS , PER SHARE * EVALUATION - JUDGEMENTAL
         FORECASTS , SPECIALIST * EVALUATION - JUDGEMENTAL FORECASTS , PROFITS *
         COMPARATIVE METHODS - JUDGEMENTAL , TREND CURVES

YA0795   CRAIG G.D.
         "Money illusion and the aggregate consumption function: note"   Am. Econ.
         Rev., vol.64, 1974, pp.195-199.
         APPL - MACRO : CONSUMPTION * EX ANTE * EVALUATION - CONSUMPTION MODELS *
         DISTRIBUTED LAG - APPL , INCOME * INCOME - EFFECT OF

YA0796   CRAIG G.D.
         "Predictive accuracy of quarterly and annual aggregate saving functions"
         J. Am. Statist. Ass., vol.65, 1970, pp.1131-1145.
         APPL - MACRO : SAVINGS * EX ANTE * EVALUATION - SAVINGS MODELS * INCOME -
         EFFECT OF * COMPARATIVE METHODS - AUTOREGRESSIVE , CAUSAL

YA0797   CRAINE R.
         "Investment, adjustment costs and uncertainty"   Int. Econ. Rev., vol.16,
         1975, pp.648-661.
         THEORY - FIRM * APPL - MACRO : EARNINGS * APPL - MACRO : INVESTMENT *
         EXOGENOUS VARIABLES - PREDICTION OF * TIME SERIES - ARIMA : APPL

YA0798   CRAINE R.
         "On the service flow from labour"   Rev. Econ. Studies, vol.40, 1973,
         pp.39-46.
         PRODUCTION FUNCTIONS - MACRO * REGRESSION - SPECIFICATION OF VARIABLES *
         DATA ERRORS - EFFECT OF * APPL - MACRO , US

YA0799   CRAINE R., HAVENNER A., BERRY J.
         "Fixed rules vs. activism in the conduct of monetary policy"   Am. Econ.
         Rev., vol.68, 1978, pp.769-783.
         MACRO MODEL - MIT , PENN , SSRC * POLICY EVALUATION - MACRO : MONETARY *
         CONTROL THEORY - STOCHASTIC , APPL * EXOGENOUS VARIABLES - PREDICTION OF ,
         EFFECT * LOSS FUNCTIONS - MACRO

YA0800   CRAINE R., HAVENNER A., TINSLEY P.
         "Optimal macro control policies"   Anns. Econ. Soc. Meas., vol.5, 1976,
         pp.191-203.
         SIMULTANEOUS SYSTEM - CONTROL * CONTROL THEORY - STOCHASTIC , APPL * LOSS
         FUNCTIONS - MACRO * POLICY EVALUATION - MACRO : FISCAL , MONETARY * MACRO
         MODEL - MIT , PENN , SSRC

YA0801   CRAMER E.M.
         "Significance tests and tests of models in multiple regression"   Am.
         Statin., vol.26:4, 1972, pp.26-30.
         REGRESSION - SUMMARY STATISTICS * REGRESSION - HYPOTHESIS TESTS * BASIC

YA0802   CRAMER J.S.
         "Interaction of income and price in consumer demand"   Int. Econ. Rev.,
         vol.14, 1973, pp.351-363.
         CONSUMER BEHAVIOUR - ECONOMIC MODELS , THEORY * PRICE - EFFECT OF * INCOME -
         EFFECT OF * APPL - SECTOR : CONSUMER NON DURABLES , FOOD * EVALUATION -
         INCOME ELASTICITIES * EVALUATION - PRICE ELASTICITIES

YA0803   CRAMER R.H., MILLER R.B.
         "Dynamic modeling of multivariate time series for use in bank analysis"
         J. Money, Credit, Banking, vol.8, 1976, pp.85-96.
         APPL - SECTOR : FINANCE , BANKS * DISTRIBUTED LAG - RATIONAL POLYNOMIAL * EX
         ANTE * COMPARATIVE METHODS - ARIMA , RATIONAL POLYNOMIAL INDICATOR * APPL -
         SECTOR : INVESTMENT

YA0804   CRANDALL R.W.
         "FCC regulation, monopsony, and network television program costs"   Bell J.
         Econ., vol.3, 1972, pp.483-508.
         APPL - FIRM : SERVICES , MEDIA , TV * COST - FIRM : SERVICES * COMPETITION -
         EFFECT OF

YA0805   CRANDALL R.W.
         "The profitability of cable television: an examination of acquisition
         prices"   J. Business, vol.47, 1974, pp.543-563.
         APPL - FIRM : SERVICES , MEDIA , TELEVISION * APPL - FIRM : FINANCE ,
         PROFITS * USE - ACQUISITION

YA0806   CRANDALL R.W., FRAY L.L.
         "A re-examination of the prophecy of doom for cable television"   Bell J.
         Econ., vol.5, 1974, pp.421-458.
         APPL - FIRM : INVESTMENT * APPL - FIRM : UTILITIES , ELECTRICITY * APPL -
         SECTOR : PRODUCTION , PLANT , ELECTRICITY GENERATION * THEORY - INVESTMENT :
         BEHAVIOUR * BAYESIAN - ESTIMATION : DISTRIBUTED LAG * EVALUATION -
         INVESTMENT MODELS * DISTRIBUTED LAG - APPL , OUTPUT

YA0807   CRANE D.B., CROTTY J.R.
         "A two stage forecasting model: exponential smoothing and multiple
         regression"   Mgmt. Sci. (B), vol.13, 1967, pp.501-507.
         EXPONENTIAL SMOOTHING - APPL * COMBINING FORECASTS - CAUSAL , TIME SERIES *
         EXOGENOUS VARIABLES - PREDICTION OF * COMBINING FORECASTS - APPL * APPL -
         FIRM : FINANCE , BANK , LIABILITIES * EX ANTE * COMPARATIVE METHODS - CAUSAL
         , EXPONENTIAL SMOOTHING

YA0808   CRANSHAW T.E.
         "The evaluation of investment performance"   J. Business, vol.50, 1977,
         pp.462-485.
         APPL - FIRM : FINANCE , MUTUAL FUNDS * USE - PORTFOLIO SELECTION * STOCK
         PRICES - INSTITUTIONAL INVESTMENT * EVALUATION - PORTFOLIO SELECTION
         PROCEDURES

YA0809   CRASK M.R., PERREAULT W.D.
         "Validation of discriminant analysis in marketing research"   J. Mktg.
         Res., vol.14, 1977, pp.60-68.
         EVALUATION - DISCRIMINANT ANALYSIS * EVALUATION - THEORY OF

YA0810   CREAN J.F.
         "Foregone earnings and the demand for education: some empirical evidence"
         Can. J. Econ., vol.6, 1973, pp.23-42.
         APPL - SECTOR : EDUCATION , SCHOOLS

YA0811   CREMEANS J.E.
         "Capacity utilisation rates - what do they really mean?"   Bus. Econ.,
         vol.13:3, 1978, pp.41-46.
         CAPACITY - ESTIMATION * APPL - MACRO : CAPACITY UTILISATION * DATA -
         SPECIFICATION OF VARIABLES

YA0812   CRICHFIELD T., DYCKMAN T., LAKONISHOK J.
         "An evaluation of security analysts' forecasts"   Acctg. Rev., vol.53,
         1978, pp.651-668.
         COMPARATIVE METHODS - AUTOREGRESSIVE , JUDGEMENTAL * EVALUATION -
         JUDGEMENTAL FORECASTS , PROFITS PER SHARE * APPL - FIRM : FINANCE , PROFITS
         , PER SHARE * EVALUATION - JUDGEMENTAL FORECASTS , SPECIALIST

YA0813   CRIPPS F., GODLEY W.
         "A formal analysis of the Cambridge Economic Policy Group Model"
         Economica, vol.43, 1976, pp.335-348.
         MACRO MODEL - UK , CAMBRIDGE

YA0814   CROCKER D.C.
         "Some interpretations of the multiple correlation coefficient"   Am.
         Stat'n., vol.26:2, 1972, pp.31-33.
         REGRESSION - SUMMARY STATISTICS * BASIC

YA0815   CROCKER D.C., ARMSTRONG J.S.
         "Comments on 'exploratory analysis of marketing data: Trees vs. regression'"
         J. Mktg. Res., vol.8, 1971, pp.509-513.
         COMPARATIVE METHODS - REGRESSION , MULTIVARIATE METHODS * REGRESSION -
         SUMMARY STATISTICS * EVALUATION - AID

YA0816   CROMARTY W.A., MYERS W.M.
         "Needed improvements in application of models for agriculture commodity
         price forecasting" with discussion   Am. J. Ag. Econ., vol.57, 1975,
         pp.172-177 & 185-187.
         EVALUATION - COMMODITY PRICE MODELS * APPL - SECTOR : COMMODITIES

YA0817   CROSTON J.D.
         "Forecasting and stock control for intermittent demands" with erratum
         Opl. Res. Q., vol.23, 1972, pp.289-303 & vo.24, 1973, pp.639-640.
         DEMAND - INTERMITTENT * EXPONENTIAL SMOOTHING - PROBABILITIES * USE -
         INVENTORY CONTROL * TIMING UNCERTAINTY

YA0818   CROTTY J.R.
         "Specification error in macro models: the influence of policy goals"   Am.
         Econ. Rev., vol.63, 1973, pp.1025-1030.
         SPECIFICATION ERROR - EFFECT OF , CONTROL BIAS * CONTROL THEORY -
         DETERMINISTIC , APPL * DECISION RULES - MACRO * DECISION RULES - FEEDBACK *
         MACRO MODELS - THEORY * DATA - CONTROL BIAS

YA0819   CROUCH R.L.
         "A model of the United Kingdom's monetary sector"   Econometrica, vol.35,
         1967, pp.398-418.
         APPL - MACRO : FLOW OF FUNDS * COMPARATIVE METHODS - ESTIMATION : OLS , 2SLS
         * APPL - MACRO , UK

YA0820   CROUCH R.L.
         "Tobin vs. Keynes on liquidity preference"   Rev. Econ. Stats., vol.53,
         1971, pp.368-371.
         THEORY - LIQUIDITY PREFERENCE * RANDOM WALK - TEST * INTEREST RATE -
         LIQUIDITY PREFERENCE

YA0821   CROWDER M., GROB P.R.
         "A logit model for infectious diseases"   Appl. Stats., vol.24, 1975,
         pp.85-94.
         MARKOV MODELS - APPL : HEALTH * HEALTH - DISEASE , INCIDENCE OF * REGRESSION
         - LIMITED DEPENDENT , LOGIT : APPL * MARKOV MODELS - METHODOLOGY

YA0822 CROWER R.T.
"Statistical vs. judgement and audience considerations in the formulation
and use of econometric models"   Am. J. Ag. Econ., vol.54, 1972,
pp.779-783.
USER REQUIREMENTS * APPL - SECTOR : COMMODITIES , LIVESTOCK , CHICKENS * EX
ANTE * COMBINING FORECASTS - CAUSAL , JUDGEMENTAL * JUDGEMENTAL FORECASTS -
INCORPORATION * EVALUATION - JUDGEMENTAL FORECASTS

YA0823 CROWSTON W.B., HAUSMAN W.H., KAMPE W.R.
"Multi stage production for stochastic seasonal demand"   Mgmt. Sci. (B),
vol.19, 1973, pp.924-935.
SEASONALITY - SINGLE SEASON * BAYESIAN - FORECASTING * USE - PRODUCTION ,
CONTROL * LP * STYLE GOODS

YA0824 CUBBIN J.
"Quality change and pricing behaviour in the UK car industry 1956-1968"
Economica, vol.42, 1975, pp.43-58.
QUALITY - PRICE * APPL - SECTOR : CONSUMER DURABLES , CARS * PRICE - SECTOR
: CONSUMER DURABLES * APPL - SECTOR : FINANCE , PROFITS * QUALITY -
ADJUSTMENTS

YA0825 CUDDY J.D.A.
"A note on projections of international trade based on coefficients of trade
intensity"   Econ. J., vol.83, 1973, pp.1222-1235.
APPL - MACRO : INTERNATIONAL TRADE * LP

YA0826 CUKIERMAN A.
"A test of expectational processes using information from the capital
markets-the Israeli case"   Int. Econ. Rev., vol.18, 1977, pp.737-753.
INFLATION - EXPECTATIONS * INTEREST RATE - EXPECTATIONS * INFLATION -
INDICATORS * DISTRIBUTED LAG - APPL , EXPECTATIONS HYPOTHESES

YA0827 CUKIERMAN A., BRANSON W.H., KLEUDRICK A.K.
"Money illusion and the aggregate consumption function: comment"   Am.
Econ. Rev., vol.62, 1972, pp.198-210.
APPL - MACRO : CONSUMPTION

YA0828 CULLISON W.E.
"An employment pressure index as an alternative measure of labor market
conditions"   Rev. Econ. Stats., vol.57, 1975, pp.115-121.
APPL - MACRO : UNEMPLOYMENT * APPL - MACRO : CAPACITY UTILISATION * INDEX
NUMBERS - MACRO : EMPLOYMENT

YA0829 CUMMING P.D., ET AL.
"A collections planning model for regional blood suppliers: description and
validation"   Mgmt. Sci, vol.22, 1976, pp.962-971.
USER - SECTOR : HEALTH * HEALTH - BLOOD AVAILABILITY * USE - SCHEDULING ,
MATERIALS SUPPLY * MARKOV MODELS - APPL : HEALTH * SIMULATION - APPL :
SECTOR , HEALTH

YA0830 CUNNINGHAM S.W.
"The predictability of British stock market prices"   Appl. Stats., vol.22,
1973, pp.315-331.
APPL - FIRM : FINANCE , STOCK PRICES * RANDOM WALK - TEST * STOCK PRICES -
BETA , VARIABLE * TIME SERIES - ARIMA : APPL

YA0831 CUNNINGHAM W.H., ANDERSON W.T., MURPHY J.H.
"Are students real people?"   J. Business, vol.47, 1974, pp.399-409.
SURVEYS - CONSUMER , RESPONSE ERROR * EVALUATION - SURVEYS , CONSUMER

YA0832 CUNNINGHAM W.H., CRISSY W.J.E.
"Market segmentation by motivation and attitudes"   J. Mktg. Res., vol.9,
1972, pp.100-102.
MARKET SEGMENTATION * CONSUMER BEHAVIOUR - PURCHASING , DETERMINANTS *
FACTOR ANALYSIS - APPL

YA0833 CURHAN R.C.
"The relationship between shelf space and unit sales in supermarkets"   J.
Mktg. Res., vol.9, 1972, pp.406-412.
USER - FIRM : RETAILING * USE - RETAIL , DISPLAY * APPL - SECTOR : CONSUMER
NON DURABLES , GROCERIES * APPL - FIRM : RETAILING , SUPERMARKETS

YA0834 CURTIS F.J., ET AL.
"Competitive bidding: viewpoint"   Opl. Res. Q., vol.25, 1974, pp.179-183.
JUDGEMENTAL FORECASTS - APPL * USE - COMPETITIVE BIDDING

YA0835 DA VANZO J.
"Does unemployment affect migration? - evidence from micro data"   Rev.
Econ. Stats., vol.60, 1978, pp.504-514.
POPULATION - MIGRATION * REGIONAL MODELS - MANPOWER PLANNING , MIGRATION *
MANPOWER PLANNING - REGIONAL - INCOME - EFFECT OF

YA0836 DA VANZO J., DE TRAY D.N., GREENBERG D.H.
"The sensitivity of male labor supply estimates to choice of assumption"
Rev. Econ. Stats., vol.53, 1976, pp.313-325.
MANPOWER PLANNING - MACRO , SUPPLY * DATA - CROSS SECTION * DATA -
SPECIFICATION OF VARIABLES * DATA ERRORS - EFFECT OF * INCOME - EFFECT OF

YA0837 DACY D.C.
"Productivity and price trends in construction since 1947"   Rev. Econ.
Stats., vol.47, 1965, pp.406-411.
APPL - SECTOR : CONSTRUCTION * APPL - SECTOR : PRODUCTIVITY * INDEX NUMBERS
- METHODOLOGY * INDEX NUMBERS - SECTOR : CONSTRUCTION

YA0838   DAGENAIS M.G.
"Application of a threshold regression model to household purchases of automobiles"   Rev. Econ. Stats., vol.57, 1975, pp.275-285.
REGRESSION - THRESHOLD * APPL - SECTOR : CONSUMER DURABLES , CARS *
COMPARATIVE METHODS - REGRESSION , LIMITED DEPENDENT * REGRESSION - LIMITED
DEPENDENT * INCOME - EFFECT OF

YA0839   DAGENAIS M.G.
"Further suggestions concerning the utilization of incomplete observations in regression analysis"   J. Am. Statist. Ass., vol.66, 1971, pp.93-98.
DATA ERRORS - MISSING OBSERVATIONS

YA0840   DAGENAIS M.G.
"Incomplete observations and simultaneous equations models"   J. Econometrics, vol.4, 1976, pp.231-241.
DATA ERRORS - MISSING OBSERVATIONS * SIMULTANEOUS SYSTEM - ESTIMATION

YA0841   DAGENAIS M.G.
"The computation of FIML estimates as iterative generalised least squares estimates in linear and non linear simultaneous equations models"
Econometrica, vol.46, 1978, pp.1351-1362.
NUMERICAL METHODS - EQUATION SOLUTION * ESTIMATION - FIML * ESTIMATION - GLS
, ITERATIVE * SIMULTANEOUS SYSTEM - ESTIMATION * SIMULTANEOUS SYSTEM - NON
LINEAR

YA0842   DAGENAIS M.G.
"The determination of newsprint prices"   Can. J. Econ., vol.9 1976, pp.442-461.
APPL - SECTOR : PRODUCTION , PAPER * PRICE - SECTOR : PRODUCTION *
REGRESSION - THRESHOLD * COMPARATIVE METHODS - REGRESSION , THRESHOLD

YA0843   DAGENAIS M.G.
"The use of incomplete observations in multiple regression analysis: a generalised least squares approach"   J. Econometrics, vol.1, 1973, pp.317-328.
DATA ERRORS - MISSING OBSERVATIONS * DATA - SIMULATION * ESTIMATION - GLS

YA0844   DAGENAIS M.G.
"Un modele annuel de prevision pour l'economie du Quebec"   Can. J. Econ., vol.6, 1973, pp.62-78.
APPL - MACRO , CANADA * REGIONAL MODELS * EX ANTE * SIMULATION - APPL :
REGIONAL MODEL

YA0845   DAGUM E.B.
"Modelling, forecasting and seasonally adjusting economic time series with the X-11 ARIMA method"   Stat'n., vol.27, 1978, pp.203-216.
SEASONALITY - ESTIMATION , CENSUS * TIME SERIES - ARIMA : APPL

YA0846   DAINTON F., ET AL.
"Comments on 'How the University Grants Committee determines allocations of university grants - a curious correlation'"   R. Statist. Soc. (A), vol.140, 1977, pp.199-209.
DECISION RULES - SECTOR * APPL - SECTOR : GOVERNMENT , EDUCATION ,
UNIVERSITIES * REGRESSION - MODEL INTERPRETATION * REGRESSION - SPURIOUS
CORRELATION

YA0847   DALRYMPLE D.J.
"Estimating price and markup elasticity for advertised clothing products"
J. Advtg. Res., vol.8:4,1968, pp.21-25.
PRICE - EFFECT OF * APPL - FIRM : RETAILING * USE - PRICING * ADVERTISING -
EFFECT OF

YA0848   DALRYMPLE D.J.
"Sales forecasting methods and accuracy"   Business Horizon, vol.18, Dec, 1975, pp.69-73.
FORECASTING - USAGE * FORECASTING - ACCURACY * EVALUATION - SALES FORECASTS
* BASIC

YA0849   DALRYMPLE D.J., HAINES G.H.
"A study of the predictive ability of market period demand-supply relations for a firm selling fashion products"   Appl. Econ., vol.1, 1970, pp.277-285.
APPL - SECTOR : CONSUMER DURABLES , CLOTHING * STYLE GOODS * COMPARATIVE
METHODS - ESTIMATION : OLS , 2SLS * COMPARATIVE METHODS - AUTOREGRESSIVE ,
CAUSAL(SIMULTANEOUS SYSTEM) * COMPARATIVE METHODS - SIMULTANEOUS SYSTEM ,
TRANSFORMATIONS

YA0850   DALTON J.A.
"Administered inflation and business pricing: another look"   Rev. Econ. Stats., vol.55, 1973, pp.516-519.
CONCENTRATION - EFFECT OF * DATA - CROSS SECTION * PRICE - SECTOR *
VOLATILITY - EFFECT OF * STABILITY OF COEFFICIENTS - REGRESSION : APPL

YA0851   DANCER R., GRAY C.
"An empirical evaluation of constant and adaptive computer forecasting models for inventory control"   Decis. Sci., vol.8, 1977, pp.228-238.
COMPARATIVE METHODS - EXPONENTIAL SMOOTHING , ADAPTIVE * APPL - SECTOR :
CONSUMER NON DURABLES , LIQUOR * EX ANTE

YA0852   DANIEL D.L., LONGBRAKE W.A., MURPHY N.B.
"The effect of technology on bank economies of scale for demand deposits"
J. Finance, vol.28, 1973, pp.131-146.
APPL - FIRM : FINANCE , BANKS * COST - SECTOR : FINANCE , BANKS * COST -
SCALE ECONOMIES * APPL - FIRM : FINANCE , BANK , LIABILITIES * TECHNOLOGY -
EFFECT OF

YA0853   DANIELSEN A.L., LEE C.F.
          "Specifying the demand equations for crude oil, coal, and natural gas'
          Appl. Econ., vol.8, 1976, pp.229-230.
          APPL - MACRO : ENERGY * PRICE - EFFECT OF * APPL - SECTOR : PRODUCTION ,
          COAL * APPL - SECTOR : COMMODITIES , OIL * APPL - SECTOR : UTILITIES , GAS

YA0854   DARBY M.R.
          "Postwar US consumption, consumer expenditures, and saving" with discussion
          Am. Econ. Ass. Proc., 1975, pp.217-224.
          APPL - MACRO : CONSUMPTION * INCOME - EFFECT OF

YA0855   DARBY M.R.
          "The allocation of transitory income among consumers' assets"   Am. Econ.
          Rev., vol.62, 1972, pp.928-941.
          APPL - MACRO : MONEY , DEMAND * APPL - SECTOR : CONSUMER DURABLES * APPL -
          MACRO : CONSUMPTION * THEORY - PERMANENT INCOME * INCOME - EFFECT OF ,
          PERMANENT

YA0856   D'ARGE R.
          "Note on customs unions and direct foreign investment" with corrections
          Econ. J., vol.79, 1969, pp.324-333, and vol.81, 1971, pp.352-355.
          APPL - MACRO : INTERNATIONAL FINANCE * APPL - MACRO : INVESTMENT ,
          INTERNATIONAL * APPL - MACRO , EEC

YA0857   DARMON R.Y.
          "Alternative models of salesmen's response to financial incentives"   Opl.
          Res. Q., vol.28, 1977, pp.37-49.
          USE - SALES FORCE MANAGEMENT * FORECASTER BEHAVIOUR

YA0858   DARMON R.Y.
          "Determinants of TV viewing"   J. Advtg. Res., vol.16:6, 1976, pp.17-20.
          APPL - FIRM : SERVICES , MEDIA , TV * REPEAT BUYING * BRAND CHOICE -
          DETERMINANTS

YA0859   DARMON R.Y.
          "Salesmen, response to financial incentives: an empirical study"   J. Mktg.
          Res., vol.11, 1974, pp.418-426.
          USE - TARGET SETTING * FORECASTER - INCENTIVE

YA0860   DARROUGH M.N.
          "A model of consumption and leisure in an intertemporal framework: a
          systematic treatment using Japanese data"   Int. Econ. Rev., vol.18, 1977,
          pp.677-696.
          APPL - MACRO , JAPAN * APPL - MACRO : CONSUMER DEMAND * DEMAND EQUATIONS -
          SYSTEMS OF

YA0861   DAS GUPTA P.
          "Age-parity-nuptiality specific stable population model that recognizes
          births to single women"   J. Am. Statist. Ass., vol.71, 1976, pp.308-314.
          POPULATION - MARRIAGE * PROBABILITY MODELS - BIRTH PROCESS

YA0862   DAUB M.
          "A comparison of the accuracy of Canadian short-term predictions of GNP"
          J. Business, vol.47, 1974, pp.173-185.
          EVALUATION - JUDGEMENTAL FORECASTS , MACRO * EVALUATION - MACRO FORECASTS *
          DATA - INTERNATIONAL * EX ANTE

YA0863   DAUB M.
          "An examination of the nature of errors in aggregate economic predictions"
          Rev. Econ. Stats., vol.59, 1977, pp.230-233.
          EVALUATION - MACRO FORECASTS

YA0864   DAUB M.
          "An international comparison of the accuracy of Canadian short-term
          predictors of gross national product"   Appl. Econ., vol.7, 1975,
          pp.235-240.
          EVALUATION - JUDGEMENTAL FORECASTS , MACRO * JUDGEMENTAL FORECASTS -
          SPECIALIST * DATA - INTERNATIONAL * APPL - MACRO , UK * APPL - MACRO ,
          CANADA

YA0865   DAUB M.
          "On the accuracy of Canadian short term economic forecasts"   Can. J.
          Econ., vol.6, 1973, pp.90-107.
          COMPARATIVE METHODS - ARIMA , JUDGEMENTAL * COMPARATIVE METHODS -
          AUTOREGRESSIVE , JUDGEMENTAL * EVALUATION - JUDGEMENTAL FORECASTS , MACRO *
          MACRO MODEL - CANADA * EX ANTE * EVALUATION - MACRO FORECASTS

YA0866   DAUB M.
          "On the cost to the firm of aggregate prediction errors"   J. Business,
          vol.47, 1974, pp.11-22.
          LOSS FUNCTIONS - FIRM * APPL - FIRM : PRODUCTION , STEEL * USER - FIRM :
          PRODUCTION * COMPARATIVE METHODS - AUTOREGRESSIVE , JUDGEMENTAL *
          FORECASTING - VALUE OF

YA0867   DAVENPORT M.
          "Leverage and the cost of capital: some tests using British data"
          Economica, vol.38, 1971, pp.136-162.
          APPL - SECTOR : FINANCE , FINANCIAL STRUCTURE , LEVERAGE

YA0868   DAVID M.
          "Measurement of the cost of living including the public sector"   Anns.
          Econ. Soc. Meas., vol.4, 1975, pp.133-152.
          INDEX NUMBERS - MACRO : CONSUMER PRICE * INDEX NUMBERS - METHODOLOGY

YA0869 DAVID P.A.
        "Just how misleading are official exchange rate conversions"   Econ. J.,
        vol.82, 1972, pp.979-990,
        APPL - MACRO : INTERNATIONAL FINANCE , EXCHANGE RATES * DATA - LDC

YA0870 DAVIDSON J.D.
        "Forecasting traffic on STOL"   Opl. Res. Q., vol.24, 1973, pp.561-569,
        APPL - SECTOR : TRANSPORT , AIR * USER - FIRM : TRANSPORT * DATA - CROSS
        SECTION * REGIONAL MODELS - SECTOR : TRANSPORT

YA0871 DAVIDSON J.E.H., ET AL.
        "Econometric modelling of the aggregate time-series relationship between
        consumers' expenditure and income in the UK   Econ. J., vol.88, 1978,
        pp.661-691.
        COMPARATIVE METHODS - ESTIMATION : SIMULTANEOUS SYSTEM * APPL - MACRO :
        CONSUMPTION * APPL - MACRO , UK * INCOME - EFFECT OF * EVALUATION -
        CONSUMPTION MODELS * EX ANTE - INFLATION - EFFECT OF * EVALUATION - EX POST
        MODELS * DATA ERRORS - EFFECT OF * STATIONARITY - TRANSFORMING TO *
        REGRESSION - MODEL CHOICE

YA0872 DAVIDSON P., FALK L.H., LEE H.
        "Oil: its time allocation and project independence" with discussion
        Brookings Paps. Econ. Activity, 1974, pp.411-448 & 479-493,
        APPL - SECTOR : PRODUCTION , PETROLEUM * SUPPLY - SECTOR : PRODUCTION * APPL
        - SECTOR : COMMODITIES , OIL

YA0873 DAVIES G.W.
        "A model of the urban residential land and housing markets"   Can. J.
        Econ., vol.10, 1977, pp.393-410,
        REGIONAL MODELS - SECTOR : CONSTRUCTION * APPL - SECTOR : CONSTRUCTION ,
        LAND * APPL - SECTOR : CONSTRUCTION , RESIDENTIAL * PRICE - SECTOR :
        CONSTRUCTION , RESIDENTIAL * PRICE - SECTOR : CONSTRUCTION , LAND * POLICY
        EVALUATION - SECTOR : CONSTRUCTRUCTION * SIMULATION - APPL : POLICY
        EVALUATION

YA0874 DAVIES P.L., CANES M.
        "Stock prices and the publication of second-hand information"   J.
        Business, vol.51, 1978, pp.43-56,
        APPL - FIRM : FINANCE , STOCK PRICES * STOCK PRICES - INFORMATION EFFECT *
        APPL - FIRM : FINANCE , STOCK BROKERS

YA0875 DAVIES R., JOHNSON D., FARROWS S.
        "Planning patient care with a Markov model"   Opl. Res. Q., vol.26, 1975,
        pp.599-607,
        HEALTH - HOSPITAL , PATIENT FACILITIES * MARKOV MODELS - APPL : HEALTH *
        USER - FIRM : HEALTH , HOSPITAL * USE - PRODUCTION , PLANNING

YA0876 DAVIES R.L.
        "Evaluation of retail store activities and sales performance"   Eur. J.
        Mktg., vol.7, 1973, pp.89-102,
        USE - SITE SELECTION , RETAIL * USE - RETAIL , SITE MONITORING * FACTOR
        ANALYSIS - APPL * MARKET POTENTIAL * APPL - FIRM : RETAILING

YA0877 DAVIES S.W.
        "The clay brick industry and the tunnel kiln industry"   Nat. Inst. Econ.
        Rev., no.58, 1971, pp.54-71,
        APPL - SECTOR : PRODUCTION , CONSTRUCTION MATERIALS * APPL - SECTOR :
        PRODUCTION , PLANT * DIFFUSION MODEL * PRICE - SECTOR : PRODUCTION

YA0878 DAVIES S.W., SCOTT T.W.K.
        "Forecasting industrial production"   Nat. Inst. Econ. Rev., no.66, 1973,
        pp.54-68 & no.69, 1974, pp.27-28,
        APPL - SECTOR : PRODUCTION * COMPARATIVE METHODS - AUTOREGRESSIVE , CAUSAL *
        EX ANTE * EVALUATION - TURNING POINT FORECASTS * STABILITY OF COEFFICIENTS -
        REGRESSION : APPL

YA0879 DAVIS B.E., CACCAPPOLO G.J., CHAUDRY M.A.
        "An econometric planning model for American Telephone & Telegraph Co."
        Bell J. Econ., vol.4, 1973, pp.29-56,
        SIMULATION - APPL : FIRM * APPL - FIRM : UTILITIES , TELEPHONE * SIMULATION
        - APPL : FINANCE * EX ANTE

YA0880 DAVIS E.G., DUNN D.M., WILLIAMS W.H.
        "Ambiguities in the cross-section analysis of pe share financial data"   J.
        Finance, vol.28, 1973, pp.1241-1248,
        APPL - FIRM : FINANCE , PROFITS , PER SHARE * APPL - FIRM : FINANCE , PE
        RATIO * DATA - TRANSFORMED , DEFLATED * DATA - SPECIFICATION OF VARIABLES *
        DATA - CROSS SECTION

YA0881 DAVIS K.
        "Relationship of hospital prices to costs"   Appl. Econ., vol.3, 1971,
        pp.115-125,
        COST - SECTOR : HEALTH * HEALTH - HOSPITAL , FINANCE * PRICE - SECTOR :
        HEALTH

YA0882 DAVIS K., RUSSELL L.B.
        "The substitution of hospital out-patient care for in-patient care"   Rev.
        Econ. Stats., vol.54, 1972, pp.109-120,
        HEALTH - HOSPITAL , PATIENT FACILITIES * SUBSTITUTE PRODUCTS * PRICE -
        EFFECT OF * COST - SECTOR : HEALTH

YA0883 DAWES R.M., CORRIGAN B.
        "Linear models in decision making"   Psychological Bull., vol.81, 1974,
        pp.95-106.
        EVALUATION - BOOTSTRAPPING * EVALUATION - JUDGEMENTAL FORECASTS *
        COMPARATIVE METHODS - BOOTSTRAPPING , JUDGEMENTAL

YA0884 DAWSON D.A.
        "Economies of scale in the Ontario public secondary schools"   Can. J.
        Econ., vol.5, 1972, pp.306-309.
        COST - SECTOR : EDUCATION * APPL - SECTOR : GOVERNMENT , EDUCATION , SCHOOLS
        * COST - SCALE ECONOMIES * APPL - SECTOR : EDUCATION , SCHOOLS

YA0885 DEACON R.T.
        "A demand model for the local public sector"   Rev. Econ. Stats., vol.60,
        1978, pp.184-192.
        DEMAND EQUATIONS - SYSTEMS OF * CONSUMER BEHAVIOUR - ECONOMIC MODELS ,
        THEORY * APPL - SECTOR : GOVERNMENT , LOCAL , SERVICES * PRICE - EFFECT OF *
        INCOME - EFFECT OF

YA0886 DEAKIN E.B.
        "A discriminant analysis of predictors of business failure"   J. Acctg.
        Res., vol.10, 1972, pp.167-179.
        USE - BANKRUPTCY PREDICTION * DISCRIMINANT ANALYSIS - APPL * EX ANTE

YA0887 DEAKIN E.B.
        "Accounting reports, policy interactions and the behaviour of securities
        returns"   Acctg. Rev., vol.51, 1976, pp.590-603.
        TIME SERIES - ARIMA : INTERVENTION * APPL - FIRM : FINANCE , STOCK PRICES *
        ACCOUNTING PRACTICE - EFFECT OF * STOCK PRICES - INFORMATION EFFECT

YA0888 DEAN A.J.H.
        Errors in National Institute forecasts of personal incomes, inflation and
        employment, 1965-75"   Nat. Inst. Econ. Rev., no.78, 1976, pp.48-57.
        MACRO MODEL - UK , NIESR * COMPARATIVE METHODS - AUTOREGRESSIVE ,
        CAUSAL(SIMULTANEOUS SYSTEM) * EVALUATION - MACRO MODELS * APPL - MACRO :
        EMPLOYMENT * APPL - MACRO : EARNINGS * EVALUATION - INFLATION MODELS *
        COMPARATIVE METHODS - MACRO MODELS

YA0889 DEANE R.T.
        "An alternative specification for participation rates"   Appl. Econ.,
        vol.9, 1977, pp.1-7.
        MANPOWER PLANNING - LABOUR PARTICIPATION , FEMALE * HEALTH - MANPOWER ,
        NURSES

YA0890 DEATON A.
        "A reconsideration of the empirical implications of additive preference"
        Econ. J., vol.84, 1974, pp.338-348.
        EVALUATION - CONSUMER BEHAVIOUR , ECONOMIC MODELS * DEMAND EQUATIONS -
        SYSTEMS OF , THEORY * CONSUMER BEHAVIOUR - ECONOMIC MODELS , THEORY *
        ADVANCED

YA0891 DEATON A.
        "Involuntary saving through unanticipated inflation"   Am. Econ. Rev.,
        vol.67, 1977, pp.899-910.
        DATA - INTERNATIONAL * APPL - MACRO , UK * APPL - MACRO : SAVINGS *
        COMPARATIVE METHODS - REGRESSION , ERROR SPECIFICATION * INFLATION - EFFECT
        OF

YA0892 DEATON A.
        "Specification and testing in applied demand analysis"   Econ. J., vol.88,
        1978, pp.524-536.
        CONSUMER BEHAVIOUR - ECONOMIC MODELS , THEORY * DEMAND EQUATIONS - SYSTEMS
        OF : METHODOLOGY * DEMAND EQUATIONS - SYSTEMS OF : THEORY * APPL - MACRO :
        CONSUMER DEMAND * APPL - MACRO , UK

YA0893 DEATON A.
        "The analysis of consumer demand in the United Kingdom 1900-1970"
        Econometrica, vol.42, 1974, pp.341-367.
        DEMAND EQUATIONS - SYSTEMS OF * COMPARATIVE METHODS - DEMAND EQUATIONS *
        APPL - MACRO : CONSUMER DEMAND * APPL - MACRO , UK

YA0894 DEATON A.
        "Wealth effects on consumption in a modified life-cycle model"   Rev. Econ.
        Studies, vol.39, 1972, pp.443-453.
        WEALTH - EFFECT OF * APPL - MACRO , UK * APPL - MACRO : CONSUMPTION * STOCK
        PRICES - EFFECT OF

YA0895 DE GRAUWE P., KOSOBUD R.F., O'NEILL W.D.
        "A cross-section model of economic growth: a comment" with discussion
        Rev. Econ. Stats., vol.54, 1972, pp.466-470.
        DATA - CROSS SECTION * APPL - MACRO : GROWTH * REGRESSION - MODEL CHOICE *
        APPL - MACRO : INVESTMENT * POPULATION

YA0896 DEHAYES D.W.
        "The analysis of rail transport performance characteristics"   Decis. Sci.,
        vol.2, 1971, pp.284-299.
        APPL - SECTOR : TRANSPORT , RAIL * TIMING UNCERTAINTY

YA0897 DELANEY J.B., HONEYCUTT T.C.
        "Determinants of research and development activity by electric utilities:
        comment   Bell J. Econ., vol.7, 1976, pp.722-725.
        APPL - FIRM : R & D * APPL - FIRM : UTILITIES , ELECTRICITY * DATA - CROSS
        SECTION

YA0898　DE LA VALLEE POUSSIN D., SAROFIM N.S.
"Leading indicators: a tool for corporate forecasting"　Sloan Mgmt. Rev.,
vol.14, no.3, 1973, pp.47-65.
APPL - FIRM : PRODUCTION ★ APPL - SECTOR : CONSUMER DURABLES , CARS ★ APPL -
SECTOR : PRODUCTION , STEEL ★ BUSINESS INDICATORS - APPL ★ STABILITY OF
COEFFICIENTS - REGRESSION , TEST ★ BASIC

YA0899　DE LEEUW F.
"The demand for housing: a review of cross-section evidence"　Rev. Econ.
Stats., vol.53, 1971, pp.1-10.
DATA - CROSS SECTION ★ APPL - SECTOR : CONSTRUCTION , RESIDENTIAL ★ INCOME -
EFFECT OF ★ DATA - GROUPED ★ PRICE - EFFECT OF

YA0900　DE LEEUW F., EKANEM N.F.
"The supply of rental housing"　Am. Econ. Rev., vol.61, 1971, pp.806-817.
APPL - SECTOR : CONSTRUCTION , RESIDENTIAL ★ DATA - CROSS SECTION

YA0901　DE MENIL G.
"Aggregate price dynamics"　Rev. Econ. Stats., vol.56, 1974, pp.129-148.
PRICE - MACRO - INFLATION - DETERMINANTS

YA0902　DE MENIL G., BHALLA S.S.
"Direct mearurement of popular price expectations"　Am. Econ. Rev.,
vol.65, 1975, pp.169-180.
EXPECTATIONS - ESTIMATING ★ INFLATION - EXPECTATIONS ★ EXPECTATIONS - DATA ★
EVALUATION - EARNINGS MODELS ★ APPL - MACRO : EARNINGS

YA0903　DEMERY D., DUCK N.W.
"The behaviour of nominal interest rates in the UK, 1961-1973"　Economica,
vol.45, 1978, pp.23-37.
INTEREST RATE - DETERMINANTS ★ INFLATION - EFFECT OF ★ COMPARATIVE METHODS -
REGRESSION , ERROR SPECIFICATION ★ ERROR SPECIFICATION - AUTOCORRELATED ★
INFLATION - EXPECTATIONS

YA0904　DEMPSTER A.P., SCHATZOFF M., WERMUTH N.
"A simulation study of alternatives to OLS" with discussion　J. Am.
Statist. Ass., vol. 72, 1977, pp.77-106.
COMPARATIVE METHODS - ESTIMATION : REGRESSION ★ COMPARATIVE METHODS -
ESTIMATION : OLS , RIDGE ★ ESTIMATION - STEIN ★ ESTIMATION - PRINCIPAL
COMPONENTS ★ DATA - SIMULATION ★ REGRESSION - ESTIMATION ★ LOSS FUNCTIONS -
THEORY ★ SIMULATION - METHODOLOGY , MODEL SPECIFICATION

YA0905　DEMSKI J.S., FELTHAM G.A.
"Forecast evaluation"　Acctg. Rev., vol.47, 1972, pp.533-548.
EVALUATION - THEORY OF ★ DATA - SIMULATION ★ EVALUATION - LOSS FUNCTIONS ★
SIMULATION - APPL : FIRM

YA0906　DEN BUTTER F.A.G.
"The use of monthly and quarterly data in an ARIMA model"　J.
Econometrics, vol.4, 1976, pp.311-324.
TIME SERIES - ARIMA : THEORY ★ INTEREST RATE - INDICATORS ★ DATA -
AGGREGATION OVER TIME ★ LEAD TIME - EFFECT OF ★ COMPARATIVE METHODS - DATA :
AGGREGATE , DISAGGREGATE ★ TIME SERIES - ARIMA : FORECASTING

YA0907　DENMAN F.L.
"The reliability of regional interindustry studies"　J. Mktg. Res., vol.3,
1966, pp.350-354.
EVALUATION - INPUT OUTPUT , REGIONAL

YA0908　DENNY M., FUSS M.
"The use of approximation analysis to test for separability and the
existence of consistent aggregates"　Am. Econ. Rev., vol.67, 1977,
pp.404-418.
PRODUCTION FUNCTIONS - METHODOLOGY ★ PRODUCTION FUNCTIONS - MACRO ★ COST -
MACRO ★ PRODUCTION FUNCTIONS - SUBSTITUTION ★ ADVANCED

YA0909　DENNY M., MAY D.
"The existence of a real value-added function in the Canadian manufacturing
sector"　J. Econometrics, vol.5, 1977, pp.55-69.
PRODUCTION FUNCTIONS - THEORY ★ PRODUCTION FUNCTIONS - MACRO ★ COST - THEORY
★ COST - MACRO ★ PRODUCTION FUNCTIONS - SUBSTITUTION ★ SUBSTITUTE FACTORS ★
APPL - MACRO , CANADA

YA0910　DENNY M., MAY J.D., PINTO C.
"The demand for energy in Canadian manufacturing: prologue to an energy
policy"　Can. J. Econ., vol.11, 1978, pp.300-313.
APPL - MACRO , CANADA ★ APPL - MACRO : ENERGY ★ APPL - MACRO : EMPLOYMENT ★
PRODUCTION FUNCTIONS - SUBSTITUTION ★ PRODUCTION FUNCTIONS - MACRO ★ PRICE -
EFFECT OF ★ APPL - MACRO : INVESTMENT

YA0911　DENT W.
"A note on Lipstein's model of consumer behaviour"　Ops. Res., vol.21,
1973, pp.650-652.
MARKOV MODELS - ESTIMATION ★ CONSUMER BEHAVIOUR - STOCHASTIC MODELS ,
ESTIMATION

YA0912　DENT W.T.
"On numerical computation in simultaneous equation systems"　Anns. Econ.
Soc. Meas., vol.6, 1977, pp.123-125.
COMPUTERISATION - ESTIMATION , SIMULTANEOUS SYSTEM MODELS , PROGRAMS ★
NUMERICAL METHODS - EQUATION SOLUTION

YA0913   DENT W.T., CASSING J.
"On Durbin's and Sims' residuals in autocorrelation tests"   Econometrica,
vol.46, 1978, pp.1489-1492.
COMPARATIVE METHODS - TESTS , AUTOCORRELATION * RESIDUALS - ANALYSIS OF ,
AUTOCORRELATION

YA0914   DENT W.T., ET AL.
"More on computational accuracy in regression" with discussion   J. Am.
Statist. Ass., vol.72, 1977, pp.598-603.
COMPUTERISATION - CALCULATION ERROR * NUMERICAL METHODS - CALCULATION ERROR
* EVALUATION - THEORY OF * COMPUTERISATION - ESTIMATION , REGRESSION MODELS

YA0915   DENT W.T., HILDRETH C.
"Maximum likelihood estimation in random coefficient models"   J. Am.
Statist. Ass., vol.72, 1977, pp.69-72.
REGRESSION - RANDOM COEFFICIENTS * COMPARATIVE METHODS - ESTIMATION :
REGRESSION , RANDOM COEFFICIENTS * DATA - SIMULATION * ESTIMATION - MAXIMUM
LIKELIHOOD

YA0916   DENT W.T., MIN A.
"A Monte Carlo study of autoregressive integrated moving average processes"
J. Econometrics, vol.7, 1978, pp.23-55.
TIME SERIES - ARIMA : ESTIMATION * COMPARATIVE METHODS - ESTIMATION : TIME
SERIES * DATA - SIMULATION * ESTIMATION - MAXIMUM LIKELIHOOD * ESTIMATION -
NON LINEAR

YA0917   DENT W.T., STYAN G.P.H.
"Uncorrelated residuals from linear models"   J. Econometrics, vol.7, 1978,
pp.211-225.
RESIDUALS - ESTIMATION , UNCORRELATED * RESIDUALS - COMPARATIVE ANALYSIS OF
* COMPARATIVE METHODS - TESTS , AUTOCORRELATION

YA0918   DENT W.T., SWANSON J.A.
"Forecasting with limited information: ARIMA models of the trailer on
flatcar transportation market"   J. Am. Statist. Ass., vol.73, 1978,
pp.293-299.
TIME SERIES - ARIMA : REVIEW * EX ANTE * APPL - SECTOR : TRANSPORT , RAIL ,
FREIGHT * TURNING POINTS - APPL * COMPARATIVE METHODS - ARIMA ,
DECOMPOSITION * COMPARATIVE METHODS - ARIMA , AUTOREGRESSIVE

YA0919   DENTON F.T.
"A simulation model of month-to-month labor force movement in Canada"
Int. Econ. Rev., vol.14, 1973, pp.293-311.
REGRESSION - LIMITED DEPENDENT , LOGIT : APPL * MANPOWER PLANNING - LABOUR
PARTICIPATION * SIMULATION - APPL : MACRO , MANPOWER PLANNING * MARKOV
MODELS - APPL : MANPOWER * APPL - MACRO , CANADA

YA0920   DENTON F.T.
"Adjustment of monthly or quarterly series to annual totals: an approach
based on quadratic minimization"   J. Am. Statist. Ass., vol.66, 1971,
pp.99-102.
DATA - INTERPOLATION

YA0921   DENTON F.T., KUIPER J.
"The effect of measurement errors on parameter estimates and forecasts: a
case study based on the Canadian preliminary national accounts"   Rev.
Econ. Stats., vol.47, 1965, pp.198-206.
DATA ERRORS - EFFECT OF * DATA ERRORS - NATIONAL ACCOUNTS , CANADA * MACRO
MODEL - CANADA * FORECAST - REVISION * DATA REVISIONS - EFFECT OF *
COMPARATIVE METHODS - ESTIMATION : OLS , 2SLS * EX ANTE

YA0922   DENTON F.T., OKSANEN E.H.
"A multi country analysis of the effects of data revisions on an econometric
model"   J. Am. Statist. Ass., vol.67, 1972, pp.286-291.
EVALUATION - MACRO MODELS * DATA REVISIONS - EFFECT OF * DATA -
INTERNATIONAL

YA0923   DENTON F.T., OKSANEN E.H.
"Measurement error and choice of econometric method: some empirical
findings"   Int. Statist. Rev., vol.41, 1973, pp.343-349.
DATA ERRORS - EFFECT OF * COMPARATIVE METHODS - ESTIMATION : OLS , 2SLS *
COMPARATIVE METHODS - ESTIMATION : OLS , 3SLS * COMPARATIVE METHODS -
ESTIMATION : SIMULTANEOUS SYSTEM , 2SLS , 3SLS * COMPARATIVE METHODS - DATA
ERRORS : ESTIMATION * DATA - INTERNATIONAL

YA0924   DENTON F.T., SPENCER B.G.
"Health care costs when the population changes"   Can. J. Econ., vol.7,
1974, pp.34-48.
POPULATION - EFFECT OF , DISTRIBUTION * COST - SECTOR : HEALTH * HEALTH -
SERVICES * SIMULATION - APPL : SECTOR , HEALTH

YA0925   DENTON F.T., SPENCER B.G.
"Household and population effects an aggregate consumption"   Rev. Econ.
Stats., vol.58, 1976, pp.86-95.
APPL - MACRO , CANADA * APPL - MACRO : CONSUMPTION * CONSUMER BEHAVIOUR -
ECONOMIC MODELS , THEORY * APPL - MACRO , OECD * REGRESSION - SPECIFICATION
OF VARIABLES * POPULATION - EFFECT OF

YA0926   DEPAMPHILIS D.M.
"Forecasting expenditure on consumer durable goods"   Bus. Econ., vol.9:3,
1974, pp.56-59.
APPL - SECTOR : CONSUMER DURABLES * EX ANTE

YA0927 DEPAMPHILIS D.M.
        "Forecasting medical care expenses"   Bus. Econ., vol.11:4, 1976, pp.21=31.
        HEALTH = SERVICES * USER = FIRM : FINANCE = PRICE = SECTOR : HEALTH *
        STABILITY OF COEFFICIENTS = REGRESSION , TEST : APPL * HEALTH = HOSPITAL

YA0928 DEPAMPHILIS D.M.
        "Long term interest rates and the anticipated rate of inflation"   Bus.
        Econ., vol.10:3, 1975, pp.11=18.
        INFLATION = EXPECTATIONS * INFLATION = EFFECT OF * INTEREST RATE =
        DETERMINANTS

YA0929 DEPAMPHILIS D.M.
        "The dynamics of household formation"   Bus. Econ., vol.12:3, 1977,
        pp.18=21.
        POPULATION = HOUSEHOLD FORMATIONS * LIFE CYCLE = FAMILY

YA0930 DEPPLER M.C., ADLER M.
        "Elasticities of demand for US exports: comments"   Rev. Econ. Stats.,
        vol.53, 1971, pp.201=204.
        APPL = MACRO : INTERNATIONAL TRADE , EXPORTS

YA0931 DESAI M.
        "Pooling as a specification error = a note"   Econometrica, vol.42, 1974,
        pp.389=391.
        DATA = CROSS SECTION , TIME SERIES * SPECIFICATION ERROR = TESTS , DATA
        SOURCES * APPL = SECTOR : CONSUMER NON DURABLES , FOOD * COMPARATIVE METHODS
        = REGRESSION , TRANSFORMATIONS

YA0932 DESAI M.
        "The Phillips curve: a revisionist interpretation"   Economica, vol.42,
        1975, pp.1=19.
        INFLATION = PHILLIPS * APPL = MACRO : EARNINGS * STABILITY OF COEFFICIENTS =
        REGRESSION : APPL * REGRESSION = MODEL CHOICE

YA0933 DESAI P.
        "The production function and technical change in postwar Soviet industry: a
        reexamination"   Am. Econ. Rev., vol.66, 1976, pp.372=381.
        APPL = MACRO , USSR * PRODUCTION FUNCTIONS = MACRO * TECHNOLOGY = EFFECT OF

YA0934 DE SALVO A.
        "Cash management converts dollars into working assets"   H.B.R., vol.50,
        May=June, 1972, pp.92=100.
        USE = CASH CONTROL * BASIC

YA0935 DE VANEY A.S.
        "The effect of price and entry regulation on airline output, capacity and
        efficiency"   Bell J. Econ., vol.6, 1975, pp.327=345.
        APPL = SECTOR : TRANSPORT , AIR * USE = FINANCIAL , REGULATION * PRICE =
        EFFECT OF * SUPPLY = SECTOR : TRANSPORT

YA0936 DE VANEY A.S.
        "The revealed value of time in air travel"   Rev. Econ. Stats., vol.56,
        1974, pp.77=82.
        TIME = VALUE OF * APPL = SECTOR : TRANSPORT , AIR * PRICE = EFFECT OF *
        DEMAND EQUATIONS = SYSTEMS OF * CONSUMER BEHAVIOUR = ECONOMIC MODELS

YA0937 DHALLA N.K.
        "How to set advertising budgets"   J. Advtg. Res., vol.17:5, 1977,
        pp.11=17.
        ADVERTISING = EFFECT OF * USE = MARKETING POLICY * ADVERTISING =
        EXPERIMENTAL DESIGN * BASIC

YA0938 DHALLA N.K., YUSPEH S.
        "Forget the product life cycle concept"   H.B.R., vol.54, Jan=Feb, 1976,
        pp.102=112 & Mar=April, pp.148ff.
        EVALUATION = PRODUCT LIFE CYCLE * BRAND CHOICE = DETERMINANTS * APPL =
        SECTOR : CONSUMER NON DURABLES * CONSUMER BEHAVIOUR = PURCHASING ,
        DETERMINANTS

YA0939 DHRYMES P.J., ET AL.
        "Criteria for evaluation of econometric models"   Anns. Econ. Soc. Meas.,
        vol.1, 1972, pp.291=324.
        COMPARATIVE METHODS = MACRO MODELS * EVALUATION = THEORY OF * LOSS FUNCTIONS
        = THEORY * MODEL SELECTION * SPECIFICATION ERROR = TESTS , CONSTRAINTS * EX
        ANTE * REGRESSION = MODEL CHOICE * TRACKING SIGNAL = APPL * STABILITY OF
        COEFFICIENTS = SIMULTANEOUS SYSTEM , TEST * SPECTRAL ANALYSIS = APPL :
        SIMULATION EVALUATION * SPECIFICATION ERROR = TESTS , REVIEW * SPECIFICATION
        ERROR=TESTS , MODEL SELECTION * MACRO MODELS = REVIEW * DATA = SAMPLE SIZE

YA0940 DICKINSON J.P.
        "Some comments on the combination of forecasts"   Opl. Res. Q., vol.26,
        1975, pp.205=210.
        COMBINING FORECASTS = THEORY

YA0941 DICKINSON J.P.
        "Some statistical results in the combination of forecasts"   Opl. Res. Q.,
        vol.24, 1973, pp.253=260.
        COMBINING FORECASTS = METHODOLOGY * EVALUATION = COMBINING FORECASTS * APPL
        = SECTOR : UTILITIES

YA0942 DICKSON H.D., STARLEAF D.R.
        "Polynomial distributed lag structures in the demand function for money"
        J. Finance, vol.27, 1972, pp.1035=1043.
        APPL = MACRO : MONEY , DEMAND * DISTRIBUTED LAG = APPL , INTEREST RATE *
        DATA = SPECIFICATION OF VARIABLES * INTEREST RATE = EFFECT OF

YA0943 DIEFFENBACH B.C.
        "A quantitive theory of risk premiums on securities with an application to
        the term structure of interest rates"   Econometrica, vol.43, 1975,
        pp.431=454.
        THEORY = EFFICIENT MARKETS * APPL = SECTOR : FINANCE , BONDS * INTEREST RATE
        = TERM STRUCTURE * INTEREST RATE = LIQUIDITY PREFERENCE

YA0944   DIETRICH J.K., GUTIERREZ A.D.
          "An evaluation of short-term forecasts of coffee and cocoa"   Am. J. Ag.
          Econ., vol.55, 1973, pp.93-99.
          APPL - SECTOR : AGRICULTURE , COFFEE * APPL - SECTOR : AGRICULTURE , COCOA *
          EVALUATION - AGRICULTURAL FORECASTS * EVALUATION - JUDGEMENTAL FORECASTS *
          SUPPLY - SECTOR : AGRICULTURE

YA0945   DIEWERT W.E.
          "Intertemporal consumer theory and the demand for durables"   Econometrica,
          vol.42, 1974, pp.497-516.
          APPL - MACRO : CONSUMER DEMAND * DEMAND EQUATIONS - SYSTEM OF * SUBSTITUTE
          PRODUCTS * CONSUMER BEHAVIOUR - ECONOMIC MODELS , THEORY * WEALTH - EFFECT
          OF * PRICE - EFFECT OF * ADVANCED

YA0946   DILLON W.R., GOLDSTEIN M., SCHIFFMAN L.G.
          "Appropriateness of linear discriminant and multinomial classification
          analysis in marketing research"   J. Mktg. Res., vol.15, 1978, pp.103-112.
          COMPARATIVE METHODS - DISCRIMINATION * DATA - CATEGORICAL * CONSUMER
          BEHAVIOUR - PURCHASING , DETERMINANTS * BIBLIOGRAPHY - DISCRIMINANT ANALYSIS

YA0947   DINGLE J.F., SPARKS G.R., WALKER M.A.
          "Monetary policy and the adjustment of chartered bank assets"   Can. J.
          Econ., vol.5, 1972, pp.494-514.
          APPL - MACRO : MONEY * APPL - SECTOR : FINANCE , BANK , ASSETS * APPL -
          SECTOR : FINANCE , BANKS * POLICY EVALUATION - MACRO : MONETARY

YA0948   DIWAN R.K.
          "Impact of education on labour efficiency"   Appl. Econ., vol.3, 1971,
          pp.127-135.
          APPL - MACRO : EFFICIENCY * PRODUCTION FUNCTIONS - MACRO * EDUCATION -
          EFFECT OF

YA0949   DOBELL A.R., ET AL.
          "Telephone communications in Canada: demand, production and investment
          decisions"   Bell J. Econ., vol.3, 1972, pp.175-219.
          APPL - FIRM : UTILITIES , TELEPHONE * INCOME - EFFECT OF * PRICE - EFFECT OF
          * APPL - FIRM : FINANCE , PROFITS * PRODUCTION FUNCTIONS - FIRM * APPL -
          FIRM : INVESTMENT * DISTRIBUTED LAG - APPL , INVESTMENT * APPL - SECTOR :
          UTILITIES , TELEPHONE

YA0950   DOBELL R., ET AL.
          "A symposium on CES production functions: extensions and comments"   Rev.
          Econ. Stats., vol.50, 1968, pp.443-479.
          PRODUCTION FUNCTIONS - SECTOR * PRODUCTION FUNCTIONS - MACRO * DATA -
          INTERNATIONAL * APPL - MACRO : PRODUCTIVITY * PRODUCTION FUNCTIONS -
          METHODOLOGY

YA0951   DOBSON S.W.
          "Estimating term structure equations with individual bond data"   J.
          Finance, vol.33, 1978, pp.75-92.
          INTEREST RATE - TERM STRUCTURE

YA0952   DOBSON S.W.
          "Reply to the critics"   Can. J. Econ., vol.9, 1976, pp.162-165.
          INTEREST RATE - TERM STRUCTURE * APPL - MACRO , CANADA

YA0953   DOBSON S.W.
          "The term structure of interest rates and the maturity composition of the
          government debt: the Canadian case"   Can. J. Econ., vol.6, 1973,
          pp.319-331.
          INTEREST RATE - TERM STRUCTURE * INTEREST RATE - EXPECTATIONS * APPL - MACRO
          , CANADA

YA0954   DOBSON S.W., SUTCH R.C., VANDERFORD D.E.
          "An evaluation of alternative empirical models of the term structure of
          interest rates"   J. Finance, vol.31, 1976, pp.1035-1065.
          INTEREST RATE - TERM STRUCTURE * DISTRIBUTED LAG - APPL , INTEREST RATES *
          EVALUATION - EXPECTATIONS * THEORY * DISTRIBUTED LAG - ALMON : APPL *
          DISTRIBUTED LAG - APPL , EXPECTATIONS HYPOTHESES * INTEREST RATE -
          EXPECTATIONS

YA0955   DODDS W.
          "An application of the Bass model in long term new product forecasting"
          J. Mktg. Res., vol.10, 1973, pp.308-311.
          LONG TERM FORECASTING * NEW PRODUCTS - DIFFUSION MODEL * APPL - SECTOR :
          SERVICES , MEDIA , TV * DIFFUSION MODEL - APPL * NEW PRODUCTS - EVALUATION

YA0956   DODSON J.A., MULLER E.
          "Models of new product diffusion through advertising and word-of-mouth"
          Mgmt. Sci., vol.24, 1978, pp.1568-1578.
          NEW PRODUCTS - DIFFUSION

YA0957   DOGAS D., HINES A.G.
          "Trade unions and wage inflation: a critique of Purdy and Zis"   Appl.
          Econ., vol.7, 1975, pp.195-211.
          UNIONISATION - EFFECT OF * APPL - MACRO : EARNINGS

YA0958   DOLDE W.
          "Forecasting the consumption effects of stabilization policies"   Int.
          Econ. Rev., vol.17, 1976, pp.431-446.
          APPL - MACRO : CONSUMPTION * INCOME - EFFECT OF * POLICY EVALUATION - MACRO
          : STABILISATION * EVALUATION - CONSUMPTION MODELS

YA0959   DOLICH I.J.
"How subscription prices affect magazine sales"   J. Advtg. Res., vol.17:2,
1977, pp.31-36.
APPL - FIRM : SERVICES , MEDIA , MAGAZINES * PRICE - EFFECT OF * MARKET
SEGMENTATION

YA0960   DOMINGUEZ L.V., PAGE A.L.
"A note on a simultaneous-equation regression study of advertising and sales
of cigarettes" with discussion   J. Mktg. Res., vol.8, 1971, pp.386-387.
ADVERTISING - EFFECT OF * MARKET SHARE - METHODOLOGY * APPL - FIRM :
CONSUMER NON DURABLES , CIGARETTES * MARKET SHARE - SECTOR : CONSUMER NON
DURABLES * SPECIFICATION ERROR - EFFECT OF , IDENTIFICATION

YA0961   DONNER A.
"Labour turnover, expectations and the determination of money wage changes
in U.S. manufacturing"   Can. J. Econ., vol.5, 1972, pp.16-34.
INFLATION - EXPECTATIONS * APPL - MACRO : EARNINGS * MANPOWER PLANNING -
LABOUR TURNOVER * INFLATION - EFFECT OF

YA0962   DONNER A.
"Labour turnover expectations and the determination of money wage changes in
US manufacturing"   Can. J. Econ., vol.5, 1972, pp.16-34.
INFLATION - DETERMINANTS , EARNINGS * APPL - MACRO : EARNINGS * MANPOWER
PLANNING - LABOUR TURNOVER

YA0963   DONNER A.W., LAZAR F.
"An econometric study of segmental labor markets and the structure of
unemployment: The Canadian experience"   Int. Econ. Rev., vol.14, 1973,
pp.312-327.
APPL - MACRO : UNEMPLOYMENT * APPL - MACRO , CANADA * MANPOWER PLANNING -
LABOUR FORCE COMPOSITION * MANPOWER PLANNING - LABOUR PARTICIPATION

YA0964   DONNER A.W., LAZAR F.
"Some comments on the Canadian Phillips curve"   Economica, vol.40, 1973,
pp.195-207.
INFLATION - PHILLIPS * APPL - MACRO : EARNINGS * APPL - MACRO , CANADA *
EVALUATION - EARNINGS MODELS * REGRESSION - MODEL CHOICE

YA0965   DOPUCH N., WATTS R.
"Using time series models to assess the significance of accounting changes"
J. Acctg. Res., vol.10, 1972, pp.180-194.
APPL - FIRM : FINANCE , PROFITS * ACCOUNTING PRACTICE - EFFECT OF * TIME
SERIES - ARIMA : APPL * APPL - FIRM : FINANCE , STOCK PRICES * STOCK PRICES
- INFORMATION EFFECT

YA0966   DORAN H.E.
"A simulation study of the small sample properties of the Hannan estimator
of a distributed lag model when the signal-to-noise ratio is constant"
Int. Econ. Rev., vol.15, 1974, pp.497-514.
DISTRIBUTED LAG - ESTIMATION * DATA - SIMULATION * ESTIMATION - HANNAN *
SPECTRAL ANALYSIS - APPL : DISTRIBUTED LAG

YA0967   DORAN H.E.
"A spectral principal components estimator of the distributed lag model"
Int. Econ. Rev., vol.17, 1976, pp.8-25.
DISTRIBUTED LAG - ESTIMATION * ESTIMATION - HANNAN * ESTIMATION - PRINCIPAL
COMPONENTS * DATA - SIMULATION

YA0968   DORAN H.E.
"Prediction of missing observations in the time series of an economic
variable"   J. Am. Statist. Ass., vol.69, 1974, pp.546-554.
DATA ERRORS - MISSING OBSERVATIONS * ADVANCED

YA0969   DORAN H.E., GRIFFITHS W.E.
"Inconsistency of the OLS estimator of the partial adjustment-adaptive
expectations model"   J. Econometrics, vol.7, 1978, pp.133-146.
COMPARATIVE METHODS - INCOME ELASTICITY , ESTIMATION * DISTRIBUTED LAG -
EXPECTATIONS HYPOTHESES * EVALUATION - ESTIMATION : OLS * COMPARATIVE
METHODS - PRICE ELASTICITY , ESTIMATION

YA0970   DORNBUSCH R., KRUGMAN P.
"Flexible exchange rates in the short run" with discussion   Brookings
Paps. Econ. Activity, 1976, pp.537-584.
EXCHANGE RATE - EFFECT OF * APPL - MACRO : INTERNATIONAL TRADE * INFLATION -
DETERMINANTS

YA0971   DORRINGTON J.C.
"A structural approach to estimating the built-in flexibility of UK taxes on
personal income"   Econ. J., vol.84, 1974, pp.576-594.
APPL - SECTOR : GOVERNMENT , REVENUES , TAX * APPL - MACRO , UK * TAX -
EFFECT OF * POLICY EVALUATION - MACRO : FISCAL

YA0972   DORY J.P., LORD R.J.
"Does T.F. really work?"   H.B.R., vol.48, Nov-Dec, 1970, pp.16-38.
EVALUATION - TECHNOLOGICAL FORECASTING * BIBLIOGRAPHY - TECHNOLOGICAL
FORECASTING * BASIC

YA0973   DOS SANTOS J.G.
"Estimating the durability of consumers' durable goods"   Rev. Econ.
Stats., vol.54, 1972, pp.475-479.
APPL - SECTOR : CONSUMER DURABLES , APPLIANCES , ELECTRICAL * APPL - SECTOR
: CONSUMER DURABLES , FURNISHINGS * PRICE - EFFECT OF * INCOME - EFFECT OF *
DEPRECIATION - ESTIMATION * QUALITY - DURABILITY * ESTIMATION - MAXIMUM
LIKELIHOOD

YA0974   DOUGHERTY C.R.S.
         "Substitution and the structure of the labour force"   Econ. J., vol.82,
         1972, pp.170-182.
         MANPOWER PLANNING - SECTOR , SUPPLY * MANPOWER PLANNING - LABOUR FORCE
         COMPOSITION * SUBSTITUTE FACTORS
YA0975   DOUGLAS E.
         "Monthly demand variability through a product's market cycle"   Appl.
         Econ., vol.9, 1977, pp.109-131.
         APPL - SECTOR : CONSUMER DURABLES , APPLIANCES , WASHERS * INCOME - EFFECT
         OF * ADVERTISING - EFFECT OF
YA0976   DOUGLAS E.
         "Secular and cyclical changes in the demand for components of a product
         cluster"   Rev. Econ. Stats., vol.49, 1967, pp.63-76; Erratum on p.272.
         APPL - SECTOR : CONSUMER DURABLES , APPLIANCES , WASHERS * LIFE CYCLE -
         PRODUCT * SUBSTITUTE PRODUCTS * EX ANTE * INCOME - EFFECT OF * STABILITY OF
         COEFFICIENTS - REGRESSION : APPL
YA0977   DOUTRIAUX J., ZIND R.G.
         "Factor input efficiency and technological bias with application to US
         agriculture"   Rev. Econ. Stats., vol.53, 1976, pp.380-382.
         APPL - SECTOR : AGRICULTURE * PRODUCTION FUNCTIONS - METHODOLOGY * APPL -
         SECTOR : PRODUCTIVITY
YA0978   DOWNES B.
         "Purchase taxes and retail prices in the UK"   Appl. Econ., vol.5, 1973,
         pp.199-218.
         TAX - EFFECT OF * APPL - MACRO : CONSUMER DEMAND * APPL - SECTOR : CONSUMER
         NON DURABLES * APPL - SECTOR : CONSUMER DURABLES
YA0979   DOYLE P.
         "Economic aspects of advertising: a survey"   Econ. J., vol.68, 1968,
         pp.570-602.
         ADVERTISING - REVIEW * BIBLIOGRAPHY - ADVERTISING
YA0980   DOYLE P., FENWICK I.
         "Sales forecasting - using a combination of approaches"   Long Range
         Planning, vol.9:3, 1976, pp.60-64.
         COMBINING FORECASTS - INTRODUCTION * FORECASTING - INTRODUCTION
YA0981   DOYLE P., FENWICK I.
         "The pitfalls of AID analysis"   J. Mktg. Res., vol.12, 1975, pp.408-413.
         APPL - SECTOR : SERVICES , MEDIA , NEWSPAPERS * AID - METHODOLOGY * CONSUMER
         BEHAVIOUR - PURCHASING , DETERMINANTS * EVALUATION - MULTIVARIATE METHODS ,
         AID * COMPARATIVE METHODS - REGRESSION , MULTIVARIATE METHODS
YA0982   DOYLE P., HUTCHINSON P.
         "The identification of target markets"   Decis. Sci., vol.7, 1976,
         pp.152-161.
         EVALUATION - MARKET SEGMENTATION * APPL - SECTOR : CONSUMER NON DURABLE ,
         FOOD * DISCRIMINANT ANALYSIS - APPL * COMPARATIVE METHODS - REGRESSION ,
         MULTIVARIATE METHODS * AID - APPL * CLUSTER ANALYSIS - APPL
YA0983   DOYLE P., WEINBERG C.B.
         "Effective new product decisions for supermarkets"   Opl. Res. Q., vol.24,
         1973, pp.45-54.
         NEW PRODUCTS - IDENTIFYING * USE - RETAIL , PRODUCT SELECTION * USER - FIRM
         : RETAILING
YA0984   DOYLE P., WEINBERG C.B.
         "Segmenting domestic and foreign car buyers"   Eur. J. Mktg., vol.8, 1974,
         pp.202-208.
         MARKET SEGMENTATION * DISCRIMINANT ANALYSIS - APPL * EX ANTE * APPL - SECTOR
         : CONSUMER DURABLES , CARS
YA0985   DRAPER N.R., COX D.R.
         "On distributions and their transformations to normality"   R. Statist.
         Soc. (B), vol.31, 1969, pp.472-476.
         EVALUATION - REGRESSION , TRANSFORMATIONS * ERROR DISTRIBUTION - NORMAL *
         ADVANCED
YA0986   DRESCH S.P., GOLDBERG R.D.
         "IDIOM: an inter-industry national-regional policy evaluation model"
         Anns. Econ. Soc. Meas., vol.2, 1973, pp.323-356.
         SIMULATION - APPL : POLICY EVALUATION * REGIONAL MODELS - INTERREGIONAL *
         POLICY EVALUATION - REGIONAL * INPUT OUTPUT - INTER REGIONAL * POLICY
         EVALUATION - MACRO : DISARMAMENT * PUBLIC EXPENDITURE - EFFECT OF
YA0987   DRETTAKIS E.G.
         "Distributed lag models for the quarterly migration flows of West Germany,
         1962-72"   R. Statist. Soc. (A), vol.139, 1976, pp.365-373.
         MANPOWER PLANNING - MIGRATION * APPL - MACRO , GERMANY
YA0988   DRETTAKIS E.G.
         "Missing data in econometric estimation"   Rev. Econ. Studies, vol.40,
         1973, pp.537-552.
         DATA ERRORS - MISSING OBSERVATIONS * DATA - INTERPOLATION * MACRO MODEL - UK
         * EX ANTE * ESTIMATION - FIML
YA0989   DRETTAKIS E.G.
         "The employment of migrant workers in West Germany, 1961-1972: an
         econometric analysis"   Appl. Econ., vol.8, 1976, pp.11-15.
         POPULATION - MIGRATION * APPL - MACRO , GERMANY * MANPOWER PLANNING -
         MIGRATION

YA0990　DREVS R.A., DURAND R.M., MATTHEISS T.H.
"Multiple discriminant analysis and several small samples - to split,
combine or treat separately"　　Decis. Sci., vol.8, 1977, pp.567-575.
USE - PERSONNEL EVALUATION * DISCRIMINANT ANALYSIS - METHODOLOGY * DATA -
SAMPLE SIZE * DATA - AGGREGATION * DATA - DISAGGREGATION * COMPARATIVE
METHODS - DATA : AGGREGATE , DISAGGREGATE

YA0991　DREZE J.H.
"Bayesian limited information analysis of the simultaneous equations model"
Econometrica, vol.44, 1976, pp.1045-1075.
BAYESIAN - ESTIMATION : SIMULTANEOUS SYSTEM * APPL - SECTOR : CONSUMER NON
DURABLES , FOOD * ADVANCED

YA0992　DRUD A.
"An optimisation code for nonlinear econometric models based on sparse
matrix techniques and reduced gradients"　　Anns. Econ. Soc. Meas., vol.6,
1978, pp.563-580.
NUMERICAL METHODS - OPTIMISATION * SIMULTANEOUS SYSTEM - NON LINEAR *
COMPUTERISATION - ESTIMATION , SIMULTANEOUS SYSTEM MODELS , PROGRAMS *
ADVANCED

YA0993　DUBBELMAN C., LOUTER A.S
"On typical characteristics of economic time series and the relative
qualities of five autocorrelation tests"　　J. Econometrics, vol.8, 1978,
pp.295-306.
COMPARATIVE METHODS - TESTS , AUTOCORRELATION * TIME SERIES -
CHARACTERISATION

YA0994　DUCK N.W., SHEPPARD D.K.
"A proposal for the control of the UK money supply"　　Econ. J., vol.88,
1978, pp.1-17.
APPL - MACRO , UK * APPL - MACRO : MONEY , SUPPLY * DECISION RULES - SECTOR
* APPL - MACRO : CONSUMER DEMAND , FINANCIAL ASSETS * POLICY EVALUATION -
MACRO : MONETARY * USER - SECTOR : GOVERNMENT

YA0995　DUDLEY L.
"Learning and productivity change in metal products"　　Am. Econ. Rev.,
vol.62, 1972, pp.662-669.
APPL - SECTOR : PRODUCTION * PRODUCTION FUNCTIONS - SECTOR * COST - SECTOR *
COST - LEARNING CURVE * APPL - SECTOR : PRODUCTIVITY

YA0996　DUESENBERRY J., BOSWORTH B.
"Policy implications of a flow of funds model" with discussion.　　J.
Finance, vol.29, 1974, pp.331-347 & 358-363.
APPL - MACRO : FLOW OF FUNDS * POLICY EVALUATION - MACRO : MONETARY * MACRO
MODEL - BROOKINGS

YA0997　DUFFY M., GOUGH T.J.
"On the short term forecasting of private housing investment in the UK" with
discussion　　Appl. Econ., vol.7, 1975, pp.119-138.
APPL - SECTOR : CONSTRUCTION , RESIDENTIAL * DISTRIBUTED LAG - VARIABLE LAG
* DISTRIBUTED LAG - APPL , ORDERS

YA0998　DUFFY M., RENTON A.
"An analysis of the UK balancing item"　　Int. Econ. Rev., vol.12, 1971,
pp.448-464.
APPL - MACRO , UK * APPL - MACRO : INTERNATIONAL TRADE * ESTIMATION -
PRINCIPAL COMPONENTS * FACTOR ANALYSIS - APPL

YA0999　DUFFY W., LEWIS K.A.
"The cyclic properties of the production-inventory process"　　Econometrica,
vol.43, 1975, pp.499-512.
BUSINESS CYCLE - IDENTIFICATION * APPL - SECTOR : AGRICULTURE , COTTON *
APPL - SECTOR : AGRICULTURE , TIMBER * APPL - SECTOR : INVENTORIES *
DECISION RULES - SECTOR

YA1000　DUGDALE M.
"Long term trend projections as an aid to management"　　Stat'n., vol.20,
1971, pp.45-54.
APPL - SECTOR : RETAILING * LONG TERM FORECASTING

YA1001　DUGGAL V.G., KLEIN L.R., McCARTHY M.D.
"The Wharton Model Mark III: a modern IS-LM construct"　　Int. Econ. Rev.,
vol.15, 1974, pp.572-594.
MACRO MODEL - WHARTON * MULTIPLIERS - MACRO * EX ANTE

YA1002　DUGGAR J.W.
"International comparisons of income levels: an additional measure"　　Econ.
J., vol.79, 1969, pp.109-116.
PROXY VARIABLES * DATA SOURCES - LDC * APPL - MACRO : DEVELOPMENT

YA1003　DUNCAN G.T., LIN L.G.
"Inference for Markov chains having stochastic entry and exit"　　J. Am.
Statist. Ass., vol.67, 1972, pp.761-767.
MARKOV MODELS - APPL * MARKOV MODELS - THEORY * APPL - SECTOR : FINANCE ,
BANKS * APPL - SECTOR : FINANCE , BANK , ASSETS * EX ANTE

YA1004　DUNCAN J.W.
"Improving economic statistics for decision makers"　　Bus. Econ., vol.10:3,
1975, pp.41-46.
DATA ERRORS - NATIONAL ACCOUNTS , US

YA1005   DUNKELBERG W.C., STAFFORD F.P.
          "Debt in the consumer portfolio: evidence from a panel study"   Am. Econ.
          Rev., vol.61, 1971, pp.598=613.
          APPL = MACRO : CONSUMER DEMAND * CONSUMER BEHAVIOUR = PURCHASING ,
          DETERMINANTS * DATA = CROSS SECTION

YA1006   DUNN D.M., WILLIAMS W.H., DeCHAINE T.L.
          "Aggregate versus subaggregate models in a local area forecasting"   J. Am.
          Statist. Ass., vol.71, 1976, pp.68=71.
          EX ANTE * COMPARATIVE METHODS = DATA : AGGREGATE , DISAGGREGATE * APPL =
          FIRM : UTILITIES , TELEPHONE * TIME SERIES = ARIMA : APPL

YA1007   DUNN D.M., WILLIAMS W.H., SPIVEY W.A.
          "Analysis and prediction of telephone demand in local geographic areas"
          Bell J. Econ., vol.2, 1971, pp.561=576.
          REGIONAL MODELS = CITY * REGIONAL MODELS = SECTOR : UTILITIES * APPL =
          SECTOR : UTILITIES , TELEPHONES * COMPARATIVE METHODS = EXPONENTIAL
          SMOOTHING , ADAPTIVE * LEAD TIME = EFFECT OF * EX ANTE * COMPARATIVE METHODS
          = BUSINESS INDICATOR , EXPONENTIAL SMOOTHING

YA1008   DURBIN J., MURPHY M.J.
          "Seasonal adjustment based on a mixed additive multiplicative model"   R.
          Statist. Soc. (A), vol.138, 1975, pp.385=410.
          SEASONALITY = MULTIPLICATIVE , ADDITIVE MODEL * REGRESSION = STEPWISE *
          SPECTRAL ANALYSIS = APPL : SEASONALITY * TIME SERIES = DECOMPOSITION * TIME
          SERIES = HARMONICS = APPL = MACRO , UK * APPL = MACRO : UNEMPLOYMENT * DATA
          ERRORS = OUTLIERS * APPL = MACRO , IRELAND * APPL = MACRO , NETHERLANDS *
          SEASONALITY = CHANGING

YA1009   DUSANSKY R., TANNER J.E.
          "The shifting of the profits tax in Canadian manufacturing 1935=1965"
          Can. J. Econ., vol.7, 1974, pp.112=121.
          APPL = MACRO : PROFITS * TAX = EFFECT OF * APPL = MACRO : EARNINGS

YA1010   DUTTA M.
          "Reexamination of the import structure of India: reply"   Rev. Econ.
          Stats., vol.53, 1976, pp.384=385.
          APPL = MACRO , INDIA * APPL = MACRO : INTERNATIONAL TRADE , IMPORTS

YA1011   DUTTA M., LYTTKENS E.
          "Iterative instrumental variables method and estimation of a large
          simultaneous system"   J. Am. Statist. Ass., vol.69, 1974, pp.977=985.
          SIMULTANEOUS SYSTEM = ESTIMATION * ESTIMATION = INSTRUMENTAL VARIABLES ,
          ITERATIVE * DATA = SAMPLE SIZE * MACRO MODEL = WEST INDIES * ADVANCED

YA1012   DUTTA M., NARGUND N.K.
          "A note on a note on Dutta's estimate of world demand for Indian tea"
          Econometrica, vol.40, 1972, pp.1165=1166.
          APPL = SECTOR : AGRICULTURE , TEA * APPL = SECTOR : INTERNATIONAL TRADE ,
          EXPORTS * PRICE = EFFECT OF

YA1013   DUTTA M., SHARMA P.L.
          "Alternative estimators and predictive power of alternative estimators: an
          econometric model of Puerto Rico"   Rev. Econ. Stats., vol.55, 1973,
          pp.381=385.
          MACRO MODEL = WEST INDIES * EX ANTE * SIMULTANEOUS SYSTEM = ESTIMATION *
          ESTIMATION = LISE * ESTIMATION = PRINCIPAL COMPONENTS * ESTIMATION =
          INSTRUMENTAL VARIABLES , ITERATIVE * COMPARATIVE METHODS = ESTIMATION :
          SIMULTANEOUS SYSTEM * COMPARATIVE METHODS = ESTIMATION : OLS , 2SLS *
          COMPARATIVE METHODS = ESTIMATION : OLS , 3SLS * COMPARATIVE METHODS =
          ESTIMATION : SIMULTANEOUS SYSTEM , 2SLS , 3SLS

YA1014   DUTTON D.S., GRAMM W.P.
          "Transaction costs, the wage rate, and the demand for money"   Am. Econ.
          Rev., vol.63, 1973, pp.652=665.
          CONSUMER BEHAVIOUR = ECONOMIC MODELS , THEORY * APPL = MACRO : MONEY ,
          DEMAND * REGRESSION = SPECIFICATION OF VARIABLES

YA1015   DUVALL R.M.
          "Time series analysis by modified least squares techniques"   J. Am.
          Statist. Ass., vol.61, 1966, pp.152=165.
          TIME SERIES = DECOMPOSITION * SEASONALITY = ESTIMATION , OLS * COMPARATIVE
          METHODS = SEASONALITY * APPL = MACRO : UNEMPLOYMENT

YA1016   DYCKMAN T.R., STEKLER H.O.
          "Probabilistic turning point forecasts"   Rev. Econ. Stats., vol.48, 1966,
          pp.288=295.
          TURNING POINTS = FORECASTING * APPL = MACRO : OUTPUT * EVALUTION = BUSINESS
          INDICATORS * EVALUATION = TURNING POINT FORECASTS

YA1017   EASTON B.H.
          "Spurious seasonal fluctuations in seasonally adjusted series"
          Econometrica, vol.40, 1972, p.929.
          EVALUATION = SEASONALITY , ESTIMATION

YA1018   EASTWOOD D.B., ANDERSON R.
          "Consumer credit and consumer demand for automobiles"   J. Finance, vol.31,
          1976, pp.113=123.
          APPL = SECTOR : CONSUMER DURABLES , CARS * APPL = SECTOR : FINANCE , HIRE
          PURCHASE

YA1019   EATHERLY B.J.
          "Summary of a simple model of mode choice"   Mgmt. Sci. (B), vol.19, 1972,
          pp.201-204.
          APPL - SECTOR : TRANSPORT * TIME - VALUE OF * BRAND CHOICE - APPL

YA1020   EATWELL J., LLEWELLYN J., TARLING R.
          "Money wage inflation in industrial countries"   Rev. Econ. Studies,
          vol.41, 1974, pp.515-523.
          DATA - CROSS SECTION * DATA - INTERNATIONAL * APPL - MACRO : EARNINGS

YA1021   EBANKS W.W.
          "A new index of the physical volume of economic activity"   Bus. Econ.,
          vol.10:3, 1975, pp.38-40.
          INDEX NUMBERS - MACRO : OUTPUT * DATA ERRORS - INDEX NUMBERS * DATA -
          TRANSFORMED , DEFLATED * INFLATION - EFFECT OF * BUSINESS INDICATORS -
          METHODOLOGY

YA1022   EBBELER D.H.
          "On the probability of correct model selection using the maximum R bar
          squared choice criterion"   Int. Econ. Rev., vol.16, 1975, pp.516-520.
          DATA - SIMULATION * REGRESSION - MODEL CHOICE * REGRESSION - SUMMARY
          STATISTICS * SPECIFICATION ERROR - TESTS , VARIABLE INCLUSION

YA1023   ECHELBERGER H.E., SHAFER E.L.
          "Snow + (X) = Use of Ski Slopes"   J. Mktg. Res., vol.7, 1970, pp.388-392.
          APPL - SECTOR : SERVICES , TOURISM * FACTOR ANALYSIS - APPL

YA1024   ECHOLS M.E., ELLIOTT J.W.
          "Rational expectations in a disequilibrium model of the term structure"
          Am. Econ. Rev., vol.66, 1976, pp.28-44.
          INTEREST RATE - TERM STRUCTURE * INTEREST RATE - LIQUIDITY PREFERENCE *
          BIBLIOGRAPHY - INTEREST RATES * EXPECTATIONS - DETERMINANTS

YA1025   ECKBO P.L., JACOBY H.D., SMITH J.L.
          "Oil supply forecasting: a disaggregated process approach"   Bell. J.
          Econ., vol.9, 1978, pp.218-235.
          APPL - SECTOR : COMMODITIES , OIL * SUPPLY - SECTOR : COMMODITIES

YA1026   ECKSTEIN O., GIROLA J.A.
          "Long-term properties of the price-wage mechanism in the US, 1891-1977"
          Rev. Econ. Stats., vol.60, 1978, pp.323-333.
          APPL - MACRO : EARNINGS * INFLATION - EFFECT OF * INFLATION - DETERMINANTS *
          STABILITY OF COEFFICIENTS - REGRESSION : APPL

YA1027   ECKSTEIN O., GREEN E., SUNDARARAJAN V.
          "New approaches in input output analysis"   Bus. Econ., vol.6:1, 1971,
          pp.73-77.
          INPUT OUTPUT - PROJECTION OF STRUCTURE * INPUT OUTPUT - REVIEW * INPUT
          OUTPUT - METHODOLOGY : COEFFICIENT ESTIMATION

YA1028   ECKSTEIN O., GREEN E.W., SINAI A.
          "The Data Resources model: uses, structure, and analysis of the US economy"
          Int. Econ. Rev., vol.15, 1974, pp.595-615.
          MACRO MODEL - DATA RESOURCES * EX ANTE

YA1029   EDELSTEIN R.
          "The determinants of value in the Philadelphia housing market: a case study
          of the Main Line, 1967-1969."   Rev. Econ. Stats., vol.56, 1974,
          pp.319-328.
          APPL - SECTOR : CONSTRUCTION , RESIDENTIAL * PRICE - SECTOR : CONSTRUCTION ,
          RESIDENTIAL * DATA - CROSS SECTION , TIME SERIES * TAX - EFFECT OF

YA1030   EDELSTEIN R.H.
          "Improving the selection of credit risks: an analysis of a commercial bank
          minority lending program"   J. Finance, vol.30, 1975, pp.37-55.
          USE - CREDIT CONTROL , COMPANY * APPL - SECTOR : FINANCE , LOANS * APPL -
          FIRM : FINANCE , BANKS * APPL - SECTOR : SOCIAL , INEQUALITY * POLICY
          EVALUATION - SECTOR : SOCIAL

YA1031   EDMISTER R.D.
          "Commision cost structure: shifts and scale economies"   J. Finance,
          vol.33, 1978, pp.477-486.
          APPL - FIRM : FINANCE , BANKS * COST - FIRM : FINANCE * APPL - FIRM :
          FINANCE , STOCK PRICES * APPL - FIRM : FINANCE , STOCK BROKERS

YA1032   EDWARDS J.B.
          "The relation between the F test and R bar squared"   Am. Stat'n.,
          vol.23:5, 1969, p.28.
          REGRESSION - SUMMARY STATISTICS

YA1033   EDWARDS J.B., ORCUTT G.H.
          "Should aggregation prior to estimation be the rule?"   Rev. Econ. Stats.,
          vol.51, 1969, pp.409-420.
          DATA - AGGREGATION * SIMULATION - METHODOLOGY , MICRO * DATA - SIMULATION *
          COMPARATIVE METHODS - DATA : AGGREGATE , DISAGGREGATE * SIMULATION - APPL :
          MICRO

YA1034   EHRENBERG A.S.C.
          "Predicting the performance of new brands"   J. Advtg. Res., vol.11:6,
          1971, pp.3-10.
          NEW PRODUCTS - NEW BRAND * REPEAT BUYING * CONSUMER BEHAVIOUR - STOCHASTIC
          MODELS * PROBABILITY MODELS - NBD

YA1035   EHRENBERG A.S.C.
          "Repetitive advertising and the consumer"   J. Advtg. Res., vol.14:2, 1974,
          pp.25-34.
          ADVERTISING - EFFECT OF * ADVERTISING - REVIEW
YA1036   EHRENBERG A.S.C.
          "The elements of lawlike relationships" with discussion   R. Statist. Soc,
          (A), vol.131, 1968, pp.280-302 & 315-325.
          REGRESSION - MODEL CHOICE * STABILITY OF COEFFICIENTS - REGRESSION * MODEL
          SELECTION * CAUSALITY - REVIEW
YA1037   EHRENBERG R.G.
          "The demand for state and local government employees"   Am. Econ. Rev.,
          vol.63, 1973, pp.366-379.
          MANPOWER PLANNING - SECTOR : GOVERNMENT , DEMAND * APPL - SECTOR :
          GOVERNMENT , LOCAL
YA1038   EHRENBERG R.G., OAXACA R.L.
          "Unemployment insurance, duration of employment, and subsequent wage gain"
          Am. Econ. Rev., vol.66, 1976, pp.754-766.
          MANPOWER PLANNING - MACRO * MANPOWER PLANNING - LABOUR FORCE COMPOSITION *
          MANPOWER PLANNING - UNEMPLOYMENT * MANPOWER PLANNING - EARNINGS * POLICY
          EVALUATION - MACRO : UNEMPLOYMENT * POLICY EVALUATION - MACRO : WELFARE
YA1039   EHRLICH I.
          "The deterrent effect of capital punishment: a question of life and death"
          Am. Econ. Rev., vol.65, 1975, pp.397-417.
          APPL - SECTOR : SOCIAL , CRIME * POLICY EVALUATION - SECTOR : SOCIAL
YA1040   EILON S., ELMALEH J.
          Adaptive limits in inventory control"   Mgmt. Sci. (B), vol.16, 1970,
          pp.533-548.
          EXPONENTIAL SMOOTHING - APPL * USE - INVENTORY CONTROL * LOSS FUNCTIONS -
          FIRM , INVENTORY * DATA SIMULATION
YA1041   EILON S., TILLEY R.P.R., GOLD B.
          "Measuring the quality of economic forecasts"   Omega, vol.1, 1973,
          pp.217-227.
          EVALUATION - THEORY OF * BASIC
YA1042   EINHORN H.J., HOGARTH R.M.
          "Unit weighting schemes for decisonmaking"   Organizational Behaviour and
          Human Performance, vol.13, 1975, pp.171-192.
          EVALUATION - REGRESSION , CONSTRAINED * EVALUATION - PRIOR INFORMATION *
          EVALUATION - REGRESSION , ESTIMATION * REGRESSION - PRIOR INFORMATION
YA1043   EISENBEIS R.A.
          "Pitfalls in the application of discriminant analysis in business, finance,
          and economics"   J. Finanace, vol.32, 1977, pp.875-900.
          DISCRIMINANT ANALYSIS - REVIEW * EVALUATION - DISCRIMINANT ANALYSIS *
          BIBLIOGRAPHY - DISCRIMINANT ANALYSIS
YA1044   EISENBEIS R.A., PINCHES G.E.
          "'A multivariate analysis of industrial bond ratings' and the use of
          subordination: comments"   J. Finance, vol.33, 1978, pp.325-344.
          APPL - FIRM : FINANCE , BONDS * USE - CREDIT CONTROL , BOND RATING *
          DISCRIMINANT ANALYSIS - APPL
YA1045   EISENPRESS H., GREENSTADT J.
          The estimation of non-linear econometric systems"   Econometrica, vol.34,
          1966, pp.851-861.
          COMPARATIVE METHODS - ESTIMATION : SIMULTANEOUS SYSTEM , NON LINEAR *
          SIMULTANEOUS SYSTEMS - ESTIMATION * SIMULTANEOUS SYSTEM - NON LINEAR
YA1046   EISNER M., PINDYCK R.S.
          "A generalized approach to estimation as implemented in the TROLL/1 system"
          Anns. Econ. Soc. Meas., vol.2, 1973, pp.29-52.
          COMPUTERISATION - ESTIMATION , SIMULTANEOUS SYSTEM MODELS , PROGRAMS *
          SIMULTANEOUS SYSTEM - ESTIMATION
YA1047   EISNER R.
          "Components of capital expenditures: replacement and modernisation versus
          expansion"   Rev. Econ. Stats., vol.54, 1972, pp.297-305.
          DATA - CROSS SECTION , TIME SERIES * SURVEYS - BUSINESS * EXPECTATIONS -
          DATA * APPL - MACRO : INVESTMENT * APPL - SECTOR : INVESTMENT * DEMAND -
          REPLACEMENT * EXPECTATIONS - DETERMINANTS
YA1048   EISNER R.
          "Non-linear estimates of the liquidity trap"   Econometrica, vol.39, 1971,
          pp.861-864.
          APPL - MACRO : MONEY , DEMAND * INTEREST RATE - EFFECT OF * ESTIMATION - NON
          LINEAR : APPL * REGRESSION - HYPOTHESIS TESTS * INTEREST RATE - DETERMINANTS
YA1049   EISNER R., NADIRI M.I.
          "Neoclassical theory of investment behaviour: a comment"   Rev. Econ.
          Stats., vol.52, 1970, pp.216-222.
          APPL - MACRO : INVESTMENT * COMPARATIVE METHODS - REGRESSION ,
          TRANSFORMATIONS * ERROR SPECIFICATION - AUTOCORRELATED * COMPARATIVE METHODS
          - DISTRIBUTED LAG , ERROR SPECIFICATION * DISTRIBUTED LAG - APPL , OUTPUT
YA1050   EKERN S.
          "Forecasting with adaptive filtering: a critical re-examination"   Opl.
          Res. Q., vol.27, 1976, pp.705-715.
          EVALUATION - EX POST MODELS * EVALUATION - TIME SERIES , ADAPTIVE FILTERING
          * EX ANTE * COMPARATIVE METHODS - ADAPTIVE FILTERING , EXPONENTIAL SMOOTHING
          * COMPARATIVE METHODS - ADAPTIVE FILTERING , TREND CURVES * COMPARATIVE
          METHODS - EXPONENTIAL SMOOTHING , TREND CURVES

YA1051 EL-SAYYAD G.M.
        "Bayesian and classical analysis of Poisson regression"   R. Statist. Soc.
        (B), vol.35, 1973, pp.445-451.
        ERROR DISTRIBUTION - NON NORMAL , POISSON * REGRESSION - ESTIMATION * APPL -
        SECTOR : SOCIAL , ACCIDENTS * COMPARATIVE METHODS - ESTIMATION : REGRESSION

YA1052 ELAM R.
        "The effect of lease data on the predictive ability of financial ratios"
        Acctg. Rev., vol.50, 1975, pp.25-43.
        USE - BANKRUPTCY PREDICTION

YA1053 ELASHOFF R.M., AFIFI A.
        "Missing values in multivariate statistics I review of the literature"   J.
        Am. Statist. Ass., vol.61, 1966, pp.595-604.
        DATA ERRORS - MISSING OBSERVATIONS * BIBLIOGRAPHY - MISSING OBSERVATIONS

YA1054 ELLERT J.C.
        "Mergers, antitrust law enforcement and stock holder returns" with
        discussion   J. Finance, vol.31, 1976, pp.715-732 & 740-751.
        APPL - FIRM : MERGERS * APPL - FIRM : FINANCE , STOCK PRICES * STOCK PRICES
        - INDUSTRIAL STRUCTURE * USE - ANTITRUST

YA1055 ELLIOTT J.W.
        "A direct comparison of short-run GNP forecasting models"   J. Business,
        vol.46, 1973, pp.33-60.
        APPL - MACRO : GNP * MACRO MODEL - FRIEND TAUBMAN * MACRO MODEL - WHARTON *
        BUSINESS INDICATORS - APPL * MACRO MODEL - OMB * EVALUATION - MACRO MODELS *
        MACRO MODEL - ST.LOUIS

YA1056 ELLIOTT J.W.
        "Measuring the expected real rate of interest: an explanation of
        macroeconomic alternatives"   Am. Econ. Rev., vol.67, 1977, pp.429-444.
        EVALUATION - EX POST MODELS * EVALUATION - INTEREST RATE MODELS * INFLATION
        - EXPECTATIONS * INTEREST RATE - INDICATORS * INFLATION - DETERMINANTS *
        INTEREST RATE - EXPECTATIONS * EX ANTE * EVALUATION - INFLATION MODELS *
        EVALUATION - MONETARIST THEORY

YA1057 ELLIOTT J.W.
        "Theories of corporate investment behaviour revisited"   Am. Econ. Rev.,
        vol.63, 1973, pp.195-207.
        THEORY - INVESTMENT BEHAVIOUR * APPL - FIRM : INVESTMENT * EVALUATION -
        INVESTMENT MODELS

YA1058 ELLIOTT J.W., ECHOLS M.E.
        "Market segmentation, speculative behaviour and the term structure of
        interest rates"   Rev. Econ. Stats., vol.58, 1976, pp.40-49
        INTEREST RATE - TERM STRUCTURE * REGRESSION - PIECEWISE * MARKET
        SEGMENTATION

YA1059 ELLIOTT J.W., UPHOFF H.L.
        "Predicting the near term profit and loss statement with an econometric
        model: a feasibility study"   J. Acctg. Res., vol.10, 1972, pp.259-274.
        EVALUATION - EXPONENTIAL SMOOTHING * EX ANTE * SIMULATION - APPL : FIRM ,
        CONSUMER NON DURABLES * SIMULATION - APPL : FINANCIAL MODELLING * APPL -
        FIRM : CONSUMER NON DURABLES * APPL - FIRM : FINANCE , PROFITS * COMPARATIVE
        METHODS - CAUSAL(SIMULTANEOUS SYSTEM) , EXPONENTIAL SMOOTHING

YA1060 ELLISON A.P., STAFFORD E.M.
        "The order delivery lag in the world's civil aircraft industry"   Appl.
        Econ., vol.5, 1973, pp.19-34.
        DISTRIBUTED LAG - VARIABLE LAG * APPL - SECTOR : PRODUCTION , AIRCRAFT *
        DISTRIBUTED LAG - ALMON : APPL * COMPARATIVE METHODS - DISTRIBUTED LAG *
        DISTRIBUTED LAG - APPL , ORDERS

YA1061 ELNICKI R.A.
        "Hospital working capital: an empirical study. (Studies on measurement and
        evaluation of the economic efficiency of public and private nonprofit
        institutions)"   J. Acctg. Res., vol.15, supplement: 1977, pp.209-240.
        HEALTH - HOSPITAL , FINANCE

YA1062 ELTON E.J., GRUBER M.J.
        "Earnings estimates and the accuracy of expectational data"   Mgmt. Sci.
        (B), vol.18, 1972, pp.409-424.
        EVALUATION - JUDGEMENTAL FORECASTS , PROFITS * COMPARATIVE METHODS -
        EXPONENTIALSMOOTHING , JUDGEMENTAL * EVALUATION - EXPONENTIAL SMOOTHING *
        COMPARATIVE METHODS - AUTOREGRESSIVE , JUDGEMENTAL * COMPARATIVE METHODS -
        AUTOREGRESSIVE , TREND CURVES * COMPARATIVE METHODS - AUTOREGRESSIVE *
        EXPONENTIAL SMOOTHING * COMPARATIVE METHODS - EXPONENTIAL SMOOTHING , TREND
        CURVES * EX ANTE * APPL - FIRM : FINANCE , PROFITS , PER SHARE

YA1063 ELTON E.J., GRUBER M.J.
        "Estimating the dependence structure of share prices-implications for
        portfolio selection"   J. Finance, vol.28, 1973, pp.1203-1232.
        APPL - FIRM : FINANCE , STOCK PRICES * STOCK PRICES - COVARIATION * STOCK
        PRICES - INDUSTRIAL STRUCTURE * EX ANTE * USE - PORTFOLIO SELECTION * APPL -
        SECTOR : FINANCE , STOCK PRICE INDEX * STOCK PRICES - MODELS , EVALUATION

YA1064 ELTON E.J., GRUBER M.J.
        "Improved forecasting through the design of homogeneous groups"   J.
        Business, vol.44, 1971, pp.432-450.
        DATA - AGGREGATION 'BIAS' * APPL - FIRM : FINANCE , PROFITS , PER SHARE *
        COMPARATIVE METHODS - DATA : AGGREGATE , DISAGGREGATE * FACTOR ANALYSIS -
        APPL * CLUSTER ANALYSIS - APPL

YA1065   ELTON E.J., GRUBER M.J., KLEINDORFER P.R.
          "A closer look at the implications of the stable paretian hypotheses"
          Rev. Econ. Stats., vol.57, 1975, pp.231-235.
          APPL - FIRM : FINANCE , STOCK PRICES * STOCK PRICES - DISTRIBUTION * ERROR
          DISTRIBUTION - STABLE * EVALUATION - PORTFOLIO SELECTION PROCEDURES *
          ADVANCED

YA1066   ELTON E.J., GRUBER M.J., URICH Y.J.
          "Are betas best?"   J. Finance, vol.33, 1978, pp.1375-1384.
          APPL - FIRM : FINANCE , STOCK PRICES * STOCK PRICES - COVARIATION * EX ANTE
          * USE - PORTFOLIO SELECTION * STOCK PRICES - MODELS , COMPARATIVE * STOCK
          PRICES - BETA , EVALUATION

YA1067   ELTON M., ROSENHEAD J.
          "Microsimulation of markets"   Opl. Res. Q., vol.22, 1971, pp.117-144.
          BIBLIOGRAPHY - SIMULATION , MICRO * CONSUMER BEHAVIOUR - STOCHASTIC MODELS ,
          REVIEW * SIMULATION - APPL : CONSUMER BEHAVIOUR * SIMULATION - APPL : MICRO
          , REVIEW

YA1068   EMERY E.D.
          "Regulated utilities and equipment manufacturers' conspiracies in the
          electric power industry"   Bell J. Econ., vol.4, 1973, pp.322-337.
          APPL - SECTOR : UTILITIES , ELECTRICITY * APPL - SECTOR : PRODUCTION , PLANT
          , ELECTRICITY GENERATION * RESIDUALS - ANALYSIS OF , ERROR DETERMINANTS

YA1069   ENGLE R.F.
          "Band spectrum regression"   Int. Econ. Rev., vol.15, 1974, pp.1-11.
          APPL - MACRO : CONSUMPTION * INCOME - EFFECT OF , PERMANENT * SPECTRAL
          ANALYSIS - APPL : DISTRIBUTED LAG * REGRESSION - ERRORS IN VARIABLES *
          ESTIMATION - HANNAN

YA1070   ENGLE R.F.
          "Interpreting spectral analyses in terms of time-domain models"   Anns.
          Econ. Soc. Meas., vol.5, 1976, pp.89-109.
          TIME SERIES - ARIMA : INTERPRETATION * DISTRIBUTED LAG - IDENTIFICATION *
          SPECTRAL ANALYSIS - APPL : LAG IDENTIFICATION * SPECTRAL ANALYSIS - APPL :
          SECTOR , CONSTRUCTIO * APPL - SECTOR : CONSTRUCTION , RESIDENTIAL * INTEREST
          RATE - EFFECT OF

YA1071   ENGLE R.F.
          "Testing price equations for stability across spectral frequency bands"
          Econometrica, vol.46, 1978, pp.869-881.
          SPECIFICATION ERROR - TESTS , SPECTRUM STABILITY * SPECIFICATION ERROR -
          TESTS , MODEL SELECTION * COMPARATIVE METHODS - ESTIMATION : DISTRIBUTED LAG
          * DISTRIBUTED LAG - IDENTIFICATION * APPL - SECTOR : CONSUMER NON DURABLES ,
          FOOD * ESTIMATION - HANNAN : APPL * PRICE - SECTOR : CONSUMER NON DURABLES *
          DISTRIBUTED LAG - APPL , EARNINGS * ADVANCED

YA1072   ENGLE R.F., ET AL.
          "An econometric simulation model of intra-metropolotan housing location:
          housing, business, transportation and local government" with discussion
          Am. Econ. Ass. Proc., 1972, pp.87-99.
          REGIONAL MODELS - CITY * SIMULATION - APPL : REGIONAL MODELS

YA1073   ENGLE R.F., FOLEY D.K.
          "An asset price model of aggregate investment"   Int. Econ. Rev., vol.16,
          1975, pp.625-647.
          APPL - MACRO : INVESTMENT * APPL - SECTOR : CONSTRUCTION , NON RESIDENTIAL *
          MACRO MODEL - FRB , MIT , PENN * EVALUATION - INVESTMENT MODELS * STOCK
          PRICES - EFFECT OF * EX ANTE * DATA REVISIONS - EFFECT OF

YA1074   ENGLE R.F., GARDNER R.
          "Some finite sample properties of spectral estimators of a linear
          regression"   Econometrica, vol. 44, 1976, pp.149-165.
          ESTIMATION - HANNAN * DATA - SIMULATION * COMPARATIVE METHODS - ESTIMATION :
          REGRESSION , ERROR SPECIFICATION

YA1075   ENKE S.
          "Economic consequences of rapid population growth"   Econ. J., vol.81,
          1971, pp.800-811.
          POPULATION - FERTILITY * SIMULATION - APPL : SECTOR , SOCIAL

YA1076   ENKE S.
          "Reducing fertility to accelerate development"   Econ. J., vol.84, 1974,
          pp.349-366.
          POPULATION - FERTILITY * POLICY EVALUATION - MACRO : POPULATION CONTROL *
          APPL - MACRO : DEVELOPMENT * SIMULATION - APPL : SECTOR , SOCIAL

YA1077   ENZLER J., JOHNSON L., PAULIS J.
          "Some problems of money demand" with discussion   Brookings Paps. Econ.
          Activity, 1976, pp.261-282.
          APPL - MACRO : MONEY , DEMAND * MACRO MODEL - MIT , PENN , SSRC * EX ANTE

YA1078   ENZLER J.J., STEKLER H.O.
          "An analysis of the 1968-69 economic forecasts"   J. Business, vol.44,
          1971, pp.271-281.
          MACRO MODEL - FRB MIT * TAX - EFFECT OF * POLICY EVALUATION - MACRO : FISCAL
          * SIMULATION - APPL : POLICY EVALUATION * POLICY EVALUATION - MACRO :
          MONETARY * EXOGENOUS VARIABLES - PREDICTION OF * EX ANTE

YA1079   EPPINK D.J., KEUNIG D., DE JONG K.
"Corporate planning in the Netherlands"   Long Range Planning, vol.9,5,
1976, pp.30-41.
FORECASTING - USAGE * USE - CORPORATE PLANNING * BASIC

YA1080   EPPS T.W.
"An econometric analysis of the effectiveness of the US army's 1971 paid
advertising campaign"   Appl. Econ., vol.5, 1973, pp.261-269.
ADVERTISING - EFFECT OF * MANPOWER PLANNING - SECTOR : GOVERNMENT , MILITARY
* APPL - SECTOR : GOVERNMENT , DEFENCE

YA1081   EPPS T.W.
"The demand for brokers' services: the relation between security trading
volume and transaction cost"   Bell J. Econ., vol.7, 1976, pp.163-194.
APPL - SECTOR : FINANCE , STOCK BROKERS * STOCK PRICES - TRADING VOLUME *
COST - SECTOR : FINANCE * COST - SCALE ECONOMIES

YA1082   EPPS T.W.
"The stochastic dependence of security price changes and transaction volumes
in a model with temporally dependent price changes"   J. Am. Statist. Ass.,
vol.71, 1976, pp.830-834.
APPL - FIRM : FINANCE , BONDS * STOCK PRICES - TRADING VOLUME * ERROR
DISTRIBUTION - COMPOUND * APPL - FIRM : FINANCE , STOCK PRICES

YA1083   EPPS T.W., EPPS M.L.
"The robustness of some standard tests for autocorrelation and
heteroscedasticity when both problems are present"   Econometrica, vol.45,
1977, pp.745-753.
COMPARATIVE METHODS - TESTS , AUTOCORRELATION * COMPARATIVE METHODS - TESTS
, HETEROSCEDASTICITY

YA1084   EPPS T.W., EPPS M.L.
"The stochastic dependence of security price changes and transaction
volumes: implications for the mixture-of-distributions hypothesis"
Econometrica, vol.44, 1976, pp.305-321.
STOCK PRICES - TRADING VOLUME * APPL - FIRM : FINANCE , STOCK PRICES * ERROR
DISTRIBUTION - COMPOUND * ADVANCED

YA1085   ERICKSEN E.P.
"A regression method for estimating population changes of local areas"   J.
Am. Statist. Ass., vol.69, 1974, pp.867-875.
REGIONAL MODELS - POPULATION * POPULATION

YA1086   ERICKSON E.W., MILLSAPS S.W., SPANN R.M.
"Oil supply and tax incentives"   Brookings Paps. Econ. Activity, 1974,
pp.449-493.
APPL - SECTOR : PRODUCTION , PETROLEUM * TAX - EFFECT OF * SUPPLY - SECTOR :
PRODUCTION * EX ANTE * POLICY EVALUATION - SECTOR : PRODUCTION * APPL -
SECTOR : COMMODITIES , OIL

YA1087   ERICKSON E.W., SPANN R.M.
"Supply response in a regulated industry: the case of natural gas"   Bell
J. Econ., vol.2, 1971, pp.94-121.
SUPPLY - SECTOR : PRODUCTION * APPL - SECTOR : PRODUCTION , GAS * DATA -
CROSS SECTION , TIME SERIES * EX ANTE * USE - FINANCIAL , REGULATION * PRICE
- EFFECT OF

YA1088   ERTEL J.E., FOWLKES E.B.
"Some algorithms for linear spline and piecewise multiple linear regression"
J. Am. Statist. Ass., vol.71, 1976, pp.640-648
SPLINE FUNCTIONS * REGRESSION - PIECEWISE * NUMERICAL METHODS - OPTIMISATION
, SEARCH * DATA - SIMULATION * APPL - FIRM : FINANCE , STOCK PRICES

YA1089   ESKEW R.K., WRIGHT W.F.
"An empirical analysis of differential capital market reactions to
extraordinary accounting items" with discussion   J. Finance, vol.31, 1976,
pp.651-677 & 680-684.
STOCK PRICES - INFORMATION EFFECT * ACCOUNTING PRACTICE - EFFECT OF * APPL -
FIRM : FINANCE , STOCK PRICES * STOCK PRICES - DETERMINANTS * TIME SERIES -
COMPARISONS * EVALUATION - TIME SERIES

YA1090   ESKIN G.J.
"Dynamic forecasts of new product demand using a depth of repeat model"
J. Mktg. Res., vol.10, 1973, pp.115-129.
NEW PRODUCTS - TESTING * REPEAT BUYING * COMPARATIVE METHODS - REGRESSION ,
ERROR SPECIFICATION

YA1091   ESPASA A., SARGAN J.D.
"The spectral estimation of simultaneous equation systems with lagged
endogenous variables"   Int. Econ. Rev., vol.18, 1977, pp.583-605.
SIMULTANEOUS SYSTEM - ESTIMATION * ESTIMATION - HANNAN * DATA - SIMULATION *
APPL - MACRO : EARNINGS * INFLATION - DETERMINANTS * COMPARATIVE METHODS -
ESTIMATION : OLS , FIML * COMPARATIVE METHODS - ESTIMATION : SIMULTANEOUS
SYSTEM * APPL - MACRO : UNEMPLOYMENT * DISTRIBUTED LAG - SIMULTANEOUS SYSTEM
* SIMULTANEOUS SYSTEM - LAGGED ENDOGENOUS

YA1092   ESPOSITO L., ESPOSITO F.F.
"Foreign competition and domestic industry profitability"   Rev. Econ.
Stats., vol.53, 1971, pp.343-353.
APPL - SECTOR : FINANCE , PROFITS * APPL - SECTOR : FINANCE , INTERNATIONAL
TRADE , IMPORTS * CONCENTRATION - EFFECT OF * SPECIFICATION ERROR - EFFECT
OF , HETEROSCEDASTICITY

YA1093   ESTRUP C.
          "The planning of a petrochemical complex"   Ind. Mktg. Mgmt., vol.2, 1972,
          pp.57-68.
          APPL - SECTOR : PRODUCTION , CHEMICALS * SIMULATION - APPL : SECTOR ,
          PRODUCTION * INPUT OUTPUT - SECTOR : PRODUCTION * BASIC

YA1094   EVANS A.
          "Notes on the changing relationship between registered unemployment and
          notified vacancies: 1961-1966 and 1966-1971"   Economica, vol.44, 1977,
          pp.179-196.
          BUSINESS INDICATORS - EMPLOYMENT VACANCIES * APPL - MACRO , UK * APPL -
          MACRO : UNEMPLOYMENT * REGIONAL MODELS - UNEMPLOYMENT

YA1095   EVANS G.J.
          "A note on trends in the relationship between unemployment and unfilled
          vacancies"   Econ. J., vol.85, 1975, pp.135-139.
          APPL - MACRO , UK * APPL - MACRO : UNEMPLOYMENT * STABILITY OF COEFFICIENTS
          - REGRESSION : APPL

YA1096   EVANS G.J., ROBERTS C.J.
          "Short-run employment functions in simulation and forecasting"   Statn.,
          vol.24, 1975, pp.262-282.
          APPL - SECTOR : PRODUCTION , ENGINEERING * APPL - SECTOR : EMPLOYMENT *
          EVALUATION - EMPLOYMENT MODELS * EX ANTE

YA1097   EVANS I.G., SHABAN S.A.
          "Point estimation of multiplicative models"   Econometrica, vol.44, 1976,
          pp.467-473.
          REGRESSION - TRANSFORMATIONS , LOGARITHMIC * ERROR DISTRIBUTION - LOGNORMAL
          * ERROR SPECIFICATION - MULTIPLICATIVE * COMPARATIVE METHODS - REGRESSION ,
          TRANSFORMATIONS * ESTIMATION - LOGARITHMIC MODEL * REGRESSION - ESTIMATION

YA1098   EVANS M.K.
          "A forecasting model application to pollution control costs" with discussion
          Am. Econ. Ass. Proc., 1973, pp.244-252 & 253-256.
          POLLUTION - CONTROLS * INPUT OUTPUT - MACRO : POLLUTION * COST - MACRO :
          POLLUTION

YA1099   EVANS M.K.
          "A study of industry investment decisions"   Rev. Econ. Stats., vol.49,
          1967, pp.151-164.
          APPL - MACRO : INVESTMENT * DISTRIBUTED LAG - APPL , OUTPUT * APPL - SECTOR
          : INVESTMENT * COMPARATIVE METHODS - DISTRIBUTED LAG * INTEREST RATE -
          EFFECT OF

YA1100   EVANS M.K.
          "Reconstruction and estimation of the balanced budget multiplier"   Rev.
          Econ. Stats., vol.51, 1969, pp.14-25.
          APPL - SECTOR : GOVERNMENT * PUBLIC EXPENDITURE - EFFECT OF * TAX - EFFECT
          OF * EVALUATION - MACRO MODELS * MULTIPLIERS - MACRO * MACRO MODEL -
          BROOKINGS * MACRO MODEL - WHARTON

YA1101   EVANS M.K., GREEN E.W.
          "The relative efficiency of investment anticipations"   J. Am. Statist.
          Ass., vol.61, 1966, pp.104-116.
          COMPARATIVE METHODS - AUTOREGRESSIVE , JUDGEMENTAL * COMPARATIVE METHODS -
          CAUSAL , JUDGEMENTAL * COMPARATIVE METHODS - AUTOREGRESSIVE , CAUSAL *
          EVALUATION - SURVEYS , BUSINESS * EVALUATION - EXPECTATIONS , DATA *
          EVALUATION - EX POST MODELS * EVALUATION - TURNING POINT FORECASTS * EX ANTE

YA1102   EVANS P.
          "Time-series analysis of the German hyperinflation"   Int. Econ. Rev.,
          vol.19, 1978, pp.195-209.
          APPL - MACRO , GERMANY * INFLATION - RAPID * INFLATION - EXPECTATIONS *
          INFLATION - DETERMINANTS * CAUSALITY - TEST : APPL * TIME SERIES - ARIMA :
          APPL

YA1103   EVANS R.G.
          "'Behavioural' cost functions for hospitals"   Can. J. Econ., vol.4, 1971,
          pp.198-215.
          HEALTH - HOSPITAL * COST - SECTOR : HEALTH * FACTOR ANALYSIS - APPL

YA1104   EVANS R.G., PARISH E.M.A., SULLY F.
          "Medical productivity, scale effects and demand generation"   Can. J.
          Econ., vol.6, 1973, pp.376-393.
          HEALTH - MANPOWER , EARNINGS * HEALTH - MANPOWER , PHYSICIANS * MANPOWER
          PLANNING - SECTOR : HEALTH

YA1105   EVANS R.G., WALKER H.D.
          "Information theory on the analysis of hospital cost structure"   Can. J.
          Econ., vol.5, 1972, pp.398-418.
          COST - FIRM : HEALTH , HOSPITAL * HEALTH - HOSPITAL

YA1106   EVANS R.H.
          "Inter-bank perceptions: a marketing application of discriminant analysis"
          J. Opl. Res. Soc., vol.29, 1978, pp.661-665.
          APPL - FIRM : FINANCE , BANKS * DISCRIMINANT ANALYSIS - APPL * MARKET
          POSITION

YA1107   EYSSELL J.H.
          "The supply response of crude petroleum - new and optimistic results"
          Bus. Econ., vol.13:3, 1978, pp.15-28.
          APPL - SECTOR : COMMODITIES , OIL * SUPPLY - SECTOR : COMMODITIES * PRICE -
          EFFECT OF

YA1108   EZZATI A,
"Forecasting market shares of alternative home heating units by market
process,using transition probabilities estimated from aggregate time series
data"   Mgmt, Sci, (B), vol,21, 1974, pp,462-473,
APPL - SECTOR : CONSUMER DURABLES , APPLIANCES , HEATING UNITS * CONSUMER
BEHAVIOUR - STOCHASTIC MODELS * MARKOV MODELS - ESTIMATION * MARKET SHARE -
SECTOR : CONSUMER DURABLES * ESTIMATION - MAXIMUM LIKELIHOOD

YA1109   FABOZZI F,J,, FRANCIS J,C,
"Stability tests for alphas and betas over bull and bear market conditions"
J, Finance, vol,32, 1977, pp,1093-1099,
STOCK PRICES - BETA , VARIABLE * BUSINESS CYCLE - EFFECT OF * APPL - FIRM :
FINANCE , STOCK PRICES

YA1110   FABRYCY M,Z,
"Multicollinearity caused by specification errors"   Appl, Stats,, vol,24,
1975, pp,250-254,
MULTICOLLINEARITY - REMOVAL OF * SPECIFICATION ERROR - EFFECT OF ,
STATIONARITY * REGRESSION - TRANSFORMATIONS * TIME SERIES - DECOMPOSITION ,
TREND REMOVAL * PRODUCTION FUNCTIONS - ESTIMATION

YA1111   FADEN A,M,, RAUSSER G,C,
"Econometric policy model construction: the post-Bayesian approach"   Anns,
Econ, Soc, Meas,, vol,5, 1976, pp,349-362,
MODEL SELECTION * CONTROL THEORY - REVIEW

YA1112   FAIR R,C,
"A comparison of alternative estimators of macroeconomic models"   Int,
Econ, Rev,, vol,14, 1973, pp,261-277,
COMPARATIVE METHODS - ESTIMATION : SIMULTANEOUS SYSTEM * COMPARATIVE METHODS
- ESTIMATION : OLS , 2SLS * COMPARATIVE METHODS - REGRESSION , ERROR
SPECIFICATION * COMPARATIVE METHODS - REGRESSION , SIMULTANEOUS SYSTEM *
COMPARATIVE METHODS - ESTIMATION : SIMULTANEOUS SYSTEM , ERROR SPECIFICATION
* COMPARATIVE METHODS - ESTIMATION : OLS , FIML * MACRO MODEL - FAIR

YA1113   FAIR R,C,
"A full information maximum likelihood program"   Econometrica, vol,40,
1972, p,773,
ESTIMATION - FIML * COMPUTERISATION - ESTIMATION , SIMULTANEOUS SYSTEM
MODELS , PROGRAMS

YA1114   FAIR R,C,
"A note on the computation of the Tobit estimator"   Econometrica, vol,45,
1978, pp,1723-1727,
REGRESSION - LIMITED DEPENDENT , TOBIT * NUMERICAL METHODS - OPTIMISATION

YA1115   FAIR R,C,
"A program to solve an econometric model"   Anns, Econ, Soc, Meas,, vol,6,
1978, p,651,
MACRO MODEL - FAIR * COMPUTERISATION - MACRO MODELLING , PROGRAMS * MACRO
MODELS - METHODOLOGY , SOLUTION

YA1116   FAIR R,C,
"An evaluation of a short-run forecasting model"   Int, Econ, Rev,, vol,15,
1974, pp,285-303,
MACRO MODEL - FAIR * EVALUATION - MACRO MODELS * EX ANTE * EVALUATION - EX
POST MODELS * COMPARATIVE METHODS - MACRO MODELS * JUDGEMENTAL FORECASTS -
ASA NBER SURVEY * EXOGENOUS VARIABLES - PREDICTION OF , EFFECT * COMPARATIVE
METHODS - CAUSAL(SIMULTANEOUS SYSTEM) , JUDGEMENTAL

YA1117   FAIR R,C,
"Disequilibrium in housing models" with discussion   J, Finance, vol,27,
1972, pp,207-221 & 226-230,
SIMULTANEOUS SYSTEM - DISEQUILIBRIUM : APPL * APPL - SECTOR : CONSTRUCTION ,
RESIDENTIAL * MACRO MODEL - SSRC , MIT , PENN * REGIONAL MODELS - SECTOR :
CONSTRUCTION

YA1118   FAIR R,C,
"Labour force participation, wage rates, and money illusion"   Rev, Econ,
Stats,, vol,53, 1971, pp,164-168,
DISTRIBUTED LAG - ALMON : APPL * APPL - MACRO : EMPLOYMENT * MANPOWER
PLANNING - LABOUR PARTICIPATION * MANPOWER PLANNING - LABOUR FORCE
COMPOSITION

YA1119   FAIR R,C,
"On the robust estimation of econometric models"   Anns, Econ, Soc, Meas,,
vol,3, 1974, pp,667-677,
SIMULTANEOUS SYSTEMS - ESTIMATION * MACRO MODEL - FAIR * COMPARATIVE METHODS
- ESTIMATION : SIMULTANEOUS SYSTEM * COMPARATIVE METHODS - ESTIMATION : OLS
, ROBUST * EX ANTE * ESTIMATION - ROBUST * COMPARATIVE METHODS - ESTIMATION
: OLS , FIML

YA1120   FAIR R,C,
"On the solution of optimal control problems as maximization problems"
Anns, Econ, Soc, Meas,, vol,3, 1974, pp,135-154,
CONTROL THEORY - DETERMINISTIC , METHODOLOGY * SIMULTANEOUS SYSTEM - CONTROL
* CONTROL THEORY - STOCHASTIC , METHODOLOGY * NUMERICAL METHODS -
OPTIMISATION * MACRO MODEL - FAIR

YA1121   FAIR R.C.
          "The estimation of simultaneous equation models with lagged endogenous
          variables and first order serially correlated errors"   Econometrica,
          vol.38, 1970, pp.507-516.
          SIMULTANEOUS SYSTEMS - LAGGED ENDOGENOUS * ERROR SPECIFICATION -
          AUTOCORRELATED * SIMULTANEOUS SYSTEM - ESTIMATION , ERROR SPECIFICATION
YA1122   FAIR R.C.
          "The sensitivity of fiscal policy effects to assumptions about the behaviour
          of the Federal Reserve"   Econometrica, vol.46, 1978, pp.1165-1179.
          CONTROL THEORY - DETERMINISTIC , APPL * POLICY EVALUATION - MACRO : FISCAL *
          DECISION RULES - MACRO * DECISION RULES - FEEDBACK * SIMULATION - APPL :
          POLICY EVALUATION
YA1123   FAIR R.C., JAFFEE D.M.
          "Methods of estimation for markets in disequilibrium"   Econometrica,
          vol.40, 1972, pp.497-514.
          SIMULTANEOUS SYSTEM - DISEQUILIBRIUM * APPL - SECTOR : CONSTRUCTION ,
          RESIDENTIAL * SIMULTANEOUS SYSTEM - ESTIMATION
YA1124   FAIR R.C., KELEJIAN H.H.
          "Methods of estimation for markets in desequilibrium: a further study"
          Econometrica, vol.42, 1974, pp.177-190.
          SIMULTANEOUS SYSTEMS - DISEQUILIBRIUM * APPL - SECTOR : CONSTRUCTION ,
          RESIDENTIAL * SIMULTANEOUS SYSTEM - ESTIMATION * ESTIMATION - MAXIMUM
          LIKELIHOOD * ADVANCED
YA1125   FALCONER R.T., SIVESIND C.M.
          "Dealing with conflicting forecasts"   Bus. Econ., vol.12:4, 1977, pp.5-11.
          APPL - MACRO : INCOME * COMBINING FORECASTS - CAUSAL , TIME SERIES * MACRO
          MODEL - FRB , MIT , PENN * LEAD TIME - EFFECT OF * EX ANTE * COMPARATIVE
          METHODS - MACRO MODELS * COMPARATIVE METHODS - ARIMA , CAUSAL(SIMULTANEOUS
          SYSTEM) * EVALUATION - COMBINING FORECASTS
YA1126   FALK H., MILLER J.C.
          "Amortisation of advertising expenditures"   J. Acctg. Res., vol.15, 1977,
          pp.12-22.
          ADVERTISING - EFFECT OF * DISTRIBUTED LAG - APPL , ADVERTISING * APPL - FIRM
          : CONSUMER DURABLES , CARS
YA1127   FAMA E.F.
          "Short term interest rates as predictors of inflation"   Am. Econ. Rev.,
          vol.65, 1975, pp.269-282.
          THEORY - MONETARY * INTEREST RATE - EXPECTATIONS * INFLATION - INDICATORS *
          THEORY - EFFICIENT MARKETS * INFLATION - EXPECTATIONS
YA1128   FAMA E.F.
          "The empirical relationships between the dividend and investment decisions
          of firms"   Am. Econ. Rev., vol.64, 1974, pp.304-318.
          APPL - FIRM : INVESTMENT * DATA - CROSS SECTION , TIME SERIES * APPL - FIRM
          : FINANCE , DIVIDENDS * EX ANTE * COMPARATIVE METHODS - ESTIMATION : OLS ,
          2SLS * CAUSALITY - TEST
YA1129   FAMA E.F., BABIAK H.
          "Dividend policy: an empirical analysis"   J. Am. Statist. Ass., vol.63,
          1968, pp.1132-1161.
          APPL - FIRM : FINANCE , DIVIDENDS * DISTRIBUTED LAG - EXPECTATIONS
          HYPOTHESES * DATA - CROSS SECTION , TIME SERIES * EX ANTE * EVALUATION -
          TEST , AUTOCORRELATION * DATA - SIMULATION * EVALUATION - REGRESSION ,
          LAGGED DEPENDENT
YA1130   FANE G.
          "Education and the managerial efficiency of farmers"   Rev. Econ. Stats.,
          vol.57, 1975, pp.452-461.
          EDUCATION - EFFECT OF * PRODUCTION FUNCTION - FIRM * APPL - FIRM :
          AGRICULTURE , FARMING * COST - FIRM : AGRICULTURE * DATA - CROSS SECTION *
          REGRESSION - MODEL CHOICE * DATA ERRORS - EFFECT OF * PRODUCTION FUNCTIONS -
          METHODOLOGY * REGRESSION - TRANSFORMATIONS , LOGARITHMIC
YA1131   FANE G., LAIDLER D.
          "Inflation in Britain: a monetarist perspective: comments"   Am. Econ.
          Rev., vol.68, 1978, pp.721-729.
          INFLATION - DETERMINANTS * POLICY EVALUATION - MACRO : MONETARY * APPL -
          MACRO , UK
YA1132   FARBER H.S.
          "Bargaining theory, wage outcomes, and the occurrence of strikes: an
          econometric analysis"   Am. Econ. Rev., vol.68, 1978, pp.262-271.
          APPL - SECTOR : SOCIAL , STRIKES * UNIONISATION - EFFECT OF * REGRESSION -
          TRUNCATED : APPL
YA1133   FARBER S., ET AL.
          "The earnings and promotion of women faculty: comments"   Am. Econ. Rev.,
          vol.67, 1977, pp.199-217.
          MANPOWER PLANNING - DISCRIMINATION , SEXUAL * MANPOWER PLANNING - EARNINGS ,
          FEMALE
YA1134   FAREBROTHER R.W.
          "A remark on the Wu test"   Econometrica, vol.44, 1976, pp.475-477.
          SPECIFICATION ERROR - TEST , INDEPENDENCE REGRESSORS , ERRORS

YA1135   FAREBROTHER R.W.
         "BLUS residuals and recursive residuals"   Appl. Stats., vol.25, 1976,
         pp.317-321.
         COMPUTERISATION - ESTIMATION , REGRESSION MODELS , PROGRAMS * RESIDUALS -
         ESTIMATION , BLUS * RESIDUALS - ESTIMATION , RECURSIVE

YA1136   FAREBROTHER R.W.
         "Minimax regret significance points for a preliminary test in regression
         analysis: comment"   Econometrica, vol.43, 1975, pp.1005-1006.
         ESTIMATION - PRE TEST * REGRESSION - HYPOTHESIS TESTS * ADVANCED

YA1137   FAREBROTHER R.W.
         "Principal components estimators and minimum mean error criteria in
         regression analysis"   Rev. Econ. Stats., vol.54, 1972, pp.332-336.
         ESTIMATION - PRINCIPAL COMPONENTS * REGRESSION - RIDGE * REGRESSION -
         ESTIMATION * ADVANCED

YA1138   FAREBROTHER R.W.
         "The graph of a k-class estimator"   Rev. Econ. Studies, vol.41, 1974,
         pp.533-538.
         ESTIMATION - K CLASS

YA1139   FAREBROTHER R.W., SAVIN N.E.
         "The graph of the k-class estimator: an algebraic and statistical
         interpretation"   J. Econometrics, vol.2, 1974, pp.373-388.
         ESTIMATION - K CLASS * COMPARATIVE METHODS - ESTIMATION : SIMULTANEOUS
         SYSTEM * COMPARATIVE METHODS - ESTIMATION : OLS , 2SLS * ADVANCED

YA1140   FARLEY J.U., ARMSTROMG J.S.
         "A note on the use of Markov chains in forecasting store choice"   Mgmt.
         Sci. (B), vol.16, 1969, pp.281-285.
         CONSUMER BEHAVIOUR - STOCHASTIC MODELS * MARKOV MODELS - APPL : BRAND CHOICE
         * BRAND CHOICE - APPL * APPL - FIRM : RETAILING * BASIC

YA1141   FARLEY J.U., HINICH M., McGUIRE T.W.
         "Some comparisons of tests for a shift in the slopes of a multivariate
         linear time series model"   J. Econometrics, vol.3, 1975, pp.297-318.
         STABILITY OF COEFFICIENTS - REGRESSION , TEST * COMPARATIVE METHODS - TESTS
         , STABILITY * DATA - SIMULATION * SPECIFICATION ERROR - TESTS , STABILITY

YA1142   FARLEY J.U., HINICH M.J.
         "A test for a shifting slope coefficient in a linear model"   J. Am.
         Statist. Ass., vol.65, 1970, pp.1320-1329.
         STABILITY OF COEFFICIENTS - REGRESSION , TEST

YA1143   FARLEY J.U., HOWARD J.A., LEHMAN D.R.
         "A 'working' system model of car buyer behaviour"   Mgmt. Sci., vol.23,
         1976, pp.235-247.
         SIMULTANEOUS SYSTEM - APPL * SIMULATION - APPL : ADVERTISING * MARKET SHARE
         - SECTOR : CONSUMER DURABLES * CONSUMER BEHAVIOUR - PURCHASING ,
         DETERMINANTS

YA1144   FARLEY J.U., LEAVITT H.J.
         "A model of the distribution of brand personal products in Jamaica"   J.
         Mktg. Res., vol.5, 1968, pp.362-368.
         APPL - SECTOR : DISTRIBUTION * APPL - SECTOR : CONSUMER NON DURABLES , HEALTH
         AIDS * COMPARATIVE METHODS - ESTIMATION : OLS , 2SLS * COMPARATIVE METHODS -
         ESTIMATION : OLS , FIML * COMPARATIVE METHODS - ESTIMATION : SIMULTANEOUS
         SYSTEMS

YA1145   FARLEY J.U., RING L.W.
         "An empirical test of the Howard-Sheth model of buyer behaviour"   J. Mktg.
         Res., vol.7, 1970, pp.427-438.
         CONSUMER BEHAVIOUR - PSYCHOLOGICAL MODELS * SIMULATION - APPL : CONSUMER
         BEHAVIOUR * APPL - SECTOR : CONSUMER NON DURABLES , GROCERIES * BRAND CHOICE
         - DETERMINANTS

YA1146   FARLEY J.U., RING L.W.
         "'Empirical' specification of a buyer behaviour model"   J. Mktg. Res.,
         vol.11, 1974, pp.89-96.
         CONSUMER BEHAVIOUR - PURCHASING , DETERMINANTS * CONSUMER BEHAVIOUR -
         PSYCHOLOGICAL MODELS * AID - APPL * CANONICAL CORRELATION - APPL * APPL -
         SECTOR : CONSUMER NON DURABLES , FOOD * BRAND CHOICE - DETERMINANTS

YA1147   FARLEY J.U., RING L.W.
         "On L and R and HAPPISIMM"   J. Mktg. Res., vol.9, 1972, pp.349-353.
         COMPARATIVE METHODS - ESTIMATION : OLS , 2SLS * EVALUATION - CONSUMER
         BEHAVIOUR , PSYCHOLOGICAL MODELS * SIMULATION - APPL : CONSUMER BEHAVIOUR *
         MODEL IDENTIFICATION - DATA - SPECIFICATION OF VARIABLES * SPECIFICATION
         ERROR - EFFECT OF , IDENTIFICATION

YA1148   FARRAR D.E., GLAUBER R.R.
         "Multicollinearity in regression analysis: the problem revisited"   Rev.
         Econ. Stats., vol.49, 1967, pp.92-107.
         MULTICOLLINEARITY - TESTS * MULTICOLLINEARITY - REVIEW

YA1149   FARRELL J. L.
         "Analysing covariation of returns to determine homogenous stock groupings"
         J. Business, vol.47, 1974, pp.186-207.
         APPL - SECTOR : FINANCE , STOCK PRICE INDEX * APPL - FIRM : FINANCE , STOCK
         PRICES * CLUSTER ANALYSIS - APPL * STOCK PRICES - INDUSTRIAL STRUCTURE

YA1150   FAUROT D.J., FON V.
"A computer program for seemingly unrelated non linear regressions"
Econometrica, vol.46, 1978, pp.479-480.
COMPUTERISATION - ESTIMATION , REGRESSION MODELS , PROGRAMS * ESTIMATION -
CONSTRAINED * ESTIMATION - NON LINEAR * REGRESSION - SEEMINGLY UNRELATED

YA1151   FEIGE E.L.
"Temporal cross-section specifications of the demand for demand deposits"
J. Finance, vol.29, 1974, pp.923-940.
APPL - MACRO : MONEY * REGRESSION - RANDOM COEFFICIENTS * REGRESSION -
COVARIANCE MODEL * COMPARATIVE METHODS - DATA : CROSS SECTION , TIME SERIES
* COMPARATIVE METHODS - REGRESSION , RANDOM COEFFICIENTS

YA1152   FEIGE E.L., WATTS H.W.
"An investigation of the consequences of partial aggregation of micro
economic data"   Econometrica, vol.40, 1972, pp.343-360.
DATA - AGGREGATION * SURVEYS - METHODOLOGY , AGGREGATION * APPL - SECTOR :
FINANCE , BANKS * COMPARATIVE METHODS - DATA : AGGREGATE , DISAGGREGATE

YA1153   FEINBERG R.M.
"Risk aversion, risk, and the duration of unemployment"   Rev. Econ.
Stats., vol.59, 1977, pp.264-271.
MANPOWER PLANNING - MACRO * RISK - EFFECT OF

YA1154   FELDSTEIN M.S.
"Hospital cost inflation: a study of non profit price dynamics"   Am. Econ.
Rev., vol.61, 1971, pp.853-872.
HEALTH - HOSPITAL * COST - SECTOR : HEALTH

YA1155   FELDSTEIN M.S.
"Multicollinearity and the mean square error of alternative estimators"
Econometrica, vol.41, 1973, pp.337-346.
MULTICOLLINEARITY - EFFECT OF * REGRESSION - RIDGE * COMPARATIVE METHODS -
MULTICOLLINEARITY * DATA - SIMULATION

YA1156   FELDSTEIN M.S.
"Personal taxation and portfolio composition: an econometric analysis"
Econometrica, vol.44, 1976, pp.631-650.
APPL - MACRO : CONSUMER DEMAND , FINANCIAL ASSETS * TAX - EFFECT OF * INCOME
- EFFECT OF

YA1157   FELDSTEIN M.S.
"Production with uncertain technology: some economic and econometric
implications"   Int. Econ. Rev., vol.12, 1971, pp.27-38.
PRODUCTION FUNCTIONS - THEORY * TECHNOLOGY - EFFECT OF * HEALTH - HOSPITAL *
PRODUCTION FUNCTIONS - SECTOR

YA1158   FELDSTEIN M.S.
"Quality change and the demand for hospital care"   Econometrica, vol.45,
1977, pp.1681-1702.
HEALTH - HOSPITAL * PRICE - SECTOR : HEALTH * APPL - SECTOR : FINANCE ,
INSURANCE * BIBLIOGRAPHY - HEALTH * QUALITY - MEASURING * CAPACITY - EFFECT
OF

YA1159   FELDSTEIN M.S.
"Social security and saving: the extended life cycle theory"   Am. Econ.
Ass. Proc., vol.66, 1976, pp.77-86.
APPL - MACRO : SAVINGS * LIFE CYCLE - CONSUMER * BASIC

YA1160   FELDSTEIN M.S.
"The effect of unemployment insurance on temporary layoff unemployment"
Am. Econ. Rev., vol.68, 1978, pp.834-846.
MANPOWER PLANNING - UNEMPLOYMENT , DURATION * MANPOWER PLANNING - LABOUR
TURNOVER * POLICY EVALUATION - MACRO : UNEMPLOYMENT * MANPOWER PLANNING -
LABOUR FORCE COMPOSITION

YA1161   FELDSTEIN M.S.
"The error of forecast in econometric models when the forecast-period
exogenous variables are stochastic"   Econometrica, vol.39 ,1971, pp.55-60.
DATA ERRORS - EFFECT OF * CONFIDENCE INTERVAL - SIMULTANEOUS SYSTEM ,
MULTIVARIATE * EXOGENOUS VARIABLES - PREDICTION OF , EFFECT * CONFIDENCE
INTERVAL - PREDICTIONS : SIMULTANEOUS SYSTEM

YA1162   FELDSTEIN M.S., AUERBACH A.
"Inventory behaviour in durable-goods manufacturing: the target-adjustment
model" with discussion   Brookings Paps. Econ. Activity, 1976, pp.351-408.
APPL - MACRO : INVENTORIES * EXPECTATIONS - DATA * EVALUATION - SALES
FORECASTS * EVALUATION - INVENTORY MODELS

YA1163   FELDSTEIN M.S., ECKSTEIN O.
"The fundamental determinants of the interest rate"   Rev. Econ. Stats.,
vol.52, 1970, pp.363-375.
INTEREST RATE - DETERMINANTS * COMPARATIVE METHODS - ESTIMATION : REGRESSION
* THEORY - LIQUIDITY PREFERENCE * INFLATION - EFFECT OF * ESTIMATION -
INSTRUMENTAL VARIABLES : APPL * DISTRIBUTED LAG - ALMON : APPL

YA1164   FELDSTEIN M.S., FANE G.
"Taxes, corporate dividend policy and personal savings: the British post-war
experience"   Rev. Econ. Stats., vol.55, 1973, pp.399-411.
TAX - EFFECT OF * DISTRIBUTED LAG - SOLOW * APPL - MACRO : CONSUMPTION *
DISTRIBUTED LAG - APPL , CONSUMPTION * APPL - MACRO : DIVIDENDS * APPL -
MACRO : SAVINGS

YA1165   FELDSTEIN M.S., FLEMMING J.S.
          "Tax policy, corporate saving and investment behaviour in Britain"   Rev.
          Econ. Studies, vol.38, 1971, pp.415-434.
          APPL - MACRO , UK * APPL - MACRO : INVESTMENT * TAX - EFFECT OF
YA1166   FELDSTEIN M.S., FOOT D.K.
          "The other half of gross investment: replacement and modernization
          expenditures"   Rev. Econ. Stats., vol.53, 1971, pp.49-59.
          DEPRECIATION * APPL - MACRO : INVESTMENT * DEMAND - REPLACEMENT
YA1167   FELDSTEIN M.S., SUMMERS L.
          "Inflation, tax rules and long-term interest rate" with discussion
          Brookings Paps. Econ. Activity, 1978, pp.61-109.
          INFLATION - EXPECTATIONS * EXPECTATIONS - ESTIMATING * TIME SERIES - ARIMA :
          APPL * INTEREST RATE - DETERMINANTS * TAX - EFFECT OF
YA1168   FELDSTEIN M.S., SUMMERS L.
          "Is the rate of profit falling?" with discussion   Brookings Paps. Econ.
          Activity, 1977, pp.211-228.
          APPL - SECTOR : FINANCE , PROFITS * APPL - MACRO : PROFITS * CAPACITY -
          EFFECT OF
YA1169   FELDSTEIN M.S., TAYLOR A.
          "The income tax and charitable contributions"   Econometrica, vol.44, 1976,
          pp.1201-1222.
          TAX - EFFECT OF * APPL - SECTOR : SERVICES , CHARITIES * PRICE - EFFECT OF *
          INCOME - EFFECT OF * POLICY EVALUATION - SECTOR : SERVICES
YA1170   FELLNER W.
          "Phillips-type approach or acceleration"   Brookings Paps. Econ. Activity,
          1971, pp.469-483.
          INFLATION - PHILLIPS CURVE
YA1171   FELLNER W., LARKINS D.
          "Interpretations of a regularity in the behaviour of M2" with discussion
          Brookings Paps. Econ. Activity, 1976, pp.741-763.
          APPL - MACRO : MONEY * APPL - MACRO : MONEY , INCOME VELOCITY
YA1172   FELS R., HINSHAW C.E., STEKLER H.O.
          "An analysis of turning point forecasts: comments"   Am. Econ. Rev.,
          vol.64, 1974, pp.724-729.
          EVALUATION - TURNING POINT FORECASTS * BUSINESS INDICATORS - APPL *
          FORECASTER BEHAVIOUR * DATA REVISIONS - EFFECT OF * JUDGEMENTAL FORECASTS -
          TURNING POINTS * BUSINESS CYCLE - TURNING POINTS * PRIOR INFORMATION
YA1173   FELSEN J.
          "Artificial intelligence techniques applied to reduction of uncertainty in
          decision analysis through learning"   Opl. Res. Q., vol.26, 1975,
          pp.581-598.
          PATTERN RECOGNITION * STOCK PRICES - DETERMINANTS
YA1174   FELSEN J.
          "Cybernetic approach to investment decision-making"   Omega, vol.6, 1978,
          pp.237-247.
          APPL - SECTOR : FINANCE , STOCK PRICE INDEX * STOCK PRICES - TRADING RULES *
          SYSTEMS THEORY - APPL
YA1175   FELTHAM G.A.
          "Cost aggregation: an information economic analysis"   J. Acctg. Res.,
          vol.15, 1977, pp.42-70.
          DATA - AGGREGATION * COMPARATIVE METHODS - DATA : AGGREGATE , DISAGGREGATE *
          BAYESIAN - ESTIMATION : REGRESSION * COMPARATIVE METHODS - ESTIMATION : OLS
          , BAYESIAN
YA1176   FERBER R.
          "Contributions of economics to the study of consumer market behaviour"
          Appl. Econ., vol.1, 1969, pp.125-136.
          CONSUMER BEHAVIOUR - ECONOMIC MODELS , REVIEW * BIBLIOGRAPHY - CONSUMER
          BEHAVIOUR * BASIC
YA1177   FERBER R., HAWKES W.J., PLOTKIN M.D.
          "How reliable are national retail sales estimates?"   J. Mktg., vol.40:4,
          1976, pp.13-22.
          APPL - MACRO : SALES * DATA ERRORS - ANALYSIS OF * DATA REVISIONS - EFFECT
          OF * BASIC
YA1178   FERNANDEZ R.B.
          "An empirical inquiry on the short-run dynamics of output and prices"   Am
          Econ. Rev., vol.67, 1977, pp.595-609.
          THEORY - MONETARY * APPL - MACRO , LATIN AMERICA * DISTRIBUTED LAG - APPL ,
          MONEY * DISTRIBUTED LAG - RATIONAL POLYNOMIAL * INFLATION - DETERMINANTS *
          APPL - MACRO : INCOME
YA1179   FERRATT T.W., MABERT V.A.
          "A description and application of the Box-Jenkins methodology"   Decis.
          Sci., vol.3:4, 1972, pp.83-107.
          APPL - FIRM : UTILITIES , ELECTRICITY * TIME SERIES - ARIMA : INTRODUCTION *
          EX ANTE
YA1180   FERREIRA P.E.
          "A Bayesian analysis of a switching regression model known number of
          regimes"   J. Am. Statist. Ass., vol.70, 1975, pp.370-374.
          TIME SERIES - SWITCHING * REGRESSION - SWITCHING * DATA - SIMULATION *
          BAYESIAN - ESTIMATION : REGRESSION , SWITCHING * ADVANCED

YA1181   FIELDS G.S.
"Labor force migration, unemployment and job turnover"   Rev. Econ. Stats.,
vol.53, 1976, pp.407-415.
MANPOWER PLANNING - MIGRATION * REGIONAL MODELS - MIGRATION * DATA - CROSS
SECTION * MANPOWER PLANNING - UNEMPLOYMENT * MANPOWER PLANNING - LABOUR
TURNOVER

YA1182   FIELITZ B.D., BHARGAVA T.N.
"The behaviour of stock prices relatives - a Markovian analysis"   Ops.
Res., vol.21, 1973, pp.1183-1199.
APPL - FIRM : FINANCE , STOCK PRICES * RANDOM WALK - TEST * RANDOM WALK -
METHODOLOGY * TURNING POINT - FORECASTING * MARKOV MODEL - APPL : STOCK
PRICES * STOCK PRICES - RUNS * TIME SERIES - NON STATIONARY

YA1183   FIELITZ B.D., SMITH E.W.
"Asymmetric stable distributions of stock price changes"   J. Am. Statist.
Ass., vol.67, 1972, pp.813-814.
STOCK PRICES - DISTRIBUTION * APPL - FIRM : FINANCE , STOCK PRICES * ERROR
DISTRIBUTION - STABLE * ERROR DISTRIBUTION - ASYMMETRICAL

YA1184   FILDES R., JALLAND M., WOOD D.
"Forecasting in conditions of uncertainty"   Long Range Planning, vol.11:4,
1978, pp.29-38.
FORECASTING - REVIEW * FORECASTING - VALUE OF * MIS * FORECASTING - USAGE *
USE - ORGANISATIONAL DESIGN * BASIC

YA1185   FILDES R., LOFTHOUSE S.
"Market share strategy and the product life cycle: a comment"   J. Mktg.,
vol.39, no.4, Oct 1975, pp.57-59.
EVALUATION - PRODUCT LIFE CYCLE * USE - CAPITAL INVESTMENT * MARKET SHARE -
EFFECT OF * APPL - FIRM : FINANCE , PROFITS

YA1186   FINGER J.M.
"Trade and domestic effects of the offshore assembly provision in the US
Tariff"   Am. Econ. Rev., vol.66, 1976, pp.598-611.
TARIFF - EFFECT OF

YA1187   FINKEL S.R., TUTTLE D.L.
"Determinants of the aggregate profits margin"   J. Finance, vol.26, 1971,
pp.1067-1075.
APPL - MACRO : PROFITS * EX ANTE * COMPARATIVE METHODS - AUTOREGRESSIVE ,
CAUSAL

YA1188   FINNERTY J.E.
"Insiders and market efficiency"   J. Finance, vol.31, 1976, pp.1141-1148.
APPL - FIRM : FINANCE , STOCK PRICES * STOCK PRICES - INFORMATION EFFECT

YA1189   FIRTH M.
"Synergism in mergers: some British results"   J. Finance, vol.33, 1978,
pp.670-672.
APPL - FIRM : MERGERS * APPL - FIRM : FINANCE , STOCK PRICES * STOCK PRICES
- INDUSTRIAL STRUCTURE

YA1190   FIRTH M.
"The impact of earnings announcements on the share price of similar type
firms"   Econ. J., vol.86, 1976, pp.296-306.
APPL - FIRM : FINANCE , STOCK PRICES * STOCK PRICES - INFORMATION EFFECT *
STOCK PRICES - INDUSTRIAL STRUCTURE

YA1191   FIRTH M.
"The information content of large investment holdings"   J. Finance,
vol.30, 1975, pp.1265-1281.
APPL - FIRM : FINANCE , STOCK PRICES * STOCK PRICES - OWNERSHIP * STOCK
PRICES - INFORMATION EFFECT

YA1192   FISHELSON G.
"Help wanted advertisements: a case study, Israel 1965-75"   J. Business,
vol.47, 1974, pp.208-217.
APPL - MACRO : UNEMPLOYMENT * INDEX NUMBERS - MACRO : EMPLOYMENT VACANCIES *
BUSINESS INDICATORS - APPL

YA1193   FISHELSON G.
"Relative shares of labor and capital in agriculture: a subarid area,
Israel, 1952-1969."   Rev. Econ. Stats., vol.56, 1974, pp.378-386.
APPL - SECTOR : AGRICULTURE * PRODUCTION FUNCTIONS - SUBSTITUTION *
PRODUCTION FUNCTIONS - SECTOR * WEATHER - EFFECT OF * DATA - CROSS SECTION ,
TIME SERIES

YA1194   FISHELSON G.
"Telecommunications, CES production function"   Appl. Econ., vol.9, 1977,
pp.9-18.
APPL - FIRM : UTILITIES , TELEPHONE * PRODUCTION FUNCTIONS - FIRM

YA1195   FISHER D.
"The speculative demand for money: an empirical test"   Economica,
vol.40, 1973, pp.174-179.
APPL - MACRO : MONEY , DEMAND * APPL - MACRO , UK * INTEREST RATE - EFFECT
OF

YA1196   FISHER F.M.
"Tests of equality between sets of coefficients in two linear regressions:
an expository note"   Econometrica, vol.38, 1970, pp.361-366.
STABILITY OF COEFFICIENTS - REGRESSION , TEST * DATA - SAMPLE SIZE

YA1197   FISHER F.M., COOTNER P.H., BAILY M.N.
"An econometric model of the world copper industry"   Bell J. Econ., vol.3,
1972, pp.568-609.
APPL - SECTOR : COMMODITIES , COPPER * SUPPLY - SECTOR : COMMODITIES *
SIMULTANEOUS SYSTEM - APPL * EX ANTE * APPL - MACRO , WORLD

YA1198   FISHER F.M., KRAFT G.
"The effect of the removal of the firemen on railroad accidents, 1962-1967"
Bell J. Econ., vol.2, 1971, pp.470-494.
APPL - SECTOR : TRANSPORT , RAILWAYS * HEALTH - ACCIDENTS * USE - HEALTH
REGULATION

YA1199   FISHER F.M., SOLOW R.M., KEARL J.M.
"Aggregate production functions: some CES experiments"   Rev. Econ.
Studies, vol.44, 1977, pp.305-320.
DATA - SIMULATION * PRODUCTION FUNCTIONS - THEORY

YA1200   FISHER L.
"The methodology of long-term forecasting of demand for industrial products"
Ind. Mktg. Res. Ass. J., vol.5, Feb, 1969, pp.3-47.
USE - MARKETING POLICY * APPL - SECTOR : PRODUCTION * FORECASTING - PRACTICE
* FORECASTING - USAGE * EVALUATION - TREND CURVES * LONG TERM FORECASTING

YA1201   FISHER R., HIRST M.
"Model building in marketing: a review of the British literature"   Eur. J.
Mktg., vol.6, 1972, pp.170-181.
USE - MARKETING POLICY * SIMULATION - APPL : MARKETING * BIBLIOGRAPHY -
MARKETING MODELS * BASIC

YA1202   FISHER R., HIRST M.
"Model building in marketing: problems, developments and the state of the
art"   Eur. J. Mktg., vol.6, 1972, pp.80-86.
USE - MARKETING POLICY * BIBLIOGRAPHY - MARKETING MODELS * SIMULATION - APPL
: MARKETING * BASIC

YA1203   FISHMAN G.S.
"Estimating sample size in computing simulation experiments"   Mgmt. Sci.
(A), vol.18, 1972, pp.21-38.
SIMULATION - EXPERIMENTAL DESIGN * TIME SERIES - ARIMA : ESTIMATION

YA1204   FITTS J.
"Testing for autocorrelation in the autoregressive moving average error
model"   J. Econometrics, vol.1, 1973, pp.363-376.
RESIDUALS - ANALYSIS OF , AUTOCORRELATION * AUTOCORRELATION - TEST * ERROR
SPECIFICATION - ARMA * SPECIFICATION ERROR - TESTS , ERROR SPECIFICATION *
ADVANCED

YA1205   FITTS R.L., MASON J.B.
"Marketing segmentation research-an application to bank services"   Omega,
vol.5, 1977, pp.207-214.
APPL - SECTOR : FINANCE , BANKS * MARKET SEGMENTATION * CONSUMER BEHAVIOUR -
PURCHASING , DETERMINANTS * CANONICAL CORRELATION - APPL

YA1206   FLANAGAN R.J
"Wage interdependence in unionized labor markets" with discussion
Brookings Paps. Econ. Activity, 1976, pp.635-681.
UNIONIZATION - EFFECT OF * APPL - MACRO : EARNINGS * EX ANTE

YA1207   FLANAGAN R.J.
"Labor force experience, job turnover, and social wage differentials"
Rev. Econ. Stats., vol.56, 1974, pp.521-530.
MANPOWER PLANNING - EARNINGS * EDUCATION - EFFECT OF * MANPOWER PLANNING -
LABOUR TURNOVER

YA1208   FLANAGAN R.J.
"The US Phillips curve and international unemployment rate differentials"
Am. Econ. Rev., vol.63, 1973, pp.114-131.
INFLATION - PHILLIPS CURVE * DATA - INTERNATIONAL * APPL - MACRO : EARNINGS
* APPL - MACRO : UNEMPLOYMENT * APPL - MACRO , UK * APPL - MACRO , SWEDEN *
MANPOWER PLANNING - UNEMPLOYMENT , DURATION

YA1209   FLAX M.
"An alternative approach to indicator development"   Mgmt. Sci., vol.22,
1975, pp.384-385.
INDEX NUMBERS - SECTOR : SOCIAL * APPL - SECTOR : SOCIAL

YA1210   FLEISHER B.M., RHODES G.
"Unemployment and labor force participation of married men and women: a
simultaneous model"   Rev. Econ. Stats., vol.53, 1976, pp.398-406.
MANPOWER PLANNING - LABOUR PARTICIPATION * DATA - CROSS SECTION *
COMPARATIVE METHODS - ESTIMATION : OLS , 2SLS

YA1211   FLEMMING R.M.
"How risky is the market"   J. Business, vol.46, 1973, pp.404-424.
STOCK PRICES - RUNS * RANDOM WALK - TEST * APPL - SECTOR : FINANCE , STOCK
PRICE INDEX * SPECTRAL ANALYSIS - APPL : SECTOR , FINANCE

YA1212   FLETCHER R.H.
"On the iterative refinement of least squares solutions"   J. Am. Statist.
Ass., vol.70, 1975, pp.109-112.
COMPUTERISATION - CALCULATION ERROR * NUMERICAL METHODS - CALCULATION ERROR
* COMPUTERISATION - ESTIMATION , REGRESSION MODELS * ESTIMATION - OLS

YA1213   FLICK W.A., LEONTIEF W.
          "Environmental repurcussions and the economic structure: an input-output
          approach: a comment"   Rev. Econ. Stats., vol.56, 1974, pp.107-110.
          INPUT OUTPUT - MACRO : POLLUTION * POLLUTION - EFFECT OF

YA1214   FOGLER H.R.
          "A note on spectral analysis of stochastic series"   Decis. Sci., vol.4,
          1973, pp.58-62.
          SPECTRAL ANALYSIS - METHODOLOGY , DATA ERRORS * DATA - SIMULATION * DATA
          ERRORS - OUTLIERS

YA1215   FOGLER H.R.
          "A pattern recognition model for forecasting"   Mgmt. Sci. (B), vol.20,
          1974, pp.1178-1189.
          PATTERN RECOGNITION * BUSINESS INDICATORS - METHODOLOGY * APPL - MACRO :
          OUTPUT * EX ANTE

YA1216   FOMBY T.B., GUILKEY D.K.
          "On choosing the optimal level of significance for the Durbin-Watson test
          and the Bayesian alternative"   J. Econometrics, vol.8, 1978, pp.203-213.
          EVALUATION - TEST , AUTOCORRELATION * DATA - SIMULATION * COMPARATIVE
          METHODS - ESTIMATION : OLS , BAYESIAN * AUTOCORRELATION - EFFECT OF * ERROR
          SPECIFICATION - AUTOCORRELATED

YA1217   FOOT D.K.
          "The demand for money in Canada: some additional evidence"   Can. J. Econ.,
          vol.10, 1977, pp.475-485.
          APPL - MACRO , CANADA * APPL - MACRO : MONEY , DEMAND * STABILITY OF
          COEFFICIENTS - REGRESSION , TEST * INCOME - EFFECT OF * INTEREST RATE -
          EFFECT OF

YA1218   FOOTE R.J., CRAVEN J.A., WILLIAMS R.R.
          "Quarterly models to predict cash prices of pork bellies"   Am. J. Ag.
          Econ., vol.54, 1972, pp.603-610.
          APPL - SECTOR : COMMODITIES , HOGS * EX ANTE * COMPARATIVE METHODS -
          AUTOREGRESSIVE , CAUSAL

YA1219   FOREMAN L.
          "Optimal control and econometric modeling: what is it?"   Bus. Econ.,
          vol.11:4, 1976, pp.51-55.
          CONTROL THEORY - REVIEW * BASIC

YA1220   FORRESTER J.W.
          "Business structure, economic cycles and national policy" with discussion
          Bus. Econ., vol.11:1, 1976, pp.13-24, and vol.11:3, 1976, pp.74-77.
          INDUSTRIAL DYNAMICS - APPL , MACRO * BUSINESS CYCLE - LONG CYCLE

YA1221   FORSYTH G.C., THOMAS D.G.
          "Models for financially healthy hospitals"   H.B.R., vol.49, July-Aug,
          1971, pp.106-117.
          HEALTH - HOSPITAL * SIMULATION - APPL : SECTOR , HEALTH * USE - CORPORATE
          PLANNING

YA1222   FORSYTHE A.B.
          "A stopping rule for variable selection in multiple regression"   J. Am.
          Statist. Ass., vol.68, 1973, pp.75-77.
          REGRESSION - STEPWISE * REGRESSION - VARIABLE INCLUSION

YA1223   FORTUNE J.N.
          "Income distribution as a determinant of imports of manufactured
          commodities"   Can. J. Econ., vol.5, 1972, pp.257-267.
          INCOME - EFFECT OF * APPL - SECTOR : INTERNATIONAL TRADE , IMPORTS * INCOME
          - EFFECT OF , DISTRIBUTION

YA1224   FORTUNE J.N.
          "Measurement of tariff elasticities"   Appl. Econ., vol.3, 1971, pp.19-34.
          APPL - SECTOR : INTERNATIONAL TRADE * TARIFF - EFFECT OF * PRICE - EFFECT OF
          * APPL - SECTOR : CONSUMER DURABLES

YA1225   FORTUNE P.
          "A theory of optimal life insurance: development and tests"   J. Finance,
          vol.28, 1973, pp.587-600.
          APPL - SECTOR : FINANCE , INSURANCE * INTEREST RATE - EFFECT OF * SURVEYS -
          CONSUMER * DISTRIBUTED LAG - ALMON : APPL * ATTITUDINAL DATA

YA1226   FORTUNE P.
          "The effect of FHLB bond operations on savings inflows at savings and
          loanassociations: comment"   J. Finance, vol.31, 1976, pp.963-972.
          APPL - SECTOR : FINANCE , BUILDING SOCIETIES * APPL - SECTOR : FINANCE ,
          SAVINGS * POLICY EVALUATION - SECTOR : FINANCE * COMPARATIVE METHODS -
          ESTIMATION : OLS , 2SLS * INTEREST RATE - EFFECT OF

YA1227   FOSTER F.G., ROSENHEAD J.V., SISKIND V.
          "The effect of the demand distribution in inventory models combining
          holding, stockout and re-order costs"   R. Statist. Soc. (B), vol.33, 1971,
          pp.312-325.
          USE - INVENTORY CONTROL * LOSS FUNCTIONS - FIRM , INVENTORY CONTROL *
          PROBABILITY MODELS - POISSON * PROBABILITY MODELS - GAMMMA

YA1228   FOSTER G.
          "Quarterly accounting data: time series properties and predictive-ability
          results"   Acctg. Rev., vol.52, 1977, pp.1-21.
          APPL - FIRM : FINANCE , PROFITS * APPL - FIRM : COST - FIRM : FINANCE * TIME
          SERIES - ARIMA : APPL * EX ANTE * STOCK PRICES - INFORMATION EFFECT * APPL -
          FIRM : FINANCE , STOCK PRICES

YA1229   FOSTER G.
          "Stock market reaction to estimates of earnings per share by company
          officials"   J. Acctg. Res., vol.11, 1973, pp.25-37.
          APPL - FIRM : FINANCE , STOCK PRICES * STOCK PRICES - INFORMATION EFFECT *
          EXPECTATIONS - ESTIMATING
YA1230   FOSTER G.
          "Valuation parameters of property-liability companies"   J. Finance,
          vol.32, 1977, pp.823-835.
          APPL - FIRM : FINANCE , INSURANCE * APPL - FIRM : FINANCE , STOCK PRICES *
          STOCK PRICES - DETERMINANTS
YA1231   FOSTER J., GREGORY M.
          "Inflation expectations: the use of qualitative survey data"   Appl. Econ.,
          vol.9, 1977, pp.319-329.
          EXPECTATIONS - DATA * EXPECTATIONS - DETERMINANTS * INFLATION - EXPECTATIONS
YA1232   FOSTER J.T., GUJARATI D.
          "The behaviour of unemployment and unfilled vacancies: Great Britain,
          1958-1971-comments"   Econ. J., vol.83, 1973, pp.192-203.
          POLICY EVALUATION - MACRO : UNEMPLOYMENT * APPL - MACRO : UNEMPLOYMENT *
          AUTOCORRELATION - EFFECT OF * REGRESSION - MODEL INTERPRETATION
YA1233   FOSTER T.W., VICKREY D.
          "The information content of stock dividend announcements"   Acctg. Rev.,
          vol.53, 1978, pp.360-370.
          APPL - FIRM : FINANCE , STOCK PRICES * STOCK PRICES - INFORMATION EFFECT *
          APPL - FIRM : FINANCE , DIVIDENDS
YA1234   FOX A.J.
          "Outliers in time series"   R. Statist. Soc. (B), vol.34, 1972, pp.350-363.
          TIME SERIES - OUTLIERS * TIME SERIES - AUTOREGRESSIVE * DATA ERRORS -
          OUTLIERS
YA1235   FOX P.D., KRAEMER H.C.
          "A probability model for the remission rate of discharged psychiatric
          patients"   Mgmt. Sci. (B), vol.17, 1971, pp.694-699.
          PROBABILITY MODELS - GAMMA * HEALTH - HOSPITAL , PSYCHIATRIC * ESTIMATION -
          MAXIMUM LIKELIHOOD : APPL
YA1236   FRANK R.E.
          "Predicting new product segments"   J. Advtg. Res., vol.12:3, 1972,
          pp.9-13.
          CANONICAL CORRELATION - APPL * APPL - SECTOR : CONSUMER NON DURABLES , FOOD
          * MARKET SEGMENTATION * USE - PROMOTION EVALUATION * LIFE CYCLE - FAMILY
YA1237   FRANK R.E., DOUGLAS S.P., POLL R.E.
          "Household correlates of "brand loyalty" for grocery products"   J.
          Business, vol.41, 1968, pp.237-245.
          REPEAT BUYING * BRAND CHOICE - DETERMINANTS * APPL - FIRM : CONSUMER NON
          DURABLES , FOOD * APPL - FIRM : CONSUMER NON DURABLES , GROCERIES * CONSUMER
          BEHAVIOUR - PURCHASING , DETERMINANTS
YA1238   FRANK R.E., MASSY W.F.
          "The effect of retail promotional activities on sales"   Decis. Sci.,
          vol.2, 1971, pp.405-431.
          APPL - FIRM : CONSUMER NON DURABLES * USE - PROMOTION EVALUATION
YA1239   FRANK R.E., MASSY W.F., LODAHL T.M.
          "Purchasing behaviour and personal attributes"   J. Advtg. Res., vol.9:4,
          1969, p.15-24.
          APPL - SECTOR : CONSUMER NON DURABLES , FOOD * APPL - SECTOR : CONSUMER NON
          DURABLES , LIQUOR * CONSUMER BEHAVIOUR - PSYCHOLOGICAL MODELS * CONSUMER
          BEHAVIOUR - PURCHASING , DETERMINANTS
YA1240   FRANK R.E., STRAIN C.E.
          "A segmentation research design using consumer panel data"   J. Mktg. Res.,
          vol.9, 1972, pp.385-390.
          MARKET SEGMENTATION * CANONICAL CORRELATION - APPL * APPL - SECTOR :
          CONSUMER NON DURABLES , FOOD * CONSUMER BEHAVIOUR - PURCHASING ,
          DETERMINANTS
YA1241   FRANK R.H.
          "How long is a spell of unemployment"   Econometrica, vol.46, 1978,
          pp.285-302.
          MANPOWER PLANNING - UNEMPLOYMENT , DURATION
YA1242   FRANK R.H.
          "why women earn less: the theory and estimation of differential
          overqualification"   Am. Econ. Rev., vol.68, 1978, pp.360-373.
          MANPOWER PLANNING - EARNINGS * MANPOWER PLANNING - DISCRIMINATION , SEXUAL
YA1243   FRANK R.H., FREEMAN R.T.
          "The distribution of the employment burden: do the last hired leave first"
          Rev. Econ. Stats., vol.60, 1978, pp.380-391.
          MANPOWER PLANNING - UNEMPLOYMENT , DURATION * BUSINESS CYCLE - EFFECT OF
YA1244   FRANK W.
          "A study of the predictive significance of two income measures"   J. Acctg.
          Res., vol.7, 1969, pp.123-136.
          APPL - FIRM : FINANCE , PROFITS * COMPARATIVE METHODS - AUTOREGRESSIVE ,
          EXPONENTIAL SMOOTHING * EX ANTE * ACCOUNTING PRACTICE - EFFECT OF * DATA -
          SPECIFICATION OF VARIABLES * BASIC

YA1245 FRANK W.G., WEYGANDT J.J.
  "A prediction model of convertible debentures" J. Acctg. Res., vol.9,
  1971, pp.116-126.
  APPL - FIRM : FINANCE , OPTIONS * DISCRIMINANT ANALYSIS - APPL * ACCOUNTING
  PRACTICE - EFFECT OF * APPL - FIRM : FINANCE , BONDS * STOCK PRICES -
  DEBENTURES

YA1246 FRANKFURTER G.M.
  "On the stability of alpha beta estimates and market portfolios in the
  Sharpe portfolio selection model" Decis. Sci., vol.9, 1978, pp.80-92.
  APPL - FIRM : FINANCE , STOCK PRICES * STOCK PRICES - BETA , VARIABLE *
  STABILITY OF COEFFICIENTS - REGRESSION : APPL * USE - PORTFOLIO SELECTION

YA1247 FRANKFURTER G.M.
  "The effect of market indexes on the ex-post performance of the Sharpe
  portfolio selection model" J. Finance, vol.31, 1976, pp.949-955.
  APPL - SECTOR : FINANCE , STOCK PRICE INDEX * APPL - FIRM : FINANCE , STOCK
  PRICES * PROXY VARIABLES * INDEX NUMBERS - SECTOR : FINANCE , STOCK PRICES *
  EVALUATION - PORTFOLIO SELECTION PROCEDURES

YA1248 FRANKFURTER G.N., KENDALL K.E., PEGELS C.C.
  "Management control of blood through a short term supply-demand forecast
  system" Mgmt. Sci. (B), vol.21, 1974, pp.444-452.
  USE - SCHEDULING , MATERIALS SUPPLY * USER - FIRM : HEALTH , HOSPITAL *
  HEALTH - BLOOD AVAILABILITY * USE - INVENTORY CONTROL * EXPONENTIAL
  SMOOTHING - APPL

YA1249 FRANKS J.R., BROYLES J.E., HECHT M.J.
  "An industry study of the profitabilty of mergers in the UK" J. Finance,
  vol.32, 1977, pp.1513-1525.
  APPL - FIRM : MERGERS * APPL - FIRM : FINANCE , STOCK PRICES * APPL - FIRM :
  CONSUMER NON DURABLES , LIQUOR * STOCK PRICES - INFORMATION EFFECT

YA1250 FRASER D.R.
  "On the accuracy and usefulness of interest rate forecasts" Bus. Econ.,
  vol.12:4, 1977, pp.38-44.
  EVALUATION - INTEREST RATE FORECASTS

YA1251 FRASER D.R., ROSE P.S.
  "Alternative monetary indicators and the 'reverse causation' problem"
  Bus. Econ., vol.11:3, 1976, pp.49-58.
  APPL - MACRO : GNP * APPL - MACRO : MONEY , SUPPLY * DATA - SPECIFICATION OF
  VARIABLES * DISTRIBUTED LAG - ALMON : APPL

YA1252 FRASER D.R., ROSE P.S.
  "Short-run portfolio behaviour: an examination of selected liquid assets"
  with discussion J. Finance, vol.28, 1973, pp.531-537 & 541-544.
  INTEREST RATE - EFFECT OF * DATA - CROSS SECTION , TIME SERIES * APPL - FIRM
  : FINANCE , BANKS * APPL - FIRM : FINANCE , FINANCIAL STRUCTURE

YA1253 FREDERICK D.G.
  "An industrial pricing decision using Bayesian multivariate analysis" J.
  Mktg. Res., vol.8, 1971, pp.199-203.
  JUDGEMENTAL FORECASTS - METHODOLOGY * BAYESIAN - PRIOR INFORMATION * APPL -
  FIRM : PRODUCTION , CHEMICALS * PRICE - FIRM : PRODUCTION * USE - PRICING *
  COMBINING FORECASTS - JUDGEMENTAL , TIME SERIES

YA1254 FREEMAN A.M.
  "Air pollution and property values: a further comment" Rev. Econ. Stats.,
  vol.56, 1974, pp.554-556.
  APPL - SECTOR : CONSTRUCTION , RESIDENTIAL * PRICE - FIRM : CONSTRUCTION ,
  RESIDENTIAL * POLLUTION - EFFECT OF

YA1255 FREEMAN A.M.
  "Air pollution and property values: a methodological comment" Rev. Econ.
  Stats., vol.53, 1971, pp.415-416.
  APPL - SECTOR : CONSTRUCTION , RESIDENTIAL * POLLUTION - EFFECT OF * MODEL
  INTERPRETATION

YA1256 FREEMAN R.B.
  "Changes in the labour market for black Americans, 1948-1972" with
  discussion Brookings Paps. Econ. Activity, 1973, pp.67-131.
  MANPOWER PLANNING - DISCRIMINATION , RACIAL

YA1257 FREEMAN R.B.
  "Job satisfaction as an economic variable" with discussion Am. Econ. Ass.
  Proc., 1978, pp.135-141 & 146-148.
  MANPOWER PLANNING - LABOUR TURNOVER * REGRESSION - LIMITED DEPENDENT , LOGIT
  : APPL * DATA - CROSS SECTION

YA1258 FREEMAN R.B.
  "Legal 'cobwebs' a recursive model of the market for new lawyers" Rev.
  Econ. Stats., vol.57, 1975, pp.171-179.
  MANPOWER PLANNING - QUALIFIED MANPOWER , PROFESSIONAL * APPL - SECTOR :
  SERVICES , LAWYERS * SUPPLY - SECTOR : SERVICES * MANPOWER PLANNING - SECTOR
  : SERVICES , SUPPLY

YA1259 FREEMAN R.B.
  "Occupational training in proprietary schools and technical institutes"
  Rev. Econ. Stats., vol.56, 1974, pp.310-318.
  APPL - SECTOR : SOCIAL , EARNINGS * EDUCATION - EFFECT OF * MANPOWER
  PLANNING - EARNINGS * MANPOWER PLANNING - EDUCATION PROGRAMS

YA1260   FREEMAN R.B.
"Supply and salary adjustments to the changing science manpower market,
physics, 1948-1973"   Am. Econ. Rev., vol.65, 1975, pp.27-39.
MANPOWER PLANNING - QUALIFIED MANPOWER , SCIENCE DEGREES * MANPOWER PLANNING
- MACRO

YA1261   FREEMAN R.B.
"The decline in the economic rewards to college education"   Rev. Econ.
Stats., vol.59, 1977, pp.18-29.
MANPOWER PLANNING - EARNINGS * EDUCATION - EFFECT OF * MANPOWER PLANNING -
LABOUR FORCE COMPOSITION

YA1262   FREIDEN A.
"A Program for the estimation of dynamic economic relations from a time
series of cross sections"   Anns. Econ. Soc. Meas., vol.2, 1973, pp.89-91.
COMPUTERISATION - ESTIMATION , REGRESSION MODELS , PROGRAMS * REGRESSION -
SEEMINGLY UNRELATED * ERROR SPECIFICATION - AUTOCORRELATED , CORRELATED

YA1263   FRENKEL J.A.
"The demand for international reserves by developed and less-developed
countries"   Economica, vol.41, 1974, pp.14-24.
APPL - MACRO : INTERNATIONAL FINANCE , FOREIGN RESERVES * DATA -
INTERNATIONAL * DATA - LDC

YA1264   FRENKEL J.A.
"The forward exchange rate, expectations, and the demand for money: the
German hyperinflation"   Am. Econ. Rev., vol.67, 1977, pp.653-670.
INFLATION - RAPID * APPL - MACRO , GERMANY * APPL - MACRO : MONEY *
EXPECTATIONS - ESTIMATING * THEORY - EXPECTATIONS * EXCHANGE RATE - FORWARD
RATE * PROXY VARIABLES * CAUSALITY - TEST * COMPARATIVE METHODS - REGRESSION
, TRANSFORMATIONS

YA1265   FRERICHS R.R., PRAWDA J.
"A computer simulation model for the control of rabies in an urban area of
Columbia"   Mgmt. Sci., vol.22, 1975, pp.411-421.
HEALTH - DISEASE , INCIDENCE OF * SIMULATION - APPL : SECTOR , HEALTH *
BIBLIOGRAPHY - EPIDEMICS

YA1266   FREUND R.J.
"Some observations on regression with grouped data"   Am. Stat'n.,
vol.25:3, 1971, pp.29-30.
REGRESSION - GROUPED OBSERVATIONS * BASIC

YA1267   FREUND R.J., DEBERTIN D.L.
"Variable selection and statistical significance: a sampling experiment"
Am. J. Ag. Econ., vol.57, 1975, pp.721-722.
EVALUATION - REGRESSION , VARIABLE INCLUSION * REGRESSION - STEPWISE * DATA
- SIMULATION

YA1268   FRIEDMAN B.M.
"Crowding out or crowding in? economic consequences of financing government
deficits"   Brookings Paps. Econ. Activity, 1978, pp.593-654.
APPL - MACRO : MONEY , DEMAND : INCOME - EFFECT OF * INTEREST RATE - EFFECT
OF * POLICY EVALUATION - MACRO : MONETARY

YA1269   FRIEDMAN B.M.
"Econometric simulation difficulties: an illustration"   Rev. Econ. Stats.,
vol.53, 1971, pp.381-384.
MACRO MODEL - WHARTON * NUMERICAL METHODS - EQUATION SOLUTION * SIMULATION -
METHODOLOGY , STABILITY * SIMULTANEOUS SYSTEM - NON LINEAR

YA1270   FRIEDMAN B.M.
"The inefficiency of short-run monetary targets for monetary policy" with
discussion   Brookings Paps. Econ. Activity, 1977, pp.293-346.
POLICY EVALUATION - MACRO : MONETARY * MACRO MODEL - US * APPL - MACRO :
MONEY

YA1271   FRIEDMAN B.M.
"Who puts the inflation premium into nominal interest rates?" with
discussion   J. Finance, vol.33, 1978, pp.833-847.
INFLATION - EXPECTATIONS * INFLATION - EFFECT OF * APPL - SECTOR : FINANCE ,
BONDS * INTEREST RATE - EFFECT OF * INTEREST RATE - DETERMINANTS

YA1272   FRIEDMAN B.M., ROLEY V.V.
"Identifying identical distributed lag structures by the use of prior sum
constraints"   Anns. Econ. Soc. Meas., vol.6, 1977, pp.429-444.
DISTRIBUTED LAG - ESTIMATION * APPL - SECTOR : FINANCE , BONDS * INTEREST
RATE - EFFECT OF * DISTRIBUTED LAG - APPL , INTEREST RATE * DISTRIBUTED LAG
- ALMON

YA1273   FRIEDMAN B.M., WACHTER M.L.
"Unemployment: Okun's Law, labor force, and productivity"   Rev. Econ.
Stats., vol.56, 1974, pp.167-176.
APPL - MACRO : UNEMPLOYMENT * INFLATION - EFFECT OF * DISTRIBUTED LAG -
ALMON : APPL * DISTRIBUTED LAG - APPL , OUTPUT * COMPARATIVE METHODS -
REGRESSION , ERROR SPECIFICATION

YA1274   FRIEDMAN L.
"Calculating T.V. reach and frequency"   J. Advtg. Res., vol.11:4, 1971,
pp.21-25.
ADVERTISING - EXPOSURE * PROBABILITY MODELS - NBD * APPL - FIRM : SERVICES ,
MEDIA , TV

YA1275   FRIEND I., BLUME M.E.
         "Competitive commission on the New York Stock Exchange"   J. Finance,
         vol.28, 1973, pp.795-819.
         APPL - SECTOR : FINANCE , STOCK BROKERS * COST - SECTOR : FINANCE * APPL -
         SECTOR : FINANCE , PROFITS * USE - FINANCIAL , REGULATION

YA1276   FRIEND I., BLUME M.E.
         "The demand for risky assets"   Am. Econ. Rev., vol.65, 1975, pp.900-922.
         APPL - MACRO : CONSUMER DEMAND , FINANCIAL ASSETS * THEORY - EFFICIENT
         MARKETS * RISK - EFFECT OF * ADVANCED

YA1277   FRIEND I., HUSIC F.
         "Efficiency of corporate investment"   Rev. Econ. Stats., vol.55, 1973,
         pp.122-127.
         APPL - FIRM : FINANCE , PROFITS * DATA - TRANSFORMED , DEFLATED * DATA -
         CROSS SECTION * DATA ERRORS - EFFECT OF

YA1278   FRIEND I., LIEBERMAN C.
         "Short run asset effects on household saving and consumption: the cross
         section evidence"   Am. Econ. Rev., vol.65, 1975, pp.624-633.
         CONSUMER BEHAVIOUR - EXPENDITURE SURVEY * APPL - MACRO : SAVINGS * WEALTH -
         EFFECT OF

YA1279   FRIEND I., WESTERFIELD R., GRANITO M.
         "New evidence on the Capital Asset Pricing Model" with discussion   J.
         Finance, vol.33, 1978, pp.903-926.
         STOCK PRICES - MODELS , CAPM * STOCK PRICES - RISK * RISK - EFFECT OF *
         STOCK PRICES - BETA * APPL - FIRM : FINANCE , STOCK PRICES * APPL - FIRM :
         FINANCE , BONDS

YA1280   FROEHLICH B.R.
         "Some estimators for a random coefficient regression model"   J. Am.
         Statist. Ass., vol.68, 1973, pp.329-335.
         DATA - SIMULATION * COMPARATIVE METHODS - ESTIMATION : REGRESSION , RANDOM
         COEFFICIENTS

YA1281   FROMM G.
         "Implications to and from economic theory in models of complex systems" with
         discussion   Am. J. Ag. Econ., vol.55, 1973, pp.259-279.
         EVALUATION - THEORY OF * THEORY - MODELLING * MACRO MODELS - REVIEW

YA1282   FROMM G., KLEIN L.R.
         "A comparison of eleven econometric models of the United States" with
         discussion   Am. Econ. Ass. Proc., 1973, pp.385-393 & 410-411.
         EVALUATION - MACRO MODELS * EX ANTE * MULTIPLIERS - MACRO

YA1283   FROMM G., KLEIN L.R.
         "The Brookings Model volume: a comment"   Rev. Econ. Stats., vol.50, 1968,
         pp.235-240.
         MACRO MODEL - BROOKINGS * EVALUATION - MACRO MODELS

YA1284   FROMM G., KLEIN L.R.
         "The NBER/NSF model comparison seminar: an analysis of results"   Anns.
         Econ. Soc. Meas., vol.5, 1976, pp.1-28.
         MULTIPLIERS - MACRO * POLICY EVALUATION - MACRO : FISCAL , MONETARY *
         EVALUATION - MACRO MODELS * EX ANTE * MACRO MODEL - BEA * MACRO MODEL -
         BROOKINGS * MACRO MODEL - DATA RESOURCES * MACRO MODEL - FAIR * MACRO MODEL
         - ST.LOUIS * MACRO MODEL - MIT , PENN , SSRC * MACRO MODEL - WHARTON * MACRO
         MODEL - LIU(MONTHLY)

YA1285   FROMM G., SCHINK G.R.
         "Aggregation and econometric models"   Int. Econ. Rev., vol.14, 1973,
         pp.1-32.
         EVALUATION - MACRO MODELS * DATA - AGGREGATION * COMPARATIVE METHODS - DATA
         : AGGREGATE , DISAGGREGATE * MACRO MODEL - BROOKINGS

YA1286   FROST P.A.
         "Some properties of the Almon lag technique when one searches for degree of
         polynomial and lag"   J. Am. Statist. Ass., vol.70, 1975, pp.606-612.
         DISTRIBUTED LAG - IDENTIFICATION * DISTRIBUTED LAG - ALMON * DATA -
         SIMULATION * ADVANCED

YA1287   FROST P.A., BAR-YOSEF S., KOLODNY R.
         "Dividend policy and capital market theory: comments"   Rev. Econ. Stats.,
         vol.60, 1978, pp.475-478.
         APPL - FIRM : FINANCE , STOCK PRICES * RISK - EFFECT OF * STOCK PRICES -
         DETERMINANTS * STOCK PRICES - BETA * APPL - FIRM : FINANCE , FINANCIAL
         STRUCTURE

YA1288   FROYEN R.T.
         "A test of the endogeneity of monetary policy"   J. Econometrics, vol.2,
         1974, pp.175-188.
         APPL - MACRO : MONEY * DECISION RULES - MACRO * CAUSALITY - TEST : APPL *
         SPECIFICATION ERROR - TESTS , SIMULTANEOUS SYSTEM BIAS

YA1289   FRY J.N.
         "Personality variables and cigarette brand choice"   J. Mktg. Res., vol.8,
         1971, pp.298-304.
         BRAND CHOICE - INDICATORS * CONSUMER BEHAVIOUR - PSYCHOLOGICAL MODELS *
         CONSUMER BEHAVIOUR - PURCHASING , DETERMINANTS * APPL - FIRM : CONSUMER NON
         DURABLES , CIGARETTES

YA1290   FRY J.N., ET AL.
"Customer loyalty to banks:a longitudinal study"   J. Business, vol.46,
1973, pp.517-525.
APPL - FIRM : FINANCE , BANKS * REPEAT BUYING

YA1291   FRY M.J.
"Turkey's first five-year development plan: an assessment"   Econ. J.,
vol.81, 1971, pp.306-326.
APPL - MACRO : DEVELOPMENT * APPL - MACRO : GROWTH * APPL - MACRO , TURKEY *
POLICY EVALUATION - MACRO

YA1292   FURGIONNE G.A.
"Management decision rules in the marketing of electricity"   Omega, vol.4,
1976, pp.228-229.
APPL - FIRM : UTILITIES , ELECTRICITY * DECISION RULES - FIRM

YA1293   FUSS M.A.
"The demand for energy in Canadian manufacturing"   J. Econometrics, vol.5,
1977, pp.89-116,, & vol.6, 1977, p.261.
APPL - MACRO : ENERGY , SOURCES * PRICE - EFFECT OF * COST - MACRO : ENERGY
* INDEX NUMBERS - THEORY * INDEX NUMBERS - MACRO : ENERGY

YA1294   GABOR A.
"Price and consumer behaviour - a review"   Omega, vol.1, 1973, pp.279-296.
PRICE - EFFECT OF * QUALITY - PRICE * CONSUMER BEHAVIOUR - REVIEW *
BIBLIOGRAPHY - PRICE EFFECTS * BASIC

YA1295   GAGAN P.
"The recent cyclical movements of interest rates in historical perspective"
Bus. Econ., vol.711, 1972, pp.43-52.
INTEREST RATE - BUSINESS CYCLE

YA1296   GAITHER N.
"The adoption of operations research techniques by manufacturing
organisations"   Decis. Sci., vol.6, 1975, pp.797-813.
FORECASTING - USAGE * BASIC

YA1297   GALATIN M.
"Optimal forecasting in models with uncertainty when the outcome is
influenced by the forecast"   Econ. J., vol.86, 1976, pp.278-295.
DECISION RULES - SECTOR * DATA - CONTROL BIAS * DECISION RULES - FEEDBACK *
FORECAST - FEEDBACK * ADVANCED

YA1298   GALE B.T.
"Market share and rate of return"   Rev. Econ. Stats., vol.54, 1972,
pp.412-423.
MARKET SHARE - EFFECT OF * APPL - FIRM : FINANCE , PROFITS , PER SHARE *
REGRESSION - NON LINEAR * CONCENTRATION - EFFECT OF

YA1299   GALLANT A.R.
"Nonlinear regression"   Am. Stat'n., vol.29, 1975, pp.73-81.
REGRESSION - ESTIMATION * ESTIMATION - NON LINEAR * DATA - SIMULATION *
REGRESSION - HYPOTHESIS TESTS * NUMERICAL METHODS - OPTIMISATION

YA1300   GALLANT A.R.
"Seemingly unrelated nonlinear regression"   J. Econometrics, vol.3, 1975,
pp.35-50.
ERROR SPECIFICATION - CORRELATED * REGRESSION - NON LINEAR * ESTIMATION -
CONSTRAINED , NON LINEAR * EVALUATION - REGRESSION , SEEMINGLY UNRELATED *
DATA - SIMULATION

YA1301   GALLANT A.R.
"Testing a nonlinear regression specification: a nonregular case"   J. Am.
Statist. Ass., vol.72, 1977, pp.523-530.
SPECIFICATION ERROR - TESTS , VARIABLE INCLUSION * REGRESSION - NON LINEAR *
REGRESSION - PIECEWISE * DATA - SIMULATION * APPL - SECTOR : NATURAL , HUMAN
PHYSIOLOGY

YA1302   GALLANT A.R.
"The power of the likelihood ratio test in nonlinear regression models"
J. Am. Statist. Ass., vol.70, 1975, pp.198-203.
EVALUATION - REGRESSION , HYPOTHESIS TESTS * REGRESSION - NON LINEAR *
ADVANCED

YA1303   GALLANT A.R., GOEBEL J.J.
"Non linear regression with autocorrelated errors"   J. Am. Statist. Ass.,
vol.71, 1976, pp.961-967.
ERROR SPECIFICATION - ARMA * TREND CURVES - EXPONENTIAL , ESTIMATION * DATA
- SIMULATION * TREND CURVES - METHODOLOGY * REGRESSION - ESTIMATION , ERROR
SPECIFICATION * ESTIMATION - NON LINEAR

YA1304   GALPER H.
"The impact of the Vietnam war on defence spending: a simulation approach"
J. Business, vol.42, 1969, pp.401-415.
APPL - SECTOR : GOVERNMENT , DEFENCE * DISTRIBUTED LAG - APPL , ORDERS *
DISTRIBUTED LAG - VARIABLE LAG * POLICY EVALUATION - MACRO : DEFENCE * EX
ANTE * SIMULATION - APPL : SECTOR , GOVERNMENT * SIMULATION - APPL : POLICY
EVALUATION

YA1305   GALPER H., ET AL.
"Alternative interest rates and the demand for money" comments   Am. Econ.
Rev., vol.59, 1969, pp.401-418.
APPL - MACRO : MONEY , DEMAND * THEORY - MONETARY * COMPARATIVE METHODS -
REGRESSION , ERROR SPECIFICATION

YA1306   GALPER H., GRAMLICH E.
"A technique for forecasting defence expenditures"   Rev. Econ. Stats.,
vol.50, 1968, pp.143-155,
DISTRIBUTED LAG - APPL , ORDERS * EX ANTE * APPL - SECTOR : GOVERNMENT ,
DEFENCE * DISTRIBUTED LAG - ALMON * DISTRIBUTED LAG - VARIABLE LAG *
EXOGENOUS VARIABLES - PREDICTION OF , EFFECT

YA1307   GAMALETSOS T.
"A generalised linear expenditure system"   Appl. Econ., vol.6, 1974,
pp.59-71,
APPL - MACRO : CONSUMER DEMAND * DEMAND EQUATIONS - SYSTEMS OF * DATA -
INTERNATIONAL * CONSUMER BEHAVIOUR - ECONOMIC MODELS , THEORY * PRICE -
EFFECT OF

YA1308   GANDOLFI A.E., LOTHIAN J.R.
"The demand for money from the Great Depression to the present"   Am. Econ.
Ass. Proc., vol.66, 1976, pp.46-51,
APPL - MACRO : MONEY , DEMAND * BUSINESS CYCLE - EFFECT OF * STABILITY OF
COEFFICIENTS - REGRESSION : APPL

YA1309   GAPINSKI J.H., HUSBY R.D.
"The Husby consumption analysis: a comment"   Rev. Econ. Stats., vol.56,
1974, pp.401-403,
APPL - MACRO : CONSUMPTION * DATA - CROSS SECTION , TIME SERIES

YA1310   GAPINSKI J.H., KUMAR T.K.
"Embodiment, putty-clay, and misspecification of the directly estimated CES"
Int. Econ. Rev., vol.17, 1976, pp.472-483,
PRODUCTION FUNCTIONS - ESTIMATION * ESTIMATION - NON LINEAR * DATA -
SIMULATION * SPECIFICATION ERROR - EFFECT OF , SPECIFICATION OF VARIABLES

YA1311   GAPINSKI J.H., TUCKMAN H.P.
"AMTRAK, AUTO-TRAIN and vacation travel to Florida: little trains that
could"   Mgmt. Sci., vol.24, 1978, pp.1109-1116
APPL - SECTOR : TRANSPORT , RAIL , PASSENGER * EX ANTE * REGRESSION - RIDGE
: APPL

YA1312   GARBADE K.
"Discretion in the choice of macro policies"   Anns. Econ. Soc. Meas.,
vol.4, 1975, pp.215-238,
CONTROL THEORY - STOCHASTIC , METHODOLOGY * POLICY EVALUATION - MACRO * LOSS
FUNCTIONS - MACRO * MACRO MODEL - US * SIMULTANEOUS SYSTEM - CONTROL

YA1313   GARBADE K.
"Two methods of examining the stability of regression coefficients"   J.
Am. Statist. Ass., vol.72, 1977, pp.54-63,
REGRESSION - RANDOM COEFFICIENTS * DATA - SIMULATION * APPL - MACRO : MONEY
, DEMAND * INTEREST RATE - EFFECT OF * INCOME - EFFECT OF * EVALUATION -
TEST , STABILITY * STABILITY OF COEFFICIENTS - REGRESSION , TEST

YA1314   GARBADE K., ROSEY K.
"Secular variations in the spread between bid and offer prices on US
Treasury coupon issues"   Bus. Econ., vol.12:4, 1977, pp.45-49,
APPL - SECTOR : FINANCE , BONDS * APPL - SECTOR : FINANCE , STOCK BROKERS *
PRICE - SECTOR : FINANCE

YA1315   GARDINER C., WARD P.W.
"A long range financial resource planning model for a local authority"
Opl. Res. Q., vol.25, 1974, pp.55-64,
LONG TERM FORECASTING * APPL - SECTOR : GOVERNMENT , LOCAL * APPL - FIRM :
FINANCE * REGIONAL MODELS - SECTOR : GOVERNMENT , LOCAL * USE - FINANCIAL ,
PLANNING

YA1316   GARDNER M.J.
"Using the environment to explain and predict mortality"   R. Statist. Soc.
(A), vol.136, 1973, pp.421-440,
POPULATION - MORTALITY * APPL - SECTOR : SOCIAL , SOCIOECONOMIC STRUCTURE

YA1317   GARDNER R., SHELDON R.
"Financial conditions and the time path of equipment expenditures"   Rev.
Econ. Stats., vol.57, 1975, pp.164-170,
APPL - MACRO : INVESTMENT * DISTRIBUTED LAG - VARIABLE LAG

YA1318   GARGANAS N.C.
"Forecasting exports to the Six: an analytic approach"   Nat. Inst. Econ.
Res., no.60, 1972, pp.56-69,
APPL - MACRO , UK * APPL - MACRO : INTERNATIONAL TRADE , EXPORTS * APPL -
SECTOR : INTERNATIONAL TRADE , EXPORTS * EX ANTE * APPL - MACRO , EEC

YA1319   GARSIDE M.J.
"Some computational procedures for the best subset problem"   Appl. Stats.,
vol. 20, 1971, pp.8-15 & 112-115,
REGRESSION - STEPWISE * REGRESSION - VARIABLE INCLUSION * COMPUTERISATION -
ESTIMATION , REGRESSION MODELS , PROGRAMS * ESTIMATION - OLS

YA1320   GART A.
"Applications of input output analysis in Commercial Banking"   Bus. Econ.,
vol.6:1, 1971, pp.78-79,
INPUT OUTPUT - SECTOR : FINANCE * APPL - SECTOR : FINANCE , BANKS * BASIC

YA1321   GAU G.W.
"A taxonomic model for the risk rating of residential mortgages"   J.
Business, vol.51, 1978, pp.687-706,
APPL - SECTOR : FINANCE , MORTGAGES * DISCRIMINANT ANALYSIS - APPL * CLUSTER
ANALYSIS - APPL * USE - CREDIT CONTROL , CONSUMER

YA1322   GAUDET G.O., MAY J.D., McFETRIDGE D.G.
          "Optimal capital accumulation: the neoclassical framework in a Canadian
          context"   Rev. Econ. Stats., vol.53, 1976, pp.269-273.
          APPL - MACRO : INVESTMENT * APPL - MACRO , CANADA

YA1323   GAVER K.M., GEISEL M.S.
          "Discriminating among linear models with interdependent disturbances"
          Econometrica, vol.44, 1976, pp.337-343.
          BAYESIAN - MODEL SELECTION * ERROR SPECIFICATION - CORRELATED * DATA -
          SIMULATION * ERROR SPECIFICATION - AUTOCORRELATED

YA1324   GAVER K.M., ZIMMERMAN J.L.
          "An analysis of competetive bidding on BART contracts"   J. Business,
          vol.50, 1977, pp.279-295.
          USE - COMPETITIVE BIDDING * APPL - SECTOR : TRANSPORT , RAILWAYS

YA1325   GAYER D.
          "The effects of wages, unearned income and taxes on the supply of labour"
          Int. Econ. Rev., vol.18, 1977, pp.181-116.
          APPL - MACRO : EARNINGS * APPL - MACRO , ISRAEL * TAX - EFFECT OF * MANPOWER
          PLANNING - MACRO , SUPPLY

YA1326   GEARING H.W.G.
          "Forecasting demand"   Stat'n., vol.20, 1971, pp.23-28.
          FORECASTING - INTRODUCTION * BASIC

YA1327   GEEHAN R.
          "Returns to scale in the life insurance industry"   Bell J. Econ., vol.8,
          1977, pp.497-514.
          APPL - FIRM : FINANCE , INSURANCE COMPANIES * COST - FIRM : FINANCE * COST -
          SCALE ECONOMIES * REGRESSION - ERRORS IN VARIABLES * DATA - CROSS SECTION *
          COMPARATIVE METHODS - ESTIMATION : REGRESSION , ERRORS IN VARIABLES

YA1328   GEEHAN R., ALLEN L.
          "Measuring the real output and productivity of savings and credit
          institutions"   Can. J. Econ., vol.11, 1978, pp.669-679.
          APPL - SECTOR : FINANCE * INDEX NUMBERS - SECTOR : FINANCE

YA1329   GEHR A., DURAND R.M.
          "ITSA: interactive time series analysis program"   J. Mktg. Res., vol.13,
          1976, p.64.
          TIME SERIES - ARIMA : APPL * COMPUTERISATION - FORECASTING , PROGRAMS *
          BASIC

YA1330   GEISEL M.S.
          "Bayesian comparisons of simple macroeconomic models"   J. Money, Credit,
          Banking, vol.5, 1973, pp.751-772.
          BAYESIAN - MODEL SELECTION * APPL - MACRO : CONSUMPTION * EX ANTE *
          EVALUATION - CONSUMPTION MODELS

YA1331   GENBERG H.
          "Constraints on the parameters in two simple simultaneous equation models"
          Econometrica, vol.40, 1972, pp.855-865.
          SIMULTANEOUS SYSTEM - CONSTRAINED * APPL - MACRO : CONSUMPTION * APPL -
          SECTOR : CONSUMER NON DURABLES , MEAT * CONFIDENCE INTERVAL - SIMULTANEOUS
          SYSTEM * ADVANCED

YA1332   GENSCH D.M., RANGANATHAN B.
          "Evaluation of television program content for the purpose of promotional
          segmentation"   J. Mktg. Res., vol.11, 1974, pp.390-398.
          APPL - SECTOR : SERVICES , MEDIA , TV * MARKET SEGMENTATION * USE - MEDIA
          PLANNING * APPL - SECTOR : CONSUMER NON DURABLES * FACTOR ANALYSIS - APPL

YA1333   GERACI V.J., PREWO W.
          "Bilateral trade flows and transport costs"   Rev. Econ. Stats., vol.59
          1977, pp.67-74.
          DATA - INTERNATIONAL * APPL - MACRO : INTERNATIONAL TRADE * SIMULTANEOUS
          SYSTEM - SPECIFICATION OF VARIABLES * APPL - SECTOR : TRANSPORT

YA1334   GERKING S.D.
          "Input-output as a simple econometric model"   Rev. Econ. Stats., vol.53,
          1976, pp.274-282.
          INPUT OUTPUT - METHODOLOGY , COEFFICIENT ESTIMATION * CONFIDENCE INTERVAL -
          INPUT OUTPUT * COMPARATIVE METHODS - ESTIMATION : SIMULTANEOUS SYSTEM *
          COMPARATIVE METHODS - ESTIMATION : OLS , 2SLS

YA1335   GERSOVITZ M., MacKINNON J.G.
          "Seasonality in regression: an application of smoothness priors"   J. Am.
          Statist. Ass., vol.73, 1978, pp.264-275.
          SEASONALITY - ESTIMATION , OLS * SEASONALITY - ESTIMATION , BAYESIAN *
          COMPARATIVE METHODS - SEASONALITY * DATA - SIMULATION * APPL - SECTOR :
          CONSUMER NON DURABLES , FOOD

YA1336   GERSTENFIELD A.
          "Technological forecasting"   J. Business, vol.44, 1971, pp.10-18.
          TECHNOLOGICAL FORECASTING - REVIEW

YA1337   GETZ M., HUANG Y.
          "Consumer revealed preference for environmental goods"   Rev. Econ. Stats.,
          vol.60, 1978, pp.449-458.
          MANPOWER PLANNING - EARNINGS * REGIONAL MODELS - MANPOWER PLANNING ,
          EARNINGS * QUALITY - EFFECT OF * MANPOWER PLANNING - REGIONAL

YA1338   GEURTS M.D., IBRAHIM I.B.
          "Comparing the Box-Jenkins approach with the exponentially smoothed
          forecasting model: application to Hawaii tourists"   J. Mktg. Res., vol.12,
          1975, pp.182-188.
          APPL - SECTOR : SERVICES , TOURISM * TIME SERIES - ARIMA : APPL *
          COMPARATIVE METHODS - ARIMA , EXPONENTIAL SMOOTHING * EX ANTE
YA1339   GEURTS M.D., TAMASHIRO R.
          "SEAFAC II: a program for estimating sales forecasting monthly seasonal
          patterns when seasonal patterns are unstable"   J. Mktg. Res., vol.11,
          1974, pp.445-446.
          COMPUTERISATION - SEASONALITY , PROGRAMS * DATA ERRORS - OUTLIERS *
          SEASONALITY - ESTIMATION , CENSUS * BASIC
YA1340   GEWEKE J.
          "Temporal aggregation in the multiple regression model"   Econometrica,
          vol.46, 1978, pp.643-661.
          DATA - AGGREGATION OVER TIME * DISTRIBUTED LAG - AGGREGATION EFFECTS *
          DISTRIBUTED LAG - APPL , EARNINGS * INFLATION - DETERMINANTS * ADVANCED
YA1341   GEWEKE J.
          "Testing the exogeneity specification in the complete dynamic symultaneous
          equation model"   J. Econometrics, vol.7, 1978, pp.163-185.
          MACRO MODEL - US : APPL * SIMULTANEOUS SYSTEM - SPECIFICATION *
          SPECIFICATION ERROR - TESTS , SIMULTANEOUS SYSTEM BIAS * SPECIFICATION ERROR
          - EFFECT OF , FILTERING * COMPARATIVE METHODS - ESTIMATION : DISTRIBUTED LAG
          * CAUSALITY - TEST
YA1342   GHALI M.
          "Pooling as a specification error: a comment"   Econometrica, vol.45, 1977,
          pp.755-757.
          DATA - CROSS SECTION , TIME SERIES * SPECIFICATION ERROR - TESTS , DATA
          SOURCES * DATA - AGGREGATION 'BIAS'
YA1343   GHALI M., AKIYAMA M., FUJIWARA J.
          "Factor mobility and regional growth"   Rev. Econ. Stats., vol.60, 1978,
          pp.78-84.
          REGIONAL MODELS - INVESTMENT * REGIONAL MODELS - GROWTH * REGIONAL MODELS -
          MANPOWER PLANNING , EMPLOYMENT
YA1344   GIBSON W.E.
          "Demand and supply functions for money in the US: theory and measurement"
          Econometrica, vol.40, 1972, pp.361-370.
          THEORY - MONETARY * APPL - MACRO : MONEY * DATA - AGGREGATION *
          SPECIFICATION ERROR - EFFECT OF , FILTERING
YA1345   GIBSON W.E.
          "Deposit demand, 'hot money', and the viability of thrift institutions" with
          discussion   Brookings Paps. Econ. Activity, 1974, pp.593-636.
          APPL - SECTOR : FINANCE , BUILDING SOCIETIES * APPL - SECTOR : FINANCE ,
          BANKS * APPL - SECTOR : FINANCE , BANK , LIABILITIES * APPL - SECTOR :
          FINANCE , SAVINGS * INTEREST RATE - EFFECT OF
YA1346   GIBSON W.E.
          "Interest rates and inflationary expectations: new evidence"   Am. Econ.
          Rev., vol.62, 1972, pp.854-865.
          INFLATION - EXPECTATIONS * INTEREST RATE - INDICATORS
YA1347   GIBSON W.E.
          "Protecting homebuilding from restrictive credit conditions" with dicussion
          Brookings Paps. Econ. Activity, 1973, pp.647-699.
          APPL - SECTOR : CONSTRUCTION , RESIDENTIAL * MANPOWER PLANNING - SECTOR :
          CONSTRUCTION * INTEREST RATE - EFFECT OF * APPL - SECTOR : EMPLOYMENT * APPL
          - SECTOR : FINANCE , PE RATIO
YA1348   GILBERT C.L.
          "Regression using mixed annual and quarterly data"   J. Econometrics,
          vol.5, 1977, pp.221-239.
          DATA - INTERPOLATION * REGRESSION - ESTIMATION * SIMULTANEOUS SYSTEM -
          ESTIMATION
YA1349   GILBERT C.L.
          "The original Phillips curve estimates"   Economica, vol.43, 1976,
          pp.51-57.
          INFLATION - PHILLIPS CURVE * ESTIMATION - NON LINEAR
YA1350   GILBERT E.S.
          "On discrimination using qualititive variables"   J. Am. Statist. Ass.,
          vol.63, 1968, pp.1399-1412.
          DISCRIMINANT ANALYSIS - METHODOLOGY * COMPARATIVE METHODS - DISCRIMINATION *
          DATA - CATEGORICAL * DATA - SIMULATION
YA1351   GILCHRIST W.
          "Statistical forecasting- the state of the art"   Omega, vol.2, 1974,
          pp.733-750.
          TIME SERIES - REVIEW * BIBLIOGRAPHY - TIME SERIES
YA1352   GILES D.E.A.
          "Current payments for New Zealand's imports: a Bayesian analysis"   Appl.
          Econ., vol.9, 1977, pp.185-201.
          EVALUATION - PRIOR INFORMATION * BAYESIAN - MODEL SELECTION * BAYESIAN -
          PRIOR INFORMATION * APPL - MACRO : INTERNATIONAL TRADE , IMPORTS * APPL -
          MACRO , NEW ZEALAND * BAYESIAN - ESTIMATION : DISTRIBUTED LAG

YA1353   GILES D.F.A.
           "Discriminating between autoregressive forms: a Monte Carlo comparison of
           Bayesian and ad hoc methods"   J. Econometrics, vol.3, 1975, pp.229=248.
           ERROR SPECIFICATION = AUTOCORRELATED * DISTRIBUTED LAG = IDENTIFICATION *
           DISTRIBUTED LAG = ERROR SPECIFICATION * BAYESIAN = MODEL SELECTION * DATA =
           SIMULATION * COMPARATIVE METHODS = TESTS , AUTOCORRELATION

YA1354   GILES D.F.A., KING M.L.
           "Fourth=order autocorrelation"   J. Econometrics, vol.8, 1978, pp.255=259.
           AUTOCORRELATION = TEST * SEASONALITY = TESTING FOR

YA1355   GILL L., BRISSIMIS S.N.
           "Polynomial operators and the asymptotic distribution of dynamic
           multipliers"   J. Econometrics, vol.7, 1978, pp.373=384.
           MACRO MODEL = KLEIN * MULTIPLIERS = MACRO * MULTIPLIERS = METHODOLOGY

YA1356   GILLEN D.W.
           "Alternative policy variables to influence urban transport demand"   Can.
           J. Econ., vol.10, 1977, pp.686=695.
           REGRESSION = LIMITED DEPENDENT , LOGIT : APPL * APPL = SECTOR : TRANSPORT *
           REGIONAL MODELS = CITY * REGIONAL MODELS = SECTOR : TRANSPORT * INCOME =
           EFFECT OF

YA1357   GILLIGAN C.T., DARLING C.
           "Delphic forecasting of the North Sea survey ship market in 1980"   Ind.
           Mktg. Mgmt., vol.4, 1975, pp.349=357.
           DELPHI * APPL = SECTOR : PRODUCTION , SHIPS * APPL = SECTOR : PRODUCTION ,
           PETROLEUM

YA1358   GILLINGHAM R.
           "Place to place rent comparisons" with discussion   Anns. Econ. Soc. Meas.,
           vol.4, 1975, pp.153=178.
           INDEX NUMBERS = SECTOR : CONSTRUCTION , RENT * QUALITY = PRICE

YA1359   GILLIVER A., GORDON H.A.
           "An analytic information system for a representative sales force = a case
           study"   J. Opl. Res. Soc., vol.29, 1978, pp.719=730.
           APPL = FIRM : RETAILING * APPL = FIRM : CONSUMER NON DURABLES , FOOD * MIS *
           USE = TARGET SETTING * USE = RETAIL , SITE MONITORING * BASIC

YA1360   GILLO M.W., SHELLY M.W.
           "Predictive modelling of multivariable and multivariate data"   J. Am.
           Statist. Ass., vol.69, 1974, pp.646=653.
           AID = THEORY * APPL = SECTOR : SOCIAL , SUCCESS * COMPARATIVE METHODS =
           DISCRIMINATION * CANONICAL CORRELATION = APPL

YA1361   GINSBURGH V.A.
           "A further note on the derivation of quarterly figures consistent with
           annual data"   Appl. Stats., vol.22, 1973, pp.368=374.
           DATA = INTERPOLATION

YA1362   GINTER J.L.
           "An experimental investigation of attitude change and choice of a new brand"
           J. Mktg. Res., vol.11, 1974, pp.30=40.
           NEW PRODUCTS = NEW BRAND * BRAND CHOICE = DETERMINANTS * CONSUMER BEHAVIOUR
           = PURCHASING , DETERMINANTS * APPL = SECTOR : CONSUMER NON DURABLES ,
           GROCERIES

YA1363   GIPE G.W.
           "Using residual analysis to search for specification errors"   Decis. Sci.,
           vol.7, 1976, pp.40=56.
           RESIDUALS = ANALYSIS OF , SPECIFICATION ERROR * SPECIFICATION ERROR = TESTS
           , REVIEW * BASIC

YA1364   GIRAO J.A., TOMEK W.G., MOUNT T.D.
           "The effect of income instability on farmers' consumption and investment"
           Rev. Econ. Stats., vol.56, 1974, pp.141=149.
           APPL = SECTOR : AGRICULTURE * APPL = SECTOR : CONSUMPTION * POLICY
           EVALUATION = SECTOR : AGRICULTURE * APPL = SECTOR : INVESTMENT * COMPARATIVE
           METHODS = ESTIMATION : OLS , GLS * COMPARATIVE METHODS = DATA : CROSS
           SECTION , TIME SERIES * INCOME = EFFECT OF , PERMANENT

YA1365   GIRTON L., ROPER D.
           "A monetary model of exchange market pressure applied to the postwar
           Canadian experience"   Am. Econ. Rev., vol.67, 1977, pp.537=548.
           APPL = MACRO , CANADA * APPL = MACRO : INTERNATIONAL FINANCE , EXCHANGE
           RATES * APPL = MACRO : MONEY * THEORY = MONETARIST

YA1366   GIVON M., HORSKY D.
           "Market share models as approximators of aggregated brand choice behaviour"
           Mgmt. Sci., vol.24, 1978, pp.1404=1416.
           EVALUATION = BRAND CHOICE MODELS * PROBABILITY MODELS = LINEAR LEARNING *
           EVALUATION = MARKET SHARE MODELS

YA1367   GLAHE F.R., HUNT J.G.
           "The small sample properties of simultaneous equation least absolute
           estimators vis a vis least squares"   Econometrica, vol.38, 1970,
           pp.742=753.
           ESTIMATION = MSAE , SIMULTANEOUS SYSTEM * SIMULTANEOUS SYSTEM = ESTIMATION *
           COMPARATIVE METHODS = ESTIMATION : SIMULTANEOUS SYSTEM * COMPARATIVE METHODS
           = ESTIMATION : OLS , MSAE * DATA = SIMULATION * ERROR SPECIFICATION =
           HETEROSCEDASTIC * SPECIFICATION ERROR = EFFECT OF , HETEROSCEDASTICITY *
           MULTICOLLINEARITY = EFFECT OF * COMPARATIVE METHODS = ESTIMATION : OLS ,
           2SLS

YA1368   GLEN J.J.
         "Length of service distributions in Markov manpower models"   Opl. Res. Q.,
         vol.28, 1977, pp.975-982.
         MARKOV MODELS - APPL : MANPOWER * MANPOWER PLANNING - FIRM
YA1369   GLOBERMAN S.
         "Technological diffusion in the Canadian tool and die industry"   Rev.
         Econ. Stats., vol.57, 1975, pp.428-434.
         DIFFUSION MODEL - APPL * APPL - FIRM : PRODUCTION , MACHINE TOOLS * USE -
         R&D * APPL - SECTOR : TECHNOLOGY * APPL - FIRM : TECHNOLOGY * MANPOWER
         PLANNING - EDUCATION PROGRAMS * NEW PRODUCTS - DIFFUSION MODELS
YA1370   GLOBERMAN S., BAESEL J.
         "Comparison of alternative inflation forecasts"   Bus. Econ., vol.11:4,
         1976, pp.60-64.
         EVALUATION - INFLATION FORECASTS * INFLATION - INDICATORS * COMPARATIVE
         METHODS - AUTOREGRESSIVE , JUDGEMENTAL
YA1371   GLOUDEMANS R.J., MILLER D.W.
         "Multiple regression analysis applied to residential properties: a study of
         structural relationships over time"   Decis. Sci., vol.7, 1976, pp.294-304.
         APPL - SECTOR : CONSTRUCTION , RESIDENTIAL * STABILITY OF COEFFICIENTS -
         REGRESSION : APPL * PRICE - SECTOR : CONSTRUCTION , RESIDENTIAL
YA1372   GLYNN D.R.
         "The C.B.I. Industrial Trends Survey"   Appl. Econ., vol.1, 1969,
         pp.183-196.
         EVALUATION - SURVEYS , BUSINESS * EVALUATION - EXPECTATIONS , DATA * BASIC
YA1373   GODFREY L.G.
         "A further note on the treatment of serial correlation"   Can. J. Econ.,
         vol.7, 1974, pp.673-676.
         AUTOCORRELATION - TEST * REGRESSION - LAGGED DEPENDENT
YA1374   GODFREY L.G.
         "A note on the treatment of serial correlation"   Can. J. Econ., vol.6,
         1973, pp.567-573.
         APPL - SECTOR : CONSUMER NON DURABLES , LIQUOR * AUTOCORRELATION - TEST
YA1375   GODFREY L.G.
         "A note on the use of Durbins h test when the equation is estimated by
         instrumental variables"   Econometrica, vol.46, 1978, pp.225-228.
         EVALUATION - AUTOCORRELATION , TEST * ESTIMATION - INSTRUMENTAL VARIABLES *
         REGRESSION - LAGGED DEPENDENT * ADVANCED
YA1376   GODFREY L.G.
         "Testing against general autoregressive and moving average error models when
         the regressors include lagged dependent variables"   Econometrica, vol.46,
         1978, pp.1293-1301.
         AUTOCORRELATION - TEST * ERROR SPECIFICATION - AUTOCORRELATED * REGRESSION -
         LAGGED DEPENDENT * ERROR SPECIFICATION - MOVING AVERAGE
YA1377   GODFREY L.G.
         "Testing for higher order serial correlation in regression equations when
         the regressors include lagged dependent variables"   Econometrica, vol.46,
         1978, pp.1303-1310.
         AUTOCORRELATION - TEST * ERROR SPECIFICATION - ARMA * REGRESSION - LAGGED
         DEPENDENT
YA1378   GODFREY L.G.
         "Testing for multiplicative heteroskedasticity"   J. Econometrics, vol.8,
         1978, pp.227-236.
         ERROR SPECIFICATION - MULTIPLICATIVE * SPECIFICATION ERROR - TESTS ,
         HETEROSCEDASTICITY * DATA - SIMULATION * EVALUATION - TEST ,
         HETEROSCEDASTICITY
YA1379   GODFREY L.G.
         "Testing for serial correlation in dynamic simultaneous equation models"
         Econometrica, vol.44, 1976, pp.1077-1084.
         AUTOCORRELATION - TEST * SIMULTANEOUS SYSTEM - ERROR SPECIFICATION *
         ADVANCED
YA1380   GODFREY L.G., POSKITT D.S.
         "Testing the restrictions of the Almon lag technique"   J. Am. Statist.
         Ass., vol.70, 1975, pp.105-108.
         DISTRIBUTED LAG - IDENTIFICATION * DISTRIBUTED LAG - ALMON * APPL - SECTOR :
         CONSUMER NON DURABLES , LIQUOR * DISTRIBUTED LAG - HYPOTHESIS TESTS
YA1381   GODOLPHIN E.J.
         "A large-sample test for detecting gaps in moving average models"   R.
         Statist. Soc. (B), vol.40, 1978, pp.290-295.
         TIME SERIES - MOVING AVERAGE * TIME SERIES - ARIMA : IDENTIFICATION
YA1382   GODOLPHIN E.J.
         "A procedure for estimating seasonal moving average models based on
         large-sample estimation of the correllogram"   R. Statist. Soc. (B),
         vol.39, 1977, pp.238-247.
         TIME SERIES - MOVING AVERAGE , ESTIMATION * SEASONALITY - ESTIMATION , ARIMA
         * ADVANCED
YA1383   GODOLPHIN E.J., HARRISON P.J.
         "Equivalence theorems for polynomial-projecting predictors"   R. Statist.
         Soc. (B), vol.37, 1975, pp.205-215.
         EXPONENTIAL SMOOTHING - HIGHER ORDER * TIME SERIES - MOVING AVERAGE * TIME
         SERIES - POLYNOMIAL * EVALUATION - TIME SERIES * EXPONENTIAL SMOOTHING -
         THEORY * ADVANCED

YA1384　　GOLD B.
　　　　　　"From backcasting towards forecasting"　　Omega, vol.2, 1974, pp.209-223.
　　　　　　EX ANTE * APPL - SECTOR * EVALUATION - THEORY OF * APPL - SECTOR :
　　　　　　AGRICULTURE * APPL - SECTOR : PRODUCTION * EVALUATION - TREND CURVES * LONG
　　　　　　TERM FORECASTING * LEAD TIME - EFFECT OF * BASIC

YA1385　　GOLDBERG L.R., LIBBY R.
　　　　　　"Man versus model of man: Just how conflicting is the evidence?"
　　　　　　Organizational Behaviour and Human Performance, vol.16, 1976, pp.13-26.
　　　　　　COMPARATIVE METHODS - DISCRIMINATION * USE - BANKRUPTCY PREDICTION *
　　　　　　EVALUATION - BOOTSTRAPPING * EVALUATION - JUDGEMENTAL FORECASTS , SPECIALIST
　　　　　　* COMPARATIVE METHODS - REGRESSION , NON LINEAR * DISCRIMINANT ANALYSIS -
　　　　　　APPL * COMPARATIVE METHODS - DATA : QUALITATIVE

YA1386　　GOLDBERG M.A.
　　　　　　"Simulation, synthesis and urban public decision making"　　Mgmt. Sci. (B),
　　　　　　vol.20, 1973, pp.629-643.
　　　　　　REGIONAL MODELS * SIMULATION - APPL : REGIONAL MODEL * INPUT OUTPUT -
　　　　　　REGIONAL

YA1387　　GOLDBERG M.A., SCAPERLANDA A.E., MAUER L.J.
　　　　　　"The determinants of US direct investment in the EEC: comments"　　Am. Econ.
　　　　　　Rev., vol.62, 1972, pp.697-704.
　　　　　　APPL - MACRO : INVESTMENT , INTERNATIONAL * APPL - MACRO , EEC

YA1388　　GOLDBERG M.A., VORA A.
　　　　　　"Spectral analysis of public utility returns"　　J. Econometrics, vol.6,
　　　　　　1977, pp.79-101.
　　　　　　USE - FINANCIAL , REGULATION * APPL - FIRM : UTILITIES * APPL - FIRM :
　　　　　　FINANCE , STOCK PRICES * SPECTRAL ANALYSIS - APPL : SECTOR , FINANCE *
　　　　　　SPECTRAL ANALYSIS - APPL : SECTOR , UTILITIES * SPECTRAL ANALYSIS - CROSS :
　　　　　　APPL * STABILITY OF COEFFICIENTS - REGRESSION , TEST

YA1389　　GOLDBERG W.H., ET AL.
　　　　　　"A method of short term profit analysis"　　Omega, vol.5, 1977, pp.309-315.
　　　　　　USE - FINANCIAL , EVALUATION * APPL - SECTOR : PRODUCTION , TEXTILES * APPL
　　　　　　- SECTOR : FINANCE , PROFITS * BASIC

YA1390　　GOLDBERGER A.S.
　　　　　　"Correlations between binary outcomes and probabilistic predictions"　　J.
　　　　　　Am. Statist. Ass., vol.68, 1973, p.84.
　　　　　　REGRESSION - SUMMARY STATISTICS * REGRESSION - QUALITATIVE DEPENDENT

YA1391　　GOLDBERGER A.S.
　　　　　　"Structural equation methods in the social sciences"　　Econometrica,
　　　　　　vol.40, 1972, pp.979-1001.
　　　　　　CAUSALITY - REVIEW * PATH ANALYSIS - REVIEW * FACTOR ANALYSIS - APPL *
　　　　　　SIMULTANEOUS SYSTEMS - ERRORS IN VARIABLES

YA1392　　GOLDBERGER A.S., LEFF N.H.
　　　　　　"Dependency rates and savings rates: further comments"　　Am. Econ. Rev.,
　　　　　　vol.63, 1973, pp.232-234.
　　　　　　APPL - MACRO : SAVINGS * DATA ERRORS - EFFECT OF

YA1393　　GOLDER E.R., SETTLE J.G.
　　　　　　"Monitoring schemes in short-term forecasting"　　Opl. Res. Q., vol.27,
　　　　　　1976, pp.489-501.
　　　　　　CONTROL CHARTS - CUSUM * TRACKING SIGNAL - METHODOLOGY * EVALUATION -
　　　　　　FORECAST MONITORING SCHEMES * DATA - SIMULATION

YA1394　　GOLDER E.R., SETTLE J.G.
　　　　　　"On adaptive filtering"　　Opl. Res. Q., vol.27, 1976, pp.857-867.
　　　　　　EVALUATION - TIME SERIES , ADAPTIVE FILTERING * DATA - SIMULATION

YA1395　　GOLDFELD S.M.
　　　　　　"The case of the missing money" with discussion　　Brookings Paps. Econ.
　　　　　　Activity, 1976, pp.683-739.
　　　　　　APPL - MACRO : MONEY , DEMAND * EX ANTE * COMPARATIVE METHODS - ESTIMATION :
　　　　　　OLS , 2SLS * MACRO MODEL - ST. LOUIS

YA1396　　GOLDFELD S.M.
　　　　　　"The demand for money revisited" with discussion　　Brookings Paps. Econ.
　　　　　　Activity, 1973, pp.577-646.
　　　　　　APPL - MACRO : MONEY , DEMAND * INCOME - EFFECT OF * INTEREST RATE - EFFECT
　　　　　　OF * CUMPARATIVE METHODS - DISTRIBUTED LAG * INFLATION - EXPECTATIONS *
　　　　　　WEALTH - EFFECT OF * COMPARATIVE METHODS - ESTIMATION : SIMULTANEOUS SYSTEM
　　　　　　, ERROR SPECIFICATION * COMPARATIVE METHODS - ESTIMATION : OLS , 2SLS

YA1397　　GOLDFELD S.M., BLINDER A.S.
　　　　　　"Some implications of endogenous stabilization policy" with discussion
　　　　　　Brookings Paps. Econ. Activity, 1972, pp.585-644.
　　　　　　FORECAST - FEEDBACK * DECISION RULES - FEEDBACK * SPECIFICATION ERROR -
　　　　　　EFFECT OF , FEEDBACK * FORECASTING - VALUE OF * MACRO MODEL - US * POLICY
　　　　　　EVALUATION - MACRO : FISCAL , MONETARY * MACRO MODELS - THEORY

YA1398　　GOLDFELD S.M., CROTTY J.R.
　　　　　　"Specification error in macro-economic models: the influence of policy -
　　　　　　comments"　　Am. Econ. Rev., vol.66, 1976, pp.662-667.
　　　　　　SPECIFICATION ERROR - EFFECT OF , CONTROL BIAS * DECISION RULES - FEEDBACK *
　　　　　　MACRO MODELS - METHODOLOGY * DATA - CONTROL BIAS * DECISION RULES - SECTOR

YA1399   GOLDFELD S.M., QUANDT R.E.
         "A Markov model for switching regressions"   J. Econometrics, vol.1, 1973,
         pp.3-15.
         REGRESSION - SWITCHING * APPL - SECTOR : CONSTRUCTION , RESIDENTIAL *
         SIMULTANEOUS SYSTEM - DISEQUILIBRIUM

YA1400   GOLDFELD S.M., QUANDT R.E.
         "Estimation in a disequilibrium model and the value of information"   J.
         Econometrics, vol.3, 1975, pp.325-348.
         ESTIMATION - MAXIMUM LIKELIHOOD * SIMULTANEOUS SYSTEM - PRIOR INFORMATION *
         COMPARATIVE METHODS - ESTIMATION : SIMULTANEOUS SYSTEM , DISEQUILIBRIUM *
         SIMULTANEOUS SYSTEM - ESTIMATION , DISEQUILIBRIUM * APPL - SECTOR :
         AGRICULTURE , FRUIT * DATA - SIMULATION

YA1401   GOLDFELD S.M., QUANDT R.E.
         "The estimation of structural shifts by switching regressions"   Anns.
         Econ. Soc. Meas., vol.2, 1973, pp.475-485.
         REGRESSION - SWITCHING * STABILITY OF COEFFICIENTS - REGRESSION *
         BIBLIOGRAPHY - REGRESSION , SWITCHING

YA1402   GOLDMAN M.B., CHENG P.L., DEETS M.K.
         "Portfolio returns and the random walk theory: comments"   J. Finance,
         vol.31, 1976, pp.153-161.
         RANDOM WALK - TEST , TRADING RULE * STOCK PRICES - TRADING RULES

YA1403   GOLDSTEIN M., KHAN M.S.
         "The supply and demand for exports: a simultaneous approach"   Rev. Econ.
         Stats., vol.60, 1978, pp.275-286.
         APPL - MACRO : INTERNATIONAL TRADE * DATA - INTERNATIONAL * APPL - MACRO :
         INTERNATIONAL TRADE , PRICE * PRICE - EFFECT OF

YA1404   GOLLOP F.M., KARLSON S.H.
         "The impact of the fuel adjustment mechanism on economic efficiency"   Rev.
         Econ. Stats., vol.60, 1978, pp.574-584.
         APPL - SECTOR : UTILITIES , ELECTRICITY * COST - SECTOR : UTILITIES *
         PRODUCTION FUNCTIONS - SECTOR * STABILITY OF COEFFICIENTS - SIMULTANEOUS
         SYSTEM : APPL * USE - FINANCIAL , REGULATION

YA1405   GOLS A.G.
         "Bridging macro forecasts to the industry level: problems and prospects in
         multi-level forecasting"   Bus. Econ., vol.8:3, 1973, pp.39-45.
         INPUT OUTPUT - PROJECTION OF STRUCTURE * TECHNOLOGICAL FORECASTING * INPUT
         OUTPUT - METHODOLOGY : COEFFICIENT ESTIMATION : JUDGEMENTAL * BASIC

YA1406   GOLS A.G.
         "The use of input output in industrial planning"   Bus. Econ., vol.10:3,
         1975, pp.19-27.
         INPUT OUTPUT - FIRM * USER - FIRM * USE - CAPACITY EXPANSION * USE -
         CORPORATE PLANNING * BASIC

YA1407   GONEDES N.J.
         "Corporate signaling, external accounting, and capital market equilibrium:
         evidence on dividends, income and extraordinary items"   J. Acctg. Res.,
         vol.16, 1978, pp.26-79.
         DATA - CROSS SECTION , TIME SERIES * APPL - FIRM : FINANCE , DIVIDENDS *
         APPL - FIRM : FINANCE , STOCK PRICES * STOCK PRICES - INFORMATION EFFECT

YA1408   GONEDES N.J., ROBERTS H.V.
         "Bayesian assessment of the unconditional mean square error of repeated
         predictions from a regression equation"   J. Econometrics, vol.2, 1974,
         pp.221-240.
         STABILITY OF COEFFICIENTS - SIMULTANEOUS SYSTEM * EX ANTE * MACRO MODEL -
         FRB , MIT , PENN * REGRESSION - SUMMARY STATISTICS * LOSS FUNCTIONS - THEORY
         * EVALUATION - THEORY OF * BAYESIAN - ESTIMATION : SIMULTANEOUS SYSTEM *
         ADVANCED

YA1409   GONEDES N.J., ROBERTS H.V.
         "Differencing of random walks and near random walks"   J. Econometrics,
         vol.6, 1977, pp.289-308.
         RANDOM WALK - METHODOLOGY * STATIONARITY - TRANSFORMING TO * TIME SERIES -
         AUTOREGRESSIVE * TIME SERIES - BAYESIAN * COMPARATIVE METHODS - ESTIMATION :
         OLS , BAYESIAN * DATA - SIMULATION

YA1410   GONIK J.
         "Tie salesmen's bonuses to their forecasts"   H.B.R., vol.56, May-June,
         1978, pp.116-123.
         USE - PERSONNEL EVALUATION * USE - TARGET SETTING * FORECASTER - INCENTIVES
         * USE - FORECASTER EVALUATION

YA1411   GOODING A.E.
         "Perceived risk and capital asset pricing"   J. Finance, vol.33, 1978,
         pp.1401-1424.
         APPL - FIRM : FINANCE , STOCK PRICES * STOCK PRICES - RISK * STOCK PRICES -
         BETA * FACTOR ANALYSIS - APPL * RISK - EFFECT OF

YA1412   GOODMAN J.L.
         "Spectral analysis of the dependence of labor force participation on
         unemployment and wages"   Rev. Econ. Stats., vol.56, 1974, pp.390-393.
         SPECTRAL ANALYSIS - APPL : MACRO , MANPOWER * MANPOWER PLANNING - LABOUR
         PARTICIPATION * APPL - MACRO : EARNINGS

YA1413   GOODMAN M.L.
         "A new look at higher order exponential smoothing"   Ops. Res., vol.22,
         1974, pp.880-888.
         EXPONENTIAL SMOOTHING - HIGHER ORDER * APPL - SECTOR : UTILITIES ,
         TELEPHONES * EXPONENTIAL SMOOTHING - THEORY * TIME SERIES - MOVING AVERAGE
YA1414   GOODNIGHT J., WALLACE T.D.
         "Operational techniques and tables for making weak MSE tests for
         restrictions in regressions"   Econometrica, vol.40, 1972, pp.699-709.
         SPECIFICATION ERROR - TESTS , CONSTRAINTS * REGRESSION - HYPOTHESIS TESTS
YA1415   GORDON N.M., MORTON T.E., BRADEN I.C.
         "Faculty salaries: is there discrimination by sex, race and discipline?"
         Am. Econ. Rev., vol.64, 1974, pp.419-427.
         MANPOWER PLANNING - SECTOR : EDUCATION , UNIVERSITIES * APPL - SECTOR :
         EDUCATION , UNIVERSITIES * MANPOWER PLANNING - DISCRIMINATION * MANPOWER
         PLANNING - EARNINGS
YA1416   GORDON R., JORGENSON D.W.
         "Investment incentives in the 1971 tax-bill"   Bus. Econ., vol.7:3, 1972,
         pp.7-13.
         MACRO MODEL - DATA RESOURCES * APPL - MACRO : INVESTMENT * POLICY EVALUATION
         - MACRO : INVESTMENT
YA1417   GORDON R.J.
         "Can the inflation of the 1970's be explained" with discussion   Brookings
         Paps. Econ. Activity, 1977, pp.253-279.
         INFLATION - DETERMINANTS * EX ANTE * EVALUATION - EX POST MODELS * APPL -
         MACRO : EARNINGS
YA1418   GORDON R.J.
         "Inflation in recession and recovery" with discussion   Brookings Paps.
         Econ. Activity, 1971, pp.105-166.
         INFLATION - DETERMINANTS * BUSINESS CYCLE - EFFECT OF * APPL - MACRO :
         EARNINGS * INFLATION - EXPECTATIONS * EXPECTATIONS - ESTIMATING
YA1419   GORDON R.J.
         "Prices in 1970: the horizontal Phillips curve"   Brookings Paps. Econ.
         Activity, 1970, pp.449-458.
         INFLATION - PHILLIPS CURVE * EX ANTE
YA1420   GORDON R.J.
         "The Brookings model in action: a review article"   J. Poliitical Economy,
         vol.78, 1970, pp.489-525.
         MACRO MODEL - BROOKINGS * EVALUATION - MACRO MODELS * EX ANTE
YA1421   GORDON R.J.
         "The impact of aggregate demand on prices" with discussion   Brookings
         Paps. Econ. Activity, 1975, pp.613-670.
         THEORY - PRICING * INFLATION - DETERMINANTS * CAPACITY - EFFECT OF * EX ANTE
YA1422   GORDON R.J.
         "The recent acceleration of inflation and its lessons for the future" with
         discussion   Brookings Paps. Econ. Activity, 1970, pp.8-41.
         EXPECTATIONS - ESTIMATING * INFLATION - DETERMINANTS * APPL - MACRO :
         EARNINGS * INFLATION - EXPECTATIONS * INTEREST RATE - DETERMINANTS * APPL -
         MACRO : UNEMPLOYMENT
YA1423   GORDON R.J.
         "The response of wages and prices to the first two years of controls" with
         discussion   Brookings Paps. Econ. Activity, 1973, pp.765-779.
         APPL - MACRO : EARNINGS * INFLATION - DETERMINANTS * INFLATION - GOVERNMENT
         CONTROLS * PRICE - CONTROLS
YA1424   GORDON R.J.
         "Wage price controls and the shifting Phillips curve" with discussion
         Brookings Paps. Econ. Activity, 1972, pp.385-430.
         INFLATION - PHILLIPS CURVE * INFLATION - DETERMINANTS , EARNINGS * INFLATION
         - GOVERNMENT CONTROLS * APPL - MACRO : EARNINGS * STABILITY OF COEFFICIENTS
         - REGRESSION * EVALUATION - INFLATION MODELS
YA1425   GORDON R.J.
         "What can stabilization policy achieve?"   Am. Econ. Ass. Proc., 1978,
         pp.335-341.
         POLICY EVALUATION - MACRO : STABILISATION
YA1426   GORDON R.J.
         "World inflation and monetary accommodation in eight countries" with
         discussion   Brookings Paps. Econ. Activity, 1977, pp.409-477.
         INFLATION - DETERMINANTS * APPL - MACRO : EARNINGS * CAUSALITY - TEST : APPL
         * DISTRIBUTED LAG - APPL , MONEY * DATA - INTERNATIONAL * EVALUATION -
         MONETARIST THEORY * EVALUATION - INFLATION MODELS
YA1427   GORECKI P.K.
         "Determinants of entry by new and diversifying enterprises in the UK
         manufacturing sector, 1958-1963: some tentative results"   Appl. Econ.,
         vol.7, 1975, pp.139-147.
         APPL - SECTOR : NEW VENTURES * ADVERTISING - EFFECT OF
YA1428   GORECKI P.K.
         "The determinants of entry by domestic and foreign enterprises in Canadian
         manufacturing industries: some comments and empirical results"   Rev. Econ.
         Stats., vol.53, 1976, pp.485-488.
         TECHNOLOGY - EFFECT OF * APPL - SECTOR : FINANCE , PROFITS * APPL - SECTOR :
         COMPANY FORMATIONS * ADVERTISING - EFFECT OF * CONCENTRATION - EFFECT OF

YA1429 GOUGH T.J.
  "Determinants of fluctuations in private housing investment" Appl. Econ.,
  vol.4, 1972, pp.135-144.
  APPL - SECTOR : CONSTRUCTION , RESIDENTIAL

YA1430 GOULD J.P., NELSON C.R.
  "The stochastic structure of the velocity of money" Am. Econ. Rev.,
  vol.64, 1974, pp.405-418.
  EX ANTE * APPL - MACRO : MONEY , VELOCITY * TIME SERIES - ARIMA : APPL

YA1431 GOULD J.P., WAUD R.N.
  "The neoclassical model of investment behaviour: another view" Int. Econ.
  Rev., vol.14, 1973, pp.33-48.
  THEORY - INVESTMENT BEHAVIOUR * APPL - SECTOR : INVESTMENT * EVALUATION -
  TURNING POINT FORECASTS * COMPARATIVE METHODS - AUTOREGRESSIVE , CAUSAL *
  EVALUATION - INVESTMENT MODELS

YA1432 GRABOWSKI H.G., MUELLER D.C.
  "Industrial research and development, intangible capital stocks, and firm
  profit rates" Bell. J. Econ., vol.9, 1978, pp.328-343.
  APPL - FIRM : R & D * APPL - FIRM : FINANCE , PROFITS * DATA - CROSS SECTION
  * RISK - EFFECT OF * STOCK PRICES - BETA

YA1433 GRABOWSKI H.G., MUELLER D.C.
  "Life cycle effects on corporate returns on retentions" Rev. Econ.
  Stats., vol.57, 1975, pp.400-409.
  APPL - FIRM : FINANCE , PROFITS * LIFE CYCLE - PRODUCT * APPL - FIRM :
  FINANCE , STOCK PRICES * APPL - SECTOR : FINANCE , STOCK PRICE INDEX * STOCK
  PRICES - DETERMINANTS * LIFE CYCLE - FIRM * STABILITY OF COEFFICIENTS -
  REGRESSION * APPL - FIRM : FINANCE , FINANCIAL STRUCTURE

YA1434 GRABOWSKI H.G., MUELLER D.C.
  "Managerial and stockholder welfare models of firm expenditures" Rev.
  Econ. Stats., vol.54, 1972, pp.9-24.
  APPL - FIRM : R & D * APPL - FIRM : FINANCE , DIVIDENDS * APPL - FIRM :
  INVESTMENT * THEORY - FIRM

YA1435 GRADY P.
  "The Canadian exemption from the interest-equalization tax: an alternative
  scenario" Can. J. Econ., vol.7, 1974, pp.100-112.
  MACRO MODEL - CANADA , RDX2 * INTEREST RATE - EFFECT OF

YA1436 GRADY P., STEPHENSON D.R.
  "Some macroeconomic effects of tax reform and indexing" Can. J. Econ.,
  vol.10, 1977, pp.378-392.
  MACRO MODEL - CANADA , RDX2 * TAX - EFFECT OF * POLICY EVALUATION - MACRO :
  TAX * SIMULATION - APPL : POLICY EVALUATION * MULTIPLIERS - MACRO

YA1437 GRAHAM D.R., HUMPHREY D.B.
  "Bank examination data as predictors of bank net loan losses" J. Money,
  Credit, Banking, vol. 10, 1978, pp.491-504.
  APPL - FIRM : FINANCE , BANKS * APPL - FIRM : FINANCE , BANK , ASSETS * USE
  - CREDIT CONTROL * EX ANTE

YA1438 GRAMLICH E.M
  "Impact of minimum wages on other wages, employment, and family incomes"
  with discussion Brookings Paps. Econ. Activity, 1976, pp.409-461.
  APPL - MACRO : EARNINGS * MANPOWER PLANNING - MACRO , DEMAND * POLICY
  EVALUATION - MACRO : EMPLOYMENT

YA1439 GRAMLICH E.M.
  "New York: ripple or tidal wave? The New York City fiscal crisis: what
  happened and what is to be done" Am. Econ. Ass. Proc., vol.66, 1976,
  pp.415-429.
  REGIONAL MODELS - CITY * REGIONAL MODELS - SECTOR : GOVERNMENT * APPL -
  SECTOR : GOVERNMENT , LOCAL , FINANCE * USE - CREDIT CONTROL , BOND RATING

YA1440 GRAMLICH E.M.
  "State and local budgets the day after it rained: why is the surplus so
  high?" with discussion Brookings Paps. Econ. Activity, 1978, pp.191-216.
  APPL - SECTOR : GOVERNMENT , LOCAL , FINANCE * EX ANTE

YA1441 GRAMLICH E.M.
  "The distributional effects of higher unemployment" with discussion
  Brookings Paps. Econ. Activity, 1974, pp.293-341.
  APPL - SECTOR : SOCIAL , INEQUALITY * APPL - MACRO : UNEMPLOYMENT * MANPOWER
  PLANNING - LABOUR FORCE COMPOSITION * DATA - CROSS SECTION * PUBLIC
  EXPENDITURE - EFFECT OF , AID PROGRAMS * MANPOWER PLANNING - DISCRIMINATION
  , RACIAL

YA1442 GRAMLICH E.M.
  "The optimal timing of unemployment in a recession" with discussion
  Brookings Paps. Econ. Activity, 1975, pp.165-181.
  APPL - MACRO : UNEMPLOYMENT * MACRO MODEL - SSRC , MIT , PENN * INFLATION -
  DETERMINANTS * POLICY EVALUATION - MACRO : UNEMPLOYMENT

YA1443 GRAMLICH E.M., GALPER H.
  "State and local fiscal behaviour and federal grant policy" with discussion
  Brookings Paps. Econ. Activity, 1973, pp.15-65.
  APPL - SECTOR : GOVERNMENT , LOCAL , EXPENDITURE * REGIONAL MODELS - SECTOR
  : GOVERNMENT , EXPENDITURE

YA1444   GRAMLICH E.M., GALPER H., LEE M.L.
           "A comment on the consistency of estimating the inventory impact of defense
           orders"   Econometrica, vol.40, 1972, pp.393-399,
           PUBLIC EXPENDITURE - EFFECT OF * APPL - SECTOR : GOVERNMENT , DEFENCE *
           POLICY EVALUATION - MACRO : DEFENCE * DISTRIBUTED LAG - APPL , ORDERS * APPL
           - SECTOR : INVENTORIES
YA1445   GRAMM W.L.
           "The labor force decision of married female teachers: a discriminant
           analysis approach"   Rev. Econ. Stats., vol.55, 1973, pp.341-348,
           DISCRIMINANT ANALYSIS - APPL * APPL - SECTOR : EDUCATION * MANPOWER PLANNING
           - SECTOR : EDUCATION , SCHOOLS * MANPOWER PLANNING - LABOUR PARTICIPATION ,
           FEMALE * MANPOWER PLANNING - SECTOR : EDUCATION , SCHOOLS
YA1446   GRANGER C.W.J.
           "Aspects of the analysis and interpretation of temporal and spatial data"
           Stat'n., vol.24, 1975, pp.197-210,
           SPATIAL ANALYSIS
YA1447   GRANGER C.W.J.
           "Investigating causal relations by econometric models and cross-spectral
           methods"   Econometrica, vol.37, 1969, pp.424-438,
           SPECTRAL ANALYSIS - APPL : CAUSALITY * CAUSALITY - REVIEW
YA1448   GRANGER C.W.J.
           "New classes of time series models"   Stat'n., vol.27, 1978, pp.237-253,
           TIME SERIES - REVIEW * TIME SERIES - NON LINEAR * TIME SERIES -
           DECOMPOSITION
YA1449   GRANGER C.W.J.
           "Prediction with a generalised cost of error function"   Opl. Res. Q.,
           vol.20, 1969, pp.199-207,
           LOSS FUNCTIONS - REVIEW
YA1450   GRANGER C.W.J.
           "The typical spectral shape of an economic variable"   Econometrica,
           vol.34, 1966, pp.150-161,
           SPECTRAL ANALYSIS - APPL : BUSINESS CYCLE * TIME SERIES - CHARACTERISATION
YA1451   GRANGER C.W.J., HUGHES A.O.
           "A new look at some old data: the Beveridge wheat price series"   R.
           Statist. Soc. (A), vol.134, 1971, pp.413-428,
           SPECTRAL ANALYSIS - APPL : BUSINESS CYCLE , LONG CYCLE * APPL - SECTOR :
           AGRICULTURE , GRAIN * TIME SERIES - AUTOREGRESSIVE * BUSINESS CYCLE - LONG
           CYCLE
YA1452   GRANGER C.W.J., MORRIS M.J.
           "Time series modelling with interpretation"   R. Statist. Soc. (A),
           vol.139, 1976, pp.246-257,
           TIME SERIES - MODEL INTERPRETATION * TIME SERIES - ARIMA : INTERPRETATION *
           DATA ERRORS - EFFECT OF * DATA - AGGREGATION
YA1453   GRANGER C.W.J., NEWBOLD P.
           "Forecasting transformed series"   R. Statist. Soc. (B), vol.38, 1976,
           pp.189-203,
           TIME SERIES - ARIMA : TRANSFORMATIONS * EVALUATION - REGRESSION ,
           TRANSFORMATIONS * ADVANCED
YA1454   GRANGER C.W.J., NEWBOLD P.
           "Some comments on the evaluation of economic forecasts"   Appl. Econ.,
           vol.5, 1973, pp.35-47,
           EVALUATION - THEORY OF * LOSS FUNCTIONS - REVIEW * EVALUATION - LOSS
           FUNCTIONS
YA1455   GRANGER C.W.J., NEWBOLD P.
           "Spurious regressions in econometrics"   J. Econometrics, vol.2, 1974,
           pp.111-120,
           ERRORS SPECIFICATION - AUTOCORRELATED * CAUSALITY - REVIEW * REGRESSION -
           SUMMARY STATISTICS * AUTOCORRELATION - EFFECT OF * EVALUATION - TEST ,
           AUTOCORRELATION
YA1456   GRANGER C.W.J., NEWBOLD P.
           "The use of R squared to determine the appropriate transformation of
           regression variables"   J. Econometrics, vol.48 1976, pp.205-210,
           REGRESSION - SUMMARY STATISTICS * REGRESSION - MODEL CHOICE * REGRESSION -
           TRANSFORMATIONS
YA1457   GRANGER C.W.J., ORR D.
           "'Infinite variance' and research strategy in time series analysis"   J.
           Am. Statist. Ass., vol.67, 1972, pp.275-285,
           APPL - SECTOR : FINANCE * ERROR DISTRIBUTION - STABLE * SPECTRAL ANALYSIS -
           APPL : SECTOR , FINANCE * SPECTRAL ANALYSIS - APPL : ERROR DISTRIBUTION *
           ADVANCED
YA1458   GRANT D., WHALEY R.
           "Transactions costs on Government bonds: a respecification"   J. Business,
           vol.51, 1978, pp.57-64,
           APPL - SECTOR : FINANCE , BONDS * APPL - SECTOR : GOVERNMENT , FINANCE *
           PRICE - SECTOR : FINANCE
YA1459   GRAY H.P., FINKEL S.R., TUTTLE D.L.
           "Determinants of the aggregate profit margin: comments"   J. Finance,
           vol.31, 1976, pp.163-168,
           APPL - MACRO : PROFITS * CAPACITY - EFFECT OF * APPL - MACRO : INTERNATIONAL
           TRADE

YA1460   GREEN D.W.
           "Capital formation in the USSR, 1959-1974: an econometric investigation of
           bureaucratic intervention in the process of capital construction"   Rev.
           Econ. Stats., vol.60, 1978, pp.39-46,
           APPL - MACRO , USSR * APPL - MACRO : INVESTMENT * POLICY EVALUATION - MACRO
           : INVESTMENT
YA1461   GREEN M., HARRISON P.J.
           "Fashion forecasting for a mail order company using a Bayesian approach"
           Opl. Res. Q., vol.24, 1973, pp.193-205,
           BAYESIAN - FORECASTING * STYLE GOODS * APPL - FIRM : RETAILING , MAIL ORDER
           * EX ANTE
YA1462   GREEN P.E.
           "An AID/logit procedure for analysing large multiway contingency tables"
           J. Mktg. Res., vol.15, 1978, pp.132-136,
           AID - METHODOLOGY * REGRESSION - LIMITED DEPENDENT , LOGIT * CONSUMER
           BEHAVIOUR - PURCHASING , DETERMINANTS * DATA - CATEGORICAL * REGRESSION -
           VARIABLE INCLUSION * MARKET SEGMENTATION * APPL - SECTOR : UTILITIES ,
           TELEPHONE
YA1463   GREEN P.E., CARMONE F.J., WACHSPRESS D.P.
           "On the analysis of qualitative data in marketing research"   J. Mktg.
           Res., vol.14, 1977, pp.52-59,
           DATA - CATEGORICAL * REGRESSION - QUALITATIVE DEPENDENT * NEW PRODUCTS -
           APPL * COMPARATIVE METHODS - DATA : QUALITATIVE * CONSUMER BEHAVIOUR -
           PURCHASING , DETERMINANTS * APPL - SECTOR : UTILITIES , TELEPHONE *
           COMPARATIVE METHODS - REGRESSION , LIMITED DEPENDENT * REGRESSION - LIMITED
           DEPENDENT , LOGIT
YA1464   GREEN P.E., CARROLL J.D., DESARBO W.S.
           "A new measure of predictor variable importance in multiple regression"
           J. Mktg. Res., vol.15, 1978, pp.356-360 & 467-468,
           REGRESSION - SUMMARY STATISTICS
YA1465   GREEN R., HASSAN Z.A., JOHNSON S.R.
           "Alternative estimates atc and dynamic demand systems for Canada"   Am. J.
           Ag. Econ., vol.40, 1978, pp.93-107,
           INCOME - EFFECT OF * PRICE - EFFECT OF * COMPARATIVE METHODS - DEMAND
           EQUATIONS * APPL - MACRO , CANADA * APPL - MACRO : CONSUMER DEMAND *
           EVALUATION - CONSUMER BEHAVIOUR , ECONOMIC MODELS
YA1466   GREEN R.D., DOLL J.P.
           "Dummy variables and seasonality- a curio"   Am. Stat'n., vol.28, 1974,
           pp.60-62
           SEASONALITY - ESTIMATION , OLS * REGRESSION - COVARIANCE MODEL *
           MULTICOLLINEARITY - EFFECT OF
YA1467   GREENBAUM S.I., ALI M.M., MERRIS R.C.
           "Monetary policy and banking profits"   J. Finance, vol.31, 1976,
           pp.89-101.
           APPL - SECTOR : FINANCE , BANKS * APPL - SECTOR : FINANCE , PROFITS * USE -
           BANK REGULATIONS * EX ANTE * SIMULATION - APPL : SECTOR , FINANCE *
           MULTIPLIERS - SECTOR * POLICY EVALUATION - MACRO : MONETARY
YA1468   GREENE J.D.
           "Personal media probabilities"   J. Advtg. Res., vol.10:5, 1970, pp.12-18,
           USE - MEDIA PLANNING * ADVERTISING - EXPOSURE * PROBABILITY MODELS - BETA *
           APPL - SECTOR : SERVICES , MEDIA * JUDGEMENTAL FORECASTS - UNCERTAINTY
YA1469   GREENE J.D., STOCK J.S.
           "A rate-frequency model of behaviour"   J. Advtg. Res., vol.11:4, 1971,
           pp.9-19,
           APPL - SECTOR : CONSUMER NON DURABLES , FOOD * PROBABILITY MODELS - NBD *
           PROBABILITY MODELS - GAMMA * REPEAT BUYING
YA1470   GREENHALGH C.
           "A labour supply function for married women in Great Britain"   Economica,
           vol.44, 1977, pp.249-265,
           MANPOWER PLANNING - LABOUR PARTICIPATION , FEMALE * MANPOWER PLANNING -
           MACRO , SUPPLY
YA1471   GREENWOOD M.J.
           "A simultaneous equations model of urban growth and migration"   J. Am.
           Statist. Ass., vol.70, 1975, pp.797-810,
           REGIONAL MODELS - CITY * REGIONAL MODELS - POPULATION * POPULATION *
           MANPOWER PLANNING - REGIONAL * REGIONAL MODELS - MANPOWER PLANNING ,
           MIGRATION * STABILITY OF COEFFICIENTS - SIMULTANEOUS SYSTEM
YA1472   GREER D.F.
           "Rate ceilings and loan turndowns"   J. Finance, vol.30, 1975,
           pp.1376-1383,
           APPL - FIRM : FINANCE , CONSUMER FINANCE COMPANIES * USE - BANK REGULATION *
           CONCENTRATION - EFFECT OF
YA1473   GREER D.F.
           "Rate ceilings, market structure and the supply of finance company personal
           loans"   J. Finance, vol.29, 1974, pp.1363-1382,
           APPL - SECTOR : FINANCE , CONSUMER CREDIT * CONCENTRATION - EFFECT OF *
           SUPPLY - SECTOR : FINANCE * USE - CREDIT CONTROL , CONSUMER * APPL - SECTOR
           : FINANCE , LOAN COMPANIES

YA1474   GREER D.F., RHOADES S.A.
"A test of the reserve labour hypothesis"   Econ. J., vol.87, 1977,
pp.290-299.
APPL - SECTOR : EMPLOYMENT * CONCENTRATION - EFFECT OF * UNIONISATION -
EFFECT OF

YA1475   GREGORY G.
"Cash flow models: a review"   Omega, vol.4, 1976, pp.643-656.
USE - FINANCIAL , CONTROL * BIBLIOGRAPHY - CASH FLOW

YA1476   GREGORY P., GRIFFIN J.M.
"Secular and cross-section industrialization patterns: some further evidence
on the Kuznets-Chenery controversy"   Rev. Econ. Stats., vol.56, 1974,
pp.360-368.
DATA - CROSS SECTION , TIME SERIES * APPL - SECTOR : GROWTH * DATA -
INTERNATIONAL

YA1477   GREGORY P.R., CAMPBELL J.M., CHENG B.
"A cost-inclusive simultaneous equation model of birth rates"
Econometrica, vol.40, 1972, pp.681-687.
POPULATION - FERTILITY * DATA - CROSS SECTION * MANPOWER PLANNING - LABOUR
PARTICIPATION

YA1478   GREGORY P.R., CAMPBELL J.M., CHENG B.S.
"A simultaneous equation model of birth rates in the U.S."   Rev. Econ.
Stats., vol.54, 1972, pp.374-380.
POPULATION - FERTILITY * MANPOWER PLANNING - LABOUR PARTICIPATION , FEMALE *
APPL - MACRO : INCOME * EDUCATION - EFFECT OF * APPL - MACRO : EMPLOYMENT *
MULTIPLIERS - MACRO

YA1479   GREGORY R.G.
"US imports and internal pressure of demand"   Am. Econ. Rev., vol.61,
1971, pp.28-47.
APPL - MACRO : INTERNATIONAL TRADE , IMPORTS * CAPACITY - EFFECT OF

YA1480   GRETHER D.M., NERLOVE M.
"Some properties of 'optimal' seasonal adjustment"   Econometrica, vol.38,
1970, pp.682-703.
SEASONALITY - REVIEW * COMPARATIVE METHODS - SEASONALITY * SPECTRAL ANALYSIS
- APPL : SEASONALITY * BIBLIOGRAPHY - SEASONALITY * DATA - SIMULATION

YA1481   GRIER P.C., ALBIN P.S.
"Non random price changes in association with trading in large blocks"   J.
Business, vol.46, 1973, pp.425-433.
STOCK PRICES - TRADING VOLUME * STOCK PRICES - TRADING RULES * STOCK PRICES
- VOLATILTY * APPL - FIRM : FINANCE , STOCK PRICES

YA1482   GRIER P.C., KATZ S.
"The differential effects of bond rating changes among industrial and public
utility bonds by maturity"   J. Business, vol.49, 1976, pp.226-239.
APPL - FIRM : FINANCE , BONDS * STOCK PRICES - INFORMATION EFFECT * USE -
CREDIT CONTROL , BOND RATING

YA1483   GRIESON R.E., DE LEEUW F., EKANEM N.F.
"The supply of rental housing: comments"   Am. Econ. Rev., vol.63, 1973,
pp.433-438.
SUPPLY - SECTOR : CONSTRUCTION * APPL - SECTOR : CONSTRUCTION , RESIDENTIAL
* MULTICOLLINEARITY - EFFECT OF

YA1484   GRIFFIN J.M.
"Inter-fuel substitution possibilities: a translog application to
intercountry data"   Int. Econ. Rev., vol.18, 1977, pp.755-770.
APPL - SECTOR : UTILITIES , ELECTRICITY * APPL - SECTOR : ENERGY , SOURCES *
SUBSTITUTE FACTORS * DEMAND EQUATIONS - SYSTEMS OF * DATA - INTERNATIONAL

YA1485   GRIFFIN J.M.
"Joint production technology: the case of petrochemicals"   Econometrica,
vol.46, 1978, pp.379-396.
PRODUCTION FUNCTIONS - THEORY , JOINT * LP * PRICE - EFFECT OF * APPL -
SECTOR : PRODUCTION , CHEMICALS

YA1486   GRIFFIN J.M.
"Long-run production modeling with pseudo data: electric power generation"
Bell J. Econ., vol.8, 1977, pp. 112-127.
APPL - SECTOR : UTILITIES , ELECTRICITY * APPL - MACRO : ENERGY , SOURCES *
SUBSTITUTE FACTORS * SIMULATION - APPL : SECTOR , UTILITIES * PRICE - EFFECT
OF * LP * COST - SECTOR : UTILITIES

YA1487   GRIFFIN J.M.
"The econometrics of joint production: another approach"   Rev. Econ.
Stats., vol.59, 1977, pp.389-397.
APPL - SECTOR : PRODUCTION , PETROLEUM * PRODUCTION FUNCTIONS - METHODOLOGY
* PRICE - EFFECT OF * PRODUCTION FUNCTIONS - JOINT * ADVANCED

YA1488   GRIFFIN J.M.
"The effects of higher prices on electricity consumption"   Bell J.
Econ. vol.5, 1974, pp.515-539.
APPL - SECTOR : UTILITIES , ELECTRICITY * APPL - SECTOR : ENERGY , SOURCES *
POLICY EVALUATION - MACRO : ENERGY * SIMULTANEOUS SYSTEM - APPL

YA1489   GRIFFIN J.M., GREGORY P.R.
"An intercountry translog model of energy substitution responses"   Am.
Econ. Rev., vol.66, 1976, pp.845-857.
PRODUCTION FUNCTIONS - MACRO * DATA - INTERNATIONAL * PRODUCTION FUNCTIONS -
SUBSTITUTION * APPL - MACRO : ENERGY * PRICE - EFFECT OF * EVALUATION -
PRODUCTION FUNCTIONS

YA1490   GRIFFIN K., NEWLYN W.T., PAPANEK G.F.
         "The effect of AID and other resourse transfers on savings and growth in
         less-developed countries: comments"   Econ. J., vol.83, 1973, pp.863-874.
         APPL - MACRO : DEVELOPMENT * APPL - MACRO : SAVINGS * APPL - MACRO :
         INTERNATIONAL FINANCE * DATA - LDC * PUBLIC EXPENDITURE - EFFECT OF , AID
         PROGRAMS

YA1491   GRIFFIN P.A.
         "Competitive information in the stock market: an empirical study of
         earnings, dividends, and analyst's forecasts" with discussion   J. Finance,
         vol.31, 1976, pp.631-650 & 680-684.
         APPL - FIRM : FINANCE , STOCK PRICES * STOCK PRICES - INFORMATION EFFECT *
         EVALUATION - JUDGEMENTAL FORECASTS , SPECIALIST * EVALUATION - JUDGEMENTAL
         FORECASTS , STOCK PRICES

YA1492   GRIFFIN P.A.
         "The association between relative risk and risk estimates derived from
         quarterly earnings and dividends"   Acctg. Rev., vol.51, 1976, pp.499-515.
         RISK - ESTIMATION * STOCK PRICES - BETA * STOCK PRICES - RISK * APPL - FIRM
         : FINANCE , STOCK PRICES * COMPARATIVE METHODS - ARIMA , AUTOREGRESSIVE

YA1493   GRIFFIN P.A.
         "The time-series behaviour of quarterly earnings: preliminary evidence"
         J. Acctg. Res., vol.15, 1977, pp.71-83.
         APPL - FIRM : FINANCE , PROFITS * EVALUATION - TIME SERIES , ARIMA *
         COMPARATIVE METHODS - ARIMA , AUTOREGRESSIVE

YA1494   GRIFFITHS D., WILLCOX M.
         "Percentile regression: a parametric approach"   J. Am. Statist. Ass.,
         vol.73, 1978, pp.284-287.
         REGRESSION - ESTIMATION * ESTIMATION - ROBUST * NON PARAMETRIC * ERROR
         SPECIFICATION - HETEROSCEDASTIC

YA1495   GRILICHES Z.
         "Cost allocation in railroad regulation"   Bell J. Econ., vol.3, 1972,
         pp.26-41.
         APPL - FIRM : TRANSPORT , RAILWAYS * COST - FIRM : TRANSPORT * DATA -
         SPECIFICATION OF VARIABLES

YA1496   GRILICHES Z.
         "Distributed lags: a survey"   Econometrica, vol.35, 1967, pp.16-49.
         COMPARATIVE METHODS - DISTRIBUTED LAG * DISTRIBUTED LAG - REVIEW *
         DISTRIBUTED LAG - IDENTIFICATION * DISTRIBUTED LAG - ESTIMATION * APPL -
         MACRO : INVESTMENT * APPL - SECTOR : PRODUCTIVITY * DISTRIBUTED LAG - ERROR
         SPECIFICATION * DISTRIBUTED LAG - SOLOW , ESTIMATION * BIBLIOGRAPHY -
         DISTRIBUTED LAG

YA1497   GRILICHES Z.
         "Errors in variables and other unobservables"   Econometrica, vol.42, 1974,
         pp.971-998.
         DATA ERRORS - EFFECT OF , REVIEW * REGRESSION - ERRORS IN VARIABLES *
         SIMULTANEOUS SYSTEM - ERRORS IN VARIABLES * APPL - SECTOR : SOCIAL , SUCCESS
         * BIBLIOGRAPHY - ERRORS IN VARIABLES

YA1498   GRILICHES Z.
         "Estimating the returns to schooling: some econometric problems"
         Econometrica, vol.45, 1977, pp.1-22.
         EDUCATION - EFFECT OF * APPL - SECTOR : SOCIAL , SUCCESS * BIBLIOGRAPHY -
         EARNINGS , EDUCATION

YA1499   GRILICHES Z.
         "The Brookings Model volume: a review article"   Rev. Econ. Stats., vol.50,
         1968, pp.215-234.
         MACRO MODEL - BROOKINGS * EVALUATION - MACRO MODELS

YA1500   GRILICHES Z., DHRYMES P.J.
         "More on CES production functions"   Rev. Econ. Stats., vol.49, 1967,
         pp.608-611.
         PRODUCTION FUNCTIONS - METHODOLOGY * PRODUCTION FUNCTIONS - SUBSTITUTION *
         EVALUATION - PRODUCTION FUNCTIONS

YA1501   GRINYER P.H.
         "Corporate financial simulation models for top management"   Omega, vol.1,
         1973, pp.465-482.
         USE - CORPORATE PLANNING * SIMULATION - APPL : FINANCIAL MODELLING * USE -
         FINANCIAL , CONTROL * BASIC

YA1502   GRINYER P.H., BATT C.D.
         "Some tentative findings on corporate financial simulation models"   Opl.
         Res. Q., vol.25, 1974, pp.149-167.
         SIMULATION - APPL : FIRM , REVIEW * USER REQUIREMENTS * USE - CORPORATE
         PLANNING

YA1503   GRINYER P.H., WHITTAKER J.D.
         "Management judgement in a competitive bidding model"   Opl. Res. Q.,
         vol.24, 1973, pp.181-191.
         JUDGEMENTAL FORECASTS - APPL * USE - COMPETITIVE BIDDING * USER - FIRM :
         CONSTRUCTION

YA1504   GROFF G.K.
         "Empirical comparison of models for short term forecasting"   Mgmt. Sci.
         (A), vol.20, 1973, pp.22-31.
         COMPARATIVE METHODS - ARIMA , EXPONENTIAL SMOOTHING * EXPONENTIAL SMOOTHING
         - HARMONIC * DATA - SIMULATION * EVALUATION - TIME SERIES , ARIMA MODELS *
         EX ANTE

YA1505   GROSS A.M.
         "Confidence intervals for bisquare regression estimates"   J. Am. Statist.
         Ass., vol.72, 1977, pp.341-354.
         ESTIMATION - ROBUST * DATA - SIMULATION * CONFIDENCE INTERVAL - PREDICTIONS
         : REGRESSION * SIMULATION - METHODOLOGY , MONTE CARLO * SIMULATION -
         EXPERIMENTAL DESIGN
YA1506   GROSS C., PETERSON R.T.
         "Some human problems in industrial sales forecasting"   Ind. Mktg. Mgmt.,
         vol.7, 1978, pp.367-368.
         FORECASTING - PRACTICE * BASIC
YA1507   GROSS C.W., NUSSBAUM H.
         "A management science application in the courtroom: a jury selection model"
         Omega, vol.6, 1978, pp.531-539.
         APPL - SECTOR : SOCIAL , CRIME * DISCRIMINANT ANALYSIS - APPL * REGRESSION -
         QUALITATIVE DEPENDENT : APPL * EX ANTE
YA1508   GROSSMAN M., FUCHS V.R.
         "Intersectoral shifts and aggregate productivity change"   Anns. Econ. Soc.
         Meas., vol.2, 1973, pp.227-243.
         APPL - SECTOR : PRODUCTIVITY
YA1509   GRUBEL H.G., MAKI D., SAX S.
         "Real and insurance-induced unemployment in Canada"   Can. J. Econ., vol.8,
         1975, pp.174-191.
         APPL - MACRO : UNEMPLOYMENT * POLICY EVALUATION - MACRO : UNEMPLOYMENT
YA1510   GRUBER A.
         "Purchase intent and purchase probability"   J. Advtg. Res., vol.10:1,
         1970, pp.23-27.
         SURVEYS - METHODOLOGY , SCALING * APPL - SECTOR : CONSUMER NON DURABLES ,
         FOOD * EVALUATION - SURVEYS , CONSUMER
YA1511   GUDMUNDSSON G.
         "Multivariate analysis of economic variables"   Appl. Stats, vol.26, 1977,
         pp.48-59.
         MACRO MODEL - UK , KLEIN * STABILITY OF COEFFICIENTS - REGRESSION : APPL *
         COMPARATIVE METHODS - MACRO MODELS * COMPARATIVE METHODS - ARIMA ,
         DISTRIBUTED LAG * COMPARATIVE METHODS - ARIMA , CAUSAL(SIMULTANEOUS SYSTEM)
YA1512   GUDMUNDSSON G.
         "Time series analysis of imports, exports and other economic variables"
         R. Statist. Soc. (A), vol.134, 1971, pp.383-412.
         APPL - MACRO : INTERNATIONAL TRADE * APPL - MACRO : GNP * SPECTRAL ANALYSIS
         - CROSS : APPL * SPECTRAL ANALYSIS : APPL * APPL - MACRO : MONEY ,
         SUPPLY * APPL - MACRO , ICELAND * BUSINESS INDICATORS - APPL * LAG , FIXED *
         INFLATION - INDICATORS * APPL - MACRO , UK * DISTRIBUTED LAG - RATIONAL
         POLYNOMIAL , IDENTIFICATION
YA1513   GUILKEY D.K.
         "A test for the presence of first-order vector autoregressive errors when
         lagged exogenous variables are present"   Econometrica, vol.43, 1975,
         pp.711-717.
         SIMULTANEOUS SYSTEM - LAGGED DEPENDENT * AUTOCORRELATION - TEST * ADVANCED
YA1514   GUILKEY D.K.
         "Alternative tests for a first order vector autoregressive error
         specification"   J. Econometrics, vol.2, 1974, pp.95-104.
         ERRORS SPECIFICATION - AUTOCORRELATED , CORRELATED * COMPARATIVE METHODS -
         TESTS , AUTOCORRELATION * DATA - SIMULATION * AUTOCORRELATION - TEST *
         SIMULTANEOUS SYSTEM - ERROR SPECIFICATION
YA1515   GUILKEY D.K., LOVELL C.A.K.
         "Secification error in generalised production function models"   Int. Econ.
         Rev., vol.16, 1975, pp.161-170.
         PRODUCTION FUNCTIONS - ESTIMATION * SPECIFICATION ERROR - EFFECT OF ,
         VARIABLE INCLUSION * REGRESSION - TRANSFORMATIONS * DATA - SIMULATION *
         SPECIFICATION ERROR - EFFECT OF , TRANSFORMATION * APPL - SECTOR :
         PRODUCTION , PLANT , TRANSPORTATION
YA1516   GUILKEY D.K., MURPHY J.L.
         "Directed ridge regression techniques in cases of multicollinearity"   J.
         Am. Statist. Ass., vol.70, 1975, pp.769-775.
         COMPARATIVE METHODS - ESTIMATION : OLS , RIDGE * DATA SIMULATION
YA1517   GUILKEY D.K., SCHMIDT P.
         "Estimation of seemingly unrelated regressions with vector autoregressive
         errors"   J. Am. Statist. Ass., vol.68, 1973, pp.642-647.
         ERROR SPECIFICATION - AUTOCORRELATED , CORRELATED * REGRESSION - SEEMINGLY
         UNRELATED * COMPARATIVE METHODS - ESTIMATION : REGRESSION , SEEMINGLY
         UNRELATED * ADVANCED
YA1518   GUJARATI D.
         "The behaviour of unemployment and unfilled vacancies: Great Britain,
         1958-1971"   Econ. J., vol.82, 1972, pp.195-204.
         POLICY EVALUATION - MACRO : UNEMPLOYMENT * APPL - MACRO : UNEMPLOYMENT * EX
         ANTE * APPL - MACRO , UK * BASIC
YA1519   GUJARATI D.
         "Use of dummy variables in testing for equality between sets of coefficients
         in two linear regressions: a note"   Am. Stat'n., vol.24:1, 1970, pp.50-52
         & vol.24:5, 1970, pp.18-22.
         BASIC * APPL - MACRO , UK * APPL - MACRO : SAVINGS * STABILITY OF
         COEFFICIENTS - REGRESSION , TEST

YA1520   GUNDERSON M.
"Logit estimates of labour force participation based on census cross-tabulations"   Can. J. Econ., vol.10, 1977, pp.453-462.
MANPOWER PLANNING - LABOUR PARTICIPATION , FEMALE * EDUCATION - EFFECT OF *
INCOME - EFFECT OF * REGRESSION - LIMITED DEPENDENT , LOGIT : APPL

YA1521   GUNDERSON M.
"Retention of trainees: a study with dichotomous dependent variables"   J.
Econometrics, vol.2, 1974, pp.79-93.
COMPARATIVE METHODS - REGRESSION , LIMITED DEPENDENT * MANPOWER PLANNING -
LABOUR TURNOVER

YA1522   GUNDERSON M.
"Training subsidies and disadvantaged workers: regression with a limited
dependent variable"   Can. J. Econ., vol.7, 1974, pp.611-624.
REGRESSION - LIMITED DEPENDENT , TOBIT * COMPARATIVE METHODS - ESTIMATION :
REGRESSION , LIMITED DEPENDENT * PUBLIC EXPENDITURE - EFFECT OF , AID
PROGRAMS * USER - SECTOR : GOVERNMENT * MANPOWER PLANNING - TRAINING
PROGRAMS * POLICY EVALUATION - MACRO : EMPLOYMENT

YA1523   GUNST R.F., MASON R.L.
"Biased estimation in regression: an evaluation using mean squared error"
J. Am. Statist. Ass., vol.72, 1977, pp.616-628.
COMPARATIVE METHODS - ESTIMATION : REGRESSION * COMPARATIVE METHODS -
ESTIMATION : OLS , RIDGE * ESTIMATION - STEIN * REGRESSION - ESTIMATION *
REGRESSION - RIDGE * ESTIMATION - PRINCIPAL COMPONENTS * DATA - SIMULATION *
MULTICOLLINEARITY - EFFECT OF

YA1524   GUPTA K.L.
"Aggregation bias in linear economic models"   Int. Econ. Rev., vol.12,
1971, pp.293-305.
REGRESSION - AGGREGATION * DATA - AGGREGATION 'BIAS' * COMPARATIVE METHODS -
DATA : AGGREGATE , DISAGGREGATE * APPL - SECTOR : EARNINGS

YA1525   GUPTA K.L.
"Factor prices,expectations and demand for labor"   Econometrica, vol.43,
1975, pp.757-770.
MANPOWER PLANNING - SECTOR , DEMAND * APPL - SECTOR : EMPLOYMENT

YA1526   GUPTA K.L., ADAMS N.A., LEFF N.H.
"Dependency rates and savings rates: comments"   Am. Econ. Rev., vol.61,
1971, pp.469-480.
DATA - LDC * APPL - MACRO : SAVINGS * POPULATION - EFFECT OF

YA1527   GUSTAFSON E.F.
"Testing unstable econometric models for stability"   J. Econometrics,
vol.8, 1978, pp.193-201.
SIMULTANEOUS SYSTEM - DYNAMIC PROPERTIES * DATA - SIMULATION * STABILITY OF
COEFFICIENTS - SIMULTANEOUS SYSTEM , TEST

YA1528   GUTH L.A., ET AL.
"The use of buyer concentration ratios in tests of oligopoly models" with
comment   Rev. Econ. Stats., vol.53, 1976, pp.488-494.
CONCENTRATION - EFFECT OF * APPL - SECTOR : FINANCE , MARGINS

YA1529   GUTHERY S.B.
"Partition regression"   J. Am. Statist. Ass., vol.69, 1974, pp.945-947.
STABILITY OF COEFFICIENTS - REGRESSION * APPL - SECTOR : CONSUMER NON
DURABLES , FOOD * APPL - SECTOR : UTILITIES , TELEPHONE * REGRESSION -
PIECEWISE * PRICE - SECTOR : CONSUMER NON DURABLES

YA1530   GUTHRIE H.W., ET AL.
"Microanalytic simulation of household behaviour"   Anns. Econ. Soc. Meas.,
vol.1, 1972, pp.141-169.
APPL - MACRO : CONSUMER DEMAND * POPULATION * LIFE CYCLE - CONSUMER * POLIC
EVALUATION - MACRO : WELFARE * TAX - EFFECT OF * SIMULATION - APPL : MICRO
SIMULATION - METHODOLOGY * POPULATION - MARRIAGES

YA1531   GUTHRIE R.S.
"A note on the Bayesian estimation of Solow's distributed lag"   J.
Econometrics, vol.4, 1976, pp.295-300.
DISTRIBUTED LAG - SOLOW , ESTIMATION * BAYESIAN - ESTIMATION : DISTRIBUTED
LAG * DATA - SIMULATION

YA1532   GUY J.R.F.
"An examination of the effects of international diversification from the
British viewpoint on both hypothetical and real portfolios"   J. Finance,
vol.33, 1978, pp.1425-1438.
APPL - FIRM : FINANCE , MUTUAL FUNDS * APPL - FIRM : FINANCE , STOCK PRICES
* STOCK PRICES - INSTITUTIONAL INVESTMENT * USE - PORTFOLIO SELECTION * APP
- FIRM : FINANCE , INVESTMENT , INTERNATIONAL

YA1533   GUY J.R.F.
"The performance of the British investment trust industry"   J. Finance,
vol.33, 1978, pp.443-455.
APPL - FIRM : FINANCE , MUTUAL FUNDS * APPL - FIRM : FINANCE , STOCK PRICES
* STOCK PRICES - INSTITUTIONAL INVESTMENT * USE - PORTFOLIO SELECTION

YA1534   HAAS R.D.
"More evidence on the role of speculation in the Canadian forward exchange
market"   Can. J. Econ., vol.7, 1974, pp.496-501.
APPL - MACRO : INTERNATIONAL FINANCE , EXCHANGE RATES * THEORY - SPECULATIO
* ERROR SPECIFICATION - AUTOCORRELATED * APPL - MACRO , CANADA * EXCHANGE
RATE - FORWARD RATE

YA1535   HABIBAGAHI H., PRATSCHKE J.L.
"A comparison of the power of the Von Neumann ratio, Durbin-Watson and Geary tests"   Rev. Econ. Stats., vol.54, 1972, pp.179-185.
AUTOCORRELATION - TEST * COMPARATIVE METHODS - TESTS , AUTOCORRELATION

YA1536   HADDAD C.L.
"Testing income series"   J. Econometrics, vol.4, 1976, pp.27-40.
FACTOR ANALYSIS - APPL * PROXY VARIABLES * APPL - MACRO , LATIN AMERICA *
APPL - MACRO , UK * INDEX NUMBERS - METHODOLOGY

YA1537   HAGERMAN R.L.
"More evidence on the distribution of security returns"   J. Finance,
vol.33, 1978, pp.1213-1221.
STOCK PRICES - DISTRIBUTION * APPL - FIRM : FINANCE , STOCK PRICES * ERROR
DISTRIBUTION - STABLE

YA1538   HAGERMAN R.L., RATCHFORD B.T.
"Some determinants of allowed rates of return on equity to electric
utilities"   Bell. J. Econ., vol.9, 1978, pp.46-55.
DECISION RULES - SECTOR * APPL - FIRM : UTILITIES * APPL - FIRM : FINANCE ,
PROFITS * RISK - EFFECT OF * STOCK PRICES - BETA * USE - FINANCIAL ,
REGULATION

YA1539   HAGERMAN R.L., RICHMOND R.D.
"Random walks,martingales and the O.T.C."   J. Finance, vol.28, 1973,
pp.897-909.
ERROR DISTRIBUTION - STABLE * APPL - SECTOR : FINANCE , STOCK PRICES *
RANDOM WALK - TEST * STOCK PRICES - MODELS , EFFICIENT MARKET * STOCK PRICES
- RUNS

YA1540   HAIG B.D.
"An analysis of changes in the distribution of employment between the
manufacturing industries, 1960-1970"   Rev. Econ. Stats., vol.57, 1975,
pp.35-42.
MACRO MODEL - AUSTRALIA * APPL - SECTOR : EMPLOYMENT * APPL - SECTOR :
GROWTH * INPUT OUTPUT - MACRO , AUSTRALIA

YA1541   HAINES G.H., SIMON L.S., ALEXIS M.
"Maximum likelihood estimation of central-city food trading areas"   J.
Mktg. Res., vol.9, 1972, pp.154-159.
APPL - SECTOR : RETAILING , FOOD * ESTIMATION - MAXIMUM LIKELIHOOD * BRAND
CHOICE - APPL

YA1542   HAITOVSKY Y.
"Missing data in regression analysis"   R. Statist. Soc. (B), vol.30, 1968,
pp.67-82.
COMPARATIVE METHODS - DATA ERRORS : ESTIMATION * DATA ERRORS - MISSING
OBSERVATIONS * DATA - SIMULATION

YA1543   HAITOVSKY Y.
"Multicollinearity in regression analysis: a comment"   Rev. Econ. Stats.,
vol.51, 1969, pp.486-489.
MULTICOLLINEARITY - TESTS * DATA - SIMULATION * MULTICOLLINEARITY - REMOVAL
OF

YA1544   HAITOVSKY Y.
"On errors of measurement in regression analysis in economics"   Int.
Statist. Rev., vol.40, 1972, pp.23-35.
REGRESSION - ERRORS IN VARIABLES * DATA ERRORS - EFFECT OF * DATA REVISIONS
- EFFECT OF * APPL - MACRO : CONSUMER DEMAND

YA1545   HAITOVSKY Y., JACOBS S.
"REGEN - Computer program to generate multivariate observations for linear
regression equations"   Anns. Econ. Soc. Meas., vol.1, 1972, pp.43-57.
SIMULATION - METHODOLOGY , RANDOM DEVIATES * COMPUTERISATION - SIMULATION ,
DATA , PROGRAMS * SIMULATION - METHODOLOGY , MODEL SPECIFICATION

YA1546   HAITOVSKY Y., TREYZ G.
"Forecasts with quarterly macroeconometric models, equation adjustments, and
benchmark predictions: the US experience"   Rev. Econ. Stats., vol.54,
1972, pp.317-325.
MACRO MODEL - OBE * MACRO MODEL - WHARTON * COMPARATIVE METHODS -
MACRO MODELS * EVALUATION - THEORY OF * COMPARATIVE METHODS -
CAUSAL(SIMULTANEOUS SYSTEM) , JUDGEMENTAL * MACRO MODEL - ST.LOUIS *
COMPARATIVE METHODS - AUTOREGRESSIVE , CAUSAL(SIMULTANEOUS SYSTEM) * MACRO
MODELS - METHODOLOGY , ADJUSTMENTS * EVALUATION - JUDGEMENTAL ADJUSTMENTS *
EX ANTE * EVALUATION - MACRO MODELS

YA1547   HAITOVSKY Y., VALENTINE T.J.
"A note on the maximisation of R bar squared"   Am. Stat'n., vol.23:1,
1969, pp.20-21 & vol.23:4, 1969, p.51.
REGRESSION - SUMMARY STATISTICS * BASIC

YA1548   HALEVI N.
"Effective devaluation and exports: some issues in empirical analysis, with
illustrations from Israel"   Economica, vol.39, 1972, pp.292-300.
APPL - MACRO , ISRAEL * APPL - MACRO : INTERNATIONAL TRADE , EXPORTS *
EXCHANGE RATE - EFFECT OF

YA1549   HALEVI N.
"The effects on investment and consumption of import surpluses of developing
countries"   Econ. J., vol.86, 1976, pp.853-858.
APPL - MACRO : INTERNATIONAL FINANCE * APPL - MACRO : DEVELOPMENT * DATA -
CROSS SECTION * DATA - LDC * APPL - MACRO : INVESTMENT * APPL - MACRO :
CONSUMPTION

YA1550   HALL R.E.
          "Investment, interest and the effects of stabilization policies" with
          discussion   Brookings Paps. Econ. Activity, 1977, pp.61-121.
          POLICY EVALUATION - MACRO : STABILISATION * APPL - MACRO : INVESTMENT *
          DISTRIBUTED LAG - APPL , INVESTMENT * EVALUATION - INVESTMENT MODELS * APPL
          - MACRO : MONEY , DEMAND * PUBLIC EXPENDITURE - EFFECT OF * THEORY -
          INVESTMENT
YA1551   HALL R.E.
          "The process of inflation in the labour market" with discussion   Brookings
          Paps. Econ. Activity, 1974, pp.343-409.
          INFLATION - DETERMINANTS , EARNINGS * APPL - FIRM : EARNINGS * UNIONIZATION
          - EFFECT OF
YA1552   HALL R.E.
          "The rigidity of wages and the persistence of unemployment" with discussion
          Brookings Paps. Econ. Activity, 1975, pp.301-349.
          APPL - SECTOR : EARNINGS * APPL - MACRO : UNEMPLOYMENT
YA1553   HALL R.E.
          "Turnover in the labour force" with discussion   Brookings Paps. Econ.
          Activity, 1972, pp.709-764.
          MANPOWER PLANNING - LABOUR TURNOVER * REGRESSION - LIMITED DEPENDENT : APPL
          * REGIONAL MODELS - MANPOWER PLANNING , LABOUR PARTICIPATION * DATA - CROSS
          SECTION
YA1554   HALL R.E.
          "Why is the unemployment rate so high at full employment" with discussion
          Brookings Paps. Econ. Activity, 1970, pp.369-410.
          APPL - MACRO : UNEMPLOYMENT
YA1555   HALL R.E., KASTEN R.A.
          "The relative occupational success of blacks and whites" with discussion
          Brookings Paps. Econ. Activity, 1973, pp.781-797.
          MANPOWER PLANNING - DISCRIMINATION , RACIAL * APPL - SECTOR : SOCIAL ,
          SUCESS
YA1556   HALPERN E.F.
          "Bayesian spline regression when the number of knots is unknown"   R.
          Statist. Soc. (B), vol.35, 1973, pp.347-360.
          REGRESSION - PIECEWISE * BAYESIAN - ESTIMATION : REGRESSION , PIECEWISE *
          SPLINE FUNCTIONS * ADVANCED
YA1557   HALPERN P.J.
          "Empirical estimates of the amount and distribution of gains to companies in
          mergers"   J. Business, vol.46, 1973, pp.554-576.
          APPL - FIRM : MERGERS * STOCK PRICES - INDUSTRIAL STRUCTURE * APPL - FIRM :
          FINANCE , STOCK PRICES * USE - ACQUISITION
YA1558   HALVORSEN R.
          "Energy substitution in US manufacturing"   Rev. Econ. Stats., vol.59,
          1977, pp.381-388.
          DEMAND EQUATIONS - SYSTEM OF * APPL - SECTOR : ENERGY , SOURCES * PRICE -
          EFFECT OF
YA1559   HALVORSEN R.
          "Residential demand for electric energy"   Rev. Econ. Stats., vol.57, 1975,
          pp.12-18.
          APPL - SECTOR : UTILITIES , ELECTRICITY * PRICE - SECTOR : UTILITIES * PRICE
          - EFFECT OF * DATA - CROSS SECTION , TIME SERIES * INCOME - EFFECT OF *
          DISTRIBUTED LAG - SOLOW : APPL * WEATHER - EFFECT OF
YA1560   HAM J.C.
          "A note on the efficient estimation of the linear expenditure system"   J.
          Am. Statist. Ass., vol.73, 1978, pp.208-210.
          DEMAND EQUATIONS - SYSTEMS OF : METHODOLOGY , ESTIMATION * ESTIMATION -
          MAXIMUM LIKELIHOOD * ESTIMATION - CONSTRAINED
YA1561   HAMADA R.S.
          "The effect of the firm's capital structure on the systematic risk of common
          stocks"   J. Finance, vol.27, 1972, pp.435-458.
          APPL - FIRM : FINANCE , STOCK PRICES * APPL - FIRM : FINANCE , FINANCIAL
          STRUCTURE , LEVERAGE * STOCK PRICES - BETA , DETERMINANTS
YA1562   HAMBOR J.C., PHILLIPS L., VOTEY H.C.
          "Optimal community educational attainment: a simultaneous equation approach"
          Rev. Econ. Stats., vol.55, 1973, pp.98-103.
          APPL - SECTOR : EDUCATION * COMPARATIVE METHODS - ESTIMATION : OLS , 2SLS *
          MANPOWER PLANNING - QUALIFIED MANPOWER * APPL - SECTOR : SOCIAL ,
          EDUCATIONAL ATTAINMENT
YA1563   HAMBURGER M.J., KOCHIN L.A.
          "Money and stock prices: the channels of influence" with discussion   J.
          Finance, vol.27, 1972, pp.231-249 & 294-298.
          APPL - SECTOR : FINANCE , STOCK PRICE INDEX * STOCK PRICES - DETERMINANTS *
          APPL - MACRO : MONEY , SUPPLY * INTEREST RATE - EFFECT OF * RISK - EFFECT OF
YA1564   HAMBURGER M.J., PLATT E.N.
          "The expectations hypothesis and the efficiency of the treasury bill market"
          Rev. Econ. Stats., vol.57, 1975, pp.190-199.
          THEORY - EFFICIENT MARKETS * INTEREST RATE - DETERMINANTS * INTEREST RATE -
          TERM STRUCTURE * INTEREST RATE - EXPECTATIONS * EXPECTATIONS - ESTIMATING

YA1565   HAMBURGER M.J., ZWICK B.
         "Instalment credit controls, consumer expenditures and the allocation of
         real resources"   J. Finance, vol.32, 1977, pp.1557-1569.
         APPL - SECTOR : CONSUMER DURABLES * APPL - SECTOR : CONSUMER DURABLES , CARS
         * APPL - MACRO : CONSUMPTION * APPL - SECTOR : FINANCE , HIRE PURCHASE

YA1566   HAMILTON J.L.
         "The demand for cigarettes: advertising, the health scare, and the cigarette
         advertising ban"   Rev. Econ. Stats., vol.54, 1972, pp.401-411.
         APPL - SECTOR : CONSUMER NON DURABLES , CIGARETTES * ADVERTISING - EFFECT OF
         * INCOME - EFFECT OF * PRICE - EFFECT OF * HEALTH - CAMPAIGNS * DISTRIBUTED
         LAG - APPL , ADVERTISING * POLICY EVALUATION - SECTOR : HEALTH

YA1567   HAMILTON W.E., MOSES M.A.
         "A computer-based corporate planning system"   Mgmt. Sci. (B), vol.21,
         1974, pp.148-159.
         SIMULATION - APPL : FIRM * USE - CORPORATE PLANNING * BASIC

YA1568   HAMLEN S.S., HAMLEN W.A.
         "Harmonic alternatives to the Almon polynomial technique"   J.
         Econometrics, vol.7, 1978, pp.57-66.
         DISTRIBUTED LAG - ALMON * DISTRIBUTED LAG - APPL , ORDERS * DISTRIBUTED LAG
         - HARMONICS

YA1569   HAMMOND E.K.
         "Evolutionary spectra in random vibrations" with discussion.   R. Statist.
         Soc. (B), vol.35, 1973, pp.167-188.
         SPECTRAL ANALYSIS - CHANGING SPECTRA * TIME SERIES - NON STATIONARY *
         ADVANCED

YA1570   HAMMOND J.S.
         "Do's and don'ts of computer models for planning"   H.B'.R., vol.52,
         Mar-April, 1974, pp.110-123.
         SIMULATION - APPL : FIRM * USER REQUIREMENTS * USE - CORPORATE PLANNING *
         USER - FIRM * BASIC

YA1571   HAMNER W.C., CARTER P.L.
         "A comparision of alternative production management coefficient decision
         rules"   Decis. Sci., vol.6, 1975, pp.324-336.
         CONTROL THEORY - DETERMINISTIC , APPL - LEAD TIME - EFFECT OF * FORECASTING
         - VALUE OF * BOOTSTRAPPING * DECISION RULES - FIRM

YA1572   HAMOVITCH W., MORGENSTERN R.D., KATZ D.A.
         "The principal cause of salary differentials: research output or
         experience?: comments"   Am. Econ. Rev., vol.65, 1975, pp.484-486.
         MANPOWER PLANNING - SECTOR : EDUCATION , UNIVERSITIES * MANPOWER PLANNING -
         EARNINGS

YA1573   HAMPTON J.M., MOORE P.G., THOMAS H.
         "Subjective probability and its measurement"   R. Statist. Soc. (A),
         vol.136, 1973, pp.21-42.
         JUDGEMENTAL FORECASTS - METHODOLOGY * DELPHI * FORECASTER BEHAVIOUR - BIAS *
         BIBLIOGRAPHY - SUBJECTIVE PROBABILITY * BAYESIAN - JUDGEMENTAL FORECASTS *
         JUDGEMENTAL FORECASTS - PROBABILITY

YA1574   HANNA M.
         An investor expectations stock price predictive model using closed-end fund
         premiums: comment"   J. Finance, vol.32, 1977, pp.1368-1371.
         APPL - SECTOR : FINANCE , STOCK PRICE INDEX * STOCK PRICES - DETERMINANTS *
         STOCK PRICES - TRADING RULES

YA1575   HANNA M., SCHNELLER M.I., EPPS T.W.
         "Security price changes and transaction volumes: additional evidence and
         comment"   Am. Econ. Rev., vol.68, 1978, pp.692-700.
         APPL - FIRM : FINANCE , STOCK PRICES * STOCK PRICES - TRADING VOLUME

YA1576   HANNAN E.J., NICHOLLS D.F.
         "The estimation of the prediction error variance"   J. Am. Statist. Ass.,
         vol.72, 1977, pp.834-840.
         ESTIMATION - HANNAN * SPECTRAL ANALYSIS - APPL : REGRESSION * ADVANCED

YA1577   HANNAN E.J., NICHOLS D.F.
         "The estimation of mixed regression, autoregression moving average and
         distributed lag models"   Econometrica, vol.40, 1972, pp.529-547.
         DISTRIBUTED LAG - ESTIMATION * DISTRIBUTED LAG - ERROR SPECIFICATION *
         DISTRIBUTED LAG - RATIONAL POLYNOMIAL * DATA - SIMULATION * ESTIMATION -
         HANNAN * ADVANCED

YA1578   HANNAN E.J., ROBINSON P.M.
         "Lagged regression with unknown lags"   R. Statist. Soc. (B), vol.35, 1973,
         pp.252-267.
         SPECTRAL ANALYSIS - APPL : LAG IDENTIFICATION * LAG , FIXED * APPL - MACRO :
         MONEY , SUPPLY

YA1579   HANSEN B.
         "On the effects of fiscal and monetary policy: a taxonomic discussion"
         Am. Econ. Rev., vol.63, 1973, pp.546-571.
         THEORY - FISCAL , MONETARY * EVALUATION - MONETARIST THEORY * MACRO MODELS -
         THEORY * ADVANCED

YA1580   HANSEN B., ET AL.
         "Fiscal and monetary policy reconsidered: comment" with discussion   Am.
         Econ. Rev., vol.61, 1971, pp.444-447, 448-457 & 500-516.
         POLICY EVALUATION - MACRO : FISCAL , MONETARY

YA1581   HANSON J.R., ENKE S.
"Economic consequences of rapid population growth-comments"   Econ, J.,
vol.83, 1973, pp.217-221.
POPULATION - FERTILITY * SIMULATION - APPL : SECTOR , SOCIAL

YA1582   HANSON J.S., VOGEL R.C.
"Inflation and monetary velocity in Latin America"   Rev, Econ, Stats.,
vol.55, 1973, pp.365-370.
INFLATION - EFFECT OF * APPL - MACRO : MONEY , INCOME VELOCITY * APPL -
MACRO , LATIN AMERICA * INFLATION - RAPID

YA1583   HANUSHEK E.A.
"Regional differences in the structure of earnings"   Rev, Econ, Stats.,
vol.55, 1973, pp.204-213.
EDUCATION - EFFECT OF * REGIONAL MODELS - MANPOWER PLANNING , EARNINGS *
MANPOWER PLANNING - REGIONAL

YA1584   HANUSHEK E.A., QUIGLEY J.M.
"Implicit investment profiles and intertemporal adjustments of relative
wages"   Am, Econ, Rev., vol.68, 1978, pp.67-79.
MANPOWER PLANNING - LABOUR FORCE COMPOSITION * MANPOWER PLANNING - EARNINGS
* EDUCATION - EFFECT OF * MANPOWER PLANNING - DISCRIMINATION , RACIAL

YA1585   HANUSHEK E.A., SONG B.N.
"The dynamics of postwar industrial location"   Rev, Econ, Stats., vol.60,
1978, pp.515-522.
APPL - SECTOR : LOCATION * REGIONAL MODELS - LOCATION * REGRESSION - ERROR
COMPONENTS : APPL

YA1586   HARDIN E.
"Michigan's employment problem and the elasticity of substitution"   J.
Business, vol.38, 1965, pp.201-206.
REGIONAL MODELS - MANPOWER PLANNING * SUBSTITUTE FACTORS * MANPOWER PLANNING
- SECTOR * COMPARATIVE METHODS - REGRESSION , SEEMINGLY UNRELATED

YA1587   HARMELINK P.J.
"An empirical examination of the predictive ability of alternate sets of
insurance company accounting data"   J, Acctg, Res,, vol.11, 1973,
pp.146-158.
APPL - FIRM : FINANCE , INSURANCE COMPANIES * USE - BANKRUPTCY PREDICTION *
DISCRIMINANT ANALYSIS - APPL * USE - CREDIT CONTROL , BOND RATING

YA1588   HARPER C.P.
"Testing for the existence of a lagged relationship with Almon's method"
Rev, Econ, Stats., vol.59, 1977, pp.204-210.
SPECIFICATION ERROR - EFFECT OF , LAG SPECIFICATION * DISTRIBUTED LAG -
MODEL CHOICE * POLICY EVALUATION - MACRO : FISCAL , MONETARY * MACRO MODEL -
ST. LOUIS * DISTRIBUTED LAG - APPL , MONEY * APPL - MACRO : GNP *
DISTRIBUTED LAG - ALMON

YA1589   HARPER C.P., FRY C.L.
"Consistent empirical results with Almon's method: implications for the
monetary versus fiscal policy debate"   J. Finance, vol.33, 1978,
pp.187-198.
DISTRIBUTED LAG - ALMON * SPECIFICATION ERROR - TESTS , MODEL CHOICE : APPL
* APPL - MACRO : GNP * POLICY EVALUATION - MACRO : FISCAL , MONETARY *
SPECIFICATION ERROR - TESTS , LAG SPECIFICATION * DISTRIBUTED LAG -
IDENTIFICATION * DISTRIBUTED LAG - APPL , MONEY

YA1590   HARRELL G.D., BENNETT P.D.
"An evaluation of the expectancy value model of attitude measurement for
physician prescribing behaviour"   J. Mktg. Res,, vol.11, 1974, pp.269-278.
CONSUMER BEHAVIOUR - PSYCHOLOGICAL MODELS * CONSUMER BEHAVIOUR - PURCHASING
, DETERMINANTS * HEALTH - MANPOWER , GPS * APPL - SECTOR : CONSUMER NON
DURABLES , PHARMACEUTICALS

YA1591   HARRIS R.
"A note on the paper: an examination of the use of adaptive filtering in
forecasting"   Opl. Res, Q., vol.24, 1973, pp.640-641.
TIME SERIES - ADAPTIVE FILTERING : APPL * EVALUATION - THEORY OF * BASIC

YA1592   HARRIS R.G.
"Economies of traffic density in the rail freight industry"   Bell J,
Econ,, vol.8, 1977, pp.556-564.
COST - SCALE ECONOMIES * APPL - FIRM : TRANSPORT , RAILWAYS , FREIGHT * COST
- FIRM : TRANSPORT

YA1593   HARRISON B.
"Education and underemployment in the urban ghetto"   Am. Econ, Rev.,
vol.62, 1972, pp.796-812.
MANPOWER PLANNING - DISCRIMINATION , RACIAL * MANPOWER PLANNING - LABOUR
FORCE COMPOSITION * MANPOWER PLANNING - UNEMPLOYMENT

YA1594   HARRISON F.B., BAKER A.
"The accountant takes to models"   Opl. Res. Q., vol.25, 1974, pp.3-18.
APPL - SECTOR : PRODUCTION , COAL * SIMULATION - APPL : SECTOR , PRODUCTION
* USER - FIRM : PRODUCTION * USE - CORPORATE PLANNING * BASIC

YA1595   HARRISON M.J.
"The power of the Durbin-Watson and Geary tests: comment and further
evidence"   Rev. Econ. Stats., vol.57, 1975, pp.377-379.
NON PARAMETRIC - TEST * COMPARATIVE METHODS - TESTS , AUTOCORRELATION *
ERROR SPECIFICATION - AUTOCORRELATED * DATA - SIMULATION

YA1596   HARRISON P.J.
"Short term sales forecasting"   Appl. Stats., vol.14, 1965, pp.102=139.
APPL - SECTOR : TRANSPORT , AIR ★ TIME SERIES - BOX JENKINS PREDICTOR ★
EVALUATION - EXPONENTIAL SMOOTHING ★ EXPONENTIAL SMOOTHING - HIGHER ORDER ★
EX ANTE ★ SEASONALITY - ESTIMATION , HARMONICS ★ TIME SERIES - HARMONICS ★
EXPONENTIAL SMOOTHING - REVIEW ★ EXPONENTIAL SMOOTHING - THEORY ★
COMPARATIVE METHODS - TIME SERIES

YA1597   HARRISON P.J., PEARCE S.F.
"The use of trend curves as an aid to market forecasting"   Ind. Mktg.
Mgmt., vol.1, 1972, pp.149-170.
TREND CURVES - REVIEW ★ APPL - SECTOR : PRODUCTION , CHEMICALS ★ LONG TERM
FORECASTING ★ APPL - SECTOR : PRODUCTION , FIBRES , ARTIFICIAL

YA1598   HARRISON P.J., STEVENS C.F.
"A Bayesian approach to short-term forecasting"   Opl. Res. Q., vol.22,
1971, pp.341-362.
BAYESIAN - FORECASTING ★ TIME SERIES - BAYESIAN ★ ESTIMATION - KALMAN FILTER
★ STABILITY OF COEFFICIENTS - TIME SERIES

YA1599   HARRISON P.J., STEVENS C.F.
"Bayesian forecasting" with discussion   R. Statist. Soc. (B), vol.38,
1976, pp.205-247.
BAYESIAN - FORECASTING ★ ESTIMATION - KALMAN FILTER ★ BAYESIAN - MODEL
SELECTION ★ STATIONARITY - TRANSFORMING TO ★ EVALUATION - THEORY OF ★ DATA
ERRORS - EFFECT OF ★ MODEL SELECTION ★ REGRESSION - STATE SPACE ★ TIME
SERIES - STATE SPACE ★ ADVANCED

YA1600   HARRISON T.
"Different market reactions to discretionary and nondiscretionary accounting
changes"   J. Acctg. Res., vol.15, 1977, pp.84-107.
STOCK PRICES - INFORMATION EFFECT ★ ACCOUNTING PRACTICE - EFFECT OF ★ APPL -
FIRM : FINANCE , STOCK PRICES ★ RISK - EFFECT OF

YA1601   HART R.A., MacKAY D.I.
"Wage inflation, regional policy and the regional earning structure"
Economica, vol.44, 1977, pp.267-281.
APPL - MACRO : EARNINGS ★ APPL - MACRO , UK ★ REGIONAL MODELS - MANPOWER
PLANNING , EARNINGS ★ INFLATION - DETERMINANTS , EARNINGS

YA1602   HARTER H.L.
"The method of least squares and some alternatives"   Int. Statist. Rev.,
vol.44, 1976, pp.113=159.
ESTIMATION - NON LINEAR ★ ESTIMATION - OLS , REVIEW ★ BIBLIOGRAPHY -
ESTIMATION , REGRESSION ★ BIBLIOGRAPHY - REGRESSION ★ ESTIMATION - MSAE ★
REGRESSION - OUTLIERS ★ REGRESSION - ROBUST ★ EXTREME VALUES ★ DATA -
CENSORED ★ EVALUATION - ERROR SPECIFICATION ★ REGRESSION - ESTIMATION ,
REVIEW

YA1603   HARTER H.L.
"The method of least squares and some alternatives: Parts I-II"   Int.
Statist. Rev., vol.42, 1974, pp.147-174 & 235-264.
ESTIMATION - OLS , REVIEW ★ REGRESSION - ESTIMATION , REVIEW ★ BIBLIOGRAPHY
- ESTIMATION , REGRESSION

YA1604   HARTER H.L.
"The method of least squares and some alternatives: Parts III-V"   Int.
Statist. Rev., vol.43, 1975, pp.1-44, 125-190, & 269-278.
ESTIMATION - OLS , REVIEW ★ REGRESSION - ESTIMATION , REVIEW ★ ESTIMATION -
ROBUST ★ EVALUATION - ERROR DISTRIBUTION ★ BIBLIOGRAPHY - ESTIMATION ,
REGRESSION

YA1605   HARTLEY K.
"Estimating military aircraft production outlays: the British experience"
Econ. J., vol.79, 1969, pp.861-881.
APPL - SECTOR : PRODUCTION , AIRCRAFT ★ COST - SECTOR : PRODUCTION ★ COST -
LEARNING CURVE ★ APPL - SECTOR : GOVERNMENT , DEFENCE

YA1606   HARTUNG P.H.
"A simple style-goods inventory model"   Mgmt. Sci. (B), vol.19, 1973,
pp.1452-1458.
STYLE GOODS ★ USE - INVENTORY CONTROL

YA1607   HARVEY A.C.
"An alternative proof and generalisation of a test for structural change"
Am. Stat'n., vol.30, 1976, pp.122-123.
RESIDUALS - ANALYSIS OF , RECURSIVE ★ STABILITY OF COEFFICIENTS - REGRESSION
, TEST

YA1608   HARVEY A.C.
"Discriminations between CES and VES production functions"   Anns. Econ.
Soc. Meas., vol.6, 1977, pp.463-471.
EVALUATION - PRODUCTION FUNCTIONS ★ REGRESSION - MODEL CHOICE ★ DATA - CROSS
SECTION ★ PRODUCTION FUNCTIONS - SECTOR ★ COMPARATIVE METHODS - MODEL
SELECTION

YA1609   HARVEY A.C.
"Some comments on multicollinearity in regression"   Appl. Stats., vol.26,
1977, pp.188-191.
MULTICOLLINEARITY - REMOVAL OF ★ PRODUCTION FUNCTIONS - METHODOLOGY

YA1610   HARVEY A.C.
          "Spectral analysis in economics"   Stat'n., vol.24, 1975, pp.1-36.
          SPECTRAL ANALYSIS - REVIEW * SPECTRAL ANALYSIS - APPL : DISTRIBUTED LAG *
          SPECTRAL ANALYSIS - APPL : REGRESSION
YA1611   HARVEY A.C., COLLIER P.
          "Testing for functional misspecification in regression analysis"   J.
          Econometrics, vol.6, 1977, pp.103-119.
          SPECIFICATION ERROR - TESTS , TRANSFORMATIONS * RESIDUALS - ANALYSIS OF ,
          SPECIFICATION ERROR * DATA - SIMULATION * REGRESSION - TRANSFORMATIONS
YA1612   HARVEY A.C., PHILLIPS G.D.A.
          "A comparison of the power of some tests for heteroskedasticity in the
          general linear model"   J. Econometrics, vol.2, 1974, pp.307-316.
          COMPARATIVE METHODS - TESTS , HETEROSCEDASTICITY * ERROR SPECIFICATION -
          HETEROSCEDASTIC * RESIDUALS - COMPARATIVE ANALYSIS OF * DATA - SIMULATION *
          HETEROSCEDASTICITY - TEST
YA1613   HASENKAMP G.
          "A study of multiple-output production functions"   J. Econometrics, vol.4,
          1976, pp.253-262.
          PRODUCTION FUNCTIONS - JOINT * APPL - SECTOR : TRANSPORT , RAILWAYS
YA1614   HASLEM J.A., LONGBRAKE W.A.
          "A note on average interest charges on bank loans, the loan mix, and
          measures of competition"   J. Finance, vol.26, 1971, pp.159-164.
          APPL - FIRM : FINANCE , BANKS * DATA - CROSS SECTION * APPL - FIRM : FINANCE
          , BANK , ASSETS * MULTICOLLINEARITY - REMOVAL OF
YA1615   HASSAN Z.A., FINLEY R.M., JOHNSON S.R.
          "The demand for food in the United States"   Appl. Econ., vol.5, 1973,
          pp.233-248.
          APPL - SECTOR : CONSUMER NON DURABLES , FOOD * DEMAND EQUATIONS - SYSTEMS OF
          * PRICE - EFFECT OF * EVALUATION - CONSUMER BEHAVIOUR , ECONOMIC MODELS
YA1616   HATANAKA M.
          "A simple suggestion to improve the Mincer-Zarnowitz criterion for the
          evaluation of forecasts"   Anns. Econ. Soc. Meas., vol.3, 1974, pp.521-524.
          EVALUATION - THEORY OF * LOSS FUNCTIONS - THEORY
YA1617   HATANAKA M.
          "The estimation of spectra and cross-spectra on short time series data"
          Int. Econ. Rev., vol.13, 1972, pp.679-704.
          DATA - SIMULATION * ESTIMATION - HANNAN * SPECTRAL ANALYSIS - METHODOLOGY *
          DATA - SAMPLE SIZE * SPECTRAL ANALYSIS - CROSS : METHODOLOGY * ADVANCED
YA1618   HATANAKA M.
          "The underestimation of variations in the forecast series: a note"   Int.
          Econ. Rev., vol.16, 1975, pp.151-160.
          EVALUATION - THEORY OF * LEAD TIME - EFFECT OF
YA1619   HATHAWAY D.E.
          "Food prices and inflation" with discussion   Brookings Paps. Econ.
          Activity, 1974, pp.63-116.
          APPL - SECTOR : AGRICULTURE * PRICE - SECTOR : AGRICULTURE
YA1620   HAUCK W.W., DONNER A.
          "Wald's test as applied to hypotheses in logit analysis"   J. Am. Statist.
          Ass., vol.72, 1977, pp.851-853.
          HEALTH - DISEASE , INCIDENCE OF * REGRESSION - LIMITED DEPENDENT , LOGIT *
          EVALUATION - REGRESSION , HYPOTHESIS TESTS
YA1621   HAUGEN R.A., LANGETEIG T.C.
          "An empirical test for synergism in mergers"   J. Finance, vol.30, 1975,
          pp.1003-1014.
          APPL - FIRM : MERGERS * APPL - FIRM : FINANCE , STOCK PRICES * STOCK PRICES
          - INDUSTRIAL STRUCTURE
YA1622   HAUGH L.D.
          "Checking the independence of two covariance-stationary time series: a
          univariate residual cross-correlation approach"   J. Am. Statist. Ass.,
          vol.71, 1976, pp.378-385.
          CROSS CORRELATIONS * TIME SERIES - AUTOREGRESSIVE * CAUSALITY - TEST * DATA
          - SIMULATION
YA1623   HAUGH L.D., BOX G.E.P.
          "Identification of dynamic regression (distributed lag) models connecting
          two time series"   J. Am. Statist. Ass., vol.72, 1977, pp.121-130.
          INTEREST RATE - COVARIATION * CROSS CORRELATIONS * DISTRIBUTED LAG -
          RATIONAL POLYNOMIAL , IDENTIFICATION * TIME SERIES - ARIMA : APPL * APPL -
          MACRO , UK * APPL - MACRO : UNEMPLOYMENT * APPL - MACRO : GDP * CAUSALITY -
          TEST * DISTRIBUTED LAG - ARIMA * DISTRIBUTED LAG - ERROR SPECIFICATION
YA1624   HAUSAFUS K.F.
          "Trade finance, capital movements and the stability of the foreign exchange
          market"   Int. Econ. Rev., vol.16, 1975, pp.404-414.
          APPL - MACRO , GERMANY * APPL - MACRO : INTERNATIONAL FINANCE , EXCHANGE
          RATES
YA1625   HAUSE J.C.
          "Spectral analysis and the detection of lead lag relations"   Am. Econ.
          Rev., vol.61, 1971, pp.213-217.
          DISTRIBUTED LAG - IDENTIFICATION * SPECTRAL ANALYSIS - APPL : LAG
          IDENTIFICATION * ADVANCED

YA1626   HAUSER J.R.
         "Testing the accuracy, usefulness and significance of probabilistic choice
         models: an information theoretic approach"   Ops. Res., vol.26, 1978,
         pp.406-421.
         REGRESSION - QUALITATIVE DEPENDENT * EVALUATION - THEORY OF * LOSS FUNCTIONS
         - INFORMATION CRITERION * REGRESSION - MODEL CHOICE * REGRESSION - LIMITED
         DEPENDENT

YA1627   HAUSMAN J.A.
         "Full information instrumental variables estimation of simultaneous
         equations systems"   Anns. Econ. Soc. Meas., vol.3, 1974, pp.641-652.
         ESTIMATION - FIML * SIMULTANEOUS SYSTEM - ESTIMATION * MACRO MODEL - KLEIN *
         COMPARATIVE METHODS - ESTIMATION : SIMULTANEOUS SYSTEM

YA1628   HAUSMAN J.A.
         "Project independence report: an appraisal of US energy needs up to 1985"
         Bell J. Econ., vol.6, 1975, pp.517-551.
         POLICY EVALUATION - MACRO : ENERGY * EVALUATION - ENERGY DEMAND FORECASTS *
         APPL - MACRO : ENERGY * APPL - SECTOR : UTILITIES , ELECTRICITY * REGIONAL
         MODELS - ENERGY * PRICE - EFFECT OF * APPL - MACRO : ENERGY , SOURCES

YA1629   HAUSMAN J.A.
         "Specification tests in econometrics"   Econometrica, vol.46, 1978,
         pp.1251-1271.
         SPECIFICATION ERROR - TESTS , REVIEW * SPECIFICATION ERROR - TESTS ,
         INDEPENDENCE REGRESSORS , ERRORS * MANPOWER PLANNING - EARNINGS * REGRESSION
         - ERRORS IN VARIABLES * REGRESSION - RANDOM COEFFICIENTS * DATA - CROSS
         SECTION , TIME SERIES * SPECIFICATION ERROR - TESTS , RANDOM COEFFICIENT
         MODEL * ADVANCED

YA1630   HAUSMAN J.A., WISE D.A.
         "A conditional probit model for qualitative choice: discrete decisions
         recognising interdependence and heterogeneous preferences"   Econometrica,
         vol.46, 1978, pp.403-426.
         SIMULTANEOUS SYSTEM - LIMITED DEPENDENT , PROBIT * APPL - SECTOR : TRANSPORT
         * USE - TRANSPORT PLANNING

YA1631   HAUSMAN J.A., WISE D.A.
         "The evaluation of results from truncated samples: the New Jersey income
         maintenance experiment"   Anns. Econ. Soc. Meas., vol.5, 1976, pp.421-445.
         POLICY EVALUATION - MACRO : UNEMPLOYMENT * MANPOWER PLANNING - EARNINGS *
         SIMULTANEOUS SYSTEM - LIMITED DEPENDENT * ESTIMATION - MAXIMUM LIKELIHOOD

YA1632   HAUSMAN W.H.
         "Sequential decision problems: a model to exploit existing forecasts"
         Mgmt. Sci. (B), vol.16, 1969, pp.93-111.
         PRIOR INFORMATION - APPL * JUDGEMENTAL FORECASTS - LEARNING * STYLE GOODS *
         APPL - SECTOR : AGRICULTURE , VEGETABLES * ERROR DISTRIBUTION - LOGNORMAL *
         LP

YA1633   HAUSMAN W.H., PETERSON R.
         "Multiproduct production scheduling for style goods with limited capacity,
         forecast revisions and terminal delivery"   Mgmt. Sci. (A), vol.18, 1972,
         pp.370-383.
         SEASONALITY - SINGLE SEASON * STYLE GOODS * JUDGEMENTAL FORECASTS - LEARNING
         * ERROR DISTRIBUTION - LOGNORMAL * USE - PRODUCTION , CONTROL * LP

YA1634   HAUSMAN W.H., SIDES R.ST.G.
         "Mail order demands for style goods: theory and data analysis"   Mgmt. Sci.
         (B), vol.20, 1973, pp.191-202.
         PROBABILITY MODELS - NBD * APPL - FIRM : RETAILING , MAIL ORDER * FORECAST -
         REVISION * SEASONALITY - SINGLE SEASON * STYLE GOODS * BIBLIOGRAPHY *
         SEASONALITY , SINGLE SEASON * ERROR DISTRIBUTION - LOGNORMAL * JUDGEMENTAL
         FORECASTS - LEARNING

YA1635   HAUSMAN W.H., WEST R.R., LARGAY J.A.
         "Stock splits, price changes and trading profits: a synthesis"   J.
         Business, vol.44, 1971, pp.69-77.
         APPL - FIRM : FINANCE , STOCK PRICES * STOCK PRICES - INFORMATION EFFECT

YA1636   HAVENNER A., HERMAN R.
         "Pooled time-series cross-section estimation"   Econometrica, vol.45, 1977,
         pp.1535-1536.
         COMPUTERISATION - ESTIMATION , REGRESSION MODELS , PROGRAMS * ESTIMATION -
         CROSS SECTION , TIME SERIES * REGRESSION - ESTIMATION

YA1637   HAWDON D.
         "Marketing models in the gas industry"   Eur. J. Mktg., vol.5, 1971,
         pp.99-109.
         APPL - SECTOR : CONSUMER DURABLES , APPLIANCES , COOKERS * APPL - SECTOR :
         CONSUMER DURABLES , HEATING UNITS * APPL - SECTOR : UTILITIES , GAS * BRAND
         CHOICE - APPL

YA1638   HAWKINS D.M.
         "On the investigation of alternative regressions by principal component
         analysis"   Appl. Stats, vol.22, 1973, pp.275-286.
         ESTIMATION - PRINCIPAL COMPONENTS * APPL - SECTOR : CONSUMER NON DURABLES ,
         LIQUOR * FACTOR ANALYSIS - APPL * REGRESSION - VARIABLE INCLUSION

YA1639 HAWKINS D.M.
  "Testing a sequence of observations for a shift in location" J. Am.
  Statist. Ass., vol.72, 1977, pp.180-186.
  TIME SERIES - PIECEWISE * STABILITY OF COEFFICIENTS - TIME SERIES , TEST *
  RANDOM WALK - TEST * APPL - SECTOR : FINANCE , STOCK PRICE INDEX

YA1640 HAWORTH C.T., REUTHER C.J.
  "Industrial concentration and interindustry wage determination" Rev.
  Econ. Stats., vol.60, 1978, pp.85-95.
  APPL - SECTOR : EARNINGS * CONCENTRATION - EFFECT OF * STABILITY OF
  COEFFICIENTS - REGRESSION : APPL

YA1641 HAWORTH J.G., GWARTNEY J., HAWORTH C.
  "Earnings, productivity, and changes in employment discrimination during the
  1960's" Am. Econ. Rev., vol.65, 1975, pp.158-168.
  MANPOWER PLANNING - DISCRIMINATION , RACIAL * MANPOWER PLANNING - EARNINGS *
  EDUCATION - EFFECT OF

YA1642 HAY G.A.
  "A note on the Stigler-Kindahl study of industrial prices" Am. Econ.
  Rev., vol.62, 1972, pp.656-658.
  DATA - SPECIFICATION OF VARIABLES * APPL - SECTOR : PRODUCTION , PAPER *
  APPL - SECTOR : AGRICULTURE , TIMBER * DECISION RULES - SECTOR * PRICE -
  SECTOR : AGRICULTURE * APPL - SECTOR : INVENTORIES * PRICE - SECTOR :
  PRODUCTION

YA1643 HAYES M.
  "Swing analysis and electoral forecasting" Opl. Res. Q., vol.27, 1976,
  pp.329-340.
  VOTING

YA1644 HAYES R.H.
  "Statistical estimation problems in inventory control" Mgmt. Sci. (A),
  vol.15, 1969, pp.686-701.
  BAYESIAN - CONTROL * LOSS FUNCTIONS - FIRM , INVENTORY * BAYESIAN -
  ESTIMATION : PROBABILITY MODEL * USE - INVENTORY CONTROL

YA1645 HAYES R.H., NOLAN R.L.
  "What kind of corporate modeling functions best?" H.B.R., vol.52,
  May-June, 1974, pp.102-113.
  SIMULATION - APPL : FIRM * USER REQUIREMENTS * BASIC

YA1646 HAZLEDINE T.
  "New specifications for employment and hours functions" Economica,
  vol.45, 1978, pp.179-193.
  APPL - SECTOR : EMPLOYMENT

YA1647 HAZLEDINE T., MORELAND R.S.
  "Population and economic growth: a world cross-section study" Rev. Econ.
  Stats., vol.59, 1977, pp.253-266.
  APPL - MACRO : GROWTH * DATA - INTERNATIONAL * POPULATION - EFFECT OF * DATA
  - LDC

YA1648 HEALD G.I.
  "The application of the automatic interaction detector (AID) programme and
  multiple regression techniques to the assessment of store performance and
  site selection" Opl. Res. Q., vol.23, 1972, pp.445-457.
  APPL - SECTOR : RETAILING * USE - SITE SELECTION , RETAIL * AID - APPL * USE
  - RETAIL , SITE MONITORING * COMPARATIVE METHODS - REGRESSION , MULTIVARIATE
  METHODS

YA1649 HEATHFIELD D.F., EVANS G.J.
  "Distribution margins in the U.K.: a quarterly analysis" Appl. Econ.,
  vol.3, 1971, pp.205-217.
  APPL - SECTOR : FINANCE , MARGINS * COST - SECTOR : RETAIL * APPL - SECTOR :
  RETAILING

YA1650 HECKMAN J.
  "Shadow prices, market wages and labor supply" Econometrica, vol.42,
  1974, pp.679-694.
  SIMULTANEOUS SYSTEM - LIMITED DEPENDENT , TOBIT * MANPOWER PLANNING - LABOUR
  PARTICIPATION , FEMALE

YA1651 HECKMAN J.J.
  "Dummy endogenous variables in a simultaneous equation system"
  Econometrica, vol.46, 1978, pp.931-959.
  PROXY VARIABLES * SIMULTANEOUS SYSTEM - THRESHOLD * SIMULTANEOUS SYSTEM -
  LIMITED DEPENDENT , PROBIT * ADVANCED

YA1652 HECKMAN J.J.
  "The common structure of statistical models of truncation, sample selection
  and limited dependent variables and a simple estimator for such models"
  Anns. Econ. Soc. Meas., vol.5, 1976, pp.475-492.
  MANPOWER PLANNING - LABOUR PARTICIPATION * REGRESSION - TRUNCATED *
  REGRESSION - LIMITED DEPENDENT * MANPOWER PLANNING - EARNINGS * REGRESSION -
  CENSORED * COMPARATIVE METHODS - REGRESSION , LIMITED DEPENDENT

YA1653 HEDRICK C.L.
  "Expectations and the labour supply" Am. Econ. Rev., vol.63, 1973,
  pp.968-974.
  APPL - MACRO : EMPLOYMENT * MANPOWER PLANNING - MACRO , SUPPLY * THEORY -
  EXPECTATIONS * COMPARATIVE METHODS - ESTIMATION : OLS , 2SLS * COMPARATIVE
  METHODS - ESTIMATION : REGRESSION , NON LINEAR

YA1654   HEELER R.M., KEARNEY M.J., MEHAFFEY B.J.
          "Modelling supermarket product selection"   J. Mktg. Res., vol.10, 1973,
          pp.34-37.
          APPL - SECTOR : RETAILING * NEW PRODUCTS - IDENTIFYING * ESTIMATION - GLS *
          REGRESSION - DISCRETE DEPENDENT * EX ANTE * USE - RETAIL , PRODUCT SELECTION
YA1655   HEFLEY G.L.
          "The value index concept for demand forecasting"   Omega, vol.4, 1976,
          pp.343-344.
          NEW PRODUCTS - APPL * CONSUMER BEHAVIOUR - ECONOMIC MODELS
YA1656   HEGGESTAD A.A.
          "Market structure, risk and profitability in commercial banking"   J.
          Finance, vol.32, 1977, pp.1207-1216.
          CONCENTRATION - EFFECT OF * APPL - FIRM : FINANCE , BANKS * APPL - FIRM :
          FINANCE , PROFITS
YA1657   HEGGESTAD A.A., MINGO J.J.
          "Capital management by holding company banks"   J. Business, vol.48, 1975,
          pp.500-505.
          APPL - FIRM : FINANCE , BANKS * APPL - FIRM : FINANCE , FINANCIAL STRUCTURE
YA1658   HEGGESTAD A.A., MINGO J.J.
          "The competitive condition of US banking markets and the impact of
          structural reform"   J. Finance, vol.32, 1977, pp.649-661.
          APPL - FIRM : FINANCE , BANKS * APPL - FIRM : FINANCE , CONSUMER CREDIT *
          APPL - FIRM : FINANCE , BANK , LIABILITIES * CONCENTRATION - EFFECT OF
YA1659   HEIEN D.
          An econometric model of the US pork economy"   Rev. Econ. Stats., vol.57,
          1975, pp.370-375.
          APPL - SECTOR : AGRICULTURE , LIVESTOCK , HOGS * PRICE - SECTOR :
          AGRICULTURE * SIMULATION - APPL : SECTOR , AGRICULTURE * EX ANTE * STABILITY
          OF COEFFICIENTS - SIMULTANEOUS SYSTEM , TEST * INCOME - EFFECT OF * PRICE -
          EFFECT OF * SUPPLY - SECTOR : AGRICULTURE * APPL - SECTOR : INTERNATIONAL
          TRADE
YA1660   HEIEN D.
          "The cost of the US dairy price support program: 1949-74"   Rev. Econ.
          Stats., vol.59 1977, pp.1-8.
          APPL - SECTOR : AGRICULTURE , DAIRY PRODUCTS * PUBLIC EXPENDITURE - EFFECT
          OF * POLICY EVALUATION - SECTOR : AGRICULTURE * EX ANTE
YA1661   HEKMAN J.S.
          "An analysis of the changing location of iron and steel production in the
          twentieth century"   Am. Econ. Rev., vol.68, 1978, pp.123-133.
          APPL - SECTOR : PRODUCTION , STEEL * PRICE - SECTOR : PRODUCTION * APPL -
          SECTOR : LOCATION * PRODUCTION FUNCTIONS - SECTOR
YA1662   HELLINGER F.J.
          "Specification of a hospital production function"   Appl. Econ., vol.7,
          1975, pp.149-160.
          PRODUCTION FUNCTIONS - SECTOR * HEALTH - HOSPITAL * EVALUATION - PRODUCTION
          FUNCTIONS
YA1663   HELLIWELL J., MAXWELL T.
          "Short-term capital flows and the foreign exchange market"   Can. J. Econ.,
          vol.5, 1972, pp.199-214.
          APPL - MACRO : INTERNATIONAL FINANCE * EX ANTE * DECISION RULES - MACRO *
          EXCHANGE RATE - EFFECT OF * APPL - MACRO , CANADA
YA1664   HELLIWELL J.F., LESTER J.M.
          "External linkages of the Canadian monetary system"   Can. J. Econ., vol.9,
          1976, pp.646-667.
          MACRO MODEL - CANADA , RDX2 * POLICY EVALUATION - MACRO : INTERNATIONAL
          FINANCE , FOREIGN EXCHANGE * SIMULATION - APPL : POLICY EVALUATION *
          EXCHANGE RATE - EFFECT OF * APPL - MACRO : INTERNATIONAL LINKAGE
YA1665   HELMER R.M., JOHANSSON J.K.
          "An exposition of the Box-Jenkins transfer function analysis with an
          application to the advertising-sales relationship"   J. Mktg. Res., vol.14,
          1977, pp.227-239.
          APPL - FIRM : CONSUMER NON DURABLES , HEALTH AIDS * ADVERTISING - EFFECT OF
          * DISTRIBUTED LAG - APPL , ADVERTISING * DISTRIBUTED LAG - RATIONAL
          POLYNOMIAL , INTRODUCTION * EX ANTE * COMPARATIVE METHODS - DISTRIBUTED LAG
          * DISTRIBUTED LAG - ERROR SPECIFICATION * DISTRIBUTED LAG - ARIMA
YA1666   HELMS J., NEWHOUSE J.P., PHELPS C.E.
          "Copayment and demand for medical care: the California medicaid experience"
          Bell. J. Econ., vol.9, 1978, pp.192-208.
          HEALTH - SERVICES * COST - SECTOR : HEALTH * POLICY EVALUATION - SECTOR :
          HEALTH * HEALTH - HOSPITAL * REGRESSION - CONSTRAINED * REGRESSION -
          SEEMINGLY UNRELATED * REGRESSION - COVARIANCE MODEL
YA1667   HELPS I.G.
          "A critique of some techniques of manpower forecasting at national and
          sectoral level"   Long Range Planning, vol.6:2, 1973, pp.75-79.
          MANPOWER PLANNING - REVIEW * BASIC
YA1668   HENDERSHOTT P.H., LEMMON R.C.
          "The financial behaviour of households: some empirical estimates"   J.
          Finance, vol.30, 1975, pp.733-759.
          APPL - MACRO : CONSUMER DEMAND , FINANCIAL ASSETS

YA1669   HENDERSHOTT P.H., ORLANDO F.S.
         "The interest-rate behaviour of flow-of-funds and bank reserves financial
         models"   J. Money, Credit, Banking, vol.8, 1976, pp.497-512.
         POLICY EVALUATION - MACRO : MONETARY * APPL - MACRO : FLOW OF FUNDS * APPL -
         SECTOR : FINANCE , BANKS * APPL - SECTOR : FINANCE , BONDS * APPL - SECTOR :
         FINANCE , MORTGAGES * INTEREST RATE - DETERMINANTS * EX ANTE
YA1670   HENDERSHOTT P.H., STARLEAF D.R., STEPHENSON J.A.
         "The full-employment interest rate and the neutralized money stock:
         comments"   J. Finance, vol.26, 1971, pp.127-143.
         APPL - MACRO : MONEY * INTEREST RATE - DETERMINANTS
YA1671   HENDERSHOTT P.H., VAN HORNE J.C.
         "Expected inflation implied by capital market rates" with discussion   J.
         Finance, vol.28, 1973, pp.301-314 & 319-320.
         INFLATION - EXPECTATIONS * APPL - SECTOR : FINANCE , BONDS * EXPECTATIONS -
         DATA * INFLATION - EFFECT OF * INTEREST RATE - EXPECTATIONS * INFLATION -
         INDICATORS * APPL - SECTOR : FINANCE , DIVIDENDS
YA1672   HENDRICKS W.
         "Regulation and labor earnings"   Bell J. Econ., vol.8, 1977, pp.483-496.
         APPL - SECTOR : EARNINGS * APPL - SECTOR : UTILITIES , ELECTRICITY *
         MANPOWER PLANNING - DISCRIMINATION , RACIAL
YA1673   HENDRICKS W.
         "The effect of regulation on collective bargaining in electric utilities"
         Bell J. Econ., vol.6, 1975, pp.451-456.
         APPL - FIRM : UTILITIES , ELECTRICITY * APPL - FIRM : EARNINGS * USE -
         FINANCIAL , REGULATION
YA1674   HENDRICKS W., KOENKER R., PODLASEK R.
         "Consumption patterns for electricity"   J. Econometrics, vol.5, 1977,
         pp.135-153.
         APPL - SECTOR : UTILITIES , ELECTRICITY * REGRESSION - PIECEWISE * INCOME -
         EFFECT OF * WEATHER - EFFECT OF
YA1675   HENDRY D.F.
         "Maximum likelihood estimation of systems of simultaneous regression
         equations with errors generated by a vector autoregressive process"   Int.
         Econ. Rev., vol.12, 1971, pp.257-272.
         COMPARATIVE METHODS - ESTIMATION : SIMULTANEOUS SYSTEM , ERROR SPECIFICATION
         * SIMULTANEOUS SYSTEM - ESTIMATION , ERROR SPECIFICATION * ESTIMATION -
         MAXIMUM LIKELIHOOD * MACRO MODEL - KLEIN * ERROR SPECIFICATION -
         AUTOCORRELATED * SIMULTANEOUS SYSTEM - HYPOTHESIS TESTS
YA1676   HENDRY D.F.
         "On asymptotic theory and finite sample experiments"   Economica, vol.40,
         1973, pp.210-217.
         SIMULATION - METHODOLOGY , EVALUATION * EVALUATION - REGRESSION , NON LINEAR
         * EVALUATION - SIMULTANEOUS SYSTEM , NON LINEAR * SIMULATION - EVALUATION OF
         RESULTS * ESTIMATION - MAXIMUM LIKELIHOOD * AUTOCORRELATION - EFFECT OF
YA1677   HENDRY D.F.
         "Stochastic specification in an aggregate demand model of the United
         Kingdom"   Econometrica, vol.42, 1974, pp.559-578.
         STABILITY OF COEFFICIENTS - SIMULTANEOUS SYSTEM * MACRO MODEL - UK * EX ANTE
         * COMPARATIVE METHODS - ESTIMATION : SIMULTANEOUS SYSTEM , 2SLS , FIML *
         COMPARATIVE METHODS - ESTIMATION : OLS , 2SLS * COMPARATIVE METHODS -
         SIMULTANEOUS SYSTEM , ERROR SPECIFICATION * COMPARATIVE METHODS - REGRESSION
         , ERROR SPECIFICATION * COMPARATIVE METHODS - ESTIMATION : OLS , FIML
YA1678   HENDRY D.F., HARRISON R.W.
         "Monte Carlo methodology and the small sample behaviour of ordinary and two
         stage least squares"   J. Econometrics, vol.2, 1974, pp.151-174.
         SIMULATION - METHODOLOGY , MONTE CARLO * SIMULATION - EXPERIMENTAL DESIGN *
         COMPARATIVE METHODS - ESTIMATION : OLS , 2SLS * ERROR SPECIFICATION -
         AUTOCORRELATED * AUTOCORRELATION - EFFECT OF
YA1679   HENDRY D.F., MIZON G.E.
         "Serial correlation as a convenient simplification, not a nuisance: a
         comment on a study of the demand for money by the Bank of England"   Econ.
         J., vol.88, 1978, pp.549-563.
         REGRESSION - MODEL CHOICE * AUTOCORRELATION - EFFECT OF , EVALUATION *
         STATIONARITY - TRANSFORMING TO * DISTRIBUTED LAG - ERROR SPECIFICATION *
         DISTRIBUTED LAG - RATIONAL POLYNOMIAL , IDENTIFICATION * APPL - MACRO :
         MONEY , DEMAND * APPL - MACRO : CONSUMER DEMAND , FINANCIAL ASSETS * APPL -
         MACRO , UK
YA1680   HENDRY D.F., SRBA F.
         "The properties of autoregressive instrumental variables estimators in
         dynamic systems"   Econometrica, vol.45, 1977, pp.969-990.
         COMPARATIVE METHODS - REGRESSION , ERROR SPECIFICATION * COMPARATIVE METHODS
         - SIMULTANEOUS SYSTEM , ERROR SPECIFICATION * SIMULTANEOUS SYSTEM -
         ESTIMATION , ERROR SPECIFICATION * SIMULATION - METHODOLOGY , MONTE CARLO *
         DATA - SIMULATION * ESTIMATION - INSTRUMENTAL VARIABLES * ERROR
         SPECIFICATION - AUTOCORRELATED * COMPARATIVE METHODS - ESTIMATION : OLS ,
         2SLS * REGRESSION - ESTIMATION , ERROR SPECIFICATION

YA1681   HENDRY D.F., TRIVEDI P.K.
           "Maximum likelihood estimation of difference equations with moving average
           errors: a simulation study"   Rev. Econ. Studies, vol.39, 1972, pp.117-145
           ESTIMATION - MAXIMUM LIKELIHOOD * REGRESSION - ESTIMATION * ERROR
           SPECIFICATION - MOVING AVERAGE * DISTRIBUTED LAG - ERROR SPECIFICATION *
           DATA - SIMULATION * SPECIFICATION ERROR - EFFECT OF , ERROR SPECIFICATION *
           EVALUATION - TEST , AUTOCORRELATION * COMPARATIVE METHODS - DISTRIBUTED LAG
           , ERROR SPECIFICATION * COMPARATIVE METHODS - ESTIMATION : REGRESSION ,
           ERROR SPECIFICATION * EVALUATION - DISTRIBUTED LAG , HYPOTHESIS TESTS

YA1682   HENDRY I.C.
           "The three-parameter approach to long range forecasting"   Long Range
           Planning, vol.5:1, 1972, pp.40-45.
           LONG TERM FORECASTING * TREND CURVES - INTRODUCTION * BASIC

YA1683   HENRY E.W.
           "An input-output model of the Irish economy"   Long Range Planning,
           vol.6:3, 1973, pp.69-73.
           INPUT OUTPUT - MACRO * IRELAND

YA1684   HENRY N.W., McDONALD J.F., STOKES H.H.
           "The estimation of dynamic economic relations from a time series of cross
           sections: a programming modification"   Anns. Econ. Soc. Meas., vol.5,
           1976, pp.153-155.
           REGRESSION - ERROR COMPONENTS * REGRESSION - ESTIMATION * COMPUTERISATION -
           ESTIMATION , REGRESSION MODELS , PROGRAMS * ESTIMATION - CROSS SECTION ,
           TIME SERIES * ERROR SPECIFICATION - AUTOCORRELATED , CORRELATED

YA1685   HENRY S.G.B.
           "The Koyck transformation and adaptive expectations: a note"   Economica,
           vol.41, 1974, pp.79-80.
           DISTRIBUTED LAG - SOLOW * DISTRIBUTED LAG - EXPECTATIONS HYPOTHESIS

YA1686   HENRY S.G.B., DESAI M.
           "Fiscal policy simulations and stabilization policy"   Rev. Econ. Studies,
           vol.42, 1975, pp.347-359.
           MACRO MODEL - UK * SIMULATION - APPL : POLICY EVALUATION * POLICY EVALUATION
           - MACRO : FISCAL * POLICY EVALUATION - MACRO : STABILISATION * COMPARATIVE
           METHODS - ESTIMATION : SIMULTANEOUS SYSTEM

YA1687   HENRY S.G.B., ORMEROD P.A.
           "Incomes policy and wage inflation: empirical evidence for the UK,
           1961-1977"   Nat. Inst. Econ. Rev., no.85, 1978, pp.31-39.
           INFLATION - GOVERNMENT CONTROLS * APPL - MACRO : EARNINGS

YA1688   HENRY S.G.B., SAWYER M.C., SMITH P.
           "Models of inflation in the UK: an evaluation   Nat. Inst. Econ. Rev.,
           no.77, 1976, pp.60-71 & no.78, 1976, p.71.
           EVALUATION - INFLATION MODELS * COMPARATIVE METHODS - REGRESSION , ERROR
           SPECIFICATION * INFLATION - DETERMINANTS * APPL - MACRO , UK * APPL - MACRO
           : EARNINGS * INFLATION - GOVERNMENT CONTROLS * STABILITY OF COEFFICIENTS -
           REGRESSION : APPL

YA1689   HENRY W.A.
           "Cultural values do correlate with consumer behaviour"   J. Mktg. Res.,
           vol.13, 1976, pp.121-127.
           CONSUMER BEHAVIOUR - PSYCHOLOGICAL MODELS * CONSUMER BEHAVIOUR - PURCHASING
           , DETERMINANTS * APPL - SECTOR : CONSUMER DURABLES , CARS * MARKET
           SEGMENTATION

YA1690   HEPBURN G.C., MAYOR T.H., STAFFORD J.E.
           "Estimation of market area population from residential electrical utility
           data"   J. Mktg. Res., vol.13, 1976, pp.230-236.
           REGIONAL MODELS - POPULATION * MARKET POTENTIAL * SIMULTANEOUS SYSTEM - APPL
           * EX ANTE

YA1691   HERBST A.F.
           "A factor analysis approach to determining the relative endogeneity of trade
           credit"   J. Finance, vol.29, 1974, pp.1087-1103.
           APPL - SECTOR : FINANCE , TRADE CREDIT * FACTOR ANALYSIS - APPL * MACRO
           MODELS - MICRO MODELS

YA1692   HERMANSON R.H., MILES C.E.
           "Fine tuning the predictive model of the American Accounting Association
           1971-72 and 1972-73 committees on future professional supply and demand"
           Acctg. Rev., vol.51, 1976, pp.875-885.
           MANPOWER PLANNING - SECTOR : EDUCATION , UNIVERSITIES * APPL - SECTOR :
           SERVICES , ACCOUNTANTS * APPL - SECTOR : EDUCATION , UNIVERSITIES * MANPOWER
           PLANNING - QUALIFIED MANPOWER , PROFESSIONAL

YA1693   HERNITER J.D.
           "A comparison of the entropy model and the Hendry model"   J. Mktg. Res.,
           vol.11, 1974, pp.21-29.
           BRAND CHOICE - APPL * EVALUATION - CONSUMER BEHAVIOUR , STOCHASTIC MODELS *
           PROBABILITY MODELS - ENTROPY

YA1694   HERNITER J.D.
           "A probabilistic market model of purchase timing and brand selection"
           Mgmt. Sci. (B), vol.18, (special issue), 1971, pp.P102-P113.
           CONSUMER BEHAVIOUR - STOCHASTIC MODELS * BRAND CHOICE - THEORY * APPL - FIRM
           : CONSUMER NON DURABLES , GROCERIES * REPEAT BUYING

YA1695 HERNITER J.D.
  "An entropy model of brand purchase behaviour" J. Mktg. Res., vol.10,
  1973, pp.361-375.
  CONSUMER BEHAVIOUR - STOCHASTIC MODELS * BRAND CHOICE - THEORY * PROBABILITY
  MODELS - ENTROPY

YA1696 HESS A.C.
  "A comparison of automobile demand equations" Econometrica, vol.45, 1977,
  pp.683-701.
  APPL - SECTOR : CONSUMER DURABLES , CARS * CONSUMER BEHAVIOUR - ECONOMIC
  MODELS * PRICE - EFFECT OF * SUBSTITUTE PRODUCTS * INCOME - EFFECT OF

YA1697 HESS A.C.
  "Household demand for durables goods: the influence of rates of return and
  wealth" Rev. Econ. Stats., vol.55, 1973, pp.9-15.
  APPL - SECTOR : CONSUMER DURABLES * PRICE - EFFECT OF * EX ANTE * ERROR
  SPECIFICATION - AUTOCORRELATED * COMPARATIVE METHODS - REGRESSION , ERROR
  SPECIFICATION * WEALTH - EFFECT OF

YA1698 HEWSON J., SAKAKIBARA E.
  "The effect of US controls on US commercial bank borrowing in the
  euro-dollar market" J. Finance, vol.30, 1975, pp.1101-1110.
  APPL - MACRO : INTERNATIONAL FINANCE * APPL - SECTOR : FINANCE , BANKS *
  APPL - SECTOR : FINANCE , INVESTMENT , INTERNATIONAL * COMPARATIVE METHODS -
  DATA : AGGREGATE , DISAGGREGATE * USE - BANK REGULATION

YA1699 HICKMAN B.G., COEN R.M., HURD M.D.
  "The Hickman-Coen annual growth model: structural characteristics and policy
  responses" Int. Econ. Rev., vol.16, 1975, pp.20-37.
  LONG TERM FORECASTING * MACRO MODEL - US

YA1700 HIGGINS C.I., FITZGERALD V.W.
  "An econometric model of the Australian economy" J. Economotrics, vol.1,
  1973, pp.229-265.
  MACRO MODEL - GOVERNMENT , AUSTRALIA * MULTIPLIERS - MACRO

YA1701 HIGGINS J.C., FINN R.
  "Planning models in the UK: a survey" Omega, vol.5, 1977, pp.133-147.
  FORECASTING - USAGE * USE - CORPORATE PLANNING * BASIC

YA1702 HIGGINS R.C.
  "Growth, dividend policy and capital costs in the electric utility industry"
  J. Finance, vol.29, 1974, pp.1189-1201.
  APPL - FIRM : UTILITIES , ELECTRICITY * APPL - FIRM : FINANCE ,
  CAPITALISATION * STOCK PRICES - DETERMINANTS

YA1703 HILL R.
  "Covariance of estimated parameters in ARMA regression models" Anns.
  Econ. Soc. Meas., vol.6, 1977, pp.109-122.
  TIME SERIES - ARIMA : FORECASTING * CONFIDENCE INTERVAL - PREDICTIONS : TIME
  SERIES * CONFIDENCE INTERVAL - TIME SERIES , MULTIVARIATE * TIME SERIES -
  ARIMA : ESTIMATION * ADVANCED

YA1704 HILL R.W., HOLLAND P.W.
  "Two robust alternatives to least squares regression" J. Am. Statist.
  Ass., vol.72, 1977, pp.828-833.
  ESTIMATION - ROBUST * ERROR DISTRIBUTION - NON NORMAL * COMPARATIVE METHODS
  - ESTIMATION : REGRESSION * COMPARATIVE METHODS - ESTIMATION : OLS , MSAE *
  REGRESSION - ESTIMATION

YA1705 HILLIARD J.E., BARKSDALE H.C.
  "The time domain implications of phase angles" Mgmt. Sci., vol.22, 1976,
  pp.1273-1281.
  SPECTRAL ANALYSIS - CROSS : METHODOLOGY * SPECTRAL ANALYSIS - APPL : LAG
  IDENTIFICATION * LAG , FIXED * ADVANCED

YA1706 HINDERLITER R.H.
  "Market access, uncertainty, and reserve-position adjustments of large
  commercial banks in the 1960's" J. Finance, vol.29, 1974, pp.41-56.
  APPL - SECTOR : FINANCE , BANKS * APPL - SECTOR : FINANCE , BANK ,
  LIABILITIES

YA1707 HINDMARSH G.W., TOWILL D.R.
  "Estimating learning time for repetitive tasks" Omega, vol.4, 1976,
  pp.234-235.
  COST - LEARNING CURVE * BASIC

YA1708 HINES A.G.
  "The Phillips curve and the distribution of unemployment" Am. Econ. Rev.,
  vol.62, 1972, pp.155-160.
  INFLATION - PHILLIPS CURVE * APPL - MACRO : EARNINGS * APPL - MACRO :
  UNEMPLOYMENT

YA1709 HINES A.G.
  "Wage inflation in the U.K. 1948-1962: a disaggregated study" Econ. J.,
  vol.79, 1969, pp.66-89.
  APPL - SECTOR : EARNINGS * MANPOWER PLANNING - EARNINGS

YA1710 HINICH M.J., TALWAR P.P.
  "A simple method for robust regression" J. Am. Statist. Ass., vol.70,
  1975, pp.113-119.
  ESTIMATION - ROBUST * ERROR DISTRIBUTION - STABLE * APPL - FIRM : FINANCE ,
  STOCK PRICES * STOCK PRICES - DISTRIBUTION * REGRESSION - ESTIMATION

YA1711   HINOMOTO H.
"Projecting consumptions of competing products"   Long Range Planning,
vol.10:5, 1977, pp.46-51.
TREND CURVES - APPL * APPL - SECTOR : PRODUCTION , FERTILISER * BASIC

YA1712   HIPPLE F.S.
"The estimation of the cost of adjustment to external disequilibria" Rev.
Econ. Stats., vol.56, 1974, pp.450-455.
APPL - MACRO : INTERNATIONAL FINANCE * DATA - INTERNATIONAL * DATA - LDC

YA1713   HIRSCH A.A., GRIMM B.T., NARASIMHAM G.V.L.
"Some multiplier and error characteristics of the BEA quarterley model"
Int. Econ. Rev., vol.15, 1974, pp.616-631.
MACRO MODEL - BEA * MULTIPLIERS - MACRO * EX ANTE * EVALUATION - EX POST
MODELS * EVALUATION - MACRO MODELS * EXOGENOUS VARIABLES - PREDICTION OF ,
EFFECT * COMPARATIVE METHODS - ARIMA , CAUSAL(SIMULTANEOUS SYSTEM) *
COMPARATIVE METHODS - MACRO MODELS

YA1714   HIRSCH A.A., HYMANS S.H., SHAPIRO H.T.
"Econometric review of alternative fiscal and monetary policies, 1971-75"
Rev. Econ. Stats., vol.60, 1978, pp.334-345.
MACRO MODEL - BEA * MACRO MODEL - FAIR * MACRO MODEL - DATA RESOURCES *
MACRO MODEL - MIT , PENN , SSRC * MACRO MODEL - MICHIGAN * MACRO MODEL -
ST.LOUIS * MACRO MODEL - WHARTON * LOSS FUNCTIONS - MACRO * EVALUATION -
CONTROL THEORY * EVALUATION - MACRO MODELS * POLICY EVALUATION - MACRO :
FISCAL , MONETARY

YA1715   HIRSHHORN R., GEEHAN R.
"Measuring the real output of the life insurance industry" Rev. Econ.
Stats., vol.59, 1977, pp.211-219.
DATA - TRANSFORMED , DEFLATED * APPL - SECTOR : FINANCE , INSURANCE
COMPANIES * INDEX NUMBERS - SECTOR : FINANCE * BASIC

YA1716   HISRICH R.D., PETERS M.P.
"Selecting the superior segmentation correlate" J. Mktg., vol.38, no.3,
July 1974, pp.60-63.
CONSUMER BEHAVIOUR - PURCHASING , DETERMINANTS * MARKET SEGMENTATION * APPL
- SECTOR : SERVICES , LEISURE * APPL - SECTOR : SERVICES , ENTERTAINMENT *
LIFE CYCLE - FAMILY

YA1717   HITIRIS T.
"Effective protection and economic performance in UK manufacturing industry,
1963-1968" Econ. J, vol.88, 1978, pp.107-120.
CONCENTRATION - EFFECT OF * ADVERTISING - EFFECT OF * TARIFF - EFFECT OF *
APPL - SECTOR : FINANCE , MARGINS * APPL - MACRO , UK

YA1718   HO D.C.C., NOTON M.
"Control computations with a Canadian econometric model" Appl. Econ.,
vol.4, 1972, pp.87-99.
MACRO MODELS - METHODOLOGY * CONTROL THEORY - DETERMINISTIC , APPL *
SIMULTANEOUS SYSTEM - CONTROL * MACRO MODEL - CANADA

YA1719   HOAGLIN D.C., WELSCH R.E.
"The hat matrix in regression and ANOVA" Am. Stat'n, vol.32, 1978,
pp.17-22 & 146.
REGRESSION - SUMMARY STATISTICS * DATA ERRORS - OUTLIERS * RESIDUALS -
ANALYSIS OF , SPECIFICATION ERROR

YA1720   HOBBS D.H.S.
"The development of a practical share evaluation model" Stat'n, vol.23,
1974, pp.31-56.
APPL - FIRM : FINANCE , DIVIDENDS * EVALUATION - SALES FORECASTS * USE -
PORTFOLIO SELECTION * USER - FIRM : FINANCE * APPL - FIRM : FINANCE , PE
RATIO * EVALUATION - JUDGEMENTAL FORECASTS , PROFITS * APPL - FIRM : FINANCE
, STOCK BROKERS * BASIC

YA1721   HODGES S.D.
"Problems in the application of portfolio selection models" Omega, vol.4,
1976, pp.699-709.
USE - PORTFOLIO SELECTION * EVALUATION - JUDGEMENTAL FORECASTS , STOCK
PRICES * APPL - FIRM : FINANCE , STOCK PRICES * STOCK PRICES - INTRODUCTION
* EVALUATION - PORTFOLIO SELECTION PROCEDURES

YA1722.   HODGES S.D., MOORE P.G.
"Data uncertainties and least squares regression" Appl. Stats., vol.21,
1972, pp.185-195.
DATA ERRORS - EFFECT OF * EVALUATION - ESTIMATION : OLS * REGRESSION -
ERRORS IN VARIABLES * APPL - SECTOR : RETAILING

YA1723   HODGINS C.D., TANNER J.E.
"Forecasting non-residential building construction" Can. J. Econ., vol.6,
1973, pp.78-89.
APPL - SECTOR : CONSTRUCTION , NON RESIDENTIAL * EVALUATION - SURVEYS ,
BUSINESS * EXPECTATIONS - DATA * DISTRIBUTED LAG - APPL , INVESTMENT *
DISTRIBUTED LAG - ALMON * APPL * COMPARATIVE METHODS - CAUSAL , SURVEYS

YA1724   HODGSON J.S., HOLMES A.B.
"Structural stability of international capital mobility: an analysis of
short term US - Canadian bank claims" Rev. Econ. Stats., vol.59, 1977,
pp.465-473.
APPL - MACRO : INTERNATIONAL FINANCE * STABILITY OF COEFFICIENTS -
REGRESSION * INTEREST RATE - EFFECT OF * APPL - MACRO , CANADA

YA1725 HODGSON J.S., PHELPS P.
  "The distributed impact of price-level variation on floating exchange rates"
  Rev. Econ. Stats., vol.57, 1975, pp.58-64.
  APPL - MACRO : INTERNATIONAL FINANCE , EXCHANGE RATES * DATA - INTERNATIONAL
  * INFLATION - EFFECT OF

YA1726 HOFFMAN E.P.
  "Faculty salaries: is there discrimination by sex, race and discipline?
  Additional evidence" Am. Econ. Rev., vol.66, 1976, pp.196-198.
  MANPOWER PLANNING - SECTOR : EDUCATION , UNIVERSITIES * APPL - SECTOR :
  EDUCATION , UNIVERSITIES * MANPOWER PLANNING - DISCRIMINATION

YA1727 HOFFMAN K.C., JORGENSON D.W.
  "Economic and technological models for evaluation of energy policy" Bell
  J. Econ., vol.8, 1977, pp.444-466.
  APPL - MACRO : ENERGY * SIMULATION - APPL : MACRO , ENERGY * POLICY
  EVALUATION - MACRO : ENERGY * APPL - SECTOR : UTILITIES , ELECTRICITY * APPL
  - MACRO : ENERGY , SOURCES

YA1728 HOGARTY T.F.
  "Price-quality relations for automobiles: a new approach" Appl. Econ.,
  vol.7, 1975, pp.41-51.
  QUALITY - PRICE * APPL - SECTOR : CONSUMER DURABLES , CARS

YA1729 HOGARTY T.F., ELZINGA K.G.
  "The demand for beer" Rev. Econ. Stats., vol.54, 1972, pp.195-198.
  DATA - CROSS SECTION , TIME SERIES * APPL - SECTOR : CONSUMER NON DURABLE ,
  LIQUOR * PRICE - EFFECT OF * INCOME - EFFECT OF

YA1730 HOLBROOK R., STAFFORD F.
  "The propensity to consume separate types of income: a generalised permanent
  income hypothesis" Econometrica, vol.39, 1971, pp.1-21.
  APPL - MACRO : CONSUMPTION * INCOME - EFFECT OF , PERMANENT * DATA -
  AGGREGATION * DATA - CROSS SECTION * REGRESSION - ERROR IN VARIABLES

YA1731 HOLBROOK R.S.
  "A practical method for controlling a large nonlinear stochastic system"
  Anns. Econ. Soc. Meas., vol.3, 1974, pp.155-175.
  MACRO MODEL - CANADA , RDX2 * MACRO MODEL - MICHIGAN * CONTROL THEORY -
  DETERMINISTIC , METHODOLOGY * SIMULTANEOUS SYSTEM - CONTROL * SIMULTANEOUS
  SYSTEM - NON LINEAR * CONTROL THEORY - STOCHASTIC , METHODOLOGY * ADVANCED

YA1732 HOLDEN K., PEEL D.A.
  "The determinants of unemployment and the 'U.V.' relationship" Appl.
  Econ., vol.7, 1975, pp.251-255.
  MANPOWER PLANNING - EMPLOYMENT VACANCIES * APPL - MACRO : UNEMPLOYMENT

YA1733 HOLLANDER M.
  "A note on Theil's test for linearity of regression" Econometrica,
  vol.42, 1974, pp.211-213.
  SPECIFICATION ERROR - TESTS , TRANSFORMATIONS * REGRESSION - TRANSFORMATIONS

YA1734 HOLMES J.M.
  "The Keynesian aggregate supply function for labour" J. Am. Statist.
  Ass., vol.67, 1972, pp.797-802.
  MANPOWER PLANNING - MACRO , SUPPLY * APPL - MACRO : EARNINGS * APPL - MACRO
  : UNEMPLOYMENT

YA1735 HOLT C.E., MODIGLIANI F., SHELTON J.P.
  "The transmission of demand fluctuations through a distribution and
  production system, the T.V. set industry" Can. J. Econ., vol.1, 1968,
  pp.718-739.
  APPL - SECTOR : CONSUMER DURABLES , APPLIANCES , TELEVISION * INDUSTRIAL
  DYNAMICS - APPL , FIRM * BUSINESS CYCLE - EFFECT OF * USE - INVENTORY
  CONTROL * DECISION RULES - FIRM * APPL - FIRM : INVENTORIES * APPL - FIRM :
  OUTPUT

YA1736 HOLTMANN A.G., BAYER A.E.
  "Determinants of professional income among recent recipients of natural
  science doctorates" J. Business, vol.43, 1970, pp.410-418.
  MANPOWER PLANNING - EARNINGS * MANPOWER PLANNING - QUALIFIED MANPOWER ,
  SCIENCE DEGREES * EDUCATION - EFFECT OF

YA1737 HOMA K.E., JAFFEE D.M.
  "The supply of money and common stock prices" J. Finance, vol.26, 1971,
  pp.1045-1066.
  APPL - MACRO : MONEY , SUPPLY * APPL - SECTOR : FINANCE , STOCK PRICE INDEX
  * USE - PORTFOLIO SELECTION * STOCK PRICES - DETERMINANTS * COMPARATIVE
  METHODS - AUTOREGRESSIVE , CAUSAL * EX ANTE * EXOGENOUS VARIABLES -
  PREDICTION OF , EFFECT

YA1738 HONG H.
  "Inflation and the market value of the firm: theory and tests" J.
  Finance, vol.32, 1977, pp.1031-1048.
  INFLATION - EFFECT OF * APPL - FIRM : FINANCE , STOCK PRICES * STOCK PRICES
  - DETERMINANTS * DATA - CROSS SECTION * RISK - EFFECT OF

YA1739 HONG H.
  "Predictability of price trends on stock exchanges: a study of some Far
  Eastern countries" Rev. Econ. Stats., vol.60, 1978, pp.619-621.
  APPL - SECTOR : FINANCE , STOCK PRICE INDEX * DATA - INTERNATIONAL * STOCK
  PRICES - RUNS

YA1740 HOOD R.D., MARTIN S.A., OSBERG L.S.
"Economic determinants of industrial charitable donations in Canada" Can.
J. Econ., vol.10, 1977, pp.653-669.
APPL - SECTOR : SERVICES , CHARITIES * TAX - EFFECT OF * DATA - CROSS
SECTION , TIME SERIES * POLICY EVALUATION - MACRO : TAX

YA1741 HOOPER P., JOY J., STOLEN J.D.
"The change in the US import demand function from the 1950's to the 1960's:
comments" Rev. Econ. Stats., vol.59, 1977, pp.250-252.
MULTICOLLINEARITY - EFFECT OF * APPL - MACRO : INTERNATIONAL TRADE , IMPORTS

YA1742 HOPEWELL M.H., KAUFMAN G.G.
"Commercial bank bidding on municipal revenue bonds: new evidence" J.
Finance, vol.32, 1977, pp.1647-1656.
APPL - SECTOR : FINANCE , BANKS * APPL - SECTOR : GOVERNMENT , LOCAL ,
FINANCE * USE - BANK REGULATION * APPL - SECTOR : FINANCE , BONDS * USE -
COMPETITIVE BIDDING * RISK - EFFECT OF

YA1743 HOPEWELL M.H., SCHWARTZ A.L.
"Temporary trading suspensions in individual NYSE securities" J. Finance,
vol.33, 1978, pp.1355-1373.
APPL - FIRM : FINANCE , STOCK PRICES * STOCK PRICES - INFORMATION EFFECT

YA1744 HOPKINS D.S.P.
"Faculty early-retirement programs" Ops. Res., vol.22, 1974, pp.455-467.
APPL - FIRM : EDUCATION , UNIVERSITIES * USER - FIRM : EDUCATION ,
UNIVERSITIES * APPL - FIRM : FINANCE , PENSIONS * MANPOWER PLANNING -
PROMOTION * MANPOWER PLANNING - SECTOR : EDUCATION , UNIVERSITIES * MANPOWER
PLANNING - FIRM

YA1745 HORAN L.J.
"Forecasting long-term interest rates - a new method" Bus. Econ.,
vol.13:4, 1978, pp.5-9.
INTEREST RATE - DETERMINANTS * EX ANTE

YA1746 HORN S.D., HORN R.A.
"Comparison of estimators of heteroscedastic variances in linear models"
J. Am. Statist. Ass., vol.70, 1975, pp.872-879.
ERROR SPECIFICATION - HETEROSCEDASTIC * RESIDUALS - ANALYSIS OF ,
HETEROSCEDASTICITY * ESTIMATION - HETEROSCEDASTIC MODELS * COMPARATIVE
METHODS - TESTS , HETEROSCEDASTICITY * ADVANCED

YA1747 HORSKY D.
"An empirical analysis of the optimal advertising policy" Mgmt. Sci.,
vol.23, 1977, pp.1037-1049.
APPL - FIRM : CONSUMER NON DURABLES , CIGARETTES * MARKET SHARE - SECTOR :
CONSUMER NON DURABLES * ADVERTISING - EFFECT OF * ADVERTISING - OPTIMALITY

YA1748 HORSKY D.
"Market share response to advertising: an example of theory testing" J.
Mktg. Res., vol.14, 1977, pp.10-21.
ADVERTISING - EFFECT OF * APPL - FIRM : CONSUMER NON DURABLES , CIGARETTES *
MARKET SHARE - SECTOR : CONSUMER NON DURABLES * DISTRIBUTED LAG - APPL ,
ADVERTISING * USER - FIRM : CONSUMER NON DURABLES

YA1749 HORST T.
"Firm and industry determinants of the decision to invest abroad: an
empirical study" Rev. Econ. Stats., vol.54, 1972, pp.258-266.
APPL - FIRM : INVESTMENT , INTERNATIONAL * APPL - SECTOR : INVESTMENT ,
INTERNATIONAL * APPL - MACRO , CANADA * APPL - FIRM TYPE : MULTINATIONALS *
CONCENTRATION - EFFECT OF * REGRESSION - QUALITATIVE DEPENDENT : APPL

YA1750 HORST T.
"The industrial composition of US exports and subsidiary sales to the
Canadian market" Am. Econ. Rev., vol.62, 1972, pp.37-45.
APPL - SECTOR : INTERNATIONAL TRADE , EXPORTS * DATA - CROSS SECTION * APPL
- MACRO , CANADA * APPL - SECTOR : R & D

YA1751 HORWITZ B., KOLODNY R.
"Line of business reporting and security prices: an analysis of an SEC
disclosure rule" Bell J. Econ., vol.8, 1977, pp.235-249.
APPL - FIRM : FINANCE , STOCK PRICES * STOCK PRICES - INFORMATION EFFECT

YA1752 HOSEK W.R.
"A test of the targets of monetary policy" Appl. Econ., vol.7, 1975,
pp.17-24.
DECISION RULES - SECTOR * APPL - SECTOR : GOVERNMENT * APPL - MACRO : MONEY

YA1753 HOUSTON F.S., WEISS D.L.
"An analysis of competitive market behaviour" J. Mktg. Res., vol.11,
1974, pp.151-155.
REGRESSION - SEEMINGLY UNRELATED * MARKET SHARE - SECTOR : CONSUMER NON
DURABLES * APPL - FIRM : CONSUMER NON DURABLES , FOOD * ADVERTISING - EFFECT
OF * PRICE - EFFECT OF

YA1754 HOUSTON F.S., WEISS D.L.
"Cumulative advertising effects: the role of serial correlation" Decis.
Sci., vol.6, 1975, pp.471-481.
APPL - FIRM : CONSUMER NON DURABLES , HEALTH AIDS * DISTRIBUTED LAG - ERROR
SPECIFICATION * ADVERTISING - EFFECT OF * DISTRIBUTED LAG - APPL ,
ADVERTISING * DISTRIBUTED LAG - SOLOW : APPL * ERROR SPECIFICATION -
AUTOCORRELATED

YA1755   HOUTHAKKER H.S.
"New evidence on demand elasticities"   Econometrica, vol.33, 1965,
pp.277-288.
PRICE - EFFECT OF * APPL - SECTOR : CONSUMER NON DURABLES * DATA -
INTERNATIONAL * APPL - SECTOR : CONSUMER DURABLES * EVALUATION - PRICE
ELASTICITIES

YA1756   HOUTHAKKER H.S., MAGEE S.P.
"Income and price elasticities in World trade"   Rev. Econ. Stats., vol.51,
1969, pp.111-125.
ERROR SPECIFICATION - AUTOCORRELATED * APPL - MACRO : INTERNATIONAL TRADE *
PRICE - EFFECT OF * INCOME - EFFECT OF * DATA - INTERNATIONAL * APPL -
SECTOR : INTERNATIONAL TRADE

YA1757   HOUTHAKKER H.S., VERLEGER P.K., SHEEHAN D.P.
"Dynamic demand analysis for gasoline and residential electricity" with
discussion   Am. J. Ag. Econ., vol.56, 1974, pp.412-418 & 427-435.
REGRESSION - ERROR COMPONENTS * COMPARATIVE METHODS - DATA : CROSS SECTION ,
TIME SERIES * COMPARATIVE METHODS - ESTIMATION : REGRESSION * APPL - SECTOR
: CONSUMER NON DURABLES , PETROL * APPL - SECTOR : UTILITIES , ELECTRICITY

YA1758   HOWARD D.H.
"Personal saving behaviour and the rate of inflation"   Rev. Econ. Stats.,
vol.60, 1978, pp.547-554.
APPL - MACRO : SAVINGS * DATA - INTERNATIONAL * INFLATION - EFFECT OF *
INCOME - EFFECT OF , PERMANENT * EVALUATION - SAVINGS MODELS

YA1759   HOWARD D.H.
"The disequilibrium model in a controlled economy: an empirical test of the
Barro-Grossman model"   Am. Econ. Rev., vol.66, 1976, pp.871-879.
APPL - MACRO , USSR : SIMULTANEOUS SYSTEM - DISEQUILIBRIUM * MANPOWER
PLANNING - MACRO , SUPPLY * APPL - MACRO : CONSUMPTION

YA1760   HOWE C.W., COCHRANE H.C.
"A decision model for adjusting to natural hazard events with application to
urban snow storms"   Rev. Econ. Stats., vol.58, 1976, pp.50-58.
WEATHER - EFFECT OF * LOSS FUNCTIONS - SECTOR : GOVERNMENT , LOCAL * APPL -
SECTOR : GOVERNMENT , LOCAL , SERVICES * REGIONAL MODELS - CITY

YA1761   HOWE J.D., McFETRIDGE D.G.
"The determinants of r & d"   Can. J. Econ., vol.9, 1976, pp.57-71.
APPL - FIRM : R & D * APPL - SECTOR : PRODUCTION , CHEMICALS * APPL - SECTOR
: PRODUCTION , ELECTRICAL MACHINERY

YA1762   HOWE W.G.
"A new look at Brown's dynamic inventory system"   Ops. Res., vol.22, 1974,
pp.848-857.
TIMING UNCERTAINTY * USE - INVENTORY CONTROL * EXPONENTIAL SMOOTHING -
THEORY

YA1763   HOWREY E.P.
"Stochastic properties of the Klein-Goldberger model"   Econometrica,
vol.39, 1971, pp.73-87.
MACRO MODEL - KLEIN GOLDBERGER * SPECTRAL ANALYSIS - APPL : SIMULTANEOUS
SYSTEM * SIMULTANEOUS SYSTEM - DYNAMIC PROPERTIES * ADVANCED

YA1764   HOWREY E.P.
"The use of preliminary data in econometric forecasting"   Rev. Econ.
Stats., vol.60, 1978, pp.193-200.
APPL - MACRO : CONSUMPTION * LEAD TIME - EFFECT OF * DATA REVISIONS - EFFECT
OF * APPL - MACRO : INCOME * ERROR SPECIFICATION - AUTOCORRELATED *
ESTIMATION - KALMAN FILTER * REGRESSION - STATE SPACE * COMPARATIVE METHODS
- DATA : REVISIONS

YA1765   HOWREY E.P., HYMANS S.H.
"The measurement and determination of loanable funds saving" with discussion
Brookings Paps. Econ. Activity, 1978, pp.655-705.
APPL - MACRO : SAVINGS * APPL - MACRO : CONSUMPTION * APPL - SECTOR :
FINANCE , SAVINGS * APPL - MACRO : CONSUMER DEMAND , FINANCIAL ASSETS *
INTEREST RATE - EFFECT OF

YA1766   HOWREY E.P., KLEIN L.R.
"Dynamic properties of nonlinear econometric models"   Int. Econ. Rev.,
vol.13, 1972, pp.599-618.
MACRO MODELS - METHODOLOGY * SIMULATION - DYNAMIC PROPERTIES * MACRO MODEL -
WHARTON * SPECTRAL ANALYSIS - APPL : SIMULATION EVALUATION * SIMULTANEOUS
SYSTEM - DYNAMIC PROPERTIES * SIMULTANEOUS SYSTEM - NON LINEAR

YA1767   HOWREY E.P., KLEIN L.R., McCARTHY M.D.
"Notes on testing the predictive performance of econometric models"   Int.
Econ. Rev., vol.15, 1974, pp.366-383.
EVALUATION - MACRO MODELS * EVALUATION - THEORY OF * COMPARATIVE METHODS -
MACRO MODELS * JUDGEMENTAL FORECASTS - INCORPORATION * MACRO MODELS -
METHODOLOGY , ADJUSTMENTS * COMPARATIVE METHODS - ARIMA ,
CAUSAL(SIMULTANEOUS SYSTEM)

YA1768   HOYLE M.H.
"Spoilt data - an introduction and bibliography"   R. Statist. Soc. (A),
vol.134, 1971, pp.429-439.
DATA ERRORS - MISSING OBSERVATIONS * BIBLIOGRAPHY - MISSING OBSERVATIONS *
BASIC

YA1769   HSU D., MILLER R.B., WICHERN D.W.
          "On the stable Paretian behaviour of stock market prices"   J. Am. Statist.
          Ass., vol.69, 1974, pp.108-113.
          APPL - FIRM : FINANCE , STOCK PRICES * ERROR DISTRIBUTION - STABLE * STOCK
          PRICES - DISTRIBUTION
YA1770   HSU D.A., HUNTER J.S.
          "Analysis of simulation-generated responses using autoregressive models"
          Mgmt. Sci., vol.24, 1977, pp.181-190.
          SIMULATION - EVALUATION OF RESULTS * TIME SERIES - ARIMA : APPL * TIME
          SERIES - COMPARISON * TIME SERIES - BAYESIAN
YA1771   HUANG C., MOON L.C., CHANG H.S.
          "A computer program using the Box-Cox transformation techniques for the
          specification of functional form"   Am. Stat'n., vol.32, 1978, p.144.
          REGRESSION - TRANSFORMATIONS , BOX COX * COMPUTERISATION - ESTIMATION ,
          REGRESSION MODELS , PROGRAMS
YA1772   HUANG C.J.
          "Bias in routine calculation of the variance of OLS estimators when the
          disturbances are autocorrelated"   Am. Stat'n., vol.30, 1976, pp.70-72.
          SEASONALITY - ESTIMATION , OLS * REGRESSION - COVARIANCE MODEL * COMPARATIVE
          METHODS - ESTIMATION : REGRESSION , ERROR SPECIFICATION * INTEREST RATE -
          SEASONALITY * SPECIFICATION ERROR - EFFECT OF , AUTOCORRELATION
YA1773   HUANG C.J., BOLCH B.W.
          "On the testing of regression disturbances for normality"   J. Am. Statist.
          Ass., vol.69, 1974, pp.330-335.
          ERROR DISTRIBUTION - NON NORMAL * RESIDUALS - COMPARATIVE ANALYSIS OF * DATA
          - SIMULATION * SPECIFICATION ERROR - TESTS , ERROR DISTRIBUTION * ERROR
          DISTRIBUTION - LOGNORMAL * COMPARATIVE METHODS - TESTS , ERROR DISTRIBUTIONS
YA1774   HUANG D.S
          "Goodness of prediction concerning binomial variables"   Appl. Stats.,
          vol.14, 1965, pp.206-209.
          REGRESSION - QUALITATIVE DEPENDENT * EVALUATION - THEORY OF * APPL - SECTOR
          : CONSUMER DURABLES , CARS
YA1775   HUANG D.S.
          "Short run instability in the single family housing starts"   J. Am.
          Statist. Ass., vol.68, 1973 pp.788-792.
          APPL - SECTOR : CONSTRUCTION , RESIDENTIAL * INTEREST RATE - EFFECT OF *
          PRICE - EFFECT OF * SUPPLY - SECTOR : CONSTRUCTION
YA1776   HUDSON E.A., JORGENSON D.W.
          "Energy policy & US economic growth" with discussion   Am. Econ. Ass.
          Proc., 1978, pp.118-130.
          APPL - MACRO : ENERGY * POLICY EVALUATION - MACRO : ENERGY * PRICE - MACRO
YA1777   HUDSON E.A., JORGENSON D.W.
          "US energy policy and economic growth, 1975-2000"   Bell J. Econ., vol.5,
          1974, pp.461-514.
          MACRO MODEL - US * POLICY EVALUATION - MACRO : ENERGY * LONG TERM
          FORECASTING * APPL - SECTOR : ENERGY , SOURCES * INPUT OUTPUT - MACRO :
          ENERGY * INPUT OUTPUT - MACRO , US * APPL - MACRO : GROWTH * TAX - EFFECT OF
YA1778   HUETTNER D.A.
          "Shifts in long run average cost curves: theoretical and managerial
          implications"   Omega, vol.1, 1973, pp.421-450.
          COST - SECTOR : UTILITIES * COST - SCALE ECONOMIES * APPL - SECTOR :
          UTILITIES , ELECTRICITY * COST - SECTOR : PRODUCTION * APPL - SECTOR :
          PRODUCTION , CEMENT
YA1779   HUGHES B.
          "Supply constraints and short-term employment functions: a comment"   Rev.
          Econ. Stats., vol.53, 1971, pp.393-397.
          DATA ERRORS - EFFECT OF * DATA - INTERNATIONAL * APPL - MACRO : UNEMPLOYMENT
YA1780   HULBERT J., FARLEY J.U., HOWARD J.A.
          "Information processing and decisionmaking in marketing organisations"   J.
          Mktg. Res., vol.9, 1972, pp.75-77.
          FORECASTING - PRACTICE * USE - ORGANISATIONAL DESIGN * FORECASTER BEHAVIOUR
          * USE - INFORMATION SYSTEMS DESIGN * BASIC
YA1781   HULETT D.T.
          "More on an empirical definition of money: note"   Am. Econ. Rev., vol.61,
          1971, pp.462-468.
          APPL - MACRO : MONEY * APPL - MACRO : GNP * DISTRIBUTED LAG - APPL , MONEY
YA1782   HULSMAN-VEJSONA M.
          "Misleading official exchange-rate conversions"   Econ. J., vol.85, 1975,
          pp.140-147.
          APPL - MACRO : INTERNATIONAL FINANCE , EXCHANGE RATES * DATA - LDC * DATA
          ERRORS - ESTIMATION OF
YA1783   HUMPHREY D.B., WOLKOWITZ B.
          "Substituting intermediates for capital and labour with alternative
          functional forms: an aggregate study"   Appl. Econ., vol.8, 1976, pp.59-68.
          PRODUCTION FUNCTIONS - THEORY * DATA - CROSS SECTION * PRODUCTION FUNCTIONS
          - SUBSTITUTION * PRODUCTION FUNCTIONS - SECTOR

268

YA1784 HUNT J.G., DOWLING J.M., GLAHE F.R.
"L1 estimation in small samples with Laplace error distributions" Decis.
Sci., vol.5, 1974, pp.22-29.
ERROR DISTRIBUTION - NONNORMAL , LAPLACE * COMPARATIVE METHODS - ESTIMATION
: OLS , MSAE * SIMULTANEOUS SYSTEMS - ESTIMATION * COMPARATIVE METHODS -
ESTIMATION : SIMULTANEOUS SYSTEMS * ESTIMATION - MSAE , SIMULTANEOUS SYSTEM
* DATA - SIMULATION

YA1785 HUNT J.W., LEWIS K.A.
"Dominance, recontracting, and the reserve clause: major league baseball"
Am. Econ. Rev., vol.66, 1976, pp.936-943.
APPL - FIRM : SERVICES , SPORT * USE - ANTITRUST

YA1786 HUNT L.H.
"Alternative econometric models for the yield on long-term corporate bonds"
Bus. Econ., vol.8:4, 1973, pp.31-38.
APPL - SECTOR : FINANCE , BONDS * INTEREST RATE - DETERMINANTS * INFLATION -
EFFECT OF

YA1787 HUNT L.H.
"Bank credit and the money stock: their roles in the determination of income
in the post accord period" J. Finance, vol.29, 1974, pp.941-954.
APPL - MACRO : GNP * APPL - MACRO : MONEY , SUPPLY * DISTRIBUTED LAG - APPL
, MONEY * STRIKE - EFFECT OF

YA1788 HUNT S.D., PAPPAS J.L.
"A crucial test for the Howard-Sheth model of buyer behaviour" J. Mktg.
Res., vol.9, 1972, pp.346-348.
CAUSALITY - TEST : APPL * MODEL INTERPRETATION * EVALUATION - CONSUMER
BEHAVIOUR , PSYCHOLOGICAL MODELS * SIMULATION - APPL : CONSUMER BEHAVIOUR

YA1789 HUNTER H.M.
"Corporate demand for cash: the influence of corporate population growth and
structure" Rev. Econ. Stats., vol.60, 1978, pp.467-471.
APPL - FIRM TYPE * APPL - SECTOR : FINANCE , FINANCIAL STRUCTURE , LIQUID
ASSETS

YA1790 HURD M.D.
"Small sample estimation of a structural equation with autocorrelated
errors" J. Am. Statist. Ass., vol.67, 1972, pp.567-573.
ERROR SPECIFICATION - AUTOCORRELATED , CORRELATED * COMPARATIVE METHODS -
ESTIMATION : REGRESSION , ERROR SPECIFICATION * COMPARATIVE METHODS -
ESTIMATION : OLS , 2SLS * COMPARATIVE METHODS - ESTIMATION : SIMULTANEOUS
SYSTEM , ERROR SPECIFICATION * DATA - SIMULATION

YA1791 HURD R.W.
"Equilibrium vacancies in a labor market dominated by non-profit firms: the
'shortage' of nurses" Rev. Econ. Stats., vol.55, 1973, pp.234-240.
HEALTH - MANPOWER , NURSES * HEALTH - HOSPITAL , MANPOWER * DATA - CROSS
SECTION - MANPOWER PLANNING - SECTOR : HEALTH

YA1792 HURDLE G.J.
"Leverage, market structure and profitability" Rev. Econ. Stats., vol.56,
1974, pp.478-485.
APPL - SECTOR : FINANCE , PROFITS * APPL - SECTOR : FINANCE , FINANCIAL
STRUCTURE , LEVERAGE * CONCENTRATION - EFFECT OF * ADVERTISING - EFFECT OF

YA1793 HURLEY K.
"A guide to evaluating forecasts" Bus. Econ., vol.11:4, 1976, pp.40-44.
EVALUATION - THEORY OF * BASIC

YA1794 HUSBY R.D.
"A nonlinear consumption function estimated from time series and
cross-section data" Rev. Econ. Stats., vol.53, 1971, pp.76-79.
DISTRIBUTED LAG - APPL , INCOME * APPL - MACRO : CONSUMPTION * COMPARATIVE
METHODS - DATA : AGGREGATE , DISAGGREGATE * REGRESSION - PRIOR INFORMATION *
ESTIMATION - CONSTRAINED

YA1795 HUTTON J.P.
"A model of short-term capital movements, the foreign exchange market and
official intervention in the UK, 1963-1970" Rev. Econ. Studies, vol.44,
1977, pp.31-41.
APPL - MACRO , UK * APPL - MACRO : INTERNATIONAL FINANCE , EXCHANGE RATES *
EXCHANGE RATE - FORWARD RATE * INTEREST RATE - DETERMINANTS * LOSS FUNCTIONS
- MACRO , EXCHANGE RATES * POLICY EVALUATION - MACRO : EXCHANGE RATES

YA1796 HYETT G.P., MCKENZIE J.R.
"Forecasting of residential telephone penetration, 1974-81 by use of the
technique of social sections" Stat'n., vol.24, 1975, pp.51-60.
APPL - SECTOR : UTILITIES , TELEPHONES * CONSUMER BEHAVIOUR - PURCHASING ,
DETERMINANTS * TREND CURVES - LOGISTIC

YA1797 HYLLEBERG S.
"A comparative study of finite sample properties of band spectrum
estimators" J. Econometrics, vol.5, 1977, pp.167-182.
COMPARATIVE METHODS - SEASONALITY * SIMULATION - METHODOLOGY , MONTE CARLO *
ESTIMATION - HANNAN * SEASONALITY - ESTIMATION , OLS

YA1798 HYMANS S.H.
"Consumer durable spending: explanations and prediction" with discussion
Brookings Paps. Econ. Activity, 1970, pp.173-206.
APPL - SECTOR : CONSUMER DURABLES * ATTITUDINAL DATA * STRIKE - EFFECT OF *
INDEX NUMBERS - MACRO : CONSUMER CONFIDENCE * STOCK PRICES - EFFECT OF *
APPL - SECTOR : CONSUMER DURABLES , CARS

YA1799   HYMANS S.H.
         "Consumption: new data and old puzzles"   Brookings Paps. Econ. Activity,
         1970, pp.117-126.
         APPL - SECTOR : CONSUMER DURABLES * MACRO MODEL - WHARTON * MACRO MODEL -
         FRB , MIT , PENN * MACRO MODEL - MICHIGAN * APPL - SECTOR : CONSUMER
         DURABLES , CARS

YA1800   HYMANS S.H.
         "On the use of leading indicators to predict cyclical turning points" with
         discussion   Brookings Paps. Econ. Activity, 1973, pp.339-384.
         TURNING POINTS - FORECASTING * SPECTRAL ANALYSIS - APPL : BUSINESS
         INDICATORS * EVALUATION - BUSINESS INDICATORS * EVALUATION - TURNING POINT
         FORECASTS

YA1801   HYMANS S.H.
         "Simultaneous confidence intervals in econometric forecasting"
         Econometrica, vol.36, 1968, pp.18-30.
         CONFIDENCE INTERVAL - SIMULTANEOUS SYSTEM , MULTIVARIATE * MACRO MODEL -
         KLEIN * CONFIDENCE INTERVAL - PREDICTIONS : SIMULTANEOUS SYSTEM

YA1802   HYMANS S.H., SHAPIRO H.T.
         "The allocation of household income to food consumption"   J. Econometrics,
         vol.4, 1976, pp.167-180.
         DATA - CROSS SECTION * INCOME - EFFECT OF * APPL - SECTOR : CONSUMER NON
         DURABLES , FOOD * REGRESSION - STABILITY OF COEFFICIENTS

YA1803   HYMANS S.H., SHAPIRO H.T.
         "The structure and properties of the Michigan quarterley econometric model
         of the US economy"   Int. Econ. Rev., vol.15, 1974, pp.632-653.
         MACRO MODEL - MICHIGAN * MULTIPLIERS - MACRO

YA1804   IBBOTSON R.C., JAFFE J.F.
         "'Hot issue' markets"   J. Finance, vol.30, 1975, pp.1027-1042.
         APPL - FIRM : FINANCE * STOCK PRICES - NEW PRODUCTS - NEW BRAND * STOCK
         PRICES - RUNS * RANDOM WALK - TEST

YA1805   IBBOTSON R.C., SINQUEFIELD R.A.
         "Stocks, bonds, bills, and inflation: simulations of the future (1976-2000)"
         J. Business, vol.49, 1976, pp.313-338.
         APPL - SECTOR : FINANCE , BONDS * APPL - SECTOR : FINANCE , STOCK PRICE
         INDEX * STOCK PRICES - COVARIATION * SIMULATION - APPL : SECTOR , FINANCE *
         LONG TERM FORECASTING

YA1806   IJIRI Y.
         "Fundamental queries in aggregation theory"   J. Am. Statist. Ass., vol.66,
         1971, pp.766-782.
         DATA - AGGREGATION , REVIEW * BIBLIOGRAPHY - AGGREGATION * SIMULATION -
         METHODOLOGY , MICRO * INPUT OUTPUT - METHODOLOGY : AGGREGATION

YA1807   IJIRI Y., KINARD J.C., PUTNEY F.B.
         "An integrated evaluation system for budget forecasting and operating
         performance with a classified budgets bibliography"   J. Acctg. Res.,
         vol.6, 1968, pp.1-28.
         USE - FORECASTER EVALUATION * LOSS FUNCTIONS - FIRM * BIBLIOGRAPHY -
         BUDGETING * BASIC

YA1808   IMEL B., HELMBERGER P.
         "Estimation of structure-profit relationships with application to the food
         processing sector"   Am. Econ. Rev., vol.61, 1971, pp.614-627.
         DATA - CROSS SECTION * REGRESSION - ERROR COMPONENTS : APPL * APPL - FIRM :
         CONSUMER NON DURABLES , FOOD , PROCESSED * APPL - FIRM : FINANCE , PROFITS *
         CONCENTRATION - EFFECT OF * ADVERTISING - EFFECT OF * MARKET SHARE - EFFECT
         OF

YA1809   IMHOFF E.A.
         "The representativeness of management earnings forecasts"   Acctg. Rev.,
         vol.53, 1978, pp.836-850.
         EVALUATION - JUDGEMENTAL FORECASTS , PROFITS * JUDGEMENTAL FORECASTS -
         SPECIALIST

YA1810   IRELAND N.J., BRISCOE G., SMYTH D.J.
         "Specification bias and short-run returns to labour: some evidence for the
         UK"   Rev. Econ. Stats., vol.55, 1973, pp.23-27.
         APPL - MACRO : EARNINGS * APPL - MACRO : OUTPUT * COMPARATIVE METHODS -
         REGRESSION , ERROR SPECIFICATION * APPL - MACRO , UK

YA1811   ISARD P.
         "How far can we push the 'Law of One Price'"   Am. Econ. Rev., vol.67,
         1977, pp.942-948.
         APPL - SECTOR : INTERNATIONAL TRADE , PRICE

YA1812   IWATA G.
         "Measurement of conjectural variations in oligopoly"   Econometrica,
         vol.42, 1974, pp.947-966.
         APPL - SECTOR : PRODUCTION , GLASS * COST - SECTOR : PRODUCTION * PRICE -
         SECTOR : PRODUCTION * THEORY - PRICING * ADVANCED

YA1813   IYENGAR N.S.
         "Some estimates of Engel elasticities based on national sample survey data"
         R. Statist. Soc. (A), vol.130, 1967, pp.84-101.
         APPL - MACRO : CONSUMER DEMAND * INCOME - EFFECT OF * COMPARATIVE METHODS -
         INCOME ELASTICITY , ESTIMATION * CONSUMER BEHAVIOUR - EXPENDITURE SURVEY

YA1814   IYOHA M.A.
"Demand for international reserves in less developed countries: a distributed lag specification"   Rev. Econ. Stats., vol.53, 1976, pp.351-355.
APPL - MACRO : INTERNATIONAL FINANCE , FOREIGN RESERVES * DATA - LDC

YA1815   JACOB N.L., SMITH K.V.
"The value of perfect market forecasts in portfolio selection" with discussion   J. Finance, vol.27, 1972, pp.355-369 & 395-398.
EX ANTE * FORECASTING - VALUE OF * USE - PORTFOLIO SELECTION * APPL - SECTOR : FINANCE , STOCK PRICE INDEX * APPL - FIRM : FINANCE , STOCK PRICES

YA1816   JAFFE J.F.
"Special information and insider trading"   J. Business, vol.47, 1974, pp.410-428.
APPL - FIRM : FINANCE , STOCK PRICES * STOCK PRICES - INFORMATION EFFECT

YA1817   JAFFE J.F.
"The effect of regulation changes on insider trading"   Bell J. Econ., vol.5, 1974, pp.93-121.
APPL - FIRM : FINANCE , STOCK PRICES * STOCK PRICES - INFORMATION EFFECT * STOCK PRICES - TRADING VOLUME * USE - STOCK MARKET REGULATION

YA1818   JAFFE J.F., MANDELKER G.
"The 'Fisher Effect' for risky assets: an empirical investigation" with discussion   J. Finance, vol.31, 1976, pp.447-458 & 438-487.
INFLATION - INDICATORS * APPL - SECTOR : FINANCE , STOCK PRICE INDEX * STOCK PRICES - DETERMINANTS * INFLATION - EXPECTATIONS * INFLATION - EFFECT OF

YA1819   JAFFEE D.M., ROSEN K.T.
"Estimates of the effectiveness of stabilisation policies in the mortgages and housing markets"   J. Finance, vol.33, 1978, pp.933-946.
APPL - SECTOR : FINANCE , BUILDING SOCIETIES * APPL - SECTOR : FINANCE , MORTGAGES * SUPPLY - SECTOR : FINANCE * SIMULTANEOUS SYSTEM - DISEQUILIBRIUM : APPL * POLICY EVALUATION - SECTOR : CONSTRUCTION * USE - LOAN REGULATION

YA1820   JAGGI B.
"A note on the information content of corporate annual earnings forecast"
Acctg. Rev., vol.53, 1978, pp.961-967.
APPL - FIRM : FINANCE , STOCK PRICES * APPL - FIRM : FINANCE , PROFITS * EXPECTATIONS - ESTIMATING * STOCK PRICES - INFORMATION EFFECT * COMPARATIVE METHODS - AUTOREGRESSIVE , CAUSAL

YA1821   JAMESON K.
"Development patterns and regional inbalance in Brazil"   Rev. Econ. Stats., vol.57, 1975, pp.361-364.
DATA - CROSS SECTION , TIME SERIES * REGIONAL MODELS - DEVELOPMENT * INCOME - EFFECT OF * APPL - MACRO , LATIN AMERICA

YA1822   JANSON J.O., SCHNEERSON D.
"Economies of scale of general cargo ships"   Rev. Econ. Stats., vol.60, 1978, pp.287-293.
APPL - SECTOR : TRANSPORT , SHIPPING * COST - SECTOR : TRANSPORT * COST - SCALE ECONOMIES

YA1823   JANTSCH E.
"Forecasting and systems approach: a frame of reference"   Mgmt. Sci. (B), vol.19, 1973, pp.1355-1367.
LONG TERM FORECASTING * FORECASTING - THEORY

YA1824   JASZI G., CARSON C.S.
"The benchmark revision of the national income and product accounts: new perspectives on the US economy"   Bus. Econ., vol.11:4, 1976, pp.7-20.
DATA - NATIONAL ACCOUNTS , US * BUSINESS CYCLE - IDENTIFICATION

YA1825   JAYATISSA W.A.
"Tests of equality between sets of coefficients in two linear regressions when disturbance variances are unequal"   Econometrica, vol.45, 1977, pp.1291-1292.
STABILITY OF COEFFICIENTS - REGRESSION , TEST * ERROR SPECIFICATION - HETEROSCEDASTIC

YA1826   JAYATISSA W.A., FAREBROTHER R.W.
"A predictive test for the reduced form model"   Anns. Econ. Soc. Meas., vol.6, 1977, pp.473-476.
STABILITY OF COEFFICIENTS - SIMULTANEOUS SYSTEM , TEST * ADVANCED

YA1827   JAYATISSA W.A., HYMANS S.H.
"Criteria for evaluation of econometric models: a correction and reply"
Anns. Econ. Soc. Meas., vol.5, 1976, pp.161-162.
STABILITY OF COEFFICIENTS - SIMULTANEOUS SYSTEM , TEST * CONFIDENCE INTERVAL - PREDICTIONS : SIMULTANEOUS SYSTEM * CONFIDENCE INTERVAL - SIMULTANEOUS SYSTEM , MULTIVARIATE

YA1828   JECKOVICH S.
"Technological forecasting as a guide for managerial planning"   Long Range Planning, vol.4:1, 1971, pp.29-34.
TECHNOLOGICAL FORECASTING * TREND CURVES - INTRODUCTION * APPL - SECTOR : PRODUCTION , GLASS

YA1829   JENSEN M.C.
"Capital markets: theory and evidence"   Bell J. Econ., vol.3, 1972, pp.357-398.
STOCK PRICES - REVIEW * THEORY - EFFICIENT MARKETS * STOCK PRICES - MODELS , COMPARATIVE * BIBLIOGRAPHY - STOCK PRICES

YA1830 JOHANSSON J.K.
"A generalised logistic function with an application to the effect of
advertising"   J. Am. Statist. Ass., vol.68, 1973, pp.824-827.
REGRESSION - NON LINEAR * BRAND CHOICE - METHODOLOGY * ADVERTISING - EFFECT
OF

YA1831 JOHNSON D.D.
"Properties of alternative seasonal adjustment techniques: a comment on the
/OMB model"   J. Business, vol.46, 1973, pp.284-303.
MULTICOLLINEARITY - EFFECT OF * MACRO MODEL - OMB * COMPARATIVE METHODS -
SEASONALITY * SEASONALITY - EFFECT OF * APPL - MACRO : MONEY , SUPPLY *
DISTRIBUTED LAG - APPL , MONEY * APPL - MACRO : GNP * STOCK PRICES - EFFECT
OF

YA1832 JOHNSON F.J.
"Forecasting problems in the gas industry"   British J. Mktg., vol.2, 1968,
pp.281-297.
APPL - SECTOR : UTILITIES , GAS * USER - FIRM : UTILITIES

YA1833 JOHNSON G.E., STAFFORD F.P.
"The earnings and promotion of women faculty"   Am. Econ. Rev., vol.64,
1974, pp.888-903.
APPL - SECTOR : EDUCATION , UNIVERSITIES * MANPOWER PLANNING - SECTOR :
EDUCATION , UNIVERSITIES * MANPOWER PLANNING - EARNINGS , FEMALE * MANPOWER
PLANNING - DISCRIMINATION , SEXUAL

YA1834 JOHNSON J.A., OKSANEN E.H.
"Estimation of demand for alcoholic beverages in Canada from pooled time
series and cross sections"   Rev. Econ. Stats., vol.59, 1977, pp.113-118.
APPL - SECTOR : CONSUMER NON DURABLES , LIQUOR * DATA - CROSS SECTION , TIME
SERIES * REGRESSION - ERROR COMPONENTS * COMPARATIVE METHODS - ESTIMATION :
REGRESSION * COMPARATIVE METHODS - ESTIMATION : OLS , GLS * COMPARATIVE
METHODS - DATA : CROSS SECTION , TIME SERIES

YA1835 JOHNSON J.A., OKSANEN E.H.
"Socio economic determinants of the consumption of alcoholic beverages"
Appl. Econ., vol.6, 1974, pp.293-301.
APPL - SECTOR : CONSUMER NON DURABLES , LIQUOR * PRICE - EFFECT OF * TAX -
EFFECT OF * CONSUMER BEHAVIOUR - PURCHASING , DETERMINANTS

YA1836 JOHNSON J.L.
"A ten year Delphi forecast in the electronics industry"   Ind. Mktg.
Mgmt., vol.5, 1976, pp.45-55.
APPL - SECTOR : PRODUCTION , ELECTRONICS * DELPHI * BASIC

YA1837 JOHNSON K., KLEIN L.R.
"Link model simulations of international trade: an evaluation of currency
realignment" with discussion   J. Finance, vol.29, 1974, pp.617-630 &
677-682.
APPL - MACRO : INTERNATIONAL LINKAGE * APPL - MACRO : INTERNATIONAL TRADE *
EXCHANGE RATE - EFFECT OF

YA1838 JOHNSON K., MARWAH K., KLEIN B.
"Competitive interest payments on bank deposits and the long-run demand for
money: comments"   INFLATION-REVIEW/APPL-MACRO,UK   Am. Econ. Rev.,
vol.66, 1976, pp.953-960.
REGRESSION - MODEL INTERPRETATION * APPL - MACRO : MONEY , DEMAND * APPL -
SECTOR : FINANCE , BANKS

YA1839 JOHNSON K.B., MORTON T.G., FINDLAY M.C.
"An empirical analysis of the flotation cost of corporate securities
1971-1972"   J. Finance, vol.30, 1975, pp.1129-1133.
APPL - FIRM : FINANCE , CAPITALISATION * COST - FIRM : FINANCING

YA1840 JOHNSON K.H., LYON H.L.
"Experimental evidence on combining cross-section and time series
information"   Rev. Econ. Stats., vol.55, 1973, pp.465-474.
DATA - SIMULATION * COMPARATIVE METHODS - DATA : CROSS SECTION , TIME SERIES
* COMPARATIVE METHODS - REGRESSION , RANDOM COEFFICIENTS * REGRESSION -
COVARIANCE MODEL * ESTIMATION - CONSTRAINED * SPECIFICATION ERROR - EFFECT
OF , RANDOM COEFFICIENTS * REGRESSION - RANDOM COEFFICIENTS * REGRESSION -
ERROR COMPONENTS

YA1841 JOHNSON K.H., SHANNON D.S.
"Effects of linear transformations of variables in regression analysis"
Decis. Sci., vol.4, 1973, pp.437-438.
REGRESSION - TRANSFORMATIONS * BASIC

YA1842 JOHNSON L.W.
"Regression with random coefficients"   Omega, vol.6, 1978, pp.71-81.
EVALUATION - REGRESSION , RANDOM COEFFICIENTS * REGRESSION - STATE SPACE *
BIBLIOGRAPHY - REGRESSION , RANDOM COEFFICIENTS

YA1843 JOHNSON L.W.
"Stochastic parameter regression: an annotated bibliography"   Int.
Statist. Rev., vol.45, 1977, pp.257-272.
REGRESSION - RANDOM COEFFICIENTS * BIBLIOGRAPHY - REGRESSION , RANDOM
COEFFICIENTS

YA1844 JOHNSON L.W., OAKENFULL E.A.
"RANPAR: a computer program for estimation of a random coefficient model
with pooled time-series and cross-section data"   J. Mktg. Res., vol.15,
1978, pp.611-612.
ESTIMATION - CROSS SECTION , TIME SERIES * REGRESSION - RANDOM COEFFICIENTS
: APPL * COMPUTERISATION - ESTIMATION , REGRESSION MODELS , PROGRAMS

YA1845   JOHNSON T.
"Qualitative and limited dependent variables in economic relationships"
Econometrica, vol.40, 1972, pp.455-462.
REGRESSION - LIMITED DEPENDENT * REGRESSION - QUALITATIVE DEPENDENT * APPL -
SECTOR : EDUCATION , UNIVERSITIES

YA1846   JOHNSON W.R.
"Racial wage discrimination and industrial structure"   Bell, J, Econ.,
vol.9, 1978, pp.70-81.
MANPOWER PLANNING - DISCRIMINATION , RACIAL * MANPOWER PLANNING - EARNINGS *
EDUCATION - EFFECT OF * MANPOWER PLANNING - LABOUR FORCE COMPOSITION *
MANPOWER PLANNING - INDUSTRIAL COMPOSITION

YA1847   JOHNSTON G.F.
"Putting forecasts to work in the corporate planning function"   Bus.
Econ., vol.11ll, 1976, pp.35-40.
USE - CORPORATE PLANNING * USER REQUIREMENTS * BASIC

YA1848   JOLLIFFE I.T.
"Discarding variables in a principal component analysis I: artificial data"
Appl, Stats., vol.19, 1970, pp.160-173.
ESTIMATION - PRINCIPAL COMPONENTS * CLUSTER ANALYSIS - APPL * DATA -
SIMULATION * REGRESSION - VARIABLE INCLUSION * REGRESSION - STEPWISE

YA1849   JOLLIFFE I.T.
"Discarding variables in a principal component analysis II: real data"
Appl, Stats., vol.22, 1973, pp.21-31.
ESTIMATION - PRINCIPAL COMPONENTS * CLUSTER ANALYSIS - APPL * APPL - SECTOR
: SOCIAL , CRIME * REGRESSION - VARIABLE INCLUSION * REGRESSION - STEPWISE

YA1850   JOLSON M.A., ROSSOW G.L.
"The Delphi process in marketing decision making"   J, Mktg, Res., vol,8,
1971, pp.443-448.
DELPHI * APPL - FIRM : SERVICES , EXPERTISE

YA1851   JONES C.L., LITTLEJOHN G.M., McPHERSON A.F.
"Predicting science-based study at university"   R, Statist, Soc, (A),
vol.137, 1974, pp.48-59.
MANPOWER PLANNING - QUALIFIED MANPOWER , SCIENCE DEGREES * MANPOWER PLANNING
- SECTOR : EDUCATION , UNIVERSITIES * APPL - SECTOR : GOVERNMENT , EDUCATION
, UNIVERSITIES

YA1852   JONES D.C., BACKUS D.K.
"British producer cooperatives in the footwear industry: an empirical
evaluation of the theory of financing"   Econ, J., vol.87, 1977,
pp.488-510.
APPL - FIRM : CONSUMER DURABLES , CLOTHING * PRODUCTION FUNCTIONS - FIRM *
EVALUATION - PRODUCTION FUNCTIONS * APPL - FIRM TYPE * APPL - FIRM : FINANCE
, FINANCIAL STRUCTURE

YA1853   JONES D.F.
"A survey technique to measure demand under various pricing strategies"
J, Mktg., vol.39, no.3, July 1975, pp.75-77.
PRICE - EFFECT OF * APPL - FIRM : CONSUMER DURABLES , APPLIANCES , STEREOS *
DATA - CROSS SECTION * BASIC

YA1854   JONES H.G.
"Subjective probability in forecasting"   Omega, vol,3, 1975, pp.321-327.
APPL - FIRM : CONSUMER NON DURABLES , LIQUOR * JUDGEMENTAL FORECASTS -
METHODOLOGY * TREND CURVES - APPL * COMBINING FORECASTS - JUDGEMENTAL , TIME
SERIES * BASIC

YA1855   JONES H.G.
"The use of forecasts in target setting"   Opl, Res, Q., vol,24, 1974,
pp.547-560.
USE - TARGET SETTING

YA1856   JONES J.C.H., LAUDADIO L., PERCY M.
"Market structure and profitability in Canadian manufacturing industry: some
cross-section results"   Can, J, Econ., vol.6, 1973, pp.356-368.
APPL - SECTOR : FINANCE , PROFITS * CONCENTRATION - EFFECT OF * DATA - CROSS
SECTION

YA1857   JONES J.M.
"A comparison of three models of brand choice"   J, Mktg, Res., vol, 7,
1970, pp.466-473.
EVALUATION - CONSUMER BEHAVIOUR , STOCHASTIC MODELS * PROBABILITY MODELS -
LINEAR LEARNING * EVALUATION - BRAND CHOICE MODELS

YA1858   JONES J.M.
"A composite heterogeneous model for brand choice behaviour"   Mgmt, Sci.
(A), vol.19, 1973, pp.499-509.
CONSUMER BEHAVIOUR - STOCHASTIC MODELS , THEORY * BRAND CHOICE - METHODOLOGY
* BRAND CHOICE - THEORY

YA1859   JONES R.H.
"Fitting autoregressions"   J, Am, Statist, Ass., vol.70, 1975, pp.590-592.
TIME SERIES - ARIMA : IDENTIFICATION * LOSS FUNCTIONS - AKAIKE'S INFORMATION
CRITERION * DATA - SIMULATION * TIME SERIES - AUTOREGRESSIVE

YA1860   JONISH J.E., WORTHLEY R.G.
"Cyclical behaviour of unemployment and the help wanted index: a cross
spectral analysis"   Decis, Sci., vol.4, 1973, pp.350-363.
SPECTRAL ANALYSIS - APPL : MACRO , MANPOWER * APPL - MACRO : EMPLOYMENT *
SPECTRAL ANALYSIS - CROSS : APPL * INDEX NUMBERS - MACRO : EMPLOYMENT
VACANCIES

YA1861   JORGENSON D.W.
"Investment behaviour and the production function"   Bell J. Econ., vol.3,
1972, pp.221-251,
APPL - SECTOR : INVESTMENT * PRODUCTION FUNCTIONS - SECTOR * PRODUCTION
FUNCTIONS - SUBSTITUTION * EVALUATION - INVESTMENT MODELS * PRODUCTION
FUNCTIONS - SCALE RETURNS * BIBLIOGRAPHY - INVESTMENT

YA1862   JORGENSON D.W., HANDEL S.S.
"Investment behaviour in US regulated industries"   Bell J. Econ., vol.2,
1971, pp.213-264,
APPL - SECTOR : INVESTMENT * APPL - SECTOR : TRANSPORT * APPL - SECTOR :
UTILITIES * THEORY - INVESTMENT BEHAVIOUR * DISTRIBUTED LAG - APPL ,
INVESTMENT * USE - FINANCIAL , REGULATION * DISTRIBUTED LAG - APPL , OUTPUT

YA1863   JORGENSON D.W., HUNTER J., NADIRI M.I.
"A comparison of alternative econometric models of quarterly investment
behaviour"   Econometrica, vol.38, 1970, pp.187-212,
APPL - SECTOR : INVESTMENT * EVALUATION - INVESTMENT MODELS * COMPARATIVE
METHODS - AUTOREGRESSIVE , CAUSAL * COMPARATIVE METHODS - CAUSAL ,
JUDGEMENTAL * COMPARATIVE METHODS - AUTOREGRESSIVE , JUDGEMENTAL * THEORY -
INVESTMENT BEHAVIOUR

YA1864   JORGENSON D.W., HUNTER J., NADIRI M.I.
"The predictive performance of econometric models of quarterly investment
behaviour"   Econometrica, vol.38, 1970, pp.213-224,
APPL - SECTOR : INVESTMENT * EVALUATION - INVESTMENT MODELS * EX ANTE *
STABILITY OF COEFFICIENTS - REGRESSION : APPL

YA1865   JORGENSON D.W., LAU L.J.
"The structure of consumer preferences"   Anns. Econ. Soc. Meas., vol.4,
1975, pp.49-101,
CONSUMER BEHAVIOUR - ECONOMIC MODELS , THEORY * DEMAND EQUATIONS - SYSTEMS
OF * APPL - MACRO : CONSUMER DEMAND * SPECIFICATION ERROR - TESTS ,
CONSTRAINTS * ADVANCED

YA1866   JORGENSON D.W., NISHIMIZU M.
"US and Japanese economic growth, 1952-1974: an international comparison"
Econ. J., vol.88, 1978, pp.767-726,
APPL - MACRO , JAPAN * DATA - INTERNATIONAL * APPL - MACRO : GROWTH * APPL -
MACRO : PRODUCTIVITY

YA1867   JORGENSON D.W., STEPHENSON J.A.
"The time structure of investment behaviour in US manufacturing, 1947-1960"
Rev. Econ. Stats., vol.49, 1967, pp.16-27,
DISTRIBUTED LAG - APPL , INVESTMENT * DISTRIBUTED LAG - SOLOW * DISTRIBUTED
LAG - RATIONAL POLYNOMIAL * APPL - SECTOR : PRODUCTION * APPL - SECTOR :
INVESTMENT

YA1868   JOSKOW P.L.
"Cartels, competition and regulation in the property liability insurance
industry"   Bell J. Econ., vol.4, 1973, pp.375-427,
APPL - FIRM : FINANCE , INSURANCE * DATA - CROSS SECTION * COST - FIRM :
FINANCE

YA1869   JOSKOW P.L.
"Pricing decisions of regulated firms: a behavioural approach"   Bell J.
Econ., vol.4, 1973, pp.119-140,
THEORY - PRICING * USE - PRICING * DECISION RULES - FIRM * APPL - FIRM :
UTILITIES * PRICE - FIRM : UTILITIES * REGRESSION - LIMITED DEPENDENT ,
PROBIT : APPL

YA1870   JOSKOW P.L.
"The determination of the allowed rate return in a formal regulatory
hearing"   Bell J. Econ., vol.3, 1972, pp.632-644,
DECISION RULES - SECTOR : GOVERNMENT * APPL - FIRM : UTILITIES * USE -
FINANCIAL , REGULATION

YA1871   JOSKOW P.L., BAUGHMAN M.L.
"The future of the US nuclear energy industry"   Bell J. Econ., vol.7,
1976, pp.3-32,
REGIONAL MODELS - ENERGY * REGIONAL MODELS - SECTOR : UTILITIES * SIMULATION
- APPL - SECTOR : UTILITIES * APPL - SECTOR : UTILITIES , ELECTRICITY ,
NUCLEAR * APPL - SECTOR : PRODUCTION , PLANT , ELECTRICITY GENERATION

YA1872   JOSKOW P.L., MISHKIN F.S.
"Electricity utility fuel choice behaviour in the US"   Int. Econ. Rev.,
vol.18, 1977, pp.719-736,
REGRESSION - LIMITED DEPENDENT , LOGIT : APPL * APPL - SECTOR : UTILITIES ,
ELECTRICITY * APPL - SECTOR : ENERGY , SOURCES * SUBSTITUTE FACTORS * PRICE
- EFFECT OF * COST - SECTOR : UTILITIES * DECISION RULES - FIRM

YA1873   JOY J., STOLEN J.D.
"The change in the US import demand function from the 1950's to the 1960's"
Rev. Econ. Stats., vol.57, 1975, pp.109-111,
APPL - MACRO : INTERNATIONAL TRADE , IMPORTS * DATA - TRANSFORMED , DEFLATED
* INCOME - EFFECT OF * PRICE - EFFECT OF * STABILITY OF COEFFICIENTS -
REGRESSION : APPL

YA1874   JOY O.M., LITZENBERGER R.H., McENALLY R.W.
"The adjustment of stock prices to announcements of unanticipated changes in
quarterly earnings"   J. Acctg. Res., vol.15, 1977, pp.207-225,
STOCK PRICES - INFORMATION EFFECT * APPL - FIRM : FINANCE , STOCK PRICES *
APPL - FIRM : FINANCE , PROFITS

YA1875　JUCKER J.V., GOMEZ J.G.
"Policy-comparing simulation experiments: design and analysis"　Decis.
Sci., vol.6, 1975, pp.631-645.
SIMULATION - METHODOLOGY , MONTE CARLO * SIMULATION - EXPERIMENTAL DESIGN *
SIMULATION - EVALUATION OF RESULTS

YA1876　JUDGE G.G., BOCK M.E., YANCEY J.A.
"Post data model evaluation"　Rev. Econ. Stats., vol.56, 1974, pp.245-253.
LOSS FUNCTIONS - THEORY * EVALUATION - REGRESSION , ESTIMATION * ESTIMATION
- PRE TEST * ESTIMATION - STEIN * EVALUATION - THEORY OF * ADVANCED

YA1877　JUDGE G.G., YANCEY T.A., BOCK M.E.
"Properties of estimators after preliminary tests of significance when
stochastic restrictions are used in regression"　J. Econometrics, vol.1,
1973, pp.29-47.
REGRESSION - PRIOR INFORMATION * REGRESSION - VARIABLE INCLUSION *
ESTIMATION - PRE TEST * ADVANCED

YA1878　JUNCKER G.R., OLDFIELD G.S.
"Projecting market structure by Monte Carlo simulations: a study of bank
expansion in New Jersey"　J. Finance, vol.27, 1972, pp.1101-1126.
APPL - SECTOR : FINANCE , BANKS * SIMULATION - APPL : SECTOR , FINANCE * USE
- BANK REGULATION * CONCENTRATION - EFFECT - OF * CONCENTRATION -
DETERMINANTS

YA1879　JUNZ H.B., RHOMBERG R.R.
"Price competitiveness in export trade among industrial countries"　Am.
Econ. Ass. Proc., 1973, pp.412-418.
APPL - MACRO : INTERNATIONAL TRADE , EXPORTS * PRICE - EFFECT OF

YA1880　JUST R.E., FLETCHER S.M.
"A program for econometric and spectral analysis - EAS"　Econometrica,
vol.44, 1976, p.835.
COMPUTERISATION - SPECTRAL ANALYSIS , PROGRAMS * COMPUTERISATION -
ESTIMATION , SIMULTANEOUS SYSTEM MODELS , PROGRAMS

YA1881　JUSTER F.T.
"An evaluation of the recent record of short term forecasting"　Bus.
Econ., vol.7:3, 1972, pp.22-26.
MACRO MODELS - METHODOLOGY , ADJUSTMENTS * MACRO MODEL - WHARTON * MACRO
MODEL - OBE * EVALUATION - MACRO MODELS * EVALUATION - JUDGEMENTAL
ADJUSTMENTS

YA1882　JUSTER F.T.
"Consumer buying intentions and purchase probability: an experiment in
survey design"　J. Am. Statist. Ass., vol.61, 1966, pp.658-696.
SURVEYS - METHODOLOGY , DESIGN * EVALUATION - EXPECTATIONS , DATA *
EVALUATION - SURVEYS , CONSUMER * APPL - SECTOR : CONSUMER DURABLES , CARS

YA1883　JUSTER F.T., TAYLOR L.D.
"Towards a theory of savings behaviour" with discussion　Am. Econ. Ass.
Proc., 1975, pp.203-209 & 224.
APPL - MACRO : SAVINGS

YA1884　JUSTER F.T., WACHTEL P.
"A note on inflation and the saving rate"　Brookings Paps. Econ. Activity,
1972, pp.765-778.
INFLATION - EXPECTATIONS * APPL - MACRO : SAVINGS * INFLATION - EFFECT OF

YA1885　JUSTER F.T., WACHTEL P.
"Anticipatory and objective models of durable goods demand"　Am. Econ.
Rev., vol.62, 1972, pp.564-579.
APPL - SECTOR : CONSUMER DURABLES * CONSUMER BEHAVIOUR - ECONOMIC MODELS *
EXPECTATIONS - DATA * COMPARATIVE METHODS - CAUSAL , JUDGEMENTAL * APPL -
SECTOR : CONSUMER DURABLES , CARS

YA1886　JUSTER F.T., WACHTEL P.
"Inflation and the consumer" with discussion　Brookings Paps. Econ.
Activity, 1972, pp.71-121 & 788-790.
APPL - MACRO : CONSUMER DEMAND * PRICE - SECTOR : CONSUMER DURABLES *
INFLATION - EFFECT OF * INFLATION - EXPECTATIONS * APPL - SECTOR : CONSUMER
DURABLES * CONSUMER BEHAVIOUR - ECONOMIC MODELS * APPL - SECTOR : CONSUMER
DURABLES , CARS * ATTITUDINAL DATA * INDEX NUMBERS - MACRO : CONSUMER
CONFIDENCE * EXPECTATIONS - DATA

YA1887　KACHERE A.J.
"Forecast error and planning"　Bus. Econ., vol.11:3, 1976, p.70.
USER REQUIREMENTS * USE - CORPORATE PLANNING * FORECASTING - VALUE OF *
BASIC

YA1888　KADIYALA K.R.
"Regressions with non Gaussian stable disturbances: some sampling results"
Econometrica, vol.40, 1972, pp.719-722.
ERROR DISTRIBUTION - STABLE * LOSS FUNCTION - ABSOLUTE ERROR * ESTIMATION -
MSAE * ADVANCED

YA1889　KADIYALA K.R.
"Testing for the independence of regression disturbances"　Econometrica,
vol.38, 1970, pp.97-117.
ERROR SPECIFICATION - AUTOCORRELATED * COMPARATIVE METHODS - TESTS ,
AUTOCORRELATION * AUTOCORRELATION - TEST * ADVANCED

YA1890   KAHN L.M.
"The returns to job search: a test of two models"   Rev. Econ. Stats.,
vol.60, 1978, pp.496-503.
HEALTH - EFFECT OF * MANPOWER PLANNING - UNEMPLOYMENT , DURATION * MANPOWER
PLANNING - LABOUR FORCE COMPOSITION

YA1891   KAHN L.M.
"Union impact: a reduced form approach"   Rev. Econ. Stats., vol.59, 1977,
pp.503-506.
UNIONIZATION - EFFECT OF * APPL - SECTOR : EARNINGS * DATA - CROSS SECTION *
COMPARATIVE METHODS - ESTIMATION : OLS , 2SLS

YA1892   KAKWANI N.C.
"A new method of estimating Engel elasticities"   J. Econometrics, vol.8,
1978, pp.103-110.
CONSUMER BEHAVIOUR - EXPENDITURE SURVEY * APPL - MACRO : CONSUMER DEMAND *
INCOME - EFFECT OF * APPL - MACRO , SOUTH EAST ASIA * COMPARATIVE METHODS -
REGRESSION , TRANSFORMATIONS

YA1893   KAKWANI N.C.
"On the estimation of consumer unit scales"   Rev. Econ. Stats., vol.59,
1977, pp.507-510.
CONSUMER UNIT SCALES * DEMAND EQUATIONS - SYSTEM OF * APPL - MACRO :
CONSUMER DEMAND * CONSUMER BEHAVIOUR - ECONOMIC MODELS

YA1894   KAKWANI N.C.
"On the estimation of Engel elasticities from grouped observations with
application to Indonesian data"   J. Econometrics, vol.6, 1977, pp.1-19.
APPL - SECTOR : CONSUMER NON DURABLES , FOOD * DATA - AGGREGATION 'BIAS' *
DATA - CROSS SECTION * APPL - MACRO , SOUTH EAST ASIA * APPL - MACRO :
CONSUMER DEMAND * INCOME - EFFECT OF * COMPARATIVE METHODS - REGRESSION ,
TRANSFORMATIONS * COMPARATIVE METHODS - INCOME ELASTICITY , ESTIMATION *
CONSUMER BEHAVIOUR - EXPENDITURE SURVEY * REGRESSION - GROUPED OBSERVATIONS
* DATA - GROUPED

YA1895   KAKWANI N.C., RAO B.B.
"An alternative econometric approach to the permanent income hypothesis: a
comment"   Rev. Econ. Stats., vol.59, 1977, pp.126-127.
EVALUATION - PERMANENT INCOME * APPL - MACRO : CONSUMPTION * EVALUATION -
ESTIMATION : NON LINEAR

YA1896   KALCHBRENNER J.A., TINSLEY P.A.
"On the use of feedback control in the design of monetary policy" with
discussion"   Am. Econ. Ass. Proc., vol.66, 1976, pp.349-360.
CONTROL THEORY - STOCHASTIC , APPL * MACRO MODEL - MIT , PENN , SSRC * MACRO
MODELS - METHODOLOGY * EXOGENOUS VARIABLES - PREDICTION OF , EFFECT *
CONTROL THEORY - ADAPTIVE

YA1897   KALDOR N., ROWTHORN R.E.
"Economic growth and the Verdoorn law - comments"   Econ. J., vol.85, 1975,
pp. pp.891-901.
APPL - MACRO : GROWTH * APPL - MACRO : PRODUCTIVITY

YA1898   KALISH L., GILBERT R.A.
"The influence of bank regulation on the operating efficiency of commercial
banks"   J. Finance, vol.28, 1973, pp.1287-1301.
APPL - FIRM : FINANCE , BANKS * COST - FIRM : FINANCE * USE - BANK
REGULATION

YA1899   KALISKI S.F.
"Unemployment and unemployment insurance: testing some corollaries"   Can.
J. Econ., vol.9, 1976, pp.705-712.
APPL - SECTOR : UNEMPLOYMENT * POLICY EVALUATION - SECTOR : UNEMPLOYMENT *
POLICY EVALUATION - MACRO : WELFARE

YA1900   KALISKI S.F., ET AL.
"Real and insurance-induced unemployment in Canada: comments"   Can. J.
Econ., vol.8, 1975, pp.600-605.
APPL - MACRO : UNEMPLOYMENT * POLICY EVALUATION - MACRO : UNEMPLOYMENT

YA1901   KALT J.P.
"Technological change and factor substitution in the US: 1929-1967"   Int.
Econ. Rev., vol.19, 1978, pp.761-775.
PRODUCTION FUNCTIONS - SUBSTITUTION * EVALUATION - PRODUCTION FUNCTIONS *
PRODUCTION FUNCTIONS - MACRO * TECHNOLOGY - EFFECT OF * COMPARATIVE METHODS
- ESTIMATION : REGRESSION , SEEMINGLY UNRELATED * BIBLIOGRAPHY - PRODUCTION
FUNCTIONS

YA1902   KALUZNY R.L.
"Determinants of household migration: a comparative study of race and
poverty level"   Rev. Econ. Stats., vol.57, 1975, pp.269-274.
REGIONAL MODELS - MANPOWER PLANNING , MIGRATION * EDUCATION - EFFECT OF *
MANPOWER PLANNING - REGIONAL

YA1903   KAMERSCHEN D.R.
"The return of target pricing"   J. Business, vol.48, 1975, pp.242-252.
APPL - FIRM : FINANCE , PROFITS * PRICE - EFFECT OF * THEORY - PRICING

YA1904   KANE E.J. MALKIEL B.G.
"The term structure of interest rates: an analysis of a survey of interest
rate expectations"   Rev. Econ. Stats., vol.49, 1967, pp.343-355.
INTEREST RATE - TERM STRUCTURE * SURVEYS - BUSINESS * EXPECTATIONS - DATA *
INTEREST RATE - EXPECTATIONS

YA1905   KANE E.J., MALKIEL B.G.
          "Autoregressive and nonautoregressive elements in cross-section forecasts of
          inflation"   Econometrica, vol.44, 1976, pp.1-16.
          EXPECTATIONS - DATA * THEORY - EXPECTATIONS * JUDGEMENTAL FORECASTS -
          DETERMINANTS * INFLATION - EXPECTATIONS

YA1906   KANUK L., BERENSON C.
          "Mail surveys and response rates: a literature review"   J. Mktg. Res.,
          vol, 12, 1975, pp.440-453.
          SURVEYS - METHODOLOGY , RESPONSE ERROR * BIBLIOGRAPHY - SURVEYS

YA1907   KAO E.P.C., POKLADNIK F.M.
          "Incorporating exogenous factors in adaptive forecasting of hospital census"
          Mgmt. Sci., vol.24, 1978, pp.1677-1686.
          EXPONENTIAL SMOOTHING - HIGHER ORDER : APPL * TIME SERIES - HARMONICS *
          INTERVENTION * COMPARATIVE METHODS - EXPONENTIAL SMOOTHING , ADAPTIVE *
          HEALTH - HOSPITAL , PATIENT FACILITIES

YA1908   KAPLAN R.S., ROLL R.
          "Investor evaluation of accounting information: some empirical evidence"
          J. Business, vol,45, 1972, pp.225-257.
          ACCOUNTING PRACTICE - EFFECT OF * APPL - FIRM : FINANCE , STOCK PRICES *
          STOCK PRICES - INFORMATION EFFECT * ERROR DISTRIBUTION - STABLE * STOCK
          PRICES - DISTRIBUTION

YA1909   KARATHANASSIS G., TZOANNOS J.
          "The demand for money by business firms: a temporal and cross-sectional
          analysis"   Appl. Econ., vol,9, 1977, pp.63-76.
          APPL - SECTOR : FINANCE , FINANCIAL STRUCTURE , LIQUID ASSETS * REGRESSION -
          ERROR COMPONENTS

YA1910   KAREKEN J.H.
          "FOMC policy: 1970 and beyond" with discussion   Brookings Paps. Econ.
          Activity, 1970, pp.474-484.
          POLICY EVALUATION - MONETARY * MACRO MODEL - FRB , MIT , PENN

YA1911   KASNAKOGLU Z.
          "A simultaneous model approach to the determinants of male earnings
          differentials in Turkey for 1968"   Rev. Econ. Stats., vol.60, 1978,
          pp.307-312.
          SPECIFICATION ERROR - TESTS , SIMULTANEOUS SYSTEM BIAS * APPL - SECTOR :
          SOCIAL , SUCCESS * MANPOWER PLANNING - EARNINGS * MANPOWER PLANNING - LABOUR
          FORCE COMPOSITION * COMPARATIVE METHODS - RECURSIVE , SIMULTANEOUS SYSTEM

YA1912   KASSARJIAN H.H.
          "Personality and behaviour: a review"   J. Mktg. Res., vol,8, 1971,
          pp.409-418.
          CONSUMER BEHAVIOUR - PSYCHOLOGICAL MODELS , REVIEW

YA1913   KASSOUF S.T.
          "The lag structure of option price"   J. Econometrics, vol,4, 1976,
          pp.303-310.
          APPL - FIRM : FINANCE , OPTIONS * STOCK PRICES - EFFECT OF * LOSS FUNCTIONS
          - SECTOR : FINANCE , TRADING RULES

YA1914   KATONA G.
          "Consumer durable spending"   Brookings Paps. Econ. Activity, 1971,
          pp.234-239.
          APPL - SECTOR : CONSUMER DURABLES * INDEX NUMBERS - MACRO : CONSUMER
          CONFIDENCE

YA1915   KATZ P.A.
          "Faculty salaries, promotions and productivity at a large university"   Am.
          Econ. Rev., vol,63, 1973, pp.469-477.
          MANPOWER PLANNING - SECTOR : EDUCATION , UNIVERSITIES * APPL - FIRM :
          EDUCATION , UNIVERSITIES * MANPOWER PLANNING - EARNINGS * APPL - FIRM :
          EARNINGS * MANPOWER PLANNING - FIRM * MANPOWER PLANNING - PROMOTION

YA1916   KAU P., HILL L.
          "A threshold model of purchasing decisions"   J. Mktg. Res., vol,9, 1972,
          pp.264-270.
          APPL - SECTOR : INVESTMENT * REGRESSION - LIMITED DEPENDENT , PROBIT * APPL
          - SECTOR : PRODUCTION , PLANT , AGRICULTURAL * CONSUMER BEHAVIOUR -
          PURCHASING , DETERMINANTS * EXPECTATIONS - DETERMINANTS

YA1917   KAUFMAN H.M., KWON J., THORNTON R.
          "An examination of the financing of Federal home loan bank advances:
          comments"   Rev. Econ. Stats., vol,55, 1973, pp.257-258.
          APPL - SECTOR : FINANCE , BUILDING SOCIETIES

YA1918   KAY N., GERSTENFELD A.
          "Technological forecasting- a note and rejoinder"   J. Business, vol,50,
          1977, pp.240-243.
          TECHNOLOGICAL FORECASTING * BASIC

YA1919   KAY R.
          "Proportional hazard regression models and analysis of censored survival
          data"   Appl. Stats., vol,26, 1977, pp.227-237.
          REGRESSION - CENSORED * ESTIMATION - MAXIMUM LIKELIHOOD

YA1920   KEARL J.R.
          "Inflation and relative price distortions: the case of housing"   Rev.
          Econ. Stats., vol,60, 1978, pp.609-614.
          INFLATION - EXPECTATIONS * INFLATION - EFFECT OF * APPL - SECTOR :
          CONSTRUCTION , RESIDENTIAL * PRICE - SECTOR : CONSTRUCTION , RESIDENTIAL

YA1921   KEARL J.R., MISHKIN F.S.
"Illiquidity, the demand for residential housing and monetary policy"   J.
Finance, vol.32, 1977, pp.1571-1586.
APPL - SECTOR : CONSTRUCTION , RESIDENTIAL * THEORY - LIQUIDITY PREFERENCE *
INCOME - EFFECT OF

YA1922   KEELER T.E.
"Airline regulation and market performance"   Bell J. Econ., vol.3, 1972,
pp.399-424.
APPL - SECTOR : PRODUCTION , AIRCRAFT * APPL - SECTOR : TRANSPORT , AIR *
COST - SECTOR : TRANSPORT * USE - FINANCIAL REGULATION * APPL - FIRM :
TRANSPORT , AIR * COST - FIRM : TRANSPORT

YA1923   KEELER T.E.
"Railroad costs, returns to scale, and excess capacity"   Rev. Econ.
Stats., vol.56, 1974, pp.201-208.
APPL - FIRM : TRANSPORT , RAILWAYS * COST - FIRM : TRANSPORT * DATA - CROSS
SECTION * ERROR SPECIFICATION - HETEROSCEDASTIC * CAPACITY - EFFECT OF

YA1924   KEELER T.E.
"The economics of passenger trains"   J. Business, vol.44, 1971,
pp.148-174.
APPL - SECTOR : TRANSPORT , RAIL , PASSENGER * COST - SECTOR : TRANSPORT

YA1925   KEELEY M.C., ET AL.
"The estimation of labour supply models using experimental data"   Am.
Econ. Rev., vol.68, 1978, pp.873-887.
MANPOWER PLANNING - MACRO , SUPPLY * REGRESSION - LIMITED DEPENDENT , TOBIT
* POLICY EVALUATION - MACRO : UNEMPLOYMENT * DATA - CROSS SECTION

YA1926   KEENAY G.A., MORGAN R.W., RAY K.H.
"An analytic model for company manpower planning"   Opl'. Res. Q., vol.28,
1977, pp.983-995.
MANPOWER PLANNING - FIRM * MANPOWER PLANNING - SECTOR : GOVERNMENT , CENTRAL
* MANPOWER PLANNING - PROMOTION

YA1927   KEESING D.B., SHERK D.R.
"Population density in patterns of trade and development"   Am. Econ. Rev.,
vol.61, 1971, pp.956-961.
POPULATION - EFFECT OF * APPL - MACRO : DEVELOPMENT * DATA - INTERNATIONAL *
APPL - MACRO : INTERNATIONAL TRADE

YA1928   KELLY J.S.
"Finite ranges and the identification problems"   Int. Econ. Rev., vol.13,
1972, pp.171-178.
SIMULTANEOUS SYSTEM - IDENTIFICATION

YA1929   KELLY T.F.
"The creation of longitudinal data from cross-section surveys: an
illustration from the current population survey"   Anns. Econ. Soc. Meas.,
vol.2, 1973, pp.209-214.
DATA - CROSS SECTION , TIME SERIES * SURVEYS - METHODOLOGY * SURVEYS -
CENSUS

YA1930   KEMP A.G., REID G.C.
"The random walk hypothesis and the recent behaviour of equity prices in
Britain"   Economica, vol.38, 1971, pp.28-51.
STOCK PRICES - RUNS * RANDOM WALK - TEST * APPL - FIRM : FINANCE , STOCK
PRICES

YA1931   KEMP K.
"Formal expressions which can be applied to cusum charts" with discussion
R. Statist. Soc. (B), vol.33, 1971, pp.331-360.
CONTROL CHARTS - CUSUM * ADVANCED

YA1932   KENDRICK D.
"Applications of control theory to macroeconomics"   Anns. Econ. Soc.
Meas., vol.5, 1976, pp.171-190.
CONTROL THEORY - REVIEW * BIBLIOGRAPHY - CONTROL THEORY

YA1933   KENEN P.B.
"New views of exchange rates and old views of policy" with discussion   Am.
Econ. Ass. Proc., 1978, pp.398-405 & 413-416.
APPL - MACRO : INTERNATIONAL FINANCE , EXCHANGE RATES * POLICY EVALUATION -
MACRO : INTERNATIONAL FINANCE , FOREIGN EXCHANGE

YA1934   KENEN P.B.
"The balance of payments and policy mix: simulations based on a US model"
with discussion   J. Finance, vol.29, 1974, pp.631-654 & 677-682.
MACRO MODEL - US * APPL - MACRO : INTERNATIONAL TRADE * POLICY EVALUATION -
MACRO

YA1935   KENKEL J.L.
"Small sample tests for serial correlation in models containing lagged
dependent variables"   Rev. Econ. Stats., vol.57, 1975, pp.383-386.
REGRESSION - LAGGED DEPENDENT * COMPARATIVE METHODS - TESTS ,
AUTOCORRELATION * DATA - SIMULATION

YA1936   KENKEL J.L.
"Some small sample properties of Durbin's tests for serial correlation in
regression models comtaining lagged dependent variables"   Econometrica,
vol.42, 1974, pp.763-769.
RESIDUALS - ANALYSIS OF , AUTOCORRELATION * COMPARATIVE METHODS - TESTS ,
AUTOCORRELATION * REGRESSION - LAGGED DEPENDENT

YA1937   KENKEL J.L., PARK S.
          "Comments on the small-sample power of Durbin's h-test"   J. Am. Statist.
          Ass., vol.71, 1976, pp.97-98.
          COMPARATIVE METHODS - TESTS , AUTOCORRELATION * DATA - SIMULATION
YA1938   KENNEDY C., THIRLWALL A.P.
          "Technical progress"   Econ. J., vol. 82, 1972, pp.11-72.
          PRODUCTION FUNCTIONS - REVIEW * TECHNOLOGY - EFFECT OF * BIBLIOGRAPHY -
          PRODUCTION FUNCTIONS * BIBLIOGRAPHY - TECHNOLOGICAL PROGRESS
YA1939   KENNEDY H.A.
          "A behavioural study of the usefulness of four financial ratios"   J.
          Acctg. Res., vol.13, 1975, pp.97-116.
          USE - BANKRUPTCY PREDICTION * BAYESIAN - JUDGEMENTAL FORECASTS * JUDGEMENTAL
          FORECASTS - SPECIALIST
YA1940   KENNEDY M.
          "An economic model of the world oil market"   Bell J. Econ., vol.5, 1974,
          pp.540-577.
          SIMULATION - APPL : SECTOR , PRODUCTION * SIMULATION - APPL : SECTOR ,
          COMMODITIES * APPL - SECTOR : COMMODITIES , OIL * LP * COST - SECTOR :
          PRODUCTION * APPL - SECTOR : CONSUMER NON DURABLES , PETROL * SUPPLY -
          SECTOR : COMMODITIES * APPL - SECTOR : PRODUCTION , PETROLEUM * APPL - MACRO
          , WORLD
YA1941   KENNEDY M.C.
          "Recent inflation and the monetarists"   Appl. Econ., vol.8, 1976,
          pp.145-156.
          INFLATION - DETERMINANTS * EVALUATION - INFLATION MODELS * THEORY - MONETARY
YA1942   KENWARD L.R.
          "Autocorrelation and dynamic methodology with an application to wage
          determination models"   J. Econometrics, vol.3, 1975, pp.179-187.
          APPL - MACRO : EARNINGS , REGRESSION - LAGGED DEPENDENT * SPECIFICATION
          ERROR - EFFECT OF , FILTERING * ERROR SPECIFICATION - AUTOCORRELATED * ERROR
          SPECIFICATION - MOVING AVERAGE * REGRESSION - ESTIMATION , ERROR
          SPECIFICATION * DISTRIBUTED LAG - ERROR SPECIFICATION * MACRO MODEL - CANADA
          , RDX1 * DISTRIBUTED LAG - IDENTIFICATION * SPECIFICATION ERROR - TESTS ,
          ERROR SPECIFICATION
YA1943   KENWARD L.R.
          "Forecasting quarterly business expenditure on non-residential construction
          in Canada: an assessment of alternative models"   Can. J. Econ., vol.9,
          1976, pp.517-529.
          COMPARATIVE METHODS - DISTRIBUTED LAG * APPL - SECTOR : CONSTRUCTION , NON
          RESIDENTIAL * EX ANTE * COMPARATIVE METHODS - ARIMA , DISTRIBUTED LAG *
          COMPARATIVE METHODS - DISTRIBUTED LAG , ERROR SPECIFICATION * DISTRIBUTED
          LAG - VARIABLE LAG * COMPARATIVE METHODS - CAUSAL , JUDGEMENTAL
YA1944   KERAN M.W.
          "Inflation, regulation, and utility stock prices"   Bell J. Econ., vol.7,
          1976, pp.268-280.
          APPL - SECTOR : UTILITIES * APPL - SECTOR : FINANCE , STOCK PRICE INDEX *
          STOCK PRICES - INDUSTRIAL STRUCTURE * USE - FINANCIAL , REGULATION * APPL -
          SECTOR : FINANCE , DIVIDENDS
YA1945   KERAN M.W.
          "Structural model of the stock market"   Bus. Econ., vol.6:4, 1971,
          pp.23-28.
          APPL - SECTOR : FINANCE , STOCK PRICE INDEX * STOCK PRICES - DETERMINANTS *
          INTEREST RATE - EFFECT OF
YA1946   KERTON R.R.
          "Price effects of market power in the Canadian newspaper industry"   Can.
          J. Econ., vol.6, 1973, pp.602-606.
          APPL - FIRM : SERVICES , MEDIA - NEWSPAPERS * PRICE - FIRM : SERVICES *
          PRICE - EFFECT OF * REGRESSION - SPECIFICATION OF VARIABLES : APPL
YA1947   KESSELMAN J.
          "The role of speculation in forward-rate determination: the Canadian
          flexible dollar 1953-1960"   Can. J. Econ., vol.4, 1971, pp.279-298.
          APPL - MACRO : INTERNATIONAL FINANCE , EXCHANGE RATES * EXCHANGE RATE -
          FORWARD RATE * ERROR SPECIFICATION - AUTOCORRELATED * THEORY - SPECULATION
YA1948   KETZ J.E.
          "The effect of general price-level adjustments on the predictive ability of
          financial ratios" with discussion   J. Acctg. Res., vol.16: supplement,
          1978, pp.273-300.
          ACCOUNTING PRACTICE - EFFECT OF * USE - BANKRUPTCY PREDICTION * INFLATION -
          EFFECT OF * DISCRIMINANT ANALYSIS - APPL
YA1949   KETZ J.E.
          "The validation of some general price level estimating models"   Acctg.
          Rev., vol.53, 1978, pp.952-960.
          SIMULATION - APPL : FINANCIAL MODELLING * APPL - FIRM : TRANSPORT , AIR
YA1950   KEYFITZ N.
          "On future population"   J. Am. Statist. Ass., vol.67, 1972, pp.347-363.
          POPULATION * EVALUATION - POPULATION FORECASTS * BIBLIOGRAPHY - POPULATION

YA1951   KHALILZADEH-SHIRAZI J.
          "Market structure and price-cost margins in UK manufacturing industries"
          Rev. Econ. Stats., vol.56, 1974, pp.67-76.
          APPL - SECTOR : FINANCE , MARGINS * CONCENTRATION - EFFECT OF

YA1952   KHAN M.S.
          "The structure and behaviour of imports of Venezuela"   Rev. Econ. Stats.,
          vol.57, 1975, pp.221-224.
          APPL - SECTOR : INTERNATIONAL TRADE , IMPORTS * COMPARATIVE METHODS -
          REGRESSION , ERROR SPECIFICATION * APPL - MACRO , LATIN AMERICA

YA1953   KHAN M.S., ROSS K.Z.
          "Cyclical and secular income elasticities of the demand for imports"   Rev.
          Econ. Stats., vol.57, 1975, pp.357-361.
          APPL - MACRO : INTERNATIONAL TRADE , IMPORTS * INCOME - EFFECT OF * PRICE -
          EFFECT OF * DATA - INTERNATIONAL

YA1954   KHAZZOOM J.D.
          "An indirect least squares estimator for overidentified equations"
          Econometrica, vol.44, 1976, pp.741-750.
          COMPARATIVE METHODS - ESTIMATION : SIMULTANEOUS SYSTEM * DATA - SIMULATION

YA1955   KHAZZOOM J.D.
          "The FPC staff's econometric model of natural gas supply in the US"   Bell
          J. Econ., vol.2, 1971, pp.51-93.
          APPL - SECTOR : PRODUCTION , GAS * SUPPLY - SECTOR : PRODUCTION * DATA -
          CROSS SECTION , TIME SERIES * MULTIPLIERS - SECTOR * PRICE - EFFECT OF

YA1956   KIDD J.B.
          "Scoring rules for subjective assessments"   Opl. Res. Q., vol.26, 1975,
          pp.183-195.
          JUDGEMENTAL FORECASTS - LEARNING * EVALUATION - JUDGEMENTAL FORECASTS ,
          STOCK PRICES * TRACKING SIGNAL - APPL * FORECASTER - INCENTIVES * USE -
          FORECASTER EVALUATION

YA1957   KIDD J.B., MORGAN J.R.
          "The use of subjective probability estimates in assessing project completion
          times"   Mgmt. Sci. (A), vol.16, 1969, pp.266-269.
          PRIOR INFORMATION - APPL * EVALUATION - JUDGEMENTAL FORECASTS , LEARNING *
          USE - PROJECT , PLANNING

YA1958   KIEFER N.M.
          "A Bayesian analysis of commodity demand and labor supply"   Int. Econ.
          Rev., vol.18, 1977, pp.209-218.
          APPL - MACRO : CONSUMER DEMAND * INCOME - EFFECT OF * COMPARATIVE METHODS -
          ESTIMATION : DEMAND EQUATIONS * BAYESIAN - ESTIMATION : DEMAND EQUATIONS *
          DEMAND EQUATIONS - SYSTEMS OF : METHODOLOGY , ESTIMATION

YA1959   KIEFER N.M.
          "Federally subsidised occupational training and the employment and earnings
          of male trainees"   J. Econometrics, vol.8, 1978, pp.111-128.
          POLICY EVALUATION - MACRO : UNEMPLOYMENT * MANPOWER PLANNING - EDUCATION
          PROGRAMS * MANPOWER PLANNING - EARNINGS * REGRESSION - LIMITED DEPENDENT :
          APPL

YA1960   KIERULFF H.E., ROBISON D.E.
          "Probabilistic forecasting for contractors"   Mgmt. Sci. (B), vol.17, 1971,
          pp.773-781.
          APPL - FIRM : CONSTRUCTION * USE - COMPETITIVE BIDDING

YA1961   KIGER J.E.
          "An empirical investigation of NYSE volume and price reactions to the
          announcement of quarterly earnings"   J. Acctg. Res., vol.10, 1972,
          pp.113-128.
          APPL - FIRM : FINANCE , STOCK PRICES * STOCK PRICES - TRADING VOLUME * STOCK
          PRICES - INFORMATION EFFECT

YA1962   KIM E.H., McCONELL J.J., GREENWOOD P.R.
          "Capital structure rearrangements and me-first rules in an efficient capital
          market"   J. Finance, vol.32, 1977, pp.789-810.
          APPL - FIRM : FINANCE , STOCK PRICES * ACCOUNTING PRACTICE - EFFECT OF *
          APPL - FIRM : FINANCE , BONDS * STOCK PRICES - INFORMATION EFFECT * STOCK
          PRICES - INDUSTRIAL STRUCTURE * APPL - FIRM : FINANCE , FINANCIAL STRUCTURE

YA1963   KING A.G.
          "Industrial structure, the flexibility of working hours, and women's labour
          force participation"   Rev. Econ. Stats., vol.60, 1978, pp.399-407.
          MANPOWER PLANNING - LABOUR PARTICIPATION , FEMALE * MANPOWER PLANNING -
          INDUSTRIAL COMPOSITION * INCOME - EFFECT OF

YA1964   KING B.F.
          "Market and industry factors in stock price behaviour"   J. Business,
          vol.39, 1966, pp.139-190.
          APPL - SECTOR : FINANCE , STOCK PRICE INDEX * STOCK PRICES - INDUSTRIAL
          STRUCTURE * APPL - FIRM : FINANCE , STOCK PRICES * BIBLIOGRAPHY - STOCK
          PRICES * FACTOR ANALYSIS - APPL * CLUSTER ANALYSIS - APPL

YA1965   KING E.P., SAMPSON C.B., SIMMS L.L.
          "An alternative to Monte Carlo sampling in stochastic models"   Mgmt. Sci.
          (B), vol.21, 1975, pp.649-657.
          SIMULATION - METHODOLOGY , MONTE CARLO

YA1966   KING M.A.
          "Corporate taxation and dividend behaviour= a comment"   Rev. Econ.
          Studies, vol.38, 1971, pp.377=380.
          APPL = SECTOR : FINANCE , DIVIDENDS * INCOME = EFFECT OF * TAX = EFFECT OF

YA1967   KING M.A., FELDSTEIN M.S.
          "Corporate taxation and dividend behaviour: comments"   Rev. Econ. Studies,
          vol.39, 1972, pp.231=240.
          APPL = SECTOR : FINANCE , DIVIDENDS * TAX = EFFECT OF * COMPARATIVE METHODS
          = ESTIMATION : REGRESSION , NON LINEAR

YA1968   KING M.L., GILES D.E.A.
          "A note on Wallis' bounds test and negative autocorrelation"
          Econometrica, vol.45, 1977, pp.1023=1026.
          SEASONALITY = TESTING * ERROR SPECIFICATION = AUTOCORRELATED

YA1969   KING W.R., DUTTA B.K., RODRIGUEZ J.T.
          "Strategic competitive information systems"   Omega, vol.6, 1978,
          pp.123=132.
          COMPETITION * MIS * USE = CORPORATE PLANNING

YA1970   KING W.R., WILSON T.A.
          "Subjective time estimates in critical path planning a preliminary analysis"
          Mgmt. Sci, (A), vol.13, 1967, pp.307=320.
          JUDGEMENTAL FORECASTS = LEARNING * EVALUATION = JUDGEMENTAL FORECASTS ,
          LEARNING * USE = PROJECT PLANNING * LOSS FUNCTIONS = FIRM , PROJECT PLANNING

YA1971   KING W.R., WITTEVRONGEL D.M., HEZEL K.D.
          "On the analysis of critical path time estimating behaviour"   Mgmt. Sci.
          (A), vol.14, 1967, pp.79=84.
          JUDGEMENTAL FORECASTS = LEARNING * USE = PROJECT PLANNING * EVALUATION =
          JUDGEMENTAL FORECASTS

YA1972   KINGSMAN B.G.
          "Commodity purchasing"   Opl. Res. Q., vol.20, 1969, pp.59=79.
          APPL = SECTOR : COMMODITIES * USE = PURCHASING , COMMODITIES * LP

YA1973   KINGSMAN B.G.
          "Forecasting and research for supply markets= commodity buying systems"
          Long Range Planning, vol.7:15, 1974, pp.24=38.
          APPL = SECTOR : COMMODITIES , COCOA * APPL = SECTOR : COMMODITIES , SUGAR *
          APPL = SECTOR : COMMODITIES , COPPER * USE = PURCHASING , COMMODITIES * APPL
          = SECTOR : COMMODITIES

YA1974   KINNEY W.R.
          "ARIMA and regression in analytical review: an empirical test"   Acctg.
          Rev., vol.53, 1978, pp.48=60.
          APPL = FIRM = TRANSPORT , RAIL * COMPARATIVE METHODS = ARIMA , INDICATOR *
          COMPARATIVE METHODS = ARIMA , RATIONAL POLYNOMIAL INDICATOR * COMBINING
          FORECASTS = ARIMA , INDICATOR

YA1975   KINNEY W.R.
          "Predicting earnings: entity versus subentity data"   J. Acctg. Res.,
          vol.9, 1971, pp.127=136.
          APPL = FIRM : FINANCE , PROFITS * COMPARATIVE METHODS = DATA : AGGREGATE ,
          DISAGGREGATE

YA1976   KIOUNTOUZIS E.A.
          "Linear programming techniques in regression analysis"   Appl. Stats.,
          vol.22, 1973, pp.69=73.
          ESTIMATION = MSAE * COMPARATIVE METHODS = ESTIMATION : OLS , MSAE * DATA =
          SIMULATION * ERROR DISTRIBUTION = NONNORMAL * ERROR DISTRIBUTION = STABLE

YA1977   KIRBY R.M.
          "A comparison of short and medium range statistical forecasting methods"
          Mgmt. Sci. (B), vol.13, 1967, pp.202=210.
          LEAD TIME = EFFECT OF * COMPARATIVE METHODS = DECOMPOSITION , EXPONENTIAL
          SMOOTHING * COMPARATIVE METHODS = DECOMPOSITION , TREND CURVES * DATA =
          SIMULATION * COMPARATIVE METHODS = EXPONENTIAL SMOOTHING , TREND CURVES

YA1978   KITCHENER A., ROWLAND D.
          "Models of a consumer product market"   Opl. Res. Q., vol.22, 1971,
          pp.67=84.
          APPL = SECTOR : CONSUMER NON DURABLES , HEALTH AIDS * ADVERTISING = EFFECT
          OF * USER = FIRM : CONSUMER NON DURABLES * USE = PROMOTION EVALUATION *
          PRICE = EFFECT OF * QUALITY = EFFECT OF * MARKET SHARE = SECTOR : CONSUMER
          NON DURABLES

YA1979   KLEIJNEN J.P.C., NAYLOR T.H., SEAKS T.G.
          "The use of multiple ranking procedures to analyze simulations of management
          systems: a tutorial"   Mgmt. Sci. (B), vol.18, 1972, pp.245=257.
          SIMULATION = EVALUATION OF RESULTS

YA1980   KLEIN B.
          "Competitive interest payments on bank deposits and the long run demand for
          money"   Am. Econ. Rev., vol.64, 1974, pp.931=949.
          APPL = MACRO : MONEY , DEMAND * INTEREST RATE = EFFECT OF * THEORY =
          MONETARY * COMPARATIVE METHODS = REGRESSION , ERROR SPECIFICATION

YA1981   KLEIN G.E.
          "Selection regression programs"   Rev. Econ. Stats., vol.50, 1968,
          pp.288=290.
          REGRESSION = SUMMARY STATISTICS * REGRESSION = VARIABLE INCLUSION *
          REGRESSION = MODEL CHOICE * REGRESSION = STEPWISE

YA1982 KLEIN L.R.
  "Whither econometrics" J. Am. Statist. Ass., vol.66, 1971, pp.415-421.
  ECONOMETRICS - REVIEW
YA1983 KLEIN L.R., LONG V.
  "Capacity utilization, concept, measurement and recent estimates" with
  discussion Brookings Paps. Econ. Activity, 1973, pp.743-763.
  CAPACITY - ESTIMATION * APPL - MACRO : CAPACITY UTILISATION
YA1984 KLEIN R.W.
  "A dynamic theory of corporate advantage" Am. Econ. Rev., vol.63, 1973,
  pp.173-184.
  APPL - SECTOR : CONSUMER NON DURABLES , PHARMACEUTICALS * APPL - SECTOR :
  INVESTMENT , INTERNATIONAL * USE - R&D
YA1985 KLEIN R.W., ET AL.
  "Decisions with estimation uncertainty" Econometrica, vol.46, 1978,
  pp.1363-1387.
  COMPARATIVE METHODS - CONTROL * LOSS FUNCTIONS - THEORY * DECISION RULES -
  METHODOLOGY , PARAMETER UNCERTAINTY * ADVANCED
YA1986 KLEMKOSKY R.C., MANESS T.S.
  "The predictability of real portfolio risk levels" J. Finance, vol.33,
  1978, pp.631-639.
  APPL - FIRM : FINANCE , MUTUAL FUNDS * STOCK PRICES - BETA , VARIABLE *
  STOCK PRICES - INSTITUTIONAL INVESTMENT * EX ANTE
YA1987 KLEMKOSKY R.C., MARTIN J.D.
  "The adjustment of beta forecasts" J. Finance, vol.30, 1975,
  pp.1123-1128.
  APPL - FIRM : FINANCE , STOCK PRICES * STOCK PRICES - BETA , VARIABLE * EX
  ANTE
YA1988 KLIMAN M.L.
  "The administered bank rate and its announcement effect" Can. J. Econ.,
  vol.7, 1974, pp.625-641.
  INTEREST RATE - EFFECT OF * APPL - SECTOR : FINANCE , STOCK PRICE INDEX *
  STOCK PRICES - INFORMATION EFFECT
YA1989 KLINOV-MALUL R.
  "Is it worthwhile to get a first" Econ. J., vol.84, 1974, pp.143-150.
  MANPOWER PLANNING - EARNINGS * EDUCATION - EFFECT OF * MANPOWER PLANNING -
  QUALIFIED MANPOWER , GRADUATES
YA1990 KLOEK T., VAN DIJK H.K.
  "Bayesian estimation of equation system parameters: an application of
  integration by Monte Carlo" Econometrica, vol.46, 1978, pp.1-19.
  BAYESIAN - ESTIMATION : SIMULTANEOUS SYSTEM * SIMULTANEOUS SYSTEM -
  ESTIMATION
YA1991 KLOTZ B.P., NEAL L.
  "Spectral and cross-spectral analysis of the long-swing hypothesis" Rev.
  Econ. Stats., vol.55, 1973, pp.291-298.
  BUSINESS CYCLE - LONG CYCLE * SPECTRAL ANALYSIS - APPL : BUSINESS CYCLE ,
  LONG CYCLE * SPECTRAL ANALYSIS - CROSS : APPL * DATA - INTERNATIONAL
YA1992 KMENTA J.
  "Small sample properties of alternative estimators of seemingly unrelated
  regressions" J. Am. Statist. Ass., vol.63, 1968, pp.1180-1200.
  COMPARATIVE METHODS - ESTIMATION : REGRESSION , SEEMINGLY UNRELATED * ERROR
  SPECIFICATION - CORRELATED * REGRESSION - ESTIMATION * ESTIMATION - GLS *
  DATA - SIMULATION
YA1993 KMENTA J., GILBERT R.F.
  "Estimation of seemingly unrelated regressions with autoregressive
  disturbances" J. Am. Statist. Ass., vol.65, 1970, pp.186-197.
  DATA - SIMULATION * ESTIMATION - NON LINEAR * ESTIMATION - GLS * ERROR
  SPECIFICATION - AUTOCORRELATED , CORRELATED * REGRESSION - SEEMINGLY
  UNRELATED * COMPARATIVE METHODS - ESTIMATION SPECIFICATION * APPL - FIRM :
  INVESTMENT * REGRESSION - ESTIMATION * COMPARATIVE METHODS - ESTIMATION :
  REGRESSION , SEEMINGLY UNRELATED * REGRESSION - ESTIMATION * COMPARATIVE
  METHODS - ESTIMATION : REGRESSION , ERROR SPECIFICATION
YA1994 KMENTA J., SMITH P.E.
  "Autonomous expenditure versus money supply: an application of dynamic
  multipliers" Rev. Econ. Stats., vol.55, 1973, pp.299-307.
  SPECIFICATION ERROR - TESTS , MODEL SELECTION : APPL * POLICY EVALUATION -
  MACRO : FISCAL , MONETARY * SIMULTANEOUS SYSTEM - DYNAMIC PROPERTIES *
  MULTIPLIERS - MACRO * MACRO MODEL - US
YA1995 KNECHT G.R.
  "Costing, technological growth, and generalised learning curves" Opl.
  Res. Q., vol.25, 1974, pp.487-491.
  COST - FIRM : PRODUCTION * LEARNING CURVE * LONG TERM FORECASTING * COST -
  LEARNING CURVE * APPL - FIRM : PRODUCTION , AIRCRAFT
YA1996 KNIESNER T.J.
  "An indirect test of complementarity in a family labor supply model"
  Econometrica, vol.44, 1976, pp.651-669.
  APPL - MACRO : EARNINGS * MANPOWER PLANNING - MACRO , SUPPLY * MANPOWER
  PLANNING - LABOUR PARTICIPATION , FEMALE

YA1997   KNIGHT M,
          "Euro-dollars, capital mobility and the forward exchange market"
          Economica, vol.44, 1977, pp.1-21,
          APPL - MACRO : INTERNATIONAL FINANCE , EXCHANGE RATES * ESTIMATION -
          CONSTRAINED * EXCHANGE RATE - FORWARD RATE

YA1998   KNOWLES J,W,
          "Long range economic forecasts or how do we bet our many tomorrows"   Bus,
          Econ,, vol.914, 1974, pp.58-62,
          LONG TERM FORECASTING * BASIC

YA1999   KOCH J,V,
          "Advertising and economic growth"   J, Advtg, Res,, vol,11:4, 1971,
          pp.36-39,
          DATA - CROSS SECTION * APPL - FIRM : GROWTH * ADVERTISING - EFFECT OF *
          CONCENTRATION - EFFECT OF

YA2000   KOEHLER R,T,
          "Forecasting profit trends in the economy"   Bus, Econ,, vol.6:4, 1971,
          pp.33-35
          APPL - MACRO : PROFITS * BUSINESS INDICATORS - APPL * BASIC

YA2001   KOERTS J,, ABRAHAMSE A,P,J,
          "On the power of the BLUS procedure"   J, Am, Statist, Ass,, vol.63, 1968,
          pp.1227-1236,
          ERROR SPECIFICATION - AUTOCORRELATED * AUTOCORRELATION - TEST * RESIDUALS -
          COMPARATIVE ANALYSIS OF * COMPARATIVE METHODS - TESTS , AUTOCORRELATION *
          RESIDUALS - ANALYSIS OF , AUTOCORRELATION

YA2002   KOFI T,A,
          "A framework for comparing the efficiencies of futures markets"   Am, J,
          Ag, Econ,, vol.55, 1973, pp.584-594,
          APPL - SECTOR : COMMODITIES * THEORY - EFFICIENT MARKETS * APPL - SECTOR :
          FINANCE : FUTURES TRADING

YA2003   KOHLHAGEN S,W,
          "The stability of exchange rate expectations and Canadian capital flows"
          J, Finance, vol.32, 1977, pp.1657-1669,
          INTEREST RATE - EFFECT OF * APPL - MACRO , CANADA * EXCHANGE RATE - EFFECT
          OF * APPL - MACRO : INTERNATIONAL FINANCE , EXCHANGE RATES * STABILITY OF
          COEFFICIENTS - REGRESSION

YA2004   KOMLI V,R,
          "A gross national product function and the derived demand for imports and
          supply of exports"   Can, J, Econ,, vol,11, 1978, pp.167-182,
          APPL - MACRO : INTERNATIONAL TRADE * PRICE - EFFECT OF * APPL - MACRO : GNP
          * APPL - MACRO , CANADA * SUBSTITUTE FACTORS

YA2005   KOHN M,G,, MANSKI C,F,, MUNDEL D,S,
          "An empirical investigation of factors which influence college-going
          behavior"   Anns, Econ, Soc, Meas,, vol.5, 1976, pp.391-419,
          APPL - FIRM : EDUCATION , UNIVERSITIES * REGRESSION - LIMITED DEPENDENT *
          CONSUMER BEHAVIOUR - ECONOMIC MODELS * PRICE - EFFECT OF * INCOME - EFFECT
          OF

YA2006   KOHN M,G,, PLESSNER Y,
          "An applicable model of optimal marketing policy"   Ops, Res,, vol,21,
          1973, pp.401-412,
          APPL - SECTOR : AGRICULTURE , FRUIT * PRICE - FIRM : AGRICULTURE * CONTROL
          THEORY - STOCHASTIC , METHODOLOGY * CONTROL THEORY - DETERMINISTIC ,
          METHODOLOGY

YA2007   KOHN R,E,
          "Price elasticities of demand and air pollution control"   Rev, Econ,
          Stats,, vol.54, 1972, pp.392-400,
          LP * POLLUTION - CONTROLS * PRICE - EFFECT OF * APPL - SECTOR : POLLUTION *
          REGIONAL MODELS - POLLUTION * COST - MACRO : POLLUTION

YA2008   KOLESAR P,
          "Square root laws for fire engine response distances"   Mgmt, Sci, (B),
          vol.19, 1973, pp.1368-1378,
          REGIONAL MODELS - SECTOR : GOVERNMENT , LOCAL , EMERGENCY * PROBABILITY
          MODELS - OTHER * APPL - SECTOR : GOVERNMENT , LOCAL , EMERGENCY SERVICES

YA2009   KON S,J,, JEN F,C,
          "Estimation of time-varying systematic risk and performance for mutual fund
          portfolios: an application of switching regression"   J, Finance, vol,33,
          1978, pp.457-475,
          REGRESSION - SWITCHING * APPL - FIRM : FINANCE , MUTUAL FUNDS * STOCK PRICES
          - INSTITUTIONAL INVESTMENT * STOCK PRICES - BETA , VARIABLE

YA2010   KOOT R,S,
          "A factor analytical approach to an empirical definition of money"   J,
          Finance, vol,30, 1975, pp.1081-1089,
          FACTOR ANALYSIS - APPL * APPL - MACRO : MONEY * REGRESSION - SPECIFICATION
          OF VARIABLES * APPL - MACRO : GNP

YA2011   KOOT R,S,
          "On economies of scale in credit unions"   J, Finance, vol,33, 1978,
          pp.1087-1094,
          APPL - FIRM : FINANCE , CREDIT UNIONS * COST - FIRM : FINANCE * COST - SCALE
          ECONOMIES * DATA - CROSS SECTION

YA2012   KOOT R.S.
"On the St. Louis equation and an alternative definition of the money
supply"   J. Finance, vol.32, 1977, pp.917-920.
APPL - MACRO : MONEY , SUPPLY * MACRO MODEL - ST. LOUIS * REGRESSION -
SPECIFICATION OF VARIABLES

YA2013   KOOT R.S., WALKER D.A.
"A reconstruction of the 'great ratios' of economics"   Decis. Sci.,
vol.313, 1972, pp.115-123.
AUTOCORRELATION - EFFECT OF * APPL - MACRO : MONEY , INCOME VELOCITY * APPL
- MACRO : CONSUMPTION * APPL - MACRO : INVESTMENT * APPL - MACRO : EARNINGS
* TREND CURVES - APPL

YA2014   KOOT R.S., WALKER D.A.
"An analysis of income stability and the money supply, 1952-1968"   Appl.
Econ., vol.3, 1971, pp.11-18.
APPL - MACRO : MONEY , SUPPLY * APPL - MACRO : INCOME * STABILITY OF
COEFFICIENTS - REGRESSION : APPL

YA2015   KOPITS G.F.
"Dividend remittance behaviour within the international firm: a
cross-country analysis"   Rev. Econ. Stats., vol.54, 1972, pp.339-342.
APPL - FIRM : FINANCE , DIVIDENDS * APPL - FIRM : FINANCE , INTERNATIONAL
FINANCE * DATA - INTERNATIONAL * TAX - EFFECT OF

YA2016   KOPITS G.F.
"Intra-firm royalties crossing frontiers and transfer pricing behaviour"
Econ. J., vol.86, 1976, pp.791-805.
APPL - SECTOR : TECHNOLOGY * APPL - SECTOR : FINANCE , INTERNATIONAL FINANCE
* APPL - FIRM TYPE : MULTINATIONALS * DATA - LDC * DATA - INTERNATIONAL

YA2017   KOPITZKE R., BOARDMAN T.J., GRAYBILL F.A.
"Least square programs- a look at the square root procedure"   Am. Stat'n.,
vol.29, 1975, pp.64-66.
ESTIMATION - OLS * COMPUTERISATION - PROGRAMS , ESTIMATION , REGRESSION
MODELS

YA2018   KOSOBUD R.F.
"Forecasting accuracy and uses of an econometric model"   Appl. Econ.,
vol.2, 1970, pp.253-263.
MACRO MODELS - MICRO MODELS * COMPARATIVE METHODS - AUTOREGRESSIVE ,
CAUSAL(SIMULTANEOUS SYSTEM) * EVALUATION - JUDGEMENTAL FORECASTS , MACRO *
COMPARATIVE METHODS - CAUSAL(SIMULTANEOUS SYSTEM) , JUDGEMENTAL *
COMPARATIVE METHODS - AUTOREGRESSIVE , JUDGEMENTAL * EX ANTE * COMPARATIVE
METHODS - MACRO MODELS * EVALUATION - MACRO FORECASTS * MACRO MODEL -
MICHIGAN , SUITS

YA2019   KOTLER P., SCHULTZ R.L.
"Marketing simulations: review and prospects"   J. Business, vol.43, 1970,
pp.237-295.
SIMULATION - APPL : MARKETING , REVIEW

YA2020   KOTTAS J.F.
"Correcting for the inherent bias in the average bidder approach to
competitive bid development"   Decis. Sci., vol.7, 1976, pp.405-410.
USE - COMPETITIVE BIDDING * EXTREME VALUES * DATA - AGGREGATION 'BIAS'

YA2021   KRAFT A.
"Piecewise approximation functions: an educational note"   Decis. Sci.,
vol.6, 1975, pp.568-580.
REGRESSION - PIECEWISE * SPLINE FUNCTIONS

YA2022   KRAFT A., KRAFT J.
"A re-estimation of the Phillips' curve for the UK"   Appl. Econ., vol.6,
1974, pp.215-227.
INFLATION - PHILLIPS CURVE * REGRESSION - PIECEWISE : APPL * STABILITY OF
COEFFICIENTS - REGRESSION * SPLINE FUNCTIONS

YA2023   KRAFT J., KRAFT A.
"Determinants of common stock prices: a time series analysis" with
discussion   J. Finance, vol.32, 1977, pp.417-425 & 442-448.
APPL - SECTOR : FINANCE , STOCK PRICE INDEX * STOCK PRICES - DETERMINANTS *
RISK - EFFECT OF * EVALUATION - FILTER CHOICE * CAUSALITY - TEST : APPL

YA2024   KRAFT J., KRAFT A.
"Empirical estimation of the value of travel time using multi mode choice
models   J. Econometrics, vol.2, 1974, pp.317-326.
APPL - SECTOR : TRANSPORT * TIME - VALUE OF * REGRESSION - LIMITED DEPENDENT
, LOGIT

YA2025   KRAUS A., LITZENBERGER R.H.
"Skewness preference and the valuation of risk assets"   J. Finance,
vol.31, 1976, pp.1085-1100.
APPL - FIRM : FINANCE , STOCK PRICES * STOCK PRICES - MODELS , COMPARATIVE *
CONSUMER BEHAVIOUR - ECONOMIC MODELS * RISK - EFFECT OF * BIBLIOGRAPHY -
STOCK PRICES * STOCK PRICES - MODELS , CAPM

YA2026   KRAUS A., STOLL H.R.
"Price impacts of block trading in the New York Stock Exchange"   J.
Finance, vol.27, 1972, pp.569-588.
APPL - FIRM : FINANCE , STOCK PRICES * STOCK PRICES - TRADING VOLUME

YA2027   KRAVIS I.B.
          "A survey of international comparisons of productivity"   Econ. J., vol.86,
          1976, pp.1-44.
          APPL - SECTOR : PRODUCTIVITY * DATA - INTERNATIONAL * BIBLIOGRAPHY -
          PRODUCTIVITY
YA2028   KRAVIS I.B., LIPSEY R.E.
          "Export prices and the transmission of inflation"   Am. Econ. Ass. Proc.,
          1977, pp.155-163.
          APPL - MACRO : INTERNATIONAL TRADE , EXPORTS * APPL - MACRO : INTERNATIONAL
          TRADE , PRICE * APPL - MACRO , GERMANY * INFLATION - EFFECT OF
YA2029   KREININ M.E.
          "A further note on the export elasticity of substitution"   Can. J. Econ.,
          vol.6, 1973, pp.606-608.
          APPL - MACRO : INTERNATIONAL TRADE , EXPORTS * PRICE - EFFECT OF *
          SUBSTITUTE PRODUCTS
YA2030   KREININ M.E.
          "Price elasticities in international trade"   Rev. Econ. Stats., vol.49,
          1967, pp.510-516.
          DATA - INTERNATIONAL * APPL - MACRO : INTERNATIONAL TRADE * PRICE - EFFECT
          OF
YA2031   KRESGE D.T., ET AL.
          "Problems of regional economic development: the case of Alaska" with
          discussion   Am. Econ. Ass. Proc., 1978, pp.99-117.
          REGIONAL MODELS * POLICY EVALUATION - REGIONAL
YA2032   KRUGMAN H.E.
          "What makes advertising effective?"   H.B.R., vol.53, Mar-April, 1975,
          pp.96-103.
          ADVERTISING - EFFECT OF * USE - MEDIA PLANNING * BASIC
YA2033   KRYZANOWSKI L.
          "Misinformation and regulatory actions in some Canadian capital markets:
          some empirical evidence"   Bell J. Econ., vol.9, 1978, pp.355-368.
          APPL - FIRM : FINANCE , STOCK PRICES * STOCK PRICES - INFORMATION EFFECT *
          USE - STOCK MARKET REGULATION
YA2034   KUBURSI A.A., WILLIAMS J.R., GEORGE P.J.
          "Sub provincial regional income multipliers in the Ontario economy: an input
          output approach"   Can. J. Econ., vol.8, 1975, pp.67-92.
          INPUT OUTPUT - REGIONAL * MULTIPLIERS - REGIONAL * POLICY EVALUATION -
          REGIONAL
YA2035   KUCH P.J., SHARIR S.
          "Added - and discouraged-worker effects in Canada, 1953-74"   Can. J.
          Econ., vol.11, 1978, pp.112-120.
          MANPOWER PLANNING - LABOUR PARTICIPATION * MANPOWER PLANNING - LABOUR FORCE
          COMPOSITION
YA2036   KUEHN A.A., ROHLOFF A.C.
          "Fitting models to aggregate data"   J. Advtg. Res., vol.7:1, 1967,
          pp.43-47.
          MODEL SELECTION * ADVERTISING - EFFECT OF , INTRODUCTION * MODEL
          INTERPRETATION * BASIC
YA2037   KUMAR T.K., ASHER E., WEITZMAN M.
          "Soviet postwar economic growth and capital-labor substitution: comments"
          Am. Econ. Rev., vol.64, 1974, pp.240-243.
          PRODUCTION FUNCTIONS - MACRO * PRODUCTION FUNCTIONS - METHODOLOGY *
          ESTIMATION - NON LINEAR * REGRESSION - SUMMARY STATISTICS * APPL - MACRO ,
          USSR
YA2038   KUMAR T.K., ET AL.
          "Multicollinearity in regression analysis"   Rev. Econ. Stats., vol.57,
          1975, pp.365-370.
          MULTICOLLINEARITY - TEST * COMPARATIVE METHODS - TESTS , MULTICOLLINEARITY
YA2039   KUMAR T.K., GAPINSKI J.H.
          "Nonlinear estimation of the CES production parameters: a monte carlo study"
          Rev. Econ. Stats., vol.56, 1974, pp.563-567.
          DATA - SIMULATION * EVALUATION - ESTIMATION : REGRESSION , NON LINEAR *
          ESTIMATION - NON LINEAR * EVALUATION - PRODUCTION FUNCTIONS , ESTIMATION
YA2040   KUMMER D.R., HOFFMEISTER J.R.
          "Valuation consequences of cash tender offers"   J. Finance, vol.33, 1978,
          pp.505-516.
          APPL - FIRM : FINANCE , STOCK PRICES * APPL - FIRM : MERGERS * STOCK PRICES
          - INDUSTRIAL STRUCTURE
YA2041   KWACK S.Y.
          "Effects of income and prices on travel and spending abroad, 1960 III-1976
          IV"   Int. Econ. Rev., vol.13, 1972, pp.245-256.
          APPL - MACRO : INTERNATIONAL TRADE , INVISIBLES * APPL - SECTOR : SERVICES ,
          TOURISM
YA2042   KWACK S.Y.
          "The structure of international interest rates: an extension of
          Hendershott's test"   J. Finance, vol.26, 1971, pp.897-900.
          APPL - MACRO : INTERNATIONAL FINANCE * INTEREST RATE - EFFECT OF * INTEREST
          RATE - DETERMINANTS

YA2043   KWAK N.K., GARRETT W.A., BARONE S.
"A stochastic model of demand forecasting for technical manpower planning"
Mgmt. Sci., vol.23, 1977, pp.1089-1098.
MANPOWER PLANNING - QUALIFIED MANPOWER

YA2044   KWEREL S.M.
"Estimating unduplicated audience and exposure distribution"   J. Advtg.
Res., vol.9:2, 1969, pp.46-53.
ADVERTISING - EXPOSURE * USE - MEDIA PLANNING * PROBABILITY MODELS - ENTROPY

YA2045   KWON J.K., THORNTON R.M.
"An evaluation of the competative effects of FHLB open market operations on
savings inflows at savings and loan associations"   J. Finance, vol.26,
1971, pp.699-712.
APPL - SECTOR : FINANCE , BUILDING SOCIETIES * APPL - SECTOR : FINANCE ,
SAVINGS * POLICY EVALUATION - SECTOR : FINANCE

YA2046   KWON J.K., THORNTON R.M.
"The Federal home loan bank and savings and loan associations: an
examination of the financing of Federal home loan bank advances"   Rev.
Econ. Stats., vol.54, 1972, pp.97-100.
SUBSTITUTE PRODUCTS * APPL - SECTOR : FINANCE , MORTGAGES * APPL - SECTOR :
FINANCE , BUILDING SOCIETIES * POLICY EVALUATION - SECTOR : CONSTRUCTION

YA2047   KYLE P.W.
"Lydia Pinkham revisited: a Box-Jenkins approach"   J. Advtg. Res.,
vol.18:2, 1978, pp.31-38.
TIME SERIES - ARIMA : INTRODUCTION * APPL - FIRM : CONSUMER NON DURABLES ,
HEALTH AIDS * EX ANTE

YA2048   KYMN K.O.
"Interindustry energy demand and aggregation of input-output tables"   Rev.
Econ. Stats., vol.59, 1977, pp.371-374.
INPUT OUTPUT - METHODOLOGY , AGGREGATION * DATA - AGGREGATION 'BIAS' * APPL
- SECTOR : ENERGY * INPUT OUTPUT - SECTOR : ENERGY

YA2049   LABYS W.C.
"The problems and challenges for international commodity models and model
builders"   Am. J. Ag. Econ., vol.57, 1975, pp.873-878.
EVALUATION - COMMODITY PRICE MODELS * APPL - SECTOR : COMMODITIES

YA2050   LABYS W.C., REES H.J.B., ELLIOTT C.M.
"Copper price behaviour and the London metal exchange"   Appl. Econ.,
vol.3, 1971, pp.99-113.
APPL - SECTOR : COMMODITIES , COPPER * SPECTRAL ANALYSIS - APPL : SECTOR :
COMMODITIES * RANDOM WALK - TEST * SPECTRAL ANALYSIS - CROSS : APPL

YA2051   LABYS W.C., THOMAS H.C.
"Speculation, hedging and commodity price behaviour: an international
comparison"   Appl. Econ., vol.7, 1975, pp.287-301.
APPL - SECTOR : FINANCE , FUTURES TRADING * SPECTRAL ANALYSIS - APPL :
FUTURES TRADING * APPL - SECTOR : COMMODITIES * VOLATILITY - EFFECT OF

YA2052   LACAVA G.J., STEINBERG E.
"The response of linear decision rule cost performance to inventory
measurement errors"   Opl. Res. Q., vol.28, 1977, pp.703-710.
USE - INVENTORY CONTROL * DECISION RULES - FIRM * FORECASTING - VALUE OF *
DATA ERRORS - EFFECT OF * USE - PRODUCTION , CONTROL * USE - SCHEDULING ,
MANPOWER

YA2053   LADD G.W.
"Linear probability functions and discriminant functions"   Econometrica,
vol.34, 1966, pp.873-885.
REGRESSION - QUALITATIVE DEPENDENT * EVALUATION - DISCRIMINANT ANALYSIS

YA2054   LADENSON M.L.
"A dynamic balance sheet approach to American direct foreign investment"
Int. Econ. Rev., vol.13, 1972, pp.531-543.
APPL - MACRO : INVESTMENT , INTERNATIONAL

YA2055   LADENSON M.L.
"A foreign exchange liquidity trap for Mexico"   Int. Econ. Rev., vol.15,
1974, pp.93-98.
APPL - MACRO , LATIN AMERICA * APPL - MACRO : INTERNATIONAL FINANCE ,
EXCHANGE RATES * INCOME - EFFECT OF , PERMANENT * APPL - MACRO : MONEY *
ESTIMATION - NON LINEAR

YA2056   LADENSON M.L.
"Pitfalls in financial model building: some extensions"   Am. Econ. Rev.,
vol.61, 1971, pp.179-186.
APPL - MACRO : FLOW OF FUNDS * SIMULTANEOUS SYSTEM - CONSTRAINED

YA2057   LAESSIG R.E., GLASSER E.R., RICCI P.F.
"A retrospective study on the influence of a state park lake on land value,
from the time of land acquisition to reservoir filling"   Decis. Sci.,
vol.6, 1975, pp.775-785.
APPL - SECTOR : CONSTRUCTION , LAND * APPL - SECTOR : SERVICES , TOURISM *
PUBLIC EXPENDITURE - EFFECT OF * PRICE - SECTOR : CONSTRUCTION , LAND

YA2058   LAFFER A.B., RANSON R.D.
"A formal model of the economy"   J. Business, vol.44, 1971, pp.247-270.
MACRO MODEL - OMB * EVALUATION - MONETARY THEORY

YA2059   LAFFONT J., GARCIA R.
          "Disequilibrium econometrics for business loans"   Econometrica, vol.45,
          1977, pp.1187-1204.
          SIMULTANEOUS SYSTEM - DISEQUILIBRIUM * APPL - SECTOR : FINANCE , BANKS ,
          ASSETS * APPL - SECTOR : FINANCE , LOANS * COMPARATIVE METHODS - ESTIMATION
          : SIMULTANEOUS SYSTEM
YA2060   LAGAKOS S.W., KUHNS M.H.
          "Maximum likelihood estimation for censored exponential survival data with
          covariates"   Appl. Stats., vol.27, 1978, pp.190-197.
          REGRESSION - CENSORED * COMPUTERISATION - ESTIMATION , REGRESSION MODELS ,
          PROGRAMS * ESTIMATION - MAXIMUM LIKELIHOOD : APPL
YA2061   LAHIRI K.
          "Inflationary expectations:their formation and interest rate effects"   Am.
          Econ. Rev., vol.66, 1976, pp.124-131.
          EXPECTATIONS - DATA * INFLATION - EXPECTATIONS * INTEREST RATE - INDICATORS
          * REGRESSION - ERRORS IN VARIABLES
YA2062   LAHIRI K.
          "Multiperiod predictions in dynamic models"   Int. Econ. Rev., vol.16,
          1975, pp.699-671.
          TIME SERIES - AUTOREGRESSIVE * COMPARATIVE METHODS - ESTIMATION : REGRESSION
          , LAGGED DEPENDENT * REGRESSION - LAGGED DEPENDENT * LEAD TIME - EFFECT OF *
          DATA - SIMULATION * AUTOCORRELATION - EFFECT OF * COMPARATIVE METHODS -
          ESTIMATION : DISTRIBUTED LAG
YA2063   LAIDLER D.
          "Inflation in Britain: a monetarist perspective"   Am. Econ. Rev., vol.66,
          1976, pp.485-500.
          INFLATION - DETERMINANTS * POLICY EVALUATION - MACRO : MONETARY * APPL -
          MACRO , UK
YA2064   LAIDLER D.
          "The 1974 report of the president's council of Economic Advisers: the
          control of inflation and the future of the international monetary system"
          Am. Econ. Rev., vol.64, 1974,pp.535-543.
          INFLATION - DETERMINANTS * EX ANTE - INFLATION - GOVERNMENT CONTROLS *
          THEORY - MONETARY * POLICY EVALUATION - MACRO : FISCAL , MONETARY
YA2065   LAIDLER D., PARKIN M.
          "Inflation: a survey"   Econ. J., vol.85, 1975, pp.741-809.
          INFLATION - REVIEW * BIBLIOGRAPHY - INFLATION
YA2066   LALL S.
          "A note on government expenditures in developing countries"   Econ. J.,
          vol.79, 1969, pp.413-417.
          APPL - MACRO : DEVELOPMENT
YA2067   LAMBERT Z.V., DURAND R.M.
          "Some precautions in using canonical analysis"   J. Mktg. Res., vol.12,
          1975, pp.468-475.
          BIBLIOGRAPHY - CANONICAL CORRELATION * CANONICAL CORRELATION - REVIEW *
          EVALUATION - MULTIVARIATE METHODS , CANONICAL CORRELATION
YA2068   LAMBIN J.J.
          "A computer on-line marketing mix model"   J. Mktg. Res., vol.9, 1972,
          pp.119-126.
          MARKET SHARE - SECTOR : CONSUMER NON DURABLES * ADVERTISING - EFFECT OF *
          USER - FIRM : RETAILING * USE - MEDIA PLANNING * DISTRIBUTED LAG - APPL ,
          ADVERTISING * JUDGEMENTAL FORECASTS - INCORPORATION * APPL - SECTOR :
          CONSUMER NON DURABLES , PETROL * COMPUTERISATION - PLANNING MODELS *
          DISTRIBUTION - EFFECT OF * COMPARATIVE METHODS - REGRESSION ,
          TRANSFORMATIONS * SIMULATION - APPL : MARKETING * SIMULATION - APPL : SECTOR
          , CONSUMER NON DURABLES * APPL - FIRM : RETAILING , PETROL
YA2069   LAMBIN J.J.
          "Advertising and competitive behaviour: a case study"   Appl. Econ., vol.2,
          1970, p.231-251.
          ADVERTISING - EFFECT OF * COMPARATIVE METHODS - ESTIMATION : OLS , 2SLS *
          APPL - FIRM : CONSUMER DURABLES , APPLIANCES , ELECTRICAL * MARKET SHARE -
          SECTOR : CONSUMER DURABLES
YA2070   LAMBIN J.J.
          "Is gasoline advertising justified"   J. Business, vol.45, 1972,
          pp.585-619.
          DISTRIBUTION - EFFECT OF * ADVERTISING - EFFECT OF * APPL - SECTOR :
          CONSUMER NON DURABLES , PETROL * APPL - FIRM : CONSUMER NON DURABLES ,
          PETROL * MARKET SHARE - SECTOR : CONSUMER NON DURABLES * ADVERTISING -
          OPTIMALITY
YA2071   LAMBIN J.J.
          "Optimal allocation of competitive marketing efforts: an empirical study"
          J. Business, vol.43, 1970, pp.468-484.
          APPL - FIRM : CONSUMER DURABLES , APPLIANCES , ELECTRICAL * MARKET SHARE -
          SECTOR : CONSUMER DURABLES * PRICE - EFFECT OF * ADVERTISING - EFFECT OF *
          ADVERTISING - OPTIMALITY
YA2072   LAMBIN J.J.
          "What is the real impact of advertising?"   H.B.R., vol.53, May-June, 1975,
          pp.139-147.
          ADVERTISING - EFFECT OF , REVIEW

YA2073　LA MOTTE L.R., McWHORTER A.
"An exact test for the presence of random walk coefficients in a linear regression model"　J. Am. Statist. Ass., vol.73, 1978, pp.816-820.
REGRESSION - STATE SPACE * REGRESSION - HYPOTHESIS TESTS * SPECIFICATION ERROR - TESTS , RANDOM COEFFICIENT MODEL

YA2074　LANCASTER T.
"Redundancy, unemployment and manpower policy: a comment"　Econ. J., vol.86, 1976, pp.335-338.
REGRESSION - SUMMARY STATISTICS * REGRESSION - MODEL INTERPRETATION * PROBABILITY MOD ELS - GAMMA * APPL - MACRO : UNEMPLOYMENT

YA2075　LANDI D.M., JOHNSON B.M.K.
"Optimal linear inventory control and first order exponential smoothing"
Ops. Res., vol.15, 1967, pp.342-347.
EXPONENTIAL SMOOTHING - COEFFICIENT CHOICE * USE - INVENTORY CONTROL

YA2076　LANFORD H.W., ROSS C.B.
"Applying the envelope curve to technological forecasting and long range planning: the evaluation of the laser"　Ind. Mktg. Mgmt., vol.4, 1975, pp.1-8.
TECHNOLOGICAL FORECASTING * TREND CURVES - APPL * APPL - SECTOR : PRODUCTION , ELECTRONICS * TREND CURVES - ENVELOPE CURVES * LONG TERM FORECASTING * BASIC

YA2077　LANGASKENS Y., VAN RIJCKEGHEM W.
"A new method to estimate measurement errors in national account statistics: the Belgian case"　Int. Statist. Rev., vol.42, 1974, pp.283-290.
APPL - MACRO , BELGIUM * DATA ERRORS - ESTIMATION OF * DATA ERRORS - NATIONAL ACCOUNTS , BELGIUM

YA2078　LANSLEY P.R.
"FOCUS: a multi-purpose interactive forecasting package"　J. Mktg. Res., vol.13, 1976, pp.64-66.
SIMULATION - APPL : FIRM * COMPUTERISATION - FORECASTING , PROGRAMS

YA2079　LAPIDUS L., KILDOYLE P.P.
"Thoughts on an investment strategy for thrift institutions"　Bus. Econ., vol.10:4, 1975, pp.72-83.
BUSINESS CYCLE - EFFECT OF * USE - PORTFOLIO SELECTION * INTEREST RATE - EFFECT OF * APPL - SECTOR : FINANCE , BANKS * APPL - SECTOR : FINANCE , BUILDING SOCIETIES

YA2080　LAPP J.S.
"Market structure and advertising in the savings and loan industry"　Rev. Econ. Stats., vol.53, 1976, pp.202-208.
ADVERTISING - DETERMINANTS * CONCENTRATION - EFFECT OF * APPL - FIRM : FINANCE , BUILDING SOCIETIES * DATA - CROSS SECTION , TIME SERIES

YA2081　LAPP J.S.
"The determination of savings and loan association deposit rates in the absence of rate ceilings: a cross section approach"　J. Finance, vol.33, 1978, pp.215-230.
APPL - FIRM : FINANCE , BUILDING SOCIETIES * INTEREST RATE - DETERMINANTS * APPL - FIRM : GROWTH * STABILITY OF COEFFICIENTS - REGRESSION : APPL * DATA - CROSS SECTION

YA2082　LARRECHE J., MONTGOMERY D.B.
"A framework for the comparison of marketing models: a delphi study"　J. Mktg. Res., vol.14, 1977, pp.487-498.
USE - MARKETING POLICY * DELPHI * USER REQUIREMENTS * EVALUATION - MARKETING MODELS

YA2083　LATANE H.A., JONES C.P.
"Standardized unexpected earnings- a progress report"　J. Finance, vol.32, 1977, pp.1457-1465.
APPL - FIRM : FINANCE , STOCK PRICES * STOCK PRICES - INFORMATION EFFECT * APPL - FIRM : FINANCE , PROFITS

YA2084　LA TOURETTE J.E.
"Economies of scale and capital utilization in Canadian manufacturing"
Can. J. Econ., vol.8, 1975, pp.448-455.
PRODUCTION FUNCTIONS - SCALE RETURNS * PRODUCTION FUNCTIONS - MACRO * APPL - MACRO , CANADA * COMPARATIVE METHODS - REGRESSION , ERROR SPECIFICATION * ERROR SPECIFICATION - AUTOCORRELATED

YA2085　LA TOURETTE J.E.
"Economies of scale in Canadian manufacturing"　Appl. Econ., vol.7, 1975, pp.275-285.
PRODUCTION FUNCTIONS - MACRO * CAPACITY - EFFECT OF * APPL - MACRO , CANADA * PRODUCTION FUNCTIONS - SCALE RETURNS

YA2086　LAU L.J., LIN W., YOTOPOULOS P.A.
"The linear logarithmic expenditure system: an application to the consumption-leisure choice"　Econometrica, vol.46, 1978, pp.843-868.
EVALUATION - CONSUMER BEHAVIOUR , ECONOMIC MODELS * DEMAND EQUATIONS - SYSTEMS OF * APPL - MACRO : CONSUMER DEMAND * APPL - MACRO , SOUTH EAST ASIA * PRICE - EFFECT OF * INCOME - EFFECT OF * ADVANCED

YA2087　LAU L.J., YOTOPOULOS P.A.
"A test for relative efficiency, and application to Indian agriculture"
Am. Econ. Rev., vol.61, 1971, pp.94-109.
APPL - FIRM : AGRICULTURE , FARMING * DATA - CROSS SECTION * APPL - FIRM : FINANCE , PROFITS * APPL - FIRM : EFFICIENCY * APPL - FIRM TYPE : SMALL BUSINESS * APPL - MACRO , INDIA

YA2088   LAU S.C., QUAY S.R., RAMSEY C.M.
          "The Tokyo stock exchange and the capital asset pricing model" with
          discussion   J. Finance, vol.29, 1974, pp.507-514 & 524-526.
          THEORY - EFFICIENT MARKETS * APPL - FIRM : FINANCE , STOCK PRICES * STOCK
          PRICES - COVARIATION * STOCK PRICES - RISK * RISK - EFFECT OF * STOCK PRICES
          - MODELS , CAPM
YA2089   LAUB P.M.
          "Some aspects of the aggregation problem in the dividend-earnings
          relationship"   J. Am. Statist. Ass., vol.67, 1972, pp.552-559.
          APPL - FIRM : FINANCE , DIVIDENDS * COMPARATIVE METHODS - DATA : AGGREGATE ,
          DISAGGREGATE * PROXY VARIABLES
YA2090   LAUB P.M., WATTS R.
          "On the informational content of dividends"   J. Business, vol.49 1976,
          pp.73-80.
          APPL - FIRM : FINANCE , PROFITS * EVALUATION - PROFIT MODELS * STOCK PRICES
          - INFORMATION EFFECT * APPL - FIRM : FINANCE , STOCK PRICES * APPL - FIRM :
          FINANCE , DIVIDENDS
YA2091   LAUFENBERG D.E.
          "Reserve measures as operating variables of monetary policy: an empirical
          analysis"   J. Finance, vol.31, 1976, pp.853-864.
          APPL - MACRO : MONEY , RESERVES * APPL - MACRO : MONEY , SUPPLY * EX ANTE
YA2092   LAUMAS G.S., MEHRA Y.P.
          "The stability of the demand for money function, 1900-1974"   J. Finance,
          vol.32, 1977, pp.911-916.
          APPL - MACRO : MONEY , DEMAND * EVALUATION - REGRESSION , STATE SPACE *
          STABILITY OF COEFFICIENTS - REGRESSION
YA2093   LAUMAS P.S.
          "Monetization, economic development and the demand for money"   Rev. Econ.
          Stats., vol.60, 1978, pp.614-618.
          APPL - MACRO , INDIA * APPL - MACRO : MONEY , DEMAND * EVALUATION -
          REGRESSION , STATE SPACE
YA2094   LAUMAS P.S., MOHABBAT K.A.
          "The permanent income hypothesis: evidence from time series data"   Am.
          Econ. Rev., vol.62, 1972, pp.730-734.
          EVALUATION - PERMANENT INCOME * APPL - MACRO : CONSUMPTION
YA2095   LAURY J.S.E., LEWIS G.R., ORMEROD P.A.
          "Properties of macroeconomic models of the UK economy: a comparative study"
          Nat. Inst. Econ. Rev., no.83, 1978, pp.52-72.
          EVALUATION - MACRO MODELS * MACRO MODEL - UK , LBS * MACRO MODEL - UK ,
          NIESR * MACRO MODEL - GOVERNMENT , UK * SIMULATION - APPL : POLICY
          EVALUATION * POLICY EVALUATION - MACRO : FISCAL * POLICY EVALUATION - MACRO
          : INTERNATIONAL FINANCE , FOREIGN EXCHANGE * INTEREST RATE - EFFECT OF
YA2096   LAVE J.R., LAVE L.B., SILVERMAN L.P.
          "Hospital cost estimation: controlling for case mix"   Appl. Econ., vol.4,
          1972, pp.165-180.
          COST - SECTOR : HEALTH * HEALTH - HOSPITAL
YA2097   LAWRENCE A.J., KOTTEGODA N.T.
          "Stochastic modelling of riverflow time series" with discussion   R.
          Statist. Soc. (A), vol.140, 1977, pp.1-47.
          APPL - SECTOR : NATURAL , HYDROLOGY * BIBLIOGRAPHY - HYDROLOGY * TIME SERIES
          - ARIMA : THEORY * TIME SERIES - AUTOREGRESSIVE
YA2098   LAWRENCE R.J.
          "Consumer brand choice - a random walk?"   J. Mktg. Res., vol.12, 1975,
          pp.314-324.
          BRAND CHOICE - THEORY * MARKET SHARE - THEORY * CONSUMER BEHAVIOUR -
          STOCHASTIC MODELS , THEORY * APPL - SECTOR : CONSUMER NON DURABLES , HEALTH
          AIDS * RANDOM WALK - APPL * CONSUMER BEHAVIOUR - PSYCHOLOGICAL MODELS *
          EVALUATION - PROBABILITY MODELS , LINEAR LEARNING
YA2099   LAWRENCE R.J.
          "Snowcrop revisted"   Eur. J. Mktg., vol.9, 1975, pp.93-108.
          BRAND CHOICE - METHODOLOGY * REPEAT BUYING * CONSUMER BEHAVIOUR - STOCHASTIC
          MODELS * PROBABILITY MODELS - LINEAR LEARNING * APPL - FIRM : CONSUMER NON
          DURABLES , FOOD
YA2100   LAWRENCE R.Z.
          "An analysis of the 1977 US trade deficit" with discussion   Brookings
          Paps. Econ. Activity, 1978, pp.159-189.
          APPL - MACRO : INTERNATIONAL TRADE , EXPORTS * PRICE - EFFECT OF *
          DISTRIBUTED LAG - ALMON : APPL
YA2101   LAZAR F.
          "Regional unemployment rate disparities in Canada: some possible
          explanations"   Can. J. Econ., vol.10, 1977, pp.112-129.
          REGIONAL MODELS - MANPOWER PLANNING , UNEMPLOYMENT * MANPOWER PLANNING -
          REGIONAL * APPL - MACRO : UNEMPLOYMENT * APPL - MACRO , CANADA
YA2102   LAZAR F.
          "The input of the 1971 unemployment insurance revisions on unemployment
          rates: another look"   Can. J. Econ., vol.11, 1978, pp.559-570.
          POLICY EVALUATION - MACRO : UNEMPLOYMENT * MANPOWER PLANNING - LABOUR
          TURNOVER * POLICY EVALUATION - MACRO : WELFARE

YA2103   LEABO D.A.
          "The declining marginal propensity to save"   Bus, Econ,, vol.6:3, 1971,
          pp.25-29,
          APPL - MACRO : SAVINGS * STABILITY OF COEFFICIENTS - REGRESSION : APPL
YA2104   LEABO D.A., ROGALSKI R.J.
          "Warrant price movements and the efficient market model"   J. Finance,
          vol.30, 1975, pp.163-177,
          STOCK PRICES - WARRANTS * RANDOM WALK - TEST * APPL - FIRM : FINANCE ,
          WARRANTS * STOCK PRICES - RUNS
YA2105   LEAMER E.E.
          "A class of informative priors and distributed lag analysis"
          Econometrica, vol.40, 1972, pp.1059-1081,
          REGRESSION - PRIOR INFORMATION * BAYESIAN - PRIOR INFORMATION * DISTRIBUTED
          LAG - ESTIMATION * APPL - MACRO : INTERNATIONAL TRADE , IMPORTS *
          MULTICOLLINEARITY - REMOVAL OF * BAYESIAN - ESTIMATION : DISTRIBUTED LAG
YA2106   LEAMER E.E.
          "A result on the sign of restricted least squares estimates"   J.
          Econometrics, vol.3, 1975, pp.387-390,
          ESTIMATION - CONSTRAINED * REGRESSION - VARIABLE INCLUSION
YA2107   LEAMER E.E.
          "Empirically weighted indexes for import demand functions"   Rev, Econ,
          Stats,, vol.55, 1973, pp.441-450,
          BAYESIAN - ESTIMATION : REGRESSION * INDEX NUMBERS - METHODOLOGY *
          SUBSTITUTE PRODUCTS * DATA - AGGREGATION * PRICE - EFFECT OF * DATA ERRORS -
          INDEX NUMBERS * BAYESIAN - SPECIFICATION OF VARIABLES * APPL - MACRO :
          INTERNATIONAL TRADE , IMPORTS * BAYESIAN - PRIOR KNOWLEDGE * COMPARATIVE
          METHODS - DATA : AGGREGATE , DISAGGREGATE
YA2108   LEAMER E.E.
          "False models and post data model construction"   J. Am. Statist. Ass.,
          vol.69, 1974, pp.122-131,
          SPECIFICATION ERROR - TESTS , MODEL SELECTION * EVALUATION - MODEL SELECTION
          * BAYESIAN - MODEL SELECTION * PRIOR INFORMATION * EVALUATION - EX POST
          MODELS * THEORY - MODELLING * MODEL IDENTIFICATION
YA2109   LEAMER E.E.
          "Multicollinearity: a Bayesian interpretation"   Rev, Econ, Stats,, vol.55,
          1973, pp.371-380,
          BAYESIAN - PRIOR INFORMATION * MULTICOLLINEARITY - REVIEW * MODEL
          INTERPRETATION
YA2110   LEBANON A.
          "An oligopolistic model of the world supply of crude petroleum"   Appl,
          Econ,, vol.7, 1975, pp.9-16,
          APPL - SECTOR : PRODUCTION , PETROLEUM * DATA - CROSS SECTION , TIME SERIES
          * EX ANTE * DATA - INTERNATIONAL * SUPPLY - SECTOR : PRODUCTION
YA2111   LEE B.S.
          "Measurement of capital depreciation within the Japanese fishing fleet"
          Rev. Econ, Stats,, vol.60, 1978, pp.225-237,
          DEPRECIATION * APPL - SECTOR : AGRICULTURE , FISHING * APPL - SECTOR :
          PRODUCTION , SHIPS
YA2112   LEE C.F.
          "Functional form and the dividend effect in the electric utility industry"
          J. Finance, vol.31, 1976, pp.1481-1486,
          APPL - FIRM : UTILITIES , ELECTRICITY * APPL - FIRM : FINANCE , STOCK PRICES
          * APPL - FIRM : FINANCE , DIVIDENDS * STOCK PRICES - DETERMINANTS *
          COMPARATIVE METHODS - REGRESSION , TRANSFORMATIONS
YA2113   LEE C.F.
          "Investment horizon and the functional form of the capital asset pricing
          model"   Rev, Econ, Stats,, vol.53, 1976, pp.356-363,
          THEORY - EFFICIENT MARKETS * REGRESSION - TRANSFORMATIONS , BOX COX : APPL *
          APPL - FIRM : FINANCE , STOCK PRICES * STOCK PRICES - MODELS , CAPM
YA2114   LEE C.F., LLOYD W.P.
          "Block recursive systems in asset pricing models: an extension"   J.
          Finance, vol.33, 1978, pp.640-644,
          CLUSTER ANALYSIS - APPL * RECURSIVE SYSTEM - APPL * APPL - FIRM : FINANCE ,
          STOCK PRICES * STOCK PRICES - COVARIATION * STOCK PRICES - INDUSTRIAL
          STRUCTURE
YA2115   LEE F.
          "Estimation of dynamic demand relations from a time series of family budget
          data"   J. Am. Statist. Ass,, vol.65, 1970, pp.586-597,
          APPL - MACRO : CONSUMER DEMAND * CONSUMER BEHAVIOUR - ECONOMIC MODELS * DATA
          - CROSS SECTION , TIME SERIES * COMPARATIVE METHODS - ESTIMATION :
          REGRESSION * COMPARATIVE METHODS - ESTIMATION : OLS , 3PLS * ERROR
          SPECIFICATION - AUTOCORRELATED * APPL - MACRO , JAPAN * REGRESSION -
          ESTIMATION
YA2116   LEE J.
          "Exports and the propensity to save in L.D.C.'s"   Econ, J,, vol.81, 1971,
          pp.341-351,
          APPL - MACRO : SAVINGS * APPL - MACRO : INTERNATIONAL TRADE , EXPORTS * DATA
          - INTERNATIONAL * DATA - LDC

YA2117   LEE J.W.
"A dynamic analysis of relative share of production labour to capital"
Appl. Econ., vol.8, 1976, pp.207-214.
PRODUCTION FUNCTIONS - THEORY * PRODUCTION FUNCTIONS - SECTOR * PRODUCTION
FUNCTIONS - SUBSTITUTION

YA2118   LEE L.
"Unionism and wage rates: a simultaneous equations model with qualitative
and limited dependent variables"   Int. Econ. Rev., vol.19, 1978,
pp.415-433.
MANPOWER PLANNING - EARNINGS * SIMULTANEOUS SYSTEM - LIMITED DEPENDENT *
SIMULTANEOUS SYSTEM - QUALITATIVE DEPENDENT * UNIONISATION - DETERMINANTS *
MANPOWER PLANNING - LABOUR FORCE COMPOSITION * UNIONISATION - EFFECT OF

YA2119   LEE L., TROST R.P.
"Estimation of some limited dependent variable models with application to
housing demand"   J. Econometrics, vol.8, 1978, pp.357-382.
REGRESSION - LIMITED DEPENDENT * SIMULTANEOUS SYSTEM - DISEQUILIBRIUM *
REGRESSION - CENSORED * ESTIMATION - MAXIMUM LIKELIHOOD * APPL - SECTOR :
CONSTRUCTION, RESIDENTIAL * COMPARATIVE METHODS - ESTIMATION : REGRESSION,
LIMITED DEPENDENT

YA2120   LEE L., TYLER W.G.
"The stochastic frontier production function and average efficiency"   J.
Econometrics, vol.7, 1978, pp.385-389.
APPL - FIRM : EFFICIENCY * PRODUCTION FUNCTIONS - FIRM * PRODUCTION
FUNCTIONS - METHODOLOGY * COMPARATIVE METHODS - ESTIMATION : REGRESSION,
ERROR SPECIFICATION * ERROR DISTRIBUTION - COMPOUND * ERROR SPECIFICATION -
PRODUCTION FUNCTIONS

YA2121   LEE R.D.
"Forecasting births in post-transition populations: stochastic renewal with
serially correlated fertility"   J. Am. Statist. Ass., vol.69, 1974,
pp.607-617.
POPULATION - FERTILITY * TIME SERIES - ARIMA : APPL * BIBLIOGRAPHY -
POPULATION * EVALUATION - TIME SERIES, ARIMA * EX ANTE - EVALUATION -
POPULATION FORECASTS * SPECIFICATION ERROR - EFFECT OF, MODEL SPECIFICAION

YA2122   LEE R.D.
"National fertility, population cycles and the spectral a°nalysis of births
and marriages"   J. Am. Statist. Ass., vol.70, 1975, pp.295-304.
POPULATION * SPECTRAL ANALYSIS - APPL : POPULATION * BIBLIOGRAPHY -
POPULATION

YA2123   LEE T.C., JUDGE G.G., CAIN R.L.
"A sampling study of the properties of estimators of transition
probabilities"   Mgmt. Sci. (A), vol 15, 1969, pp.374-398.
MARKOV MODELS - ESTIMATION * ESTIMATION - MAXIMUM LIKELIHOOD : APPL *
BIBLIOGRAPHY - MARKOV MODELS * ESTIMATION - CONSTRAINED : APPL * COMPARATIVE
METHODS - ESTIMATION : MARKOV MODELS * DATA - SIMULATION

YA2124   LEE T.H.
"Housing and permanent income: tests based on a three-year reinterview
survey"   Rev. Econ. Stats., vol.50, 1968, pp.480-490.
INCOME - EFFECT OF, PERMANENT * APPL - SECTOR : CONSTRUCTION, RESIDENTIAL
* REGRESSION - ERRORS IN VARIABLES : APPL * COMPARATIVE METHODS - INCOME
ELASTICITY, ESTIMATION * COMPARATIVE METHODS - ESTIMATION : REGRESSION,
ERRORS IN VARIABLES * DATA ERRORS - EFFECT OF

YA2125   LEE T.H., ET AL.
"On measuring the nearness of near moneys: comments"   Am. Econ. Rev.,
vol.62, 1972, pp.217-229.
APPL - MACRO : MONEY * DATA - SPECIFICATION OF VARIABLES

YA2126   LEE Y.
"Some results on the sampling distribution of the multiple correlation
coefficient"   R. Statist. Soc. (B), vol.33, 1971, pp.117-130.
REGRESSION - SUMMARY STATISTICS * ADVANCED

YA2127   LEECH D.
"Testing the error specification in non linear regression"   Econometrica,
vol.43, 1975, pp.719-725.
ERROR SPECIFICATION - NON LINEAR MODEL * SPECIFICATION ERROR - TESTS, ERROR
SPECIFICATION * PRODUCTION FUNCTIONS - MACRO * ERROR SPECIFICATION -
MULTIPLICATIVE * REGRESSION - TRANSFORMATIONS * APPL - MACRO, USSR *
REGRESSION - NON LINEAR

YA2128   LEGER A.S.St.
"Comparison of two tests for seasonality in epidemiological data"   Appl.
Stats., vol.25, 1976, pp.280-286.
SEASONALITY - TESTING * HEALTH - DISEASE, INCIDENCE OF

YA2129   LEHMANN D.R.
"Judged similarity, and brand-switching data as similarity measures"   J.
Mktg. Res., vol.9, 1972, pp.331-334.
BRAND CHOICE - METHODOLOGY * CONSUMER BEHAVIOUR - STOCHASTIC MODEL,
METHODOLOGY * MARKET SEGMENTATION * MULTIDIMENSIONAL SCALING

YA2130   LEIGH D.E., RAWLINS V.L.
"Racial differentials in male unemployment rates: evidence from low-income
urban areas"   Rev. Econ. Stats., vol.56, 1974, pp.150-157.
MANPOWER PLANNING - UNEMPLOYMENT * DATA - CROSS SECTION * EDUCATION - EFFECT
OF * PUBLIC EXPENDITURE - EFFECT OF, AID PROGRAMS * MANPOWER PLANNING -
LABOUR FORCE COMPOSITION * MANPOWER PLANNING - DISCRIMINATION, RACIAL

YA2131 LEIPZIGER P.M.
"Capital movements and economic policy: Canada under a flexible exchange rate" Can. J. Econ., vol.7, 1974, pp.59-74.
APPL - MACRO : INTERNATIONAL FINANCE * EXCHANGE RATE - EFFECT OF * POLICY EVALUATION - MACRO : FISCAL , MONETARY

YA2132 LEITCH R.A., PAULSON A.S.
"Estimation of stable law parameters: stock price behaviour application" J. Am. Statist. Ass., vol.70, 1975, pp.690-697.
ERROR DISTRIBUTION - STABLE * APPL - FIRM : FINANCE , STOCK PRICES * STOCK PRICES - DISTRIBUTION * ESTIMATION - ERROR DISTRIBUTION , STABLE

YA2133 LEONTIEF W.
"Structure of the world economy" Am. Econ. Rev., vol.64, 1974, pp.823-834.
INPUT OUTPUT - MACRO , WORLD

YA2134 LeROY S.F., WAUD R.N.
"Applications of the Kalman filter in short run monetary control" Int. Econ. Rev., vol.18, 1977, pp.195-207.
POLICY EVALUATION - MACRO : MONETARY * ESTIMATION - KALMAN FILTER

YA2135 LERVIKS A.
"Forecasting new consumer durables by market segmentation" Eur. J. Mktg., vol.10, 1976, pp.257-265.
NEW PRODUCTS - EVALUATION * MARKET SEGMENTATION * APPL - FIRM : CONSUMER DURABLES - SIMULATION - APPL : NEW PRODUCTS * SIMULATION - APPL : MARKETING * PRICE - EFFECT OF * ADVERTISING - EFFECT OF

YA2136 L'ESPERANCE W.L., CHALL D., TAYLOR D.
"An algorithm for determining the distribution function of the Durbin-Watson test statistic" Econometrica, vol.44, 1976, pp.1325-1326.
COMPUTERISATION - DIAGNOSTIC TESTS , PROGRAMS * AUTOCORRELATION - TEST

YA2137 L'ESPERANCE W.L., TAYLOR D.
"The power of four tests of autocorrelation in the linear regression model" J. Econometrics, vol.3, 1975, pp.1-21 & 405.
COMPARATIVE METHODS - TESTS , AUTOCORRELATION * ERROR SPECIFICATION - AUTOCORRELATED

YA2138 LESSARD D.R.
"World, national and industry factors in equity returns" J. Finance, vol.29, 1974, pp.379-398.
STOCK PRICES - COVARIATION * EX ANTE * FACTOR ANALYSIS - APPL * THEORY - EFFICIENT MARKETS * STOCK PRICES - INDUSTRIAL STRUCTURE * STOCK PRICES - MODELS , INTERNATIONAL

YA2139 LEUTHOLD R.M.
"On the use of Theil's inequality coefficients" Am. J. Ag. Econ., vol.57, 1975, pp.344-346.
LOSS FUNCTIONS - THEIL

YA2140 LEUTHOLD R.M.
"Random walk and price trends: the live cattle futures market" J. Finance, vol.27, 1972, pp.879-889.
SPECTRAL ANALYSIS - APPL : SECTOR , COMMODITIES * APPLICATION - SECTOR : COMMODITIES , LIVESTOCK * RANDOM WALK - TEST * LOSS FUNCTIONS - SECTOR : FINANCE , TRADING RULES

YA2141 LEUTHOLD R.M., ET AL.
"Forecasting daily hog prices and quantities: a study of alternative forecasting models" J. Am. Statist. Ass., vol.65, 1970, pp.90-107.
APPL - SECTOR : AGRICULTURE , LIVESTOCK , HOGS * TIME SERIES - ARIMA : APPL * COMPARATIVE METHODS - ARIMA , CAUSAL * PRICE - SECTOR : AGRICULTURE

YA2142 LEV B.
"A note on the analysis of peak demand forecasts of an electrical utility" Ops. Res., vol.18, 1970, pp.174-179.
EVALUATION - ELECTRICITY DEMAND FORECASTS * EXTREME VALUES * APPL - FIRM : UTILITIES , ELECTRICITY * EX ANTE * LEAD TIME - EFFECT OF

YA2143 LEV B.
"The RAS method for two dimensional forecasts" J. Mktg. Res., vol.10, 1973, pp.153-159.
FORECASTING - MULTISTAGE * INPUT OUTPUT - PROJECTION OF STRUCTURE * DATA - DISAGGREGATION * LOSS FUNCTIONS - INFORMATION CRITERION : APPL * FORECAST - AGGREGATION

YA2144 LEV B., PEKELMAN D.
"A multiperiod adjustment model for the firm's capital structure" J. Finance, vol.30, 1975, pp.75-91.
SIMULATION - APPL : FINANCE * APPL - FIRM : FINANCE

YA2145 LEVHARI D., LEVY H.
"The Capital Asset Pricing Model and the investment horizon" Rev. Econ. Stats., vol.59, 1977, pp.92-104.
STOCK PRICES - BETA * APPL - FIRM : FINANCE , STOCK PRICES * STOCK PRICES - THEORY * STOCK PRICES - MODELS , CAPM

YA2146 LEVHARI D., SHESHINSKI E.
"Experience and productivity in the Israeli diamond industry" Econometrica, vol.41, 1973, pp.239-253.
APPL - SECTOR : PRODUCTION , DIAMONDS * LEARNING CURVE * PRODUCTION FUNCTIONS - SECTOR

YA2147   LEVI M.D.
"Errors in the variables bias in the presence of correctly measured
variables" Econometrica, vol.41, 1973, pp.985-986.
DATA ERRORS - EFFECT OF * REGRESSION - ERRORS IN VARIABLES

YA2148   LEVI M.D.
"The weekend game: clearing house vs. federal funds" Can. J. Econ.,
vol.11, 1978, pp.750-757.
APPL - MACRO : INTERNATIONAL FINANCE , EXCHANGE RATES * APPL - MACRO ,
CANADA

YA2149   LEVIN F.J.
"Examination of the money-stock control approach of Burger, Kalish and Babb"
J. Money, Credit, Banking, vol.5, 1973, pp.924-938.
APPL - MACRO : MONEY , SUPPLY * EX ANTE * EVALUATION - MONEY SUPPLY , MODELS
OF * EX ANTE * EXOGENOUS VARIABLES - PREDICTION OF , EFFECT

YA2150   LEVIN R.C.
"Allocation in surface freight transportation: does rate regulation matter?"
Bell, J. Econ., vol.9, 1978, pp.18-45.
-REGRESSION - LIMITED DEPENDENT, LOGIT * APPL - SECTOR : TRANSPORT , RAIL *
APPL - SECTOR : TRANSPORT , ROAD , FREIGHT * TIME - VALUE OF * USE -
TRANSPORT PLANNING * USE - FINANCIAL , REGULATION

YA2151   LEVY F.K., MANSFIELD E., BRANDENBURG R.
"The allocation, characteristics and outcome of the firm's research and
development portfolio" J. Business, vol.41, 1968, pp.89-93.
APPL - FIRM : R & D * EVALUATION - JUDGEMENTAL FORECASTS , R & D

YA2152   LEVY M.B., WADYCKI W.J.
"Education and the decision to migrate: an econometric analysis of migration
in Venezuela" Econometrica, vol.42, 1974, pp.377-388.
MANPOWER PLANNING - REGIONAL * COMPARATIVE METHODS - REGRESSION , SEEMINGLY
UNRELATED * REGIONAL MODELS - MANPOWER PLANNING , MIGRATION * EDUCATION -
EFFECT OF

YA2153   LEVY M.B., WADYCKI W.J.
"The influence of family and friends on geographical labour mobility: an
international comparison" Rev. Econ. Stats., vol.55, 1973, pp.198-203.
MANPOWER PLANNING - REGIONAL * REGIONAL MODELS - MANPOWER PLANNING ,
MIGRATION * APPL - MACRO , INDIA * APPL - MACRO , LATIN AMERICA

YA2154   LEVY R.A.
"The predictive significance of five-point chart patterns" J. Business,
vol.44, 1971, pp.316-323.
STOCK PRICES - TECHNICAL ANALYSIS * EVALUATION - JUDGEMENTAL FORECASTS ,
STOCK PRICES * APPL - FIRM : FINANCE , STOCK PRICES

YA2155   LEWANDOWSKI R.
"INCOM: A general system for medium and long-range forecasting" Ind.
Mktg. Mgmt., vol.1, 1971, pp.103-121, 132-142, & 377-385.
COMPUTERISATION - FORECASTING , PROGRAMS * TREND CURVES - APPL * FORECASTING
- REVIEW

YA2156   LEWANDOWSKI R.
"Life cycle forecasting methods" Ind. Mktg. Mgmt., vol.2, 1972, pp.87-91
& 208-215.
LIFE CYCLE - PRODUCT * TREND CURVES - REVIEW

YA2157   LEWIS C.D.
"Monitoring a forecasting system - letter" Opl. Res. Q., vol.19, 1968,
p.96.
EXPONENTIAL SMOOTHING - ADAPTIVE COEFFICIENTS * TRACKING SIGNAL - APPL *
BASIC

YA2158   LEWIS C.D.
"This year's non-deliberate mistake creates a generalised gamma periods
ahead forecast nomogram" Opl. Res. Q., vol.23, 1972, pp.87-89.
EXPONENTIAL SMOOTHING - GRAPHICAL

YA2159   LEWIS K.A.
"An econometric analysis of the demand for textile fibres" Am. J. Ag.
Econ., vol.54, 1972, pp.238-244.
APPL - SECTOR : PRODUCTION , TEXTILES * EX ANTE * PRICE - EFFECT OF * INCOME
- EFFECT OF

YA2160   LEWIS K.A., BREEN F.F.
"Empirical issues in the demand for currency: a multinational study" J.
Finance, vol.30, 1975, pp.1065-1079.
APPL - MACRO : MONEY , DEMAND * DATA - INTERNATIONAL * INCOME - EFFECT OF *
INFLATION - EFFECT OF

YA2161   LEWIS S.D.
"Factor input demand and implied production functions" Appl. Econ.,
vol.4, 1972, pp.1-9.
EX ANTE * EVALUATION - PRODUCTION FUNCTIONS * PRODUCTION FUNCTIONS - MACRO *
APPL - MACRO : EARNINGS

YA2162   LI M.M.
"A logit model of homeownership" Econometrica, vol.45, 1977,
pp.1081-1097.
APPL - SECTOR : CONSTRUCTION , RESIDENTIAL * LIFE CYCLE - CONSUMER *
REGRESSION - LIMITED DEPENDENT , LOGIT

YA2163   LIANOS T.P., RAUSSER G.C.
         "Approximate distribution of parameters in a distributed lag model"   J.
         Am. Statist. Ass., vol.67, 1972, pp.64-67.
         DISTRIBUTED LAG - HYPOTHESIS TESTS * DATA - SIMULATION * REGRESSION -
         HYPOTHESIS TESTS

YA2164   LIBBY R.
         "Accounting ratios and the prediction of failure: some behavioural evidence"
         J. Acctg. Res., vol.13, 1975, pp.150-161.
         USE - BANKRUPTCY PREDICTION * JUDGEMENTAL FORECASTS - AGGREGATION *
         EVALUATION - JUDGEMENTAL FORECASTS

YA2165   LIEBERMAN C.
         "The transactions demand for money and technological change"   Rev. Econ.
         Stats., vol.59, 1977, pp.307-317.
         APPL - MACRO : MONEY , DEMAND * REGRESSION - SPECIFICATION OF VARIABLES *
         WEALTH - EFFECT OF * INCOME - EFFECT OF , PERMANENT

YA2166   LIEBLING H.I., BIDWELL P.T., HALL K.E.
         "The recent performance of anticipations surveys and econometric model
         projections of investment spending in the US"   J. Business, vol.49, 1976,
         pp.451-477.
         MACRO MODEL - DATA RESOURCES * APPL - MACRO : INVESTMENT * MACRO MODEL -
         CHASE * MACRO MODEL - WHARTON * EVALUATION - INVESTMENT MODELS * EVALUATION
         - INVESTMENT FORECASTS * EX ANTE * LEAD TIME - EFFECT OF * EVALUATION -
         EXPECTATIONS , DATA * EVALUATION - SURVEYS , BUSINESS * EVALUATION - MACRO
         MODELS * COMPARATIVE METHODS - MACRO MODELS * COMPARATIVE METHODS -
         CAUSAL(SIMULTANEOUS SYSTEM) , SURVEYS

YA2167   LIEBMAN L., LEE E.
         "Reach and frequency estimating services"   J. Advtg. Res., vol.14:4, 1974,
         pp.23-25.
         EVALUATION - ADVERTISING EXPOSURE MODELS

YA2168   LIEW C.K.
         "A computer program for dynamic multipliers"   Econometrica, vol.41, 1973,
         p.1207.
         COMPUTERISATION - SIMULATION , PROGRAMS * SIMULATION - DYNAMIC PROPERTIES *
         MULTIPLIERS - METHODOLOGY

YA2169   LIEW C.K.
         "Inequality constrained least squares estimation"   J. Am. Statist. Ass.,
         vol.71, 1976, pp.746-751.
         ESTIMATION - CONSTRAINED * DATA - SIMULATION * COMPARATIVE METHODS -
         ESTIMATION : REGRESSION , CONSTRAINED * APPL - SECTOR : UTILITIES ,
         ELECTRICITY

YA2170   LIEW C.K., SHIM J.K.
         "A computer program for inequality constrained least squares estimation"
         Econometrica, vol.46, 1978, pp.237-239.
         COMPUTERISATION - ESTIMATION , REGRESSION MODELS , PROGRAMS * ESTIMATION -
         CONSTRAINED * REGRESSION - ESTIMATION

YA2171   LILIEN G.L.
         "Application of a modified linear learning model of buyer behaviour"   J.
         Mktg. Res., vol.11, 1974, pp.279-285.
         PROBABILITY MODELS - BERNOULLI , COMPOUND * CONSUMER BEHAVIOUR - STOCHASTIC
         MODELS * BRAND CHOICE - METHODOLOGY * EX ANTE * APPL - SECTOR : RETAILING ,
         GASOLINE * PRICE - EFFECT OF * CONSUMER BEHAVIOUR - PURCHASING ,
         DETERMINANTS * PROBABILITY MODELS - LINEAR LEARNING * USE - PRICING *
         EVALUATION - CONSUMER BEHAVIOUR , STOCHASTIC MODELS

YA2172   LILIEN G.L., RAO A.G.
         "A model for manpower management"   Mgmt. Sci. (B), vol.21, 1975,
         pp.1447-1457.
         MANPOWER PLANNING - FIRM * MANPOWER PLANNING - QUALIFIED MANPOWER * MARKOV
         MODELS - APPL : MANPOWER

YA2173   LIM D.
         "Capital utilisation of local and foreign establishments in Malaysian
         manufacturing"   Rev. Econ. Stats., vol.53, 1976, pp.209-217.
         APPL - MACRO : CAPACITY UTILISATION * APPL - MACRO , SOUTH EAST ASIA

YA2174   LIN T.
         "The identification problem with the Houthakker-Taylor model"   Rev. Econ.
         Stats., vol.56, 1974, pp.406-409.
         ESTIMATION - CONSTRAINED * COMPARATIVE METHODS - ESTIMATION : REGRESSION *
         COMPARATIVE METHODS - ESTIMATION : OLS , 3PLS

YA2175   LINDLEY D.V., SMITH A.F.M.
         "Bayes estimates for the linear model" with discussion   R. Statist. Soc.
         (B), vol.34, 1972, pp.1-41.
         BAYESIAN - ESTIMATION : REGRESSION * REGRESSION - RIDGE * COMPARATIVE
         METHODS - ESTIMATION : REGRESSION * COMPARATIVE METHODS - ESTIMATION : OLS ,
         BAYES * REGRESSION - ESTIMATION * COMPARATIVE METHODS - ESTIMATION : OLS ,
         RIDGE * ADVANCED

YA2176   LINDLEY R.M.
         "Inter-industry mobility of male employees in Great Britain, 1959-68"   R.
         Statist. Soc. (A), vol.139, 1976, pp.56-79.
         MARKOV MODELS - APPL : MANPOWER * MANPOWER PLANNING - INDUSTRIAL MOBILITY

YA2177 LINDVALL J.R.
"New issue corporate bonds, seasoned market efficiency and yield spreads"
J. Finance, vol.32, 1977 pp.1057-1067.
APPL - FIRM : FINANCE , BONDS * BUSINESS CYCLE - EFFECT OF * COMPARATIVE
METHODS - REGRESSION , ERROR SPECIFICATION * NEW PRODUCTS - NEW BRANDS

YA2178 LING R.F., ROBERTS H.V.
"IDA: an approach to interactive data analysis in teaching and research"
J. Business, vol.48, 1975, pp.411-451.
COMPUTERISATION - ESTIMATION , REGRESSION MODELS , PROGRAMS * MIS * DATA -
HANDLING

YA2179 LINGLE R.C., JONES E.B.
"Women's increasing unemployment: a cross-sectional analysis" with
discussion Am. Econ. Ass. Proc., 1978, pp.84-89 & 95-98.
APPL - MACRO * UNEMPLOYMENT * MANPOWER PLANNING - UNEMPLOYMENT * MANPOWER
PLANNING - DISCRIMINATION , SEXUAL * STABILITY OF COEFFICIENTS - REGRESSION
: APPL * DATA - CROSS SECTION

YA2180 LINK C.R.
"Graduate education, school quality, experience, student ability and
earnings" J. Business, vol.48, 1975, pp.477-491.
EDUCATION - EFFECT OF * MANPOWER PLANNING - EARNINGS * MANPOWER PLANNING -
QUALIIFIED MANPOWER , GRADUATES

YA2181 LINK C.R.
"The quantity and quality of education and their influence on earnings: the
case of chemical engineers" Rev. Econ. Stats., vol.55, 1973, pp.241-247.
MANPOWER PLANNING - SECTOR : PRODUCTION * APPL - SECTOR : PRODUCTION ,
CHEMICALS * MANPOWER PLANNING - EARNINGS * APPL - SECTOR : EARNINGS -
EDUCATION - EFFECT OF * MANPOWER PLANNING - QUALIFIED MANPOWER , ENGINEERS

YA2182 LINK C.R, RATLEDGE E.C.
"The influence of the quantity and quality of education on black-white
earnings differentials: some new evidence" Rev. Econ. Stats., vol.57,
1975, pp.346-350.
EDUCATION - EFFECT OF * MANPOWER PLANNING - EARNINGS * MANPOWER PLANNING -
DISCRIMINATION , RACIAL

YA2183 LINK C.R., RATLEDGE E.C.
"Useful interactions in econometric models: the case of black/white earnings
differentials" Appl. Econ., vol.9, 1977, pp.83-91.
MANPOWER PLANNING - DISCRIMINATION , RACIAL * AID - APPL * COMPARATIVE
METHODS - REGRESSION , MULTIVARIATE METHODS * EDUCATION - EFFECT OF *
MANPOWER PLANNING - EARNINGS

YA2184 LINNEMAN R.E., KENNEL J.D.
"Shirt-sleeve approach to long-range plans" H.B.R., vol.55, Mar-April,
1977, pp.141-150.
USE - CORPORATE PLANNING * TECHNOLOGICAL FORECASTING * LONG TERM FORECASTING
* BASIC

YA2185 LINTNER J.
"Inflation and security returns" J. Finance, vol.30, 1975, pp.259-280.
STOCK PRICES - REVIEW * INFLATION - EFFECT OF

YA2186 LIPSTEIN B.
"Modelling and new product birth" J. Advtg. Res., vol.10:5, 1970,
pp.3-11.
NEW PRODUCTS - NEW BRAND * BRAND CHOICE - INTRODUCTION * CONSUMER BEHAVIOUR
- STOCHASTIC MODELS * APPL - FIRM : CONSUMER NON DURABLES , GROCERIES *
MARKOV MODELS - APPL : BRAND CHOICE

YA2187 LISSITZ R.W.
"Comparison of the small sample power of the chi-square and likelihood ratio
tests of the assumption for stochastic models" J. Am. Statist. Ass.,
vol.67, 1972, pp.574-577.
COMPARATIVE METHODS - ESTIMATION : MARKOV MODELS * MARKOV MODELS -
ESTIMATION

YA2188 LITTLE B., MOORE R.A.
"Sales forecast errors for new product projects" Ind. Mktg. Mgmt., vol.7,
1978, pp.49-53.
EVALUATION - NEW PRODUCT FORECASTS * BASIC

YA2189 LITTLE J.D.C.
"BRANDAID: A marketing mix model" Ops. Res., vol.23, 1975, pp.628-673.
ADVERTISING - EFFECT OF * DISTRIBUTION - EFFECT OF * USE - PROMOTION
EVALUATION * MARKET SHARE - METHODOLOGY * APPL - FIRM : CONSUMER NON
DURABLES , GROCERIES * USE - MARKETING POLICY * STRIKE - EFFECT OF * USER
REQUIREMENTS * PRICE - EFFECT OF * USE - MEDIA PLANNING * USE - SALES FORCE
MANAGEMENT

YA2190 LITTLE J.D.C., LODISH L.M.
"A media planning calculus" Ops. Res., vol.17, 1969, pp.1-35.
USE - MEDIA PLANNING * BIBLIOGRAPHY - ADVERTISING , MEDIA PLANNING *
ADVERTISING - EXPOSURE

YA2191 LITZENBERGER R.H., RAO C.V.
"Estimates of the marginal rate of time preference and average risk aversion
of investors in electric utility shares: 1960-66. Bell J. Econ., vol.2,
1971, pp.265-277.
APPL - FIRM : FINANCE , CAPITALISATION * APPL - FIRM : UTILITIES ,
ELECTRICITY * STOCK PRICES - RISK

YA2192   LIU B.
"Differential net migration rates and the quality of life"   Rev. Econ.
Stats., vol.57, 1975, pp.329-337.
QUALITY - EFFECT OF * REGIONAL MODELS - MANPOWER PLANNING , MIGRATION *
EDUCATION - EFFECT OF * INDEX NUMBERS - SECTOR : SOCIAL * MANPOWER PLANNING
- REGIONAL

YA2193   LIU T.
"A monthly recursive econometric model of US: a test of feasibility"   Rev.
Econ. Stats., vol.51, 1969, pp.1-13.
MACRO MODEL - LIU(MONTHLY) * ERROR SPECIFICATION - AUTOCORRELATED

YA2194   LIU T., HWA E.
"A monthly econometric model of the US economy"   Int. Econ. Rev., vol.15,
1974, pp.38-365.
MACRO MODEL - LIU(MONTHLY) * EVALUATION - MACRO MODELS * EX ANTE * LEAD TIME
- EFFECT OF * EVALUATION - EX POST MODELS * MACRO MODEL - BEA * MACRO MODEL
- * WHARTON

YA2195   LIVESEY D.A.
"Optimising short-term economic policy"   Econ. J., vol.81, 1971,
pp.525-546.
MACRO MODEL - UK * DIFFERENTIAL EQUATIONS - STOCHASTIC * SIMULTANEOUS SYSTEM
- CONTINUOUS * ESTIMATION - NON LINEAR * EX ANTE * CONTROL THEORY -
STOCHASTIC , METHODOLOGY * POLICY EVALUATION - MACRO * SIMULTANEOUS SYSTEM -
CONTROL * SIMULATION - APPL : POLICY EVALUATION

YA2196   LIVESEY F.
"A note on forecasting the market demand for waste paper"   Long Range
Planning, vol.11:1, 1978, pp.87-88.
APPL - SECTOR : PRODUCTION , PAPER , WASTE

YA2197   LIVIATAN N.
"Estimates of distributed lag consumption functions from cross section data"
Rev. Econ. Stats., vol.47, 1965, pp.44-53.
APPL - MACRO : CONSUMPTION * COMPARATIVE METHODS - ESTIMATION : DISTRIBUTED
LAG * INCOME - EFFECT OF * ESTIMATION - INSTRUMENTAL VARIABLES * DISTRIBUTED
LAG - CROSS SECTION DATA * DATA - CROSS SECTION

YA2198   LIVINGSTON M.
"Industry movements of common stocks"   J. Finance, vol.32, 1977,
pp.861-874.
APPL - FIRM : FINANCE , STOCK PRICES * STOCK PRICES - INDUSTRIAL STRUCTURE *
FACTOR ANALYSIS - APPL * STOCK PRICES - COVARIATION

YA2199   LLEWELLYN G.E.J.
"The determinants of UK import prices"   Econ. J., vol.84, 1974, pp.18-31.
APPL - MACRO , UK * APPL - MACRO : INTERNATIONAL TRADE , IMPORTS * INFLATION
- EFFECT OF * APPL - MACRO : INTERNATIONAL TRADE , PRICE

YA2200   LLEWELLYN G.E.J., PESARAN M.H.
"The determinants of UK import prices - a note"   Econ. J., vol.86, 1976,
pp.315-320.
APPL - MACRO , UK * APPL - MACRO : INTERNATIONAL TRADE , IMPORTS * APPL -
MACRO : INTERNATIONAL TRADE , PRICE

YA2201   LLOYD C.B., NIEMI B.
"Sex differences in labour supply elasticity: the implications of sectoral
shifts in demand" with discussion   Am. Econ. Ass. Proc., 1978, pp.78-83 &
95-98.
MANPOWER PLANNING - MACRO , SUPPLY * MANPOWER PLANNING - LABOUR
PARTICIPATION , FEMALE * MANPOWER PLANNING - LABOUR FORCE COMPOSITION *
MANPOWER PLANNING - EARNINGS

YA2202   LLOYD R.A.
"Combine forecasting methods for demand estimates"   Ind. Mktg. Mgmt.,
vol.5, 1976, pp.89-93.
FORECASTING - INTRODUCTION * BASIC

YA2203   LLOYD W.P., LEE C.F.
"Block recursive systems in asset pricing models"   J. Finance, vol.31,
1976, pp.1101-1113.
APPL - FIRM : FINANCE , STOCK PRICES * FACTOR ANALYSIS - APPL * STOCK PRICES
- INDUSTRIAL STRUCTURE * RECURSIVE SYSTEMS - APPL * STOCK PRICES -
COVARIATION

YA2204   LLUCH C., WILLIAMS R.
"Consumer demand systems and aggregate consumption in the USA: an
application of the extended linear expenditure system"   Can. J. Econ.,
vol.8, 1975, pp.49-66.
APPL - MACRO : CONSUMER DEMAND * DEMAND EQUATIONS - SYSTEMS OF * COMPARATIVE
METHODS - ESTIMATION : DEMAND EQUATIONS * CONSUMER BEHAVIOUR - ECONOMIC
MODELS * INCOME - EFFECT OF * PRICE - EFFECT OF

YA2205   LLUCH C., WILLIAMS R.
"Cross-country demand and savings patterns: an application of the extended
linear expenditure system"   Rev. Econ. Stats., vol.57, 1975, pp.320-328.
DATA - LDC * DEMAND EQUATIONS - SYSTEMS OF * CONSUMER BEHAVIOUR - ECONOMIC
MODELS * DATA - INTERNATIONAL * DATA - CROSS SECTION , TIME SERIES * INCOME
- EFFECT OF * PRICE - EFFECT OF * PRICE - EFFECT OF , DETERMINANTS * INCOME
- EFFECT OF , DETERMINANTS * APPL - MACRO : SAVINGS

YA2206   LODISH L.M.
          "A note on modelling the relationship of diminishing returns to media
          overlap for the media planning problem"   Mgmt. Sci., vol.22, 1976,
          pp.111=115.
          USE = MEDIA PLANNING * CONSUMER BEHAVIOUR = STOCHASTIC MODELS
YA2207   LODISH L.M.
          "Exposure interactions among media schedules"   J. Advtg. Res., vol.13:2,
          1973, pp.31=34.
          ADVERTISING = EXPOSURE
YA2208   LODISH L.M.
          "'Vaguely right' approach to sales force allocations"   H.B.R., vol.52,
          Jan=Feb, 1974, pp.119=124.
          USE = SALES AREA ALLOCATION * BASIC
YA2209   LODISH L.M., PEKELMAN D.
          "Increasing precision of marketing experiments by matching sales areas"
          J. Mktg. Res., vol.15, 1978, pp.449=455.
          USE = PROMOTION EVALUATION * USE = TARGET SETTING * USE = SALES AREA
          ALLOCATION * ADVERTISING = EXPERIMENTAL DESIGN * ADVERTISING = EFFECT OF
YA2210   LOEB M.
          "Comments on budget forecasting and operating performance"   J. Acctg.
          Res., vol.12, 1974, pp.362=366.
          LOSS FUNCTIONS = FIRM * USE = FORECASTER EVALUATION * BASIC
YA2211   LOEB P.D.
          "Specification error tests and investment functions"   Econometrica,
          vol.44, 1976, pp.185=194.
          APPL = SECTOR : INVESTMENT * SPECIFICATION ERROR = TESTS , MODEL SELECTION *
          EVALUATION = INVESTMENT MODELS
YA2212   LOGUE D.E., SWEENEY R.J.
          "'White noise' in imperfect markets: the case of the franc/dollar exchange
          rate"   J. Finance, vol.32, 1977, pp.761=768.
          APPL = MACRO , FRANCE & APPL = MACRO : INTERNATIONAL FINANCE , EXCHANGE
          RATES * EVALUATION = SPECTRAL ANALYSIS3 * RANDOM WALK = TEST , TRADING RULE
YA2213   LOGUE D.E., WILLETT T.D.
          "A note on the relation between the rate and variability of inflation"
          Economica, vol.43, 1976, pp.151=158.
          INFLATION = INDICATORS * VOLATILITY = EFFECT OF * DATA = INTERNATIONAL
YA2214   LOMBRA R., KAUFMAN H.M.
          "Interest rate seasonality and the specification of money demand functions"
          Rev. Econ. Stats., vol.57, 1975, pp.252=255.
          INTEREST RATE = SEASONALITY * APPL = MACRO : MONEY , REAL CASH BALANCES *
          INTEREST RATE = EFFECT OF
YA2215   LOMBRA R., TORTO R.G.
          "Measuring the impact of monetary and fiscal actions: a new look at the
          specification problems"   Rev. Econ. Stats., vol.56, 1974, pp.104=106.
          APPL = MACRO : GNP * APPL = MACRO : MONEY , SUPPLY * MODEL INTERPRETATION *
          POLICY EVALUATION = MACRO : FISCAL , MONETARY
YA2216   LONG R.
          "Forecasting specific turning points"   J. Am. Statist. Ass., vol.65, 1970,
          pp.520=521.
          EVALUATION = BUSINESS INDICATORS * EVALUATION = TURNING POINT FORECASTS
YA2217   LONGBOTTOM D.A.
          "The application of decision analysis to a new product planning decision"
          Opl. Res. Q., vol.24, 1973, pp.9=17.
          APPL = SECTOR : PRODUCTION , REFRIGERATION * NEW PRODUCTS = EVALUATION *
          MARKET SHARE = SECTOR : PRODUCTION * JUDGEMENTAL FORECASTS = METHODOLOGY *
          USER = FIRM : PRODUCTION
YA2218   LONGBRAKE W.A.
          "Computers and the cost of producing various types of banking services"
          J. Business, vol.47, 1974, pp.363=381.
          APPL = FIRM : FINANCE , BANKS * COST = SECTOR : FINANCE , BANKS *
          COMPUTERISATION = EFFECT OF * APPL = FIRM : FINANCE , BANK , LIABILITIES *
          APPL = FIRM : FINANCE , BANK , ASSETS * APPL = FIRM : FINANCE , CONSUMER
          CREDIT
YA2219   LONGLEY J.W.
          "An appraisal of least squares programs for the electronic computer from the
          point of view of the user"   J. Am. Statist. Ass., vol.62, 1967,
          pp.819=841.
          COMPUTERISATION = CALCULATION ERROR * MULTICOLLINEARITY = EFFECT OF *
          COMPUTERISATION = ESTIMATION , REGRESSION MODELS
YA2220   LOOKABILL L.L.
          "Some additional evidence on time series properties of accounting earnings"
          Acctg. Rev., vol.51, 1976, pp.724=738.
          APPL = FIRM : FINANCE , PROFITS * TIME SERIES = ARIMA : APPL
YA2221   LORANGER J.
          "Elasticite de substitution et rendements dans l'industrie manufacturiere
          Canadienne"   Can. J. Econ., vol.8, 1975, pp.520=535.
          DISTRIBUTED LAG = IDENTIFICATION * ERROR SPECIFICATION = AUTOCORRELATED *
          DISTRIBUTED LAG = ALMON * COMPARATIVE METHODS = DISTRIBUTED LAG , ERROR
          SPECIFICATION * PRODUCTION FUNCTIONS = SUBSTITUTION * PRODUCTION FUNCTIONS =
          MACRO * EVALUATION = DISTRIBUTED LAG , MODEL SPECIFICATION * APPL = MACRO ,
          CANADA *

YA2222 LORANGER J.
"Problems of identification and estimation of the demand for capital"
Rev. Econ. Stats., vol.53, 1976, pp.173-188.
APPL - MACRO , CANADA * APPL - MACRO : INVESTMENT * PRODUCTION FUNCTIONS -
MACRO * SUBSTITUTE FACTORS

YA2223 LOREK K.S., McDONALD C.L., PATZ D.H.
"A comparative examination of management forecasts and Box-Jenkins forecasts
of earnings"   Acctg. Rev., vol.51, 1976, pp.321-329.
TIME SERIES - ARIMA : APPL * APPL - FIRM : FINANCE , PROFITS * COMPARATIVE
METHODS - ARIMA , JUDGEMENTAL * EVALUATION - JUDGEMENTAL FORECASTS , PROFITS
* EX ANTE

YA2224 LOREK K.S., McKEOWN J.C.
"The effect on predictive ability of reducing the number of observations on
a time-series analysis of quarterly earnings data"   J. Acctg. Res.,
vol.16, 1978, pp.204-214.
DATA - SAMPLE SIZE * TIME SERIES - ARIMA : ESTIMATION * TIME SERIES - ARIMA
: FORECASTING * EVALUATION - TIME SERIES , ARIMA * EX ANTE

YA2225 LOTHIAN J.R.
"The demand for high-powered money"   Am. Econ. Rev., vol.66, 1976,
pp.56-68.
APPL - MACRO : MONEY , DEMAND * DATA - INTERNATIONAL

YA2226 LOTSHAW E.
"Aall the economics you need for industrial market planning - and no more"
Ind. Mktg. Mgmt., vol.7, 1978, pp.1-8.
FORECASTING - INTRODUCTION * USE - MARKETING POLICY * BASIC

YA2227 LOVE P.E.
"Long-range forecasting in advanced technology"   Ind. Mktg. Mgmt., vol.3,
1973, pp.91-105.
APPL - SECTOR : PRODUCTION , PLANT , TRANSPORTATION * APPL - SECTOR :
TRANSPORT * APPL - SECTOR : PRODUCTION , AEROSPACE * LONG TERM FORECASTING

YA2228 LOVELL C.A.K.
"A note on aggregation bias and loss"   J. Econometrics, vol.1, 1973,
pp.301-311.
DATA - AGGREGATION 'BIAS' * PRODUCTION FUNCTIONS - MACRO * DATA ERRORS -
EFFECT OF

YA2229 LOVELL C.A.K.
"Estimation and prediction with CES and VES production functions"   Int.
Econ. Rev., vol.14, 1973, pp.676-692.
EVALUATION - PRODUCTION FUNCTIONS * COMPARATIVE METHODS - REGRESSION ,
TRANFORMATIONS * EX ANTE * PRODUCTION FUNCTIONS - MACRO

YA2230 LOVELL M.C.
"Alternative axiomatizations of seasonal adjustment"   J. Am. Statist.
Ass., vol.61, 1966, pp.800-802.
SEASONALITY - ESTIMATION , OLS * COMPARATIVE METHODS - SEASONALITY

YA2231 LOVELL M.C.
"Least-squares seasonally adjusted unemployment data" with discussion
Brookings Paps. Econ. Activity, 1976, pp.225-245.
APPL - MACRO : UNEMPLOYMENT * SEASONALITY - ESTIMATION , OLS

YA2232 LOVELL M.C.
"Spending for education: the exercise of public choice"   Rev. Econ.
Stats., vol.60, 1978, pp.487-495.
APPL - SECTOR : EDUCATION * APPL - SECTOR : GOVERNMENT , EDUCATION *
COMPARATIVE METHODS - REGRESSION , TRANSFORMATIONS * POLICY EVALUATION -
SECTOR : EDUCATION * EVALUATION - PRODUCTION FUNCTIONS

YA2233 LOVELL M.C.
"The profit picture: trends and cycles"   Brookings Paps. Econ. Activity,
1978, pp.769-789.
APPL - MACRO : PROFITS * BUSINESS CYCLE - EFFECT OF * DATA - SPECIFICATION
OF VARIABLES * INFLATION - EFFECT OF

YA2234 LOVELL M.C.
"Why was the consumer feeling so sad?"   Brookings Paps. Econ. Activity,
1975, pp.473-479.
ATTITUDINAL DATA * INDEX NUMBERS - MACRO : CONSUMER CONFIDENCE * SURVEYS -
CONSUMER , DETERMINANTS * BUSINESS INDICATORS - APPL

YA2235 LOWENHAR J.A., STANTON J.L.
"Forecasting competitive advertising expenditures"   J. Advtg. Res.,
vol.16:3, 1976, pp.37-42.
COMPETITION - ESTIMATING * APPL - FIRM : CONSUMER NON DURABLES * ADVERTISING
- DETERMINANTS

YA2236 LUCAS H.C., WEINBERG C.B., CLOWES K.W.
"Sales response as a function of territorial potential and sales
representation workload"   J. Mktg. Res, vol.12, 1975, pp.298-305.
USE - SALES FORCE MANAGEMENT * APPL - FIRM : CONSUMER DURABLES , CLOTHING *
MULTICOLLINEARITY - EFFECT OF * USE - SALES AREA ALLOCATION

YA2237 LUCAS R.E.
"Some international evidence on output-inflation trade offs"   Am. Econ.
Rev., vol.63, 1973, pp.326-334.
APPL - MACRO : GNP * DATA - INTERNATIONAL * INFLATION - EFFECT OF

YA2238   LUCK G.M., ET AL.
         "The management of capital investment"   R. Statist. Soc. (A), vol.134,
         1971, pp.485-533.
         USE - CORPORATE PLANNING * USE - CAPITAL INVESTMENT
YA2239   LUEY P., ET AL.
         "On Naya and Morgan's criterion of accuracy in trade recording: comments"
         J. Am. Statist. Ass., vol.66, 1971, pp.763-765.
         APPL - MACRO : INTERNATIONAL TRADE * DATA ERRORS - IDENTIFICATION
YA2240   LUFT H.S.
         "The impact of poor health on earnings"   Rev. Econ. Stats., vol.57, 1975,
         pp.43-57.
         HEALTH - EFFECT OF * EDUCATION - EFFECT OF * MANPOWER PLANNING - EARNINGS
YA2241   LUND P.J., MINER D.A.
         "The nature of the error term in distributed lag models"   Appl. Econ.,
         vol.7, 1975, pp.185-194.
         DISTRIBUTED LAG - ERROR SPECIFICATION
YA2242   LURY D.A.
         "The analysis and forecasting of the British economy: some recent
         publications"   Stat'n., vol.21, 1972, pp.132-140.
         MACRO MODEL - UK
YA2243   LUSTGARTEN S.H.
         "The impact of buyer concentration in manufacturing industries"   Rev.
         Econ. Stats., vol.57, 1975, pp.125-132.
         APPL - SECTOR : FINANCE , MARGINS * CONCENTRATION - EFFECT OF * ADVERTISING
         - EFFECT OF * ADVERTISING - DETERMINANTS * DATA - CROSS SECTION
YA2244   LUTZ R.J., RESEK R.W.
         "More on testing the Howard-Sheth model of buyer behaviour"   J. Mktg.
         Res., vol.9, 1972, pp.338-345.
         CONSUMER BEHAVIOUR - PSYCHOLOGICAL MODELS * SIMULATION - APPL : CONSUMER
         BEHAVIOUR * SPECIFICATION ERROR - EFFECT OF , IDENTIFICATION
YA2245   LYBECK J.A.
         "The monetary sector of RDX2: a note of some puzzling features"   Can. J.
         Econ., vol.6, 1973, pp.595-598.
         APPL - MACRO : FLOW OF FUNDS * MACRO MODEL - CANADA , RDX2
YA2246   LYNCH M., CURHAN R.C.
         "A comment on Curhan's 'the relationship between shelf space and unit sales
         in supermarkets'"   J. Mktg. Res., vol.11, 1974, pp.218-222.
         USE - RETAIL , DISPLAY * APPL - SECTOR : RETAILING , GROCERIES *
         SPECIFICATION ERROR - EFFECT OF , SIMULTANEOUS SYSTEM BIAS
YA2247   LYTTKENS E.
         "The fixpoint method for estimating interdependent systems with the
         underlying model specification" with discussion   R. Statist. Soc. (A),
         vol.136, 1973, pp.353-394.
         SIMULTANEOUS SYSTEM - ESTIMATION * ESTIMATION - FIXED POINT * APPL - MACRO ,
         UK * COMPARATIVE METHODS - ESTIMATION : SIMULTANEOUS SYSTEM * ESTIMATION -
         OLS , ITERATIVE * EX ANTE
YA2248   MABERT V.A.
         "Forecast modification based upon residual analysis: a case study of check
         volume estimation"   Decis. Sci., vol.9, 1978, pp.285-296.
         APPL - FIRM : FINANCE , BANKS * RESIDUALS - ANALYSIS OF , AUTOCORRELATION *
         FORECASTING - MULTISTAGE * COMPARATIVE METHODS - EXPONENTIAL SMOOTHING ,
         ADAPTIVE * EVALUATION - EXPONENTIAL SMOOTHING * EVALUATION - EXPONENTIAL
         SMOOTHING , ADAPTIVE
YA2249   MABERT V.A.
         "Statistical versus sales force - executive opinion short range forecasts: a
         time series analysis case study"   Decis. Sci., vol.7, 1976, pp.310-318.
         COMPARATIVE METHODS - EXPONENTIAL SMOOTHING , JUDGEMENTAL * COMPARATIVE
         METHODS - ARIMA , JUDGEMENTAL * COMPARATIVE METHODS - EXPONENTIAL SMOOTHING
         , HARMONIC * COMPARATIVE METHODS - ARIMA , EXPONENTIAL SMOOTHING *
         COMPARATIVE METHODS - TIME SERIES * EX ANTE * FORECASTING - COST OF
YA2250   MABERT V.A., RADCLIFFE R.C.
         "A forecasting methodology as applied to financial time series"   Acctg
         Rev., vol.49, 1974, pp.61-65.
         TIME SERIES - ARIMA : INTRODUCTION * APPL - FIRM : UTILITIES , ELECTRICITY *
         EX ANTE
YA2251   MACAVOY P.W., NOLL R.
         "Relative prices on regulated transactions of the natural gas pipelines"
         Bell J. Econ., vol.4, 1973, pp.212-234.
         APPL - SECTOR : UTILITIES , GAS * APPL - SECTOR : ENERGY , SOURCES * APPL -
         FIRM : UTILITIES , GAS
YA2252   MACAVOY P.W., PINDYCK R.S.
         "Alternative regulatory policies for dealing with the natural gas shortage"
         Bell J. Econ., vol.4, 1973, pp.454-498.
         APPL - SECTOR : UTILITIES , GAS * DATA - CROSS SECTION , TIME SERIES * LONG
         TERM FORECASTING * POLICY EVALUATION - MACRO : ENERGY * USE - FINANCIAL ,
         REGULATION

YA2253　McCALL A.S., PETERSON M.O.
"The impact of de novo commercial bank entry"　J. Finance, vol.32, 1977, pp.1587-1604.
NEW PRODUCT - NEW BRAND * APPL - FIRM : FINANCE , BANKS * APPL - FIRM : FINANCE , PROFITS * COMPETITION - EFFECT OF * USE - BANK REGULATION

YA2254　McCALL J.J.
"A Markovian model of income dynamics"　J. Am. Statist. Ass., vol.66, 1971, pp.439-447.
MANPOWER PLANNING - EARNINGS * MARKOV MODEL - APPL : MANPOWER * REGRESSION - LIMITED DEPENDENT , LOGIT : APPL * APPL - SECTOR : SOCIAL , SUCCESS

YA2255　McCALLUM B.T.
"Competitive price adjustments: an empirical study"　Am. Econ. Rev., vol.64, 1974, pp.56-65.
EVALUATION - PRICING MODELS * APPL - SECTOR : AGRICULTURE , TIMBER * PRICE - SECTOR : AGRICULTURE

YA2256　McCALLUM B.T.
"Money wage changes and the excess demand for labour: international evidence on a new approach"　Appl. Econ., vol.6, 1974, pp.205-213.
INFLATION - EFFECT OF * APPL - MACRO : EARNINGS * DATA - INTERNATIONAL

YA2257　McCALLUM B.T.
"Rational expectations and the natural rate hypothesis: some consistent estimates"　Econometrica, vol.44, 1976, pp.43-52.
INFLATION - DETERMINANTS , EARNINGS * EXPECTATIONS - METHODOLOGY * ESTIMATION - INSTRUMENTAL VARIABLES * APPL - MACRO : EARNINGS

YA2258　McCALLUM B.T.
"Relative asymptotic bias from errors of ommission and measurement"　Econometrica, vol.40, 1972, pp.757-758.
REGRESSION - ERROR IN VARIABLES * SPECIFICATION ERROR - EFFECT OF , SPECIFICATION OF VARIABLES * DATA ERRORS - EFFECT OF * PROXY VARIABLES

YA2259　McCALLUM B.T.
"The relative impact of monetary and fiscal policy instruments: some structure-based estimates"　J. Econometrics, vol.2, 1974, pp.283-299.
POLICY EVALUATION - MACRO : FISCAL , MONETARY * MACRO MODEL - US * EVALUATION - MACRO MODELS * MACRO MODEL - ST.LOUIS

YA2260　McCALLUM B.T.
"The role of speculation in the Canadian forward exchange market: some estimates assuming rational expectations"　Rev. Econ. Stats., vol.59, 1977, pp.145-151.
COMPARATIVE METHODS - ESTIMATION : REGRESSION , ERROR SPECIFICATION * APPL - MACRO , CANADA * APPL - MACRO : INTERNATIONAL FINANCE , EXCHANGE RATES * EXCHANGE RATE - FORWARD RATE * THEORY - EXPECTATIONS * EVALUATION - EXPECTATIONS , THEORY

YA2261　McCALLUM B.T.
"Wage rate changes and the excess demand for labour: an alternative formulation"　Economica, vol.41, 1974, pp.269-277.
INFLATION - PHILLIPS CURVE * APPL - MACRO : EARNINGS

YA2262　McCANN J.M.
"Market segment response to the marketing decision variables"　J. Mktg. Res., vol.11, 1974, pp.399-412.
USER - FIRM : RETAILING * MARKET SEGMENTATION * USE - PROMOTION EVALUATION * PRICE - EFFECT OF * ESTIMATION - CROSS SECTION , TIME SERIES * ADVERTISING - EFFECT OF * APPL - SECTOR : CONSUMER NON DURABLES * CONSUMER BEHAVIOUR - PURCHASING , DETERMINANTS

YA2263　McCARTHY C., RYAN T.M.
"Estimates of voter transition probabilities from the British General Election of 1974"　R. Statist. Soc. (A), vol.140, 1977, pp.78-85.
VOTING * MARKOV MODELS - ESTIMATION * MARKOV MODELS - APPL : VOTING * LP

YA2264　McCARTHY M.D.
"The US productivity growth recession: history and prospects for the future" with discussion　J. Finance, vol.33, 1978, pp.977-988 & 1001-1010.
APPL - MACRO : PRODUCTIVITY

YA2265　MACCINI L.J.
"The impact of demand and price expectations on the behaviour of prices"　Am. Econ. Rev., vol.68, 1978, pp.134-145.
THEORY - PRICING * PRICE - MACRO * PRICE - SECTOR : PRODUCTION * PRICE - EXPECTATIONS * DISTRIBUTED LAG - ALMON : APPL

YA2266　McCLAIN J.O.
"Dynamics of exponential smoothing with trend and seasonal terms"　Mgmt. Sci. (A), vol.20, 1974, pp.1300-1304.
EXPONENTIAL SMOOTHING - HIGHER ORDER * SEASONALITY - EFFECT OF * EVALUATION - EXPONENTIAL SMOOTHING * ADVANCED

YA2267　McCLAIN J.O., THOMAS L.J.
"Response-variance tradeoffs in adaptive forecasting"　Ops. Res., vol.21, 1973, pp.554-568.
EXPONENTIAL SMOOTHING - THEORY * EVALUATION - EXPONENTIAL SMOOTHING * EXPONENTIAL SMOOTHING - COEFFICIENT CHOICE * ADVANCED

YA2268   McCLAVE J.T.
"Estimating the order of autoregressive models: the max chi-squared method"
J. Am. Statist. Ass., vol.73, 1978, pp.122-128.
TIME SERIES - ARIMA : IDENTIFICATION * DATA - SIMULATION * EVALUATION - LOSS
FUNCTIONS * LOSS FUNCTIONS - AKAIKE'S FPE

YA2269   McCLEAN S.
"Some models for company growth"   R. Statist. Soc. (A), vol.139, 1976,
pp.501-507.
APPL - FIRM : GROWTH * PROBABILITY MODELS - BIRTH PROCESS * MANPOWER
PLANNING - FIRM

YA2270   McCLEAN S.
"The steady-state behaviour of a manpower planning model in which class
corresponds to length of service"   Opl. Res. Q., vol.28, 1977, pp.305-311.
MARKOV MODELS - APPL : MANPOWER * MANPOWER PLANNING - FIRM

YA2271   McCLEAN S.
"The two stage model of personnel behaviour"   R. Statist. Soc. (A),
vol.139, 1976, pp.205-217.
MANPOWER PLANNING - LABOUR TURNOVER * PROBABILITY MODELS - GAMMA , COMPOUND
* MANPOWER PLANNING - FIRM

YA2272   McCLEMENTS L.D.
"An analysis of retail meat pricing behaviour in Britain"   Appl. Econ.,
vol.4, 1972, pp.291-300.
APPL - SECTOR : CONSUMER NON DURABLES , FOOD , MEAT * APPL - SECTOR :
FINANCE , MARGINS * APPL - SECTOR : RETAILING , FOOD

YA2273   McCLEMENTS L.D.
"Econometric forecasts of pig supply"   Appl. Econ., vol.2, 1970, pp.27-34.
APPL - SECTOR : AGRICULTURE , LIVESTOCK , HOGS * EX ANTE * COMPARATIVE
METHODS - AUTOREGRESSIVE , CAUSAL * COMPARATIVE METHODS - AUTOREGRESSIVE ,
JUDGEMENTAL * COMPARATIVE METHODS - CAUSAL , JUDGEMENTAL

YA2274   McCOLLUM J.F., GIBSON W.E.
"Price-expectations effects on interest rates: comments"   J. Finance,
vol.28, 1973, pp.746-753.
INTEREST RATE - INDICATORS * INFLATION - EXPECTATIONS * INFLATION - EFFECT
OF

YA2275   McCROHAN K.
"Forecasting business needs in the telephone market"   Ind. Mktg. Mgmt.,
vol.7, 1978, pp.109-113.
USER - FIRM : UTILITIES * APPL - FIRM : UTILITIES , TELEPHONE * FORECASTING
- PRACTICE * BASIC

YA2276   McCULLOCH J.H., ET AL.
"Spline estimation of the liquidity trap: comments"   Rev. Econ. Stats.,
vol.60, 1978, pp.318-321.
INTEREST RATE - EFFECT OF * APPL - MACRO : MONEY , DEMAND * REGRESSION -
PIECEWISE * SPLINE FUNCTIONS

YA2277   McDONALD G.C., GALARNEAU D.I.
"A Monte Carlo evaluation of some ridge-type estimators"   J. Am. Statist.
Ass., vol.70, 1975, pp.407-416.
EVALUATION - REGRESSION , RIDGE * DATA - SIMULATION * COMPARATIVE METHODS -
ESTIMATION : OLS , RIDGE * COMPARATIVE METHODS - ESTIMATION : OLS , BAYES

YA2278   McDONALD J.
"An analysis of the significance of revisions to some quarterly UK National
Income time series"   R. Statist. Soc. (A), vol.138, 1975, pp.242-256.
DATA ERRORS - EFFECT OF * DATA ERRORS - ESTIMATION OF * DATA REVISIONS -
EFFECTS OF * DATA REVISIONS - ESTIMATION OF * TIME SERIES - ARIMA : APPL *
APPL - MACRO , UK

YA2279   McDONALD J.
"On the insenitivity of the autoregressive moving average representations of
some Australian quarterly time series"   Econometrica, vol.44, 1976,
pp.1277-1287.
TIME SERIES - ARIMA : APPL * APPL - MACRO , AUSTRALIA * DATA REVISIONS -
EFFECT OF * APPL - MACRO : GDP * APPL - MACRO : CONSUMPTION

YA2280   McDONALD J.
"The residual error in the quarterly national accounts of the UK"   Appl.
Stats., vol.22, 1973, pp.354-368.
DATA ERRORS - NATIONAL ACCOUNTS , UK * TIME SERIES - ARIMA : APPL

YA2281   McDONALD J.G.
"French Mutual Fund performance:evaluation of internationally-diversified
portfolios"   J. Finance, vol.28, 1973, pp.1161-1180.
USE - PORTFOLIO SELECTION * APPL - FIRM : FINANCE , MUTUAL FUNDS * STOCK
PRICES - RISK * APPL - FIRM : FINANCE , STOCK PRICES * STOCK PRICES - MODELS
, INTERNATIONAL

YA2282   McDONALD J.G.
"Required return on public utility equities: a national and regional
analysis"   Bell J. Econ., vol.2, 1971, pp.503-514.
APPL - FIRM : UTILITIES * APPL - FIRM : FINANCE , CAPITALISATION * DATA -
CROSS SECTION * STABILITY OF COEFFICIENTS - REGRESSION : APPL

YA2283　McDONALD J.G., BARON D.C.
"Risks and return on short positions in common stocks"　J. Finance,
vol.28, 1973, pp.97-107
APPL - FIRM : FINANCE , STOCK PRICES * STOCK PRICES - RISK * USE -
SPECULATION

YA2284　MACDONALD K.H.
"Use of computers in ICL for short and long-term sales projections"　Ind.
Mktg. Mgmt., vol.1, 1971, pp.81-94.
APPL - SECTOR : PRODUCTION , COMPUTERS * APPL - FIRM : PRODUCTION ,
COMPUTERS * BASIC

YA2285　McDONOUGH C.C.
"A simultaneous equation model of the demand for manuscript review"　Rev.
Econ. Stats., vol.60, 1978, pp.153-158.
APPL - SECTOR : SERVICES , MEDIA , MAGAZINES * QUALITY - EFFECT OF

YA2286　MACE J.R.
"Criteria for the selection of reporting method"　Omega, vol.5, 1973,
pp.567-582.
ACCOUNTING PRACTICE - EFFECT OF * EVALUATION - THEORY OF * BASIC

YA2287　McELROY M.B.
"A spliced CES expenditure system"　Int. Econ. Rev., vol.16, 1975,
pp.765-780.
APPL - MACRO : CONSUMER DEMAND * APPL - MACRO , SOUTH EAST ASIA * DEMAND
EQUATIONS - SYSTEMS OF , THEORY * CONSUMER BEHAVIOUR - ECONOMIC MODELS ,
THEORY

YA2288　McELROY M.B.
"Goodness of fit for seemingly unrelated regressions"　J. Econometrics,
vol.6, 1977, pp.381-387.
REGRESSION - SUMMARY STATISTICS * REGRESSION - SEEMINGLY UNRELATED * APPL -
FIRM : INVESTMENT

YA2289　McELROY M.B., POINDEXTER J.C., BHATIA K.B.
"Capital gains and the aggregate consumption function: comments"　Am.
Econ. Rev., vol.65, 1975, pp.705-707.
WEALTH - EFFECT OF * APPL - MACRO : CONSUMPTION

YA2290　McFADDEN D.
"A comment on discriminant analysis 'versus' logit analysis"　Anns. Econ.
Soc. Meas., vol.5, 1976, pp.511-523.
COMPARATIVE METHODS - DISCRIMINATION * EVALUATION - DISCRIMINANT ANALYSIS *
REGRESSION - LIMITED DEPENDENT , LOGIT * ADVANCED

YA2291　McFADDEN D.
"Quantal choice analysis: a survey"　Anns. Econ. Soc. Meas., vol.5, 1976,
pp.363-390.
REGRESSION - LIMITED DEPENDENT , REVIEW * REGRESSION - QUALITATIVE DEPENDENT
, REVIEW * BIBLIOGRAPHY - REGRESSION , QUALITATIVE DEPENDENT * SIMULTANEOUS
SYSTEM - QUALITATIVE DEPENDENT * SIMULTANEOUS SYSTEM - LIMITED DEPENDENT

YA2292　McFADDEN D.
"The revealed preference of a government bureaucracy: empirical evidence"
Bell J. Econ., vol.7, 1976, pp.55-72.
REGRESSION - LIMITED DEPENDENT , LOGIT : APPL * DECISION RULES - SECTOR :
GOVERNMENT * APPL - SECTOR : CONSTRUCTION , ROADS * APPL - SECTOR :
GOVERNMENT , ROADS

YA2293　McFADYEN S., HOBART R.
"An alternative measurement of housing costs and the Consumer Price Index"
Can. J. Econ., vol.11, 1978, pp.105-112.
INDEX NUMBERS - SECTOR : CONSTRUCTION * INDEX NUMBERS - MACRO : CONSUMER
PRICE * APPL - SECTOR : CONSTRUCTION , RESIDENTIAL

YA2294　McFETRIDGE D.G.
"Market structure and price-cost margins: an analysis of the Canadian
manufacturing sector"　Can. J. Econ., vol.6, 1973, pp.344-355.
DATA - CROSS SECTION * APPL - SECTOR : FINANCE , MARGINS * CONCENTRATION -
EFFECT OF

YA2295　McFETRIDGE D.G.
"The efficiency implications of earnings retentions"　Rev. Econ. Stats.,
vol.60, 1978, pp.218-224.
APPL - FIRM : FINANCE , PROFITS * ERROR SPECIFICATION - HETEROSCEDASTIC *
APPL - FIRM : FINANCE , FINANCIAL STRUCTURE * APPL - FIRM : GROWTH

YA2296　McGILLIVRAY R.G.
"Binary choice of urban transport mode in the San Francisco Bay region"
Econometrica, vol.40, 1972, pp.827-848.
APPL - SECTOR : TRANSPORT * REGIONAL MODELS - CITY * REGIONAL MODELS -
SECTOR : TRANSPORT * DISCRIMINANT ANALYSIS - APPL * PRICE - SECTOR :
TRANSPORT * USE - TRANSPORT PLANNING

YA2297　McGILVRAY J., SIMPSON D.
"Some tests of stability in interindustry coefficients"　Econometrica,
vol.37, 1969, pp.204-221.
APPL - SECTOR : CONSUMER DURABLES : TEXTILES , CLOTHING * STABILITY OF
COEFFICIENTS - INPUT OUTPUT * INPUT OUTPUT - MACRO , IRELAND * INPUT OUTPUT
- PROJECTION OF STRUCTURE

YA2298   McGREGOR A.
         "Unemployment duration and re-employment probability"   Econ. J., vol.88,
         1978, pp.693-706.
         MANPOWER PLANNING - UNEMPLOYMENT , DURATION * REGRESSION - QUALITATIVE
         DEPENDENT : APPL * REGRESSION - LIMITED DEPENDENT , LOGIT : APPL *
         COMPARATIVE METHODS - REGRESSION , QUALITATIVE DEPENDENT * COMPARATIVE
         METHODS - REGRESSION , LIMITED DEPENDENT

YA2299   McGUIRE T.W.
         "Measuring and testing relative advertising effectiveness with split-cable
         TV panel data"   J. Am. Statist. Ass., vol.72, 1977, pp.736-745.
         ADVERTISING - EFFECT OF * ADVERTISING - EXPERIMENTAL DESIGN * DATA ERRORS -
         MISSING OBSERVATIONS * APPL - FIRM : CONSUMER NON DURABLES , FOOD * APPL -
         SECTOR : SERVICES , MEDIA , TV * ADVANCED

YA2300   McGUIRE T.W., WEISS D.L.
         "Logically consistent market share models"   J. Mktg. Res., vol.14, 1976,
         pp.296-302.
         MARKET SHARE - THEORY

YA2301   MACKAY D.B.
         "A microanalytic approach to store location analysis"   J. Mktg. Res.,
         vol.9, 1972, pp.134-140.
         USE - SITE SELECTION , RETAIL * APPL - FIRM : RETAILING , GROCERIES *
         DISCRIMINANT ANALYSIS - APPL

YA2302   MACKAY D.B.
         "Spatial measurement of retail store demand"   J. Mktg. Res., vol.10, 1973,
         pp.447-453.
         USE - RETAIL , SITE MONITORING * SPATIAL ANALYSIS * MARKET POSITION *
         ADVANCED

YA2303   MACKAY D.I., REID G.L.
         "Redundancy, unemployment and manpower policies"   Econ. J., vol. 82, 1972,
         pp.1256-1368.
         APPL - SECTOR : PRODUCTION , ENGINEERING * MANPOWER PLANNING - SECTOR :
         PRODUCTION * APPL - SECTOR : UNEMPLOYMENT * POLICY EVALUATION - UNEMPLOYMENT

YA2304   McKAY R.J.
         "A graphical aid to selection of variables in two-group discriminant
         analysis"   Appl. Stats., vol.27, 1978, pp.259-263.
         DISCRIMINANT ANALYSIS - METHODOLOGY * APPL - SECTOR : NATURAL , ANIMAL
         POPULATIONS

YA2305   MACKAY R.R., MOORE B., RHODES J.
         "Evaluating the effects of British regional economic policy-comments"
         Econ. J., vol.84, 1974, pp.367-374.
         REGIONAL MODELS - EMPLOYMENT * POLICY EVALUATION - REGIONAL

YA2306   McKENZIE E.
         "A comparison of some standard seasonal forecasting systems"   Stat'n,,
         vol.25, 1976, pp.3-14.
         EVALUATION - TIME SERIES , SEASONALITY * EVALUATION - SEASONALITY

YA2307   McKENZIE E.
         "A comparison of standard forecasting systems with the Box-Jenkins approach"
         Stat'n., vol.23, 1974, pp.107-116.
         TIME SERIES - REVIEW

YA2308   McKENZIE E.
         "The monitoring of exponentially weighted forecasts"   J. Opl. Res. Soc.,
         vol.29, 1978, pp.449-458.
         EXPONENTIAL SMOOTHING - ADAPTIVE COEFFICIENTS

YA2309   McKENZIE E., PETERSON M.M.
         "A note on a matrix inversion in multiple exponential smoothing"   R.
         Statist. Soc. (B), vol.40, 1978, pp.182-183.
         EXPONENTIAL SMOOTHING - THEORY * ADVANCED

YA2310   McKEOWN J.C., LOREK K.S.
         "A comparative analysis of the predictive ability of adaptive forecasting,
         re-estimation, and re-identification using Box-Jenkins time-series analysis
         on quarterly earnings data"   Decis. Sci., vol.9, 1978, pp.658-672.
         APPL - FIRM : FINANCE , PROFITS * TIME SERIES - ARIMA : IDENTIFICATION *
         STABILITY OF COEFFICIENTS - TIME SERIES : APPL * TIME SERIES - ARIMA :
         FORECASTING * EX ANTE * FORECASTING - COST OF

YA2311   McKEOWN J.J., MILLER A.L.
         "Non-linear parameter estimation"   Opl. Res. Q., vol.23, 1972, pp.81-83 &
         pp.393-394.
         REGRESSION - ESTIMATION * ESTIMATION - NON LINEAR * REGRESSION -
         TRANSFORMATIONS

YA2312   McKIBBEN W
         "Econometric forecasting of common stock investment returns: a new
         methodology using fundamental operating data"   J. Finance, vol.27, 1972,
         pp.371-380 & 392-395.
         APPL - FIRM : FINANCE , STOCK PRICES * STOCK PRICES - DETERMINANTS * APPL -
         FIRM : FINANCE , PE RATIO * USE - PORTFOLIO SELECTION

YA2313   McKINNEY G.W.
         "Pitfalls and pratfalls of econometric forecasting"   Bus. Econ., vol.11:3,
         1976, pp.5-10.
         EVALUATION - MACRO MODELS * USE - CORPORATE PLANNING * USER - FIRM * BASIC

YA2314   MACLACHLAN D.L.
"A model of intermediate market response"   J. Mktg. Res., vol.9, 1972,
pp.378-384.
APPL - FIRM : CONSUMER NON DURABLES , FOOD * MARKOV MODELS - METHODOLOGY *
MARKET SHARE - SECTOR : CONSUMER NON DURABLES * ADVERTISING - EFFECT OF *
PRICE - EFFECT OF * EX ANTE * USE - PROMOTION EVALUATION

YA2315   McLAGAN D.L.
"A non-econometrician's guide to econometrics"   Bus. Econ., vol.8:3, 1973,
pp.38-45.
REGRESSION - INTRODUCTION * REGRESSION - MODEL CHOICE

YA2316   McLAUGHLIN R.L.
"A new five phase economic forecasting system"   Bus. Econ., vol.10:4,
1975, pp.49-60.
BUSINESS CYCLE - DETERMINANTS * TURNING POINTS - FORECASTING * INDEX NUMBERS
- MACRO : MONETARY , FISCAL POLICY * BUSINESS INDICATORS - METHODOLOGY

YA2317   McLAUGHLIN R.L.
"Leading indicators: a new approach for corporate planning"   Bus. Econ.,
vol.6:3, 1971, pp.7-12.
BUSINESS INDICATORS - REVIEW * USE - CORPORATE PLANNING

YA2318   McLAUGHLIN R.L.
"Measuring the accuracy of forecasts"   Bus. Econ., vol.7:3, 1972,
pp.27-35.
EVALUATION - THEORY OF * EVALUATION - MACRO FORECASTS * EX ANTE * EVALUATION
- MACRO MODELS * LOSS FUNCTIONS - THEIL

YA2319   McLAUGHLIN R.L.
"The real record of the economic forecasts"   Bus. Econ., vol.10:3, 1975,
pp.28-36.
COMPARATIVE METHODS - CAUSAL , JUDGEMENTAL * MACRO MODEL - FAIR *
COMPARATIVE METHODS - MACRO MODELS * EVALUATION - JUDGEMENTAL FORECASTS ,
MACRO * BASIC

YA2320   McLEOD A.I.
"On the distribution of residual autocorrelations in Box-Jenkins models"
R. Statist. Soc. (B), vol.40, 1978, pp.296-302.
TIME SERIES - ARIMA : DIAGNOSTICS * AUTOCORRELATION - COEFFICIENTS * TIME
SERIES - ARIMA : INTERVENTION * ADVANCED

YA2321   McMENAMIN J.S., PINARD J.
"Specification and estimation of dynamic demand systems incorporating
polynomial price response functions"   J. Econometrics, vol.7, 1978,
pp.147-162.
DEMAND EQUATIONS - SYSTEMS OF : METHODOLOGY , DISTRIBUTED LAG * PRICE -
EFFECT OF * APPL - SECTOR : INTERNATIONAL TRADE * APPL - SECTOR CONSUMER
DURABLES , CLOTHING * DISTRIBUTED LAG - ALMON

YA2322   McNEES S.K.
"How accurate are economic forecasts"   New England economic Review,
Federal Reserve Bank of Boston, Nov-Dec, 1974, pp.2-19.
COMPARATIVE METHODS - MACRO MODELS * EVALUATION - MACRO FORECASTS

YA2323   McNEES S.K.
"The 'rationality' of economic forecasts" with discussion   Am. Econ. Ass.
Proc., 1978, pp.301-305 & 320-321.
MACRO MODEL - CHASE * MACRO MODEL - DATA RESOURCES * MACRO MODEL - WHARTON *
COMPARATIVE METHODS - ESTIMATION : OLS , GLS * EVALUATION - MACRO MODELS *
EX ANTE * LEAD TIME - EFFECT OF

YA2324   McNEILL G., MILLER M.
"Inputs to corporate planning: forecasting the external environment"   Ind.
Mktg. Mgmt., vol.1, 1972, pp.233-245.
USE - CORPORATE PLANNING * FORECASTING - REVIEW

YA2325   McNICOL D.L.
"The two price systems in the copper industry"   Bell J. Econ., vol.6,
1975, pp.50-73.
THEORY - PRICING * APPL - SECTOR : COMMODITIES , COPPER

YA2326   McPHETERS L.R., STRONGE W.B.
"Canadian response to fluctuations in US prices"   Rev. Econ. Stats.,
vol.58, 1976, pp.69-74.
SPECTRAL ANALYSIS - CROSS : APPL * APPL - MACRO , CANADA * SPECTRAL ANALYSIS
- APPL : MACRO * INFLATION - INDICATORS * APPL - MACRO : INTERNATIONAL
LINKAGE

YA2327   MACRAE C.D.
"The relation between unemployment and inflation in the Laffer-Ranson model"
J. Business, vol.45, 1972, pp.513-518.
MACRO MODEL - OMB * APPL - MACRO : UNEMPLOYMENT * INFLATION - PHILLIPS CURVE
* STOCK PRICES - EFFECT OF * INFLATION - DETERMINANTS

YA2328   McWHORTER A., NARASIMHAM G.V.L., SIMONDS R.R.
"An empirical examination of the predictive performance of an econometric
model with random coefficients"   Int. Statist. Rev., vol.45, 1977,
pp.243-256.
MACRO MODEL - KLEIN * COMPARATIVE METHODS - ESTIMATION : SIMULTANEOUS SYSTEM
* COMPARATIVE METHODS - ESTIMATION : OLS , 2SLS * COMPARATIVE METHODS -
ESTIMATION : OLS , 3SLS * ESTIMATION - KALMAN FILTER * COMPARATIVE METHODS -
ARIMA , CAUSAL(SIMULTANEOUS SYSTEM) * COMPARATIVE METHODS - MACRO MODELS *
COMPARATIVE METHODS - SIMULTANEOUS SYSTEM , RANDOM COEFFICIENTS * LEAD TIME
- EFFECT OF * EX ANTE

YA2329   McWHORTER A., SPIVEY W.A., WROBESKI W.J.
"A sensitivity analysis of varying parameter econometric models"   Int.
Statist. Rev., vol.44, 1976, pp.265-282.
EVALUATION - ESTIMATION , KALMAN FILTER * REGRESSION - STATE SPACE *
ESTIMATION - KALMAN FILTER * DATA - SIMULATION * EVALUATION - PRIOR
INFORMATION

YA2330   MADANSKY A.
"Introduction to symposium on forecasting with econometric methods"   J.
Business, vol.51, 1978, p.547.
ECONOMETRICS - REVIEW * FORECASTING - REVIEW

YA2331   MADDALA G.S.
"Some small sample evidence on tests of significance in simultaneous
equations models"   Econometrica, vol.42, 1974, pp.841-851.
COMPARATIVE METHODS - TESTS , REGRESSION COEFFICIENTS * SIMULTANEOUS SYSTEM
- HYPOTHESIS TESTS

YA2332   MADDALA G.S.
"The likelihood approach to pooling cross section and time series data"
Econometrica, vol.39, 1971, pp.939-953.
APPL - SECTOR : CONSUMER NON DURABLES , FOOD * ESTIMATION - CROSS SECTION ,
TIME SERIES * SPECIFICATION ERROR - TESTS , DATA SOURCES * BAYESIAN -
ESTIMATION : CROSS SECTION , TIME SERIES

YA2333   MADDALA G.S.
"The use of variance components models in pooling cross section and time
series data"   Econometrica, vol.39, 1971, pp.341-358.
ESTIMATION - CROSS SECTION , TIME SERIES * REGRESSION - ERROR COMPONENTS *
DATA - SIMULATION * ESTIMATION - MAXIMUM LIKELIHOOD

YA2334   MADDALA G.S.
"Weak priors and sharp posteriors in simultaneous equation models"
Econometrica, vol. 44, 1976, pp.345-351.
BAYESIAN - ESTIMATION : SIMULTANEOUS SYSTEM * SIMULTANEOUS SYSTEM -
IDENTIFICATION * SIMULTANEOUS SYSTEM - ESTIMATION

YA2335   MADDALA G.S., ENGLE R.F., ZELLNER A.
"Constraints often overlooked in analysis of simultaneous equation models:
comments"   Econometrica, vol.44, 1976, pp.615-628.
SIMULTANEOUS SYSTEM - CONSTRAINED

YA2336   MADDALA G.S., KADANE J.A.
"Some notes on the estimation of the constant elasticity of substitution
production function"   Rev. Econ. Stats., vol.48, 1966, pp.340-344.
PRODUCTION FUNCTIONS - ESTIMATION

YA2337   MADDALA G.S., LEE L.
"Recursive models with qualitative endogenous variables"   Anns. Econ. Soc.
Meas., vol.5, 1976, pp.525-545.
RECURSIVE SYSTEMS - THEORY * SIMULTANEOUS SYSTEM - QUALITATIVE DEPENDENT *
SIMULTANEOUS SYSTEM - LIMITED DEPENDENT * MANPOWER PLANNING - EDUCATION
PROGRAMS * COMPARATIVE METHODS - SIMULTANEOUS SYSTEM , LIMITED DEPENDENT *
ADVANCED

YA2338   MADDALA G.S., NELSON F.D.
"Maximum likelihood methods for models of markets in disequilibrium"
Econometrica, vol.42, 1974, pp.1013-1030.
APPL - SECTOR : CONSTRUCTION , RESIDENTIAL * SIMULTANEOUS SYSTEMS -
DISEQUILIBRIUM * SIMULTANEOUS SYSTEM - LIMITED DEPENDENT * COMPARATIVE
METHODS - SIMULTANEOUS SYSTEM , DISEQUILIBRIUM * COMPARATIVE METHODS -
SIMULTANEOUS SYSTEM , LIMITED DEPENDENT * COMPARATIVE METHODS - ESTIMATION :
SIMULTANEOUS SYSTEM * ESTIMATION - MAXIMUM LIKELIHOOD

YA2339   MADDALA G.S., RAO A.S.
"Maximum likelihood estimation of Solow's and Jorgenson's distributed lag
models"   Rev. Econ. Stats., vol.53, 1971, pp.80-88.
DISTRIBUTED LAG - SOLOW , ESTIMATION * APPL - MACRO : INVESTMENT * ERROR
SPECIFICATION - AUTOCORRELATED * COMPARATIVE METHODS - DISTRIBUTED LAG ,
ERROR SPECIFICATION * DISTRIBUTED LAG - RATIONAL POLYNOMIAL , ESTIMATION *
COMPARATIVE METHODS - DISTRIBUTED LAG * DISTRIBUTED LAG - APPL , ORDERS *
DISTRIBUTED LAG - ESTIMATION * ESTIMATION - MAXIMUM LIKELIHOOD

YA2340   MADDALA G.S., RAO A.S.
"Tests for serial correlation in regression models with lagged dependent
variables and serially correlated errors"   Econometrica, vol.41, 1973,
pp.761-774.
RESIDUALS - ANALYSIS OF , AUTOCORRELATION * REGRESSION - LAGGED DEPENDENT *
AUTOCORRELATION - TEST * COMPARATIVE METHODS - TESTS , AUTOCORRELATION *
DATA - SIMULATION

YA2341   MAESHIRO A.
"Autoregressive transformation; trended independent variables and
autocorrelated disturbances"   Rev. Econ. Stats., vol.53, 1976, pp.497-500.
COMPARATIVE METHODS - ESTIMATION : REGRESSION , ERROR SPECIFICATION *
STATIONARITY - TRANSFORMING TO

YA2342   MAGEE R.P.
"Industry wide commonalities in earnings"   J. Acctg. Res., vol.12, 1974,
pp.270-287.
APPL - FIRM : FINANCE , PROFITS * APPL - FIRM : FINANCE , STOCK PRICES *
STOCK PRICES - INDUSTRIAL STRUCTURE

YA2343   MAHAJAN V., JAIN A.K., BERGIER M.
          "Parameter estimation in marketing models in the presence of
          multicollinearity: an application of ridge regression" with computer program
          J. Mktg. Res., vol.14, -1977, pp.561 & 586-591.
          COMPUTERISATION - ESTIMATION , REGRESSION MODELS , PROGRAM * COMPARATIVE
          METHODS - ESTIMATION : OLS , RIDGE * APPL - FIRM : RETAILING *
          MULTICOLLINEARITY - REMOVAL OF
YA2344   MAHAJAN V., PETERSON R.A.
          "Innovation diffusion in a dynamic potential adopter population"   Mgmt.
          Sci., vol.24, 1978, pp.1589-1597.
          NEW PRODUCTS - DIFFUSION
YA2345   MAINDONALD J.H.
          "Least squares programs- a second look" letter   Am. Stat'n., vol.30, 1976,
          pp.202-203.
          COMPUTERISATION - PROGRAMS , ESTIMATION , REGRESSION MODELS * NUMERICAL
          METHODS - CALCULATION ERROR * ESTIMATION - OLS
YA2346   MAINS N.E.
          "Risk, the pricing of capital assets, and the evaluation of investment
          portfolios: comment"   J. Business, vol.50, 1977, pp.371-384.
          STOCK PRICES - INSTITUTIONAL INVESTMENT * APPL - FIRM : FINANCE , MUTUAL
          FUNDS
YA2347   MAISEL S.J., BURNHAM J.B.
          "The demand for housing: a comment"   Rev. Econ. Stats., vol.53, 1971,
          pp.410-413.
          DATA - CROSS SECTION * APPL - SECTOR : CONSTRUCTION , RESIDENTIAL * INCOME -
          EFFECT OF * PRICE - EFFECT OF * COMPARATIVE METHODS - DATA : AGGREGATE ,
          DISAGGREGATE
YA2348   MAJANI B., MAKRIDAKIS S.
          "Can recessions be predicted?"   Long Range Planning, vol.10:2, 1977,
          pp.31-41.
          BUSINESS CYCLE - PREDICTION * APPL - SECTOR : PRODUCTION , PAPER * APPL -
          SECTOR : PRODUCTION , STEEL * APPL - SECTOR : CONSUMER DURABLES , FURNITURE
          * APPL - MACRO , FRANCE * BASIC
YA2349   MAKIN J.H.
          "Demand and supply functions for stocks of Euro-dollar deposits: an
          empirical study"   Rev. Econ. Stats., vol.54, 1972, pp.381-390.
          APPL - MACRO : INTERNATIONAL FINANCE * COMPARATIVE METHODS - DISTRIBUTED LAG
YA2350   MAKIN J.H.
          "Identifying a reserve base for the Euro-dollar system"   J. Finance,
          vol.28, 1973, pp.609-617.
          APPL - MACRO : INTERNATIONAL FINANCE * APPL - SECTOR : FINANCE , BANKS *
          APPL - SECTOR : FINANCE , BANK , LIABILITIES * APPL - SECTOR : FINANCE ,
          INTERNATIONAL FINANCE
YA2351   MAKIN J.H.
          "Portfolio theory and the problem of foreign exchange risk"   J. Finance,
          vol.33, 1978, pp.517-534.
          USE - FINANCIAL , CONTROL * APPL - MACRO : INTERNATIONAL FINANCE , EXCHANGE
          RATES * EXCHANGE RATE - EFFECT OF
YA2352   MAKIN J.H.
          "The composition of international reserve holdings: a problem of choice
          involving risk"   Am. Econ. Rev., vol.61, 1971, pp.818-832.
          APPL - MACRO : INTERNATIONAL FINANCE , FOREIGN RESERVES * DATA -
          INTERNATIONAL
YA2353   MAKRIDAKIS S.
          "A survey of time series"   Int. Statist. Rev., vol.44, 1976, pp.29-70.
          TIME SERIES - REVIEW * SEASONALITY - ESTIMATION , CENSUS * BIBLIOGRAPHY -
          TIME SERIES * EVALUATION - TIME SERIES * FORECASTING - COST OF * DATA -
          REQUIREMENT
YA2354   MAKRIDAKIS S.
          "SIBYL/RUNNER: an interactive forecasting system"   J. Mktg. Res., vol.15,
          1978, pp.270-271.
          COMPUTERISATION - FORECASTING , PROGRAMS * COMPUTERISATION - ESTIMATION ,
          TIME SERIES , PROGRAMS
YA2355   MAKRIDAKIS S.
          "Time-series analysis and forecasting: an update and evaluation"   Int.
          Statist. Rev., vol.46, 1978, pp.255-278.
          TIME SERIES - REVIEW * TIME SERIES - ARIMA : TRANSFORMATIONS * LEAD TIME -
          EFFECT OF * EVALUATION - TIME SERIES , ARIMA * STABILITY OF COEFFICIENTS -
          TIME SERIES : APPL * BIBLIOGRAPHY - TIME SERIES
YA2356   MAKRIDAKIS S., HODGDON A., WHEELWRIGHT S.C.
          "An interactive forecasting system"   Am. Stat'n., vol.28, 1974,
          pp.153-158.
          MIS * COMPUTERISATION - PROGRAMS , FORECASTING * FORECASTING - REVIEW *
          BASIC
YA2357   MAKRIDAKIS S., WHEELWRIGHT S.C.
          "Adaptive filtering: an integrated autoregressive moving average filter for
          time series forecasting"   Opl. Res. Q., vol.28, 1977, pp.425-437.
          EVALUATION - TIME SERIES , ADAPTIVE FILTERING * COMPARATIVE METHODS -
          ADAPTIVE FILTERING , ARIMA * EX ANTE

YA2358   MAKRIDAKIS S., WHEELWRIGHT S.C.
          "Forecasting: issues and challenges for marketing management"   J. Mktg.,
          vol.4114, 1977, pp.24-38,
          FORECASTING - USAGE * FORECASTING - REVIEW * USE - MARKETING POLICY
YA2359   MAKRIDAKIS S., WHEELWRIGHT S.C.
          "Integrating forecasting and planning"   Long Range Planning, vol.6:3,
          1973, pp.53-63,
          FORECASTING - REVIEW * FORECASTING - COST OF * DATA - SAMPLE SIZE * USE -
          REVIEW * BASIC
YA2360   MAKRIDAKIS S., WHEELWRIGHT S.C.
          "The new SIBYL/RUNNER interactive forecasting package"   Am. Stat'n.,
          vol.32, 1978, pp.109-110,
          COMPUTERISATION - FORECASTING , PROGRAMS * COMPUTERISATION - ESTIMATION ,
          TIME SERIES , PROGRAMS * BASIC
YA2361   MALIZIA E.E.
          "Comparative evaluation of two sets of social indicators"   Mgmt. Sci.,
          vol.22, 1975, pp.376-383,
          INDEX NUMBERS - SECTOR : SOCIAL * APPL - SECTOR : SOCIAL
YA2362   MALKIEL B.G.
          "The valuation of closed-end investment company shares"   J. Finance,
          vol.32, 1977, pp.847-859,
          APPL - FIRM : FINANCE , MUTUAL FUNDS * APPL - FIRM : FINANCE , STOCK PRICES
          * STOCK PRICES - INSTITUTIONAL INVESTMENT
YA2363   MALKIEL B.G., CRAGG J.G.
          "Expectations and the structure of share prices"   Am. Econ. Rev., vol.60,
          1970, pp.601-617,
          APPL - FIRM : FINANCE , PE RATIO * EVALUATION - EXPECTATIONS , THEORY * DATA
          - CROSS SECTION * RISK - EFFECT OF * STABILITY OF COEFFICIENTS - REGRESSION
          , TEST : APPL * USE - PORTFOLIO SELECTION * EVALUATION - EXPECTATIONS , DATA
YA2364   MALKIEL B.G., MALKIEL J.A.
          "Male-female pay differentials in professional employment"   Am. Econ.
          Rev., vol.63, 1973, pp.693-705,
          MANPOWER PLANNING - DISCRIMINATION , SEXUAL * MANPOWER PLANNING - EARNINGS *
          MANPOWER PLANNING - FIRM
YA2365   MALKIEL B.G., QUANDT R.E.
          "The supply of money and common stock prices: comment"   J. Finance,
          vol.27, 1972, pp.921-926,
          APPL - SECTOR : FINANCE , STOCK PRICES * STOCK PRICES - DETERMINANTS * APPL
          - MACRO : MONEY , SUPPLY * STOCK PRICES - MODELS , EVALUATION
YA2366   MAMMEN T.
          "Indian money market: an econometric study"   Int. Econ. Rev., vol.14,
          1973, pp.49-68,
          APPL - MACRO : MONEY * APPL - MACRO , INDIA * EX ANTE * PUBLIC EXPENDITURE -
          EFFECT OF * APPL - MACRO : FLOW OF FUNDS
YA2367   MANDELBROT B.B.
          "Comments on 'A subordinated stochastic process model with finite variance
          for speculative prices', by P.K. Clark"   Econometrica, vol.41, 1973,
          pp.157-159,
          APPL - SECTOR : FINANCE , VOLATILITY * RANDOM WALK - THEORY * ERROR
          DISTRIBUTION - STABLE * THEORY - MODELLING * ERROR DISTRIBUTION - LOGNORMAL
          * COMPARATIVE METHODS - ERROR DISTRIBUTIONS
YA2368   MANDELBROT B.B.
          "Correction of an error in 'The variation of certain speculative prices'
          (1963)"   J. Business, vol.45, 1972, pp.542-543,
          APPL - SECTOR : COMMODITIES , COTTON * ERROR DISTRIBUTION - NON NORMAL *
          DATA ERRORS - EFFECT OF
YA2369   MANDELBROT B.B.
          "Statistical methodology for nonperiodic cycles: from the covariance to R/S
          analysis"   Anns. Econ. Soc. Meas., vol.2, 1973, pp.259-290,
          ERROR DISTRIBUTION - STABLE * BUSINESS CYCLE - METHODOLOGY * TIME SERIES -
          IDENTIFICATION * RANDOM WALK - TEST * TIME SERIES - RANGE , STANDARD
          DEVIATION * ERROR DISTRIBUTION - NON NORMAL * MODEL SELECTION * TIME SERIES
          - AUTOREGRESSIVE * CONTROL CHARTS - CUSUM * EVALUATION - SPECTRAL ANALYSIS *
          AUTOCORRELATION - TEST * ADVANCED
YA2370   MANDELBROT B.B.
          "When can price be arbitrated efficiently? A limit to the validity of the
          Random Walk and Martingale models"   Rev. Econ. Stats., vol.53, 1971,
          pp.225-236,
          THEORY - SPECULATION * RANDOM WALK - THEORY * STOCK PRICES - THEORY *
          PROBABILITY MODELS - MARTINGALE * THEORY - EFFICIENT MARKETS * ADVANCED
YA2371   MANLY B.F.J.
          "Exponential data transformations"   Stat'n., vol.25, 1976, pp.37-42,
          REGRESSION - TRANSFORMATION , EXPONENTIAL
YA2372   MANN D.H.
          "Implications of modal - delayed distributed lag response to advertising
          expenditure"   Decis. Sci., vol.6, 1975, pp.646-661.
          ADVERTISING - EFFECT OF * DISTRIBUTED LAG - APPL , ADVERTISING * APPL - FIRM
          : CONSUMER NON DURABLES , HEALTH AIDS * COMPARATIVE METHODS - DISTRIBUTED
          LAG * DISTRIBUTED LAG - SOLOW * ADVERTISING - OPTIMALITY

YA2373   MANN J.K., YETT D.E.,
          "The analysis of hospital costs: a review"   J. Business, vol.41, 1968,
          pp.191-202.
          HEALTH - HOSPITAL * COST - SECTOR : HEALTH , HOSPITALS
YA2374   MANSFIELD E., WAGNER S,
          "Organisational and strategic factors associated with probabilities of
          success in industrial r & d"   J. Business, vol.48, 1975, pp.179-198,
          APPL - FIRM : R & D * USE - R&D
YA2375   MANSFIELD E.R.
          "PCR: principal component regression analysis"   J. Mktg. Res., vol.15,
          1978, pp.471-472,
          ESTIMATION - PRINCIPAL COMPONENTS * COMPUTERISATION - ESTIMATION ,
          REGRESSION MODELS , PROGRAMS
YA2376   MANSFIELD E.R., WEBSTER J.T., GUNST R.F.
          "An analytic selection technique for principal components regression"
          Appl. Stats., vol.26, 1977, pp.34-40.
          ESTIMATION - PRINCIPAL COMPONENTS * REGRESSION - ESTIMATION * REGRESSION -
          PRINCIPAL COMPONENTS
YA2377   MANTEL N., MYERS M,
          "Problems of convergence of maximum likelihood iterative procedures in
          multiparameter situations"   J. Am. Statist. Ass., vol.66, 1971,
          pp.484-491,
          ESTIMATION - MAXIMUM LIKELIHOOD , ITERATIVE * DATA - SIMULATION * NUMERICAL
          METHODS - OPTIMISATION
YA2378   MANTELL E.H.
          "Discrimination based on education in the labor market for engineers"
          Rev. Econ. Stats., vol.56, 1974, pp.158-166,
          EDUCATION - EFFECT OF * MANPOWER PLANNING - QUALIFIED MANPOWER , ENGINEERS *
          MANPOWER PLANNING - EARNINGS
YA2379   MANTELL E.H.
          "Factors affecting labour productivity in post offices"   J. Am. Statist,
          Ass., vol.69, 1974, pp.303-309,
          PRODUCTION FUNCTIONS - THEORY , JOINT * PRODUCTION FUNCTIONS - SECTOR * APPL
          - SECTOR : GOVERNMENT , POSTAL SERVICES * CANONICAL CORRELATION - APPL *
          APPL - FIRM : PRODUCTIVITY
YA2380   MANTELL E.H.
          "Forecasting aggregate changes in US manufacturing and nonmanufacturing
          inventory investment"   J. Business, vol.50, 1977, pp.40-49,
          APPL - MACRO : INVENTORIES * CANONICAL CORRELATION - APPL * EX ANTE *
          EXPECTATIONS - ESTIMATING
YA2381   MARCHANT L.J., HOCKLEY D.J.
          "A comparison of two forecasting techniques"   Stat'n., vol.20, 1971,
          pp.35-44.
          APPL - SECTOR : CONSUMER DURABLES , CARS * COMPARATIVE METHODS - EXPONENTIAL
          SMOOTHING , JUDGEMENTAL
YA2382   MARCIS R.G., SMITH V.K.
          "Efficient estimation of multivariate financial relationships"   J.
          Finance, vol.29, 1974, pp.1415-1423.
          REGRESSION - SEEMINGLY UNRELATED * INTEREST RATE - DETERMINANTS * DATA -
          INTERNATIONAL * COMPARATIVE METHODS - REGRESSION , SEEMINGLY UNRELATED
YA2383   MARITZ A.
          "A note of correction to Guilkey's test for serial independence in
          simultaneous equation models"   Econometrica, vol.46, 1978, p.471,
          AUTOCORRELATION - TEST * SIMULTANEOUS SYSTEM - LAGGED DEPENDENT * ADVANCED
YA2384   MARQUARDT D.W., SNEE R.D.
          "Ridge regression in practice"   Am. Stat'n., vol.29, 1975, pp.3-20,
          REGRESSION - RIDGE * MULTICOLLINEARITY - REMOVAL OF
YA2385   MARSCHNER D.C.
          "DAGMAR revisited - eight years later"   J. Advtg. Res., vol.11:2, 1971,
          pp.27-33.
          ADVERTISING - EFFECT OF * APPL - FIRM : PRODUCTION , PETROLEUM * APPL - FIRM
          : FINANCE , PROFITS * APPL - FIRM : FINANCE , STOCK PRICES * STOCK PRICES -
          DETERMINANTS * BASIC
YA2386   MARSCHNER D.C.
          "Theory versus practice in allocating advertising money"   J. Business,
          vol.40, 1967, pp.286-302,
          ADVERTISING - REVIEW * ADVERTISING - DETERMINANTS
YA2387   MARSDEN J.R., ET AL.
          "The process analysis alternative to statistical cost functions: comments"
          Am. Econ. Rev., vol.64, 1974, pp.773-779,
          COST - METHODOLOGY
YA2388   MARSHALL K.T.
          "A comparison of two personnel prediction models"   Ops. Res., vol.21,
          1973, pp.810-822,
          MARKOV MODELS - APPL : MANPOWER * APPL - FIRM : EDUCATION , UNIVERSITIES *
          EVALUATION - MANPOWER PLANNING MODELS * EX ANTE * MANPOWER PLANNING - SECTOR
          : EDUCATION , UNIVERSITIES * MANPOWER PLANNING - PROMOTION * MANPOWER
          PLANNING - FIRM

YA2389   MARSHALL M.L.
         "Equilibrium age distributions for graded systems"   R. Statist. Soc. (A),
         vol.138, 1975, pp.62-69.
         MANPOWER PLANNING - PROMOTION * PROBABILITY MODELS - RENEWAL THEORETIC
YA2390   MARSHALL M.L.
         "Some statistical methods for forecasting wastage"   Stat'n., vol.28, 1971,
         pp.53-68.
         MANPOWER PLANNING - FIRM * MANPOWER PLANNING - LABOUR TURNOVER * MANPOWER
         PLANNING - SECTOR : MILITARY * EX ANTE * PROBABILITY MODELS - LOGNORMAL
YA2391   MARTELL T.F.
         "Adaptive trading rules for commodity futures"   Omega, vol.4, 1976,
         pp.407-416.
         APPL - SECTOR : COMMODITIES , GRAIN * APPL - SECTOR : COMMODITIES , SOYBEAN
         * PROBABILITY MODELS - ENTROPY * USE - PURCHASING , COMMODITIES * RANDOM
         WALK - TEST * EX ANTE
YA2392   MARTELL T.F., PHILLIPPATOS G.C.
         "Adaption, information and dependence in commodity markets" with discussion
         J. Finance, vol.29, 1974, pp.493-498 & 523-524.
         APPL - SECTOR : COMMODITIES , GRAIN * APPL - SECTOR : COMMODITIES , SOYBEAN
         * PROBABILITY MODELS - ENTROPY * USE - COMMODITY PURCHASE * LOSS FUNCTIONS -
         SECTOR : FINANCE , TRADING RULES
YA2393   MARTIN C.R., WRIGHT R.L.
         "Profit-orientated data analysis for market segmentation; an alternative to
         AID"   J. Mktg. Res., vol.11, 1974, pp.237-242.
         AID - METHODOLOGY * EVALUATION - MARKET SEGMENTATION * APPL - SECTOR :
         CONSUMER DURABLES , CLOTHING * CONSUMER BEHAVIOUR - PURCHASING ,
         DETERMINANTS
YA2394   MARTIN J.D., KLEMKOSKY R.C.
         "Evidence of heteroscedasticity in the market model"   J. Business, vol.48,
         1975, pp.81-86.
         APPL - FIRM : FINANCE , STOCK PRICES * STOCK PRICES - MODELS , CAPM *
         SPECIFICATION ERROR - TESTS , HETEROSCEDASTICITY
YA2395   MARTIN W.S.
         "The effects of scaling on the correlation coefficient; a test of validity"
         J. Mktg. Res., vol.10, 1973, pp.316-318.
         REGRESSION - DISCRETE DEPENDENT * REGRESSION - SUMMARY STATISTICS * DATA -
         ORDINAL
YA2396   MARVEL H.P.
         "Competition and price levels in the retail gasoline market"   Rev. Econ.
         Stats., vol.60, 1978, pp.252-258.
         APPL - SECTOR : RETAILING , GASOLINE * CONCENTRATION - EFFECT OF * PRICE -
         SECTOR : RETAILING
YA2397   MASON J.M.
         "A structural study of the income velocity of circulation"   J. Finance,
         vol.29, 1974, pp.1077-1086.
         MACRO MODEL - US * APPL - MACRO : MONEY , INCOME VELOCITY * MULTIPLIERS -
         MACRO * APPL - MACRO : MONEY , SUPPLY
YA2398   MASON P.F.
         "Long term forecasting of consumer durable markets"   British J. Mktg.,
         vol.4, 1970, pp.34-41.
         APPL - SECTOR : CONSUMER DURABLES * LONG TERM FORECASTING
YA2399   MASON R.H., SAKONG I.
         "Level of economic development and capital-labour ratios in manufacturing"
         Rev. Econ. Stats., vol.53, 1971, pp.176-178.
         APPL - MACRO : DEVELOPMENT * DATA - CROSS SECTION * DATA - INTERNATIONAL
YA2400   MASSARO V.G., BLACK S.W.
         "An econometric study of eurodollar borrowing by New York banks and the rate
         of interest on eurodollars: comments"   J. Finance, vol.27, 1972,
         pp.927-932.
         APPL - MACRO : INTERNATIONAL FINANCE * INTEREST RATE - EFFECT OF
YA2401   MASSELL B.F., PEARSON S.R., FITCH J.B.
         "Foreign exchange and economic development; an empirical study of selected
         Latin American countries"   Rev. Econ. Stats., vol.54, 1972, pp.208-212.
         APPL - MACRO : DEVELOPMENT * APPL - MACRO : INTERNATIONAL TRADE , IMPORTS *
         APPL - MACRO : GNP * DATA - CROSS SECTION , TIME SERIES * APPL - MACRO :
         INTERNATIONAL FINANCE * APPL - MACRO , LATIN AMERICA
YA2402   MASSON P.R.
         "Structural models of the demand for bonds and the term structure of
         interest rates"   Economica, vol.45, 1978, pp.363-377.
         APPL - SECTOR : FINANCE , BONDS * INTEREST RATE - TERM STRUCTURE * INTEREST
         RATE - DETERMINANTS
YA2403   MASSON R.T., ORNSTEIN S.I.
         "'Concentration and profits' by Stanley I. Ornstein: comments"   J.
         Business, vol.50, 1977, pp.529-536.
         APPL - SECTOR : FINANCE , PROFITS * CONCENTRATION - EFFECT OF
YA2404   MASSY W.F.
         "Principal components regression in exploratory statistical research"   J.
         Am. Statist. Ass., vol.60, 1965, pp.234-256.
         APPL - SECTOR : CONSUMER DURABLES , APPLIANCES , HEATING UNITS * REGRESSION
         - ESTIMATION * ESTIMATION - PRINCIPAL COMPONENTS * MULTICOLLINEARITY -
         REMOVAL OF * MARKET SEGMENTATION * APPL - SECTOR : CONSUMER DURABLES ,
         APPLIANCES , REFRIDGERATORS * COMPARATIVE METHODS - DATA : AGGREGATE ,
         DISAGGREGATE * FACTOR ANALYSIS - THEORY * CONSUMER BEHAVIOUR - PURCHASING ,
         DETERMINANTS * INCOME - EFFECT OF * EDUCATION - EFFECT OF

YA2405   MASSY W.F., MORRISON D.G., EHRENBERG A.S.C.
         "Comments on Ehrenberg's appraisal of brand switching models"   J. Mktg.
         Res., vol.5, 1968, pp.225-229.
         EVALUATION - MARKOV MODELS * BRAND CHOICE - THEORY

YA2406   MATHEWSON G.F.
         "A consumer theory of demand for the media"   J. Business, vol.45, 1972,
         pp.212-224.
         CONSUMER BEHAVIOUR - ECONOMIC MODELS , THEORY * APPL - SECTOR : SERVICES ,
         MEDIA

YA2407   MATHEWSON G.F.
         "A note on the price effects of market power in the Canadian newspaper
         industry"   Can. J. Econ., vol.5, 1972, pp.298-301.
         APPL - FIRM : SERVICES , MEDIA , NEWSPAPERS * PRICE - FIRM : SERVICES

YA2408   MATHEWSON G.F.
         "Price effects of market power in the Canadian newspaper industry: a reply"
         Can. J. Econ., vol.7, 1974, pp.130-132.
         APPL - FIRM : SERVICES , MEDIA , NEWSPAPERS * PRICE - FIRM : SERVICES *
         PRICE - EFFECT OF * REGRESSION - SPECIFICATION OF VARIABLES : APPL

YA2409   MATHUR S.S., PADLEY H.
         "Forecasting first order sales of consumer durables"   Ind. Mktg. Mgmt.,
         vol.3, 1974, pp.137-151.
         APPL - SECTOR : CONSUMER DURABLES , APPLIANCES , TV * LIFE CYCLE - PRODUCT

YA2410   MATHUR V.K.
         "Economics of crime: an investigation of the deterrent hypothesis for urban
         areas"   Rev. Econ. Stats., vol.60, 1978, pp.459-466.
         APPL - SECTOR : SOCIAL , CRIME * DATA - CROSS SECTION

YA2411   MATTHEWS K.G.P., ORMEROD P.A.
         "St. Louis models of the UK economy"   Nat. Inst. Econ. Rev., no.84, 1978,
         pp.65-69.
         MACRO MODEL - ST.LOUIS * MACRO MODEL - UK * APPL - MACRO : GNP * POLICY
         EVALUATION - MACRO : FISCAL , MONETARY * MULTIPLIERS - MACRO * DATA -
         SPECIFICATION OF VARIABLES

YA2412   MAYER C.S.
         "Assessing the accuracy of marketing research"   J. Mktg. Res., vol.7,
         1970, pp.285-291.
         DATA ERRORS - ESTIMATION OF * SURVEYS - METHODOLOGY , RESPONSE ERROR * BASIC

YA2413   MAYER L.S., YOUNGER M.S.
         "Estimation of standardized regression coefficients"   J. Am. Statist.
         Ass., vol.71, 1976, pp.154-157.
         REGRESSION - MODEL INTERPRETATION * EVALUATION - REGRESSION , COEFFICIENTS

YA2414   MAYER T.
         "Selecting economic hypotheses by goodness of fit"   Econ. J., vol.85,
         1975, pp.877-883.
         EX ANTE * EVALUATION - THEORY OF * EVALUATION - MODEL SELECTION * EVALUATION
         - EX POST MODELS

YA2415   MAYNE L.S.
         "Supervisory influence on bank capital"   J. Finance, vol.27, 1972,
         pp.637-651.
         APPL - FIRM : FINANCE , BANKS * APPL - FIRM : FINANCE , BANK , LIABILITIES *
         USE - BANK REGULATION

YA2416   MAYOR T.H.
         "Equipment expenditures by input-output industries"   Rev. Econ. Stats.,
         vol.53, 1971, pp.26-36.
         DISTRIBUTED LAG - APPL , INVESTMENT * APPL - SECTOR : INVESTMENT * TAX -
         EFFECT OF * PRODUCTION FUNCTIONS - SECTOR * PRODUCTION FUNCTIONS -
         SUBSTITUTION

YA2417   MEADOWS D.H., RANDERS J.
         "The carrying capacity of the globe"   Sloan Mgmt. Rev., vol.13, no.2,
         1972, pp.11-27.
         SIMULATION - APPL : WORLD MODELS * INDUSTRIAL DYNAMICS - APPL , WORLD * APPL
         - MACRO , WORLD

YA2418   MEEKER W.Q.
         "TSERIES - a user-orientated computer program for time series analysis"
         Am. Stat'n., vol.32, 1978, pp.111-112.
         COMPUTERISATION - ESTIMATION , TIME SERIES , PROGRAMS * TIME SERIES - ARIMA
         : APPL

YA2419   MEEUSEN W., VAN DEN BROECK J.
         "Efficiency estimation from Cobb-Douglas production functions with composed
         error"   Int. Econ. Rev., vol.18, 1977, pp.435-444 & 790.
         APPL - SECTOR : EFFICIENCY * PRODUCTION FUNCTIONS - ESTIMATION * PRODUCTION
         FUNCTIONS - SECTOR * ERROR DISTRIBUTION - GAMMA

YA2420   MEHRA R.K.
         "Identification in control and econometrics: similarities and differences"
         Anns. Econ. Soc. Meas., vol.3, 1974, pp.21-47.
         CONTROL THEORY - STOCHASTIC , REVIEW * ESTIMATION - KALMAN FILTER *
         SIMULTANEOUS SYSTEM - MODEL IDENTIFICATION * ECONOMETRICS - REVIEW *
         REGRESSION - REVIEW * SIMULTANEOUS SYSTEM - MODEL CHOICE * REGRESSION -
         STATE SPACE * ADVANCED

YA2421   MEHRA Y.P.
         "Spillovers in wage determination in US manufacturing industries"   Rev.
         Econ. Stats., vol.53, 1976, pp.300-312.
         APPL - SECTOR : EARNINGS * RESIDUAL - ANALYSIS OF , SPECIFICATION ERROR *
         MANPOWER PLANNING - INDUSTRIAL STRUCTURE
YA2422   MEHTA J.S., NARASIMHAM G.V.L., SWAMY P.A.V.B.
         "Estimation of a dynamic demand function for gasoline with different schemes
         of parameter variation"   J. Econometrics, vol.7, 1978, pp.263-279.
         REGRESSION - RANDOM COEFFICIENTS * STABILITY OF COEFFICIENTS - REGRESSION ,
         TEST * COMPARATIVE METHODS - DATA : CROSS SECTION , TIME SERIES * REGRESSION
         - ERROR COMPONENTS * PRICE - EFFECT OF * INCOME - EFFECT OF * DATA -
         AGGREGATION * ESTIMATION - MAXIMUM LIKELIHOOD * ADVANCED
YA2423   MEHTA J.S., SWAMY P.A.V.B.
         "Further evidence on the relative efficiencies of Zellner's seemingly
         uncorrelated regressions estimator"   J. Am. Statist. Ass., vol.71, 1976,
         pp.634-639.
         ESTIMATION - GLS * EVALUATION - REGRESSION , SEEMINGLY UNRELATED * ADVANCED
YA2424   MELLER P.
         "Production functions for industrial establishments of different sizes: the
         Chilean case"   Anns. Econ. Soc. Meas., vol.4, 1975, pp.595-634.
         APPL - MACRO , LATIN AMERICA * PRODUCTION FUNCTIONS - SCALE RETURNS *
         STABILITY OF COEFFICIENTS - REGRESSION : APPL * PRODUCTION FUNCTIONS -
         SECTOR * DATA - CROSS SECTION
YA2425   MELLICHAMP J.M., LOVE R.M.
         "Production switching heuristics for the aggregate planning problem"
         Mgmt. Sci., vol.24, 1978, pp.1242-1251.
         USE - PRODUCTION , PLANNING * USE - INVENTORY CONTROL * USE - SCHEDULING ,
         MANPOWER * FORECASTING - VALUE OF
YA2426   MELNICK E.L., MOUSSOURAKIS J.
         "Seasonal adjustment for the decisionmaker"   Decis. Sci., vol.6, 1975,
         pp.252-258.
         TIME SERIES - DECOMPOSITION * SEASONALITY - ESTIMATION , HARMONICS
YA2427   MELROSE K.B.
         "An empirical study of optimising advertising policy"   J. Business,
         vol.42, 1969, pp.282-292.
         ADVERTISING - OPTIMALITY * APPL - SECTOR : CONSUMER NON DURABLES , GROCERIES
         * ADVERTISING - DETERMINANTS
YA2428   MELTZER A.H.
         "Credit availabilty and economic decisions; some evidence from the mortgage
         and housing markets"   J. Finance, vol.29, 1974, pp.763-777.
         APPL - SECTOR : CONSTRUCTION , RESIDENTIAL * APPL - SECTOR : FINANCE ,
         MORTGAGES
YA2429   MELVIN J.R.
         "The effects of Tariff Preferences on Canadian Imports: an empirical
         analysis"   Can. J. Econ., vol.5, 1972, pp.48-69.
         TARIFF - EFFECT OF * APPL - SECTOR : INTERNATIONAL TRADE , IMPORTS
YA2430   MENDELSON R.C.
         "The table producing language of the bureau of labour statistics"   Anns.
         Econ. Soc. Meas., vol.4, 1975, pp.357-361.
         COMPUTERISATION - DATA , PRESENTATION , PROGRAMS
YA2431   MENEZES O.J.
         "The dummy variable method for jointly estimating seasonal indexes and
         regression on non-seasonal variables"   Am. Stat'n., vol.25:5, 1971,
         pp.32-36.
         SEASONALITY - ESTIMATION , OLS
YA2432   MENNIS E.A.
         "The practical use of economic analysis in investment management"   Bus.
         Econ., vol.10:4, 1975, pp.38-44.
         USE - PORTFOLIO SELECTION
YA2433   MERCER A., RUSSELL J.I.T.
         "Recurrent competitive bidding"   Opl. Res. Q., vol.20, 1969, pp.209-221.
         EXPONENTIAL SMOOTHING - APPL * PROBABILITIES - FORECAST OF * USE -
         COMPETITIVE BIDDING
YA2434   MEREDITH J.
         "Markovian analysis of a geriatric ward"   Mgmt. Sci. (B), vol.19, 1973,
         pp.604-612.
         USER - FIRM : HEALTH , HOSPITAL * HEALTH - HOSPITAL , PSYCHIATRIC * MARKOV
         MODELS - APPL : MANPOWER * MANPOWER PLANNING - FIRM : HEALTH
YA2435   MEREWITZ L.
         "Costs and returns to scale in US post offices"   J. Am. Statist. Ass.,
         vol.66, 1971, pp.504-509.
         APPL - SECTOR : GOVERNMENT , POSTAL SERVICES * COST - SECTOR : GOVERNMENT *
         COST - SCALE ECONOMIES * APPL - SECTOR : PRODUCTIVITY
YA2436   MERRITT T.P.
         "Forecasting the future business environment - the state of the art"   Long
         Range Planning, vol.7:3, 1974, pp.54-62.
         FORECASTING - INTRODUCTION * BASIC

YA2437 MESSENGER R., MANDELL L.
"A model search technique for predictive nominal scale multivariate
analysis" J. Am. Statist. Ass., vol.67, 1972, pp.768=772.
APPL = SECTOR : CONSUMER DURABLES , CARS * COMPARATIVE METHODS =
DISCRIMINATION * CONSUMER BEHAVIOUR = PURCHASING , DETERMINANTS * AID =
METHODOLOGY

YA2438 METCALF D.
"Pay dispersion, information, and returns to search in a professional labour
market" Rev. Econ. Studies, vol.40, 1973, pp.491=505.
APPL = SECTOR : EDUCATION , UNIVERSITIES * MANPOWER PLANNING = SECTOR :
EDUCATION , UNIVERSITIES * EDUCATION = EFFECT OF * MANPOWER PLANNING =
EARNINGS * MANPOWER PLANNING = QUALIFIED MANPOWER

YA2439 METCALF D.
"The determinants of earnings changes: a regional analysis for the UK,
1960=68" Int. Econ. Rev., vol.12, 1971, pp.273=282.
APPL = MACRO : EARNINGS * APPL = MACRO , UK * REGIONAL MODELS = MANPOWER
PLANNING , EARNINGS

YA2440 METCALF D.
"Urban unemployment in England" Econ. J., vol.85, 1975, pp.578=589.
APPL = MACRO : UNEMPLOYMENT * APPL = MACRO , UK

YA2441 METWALLY M.M.
"Advertising and competition behaviour of related Australian firms" Rev.
Econ. Stats., vol.57, 1975, pp.417=427.
ADVERTISING = EFFECT OF * ADVERTISING = OPTIMALITY * APPL = FIRM : CONSUMER
NON DURABLES , CIGARETTES * APPL = FIRM : CONSUMER NON DURABLES , GROCERIES
* APPL = FIRM : CONSUMER NON DURABLES , LIQUOR * APPL = SECTOR : CONSUMER
NON DURABLES * MARKET SHARE = SECTOR : CONSUMER NON DURABLES * APPL = SECTOR
: CONSUMER NON DURABLES , HEALTH AIDS * EVALUATION = MARKET SHARE MODELS

YA2442 METWALLY M.M.
"Optimal advertising and traders' margins: a case study" Ind. Mktg.
Mgmt., vol.4, 1975, pp.227=233.
APPL = FIRM : CONSUMER DURABLES , CARS * MARKET SHARE = SECTOR : CONSUMER
DURABLES * ADVERTISING = EFFECT OF * ADVERTISING = OPTIMALITY * DECISION
RULES = FIRM * PRICE = EFFECT OF * COMPARATIVE METHODS = REGRESSION , MODEL
SPECIFICATION

YA2443 MEULENDYKE A., MAKIN J.
"Demand and supply functions for stocks of Euro=dollar deposits: an
empirical study: comments" Rev. Econ. Stats., vol.57, 1975, pp.350=356.
APPL = MACRO : INTERNATIONAL FINANCE

YA2444 MEYER J.A.
"The impact of welfare benefit levels and tax rates on the labor supply of
poor women" Rev. Econ. Stats., vol.57, 1975, pp.236=238.
POLICY EVALUATION = MACRO : WELFARE * MANPOWER PLANNING = LABOUR
PARTICIPATION , FEMALE * EDUCATION = EFFECT OF

YA2445 MEYER L.H., HART W.R.
"On the effects of fiscal and monetary policy: completing the taxonomy"
Am. Econ. Rev., vol.65, 1975, pp.762=767.
THEORY = FISCAL , MONETARY * POLICY EVALUATION = MACRO : FISCAL , MONETARY *
ADVANCED

YA2446 MEYER P.A., NERI J.A.
"A Keynes=Friedman money demand function" Am. Econ. Rev., vol.65, 1975,
pp.610=623.
APPL = MACRO : MONEY , DEMAND * THEORY = MONETARY * INTEREST RATE = EFFECT
OF * EVALUATION = SPECIFICATION OF VARIABLES * EVALUATION = MONEY DEMAND ,
MODELS OF * INCOME = EFFECT OF * EX ANTE

YA2447 MEYER R.A.
"Publicly owned versus privately owned utilities: a policy choice" Rev.
Econ. Stats., vol.57, 1975, pp.391=399.
APPL = SECTOR : UTILITIES , ELECTRICITY * STABILITY OF COEFFICIENTS =
REGRESSION : APPL = SECTOR : UTILITIES * APPL = SECTOR : GOVERNMENT ,
NATIONALISED INDUSTRIES * POLICY EVALUATION = MACRO : INDUSTRIAL STRUCTURE

YA2448 MEYER R.R., ET AL.
"Comments on 'fitting parameters to complex models by direct search'" J.
Mktg. Res., vol.8, 1971, pp.518=519.
EVALUATION = ESTIMATION , NON LINEAR * BASIC

YA2449 MEYERS S.L.
"A re=examination of market and industry factors in stock price behaviour"
J. Finance, vol.28, 1973, pp.695=705.
APPL = SECTOR : FINANCE , STOCK PRICES * STOCK PRICES = INDUSTRIAL STRUCTURE
* APPL = FIRM : FINANCE , STOCK PRICES * CLUSTER ANALYSIS = APPL * FACTOR
ANALYSIS = APPL

YA2450 MICHAEL G.C.
"A computer simulation model for forecasting catalog sales" J. Mktg.
Res., vol.8, 1971, pp.224=229.
APPL = FIRM : RETAILING , MAIL ORDER * BOOTSTRAPPING = APPL * COMPARATIVE
METHODS = BOOTSTRAPPING , JUDGEMENTAL * STYLE GOODS * EX ANTE

YA2451   MICHELINI C.
         "Estimating the exponential growth model by direct least squares: a comment"
         Appl. Stats., vol.21, 1972, pp.233-235.
         TREND CURVES - EXPONENTIAL , ESTIMATION * APPL - MACRO : INVESTMENT *
         ESTIMATION - NON LINEAR * NUMERICAL METHODS - OPTIMISATION , SEARCH

YA2452   MIHRAM G.A.
         "Some practical aspects of the verification and validation of simulation
         models"   Opl. Res. Q., vol.23, 1972, pp.17-29.
         SIMULATION - EVALUATION OF RESULTS * SIMULATION - EXPERIMENTAL DESIGN

YA2453   MIKHAIL W.M.
         "A comparative Monte Carlo study of the properties of econometric
         estimators"   J. Am. Statist. Ass., vol.70, 1975, pp.94-103.
         ESTIMATION - LISE * SIMULATION - METHODOLOGY , MONTE CARLO * ESTIMATION -
         FIML * ESTIMATION - MAXIMUM LIKELIHOOD , LINEARIZED * COMPARATIVE METHODS -
         ESTIMATION : SIMULTANEOUS SYSTEM * COMPARATIVE METHODS - ESTIMATION : OLS ,
         2SLS * COMPARATIVE METHODS - ESTIMATION : OLS , FIML * COMPARATIVE METHODS -
         ESTIMATION : OLS , 3SLS * DATA - SIMULATION * COMPARATIVE METHODS -
         ESTIMATION : SIMULTANEOUS SYSTEM , 2SLS , 3SLS * ADVANCED

YA2454   MIKHAIL W.M.
         "Simulating the small sample properties of econometric estimators"   J. Am.
         Statist. Ass., vol.67, 1972, pp.620-625.
         EVALUATION - ESTIMATION : 2SLS * DATA - SIMULATION * SIMULATION -
         METHODOLOGY , MONTE CARLO

YA2455   MILBOURNE R.H.
         "Wisconsin's econometric model"   Bus. Econ., vol.13:4, 1978, pp.42-45.
         REGIONAL MODELS * USER - SECTOR : GOVERNMENT , LOCAL

YA2456   MILES M.A.
         "Currency substitution, flexible exchange rates, and monetary independence"
         Am. Econ. Rev., vol.68, 1978, pp.428-436.
         APPL - MACRO : INTERNATIONAL FINANCE , EXCHANGE RATES * APPL - MACRO ,
         CANADA * INTEREST RATE - EFFECT OF * PRODUCTION FUNCTIONS - SUBSTITUTION *
         PRODUCTION FUNCTIONS - MACRO

YA2457   MILKOVICH G.T., ANNONI A.J., MAHONEY T.A.
         "The use of the Delphi procedure in manpower forecasting"   Mgmt. Sci. (B),
         vol.19, 1972, pp.381-388.
         DELPHI * MANPOWER PLANNING - QUALIFIED MANPOWER * COMPARATIVE METHODS -
         CAUSAL , JUDGEMENTAL * LONG TERM FORECASTING * JUDGEMENTAL FORECASTS -
         SPECIALIST

YA2458   MILLER B.R., MASTERS G.C.
         "A short-run price prediction model for eggs"   Am. J. Ag. Econ., vol.55,
         1973, pp.484-489.
         APPL - SECTOR : AGRICULTURE , EGGS * EX ANTE

YA2459   MILLER J.G., BERRY W.L., LAI C.F.
         "A comparison of alternative forecasting strategies for multi-stage
         production-inventory systems"   Decis. Sci., vol.7, 1976, pp.714-724.
         USE - PRODUCTION , CONTROL * USE - INVENTORY CONTROL * FORECASTING -
         MULTISTAGE * COMPARATIVE METHODS - DATA : AGGREGATE , DISAGGREGATE

YA2460   MILLER J.G., SPRAGUE L.G.
         "Behind the growth in MRP"   H.B.R., vol.53, Sept-Oct, 1975, pp.83-91.
         USE - INVENTORY CONTROL * USE - PRODUCTION PLANNING

YA2461   MILLER M.H.
         "Can a rise in import prices be inflationary and deflationary? economists
         and UK inflation, 1973-74"   Am. Econ. Rev., vol.66, 1976, pp.501-519.
         INFLATION - REVIEW * APPL - MACRO , UK

YA2462   MILLER N.C., WHITMAN M.V.N.
         "Alternative theories and tests of US short-term foreign investment"   J.
         Finance, vol.28, 1973, pp.1131-1150.
         THEORY - INVESTMENT BEHAVIOUR * APPL - MACRO : INVESTMENT * APPL - MACRO :
         INTERNATIONAL FINANCE * COMPARATIVE METHODS - ESTIMATION : OLS , 2SLS

YA2463   MILLER R.A.
         "Marginal concentration ratios as market structure variables"   Rev. Econ.
         Stats., vol.53, 1971, pp.289-293.
         APPL - SECTOR : FINANCE , PROFITS * DATA - CROSS SECTION * CONCENTRATION -
         EFFECT OF

YA2464   MILLER R.L.
         "A short term econometric model of textile industries"   Am. Econ. Rev.,
         vol.61, 1971, pp.279-289.
         APPL - SECTOR : CONSUMER DURABLES , TEXTILES * MANPOWER PLANNING - SECTOR :
         PRODUCTION * ESTIMATION - 3SLS : APPL * APPL - SECTOR : PRODUCTION ,
         TEXTILES

YA2465   MILLER R.L.R.
         "The reserve Labour hypothesis: some tests of its implications"   Econ. J.,
         vol.81, 1971, pp.17-35.
         APPL - SECTOR : EMPLOYMENT * MANPOWER PLANNING - LABOUR TURNOVER *
         COMPARATIVE METHODS - ESTIMATION : REGRESSION , SEEMINGLY UNRELATED

YA2466   MILLS T.C.
         "The functional form of the UK demand for money"   Appl. Stats., vol.27,
         1978, pp.52-57.
         REGRESSION - TRANSFORMATIONS , BOX COX : APPL * APPL - MACRO , UK * APPL -
         MACRO : MONEY , DEMAND * INTEREST RATE - EFFECT OF * STABILITY OF
         COEFFICIENTS - REGRESSION : APPL

YA2467   MILSUM J.M., TURBAN E., VERTINSKY I.
"Hospital admissions systems: their evaluation and management"   Mgmt. Sci.
(B), vol.19, 1973, pp.646-666.
USER - FIRM : HEALTH , HOSPITALS * USE - SCHEDULING , SERVICES * HEALTH -
HOSPITAL * HEALTH - HOSPITAL , PATIENT FACILITIES

YA2468   MILTON H.S.
"Cost of research index, 1920-1970"   Ops. Res., vol.20, 1972, pp.1-18.
USE - R&D * COST - FIRM : R&D

YA2469   MINGO J.J.
"Regulatory influence on bank capital investment"   J. Finance, vol.30,
1975, pp.1111-1121.
USE - BANK REGULATION * APPL - FIRM : FINANCE , BANKS * DATA - CROSS SECTION
* APPL - FIRM : FINANCE , BANK , LIABILITIES

YA2470   MIRER T.W., PECK J.K., BERGMANN B.R.
"Combining microsimulation and regression: comments"   Econometrica,
vol.43, 1975, pp.523-531.
APPL - MACRO : UNEMPLOYMENT * SIMULATION - METHODOLOGY , MICRO * APPL -
SECTOR : SOCIAL , POVERTY * REGRESSION - LIMITED DEPENDENT , PROBIT : APPL *
THEORY - MODELLING * COMPARATIVE METHODS - REGRESSION , SIMULATION

YA2471   MIRUS R.
"The impact of bank portfolio decisions on the balance of payments: the
German experience"   J. Finance, vol.29, 1974, pp.1513-1522.
APPL - MACRO : INTERNATIONAL FINANCE * APPL - SECTOR : FINANCE , BANKS *
APPL - SECTOR : FINANCE , INTERNATIONAL FINANCE * APPL - MACRO , GERMANY

YA2472   MISHKIN F.S.
"A note on short-run asset effects on household saving and consumption"
Am. Econ. Rev., vol.67, 1977, pp.246-248.
MACRO MODEL - MIT , PENN , SSRC * APPL - MACRO : CONSUMPTION * STOCK PRICES
- EFFECT OF

YA2473   MISHKIN F.S.
"Consumer sentiment and spending on durable goods"   Brookings Paps. Econ.
Activity, 1978, pp.215-232.
EVALUATION - ATTITUDINAL DATA * APPL - SECTOR : CONSUMER DURABLES , CARS *
INDEX NUMBERS - MACRO : CONSUMER CONFIDENCE * APPL - SECTOR : CONSUMER
DURABLES * ESTIMATION - INSTRUMENTAL VARIABLES : APPL * ERROR SPECIFICATION
- AUTOCORRELATED : APPL

YA2474   MISHKIN F.S.
"Efficient-markets theory: implication for monetary policy" with discussion
Brookings Paps. Econ. Activity, 1978, pp.707-768.
POLICY EVALUATION - MACRO : MONETARY * POLICY EVALUATION - METHODOLOGY *
INTEREST RATE - TERM STRUCTURE * THEORY - EFFICIENT MARKETS * STOCK PRICES -
DETERMINANTS * INTEREST RATE - EFFECT OF * INTEREST RATE - EXPECTATIONS *
APPL - SECTOR : FINANCE , STOCK PRICE INDEX * MACRO MODEL - MIT , PENN ,
SSRC * MACRO MODELS - METHODOLOGY * EVALUATION - INTEREST RATE FORECASTS *
EVALUATION - EXPECTATIONS , THEORY

YA2475   MISHKIN F.S.
"Household liabilities and the generalised stock-adjustment model"   Rev.
Econ. Stats., vol.53, 1976, pp.481-485.
APPL - MACRO : CONSUMER DEMAND , FINANCIAL LIABILITIES

YA2476   MISHKIN F.S.
"Illiquidity, consumer durable expenditure and monetary policy"   Am. Econ.
Rev., vol.66, 1976, pp.642-654.
APPL - SECTOR : CONSUMER DURABLES * APPL - SECTOR : CONSUMER DURABLES , CARS
* THEORY - MONETARY * THEORY - LIQUIDITY PREFERENCE

YA2477   MISHKIN F.S.
"What depressed the consumer? The household balance sheet and the 1973-75
recession" with discussion   Brookings Paps. Econ. Activity, 1977,
pp.123-174.
APPL - MACRO : CONSUMPTION * APPL - MACRO : CONSUMER DEMAND * EX ANTE *
INCOME - EFFECT OF , PERMANENT * DISTRIBUTED LAG - APPL , CONSUMPTION *
COMPARATIVE METHODS - DISTRIBUTED LAG * APPL - SECTOR : CONSTRUCTION ,
RESIDENTIAL * INTEREST RATE - EFFECT OF * EVALUATION - DISTRIBUTED LAG ,
SPECIFICATION * STOCK PRICES - EFFECT OF * WEALTH - EFFECT OF

YA2478   MITCHELL B.M.
"Estimation of large econometric models by principal component and
instrumental variable methods"   Rev. Econ. Stats., vol.53, 1971,
pp.140-146.
DATA - SAMPLE SIZE * SIMULTANEOUS SYSTEM - ESTIMATION * MACRO MODEL -
BROOKINGS * COMPARATIVE METHODS - ESTIMATION : SIMULTANEOUS SYSTEM *
ESTIMATION - PRINCIPAL COMPONENTS * ESTIMATION - INSTRUMENTAL VARIABLES

YA2479   MITCHELL D.J.B.
"Union wage determination: policy implications and outlook" with discussion
Brookings Paps. Econ. Activity, 1978, pp.538-591.
UNIONISATION - EFFECT OF * APPL - MACRO : EARNINGS

YA2480   MIZON G.E.
"Inferential procedures in nonlinear models: an application in a UK
industrial cross section study of factor substitution and returns to scale"
Econometrica, vol.45, 1977, pp.1221-1242.
EVALUATION - ERROR SPECIFICATION , MULTIPLICATIVE * PRODUCTION FUNCTIONS -
METHODOLOGY * MODEL SELECTION * REGRESSION - HYPOTHESIS TESTS * REGRESSION -
TRANSFORMATIONS * REGRESSION - MODEL SELECTION * PRODUCTION FUNCTIONS -
SECTOR

YA2481 MIZON G.E.
"The estimation on non-linear econometric equations: an application to the
specification and estimation of an aggregate putty-clay relation for the UK"
Rev. Econ. Studies, vol.41, 1974, pp.353-369,
APPL - MACRO , UK * APPL - MACRO : OUTPUT * ESTIMATION - NON LINEAR

YA2482 MODIGLIANI F., FARANTELLI E.
"A generalization of the Phillips curve for a developing country"   Rev.
Econ. Studies, vol.40, 1973, pp.203-223,
PRIOR INFORMATION - APPL * APPL - MACRO , ITALY * APPL - MACRO : DEVELOPMENT
* APPL - MACRO : EARNINGS * INFLATION - PHILLIPS CURVE * INFLATION - EFFECT
OF * REGRESSION - SPECIFICATION OF VARIABLES

YA2483 MODIGLIANI F., PAPADEMOS L.
"Targets for monetary policy in the coming year" with discussion
Brookings Paps. Econ. Activity, 1975, pp.141-165,
INFLATION - PHILLIPS * INFLATION - DETERMINANTS * POLICY EVALUATION - MACRO
: MONETARY

YA2484 MODIGLIANI F., SHILLER R.J.
"Inflation, rational expectations and the term structure of interest rates"
Economica, vol.40, 1973, pp.12-43,
INTEREST RATE - INDICATORS * INFLATION - EXPECTATIONS * INTEREST RATE - TERM
STRUCTURE * DISTRIBUTED LAG - APPL , INTEREST RATE * INTEREST RATE - LONG
TERM * BAYESIAN - ESTIMATION : DISTRIBUTED LAG * THEORY - EXPECTATIONS *
INTEREST RATE - LIQUIDITY PREFERENCE

YA2485 MODIGLIANI F., STEINDEL C.
"Is a tax rebate an effective tool for stabilization policy" with discussion
Brookings. Paps. Econ. Activity, 1977, pp.175-209,
POLICY EVALUATION - MACRO : STABILISATION * TAX - EFFECT OF * MACRO MODEL -
DATA RESOURCES * MACRO MODEL - MICHIGAN * MACRO MODEL - WHARTON * EX ANTE *
EVALUATION - ESTIMATION : SIMULTANEOUS SYSTEM , ERROR SPECIFICATION * APPL -
MACRO : CONSUMPTION * EVALUATION - ESTIMATION : REGRESSION , ERROR
SPECIFICATION * APPL - MACRO : CONSUMER DEMAND * EVALUATION - MACRO MODELS

YA2486 MODIGLIANI F., TARANTELLI E.
"The consumption function in a developing economy and the Italian
experience"   Am. Econ. Rev., vol.65, 1975, pp.825-842,
APPL - MACRO : CONSUMPTION * EVALUATION - CONSUMPTION MODELS * APPL - MACRO
, ITALY

YA2487 MOELLER J.F.
"Development of a microsimulation model for evaluating economic implications
of income transfer and tax policies"   Anns. Econ. Soc. Meas., vol.2, 1973,
pp.183-187,
TAX - EFFECT OF * APPL - SECTOR : SOCIAL , POVERTY * POLICY EVALUATION -
MACRO : WELFARE * PUBLIC EXPENDITURE - EFFECT OF , AID PROGRAMS

YA2488 MONROE K.B.
"The information content of prices: a preliminary model for estimating buyer
response"   Mgmt. Sci. (B), vol.17, 1971, pp.519-533,
CONSUMER BEHAVIOUR - PSYCHOLOGICAL MODELS * PRICE - EFFECT OF * REGRESSION -
LIMITED DEPENDENT , PROBIT : APPL * REGRESSION - THRESHOLD : APPL

YA2489 MONROE K.B., DELLA BITTA A.J.
"Models for pricing decisions"   J. Mktg. Res., vol.15, 1978, pp.413-428,
USE - PRICING * THEORY - PRICING * BIBLIOGRAPHY - PRICING

YA2490 MONTGOMERY D.B.
"Consumer characteristics associated with dealing: an empirical example"
J. Mktg. Res., vol.8, 1971, pp.118-120,
USE - PROMOTION EVALUATION * CONSUMER BEHAVIOUR - PURCHASING , DETERMINANTS
* APPL - SECTOR : CONSUMER NON DURABLES , HEALTH AIDS

YA2491 MONTGOMERY D.B.
"New product distribution: an analysis of supermarket buyer decisions"   J.
Mktg. Res., vol.12, 1975, pp.255-264,
NEW PRODUCTS - EVALUATION * APPL - SECTOR : RETAILING , SUPERMARKETS *
DISTRIBUTION - EFFECT OF * DISCRIMINANT ANALYSIS - METHODOLOGY * USE -
RETAIL , PRODUCT SELECTION * COMPARATIVE METHODS - DISCRIMINATION

YA2492 MONTGOMERY D.B.
"The outlook for MIS"   J. Advtg. Res., vol.13:3, 1973, pp.5-11,
MIS * USE - MARKETING PLANNING * BASIC

YA2493 MONTGOMERY D.B., ARMSTRONG J.S.
"Brand trial after a credibility change"   J. Advtg. Res., vol.10:5, 1970,
pp.26-32,
USE - PROMOTION , EVALUATION * APPL - FIRM : CONSUMER NON DURABLES , HEALTH
AIDS * AID - APPL * COMPARATIVE METHODS - REGRESSION , MULTIVARIATE METHODS

YA2494 MONTGOMERY D.B., MORRISON D.C.
"A note on adjusting R squared"   J. Finance, vol.28, 1973, pp.1009-1013,
REGRESSION - SUMMARY STATISTICS

YA2495 MONTGOMERY D.B., SILK A.J.
"Estimating dynamic effects of market communication expenditures"   Mgmt.
Sci. (B), vol.18, 1972, pp.485-501,
DISTRIBUTED LAG - APPL , ADVERTISING * ADVERTISING - EFFECT OF * DISTRIBUTED
LAG - SOLOW * COMPARATIVE METHODS - DISTRIBUTED LAG * USE - PROMOTION
EVALUATION

YA2496   MONTGOMERY D.B., URBAN G.L.
     "Marketing decision-information systems: an emerging view"   J. Mktg. Res.,
     vol.7, 1970, pp.226-234.
     USE - MARKETING POLICY * USER REQUIREMENTS * MIS * COMPUTERISATION - DATA ,
     SOURCES * BASIC

YA2497   MONTGOMERY D.C., CONTRERAS L.E.
     "A note on forecasting with adaptive filtering"   Opl. Res. Q., vol.28,
     1977, pp.87-91.
     EVALUATION - TIME SERIES , ADAPTIVE FILTERING * COMPARATIVE METHODS -
     ADAPTIVE FILTERING , EXPONENTIAL SMOOTHING * COMPARATIVE METHODS - ADAPTIVE
     FILTERING , ARIMA * COMPARATIVE METHODS - ARIMA , EXPONENTIAL SMOOTHING

YA2498   MOORE B., RHODES J.
     "Regional economic policy and the movement of manufacturing firms to
     development areas"   Economica, vol.43, 1976, pp.17-31.
     REGIONAL MODELS - LOCATION * POLICY EVALUATION - REGIONAL

YA2499   MOORE G.H.
     "Economic indicators and econometric models"   Bus. Econ., vol.1014, 1975,
     pp.45-48.
     BUSINESS CYCLE - IDENTIFICATION * EVALUATION - BUSINESS INDICATORS *
     COMBINING FORECASTS - BUSINESS INDICATORS , MACRO MODELS * EVALUATION -
     TURNING POINT FORECASTS * DATA - INTERNATIONAL * BASIC

YA2500   MOORE J.R.
     "Forecasting and scheduling for past-model replacement parts"   Mgmt. Sci.
     (B), vol.18, 1971, pp.200-213.
     DEMAND - CUMULATIVE * LIFE CYCLE - PRODUCT , DECLINING * STYLE GOODS *
     EXPONENTIAL SMOOTHING - HIGHER ORDER : APPL * APPL - SECTOR : CONSUMER
     DURABLES , CARS , SPARES * USER - FIRM : CONSUMER DURABLES * DEMAND -
     REPLACEMENT * USE - INVENTORY CONTROL

YA2501   MOORE P.G., THOMAS H.
     "Measuring uncertainty"   Omega, vol.3, 1975, pp.657-672.
     JUDGEMENTAL FORECASTS - UNCERTAINTY * DELPHI * JUDGEMENTAL FORECASTS -
     PROBABILITIES

YA2502   MOORE T.G.
     "The demand for Broadway theatre tickets"   Rev. Econ. Stats., vol.48,
     1966, pp.79-87.
     APPL - SECTOR : SERVICES , ENTERTAINMENT * TIME - VALUE OF * INCOME - EFFECT
     OF * PRICE - EFFECT OF

YA2503   MOOSA S.A.
     "Dynamic portfolio-balance behaviour of time deposits and 'money'"   J.
     Finance, vol.32, 1977, pp.709-717.
     WEALTH - EFFECT OF * INCOME - EFFECT OF * EX ANTE * APPL - SECTOR : FINANCE
     , BANKS * APPL - SECTOR : FINANCE , BANK , LIABILITIES * APPL - MACRO :
     MONEY * INFLATION - EFFECT OF * BIBLIOGRAPHY - MONEY * INTEREST RATE -
     EFFECT OF

YA2504   MORAWETZ D.
     "Employment implications of industrialisation in developing countries: a
     survey"   Econ. J., vol. 84, 1974, pp.491-542.
     APPL - MACRO : DEVELOPMENT * APPL - MACRO : EMPLOYMENT * BIBLIOGRAPHY -
     DEVELOPMENT

YA2505   MORAWETZ D.
     "The sensitivity of the yield of personal income tax in the UK: a note"
     Econ. J., vol.81, 1971, pp.612-616.
     TAX - EFFECT OF * APPL - SECTOR : GOVERNMENT , REVENUES , TAX

YA2506   MORAWETZ D., BECKERMAN W., BACON R.
     "International comparisons of income levels: comments"   Econ. J., vol.80,
     1970, pp.977-982.
     SPECIFICATION ERROR - EFFECT OF , VARIABLE INCLUSION * DATA - SAMPLE SIZE *
     PROXY VARIABLES * DATA SOURCES - LDC

YA2507   MORGAN A., VANDAELE W.
     "On testing hypotheses in simultaneous equation models"   J. Econometrics,
     vol.2, 1974, pp.55-65.
     SIMULTANEOUS SYSTEM - HYPOTHESIS TESTS * COMPARATIVE METHODS - TESTS ,
     REGRESSION COEFFICIENTS * MACRO MODEL - ST.LOUIS

YA2508   MORGAN A.D., MARTIN D.
     "Tariff reductions and UK imports of manufactures: 1955-1971"   Nat. Inst.
     Econ. Rev., no.72, 1975, pp.38-54.
     TARIFF - EFFECT OF * APPL - MACRO : INTERNATIONAL TRADE , IMPORTS * APPL -
     MACRO , UK * PRICE - EFFECT OF

YA2509   MORGAN I., SAINT-PIERRE J.
     "Dividend and investment decisions of Canadian firms"   Can. J. Econ.,
     vol.11, 1978, pp.20-37.
     APPL - FIRM : FINANCE , DIVIDENDS * APPL - FIRM : INVESTMENT * COMPARATIVE
     METHODS - ESTIMATION : OLS , 2SLS

YA2510   MORGAN I.G.
     "Stock prices and heteroscedasticity"   J. Business, vol.49, 1976,
     pp.496-508.
     STOCK PRICES - TRADING VOLUME * APPL - FIRM : FINANCE , STOCK PRICES *
     HETEROSCEDASTICITY - TEST * EX ANTE

YA2511   MORGAN J.A., ET AL.
        Letters to the editor on multiple regression   Am. Stat'n., vol.26:3, 1972,
        pp.62-64.
        REGRESSION - SUMMARY STATISTICS * COMPUTERISATION - ESTIMATION , REGRESSION
        MODELS * BASIC

YA2512   MORGENSTERN R.D.
        "Direct and indirect effects on earnings of schooling and socio-economic
        background"   Rev. Econ. Stats., vol.55, 1973, pp.225-233.
        MANPOWER PLANNING - EARNINGS * APPL - SECTOR : SOCIAL , EDUCATIONAL
        ATTAINMENT * EDUCATION - EFFECT OF * MANPOWER PLANNING - LABOUR FORCE
        COMPOSITION

YA2513   MORIARTY M.
        "Cross-sectional, time series issues in the analysis of marketing decision
        variables"   J. Mktg. Res., vol.12, 1975, pp.141-151.
        MARKET SHARE - SECTOR : CONSUMER NON DURABLES * ESTIMATION - GLS * PRICE -
        EFFECT OF * ADVERTISING - EFFECT OF * REGRESSION - ERROR COMPONENTS *
        ESTIMATION - CROSS SECTION , TIME SERIES * APPL - FIRM : CONSUMER NON
        DURABLES

YA2514   MORIGUCHI C.
        "Forecasting and simulation analysis of the World economy"   Am. Econ. Ass.
        Proc., 1973, pp.402-409.
        APPL - MACRO : INTERNATIONAL LINKAGE * APPL - MACRO : INTERNATIONAL TRADE *
        PRICE - EFFECT OF

YA2515   MORKRE M.E.
        "Short-term price change in the steel industry"   Rev. Econ. Stats.,
        vol.52, 1970, pp.26-33.
        APPL - SECTOR : PRODUCTION , STEEL * PRICE - SECTOR : PRODUCTION * THEORY -
        PRICING

YA2516   MORRIS M.J.
        "Forecasting the sunspot cycle" with discussion   R. Statist. Soc. (A),
        vol.140, 1977, pp.437-468.
        APPL - SECTOR : NATURAL , SUNSPOTS * TIME SERIES - NON LINEAR * COMBINING
        FORECASTS - TIME SERIES * EX ANTE

YA2517   MORRIS P.A.
        "Combining experts judgements: a Bayesian approach"   Mgmt. Sci., vol.23,
        1977, pp.679-693.
        BAYESIAN - PRIOR INFORMATION * JUDGEMENTAL FORECASTS - METHODOLOGY

YA2518   MORRISON D.G.
        "Evaluation market segmentation studies: the properties of R squared"
        Mgmt. Sci. (A), vol.19, 1973, pp.1213-1221.
        EVALUATION - CONSUMER BEHAVIOUR , PURCHASING MODELS * REGRESSION - SUMMARY
        STATISTICS * MARKET SEGMENTATION * EVALUATION - CONSUMER BEHAVIOUR ,
        PSYCHOLOGICAL MODELS

YA2519   MORRISON D.G.
        "On the interpretation of discriminant analysis"   J. Mktg. Res., vol.6,
        1969, pp.156-163.
        EVALUATION - DISCRIMINANT ANALYSIS * BASIC

YA2520   MORRISON D.G.
        "Regression with discrete dependent variables: the effect on R squared"
        J. Mktg. Res., vol.9, 1972, pp.338-340
        REGRESSION - DISCRETE DEPENDENT * REGRESSION - SUMMARY STATISTICS

YA2521   MORRISON D.G.
        "Reliability of tests: a technique using the 'regression to the mean'
        fallacy"   J. Mktg. Res., vol.10, 1973, pp.91-93
        REGRESSION - ERROR COMPONENTS * REGRESSION - MODEL INTERPRETATION * SURVEYS
        - METHODOLOGY , RESPONSE ERROR * BASIC

YA2522   MORRISON D.G.
        "Upper bounds for correlations between binary outcomes and probabilistic
        predictions"   J. Am. Statist. Ass., vol.67, 1972, pp.68-70.
        REGRESSION - SUMMARY STATISTICS * REGRESSION - QUALITATIVE DEPENDENT

YA2523   MORRISON D.G., GLUCK D.J.
        "Spurious correlations that result from 'awareness vs. usage' type
        regressions"   J. Mktg. Res., vol.7, 1970, pp.381-384.
        REGRESSION - SUMMARY STATISTICS * REGRESSION - MODEL INTERPRETATION

YA2524   MORRISON G.W., PIKE D.H.
        "Kalman filtering applied to statistical forecasting"   Mgmt. Sci., vol.23,
        1977, pp.768-774.
        BAYESIAN - FORECASTING * ESTIMATION - KALMAN FILTER * APPL - SECTOR :
        UTILITIES , ELECTRICITY * COMPARATIVE METHODS - KALMAN , TREND CURVES * TIME
        SERIES - FILTER , KALMAN

YA2525   MORRISSEY T.F.
        "A model of Federal Home Loan Bank Systems and Federal National Mortgage
        Association behaviour: a comment"   Rev. Econ. Stats., vol.57, 1975,
        pp.121-123.
        APPL - SECTOR : FINANCE , MORTGAGES * POLICY EVALUATION - SECTOR :
        CONSTRUCTION

YA2526 MOSKOWITZ H.
"Regression models of behaviour for managerial decision making" Omega,
vol.2, 1974, pp.677-690.
BOOTSTRAPPING * DECISION RULES - FIRM * LEAD TIME - EFFECT OF

YA2527 MOSKOWITZ H.
"Robustness of linear models for decision making: some comments" Omega,
vol.4, 1976, pp.743-746.
JUDGEMENTAL FORECASTS - REVIEW * EVALUATION - BOOTSTRAPPING * DECISION RULES
- METHODOLOGY

YA2528 MOSKOWITZ H., MILLER J.G.
"Information and decision systems for production planning" Mgmt, Sci.,
vol.22, 1975, pp.359-370.
EVALUATION - BOOTSTRAPPING * DECISION RULES - FIRM * USE - SCHEDULING ,
PRODUCTION * USE - SCHEDULING , MANPOWER * COMPARATIVE METHODS -
BOOTSTRAPPING , JUDGEMENTAL

YA2529 MOSKOWITZ H., SCHAEFER R.E., BORCHERDING K.
"'Irrationality' of managerial judgements: implications for information
systems" Omega, vol.4, 1976, pp.125-140.
MIS * USER REQUIREMENTS * APPL - FIRM : FINANCE , BANKS * USE - CREDIT
CONTROL , CONSUMER * EVALUATION - JUDGEMENTAL FORECASTS

YA2530 MUELLBAUER J.
"Identification and consumer unit scales" Econometrica, vol.43, 1975,
pp.807-809.
CONSUMER UNIT SCALES * SIMULTANEOUS SYSTEM - IDENTIFICATION

YA2531 MUELLBAUER J.
"Testing the Barten model of household composition effects and the cost of
children" Econ. J., vol.87, 1977, pp.460-487.
DEMAND EQUATIONS - SYSTEMS OF * CONSUMER UNIT SCALES * PRICE - EFFECT OF *
APPL - MACRO , UK * APPL - MACRO : CONSUMER DEMAND * CONSUMER BEHAVIOUR -
ECONOMIC MODELS

YA2532 MUENCH T., ET AL.
"Tests for structural change and prediction intervals for the reduced forms
of two structural models of the US: the FRB-MIT and Michigan quarterly
models" Anns. Econ. Soc. Meas., vol.3, 1974, pp.491-519.
MACRO MODEL - MICHIGAN * MACRO MODEL - FRB , MIT * STABILITY OF COEFFICIENTS
- SIMULTANEOUS SYSTEM , TEST * CONFIDENCE INTERVAL - SIMULTANEOUS SYSTEM ,
MULTIVARIATE * CONFIDENCE INTERVAL - PREDICTIONS : SIMULTANEOUS SYSTEM * EX
ANTE * SIMULATION - EVALUATION OF RESULTS * MACRO MODEL - METHODOLOGY ,
STABILITY

YA2533 MULLER R.A.
"Econometric analysis of environmental policy: estimation of a model of the
Canadian pulp and paper industry" Can. J. Econ., vol.11, 1978,
pp.263-286.
APPL - SECTOR : PRODUCTION , PAPER * POLLUTION - CONTROLS * PRICE - SECTOR :
PRODUCTION * APPL - SECTOR : EARNINGS * APPL - SECTOR : INTERNATIONAL TRADE
, EXPORTS * APPL - SECTOR : CAPACITY * SIMULATION - APPL : POLICY EVALUATION

YA2534 MULLET G.M., MORGAN D.L.
"Using dummy variables to check for rounding error in computerized
regression programs" Decis. Sci., vol.7, 1976, pp.66-70.
COMPUTERISATION - CALCULATION ERROR * NUMERICAL METHODS - CALCULATION ERROR

YA2535 MULLET G.M., MURRAY T.W.
"A new method for examining rounding error in least-squares regression
computer programs" J. Am. Statist. Ass., vol.66, 1971, pp.496-498.
COMPUTERISATION - ESTIMATION : REGRESSION MODELS * COMPUTERISATION -
CALCULATION ERROR

YA2536 MULLICK S.K., BURROUGHS M.O.
"The role of econometrics in product forecasting" Bus. Econ., vol.11;4,
1976, pp.45-50.
APPL - FIRM : PRODUCTION , ELECTRONICS * FORECASTING - INTRODUCTION

YA2537 MULLINEAUX D.J.
"Banking restrictions and commercial-bank costs" J. Business, vol.49,
1976, pp.402-407.
APPL - FIRM : FINANCE , BANKS * COST - FIRM : FINANCE , BANKS * DATA - CROSS
SECTION * USE - BANK REGULATION

YA2538 MULLINEAUX D.J.
"Economies of scale and organisational efficiency in banking: a
profit-function approach" J. Finance, vol.33, 1978, pp.258-280.
APPL - FIRM : FINANCE , BANKS * APPL - FIRM : FINANCE , PROFITS * STABILITY
OF COEFFICIENTS - REGRESSION : APPL

YA2539 MULVEY C.
"Collective agreements and relative earnings in UK manufacturing in 1973"
Economica, vol.43, 1976, pp.419-427.
APPL - SECTOR : EARNINGS * UNIONIZATION - EFFECT OF

YA2540 MUNASINGHE M., CORBO V
"The demand for CATV services in Canada" Can. J. Econ., vol.11, 1978,
pp.506-520.
APPL - SECTOR : SERVICES , MEDIA , TV * DISTRIBUTION - EFFECT OF

YA2541 MUNDLAK Y.
"Occupational migration out of agriculture - a cross-country analysis"
Rev. Econ. Stats., vol.60, 1978, pp.392-398.
REGIONAL MODELS - MANPOWER PLANNING , MIGRATION * MANPOWER PLANNING -
REGIONAL * DATA - INTERNATIONAL * DATA - CROSS SECTION * REGIONAL MODELS -
SECTOR : AGRICULTURE

YA2542 MUNDLAK Y.
"On the pooling of time series and cross section data"   Econometrica,
vol.46, 1978, pp.69-85.
ESTIMATION - CROSS SECTION , TIME SERIES * REGRESSION - ERROR COMPONENTS *
ADVANCED

YA2543 MURPHY A.H.
"Expressing the uncertainty in weather forecasts"   Stat'n., vol.24, 1975,
pp.69-71.
WEATHER * EVALUATION - CONFIDENCE INTERVALS

YA2544 MURPHY A.H., WINKER R.L.
"Reliability of subjective probability forecasts of precipitation and
temperature"   Appl. Stats., vol.26, 1977, pp.41-47.
EVALUATION - JUDGEMENTAL FORECASTS * APPL - SECTOR : NATURAL , WEATHER *
JUDGEMENTAL FORECASTS - UNCERTAINTY

YA2545 MURPHY N.B.
"The demand for New York State mutual savings bank deposits"   J. Finance,
vol.26, 1971, pp.713-718.
APPL - FIRM : FINANCE , BANKS * APPL - FIRM : FINANCE , SAVINGS * EX ANTE *
APPL - FIRM : FINANCE , BANK , ASSETS * INCOME - EFFECT OF * INTEREST RATE -
EFFECT OF

YA2546 MURRAY G.D.
"A cautionary note on selection of variables in discriminant analysis"
Appl Stats., vol.26, 1977, pp.246-250.
DISCRIMINANT ANALYSIS - METHODOLOGY * EVALUATION - DISCRIMINANT ANALYSIS

YA2547 MURRAY G.R., SILVER E.A.
"A Bayesian analysis of the style goods inventory problem"   Mgmt. Sci.,
(a), vol.12, 1966, pp.785-797.
BAYESIAN - STYLE GOODS * LOSS FUNCTIONS - FIRM , INVENTORY * USE - INVENTORY
CONTROL * LP * STYLE GOODS

YA2548 MURRAY J.A.
"Canadian consumer expectational data: an evaluation"   J. Mktg. Res.,
vol.6, 1969, pp.54-61.
EVALUATION - EXPECTATIONS , DATA * APPL - SECTOR : CONSTRUCTION ,
RESIDENTIAL * APPL - SECTOR : CONSUMER DURABLES * EVALUATION - SURVEYS ,
CONSUMER * APPL - SECTOR : CONSUMER DURABLES , CARS * DATA - DISAGGREGATION
, GEOGRAPHICAL

YA2549 MURRAY M.P.
"The demand for electricity in Virginia"   Rev. Econ. Stats., vol.60, 1978,
pp.585-600.
APPL - SECTOR : UTILITIES , ELECTRICITY * WEATHER - EFFECT OF * INCOME -
EFFECT OF * PRICE - EFFECT OF * COMPARATIVE METHODS - ARIMA , CAUSAL * EX
ANTE

YA2550 MURRAY T., GINMAN P.J.
"An empirical examination of the traditional aggregate import demand model"
Rev. Econ. Stats., vol.58, 1976, pp.75-80.
APPL - MACRO : INTERNATIONAL TRADE , IMPORTS * SPECIFICATION ERROR - TESTS ,
CONSTRAINTS

YA2551 MURRAY T.W.
"An empirical example of the classical assumptions concerning errors in
data"   J. Am. Statist. Ass., vol.67, 1972, pp.530-537.
APPL - MACRO : INTERNATIONAL TRADE * EVALUATION - ERROR SPECIFICATION * DATA
ERRORS - ANALYSIS OF * DATA ERROR - ESTIMATION OF

YA2552 MUSGRAVE P.B.
"Foreign investment in the national income accounts"   Rev. Econ. Stats.,
vol.59, 1977, pp.220-224.
DATA ERRORS - NATIONAL ACCOUNTS , US * APPL - MACRO : INVESTMENT ,
INTERNATIONAL

YA2553 MUSGROVE P.
"Detecting errors in economic survey data: multivariate vs. univariate
procedures"   Anns. Econ. Soc. Meas., vol.3, 1974, pp.333-345.
DATA ERRORS - IDENTIFICATION * SURVEYS - METHODOLOGY , VALIDATION *
COMPARATIVE METHODS - DATA ERRORS : IDENTIFICATION

YA2554 MYERS C.L.
"Forecasting electricity sales"   Stat'n., vol.20, 1971, pp.15-22.
APPL - SECTOR : UTILITIES , ELECTRICITY * BASIC

YA2555 MYERS J.H.
"Finding determinant buying attitudes"   J. Advtg. Res., vol.10:6, 1970,
pp.9-12.
BRAND CHOICE - DETERMINANTS * APPL - FIRM : CONSUMER NON DURABLES ,
GROCERIES * APPL - FIRM : CONSUMER NON DURABLES , FOOD * CONSUMER BEHAVIOUR
- PURCHASING , DETERMINANTS

YA2556   MYERS J.H., MOUNT J.F.
       "More on social class vs. income as correlates of buying behaviour"   J.
       Mktg., vol.37, no.2, April 1973, pp.71-73.
       CONSUMER BEHAVIOUR - PURCHASING , DETERMINANTS * INCOME - EFFECT OF * APPL -
       SECTOR : CONSUMER DURABLES

YA2557   MYERS J.H., STANTON R.R., HAUG A.F.
       "Correlates of buying brhaviour: social class vs. income"   J. Mktg.,
       vol.35, no.2, April 1971, pp.8-15.
       APPL - SECTOR : CONSUMER NON DURABLES * MARKET SEGMENTATION * INCOME -
       EFFECT OF * CONSUMER BEHAVIOUR - PURCHASING , DETERMINANTS * BASIC

YA2558   N.I.E.S.R.
       "Imports of manufactures into the UK and other industrial countries"   Nat.
       Inst. Econ. Rev., no.56, 1971, pp.41-63.
       APPL - MACRO , OECD * APPL - MACRO : INTERNATIONAL TRADE , IMPORTS * PRICE -
       EFFECT OF * TARIFF - EFFECT OF

YA2559   N.I.E.S.R.
       "Some aspects of the medium term management of the economy"   Nat. Inst.
       Econ. Rev., no.79, 1979, pp.39-57.
       CAPACITY - ESTIMATION OF * APPL - MACRO : ENERGY * APPL - SECTOR :
       PRODUCTION , PETROLEUM * APPL - MACRO : GNP , POTENTIAL

YA2560   N.I.E.S.R.
       "Some aspects of the present inflation"   Nat. Inst. Econ. Rev., no.55,
       1971, pp.38-51.
       INFLATION - EXPECTATIONS * INFLATION - DETERMINANTS * APPL - MACRO , UK *
       APPL - MACRO : EARNINGS * EX ANTE

YA2561   N.I.E.S.R.
       "The economic situation: the home economy"   Nat. Inst. Econ. Rev., no.60,
       1972, pp.14-16.
       MACRO MODEL - UK , NIESR * MACRO MODEL - GOVERNMENT , UK * MACRO MODEL - UK
       , LBS * EVALUATION - MACRO FORECASTS

YA2562   N.I.E.S.R.
       "The economic situation: the home economy"   Nat. Inst. Econ. Rev., no.56,
       1971, pp.20-21.
       MACRO MODEL - UK , NIESR * MACRO MODEL - GOVERNMENT , UK * MACRO MODEL - UK
       , LBS * EVALUATION - MACRO FORECASTS

YA2563   N.I.E.S.R.
       "The economy in 1976"   Nat. Inst. Econ. Rev., no.79, 1977, pp.22-25.
       MACRO MODEL - UK , NIESR * MACRO MODEL - UK , LBS * MACRO MODEL - GOVERNMENT
       , UK * EVALUATION - MACRO FORECASTS

YA2564   N.I.E.S.R.
       "The economy in 1977"   Nat. Inst. Econ. Rev., no.84, 1978, pp.19-21.
       EVALUATION - MACRO MODELS * MACRO MODEL - UK , LBS * MACRO MODEL - UK ,
       NIESR * MACRO MODEL - GOVERNMENT , UK

YA2565   N.I.E.S.R.
       "The effects of the devaluation of 1967 on the current balance of payments"
       Econ. J., vol. 82, 1972, pp.442-464.
       APPL - MACRO : INTERNATIONAL TRADE * APPL - MACRO , UK * EXCHANGE RATE -
       EFFECT OF

YA2566   N.I.E.S.R.
       "The home economy"   Nat. Inst. Econ. Rev., no.72, 1975, pp.14-15.
       MACRO MODEL - UK , NIESR * MACRO MODEL - GOVERNMENT , UK * MACRO MODEL - UK
       , LBS * EVALUATION - MACRO FORECASTS

YA2567   N.I.E.S.R.
       "The home economy"   Nat. Inst. Econ. Rev., no.83, 1978, pp.7-23, and
       no.84, 1978, pp.22-34.
       MACRO MODEL - UK , NIESR * RESIDUALS - ANALYSIS OF , SPECIFICATION ERROR *
       FORECASTING - MULTISTAGE

YA2568   N.I.E.S.R.
       "The home economy"   Nat. Inst. Econ. Rev., no.80, 1977, pp.18-20.
       MACRO MODEL - UK , NIESR * MACRO MODEL - UK , LBS * MACRO MODEL - GOVERNMENT
       , UK

YA2569   N.I.E.S.R.
       "The productivity effects of selective employment tax"   Nat. Inst. Econ.
       Rev., no.56, 1971, pp.36-40.
       TAX - EFFECT OF * APPL - SECTOR : PRODUCTIVITY * APPL - MACRO , UK * APPL -
       MACRO : PRODUCTIVITY * APPL - SECTOR : RETAILING

YA2570   NADIRI M.I.
       "An alternative model of business investment spending" with discussion
       Brookings Paps. Econ. Activity, 1972, pp.547-583.
       APPL - MACRO : INVESTMENT * PRODUCTION FUNCTION - MACRO * EVALUATION -
       INVESTMENT MODELS * EX ANTE

YA2571   NAGAR A.L., CARTER R.A.L.
       "Minimum second moment estimation in simultaneous equation systems"   Int.
       Econ. Rev., vol.15, 1974, pp.31-38.
       ESTIMATION - K CLASS * DATA - SIMULATION

YA2572   NAGATA E.A.
       "The cost structure of consumer finance small-loan operators"   J. Finance,
       vol.28, 1973, pp.1327-1337.
       APPL - FIRM : FINANCE , LOAN COMPANIES * COST - FIRM : FINANCE

YA2573   NAKAMURA A.O., NAKAMURA M.
"On the impact of the tests for serial correlation upon the test for
significance for the regression coefficient"   J. Econometrics, vol.7,
1978, pp.199-210.
BIBLIOGRAPHY - AUTOCORRELATION * TIME SERIES - HYPOTHESIS TESTS * DATA -
SIMULATION * COMPARATIVE METHODS - TESTS , AUTOCORRELATION * EVALUATION -
REGRESSION , HYPOTHESIS TESTS * ESTIMATION - PRE TEST * ERROR SPECIFICATION
- EFFECT OF

YA2574   NAKAMURA A.O., NAKAMURA M., ORCUTT G.H.
"Testing the relationship between time series"   J. Am. Statist. Ass.,
vol.71, 1976, pp.214-222.
COMPARATIVE METHODS - TESTS , INDEPENDENCE * TIME SERIES - AUTOREGRESSIVE *
CAUSALITY - TEST * CROSS CORRELATIONS * REGRESSION - VARIABLE INCLUSION

YA2575   NAKANISHI M.
"Advertising and promotion effects on consumer response to new products"
J. Mktg. Res., vol.10, 1973, pp.242-249.
NEW PRODUCTS - ADVERTISING * APPL - FIRM : CONSUMER NON DURABLES , FOOD *
REPEAT BUYING * ADVERTISING - EFFECT OF * USE - PROMOTION EVALUATION

YA2576   NAKANISHI M., COOPER L.G.
"Parameter estimation for a multiplicative competitive interaction model:
least squares approach"   J. Mktg. Res., vol.11, 1974, pp.303-311.
ERROR SPECIFICATION - CORRELATED * MARKET SHARE - METHODOLOGY * ESTIMATION -
GLS * DATA - SIMULATION * REGRESSION - TRANSFORMATIONS , LOGARITHMIC *
COMPARATIVE METHODS - ESTIMATION : OLS , GLS * COMPARATIVE METHODS - DATA :
CROSS SECTION , TIME SERIES

YA2577   NAKAO T.
"Application of Duesenberry's model to the growth in stocks of consumer
durable goods in Japan"   Rev. Econ. Stats., vol.60, 1978, pp.33-38.
APPL - SECTOR : CONSUMER DURABLES , APPLIANCES , REFRIDGERATORS * APPL -
SECTOR : CONSUMER DURABLES , APPLIANCES , TELEVISION * APPL - SECTOR :
CONSUMER DURABLES , APPLIANCES , WASHERS * PRICE - EFFECT OF * NEW PRODUCTS
- DIFFUSION MODEL

YA2578   NARODICK K.G.
"Determinants of airline market share"   J. Advtg. Res., vol.12:5, 1972,
pp.31-36.
APPL - FIRM : TRANSPORT * MARKET SHARE - SECTOR : TRANSPORT * ADVERTISING -
EFFECT OF

YA2579   NARULA S.C.
"Predictive mean square error and stochastic regressor variables"   Appl.
Stats., vol.23, 1974, pp.11-17.
REGRESSION - ERRORS IN VARIABLES * CONFIDENCE INTERVAL - PREDICTIONS :
REGRESSION * APPL - SECTOR : SOCIAL , EDUCATIONAL TESTING * ESTIMATION -
STEIN

YA2580   NARULA S.C., WELLINGTON J.F.
"Multiple linear regression with minimum sum of absolute errors"   Appl.
Stats., vol.26, 1977, pp.106-111.
COMPUTERISATION - ESTIMATION , REGRESSION MODELS , PROGRAMS * ESTIMATION -
MSAE

YA2581   NASH J.C.
"A discrete alternative to the logistic growth function"   Appl. Stats.,
vol.26, 1977, pp.9-14.
TREND CURVES - LOGISTIC

YA2582   NASH J.C.
"Small computer programs for OLS and principal components regression
calculations"   Econometrica, vol.44, 1976, p.833.
COMPUTERISATION - ESTIMATION , REGRESSION MODELS , PROGRAMS

YA2583   NASSE P.
"Un systeme complet de fonctions de demande: les equations de Fourgeaud et
Nataf"   Econometrica, vol.41, 1973, pp.1137-1158.
DEMAND EQUATIONS - SYSTEMS OF : METHODOLOGY , ESTIMATION * APPL - MACRO :
CONSUMER DEMAND * APPL - MACRO , FRANCE * PRICE - EFFECT OF

YA2584   NATAKANI I.
"Production functions with variable elasticity of substitution: a comment"
Rev. Econ. Stats., vol.55, 1973, pp.394-396.
PRODUCTION FUNCTIONS - SUBSTITUTION * PRODUCTION FUNCTIONS - METHODOLOGY *
PRODUCTION FUNCTIONS - MACRO * DATA - INTERNATIONAL

YA2585   NAYLOR T.H.
"A conceptual framework for corporate modeling and the results of a survey
of current practice"   Opl. Res. Q., vol.27, 1976, pp.671-682.
FORECASTING - USAGE * USE - CORPORATE PLANNING * SIMULATION - APPL : FIRM *
USER REQUIREMENTS

YA2586   NAYLOR T.H.
"Integrating models into the planning process"   Long Range Planning,
vol.1016, 1977, pp.11-15.
USE - CORPORATE PLANNING * SIMULATION - APPL : FIRM * USER REQUIREMENTS *
COMPUTERISATION - PLANNING MODELS * BASIC

YA2587   NAYLOR T.H., MANSFIELD M.J.
"The design of computer based planning and modeling systems"   Long Range
Planning, vol.10:1, 1977, pp.16-25.
SIMULATION - APPL : FIRM * USE - CORPORATE PLANNING * COMPUTERISATION -
PLANNING MODELS * MIS * BASIC

YA2588   NAYLOR T.H., SCHAULAND H.
"A survey of uses of corporate planning models"   Mgmt. Sci., vol.22, 1976,
pp.927-937.
SIMULATION - APPL : FIRM * FORECASTING - USAGE * USE - CORPORATE PLANNING *
BASIC

YA2589   NAYLOR T.H., SCHAULAND H.
"Experience with corporate simulation models - a survey"   Long Range
Planning, vol.9:2, 1976, pp.94-100.
SIMULATION - APPL : FIRM * USE - CORPORATE PLANNING * FORECASTING - USAGE *
BASIC

YA2590   NAYLOR T.H., SEAKS T.G., WICHERN D.W.
"Box-Jenkins methods: an alternative to econometric methods"   Int.
Statist. Rev., vol.40, 1972, pp.123-137.
MACRO MODEL - WHARTON * COMPARATIVE METHODS - ARIMA , CAUSAL(SIMULTANEOUS
SYSTEM) * COMPARATIVE METHODS - MACRO MODELS * EX ANTE

YA2591   NAYLOR T.H., WERTZ K., WONNACOTT T.H.
"Spectral analysis of data generated by simulation experiments with
econometric models"   Econometrica, vol.37, 1969, pp.333-352.
SPECTRAL ANALYSIS - APPL : SIMULATION EVALUATION * SIMULATION - EVALUATION
OF RESULTS * MACRO MODEL - US * CONFIDENCE INTERVAL - PREDICTIONS : TIME
SERIES * TIME SERIES - COMPARISON * EVALUATION - THEORY OF * CONFIDENCE
INTERVAL - SPECTRA , MULTIVARIATE

YA2592   NAZEM S.M.
"Forecasting rail freight transportation demand"   Bus. Econ., vol.11:4,
1976, pp.65-69.
APPL - SECTOR : TRANSPORT , RAIL , FREIGHT * BASIC

YA2593   NEART P.A., BULTEZ A.
"Logically consistent market share models"   J. Mktg. Res., vol.10, 1973,
pp.334-340.
MARKET SHARE - METHODOLOGY * SIMULTANEOUS SYSTEM - CONSTRAINED * REGRESSION
- NON LINEAR

YA2594   NEAVE E.H., WIGINTON J.C.,
"Evaluating security performance forecasts"   Mgmt Sci., vol.23, 1976,
pp.371-379.
JUDGEMENTAL FORECASTS - SPECIALIST * EVALUATION - JUDGEMENTAL FORECASTS ,
STOCK PRICES * LOSS FUNCTIONS - INFORMATION CRITERION * APPL - FIRM :
FINANCE , STOCK PRICES

YA2595   NEHLAWI J.E.
"Consistent estimation of real econometric models with undersized samples:
study of the Trace (MKIIIR) econometric model of the Canadian economy"
Int. Econ. Rev., vol.18, 1977, pp.163-179.
MACRO MODEL - CANADA , TRACE * EX ANTE * COMPARATIVE METHODS - ESTIMATION :
SIMULTANEOUS SYSTEM * SIMULTANEOUS SYSTEM - ESTIMATION * COMPARATIVE METHODS
- REGRESSION , SIMULTANEOUS SYSTEM * DATA - SAMPLE SIZE * ESTIMATION - 2SLS
, PRINCIPAL COMPONENTS

YA2596   NELDER J.A.
"Regression, model building and invariance"   R. Statist. Soc. (A),
vol.131, 1968, pp.303-329.
DATA ERRORS - EFFECT OF * REGRESSION - RANDOM COEFFICIENTS * STABILITY OF
COEFFICIENTS - REGRESSION

YA2597   NELSON C.R.
"Estimation of term premiums from average yield differentials in the term
structure of interest rates"   Econometrica, vol.40, 1972, pp.277-287.
INTEREST RATE - TERM STRUCTURE * INTEREST RATE - LIQUIDITY PREFERENCE

YA2598   NELSON C.R.
"Gains in efficiency from joint estimation of systems of
autoregressive-moving average processes"   J. Econometrics, vol.4, 1976,
pp.331-348.
EX ANTE * MACRO MODEL - FRB , MIT , PENN * TIME SERIES - MULTIVARIATE * TIME
SERIES - ARIMA : ESTIMATION * DATA - SIMULATION * TIME SERIES - SEEMINGLY
UNRELATED * COMPARATIVE METHODS - ARIMA , CAUSAL(SIMULTANEOUS SYSTEM) *
COMPARATIVE METHODS - MACRO MODELS * INTEREST RATE - INDICATORS * ADVANCED

YA2599   NELSON C.R.
"Inflation and rates of return on common stocks" with discussion   J.
Finance, vol.31, 1976, pp.471-487.
INFLATION - INDICATORS * APPL - SECTOR : FINANCE , STOCK PRICE INDEX * EX
ANTE * STOCK PRICES - DETERMINANTS * INFLATION - EXPECTATIONS * INFLATION -
EFFECT OF

YA2600   NELSON C.R.
"Rational expectations and the predictive efficiency of economic models"
J. Business, vol.48, 1975, pp.331-343.
THEORY - EXPECTATIONS * FORECASTING - THEORY

YA2601   NELSON C.R.
          "Testing a model of the term structure of interest rates by simulation of
          market forecasts"   J. Am. Statist. Ass., vol.65, 1970, pp.1163-1179.
          INTEREST RATE - TERM STRUCTURE * INTEREST RATE - EXPECTATIONS * EXPECTATIONS
          - DATA * EXPECTATIONS - ESTIMATING

YA2602   NELSON C.R.
          "The first order moving average process: indentification, estimation and
          prediction"   J. Econometrics, vol.2, 1974, pp.121-141.
          TIME SERIES - MOVING AVERAGE * COMPARATIVE METHODS - ESTIMATION : TIME
          SERIES * DATA - SIMULATION

YA2603   NELSON C.R.
          "The interpretation of R squared in autoregressive-moving average time
          series models"   Am. Stat'n., vol.30, 1976, pp.175-180.
          TIME SERIES - SUMMARY STATISTICS * TIME SERIES - ARIMA : DIAGNOSTICS

YA2604   NELSON C.R.
          "The prediction performance of the FRB-MIT-PENN model of the US economy"
          Am. Econ. Rev., vol.62, 1972, pp.902-917.
          MACRO MODEL - FRB , MIT , PENN * EVALUATION - MACRO MODELS * COMPARATIVE
          METHODS - ARIMA , CAUSAL(SIMULTANEOUS SYSTEM) * COMPARATIVE METHODS - MACRO
          MODELS * EX ANTE

YA2605   NELSON C.R., SCHWERT G.W.
          "Estimating the parameters of a distributed lag model from cross section
          data: the case of hospital admissions and discharge"   J. Am. Statist.
          Ass., vol.69, 1974, pp.627-633.
          DATA - CROSS SECTION * DISTRIBUTED LAG - ESTIMATION * DISTRIBUTED LAG -
          CROSS SECTION DATA * HEALTH - HOSPITAL , PATIENT FACILITIES * ADVANCED

YA2606   NELSON C.W., KRISBERGH H.M.
          "A search procedure for policy oriented simulations: applications to urban
          dynamics"   Mgmt. Sci. (B), vol.20, 1974, pp.1164-1177.
          SIMULATION - METHODOLOGY * CONTROL THEORY - DETERMINISTIC , APPL *
          INDUSTRIAL DYNAMICS - APPL , URBAN * REGIONAL MODELS - CITY * POLICY
          EVALUATION - REGIONAL

YA2607   NELSON F., OLSON L.
          "Specification and estimation of a simultaneous-equation model with limited
          dependent variables"   Int. Econ. Rev., vol.19, 1978, pp.695-709.
          MANPOWER PLANNING - EDUCATION PROGRAMS * SIMULTANEOUS SYSTEM - LIMITED
          DEPENDENT * DATA - SIMULATION * COMPARATIVE METHODS - ESTIMATION :
          SIMULTANEOUS SYSTEM , LIMITED DEPENDENT

YA2608   NELSON F.D.
          "Censored regression models with unobserved stochastic censoring thresholds"
          J. Econometrics, vol.6, 1977, pp.309-327.
          REGRESSION - CENSORED * TIME - VALUE OF * COMPARATIVE METHODS - REGRESSION ,
          CENSORED * MANPOWER PLANNING - LABOUR PARTICIPATION , FEMALE

YA2609   NELSON F.D.
          "On a general computer algorithm for the analysis of models with limited
          dependent variables"   Anns. Econ. Soc. Meas., vol.5, 1976, pp.493-509.
          REGRESSION - LIMITED DEPENDENT * COMPUTERISATION - ESTIMATION , REGRESSION
          MODELS , PROGRAMS * ADVANCED

YA2610   NELSON G., SPREEN T.
          "Monthly steer and heifer supply"   Am. J. Ag. Econ., vol.40, 1978,
          pp.117-125.
          APPL - SECTOR : AGRICULTURE , LIVESTOCK , CATTLE * SUPPLY - SECTOR :
          AGRICULTURE * STABILITY OF COEFFICIENTS - REGRESSION , TEST : APPL * EX ANTE

YA2611   NELSON J.P.
          "The demand for space heating energy"   Rev. Econ. Stats., vol.57, 1975,
          pp.508-512.
          DATA - CROSS SECTION * APPL - SECTOR : ENERGY * REGRESSION - MODEL CHOICE *
          REGRESSION - TRANSFORMATIONS , LOGARITHMIC

YA2612   NELSON P.
          "The economic consequences of advertising"   J. Business, vol.48, 1975,
          pp.213-241.
          ADVERTISING - REVIEW

YA2613   NELSON W.G.
          "The office of economic forecasting - its purposes and functions"   Bus.
          Econ., vol.11:3, 1976, pp.64-69.
          USER REQUIREMENTS * USE - CORPORATE PLANNING * BASIC

YA2614   NEPOMIASICHY P., RAVELLI A.
          "Adapted methods for solving and optimising quasi-triangular econometric
          models"   Anns. Econ. Soc. Meas., vol.6, 1978, pp.555-562.
          NUMERICAL METHODS - EQUATION SOLUTION * MACRO MODELS - METHODOLOGY ,
          SOLUTION

YA2615   NERI J.A.
          "An evaluation of two alternative supply models of natural gas"   Bell J.
          Econ., vol.8, 1977, pp.289-302.
          APPL - SECTOR : PRODUCTION , GAS * EX ANTE * EVALUATION - GAS SUPPLY ,
          MODELS OF * SUPPLY - SECTOR : PRODUCTION

YA2616   NERLOVE M.
"A comparison of a modified 'Hannan' and the BLS seasonal adjustment
filters"   J. Am. Statist. Ass., vol.60, 1965, pp.442-491.
SPECTRAL ANALYSIS - APPL : SEASONALITY * SEASONALITY - ESTIMATION ,
HARMONICS * COMPARATIVE METHODS - SEASONALITY * TIME SERIES - DECOMPOSITION
* ADVANCED

YA2617   NERLOVE M.
"Factors affecting differences among rates of return on investments in
individual common stocks"   Rev. Econ. Stats., vol.50, 1968, pp.312-331.
APPL - FIRM : FINANCE , STOCK PRICES * STOCK PRICES - DETERMINANTS * DATA -
CROSS SECTION , TIME SERIES * STABILITY OF COEFFICIENTS - REGRESSION : APPL

YA2618   NERLOVE M.
"Further evidence on the estimation of dynamic economic relations from a
time series of cross sections"   Econometrica, vol.39, 1971, pp.359-382.
REGRESSION - ERROR COMPONENTS * ERROR SPECIFICATION - CORRELATED *
COMPARATIVE METHODS - DATA : CROSS SECTION , TIME SERIES * DATA - SIMULATION
* COMPARATIVE METHODS - ESTIMATION : REGRESSION , ERROR COMPONENTS

YA2619   NERLOVE M.
"Lags in economic behaviour"   Econometrica, vol.40, 1972, pp.221-251.
DISTRIBUTED LAG - REVIEW * DISTRIBUTED LAG - IDENTIFICATION * BIBLIOGRAPHY -
DISTRIBUTED LAG * DISTRIBUTED LAG - APPL , INVESTMENT

YA2620   NETER J.
"Measurement errors in reports of consumer expenditures"   J. Mktg. Res.,
vol.7, 1970, pp.11-25.
DATA ERRORS - ESTIMATION OF * SURVEYS - METHODOLOGY , RESPONSE ERROR *
BIBLIOGRAPHY - SURVEYS * EVALUATION - SURVEYS , CONSUMER

YA2621   NETER J., MAYNES E.S.
"On the appropriateness of the correlation coefficient with a 0,1 dependent
variable"   J. Am. Statist. Ass., vol.65, 1970, pp.501-509.
REGRESSION - DISCRETE DEPENDENT * REGRESSION - SUMMARY STATISTICS * APPL -
SECTOR : CONSUMER DURABLES , CARS * EVALUATION - THEORY OF * EVALUATION -
LOSS FUNCTIONS * REGRESSION - QUALITATIVE DEPENDENT

YA2622   NEUBERG L.G.
"Two issues in the municipal ownership of electric power distribution
systems"   Bell J. Econ., vol.8, 1977, pp.303-323.
APPL - FIRM : UTILITIES , ELECTRICITY * APPL - FIRM TYPE * APPL - FIRM :
EFFICIENCY * COST - FIRM : UTILITIES

YA2623   NEVERS J.V.
"Extensions of a new product growth model"   Sloan Mgmt. Rev., vol.13,
no.2, 1972, pp.76-91.
NEW PRODUCTS - DIFFUSION MODELS * APPL - SECTOR * APPL - FIRM

YA2624   NEVIN J.R.
"Laboratory experiments for estimating consumer demand: a validation study"
J. Mktg. Res., vol.11, 1974, pp.261-268.
PRICE - EFFECT OF * APPL - SECTOR : RETAILING , GROCERIES * USE - PROMOTION
EVALUATION * SURVEYS - METHODOLOGY , VALIDATION * EVALUATION - SURVEYS ,
CONSUMER

YA2625   NEWBOLD P.
"Bayesian estimation of Box-Jenkins transfer function - noise models"   R.
Statist. Soc. (B), vol.35, 1973, pp.323-336.
DISTRIBUTED LAG - ESTIMATION * DISTRIBUTED LAG - RATIONAL POLYNOMIAL ,
ESTIMATION * DISTRIBUTED LAG - ERROR SPECIFICATION * BAYESIAN - ESTIMATION :
DISTRIBUTED LAG * ERROR SPECIFICATION - ARMA * DISTRIBUTED LAG - ARIMA *
DISTRIBUTED LAG - ERROR SPECIFICATION * DATA - SIMULATION * ADVANCED

YA2626   NEWBOLD P.
"Feedback induced by measurement errors"   Int. Econ. Rev., vol.19, 1978,
pp.787-791.
DATA ERRORS - EFFECT OF * CAUSALITY - TEST

YA2627   NEWBOLD P.
"On testing for forecast bias"   Bus. Econ., vol.7:3, 1972, pp.60-61.
EVALUATION - THEORY OF * CONFIDENCE INTERVAL - PREDICTIONS : TIME SERIES *
BASIC

YA2628   NEWBOLD P.
"Testing for forecast bias: revisited"   Bus. Econ., vol.9:3, 1974,
pp.74-75.
EVALUATION - THEORY OF * CONFIDENCE INTERVAL - PREDICTIONS : TIME SERIES

YA2629   NEWBOLD P.
"The principles of the Box-Jenkins approach"   Opl. Res. Q., vol.26, 1975,
pp.397-412.
TIME SERIES - ARIMA : INTRODUCTION * DISTRIBUTED LAG - RATIONAL POLYNOMIAL ,
INTRODUCTION * DISTRIBUTED LAG - ARIMA * COMPARATIVE METHODS - ARIMA ,
EXPONENTIAL SMOOTHING * LEAD TIME - EFFECT OF * EX ANTE * DISTRIBUTED LAG -
ERROR SPECIFICATION

YA2630   NEWBOLD P. GRANGER C.W.J.
"Experience with forecasting univariate time series and the combination of
forecasts" with discussion   R. Statist., Soc. (A), vol.137, 1974,
pp.131-164.
COMPARATIVE METHODS - AUTOREGRESSIVE , EXPONENTIAL SMOOTHING * COMBINING
FORECASTS - TIME SERIES * COMBINING FORECASTS - METHODOLOGY * COMPARATIVE
METHODS - ARIMA , EXPONENTIAL SMOOTHING * COMPARATIVE METHODS - ARIMA ,
AUTOREGRESSIVE * MODEL SELECTION * LEAD TIME - EFFECT OF * EX ANTE

YA2631   NEWBOLD P., DAVIES N.
        "Error mis-specification and spurious regression"   Int. Econ. Rev.,
        vol.19, 1978, pp.513-519.
        DATA - SIMULATION * REGRESSION - SPURIOUS * ERROR SPECIFICATION - MOVING
        AVERAGE

YA2632   NEWELL G.E.
        "Revisions of reported quarterly earnings"   J. Business, vol.44, 1971,
        pp.282-285.
        DATA REVISIONS - BIAS * APPL - FIRM : FINANCE , PROFITS

YA2633   NEWMAN H.H.
        "Strategic groups and the structure-performance relationship"   Rev. Econ.
        Stats., vol.60, 1978, pp.417-427.
        APPL - FIRM TYPE * CONCENTRATION - EFFECT OF * APPL - SECTOR : FINANCE ,
        MARGINS

YA2634   NIARCHOS N.A., GRANGER C.W.J.
        "The gold sovereign market in Greece- an unusual speculative market"   J.
        Finance, vol.27, 1972, pp.1127-1135.
        APPL - SECTOR : COMMODITIES , GOLD

YA2635   NICCOLI A., ET AL.
        "Real money balances: an omitted variable from the production function:
        comment"   Rev. Econ. Stats., vol.57, 1975, pp.241-252.
        APPL - MACRO : MONEY , REAL CASH BALANCES * PRODUCTION FUNCTIONS - THEORY *
        PRODUCTION FUNCTIONS - MACRU * AUTOCORRELATION - EFFECT OF

YA2636   NICHOLLS D.F., PAGAN A.R., TERRELL R.D.
        "The estimation and use of models with moving average disturbance terms: a
        survey"   Int. Econ. Rev., vol.16, 1975, pp.113-134.
        ERROR SPECIFICATION - MOVING AVERAGE * DISTRIBUTED LAG - RATIONAL POLYNOMIAL
        * SIMULTANEOUS SYSTEM - ESTIMATION , ERROR SPECIFICATION * BIBLIOGRAPHY -
        ERROR SPECIFICATION * DISTRIBUTED LAG - ERROR SPECIFICATION * DISTRIBUTED
        LAG - ARIMA

YA2637   NICHOLSON R.J., TOPHAM N.
        "The determinants of investment in housing by local authorities: an
        econometric approach" with discussion   R. Statist. Soc. (A), vol.134,
        1971, pp.273-320.
        APPL - SECTOR : CONSTRUCTION , RESIDENTIAL * APPL - SECTOR : GOVERNMENT ,
        LOCAL , HOUSING * REGIONAL MODELS - SECTOR : CONSTRUCTION

YA2638   NICKELL S., METCALF D.
        "Monopolistic industries and monopoly profits or, are Kellog's Cornflakes
        overpriced"   Econ. J., vol.88, 1978, pp.254-268.
        APPL - SECTOR : FINANCE , MARGINS * CONCENTRATION - EFFECT OF * ADVERTISING
        - EFFECT OF * DATA - CROSS SECTION

YA2639   NICOL D.J.
        "The influence of aircraft size on airlines' operating costs"   Omega,
        vol.6, 1978, pp.15-24.
        APPL - SECTOR : TRANSPORT , AIR * COST - SECTOR : TRANSPORT * COST - SCALE
        ECONOMIES

YA2640   NICOLAOU G.B.
        "The place of petroleum in the UK fuel market"   Appl. Econ., vol.9, 1977,
        pp.167-172.
        SUBSTITUTE PRODUCTS * APPL - SECTOR : PRODUCTION , PETROLEUM * PRICE -
        EFFECT OF

YA2641   NIEHANS J., SCHELBERT-SYFRIG H.
        "Simultaneous determination of interest and prices in Switzerland by a two
        market model for money and bonds"   Econometrica, vol.34, 1966, pp.408-423.
        INFLATION - DETERMINANTS * DATA - INTERPOLATION * INTEREST RATE - EFFECT OF
        * APPL - MACRO : MONEY * COMPARATIVE METHODS - ESTIMATION : OLS , 2SLS *
        APPL - SECTOR : FINANCE , BONDS * INTEREST RATE - DETERMINANTS

YA2642   NILAND P.
        "Developing standards for library expenditures"   Mgmt. Sci. (B), vol.13,
        1967, pp.797-808.
        APPL - SECTOR : GOVERNMENT , LIBRARIES * USER - SECTOR : GOVERNMENT * USE -
        TARGET SETTING * USE - FINANCIAL PLANNING * COST - SECTOR : GOVERNMENT

YA2643   NISBET C.T., VAKIL F.
        "Some estimates of price and expenditures elasticities of demand for
        marijuana among UCLA students"   Rev. Econ. Stats., vol.54, 1972,
        pp.473-475.
        PRICE - EFFECT OF * INCOME - EFFECT OF * DATA - CROSS SECTION * APPL -
        SECTOR : CONSUMER NON DURABLES , DRUGS * EVALUATION - SURVEYS , CONSUMER

YA2644   NORDHAUS W.D.
        "The falling share of profits" with discussion   Brookings Paps. Econ.
        Activity, 1974, pp.169-217.
        APPL - SECTOR : FINANCE , PROFITS * APPL - SECTOR : FINANCE , COST OF
        CAPITAL

YA2645   NORDHAUS W.D.
        "The recent productivity slowdown"   Brookings Paps. Econ. Activity, 1972,
        pp.493-545.
        APPL - SECTOR : PRODUCTIVITY

YA2646   NORDHAUS W.D.
          "The worldwide wage explosion" with discussion   Brookings Paps, Econ,
          Activity, 1972, pp.431-465,
          APPL - MACRO : EARNINGS * DATA - INTERNATIONAL * INFLATION - PHILLIPS CURVE
          * THEORY - MONETARY * INFLATION - EXPECTATIONS * INFLATION - REVIEW

YA2647   NORDHAUS W.D.
          "World dynamics: measurement without data"   Econ, J,, vol,83, 1973,
          pp.1156-1183,
          APPL - MACRO , WORLD * SIMULATION - APPL : WORLD MODELS * EVALUATION -
          INDUSTRIAL DYNAMICS * POPULATION - EFFECT OF * SPECIFICATION ERROR - EFFECT
          OF , SIMULATION MODEL SPECIFICATION * INDUSTRIAL DYNAMICS - APPL , WORLD

YA2648   NORDHAUS W.D., GODLEY W.
          "Pricing in the trade cycle"   Econ, J,, vol,82, 1972, pp.853-882,
          PRICE - MACRO * BUSINESS CYCLE - EFFECT OF * PRICE - SECTOR * APPL - MACRO :
          EMPLOYMENT * COST - SECTOR * APPL - MACRO , UK * APPL - MACRO : EARNINGS *
          COMPARATIVE METHODS - REGRESSION , MODEL SPECIFICATION * APPL - MACRO :
          PRODUCTIVITY * DISTRIBUTED LAG - EFFECT OF * THEORY - PRICING

YA2649   NORMAN A.L.
          "First order dual control"   Anns, Econ, Soc, Meas,, vol,5, 1976,
          pp.311-321,
          COMPARATIVE METHODS - CONTROL * CONTROL THEORY - STOCHASTIC , METHODOLOGY *
          DATA - SIMULATION * SIMULTANEOUS SYSTEM - CONTROL

YA2650   NORUSIS M.J., ET AL,
          "Accuracy of sample moments calculations among widely used statistical
          programs"   Am, Stat'n,, vol,32, 1978, pp.113-114,
          COMPUTERISATION - ESTIMATION , REGRESSION MODELS * COMPUTERISATION -
          CALCULATION ERROR

YA2651   NUGENT J.B.
          "Policy-orientated macroeconometric models for development and planning"
          Anns. Econ, Soc, Meas,, vol,4, 1975, pp.509-529,
          MACRO MODEL - LATIN AMERICA * APPL - MACRO : INTERNATIONAL LINKAGE * LP *
          POLICY EVALUATION - MACRO

YA2652   NUTT A.B., ET AL,
          "Data sources for trend extrapolation in technological forecasting"   Long
          Range Planning, vol,9:1, 1976, pp,72-76,
          TREND CURVES - APPL * TECHNOLOGICAL FORECASTING * DATA SOURCES - TECHNOLOGY
          * BASIC

YA2653   OAKLAND W.H.
          "Corporate earnings and tax shifting in US manufacturing, 1930-1968"   Rev,
          Econ, Stats,, vol,54, 1972, pp,235-244,
          TAX - EFFECT OF * APPL - MACRO : PROFITS

YA2654   OAXACA R.
          "Male-female wage differentials in urban labor markets"   Int, Econ, Rev,,
          vol,14, 1973, pp,693-709,
          MANPOWER PLANNING - DISCRIMINATION * MANPOWER PLANNING - EARNINGS * MANPOWER
          PLANNING - SECTOR * EDUCATION - EFFECT OF * APPL - SECTOR : EARNINGS

YA2655   OBERHOFER W., KMENTA J.
          "Estimation of standard errors of the characteristic roots of a dynamic
          econometric model"   Econometrica, vol,41, 1973, pp,171-177,
          SIMULTANEOUS SYSTEM - DYNAMIC PROPERTIES * SIMULTANEOUS SYSTEM - HYPOTHESIS
          TESTS * ADVANCED

YA2656   O'BRIEN J.M.
          "The covariance measure of substitution: an application to financial assets"
          Rev. Econ, Stats,, vol,56, 1974, pp,456-467,
          SUBSTITUTE PRODUCTS * CONSUMER BEHAVIOUR - ECONOMIC MODELS * APPL - MACRO :
          CONSUMER DEMAND , FINANCIAL ASSETS

YA2657   O'CARROLL F.M.
          "Subjective probabilities and short-term economic forecasts: an empirical
          investigation"   Appl, Stats,, vol,26, 1977, pp,269-278,
          APPL - MACRO : INTERNATIONAL FINANCE , EXCHANGE RATES * APPL - MACRO , UK *
          APPL - SECTOR : FINANCE , STOCK PRICE INDEX * APPL - SECTOR : PRODUCTION ,
          PETROLEUM * PRICE - SECTOR : PRODUCTION * JUDGEMENTAL FORECASTS - SPECIALIST
          * ERROR DISTRIBUTION - LOGNORMAL * EVALUATION - JUDGEMENTAL FORECASTS *
          JUDGEMENTAL FORECASTS - UNCERTAINTY

YA2658   O'CONNOR M.C.
          "On the usefulness of financial ratios to investors in common stock"
          Acctg. Rev,, vol,48, 1973, pp,339-352,
          STOCK PRICES - INDICATORS * APPL - FIRM : FINANCE , STOCK PRICES * BUSINESS
          INDICATORS - APPL

YA2659   ODAGIRI H.
          "Demand for economics journals: a cross section analysis"   Rev, Econ.
          Stats,, vol,59, 1977, pp.493-499,
          APPL - FIRM : SERVICES , MEDIA , MAGAZINES * QUALITY - EFFECT OF * DATA -
          CROSS SECTION

YA2660   OFER A.R.
          "Investors' expectations of earnings growth, their accuracy and effects on
          the structure of realized rates of return" with discussion   J, Finance,
          vol,30, 1975, pp,509-523 & 548-550,
          APPL - FIRM : FINANCE , PE RATIO * RISK - EFFECT OF * DATA - CROSS SECTION ,
          TIME SERIES * STOCK PRICES - DETERMINANTS * APPL - FIRM : FINANCE , STOCK
          PRICES * EX ANTE * APPL - FIRM : FINANCE , PROFITS , PER SHARE

YA2661   OFER A.R., MELNICK A.
"Price deregulation in the brokerage industry: an empirical analysis"
Bell J. Econ, vol.9, 1978, pp.633-641.
APPL - FIRM : FINANCE , STOCK BROKERS * CUST - FIRM : FINANCE * SCALE
ECONOMIES * PRICE - FIRM : FINANCE

YA2662   OFFICER L.H.
"The relationship between absolute and relative purchasing power parity"
Rev. Econ. Stats., vol.60, 1978, pp.562-568.
APPL - MACRO : INTERNATIONAL FINANCE , EXCHANGE RATES * INFLATION - EFFECT
OF * EVALUATION - EXCHANGE RATE MODELS

YA2663   OFFICER R.R.
"The distribution of stock returns"   J. Am. Statist. Ass., vol.67, 1972,
pp.807-812.
STOCK PRICES - DISTRIBUTION * APPL - FIRM : FINANCE , STOCK PRICES * ERROR
DISTRIBUTION - STABLE * ERROR DISTRIBUTION - ASYMMETRICAL

YA2664   OFFICER R.R.
"The variability of the market factor of the New York Stock Exchange"   J.
Business, vol.46, 1973, pp.434-453
APPL - SECTOR : FINANCE , STOCK PRICE INDEX * STOCK PRICES - VOLATILITY *
BUSINESS INDICATORS - APPL

YA2665   O'HERLIHY C. St. J.
"Demand for cars in Great Britain"   Appl. Stats., vol.14, 1965,
pp.162-195.
APPL - SECTOR : CONSUMER DURABLES , CARS * DEPRECIATION - ESTIMATION

YA2666   O'HERLIHY C. St. J., SPENCER J.E.
"Building societies' behaviour, 1955-70"   Nat. Inst. Econ. Rev., no.61,
1972, pp.40-52.
APPL - SECTOR : FINANCE , BUILDING SOCIETIES * APPL - SECTOR : FINANCE ,
MORTGAGES * INTEREST RATE - DETERMINANTS * APPL - SECTOR : FINANCE , SAVINGS
* EX ANTE

YA2667   OHLS J.C., WALES T.J.
"Supply and demand for state and local services"   Rev. Econ. Stats.,
vol.54, 1972, pp.424-430.
DATA - CROSS SECTION * APPL - SECTOR : GOVERNMENT , LOCAL * APPL - SECTOR :
GOVERNMENT , ROADS * APPL - SECTOR : GOVERNMENT , EDUCATION * APPL - SECTOR
: GOVERNMENT , LOCAL , SERVICES * SUPPLY - SECTOR : GOVERNMENT

YA2668   OKNER B.A., ET AL.
"Data matching and merging: a workshop"   Anns. Econ. Soc. Meas., vol.3,
1974, pp.347-437.
DATA - HANDLING * SURVEYS - METHODOLOGY , EDITING * SURVEYS - CONSUMER

YA2669   OKSANEN E.H., SPENCER B.G.
"International consumption behaviour: tests of alternative consumption
function hypotheses using national accounting data for twelve countries"
Int. Statist. Rev., vol.41, 1973, pp.69-76.
DATA - INTERNATIONAL * APPL - MACRO : CONSUMPTION * EVALUATION - CONSUMPTION
MODELS

YA2670   OKSANEN E.H., SPENCER B.G.
"Testing an aggregate consumption model for Canada"   Can. J. Econ, vol.5,
1972, pp.96-109.
APPL - MACRO , CANADA * APPL - MACRO : CONSUMPTION * APPL - MACRO : CONSUMER
DEMAND * PRICE - EFFECT OF * INCOME - EFFECT OF , PERMANENT

YA2671   OKSANEN E.H., WILLIAMS J.R.
"A principal component analysis of national accounting data of eighteen OECD
countries"   Rev. Econ. Stats., vol.56, 1974, pp.559-562.
FACTOR ANALYSIS - APPL * MULTICOLLINEARITY - TESTS

YA2672   OKUN A.M.
"Fiscal-monetary activism: some analytical issues" with discussion
Brookings Paps. Econ. Activity, 1972, pp.123-172.
POLICY EVALUATION - MACRO * DECISION RULES - MACRO * MULTIPLIERS - MACRO *
MACRO MODEL - ST.LOUIS

YA2673   OKUN A.M.
"The personal tax surcharge and consumer demand, 1968-1970" with discussion
Brookings Paps. Econ. Activity, 1971, pp.167-211.
MACRO MODEL - US * MACRO MODEL - WHARTON * MACRO MODEL - OBE * MACRO MODEL -
MICHIGAN * EX ANTE * TAX - EFFECT OF * APPL - MACRO : CONSUMER DEMAND

YA2674   OKUN A.M.
"Unemployment and output in 1974" with discussion   Brookings Paps. Econ.
Activity, 1974, pp.495-505.
APPL - MACRO : UNEMPLOYMENT * APPL - MACRO : GNP

YA2675   OKUN A.M.
"Upward mobility in a high-pressure economy" with discussion   Brookings
Paps. Econ. Activity, 1973, pp.207-261.
MANPOWER PLANNING - LABOUR FORCE COMPOSITION * MANPOWER PLANNING - SECTOR ,
DEMAND * MANPOWER PLANNING - INDUSTRIAL COMPOSITION

YA2676   OKUN A.M., PERRY G.L.
"Notes and numbers on the profits squeeze?" with discussion   Brookings
Paps. Econ. Activity, 1970, pp.466-473.
APPL - SECTOR : FINANCE , PROFITS

YA2677 OKUN A.M., SPRINGER W.L.
"Did the 1968 surcharge really work? comments"   Am. Econ. Rev., vol.67,
1977, pp.166-172.
POLICY EVALUATION - MACRO : FISCAL * APPL - MACRO : CONSUMPTION * INCOME -
EFFECT OF * TAX - EFFECT OF * THEORY - MODELLING * POLICY EVALUATION -
METHODOLOGY

YA2678 OLIVEIRA R.A., RAUSSER G.C.
"Daily fluctuations in campground use: an environmental analysis"   Am. J.
Ag. Econ., vol.59, 1977, pp.283-293.
COMPARATIVE METHODS - ARIMA , CAUSAL * APPL - SECTOR : SERVICES , TOURISM *
EX ANTE * USE - TOURISM DEVELOPMENT

YA2679 OLIVER F.R.
"The effectiveness of the UK travel allowance"   Appl. Econ., vol.3, 1971,
pp.219-226.
APPL - MACRO : INTERNATIONAL TRADE , INVISIBLES * APPL - SECTOR : SERVICES ,
TOURISM * POLICY EVALUATION - MACRO : INTERNATIONAL FINANCE * EX ANTE

YA2680 OLIVER R.M., HOPKINS D.S.P.
"An equilibrium flow model of the university campus"   Ops. Res., vol.20,
1972, pp.249-264.
APPL - SECTOR : EDUCATION , UNIVERSITIES * APPL - FIRM : EDUCATION ,
UNIVERSITIES * MANPOWER PLANNING - FIRM * MANPOWER PLANNING - SECTOR :
EDUCATION , UNIVERSITIES

YA2681 OLLER L.
"A method for pooling forecasts"   J. Opl. Res. Soc., vol.29, 1978,
pp.55-63.
JUDGEMENTAL FORECASTS - METHODOLOGY * COMBINING FORECASTS - METHODOLOGY *
JUDGEMENTAL FORECASTS - UNCERTAINTY

YA2682 OLSEN R.J.
"Comment on 'The effect of unions on earnings and earnings on unions: a
mixed logit approach'"   Int. Econ. Rev., vol.19, 1978 pp.259-261.
UNIONISATION - DETERMINANTS * UNIONISATION - EFFECT OF * MANPOWER PLANNING -
EARNINGS * MANPOWER PLANNING - LABOUR FORCE COMPOSITION * REGRESSION -
LIMITED DEPENDENT , LOGIT

YA2683 OLSON J.E.
"Price discrimination by regulated motor carriers"   Am. Econ. Rev.,
vol.62, 1972, pp.395-402.
APPL - SECTOR : TRANSPORT , ROAD , FREIGHT * PRICE - SECTOR : TRANSPORT *
POLICY EVALUATION - SECTOR : TRANSPORT

YA2684 O'NEILL D.M.
"A note on product price and aggregation biases in cross-sectional
estimation of the elasticity of substitution"   Rev. Econ. Stats., vol.49,
1967, pp.268-271.
DATA - CROSS SECTION * DATA - AGGREGATION 'BIAS' * PRODUCTION FUNCTIONS -
SUBSTITUTION * PRODUCTION FUNCTIONS - SECTOR * PRODUCTION FUNCTIONS -
METHODOLOGY

YA2685 ORAL M., ET AL.
"On the evaluation of shortage costs for inventory control of finished
goods"   Mgmt. Sci. (B), vol.18, 1972, pp.344-351.
LOSS FUNCTIONS - FIRM , INVENTORY * USE - INVENTORY CONTROL

YA2686 ORCUTT G.H., WINOKUR H.S.
"First order autoregression: inference, estimation and prediction"
Econometrica, vol.37, 1969, pp.1-14.
TIME SERIES - AUTOREGRESSIVE * COMPARATIVE METHODS - ESTIMATION : TIME
SERIES

YA2687 ORD K.
"Estimation methods for models of spatial interaction"   J. Am. Statist.
Ass., vol.70, 1975, pp.120-126.
SPATIAL ANALYSIS * COMPARATIVE METHODS - ESTIMATION : OLS , MLE

YA2688 ORGLER Y.E.
"Capital adequacy and recoveries from failed banks"   J. Finance, vol.30,
1975, pp.1366-1375.
APPL - FIRM : FINANCE , BANKS * USE - BANKRUPTCY PREDICTION * APPL - FIRM :
FINANCE , BANK , LIABILITIES

YA2689 ORMEROD P.
"Activity rates and unemployment in GB: an empirical rejoinder"   Appl.
Econ., vol.8, 1976, pp.91-98.
APPL - MACRO : UNEMPLOYMENT * APPL - MACRO , UK * MANPOWER PLANNING - LABOUR
PARTICIPATION * COMPARATIVE METHODS - ESTIMATION : REGRESSION , ERROR
SPECIFICATION

YA2690 ORNSTEIN S.I
"Concentration and profits"   J. Business, vol.45, 1972, pp.519-541.
CONCENTRATION - EFFECT OF * APPL - SECTOR : FINANCE , PROFITS

YA2691 ORR D.
"A note on the uselessness of transaction demand models"   J. Finance,
vol.29, 1974, pp.1565-1572.
APPL - FIRM : FINANCE , FINANCIAL STRUCTURE , LIQUID ASSETS * EX ANTE *
EVALUATION - CASH FLOW MODELS

YA2692 ORR D.
  "The determinants of entry: a study of Canadian manufacturing industries"
  Rev. Econ. Stats., vol.56, 1974, pp.58-66.
  APPL - SECTOR : FINANCE , PROFITS * APPL - SECTOR : COMPANY FORMATIONS *
  ADVERTISING - EFFECT OF * TECHNOLOGY - EFFECT OF * CONCENTRATION - EFFECT OF

YA2693 ORR D.
  "The economic determinants of entry into Canadian banking: 1963-7" Can.
  J. Econ., vol.7, 1974, pp.87-89
  APPL - FIRM : FINANCE , BANKS * APPL - FIRM : FINANCE , PROFITS *
  ADVERTISING - EFFECT OF * CONCENTRATION - EFFECT OF

YA2694 ORR D., HORST T.
  "The industrial composition of US exports, and subsidiary sales to the
  Canadian market: comment" Am. Econ. Rev., vol.65, 1975, pp.230-235.
  APPL - SECTOR : INTERNATIONAL TRADE , EXPORTS * TARIFF - EFFECT OF * DATA -
  CROSS SECTION * APPL - SECTOR : R & D * APPL - MACRO , CANADA

YA2695 OSBORN D.R.
  "Maximum likelihood estimation of moving average processes" Anns. Econ.
  Soc. Meas., vol.5, 1976, pp.75-87.
  ESTIMATION - MAXIMUM LIKELIHOOD * COMPARATIVE METHODS - ESTIMATION : TIME
  SERIES * TIME SERIES - ARIMA : ESTIMATION * ERROR SPECIFICATION - MOVING
  AVERAGE * TIME SERIES - MOVING AVERAGE

YA2696 OSBORNE M.F.M.
  "Some quantitative tests for stock price generating models and trading
  folklore" J. Am. Statist. Ass., vol.62, 1967, pp.321-340.
  APPL - FIRM : FINANCE , STOCK PRICES * STOCK PRICES - TRADING VOLUME * STOCK
  PRICES - RUNS * STOCK PRICES - TECHNICAL ANALYSIS

YA2697 OSTAS J.R.
  "Effects of usury ceilings in the mortgage market" J. Finance, vol.31,
  1976, pp.821-834.
  APPL - SECTOR : CONSTRUCTION , RESIDENTIAL * APPL - SECTOR : FINANCE ,
  MORTGAGES * USE - LOAN REGULATION * DATA - CROSS SECTION , TIME SERIES

YA2698 OSTAS J.R.
  "Regional differences in mortgage financing costs: a reexamination" J.
  Finance, vol.32, 1977, pp.1774-1778.
  APPL - SECTOR : FINANCE , MORTGAGES * DATA - CROSS SECTION * REGIONAL MODELS
  - SECTOR : CONSTRUCTION * APPL - SECTOR : CONSTRUCTION , RESIDENTIAL * PRICE
  - SECTOR : CONSTRUCTION , RESIDENTIAL

YA2699 OSTLUND L.C.
  "Identifying early buyers" J. Advtg. Res., vol.12:2, 1972, pp.25-30.
  CONSUMER BEHAVIOUR - PSYCHOLOGICAL MODELS * DISCRIMINANT ANALYSIS - APPL *
  APPL - FIRM : CONSUMER NON DURABLES , GROCERIES * USE - MEDIA PLANNING

YA2700 OTTANI I.
  "Real wages and business cycles revisited" Rev. Econ. Stats., vol.60,
  1978, pp.301-304.
  APPL - MACRO : EARNINGS * BUSINESS CYCLE - EFFECT OF * DATA - INTERNATIONAL

YA2701 OTTESTAD P.
  "Discrimination analysis" Int. Statist. Rev., vol.43, 1975, pp.301-315.
  DISCRIMINANT ANALYSIS - REVIEW * REGRESSION - QUALITATIVE DEPENDENT *
  REGRESSION - LIMITED DEPENDENT

YA2702 OU C.C.F.
  "Demand for short-term foreign assets by the German banks" J. Finance,
  vol.27, 1972, pp.653-662.
  APPL - MACRO , GERMANY * APPL - MACRO : INTERNATIONAL FINANCE , FOREIGN
  RESERVES * APPL - SECTOR : FINANCE , BANKS

YA2703 OUDET B.A.
  "Use of the linear quadratic approach to study the dynamic policy responses
  of a nonlinear model of the French economy" Anns. Econ. Soc. Meas.,
  vol.5, 1976, pp.205-210.
  MACRO MODEL - GOVERNMENT , FRANCE * LOSS FUNCTIONS - MACRO * CONTROL THEORY
  - STOCHASTIC , APPL * SIMULTANEOUS SYSTEM - NON LINEAR * SIMULTANEOUS SYSTEM
  - DYNAMIC PROPERTIES

YA2704 OZAKI T.
  "On the order determination of ARIMA models" Appl. Stats., vol.26, 1977,
  pp.290-301.
  TIME SERIES - ARIMA : IDENTIFICATION * LOSS FUNCTIONS - AKAIKE'S INFORMATION
  CRITERION * EVALUATION - TIME SERIES , ARIMA MODELS

YA2705 PACK D.J.
  "Revealing time series interrelationships" Decis. Sci., vol.8, 1977,
  pp.377-402.
  DISTRIBUTED LAG - IDENTIFICATION * DISTRIBUTED LAG - ARIMA * DISTRIBUTED LAG
  - ERROR SPECIFICATION * ERROR SPECIFICATION - ARMA * DISTRIBUTED LAG -
  RATIONAL POLYNOMIAL , IDENTIFICATION * TIME SERIES - ARIMA : APPL

YA2706 PACKER A.H.
  "Simulation and adaptive forecasting as applied to inventory control"
  Ops. Res., vol.15, 1967, pp.660-679.
  EXPONENTIAL SMOOTHING - COEFFICIENT CHOICE * USE - INVENTORY CONTROL * COST
  - FIRM : INVENTORY * BASIC

YA2707 PACKER A.H., PARK S.H.
"Distortions in relative wages and shifts in the Phillips curve" Rev.
Econ. Stats., vol.55, 1973, pp.16-22.
INFLATION - DETERMINANTS , EARNINGS * APPL - MACRO : EARNINGS * INFLATION -
PHILLIPS CURVE * COMPARATIVE METHODS - REGRESSION , ERROR SPECIFICATION

YA2708 PAGAN A.
"A note on the extraction of components from time series" Econometrica,
vol.43, 1975, pp.163-168.
TIME SERIES - STATE SPACE * ESTIMATION - KALMAN FILTER * TIME SERIES -
DECOMPOSITION * APPL - MACRO : CONSUMPTION * STABILITY OF COEFFICIENTS -
TIME SERIES

YA2709 PAGAN A.
"Efficient estimation of models with composite disturbance terms" J.
Econometrics, vol.1, 1973, pp.329-340.
PRODUCTION FUNCTIONS - ESTIMATION * DATA ERRORS - EFFECT OF * ERROR
SPECIFICATION - AUTOCORRELATED * DISTRIBUTED LAG - RATIONAL POLYNOMIAL ,
ESTIMATION * APPL - SECTOR : NATURAL , SUNSPOTS * DISTRIBUTED LAG - ERROR
SPECIFICATION * REGRESSION - STATE SPACE * TIME SERIES - STATE SPACE *
COMPARATIVE METHODS - REGRESSION , ERROR SPECIFICATION

YA2710 PAGAN A.
"Rational and polynomial lag" J. Econometrics, vol.8, 1978, pp.247-254.
DISTRIBUTED LAG - ALMON * DISTRIBUTED LAG - RATIONAL POLYNOMIAL *
COMPARATIVE METHODS - DISTRIBUTED LAG * DISTRIBUTED LAG - ESTIMATION *
ESTIMATION - NON LINEAR

YA2711 PAGAN A., NICHOLLS D.F.
"Exact maximum likelihood estimation of regression models with finite order
moving average errors" Rev. Econ. Studies, vol.43, 1976, pp.383-387.
ESTIMATION - MAXIMUM LIKELIHOOD * ERROR SPECIFICATION - MOVING AVERAGE *
COMPARATIVE METHODS - ESTIMATION : REGRESSION , ERROR SPECIFICATION * APPL -
MACRO : EMPLOYMENT

YA2712 PAGE S.A.B.
"Errors in National Institute forecasts for the world economy" Nat. Inst.
Econ. Rev., no.68, 1974, pp.65-76.
APPL - MACRO : INTERNATIONAL TRADE * APPL - MACRO , OECD * APPL - MACRO :
GNP * APPL - SECTOR : COMMODITIES * EVALUATION - MACRO FORECASTS *
COMPARATIVE METHODS - MACRO MODELS * APPL - MACRO , WORLD * COMPARATIVE
METHODS - AUTOREGRESSIVE , CAUSAL(SIMULTANEOUS SYSTEM)

YA2713 PAGE S.A.B.
"The effect of exchange rates on export market shares" Nat. Inst. Econ.
Rev., no.74, 1975, pp.71-82.
APPL - MACRO : INTERNATIONAL TRADE , EXPORTS * PRICE - EFFECT OF * EXCHANGE
RATE - EFFECT OF

YA2714 PALDA K.S., BLAIR L.M.
"A moving cross-section analysis of demand for toothpaste" J. Mktg. Res.,
vol.7, 1970, pp.439-449.
APPL - SECTOR : CONSUMER NON DURABLES , HEALTH AIDS * DATA - CROSS SECTION ,
TIME SERIES * REGRESSION - COVARIANCE MODEL * CONSUMER BEHAVIOUR -
PURCHASING , DETERMINANTS * INCOME - EFFECT OF * BASIC

YA2715 PALMER J.
"A further analysis of provincial trucking regulation" Bell J. Econ.,
vol.4, 1973, pp.655-664.
APPL - SECTOR : TRANSPORT , ROAD , FREIGHT * USE - FINANCIAL , REGULATION

YA2716 PANDIT S.M., WU S.M.
"Exponential smoothing as a special case of a linear stochastic system"
Ops. Res., vol.22, 1974, pp.868-879.
TIME SERIES - ARIMA : CONTINUOUS * EXPONENTIAL SMOOTHING - THEORY * APPL -
FIRM : FINANCE , STOCK PRICES * EXPONENTIAL SMOOTHING - COEFFICIENT CHOICE

YA2717 PANIK M.J.
"Factor learning and biased factor-efficiency growth in the US, 1929-1966"
Int. Econ. Rev., vol.17, 1976, pp.733-739.
PRODUCTION FUNCTIONS - MACRO * APPL - MACRO : PRODUCTIVITY

YA2718 PANKOFF L.D.
"Market efficiency and football betting" J. Business, vol.41, 1968,
pp.203-214.
APPL - FIRM : SERVICES , SPORTS * JUDGEMENTAL FORECASTS - SPECIALIST *
EVALUATION - EFFICIENT MARKET THEORY

YA2719 PANTON D.
"Chicago board call options as predictors of common stock price changes"
J. Econometrics, vol.4, 1976, pp.101-113.
APPL - FIRM : FINANCE , OPTIONS * APPL - FIRM : FINANCE , STOCK PRICES *
STOCK PRICES - INDICATORS

YA2720 PAPADOPOULOS D.
"On testing for forecast bias and underestimation" Bus. Econ., vol.8:4,
1973, pp.54-58.
LOSS FUNCTIONS - THEIL * EVALUATION - THEORY OF * CONFIDENCE INTERVAL -
PREDICTIONS : TIME SERIES

YA2721   PAPAKYRIAZIS P.A.
          "Optimal experimental design in econometrics"   J. Econometrics, vol.7,
          1978, pp.351-372.
          REGRESSION - EXPERIMENTAL DESIGN * SIMULATION - EXPERIMENTAL DESIGN * ERROR
          SPECIFICATION - ARMA * DISTRIBUTED LAG - RATIONAL POLYNOMIAL
YA2722   PAPANEK G.F.
          "The effect of aid and other resource transfers in savings and growth in
          less developed countries"   Econ. J., vol.82, 1972, pp.934-950.
          APPL - MACRO : DEVELOPMENT * APPL - MACRO : SAVINGS * APPL - MACRO :
          INTERNATIONAL FINANCE * DATA - LDC * PUBLIC EXPENDITURE - EFFECT OF , AID
          PROGRAMS
YA2723   PARFITT J.H., COLLINS B.J.K.
          "Use of consumer panels for brand-share prediction"   J. Mktg. Res., vol.5,
          1968, pp.131-145.
          MARKET SHARE - SECTOR : CONSUMER NON DURABLES * APPL - FIRM : CONSUMER NON
          DURABLES , HEALTH AIDS * NEW PRODUCTS - NEW BRAND * BRAND CHOICE - APPL *
          REPEAT BUYING * PRICE - EFFECT OF * NEW PRODUCTS - EVALUATION
YA2724   PARIKH A.
          "A model of the world coffee economy: 1950-1968"   Appl. Econ., vol.6,
          1974, pp.23-43.
          APPL - SECTOR : AGRICULTURE , COFFEE * SIMULATION - APPL : SECTOR ,
          AGRICULTURE * PRICE - SECTOR : AGRICULTURE * EX ANTE
YA2725   PARIKH A.
          "Differences in growth rates and Kaldor's laws"   Economica, vol.45, 1978,
          pp.83-91.
          DATA - INTERNATIONAL * SPECIFICATION ERROR - EFFECT OF , SIMULTANEOUS SYSTEM
          BIAS * APPL - MACRO : PRODUCTIVITY * APPL - MACRO : GROWTH * ESTIMATION -
          2SLS : APPL
YA2726   PARIKH A., HOLDEN K., PEEL D.A.
          "The relationship between unemployment and vacancies: comments"   Appl.
          Econ., vol.9, 1977, pp.77-82.
          APPL - MACRO : UNEMPLOYMENT * MANPOWER PLANNING - EMPLOYMENT VACANCIES
YA2727   PARK R.E.
          "Prospects for cable in the 100 largest television markets"   Bell J.
          Econ., vol.3, 1972, pp.130-150.
          APPL - SECTOR : SERVICES , MEDIA , TV * APPL - SECTOR : FINANCE , PROFITS
YA2728   PARK S.
          "On the small-sample power of Durbin's h test"   J. Am. Statist. Ass.,
          vol.70, 1975, pp.60-63.
          COMPARATIVE METHODS - TESTS , AUTOCORRELATION
YA2729   PARKER G.G.C., SEGURA E.L.
          "How to get a better forecast"   H.B.R., vol.49, Mar-April, 1971,
          pp.99-109.
          APPL - SECTOR : CONSUMER DURABLES , FURNISHINGS * EVALUATION - REGRESSION *
          COMPARATIVE METHODS - CAUSAL , TREND CURVES * BASIC
YA2730   PARKIN M.
          "A 'Monetarist' analysis of the generation and transmission of inflation:
          1958-71"   Am. Econ. Ass. Proc., 1977, pp.164-171.
          INFLATION - DETERMINANTS * EVALUATION - INFLATION MODELS * BIBLIOGRAPHY -
          INFLATION
YA2731   PARKINSON M.
          "Empirical warrant-stock relationships"   J. Business, vol.45, 1972,
          pp.563-569.
          VOLATILITY - EFFECT OF * APPL - FIRM : FINANCE , WARRANTS * STOCK PRICES -
          WARRANTS
YA2732   PARKINSON M.
          "Option pricing: the American put"   J. Business, vol.50, 1977, pp.21-36.
          APPL - FIRM : FINANCE , OPTIONS * EX ANTE
YA2733   PARKS R.W.
          "Determinants of scrapping rates for postwar vintage automobiles"
          Econometrica, vol.45, 1977, pp.1099-1115.
          APPL - FIRM : CONSUMER DURABLES , CARS * DEPRECIATION * EX ANTE * REGRESSION
          - LIMITED DEPENDENT , LOGIT
YA2734   PARKS R.W.
          "Price responsiveness of factor utilization in Swedish manufacturing,
          1870-1950"   Rev. Econ. Stats., vol.53, 1971, pp.129-139.
          PRODUCTION FUNCTIONS - SECTOR * ERROR SPECIFICATION - AUTOCORRELATED ,
          CORRELATED * REGRESSION - SEEMINGLY UNRELATED : APPL * APPL - MACRO , SWEDEN
          * PRICE - EFFECT OF * SIMULTANEOUS SYSTEM - CONSTRAINED * PRODUCTION
          FUNCTIONS - SUBSTITUTION * DEMAND EQUATIONS - SYSTEMS OF * ADVANCED
YA2735   PARKS R.W.
          "Systems of demand equations: an empirical comparison of alternative
          functional forms"   Econometrica, vol.37, 1969, pp.629-650.
          DEMAND EQUATIONS - SYSTEMS OF : METHODOLOGY * COMPARATIVE METHODS - DEMAND
          EQUATIONS * APPL - MACRO : CONSUMER DEMAND
YA2736   PARKS R.W., BARTEN A.P.
          "A cross-country comparison of the effects of prices, income and population
          composition on consumption patterns"   Econ. J., vol.83, 1973, pp.834-852.
          INCOME - EFFECT OF * PRICE - EFFECT OF * DATA - INTERNATIONAL * APPL - MACRO
          : CONSUMER DEMAND * CONSUMER BEHAVIOUR - ECONOMIC MODELS , THEORY

YA2737 PARSONS D.O.
        "Quit rates over time: a search and information approach"   Am. Econ. Rev.,
        vol.63, 1973, pp.390-401.
        MANPOWER PLANNING - LABOUR TURNOVER * MANPOWER PLANNING - SECTOR , SUPPLY

YA2738 PARSONS L.J.
        "A rachet model of advertising carryover effects"   J. Mktg. Res., vol.13,
        1976, pp.76-79.
        APPL - FIRM : CONSUMER NON DURABLES , HEALTH AIDS * ADVERTISING - EFFECT OF
        * REGRESSION - MODEL CHOICE

YA2739 PARSONS L.J.
        "An econometric analysis of advertising, retail availability and sales of a
        new brand"   Mgmt. Sci. (B), vol.20, 1974, pp.938-947.
        ADVERTISING - EFFECT OF * APPL - SECTOR : RETAILING * DATA - CROSS SECTION ,
        TIME SERIES * NEW PRODUCTS - ADVERTISING * APPL - FIRM : CONSUMER NON
        DURABLES * NEW PRODUCTS - NEW BRAND

YA2740 PARSONS L.J.
        "The product life cycle and time-varying advertising elasticities"   J.
        Mktg. Res., vol.12, 1975, pp.476-480.
        STABILITY OF COEFFICIENTS - REGRESSION * REGRESSION - SHIFTING COEFFICIENTS
        * APPL - FIRM : CONSUMER NON DURABLES , GROCERIES * ADVERTISING - OPTIMALITY
        * ADVERTISING - EFFECT OF * LIFE CYCLE - PRODUCT

YA2741 PARSONS L.J., HENRY W.A.
        "Testing equivalence of observed and generated time series data using
        spectral analysis"   J. Mktg. Res., vol.9, 1972, pp.391-395.
        SPECTRAL ANALYSIS - APPL : SIMULATION EVALUATION * EVALUATION - MARKET SHARE
        MODELS * APPL - FIRM : CONSUMER NON DURABLES , GROCERIES * MARKET SHARE -
        SECTOR : CONSUMER NON DURABLES * ADVERTISING - DETERMINANTS

YA2742 PASSELL P., TAYLOR J.B., EHRLICH I.
        "The deterrent effect of capital punishment: another view"   Am. Econ.
        Rev., vol.67, 1977, pp.445-458.
        APPL - SECTOR : SOCIAL , CRIME * POLICY EVALUATION - SECTOR : SOCIAL

YA2743 PASTORE A.C.
        "Notes on the recent monetary policy in Brazil"   Anns. Econ. Soc. Meas.,
        vol.4, 1975, pp.489-508.
        APPL - MACRO , LATIN AMERICA * THEORY - MONETARY * POLICY EVALUATION - MACRO
        : MONETARY * INFLATION - DETERMINANTS * INFLATION - RAPID

YA2744 PATTON R.A., SMITH V.K.
        Identification: it's performance that counts"   Decis. Sci., vol.3:2, 1972,
        pp.76-86.
        SIMULTANEOUS SYSTEM - IDENTIFICATION * DATA - SIMULATION * ERROR
        SPECIFICATION - EFFECT OF

YA2745 PAULL A.E.
        "A generalised compound Poisson model for consumer purchase panel data
        analysis"   J. Am. Statist. Ass., vol.73, 1978, pp.706-713.
        PROBABILITY MODELS - NBD * BRAND CHOICE - METHODOLOGY * REGRESSION - LIMITED
        DEPENDENT , LOGIT * BRAND CHOICE - APPL

YA2746 PAULUS J.D.
        "Mixed estimation of a complete system of consumer demand equations"
        Anns. Econ. Soc. Meas., vol.4, 1975, pp.117-131.
        DEMAND EQUATIONS - SYSTEMS OF : METHODOLOGY , ESTIMATION * ESTIMATION -
        THEIL GOLDBERGER * APPL - MACRO : CONSUMER DEMAND * SIMULTANEOUS SYSTEM -
        PRIOR INFORMATION * SPECIFICATION ERROR - TESTS , DATA SOURCES * PRICE -
        EFFECT OF * INCOME - EFFECT OF

YA2747 PAUNIO J.J., SUVANTO A.
        "Changes in price expectations: some tests using data on indexed and
        non-indexed bonds"   Economica, vol.44, 1977, pp.37-55.
        EXPECTATIONS - ESTIMATING * EXPECTATIONS - DATA * INFLATION - EXPECTATIONS *
        DISTRIBUTED LAG - APPL , EXPECTATIONS HYPOTHESES * APPL - SECTOR : FINANCE ,
        BONDS * INFLATION - EFFECT OF

YA2748 PEARMAN A.D., BUTTON K.J.
        "Regional variations in car ownership"   Appl. Econ., vol.8, 1976,
        pp.231-233.
        APPL - SECTOR : CONSUMER DURABLES , CARS * REGIONAL MODELS - SECTOR :
        CONSUMER DURABLES * DATA - CROSS SECTION , TIME SERIES * INCOME - EFFECT OF

YA2749 PEARSON A.S.
        "How to compare new product programs"   J. Advtg. Res., vol.11:3, 1971,
        pp.3-8.
        SIMULATION - APPL : NEW PRODUCTS * NEW PRODUCTS - EVALUATION * JUDGEMENTAL
        FORECASTS - APPL * MARKET SHARE - SECTOR * USER - FIRM

YA2750 PECHMAN J.A.
        "Responsiveness of the Federal individual income tax to changes in income"
        with discussion   Brookings Paps. Econ. Activity, 1973, pp.385-427.
        APPL - SECTOR : GOVERNMENT , REVENUES , TAX * INCOME - EFFECT OF

YA2751 PECK S.C.
        "Alternative investment models for firms in the electric utilities"   Bell
        J. Econ., vol.5, 1974, pp.421-458.
        APPL - FIRM : INVESTMENT * APPL - FIRM : UTILITIES , ELECTRICITY * APPL -
        SECTOR : PRODUCTION , PLANT , ELECTRICITY GENERATION * THEORY - INVESTMENT
        BEHAVIOUR * BAYESIAN - ESTIMATION : DISTRIBUTED LAG * EVALUATION -
        INVESTMENT MODELS * DISTRIBUTED LAG - APPL , OUTPUT

YA2752 PEDERSON P.J.
  "A note on estimation of aggregate CES production function with the use of
  capital data" Rev. Econ. Stats., vol.54, 1972, pp.336-337.
  PRODUCTION FUNCTIONS - ESTIMATION * PRODUCTION FUNCTIONS - SECTOR *
  PRODUCTION FUNCTIONS - SUBSTITUTION

YA2753 PEEL D.A., WALKER I.
  "Short-run employment functions, excess supply and the speed of adjustment:
  a note" Economica, vol.45, 1978, pp.195-202
  APPL - MACRO : EMPLOYMENT * APPL - MACRO , UK

YA2754 PEERA N.
  "Measuring the price sensitivity of Indian tea exports: a comment"
  Econometrica, vol.39, 1971, pp.177-178.
  APPL - SECTOR : AGRICULTURE , TEA * APPL - SECTOR : INTERNATIONAL TRADE ,
  EXPORTS * PRICE - EFFECT OF

YA2755 PEGELS C.C.
  "Exponential forecasting: some new variations" Mgmt. Sci. (A), vol.15,
  1969, pp.311-315.
  EXPONENTIAL SMOOTHING - REVIEW

YA2756 PEGELS C.C.
  "Start up or learning curves-some new approaches" Decis. Sci., vol.7,
  1976, pp.705-713.
  COST - LEARNING CURVE * TREND CURVES - EXPONENTIAL * BASIC

YA2757 PELES Y.
  "Economies of scale in advertising beer and cigarettes" J. Business,
  vol.44, 1971, pp.32-37.
  APPL - SECTOR : CONSUMER NON DURABLES , LIQUOR * APPL - SECTOR : CONSUMER
  NON DURABLES , CIGARETTES * APPL - FIRM : CONSUMER NON DURABLES , CIGARETTES
  * COST - SCALE ECONOMIES * APPL - FIRM : CONSUMER NON DURABLES , LIQUOR *
  ADVERTISING - EFFECT OF

YA2758 PELZMAN J.
  "Trade creation and trade diversion in the Council of Mutual Economic
  Assistance: 1954-1970" Am. Econ. Rev., vol.67, 1977, pp.713-722.
  APPL - MACRO : INTERNATIONAL TRADE , EXPORTS * APPL - SECTOR : INTERNATIONAL
  TRADE , EXPORTS * TARIFF - EFFECT OF * DATA - INTERNATIONAL

YA2759 PENCAVEL J.H.
  "A note on the comparative predictive performance of wage inflation models
  of the British Economy" Econ. J., vol.81, 1971, pp.113-119.
  APPL - MACRO , UK * APPL - MACRO : EARNINGS * EX ANTE - EVALUATION -
  EARNINGS MODELS * COMPARATIVE METHODS - ESTIMATION : OLS , 2SLS *
  COMPARATIVE METHODS - AUTOREGRESSIVE , CAUSAL * INFLATION - DETERMINANTS ,
  EARNINGS

YA2760 PENCAVEL J.H.
  "Relative wages and trade unions in the UK" Economica, vol.41, 1974,
  pp.194-210.
  UNIONIZATION - EFFECT OF * APPL - SECTOR : EARNINGS * DATA - CROSS SECTION *
  MANPOWER PLANNING - DISCRIMINATION , SEX * COMPARATIVE METHODS - ESTIMATION
  : SIMULTANEOUS SYSTEM

YA2761 PENCAVEL J.H.
  "Wages, specific training, and labor turnover in US manufacturing
  industries" Int. Econ. Rev., vol.13, 1972, pp.53-64.
  APPL - SECTOR : EARNINGS * MANPOWER PLANNING - LABOUR TURNOVER * EDUCATION -
  EFFECT OF * COMPARATIVE METHODS - ESTIMATION : OLS , 2SLS

YA2762 PERCIVAL J.
  "On the selective use of spectral analysis" Rev. Econ. Stats., vol.57,
  1975, pp.106-109.
  BUSINESS CYCLE - LONG CYCLE * SPECTRAL ANALYSIS - APPL : BUSINESS CYCLE ,
  LONG CYCLE * SPECTRAL ANALYSIS - METHODOLOGY

YA2763 PEREIRA B. de B.
  "Discriminating among seperate models: a bibliography" Int. Statist.
  Rev., vol.45, 1977, pp.163-172.
  BIBLIOGRAPHY - MODEL SELECTION * MODEL SELECTION * REGRESSION - MODEL CHOICE
  * BASIC

YA2764 PERKINS W.C., PASHKE P.E.
  "A simulation model of the higher education system of a state" Decis.
  Sci., vol.4, 1973, pp.194-215.
  SIMULATION - APPL : SECTOR , EDUCATION * APPL - SECTOR : EDUCATION ,
  UNIVERSITIES * USE - CAPACITY EXPANSION * POLICY EVALUATION - SECTOR :
  EDUCATION * COST - SECTOR : EDUCATION

YA2765 PERRY G.L.
  "Capacity in manufacturing" with discussion Brookings Paps. Econ.
  Activity, 1973, pp.701-742 & 757-763.
  CAPACITY - EFFECT OF * REGRESSION - SPECIFICATION OF VARIABLES * APPL -
  MACRO : INVESTMENT * CAPACITY - ESTIMATION * APPL - MACRO : CAPACITY
  UTILISATION * DATA - SPECIFICATION OF VARIABLES * PRICE - SECTOR

YA2766 PERRY G.L.
  "Changing labour markets and inflation" with discussion Brookings Paps.
  Econ. Activity, 1970, pp.411-448.
  INFLATION - EFFECT OF * MANPOWER PLANNING - MACRO * MANPOWER PLANNING -
  LABOUR FORCE COMPOSITION * EX ANTE * APPL - MACRO : EARNINGS * DATA -
  SPECIFICATION OF VARIABLES

YA2767 PERRY G.L.
  "Determinants of wage inflation around the world" with discussion
  Brookings Paps. Econ Activity, 1975, pp.403-447,
  INFLATION - PHILLIPS * DATA - INTERNATIONAL * APPL - MACRO : EARNINGS

YA2768 PERRY G.L.
  "Labor force structure, potential output and productivity" with discussion
  Brookings Paps. Econ. Activity, 1971, pp.533-578,
  APPL - MACRO : GNP , POTENTIAL * MANPOWER PLANNING - LABOUR PARTICIPATION *
  APPL - MACRO : PRODUCTIVITY * APPL - MACRO : EMPLOYMENT

YA2769 PERRY G.L.
  "Potential output and productivity" with discussion Brookings Paps. Econ.
  Activity, 1977, pp.11-60.
  MANPOWER PLANNING - LABOUR FORCE COMPOSITION * MANPOWER PLANNING - LABOUR
  PARTICIPATION * APPL - MACRO : EMPLOYMENT * APPL - MACRO : PRODUCTIVITY *
  APPL - MACRO : GNP , POTENTIAL

YA2770 PERRY G.L.
  "Slowing the wage-price spiral: the macroeconomic view" with discussion
  Brookings Paps. Econ. Activity, 1978, pp.259-299,
  INFLATION - DETERMINANTS * INFLATION - PHILLIPS CURVE * APPL - SECTOR :
  EARNINGS * EX ANTE

YA2771 PERRY G.L.
  "The success of anti-inflation policies in the US" J. Money, Credit,
  Banking, vol.5, 1973, pp.569-593.
  INFLATION - DETERMINANTS * APPL - MACRO : EARNINGS * EX ANTE

YA2772 PERRY G.L.
  "Unemployment flows in the US labour market" with discussion Brookings
  Paps. Econ. Activity, 1972, pp.245-292.
  APPL - MACRO : UNEMPLOYMENT * MANPOWER PLANNING - LABOUR FORCE COMPOSITION

YA2773 PESANDO J.E.
  "Alternative models of the determination of nominal interest rates" J.
  Money, Credit, Banking, vol.8, 1976, pp.209-218,
  EVALUATION - INTEREST RATE MODELS * INTEREST RATE - DETERMINANTS * APPL -
  MACRO , CANADA

YA2774 PESANDO J.E.
  "Determinants of term premiums in the market for US Treasury bills" J.
  Finance, vol.30, 1975, pp.1317-1327,
  INTEREST RATE - TERM STRUCTURE * INTEREST RATE - LIQUIDITY PREFERENCE *
  DISTRIBUTED LAG - APPL , EXPECTATIONS HYPOTHESES

YA2775 PESANDO J.E.
  "On the accuracy and formation of life insurance company cash flow
  forecasts" J. Business, vol.48, 1975, pp.20-26,
  USER - FIRM : FINANCE * APPL - SECTOR : FINANCE , FINANCIAL STRUCTURE ,
  LIQUID ASSETS * APPL - SECTOR : FINANCE , MORTGAGES * EVALUATION - CASH FLOW
  FORECASTS * JUDGEMENTAL FORECASTS - DETERMINANTS * COMPARATIVE METHODS -
  AUTOREGRESSIVE , JUDGEMENTAL * APPL - SECTOR : FINANCE , INSURANCE COMPANIES

YA2776 PESANDO J.E.
  "Rational expectations and distributed lag expectations proxies" J. Am.
  Statist. Ass., vol.71, 1976, pp.36-42,
  EVALUATION - EXPECTATIONS , DATA * EVALUATION - EXPECTATIONS , THEORY *
  DISTRIBUTED LAG - APPL , EXPECTATIONS HYPOTHESES * APPL - SECTOR : FINANCE ,
  INSURANCE COMPANIES * APPL - SECTOR : FINANCE , FINANCIAL STRUCTURE

YA2777 PESANDO J.E.
  "Seasonal variability in distributed lag models" J. Am. Statist. Ass.,
  vol.67, 1972, pp.311-312.
  APPL - SECTOR : FINANCE , MORTGAGES * DISTRIBUTED LAG - SEASONALITY

YA2778 PESANDO J.E.
  "The impact of the conversion loan on the term structure of interest rates
  in Canada: some additional evidence" Can. J. Econ., vol.8, 1975,
  pp.281-288.
  INTEREST RATE - EXPECTATIONS * INFLATION - EFFECT OF * INTEREST RATE - TERM
  STRUCTURE * APPL - MACRO , CANADA

YA2779 PESANDO J.E.
  "The interest sensitivity of Canadian mortgage flows: a comment" Can. J.
  Econ., vol.4, 1971, pp.401-424.
  APPL - SECTOR : FINANCE , MORTGAGES * INTEREST RATE - EFFECT OF

YA2780 PESANDO J.E.
  "The interest sensitivity of the flow of funds through life insurance
  companies: an econometric analysis" J. Finance, vol.29, 1974,
  pp.1105-1121.
  APPL - SECTOR : FINANCE , INSURANCE COMPANIES * INTEREST RATE - EFFECT OF *
  APPL - SECTOR : FINANCE , FINANCIAL STRUCTURE

YA2781 PESANDO J.E.
  "The supply of money and common stock prices: further observations on the
  economic evidence" J. Finance, vol.29, 1974, pp.909-921.
  EX ANTE * APPL - SECTOR : FINANCE , STOCK PRICE INDEX * STOCK PRICES -
  DETERMINANTS * AUTOCORRELATION - EFFECT OF

YA2782   PESARAN M.H.
"Exact maximum likelihood estimation of a regression equation with a first order moving-average error"   Rev. Econ. Studies, vol.40, 1973, pp.529-535.
COMPARATIVE METHODS - ESTIMATION : REGRESSION , ERROR SPECIFICATION *
ESTIMATION - MAXIMUM LIKELIHOOD * ERROR SPECIFICATION - MOVING AVERAGE *
APPL - MACRO , UK * APPL - MACRO : EARNINGS

YA2783   PESARAN M.H.
"On the general problem of model selection"   Rev. Econ. Studies, vol.41, 1974, pp.153-171.
REGRESSION - MODEL CHOICE * DATA - SIMULATION

YA2784   PESARAN M.H.
"The small sample problem of truncation remainders in the estimation of distributed lag models with autocorrelated errors"   Int. Econ. Rev., vol.14, 1973, pp.120-131.
DATA ERRORS - MISSING OBSERVATIONS * DISTRIBUTED LAG - SOLOW , ESTIMATION *
APPL - MACRO : INTERNATIONAL TRADE , IMPORTS * DISTRIBUTED LAG - ERROR
SPECIFICATION * ERROR SPECIFICATION - AUTOCORRELATED * COMPARATIVE METHODS -
ESTIMATION : DISTRIBUTED LAG * COMPARATIVE METHODS - ESTIMATION : REGRESSION
, ERROR SPECIFICATION * COMPARATIVE METHODS : DATA ERRORS - MISSING
OBSERVATIONS

YA2785   PESARAN M.H., DEATON A.S.
"Testing non-nested non linear regression models"   Econometrica, vol.46, 1978, pp.677-694.
MODEL SELECTION * REGRESSION - NON LINEAR * REGRESSION - MODEL CHOICE * APPL
- MACRO : CONSUMPTION * EVALUATION - CONSUMPTION MODELS

YA2786   PESARAN M.H., RAO B.B.
"An alternative econometric approach to the permanent income hypothesis: an international comparison: comments"   Rev. Econ. Stats., vol.55, 1973, pp.259-261.
EVALUATION - PERMANENT INCOME * DATA - INTERNATIONAL * APPL - MACRO :
CONSUMPTION * INCOME - EFFECT OF , PERMANENT * EVALUATION - ESTIMATION : NON
LINEAR , ITERATIVE

YA2787   PESTON M.H.
"On optimal control and macroeconomic policy"   Omega, vol.6, 1978, pp.117-121.
CONTROL THEORY - INTRODUCTION * EVALUATION - CONTROL THEORY * BASIC

YA2788   PESTON M.H.
"The correlation between targets and instruments"   Economica, vol.39, 1972, pp.427-431.
POLICY EVALUATION - METHODOLOGY * DECISION RULES - FEEDBACK

YA2789   PETERSEN H.C.
"An empirical test of regulatory effects"   Bell J. Econ. vol.6, 1975, pp.111-126.
USE - FINANCIAL REGULATION * APPL - FIRM : UTILITIES , ELECTRICITY * COST -
FIRM : UTILITIES * DATA - CROSS SECTION

YA2790   PETERSEN H.C.
"The effect of 'fair value' rate base valuation in electric utility regulation"   J. Finance, vol.31, 1976, pp.1487-1490.
APPL - FIRM : UTILITIES , ELECTRICITY * APPL - FIRM : FINANCE , PROFITS *
USE - FINANCIAL , REGULATION

YA2791   PETERSEN H.J.S.
"Forecasting Danish nitrogen fertilizer consumption"   Ind. Mktg. Mgmt., vol.6, 1977, pp.211-222.
APPL - SECTOR : PRODUCTION , FERTILIZER * EVALUATION - TREND CURVES *
COMPARATIVE METHODS - CAUSAL , JUDGEMENTAL

YA2792   PETERSON R.A.
"Trade area analysis using trend surface mapping"   J. Mktg. Res., vol.11, 1974, pp.338-342.
APPL - SECTOR : RETAILING * SPATIAL ANALYSIS * MARKET POTENTIAL * USE -
RETAIL , SITE MONITORING

YA2793   PETERSON R.A., MAHAJAN V.
"Practical significance and partitioning variance in discriminant analysis"   Decis. Sci., vol.7, 1976, pp.649-658.
DISCRIMINANT ANALYSIS - METHODOLOGY * APPL - SECTOR : FINANCE , BANKS *
HEALTH - HOSPITAL * APPL - SECTOR : PRODUCTION , COMPUTERS * MARKET
SEGMENTATION * REGRESSION - SUMMARY STATISTICS

YA2794   PETERSON R.E.
"A cross section study of the demand for money: the US, 1960-62"   J. Finance, vol.29, 1974, pp.73-88.
APPL - MACRO : MONEY , DEMAND * DATA - CROSS SECTION * INCOME - EFFECT OF *
WEALTH - EFFECT OF * EVALUATION - PERMANENT INCOME * EDUCATION - EFFECT OF

YA2795   PETERSON R.E.
"The permanent incomes hypothesis of the demand for money"   Rev. Econ. Stats., vol.54, 1972, pp.364-373.
THEORY - PERMANENT INCOME * REGRESSION - ERRORS IN VARIABLES * DATA ERRORS -
EFFECT OF * APPL - MACRO : CONSUMER DEMAND , FINANCIAL ASSETS * EVALUATION -
PERMANENT INCOME * INCOME - EFFECT OF , PERMANENT

YA2796   PETERSON R.L.
          "Factors affecting the growth of bank credit card and check credit" with
          discussion   J. Finance, vol.32, 1977, pp.553-564 & 588-589.
          APPL - SECTOR : FINANCE , BANKS * APPL - SECTOR : FINANCE , CONSUMER CREDIT
          * CONSUMER BEHAVIOUR - PURCHASING , DETERMINANTS
YA2797   PETHYBRIDGE R.J.
          "Maximum likelihood estimation of a linear regression function with grouped
          data"   Appl. Stats., vol.24, 1975, pp.28-41.
          REGRESSION - GROUPED OBSERVATIONS * DATA - GROUPED * ESTIMATION - MAXIMUM
          LIKELIHOOD * SPECIFICATION ERROR - EFFECT OF , ERROR DISTRIBUTION
YA2798   PETTIT R.R.
          "Dividend announcements, security performance and capital market efficiency"
          J. Finance, vol.27, 1972, pp.993-1007.
          APPL - FIRM : FINANCE , STOCK PRICES * STOCK PRICES - INFORMATION EFFECT *
          APPL - FIRM : FINANCE , DIVIDENDS
YA2799   PETTIT R.R., WATTS R.
          "The impact of dividend and earnings announcements: a reconciliation" with
          comments   J. Business, vol.49, 1976, pp.86-101.
          APPL - FIRM : FINANCE , DIVIDENDS * APPL - FIRM : FINANCE , PROFITS , PER
          SHARE * STOCK PRICES - INFORMATION EFFECT
YA2800   PETTWAY R.H.
          "Market tests of capital adequacy of large commercial banks"   J. Finance,
          vol.31, 1976, pp.865-875.
          STOCK PRICES - BETA , DETERMINANTS * APPL - FIRM : FINANCE , BANKS * APPL -
          FIRM , FINANCE , PE RATIO * APPL - FIRM : FINANCE , STOCK PRICES * DATA -
          CROSS SECTION * MULTICOLLINEARITY - EFFECT OF
YA2801   PETTWAY R.H.
          "On the use of beta in regulatory proceedings: an empirical examination"
          Bell. J. Econ., vol.9, 1978, pp.239-248.
          APPL - FIRM : UTILITIES , ELECTRICITY * STABILITY OF COEFFICIENTS -
          REGRESSION , TEST * STOCK PRICES - BETA , VARIABLE * APPL - FIRM : FINANCE ,
          STOCK PRICES * USE - FINANCIAL , REGULATION
YA2802   PFAFF P.
          "Evaluation of some money stock forecasting models"   J. Finance, vol.32,
          1977, pp.1639-1646.
          APPL - MACRO : MONEY , SUPPLY * EX ANTE * COMPARATIVE METHODS -
          AUTOREGRESSIVE , CAUSAL * EVALUATION - MONEY SUPPLY , MODELS OF
YA2803   PHADKE M.S., WU S.M.
          "Modelling of continuous stochastic processes from discrete observations
          with applications to sunspots data"   J. Am. Statist. Ass., vol.69, 1974,
          pp.325-329.
          TIME SERIES - CONTINUOUS * TIME SERIES - ARIMA : CONTINUOUS * APPL - SECTOR
          : NATURAL , SUNSPOTS * ADVANCED
YA2804   PHELPS C.E., NEWHOUSE J.P.
          "Coinsurance, the price of time and the demand for medical services"   Rev.
          Econ. Stats., vol.56, 1974, pp.334-342.
          PRICE - SECTOR : HEALTH * HEALTH - SERVICES * HEALTH - MANPOWER , EARNINGS *
          PRICE - EFFECT OF
YA2805   PHILIPPATOS G.C., WILSON C.J.
          "Information theory and risk in capital markets"   Omega, vol.2, 1974,
          pp.523-532.
          APPL - FIRM : FINANCE , STOCK PRICES * STOCK PRICES - RISK * PROBABILITY
          MODELS - ENTROPY * STABILITY OF COEFFICIENTS - PROBABILITY MODELS : APPL
YA2806   PHILLIPS G.D.A., HARVEY A.C.
          "A simple test for serial correlation in regression analysis"   J. Am.
          Statist. Ass., vol.69, 1974, pp.935-939.
          RESIDUALS - ESTIMATION , RECURSIVE * DATA - SIMULATION * RESIDUALS -
          COMPARATIVE ANALYSIS OF * COMPARATIVE METHODS - TESTS , AUTOCORRELATION *
          ADVANCED
YA2807   PHILLIPS L., ET AL.
          "A spectral analysis of post-accord Federal open market operations:
          comments"   Am. Econ. Rev., vol.62, 1972, pp.988-996.
          SPECTRAL ANALYSIS - APPL : SECTOR , FINANCE * SPECTRAL ANALYSIS - CROSS :
          APPL * DATA - SPECIFICATION OF VARIABLES * POLICY EVALUATION - SECTOR :
          FINANCE
YA2808   PHILLIPS P.
          "A forecasting model for the UK invisible account"   Nat. Inst. Econ. Rev.,
          no.69, 1974, pp.58-76.
          APPL - MACRO , UK * EX ANTE * APPL - MACRO : INTERNATIONAL TRADE ,
          INVISIBLES * APPL - SECTOR : SERVICES * APPL - MACRO : INTERNATIONAL FINANCE
          * COMPARATIVE METHODS - AUTOREGRESSIVE , CAUSAL
YA2809   PHILLIPS P.C.B.
          "The structural estimation of a stochastic differential equation systems"
          Econometrica, vol.40, 1972, pp.1021-1041.
          DIFFERENTIAL EQUATIONS - ESTIMATION * SIMULTANEOUS SYSTEM - CONTINUOUS *
          COMPARATIVE METHODS - ESTIMATION : SIMULTANEOUS SYSTEM * DATA - SIMULATION

YA2810   PHIPPS D.F.
         "The logistic curve: a fitting technique"   Stat'n., vol,24, 1975,
         pp.129-136 & 232-233.
         TREND CURVES - LOGISTIC , ESTIMATION

YA2811   PHLIPS L.
         "A dynamic version of the linear expenditure model"   Rev, Econ, Stats,,
         vol.54, 1972, pp.450-458.
         PRICE - EFFECT OF * APPL - MACRO : CONSUMER DEMAND * DEMAND EQUATIONS -
         SYSTEMS OF : METHODOLOGY , ESTIMATION * CONSUMER BEHAVIOUR - ECONOMIC MODELS
         , THEORY

YA2812   PHLIPS L.
         "The demand for leisure and money"   Econometrica, vol.46, 1978,
         pp.1025-1043.
         CONSUMER BEHAVIOUR - ECONOMIC MODELS , THEORY * APPL - MACRO : CONSUMER
         DEMAND * PRICE - EFFECT OF * INCOME - EFFECT OF

YA2813   PICCONI M.J.
         "A reconsideration of the recognition of advertising assets on financial
         statements"   J. Acctg. Res., vol,15, 1977, pp,317-326.
         ADVERTISING - EFFECT OF * APPL - FIRM : CONSUMER NON DURABLES , FOOD *
         MARKET SHARE - SECTOR : CONSUMER NON DURABLES

YA2814   PICCONI M.J., OLSON C.L.
         "Advertising decision rules in a multibrand environment: optimal control
         theeory and evidence"   J. Mktg. Res,, vol.15, 1978, pp.82-92.
         REGRESSION - SEEMINGLY UNRELATED : APPL * APPL - FIRM : CONSUMER NON
         DURABLES , FOOD * ADVERTISING - OPTIMALITY * MARKET SHARE - SECTOR :
         CONSUMER NON DURABLES * WEATHER - EFFECT OF * PRICE - EFFECT OF *
         DISTRIBUTED LAG - APPL , ADVERTISING * ADVERTISING - EFFECT OF

YA2815   PICKERING J.F., HARRISON J.A., COHEN C.D.
         "Identification and measurement of consumer confidence: methodology and some
         preliminary results"   R. Statist. Soc. (A), vol,136, 1973, pp,43-63.
         APPL - SECTOR : CONSUMER DURABLES * ATTITUDINAL DATA * FACTOR ANALYSIS -
         APPL * INDEX NUMBERS - MACRO : CONSUMER CONFIDENCE * SURVEYS - CONSUMER ,
         METHODOLOGY

YA2816   PICKERING J.F., ISHERWOOD B.C.
         "Determinants of expenditure on consumer durables"   R. Statist. Soc. (A),
         vol.138, 1975, pp.504-530.
         APPL - SECTOR : CONSUMER DURABLES * CONSUMER BEHAVIOUR - PURCHASING ,
         DETERMINANTS * COMPARATIVE METHODS - DISCRIMINATION * ATTITUDINAL DATA *
         EXPECTATIONS - DATA * DISCRIMINANT ANALYSIS - APPL

YA2817   PICKERSGILL J.
         "Soviet household saving behaviour"   Rev. Econ. Stats., vol.58, 1976,
         pp.139-147.
         APPL - MACRO : SAVINGS * INCOME - EFFECT OF , PERMANENT * APPL - MACRO ,
         USSR

YA2818   PICKFORD M.
         "A statistical analysis of university administration expenditure"   R.
         Statist. Soc. (A), vol.137, 1974, pp.35-47.
         COST - SECTOR : EDUCATION * APPL - SECTOR : GOVERNMENT , EDUCATION ,
         UNIVERSITIES

YA2819   PIERCE D.A.
         "Distribution of residual autocorrelations in the regression model with
         autoregression model with autoregressive moving average errors"   R.
         Statist. Soc. (B), vol.33, 1971, pp.140-146.
         TIME SERIES - ARIMA : DIAGNOSTICS * ERROR SPECIFICATION - ARIMA *
         SPECIFICATION ERROR - TESTS , ERROR SPECIFICATION * RESIDUALS - ANALYSIS OF
         , AUTOCORRELATION * AUTOCORRELATION - TEST

YA2820   PIERCE D.A.
         "Forecasting in dynamic models with stochastic regressors"   J.
         Econometrics, vol.3, 1975, pp.349-374.
         DISTRIBUTED LAG - RATIONAL POLYNOMIAL , IDENTIFICATION * COMPARATIVE METHODS
         - ARIMA , CAUSAL * EXOGENOUS VARIABLES - PREDICTION OF , EFFECT * EX ANTE *
         LAG , FIXED * MODEL SELECTION * EVALUATION - THEORY OF * APPL - MACRO :
         INVESTMENT * APPL - MACRO : GDP * FORECASTING - THEORY * ADVANCED

YA2821   PIERCE D.A.
         "Money supply control: reserves as the instrument under lagged accounting"
         J. Finance, vol.31, 1976, pp.845-852.
         APPL - MACRO : MONEY , RESERVES * CAUSALITY - TEST * APPL - MACRO : MONEY ,
         SUPPLY * DISTRIBUTED LAG - APPL , MONEY * DISTRIBUTED LAG - RATIONAL
         POLYNOMIAL * ACCOUNTING PRACTICE - EFFECT OF * CROSS CORRELATIONS * TIME
         SERIES - ARIMA : APPL

YA2822   PIERCE D.A.
         "Relationships - and the lack thereof - between economic time series, with
         special reference to money and interest rates" with discussion   J, Am.
         Statist. Ass., vol.72, 1977, pp.11-26.
         CAUSALITY - TEST * CROSS CORRELATIONS * TIME SERIES - ARIMA : DIAGNOSTICS *
         APPL - MACRO : MONEY * APPL - SECTOR : RETAILING * INTEREST RATE -
         INDICATORS

YA2823   PIERCE D.A.
"Residual correlations and diagnostic checking in dynamic disturbance time
series models"   J. Am. Statist. Ass., vol,67, 1972, pp.636-640,
RESIDUALS - ANALYSIS OF , ERROR SPECIFICATION * DISTRIBUTED LAG - RATIONAL
POLYNOMIAL , DIAGNOSTICS * SPECIFICATION ERROR - TESTS , ERROR SPECIFICATION
* SPECIFICATION ERROR - TESTS , LAG SPECIFICATION * DISTRIBUTED LAG - ARIMA
* DISTRIBUTED LAG - ERROR SPECIFICATION

YA2824   PIERCE D.A., HAUGH L.D.
"Causality in temporal systems: characterizations and a survey"   J.
Econometrics, vol,5, 1977, pp.265-293,
CAUSALITY - REVIEW * BIBLIOGRAPHY - CAUSALITY

YA2825   PIERCE J.L.
"Interest rates and their prospect in the recovery" with discussion
Brookings Paps.Econ. Activity, 1975, pp.89-122,
APPL - MACRO : MONEY , DEMAND * INTEREST RATE - DETERMINANTS

YA2826   PIERCE J.L.
"Quantitative analysis for decisions at the Federal Reserve"   Anns, Econ.
Soc. Meas., vol,3, 1974, pp.11-19,
FORECASTING - PRACTICE * USER - SECTOR : GOVERNMENT , CENTRAL BANK * POLICY
EVALUATION - MACRO : MONETARY

YA2827   PIERCE J.L., ENZLER J.J.
"The effects of external inflationary shocks" with discussion   Brookings
Paps. Econ Activity, 1974, pp.13-61,
INFLATION - DETERMINANTS * MACRO MODEL - MIT , PENN , SSRC * APPL - MACRO :
MONEY , DEMAND * APPL - MACRO : EARNINGS * INFLATION - GOVERNMENT CONTROLS *
SIMULATION - APPL : POLICY EVALUATION * PRICE - EFFECT OF * POLICY
EVALUATION - MACRO * PRICE - CONTROLS

YA2828   PIERCE J.L., THOMSON T.D.
"Short-term financial models at the Federal Reserve Board" with discussion
J. Finance, vol,29, 1974, pp.349-363,
APPL - MACRO : FLOW OF FUNDS * MACRO MODEL - FRB , MIT

YA2829   PIERSOL R.J.
"Accuracy of estimating markets for industrial products by size of consuming
industries"   J. Mktg. Res., vol,5, 1968, pp.147-154,
EVALUATION - MARKET POTENTIAL * DATA - DISAGGREGATION , GEOGRAPHICAL * APPL
- SECTOR : PRODUCTION * BASIC

YA2830   PINCHES G.E., MINGO K.A.
"A multivariate analysis of industrial bond ratings"   J. Finance, vol,28,
1973, pp.1-18,
APPL - FIRM : FINANCE , BONDS * USE - CREDIT CONTROL , BOND RATING * FACTOR
ANALYSIS - APPL * DISCRIMINANT ANALYSIS - APPL

YA2831   PINCHES G.E., MINGO K.A.
"The role of subordination and industrial bond ratings"   J. Finance,
vol,30, 1975, pp.201-206,
APPL - FIRM : FINANCE , BONDS * RISK - ESTIMATION * DISCRIMINANT ANALYSIS -
APPL * USE - CREDIT CONTROL , BOND RATING

YA2832   PINCHES G.E., SINGLETON J.C.
"The adjustment of stock prices to land rating changes"   J. Finance,
vol,33, 1978, pp.29-44,
APPL - FIRM : FINANCE , STOCK PRICES * STOCK PRICES - INFORMATION EFFECT *
APPL - FIRM : FINANCE , BONDS

YA2833   PINDYCK R.S.
"Optimal policies for economic stabilization"   Econometrica, vol,41, 1973,
pp.529-560,
CONTROL THEORY - DETERMINISTIC , APPL * MACRO MODEL - US * POLICY EVALUATION
- MACRO : STABILISATION * SIMULTANEOUS SYSTEM - CONTROL

YA2834   PINDYCK R.S.
"The regulatory implications of three alternative econometric supply models
of natural gas"   Bell J. Econ. vol,5, 1974, pp.633-645,
SUPPLY - SECTOR : PRODUCTION * APPL - SECTOR : PRODUCTION , GAS * EVALUATION
- GAS SUPPLY , MODELS OF

YA2835   PINDYCK R.S., ROBERTS S.M.
"Instruments, intermediate targets, and monetary controllability"   Int.
Econ. Rev., vol,17, 1976, pp.627-650,
POLICY EVALUATION - MACRO : MONETARY * CONTROL THEORY - DETERMINISTIC : APPL
* APPL - MACRO : MONEY

YA2836   PINDYCK R.S., ROBERTS S.M.
"Optimal policies for monetary control"   Anns, Econ, Soc, Meas,, vol,3,
1974, pp.207-237,
APPL - MACRO : MONEY * POLICY EVALUATION - MACRO : MONETARY * SIMULATION -
APPL : POLICY EVALUATION * CONTROL THEORY - STOCHASTIC , APPL * COMPARATIVE
METHODS - CONTROL

YA2837   PIPPINGER J.E.
"Interest arbitrage between Canada and the US: a new perspective"   Can. J.
Econ., vol,11, 1978, pp.183-193,
INTEREST RATE - COVARIATION * APPL - MACRO : INTERNATIONAL LINKAGE *
SPECTRAL ANALYSIS - CROSS : APPL * BIBLIOGRAPHY - INTEREST RATES * SPECTRAL
ANALYSIS - APPL : INTEREST RATE

YA2838   PIPPINGER J.E., PHILLIPS L.
"Stabilization of the Canadian dollar: 1952-1960"   Econometrica, vol.41, 1973, pp.797-815.
APPL - MACRO : INTERNATIONAL FINANCE , EXCHANGE RATES * POLICY EVALUATION - MACRO : STABILISATION * SPECTRAL ANALYSIS - APPL : MACRO * SPECTRAL ANALYSIS - CROSS : APPL * INTERVENTION

YA2839   PITTS J.E., WHITAKER W.M.
"The impact of tax policy on investment behaviour in the chemical industry, 1951-1965"   Decis. Sci., vol.2, 1971, pp.53-63.
APPL - SECTOR : PRODUCTION , CHEMICALS * APPL - SECTOR : INVESTMENT * TAX - EFFECT OF

YA2840   PLATT R.B.
"A monetarist approach to forecasting: issues and results"   Bus. Econ., vol.7:4, 1972, pp.12-22.
EVALUATION - MACRO MODEL * MACRO MODEL - ST.LOUIS * EX ANTE * MACRO MODEL - FRIEND TAUBMANN JONES

YA2841   PLATT R.B.
"Forecasting industry profits"   Bus. Econ., vol.9:1, 1974, pp.47-50.
APPL - SECTOR : FINANCE , PROFITS * BASIC

YA2842   PLATT R.B.
"Some measures of forecast accuracy"   Bus. Econ., vol.6:3, 1971, pp.30-39.
LOSS FUNCTIONS - REVIEW * CONTROL CHARTS - CUSUM * EVALUATION - THEORY OF * BASIC

YA2843   PLOSSER C.I., SCHWERT G.W.
"Estimation of a non-invertible moving average process"   J. Econometrics, vol.6, 1977, pp.199-224.
STATIONARITY - TRANSFORMING TO * ERROR SPECIFICATION - MOVING AVERAGE * REGRESSION - ESTIMATION * TIME SERIES - MOVING AVERAGE * DATA - SIMULATION

YA2844   POCOCK S.J.
"Daily variations in sickness absence"   Appl. Stats., vol.22, 1973, pp.375-391.
MANPOWER PLANNING - ABSENCE * PROBABILITY MODELS - OTHER * SEASONALITY - ESTIMATION , OTHER

YA2845   POCOCK S.J.
"Harmonic analysis applied to seasonal variations in sickness absence"   Appl. Stats., vol.23, 1974, pp.103-120.
SPECTRAL ANALYSIS - APPL : FIRM , MANPOWER PLANNING * SPECTRAL ANALYSIS - APPL : SEASONALITY * MANPOWER PLANNING - ABSENCE * HEALTH - DISEASE , INCIDENCE OF * SEASONALITY - ESTIMATION , HARMONICS

YA2846   POIRIER D.J.
"On the use of bilinear splines in economics"   J. Econometrics, vol.3, 1975, pp.23-34.
REGRESSION - PIECEWISE * APPL - MACRO : EARNINGS * SPLINE FUNCTIONS

YA2847   POIRIER D.J.
"On the use of Cobb-Douglas splines"   Int. Econ. Rev., vol.16, 1975, pp.733-744.
REGRESSION - PIECEWISE * PRODUCTION FUNCTIONS - THEORY * SPLINE FUNCTIONS * APPL - FIRM : UTILITIES , ELECTRICITY * DATA - CROSS SECTION * PRODUCTION FUNCTIONS - ESTIMATION

YA2848   POIRIER D.J.
"Piecewise regression using cubic splines"   J. Am. Statist. As., vol.68, 1973, pp.515-524.
STABILITY OF COEFFICIENTS - REGRESSION , TEST * REGRESSION - PIECEWISE * SPLINE FUNCTIONS

YA2849   POIRIER D.J.
"The effect of the first observation in regression models with first order autoregressive disturbances"   Appl. Stats., vol.27, 1978, pp.67-68.
DISTRIBUTED LAG - ERROR SPECIFICATION * ESTIMATION - KALMAN FILTER : APPL * ERROR SPECIFICATION - AUTOCORRELATED * REGRESSION - ESTIMATION , ERROR SPECIFICATION

YA2850   POIRIER D.J.
"The use of the Box-Cox transformation in limited dependent variable models"   J. Am. Statist. Ass., vol.73, 1978, pp.284-287.
REGRESSION - TRANSFORMATIONS , BOX COX * REGRESSION - LIMITED DEPENDENT * DECISION RULES - SECTOR * APPL - SECTOR : GOVERNMENT , FOREIGN AID

YA2851   POLACHEK S.W.
"Differences in expected post-school investment as a determinant of market wage differentials"   Int. Econ. Rev., vol.16, 1975, pp.451-470.
APPL - SECTOR : EARNINGS * EDUCATION - EFFECT OF * MANPOWER PLANNING - DISCRIMINATION , SEX

YA2852   POLINSKY A.M.
"The demand for housing: a study in specification and grouping"   Econometrica, vol.45, 1977, pp.447-461.
INCOME - EFFECT OF * PRICE - EFFECT OF * APPL - SECTOR : CONSTRUCTION , RESIDENTIAL

YA2853   POLINSKY A.M., SHAVELL S., SMALL K.A.
"The air pollution and property value debate"   Rev. Econ. Stats., vol.57, 1975, pp.100-107.
APPL - SECTOR : CONSTRUCTION , RESIDENTIAL * POLLUTION - EFFECT OF * LP * THEORY - MODELLING * CONSUMER BEHAVIOUR - ECONOMIC MODELS , THEORY * PRICE - SECTOR : CONSTRUCTION , RESIDENTIAL

YA2854   POLLACK E.D., SNYDER C.
       "Bank forecasting models: coming of age?"   Bus. Econ., vol.13:1, 1978,
       pp.31-35.
       USER - FIRM : FINANCE * APPL - FIRM : FINANCE , BANKS * USER REQUIREMENTS

YA2855   POLLAK R.A., WALES T.J.
       "Estimation of complete demand systems from household budget data: the
       linear and quadratic expenditure system"   Am. Econ. Rev., vol.68, 1978,
       pp.348-359.
       COMPARATIVE METHODS - DEMAND EQUATIONS * DEMAND EQUATIONS - SYSTEMS OF :
       METHODOLOGY , ESTIMATION * CONSUMER BEHAVIOUR - EXPENDITURE SURVEY * PRICE -
       EFFECT OF * APPL - MACRO : CONSUMER DEMAND

YA2856   POLLAK R.A., WALES T.J.
       "Estimation of the linear expenditure system"   Econometrica, vol.37, 1969,
       pp.611-628.
       DEMAND EQUATIONS - SYSTEMS OF : METHODOLOGY : ESTIMATION * COMPARATIVE
       METHODS - ESTIMATION : DEMAND EQUATIONS * APPL - MACRO : CONSUMER DEMAND

YA2857   POLLI R., COOK V.
       "Validity of the product life cycle"   J. Business, vol.42, 1969,
       pp.385-400.
       EVALUATION - LIFE CYCLE , PRODUCT * APPL - SECTOR : CONSUMER NON DURABLE ,
       CIGARETTES * APPL - SECTOR : CONSUMER NON DURABLES , GROCERIES * APPL -
       SECTOR : CONSUMER NON DURABLES , FOOD

YA2858   POOLE W.
       "Gradualism: a mid-course view" with discussion   Brookings Paps. Econ.
       Activity, 1970, pp.271-301.
       POLICY EVALUATION - MACRO * MACRO MODEL - FRB , MIT , PENN

YA2859   POOLE W.
       "Rational expectations in the macro model" with discussion   Brookings
       Paps. Econ. Activity, 1976, pp.463-514.
       THEORY - EXPECTATIONS * FORECAST - FEEDBACK

YA2860   POOLE W.
       "Reflections on US macroeconomic policy" with discussion   Brookings
       Paps. Econ. Activity, 1974, pp.233-248.
       POLICY EVALUATION - MACRO * EX ANTE * EVALUATION - MACRO MODELS * MACRO
       MODEL - FRB , MIT , PENN

YA2861   POOLE W.
       "The relationship of monetary decelerations to business cycle peaks: another
       look at the evidence"   J. Finance, vol.30, 1975, pp.697-712.
       APPL - MACRO : MONEY , SUPPLY * INFLATION - INDICATORS * BUSINESS CYCLE -
       PREDICTION , TURNING POINTS * BASIC

YA2862   POOLE W.
       "The role of interest rates and inflation in the consumption function"
       Brookings Paps. Econ. Activity, 1972, pp.211-220.
       APPL - MACRO : CONSUMPTION * INFLATION - EFFECT OF * INTEREST RATE - EFFECT
       OF * EX ANTE

YA2863   POOLE W.
       "Whither money demand?" with discussion   Brookings Paps. Econ. Activity,
       1970, pp.485-501.
       APPL - MACRO : MONEY , DEMAND * INCOME - EFFECT OF * INTEREST RATE - EFFECT
       OF * STABILITY OF COEFFICIENTS - REGRESSION : APPL

YA2864   POOLE W., KORNBLITH E.B.F.
       "The Friedman-Meiselman CMC paper: new evidence on an old controversy"
       Am. Econ. Rev., vol.63, 1973, pp.908-917.
       EVALUATION - MONETARIST THEORY * POLICY EVALUATION - MACRO : FISCAL ,
       MONETARY * EX ANTE * MACRO MODEL - ST.LOUIS

YA2865   POOLE W., LIEBERMAN C.
       "Improving monetary control" with discussion   Brookings Paps. Econ.
       Activity, 1972, pp.293-342.
       APPL - MACRO : MONEY * POLICY EVALUATION - MACRO : MONETARY * EVALUATION -
       SEASONAL ADJUSTMENT * DATA ERRORS - EFFECT OF

YA2866   POPKIN J.
       "An integrated model of final and intermediate demand by stage of process: a
       progress report"   Am. Econ. Ass. Proc., 1977, pp.141-147.
       INFLATION - DETERMINANTS * APPL - MACRO : INTERMEDIATE GOODS * APPL - MACRO
       : RAW MATERIALS * APPL - MACRO : FINISHED GOODS

YA2867   POPKIN J.
       "Comment on 'The distributed lag between capital appropriations and
       expenditures'"   Econometrica, vol.34, 1966, pp.719-723.
       DISTRIBUTED LAG - VARIABLE LAG * DISTRIBUTED LAG - ALMON * COMPARATIVE
       METHODS - DISTRIBUTED LAG * APPL - MACRO : INVESTMENT * DISTRIBUTED LAG -
       APPL , ORDERS

YA2868   POPKIN J.
       "Commodity prices and the US price level"   Brookings Paps. Econ. Activity,
       1974, pp.249-259.
       INFLATION - DETERMINANTS * INPUT OUTPUT - MACRO : RAW MATERIALS * APPL -
       SECTOR : COMMODITIES * APPL - MACRO : RAW MATERIALS * PRICE - EFFECT OF

YA2869　POPKIN J.
"Consumer and wholesale prices in a model of price behaviour by stage of processing"　Rev. Econ. Stats., vol.56, 1974, pp.486-501.
THEORY - PRICING * PRICE - SECTOR * INFLATION - DETERMINANTS * APPL - MACRO : EARNINGS

YA2870　POPKIN J.
"Price forecasting"　Bus. Econ., vol.12:1, 1977, pp.33-37.
PRICE - SECTOR * BASIC

YA2871　POPKIN J.
"Some avenues for the improvement of price forecasts generated by macroeconometric models"　Am. J. Ag. Econ., vol.57, 1975, pp.157-163.
EVALUATION - INFLATION MODELS * EVALUATION - MACRO MODELS * EX ANTE * INFLATION - DETERMINANTS

YA2872　PORTER M.E.
"Consumer behaviour, retailer power and market performance in consumer goods industries"　Rev. Econ. Stats., vol.56, 1974, pp.419-436.
APPL - SECTOR : FINANCE , PROFITS * DISTRIBUTION - EFFECT OF * APPL - SECTOR : CONSUMER DURABLES * APPL - SECTOR : CONSUMER NON DURABLES * CONCENTRATION - EFFECT OF * ADVERTISING - EFFECT OF

YA2873　PORTER M.E.
"Interbrand choice, media mix and market performance"　Am. Econ. Ass. Proc., vol.66, 1976, pp.398-406.
ADVERTISING - EFFECT OF * APPL - SECTOR : CONSUMER DURABLES * APPL - SECTOR : CONSUMER NON DURABLES * CONCENTRATION - EFFECT OF * APPL - SECTOR : FINANCE , PROFITS

YA2874　PORTER R.C.
"A growth model forecast of faculty size and salaries in US higher education"　Rev. Econ. Stats., vol.47, 1965, pp.191-197.
APPL - SECTOR : EDUCATION , UNIVERSITIES * EX ANTE

YA2875　PORTES R., WINTER D.
"The demand for money and for consumption goods in centrally planned economies"　Rev. Econ. Stats., vol.60, 1978, pp.8-18.
APPL - MACRO : MONEY , DEMAND * APPL - MACRO , EASTERN EUROPE * APPL - MACRO : SAVINGS * DATA - INTERNATIONAL

YA2876　POSSENTI P.
"A new statistical model for short-term and medium range forecasting"　Ind. Mktg. Mgmt., vol.4, 1975, pp.69-80.
APPL - FIRM : CONSUMER NON DURABLES , PHARMACEUTICALS * EVALUATION - EXPONENTIAL SMOOTHING * EX ANTE

YA2877　POWELL N.K., WESTWOOD J.B.
"Buyer behaviour in management education"　Appl. Stats., vol.27, 1978, pp.69-72.
REPEAT BUYING * MANPOWER PLANNING - EDUCATION PROGRAMS * APPL - FIRM : EDUCATION , UNIVERSITIES * EX ANTE

YA2878　POWER P.D.
"Computers and financial planning"　Long Range Planning, vol. 8:6, 1975, pp.52-59.
USE - CORPORATE PLANNING * SIMULATION - APPL : FINANCE * COMPUTERISATION - PLANNING MODELS * USER REQUIREMENTS * BASIC

YA2879　PRAETZ P.D.
"Rates of return on filter tests"　J. Finance, vol.31, 1978, pp.71-75.
STOCK PRICES - TRADING RULES * RANDOM WALK - TEST , TRADING RULE

YA2880　PRAETZ P.D.
"The distribution of share price changes"　J. Business, vol.45, 1972, pp.49-55.
APPL - SECTOR : FINANCE , STOCK PRICE INDEX * STOCK PRICES - DISTRIBUTION * ERROR DISTRIBUTION - T * ERROR DISTRIBUTION - STABLE

YA2881　PRAETZ P.D., BLATTBERG R.C., GONEDES N.J.
"A comparison of stable and Student distributions as statistical models of stock prices: comment"　J. Business, vol.50, 1977, pp.76-79.
STOCK PRICES - DISTRIBUTION * ERROR DISTRIBUTION - STABLE * ERROR DISTRIBUTION - T

YA2882　PRAETZ P.D., ET AL.
"On the methodology of testing for independence in future prices: comment"　J. Finance, vol.31, 1976, pp.977-985.
ERROR SPECIFICATION - AUTOCORRELATED * APPL - SECTOR : COMMODITIES * LOSS FUNCTIONS - SECTOR : FINANCE , TRADING RULES * RANDOM WALK - TEST , TRADING RULES

YA2883　PRAS B., SUMMERS J.
"A comparison of linear and nonlinear evaluation process models"　J. Mktg. Res., vol.12, 1975, pp.276-281.
EVALUATION - CONSUMER BEHAVIOUR , PSYCHOLOGICAL MODELS

YA2884　PRASAD V.K., RING L.W.
"Measuring sales effects of some marketing mix variables and their interactions"　J. Mktg. Res., vol.13, 1976, pp.391-396.
ADVERTISING - EXPERIMENTAL DESIGN * APPL - FIRM : CONSUMER NON DURABLES , FOOD , PROCESSED * ADVERTISING - EFFECT OF * MARKET SHARE - SECTOR : CONSUMER NON DURABLES * PRICE - EFFECT OF

YA2885 PRATSCHKE J.L.
        "Adjusted and unadjusted R squared- further evidence from Irish data"
        Int. Statist. Rev., vol.39, 1971, pp.4-8.
        REGRESSION - MODEL CHOICE * REGRESSION - SUMMARY STATISTICS * APPL - MACRO ,
        IRELAND * APPL - MACRO : CONSUMER DEMAND * DATA - CROSS SECTION
YA2886 PRESS S.J., SCOTT A.J.
        "Missing observations in Bayesian regression, II"   J. Am. Statist. Ass.,
        vol.71, 1976, pp.366-369.
        BAYESIAN - ESTIMATION : REGRESSION , DATA ERRORS * DATA ERRORS - MISSING
        OBSERVATIONS * REGRESSION - OUTLIERS * ADVANCED
YA2887 PRESS S.J., WILSON S.
        "Choosing between logistic regression and discriminant analysis"   J. Am.
        Statist. Ass., vol.73, 1978, pp.699-705.
        EVALUATION - REGRESSION , LIMITED DEPENDENT , LOGIT * COMPARATIVE METHODS -
        DISCRIMINATION * EX ANTE * REGRESSION - QUALITATIVE DEPENDENT * DATA -
        CATEGORICAL
YA2888 PRESS S.J., ZELLNER A.
        "Posterior distribution for the multiple correlation coefficient with fixed
        regressors"   J. Econometrics, vol.8, 1978, pp.307-321.
        REGRESSION - SUMMARY STATISTICS * BAYESIAN - ESTIMATION : REGRESSION *
        CONFIDENCE INTERVAL - REGRESSION , SUMMARY STATISTICS * ADVANCED
YA2889 PRESTON R.S.
        "The Wharton long term model: input output within the context of a macro
        forecasting model"   Int. Econ. Rev., vol.16, 1975, pp.3-19.
        MACRO MODEL - WHARTON * LONG TERM FORECASTING * INPUT OUTPUT - MACRO , US *
        MULTIPLIERS - MACRO * MACRO MODEL - METHODOLOGY
YA2890 PRICE R.W.R.
        "Some aspects of the progressive income tax structure in the UK"   Nat.
        Inst. Econ. Rev., no.65, 1973, pp.52-63.
        APPL - SECTOR : GOVERNMENT , REVENUES , TAX * INCOME - EFFECT OF
YA2891 PRIESTLEY M.B.
        "Non-linear models in time series analysis"   Stat'n., vol.27, 1978,
        pp.159-176.
        TIME SERIES - NON STATIONARY * TIME SERIES - NON LINEAR * TIME SERIES -
        REVIEW
YA2892 PRIESTLEY M.B., SUBBA RAO T.
        "A test for non-stationarity of time-series"   R. Statist. Soc. (B),
        vol.31, 1969, pp.140-149.
        TIME SERIES - NON STATIONARY * TIME SERIES - STATIONARY * SPECTRAL ANALYSIS
        - CHANGING SPECTRA * STABILITY OF COEFFICIENTS - TIME SERIES * STATIONARITY
        - TESTING * ADVANCED
YA2893 PRIESTLEY M.B., TONG H.
        "On the analysis of bivariate non-stationary processes" with discussion
        R. Statist. Soc. (B), vol.35, 1973, pp.153-166 & 179-188.
        DATA - SIMULATION * TIME SERIES - NON STATIONARY * DISTRIBUTED LAG -
        VARIABLE LAG * REGRESSION - STATE SPACE * REGRESSION - ESTIMATION * SPECTRAL
        ANALYSIS - CHANGING SPECTRA * SPECTRAL ANALYSIS - CROSS : METHODOLOGY * TIME
        SERIES - FILTER , TIME DEPENDENT * ADVANCED
YA2894 PROTHERO D.L., WALLIS K.F.
        "Modelling macroeconomic time series" with discussion   R. Statist. Soc.
        (A), vol.139, 1976, pp.468-500.
        TIME SERIES - ARIMA : APPL * COMPARATIVE METHODS - MACRO MODELS * MACRO
        MODEL - UK * COMPARATIVE METHODS - ARIMA , CAUSAL(SIMULTANEOUS SYSTEM)
YA2895 PUNJ G.N., STAELIN R.
        "The choice process for graduate business schools"   J. Mktg. Res., vol.15,
        1978, pp.588-598.
        REGRESSION - LIMITED DEPENDENT , LOGIT : APPL * APPL - FIRM : EDUCATION ,
        UNIVERSITIES * EX ANTE
YA2896 PURDY D.L., ZIS G.
        "Trade unions and wage inflation in the UK: a reply to Dogas and Hines"
        Appl. Econ., vol.8, 1976, pp.249-265.
        UNIONISATION - EFFECT OF * INFLATION - DETERMINANTS
YA2897 PURVIS D.D., SMITH G.
        "Dynamic models of portfolio behaviour: more on pitfalls on financial
        modelling" with comments   Am. Econ. Rev., vol.68, 1978, pp.403-416.
        APPL - MACRO : FLOW OF FUNDS * SIMULTANEOUS SYSTEM - CONSTRAINED * APPL -
        MACRO : CONSUMER DEMAND , FINANCIAL ASSETS
YA2898 PYLE D.H.
        "Observed price expectations and interest rates"   Rev. Econ. Stats.,
        vol.54, 1972, pp.275-280.
        EXPECTATIONS - DATA * INTEREST RATE - INDICATORS * INFLATION - EFFECT OF *
        INFLATION - EXPECTATIONS * DISTRIBUTED LAG - POLYNOMIAL : APPL * DISTRIBUTED
        LAG - APPL , INTEREST RATE
YA2899 PYLE D.H.
        "The losses on savings deposits from interest rate regulation"   Bell J.
        Econ., vol.5, 1974, pp.614-622.
        APPL - SECTOR : FINANCE , BANKS * APPL - SECTOR : FINANCE , BUILDING
        SOCIETIES * INTEREST RATE - COVARIATION * EX ANTE * USE - BANK REGULATION

YA2900   QUANDT R.E.
         "A comparison of methods for testing nonnested hypotheses"   Rev. Econ.
         Stats., vol.56, 1974, pp.92-99.
         MODEL SELECTION * SPECIFICATION ERROR - TESTS , MODEL SELECTION * MACRO
         MODEL - KLEIN * APPL - SECTOR : PRODUCTION , COMPUTERS * COMPARATIVE METHODS
         - TESTS , MODEL SELECTION
YA2901   QUANDT R.E.
         "A new approach to estimating switching regressions"   J. Am. Statist.
         Ass., vol.67, 1972, pp.306-310.
         REGRESSION - SWITCHING * DATA - SIMULATION * APPL - SECTOR : CONSTRUCTION ,
         RESIDENTIAL * COMPARATIVE METHODS - ESTIMATION : REGRESSION , SWITCHING *
         ESTIMATION - MAXIMUM LIKELIHOOD : APPL
YA2902   QUANDT R.E.
         "Tests of the equilibrium vs. disequilibrium hypotheses"   Int. Econ. Rev.,
         vol.19, 1978, pp.435-452.
         SIMULTANEOUS SYSTEM - DISEQUILIBRIUM * DATA - SIMULATION * SIMULTANEOUS
         SYSTEM - MODEL CHOICE
YA2903   QUANDT R.E., RAMSEY J.B.
         "Estimating mixtures of normal distributions and switching regressions" with
         discussion   J. Am. Statist. Ass., vol.73, 1978, pp.730-752.
         REGRESSION - SWITCHING * ERROR DISTRIBUTION - MIXTURE * ESTIMATION - METHOD
         OF MOMENTS * DATA - SIMULATION * ADVANCED
YA2904   RACETTE G.A., ET AL.
         "Earnings retention, new capital and the growth of the firm: comments"
         Rev. Econ. Stats., vol.55, 1973, pp.127-131.
         APPL - FIRM : FINANCE , PROFITS * APPL - FIRM : GROWTH
YA2905   RADICE H.K.
         "Control type, profitability and growth in large firms: an empirical study"
         Econ. J., vol.81,1971, pp.547-562.
         APPL - FIRM TYPE * APPL - FIRM : CONSUMER NON DURABLES , FOOD * APPL - FIRM
         : FINANCE , PROFITS * APPL - FIRM : PRODUCTION , TEXTILES * APPL - FIRM :
         PRODUCTION , ENGINEERING , ELECTRICAL * APPL - FIRM : EARNINGS
YA2906   RAGAN J.F.
         "Minimum wages and the youth labor market"   Rev. Econ. Stats., vol.59,
         1977, pp.129-136.
         MANPOWER PLANNING - LABOUR FORCE COMPOSITION * MANPOWER PLANNING - LABOUR
         PARTICIPATION * POLICY EVALUATION - MACRO : UNEMPLOYMENT * MANPOWER PLANNING
         - MACRO
YA2907   RAGAN J.F.
         "Projecting capacity utilisation in manufacturing"   Bus. Econ., vol.13:4,
         1978, pp.15-20.
         APPL - MACRO : CAPACITY UTILISATION * ERROR SPECIFICATION - AUTOCORRELATED
YA2908   RAINE J.E.
         "Self adaptive forecasting reconsidered"   Decis. Sci., vol.2, 1971,
         pp.181-191 & 503.
         EXPONENTIAL SMOOTHING - ADAPTIVE COEFFICIENTS * COMPARATIVE METHODS -
         EXPONENTIAL SMOOTHING , ADAPTIVE
YA2909   RAJ B.
         "Linear regression with random coefficients: the finite sample and
         convergence properties"   J. Am. Statist. Ass., vol.70, 1975, pp.127-137.
         COMPARATIVE METHODS - ESTIMATION : REGRESSION , RANDOM COEFFICIENTS *
         REGRESSION - RANDOM COEFFICIENTS
YA2910   RAMSAY J.O.
         "A comparative study of several robust estimates of slope, intercept, and
         scale in linear regression"   J. Am. Statist. Ass., vol.72, 1977,
         pp.608-615.
         EVALUATION - ESTIMATION : ROBUST * DATA - SIMULATION * COMPARATIVE METHODS -
         ESTIMATION : REGRESSION
YA2911   RAMSEY J.B.
         "Limiting forms for demand functions: tests of some specific hypotheses"
         Rev. Econ. Stats., vol.56, 1974, pp.468-477.
         APPL - SECTOR : CONSUMER NON DURABLES * INCOME - EFFECT OF * PRICE - EFFECT
         OF * SPECIFICATION ERROR - TESTS , MODEL SELECTION
YA2912   RAMSEY J.B.
         "Tests for specification errors in classical linear least squares regression
         analysis"   R. Statist. Soc. (B), vol.31, 1969, pp.350-371.
         SPECIFICATION ERROR - TESTS , EVALUATION * SPECIFICATION ERROR - TESTS ,
         HETEROSCEDASTICITY * SPECIFICATION ERROR - TESTS , MODEL SELECTION *
         AUTOCORRELATION - TEST * SPECIFICATION ERROR - TESTS , SIMULTANEOUS SYSTEM
         BIAS
YA2913   RAMSEY J.B., GILBERT R.
         "A Monte Carlo study of some small sample properties of tests for
         specification error"   J. Am. Statist. Ass., vol.67, 1972, pp.180-186.
         SPECIFICATION ERROR - TESTS , EVALUATION * DATA - SIMULATION * RESIDUALS -
         COMPARATIVE ANALYSIS OF * SPECIFICATION ERROR - TESTS , HETEROSCEDASTICITY *
         SPECIFICATION ERROR - TESTS , VARIABLE INCLUSION * SPECIFICATION ERROR -
         TESTS , TRANSFORMATIONS * SPECIFICATION ERROR - TESTS , SIMULTANEOUS SYSTEM
         BIAS

YA2914   RAMSEY J.B., RASCHE R., ALLEN B.
"An analysis of the private and commercial demand for gasoline"   Rev.
Econ. Stats., vol.57, 1975, pp.502-507.
APPL - SECTOR : PRODUCTION , PETROLEUM * APPL - SECTOR : CONSUMER NON
DURABLES , PETROL * INCOME - EFFECT OF * PRICE - EFFECT OF * SUPPLY - SECTOR
: PRODUCTION

YA2915   RAMSEY J.B., SCHMIDT P.
"Some further results on the use of OLS and BLUS residuals in specification
error tests"   J. Am. Statist. Ass., vol.71, 1976, pp.389-390.
RESIDUALS - COMPARATIVE ANALYSIS OF * SPECIFICATION ERROR - TESTS ,
EVALUATION

YA2916   RAMSEY J.B., ZAREMBKA P.
"Specification error tests and alternative functional forms of the aggregate
production function"   J. Am. Statist. Ass., vol.66, 1971, pp.471-477.
PRODUCTION FUNCTIONS - MACRO * SPECIFICATION ERROR - TESTS , MODEL SELECTION
* EVALUATION - PRODUCTION FUNCTIONS

YA2917   RANARD E.D.
"Use of input-output concepts in sales forecasting"   J. Mktg. Res., vol.9,
1972, pp.53-58.
INPUT OUTPUT - SECTOR : PRODUCTION * APPL - SECTOR : PRODUCTION , STEEL *
APPL - SECTOR : PRODUCTION , REFRACTORIES * INPUT OUTPUT - MACRO :
INTERMEDIATE GOODS * APPL - MACRO : INTERMEDIATE GOODS

YA2918   RANDLES R.H., ET AL.
"Discriminant analysis based on ranks"   J. Am. Statist. Ass, vol.73, 1978,
pp.373-384.
DISCRIMINANT ANALYSIS - THEORY * DATA - ORDINAL * COMPARATIVE METHODS -
DISCRIMINATION * DATA - SIMULATION * ADVANCED

YA2919   RANDLES R.H., ET AL.
"Generalised linear and quadratic discriminant functions using robust
estimation"   J. Am. Statist. Ass., vol.73, 1978, pp.564-568.
DISCRIMINANT ANALYSIS - METHODOLOGY * COMPARATIVE METHODS - DISCRIMINATION *
DATA - SIMULATION * ERROR DISTRIBUTION - STABLE * DISCRIMINANT ANALYSIS -
THEORY * DATA ERRORS - EFFECT OF * ERROR DISTRIBUTION - LOGNORMAL

YA2920   RANGARAJAN C., CHATTERJEE S.
"A note on comparison between correlation coefficients of original and
transformed variables"   Am. Stat'n., vol.23:4, 1969, pp.28-29.
DATA - TRANSFORMED , DEFLATED * REGRESSION - TRANSFORMATION , RATIO *
REGRESSION - SPURIOUS CORRELATION

YA2921   RANGARAJAN C., SUNDARAJAN V.
"Impact of export fluctuations on income- a cross country analysis"   Rev.
Econ. Stats., vol.53, 1976, pp.368-372.
APPL - MACRO : INTERNATIONAL TRADE , EXPORTS * APPL - MACRO : GROWTH

YA2922   RAO A.G., LILIEN G.
"A system of promotional models"   Mgmt. Sci. (B), vol.19, 1972,
pp.152-160.
CONSUMER BEHAVIOUR - STOCHASTIC MODELS * MARKET SHARE - SECTOR : RETAILING *
ADVERTISING - EFFECT OF * COMPARATIVE METHODS - AUTOREGRESSIVE , CAUSAL *
REGRESSION - NON LINEAR : APPL * APPL - FIRM : RETAILING , PETROL * USE -
PROMOTION EVALUATION

YA2923   RAO A.G., MILLER P.B.
"Advertising/sales response functions"   J. Advtg. Res., vol.15:2, 1975,
pp.7-15.
ADVERTISING - EFFECT OF * DATA - CROSS SECTION , TIME SERIES * DISTRIBUTED
LAG - APPL , ADVERTISING * USE - MARKETING POLICY

YA2924   RAO A.V.
"A comment on: forecasting and stock control for intermittent demand"
Opl. Res. Q., vol.24, 1973, pp.639-640.
DEMAND - INTERMITTENT * EXPONENTIAL SMOOTHING - PROBABILITIES * TIMING
UNCERTAINTY

YA2925   RAO C.U., ET AL.
"Leverage and the cost of capital in a less developed capital market:
comments"   J. Finance, vol.26, 1971, pp.777-785.
APPL - FIRM : UTILITIES * APPL - FIRM : FINANCE , PROFITS * APPL - FIRM :
FINANCE , FINANCIAL STRUCTURE , LEVERAGE

YA2926   RAO M.R., SRINIVASAN V.
"A note on Sharpe's algorithm for minimizing the sum of absolute deviations
in a simple regression problem" with erratum.   Mgmt. Sci. (B), vol.19,
1972, pp.222-225. & 1334.
ESTIMATION - MSAE * NUMERICAL METHODS - OPTIMISATION

YA2927   RAO P.
"On a correspondence between t and F in values in multiple regressions"
Am. Stat'n., vol.30, 1976, pp.190-191.
REGRESSION - SUMMARY STATISTICS * REGRESSION - HYPOTHESIS TESTS

YA2928   RAO P.
"Some notes on the errors in variables model"   Am. Stat'n., vol.27, 1973,
pp.217-218.
REGRESSION - ERRORS IN VARIABLES * BASIC

YA2929   RAO P., CROCKER D.C.
          "Some notes on misspecification in multiple regressions"   Am. Stat'n.,
          vol.25:5, 1971, pp.37-39 & vol.26:5, 1972, pp.41-42.
          SPECIFICATION ERROR - EFFECT OF , VARIABLE INCLUSION
YA2930   RAO T.R.
          "Is brand loyalty a criterion for market segmentation?"   Decis. Sci.,
          vol.4, 1973, pp.395-404.
          MARKET SEGMENTATION * DISCRIMINANT ANALYSIS - APPL * REPEAT BUYING *
          CONSUMER BEHAVIOUR - PURCHASING , DETERMINANTS
YA2931   RAO T.R.
          "Time between purchases and consumer brand choice"   Decis. Sci., vol.3:1,
          1972, pp.47-55.
          BRAND CHOICE - THEORY * CONSUMER BEHAVIOUR - STOCHASTIC MODELS , THEORY *
          APPL - FIRM : CONSUMER NON DURABLES , GROCERIES
YA2932   RAO T.R.
          "Time between purchases and consumer brand choice"   Decis. Sci., vol.3:1,
          1972, pp.47-55.
          BRAND CHOICE - METHODOLOGY * CONSUMER BEHAVIOUR - STOCHASTIC MODELS * APPL -
          FIRM : CONSUMER NON DURABLES , GROCERIES
YA2933   RAO U.L.G.
          "Estimated residual covariance matrix of two stage least squares and
          computation of three stage least squares estimates"   Int. Econ. Rev.,
          vol.15, 1974, pp.693-698.
          DATA - SIMULATION * SIMULTANEOUS SYSTEM - ESTIMATION * ESTIMATION - 2SLS *
          ESTIMATION - 3SLS * ADVANCED
YA2934   RAO V.R.
          "Alternative econometric models of sales-advertising relationship"   J.
          Mktg. Res., vol.9, 1972, pp.177-181.
          MARKET SHARE - SECTOR : CONSUMER NON DURABLES * ADVERTISING - EFFECT OF *
          COMPARATIVE METHODS - DISTRIBUTED LAG , ERROR SPECIFICATION * APPL - FIRM :
          CONSUMER NON DURABLES , CIGARETTES * COMPARATIVE METHODS - ESTIMATION : OLS
          , 2SLS * COMPARATIVE METHODS - REGRESSION , MODEL SPECIFICATION * REGRESSION
          - SPECIFICATION OF VARIABLES
YA2935   RAO V.R., SOUTAR G.N.
          "Subjective evaluations for product design decisions"   Decis. Sci., vol.6,
          1975, pp.120-134.
          NEW PRODUCTS - IDENTIFYING * JUDGEMENTAL FORECASTS - INCORPORATION * APPL -
          SECTOR : CONSUMER DURABLES , CARS * APPL - SECTOR : CONSUMER DURABLES ,
          TYPEWRITERS * APPL - SECTOR : CONSUMER DURABLES , APPLIANCES
YA2936   RAO V.R., WINTER F.W.
          "An application of the multivariate probit model to market segmentation and
          product design"   J. Mktg. Res., vol.15, 1978, pp.361-368.
          MARKET SEGMENTATION * REGRESSION - LIMITED DEPENDENT , PROBIT : APPL * NEW
          PRODUCTS - IDENTIFYING * APPL - SECTOR : CONSUMER DURABLES , CAMERAS
YA2937   RASCHE R.H.
          "Impact of the stock market on private demand" with discussion   Am. Econ.
          Ass. Proc., 1972, pp.220-233.
          APPL - MACRO : CONSUMPTION * LIFE CYCLE - CONSUMER * STOCK PRICES - EFFECT
          OF
YA2938   RASMUSSEN J.A.
          "Application of a model of endogenous technical change to US industry data"
          Rev. Econ. Studies, vol.40, 1973, pp.225-238.
          APPL - SECTOR : R & D
YA2939   RATCHFORD B.T., FORD G.T.
          "A study of prices and market shares in the computer mainframe industry"
          J. Business, vol.49, 1976, pp.194-218.
          APPL - FIRM : PRODUCTION , COMPUTERS * MARKET SHARE - SECTOR : PRODUCTION *
          QUALITY - PRICE * DATA - CROSS SECTION * PRICE - EFFECT OF
YA2940   RATKOWSKY D.A., DOLBY G.R.
          "Taylor series linearization and scoring for parameters in nonlinear
          regression"   Appl. Stats., vol.24, 1975, pp.109-111.
          ESTIMATION - MAXIMUM LIKELIHOOD * ESTIMATION - LOGARITHMIC MODEL *
          REGRESSION - ESTIMATION * NUMERICAL METHODS - OPTIMISATION , SEARCH *
          REGRESSION - NON LINEAR
YA2941   RAUSSER G.C., FREEBAIRN J.W.
          "Approximate adaptive control solutions to US beef trade policy"   Anns.
          Econ. Soc. Meas., vol.3, 1974, pp.177-205.
          APPL - SECTOR : AGRICULTURE , LIVESTOCK , BEEF * CONTROL THEORY - STOCHASTIC
          , APPL * COMPARATIVE METHODS - CONTROL * ADVANCED
YA2942   RAUSSER G.C., FREEBAIRN J.W.
          "Estimation of policy preference functions: an application to US beef"
          Rev. Econ. Stats., vol.56, 1974, pp.437-449.
          DECISION RULES - ESTIMATION * DECISION RULES - SECTOR : AGRICULTURE * APPL -
          SECTOR : AGRICULTURE , LIVESTOCK , BEEF * CONTROL THEORY - DETERMINISTIC ,
          APPL * LOSS FUNCTIONS - SECTOR : AGRICULTURE
YA2943   RAUSSER G.C., OLIVEIRA R.A.
          "An econometric analysis of wilderness area use"   J. Am. Statist. Ass.,
          vol.71, 1976, pp.276-285.
          APPL - SECTOR : SERVICES , TOURISM * APPL - SECTOR : GOVERNMENT , LOCAL ,
          SERVICES , LEASURE * EX ANTE * COMPARATIVE METHODS - ARIMA , CAUSAL * LEAD
          TIME - EFFECT OF * COMBINING FORECASTS - CAUSAL , TIME SERIES * EVALUATION -
          COMBINING FORECASTS

YA2944   RAVINDRAN A.
"Management of seasonal style-goods inventories" Ops. Res., vol.20, 1972,
pp.265-275.
STYLE GOODS * USE - INVENTORY CONTROL * SEASONALITY - SINGLE SEASON * APPL -
SECTOR : CONSUMER DURABLES , TEXTILES

YA2945   RAY G.F.
"Medium-term forecasts reassessed: III. energy" Nat. Inst. Econ. Rev.,
no.62, 1972, pp.61-74.
APPL - SECTOR : ENERGY * APPL - MACRO , UK * APPL - MACRO : ENERGY

YA2946   RAY G.F., DAVIES S.W.
"Medium term forecasts reassessed: II. paper and board" Nat. Inst. Econ.
Rev., no.62, 1972, pp.44-61.
APPL - SECTOR : PRODUCTION , PACKAGING * APPL - SECTOR : PRODUCTION , PAPER
* APPL - SECTOR : SERVICES , MEDIA , NEWSPAPERS

YA2947   RAY M.L., SAWYER A.G.
"Behavioural measurement for marketing models: estimating the effects of
advertising repetition for media planning" Mgmt. Sci. (B), vol.18,
(special issue), 1971, pp.P73-P89.
ADVERTISING - EFFECT OF * CONSUMER BEHAVIOUR - STOCHASTIC MODELS * BRAND
CHOICE - APPL * ADVERTISING - EXPOSURE * USE - MEDIA PLANNING * APPL -
SECTOR : SERVICES , MEDIA , MAGAZINES

YA2948   REA J.D.
"Indeterminacy of the Chow test when the number of observations is
insufficient" Econometrica, vol.46, 1978, p.229.
STABILITY OF COEFFICIENTS - REGRESSION , TEST * DATA - SAMPLE SIZE

YA2949   REA S.A.
"Unemployment insurance and labour supply: a simulation of the 1971
unemployment act" Can. J. Econ., vol.10, 1977, pp.263-278.
POLICY EVALUATION - MACRO : UNEMPLOYMENT * MANPOWER PLANNING - UNEMPLOYMENT
* POLICY EVALUATION - MACRO : WELFARE

YA2950   REBACK R., GRIER P.
"Non random price changes in association with trading in large blocks: a
comment" J. Business, vol.47, 1974, pp.564-567.
STOCK PRICES - RUNS * STOCK PRICES - TRADING RULES * STOCK PRICES - TRADING
VOLUME * APPL - FIRM : FINANCE , STOCK PRICES

YA2951   REDDAWAY W.B.
"The productivity effects of selective employment tax" Nat. Inst. Econ.
Rev., no.57, 1971, pp.62-68.
APPL - MACRO , UK * APPL - SECTOR : PRODUCTIVITY * APPL - SECTOR : RETAILING
* APPL - MACRO : PRODUCTIVITY * TAX - EFFECT OF * POLICY EVALUATION - MACRO
: EMPLOYMENT

YA2952   REDER M.W.
"An analysis of a small, closely observed labour market: starting salaries
for University of Chicago M.B.A's" J. Business, vol.51, 1978, pp.263-297.
EDUCATION - EFFECT OF * MANPOWER PLANNING - EDUCATION * MANPOWER PLANNING -
QUALIFIED MANPOWER * MANPOWER PLANNING - EARNINGS * COMPARATIVE METHODS -
REGRESSION , TRANSFORMATIONS

YA2953   REEKIE W.D.
"The price elasticity of demand for evening newspapers" Appl. Econ.,
vol.8, 1976, pp.69-79.
APPL - FIRM : SERVICES , MEDIA , NEWSPAPERS * PRICE - EFFECT OF

YA2954   REID D.J.
"The C.B.I. Industrial Trends Survey - a statistical note" Appl. Econ.,
vol.1, 1969, pp.197-203.
SPECTRAL ANALYSIS - APPL : BUSINESS INDICATORS * SURVEYS - BUSINESS *
SPECTRAL ANALYSIS - APPL : SEASONALITY * SPECTRAL ANALYSIS - CROSS : APPL *
EVALUATION - EXPECTATIONS , DATA * EVALUATION - ATTITUDINAL DATA

YA2955   REID F.
"Dummy variables with a transitional phase" Can. J. Econ., vol.10, 1977,
pp.326-329.
REGRESSION - SHIFTING COEFFICIENTS

YA2956   REILLY F.K.
"Evidence regarding a segmented stock market" J. Finance, vol.27, 1972,
pp.607-625.
APPL - SECTOR : FINANCE , STOCK PRICE INDEX * STOCK PRICES - COVARIATION

YA2957   REILLY F.K., JOEHNK M.D.
"The association between market-determined risk measures for bonds and bond
ratings" J. Finance, vol.31, 1976, pp.1387-1403.
INDEX NUMBERS - SECTOR : FINANCE , STOCK PRICES * APPL - FIRM : FINANCE ,
BONDS * USE - CREDIT CONTROL , BOND RATING * STOCK PRICES - BETA * STOCK
PRICES - RISK * APPL - FIRM : FINANCE , STOCK PRICES

YA2958   REINHARDT U.
"A production function for physician services" Rev. Econ. Stats., vol.54,
1972, pp.55-66.
DATA - CROSS SECTION * PRODUCTION FUNCTIONS - SECTOR * HEALTH - MANPOWER ,
PHYSICIANS * MANPOWER PLANNING - SECTOR : HEALTH * APPL - SECTOR :
PRODUCTIVITY

YA2959   REINMUTH J.E., GEURTS M.D.
          "A Bayesian approach to forecasting the effects of atypical situations"
          J. Mktg. Res., vol.9, 1972, pp.292-297.
          APPL - SECTOR : CONSUMER NON DURABLES , FOOD , FROZEN * STRIKE - EFFECT OF *
          JUDGEMENTAL FORECASTS - METHODOLOGY * BAYESIAN - PRIOR INFORMATION * DATA
          ERRORS - OUTLIERS * DATA - ATYPICAL EVENTS * DATA - SMOOTHING
YA2960   REINMUTH J.E., GEURTS M.D.
          "Using spectral analysis for forecast model selection"   Decis. Sci.,
          vol.8, 1977, pp.134-150.
          EVALUATION - EXPONENTIAL SMOOTHING * MODEL SELECTION * APPL - SECTOR :
          SERVICES , TOURISM
YA2961   REINMUTH J.E., HAWKINS D.I.
          "Qualitative variable discriminant analysis and its use in product version
          selection"   Decis. Sci., vol.8, 1977, pp.478-488.
          DISCRIMINANT ANALYSIS - METHODOLOGY * DATA - CATEGORICAL * NEW PRODUCTS -
          IDENTIFYING * APPL - FIRM : CONSUMER NON DURABLES , FOOD
YA2962   REISMAN A., ET AL.
          "Physician supply and surgical demand forecasting: a regional manpower
          study"   Mgmt. Sci. (B), vol.19, 1973, pp.1345-1354.
          MANPOWER PLANNING - SECTOR : HEALTH , SUPPLY * MANPOWER PLANNING - QUALIFIED
          MANPOWER , PROFESSIONAL * LONG TERM FORECASTING * MANPOWER PLANNING -
          REGIONAL * DELPHI * COMPARATIVE METHODS - CAUSAL , TREND CURVES *
          COMPARATIVE METHODS - CAUSAL , JUDGEMENTAL * REGIONAL MODELS - SECTOR :
          HEALTH * HEALTH - HOSPITAL , MANPOWER
YA2963   RELLES D.A., ROGERS W.H.
          "Statisticians are fairly robust estimators of location"   J. Am. Statist.
          Ass., vol.72, 1977, pp.107-111.
          DATA ERRORS - OUTLIERS * ESTIMATION - ROBUST * REGRESSION - OUTLIERS *
          EVALUATION - JUDGEMENTAL FORECASTS * JUDGEMENTAL FORECASTS - SPECIALIST
YA2964   RENAUD B.
          "The economic determinants of internal migration in Korea"   Appl. Econ.,
          vol.9, 1977, pp.307-318.
          APPL - MACRO , SOUTH EAST ASIA * REGIONAL MODELS - MIGRATION
YA2965   RENSHAW E.F.
          "Money, prices and output"   J. Finance, vol.31, 1976, pp.956-959.
          APPL - MACRO : MONEY , SUPPLY * INFLATION - DETERMINANTS * THEORY - MONETARY
          * CAPACITY - EFFECT OF
YA2966   RHOADES S.A.
          "A further evaluation of the effect of diversification on industry profit
          performance"   Rev. Econ. Stats., vol.56, 1974, pp.557-559.
          APPL - SECTOR : FINANCE , PROFITS * DATA - CROSS SECTION * CONCENTRATION -
          EFFECT OF
YA2967   RHOADES S.A.
          "The effect of diversification on industry profit performance in 241
          manufacturing industries"   Rev. Econ. Stats., vol.55, 1973, pp.146-155.
          DATA - CROSS SECTION * APPL - SECTOR : FINANCE , MARGINS * APPL - FIRM TYPE
          : DIVERSIFIED * CONCENTRATION - EFFECT OF
YA2968   RICE P., SMITH V.K.
          "An econometric model of the petroleum industry"   J. Econometrics, vol.6,
          1977, pp.263-287.
          PRICE - EFFECT OF * INCOME - EFFECT OF * APPL - SECTOR : PRODUCTION ,
          PETROLEUM * APPL - SECTOR : RETAILING , PETROL * EX ANTE * PRICE CONTROLS -
          EFFECT OF * SUPPLY - SECTOR : PRODUCTION * PRICE - SECTOR : PRODUCTION *
          EVALUATION - PETROLEUM MODELS * APPL - SECTOR : COMMODITIES , OIL *
          SIMULATION - APPL : SECTOR , PRODUCTION
YA2969   RICE S.J.
          "The information content of fully diluted earnings per share"   Acctg.
          Rev., vol.53, 1978, pp.429-438.
          APPL - FIRM : FINANCE , STOCK PRICES * STOCK PRICES - INFORMATION EFFECT *
          APPL - FIRM : FINANCE , PROFITS , PER SHARE
YA2970   RICHARDS L.E.
          "Detection and incorporation of interactive effects in discriminant
          analysis"   Decis. Sci., vol.6, 1975, pp.508-512.
          DISCRIMINANT ANALYSIS - METHODOLOGY * SPECIFICATION ERROR - TESTS , VARIABLE
          INCLUSION * BASIC
YA2971   RICHARDS L.E.
          "Detection of unexplained joint effect residual through an analysis of
          residuals"   Decis. Sci., vol.4, 1973, pp.40-43.
          RESIDUALS - ANALYSIS OF , SPECIFICATION ERROR * SPECIFICATION ERROR - TESTS
          , VARIABLE INCLUSION * BASIC
YA2972   RICHARDS L.E.
          "Distribution-free significance tests for choosing among prediction
          equations"   Decis. Sci., vol.6, 1975, pp.270-273.
          MODEL SELECTION * NON PARAMETRIC - TEST
YA2973   RICHARDS R.M.
          "Analysts' performance and the accuracy of corporate earnings forecasts"
          J. Business, vol.49, 1976, pp.350-357.
          EVALUATION - JUDGEMENTAL FORECASTS , SPECIALIST * APPL - FIRM : FINANCE ,
          PROFITS * JUDGEMENTAL FORECASTS - PROFITS * COMPARATIVE METHODS -
          AUTOREGRESSIVE , JUDGEMENTAL

YA2974   RICHARDSON D.H., ROHR R.J.
"A program for estimating econometric models ECOMP 3"   Econometrica,
vol.43, 1975, pp.177-178,
ESTIMATION - 2SLS : APPL * ESTIMATION - 3SLS : APPL * COMPUTERISATION -
ESTIMATION , SIMULTANEOUS SYSTEM MODELS , PROGRAMS

YA2975   RICHARDSON D.H., WU D.
"A note on the comparison of ordinary and two stage least squares
estimators"   Econometrica, vol.39, 1971, pp.973-981,
COMPARATIVE METHODS - ESTIMATION : OLS , 2SLS * ADVANCED

YA2976   RICHARDSON J.D.
"On improving the estimate of the export elasticity of substitution"   Can.
J. Econ., vol.5, 1972, pp.349-357,
APPL - MACRO : INTERNATIONAL TRADE , EXPORTS * PRICE - EFFECT OF * DATA -
CROSS SECTION , TIME SERIES * SUBSTITUTE PRODUCTS * DATA ERRORS - EFFECT OF

YA2977   RICHARDSON P.W.
"A short run econometric analysis of the demand and import supply of a
horticultural good: tomatoes"   Appl. Econ., vol.6, 1974, pp.157-169,
TARIFF - EFFECT OF * APPL - SECTOR : CONSUMER NON DURABLES , FOOD * APPL -
SECTOR : AGRICULTURE , VEGETABLES * COMPARATIVE METHODS - ESTIMATION : OLS ,
2SLS * APPL - SECTOR : INTERNATIONAL TRADE , IMPORTS

YA2978   RICHMOND J.
"Estimating the efficiency of production"   Int. Econ. Rev., vol.15, 1974,
pp.515-521,
APPL - SECTOR : EFFICIENCY * PRODUCTION FUNCTIONS - ESTIMATION * ERROR
DISTRIBUTION - GAMMA * PRODUCTION FUNCTIONS - SECTOR

YA2979   RIDER K.L.
"An examination of four housing policies for New York City"   Omega, vol.1,
1973, pp.577-589,
INDUSTRIAL DYNAMICS - APPL , URBAN * REGIONAL MODELS - CITY * POLICY
EVALUATION - SECTOR : CONSTRUCTION

YA2980   RIDLER M., STEVENS G.V.G.
"The trade effects of direct investment" with discussion   J. Finance,
vol.29, 1974, pp.655-676 & 677-682,
APPL - SECTOR : PRODUCTION * COST - SECTOR * EXCHANGE RATE - EFFECT OF *
COST - SCALE ECONOMIES * APPL - FIRM : INVESTMENT * APPL - FIRM TYPE :
MULTINATIONALS * APPL - SECTOR : PRODUCTION , ELECTRICAL MACHINERY * APPL -
MACRO : INTERNATIONAL FINANCE

YA2981   RIEW J.
"Scale economies in public schools"   Rev. Econ. Stats., vol.54, 1972,
p.100,
COST - SECTOR : EDUCATION * APPL - SECTOR : GOVERNMENT , EDUCATION , SCHOOLS
* COST - METHODOLOGY

YA2982   RIMBARA Y., SANTOMERO A.M.
"A study of credit rationing in Japan"   Int. Econ. Rev., vol.17, 1976,
pp.567-580,
APPL - SECTOR : FINANCE , BANKS * INTEREST RATE - INDICATORS * APPL - SECTOR
: FINANCE , BANK , ASSETS

YA2983   RINGSTAD V.
"Some empirical evidence on the decreasing scale elasticity"
Econometrica, vol.42, 1974, pp.87-101,
PRODUCTION FUNCTIONS - SECTOR * COST - SECTOR * PRODUCTION FUNCTIONS - SCALE
RETURNS * COST - SCALE ECONOMIES * PRODUCTION FUNCTIONS - METHODOLOGY *
ESTIMATION - MAXIMUM LIKELIHOOD

YA2984   RIPLEY D.M.
"Systematic elements in the linkage of national stock market indices"
Rev. Econ. Stats., vol.55, 1973, pp.356-361,
APPL - SECTOR : FINANCE , STOCK PRICES * STOCK PRICES - COVARIATION * DATA -
INTERNATIONAL * FACTOR ANALYSIS - APPL * APPL - MACRO : INTERNATIONAL
FINANCE , STOCK PRICES * APPL - MACRO : INTERNATIONAL LINKAGE

YA2985   RIPLEY F.C., SEGAL L.
"Price determination in 395 manufacturing industries"   Rev. Econ. Stats.,
vol.55, 1973, pp.263-271,
PRICE - SECTOR * DATA - CROSS SECTION , TIME SERIES

YA2986   RIPPE R.D., FELDMAN R.L.
"The impact of residential construction on the demand for automobiles; an
omitted variable"   J. Business, vol.49, 1976, pp.389-401,
APPL - SECTOR : CONSUMER DURABLES , CARS * SUBSTITUTE PRODUCTS * APPL -
SECTOR : CONSTRUCTION , RESIDENTIAL * PRICE - EFFECT OF * INCOME - EFFECT OF
* EX ANTE

YA2987   RIPPE R.D., WILKINSON M.
"Forecasting accuracy of the McGraw Hill anticipatory data"   J. Am.
Statist. Ass., vol.69, 1974, pp.849-858,
EXPECTATIONS - DATA * COMPARATIVE METHODS - AUTOREGRESSIVE , CAUSAL * APPL -
MACRO : INVESTMENT * APPL - SECTOR : PRODUCTION * APPL - SECTOR : INVESTMENT
* APPL - SECTOR : CAPACITY * LEAD TIME - EFFECT OF * COMPARATIVE METHODS -
CAUSAL , JUDGEMENTAL * EVALUATION - INVESTMENT MODELS * EVALUATION - SURVEYS
, BUSINESS * COMPARATIVE METHODS - AUTOREGRESSIVE , JUDGEMENTAL

YA2988   RIPPE R.D., WILKINSON M., MORRISON D.
"Industrial market forecasting with anticipation data"   Mgmt. Sci.,
vol.22, 1976, pp.639-651.
EXOGENOUS VARIABLES - PREDICTION OF * EX ANTE * INPUT OUTPUT - FIRM *
COMPARATIVE METHODS - AUTOREGRESSIVE , INPUT OUTPUT * APPL - SECTOR :
PRODUCTION , STEEL * EVALUATION - EXPECTATIONS , DATA

YA2989   RO B.T.
"The disclosure of capitalised lease information and stock prices"   J.
Acctg. Res., vol.16, 1978, pp.315-340.
ACCOUNTING PRACTICE - EFFECT OF * APPL - FIRM : FINANCE , STOCK PRICES *
STOCK PRICES - INFORMATION EFFECT

YA2990   ROBERTS P.
"Models of the future"   Omega, vol.1, 1973, pp.591-601.
APPL - MACRO , WORLD * SIMULATION - APPL : WORLD MODELS * APPL - MACRO :
ENERGY

YA2991   ROBERTS R.B., MADDALA G.S., ENHOLM G.
"Determinants of the requested rate of return and the rate of return granted
in a formal regulatory process"   Bell J. Econ., vol.9, 1978, pp.611-621.
COMPARATIVE METHODS - SIMULTANEOUS SYSTEM , LIMITED DEPENDENT * APPL - FIRM
: UTILITIES , ELECTRICITY * APPL - FIRM : FINANCE , PROFITS * DECISION RULES
- FIRM * USE - FINANCIAL , REGULATION * SIMULTANEOUS SYSTEM - LIMITED
DEPENDENT , TOBIT * DECISION RULES - SECTOR

YA2992   ROBICHEK A.A., COHN R.A.
"The economic determinants of systematic risk" with discussion   J.
Finance, vol.29, 1974, pp.439-447 & 489-492.
APPL - FIRM : FINANCE , STOCK PRICES * STOCK PRICES - BETA , VARIABLE *
STOCK PRICES - BETA , DETERMINANTS

YA2993   ROBICHEK A.A., EAKER M.R.
"Foreign exchange hedging and the Capital Asset Pricing Model" with
discussion   J. Finance, vol.33, 1978, pp.1011-1018 & 1031.
APPL - MACRO : INTERNATIONAL FINANCE , EXCHANGE RATES * USE - FINANCIAL ,
CONTROL * USER - FIRM * DATA - INTERNATIONAL

YA2994   ROBICHEK A.A., HIGGINS R.C., KINSMAN M.
"The effect of leverage on the cost of equity capital of electric utility
firms" with discussion   J. Finance, vol.28, 1973, pp.353-372.
APPL - FIRM : FINANCE , FINANCIAL STRUCTURE , LEVERAGE * APPL - FIRM :
FINANCE , COST OF CAPITAL * APPL - FIRM : UTILITIES , ELECTRICITY

YA2995   ROBINS P.K.
"The effects of state usury ceilings on single family home building"   J.
Finance, vol.29, 1974, pp.227-235.
APPL - SECTOR : CONSTRUCTION , RESIDENTIAL * INCOME - EFFECT OF * DATA -
CROSS SECTION * USE - LOAN REGULATION * INTEREST RATE - EFFECT OF

YA2996   ROBINS P.K., WEST R.W.
"Measurement error in the estimation of home value"   J. Am. Statist. Ass.,
vol.72, 1977, pp.290-294.
APPL - SECTOR : CONSTRUCTION , RESIDENTIAL * PRICE - SECTOR : CONSTRUCTION ,
RESIDENTIAL * FORECASTER - BIAS * REGRESSION - ERRORS IN VARIABLES ,
UNOBSERVABLES * DATA ERRORS - ANALYSIS OF

YA2997   ROBINSON D.
"Divination in ancient China"   Appl. Stats., vol.24, 1975, pp.329-322.
JUDGEMENTAL FORECASTS - OCCULT

YA2998   ROBINSON R.V.F., VICKERMAN R.W.
"The demand for shopping travel: a theoretical and empirical study"   Appl.
Econ., vol.8, 1976, pp.267-281.
TIME - VALUE OF * APPL - SECTOR : RETAILING

YA2999   RODGER A.A.S., RAWLINGS W.J., SIMPSON J.M.
"Forecasting in an Area Gas Board"   Stat'n., vol.20, 1971, pp.3-14.
APPL - SECTOR : UTILITIES , GAS * BASIC

YA3000   ROEMER J.E.
"The effect of sphere of influence and economic distance on the commodity
composition of trade in manufactures"   Rev. Econ. Stats., vol.59, 1977,
pp.318-327.
APPL - MACRO , GERMANY * APPL - MACRO , CANADA * APPL - MACRO :
INTERNATIONAL TRADE * DATA - INTERNATIONAL * DATA - LDC * APPL - MACRO , EEC
* APPL - MACRO , JAPAN * APPL - MACRO , UK

YA3001   ROGALSKI R.J.
"Bond yields: trends or random walks?"   Decis. Sci., vol.6, 1975,
pp.688-699.
APPL - FIRM : FINANCE , BONDS * RANDOM WALK - TEST : APPL * TIME SERIES -
ARIMA : APPL * STOCK PRICES - RUNS

YA3002   ROGALSKI R.J.
"The dependence of prices and volume"   Rev. Econ. Stats., vol.60, 1978,
pp.268-274.
APPL - FIRM : FINANCE , STOCK PRICES * STOCK PRICES - TRADING VOLUME *
CAUSALITY - TEST : APPL

YA3003   ROGALSKI R.J.
"Trading in warrants by mechanical systems"   J. Finance, vol.32, 1977,
pp.87-101.
APPL - FIRM : FINANCE , STOCK PRICES * STOCK PRICES - WARRANTS * STOCK
PRICES - TRADING RULES

YA3004   ROGALSKI R.J., VINSO J.D.
"Stock returns, money supply and the direction of causality"   J. Finance,
vol.32, 1977, pp.1017-1030.
CAUSALITY - TEST : APPL * APPL - MACRO : MONEY , SUPPLY * APPL - SECTOR :
FINANCE , STOCK PRICE INDEX * STOCK PRICES - DETERMINANTS * TIME SERIES -
ARIMA : APPL

YA3005   ROLL R.
"Evidence on the 'growth-optimum' model"   J. Finance, vol.28, 1973,
pp.551-566.
APPL - FIRM : FINANCE , STOCK PRICES * STOCK PRICES - MODELS , COMPARATIVE *
RISK - EFFECT OF

YA3006   ROLL R.
"Interest rates on monetary assets and commodity price index changes" with
discussion   J. Finance, vol.27, 1972, pp.251-277 & 298-302.
INTEREST RATE - EFFECT OF * INFLATION - EXPECTATIONS * INTEREST RATE -
DETERMINANTS * EXPECTATIONS - DATA * EXPECTATIONS - ESTIMATING * INTEREST
RATE - INDICATORS

YA3007   ROLL R.
"Investment diversification and bond maturity"   J. Finance, vol.26, 1971,
pp.51-66.
INTEREST RATE - TERM STRUCTURE * THEORY - EFFICIENT MARKETS

YA3008   ROMEO A.A.
"Interindustry and interfirm differences in the rate of diffusion of an
innovation"   Rev. Econ. Stats., vol.57, 1975, pp.311-319.
DIFFUSION MODEL - APPL * USE - R&D * APPL - FIRM : TECHNOLOGY * APPL -
SECTOR : TECHNOLOGY * NEW PRODUCTS - DIFFUSION MODELS * APPL - SECTOR :
PRODUCTION , MACHINE TOOLS * APPL - FIRM : PRODUCTION

YA3009   ROMEO A.A.
"The rate of imitation of a capital-embodied process innovation"
Economica, vol.44, 1977, pp.63-69.
APPL - FIRM : PRODUCTION , MACHINE TOOLS * APPL - FIRM : TECHNOLOGY *
DIFFUSION MODEL * REGRESSION - SHIFTING COEFFICIENTS

YA3010   RONINGEN V.O.
"The effect of exchange rate, payments, and trade restrictions on the trade
between OECD countries, 1967-1973"   Rev. Econ. Stats., vol.60, 1978,
pp.471-475.
APPL - MACRO , OECD * APPL - MACRO : INTERNATIONAL TRADE * EXCHANGE RATE -
EFFECT OF * STABILITY OF COEFFICIENTS - REGRESSION : APPL

YA3011   ROODMAN G.M.
"A procedure for optimal stepwise MSAE regression analysis"   Ops. Res.,
vol.22, 1974, pp.393-399.
REGRESSION - STEPWISE - ESTIMATION - MSAE * COMPUTERISATION - ESTIMATION ,
REGRESSION MODELS , PROGRAMS

YA3012   ROSE D.E.
"Forecasting aggregates of independent ARIMA processes"   J. Econometrics,
vol.5, 1977, pp.323-345.
TIME SERIES - ARIMA : THEORY * DATA - AGGREGATION 'BIAS' * TIME SERIES -
ARIMA : FORECASTING

YA3013   ROSE P.S.
"Policy variables and the components of private spending in the US economy"
Bus. Econ., vol.7:3, 1972, pp.41-48.
APPL - MACRO : INVESTMENT * APPL - MACRO : INVENTORIES * POLICY EVALUATION -
MACRO : FISCAL , MONETARY * DISTRIBUTED LAG - APPL , MONEY * DISTRIBUTED LAG
- ALMON : APPL * APPL - MACRO : CONSUMPTION * APPL - SECTOR : CONSUMER NON
CURABLES * APPL - SECTOR : CONSUMER DURABLES * APPL - SECTOR : CONSTRUCTION

YA3014   ROSE P.S., HUNT L.H.
"The relative importance of monetary and fiscal variables in determining
price level movements: a note"   J. Finance, vol.26, 1971, pp.31-37.
INFLATION - DETERMINANTS * POLICY EVALUATION - MACRO : FISCAL , MONETARY

YA3015   ROSEFIELDE S., KNOX LOVELL C.A.
"The impact of adjusted factor cost valuation on the CES interpretation of
postwar Soviet economic growth"   Economica, vol.44, 1977, pp.381-392.
APPL - MACRO , USSR * PRODUCTION FUNCTIONS - SECTOR

YA3016   ROSEN H.3.
"Tax illusion and the labor supply of married women"   Rev. Econ. Stats.,
vol.53, 1976, pp.167-172
MANPOWER PLANNING - LABOUR PARTICIPATION , FEMALE * TAX - EFFECT OF

YA3017   ROSEN H.S.
"Taxes in a labor supply model with joint wage hours determination"
Econometrica, vol.44, 1976, pp.485-507.
INCOME - EFFECT OF * APPL - MACRO : EARNINGS * MANPOWER PLANNING - MACRO ,
SUPPLY * COMPARATIVE METHODS - REGRESSION , LIMITED DEPENDENT * TAX - EFFECT
OF * MANPOWER PLANNING - LABOUR PARTICIPATION , FEMALE

YA3018   ROSEN H.S., QUANDT R.E.
"Estimation of a disequilibrium aggregate labour market"   Rev. Econ.
Stats., vol.60, 1978, pp.371-379.
APPL - MACRO : EMPLOYMENT * SIMULTANEOUS SYSTEM - DISEQUILIBRIUM : APPL

YA3019   ROSEN S., NADIRI M.I.
         "A disequilibrium model of demand for factors of production"   Am. Econ.
         Assn. Proc., 1974, pp.264-270.
         PRODUCTION FUNCTIONS - SECTOR * APPL - SECTOR : INVENTORIES * APPL - SECTOR
         : EMPLOYMENT * APPL - SECTOR : CAPACITY UTILISATION * APPL - SECTOR :
         INVESTMENT * APPL - SECTOR : CONSUMER DURABLES * APPL - SECTOR : CONSUMER
         NON DURABLES
YA3020   ROSEN S., WELCH F.
         "Labour supply and income redistribution"   Rev. Econ. Stats., vol.53,
         1971, pp.278-282.
         DATA - CROSS SECTION * MANPOWER PLANNING - MACRO , SUPPLY * APPL - SECTOR :
         SOCIAL , POVERTY * TAX - EFFECT OF * POLICY EVALUATION - MACRO : WELFARE
YA3021   ROSENBERG B.
         "A survey of stochastic parameter regression"   Anns. Econ. Soc. Meas.,
         vol.2, 1973, pp.381-397.
         STABILITY OF COEFFICIENTS - REVIEW * REGRESSION - RANDOM COEFFICIENTS *
         BIBLIOGRAPHY - REGRESSION , RANDOM COEFFICIENTS * ESTIMATION - CROSS SECTION
         , TIME SERIES * REGRESSION - PIECEWISE * ESTIMATION - KALMAN FILTER
YA3022   ROSENBERG B.
         "Estimation error covariance in regression with sequentially varying
         parameters"   Anns. Econ. Soc. Meas., vol.6, 1977, pp.457-462.
         REGRESSION - STATE SPACE * ESTIMATION - KALMAN FILTER * ADVANCED
YA3023   ROSENBERG B.
         "Random coefficient models: the analysis of a cross section of time series
         by stochastically convergent parameter regression"   Anns. Econ. Soc.
         Meas., vol2, 1973, pp.399-428.
         STABILITY OF COEFFICIENTS - REGRESSION * ESTIMATION - CROSS SECTION , TIME
         SERIES * ESTIMATION - MAXIMUM LIKELIHOOD * REGRESSION - RANDOM COEFFICIENTS
         * BAYESIAN - ESTIMATION : REGRESSION , RANDOM COEFFICIENTS * DATA -
         SIMULATION * COMPARATIVE METHODS - ESTIMATION : REGRESSION , RANDOM
         COEFFICIENTS * ADVANCED
YA3024   ROSENBERG B., HOUGLET M.
         "Error rates in CRSP and COMPUSTAT data bases and their implications"   J.
         Finance, vol.29, 1974, pp.1303-1310.
         DATA ERRORS - EFFECT OF * DATA ERRORS - ESTIMATION OF * APPL - FIRM :
         FINANCE , STOCK PRICES * STOCK PRICES - DATA ERRORS
YA3025   ROSENBLATT H.M.
         "Spectral evaluation of BLS and census revised seasonal adjustment
         procedures"   J. Am. Statist. Ass., vol.63, 1968, pp.472-501.
         SPECTRAL ANALYSIS - APPL : SEASONALITY * COMPARATIVE METHODS - SEASONALITY *
         SEASONALITY - ESTIMATION , CENSUS
YA3026   ROSENFELD G.
         "Identification of time series with infinite variance"   Appl. Stats.,
         vol.25, 1976, pp.147-153.
         TIME SERIES - ARIMA : IDENTIFICATION * ERROR DISTRIBUTION - STABLE * DATA -
         SIMULATION * DATA ERRORS - OUTLIERS
YA3027   ROSENZWEIG M.R.
         "Rural wages, labour supply, and land reform: a theoretical and empirical
         analysis"   Am. Econ. Rev., vol.68, 1978, pp.847-861.
         APPL - SECTOR : AGRICULTURE * APPL - SECTOR : EARNINGS * POLICY EVALUATION -
         SECTOR : AGRICULTURE * MANPOWER PLANNING - LABOUR FORCE COMPOSITION *
         MANPOWER PLANNING - EARNINGS * APPL - MACRO , INDIA
YA3028   ROSETT R.N., NELSON F.D.
         "Estimation of the two-limit probit regression model"   Econometrica,
         vol.43, 1975, pp.141-146.
         REGRESSION - LIMITED DEPENDENT , PROBIT * DATA - SIMULATION
YA3029   ROSHWALB I.
         "A consideration of probability estimates provided by respondent"   J.
         Mktg. Res., vol.12, 1975, pp.100-103.
         JUDGEMENTAL FORECASTS - METHODOLOGY * SURVEYS - CONSUMER : APPL * SURVEYS -
         METHODOLOGY * EVALUATION - EXPECTATIONS , DATA * JUDGEMENTAL FORECASTS -
         UNCERTAINTY
YA3030   ROSKAMP K.W.
         "Labor productivity and the elasticity of factor substitution in west German
         industries"   Rev. Econ. Stats., vol.59, 1977, pp.366-371.
         APPL - SECTOR : PRODUCTIVITY * PRODUCTION FUNCTIONS - SUBSTITUTION *
         PRODUCTION FUNCTIONS - SECTOR
YA3031   ROSSE J.N.
         "Estimating cost function parameters without using cost data: illustrated
         methodology"   Econometrica, vol.38, 1970, pp.256-275.
         DATA - CROSS SECTION * APPL - SECTOR : SERVICES , MEDIA , NEWSPAPERS * COST
         - SECTOR : SERVICES * COMPARATIVE METHODS - ESTIMATION : SIMULTANEOUS SYSTEM
         * COMPARATIVE METHODS - ESTIMATION : OLS , 2SLS
YA3032   ROTHE J.T.
         "Effectiveness of sales forecasting methods"   Ind. Mktg. Mgmt., vol.7,
         1978, pp.114-118.
         FORECASTING - USAGE * FORECASTING - PRACTICE * EVALUATION - SALES FORECASTS
         * BASIC

YA3033   ROTHKOPF M.H.
      "An economic model of world energy: 1900-2020"   Long Range Planning,
      vol.6:2, 1973, pp.43-51.
      APPL - MACRO : ENERGY , SOURCES * BASIC

YA3034   ROWE R.D.
      "The effects of aggregation over time on t-ratios and R squared's"   Int.
      Econ. Rev., vol.17, 1976, pp.751-757.
      REGRESSION - AGGREGATION * DATA - AGGREGATION OVER TIME * REGRESSION -
      SUMMARY STATISTICS * REGRESSION - HYPOTHESIS TESTS

YA3035   ROWLEY J.C.R.
      "Fixed capital formation in the British economy, 1956-1965"   Economica,
      vol.39, 1972, pp.177-189.
      APPL - MACRO : INVESTMENT * APPL - MACRO , UK

YA3036   ROWLEY J.C.R.
      "Investment and neoclassical production functions"   Can. J. Econ., vol.5,
      1972, pp.430-435.
      APPL - MACRO : INVESTMENT * PRODUCTION FUNCTIONS - THEORY

YA3037   ROWLEY J.C.R., WILTON D.A.
      "Empirical foundations for the Canadian Phillips curve"   Can. J. Econ.,
      vol.7, 1974, pp.240-259.
      INFLATION - PHILLIPS CURVE * APPL - MACRO : EARNINGS * DATA - SPECIFICATION
      OF VARIABLES * APPL - MACRO , CANADA * ERROR SPECIFICATION - AUTOCORRELATED
      * COMPARATIVE METHODS - REGRESSION , ERROR SPECIFICATION * STABILITY OF
      COEFFICIENTS - REGRESSION : APPL * DATA ERRORS - EFFECT OF

YA3038   ROWLEY J.C.R., WILTON D.A.
      "Quarterly models of wage determination: some new efficient estimates"
      Am. Econ. Rev., vol.63, 1973, pp.380-389.
      MACRO MODEL - CANADA , RDX1 * COMPARATIVE METHODS - ESTIMATION : OLS , GLS *
      EVALUATION - EARNINGS MODELS * APPL - MACRO : EARNINGS * APPL - MACRO ,
      CANADA * BIBLIOGRAPHY - EARNINGS

YA3039   ROWTHORN R.E.
      "What remains of Kaldor's Law"   Econ. J., vol.85, 1975, pp.10-19.
      APPL - MACRO : GROWTH * APPL - MACRO : PRODUCTIVITY * DATA ERRORS - OUTLIERS
      * DATA ERRORS - EFFECT OF

YA3040   ROY S.K., IRELAND M.E.
      "An econometric analysis of the sorghum market"   Am. J. Ag. Econ., vol.57,
      1975, pp.513-516.
      COMPARATIVE METHODS - ESTIMATION : SIMULTANEOUS SYSTEM , 2SLS , 3SLS * APPL
      - SECTOR : AGRICULTURE , FEED * TURNING POINT FORECASTS - APPL

YA3041   RUBENSTEIN A.H., SHRODER H.
      "Managerial differences in assessing probabilities of technical success for
      R & D projects"   Mgmt. Sci., vol.24, 1977, pp.137-148.
      JUDGEMENTAL FORECASTS - DETERMINANTS * FORECASTER BEHAVIOUR * FORECASTER -
      BIAS * JUDGEMENTAL FORECASTS - BIAS * APPL - FIRM : R & D * EVALUATION -
      JUDGEMENTAL FORECASTS , R & D

YA3042   RUGG D.
      "The choice of journey destination: a theoretical and empirical analysis"
      Rev. Econ. Stats., vol.55, 1973, pp.64-72.
      APPL - SECTOR : TRANSPORT , AIR * APPL - SECTOR : SERVICES , TOURISM * PRICE
      - EFFECT OF * INCOME - EFFECT OF

YA3043   RUGGINS L.F.
      "A short term forecasting model for R & D expenses"   Omega, vol.1, 1973,
      pp.483-491
      USE - R&D * APPL - FIRM : R & D * COST - FIRM : R & D * CONFIDENCE INTERVAL
      - EX ANTE : APPL

YA3044   RUGGLES N., RUGGLES R., WOLFF E.
      "Merging microdata: rationale, practice and testing"   Anns. Econ. Soc.
      Meas., vol.6, 1977, pp.407-428.
      DATA - HANDLING

YA3045   RULAND W.
      "The accuracy of forecasts by management and by financial analysts"
      Acctg. Rev., vol.53, 1978, pp.439-447.
      EVALUATION - JUDGEMENTAL FORECASTS , PROFITS PER SHARE * APPL - FIRM :
      FINANCE , PROFITS , PER SHARE * COMPARATIVE METHODS - JUDGEMENTAL FORECASTS
      , TREND CURVES * EVALUATION - JUDGEMENTAL FORECASTS , SPECIALIST * BASIC

YA3046   RUSH D.F., MELICHER R.W.
      "An empirical examination of factors which influence warrant prices"   J.
      Finance, vol.29, 1974, pp.1449-1466.
      APPL - FIRM : FINANCE , WARRANTS * STOCK PRICES - EFFECT OF * RISK - EFFECT
      OF

YA3047   RUSSELL A.H.
      "Estimation of beta in the Sharpe/Tobin capital asset evaluation model"
      Stat'n., vol.23, 1974, pp.17-30.
      APPL - FIRM : FINANCE * STOCK PRICES * STOCK PRICES - BETA * STOCK PRICES -
      MODELS , CAPM * DATA - AGGREGATION OVER TIME

YA3048   RYANS A.B.
      "Estimating consumer preferences for a new durable brand in an established
      product class"   J. Mktg. Res., vol.11, 1974, pp.434-443.
      NEW PRODUCTS - NEW BRAND * EX ANTE * APPL - SECTOR : CONSUMER DURABLES ,
      APPLIANCES , ELECTRICAL * MULTIDIMENSIONAL SCALING * CLUSTER ANALYSIS - APPL
      * BRAND CHOICE - APPL

YA3049   SABAVALA D.J., MORRISON D.G.
          "A model of TV show loyalty"   J. Advtg. Res., vol.17:6, 1977, pp.35-43.
          APPL - FIRM : SERVICES , MEDIA , TV * USE - MEDIA PLANNING * REPEAT BUYING *
          PROBABILITY MODELS - BETA
YA3050   SABOIA J.L.M.
          "Autoregressive integrated moving average (ARIMA) models for birth
          forecasting"   J. Am. Statist. Ass., vol.72, 1977, pp.264-270.
          POPULATION - FERTILITY * TIME SERIES - ARIMA : THEORY
YA3051   SADAN E., TROPP Z.
          "Consumption function analysis in a communal household: cross section and
          time series"   Rev. Econ. Stats., vol.55, 1973, pp.475-481.
          DATA - CROSS SECTION , TIME SERIES * APPL - MACRO : CONSUMPTION * APPL -
          MACRO , ISRAEL
YA3052   SAMIN I., HENDRICK D.J.
          "On strike durations and a measure of termination"   Appl. Stats., vol.27,
          1978, pp.319-324.
          PROBABILITY MODELS - GAMMA , COMPOUND * APPL - SECTOR : SOCIAL , STRIKES
YA3053   SAHLING L.
          "Price behaviour in US manufacturing: an empirical analysis of the speed of
          adjustment"   Am. Econ. Rev., vol.67, 1977, pp.911-925.
          THEORY - PRICING * PRICE - MACRO * EVALUATION - PRICING MODELS
YA3054   SAITO M.
          "An interindustry study of price formation"   Rev. Econ. Stats., vol.53,
          1971, pp.11-25.
          INPUT OUTPUT - MACRO , JAPAN * PRODUCTION FUNCTIONS - SECTOR * APPL - MACRO
          : CONSUMER DEMAND * PRICE - SECTOR * APPL - SECTOR : INTERNATIONAL TRADE ,
          IMPORTS * PRICE - EFFECT OF * APPL - SECTOR : EARNINGS
YA3055   SALAMON G.L., ET AL.
          "Additional evidence on the time series properties of reported earnings per
          share: comments"   J. Finance, vol.32, 1977, pp.1795-1808.
          APPL - FIRM : FINANCE , PROFITS , PER SHARE * EXPONENTIAL SMOOTHING - APPL *
          ACCOUNTING PRACTICE - EFFECT OF * EX ANTE * EVALUATION - EXPONENTIAL
          SMOOTHING
YA3056   SALANT W.S., HELLER H.R.
          "Projecting, forecasting, and hindcasting: comments on 'the US balance of
          payments in 1968'"   J. Money, Credit, Banking, vol.3, 1971, pp.281-292.
          EVALUATION - MACRO FORECASTS * EX ANTE * APPL - MACRO : INTERNATIONAL TRADE
YA3057   SALEM B.K.
          "Savings deposits forecasts: a critical planning tool for financial
          institutions"   Bus. Econ., vol.13:1, 1978, pp.25-30.
          DISTRIBUTED LAG - RATIONAL POLYNOMIAL : APPL * APPL - MACRO : SAVINGS
YA3058   SALES P.
          "The validity of the Markov chain model for a class of the civil service"
          Stat'n., vol.20, 1971, pp.85-110.
          MARKOV MODELS - APPL : MANPOWER * MANPOWER PLANNING - SECTOR : GOVERNMENT ,
          CENTRAL * APPL - SECTOR : GOVERNMENT , CENTRAL * EX ANTE
YA3059   SALKEVER D.S.
          "The use of dummy variables to compute predictions, prediction errors, and
          confidence intervals"   J. Econometrics, vol.4, 1976, pp.393-397.
          CONFIDENCE INTERVAL - PREDICTIONS : REGRESSION * REGRESSION - COVARIANCE
          MODEL * COMPUTERISATION - ESTIMATION , REGRESSION MODELS * COMPUTERISATION -
          FORECASTING
YA3060   SAMETZ A.W., KAVESH R.A., PAPADOPOULOUS D.
          "The financial environment and the structure of capital markets in 1985"
          Bus. Econ., vol.10:1, 1975, pp.34-46.
          APPL - MACRO : MONEY * LONG TERM FORECASTING * APPL - MACRO : FLOW OF FUNDS
          * BASIC
YA3061   SAN MIGUEL J.G.
          "The reliability of R&D data in COMPUSTAT and 10-K reports"   Acctg. Rev.,
          vol.52, 1977, pp.638-641.
          APPL - FIRM : R & D * DATA ERRORS - ESTIMATION OF
YA3062   SANDELL S.H.
          "Women and the economics of family migration"   Rev. Econ. Stats., vol.59,
          1977, pp.406-414.
          MANPOWER PLANNING - MIGRATION * EDUCATION - EFFECT OF
YA3063   SANDOR R.L., SOSIN H.B.
          "The determinants of mortgage risk premiums: a case study of the portfolio
          of a savings and loan association"   J. Business, vol.48, 1975, pp.27-38.
          APPL - SECTOR : FINANCE , MORTGAGES * APPL - SECTOR : FINANCE , BUILDING
          SOCIETIES * INTEREST RATE - DETERMINANTS
YA3064   SANKAR U.
          "Investment behaviour in the US electric utility industry, 1949-1968"
          Bell J. Econ., vol. 3, 1972, pp.645-664.
          APPL - SECTOR : UTILITIES , ELECTRICITY * APPL - SECTOR : INVESTMENT *
          DISTRIBUTED LAG - APPL , INVESTMENT * DISTRIBUTED LAG - APPL , OUTPUT
YA3065   SANKAR U.
          "Investment behaviour in the US telephone industry- 1949 to 1968"   Bell J.
          Econ., vol.4, 1973, pp.665-678.
          APPL - SECTOR : INVESTMENT * APPL - SECTOR : UTILITIES , TELEPHONE *
          DISTRIBUTED LAG - APPL , OUTPUT * DISTRIBUTED LAG - POLYNOMIAL : APPL

YA3066   SANTHANAM K.V., PATIL R.H.
          "A study of the production structure of the Indian economy: an international
          comparison"   Econometrica, vol.40, 1972, pp.159-176.
          DATA - INTERNATIONAL * INPUT OUTPUT - MACRO , INDIA

YA3067   SANTOMERO A.M.
          "The error-learning hypothesis and the term structure of interest rates in
          eurodollars"   J. Finance, vol.30, 1975, pp.773-783.
          INTEREST RATE - TERM STRUCTURE * INTEREST RATE - EXPECTATIONS * APPL - MACRO
          : INTERNATIONAL FINANCE * INTEREST RATE - LIQUIDITY PREFERENCE

YA3068   SARGAN J.D.
          "Some discrete approximations to continuous time stochastic models"   R.
          Statist. Soc. (B), vol.36, 1974, pp.74-90.
          DIFFERENTIAL EQUATIONS * SIMULTANEOUS SYSTEM - CONTINUOUS * ADVANCED

YA3069   SARGEN N.P.
          "Exchange rate flexibility and demand for money" with discussion   J.
          Finance, vol.32, 1977, pp.531-551.
          APPL - MACRO , UK * INTEREST RATE - EFFECT OF * APPL - MACRO : EXCHANGE
          RATES * APPL - MACRO : MONEY , SUPPLY * APPL - MACRO , CANADA * APPL - MACRO
          , GERMANY

YA3070   SARGENT T.J.
          "Rational expectations, the real rate of interest and the natural rate of
          unemployment" with discussion   Brookings Paps, Econ, Activity, 1973,
          pp.429-480.
          INTEREST RATE - INDICATORS * APPL - MACRO : UNEMPLOYMENT * DISTRIBUTED LAG -
          APPL , EXPECTATIONS HYPOTHESES * DISTRIBUTED LAG - RATIONAL POLYNOMIAL *
          COMPARATIVE METHODS - ARIMA , DISTRIBUTED LAG * DECISION RULES - FEEDBACK *
          THEORY - EXPECTATIONS

YA3071   SARGENT T.J.
          "Some evidence on the small sample properties of distributed lag estimators
          in the presence of autocorrelated disturbances"   Rev, Econ, Stats,,
          vol.50, 1968, pp.87-95.
          DISTRIBUTED LAG - ERROR SPECIFICATION * COMPARATIVE METHODS - ESTIMATION :
          DISTRIBUTED LAG * REGRESSION - ERRORS IN VARIABLES * DATA - SIMULATION *
          COMPARATIVE METHODS - ESTIMATION : REGRESSION , ERROR SPECIFICATION *
          COMPARATIVE METHODS - ESTIMATION : OLS , 2SLS * COMPARATIVE METHODS -
          ESTIMATION : OLS , 3PLS * ESTIMATION - OLS , ITERATIVE * ESTIMATION -
          MAXIMUM LIKELIHOOD : APPL * ERROR SPECIFICATION - AUTOCORRELATED *
          AUTOCORRELATION - EFFECT OF

YA3072   SARGENT T.J.
          "The demand for money during hyperinflations under rational expectations"
          Int. Econ. Rev., vol.18, 1977, pp.59-82.
          INFLATION - RAPID * APPL - MACRO : MONEY , DEMAND * DATA - INTERNATIONAL *
          INFLATION - EFFECT OF * THEORY - EXPECTATIONS * INFLATION - EXPECTATIONS *
          DISTRIBUTED LAG - SIMULTANEOUS SYSTEM * ESTIMATION - MAXIMUM LIKELIHOOD *
          ADVANCED

YA3073   SARGENT T.J.
          "The fundamental determinants of the interest rate: a comment"   Rev, Econ,
          Stats., vol.55, 1973, pp.391-393.
          INTEREST RATE - DETERMINANTS * THEORY - LIQUIDITY PREFERENCE * APPL - MACRO
          : MONEY

YA3074   SARGENT T.J.
          "What do regressions of interest on inflation show?"   Anns, Econ, Soc,
          Meas., vol.2, 1973, pp.289-301.
          INFLATION - EXPECTATIONS * INFLATION - EFFECT OF * THEORY - EXPECTATIONS *
          DISTRIBUTED LAG - RATIONAL POLYNOMIAL * DISTRIBUTED LAG - IDENTIFICATION *
          INTEREST RATE - INDICATORS * ADVANCED

YA3075   SARGENT T.J., WALLACE N.
          "Rational expectations and the dynamics of hyperinflation"   Int, Econ,
          Rev., vol.14, 1973, pp.328-350.
          DISTRIBUTED LAG - EXPECTATIONS HYPOTHESES * INFLATION - RAPID * INFLATION -
          EXPECTATIONS * APPL - MACRO : MONEY * DISTRIBUTED LAG - APPL , MONEY *
          THEORY - EXPECTATIONS * ADVANCED

YA3076.   SARNAT M.
          "A note on the prediction of portfolio performance from ex ante data"   J,
          Finance, vol.27, 1972, pp.903-906.
          EVALUATION - PORTFOLIO SELECTION PROCEDURES * EX ANTE * USE - PORTFOLIO
          SELECTION

YA3077   SARRIS A.H.
          "Kalman filter models: a Bayesian approach to estimation of time varying
          regression coefficients"   Anns, Econ, Soc, Meas,, vol.2, 1973, pp.501-523
          & vol.6, 1978, pp.652-653.
          ESTIMATION - KALMAN FILTER * BAYESIAN - ESTIMATION : REGRESSION , STATE
          SPACE * ADVANCED

YA3078   SASAKI K.
          "An empirical analysis of linear aggregation problems"   J, Econometrics,
          vol.7, 1978, pp.313-331.
          DATA - AGGREGATION 'BIAS' * APPL - FIRM : INVESTMENT * APPL - SECTOR :
          INVESTMENT * COMPARATIVE METHODS - DATA : AGGREGATE , DISAGGREGATE

YA3079   SATO K.
"A note on factor substitutions and efficiency"   Rev. Econ. Stats.,
vol.59, 1977, pp.360-366.
DATA - LDC * PRODUCTION FUNCTIONS - METHODOLOGY * DATA - INTERNATIONAL *
PRODUCTION FUNCTIONS - SUBSTITUTION * PRODUCTION FUNCTIONS - SECTOR

YA3080   SATO K.
"The demand function for industrial exports: a cross-country analysis"
Rev. Econ. Stats., vol.59, 1977, pp.456-464.
APPL - MACRO : INTERNATIONAL TRADE , EXPORTS * DATA - INTERNATIONAL *
CAPACITY - EFFECT OF

YA3081   SATO R.
"Homothetic and non-homothetic CES production functions"   Am. Econ. Rev.,
vol.67, 1977, pp.559-569.
PRODUCTION FUNCTIONS - THEORY * PRODUCTION FUNCTIONS - SECTOR

YA3082   SAVAGE D.
"Interpreting the investment intentions data"   Nat. Inst. Econ. Rev.,
no.73, 1975, pp.41-46.
EVALUATION - EXPECTATIONS , DATA * EVALUATION - SURVEYS , BUSINESS * APPL -
MACRO : INVESTMENT * APPL - MACRO , UK

YA3083   SAVAGE D.
"The channels of monetary influence: a survey of the empirical evidence"
Nat. Inst. Econ. Rev., no.83, 1978, pp.73-89.
INTEREST RATE - EFFECT OF * EVALUATION - INVESTMENT MODELS * APPL - MACRO :
INVESTMENT * APPL - MACRO : CONSUMPTION * APPL - SECTOR : FINANCE , CONSUMER
CREDIT * APPL - MACRO : INVENTORIES * APPL - MACRO , UK

YA3084   SAVIN N.E.
"Conflict among testing procedures in a linear regression model with
autoregressive disturbances"   Econometrica, vol.44, 1976, pp.1303-1315.
ERROR SPECIFICATION - AUTOCORRELATED * SPECIFICATION ERROR - TESTS ,
CONSTRAINTS * REGRESSION - CONSTRAINED * APPL - MACRO : CONSUMPTION *
COMPARATIVE METHODS - TESTS , MODEL CONSTRAINTS

YA3085   SAVIN N.E.
"The Koopmans and Hood test: a comment"   Econometrica, vol.43, 1975,
pp.521-522.
SPECIFICATION ERROR - TESTS , VARIABLE INCLUSION * SPECIFICATION ERROR -
TESTS , IDENTIFICATION

YA3086   SAVIN N.E., WHITE K.J.
"Estimation and testing for functional form and autocorrelation"   J.
Econometrics, vol.8, 1978, pp.1-12.
ERROR SPECIFICATION - AUTOCORRELATED * REGRESSION - TRANSFORMATIONS , BOX
COX * REGRESSION - HYPOTHESIS TESTS * APP - MACRO : MONEY , DEMAND *
COMPARATIVE METHODS - REGRESSION , TRANSFORMATIONS * COMPARATIVE METHODS -
REGRESSION , ERROR SPECIFICATION

YA3087   SAVIN N.E., WHITE K.J.
"Testing for correlation with missing observations"   Econometrica, vol.46,
1978, pp.59-67.
DATA ERRORS - MISSING OBSERVATIONS * AUTOCORRELATION - TEST

YA3088   SAVIN N.E., WHITE K.J.
"The Durbin-Watson test for serial correlation with extreme sample sizes or
many regressors"   Econometrica, vol.45, 1977, pp.1989-1996.
AUTOCORRELATION - TEST

YA3089   SAWA T.
"Information criteria for discriminating among alternative regression
models"   Econometrica, vol.46, 1978, pp.1273-1291.
REGRESSION - MODEL CHOICE * LOSS FUNCTION - AKAIKE'S INFORMATION CRITERION *
BAYESIAN - MODEL SELECTION * ADVANCED

YA3090   SAWA T.
"The mean square error of a combined estimator and numerical comparison with
the TSLS estimator"   J. Econometrics, vol.1, 1973, pp.115-132.
SIMULTANEOUS SYSTEM - ESTIMATION * EVALUATION - ESTIMATION : 2SLS *
COMPARATIVE METHODS - ESTIMATION : SIMULTANEOUS SYSTEM * COMPARATIVE METHODS
- ESTIMATION : OLS , 2SLS

YA3091   SAWA T., HIROMATSU T.
"Minimax regret significance points for a preliminary test in regression
analysis"   Econometrica, vol.41, 1973, pp.1093-1101.
REGRESSION - HYPOTHESIS TESTS * ESTIMATION - PRE TEST * MULTICOLLINEARITY -
EFFECT OF * ADVANCED

YA3092   SAXONHOUSE G.R.
"Estimated parameters as dependent variables"   Am. Econ. Rev., vol.66,
1976, pp.178-183.
REGRESSION - STATE SPACE * COST - METHODOLOGY

YA3093   SCANLON W.J., STRAUSS R.P.
"The geographical heterogeneity of public expenditure functions"   Rev.
Econ. Stats., vol.54, 1972, pp.191-194.
APPL - SECTOR : GOVERNMENT , LOCAL * APPL - SECTOR : GOVERNMENT , LOCAL ,
EXPENDITURE * REGIONAL MODELS - SECTOR : GOVERNMENT , EXPENDITURE * PUBLIC
EXPENDITURE - EFFECT OF

YA3094   SCAPERLANDA A., REILING E., D'ARGE R.C.
          "A comment on a note on customs unions and direct foreign investment"
          Econ. J., vol81, 1971, pp.355-360.
          APPL - MACRO : INTERNATIONAL FINANCE * APPL - MACRO : INVESTMENT ,
          INTERNATIONAL * APPL - MACRO , EEC
YA3095   SCAPERLANDA A.E., MAUER L.J.
          "The determinants of US direct investments in the EEC: errata"   Am. Econ.
          Rev., vol.61, 1971, pp.509-510.
          APPL - MACRO : INVESTMENT , INTERNATIONAL * APPL - MACRO , EEC
YA3096   SCARTH W.M.
          "The financing of stabilisation policies: evidence for the Canadian economy"
          Can. J. Econ., vol.6, 1973, pp.301-318.
          MACRO MODEL - CANADA * POLICY EVALUATION - MACRO : MONETARY * POLICY
          EVALUATION - MACRO : STABILISATION
YA3097   SCHENDEL D., PATTON G.R.
          "A simultaneous equation model of corporate strategy"   Mgmt. Sci., vol.24,
          1978, pp.1611-1621.
          APPL - FIRM : CONSUMER NON DURABLES , LIQUOR * MARKET SHARE - EFFECT OF *
          APPL - FIRM : FINANCE , PROFITS * APPL - FIRM : EFFICIENCY * MARKET SHARE -
          SECTOR : CONSUMER NON DURABLES * ADVERTISING - EFFECT OF * CONCENTRATION -
          EFFECT OF
YA3098   SCHILBRED C.M.
          "The market price of risk"   Rev. Econ. Studies, vol.40, 1973, pp.283-292.
          APPL - SECTOR : FINANCE , BONDS * STOCK PRICES - RISK * RISK - EFFECT OF
YA3099   SCHIM VAN DER LOEFF S., HARKEMA R.
          "Three models of firm behaviour: theory and estimation, with an application
          to the Dutch manufacturing sector"   Rev. Econ. Stats., vol.53, 1976,
          pp.13-21.
          APPL - SECTOR : FINANCE , PROFITS * THEORY - FIRM
YA3100   SCHINK G.R.
          "The Brookings quarterly model as an aid to longer term economic policy
          analysis"   Int. Econ. Rev., vol.16, 1975, pp.39-53.
          MACRO MODEL - BROOKINGS * LONG TERM FORECASTING * TAX - EFFECT OF * PUBLIC
          EXPENDITURE - EFFECT OF
YA3101   SCHLARBAUM G.G., LEWELLEN W.G., LEASE R.C.
          "The common-stock-portfolio performance record of individual investors:
          1964-1970"   J. Finance, vol.33, 1978, pp.429-441.
          APPL - FIRM : FINANCE , STOCK PRICES * STOCK PRICES - INSTITUTIONAL
          INVESTMENT * USE - PORTFOLIO SELECTION
YA3102   SCHMALENSEE R.
          "An experimental study of expectation formation"   Econometrica, vol.44,
          1976, pp.17-41.
          APPL - SECTOR : COMMODITIES , GRAIN * JUDGEMENTAL FORECASTS - DETERMINANTS *
          JUDGEMENTAL FORECASTS - UNCERTAINTY * EXPECTATIONS - ESTIMATING
YA3103   SCHMALENSEE R.
          "Using the H-index of concentration with published data"   Rev. Econ.
          Stats., vol.59, 1977, pp.186-193.
          CONCENTRATION - MEASURING * PROXY VARIABLES * DATA - SPECIFICATION OF
          VARIABLES
YA3104   SCHMALENSEE R., TRIPPI R.R.
          "Common stock volatility expectations implied by options premia"   J.
          Finance, vol.33, 1978, pp.129-147.
          APPL - FIRM : FINANCE , OPTIONS * APPL - FIRM : FINANCE , STOCK PRICES *
          STOCK PRICES - VOLATILITY
YA3105   SCHMENNER R.W.
          "The determination of municipal employee wages"   Rev. Econ. Stats.,
          vol.55, 1973, pp.83-90.
          APPL - SECTOR : EARNINGS * APPL - SECTOR : GOVERNMENT , LOCAL * MANPOWER
          PLANNING - SECTOR : GOVERNMENT , LOCAL * APPL - SECTOR : GOVERNMENT ,
          EDUCATION * MANPOWER PLANNING - SECTOR : EDUCATION , SCHOOLS
YA3106   SCHMIDT P.
          "A modification of the Almon distributed lag"   J. Am. Statist. Ass.,
          vol.69, 1974, pp.679-681.
          COMPARATIVE METHODS - DISTRIBUTED LAG * DISTRIBUTED LAG - ALMON * ADVANCED
YA3107   SCHMIDT P.
          "A note on dynamic simulation forecasts and stochastic forecast-period
          exogenous variables"   Econometrica, vol.46, 1978, pp.1227-1230.
          EXOGENOUS VARIABLES - PREDICTION OF , EFFECT * CONFIDENCE INTERVAL -
          PREDICTIONS : SIMULTANEOUS SYSTEM * ADVANCED
YA3108   SCHMIDT P.
          "A note on the treatment of the truncation remainder in the gamma
          distributed lag"   Int. Econ. Rev., vol.16, 1975, pp.800-801.
          DISTRIBUTED LAG - SOLOW , ESTIMATION
YA3109   SCHMIDT P.
          "A note on Theil's minimum standard error criterion when the disturbances
          are autocorrelated"   Rev. Econ. Stats., vol.56, 1974, pp.122-123.
          REGRESSION - MODEL CHOICE * REGRESSION - MODEL INTERPRETATION * REGRESSION -
          SUMMARY STATISTICS * ERROR SPECIFICATION - AUTOCORRELATED

YA3110   SCHMIDT P.
"An argument for the usefulness of the gamma distributed lag model"   Int.
Econ. Rev., vol.15, 1974, pp.246-250.
DISTRIBUTED LAG - SOLOW * DISTRIBUTED LAG - HYPOTHESIS TESTS * DISTRIBUTED
LAG - IDENTIFICATION * DISTRIBUTED LAG - APPL , ORDERS

YA3111   SCHMIDT P.
"Calculating the power of the minimum standard error choice criterion"
Int. Econ. Rev., vol.14, 1973, pp.253-255.
REGRESSION - SUMMARY STATISTICS * REGRESSION - MODEL CHOICE * SPECIFICATION
ERROR - TESTS , VARIABLE INCLUSION

YA3112   SCHMIDT P.
"Estimation of a distributed lag model with second order autoregressive
disturbances: a Monte Carlo experiment"   Int. Econ. Rev., vol.12, 1971,
pp.372-380.
DATA - SIMULATION * DISTRIBUTED LAG - ERROR SPECIFICATION * ERROR
SPECIFICATION - AUTOCORRELATED * DISTRIBUTED LAG - SOLOW , ESTIMATION *
EVALUATION - DISTRIBUTED LAG , ESTIMATION * COMPARATIVE METHODS - ESTIMATION
: DISTRIBUTED LAG , ERROR SPECIFICATION

YA3113   SCHMIDT P.
"Estimation of a simultaneous equations model with jointly dependent
continuous and qualitatitive variables: the union-earnings question
revisited"   Int. Econ. Rev., vol.19, 1978, pp.453-465.
SIMULTANEOUS SYSTEM - LIMITED DEPENDENT , LOGIT * ESTIMATION - MAXIMUM
LIKELIHOOD * SIMULTANEOUS SYSTEM - ESTIMATION * MANPOWER PLANNING - EARNINGS
* UNIONISATION - DETERMINANTS * UNIONISATION - EFFECT OF * MANPOWER PLANNING
- LABOUR FORCE COMPOSITION

YA3114   SCHMIDT P.
"Estimation of seemingly unrelated regressions with unequal numbers of
observations"   J. Econometrics, vol.5, 1977, pp.365-377.
REGRESSION - SEEMINGLY UNRELATED * COMPARATIVE METHODS - ESTIMATION : OLS ,
MLE * DATA ERRORS - MISSING OBSERVATIONS * DATA - SIMULATION

YA3115   SCHMIDT P.
"On the difference between conditional and unconditional asymptotic
distributions of estimates in distributed lag models with integer valued
parameters"   Econometrica, vol.41, 1973, pp.165-169.
DISTRIBUTED LAG - IDENTIFICATION * CONFIDENCE INTERVAL - REGRESSION ,
MULTIVARIATE * DISTRIBUTED LAG - SOLOW , ESTIMATION * DISTRIBUTED LAG -
HYPOTHESIS TESTS * ADVANCED

YA3116   SCHMIDT P.
"On the statistical estimation of frontier production functions"   Rev.
Econ. Stats., vol.53, 1976, pp.238-239.
PRODUCTION FUNCTIONS - ESTIMATION * PRODUCTION FUNCTIONS - METHODOLOGY *
ERROR DISTRIBUTION - NONNORMAL , GAMMA * ERROR DISTRIBUTION - ASYMMETRICAL *
ERROR SPECIFICATION - PRODUCTION FUNCTIONS

YA3117   SCHMIDT P.
"Some small sample evidence on the distribution of dynamic simulation
forecasts"   Econometrica, vol.45, 1977, pp.997-1005.
CONFIDENCE INTERVAL - PREDICTIONS : SIMULTANEOUS SYSTEM * DATA - SIMULATION

YA3118   SCHMIDT P.
"The asymptotic distribution of dynamic multipliers"   Econometrica,
vol.41, 1973, pp.161-164.
SIMULATION - DYNAMIC PROPERTIES * MACRO MODEL - KLEIN * MULTIPLIERS -
METHODOLOGY * ADVANCED

YA3119   SCHMIDT P.
"The small sample effects of various treatments of truncation remainders in
the estimation of distributed lag models"   Rev. Econ. Stats., vol.57,
1975, pp.387-389.
DISTRIBUTED LAG - SOLOW , ESTIMATION * COMPARATIVE METHODS - ESTIMATION :
DISTRIBUTED LAG * DATA - SIMULATION

YA3120   SCHMIDT P., GUILKEY D.K.
"Some further evidence on the power of the Durbin-Watson and Geary tests"
Rev. Econ. Stats., vol.57, 1975, pp.379-382.
NON PARAMETRIC - TEST * COMPARATIVE METHODS - TESTS , AUTOCORRELATION * DATA
- SIMULATION * ERROR SPECIFICATION - AUTOCORRELATED

YA3121   SCHMIDT P., GUILKEY D.K.
"The effects of various treatments of truncation remainders on tests of
hypothesis in distributed lag models"   J. Econometrics, vol.4, 1976,
pp.211-230.
DISTRIBUTED LAG - SOLOW , ESTIMATION * DATA - SIMULATION * DISTRIBUTED LAG -
HYPOTHESIS TESTS

YA3122   SCHMIDT P., SICKLES R.
"Some further evidence on the use of the Chow test under heteroscedasticity"
Econometrica, vol.45, 1977, pp.1293-1298.
STABILITY OF COEFFICIENTS - REGRESSION , TEST * ERROR SPECIFICATION -
HETEROSCEDASTIC

YA3123   SCHMIDT P., STAUSS R.P.
"The effect of unions on earnings and earnings on unions"   Int. Econ.
Rev., vol.17, 1976, pp.204-212.
SIMULTANEOUS SYSTEM - LIMITED DEPENDENT , LOGIT * UNIONISATION - EFFECT OF *
APPL - MACRO : EARNINGS * EDUCATION - EFFECT OF * COMPARATIVE METHODS -
SIMULTANEOUS SYSTEM , LIMITED DEPENDENT

YA3124   SCHMIDT P., STRAUSS R.P.
          "Estimation of models with jointly dependent qualitive variables: a
          simultaneous logit approach"   Econometrica, vol.43, 1975, pp.745-755.
          SIMULTANEOUS SYSTEM - LIMITED DEPENDENT , LOGIT * APPL - SECTOR : SOCIAL ,
          OCCUPATION * EDUCATION - EFFECT OF * MANPOWER PLANNING - DISCRIMINATION
YA3125   SCHMIDT P., STRAUSS R.P.
          "The prediction of occupation using multiple logit models"   Int. Econ.
          Rev., vol.16, 1975, pp.471-486.
          APPL - SECTOR : SOCIAL , OCCUPATION * EDUCATION - EFFECT OF * REGRESSION -
          LIMITED DEPENDENT , LOGIT
YA3126   SCHMIDT P., WAUD R.N.
          "The Almon lag technique and the monetary versus fiscal debate"   J. Am.
          Statist. Ass., vol.68, 1973, pp.11-19.
          DISTRIBUTED LAG - IDENTIFICATION * SPECIFICATION ERROR - TESTS , LAG
          SPECIFICATION * POLICY EVALUATION - MACRO : FISCAL , MONETARY * DISTRIBUTED
          LAG - APPL , MONEY * EVALUATION - DISTRIBUTED LAG , ALMON
YA3127   SCHNEE J.E.
          "Development cost: determinants and overruns"   J. Business, vol.45, 1972,
          pp.347-374.
          USE - R&D * EVALUATION - JUDGEMENTAL FORECASTS , R&D * EVALUATION - R&D
          FORECASTS * JUDGEMENTAL FORECASTS - DETERMINANTS * APPL - SECTOR : CONSUMER
          NON DURABLES , PHARMACEUTICALS * COMPARATIVE METHODS - CAUSAL , JUDGEMENTAL
YA3128   SCHOEFFLER S., BUZZELL R.D., HEANY D.F.
          "Impact of strategic planning on profit performance"   H.B.R., vol.52,
          March-April, 1974, pp.137-145.
          USE - CORPORATE PLANNING * SIMULATION - APPL : FINANCIAL MODELLING * APPL -
          FIRM : FINANCE , PROFITS * MARKET SHARE - EFFECT OF * QUALITY - EFFECT OF
YA3129   SCHOLES M.S.
          "The market for securities: substitution versus price pressure and the
          effects of information on share prices"   J. Business, vol.45, 1972,
          pp.179-211.
          APPL - FIRM : FINANCE , STOCK PRICES * STOCK PRICES - INFORMATION EFFECT *
          STOCK PRICES - TRADING VOLUME
YA3130   SCHOTT F.H.
          "Disintermediation through policy loans at life insurance companies"   J.
          Finance, vol.26, 1971, pp.719-729.
          APPL - SECTOR : FINANCE , INSURANCE COMPANIES
YA3131   SCHOTT F.H.
          "Forecasting long term interest rates"   Bus. Econ., vol.8:3, 1973,
          pp.46-53.
          INTEREST RATE - INDICATORS * INFLATION - EFFECT OF
YA3132   SCHOTT F.H.
          "Interest rate forecasting in theory and practice"   Bus. Econ., vol.12:4,
          1977, pp.55-60.
          INTEREST RATE - DETERMINANTS * BASIC
YA3133   SCHOTT K.
          "The relations between industrial research and development and factor
          demands"   Econ. J., vol.88, 1978, pp.85-106.
          APPL - MACRO : EMPLOYMENT * APPL - MACRO : INVESTMENT * APPL - MACRO : R & D
          * EX ANTE * COMPARATIVE METHODS - AUTOREGRESSIVE , CAUSAL * TAX - EFFECT OF
          * POLICY EVALUATION - MACRO : R&D * APPL - MACRO : CAPACITY UTILISATION *
          APPL - MACRO , UK
YA3134   SCHRAMM R.
          "Neoclassical investment models and French private manufacturing investment"
          Am. Econ. Rev., vol.62, 1972, pp.553-563.
          THEORY - INVESTMENT BEHAVIOUR * APPL - SECTOR : INVESTMENT
YA3135   SCHRANK W.E.
          "Sex discrimination in faculty salaries: a case study"   Can. J. Econ.,
          vol.10, 1977, pp.411-433.
          MANPOWER PLANNING - SECTOR : EDUCATION , UNIVERSITIES * MANPOWER PLANNING -
          DISCRIMINATION , SEX * APPL - FIRM : EDUCATION , UNIVERSITIES * MANPOWER
          PLANNING - FIRM * MANPOWER PLANNING - EARNINGS * MANPOWER PLANNING -
          QUALIFIED MANPOWER
YA3136   SCHREIBER R.J.
          "The Metheringham method for media mix: an evaluation"   J. Advtg. Res.,
          vol.9:2, 1969, pp.54-57.
          ADVERTISING - EXPOSURE * USE - MEDIA PLANNING * PROBABILITY MODELS - BETA *
          APPL - SECTOR : SERVICES , MEDIA , MAGAZINES
YA3137   SCHRUBEN L.W., MARGOLIN B.H.
          "Pseudorandom number assignment in statistically designed simulation and
          distribution sampling experiment" with discussion   J. Am. Statist. Ass.,
          vol.73, 1978, pp.504-525.
          SIMULATION - METHODOLOGY , MONTE CARLO
YA3138   SCHULTZ R.L.
          "Market measurement and planning with a simultaneous equation model"   J.
          Mktg. Res., vol.8, 1971, pp.153-164.
          MARKET POTENTIAL - ADVERTISING - EFFECT OF * USE - SCHEDULING , SERVICES *
          APPL - SECTOR : TRANSPORT , AIR * MARKET SHARE - SECTOR : TRANSPORT *
          COMPARATIVE METHODS - ESTIMATION : OLS , 3SLS * COMPARATIVE METHODS -
          REGRESSION , TRANSFORMATIONS * APPL - FIRM : TRANSPORT , AIR * REGIONAL
          MODELS - SECTOR : TRANSPORT

YA3139   SCHULTZ R.L.
"Methods for handling competition in dynamic market models"   Eur. J.
Mktg., vol.7, 1973, pp.18-27.
MARKET SHARE - INTRODUCTION * USE - MARKETING POLICY * COMPETITION - EFFECT
OF * BASIC

YA3140   SCHULTZ R.L., ET AL.
"Evaluating airline advertising: comments"   J. Advtg. Res., vol.13:4,
1973, pp.47-51.
APPL - SECTOR : TRANSPORT , AIR * MARKET SHARE - SECTOR : TRANSPORT *
ADVERTISING - EFFECT OF

YA3141   SCHULTZ T.P.
"Fertility and child mortality over the life cycle: aggregate and individual
evidence"   Am. Econ. Ass. Proc., 1978, pp.208-215.
POPULATION - FERTILITY * POPULATION - MORTALITY

YA3142   SCHULTZ T.P.
"Rural-urban migration in Columbia"   Rev. Econ. Stats., vol.53, 1971,
pp.157-163.
REGIONAL MODELS - MANPOWER PLANNING , MIGRATION * MANPOWER PLANNING -
REGIONAL * APPL - MACRO , LATIN AMERICA

YA3143   SCHULTZE C.L.
"Falling profits, rising profit margins, and the full-employment profit
rate" with discussion   Brookings Paps. Econ. Activity, 1975, pp.449-471.
INFLATION - DETERMINANTS * EX ANTE * APPL - MACRO : PROFITS

YA3144   SCHULTZE C.L.
"Has the Phillips curve shifted? some additional evidence" with discussion
Brookings Paps. Econ. Activity, 1971, pp.452-467.
INFLATION - PHILLIPS CURVE * MANPOWER PLANNING - LABOUR TURNOVER * EX ANTE *
STABILITY OF COEFFICIENTS - REGRESSION

YA3145   SCHULZ J.H.
"Comparative simulation analysis of social security systems"   Anns. Econ.
Soc. Meas., vol.1, 1972, pp.109-127.
POLICY EVALUATION - MACRO : WELFARE

YA3146   SCHWARTZ L.B., JOHNSON R.E.
"An appraisal of the linear decision rule for aggregate planning"   Mgmt.
Sci., vol.24, 1978, pp.844-849.
USE - INVENTORY CONTROL * USE - SCHEDULING , MANPOWER * USE - PRODUCTION ,
PLANNING * FORECASTING - VALUE OF

YA3147   SCHWARTZ R.A., WHITCOMB D.K.
"The time-variance relationship: evidence on autocorrelation in common stock
returns"   J. Finance, vol.32, 1977, pp.41-55.
APPL - FIRM : FINANCE , STOCK PRICES * STOCK PRICES - VOLATILITY * RANDOM
WALK - TEST * STOCK PRICES - RUNS * AUTOCORRELATION - TEST * DATA -
AGGREGATION OVER TIME

YA3148   SCHWARTZ S.L., VERTINSKY I.
"Multi-attribute investment decisions: a study of r & d project selection"
Mgmt. Sci., vol.24, 1977, pp.285-301.
USE - R&D * JUDGEMENTAL FORECASTS - DETERMINANTS * DISCRIMINANT ANALYSIS -
APPL * USE - PROJECT , SELECTION

YA3149   SCHWEDER T.
"Some 'optimal' methods to detect structural shift or outliers in
regression"   J. Am. Statist. Ass., vol.71, 1976, pp.491-501.
REGRESSION - OUTLIERS * CONTROL CHARTS - CUSUM * DATA ERRORS - OUTLIERS *
STABILITY OF COEFFICIENTS - REGRESSION , TESTS

YA3150   SCHWENDIMAN C.J., PINCHES G.E.
"An analysis of alternative measures of investment risk"   J. Finance,
vol.30, 1975, pp.193-200.
APPL - FIRM : FINANCE , BONDS * APPL - FIRM : FINANCE , STOCK PRICES * STOCK
PRICES - RISK * STOCK PRICES - BETA * RISK - ESTIMATION

YA3151   SCHWERT G.W.
"Public regulation of national securities exchanges: a test of the capture
hypothesis"   Bell J. Econ., vol.8, 1977, pp.129-150.
APPL - SECTOR : FINANCE , STOCK BROKERS * STOCK PRICES - TRADING VOLUME *
TIME SERIES - ARIMA : INTERVENTION * USE - STOCK MARKET REGULATION

YA3152   SCHYDLOWSKY D.M., SYRQUIN M.
"The estimation of CES production functions and neutral efficiency levels
using effective rates of protection as price deflators"   Rev. Econ.
Stats., vol.54, 1972, pp.79-83.
PRODUCTION FUNCTIONS - SECTOR * TARIFF - EFFECT OF * DATA - INTERNATIONAL *
PRODUCTION FUNCTIONS - METHODOLOGY * EVALUATION - PRODUCTION FUNCTIONS *
SPECIFICATION ERROR - EFFECT OF , VARIABLE INCLUSION

YA3153   SCOBIE G.M., JOHNSON P.R.
"Estimation of the elasticity of substitution in the presence of errors of
measurement"   J. Econometrics, vol.3, 1975, pp.51-56.
SUBSTITUTE PRODUCTS * DATA ERRORS - EFFECT OF * PRICE - EFFECT OF * APPL -
MACRO : INTERNATIONAL TRADE , EXPORTS * DATA ERRORS - ANALYSIS OF , BIAS

YA3154   SCOTT A.J., SMITH T.M.F.
"Analysis of repeated surveys using time series methods"   J. Am. Statist.
Ass., vol.69, 1974, pp.674-678.
TIME SERIES - ARIMA : THEORY * SURVEYS - METHODOLOGY , PREDICTION OF *
ADVANCED

YA3155   SCOTT A.J., SMITH T.M.F., JONES R.C.
"The application of time series methods to the analysis of repeated surveys"
Int. Statist. Rev., vol.45, 1977, pp.13-28.
SURVEYS - METHODOLOGY , PREDICTION OF * TIME SERIES - ARIMA : THEORY

YA3156   SCOTT J.R.
"A regression assessment statistic"   Appl. Stats., vol.24, 1975, pp.42-45.
REGRESSION - VARIABLE INCLUSION * REGRESSION - SUMMARY STATISTICS *
REGRESSION - HYPOTHESIS TESTS

YA3157   SCOTT J.T.
"Factor analysis and regression"   Econometrica, vol.34, 1966, pp.552-562.
MULTICOLLINEARITY - REMOVAL OF * ESTIMATION - PRINCIPAL COMPONENTS * FACTOR
ANALYSIS - APPL * APPL - SECTOR : AGRICULTURE , FARMING * APPL - SECTOR :
INVESTMENT * REGRESSION - ESTIMATION * COMPARATIVE METHODS - REGRESSION ,
PRINCIPAL COMPONENTS

YA3158   SCRUGGS L.S.
"A note on scale economies in investment advising"   J. Business, vol.49,
1976, pp.408-411.
APPL - SECTOR : FINANCE , STOCK BROKERS * COST - SECTOR : FINANCE * COST -
SCALE ECONOMIES

YA3159   SCULLY G.W.
"Business cycles and industrial strike activity"   J. Business, vol.44,
1971, pp.359-374.
STRIKE * BUSINESS CYCLE - EFFECT OF * SPECTRAL ANALYSIS - APPL : BUSINESS
CYCLE * SPECTRAL ANALYSIS - CROSS : APPL * APPL - MACRO : STRIKES

YA3160   SCULLY G.W.
"Pay and performance in major league baseball"   Am. Econ. Rev., vol.64,
1974, pp.915-930.
APPL - FIRM : SERVICES , SPORTS * APPL - FIRM : EARNINGS * MANPOWER PLANNING
- EARNINGS * MANPOWER PLANNING - SECTOR : SERVICES

YA3161   SCULLY G.W.
"Static vs. dynamic Phillips curves"   Rev. Econ. Stats., vol.56, 1974,
pp.387-390.
SPECTRAL ANALYSIS - CROSS * SPECTRAL ANALYSIS - APPL : MACRO , EARNINGS *
INFLATION - PHILLIPS CURVE * APPL - MACRO : EARNINGS * INFLATION -
DETERMINANTS , EARNINGS

YA3162   SCULLY G.W., GALLAWAY L.E.
"A spectral analysis of the demographic structure of American unemployment"
J. Business, vol.46, 1973, pp.87-102.
APPL - MACRO : UNEMPLOYMENT * SPECTRAL ANALYSIS - APPL : MACRO , MANPOWER
PLANNING

YA3163   SEALEY C.W.
"Changing seasonal movements in interest rates and their implications for
interest rate forecasting"   Bus. Econ., vol.12:4, 1977, pp.67-73.
INTEREST RATE - SEASONALITY

YA3164   SEELIG S.A.
"Rising interest rates and cost plus inflation"   J. Finance, vol.29, 1974,
pp.1049-1061.
INTEREST RATE - EFFECT OF * INFLATION - DETERMINANTS * COST - SECTOR

YA3165   SEGUY R.M., RAMIREZ J.A.
"The use of input-output analysis in an econometric model of the Mexican
economy"   Anns. Econ. Soc. Meas., vol.4, 1975, pp.531-552.
INPUT OUTPUT - MACRO , LATIN AMERICA * INPUT OUTPUT - PROJECTION OF
STRUCTURE - SIMULATION - APPL : POLICY EVALUATION * MULTIPLIERS - MACRO *
MACRO MODEL - LATIN AMERICA

YA3166   SEIDMAN L.S.
"Tax-based incomes policies" with discussion   Brookings Paps. Econ.
Activity, 1978, pp.301-361.
APPL - MACRO : EARNINGS * INFLATION - GOVERNMENT CONTROLS * POLICY
EVALUATION - MACRO : TAX

YA3167   SELODY J.
"On the definition of money: some Canadian evidence"   Can. J. Econ.,
vol.11, 1978, pp.594-602.
APPL - MACRO : MONEY , SUPPLY * DATA - SPECIFICATION OF VARIABLES *
REGRESSION - SPECIFICATION OF VARIABLES : APPL - MACRO : GNP * APPL - MACRO
, CANADA * STABILITY OF COEFFICIENTS - REGRESSION : APPL * EVALUATION - EX
POST MODELS * CONFIDENCE INTERVAL - EX ANTE : APPL * EX ANTE

YA3168   SENECA J.J., TAUSSIG M.K.
"Family equivalence scales and personal income tax exceptions for children"
Rev. Econ. Stats., vol.53, 1971, pp.253-262.
INCOME - EFFECT OF * DATA - CROSS SECTION * APPL - SECTOR : SOCIAL , POVERTY
* APPL - SECTOR : CONSUMER NON DURABLES * APPL - SECTOR : CONSUMER DURABLES
* TAX - EFFECT OF * CONSUMER UNIT SCALES * POLICY EVALUATION - MACRO :
WELFARE

YA3169   SERFATY A.
"The determinants of net savings flow in financial intermediaries - an
additional note"   Bus. Econ., vol.11:3, 1976, pp.78-79.
APPL - SECTOR : FINANCE , SAVINGS * APPL - SECTOR : FINANCE , BANKS *
INTEREST RATE - EFFECT OF

YA3170 SERFATY A.
"The determinants of net savings flows in financial intermediaries" Bus.
Econ., vol.10:3, 1975, pp.66-70.
APPL - SECTOR : FINANCE , SAVINGS * APPL - SECTOR : FINANCE , BANKS *
INTEREST RATE - EFFECT OF

YA3171 SEXTON D.E.
"A cluster analytic approach to market response functions" J. Mktg. Res.,
vol.11, 1974, pp.109-114.
MARKET SEGMENTATION * CLUSTER ANALYSIS - APPL * APPL - SECTOR : CONSUMER NON
DURABLES , FOOD * EX ANTE * FORECAST - AGGREGATION * APPL - FIRM : CONSUMER
NON DURABLES , FOOD

YA3172 SEXTON D.E.
"A microeconomic model of the effects of advertising" J. Business,
vol.45, 1972, pp.29-41.
ADVERTISING - EFFECT OF * APPL - FIRM : CONSUMER NON DURABLES , GROCERIES *
MARKET SHARE - SECTOR : CONSUMER NON DURABLES * COMPARATIVE METHODS -
REGRESSION , MODEL SPECIFICATION * COMPARATIVE METHODS - REGRESSION ,
TRANSFORMATIONS

YA3173 SEXTON D.E.
"Determining good and bad credit risks among high- and low-income families"
J. Business, vol.50, 1977, pp.226-239.
APPL - FIRM : RETAILING * USE - CREDIT CONTROL , CONSUMER

YA3174 SEXTON D.E.
"Estimating marketing policy effects on sales of a frequently purchased
product" J. Mktg. Res., vol.7, 1970, pp.338-347.
MARKET SHARE - SECTOR : CONSUMER NON DURABLES * ADVERTISING - EFFECT OF *
DISTRIBUTED LAG - APPL , ADVERTISING * COMPARATIVE METHODS - REGRESSION ,
TRANSFORMATIONS * BIBLIOGRAPHY - ADVERTISING * COMPARATIVE METHODS -
AUTOREGRESSIVE , CAUSAL

YA3175 SHABIRO H.T., HALABUK L.
"Macroeconometric model building in socialist and non-socialist countries: a
comparative study" Int. Econ. Rev., vol.17, 1976, pp.529-565.
MACRO MODELS - REVIEW * APPL - MACRO, USSR * APPL - MACRO , EASTERN EUROPE
* USE - NATIONAL PLANNING * BIBLIOGRAPHY - MACRO MODELS * POLICY EVALUATION
- MACRO

YA3176 SHAIKH A., SOLOW R.
"Laws of production and laws of algebra: the Humbug production function: a
comment" Rev. Econ. Stats., vol.56, 1974, pp.115-121.
PRODUCTION FUNCTIONS - THEORY

YA3177 SHALIT S.S.
"A doctor-hospital cartel theory" J. Business, vol.50, 1977, pp.1-20.
MANPOWER PLANNING - SECTOR : HEALTH * COMPETITION - EFFECT OF * HEALTH -
MANPOWER , PHYSICIANS * HEALTH - HOSPITAL * DATA - CROSS SECTION * PRICE -
SECTOR : HEALTH

YA3178 SHALIT S.S., BEN-ZION U.
"The expected impact of the wage-price freeze on relative shares" Am.
Econ. Rev., vol.64, 1974, pp.904-930.
APPL - FIRM : FINANCE , STOCK PRICES * INFLATION - GOVERNMENT CONTROLS

YA3179 SHALIT S.S., SANKAR U.
"The measurement of firm size" Rev. Econ. Stats., vol.59, 1977,
pp.290-298.
APPL - FIRM * REGRESSION - ERRORS IN VARIABLES * REGRESSION - SPECIFICATION
OF VARIABLES

YA3180 SHANE H.D.
"Mathematical models for economic and political advertising campaigns"
Ops. Res., vol.25, 1977, pp.1-14.
VOTING * ADVERTISING - EFFECT OF * ADVANCED

YA3181 SHAPIRO A.A.
"Inflation, lags and the demand for money" Int. Econ. Rev., vol.14, 1973,
pp.81-96.
APPL - MACRO : MONEY , DEMAND * INTEREST RATE - EFFECT OF * INFLATION -
EFFECT OF * DISTRIBUTED LAG - APPL , INFLATION * INCOME - EFFECT OF *
DISTRIBUTED LAG - APPL , INTEREST RATE

YA3182 SHAPIRO A.A.
"The demand for liquid assets by Canadian manufacturing corporations"
Can. J. Econ., vol.5, 1972, pp.140-144.
DATA - CROSS SECTION , TIME SERIES * APPL - FIRM : FINANCE , FINANCIAL
STRUCTURE , LIQUID ASSETS * REGRESSION - COVARIANCE MODEL : APPL

YA3183 SHAPIRO D.
"Economy of scale as a cost factor in the operation of school districts in
Alberta" Can. J. Econ., vol.6, 1973, pp.114-121.
APPL - SECTOR : GOVERNMENT , EDUCATION , SCHOOLS * COST - SECTOR : EDUCATION
* COST - SCALE ECONOMIES * APPL - SECTOR : EDUCATION , SCHOOLS

YA3184 SHAPIRO H.T.
"Is verification possible? the evaluation of large econometric models" with
discussion Am. J. Ag. Econ., vol.55, 1973, pp.250-258 & 271-279.
EVALUATION - THEORY OF * EVALUATION - MACRO MODELS

YA3185   SHAPIRO H.T.
          "Macroeconomic models of the Soviet Union and Eastern European economies"
          Econometrica, vol.45, 1977, pp.1747-1766.
          MACRO MODEL - USSR , REVIEW * BIBLIOGRAPHY - MACRO MODELS , USSR

YA3186   SHAPIRO H.T., ANGEVINE G.E.
          "Consumer attitudes, buying intentions and expenditures: an analysis of
          Canadian data"   Can. J. Econ., vol.2, 1969, pp.230-249.
          SURVEYS - CONSUMER * EVALUATION - EXPECTATIONS , DATA * APPL - SECTOR :
          CONSUMER DURABLES * EVALUATION - ATTITUDINAL DATA * EX ANTE * APPL - SECTOR
          : CONSUMER DURABLES , CARS

YA3187   SHAPIRO S.S., WILKS M.B., CHEN H.J.
          "A comparative study of various tests for normality"   J. Am. Statist.
          Ass., vol.63, 1968, pp.1343-1372.
          COMPARATIVE METHODS - TESTS , ERROR DISTRIBUTIONS * DATA - SIMULATION

YA3188   SHARIR S.
          "Brand loyalty and the household's cost of time"   J. Business, vol.47,
          1974, pp.53-55.
          CONSUMER BEHAVIOUR - PURCHASING , DETERMINANTS * TIME - VALUE OF * PROXY
          VARIABLES * REPEAT BUYING

YA3189   SHARPE B.C., MILLER M.B.
          "The role of money in the Canadian economy"   Can. J. Econ., vol.8, 1975,
          pp.289-290.
          APPL - MACRO : MONEY , SUPPLY * APPL - MACRO , CANADA

YA3190   SHARPE I.G., WALKER R.G.
          "Asset revaluations and stock market prices"   J. Acctg. Res., vol.13,
          1975, pp.293-310.
          APPL - FIRM : FINANCE , STOCK PRICES * ACCOUNTING PRACTICE - EFFECT OF *
          STOCK PRICES - INFORMATION EFFECT

YA3191   SHARPE J.A.
          "System dynamics applications to industrial and other systems"   Opl. Res.
          Q., vol.28, 1977, pp.489-504.
          INDUSTRIAL DYNAMICS - REVIEW * FORECASTING - VALUE OF * SYSTEMS THEORY -
          REVIEW

YA3192   SHASHUA L., GOLDSCHMIDT Y.
          An index for evaluating financial performance"   J. Finance, vol.29, 1974,
          pp.797-814.
          USE - FINANCIAL , EVALUATION

YA3193   SHEARER R.A.
          "A critical note on two sectors of the financial flow charts"   Can. J.
          Econ., vol.5, 1972, pp.541-553.
          DATA ERRORS - NATIONAL ACCOUNTS , CANADA

YA3194   SHEEHAN R.G.
          "The interaction between the actual and the potential rates of growth:
          comment"   Rev. Econ. Stats., vol.53, 1976, pp.494-496.
          PRODUCTION FUNCTIONS - METHODOLOGY * TECHNOLOGY - EFFECT OF

YA3195   SHEN T.Y.
          "Technology diffusion,substitution and X-efficiency"   Econometrica,
          vol.41, 1973, pp.263-284.
          PRODUCTION FUNCTIONS - FIRM * APPL - FIRM : TECHNOLOGY * PRODUCTION
          FUNCTIONS - SUBSTITUTION

YA3196   SHEPHERD W.G.
          "The elements of market structure"   Rev. Econ. Stats., vol.54, 1972,
          pp.25-37.
          APPL - FIRM : FINANCE , PROFITS * ADVERTISING - EFFECT OF * CONCENTRATION -
          EFFECT OF * MARKET SHARE - EFFECT OF

YA3197   SHERIFF T.D.
          "Some empirical evidence on the effectiveness of income policy in the UK"
          Appl. Econ., vol.9, 1977, pp.253-263.
          INFLATION - GOVERNMENT CONTROLS * INFLATION - DETERMINANTS * APPL - MACRO :
          EARNINGS * APPL - MACRO , UK

YA3198   SHERMAN R., ET AL.
          "Advertising and profitability"   Rev. Econ. Stats., vol.53, 1971,
          pp.397-410.
          DATA - CROSS SECTION * APPL - SECTOR : FINANCE , PROFITS * ADVERTISING -
          EFFECT OF * CONCENTRATION - EFFECT OF * COMPARATIVE METHODS - REGRESSION ,
          TRANSFORMATIONS

YA3199   SHERMAN R., HOFFER G.
          "Does automobile style change payoff?"   Appl. Econ., vol.3, 1971,
          pp.153-165.
          APPL - SECTOR : CONSUMER DURABLES , CARS * MARKET SHARE - SECTOR : CONSUMER
          DURABLES * QUALITY - EFFECT OF * PRICE - EFFECT OF

YA3200   SHILLER R.J.
          "A distributed lag estimator derived from smoothness priors"
          Econometrica, vol.41, 1973, pp.775-788.
          DISTRIBUTED LAG - ESTIMATION * BAYESIAN - ESTIMATION : DISTRIBUTED LAG *
          BAYESIAN - PRIORINFORMATION * APPL - SECTOR : FINANCE , BONDS * DATA -
          SIMULATION * COMPARATIVE METHODS - DISTRIBUTED LAG

YA3201   SHINJO K.
"Business pricing policies and inflation: the Japanese case"   Rev. Econ.
Stats., vol.59, 1977, pp.447-455.
PRICE - SECTOR * DATA - CROSS SECTION * CONCENTRATION - EFFECT OF

YA3202   SHINJO K.
"Predictive ability and dynamic multiplier properties of alternative
treatments of the monetary mechanism" with discussion   J. Finance, vol.27,
1972, pp.481-493 & 510.
MACRO MODEL - ST LOUIS * MACRO MODEL - MIT , PENN , SSRC * EX ANTE * MACRO
MODEL - WHARTON * POLICY EVALUATION - MACRO , MONETARY * MULTIPLIERS - MACRO
* EVALUATION - TURNING POINT FORECASTS * EVALUATION - MACRO MODELS *
COMPARATIVE METHODS - ESTIMATION : SIMULTANEOUS SYSTEM , ERROR STRUCTURE

YA3203   SHINKAI Y.
"A note on the role of demand in the price formation"   Appl. Econ., vol.9,
1977, pp.271-276.
PRICE - SECTOR * DATA - CROSS SECTION , TIME SERIES

YA3204   SHINKAI Y.
"Elasticities of substitution for the Japanese imports"   Rev. Econ.
Stats., vol.54, 1972, pp.198-202.
TARIFF - EFFECT OF * APPL - MACRO : INTERNATIONAL TRADE , IMPORTS *
SUBSTITUTE PRODUCTS * APPL - MACRO , JAPAN

YA3205   SHINKAI Y.
"Price elasticities of the Japanese exports: a cross-section study"   Rev.
Econ. Stats., vol.50, 1968, pp.268-273.
APPL - MACRO : INTERNATIONAL TRADE , EXPORTS * PRICE - EFFECT OF * APPL -
SECTOR : INTERNATIONAL TRADE , EXPORTS * DATA ERRORS - EFFECT OF

YA3206   SHISHKO R., ROSTKER B.
"The economics of multiple job holding"   Am. Econ. Rev., vol.66, 1976,
pp.298-308.
MANPOWER PLANNING - SECONDARY LABOUR MARKETS * REGRESSION - LIMITED
DEPENDENT , TOBIT

YA3207   SHISKIN J.
"Measuring current economic fluctuations"   Anns. Econ. Soc. Meas., vol.2,
1973, pp.1-15.
DATA REVISIONS - EFFECT OF * BUSINESS INDICATORS - REVIEW

YA3208   SHISKIN J.
"Modernizing business cycle concepts"   Am. Stat'n., vol.25:4, 1971,
pp.17-19.
BUSINESS CYCLE - INTRODUCTION * BASIC

YA3209   SHISKIN J.
"Recent trends in wages and industrial relations and problems of
measurement"   Bus. Econ., vol.10:1, 1975, pp.64-71.
INFLATION - MEASUREMENT OF * INDEX NUMBERS - METHODOLOGY * DATA ERRORS -
INDEX NUMBERS

YA3210   SHISKIN J.
"The consumer price index: how will the 1977 revision affect it?"   Bus.
Econ., vol.11:2, 1976, pp.1-9.
INDEX NUMBERS - MACRO : CONSUMER PRICE

YA3211   SHISKIN J., PLEWES T.J.
"Seasonal adjustment of the US employment rate"   Stat'n., vol.27, 1978,
pp.177-202.
SEASONALITY - ESTIMATION , CENSUS * APPL - MACRO : UNEMPLOYMENT *
COMPARATIVE METHODS - SEASONALITY * SPECIFICATION ERROR - TESTS *
SEASONALITY * SEASONALITY - MULTIPLICATIVE , ADDITIVE MODEL * EVALUATION -
SEASONALITY

YA3212   SHOEMAKER R., STAELIN R.
"The effects of sampling variations on sales forecasts for new consumer
products"   J. Mktg. Res., vol.13, 1976, pp.138-143.
CONFIDENCE INTERVAL - PREDICTIONS : SIMULATION MODEL * TREND CURVES - APPL *
MARKET SHARE - METHODOLOGY * REPEAT BUYING * DATA - SAMPLE SIZE * NEW
PRODUCTS - EVALUATION * SIMULATION - APPL : NEW PRODUCTS * APPL - SECTOR :
CONSUMER NON DURABLES * EX ANTE * MARKET SHARE - SECTOR : CONSUMER NON
DURABLES

YA3213   SHOEMAKER R.W., ET AL.
"Relation of brand choice to purchase frequency"   J. Mktg. Res., vol.14,
1977, pp.458-468.
REPEAT BUYING * BRAND CHOICE - INDICATORS * PROBABILITY MODELS - DIRICHLET *
APPL - FIRM : CONSUMER NON DURABLES , FOOD * APPL - FIRM : CONSUMER NON
DURABLES , GROCERIES

YA3214   SHOEMAKER R.W., SHOAF F.R.
"Repeat rates of deal purchases"   J. Advtg. Res., vol.17:2, 1977,
pp.47-53.
USE - PROMOTION EVALUATION * REPEAT BUYING * APPL - FIRM : CONSUMER NON
DURABLES

YA3215   SHONE M.L.
"Exponential smoothing with an adaptive response rate"   Opl. Res. Q.,
vol.18, 1967, pp.318-319.
EXPONENTIAL SMOOTHING - ADAPTIVE COEFFICIENTS * TRACKING SIGNAL - APPL

YA3216   SHOREY J.
"An inter-industry analysis of strike frequency"   Economica, vol,43, 1977,
pp,349-365.
STRIKE - DETERMINANTS * APPL - SECTOR : STRIKES * DATA - CROSS SECTION

YA3217   SHORT B.K.
"The demand for money in Canada: a comment"   Economica, vol,39, 1972,
pp,442-446.
APPL - MACRO : MONEY , DEMAND * APPL - MACRO , CANADA * INTEREST RATE -
EFFECT OF

YA3218   SHRINER R.D.
"Control reversal in economics: US scrap export restrictions"   Bus, Econ,,
vol,12:3, 1977, pp,14-17.
APPL - SECTOR : PRODUCTION , SCRAP METAL * PRICE - SECTOR : PRODUCTION *
POLICY EVALUATION - SECTOR : PRODUCTION * POLICY EVALUATION - MACRO :
INTERNATIONAL TRADE * APP - SECTOR : INTERNATIONAL TRADE * APPL - SECTOR :
INTERNATIONAL TRADE , EXPORTS

YA3219   SHUCHMAN A., RIESZ P.C.
"Correlates of persuasibility: the Crest case"   J, Mktg,, Res,, vol,12,
1975, pp,7-11.
APPL - FIRM : CONSUMER NON DURABLES , HEALTH AIDS * CONSUMER BEHAVIOUR -
PURCHASING , DETERMINANTS * DISCRIMINANT ANALYSIS - APPL

YA3220   SHUPP F.R.
"Optimal policy rules for a temporal incomes policy"   Rev, Econ, Studies,
vol,43, 1976, pp,249-259.
APPL - MACRO : EARNINGS * INFLATION - DETERMINANTS , EARNINGS * CONTROL
THEORY - DETERMINISTIC , APPL * LOSS FUNCTIONS - MACRO , INFLATION

YA3221   SIDHU S.S.
"Relative efficiency in wheat production in the Indian Punjab"   Am, Econ,
Rev,, vol,64, 1974, pp,742-751.
APPL - FIRM : AGRICULTURE , FARMING * APPL - FIRM : EFFICIENCY * APPL -
MACRO , INDIA * PRODUCTION FUNCTIONS - FIRM * APPL - FIRM : FINANCE ,
PROFITS * COMPARATIVE METHODS - REGRESSION , SEEMINGLY UNRELATED

YA3222   SIEGFRIED J.J., WEISS L.W.
"Advertising, profits and corporate taxes revisited"   Rev, Econ, Stats,,
vol,56, 1974, pp,195-200.
ADVERTISING - EFFECT OF * DEPRECIATION * APPL - SECTOR : FINANCE , PROFITS *
TAX - EFFECT OF

YA3223   SILBER W.L.
"A model of Federal Home Loan Bank System and Federal National Mortgage
Association behaviour"   Rev, Econ, Stats,, vol,55, 1973, pp,308-320.
APPL - SECTOR : FINANCE , MORTGAGES * POLICY EVALUATION - SECTOR :
CONSTRUCTION

YA3224   SILBER W.L.
"The market for Federal agency securities: is there an optimum size of
issue?"   Rev, Econ, Stats,, vol,56, 1974, pp,14-22.
APPL - SECTOR : FINANCE , BONDS * REGRESSION - PIECEWISE * EX ANTE *
SPECIFICATION ERROR - ANALYSIS , SIMULTANEOUS SYSTEM BIAS * APPL - SECTOR :
GOVERNMENT , FINANCE

YA3225   SILBER W.L.
"The St. Louis equation: 'Democratic' and 'Republican' versions"   Rev,
Econ, Stats,, vol,53, 1971, pp,362-367.
MACRO MODEL - ST.LOUIS * DISTRIBUTED LAG - APPL , MONEY * DISTRIBUTED LAG -
ALMON : APPL * STABILITY OF COEFFICIENTS - REGRESSION * POLICY EVALUATION -
MACRO : FISCAL , MONETARY

YA3226   SILK A.J., URBAN G.L.
"Pre-test-market evaluation of new packaged goods: a model and measurement
methodology"   J, Mktg, Res,, vol,15, 1978, pp,171-191.
APPL - SECTOR : CONSUMER NON DURABLES * NEW PRODUCTS - EVALUATION * NEW
PRODUCTS - NEW BRAND * EX ANTE * BIBLIOGRAPHY - NEW PRODUCTS

YA3227   SILVERBERG S.C.
"Deposit costs and bank portfolio policy"   J, Finance, vol,28, 1973,
pp,881-895.
COST - FIRM : FINANCE * APPL - FIRM : FINANCE , BANKS * APPL - SECTOR :
FINANCE , FINANCIAL STRUCTURE * INTEREST RATE - EFFECT OF

YA3228   SILVERS J.B.
"An alternative to the yeild spread as a measure of risk"   J, Finance,
vol,28, 1973, pp,933-955.
APPL - SECTOR : FINANCE , BONDS * RISK - ESTIMATION * APPL - FIRM : FINANCE
, BONDS

YA3229   SILVEY S.D.
"Multicollinearity and imprecise estimation"   R. Statist. Soc, (B),
vol,31, 1969, pp,539-552.
MULTICOLLINEARITY - TESTS * ADVANCED

YA3230   SIMKOWITZ M.A., JONES C.P.
"A note on the simultaneous nature of finance methodology"   J, Finance,
vol,27, 1972, pp,103-108.
APPL - SECTOR : FINANCE * SIMULTANEOUS SYSTEM - APPL

YA3231   SIMON J.L.
"New evidence for no effect of scale in advertising"   J. Advtg. Res.,
vol.9:1, 1969, pp.38-41.
ADVERTISING - SCALE ECONOMIES * APPL - SECTOR : CONSUMER NON DURABLES , FOOD
* APPL - SECTOR : CONSUMER NON DURABLES , LIQUOR * USE - MEDIA PLANNING *
NEW PRODUCTS - ADVERTISING

YA3232   SIMON J.L.
"The effect of advertising on liquor brand sales"   J. Mktg. Res., vol.6,
1969, pp.301-313.
APPL - FIRM : CONSUMER NON DURABLES , LIQUOR * ADVERTISING - EFFECT OF *
DISTRIBUTED LAG - APPL , ADVERTISING * ADVERTISING - OPTIMALITY * MARKET
SHARE - SECTOR : CONSUMER NON DURABLES * COMPARATIVE METHODS - REGRESSION ,
TRANSFORMATIONS * REGRESSION - MODEL CHOICE

YA3233   SIMON J.L.
"The positive effect of population growth on agricultural saving in
irrigation systems"   Rev. Econ. Stats., vol.57, 1975, pp.71-79.
DATA - LDC * DATA - CROSS SECTION * APPL - SECTOR : INVESTMENT * APPL -
SECTOR : AGRICULTURE * POPULATION - EFFECT OF * APPL - MACRO : DEVELOPMENT

YA3234   SIMONDS R.R., ET AL.
"Line of business reporting and security prices: an analysis of an SEC
disclosure rule: comments"   Bell J. Econ., vol.9, 1978, pp.646-663.
APPL - FIRM : FINANCE , STOCK PRICES * STOCK PRICES - INFORMATION EFFECT *
STOCK PRICES - BETA , VARIABLE * STABILITY OF COEFFICIENTS - REGRESSION

YA3235   SIMONSON D.G.
"The speculative behaviour of mutual funds"   J. Finance, vol.27, 1972,
pp.381-395.
APPL - FIRM : FINANCE , MUTUAL FUNDS * STOCK PRICES - INSTITUTIONAL
INVESTMENT

YA3236   SIMS C.A.
"A note on exact tests for serial correlation"   J. Am. Statist. Ass.,
vol.70, 1975, pp.162-165.
AUTOCORRELATION - TEST * RESIDUALS - ANALYSIS OF , AUTOCORRELATION *
ADVANCED

YA3237   SIMS C.A.
"Are there exogenous variables in short run production relationships?"
Anns. Econ. Soc. Meas., vol.1, 1972, pp.17-36.
DISTRIBUTED LAG - SEASONALITY * CAUSALITY - TEST * SPECIFICATION ERROR -
TESTS , SIMULTANEOUS SYSTEM BIAS * DISTRIBUTED LAG - APPL , INVESTMENT *
APPL - MACRO : EMPLOYMENT * APPL - MACRO : SALES * ESTIMATION - HANNAN :
APPL * DISTRIBUTED LAG - APPL , ORDERS

YA3238   SIMS C.A.
"Evaluating short term macro forecasts: the Dutch performance"   Rev. Econ.
Stats., vol.49, 1967, pp.225-236.
MACRO MODEL - GOVERNMENT , NETHERLANDS * EVALUATION - GOVERNMENT FORECASTS *
COMPARATIVE METHODS - AUTOREGRESSIVE , CAUSAL * EXOGENOUS VARIABLES -
PREDICTION OF * EX ANTE * MACRO MODEL - GOVERNMENT , NORWAY

YA3239   SIMS C.A.
"Money, income and causality"   Am. Econ. Rev., vol.62, 1972, pp.540-552.
APPL - MACRO : MONEY * APPL - MACRO : GNP * CAUSALITY - TEST * DISTRIBUTED
LAG - APPL , MONEY

YA3240   SIMS C.A.
"Optimal stable policies for unstable instruments"   Anns. Econ. Soc.
Meas., vol.3, 1974, pp.257-261.
EVALUATION - CONTROL THEORY * POLICY EVALUATION - METHODOLOGY

YA3241   SIMS C.A.
"Output and labour input in manufacturing" with discussion   Brookings
Paps. Econ. Activity, 1974, pp.695-736.
APPL - SECTOR : EMPLOYMENT * APPL - SECTOR : OUTPUT * DISTRIBUTED LAG - APPL
, OUTPUT * SEASONALITY - TESTING : APPL * CAUSALITY - TEST : APPL * APPL -
MACRO : OUTPUT * APPL - MACRO : EMPLOYMENT

YA3242   SIMS C.A.
"Seasonality in regression"   J. Am. Statist. Ass., vol.69, 1974,
pp.618-626.
SEASONALITY - REVIEW * DISTRIBUTED LAG - SEASONALITY * SPECTRAL ANALYSIS -
APPL : SEASONALITY * ADVANCED

YA3243   SIMS C.A., MANDELBROT B.
"Linear regression with non-normal error terms: a comment"   Rev. Econ.
Stats., vol.53, 1971, pp.204-206.
SPECIFICATION ERROR - EFFECT OF , HETEROSCEDASTICITY * ERROR DISTRIBUTION -
NON NORMAL * ERROR DISTRIBUTION - STABLE * REGRESSION - ESTIMATION *
ESTIMATION - ERROR DISTRIBUTION

YA3244   SIMS H.P., WILKERSON D.A.
"Time-lags in cross-lag correlation studies: a computer simulation"
Decis. Sci., vol.8, 1977, pp.630-644.
BIBLIOGRAPHY - CAUSAL CORRELATIONS * CAUSALITY - TEST * CROSS CORRELATIONS *
LAG , FIXED * SPECIFICATION ERROR - EFFECT OF , LAG SPECIFICATION

YA3245   SINAI A., STOKES H.H.
         "Real money balances: an omitted variable from the production function"
         Rev. Econ. Stats., vol.54, 1972, pp.290-296.
         PRODUCTION FUNCTIONS - MACRO * PRODUCTION FUNCTIONS - THEORY * APPL - MACRO
         : MONEY , REAL CASH BALANCES * PRODUCTION FUNCTIONS - SCALE RETURNS

YA3246   SINGER B., SPILERMAN S.
         "Some methodological issues in the analysis of longitudinal surveys"
         Anns. Econ. Soc. Meas., vol.5, 1976, pp.447-474.
         SURVEYS - METHODOLOGY * SPECIFICATION ERROR - TESTS , DATA SOURCES * DATA -
         CROSS SECTION , TIME SERIES * ADVANCED

YA3247   SINGH A.
         "Take-overs, economic natural selection, and the theory of the firm:
         evidence from the postwar UK experience"   Econ. J., vol.85, 1975,
         pp.497-515.
         APPL - FIRM : MERGERS * USE - BANKRUPTCY PREDICTION * USE - ACQUISITION

YA3248   SINGH A., WHITTINGTON G.
         "The size and growth of firms"   Rev. Econ. Studies, vol.42, 1975,
         pp.15-26.
         APPL - FIRM : GROWTH

YA3249   SINGH B.
         "Maximum likelihood estimation of the Friedman consumption function"   Rev.
         Econ. Stats., vol.57, 1975, pp.94-100 & 522.
         EVALUATION - PERMANENT INCOME * APPL - MACRO : CONSUMPTION * DATA -
         INTERNATIONAL * COMPARATIVE METHODS - ESTIMATION : REGRESSION * REGRESSION -
         ERRORS IN VARIABLES * ESTIMATION - MAXIMUM LIKELIHOOD * EVALUATION -
         ESTIMATION : NON LINEAR , ITERATIVE * INCOME - EFFECT OF , PERMANENT

YA3250   SINGH B.
         "On the determination of economies of scale in household consumption"
         Int. Econ. Rev., vol.13, 1972, pp.257-270.
         APPL - MACRO : CONSUMER DEMAND * APPL - MACRO , INDIA * CONSUMER BEHAVIOUR -
         ECONOMIC MODELS , THEORY * COMPARATIVE METHODS - ELASTICITY , ESTIMATION *
         DATA - CROSS SECTION * CONSUMER BEHAVIOUR - EXPENDITURE SURVEY * SCALE
         ECONOMIES

YA3251   SINGH B., DROST H.
         "An alternative econometric approach to the permanent income hypothesis: an
         international comparison"   Rev. Econ. Stats., vol.53, 1971, pp.326-334.
         THEORY - PERMANENT INCOME * DATA - INTERNATIONAL * APPL - MACRO :
         CONSUMPTION * REGRESSION - ERRORS IN VARIABLES * INCOME - EFFECT OF ,
         PERMANENT * ESTIMATION - NON LINEAR , ITERATIVE * EVALUATION - PERMANENT
         INCOME

YA3252   SINGH B., ET AL.
         "On the estimation of structural change: a generalisation of the random
         coefficients regression model"   Int. Econ. Rev., vol.17, 1976, pp.340-361.
         REGRESSION - SHIFTING COEFFICIENTS * REGRESSION - RANDOM COEFFICIENTS * APPL
         - MACRO : CONSUMPTION * DATA - INTERNATIONAL * COMPARATIVE METHODS -
         ESTIMATION : REGRESSION , RANDOM COEFFICIENTS * STABILITY OF COEFFICIENTS -
         REGRESSION

YA3253   SINGH B., NAGAR A.L.
         "Determination of consumer unit scales"   Econometrica, vol.41, 1973,
         pp.347-355.
         DATA - SPECIFICATION OF VARIABLES * DATA - CROSS SECTION * APPL - MACRO :
         CONSUMER DEMAND * CONSUMER UNIT SCALES * CONSUMER BEHAVIOUR - EXPENDITURE
         SURVEY * APPL - MACRO , INDIA

YA3254   SINGH B., NAGAR A.L.
         "Identification and estimation of consumer unit scales"   Econometrica,
         vol.46, 1978, pp.231-233.
         CONSUMER UNIT SCALES * ADVANCED

YA3255   SINKEY J.F.
         "A multivariate statistical analysis of the characteristics of problem
         banks"   J. Finance, vol.30, 1975, pp.21-36.
         APPL - FIRM : FINANCE , BANKS * USE - BANK REGULATION * DISCRIMINANT
         ANALYSIS - APPL * EX ANTE

YA3256   SIRKIN G.W.
         "Business structure, economic cycles and national policy"   Bus. Econ.,
         vol.11:2, 1976, pp.12-14.
         EVALUATION - BUSINESS CYCLES * BUSINESS CYCLE - LONG CYCLE

YA3257   SJOQUIST D.L.
         "Property crime and economic behaviour: some empirical results"   Am. Econ.
         Rev., vol.63, 1973, pp.439-446.
         APPL - SECTOR : SOCIAL , CRIME

YA3258   SKOVSEN K.F.
         "A control model to assist in forecasting state tax revenues"   Decis.
         Sci., vol.4, 1973, pp.559-562.
         APPL - SECTOR : GOVERNMENT , LOCAL , REVENUES , TAX * APPL - SECTOR :
         GOVERNMENT , REVENUES , TAX * USE - FINANCIAL CONTROL * REGIONAL MODELS -
         TAX * BASIC

YA3259   SLATER C.C., WALSHAM G.
"A systems simulation model of the Kenyan economy"   Omega, vol.3, 1975, pp.557-567.
SIMULATION - APPL : MACRO * APPL - MACRO , AFRICA * MACRO MODEL - AFRICA

YA3260   SLATER P.B.
"Disaggregated spatial-temporal analyses of residential sales prices"   J. Am. Statist. Ass., vol.69, 1974, pp.359-363.
APPL - SECTOR : CONSTRUCTION , RESIDENTIAL * REGIONAL MODELS - CITY * PRICE - SECTOR : CONSTRUCTION , RESIDENTIAL * REGIONAL MODELS - SECTOR : TRANSPORT

YA3261   SLATER P.B.
"Spatial and temporal effects in residential sales prices"   J. Am. Statist. Ass., vol.68, 1973, pp.554-561.
APPL - SECTOR : CONSTRUCTION , RESIDENTIAL * REGIONAL MODELS - CITY * PRICE - SECTOR : CONSTRUCTION , RESIDENTIAL * REGIONAL MODELS - SECTOR : TRANSPORT

YA3262   SLOSS,J.
"The demand for intercity motor freight transport:a macro analysis"   J. Business, vol.44, 1971, pp.62-68.
APPL - SECTOR : TRANSPORT , ROAD * PRICE - EFFECT OF

YA3263   SLOVIC P.
"Psychological study of human judgement: implications for investment decision making"   J. Finance, vol.27, 1972, pp.779-799.
JUDGEMENTAL FORECASTS - REVIEW * BOOTSTRAPPING * BIBLIOGRAPHY - JUDGEMENTAL FORECASTING

YA3264   SLOVIN M.B.
"On the relationships among monetary aggregates"   J. Money, Credit, Banking, vol, 6, 1974, pp.353-366.
EX ANTE * APPL - MACRO : MONEY

YA3265   SLOVIN M.B., SUSHKA M.E.
"The structural shift in the demand for money"   J. Finance, vol.30, 1975, pp.721-731.
APPL - MACRO : MONEY , DEMAND * STABILITY OF COEFFICIENTS - REGRESSION

YA3266   SLY D.F.
"Evaluating estimates of net migration and net migration rates based on survival ratios corrected in varying degrees"   J.Am. Statist. Ass., vol.67, 1972, pp.313-318.
POPULATION - MIGRATION * DATA ERRORS - EFFECTS OF

YA3267   SMIL V., KUZ T.
"Energy and the economy - a global and national analysis"   Long Range Planning, vol. 9:3, 1976, pp.65-74.
APPL - MACRO : ENERGY * DATA - INTERNATIONAL * BASIC

YA3268   SMITH A.F.M.
"A general Bayesian linear model"   R. Statist. Soc. (B), vol.35, 1973, pp.67-75.
BAYESIAN - ESTIMATION : REGRESSION * APPL - FIRM : FINANCE , INVESTMENT * COMPARATIVE METHODS - ESTIMATION : REGRESSION , RANDOM COEFFICIENTS

YA3269   SMITH A.F.M., ET AL.
"Ridge regression: some comments on a paper of Conniffe and Stone"   Stat'n., vol.24, 1975, pp.61-68.
EVALUATION - REGRESSION , RIDGE

YA3270   SMITH B., CAMPBELL J.M.
"Aggregation bias and the demand for housing"   Int. Econ. Rev., vol.19, 1978, pp.495-505.
INCOME - EFFECT OF * APPL - SECTOR : CONSTRUCTION , RESIDENTIAL * COMPARATIVE METHODS - INCOME ELASTICITY , ESTIMATION * DATA - AGGREGATION 'BIAS' * PRICE - SECTOR : CONSTRUCTION , RESIDENTIAL

YA3271   SMITH D.E.
"Adaptive response for exponential smoothing: comparative system analysis"   Opl. Res. Q., vol.25, 1974, pp.421-435.
EVALUATION - EXPONENTIAL SMOOTHING , ADAPTIVE COEFFICIENTS * COMPARATIVE METHODS - EXPONENTIAL SMOOTHING , ADAPTIVE * DATA - SIMULATION

YA3272   SMITH D.M.
"Regional growth: interstate and intersectoral factor reallocations"   Rev. Econ. Stats., vol.56, 1974, pp.353-359.
REGIONAL MODELS - MANPOWER PLANNING , MIGRATION * REGIONAL MODELS - MANPOWER PLANNING , EARNINGS * APPL - SECTOR : GROWTH * REGIONAL MODELS - GROWTH * REGIONAL MODELS - INTERREGIONAL * DATA - CROSS SECTION * MANPOWER PLANNING - MIGRATION

YA3273   SMITH G.
"Pitfalls in financial model building: a clarification"   Am. Econ. Rev., vol.65, 1975, pp.510-516.
APPL - MACRO : FLOW OF FUNDS * SIMULTANEOUS SYSTEM - IDENTIFICATION : APPL * SIMULTANEOUS SYSTEM - CONSTRAINED

YA3274   SMITH G., BRAINARD W.
"The value of a priori information in estimating a financial model"   J. Finance, vol.31, 1976, pp.1299-1322.
REGRESSION - PRIOR INFORMATION : APPL * APPL - SECTOR : FINANCE , BUILDING SOCIETIES * INTEREST RATE - EFFECT OF * EVALUATION - EX POST MODELS * APPL - SECTOR : FINANCE , BANKS * COMPARATIVE METHODS - AUTOREGRESSIVE , CAUSAL * EX ANTE * EVALUATION - EX POST MODELS * EVALUATION - PRIOR INFORMATION * COMPARATIVE METHODS - ESTIMATION : OLS , BAYESIAN * LEAD TIME - EFFECT OF

YA3275   SMITH G.W., SCHINK G.R.
"The international tin agreement: a reassessment"   Econ. J., vol.86,, 1976, pp.715-728,
APPL - SECTOR : COMMODITIES , TIN * POLICY EVALUATION - SECTOR : COMMODITIES * SIMULATION - APPL : POLICY EVALUATION * SIMULATION - APPL : SECTOR , COMMODITIES * APPL - SECTOR : PRODUCTION , TIN

YA3276   SMITH J.H.
"Families of transformations for use in regression analysis"   Am. Stat'n., vol.26:3, 1972, pp.59-61,
REGRESSION - TRANSFORMATIONS * BASIC

YA3277   SMITH J.P., WELCH F.R.
"Black-white male wage ratios: 1960-70"   Am. Econ. Rev., vol.67, 1977, pp.323-338,
MANPOWER PLANNING - EARNINGS * MANPOWER PLANNING - DISCRIMINATION , RACIAL * EDUCATION - EFFECT OF

YA3278   SMITH L.B.
"A note on the price adjustment mechanism for rental housing"   Am. Econ. Rev., vol.64, 1974, pp.478-481,
APPL - SECTOR : CONSTRUCTION , RESIDENTIAL * PRICE - SECTOR : CONSTRUCTION , RESIDENTIAL * DATA - CROSS SECTION , TIME SERIES

YA3279   SMITH L.B., CHOUDHRY N.K.
"Academic salaries in economics and the returns to academic productivity: a case study"   Can. J. Econ., vol.11, 1978, pp.603-613,
APPL - SECTOR : EDUCATION , UNIVERSITIES * MANPOWER PLANNING - EARNINGS * MANPOWER PLANNING - SECTOR : EDUCATION , UNIVERSITIES * MANPOWER PLANNING - QUALIFIED MANPOWER

YA3280   SMITH L.B., SPARKS G.R.
"Specification and estimation of financial stock adjustment models, with special reference to life insurance company mortgage investment"   Int. Econ. Rev., vol.12, 1971, pp.14-26,
APPL - SECTOR : FINANCE , INSURANCE COMPANIES * APPL - SECTOR : FINANCE , MORTGAGES * EVALUATION - DISTRIBUTED LAG MODEL SPECIFICATION * ERROR SPECIFICATION - AUTOCORRELATED * COMPARATIVE METHODS - REGRESSION , ERROR SPECIFICATION

YA3281   SMITH L.B., WINDER J.W.L.
"Price and interest rate expectations and the demand for money in Canada" J. Finance, vol.26, 1971, pp.671-682,
APPL - MACRO , CANADA * APPL - MACRO : MONEY , DEMAND * INFLATION - EXPECTATIONS * DISTRIBUTED LAG - EXPECTATIONS HYPOTHESES * DISTRIBUTED LAG - APPL , INTEREST RATE * DISTRIBUTED LAG - ALMON : APPL * INTEREST RATE - EXPECTATIONS

YA3282   SMITH P.E., TANNER J.E.
"Lags in the effect of monetary policy: comments"   Am. Econ. Rev., vol.62, 1972, pp.230-237,
APPL - MACRO : MONEY * POLICY EVALUATION - MACRO : MONETARY * DISTRIBUTED LAG - APPL , MONEY * APPL - MACRO : INVESTMENT

YA3283   SMITH P.M., WILTON D.A.
"Wage changes: the frequency of wage settlements, the variability of contract length and 'locked-in' wage adjustments"   Economica, vol.45, 1978, pp.305-310,
APPL - MACRO : EARNINGS * APPL - MACRO , CANADA * INFLATION - PHILLIPS CURVE

YA3284   SMITH R.E., VANSKI J.E., HOLT C.C.
"Recession and the employment of demographic groups" with discussion
Brookings Paps. Econ. Activity, 1974, pp.737-760,
MANPOWER PLANNING - LABOUR PARTICIPATION * MANPOWER PLANNING - LABOUR FORCE COMPOSITION * APPL - MACRO : EMPLOYMENT * APPL - MACRO : UNEMPLOYMENT

YA3285   SMITH R.J.
"Medium-term forecasts reassessed IV: domestic appliances"   Nat. Inst. Econ. Rev., no.64, 1973, pp.68-83,
APPL - SECTOR : CONSUMER DURABLES , APPLIANCES * INCOME - EFFECT OF * DATA - INTERNATIONAL

YA3286   SMITH R.P.
"A note on car replacement"   Rev. Econ. Studies, vol.41, 1974, pp.567-570,
APPL - SECTOR : CONSUMER DURABLES , CARS * DEMAND - REPLACEMENT

YA3287   SMITH R.P.
"Demand management and the 'New School'"   Appl. Econ., vol.8, 1976, pp.193-205,
MACRO MODEL - UK , CAMBRIDGE

YA3288   SMITH V.K.
"A note on ridge regression"   Decis. Sci., vol.7, 1976, pp.562-566,
REGRESSION - RIDGE

YA3289   SMITH V.K.
"A simulation analysis of the power of several tests for detecting heavy-tailed distributions"   J. Am. Statist. Ass., vol.70, 1975, pp.662-665,
ERROR DISTRIBUTION - STABLE * COMPARATIVE METHODS - TESTS , ERROR DISTRIBUTIONS

YA3290   SMITH V.K.
"A tabular review of sampling studies with problems of autocorrelation and
distributed lag models"   Int. Statistl Rev., vol.41, 1973, pp.351-355.
COMPARATIVE METHODS - ESTIMATION : REGRESSION , ERROR SPECIFICATION *
COMPARATIVE METHODS - ESTIMATION : DISTRIBUTED LAG * REGRESSION - ESTIMATION
, ERROR SPECIFICATION , REVIEW * EVALUATION - ERROR SPECIFICATION ,
AUTOCORRELATED * DISTRIBUTED LAG - ERROR SPECIFICATION

YA3291   SMITH V.K.
"Economic anonymity and Monte Carlo studies"   Appl. Econ., vol.3, 1971,
pp.35-45.
COMPARATIVE METHODS - ESTIMATION : OLS , 2SLS * EVALUATION - ESTIMATION :
SIMULTANEOUS SYSTEM , CONSTRAINED * DATA - SIMULATION * ESTIMATION - LISE *
COMPARATIVE METHODS - ESTIMATION : SIMULTANEOUS SYSTEM , 2SLS , LISE

YA3292   SMITH V.K.
"Some aspects of the dynamic properties of econometric models"   Decis.
Sci., vol.5, 1974, pp.115-127.
APPL - SECTOR : AGRICULTURE , FRUIT * SIMULTANEOUS SYSTEMS - DYNAMIC
PROPERTIES * SIMULATION - APPL : SECTOR , AGRICULTURE * SIMULATION - DYNAMIC
PROPERTIES * MULTIPLIERS - METHODOLOGY

YA3293   SMITH V.K.
"The estimated power of several tests for autocorrelation with
non-first-order alternatives"   J. Am. Statist. Ass., vol.71, 1976,
pp.879-883.
COMPARATIVE METHODS - TESTS , AUTOCORRELATION * ERROR SPECIFICATION - ARMA *
DATA - SIMULATION

YA3294   SMITH V.K., FIBIGER W.W.
"An approach for efficient estimation of state and local government
expenditure determinants"   Appl. Econ., vol.4, 1972, pp.101-123.
APPL - SECTOR : GOVERNMENT , LOCAL , EXPENDITURE * REGRESSION - SEEMINGLY
UNRELATED : APPL * BIBLIOGRAPHY - LOCAL GOVERNMENT

YA3295   SMITH V.K., HALL T.W.
"A comparison of maximum likelihood versus BLUE estimation"   Rev. Econ.
Stats., vol.54, 1972, pp.186-190.
ERROR DISTRIBUTION - NON NORMAL , LAPLACE * DATA - SIMULATION * COMPARATIVE
METHODS - ESTIMATION : OLS , MSAE * SPECIFICATION ERROR - EFFECT OF , ERROR
DISTRIBUTION

YA3296   SMITH V.K., LOEB P.D.
"Mis specification and the small sample properties of econometric
estimators"   Appl. Econ., vol.5, 1973, pp.167-179.
COMPARATIVE METHODS - ESTIMATION : OLS , 2SLS * SPECIFICATION ERROR - EFFECT
OF , VARIABLE INCLUSION * DATA - SIMULATION * ESTIMATION - LISE *
COMPARATIVE METHODS - ESTIMATION : SIMULTANEOUS SYSTEM , 2SLS , LISE

YA3297   SMITH V.K., MARCIS R.G.
"A time series analysis of post-accord interest rates"   J. Finance,
vol.27, 1972, pp.589-605.
INTEREST RATE - TERM STRUCTURE *'SPECTRAL ANALYSIS - APPL : INTEREST RATE *
SPECTRAL ANALYSIS - CROSS : APPL

YA3298   SMITH V.K., MARCIS R.G.
"Applications of spectral analysis: some further considerations"   Decis.
Sci., vol.4, 1973, pp.44-57.
SPECTRAL ANALYSIS - REVIEW

YA3299   SMYTH D.J.
"Unemployment and inflation: a cross-country analysis of the Phillips curve"
Am. Econ. Rev., vol.61, 1971, pp.426-429.
DATA - INTERNATIONAL * INFLATION - PHILLIPS CURVE

YA3300   SNELLA J.J.
"A program for nonlinear multivariate regressions - GCM"   Econometrica,
vol.46, 1978, p.481.
ESTIMATION - NON LINEAR * COMPUTERISATION - ESTIMATION , REGRESSION MODELS ,
PROGRAMS * REGRESSION - ESTIMATION

YA3301   SNYDER W., TANAKA T.
"Budget policy and economic stability in postwar Japan"   Int. Econ. Rev.,
vol.13, 1972, pp.85-116.
APPL - MACRO , JAPAN * POLICY EVALUATION - MACRO : STABILISATION * PUBLIC
EXPENDITURE - EFFECT OF

YA3302   SOBEK R.S.
"A manager's primer on forecasting"   H.B.R., vol.51, May-June, 1973,
pp.6-28 & 181-183.
BUSINESS INDICATORS - INTRODUCTION * FORECASTING - INTRODUCTION * BASIC

YA3303   SOLNIK B.H.
"Note on the validity of the random walk for European stock prices"   J.
Finance, vol.28, 1973, pp.1151-1159
APPL - FIRM : FINANCE , STOCK PRICES * STOCK PRICES - MODELS , EFFICIENT
MARKET * RANDOM WALK - TEST * DATA - INTERNATIONAL

YA3304   SOLNIK B.H.
"The international pricing of risk: an empirical investigation of the world
capital market structure" with discussion   J. Finance, vol.29, 1974,
pp.365-378 & 392-398.
THEORY - EFFICIENT MARKETS * APPL - FIRM : FINANCE , STOCK PRICES * STOCK
PRICES - COVARIATION * STOCK PRICES - MODELS , INTERNATIONAL * APPL - MACRO
: INTERNATIONAL FINANCE

YA3305   SOMERMEYER W,H,, JANSEN R,, LOUTER A,S,
"Estimating quarterly values of annually known variables in quarterly
relationships"   J, Am, Statist, Ass,, vol,71, 1976, pp,588=595,
DATA - INTERPOLATION * COMPARATIVE METHODS - DATA : INTERPOLATED * APPL -
MACRO : CONSUMPTION * APPL - MACRO : INCOME * APPL - MACRO , NETHERLANDS

YA3306   SOMMERS P,M, SUITS D,B,
"A cross=section model of economic growth"   Rev, Econ, Stats,, vol,53,
1971, pp,121=128,
DATA - CROSS SECTION * APPL - MACRO : GROWTH * DATA - INTERNATIONAL

YA3307   SORENSON E,E,, GILHEANY J,F,
"A simulation model for harvest operations under stochastic conditions"
Mgmt, Sci, (B), vol,16, 1970, pp,549=565,
APPL - SECTOR : AGRICULTURE * SIMULATION - APPL : SECTOR , AGRICULTURE *
WEATHER - EFFECT OF * APPL - SECTOR : AGRICULTURE , SUGAR * USE - PRODUCTION
, CONTROL * USE - CAPACITY EXPANSION * USE - SCHEDULING , MANPOWER

YA3308   SOVEREIGN M,G,, NOLAN R,L,, MANDEL J,P,
"Applications of spectral analysis"   Decis, Sci,, vol,2, 1971, pp,81=105,
SPECTRAL ANALYSIS - INTRODUCTION * SPECTRAL ANALYSIS - APPL : SECTOR ,
FINANCE * APPL - SECTOR : FINANCE , STOCK PRICE INDEX * STOCK PRICES -
INFORMATION EFFECT

YA3309   SOWEY E,R,
"A classified bibliography of Monte Carlo studies in econometrics"   J,
Econometrics, vol,1, 1973, pp,377=395,
BIBLIOGRAPHY - MONTE CARLO , APPLS * BIBLIOGRAPHY - SIMULATION *
BIBLIOGRAPHY - ESTIMATION * BIBLIOGRAPHY - SIGNIFICANCE TESTS

YA3310   SPADY R,H,, FRIEDLAENDER A,F,
"Hedonic cost functions for the regulated trucking industry"   Bell, J,
Econ,, vol,9, 1978, pp,159=179,
APPL - FIRM : TRANSPORT , ROAD , FREIGHT * DATA - CROSS SECTION * QUALITY -
ADJUSTMENTS * COST - SCALE ECONOMIES * COST - FIRM : TRANSPORT

YA3311   SPANN R,M,
"Rate of return regulation and efficiency in production; an empirical test
of the Averch-Johnson thesis   Bell J, Econ,, vol,5, 1974, pp,38=52,
PRODUCTION FUNCTIONS - FIRM * APPL - FIRM : UTILITIES , ELECTRICITY * APPL -
FIRM : EFFICIENCY * USE - FINANCIAL , REGULATION

YA3312   SPARKS G,, GORBET F,, HELLIWELL J,
"The monetary sector of RDX2: reply"   Can, J, Econ,, vol,7, 1974,
pp,126=130,
APPL - MACRO : FLOW OF FUNDS * MACRO MODEL - CANADA , RDX2

YA3313   SPARKS G,R,, WILTON D,A,
"Determinants of negotiated wage increases: an empirical analysis"
Econometrica, vol,39, 1971, pp,739=750,
DATA - CROSS SECTION , TIME SERIES * APPL - SECTOR : EARNINGS * INFLATION -
PHILLIPS CURVE

YA3314   SPENCE M,
"Tacit co=ordination and imperfect information"   Can, J, Econ,, vol,11,
1978, pp,490=505,
APPL - SECTOR : FINANCE , PROFITS * DATA - CROSS SECTION * CONCENTRATION -
EFFECT OF * ADVERTISING - EFFECT OF

YA3315   SPENCER B,G,
"The small sampl bias of Durbin's test for serial correlation when one of
the regressors is the lagged dependent variable and the null hypothesis is
true"   J, Econometrics, vol,3, 1975, pp,249=254,
DISTRIBUTED LAG - ERROR SPECIFICATION * EVALUATION - TEST , AUTOCORRELATION
* REGRESSION - LAGGED DEPENDENT * DATA - SIMULATION

YA3316   SPIES R,R,
"The dynamics of corporate capital budgeting"   J, Finance, vol,29, 1974,
pp,825=845,
APPL - SECTOR : FINANCE , FINANCIAL STRUCTURE * APPL - SECTOR : INVESTMENT *
APPL - SECTOR : FINANCE , DIVIDENDS

YA3317   SPITZER J,J,
"A Monte Carlo investigation of the Box=Cox transformation in small sample"
J, Am, Statist, Ass,, vol,73, 1978, pp,488=495,
EVALUATION - REGRESSION , TRANSFORMATIONS , BOX COX * DATA - SIMULATION *
REGRESSION - HYPOTHESIS TESTS

YA3318   SPITZER J,J,
"A simultaneous equations system of money demand and supply using
generalised functional forms"   J, Econometrics, vol,5, 1977, pp,117=128,
APPL - MACRO : MONEY * INTEREST RATE - EFFECT OF * INTEREST RATE -
DETERMINANTS * COMPARATIVE METHODS - REGRESSION , TRANSFORMATIONS * INCOME -
EFFECT OF * COMPARATIVE METHODS - REGRESSION , SIMULTANEOUS SYSTEM

YA3319   SPITZER J,J,
"The demand for money, the liquidity trap, and functional forms"   Int,
Econ, Rev,, vol,17, 1976, pp,220=227,
APPL - MACRO : MONEY , DEMAND * REGRESSION - TRANSFORMATIONS , BOX COX *
COMPARATIVE METHODS - REGRESSION , TRANSFORMATIONS

YA3320 SPRAGUE R.H., WATSON H.J.
        "A decision support system for banks" Omega, vol.4 1976, pp.657-671.
        USER - FIRM : FINANCE , BANKS * APPL - FIRM : FINANCE , BANKS * MIS * BASIC

YA3321 SPRENKLE C.M.
        "The uselessness of transaction demand models: comment" J. Finance,
        vol.32, 1977, pp.227-230.
        APPL - FIRM : FINANCE , FINANCIAL STRUCTURE , CASH FLOW

YA3322 SPRINGER W.L.
        "Consumer spending and the rate of inflation" Rev. Econ. Stats., vol.59,
        1977, pp.299-306.
        APPL - MACRO : CONSUMER DEMAND * EVALUATION - EXPECTATIONS , DATA *
        INFLATION - EFFECT OF * EX ANTE

YA3323 SPRINGER W.L.
        "Did the 1968 surcharge really work?" Am. Econ. Rev., vol.65, 1975,
        pp.644-659.
        POLICY EVALUATION - MACRO : FISCAL * APPL - MACRO : CONSUMPTION * APPL -
        SECTOR : CONSUMER DURABLES * TAX - EFFECT OF * POLICY EVALUATION -
        METHODOLOGY

YA3324 STAELIN R., TURNER R.E.
        "Error in judgemental sales forecasts: theory and results" J. Mktg. Res.,
        vol.10, 1973, pp.10-16.
        JUDGEMENTAL FORECASTS - SPECIALIST * JUDGEMENTAL FORECASTS - AGGREGATION *
        FORECAST - AGGREGATION * FORECASTING - PRACTICE

YA3325 STANLEY T.J., SEWALL M.A.
        "Image inputs to a probabilistic model: predicting retail potential" J.
        Mktg., vol.40:3, 1976, pp.48-53.
        QUALITY - EFFECT OF * MARKET POTENTIAL * USE - SITE SELECTION , RETAIL *
        APPL - SECTOR : RETAILING , SUPERMARKETS

YA3326 STANSELL S.R., WILDER R.P.
        "Lagged effects of annual advertising budgets" J. Advtg. Res., vol.16:5,
        1976, pp.35-40.
        ADVERTISING - EFFECT OF * DISTRIBUTED LAG - APPL , ADVERTISING * APPL -
        SECTOR : CONSUMER DURABLES * APPL - SECTOR : CONSUMER NON DURABLES

YA3327 STAUFFER C.H., VOGEL R.C.
        "Parameters of mutual fund performance" Bus. Econ., vol.6:4, 1971,
        pp.58-63.
        APPL - FIRM : FINANCE , PROFITS * APPL - FIRM : FINANCE , MUTUAL FUNDS *
        RISK - EFFECT OF

YA3328 STEHLE R.
        "An empirical test of the alternative hypotheses of national and
        international pricing of risky assets" with discussion J. Finance,
        vol.32, 1977, pp.493-502 & 515-517.
        APPL - SECTOR : FINANCE , STOCK PRICE INDEX * DATA - INTERNATIONAL * STOCK
        PRICES - COVARIATION * STOCK PRICES - MODELS , INTERNATIONAL

YA3329 STEIB S.B.
        "The demand for euro-dollar borrowings by US banks" J. Finance, vol.28,
        1973, pp.875-879.
        APPL - SECTOR : FINANCE , BANKS * APPL - SECTOR : FINANCE , INTERNATIONAL
        FINANCE * APPL - MACRO : INTERNATIONAL FINANCE

YA3330 STEIGMANN A.J.
        "A partial recursive model of automobile demand" Bus. Econ., vol.8:4,
        1973, pp.28-30.
        APPL - SECTOR : CONSUMER DURABLES , CARS

YA3331 STEIGMANN A.J.
        "On inflation and interest rates" Bus. Econ., vol.10:3, 1975, pp.72-73.
        INFLATION - EFFECT OF * INTEREST RATE - DETERMINANTS

YA3332 STEIN J.L., TOWER E.
        "The short run stability of the foreign exchange market" Rev. Econ.
        Stats., vol.49, 1967, pp.173-185.
        APPL - MACRO : INTERNATIONAL FINANCE , EXCHANGE RATES * APPL - MACRO ,
        CANADA * APPL - MACRO , UK * EX ANTE

YA3333 STEINWALD B., SLOAN F.A.
        "Determinants of physicians' fees" J. Business, vol.47, 1974, pp.493-511.
        HEALTH - MANPOWER , EARNINGS * HEALTH - MANPOWER , PHYSICIANS

YA3334 STEKLER H.O.
        "An analysis of turning point forecasts" Am. Econ. Rev., vol.62, 1972,
        pp.724-729.
        BUSINESS CYCLE - TURNING POINTS * BUSINESS INDICATORS - APPL * EVALUATION -
        TURNING POINT FORECASTS * JUDGEMENTAL FORECASTS - TURNING POINTS *
        EVALUATION - JUDGEMENTAL FORECASTS * BAYESIAN - JUDGEMENTAL FORECASTS

YA3335 STEKLER H.O.
        "An evaluation of quarterly judgemental economic forecasts" J. Business,
        vol.41, 1968, pp.329-339.
        EVALUATION - MACRO FORECASTS * EVALUATION - JUDGEMENTAL FORECASTS , MACRO *
        BASIC

YA3336 STEKLER H.O.
        "Evaluation of econometric inventory forecasts" Rev. Econ. Stats.,
        vol.51, 1969, pp.77-83.
        EVALUATION - INVENTORY FORECASTS * EX ANTE * COMPARATIVE METHODS - CAUSAL ,
        JUDGEMENTAL * APPL - MACRO : INVENTORIES * STABILITY OF COEFFICIENTS -
        REGRESSION : APPL

YA3337　STEKLER H.O.
"Forecasting and analysis with an econometric model: comment"　Am, Econ,
Rev., vol.56, 1966, pp.1241-1248.
EVALUATION - MACRO MODELS * MACRO MODEL - MICHIGAN * EX ANTE

YA3338　STEKLER H.O.
"Forecasting the gnp deflator"　J, Business, vol.41, 1968, pp.431-438.
INFLATION - DETERMINANTS * EX ANTE

YA3339　STEKLER H.O.
"Forecasting with econometric models: an evaluation"　Econometrica,
vol.36, 1968, pp.437-463.
EVALUATION - THEORY OF * COMPARATIVE METHODS - MACRO MODELS * MACRO MODEL -
KLEIN * MACRO MODEL - OBE * MACRO MODEL - FROMM * MACRO MODEL - LIU * MACRO
MODEL - FRIEND JONES * MACRO MODEL - FRIEND TAUBMAN * COMPARATIVE METHODS -
AUTOREGRESSIVE , CAUSAL(SIMULTANEOUS SYSTEM) * EX ANTE

YA3340　STEKLER H.O.
"The Federal budget as a short-term forecasting tool"　J, Business,
vol.40, 1967, pp.280-285.
APPL - SECTOR : GOVERNMENT , EXPENDITURE * EVALUATION - GOVERNMENT FORECASTS

YA3341　STEKLER H.O.
"The savings rate as a tool of economic analysis"　J, Business, vol.49,
1976, pp.189-193.
DATA REVISIONS - EFFECT OF * APPL - MACRO : SAVINGS * JUDGEMENTAL FORECASTS
- DETERMINANTS

YA3342　STEKLER H.O., SCHEPSMAN M,
"Forecasting with an index of leading series"　J, Am, Statist Ass,,
vol.68, 1973, pp.291-296.
EVALUATION - BUSINESS INDICATORS * TURNING POINTS - FORECASTING

YA3343　STEPHENSON J,A,, FARR H,T,
"Seasonal adjustment of economic data by the general linear statistical
model"　J, Am, Statist, Ass,, vol.67, 1972, pp.37-45.
SEASONALITY - ESTIMATION , OLS * SEASONALITY - CHANGING * COMPARATIVE
METHODS - SEASONALITY * TIME SERIES - DECOMPOSITION * DATA - SIMULATION

YA3344　STEPHENSON S,P,
"The economics of youth job search behaviour"　Rev, Econ, Stats,, vol.53,
1976, pp.104-111.
MANPOWER PLANNING - UNEMPLOYMENT , DURATION

YA3345　STERN A,
"Fluctuations in residential construction: some evidence from the spectral
estimates"　Rev, Econ, Stats,, vol.54, 1972, pp.328-332.
APPL - SECTOR : CONSTRUCTION , RESIDENTIAL * BUSINESS CYCLE - LONG CYCLE *
SPECTRAL ANALYSIS - APPL : SECTOR , CONSTRUCTION * SPECTRAL ANALYSIS - APPL
: BUSINESS CYCLE , LONG CYCLE * SPECTRAL ANALYSIS - CROSS : APPL

YA3346　STEVENS B,J,
"Scale, market structure, and the cost of refuse collection"　Rev, Econ,
Stats,, vol.60, 1978, pp.438-448.
APPL - FIRM : GOVERNMENT , LOCAL , SERVICES * REGIONAL MODELS - SECTOR :
GOVERNMENT , LOCAL * COST - FIRM : GOVERNMENT , LOCAL * COST - SCALE
ECONOMIES

YA3347　STEVENS C,F,
"On the variability of demand for families of items"　Opl, Res, Q,,
vol.25, 1974, pp.411-419.
ERROR SPECIFICATION - HETEROSCEDASTIC * ERROR DISTRIBUTION - POWER LAW * USE
- INVENTORY CONTROL

YA3348　STEVENSON W,J,, BERRA P,B,
"Predicting changes in NASA satellite contracts"　Mgmt, Sci, (B), vol.21,
1975, pp.626-637.
APPL - SECTOR : PRODUCTION , SPACECRAFT * USE - PROJECT , CONTROL * USE -
COST CONTROL * COST - SECTOR : PRODUCTION

YA3349　STEWMAN S,
"Markov and renewal models for total manpower system"　Omega, vol.6, 1978,
pp.341-351.
LONG TERM FORECASTING * EX ANTE * APPL - SECTOR : GOVERNMENT , LOCAL ,
SERVICES * MANPOWER PLANNING - SECTOR : GOVERNMENT , LOCAL * MARKOV MODEL -
APPL : MANPOWER * PROBABILITY MODEL - RENEWAL THEORETIC * COMPARATIVE
METHODS - PROBABILITY MODELS

YA3350　STICKNEY C,P,
"Window dressing the interim-earnings report: an empirical assesment for
firms initially going public"　J, Business, vol.48, 1975, pp.87-97.
JUDGEMENTAL FORECASTS - BIAS * APPL - FIRM : FINANCE , PROFITS * COMPARATIVE
METHODS - AUTOREGRESSIVE , JUDGEMENTAL * EVALUATION - JUDGEMENTAL FORECASTS
, PROFITS

YA3351　STIGUM M,L,
"Some further implications of profit maximization by a savings and loan
association"　J, Finance, vol.31, 1976, pp.1405-1426.
APPL - FIRM : FINANCE , BUILDING SOCIETIES * APPL - FIRM : FINANCE , SAVINGS
* DATA - CROSS SECTION * THEORY - FIRM * RISK - EFFECT OF

YA3352　STOBAUGH R.B., TOWNSEND P.L.
　　　　　"Price forecasting and strategic planning; the case of petrochemicals"　J.
　　　　　Mktg. Res., vol.12, 1975, pp.19-29.
　　　　　APPL - SECTOR : PRODUCTION , CHEMICALS * PRICE - SECTOR : PRODUCTION *
　　　　　COMPETITION - EFFECT OF * LEARNING CURVE * LIFE CYCLE - PRODUCT * COST -
　　　　　SCALE ECONOMIES

YA3353　STOLL H.R.
　　　　　"The pricing of security dealer services; an empirical study of NASDAQ
　　　　　stocks"　J. Finance, vol.33, 1978, pp.1153-1172.
　　　　　APPL - SECTOR : FINANCE , STOCK BROKERS * RISK - EFFECT OF * PRICE - SECTOR
　　　　　: FINANCE * VOLATILITY - EFFECT OF

YA3354　STONE M.
　　　　　"Cross-validatory choice and the assessment of statistical predictions" with
　　　　　discussion　R. Statist. Soc. (B), vol.36, 1974, pp.111-147.
　　　　　EX ANTE * MODEL SELECTION * EVALUATION - THEORY OF * THEORY - MODELLING

YA3355　STONEBRAKER R.J.
　　　　　"Corporate profits and the risk of entry"　Rev. Econ. Stats., vol.53,
　　　　　1976, pp.33-39.
　　　　　RISK - EFFECT OF * APPL - SECTOR : FINANCE , PROFITS * RISK - DETERMINANTS

YA3356　STONEMAN P.
　　　　　"The effect of computers on the demand for labour in the UK"　Econ. J.,
　　　　　vol.85, 1975, pp.590-606.
　　　　　APPL - SECTOR : PRODUCTION , COMPUTERS * DIFFUSION MODEL - APPL * QUALITY -
　　　　　PRICE * MANPOWER PLANNING - TECHNOLOGY * COMPUTERISATION - EFFECT OF

YA3357　STRASZHEIM D.H., STRASZHEIM M.R.
　　　　　"An econometric analysis of the determination of prices in manufacturing
　　　　　industries"　Rev. Econ. Stats., vol.53, 1976, pp.191-201.
　　　　　PRICE - SECTOR * ERROR SPECIFICATION - AUTOCORRELATED : APPL * EVALUATION -
　　　　　REGRESSION , LAGGED DEPENDENT

YA3358　STRASZHEIM M.R.
　　　　　"Estimation of the demand for urban housing services from household
　　　　　interview data"　Rev. Econ. Stats., vol.55, 1973, pp.1-8.
　　　　　APPL - SECTOR : CONSTRUCTION , RESIDENTIAL * PRICE - EFFECT OF * INCOME -
　　　　　EFFECT OF * PRICE - SECTOR : CONSTRUCTION , RESIDENTIAL * DATA - CROSS
　　　　　SECTION

YA3359　STROBER M.H.
　　　　　"Wives' labor force behaviour and family consumption patterns"　Am. Econ.
　　　　　Ass. Proc., 1977, pp.410-417.
　　　　　APPL - MACRO : CONSUMPTION * APPL - SECTOR : CONSUMER DURABLES * MANPOWER
　　　　　PLANNING - LABOUR PARTICIPATION , FEMALE

YA3360　STRUYK R.J., MARSHALL S.A.
　　　　　"Income and urban home ownership"　Rev. Econ. Stats., vol.57, 1975,
　　　　　pp.19-26.
　　　　　APPL - SECTOR : CONSTRUCTION , RESIDENTIAL * INCOME - EFFECT OF * REGRESSION
　　　　　- LIMITED DEPENDENT * LIFE CYCLE - FIRM

YA3361　SU V.
　　　　　"An error analysis of econometric and noneconometric forecasts" with
　　　　　discussion　Am. Econ. Ass. Proc., 1978, pp.306-312 & 320-321.
　　　　　JUDGEMENTAL FORECASTS - ASA NBER SURVEY * EX ANTE * COMPARATIVE METHODS -
　　　　　MACRO MODELS * COMPARATIVE METHODS - CAUSAL(SIMULTANEOUS SYSTEM) ,
　　　　　JUDGEMENTAL * FORECAST - REVISION * MACRO MODEL - WHARTON * EVALUATION -
　　　　　MACRO MODELS

YA3362　SUBBA RAO T.
　　　　　"The fitting of non-stationary time series models with time-dependent
　　　　　parameters"　R. Statist. Soc. (B), vol.32, 1970, pp.312-322.
　　　　　TIME SERIES - NON STATIONARY * SPECTRAL ANALYSIS - CHANGING SPECTRA *
　　　　　STABILITY OF COEFFICIENTS - TIME SERIES * ADVANCED

YA3363　SUBBA RAO T., TONG H.
　　　　　"A test for time dependence of linear open-loop systems"　R. Statist. Soc.
　　　　　(B), vol.34, 1972, pp.235-250.
　　　　　SPECTRAL ANALYSIS - CHANGING SPECTRA * STATIONARITY - TESTING * ADVANCED

YA3364　SUDIT E.F.
　　　　　"Additive nonhomogenous production functions in telecommunications"　Bell
　　　　　J. Econ., vol.4, 1973, pp.499-514.
　　　　　PRODUCTION FUNCTIONS - FIRM * APPL - FIRM : UTILITIES , TELEPHONE * DATA -
　　　　　CROSS SECTION , TIME SERIES * STABILITY OF COEFFICIENTS - REGRESSION : APPL
　　　　　* TECHNOLOGY - EFFECT OF * PRODUCTION FUNCTIONS - SUBSTITUTION * PRODUCTION
　　　　　FUNCTIONS - SCALE RETURNS * PRODUCTION FUNCTIONS - THEORY * EVALUATION -
　　　　　PRODUCTION FUNCTIONS

YA3365　SUDMAN S., FERBER R.
　　　　　"A comparison of alternative procedures for collecting consumer expenditure
　　　　　data for frequently purchased products"　J. Mktg. Res., vol.11, 1974,
　　　　　pp.128-135.
　　　　　EVALUATION - SURVEYS , CONSUMER * SURVEYS - METHODOLOGY * APPL - SECTOR :
　　　　　CONSUMER NON DURABLES

YA3366　SUITS D.B., ET AL.
　　　　　"Birth control in an econometric simulation"　Int. Econ. Rev., vol.16,
　　　　　1975, pp.92-111.
　　　　　POPULATION - FERTILITY * APPL - MACRO , LDC * APPL - MACRO , OECD * APPL -
　　　　　MACRO : GROWTH * DATA - INTERNATIONAL * POPULATION - EFFECT OF

YA3367   SUITS D.B., MASON A., CHAN L.
          "Spline functions fitted by standard regression methods"   Rev. Econ.
          Stats., vol.60, 1978, pp.132-139.
          REGRESSION - PIECEWISE * SPLINE FUNCTIONS * INTEREST RATE - DETERMINANTS
YA3368   SULLIVAN J.A., MARCIS R.G.
          "Forecasting consumer instalment credit: an application of parametric time
          series modelling"   J. Business, vol.48, 1975, pp.98-107.
          APPL - SECTOR : FINANCE , CONSUMER CREDIT , HIRE PURCHASE * EX ANTE * TIME
          SERIES - ARIMA : INTRODUCTION
YA3369   SULLIVAN T.G.
          "A note on market power and returns to stockholders"   Rev. Econ. Stats.,
          vol.59, 1977, pp.108-113.
          CONCENTRATION - EFFECT OF * APPL - FIRM : FINANCE , PROFITS * APPL - FIRM :
          FINANCE , CAPITALISATION
YA3370   SUMMERS B.J.
          "Interest rate expectations and the demand for short-term business credit"
          Bus. Econ., vol.13:3, 1978, pp.63-67.
          INTEREST RATE - EFFECT OF * ERROR SPECIFICATION - AUTOCORRELATED : APPL *
          INTEREST RATE - EXPECTATIONS * APPL - SECTOR : FINANCE , FINANCIAL STRUCTURE
YA3371   SUNOO D., LIN L.Y.S.
          "Sales effects of promotion and advertising"   J. Advtg. Res., vol.18:5,
          1978, pp.37-40.
          ADVERTISING - EXPERIMENTAL DESIGN * ADVERTISING - EFFECT OF * APPL - FIRM :
          CONSUMER NON DURABLES * BRAND CHOICE - APPL * BASIC
YA3372   SURREY M.J.C., OMEROD P.A.
          "Formal and informal aspects of forecasting with an econometric model"
          Nat. Inst. Econ. Rev., no.81, 1977, pp.67-71.
          MACRO MODELS - METHODOLOGY , ADJUSTMENTS * JUDGEMENTAL FORECASTS -
          INCORPORATION
YA3373   SUSHKA M.E., SLOVIN M.B.
          "The macroeconomic impact of changes in the ceilings on deposit rates"   J.
          Finance, vol.32, 1977, pp.117-130.
          POLICY EVALUATION - MACRO : MONETARY * MACRO MODEL - FRB , MIT , PENN * APPL
          - MACRO : MONEY * INTEREST RATE - EFFECT OF * SIMULATION - APPL : MACRO ,
          MONEY
YA3374   SUTHERLAND R.J.
          "Income velocity and commercial bank portfolios"   J. Finance, vol.32,
          1977, pp.1752-1758.
          APPL - MACRO : MONEY , INCOME VELOCITY * INTEREST RATE - EFFECT OF * APPL -
          SECTOR : FINANCE , BANKS * APPL - SECTOR : FINANCE , BONDS * APPL - SECTOR :
          FINANCE , FINANCIAL STRUCTURE
YA3375   SVEIKAUSKAS L.
          "Bias in cross-section estimates of the elasticity substitution"   Int.
          Econ. Rev., vol.15, 1974, pp.522-528.
          PRODUCTION FUNCTIONS - SECTOR * REGRESSION - COVARIANCE MODEL * PRODUCTION
          FUNCTIONS - SUBSTITUTION * SPECIFICATION ERROR - EFFECT OF , INDEPENDENCE ,
          REGRESSORS , ERRORS
YA3376   SWAMY P.A.V.B.
          "Criteria, constraints and multicollinearity in random coefficient
          regression models"   Anns. Econ. Soc. Meas., vol.2, 1973, pp.429-450.
          MULTICOLLINEARITY - EFFECT OF * REGRESSION - RIDGE * REGRESSION - RANDOM
          COEFFICIENTS * COMPARATIVE METHODS - ESTIMATION : REGRESSION , RANDOM
          COEFFICIENTS * ESTIMATION - STEIN * ADVANCED
YA3377   SWAMY P.A.V.B., MEHTA J.S.
          "Bayesian and non Bayesian analysis of switching regressions and of random
          coefficient regression models"   J. Am. Statist. Ass., vol.70, 1975,
          pp.593-602.
          BAYESIAN - ESTIMATION : REGRESSION , SWITCHING * DATA ERRORS - EFFECT OF *
          REGRESSION - SWITCHING * REGRESSION - RANDOM COEFFICIENTS * APPL - FIRM :
          FINANCE , BANK , DEBITS * REGRESSION - ESTIMATION * ADVANCED
YA3378   SWAMY P.A.V.B., MEHTA J.S.
          "Estimation of linear models with time and cross-sectionally varying
          coefficients"   J. Am. Statist. Ass., vol.72, 1977, pp.890-898.
          REGRESSION - RANDOM COEFFICIENTS * ESTIMATION - CROSS SECTION , TIME SERIES
          * APPL - MACRO : MONEY , DEMAND * ADVANCED
YA3379   SWAMY P.A.V.B., MEHTA J.S.
          "On Bayesian estimation of seemingly unrelated regressions when some
          observations are missing"   J. Econometrics, vol.3, 1975, pp.157-169.
          DATA ERROR - MISSING OBSERVATIONS * REGRESSION - SEEMINGLY UNRELATED *
          ERRORR SPECIFICATION - CORRELATED * BAYESIAN - ESTIMATION : REGRESSION ,
          SEEMINGLY UNRELATED * ADVANCED
YA3380   SWAMY P.A.V.B., RAPPOPORT P.N.
          "Relative efficiencies of some simple Bayes estimators of coefficients in a
          dynamic equation with serially correlated errors-II"   J. Econometrics,
          vol.7, 1978, pp.245-258.
          EVALUATION - REGRESSION , RIDGE * ERROR SPECIFICATION - AUTOCORRELATED *
          COMPARATIVE METHODS - ESTIMATION : REGRESSION , ERROR SPECIFICATION *
          BAYESIAN - ESTIMATION : REGRESSION , ERROR SPECIFICATION

YA3381   SWAMY P.A.V.B., RAPPOPORT P.N.
          "Relative efficiencies of some simple Bayes estimators of coefficients in
          dynamic models-I"   J. Econometrics, vol.3, 1975, pp.273-296.
          REGRESSION - LAGGED DEPENDENT * ESTIMATION - STEIN * REGRESSION - RIDGE *
          BAYESIAN - ESTIMATION : REGRESSION * BAYESIAN - ESTIMATION : DISTRIBUTED LAG
          * DATA - SIMULATION * REGRESSION - PRIOR INFORMATION * MULTICOLLINEARITY -
          EFFECT OF * COMPARATIVE METHODS - ESTIMATION : REGRESSION * COMPARATIVE
          METHODS - ESTIMATION : OLS , BAYES * COMPARATIVE METHODS - ESTIMATION : OLS
          , RIDGE

YA3382   SWAN C.
          "Homebuilding: a review of experience" with discussion   Brookings Paps.
          Econ. Activity, 1970, pp.48-76.
          APPL - SECTOR : CONSTRUCTION , RESIDENTIAL

YA3383   SWAN C.
          "Labor and material requirements for housing" with discussion   Brookings
          Paps. Econ. Activity, 1971, pp.347-382.
          APPL - SECTOR : CONSTRUCTION , RESIDENTIAL * APPL - SECTOR : EMPLOYMENT *
          APPL - SECTOR : AGRICULTURE , TIMBER * APPL - SECTOR : FINANCE , MORTGAGES

YA3384   SWAN N.
          "Differences in the response of the demand for labour to variations in
          output among Canadian regions"   Can. J. Econ., vol.5, 1972, pp.373-385.
          MANPOWER PLANNING - REGIONAL * REGIONAL MODELS - MANPOWER PLANNING ,
          EMPLOYMENT * BUSINESS CYCLE - REGIONAL

YA3385   SWAN N.
          "The response of labour supply to demand in Canadian regions"   Can. J.
          Econ., vol.7, 1974, pp.418-433.
          REGIONAL MODELS - MANPOWER PLANNING , LABOUR PARTICIPATION * MANPOWER
          PLANNING - REGIONAL * MANPOWER PLANNING - LABOUR PARTICIPATION

YA3386   SWAN P.L.
          "National rubber trade: the implications of synthetic rubber innovations"
          Appl. Econ., vol.3, 1971, pp.57-66.
          APPL - SECTOR : PRODUCTION , RUBBER * PRICE - EFFECT OF * APPL - SECTOR :
          INTERNATIONAL TRADE

YA3387   SWEENEY J.C.
          "Energy modeling and forecasting: implications for strategic planning"
          Bus. Econ., vol.13:4, 1978, pp.21-27.
          APPL - MACRO : ENERGY * FORECASTING - INTRODUCTION * BASIC

YA3388   SWEENEY R.E., ULVELING E.F.
          "A transformation for simplifying the interpretation of coefficients of
          binary variables in regression analysis"   Am. Stat'n., vol.26:5, 1972,
          pp.30-32.
          REGRESSION - COVARIANCE MODEL * REGRESSION - MODEL INTERPRETATION * BASIC

YA3389   SYRON R.F.
          "Administered prices and the market reaction: the case of urban core
          property insurance"   J. Finance, vol.28, 1973, pp.147-156.
          APPL - SECTOR : FINANCE , INSURANCE * REGIONAL MODELS - CITY

YA3390   SYRQUIN M.
          "Efficient input frontiers for the manufacturing sector in Mexico 1965-1980"
          Int. Econ. Rev., vol.14, 1973, pp.657-675.
          APPL - MACRO , LATIN AMERICA * APPL - SECTOR : EFFICIENCY * PRODUCTION
          FUNCTIONS - SECTOR

YA3391   SZROETER J.
          "A class of parametric tests for heteroscedasticity in linear econometric
          models"   Econometrica, vol.46, 1978, pp.1311-1327.
          HETEROSCEDASTICITY - TEST * ADVANCED

YA3392   SZROETER J.
          "Generalised variance-ratio tests for serial correlation in multivariate
          models"   J. Econometrics, vol.8, 1978, pp.47-59.
          AUTOCORRELATION - TEST * ERROR SPECIFICATION - AUTOCORRELATED * ADVANCED

YA3393   TACHIBANAKI T.
          "Wage determinations in Japanese manufacturing industries-structural change
          and wage differentials"   Int. Econ. Rev., vol.16, 1975, pp.562-586.
          MANPOWER PLANNING - DISCRIMINATION , SEX * APPL - SECTOR : EARNINGS *
          MANPOWER PLANNING - LABOUR FORCE COMPOSITION

YA3394   TAGGART R.A.
          "A model of corporate financing decisions"   J. Finance, vol.32, 1977
          pp.1467-1484.
          APPL - SECTOR : FINANCE , FINANCIAL STRUCTURE * SIMULTANEOUS SYSTEM - APPL *
          COMPARATIVE METHODS - REGRESSION , SEEMINGLY UNRELATED * COMPARATIVE METHODS
          - REGRESSION , ERROR SPECIFICATION

YA3395   TALLEY R.J.
          "The true condition of profits as reflected in stock prices and the rate of
          capital formation"   Bus. Econ., vol.13:4, 1978, pp.33-41.
          APPL - SECTOR : FINANCE , STOCK PRICE INDEX * STOCK PRICES - DETERMINANTS *
          APPL - MACRO : INVESTMENT * APPL - MACRO : PROFITS

YA3396   TALPAZ H.
          "Nonlinear estimation by an efficient numerical search"   Rev. Econ.
          Stats., vol.53, 1976, pp.501-504.
          NUMERICAL METHODS - OPTIMISATION * ESTIMATION - NON LINEAR * COMPARATIVE
          METHODS - ESTIMATION : REGRESSION , NON LINEAR

YA3397   TANNER J.C.
"Long term forecasting of vehicle ownership and road traffic" with
discussion   R. Statist, Soc. (A), vol.141, 1978, pp.14-62.
APPL - SECTOR : CONSUMER DURABLES , CARS * APPL - SECTOR : GOVERNMENT ,
ROADS * APPL - SECTOR : TRANSPORT , ROAD * REGRESSION - NON LINEAR * LONG
TERM FORECASTING * DATA - INTERNATIONAL * EX ANTE

YA3398   TANNER J.E.
"The determinants of interest cost on new municipal bonds: a reevaluation"
J. Business, vol.48, 1975, pp.74-80.
APPL - SECTOR : FINANCE , BONDS * USER - SECTOR : GOVERNMENT , LOCAL *
INTEREST RATE - DETERMINANTS * APPL - SECTOR : GOVERNMENT , LOCAL , FINANCE

YA3399   TANNER J.E.
"Variable distributed lags and forecasting non-residential construction"
Can. J. Econ., vol.7, 1974, pp.642-654.
APPL - SECTOR : CONSTRUCTION , NON RESIDENTIAL * DISTRIBUTED LAG - VARIABLE
LAG * DISTRIBUTED LAG - APPL , ORDERS * EVALUATION - SURVEYS , BUSINESS *
COMPARATIVE METHODS - CAUSAL , SURVEYS

YA3400   TANNER J.E., KOCHIN L.A.
"The determinants of the difference between bid and ask prices on Government
bonds"   J. Business, vol.44, 1971, pp.375-379.
APPL - SECTOR : GOVERNMENT , FINANCE * APPL - SECTOR : FINANCE , BONDS *
PRICE - SECTOR : FINANCE

YA3401   TANZI V., HART T.P.
"The effect of the 1964 revenue act on the sensitivity of the Federal income
tax"   Rev. Econ. Stats., vol.54, 1972, pp.326-328.
APPL - SECTOR : GOVERNMENT , TAX * DATA - CROSS SECTION , TIME SERIES *
REGIONAL MODELS - TAX * INCOME - EFFECT OF

YA3402   TAPIERO C.S.
"On line and adaptive optimum advertising control by a diffusion
approximation"   Ops. Res., vol.23, 1975, pp.890-907.
DIFFERENTIAL EQUATIONS * ADVERTISING - OPTIMALITY * CONTROL THEORY -
STOCHASTIC , THEORY * CONTROL THEORY - STOCHASTIC , METHODOLOGY * USE -
MEDIA PLANNING * PROBABILITY MODELS - DIFFUSION * ADVANCED

YA3403   TAPIERO C.S.
"Random walk models of advertising: their diffusion approximation and
hypothesis testing"   Anns. Econ. Soc. Meas., vol.4, 1975, pp.293-310.
ADVERTISING - EFFECT OF * PROBABILITY MODELS - BIRTH PROCESS * RANDOM WALK -
METHODOLOGY * APPL - FIRM : CONSUMER NON DURABLES , HEALTH AIDS * ADVANCED

YA3404   TAUB A.J.
"Determinants of the firm's capital structure"   Rev. Econ. Stats., vol.57,
1975, pp.410-416.
APPL - FIRM : FINANCE , FINANCIAL STRUCTURE * REGRESSION - LIMITED DEPENDENT
, PROBIT * TAX - EFFECT OF * RISK - EFFECT OF * VOLATILITY - EFFECT OF

YA3405   TAUBER E.M.
"Forecasting sales prior to test market"   J. Mktg., vol.41:1, 1977,
pp.80-84.
NEW PRODUCTS - EVALUATION * BASIC

YA3406   TAUBER E.M.
"Why concept and product tests fail to predict new product results"   J.
Mktg., vol.39, no.4, Oct 1975, pp.69-71.
NEW PRODUCTS - IDENTIFICATION * EVALUATION - NEW PRODUCT FORECASTS * BASIC

YA3407   TAUBMAN P.
"Personal saving: a time series analysis of three measures of the same
conceptual series"   Rev. Econ. Stats., vol.50, 1968, pp.125-129.
DATA ERRORS - EFFECT OF * APPL - MACRO : SAVINGS * SPECIFICATION ERROR -
EFFECT OF , SPECIFICATION OF VARIABLES * DATA ERRORS - ESTIMATION OF *
REGRESSSION - SPECIFICATION OF VARIABLES

YA3408   TAUBMAN P., GOTTSCHALK P.
"The average workweek of capital in manufacturing"   J. Am. Statist. Assn.,
vol.66, 1971, pp.448-455.
CAPACITY - ESTIMATION

YA3409   TAYLOR A.J.
"System dynamics in shipping"   Opl. Res. Q., vol.27, 1976, pp.41-56.
INDUSTRIAL DYNAMICS - APPL , SECTOR * APPL - SECTOR : TRANSPORT , SHIPPING *
BASIC

YA3410   TAYLOR A.J.
"The modelling of supply in the shipping industry"   Omega, vol.4, 1976,
pp.175-180.
APPL - SECTOR : TRANSPORT , SHIPPING * SUPPLY - SECTOR : TRANSPORT *
INDUSTRIAL DYNAMICS - APPL , SECTOR * BASIC

YA3411   TAYLOR J., GUJARATI D.
"The behaviour of unemployment and unfilled vacancies: Great Britain,
1958-1971: Alternative views"   Econ. J., vol.82, 1972, pp.1352-
POLICY EVALUATION - MACRO : UNEMPLOYMENT * APPL - MACRO : UNEMPLOYMENT *
APPL - MACRO , UK * CAPACITY - EFFECT OF * APPL - SECTOR : UNEMPLOYMENT

YA3412   TAYLOR J.B.
"Methods of efficient parameter estimation in control problems"   Anns.
Econ. Soc. Meas., vol.5, 1976, pp.339-347.
DATA - CONTROL BIAS * REGRESSION - ESTIMATION * REGRESSION - CONTROL *
CONTROL THEORY - STOCHASTIC , METHODOLOGY

YA3413   TAYLOR J.W., HOULAHAN J.J., GABRIEL A.C.
"The purchase intention question in new product development: a field test"
J. Mktg., vol.39, no.1, Jan 1975, pp.90-92.
EVALUATION - EXPECTATIONS , DATA * NEW PRODUCTS - TESTING * EVALUATION -
SURVEYS , CONSUMER

YA3414   TAYLOR L.D.
"Saving out of different kinds of income" with discussion   Brookings Paps,
Econ. Activity, 1971, pp.383-416.
APPL - MACRO : SAVINGS * STABILITY OF COEFFICIENTS - REGRESSION

YA3415   TAYLOR L.D.
"The demand for electricity: a survey"   Bell J. Econ., vol.6, 1975,
pp.74-110.
APPL - SECTOR : UTILITIES , ELECTRICITY * PRICE - EFFECT OF * INCOME -
EFFECT OF * BIBLIOGRAPHY - ELECTRICITY * EVALUATION - ELECTRICITY DEMAND
MODELS

YA3416   TAYLOR L.D., WEISERBS D.
"Advertising and the aggregate consumption function"   Am. Econ. Rev.,
vol.62, 1972, pp.642-655.
APPL - MACRO : SAVINGS * ADVERTISING - EFFECT OF

YA3417   TAYLOR L.D., WEISERBS D.
"On the estimation of dynamic demand functions"   Rev. Econ. Stats.,
vol.54, 1972, pp.459-465.
CONSUMER BEHAVIOUR - ECONOMIC MODELS * EX ANTE * APPL - MACRO : CONSUMER
DEMAND * COMPARATIVE METHODS - ESTIMATION : DEMAND EQUATIONS * DEMAND
EQUATIONS - SYSTEMS OF : METHODOLOGY , ESTIMATION

YA3418   TAYLOR R.A.
"Economies of scale in large credit unions"   Appl. Econ., vol.4, 1972,
pp.33-40.
APPL - FIRM : FINANCE , BANKS * COST - FIRM : FINANCE , BANKS * COST - SCALE
ECONOMIES

YA3419   TAYLOR S.J., KINGSMAN B.G.
"Non-stationarity in sugar prices"   J. Opl. Res. Soc., vol.29, 1978,
pp.971-980.
APPL - SECTOR : COMMODITIES , SUGAR * APPL - SECTOR : FINANCE , FUTURES
TRADING * TIME SERIES - ARIMA : TRANSFORMATIONS * TIME SERIES - NON
STATIONARY * TIME SERIES - STATE SPACE

YA3420   TAYLOR W.H.
"The heteroscedastic linear model: exact finite sample results"
Econometrica, vol.46, 1978, pp.663-675.
SPECIFICATION ERROR - EFFECT OF , HETEROSCEDASTICITY * ESTIMATION -
HETEROSCEDASTIC MODELS * ESTIMATION - GLS * APPL - FIRM : INVESTMENT

YA3421   TEECE D.
"Time-cost tradeoffs: elasticity estimates and determinants for
international technology transfer projects"   Mgmt. Sci., vol.23, 1977,
pp.830-837.
APPL - FIRM : TECHNOLOGY * TIME - VALUE OF * USE - PROJECT , PLANNING

YA3422   TEEKENS R., KOERTS J.
"Some statistical implications of the log transformation of multiplicative
models"   Econometrica, vol.40, 1972, pp.793-819.
REGRESSION - TRANSFORMATIONS , LOGARITHMIC * ERROR DISTRIBUTION - LOGNORMAL
* COMPARATIVE METHODS - ESTIMATION : REGRESSION , TRANSFORMATIONS *
REGRESSION - ESTIMATION - ESTIMATION - LOGARITHMIC MODEL * ERROR
SPECIFICATION - MULTIPLICATIVE

YA3423   TEETERS N.H.
"Built-in flexibility of Federal expenditures" with discussion   Brookings
Paps, Econ. Activity, 1971, pp.615-657.
APPL - SECTOR : GOVERNMENT , EXPENDITURE

YA3424   TEICHMOELLER J.
"A note on the distribution of stock price changes"   J. Am. Statist. Ass.,
vol.66, 1971, pp.282-284.
STOCK PRICES - DISTRIBUTION * APPL - FIRM : FINANCE , STOCK PRICES * ERROR
DISTRIBUTION - COMPOUND * ERROR DISTRIBUTION - STABLE

YA3425   TEIGEN R.L., GIBSON W.E.
"Demand and supply functions for money: another look at theory and
measurement"   Econometrica, vol.44, 1976, pp.377-389.
APPL - MACRO : MONEY * INCOME - EFFECT OF * INTEREST RATE - EFFECT OF *
EVALUATION - MONEY SUPPLY , MODELS OF * EVALUATION - MONEY DEMAND , MODELS
OF

YA3426   TERASVIRTA T.
"A note on bias in the Almon distributed lag estimator"   Econometrica,
vol.44, 1976, pp.1317-1321.
EVALUATION - DISTRIBUTED LAG , MODEL SPECIFICATION * SPECIFICATION ERROR -
EFFECT OF , LAG STRUCTURE * COMPARATIVE METHODS - ESTIMATION : DISTRIBUTED
LAG * DISTRIBUTED LAG - ALMON , ESTIMATION

YA3427   TERRELL R.D., TUCKWELL N.E.
"The efficiency of least squares in estimating a stable seasonal pattern"
J. Am. Statist. Ass., vol.66, 1971, pp.354-362.
SEASONALITY - ESTIMATION , OLS * ERROR SPECIFICATION - AUTOCORRELATED *
SPECIFICATION ERROR - EFFECT OF , FILTERING

YA3428   THATCHER A.R.
         "Year-to-year variations in the earnings of individuals"   R. Statist. Soc.
         (A), vol.134, 1971, pp.374-382.
         APPL - MACRO : EARNINGS * MANPOWER PLANNING - EARNINGS
YA3429   THEIL H., KOSOBUD R.F.
         "How informative are consumer buying intentions surveys"   Rev. Econ.
         Stats., vol.50, 1968, pp.50-59.
         EVALUATION - THEORY OF * EVALUATION - SURVEYS , CONSUMER * EXPECTATIONS -
         DATA * REGRESSION - LIMITED DEPENDENT , LOGIT * APPL - SECTOR : CONSUMER
         DURABLES , CARS
YA3430   THEIL H., SCHOLES M.
         "Forecast evaluation based on a multiplicative decomposition of mean square
         errors"   Econometrica, vol.35, 1967, pp.70-88.
         EVALUATION - THEORY OF * INPUT OUTPUT - PROJECTION OF STRUCTURE * EVALUATION
         - INPUT OUTPUT * STABILITY OF COEFFICIENTS - INPUT OUTPUT * INPUT OUTPUT -
         MACRO , NETHERLANDS
YA3431   THEOBALD C.M.
         "Generalisations of mean square error applied to ridge regression"   R.
         Statist. Soc. (B), vol.36, 1974, pp.103-106.
         REGRESSION - RIDGE * LOSS FUNCTIONS - THEORY
YA3432   THOMADAKIS S.B.
         "A value-based test of profitability and market structure"   Rev. Econ.
         Stats., vol.59, 1977, pp.179-185.
         APPL - FIRM : FINANCE , CAPITALISATION * CONCENTRATION - EFFECT OF
YA3433   THOMAS J., CHHABRIA P.
         "Bayesian models for new product pricing"   Decis. Sci., vol.6, 1975,
         pp.51-64.
         BAYESIAN - ESTIMATION : PROBABILITY MODEL * NEW PRODUCTS - PRICING *
         BAYESIAN - CONTROL * CONSUMER BEHAVIOUR - STOCHASTIC MODELS * CONTROL THEORY
         - STOCHASTIC , APPL * LP * USE - PRICING * LOSS FUNCTIONS - FIRM
YA3434   THOMAS M.U., BARR D.R.
         "An approximate test of Markov chain lumpability"   J. Am. Statist. Ass.,
         vol.72, 1977, pp.175-179.
         MARKOV MODELS - THEORY * MARKOV MODELS - APPL : MANPOWER * MANPOWER PLANNING
         - SECTOR : EDUCATION , UNIVERSITIES * MANPOWER PLANNING - PROMOTION *
         MANPOWER PLANNING - FIRM
YA3435   THOMAS R.L.
         "Money wage inflation in industrial countries: an alternative explanation"
         Rev. Econ. Studies, vol.43, 1976, pp.551-552.
         DATA - CROSS SECTION * DATA - INTERNATIONAL * APPL - MACRO : EARNINGS *
         UNIONIZATION - EFFECT OF * INFLATION - PHILLIPS
YA3436   THOMAS R.L.
         "Unionization and the Phillips curve- time series evidence from seven
         industrial countries"   Appl. Econ., vol.9, 1977, pp.33-49.
         INFLATION - PHILLIPS CURVE * UNIONISATION - EFFECT OF * DATA - INTERNATIONAL
YA3437   THOMAS R.W.
         "The effect of averaging components on the predictability of the index of
         consumer sentiment"   Rev. Econ. Stats., vol.57, 1975, pp.84-91.
         ATTITUDINAL DATA * SURVEYS - CONSUMER , DETERMINANTS * SPECTRAL ANALYSIS -
         CROSS : APPL * APPL - SECTOR : CONSUMER DURABLES , CARS * BUSINESS
         INDICATORS - APPL * ERROR SPECIFICATION - AUTOCORRELATED * ESTIMATION - GLS
         * SPECTRAL ANALYSIS - APPL : BUSINESS INDICATORS * INDEX NUMBERS - MACRO :
         CONSUMER CONFIDENCE
YA3438   THOMPSON D.J.
         "Sources of systematic risk in common stock"   J. Business, vol.49, 1976,
         pp.173-188.
         APPL - FIRM : FINANCE , STOCK PRICES * STOCK PRICES - BETA , DETERMINANTS
YA3439   THOMPSON H.E., KRAJEWSKI L.J.
         "A behavioural test of adaptive forecasting"   Decis. Sci., vol.3:4, 1972,
         pp.108-119.
         APPL - FIRM : UTILITIES , ELECTRICITY * TIME SERIES - ARIMA : APPL *
         COMPARATIVE METHODS - ARIMA , JUDGEMENTAL
YA3440   THOMPSON H.E., TIAO G.C.
         "Analysis of telephone data: a case study of forecasting seasonal time
         series   Bell J. Econ., vol.2, 1971, pp.515-541.
         TIME SERIES - ARIMA : INTRODUCTION * APPL - FIRM : UTILITIES , TELEPHONE
YA3441   THOMPSON M.L.
         "Selection of variables in multiple regression: part i, A review and
         evaluation"   Int. Statist. Rev., vol.46, 1978, pp.1-19 & 146.
         REGRESSION - VARIABLE INCLUSION * REGRESSION - STEPWISE * LOSS FUNCTIONS -
         CP * BIBLIOGRAPHY - REGRESSION
YA3442   THOMPSON M.L.
         "Selection of variables in multiple regression: Part ii, Chosen procedures
         and examples"   Int. Statist. Rev., vol.46, 1978, pp.129-146.
         REGRESSION - VARIABLE INCLUSION * LOSS FUNCTIONS - CP
YA3443   THOMPSON R.G., ET AL.
         "A stochastic investment model for a survival conscious firm applied to
         shrimp fishing"   Appl. Econ., vol.5, 1973, pp.75-87.
         APPL - FIRM : AGRICULTURE , FISHIING * USE - CAPITAL INVESTMENT * SIMULATION
         - APPL : FIRM , AGRICULTURE

YA3444   THOMPSON T.D.
"Interest rate forecasting: an eclectic approach"   Bus. Econ., vol.12:1,
1977, pp.28-32.
INTEREST RATE - DETERMINANTS * EX ANTE * POLICY EVALUATION - MACRO :
MONETARY * BASIC

YA3445   THOMPSON W., VERTINSKY I., KANE J.
"Canadian industrial policy - simulation and analysis"   Long Range
Planning, vol.6:4, 1973, pp.66-73.
SIMULATION - APPL : MACRO * POLICY EVALUATION - MACRO * SIMULATION -
METHODOLOGY

YA3446   THORNBER H.
"Finite sample Monte Carlo studies: an autoregressive illustration"   J.
Am. Statist. Ass., vol.62, 1967, pp.801-818.
SIMULATION - EXPERIMENTAL DESIGN * SIMULATION - EVALUATION OF RESULTS * TIME
SERIES - AUTOREGRESSIVE * LOSS FUNCTIONS - METHODOLOGY * COMPARATIVE METHODS
- ESTIMATION : TIME SERIES * EVALUATION - THEORY OF * TIME SERIES - BAYESIAN
* ADVANCED

YA3447   THURSBY J.G., LOVELL C.A.K.
"An investigation of the Kmenta approximation to the CES function"   Int.
Econ. Rev., vol 19, 1978, pp.363-377.
PRODUCTION FUNCTIONS - ESTIMATION * DATA - SIMULATION * EVALUATION -
PRODUCTION FUNCTIONS

YA3448   THURSBY J.G., SCHMIDT P.
"Some properties of tests for specification error in a linear regression
model"   J. Am. Statist. Ass., vol.72, 1977, pp.635-641.
DATA - SIMULATION * SPECIFICATION ERROR - TESTS , VARIABLE INCLUSION *
SPECIFICATION ERROR - TESTS , TRANSFORMATIONS * SPECIFICATION ERROR - TESTS
, EVALUATION

YA3449   THURSTON P.H.
"Make T.F. serve corporate planning"   H.B.R., vol.49, Sept-Oct, 1971,
pp.98-102.
TECHNOLOGICAL FORECASTING * USE - CORPORATE PLANNING * BASIC

YA3450   THURSTON P.H.
"Requirements planning for inventory control"   H.B.R., vol.50, May-June,
1972, pp.67-71.
USE - INVENTORY CONTROL * BASIC

YA3451   THURSTON T.B.
"Regional interaction and the reserve adjustment lag within the commercial
banking sector"   J. Finance, vol.31, 1976, pp.1443-1456.
APPL - SECTOR : FINANCE , BANK , LIABILITIES * DATA - AGGREGATION OVER TIME
* DISTRIBUTED LAG - AGGREGATION EFFECT * REGIONAL MODELS - SECTOR : FINANCE
* APPL - SECTOR : FINANCE , BANKS

YA3452   TILLMAN J.A.
"The power of the Durbin-Watson test"   Econometrica, vol.43, 1975,
pp.959-974.
EVALUATION - TEST , AUTOCORRELATION * ERROR SPECIFICATION - AUTOCORRELATED

YA3453   TILLMAN J.A., BELSLEY D.A.
"The relative power of the tau-test: a comment"   Rev. Econ. Stats.,
vol.56, 1974, pp.416-418.
COMPARATIVE METHODS - TESTS , AUTOCORRELATION * EVALUATION - TEST ,
AUTOCORRELATION * NON PARAMETRIC - TEST

YA3454   TINIC S.M., HARNDEN B.M., JANNSEN C.T.L.
"Estimation of rural demand for natural gas"   Mgmt. Sci. (B), vol.20,
1973, pp.604-615.
APPL - SECTOR : UTILITIES , GAS * PRICE - EFFECT OF * DATA - CROSS SECTION

YA3455   TINSLEY P.A.
"A variable adjustment model of labour demand"   Int. Econ. Rev., vol.12,
1971, pp.482-510.
DISTRIBUTED LAG - VARIABLE LAG * APPL - MACRO : EMPLOYMENT * CAPACITY -
EFFECT OF * MANPOWER PLANNING - MACRO , DEMAND * ADVANCED

YA3456   TINSLEY P.A.
"An application of variable weight distributed lag"   J. Am. Statist. Ass.,
vol.62, 1967, pp.1277-1289.
DISTRIBUTED LAG - VARIABLE LAG * APPL - MACRO : OUTPUT * DISTRIBUTED LAG -
APPL , ORDERS * EX ANTE * COMPARATIVE METHODS - DISTRIBUTED LAG * ESTIMATION
- CONSTRAINED : APPL

YA3457   TOBIN J.
"Monetary policy in 1974 and beyond" with discussion   Brookings Paps,
Econ. Activity, 1974, pp.219-232 & 246-248.
POLICY EVALUATION - MACRO : MONETARY * APPL - MACRO : MONEY , DEMAND * APPL
- MACRO : INVESTMENT * INFLATION - DETERMINANTS , EARNINGS

YA3458   TODA Y.
"Estimation of a cost function when the cost is not minimum: the case of
Soviet manufacturing, 1958-1971"   Rev. Econ. Stats., vol.53, 1976,
pp.259-268.
COST - METHODOLOGY * COST - SECTOR * APPL - MACRO , USSR

YA3459   TODA Y.
"Substitutability and price distortation in the demand for factors of
production: an empirical estimation"   Appl. Econ. vol.9, 1977, pp.203-217.
COST - THEORY * COST - SECTOR * SUBSTITUTE FACTORS

YA3460   TOIKKA R.S.
"A Markovian model of labour market decisions by workers"   Am. Econ. Rev.,
vol.66, 1976, pp.821-834.
MARKOV MODELS - APPL : MANPOWER * SIMULATION - APPL : MACRO , MANPOWER *
MANPOWER PLANNING - LABOUR PARTICIPATION * MANPOWER PLANNING - LABOUR
TURNOVER

YA3461   TOIKKA R.S., HOLT C.C.
"Labour force participation and earnings in a demographic model of the
labour market"   Am. Econ. Ass. Proc., vol.66, 1976, pp.295-301.
MANPOWER PLANNING - LABOUR FORCE COMPOSITION * MANPOWER PLANNING - LABOUR
PARTICIPATION * MANPOWER PLANNING - LABOUR TURNOVER * SIMULATION - APPL :
MACRO , MANPOWER

YA3462   TOLLEY G.S., WANG Y., FLETCHER R.G.
"Reexamination of the time series evidence on food demand"   Econometrica,
vol.37, 1969, pp.695-705.
APPL - SECTOR : CONSUMER NON DURABLES , FOOD * EVALUATION - INDEX NUMBERS *
DATA - SPECIFICATION OF VARIABLES * PRICE - EFFECT OF * SUPPLY - SECTOR :
CONSUMER NON DURABLES * EVALUATION - PRICE ELASTICITIES * COMPARATIVE
METHODS - REGRESSION , MODEL SPECIFICATION * INDEX NUMBERS - SECTOR :
CONSUMER NON DURABLES

YA3463   TOMEK W.G.
"R squared in TSLS and GLS estimation"   Am. J Ag. Econ., vol.55, 1973,
p.670.
REGRESSION - SUMMARY STATISTICS * SIMULTANEOUS SYSTEM - SUMMARY STATISTICS *
ESTIMATION - 2SLS * ESTIMATION - GLS * BASIC

YA3464   TONG H.
"Some comments on the Canadian lynx data" with discussion   R. Statist.
Soc. (A) vol.140, 1977, pp.432-436, & 448-468.
APPL - SECTOR : NATURAL , ANIMAL POPULATIONS * TIME SERIES - ARIMA : APPL *
LOSS FUNCTIONS - AKAIKE'S INFORMATION CRITERION * TIME SERIES - HARMONICS

YA3465   TORRANCE G.W.
"Health status index models: a unified mathematical view"   Mgmt. Sci.,
vol.22, 1976, pp.990-1001.
INDEX NUMBERS - SECTOR : HEALTH

YA3466   TOYODA T.
"Price expectations and the short-run and long-run Phillips curves in Japan,
1956-1968"   Rev. Econ. Stats., vol.54, 1972, pp.267-274.
APPL - MACRO : EARNINGS * INFLATION - EFFECT OF * THEORY - EXPECTATIONS *
INFLATION - EXPECTATIONS * INFLATION - PHILLIPS CURVE * APPL - MACRO , JAPAN

YA3467   TOYODA T.
"Use of the Chow test under heteroscedasticity"   Econometrica, vol.42,
1974, pp.601-608.
STABILITY OF COEFFICIENTS - REGRESSION , TEST * SPECIFICATION ERROR - TESTS
, HETEROSCEDASTICITY * EVALUATION - TEST , STABILITY

YA3468   TREYZ G.I.
"An econometric procedure for ex post policy evaluation"   Int. Econ. Rev.,
vol.13, 1972, pp.212-222.
MACRO MODELS - METHODOLOGY * POLICY EVALUATION - METHODOLOGY * MACRO MODEL -
WHARTON , EFU * APPL - MACRO : UNEMPLOYMENT * INFLATION - DETERMINANTS

YA3469   TRIGG D.W., LEACH A.G.
"Exponential smoothing with an adaptive response rate"   Opl. Res. Q.,
vol.18, 1967, pp.53-59.
EXPONENTIAL SMOOTHING - ADAPTIVE COEFFICIENTS * TRACKING SIGNAL - APPL *
BASIC

YA3470   TRINKL F.H.
"A stochastic analysis of programs for the mentally retarded"   Ops. Res.,
vol.22, 1974, pp.1175-1191.
MARKOV MODELS - APPL : MANPOWER * HEALTH - HOSPITAL , PSYCHIATRIC * POLICY
EVALUATION - SECTOR : HEALTH

YA3471   TRIPLETT J.E., MERCHANT S.M.
"The CPI and the PCE deflator: an econometric analysis of true price
measures" with discussion.   Anns. Econ. Soc. Meas., vol.2, 1973,
pp.263-288.
INDEX NUMBERS - METHODOLOGY * INDEX NUMBERS - MACRO : CONSUMER PRICE *
EVALUATION - INDEX NUMBERS * DATA ERRORS - INDEX NUMBERS

YA3472   TRIPPI R.R.
"Estimating the relationship between price and time to sale for investment
property"   Mgmt. Sci., vol.23, 1977, pp.838-842.
USE - REAL ESTATE APPRAISAL * APPL - SECTOR : CONSTRUCTION , RESIDENTIAL *
CANONICAL CORRELATION - APPL

YA3473   TRIVEDI P.K.
"Retail inventory investments behaviour"   J. Econometrics, vol.1, 1973,
pp.61-80.
APPL - SECTOR : RETAILING * APPL - SECTOR : INVENTORIES * DISTRIBUTED LAG -
RATIONAL POLYNOMIAL

YA3474   TRIVEDI P.K.
         "Time series versus structural models: a case study of Canadian
         manufacturing inventory behaviour."   Int. Econ. Rev., vol.16, 1975,
         pp.587-608.
         APPL - SECTOR : INVENTORIES * APPL - MACRO , CANADA * APPL - MACRO :
         INVENTORIES * ERROR SPECIFICATION - ARMA * COMPARATIVE METHODS - ARIMA ,
         CAUSAL

YA3475   TSAO C.S.
         "The linearity property in the consumption function: estimation, tests and
         some related results"   Rev. Econ. Stats., vol.57, 1975, pp.214-220.
         APPL - MACRO : CONSUMPTION * EX ANTE * WEALTH - EFFECT OF * REGRESSION -
         TRANSFORMATIONS , BOX COX

YA3476   TSAO C.S., DAY R.H.
         "A process analysis model of the U.S. steel industry"   Mgmt. Sci. (8),
         vol.17, 1971, pp.588-608.
         INPUT OUTPUT - SECTOR : PRODUCTION * COST - SECTOR : PRODUCTION * SIMULATION
         - APPL : SECTOR , PRODUCTION * APPL - SECTOR : PRODUCTION , STEEL * LP

YA3477   TSE E.
         "Adaptive dual control methods"   Anns. Econ. Soc. Meas., vol.3, 1974,
         pp.65-83.
         CONTROL THEORY - STOCHASTIC , THEORY * BIBLIOGRAPHY - CONTROL THEORY *
         COMPARATIVE METHODS - CONTROL

YA3478   TSURUMI H.
         "A Bayesian test of the product cycle hypothesis applied to Japanese crude
         steel production"   J. Econometrics, vol.4, 1976, pp.371-392.
         PRODUCTION FUNCTIONS - SECTOR * APPL - SECTOR : PRODUCTION , STEEL *
         BAYESIAN - ESTIMATION : REGRESSION , PIECEWISE * TECHNOLOGY - EFFECT OF *
         LIFE CYCLE - PRODUCT * PRODUCTION FUNCTIONS - ESTIMATION * PRODUCTION
         FUNCTIONS - METHODOLOGY * REGRESSION - PIECEWISE * REGRESSION - SHIFTING
         COEFFICIENTS

YA3479   TSURUMI H.
         "A comparison of alternative optimal models of advertising expenditures:
         stock adjustment vs. control theoretic approaches"   Rev. Econ. Stats.,
         vol.55, 1973, pp.156-168.
         APPL - FIRM : CONSUMER NON DURABLES , PHARMACEUTICALS * DISTRIBUTED LAG -
         APPL , ADVERTISING * ADVERTISING - EFFECT OF * ADVERTISING - OPTIMALITY *
         CONTROL THEORY - DETERMINISTIC , APPL * DISTRIBUTED LAG - GAMMA *
         COMPARATIVE METHODS - AUTOREGRESSIVE , CAUSAL

YA3480   TSURUMI H.
         "A comparison of econometric macro models in three countries" with
         discussion   Am. Econ. Ass. Proc., 1973, pp.394-401 & 410-411.
         MACRO MODEL - WHARTON * MACRO MODEL - CANADA , RDX 2 * MACRO MODEL - JAPAN *
         MACRO MODELS - REVIEW * EVALUATION - MACRO MODELS * COMPARATIVE METHODS -
         DISTRIBUTED LAG

YA3481   TSURUMI H.
         "A note on gamma distributed lags"   Int. Econ. Rev., vol.12, 1971,
         pp.317-324.
         DISTRIBUTED LAG - SOLOW * DISTRIBUTED LAG - APPL , OUTPUT * APPL - MACRO,
         CANADA * APPL - MACRO : INVESTMENT * COMPARATIVE METHODS - DISTRIBUTED LAG

YA3482   TSURUMI H.
         "A survey of recent Canadian macro econometric models"   Can. J. Econ.,
         vol.6, 1973, pp.409-428.
         COMPARATIVE METHODS - MACRO MODELS * BIBLIOGRAPHY - MACRO MODELLING * MACRO
         MODEL - CANADA * MACRO MODEL - CANADA , RDX2

YA3483   TSURUMI H.
         "Effects of wage-parity and price synchronization between Canada and the US
         on Canadian economic growth: simulation experiments with a macro-model"
         Int. Econ. Rev., vol.13, 1972, pp. 644-678.
         MACRO MODEL - CANADA * APPL - MACRO : INTERNATIONAL LINKAGE

YA3484   TSURUMI H., TSURUMI Y.
         "A Bayesian estimation of macro and micro CES production functions"   J.
         Econometrics, vol.4, 1976, pp.1-25.
         PRODUCTION FUNCTIONS - ESTIMATION * BAYESIAN - ESTIMATION : PRODUCTION
         FUNCTIONS * PRODUCTION FUNCTIONS - MACRO * PRODUCTION FUNCTIONS - FIRM *
         APPL - MACRO , JAPAN * APPL - FIRM : PRODUCTION , ELECTRONICS

YA3485   TUCKMAN H.P., GAPINSK J.H., HAGEMANN R.P.
         "Faculty skills and the salary structure in academe: a market perspective"
         Am. Econ. Rev., vol.67, 1977, pp.692-702.
         MANPOWER PLANNING - SECTOR : EDUCATION , UNIVERSITIES * MANPOWER PLANNING -
         EARNINGS

YA3486   TULL D.S.
         "The relationship of actual and predicted sales and profits in new-product
         introductions"   J. Business, vol.40, 1967, pp.233-250.
         NEW PRODUCTS - EVALUATION * EVALUATION - NEW PRODUCT FORECASTS * NEW
         PRODUCTS - NEW BRAND * JUDGEMENTAL FORECASTS - BIAS

YA3487   TULL D.S., RUTEMILLER H.C.
         "A note on the relationship of actual and predicted sales and profits in
         new-product introductions"   J. Business, vol.41, 1968, pp.385-387.
         NEW PRODUCTS - EVALUATION * EVALUATION - NEW PRODUCT FORECASTS *
         SPECIFICATION ERROR - EFFECT OF , HETEROSCEDASTICITY

YA3488   TUNNICLIFFE WILSON G.
          "The estimation of parameters in multivariate time series models"   R.
          Statist. Soc. (B), vol.35, 1973, pp.76-85.
          TIME SERIES - MULTIVARIATE * ERROR SPECIFICATION - ARMA
YA3489   TURNBULL P., WILLIAMS G.
          "Sex differentials in teacher's pay"   R. Statist. Soc. (A), vol.137, 1974,
          pp.245-258.
          APPL - SECTOR : GOVERNMENT , EDUCATION , SCHOOLS * MANPOWER PLANNING -
          DISCRIMINATION , SEX * MANPOWER PLANNING - SECTOR : EDUCATION , SCHOOLS *
          DATA - CROSS SECTION * MANPOWER PLANNING - EARNINGS
YA3490   TURNER R.E., WIGINTON J.C.
          "Advertising expenditure trajectories: an empirical study for filter
          cigarettes 1953-1963"   Decis. Sci., vol.7, 1976, pp.496-509.
          ADVERTISING - OPTIMALITY * APPL - SECTOR : CONSUMER NON DURABLES ,
          CIGARETTES * MARKET SHARE - SECTOR : CONSUMER NON DURABLES * ERROR
          SPECIFICATION - AUTOCORRELATED * ESTIMATION - NON LINEAR * USE - MEDIA
          PLANNING * ADVERTISING - EFFECT OF
YA3491   TURNER R.K., GRACE R.P.
          "Forecasting the market demand for waste paper"   Long Range Planning,
          vol.10:3, 1977, pp.30-36.
          APPL - SECTOR : PRODUCTION , PAPER , WASTE
YA3492   TURNOVSKY S.J.
          "Empirical evidence on the formation of price expectations"   J. Am.
          Statist. Ass., vol.65, 1970, pp.1441-1454.
          INFLATION - EXPECTATIONS * EVALUATION - EXPECTATIONS , THEORY * EXPECTATIONS
          - DATA * COMPARATIVE METHODS - AUTOREGRESSIVE , JUDGEMENTAL
YA3493   TURNOVSKY S.J.
          "The expectations hypothesis and the aggregate wage equation: some
          empiricalevidence for Canada"   Economica, vol.39, 1972, pp.1-17.
          EXPECTATIONS - DATA * INFLATION - PHILLIPS CURVE * APPL - MACRO , CANADA *
          APPL - MACRO : EARNINGS
YA3494   TURNOVSKY S.J., WACHTER M.L.
          "A test of the 'expectations hypothesis' using directly observed wage and
          price expectations"   Rev. Econ. Stats., vol.54, 1972, pp.47-54.
          APPL - MACRO : EARNINGS * EXPECTATIONS - ESTIMATING * INFLATION -
          EXPECTATIONS * EXPECTATIONS - DATA * DISTRIBUTED LAG - APPL , EXPECTATIONS
          HYPOTHESES * EVALUATION - EXPECTATIONS , THEORY
YA3495   TYDEMAN J.
          "A note on shrt-term forecasting using an irregular time interval"   Opl.
          Res. Q., vol.23, 1972, pp.381-383.
          EXPONENTIAL SMOOTHING - THEORY * USE - PRODUCTION , CONTROL * DATA -
          IRREGULAR SAMPLING INTERVAL
YA3496   TYDEMAN J., MITCHELL R.B.
          "Subjective information modelling"   Opl. Res. Q., vol.28, 1977, pp.1-19.
          JUDGEMENTAL FORECASTS - METHODOLOGY * TECHNOLOGICAL FORECASTING * USE -
          CAPITAL INVESTMENT * BASIC
YA3497   TYSON L.D.
          "A permanent income hypothesis for the Yugoslav firm"   Economica, vol.44,
          1977, pp.393-408.
          APPL - SECTOR : EARNINGS * INCOME - EFFECT OF , PERMANENT * APPL - MACRO ,
          YUGOSLAVIA
YA3498   TZOANNOS J.
          "An emperical study of peak-load pricing and investment policies for the
          domestic market of gas in GB"   Appl. Econ., vol.9, 1977, pp.133-153.
          APPL - SECTOR : UTILITIES , GAS * COST - SECTOR : UTILITIES * THEORY -
          PRICING
YA3499   UCHE P.I.
          "Statistical analysis of recurrent expenditure of universities in a
          developing country: a Nigerian example"   R. Statist. Soc. (A), vol.141,
          1978, pp.394-400.
          APPL - FIRM : EDUCATION , UNIVERSITIES * COST - FIRM : EDUCATION
YA3500   UENO H.
          "A long-term model of economic growth of Japan, 1906-1968"   Int. Econ.
          Rev., vol.13, 1968, pp.619-643.
          MACRO MODEL - JAPAN * LONG TERM FORECASTING * APPL - MACRO : GROWTH * APPL -
          MACRO , JAPAN * EX ANTE
YA3501   UHLER R.S.
          "Costs and supply in petroleum exploration: the case of Alberta"   Can. J.
          Econ., vol.9, 1976, pp.72-90.
          APPL - SECTOR : PRODUCTION , PETROLEUM * APPL - SECTOR : COMMODITIES , OIL *
          COST - SECTOR : PRODUCTION * PROBABILITY MODELS - POISSON * APPL - SECTOR :
          PRODUCTION , GAS
YA3502   UHLER R.S., CRAGG J.C.
          "The structure of the asset portfolios of households"   Rev. Econ. Studies,
          vol.38, 1971, pp.341-357.
          APPL - MACRO : CONSUMER DEMAND , FINANCIAL ASSETS * REGRESSION - LIMITED
          DEPENDENT , LOGIT

YA3503   UMSTEAD D.
"Forecasting stock prices" with discussion   J. Finance, vol.32, 1977,
pp.427-441 & 442-448.
APPL - SECTOR : FINANCE , STOCK PRICE INDEX * BUSINESS INDICATORS - APPL *
STOCK PRICES - DETERMINANTS * DISTRIBUTED LAG - RATIONAL POLYNOMIAL * EX
ANTE

YA3504   UNWIN D.J., HEPPLE L.W.
"The statistical analysis of spatial series"   Stat'n., vol.23, 1974,
pp.211-227.
SPATIAL ANALYSIS - REVIEW * BIBLIOGRAPHY - SPATIAL , ANALYSIS

YA3505   UPTON G.J.G.
"A memory model for voting transitions in British elections"   R. Statist.
Soc. (A), vol.140, 1977, pp.86-94.
VOTING * MARKOV MODELS - APPL : VOTING * EVALUATION - VOTING MODELS * REPEAT
BUYING

YA3506   URBAN G.L.
"A mathematical approach to product line decisions"   J. Mktg. Res., vol.6,
1969, pp.40-47.
MARKET SHARE - THEORY * SUBSTITUTE PRODUCTS * PRICE - EFFECT OF * APPL -
FIRM : CONSUMER NON DURABLES , FOOD * COMPETITION - EFFECT OF * USE -
PRICING * USE - PROMOTION POLICY * MARKET SHARE - SECTOR : CONSUMER NON
DURABLES

YA3507   URBAN G.L.
"A model for managing a family-planning system"   Ops. Res., vol.22, 1974,
pp.205-233.
POPULATION - FERTILITY * HEALTH - FAMILY PLANNING * SIMULATION - APPL :
SECTOR , HEALTH * EX ANTE * USER - SECTOR : HEALTH

YA3508   URBAN G.L.
"Allocating ad budgets geographically"   J. Advtg. Res., vol.15:6, 1975,
pp.7-16.
ADVERTISING - DETERMINANTS * MARKET POTENTIAL * USE - MARKETING POLICY *
ADVERTISING - EFFECT OF * DATA - DISAGGREGATION , GEOGRAPHICAL

YA3509   URBAN G.L.
"PERCEPTOR: a model for product positioning"   Mgmt. Sci. (B), vol.21,
1975, pp.858-871.
CONSUMER BEHAVIOUR - PSYCHOLOGICAL MODELS * NEW PRODUCTS - IDENTIFYING *
BRAND CHOICE - THEORY * APPL - SECTOR : CONSUMER NON DURABLES * MARKET SHARE
- SECTOR : CONSUMER NON DURABLES * MARKET POSITION * MULTIDIMENSIONAL
SCALING * NEW PRODUCTS - NEW BRAND * MARKOV MODELS - APPL : BRAND CHOICE

YA3510   URBAN G.L.
"SPRINTER Mod. III: a model for the analysis of new frequently purchased
consumer products"   Ops. Res., vol.18, 1970, pp.805-854.
REPEAT BUYING * BRAND CHOICE - THEORY * APPL - FIRM : CONSUMER NON DURABLES
* NEW PRODUCTS - TESTING * MARKET SHARE - SECTOR : CONSUMER NON DURABLES

YA3511   URBAN G.L., KARASH R.
"Evolutionary model building"   J. Mktg. Res., vol.8, 1971, pp.62-66.
USE - MARKETING POLICY * NEW PRODUCTS - EVALUATION * THEORY - MODELLING *
BASIC

YA3512   URI N.D.
"Forecasting: a hybrid approach"   Omega, vol.5, 1977, pp.463-472.
APPL - SECTOR : UTILITIES , ELECTRICITY * TIME SERIES - ARIMA : APPL *
COMBINING MODELS - ARIMA , CAUSAL * EX ANTE * COMPARATIVE METHODS - ARIMA ,
CAUSAL

YA3513   URI N.D., MIXON J.W.
"The distribution of changes in manufacturing employment and the impact of
the minimum wage"   J. Econometrics, vol.7, 1978, pp.103-114.
POLICY EVALUATION - MACRO : EMPLOYMENT * APPL - SECTOR : EMPLOYMENT * DATA -
CROSS SECTION , TIME SERIES

YA3514   URIBE P.
"Some 'RAS' experiments with the Mexican input output model"   Anns. Econ.
Soc. Meas., vol.4, 1975, pp.553-570.
INPUT OUTPUT - MACRO , LATIN AMERICA * STABILITY OF COEFFICIENTS - INPUT
OUTPUT * INPUT OUTPUT - PROJECTION OF STRUCTURE * EX ANTE

YA3515   VALENTI J.J., HUNT L.H., BLACK S.W.
"Eurodollar borrowing by New York banks and the rate of interest on
Eurodollars: comment"   J. Finance, vol.27, 1972, pp.130-135.
APPL - MACRO : INTERNATIONAL FINANCE * SIMULTANEOUS SYSTEM - IDENTIFICATION
* APPL - SECTOR : FINANCE , BANKS * COMPARATIVE METHODS - ESTIMATION : OLS ,
2SLS * INTEREST RATE - EFFECT OF

YA3516   VALENTINE T.J.
"The demand for money and price expectations in Australia"   J. Finance,
vol.32, 1977, pp.735-748.
APPL - MACRO : MONEY , DEMAND * INFLATION - EFFECT OF * APPL - MACRO ,
AUSTRALIA * ERROR SPECIFICATION - MOVING AVERAGE * INTEREST RATE - EFFECT OF

YA3517   VALENTINI J.J., HUNT L.H.
"Monetary and fiscal policy influences on the unemployment rate"   Bus.
Econ., vol.6:3, 1971, pp.21-24.
APPL - MACRO : UNEMPLOYMENT * POLICY EVALUATION - MACRO : FISCAL , MONETARY
* DISTRIBUTED LAG - ALMON : APPL

YA3518   VALLIANT R., MILKOVITCH G.
"Comparison of semi-Markov and Markov models in a personnel forecasting
appl"   Decis. Sci., vol.8, 1977, pp.465-477,
MARKOV MODELS - APPL : MANPOWER * MANPOWER PLANNING - FIRM * MANPOWER
PLANNING - SECTOR : SERVICES * EVALUATION - MANPOWER PLANNING MODELS

YA3519   VAN ALPHEN H.J., MERKIES A.H.Q.M.
"Distributed lags in construction: an empirical study"   Int. Econ. Rev.,
vol.17, 1976, pp.411-430,
APPL - SECTOR : CONSTRUCTION , RESIDENTIAL * DISTRIBUTED LAG - APPL , ORDERS
* DISTRIBUTED LAG - ALMON : APPL * DISTRIBUTED LAG - SOLOW : APPL *
COMPARATIVE METHODS - DISTRIBUTED LAG

YA3520   VAN HORN R.L.
"Validation of simulation results"   Mgmt. Sci, (A), vol.17, 1971,
pp.247-258,
SIMULATION - METHODOLOGY * SIMULATION - EVALUATION OF RESULTS

YA3521   VAN HORNE J.C., ET AL.
"The effect of FLHB bond operations on savings inflows at savings and loan
associations: comments"   J. Finance, vol.28, 1973, pp.194-206,
APPL - SECTOR : FINANCE , BUILDING SOCIETIES * APPL - SECTOR : FINANCE ,
SAVINGS * POLICY EVALUATION - SECTOR : FINANCE * COMPARATIVE METHODS -
REGRESSION , ERROR SPECIFICATION

YA3522   VAN HORNE J.C., McDONALD J.G.
"Dividend policy and new equity financing" with discussion   J. Finance,
vol.26, 1971, pp.507-519 & 540-542,
DATA - CROSS SECTION * APPL - FIRM : UTILITIES , ELECTRICITY * APPL - FIRM :
PRODUCTION , ELECTRONICS * APPL - FIRM : FINANCE , PE RATIO * APPL - FIRM :
FINANCE , DIVIDENDS

YA3523   VAN LOO F.
"The effect of foreign direct investment on investment in Canada"   Rev.
Econ. Stats., vol.59, 1977, pp.474-481,
APPL - MACRO , CANADA * APPL - MACRO : INVESTMENT * APPL - MACRO :
INVESTMENT , INTERNATIONAL

YA3524   VAN ORDER R.
"On the bias in estimates of the effects of monetary and fiscal policy"
Rev. Econ. Stats., vol.60, 1978, pp.304-306,
POLICY EVALUATION - MACRO : FISCAL , MONETARY * DATA ERRORS - CONTROL BIAS *
POLICY EVALUATION - METHODOLOGY

YA3525   VANCIL R.F.
"The accuracy of long-range planning"   H.B.R., vol.48, Sept-Oct, 1970,
pp.98-101,
APPL - FIRM : FINANCE , PROFITS * USE - CORPORATE PLANNING * EX ANTE *
CONFIDENCE INTERVAL - EX ANTE * BASIC

YA3526   VANDERKAMP J.
"Industrial mobility: some further results"   Can. J. Econ., vol.10, 1977,
pp.462-472,
MANPOWER PLANNING - INDUSTRIAL MOBILITY * EVALUATION - EX POST MODELS *
COMPARATIVE METHODS - REGRESSION , TRANSFORMATIONS

YA3527   VANDERKAMP J.
"Wage adjustment, productivity and price change expectations"   Rev. Econ.
Studies, vol.39, 1972, pp.61-72,
APPL - MACRO : EARNINGS , INFLATION - EFFECT OF * INFLATION - PHILLIPS CURVE
* INFLATION - EXPECTATIONS

YA3528   VANNESS P.H.
"Adjusting polynomial trend functions"   Decis. Sci., vol.4, 1973,
pp.563-568,
DATA - AGGREGATION * DATA - DISAGGREGATION * TREND CURVES - POLYNOMIAL *
DEMAND - CUMULATIVE

YA3529   VASSILIOU P.C.G.
"A high order non-linear markovian model for promotion in manpower systems"
R. Statist. Soc. (A), vol.141, 1978, pp.86-94,
MARKOV MODEL - APPL : MANPOWER * EX ANTE * MANPOWER PLANNING - FIRM

YA3530   VASSILIOU P.C.G.
"A Markov chain model for wasteage in manpower systems"   Opl. Res. Q.,
vol.27, 1976, pp.57-70,
MANPOWER PLANNING - LABOUR TURNOVER * MARKOV MODEL - APPL : MANPOWER *
MANPOWER PLANNING - FIRM

YA3531   VENIERIS Y.P., SEBOLD F.D., HARPER R.D.
"The impact of economic, technological and demographic factors on aggregate
births"   Rev. Econ. Stats., vol.55, 1973, pp.493-497,
POPULATION - FERTILITY * INCOME - EFFECT OF , PERMANENT

YA3532   VERBRUGGE J.A., SHICK R.A., THYGERSON K.J.
"An analysis of savings and loan profit performance"   J. Finance, vol.31,
1976,1427-1442,
APPL - FIRM : FINANCE , BUILDING SOCIETIES * APPL - FIRM : FINANCE , PROFITS
* STABILITY OF COEFFICIENTS - REGRESSION * DATA - CROSS SECTION , TIME
SERIES

YA3533   VERLEGER P.K.
"Models of the demand for air transport"   Bell J. Econ., vol.3, 1972, pp.437-457,
APPL - SECTOR : TRANSPORT , AIR * INCOME - EFFECT OF * REGIONAL MODELS - INTERREGIONAL * REGIONAL MODELS - SECTOR : TRANSPORT

YA3534   VERNON J.M., ET AL,
"Estimation of structure-profit relationship: comments"   Am. Econ. Rev., vol.63, 1973, pp.763-769,
APPL - FIRM : FINANCE , PROFITS * COOCENTRATION - EFFECT OF * REGRESSION - ERROR COMPONENTS

YA3535   VERNON J.M., GUSEN P,
"Technical changes and firm size: the pharmaceutical industry"   Rev. Econ. Stats., vol.56, 1974, pp.294-302,
APPL - FIRM : CONSUMER NON DURABLES , PHARMACEUTICALS * USE - R&D * ADVERTISING - EFFECT OF * REGRESSION - LIMITED DEPENDENT : APPL

YA3536   VERNON R,
"Comprehensive model-building in the planning process: the case of the less-developed countries"   Econ. J., vol.76, 1966, pp.57-69,
USER REQUIREMENTS * POLICY EVALUATION - METHODOLOGY * DATA - LDC

YA3537   VERRY D.W., LAYARD P.R.G,
"Cost functions for university teaching and research"   Econ. J., vol.85, 1975, pp.55-74,
APPL - SECTOR : EDUCATION , UNIVERSITIES * COST - SECTOR : EDUCATION

YA3538   VICKERY C,
"The impact of turnover on group unemployment rates"   Rev. Econ. Stats., vol.59, 1977, pp.415-426,
MANPOWER PLANNING - LABOUR TURNOVER * SIMULATION - APPL : MACRO , MANPOWER PLANNING * MANPOWER PLANNING - DISCRIMINATION

YA3539   VIGDERHOUS G,
"Statistical test of multicollinearity: a computer program"   J. Mktg. Res., vol.12, 1975, p.83,
MULTICOLLINEARITY - TESTS * COMPUTERISATION - DIAGNOSTIC TESTS , PROGRAMS

YA3540   VINOD H.D
"Non homogeneous production functions and applications to telecommunications"   Bell J. Econ., vol.3, 1972, pp.531-543,
PRODUCTION FUNCTIONS - THEORY * APPL - FIRM : PRODUCTION , ELECTRONICS * APPL - FIRM : UTILITIES , TELEPHONE * PRODUCTION FUNCTIONS - FIRM

YA3541   VINOD H.D.
"A ridge estimator whose MSE dominates OLS"   Int. Econ. Rev., vol.19, 1978, pp.727-737,
REGRESSION - RIDGE * DATA - SIMULATION * ESTIMATION - STEIN

YA3542   VINOD H.D.
"A survey of ridge regression and related techniques for improvements over ordinary least squares"   Rev. Econ. Stats., vol.60, 1978, pp.121-131,
REGRESSION - ESTIMATION * EVALUATION - REGRESSION , RIDGE * BIBLIOGRAPHY - REGRESSION , RIDGE * ESTIMATION - PRINCIPAL COMPONENTS * COMPARATIVE METHODS - MULTICOLLINEARITY

YA3543   VINOD H.D.
"Application of new ridge regression methods to a study of Bell system scale economies"   J. Am. Statist. Ass., vol.71, 1976, pp.835-841,
COMPARATIVE METHODS - ESTIMATION : OLS , RIDGE * MULTICOLLINEARITY - EFFECT OF * EVALUATION - REGRESSION , RIDGE * APPL - FIRM : UTILITIES , TELEPHONE * APPL - FIRM : FINANCE , PROFITS * PRODUCTION FUNCTIONS - SCALE ECONOMIES

YA3544   VINOD H.D.
"Canonical ridge regression and econometrics of joint production"   J. Econometrics, vol.4, 1976, pp.147-166,
PRODUCTION FUNCTIONS - THEORY , JOINT * PRODUCTION FUNCTIONS - METHODOLOGY * PRODUCTION FUNCTIONS - MACRO * CANONICAL CORRELATION - APPL * REGRESSION - RIDGE

YA3545   VINOD H.D.
"Econometrics of joint production"   Econometrica, vol.36, 1968, pp.322-336,
PRODUCTION FUNCTIONS - ESTIMATION * PRODUCTION FUNCTIONS - SECTOR * COMPARATIVE METHODS - ESTIMATION : PRODUCTION FUNCTIONS * CANONICAL CORRELATION - APPL * PRODUCTION FUNCTIONS - JOINT * APPL - SECTOR : AGRICULTURE , WOOL * APPL - SECTOR : AGRICULTURE , LIVESTOCK , SHEEP

YA3546   VINOD H.D.
"Effects of ARMA errors on the significance tests for regression coefficients"   J. Am. Statist. Ass., vol.71, 1976, pp.929-933,
EVALUATION - REGRESSION , HYPOTHESIS TESTS * ERROR SPECIFICATION - ARMA

YA3547   VINSON C.E.
"The cost of ignoring lead time unreliability in inventory control"   Decis. Sci., vol.3:2, 1972, pp.87-105,
TIMING UNCERTAINTY * USE - INVENTORY CONTROL

YA3548   VIRTS J.R.
"US health care spending: a macro analysis   Bus. Econ., vol.12:4, 1977, pp.26-37,
HEALTH - SERVICES * PRICE - SECTOR : HEALTH * INCOME - EFFECT OF

YA3549   VISCUSSI W.K.
"Wealth effects and earnings premiums for job hazards"   Rev. Econ. Stats.,
vol.60, 1978, pp.408-416.
MANPOWER PLANNING - EARNINGS * UNIONISATION - EFFECT OF * APPL - SECTOR :
SOCIAL , ACCIDENTS

YA3550   VOGEL R.C.
"The dynamics of inflation in Latin America, 1950-1969"   Am. Econ. Rev.,
vol.64, 1974, pp.102-114.
INFLATION - RAPID * THEORY - MONETARY * INFLATION - DETERMINANTS * APPL -
MACRO , LATIN AMERICA * DATA - INTERNATIONAL

YA3551   VOIVODAS C.S.
"The effect of foreign exchange instability on growth"   Rev. Econ. Stats.,
vol.56, 1974, pp.410-412.
DATA - INTERNATIONAL * DATA - CROSS SECTION * APPL - MACRO : GROWTH * APPL -
MACRO : INTERNATIONAL FINANCE , EXCHANGE RATES * EXCHANGE RATE - EFFECT OF

YA3552   VON FURSTENBERG G.M.
"Corporate investment: does market valuation matter in the aggregate" with
discussion   Brookings Paps. Econ. Activity, 1977, pp.347-408.
DISTRIBUTED LAG - APPL , ORDERS * APPL - MACRO : SHIPMENTS * REGRESSION -
SHIFTING COEFFICIENTS * APPL - SECTOR : FINANCE , FINANCIAL STRUCTURE * APPL
- MACRO : INVESTMENT * APPL - MACRO : ORDERS * CAPACITY - EFFECT OF

YA3553   VON FURSTENBERG G.M.
"Flow-of-funds analysis and the economic outlook"   Anns. Econ. Soc. Meas.,
vol.6, 1977, pp.1-25.
APPL - MACRO : FLOW OF FUNDS * FORECAST - AGGREGATION

YA3554   VON FURSTENBERG G.M., GREEN R.J.
"Home mortgage delinquencies: a cohort analysis"   J. Finance, vol.29,
1974, pp.1545-1548
APPL - SECTOR : FINANCE , MORTGAGES * APPL - SECTOR : CONSTRUCTION ,
RESIDENTIAL * USE - CREDIT CONTROL , CONSUMER * INCOME - EFFECT OF

YA3555   VON FURSTENBURG G.M.
"An appraisal of recent forecasts of housing starts"   Bus. Econ., vol.9:3,
1974, pp.60-63.
APPL - SECTOR : CONSTRUCTION , RESIDENTIAL * LEAD TIME - EFFECT OF *
EVALUATION - JUDGEMENTAL FORECASTS

YA3556   VROMAN W.
"Employer payroll taxes and money wage behaviour"   Appl. Econ., vol.6,
1974, pp.189-204.
TAX - EFFECT OF * APPL - MACRO : EARNINGS

YA3557   WABE J.S.
"A study of house prices as a means of establishing the value of journey
time, the rate of time preference and the valuation of some aspects of
environment in the London Metropolitan Region"   Appl. Econ., vol.3, 1971,
pp.247-255.
DATA - CROSS SECTION * APPL - SECTOR : CONSTRUCTION , RESIDENTIAL * PRICE -
SECTOR : CONSTRUCTION , RESIDENTIAL * TIME - VALUE OF

YA3558   WABE J.S., COLES O.B.
"The peak and off peak demand for bus transport: a cross sectional analysis
of British municipal operators"   Appl. Econ., vol.7, 1975, pp.25-30.
APPL - SECTOR : TRANSPORT , ROAD , PASSENGER * DATA - CROSS SECTION *
REGIONAL MODELS - CITY * REGIONAL MODELS - SECTOR : TRANSPORT * BASIC

YA3559   WABE S., LEECH D.
"Relative earnings in UK manufacturing - a reconsideration of the evidence"
Econ. J., vol.88, 1978, pp.296-313.
MANPOWER PLANNING - EARNINGS * DATA - CROSS SECTION * MANPOWER PLANNING -
SECTOR * MANPOWER PLANNING - INDUSTRIAL COMPOSITION

YA3560   WACHTEL H.M., BETSEY C.
"Employment at low wages"   Rev. Econ. Stats., vol.54, 1972, pp.121-129.
APPL - SECTOR : SOCIAL , POVERTY * MANPOWER PLANNING - EARNINGS * DATA -
CROSS SECTION * EDUCATION - EFFECT OF * MANPOWER PLANNING - LABOUR FORCE
COMPOSITION

YA3561   WACHTEL P.
"A model of interrelated demand for assets by households"   Anns. Econ.
Soc. Meas., vol.1, 1972, pp.129-140.
APPL - MACRO : CONSUMER DEMAND * INTEREST RATE - EFFECT OF * PRICE - EFFECT
OF * INCOME - EFFECT OF , PERMANENT

YA3562   WACHTEL P.
"Interpolated models of household behaviour: a summary and an extension"
J. Finance, vol.27, 1972, pp.503-506 & 510.
APPL - MACRO : CONSUMER DEMAND * CONSUMER BEHAVIOUR - ECONOMIC MODELS ,
THEORY

YA3563   WACHTEL P.
"The effect of earnings of school and college investment expenditures"
Rev. Econ. Stats., vol.53, 1976, pp.326-331.
DATA - CROSS SECTION * MANPOWER PLANNING - EARNINGS * EDUCATION - EFFECT OF

YA3564   WACHTEL P., SAMETZ A., SHUFORD H.
"Capital shortages: myth or reality" with discussion   J. Finance, vol.31,
1976, pp.269-286 & 312-318
EVALUATION - FLOW OF FUNDS FORECASTS * EX ANTE * APPL - MACRO : FLOW OF
FUNDS

YA3565   WACHTER M.L.
"A labor supply model for secondary workers"   Rev. Econ. Stats., vol.54, 1972, pp.141-151.
MANPOWER PLANNING - LABOUR PARTICIPATION * MANPOWER PLANNING - MACRO , SUPPLY * EX ANTE * EVALUATION - EX POST MODELS * MANPOWER PLANNING - LABOUR FORCE COMPOSITION

YA3566   WACHTER M.L.
"A new approach to the equilibrium labour force"   Economica, vol.41, 1974, pp.35-51.
MANPOWER PLANNING - MACRO * MANPOWER PLANNING - LABOUR PARTICIPATION * BIBLIOGRAPHY - MANPOWER PLANNING , LABOUR PARTICIPATION * APPL - MACRO : EMPLOYMENT

YA3567   WACHTER M.L.
"A time-series fertility equation: the potential for a baby-boom in the 1980's"   Int. Econ. Rev., vol.16, 1975, pp.609-624.
POPULATION - FERTILITY * INCOME - EFFECT OF

YA3568   WACHTER M.L.
"Intermediate swings in labor-force participation" with discussion
Brookings Paps. Econ. Activity, 1977, pp.545-576.
MANPOWER PLANNING - LABOUR PARTICIPATION * MANPOWER PLANNING - LABOUR FORCE COMPOSITION

YA3569   WACHTER M.L.
"Phase ii, cost-push inflation, and relative wages"   Am. Econ. Rev., vol.64, 1974, pp.482-491.
INFLATION - GOVERNMENT CONTROLS * APPL - SECTOR : EARNINGS * INFLATION - EFFECT OF

YA3570   WACHTER M.L.
"The changing cyclical responsiveness of wage inflation" with discussion
Brookings Paps. Econ. Activity, 1976, pp.115-167.
INFLATION - DETERMINANTS , EARNINGS * APPL - MACRO : EARNINGS * APPL - MACRO : UNEMPLOYMENT * MANPOWER PLANNING - LABOUR FORCE COMPOSITION * INFLATION - PHILLIPS * BUSINESS CYCLE - EFFECT OF

YA3571   WACHTER M.L.
"The wage process: an analysis of the early 1970's" with discussion
Brookings Paps. Econ. Activity, 1974, pp.507-525.
INFLATION - DETERMINANTS , EARNINGS * APPL - MACRO : EARNINGS * UNIONIZATION - EFFECT OF * DISTRIBUTED LAG - APPL , INFLATION

YA3572   WACHTER S.M.
"The impact of agricultural prices on inflation"   Bus. Econ., vol.10:4, 1975, pp.84-88.
INFLATION - SECTOR : AGRICULTURE * APPL - SECTOR : AGRICULTURE * DATA - INTERNATIONAL * PRICE - EFFECT OF * INFLATION - DETERMINANTS

YA3573   WADYCKI W.J.
"Alternative opportunities and interstate migration: some additional results"   Rev. Econ. Stats., vol.56, 1974, pp.254-257.
REGIONAL MODELS - INTERREGIONAL * REGIONAL MODELS - MANPOWER PLANNING , MIGRATION * MANPOWER PLANNING - MIGRATION

YA3574   WAGLE B., RAPPOPORT J., DOWNES V.A.
"A program for short-term sales forecasting"   Stat'n., vol.18, 1968, pp.141-147.
COMPARATIVE METHODS - EXPONENTIAL SMOOTHING , TREND CURVES * EX ANTE * EVALUATION - EXPONENTIAL SMOOTHING * BASIC

YA3575   WAGNER H.M.
"The design of production and inventory systems for multifacility and multiwarehouse companies"   Ops. Res., vol.22, 1974, pp.278-291.
USE - PRODUCTION , CONTROL * USE - INVENTORY CONTROL

YA3576   WAHLBIN C.
"Analyzing variations in demand for an industrial good"   Ind. Mktg. Mgmt., vol.6, 1977, pp.223-230.
APPL - SECTOR : PRODUCTION , PLANT , PUMPS * APPLICATION - SECTOR : PRODUCTION , WOOD , PULP * APPL - SECTOR : INVESTMENT

YA3577   WAINSTEIN B.M., SICHEL H.S.
"The price-quality relationship: a heuristic model"   Omega, vol.4, 1976, pp.417-436.
APPL - FIRM : CONSUMER NON DURABLES , GROCERIES * DATA - CROSS SECTION * PRICE - EFFECT OF * QUALITY - PRICE

YA3578   WALDRON D.G.
"The image of craftmanship: a predictor variable influencing the purchase of European automobiles by Americans"   Eur. J. Mktg., vol.12, 1978, pp.554-561.
QUALITY - EFFECT OF * FACTOR ANALYSIS - APPL * BRAND CHOICE - DETERMINANTS * APPL - SECTOR : CONSUMER DURABLES , CARS

YA3579   WALES T.J.
"A generalized linear expenditure model of the demand for non durable goods in Canada"   Can. J. Econ., vol.4, 1971, pp.471-484.
APPL - MACRO : CONSUMER DEMAND * DEMAND EQUATIONS - SYSTEMS OF * APPL - MACRO , CANADA * APPL - SECTOR : CONSUMER NON DURABLES * COMPARATIVE METHODS - DEMAND EQUATIONS

YA3580   WALES T.J.
"Labour supply and commuting time"   J. Econometrics, vol.8, 1978,
pp.215-226.
CONSUMER BEHAVIOUR - ECONOMIC MODELS , THEORY * TIME - VALUE OF * DEMAND
EQUATIONS - SYSTEMS OF * APPL - MACRO : CONSUMER DEMAND * MANPOWER PLANNING
- MACRO , SUPPY

YA3581   WALES T.J.
"The effect of school and district size on education costs in British
Columbia"   Int. Econ. Rev., vol.14, 1973, pp.710-720.
COST - SECTOR : EDUCATION , SCHOOLS * APPL - SECTOR : EDUCATION , SCHOOLS *
COST - SCALE ECONOMIES

YA3582   WALES T.J., WIENS E.G.
"Capitalisation of residential property taxes: an empirical study"   Rev.
Econ. Stats., vol.56, 1974, pp.329-333.
APPL - SECTOR : CONSTRUCTION , RESIDENTIAL * PRICE - SECTOR : CONSTRUCTION ,
RESIDENTIAL * TAX - EFFECT OF

YA3583   WALES T.J., WOODLAND A.D.
"Estimation of household utility functions and labour supply response"
Int. Econ. Rev., vol.17, 1976, pp.397-410.
CONSUMER BEHAVIOUR - ECONOMIC MODELS , THEORY * APPL - MACRO : EMPLOYMENT *
EDUCATION - EFFECT OF

YA3584   WALKER D.A.
"The estimation of linear production functions having multicollinear inputs"
Decis. Sci., vol.2, 1971, pp.448-459.
MULTICOLLINEARITY - REMOVAL OF * PRODUCTION FUNCTIONS - FIRM

YA3585   WALL K.D.
"FIML estimation of rational distributed lag structural form models"
Anns. Econ. Soc. Meas., vol.5, 1976, pp.53-63.
DISTRIBUTED LAG - RATIONAL POLYNOMIAL , ESTIMATION * ESTIMATION - FIML *
SIMULTANEOUS SYSTEM - ESTIMATION * COMPARATIVE METHODS - ESTIMATION : OLS ,
FIML * DISTRIBUTED LAG - SIMULTANEOUS SYSTEM

YA3586   WALLACE J.B.
"Subjective estimation bias and PERT statistical procedures"   Omega,
vol.3, 1975, pp.79-85.
TIMING UNCERTAINTY * USE - PROJECT , PLANNING * JUDGEMENTAL FORECASTS - BIAS
* BASIC

YA3587   WALLACE T.D.
"Pretest estimation in regression: a survey"   Am. J. Ag. Econ., vol.59,
1977, pp.431-443.
REGRESSION - HYPOTHESES TESTS * REGRESSION - MODEL CHOICE * EVALUATION -
THEORY OF * EVALUATION - EX POST MODELS * ESTIMATION - PRE TEST * REGRESSION
- ESTIMATION

YA3588   WALLACE T.D.
"Weaker criteria and tests for linear restrictions in regression"
Econometrica, vol.40, 1972, pp.689-698.
REGRESSION - HYPOTHESIS TESTS * SPECIFICATION ERROR - TESTS , CONSTRAINTS *
ADVANCED

YA3589   WALLACE T.D., ASHAR V.G.
"Sequential methods in model construction"   Rev. Econ. Stats., vol.54,
1972, pp.172-178.
THEORY - MODELLING * MODEL IDENTIFICATION * REGRESSION - MODEL CHOICE *
REGRESSION - STEPWISE * ESTIMATION - PRE TEST

YA3590   WALLIS K.F.
"Lagged dependent variables and serially correlated residuals: a reappraisal
of three-pass least squares"   Rev. Econ. Stats., vol.49, 1967, pp.555-567.
REGRESSION - LAGGED DEPENDENT * ERROR SPECIFICATION - AUTOCORRELATED *
ESTIMATION - 3PLS * DATA - SIMULATION * COMPARATIVE METHODS - ESTIMATION :
OLS , 3PLS * COMPARATIVE METHODS - ESTIMATION : OLS , GLS * COMPARATIVE
METHODS - ESTIMATION : REGRESSION , ERROR SPECIFICATION

YA3591   WALLIS K.F.
"Multiple time series analysis and the final form of econometric models"
Econometric, vol.45, 1977, pp.1481-1497.
DISTRIBUTED LAG - SIMULTANEOUS SYSTEM * DISTRIBUTED LAG - ARIMA * APPL -
SECTOR : AGRICULTURE , LIVESTOCK , HOGS * APPL - MACRO : CONSUMPTION * APPL
- MACRO : INCOME * APPL - MACRO : INVESTMENT

YA3592   WALLIS K.F.
"Seasonal adjustment and relations between variables"   J. Am. Statist.
Ass., vol.69, 1974, pp.18-31.
DISTRIBUTED LAG - SEASONALITY * EVALUATION - SEASONAL ADJUSTMENT * DATA -
SIMULATION

YA3593   WALLIS K.F.
"Testing for fourth order autocorrelation in quarterly regression equations"
Econometrica, vol.40, 1972, pp.617-636.
REGRESSION - LAGGED DEPENDENT * AUTOCORRELATION - TEST * ESTIMATION - NON
LINEAR * RESIDUALS - ANALYSIS OF , AUTOCORRELATION * SEASONALITY * TESTING *
APPL - MACRO : MONEY * APPL - SECTOR : CONSUMER NON DURABLES , LIQUOR *
INFLATION - DETERMINANTS * DATA ERRORS - MISSING OBSERVATIONS * APPL -
SECTOR : PRODUCTION , CEMENT * ERROR SPECIFICATION - AUTOCORRELATED *
COMPARATIVE METHODS - REGRESSION , ERROR SPECIFICATION

YA3594 WALLIS K.F.
"Wage, prices and incomes policy: some comments" Economica, vol.38, 1971, pp.304-310.
APPL - MACRO : EARNINGS * APPL - MACRO , UK * INFLATION - DETERMINANTS , EARNINGS * INFLATION - GOVERNMENT CONTROLS

YA3595 WALLIS K.F., THOMAS J.J.
"Seasonal variations in regression analysis" R. Statist. Soc. (A), vol.134, 1971, pp.57-72.
SEASONALITY - TESTS * SEASONALITY - ESTIMATION , OLS * SPECIFICATION ERROR - EFFECT OF , SEASONALITY * SPECIFICATION ERROR - TESTS , SEASONALITY * APPL - SECTOR : CONSUMER NON DURABLES , LIQUOR * REGRESSION - ESTIMATION , ERROR SPECIFICATION * ERROR SPECIFICATION - AUTOCORRELATED * AUTOCORRELATION - TEST

YA3596 WALSH C.F.
"Does listing increase the market price of common stocks? - comment" J. Business, vol.46, 1973, pp.616-620.
STOCK PRICES - DETERMINANTS * APPL - FIRM : FINANCE , STOCK PRICES

YA3597 WALSH P., CRUZ J.B.
"Neighboring stochastic control of an econometric model" with discussion Anns. Econ. Soc. Meas., vol.5, 1976, pp.211-224.
CONTROL THEORY - STOCHASTIC , METHODOLOGY * ESTIMATION - KALMAN FILTER

YA3598 WALTER J.E., QUE A.V.
"The valuation of convertible bonds" J. Finance, vol.28, 1973, pp.713-732.
APPL - FIRM : FINANCE , BONDS

YA3599 WALTERS A.A.
"Consistent expectations, distributed lags and the Quantity Theory" Econ. J., vol.81, 1971, pp.273-281.
THEORY - EXPECTATIONS * DECISION RULES - FEEDBACK * APPL - MACRO : MONEY * DISTRIBUTED LAG - APPL , MONEY

YA3600 WALZER N.
"Economies of scale and municipal police services: the Illinois exerience" Rev. Econ. Stats., vol.54, 1972, pp.431-438.
APPL - SECTOR : GOVERNMENT , LOCAL , SERVICES * APPL - SECTOR : SOCIAL , CRIME * DATA - CROSS SECTION * COST - SECTOR : GOVERNMENT , LOCAL * COST - SCALE ECONOMIES

YA3601 WAMPER R.H.
"On least squares algorithms" letter Am. Stat'n., vol.31, 1977, pp.52-53.
COMPUTERISATION - ESTIMATION , REGRESSION MODELS , PROGRAMS * NUMERICAL METHODS - CALCULATION ERROR * ESTIMATION - OLS

YA3602 WARD R.W.
"Measuring advertising decay" J. Advtg. Res., vol.16:4, 1976, pp.37-41.
ADVERTISING - EFFECT OF * DISTRIBUTED LAG - APPL , ADVERTISING * APPL - SECTOR : CONSUMER NON DURABLES , FOOD * DISTRIBUTED LAG - ALMON

YA3603 WARNER J.C.
"Unfilled long-term interest rate expectation and changes in business fixed investment" Am. Econ. Rev., vol.68, 1978, pp.339-347.
INTEREST RATE - EFFECT OF * APPL - MACRO : INVESTMENT * INTEREST RATE - EXPECTATIONS

YA3604 WARREN J.M., SHELTON J.P.
"A simultaneous equation approach to financial planning" J. Finance, vol.26, 1971, pp.1123-1142.
USE - FINANCIAL , PLANNING * SIMULATION - APPL : FINANCE * BASIC

YA3605 WARREN R.D., WHITE J.K., FULLER W.A.
"An error-in-variables analysis of managerial role performance" J. Am. Statist. Ass., vol.69, 1974, pp.886-893.
COMPARATIVE METHODS - REGRESSION , ERRORS IN VARIABLES

YA3606 WARREN R.S.
"The behaviour of unemployment and unfilled vacancies in GB: a search-turnover view" Appl. Econ., vol.9, 1977, pp.237-242.
APPL - MACRO : UNEMPLOYMENT * MANPOWER PLANNING - EMPLOYMENT VACANCIES * STABILITY OF COEFFICIENTS - REGRESSION : APPL

YA3607 WATTS R.
"The information content of dividends" J. Business, vol.46, 1973, pp.191-211.
APPL - FIRM : FINANCE , PROFITS * APPL - FIRM : FINANCE , DIVIDENDS * APPL - FIRM : FINANCE , STOCK PRICES * STOCK PRICES - INFORMATION EFFECT

YA3608 WATTS R.L., LEFTWICH R.W.
"The time series of annual accounting earnings" J. Acctg. Res., vol.15, 1977, pp.253-271.
EX ANTE * COMPARATIVE METHODS - ARIMA , AUTOREGRESSIVE * APPL - FIRM : FINANCE , PROFITS

YA3609 WAUD R.N.
"Monetary and fiscal effects on economic activity: a reduced form examination of their relative importance" Rev. Econ. Stats., vol.56, 1974, pp.177-187.
MULTICOLLINEARITY - EFFECT OF * ERROR SPECIFICATION - AUTOCORRELATED * APPL - SECTOR : EMPLOYMENT * ESTIMATION - NON LINEAR : APPL * SPECIFICATION ERROR - EFFECT OF , SIMULTANEOUS SYSTEM BIAS * POLICY EVALUATION - MACRO : FISCAL , MONETARY

YA3610 WEBB M., STEVENS G., BRAMSON C.
"An approach to the control of bed occupancy in a general hospital" Opl.
Res. Q., vol.28, 1977, pp.391-399.
HEALTH - HOSPITAL , PATIENT FACILITIES * USE - UTILISATION CONTROL * LEAD
TIME - EFFECT OF * COMPARATIVE METHODS - AUTOREGRESSIVE , JUDGEMENTAL *
JUDGEMENTAL FORECASTS - SPECIALIST

YA3611 WEBB S.
"Measurement of the effect of wool advertising"   Omega, vol.1, 1973,
pp.757-770.
APPL - SECTOR : AGRICULTURE , WOOL * ADVERTISING - EFFECT OF

YA3612 WEBER D.C.
"Accident rate potential: an application of multiple regression analysis of
a Poisson process"   J. Am. Statist. Ass., vol.66, 1971, pp.285-288.
APPL - SECTOR : SOCIAL , ACCIDENTS * REGRESSION - DISCRETE DEPENDENT *
ESTIMATION - MAXIMUM LIKELIHOOD * ERROR DISTRIBUTION - NONNORMAL , POISSON

YA3613 WEBER J.E., MONARCHI D.E.
"Graphical representation of the effects of multicollinearity"   Decis.
Sci., vol.8, 1977, pp.534-547.
MULTICOLLINEARITY - EFFECT OF * REGRESSION - HYPOTHESIS TESTING * REGRESSION
- SUMMARY STATISTICS

YA3614 WEBER W.E.
"Interest rates and the short run consumption function"   Am. Econ. Rev.,
vol.61, 1971, pp.421-425.
INTEREST RATE - EFFECT OF * APPL - MACRO : CONSUMPTION * COMPARATIVE METHODS
- DATA : AGGREGATE , DISAGGREGATE

YA3615 WEBER W.E.
"Interest rates, inflation and consumer expenditures"   Am. Econ. Rev.,
vol.65, 1975, pp.843-858.
INFLATION - EFFECT OF * MACRO MODELS - THEORY * CONSUMER BEHAVIOUR -
ECONOMIC MODELS * ESTIMATION - MAXIMUM LIKELIHOOD : APPL * INTEREST RATE -
EFFECT OF * EXPECTATIONS - ESTIMATING * APPL - MACRO : CONSUMER DEMAND

YA3616 WECKER W.E.
"Predicting demand from sales data in the presence of stockouts"   Mgmt.
Sci., vol.24, 1978, pp.1043-1054.
DATA - CENSORED * DEMAND - STOCK OUT * TIME SERIES - AUTOREGRESSIVE * DATA
ERRORS - MISSING OBSERVATIONS * DATA - ATYPICAL EVENTS

YA3617 WEGGE L.L.
"Constrained indirect least squares estimators"   Econometrica, vol.46,
1978, pp.435-449.
ESTIMATION - CONSTRAINED * SIMULTANEOUS SYSTEM - ESTIMATION * MACRO MODEL -
KLEIN * ADVANCED

YA3618 WEI W.W.S.
"The effect of temporal aggregation on parameter estimation in distributed
lag model"   J. Econometrics, vol.8, 1978, pp.237-246.
DISTRIBUTED LAG - AGGREGATION EFFECT * DATA - AGGREGATION OVER TIME

YA3619 WEINBERG C.B.
"Advertising decision rules for market share models"   Decis. Sci., vol.6,
1975, pp.25-36.
ADVERTISING - OPTIMALITY * CONTROL THEORY - STOCHASTIC , APPL * FORECASTING
- VALUE OF

YA3620 WEINBERG C.B.
"Dynamic correction in marketing planning models"   Mgmt. Sci., vol.22,
1976, pp.677-687.
ADVERTISING - EFFECT OF * DISTRIBUTED LAG - APPL , ADVERTISING * ADVERTISING
- OPTIMALITY

YA3621 WEINBERG C.B.
"Response curves for a leaflet distribution - further analysis of the
Defleur data"   Opl. Res. Q., vol.22, 1971, pp.177-179.
EVALUATION - REGRESSION , TRANSFORMATIONS

YA3622 WEINBERG C.B., ET AL.
"Carry-over is important"   J. Advtg. Res., vol.15:3, 1975, pp.41-45.
ADVERTISING - EFFECT OF * ADVERTISING - OPTIMALITY * DISTRIBUTED LAG - APPL
, ADVERTISING

YA3623 WEINBERG C.B., SHACHMUT K.M.
"ARTS PLAN: a model based system for use in planning a performing arts
series"   Mgmt. Sci., vol.24,1978, pp.654-664.
APPL - FIRM : SERVICES , ENTERTAINMENT * USE - MARKETING PLANNING *
SIMULATION - APPL : MARKETING

YA3624 WEINROBE M.
"An analysis of the effectiveness of FHLBB liquidity policy, 1971-1975"
J. Finance, vol.32, 1977, pp.1617-1637.
APPL - SECTOR : FINANCE , BUILDING SOCIETIES * APPL - SECTOR : FINANCE ,
MORTGAGES * APPL - SECTOR : FINANCE , FINANCIAL STRUCTURE , LIQUID ASSETS *
USE - FINANCIAL , REGULATION * POLICY EVALUATION - SECTOR : FINANCE

YA3625 WEINSTEIN M.I.
"The seasoning process of new corporate bond issues"   J. Finance, vol.33,
1978, pp.1343-1354.
APPL - FIRM : FINANCE , BONDS * NEW PRODUCTS - NEW BRANDS

YA3626　　WEISER L., JAY K., BALDWIN R.E.
　　　　　　"Determinants of the commodity structure of US trade"　　Am. Econ. Rev.,
　　　　　　vol.62, 1972, pp.459-465.
　　　　　　APPL - SECTOR : INTERNATIONAL TRADE , EXPORTS

YA3627　　WEISS D.L.
　　　　　　"An analysis of the demand structure for branded consumer products"　　Appl.
　　　　　　Econ., vol.1, 1969, pp.37-49.
　　　　　　APPL - FIRM : CONSUMER NON DURABLES , FOOD * ADVERTISING - EFFECT OF *
　　　　　　MARKET SHARE - SECTOR : CONSUMER NON DURABLES * PRICE - EFFECT OF

YA3628　　WEISS D.L., HOUSTON F.S., WINDAL P.
　　　　　　"The periodic pain of Lydia E. Pinkham"　　J. Business, vol.51, 1978,
　　　　　　pp.91-101.
　　　　　　APPL - FIRM : CONSUMER NON DURABLES , HEALTH AIDS * ADVERTISING - EFFECT OF
　　　　　　* DISTRIBUTED LAG - APPL , ADVERTISING * COMPARATIVE METHODS - DISTRIBUTED
　　　　　　LAG * REGRESSION - MODEL CHOICE * DISTRIBUTED LAG - ERROR SPECIFICATION *
　　　　　　ERROR SPECIFICATION - AUTOCORRELATED

YA3629　　WEISS L.W.
　　　　　　"The geographical size of markets in manufacturing"　　Rev. Econ. Stats.,
　　　　　　vol.54, 1972, pp.245-257.
　　　　　　APPL - SECTOR : LOCATION * MARKET SEGMENTATION * DATA - SPECIFICATION OF
　　　　　　VARIABLES

YA3630　　WEISS R.D.
　　　　　　"Elasticities of substitution among capital and occupations in US
　　　　　　manufacturing"　　J. Am. Statist. Ass., vol.72, 1977, pp.764-771.
　　　　　　PRODUCTION FUNCTIONS - SECTOR * PRODUCTION FUNCTIONS - METHODOLOGY * DATA -
　　　　　　CROSS SECTION * PRODUCTION FUNCTIONS - SUBSTITUTION * MANPOWER PLANNING -
　　　　　　QUALIFIED MANPOWER * ESTIMATION - 3SLS , ITERATIVE

YA3631　　WEISSKOPF R., WOLFF E.
　　　　　　"Development and trade dependence: the case of Puerto Rico, 1948-1963"
　　　　　　Rev. Econ. Stats., vol.57, 1975, pp.470-477.
　　　　　　INPUT OUTPUT - MACRO , WEST INDIES * APPL - MACRO : DEVELOPMENT * APPL -
　　　　　　MACRO : INTERNATIONAL TRADE

YA3632　　WELCH F., CUNNINGHAM J.
　　　　　　"Effects of minimum wages on the level and age composition of youth
　　　　　　employment"　　Rev. Econ. Stats., vol.60, 1978, pp.140-145.
　　　　　　POLICY EVALUATION - MACRO : EMPLOYMENT * DATA - CROSS SECTION

YA3633　　WELCH T.H., ET AL.
　　　　　　"Meeting seasonal peak demands for natural gas"　　Opl. Res. Q., vol.22,
　　　　　　(conference issue), 1971, pp.93-106.
　　　　　　APPL - SECTOR : UTILITIES , GAS * SEASONALITY - EFFECT OF * USE - PRODUCTION
　　　　　　, PLANNING * USER - FIRM : UTILITIES * USER REQUIREMENTS

YA3634　　WELLAND J.D.
　　　　　　"Cognitive abilities, schooling and earnings: the question of functional
　　　　　　form"　　Rev. Econ. Stats., vol.60, 1978, pp.622-627.
　　　　　　EDUCATION - EFFECT OF * MANPOWER PLANNING - EARNINGS * MANPOWER PLANNING -
　　　　　　LABOUR FORCE COMPOSITION * COMPARATIVE METHODS - REGRESSION ,
　　　　　　TRANSFORMATIONS * REGRESSION - TRANSFORMATIONS , BOX COX

YA3635　　WELLS J.D.
　　　　　　"Computerised industrial forecasting for planning in central government"
　　　　　　Long Range Planning, vol.4:2, 1971, pp.41-46.
　　　　　　MACRO MODEL - GOVERNMENT , UK * INPUT OUTPUT - APPL , UK * BASIC

YA3636　　WELLS W.D.
　　　　　　"Psychographics: a critical review"　　J. Mktg. Res., vol.12, 1975,
　　　　　　pp.196-213.
　　　　　　CONSUMER BEHAVIOUR - PSYCHOLOGICAL MODELS , REVIEW * BIBLIOGRAPHY - CONSUMER
　　　　　　BEHAVIOUR , PSYCHOLOGICAL MODELS

YA3637　　WENGLOWSKI G.M.
　　　　　　"Industry profit forecasting"　　Bus. Econ., vol.7:1, 1972, pp.61-66.
　　　　　　APPL - SECTOR : FINANCE , PROFITS * BASIC

YA3638　　WEST R.R., ET AL.
　　　　　　"Portfolio returns and the random walk theory: comments"　　J. Finance,
　　　　　　vol.28, 1973, pp.733-745.
　　　　　　STOCK PRICES - RUNS * STOCK PRICES - TRADING RULES * RANDOM WALK - TEST ,
　　　　　　TRADING RULE * APPL - FIRM : FINANCE , STOCK PRICES * USE - PORTFOLIO
　　　　　　SELECTION * STOCK PRICES - MODELS , EFFICIENT MARKET

YA3639　　WEST R.R., ET AL.
　　　　　　"Premiums on convertible bonds: comment　　J. Finance, vol.27, 1972,
　　　　　　pp.1156-1170.
　　　　　　APPL - FIRM : FINANCE , BONDS * APPL - FIRM : FINANCE , OPTIONS

YA3640　　WEST R.R., TINIC S.M.
　　　　　　"Minimum commission rates on New York Stock Exchange transactions"　　Bell
　　　　　　J. Econ., vol.2, 1971, pp.577-605.
　　　　　　APPL - FIRM : FINANCE , STOCK BROKER * COST - FIRM : FINANCE * COST - SCALE
　　　　　　ECONOMIES

YA3641　　WESTIN R.B.
　　　　　　"Empirical implications of infrequent purchase behaviour in a stock
　　　　　　adjustment model"　　Am. Econ. Rev., vol.65, 1975, pp.384-395.
　　　　　　THEORY - STOCK ADJUSTMENT * APPL - SECTOR : CONSUMER DURABLES , CARS *
　　　　　　DEMAND - INTERMITTENT * INCOME - EFFECT OF * PRICE - EFFECT OF

YA3642   WESTIN R.B.
         "Predictions from binary choice models"   J. Econometrics, vol.2, 1974,
         pp.1-16.
         TIME - VALUE OF * APPL - SECTOR : TRANSPORT * EVALUATION - REGRESSION ,
         LIMITED DEPENDENT * EVALUATION - REGRESSION , QUALITATIVE DEPENDENT *
         EVALUATION - THEORY OF
YA3643   WESTIN R.B., GILLEN D.W.
         "Parking location and transit demand: a case study in endogenous attributes
         in disaggregate mode choice models"   J. Econometrics, vol.8, 1978,
         pp.75-101.
         REGRESSION - LIMITED DEPENDENT , PROBIT * APPL - SECTOR : TRANSPORT , ROAD *
         REGIONAL MODELS * - CITY * REGIONAL MODELS - SECTOR : TRANSPORT * USE -
         TRANSPORT PLANNING * TIME - VALUE OF
YA3644   WESTIN R.B., WATSON P.L.
         "Reported and revealed preferences as determinants of mode choice behaviour"
         J. Mktg. Res., vol.12, 1975, pp.282-289.
         REGRESSION - LIMITED DEPENDENT , LOGIT * TIME - VALUE OF * APPL - SECTOR :
         TRANSPORT * USE - TRANSPORT PLANNING
YA3645   WESTLAKE M.J.
         "British company taxation and automatic stabilisation"   Appl. Econ.,
         vol.3, 1971, pp.257-274.
         TAX - EFFECT OF * APPL - SECTOR : FINANCE , PROFITS * APPL - SECTOR :
         INVESTMENT
YA3646   WESTON J.F., SMITH V.K., SHRIEVES R.E.
         "Conglomerate performance using the capital asset pricing model"   Rev.
         Econ. Stats., vol.54, 1972, pp.357-363.
         THEORY - EFFICIENT MARKETS * APPL - SECTOR : FINANCE , STOCK PRICES * STOCK
         PRICES - INDUSTRIAL STRUCTURE * BIBLIOGRAPHY - INDUSTRIAL STRUCTURE * APPL -
         FIRM TYPE : CONGLOMERATES * STOCK PRICES - RISK
YA3647   WHARTON F.
         "On estimating aggregate inventory characteristics"   Opl. Res. Q., vol.26,
         1975, pp.543-551.
         USE - INVENTORY CONTROL * ERROR DISTRIBUTION - LOGNORMAL * ERROR
         DISTRIBUTION - POWER LAW * ERROR SPECIFICATION - HETEROSCEDASTIC
YA3648   WHEATON W.C.
         "Income and urban residence: an analysis of consumer demand for location"
         Am. Econ. Rev., vol.67, 1977, pp.620-631.
         APPL - SECTOR : CONSTRUCTION , LAND * APPL - SECTOR : LOCATION * PRICE -
         SECTOR : CONSTRUCTION , LAND * CONSUMER BEHAVIOUR - ECONOMIC MODELS , THEORY
         * POLICY EVALUATION - REGIONAL * DATA - CROSS SECTION * APPL - SECTOR :
         CONSTRUCTION , RESIDENTIAL
YA3649   WHEELWRIGHT S.C., CLARKE D.G.
         "Corporate forecasting: promise and reality"   H.B.R., vol.54, Nov-Dec,
         1976, pp.40ff.
         USE - ORGANISATIONAL DESIGN * FORECASTING - PRACTICE * FORECASTING - USAGE *
         BASIC
YA3650   WHEELWRIGHT S.C., MAKRIDAKIS S.
         "An examination of the use of adaptive filtering in forecasting"   Opl.
         Res. Q., vol.24, 1973, pp.55-64.
         TIME SERIES - ADAPTIVE FILTERING * COMPARATIVE METHODS - ADAPTIVE FILTERING
         , TREND CURVES * COMPARATIVE METHODS - ADAPTIVE FILTERING , DECOMPOSITION *
         COMPARATIVE METHODS - DECOMPOSITION , TREND CURVES * APPL - SECTOR :
         CONSUMER NON DURABLES , LIQUOR
YA3651   WHITAKER D.
         "The derivation of a measure of brand loyalty using a Markov brand switching
         model"   J. Opl. Res. Soc., vol.29, 1978, pp.959-970.
         MARKOV MODELS - APPL : BRAND CHOICE * APPL - FIRM : SERVICES , MEDIA ,
         NEWSPAPERS * MARKOV MODELS - ESTIMATION * BRAND CHOICE - APPL * MARKOV
         MODELS - METHODOLOGY
YA3652   WHITE H., THIRLWALL A.P.
         "US merchandise imports and the dispersion of demand"   Appl. Econ., vol.6,
         1974, pp.275-292.
         APPL - MACRO : INTERNATIONAL TRADE , IMPORTS * COMPARATIVE METHODS -
         REGRESSION , ERROR SPECIFICATION
YA3653   WHITE K.J.
         "A general computer program for econometric methods - SHAZAM"
         Econometrica, vol.46, 1978, pp.239-240.
         COMPUTERISATION - ESTIMATION , REGRESSION MODELS , PROGRAM * SIMULTANEOUS
         SYSTEM - ESTIMATION * ERROR SPECIFICATION - AUTOCORRELATED * COMPUTERISATION
         - ESTIMATION , SIMULTANEOUS SYSTEM MODELS , PROGRAMS * REGRESSION -
         ESTIMATION
YA3654   WHITE K.J.
         "Estimation of the liquidity trap with a generalised functional form"
         Econometrica, vol.40, 1972, pp.193-199.
         APPL - MACRO : MONEY , DEMAND * INTEREST RATE - EFFECT OF * REGRESSION -
         TRANSFORMATIONS , BOX , COX * COMPARATIVE METHODS - REGRESSION ,
         TRANSFORMATIONS

YA3655   WHITE L.A., ELLIS J.B.
        "A system construct for evaluating retail market locations"   J. Mktg.
        Res., vol.8, 1971, pp.43-46.
        APPL - FIRM : RETAILING , SUPERMARKETS * USE - SITE SELECTION , RETAIL

YA3656   WHITE W.L.
        "Debt management and the form of business financing" with discussion   J.
        Finance, vol.29, 1974, pp.565-577 & 614-616.
        APPL - SECTOR : FINANCE , FINANCIAL STRUCTURE * EX ANTE * APPL - FIRM :
        FINANCE , FINANCIAL STRUCTURE

YA3657   WHITLEY J.D., WORSWICK G.D.N.
        "The productivity effects of selective employment tax"   Nat. Inst. Econ.
        Rev., no.58, 1971, pp.72-75.
        APPL - MACRO : PRODUCTIVITY * APPL - SECTOR : RETAILING * APPL - SECTOR :
        PRODUCTIVITY * APPL - MACRO , UK * TAX - EFFECT OF * POLICY EVALUATION -
        MACRO : EMPLOYMENT

YA3658   WHITTINGTON G.
        "The profitability of alternative sources of finance - some further
        evidence"   Rev. Econ. Stats., vol.60, 1978, pp.632-634.
        APPL - FIRM : FINANCE , PROFITS * APPL - FIRM : FINANCE , FINANCIAL
        STRUCTURE

YA3659   WHITTINGTON G.
        "The profitability of retained earnings"   Rev. Econ. Stats., vol.54, 1972,
        pp.152-160.
        DATA - CROSS SECTION * APPL - FIRM : FINANCE , PROFITS * APPL - FIRM :
        GROWTH

YA3660   WHYBARK D.C., WILLIAMS J.G.
        "Material requirements planning under uncertainty"   Decis. Sci., vol.7,
        1976, pp.595-606.
        USE - INVENTORY CONTROL * USE - PRODUCTION , CONTROL * USE - SCHEDULING ,
        MATERIALS SUPPLY * TIMING UNCERTAINTY

YA3661   WICHERN D.W., JONES R.H.
        "Assessing the impact of market disturbances using intervention analysis"
        Mgmt. Sci., vol.24, 1977, pp.329-337.
        TIME SERIES - ARIMA : INTERVENTION * APPL - FIRM : CONSUMER NON DURABLES ,
        GROCERIES * COMPETITION - EFFECT OF

YA3662   WICHERN D.W., MILLER R.B., HSU D.
        "Changes of variance in first-order auto regressive time series models- with
        an application"   Appl. Stats., vol.25, 1976, pp.248-256.
        SPECIFICATION ERROR - TESTS , HETEROSCEDASTICITY * TIME SERIES -
        AUTOREGRESSIVE * APPL - FIRM : FINANCE , STOCK PRICES * STOCK PRICES -
        VOLATILITY

YA3663   WICKENS M.R.
        "A note on the use of proxy variables"   Econometrica, vol.40, 1972,
        pp.759-761.
        REGRESSION - ERROR IN VARIABLES * SPECIFICATION ERROR - EFFECT OF ,
        SPECIFICATION OF VARIABLES * DATA ERRORS - EFFECT OF * PROXY VARIABLES

YA3664   WICKENS M.R., GREENFIELD J.N.
        "The econometrics of agricultural supply: an application to the world coffee
        market"   Rev. Econ. Stats., vol.55, 1973, pp.433-440.
        SUPPLY - SECTOR : AGRICULTURE * APPL - SECTOR : AGRICULTURE , COFFEE *
        DISTRIBUTED LAG - ALMON : APPL

YA3665   WIERENGA B.
        "A least squares estimation method for the linear learning model"   J.
        Mktg. Res., vol.15, 1978, pp.145-153.
        ESTIMATION - MINIMUM CHI - SQUARE : APPL * PROBABILITY MODELS - LINEAR
        LEARNING * APPL - FIRM : CONSUMER NON DURABLES * ESTIMATION - OLS ,
        ITERATIVE * COMPARATIVE METHODS - ESTIMATION : PROBABILITY MODELS

YA3666   WIGINTON J.C.
        "A Bayesian approach to discrimination among economic models"   Decis.
        Sci., vol.5, 1974, pp.182-191.
        APPL - MACRO : CONSUMPTION * BAYESIAN - MODEL SELECTION

YA3667   WIGINTON J.C.
        "Alternative estimators of line securities"   Omega, vol.4, 1976,
        pp.109-110.
        COMPARATIVE METHODS - ESTIMATION : OLS , MSAE * EX ANTE * APPL - FIRM :
        FINANCE , STOCK PRICES * STOCK PRICES - BETA

YA3668   WIGINTON J.C.
        "MSAE estimation: an alternative approach to regression analysis for
        economic forecasting applications"   Appl. Econ., vol.4, 1972, pp.11-21.
        ESTIMATION - MSAE * EX ANTE * COMPARATIVE METHODS - ESTIMATION : OLS , MSAE
        * INFLATION - RAPID * APPL - MACRO : MONEY , CASH BALANCES

YA3669   WILBRATTE B.J.
        "Some essential differences in the demand for money by households and by
        firms"   J. Finance, vol.30, 1975, pp.1091-1099.
        APPL - MACRO : MONEY , DEMAND * DATA - SPECIFICATION OF VARIABLES * APPL -
        SECTOR : FINANCE , FINANCIAL STRUCTURE * APPL - MACRO : CONSUMER DEMAND ,
        FINANCIAL ASSETS

YA3670   WILDER R.P., STANSELL S.R.
          "Determinants of research and development activity by electric utilities"
          Bell J. Econ, vol.5, 1974, pp.646-650.
          APPL - FIRM : R & D * APPLICATION - FIRM : UTILITIES , ELECTRICITY
YA3671   WILDER R.P., WILLIAMS C.G., SINGH D.
          "The price equation: a cross-section approach"   Am, Econ, Rev,, vol.67,
          1977, pp.732-740.
          DATA - CROSS SECTION , TIME SERIES * CONCENTRATION - EFFECT OF * STABILITY
          OF COEFFICIENTS - REGRESSION : APPL * PRICE - SECTOR
YA3672   WILDT A.R.
          "Estimating models of seasonal market response using dummy variables"   J.
          Mktg. Res,, vol.14, 1977, pp.34-41.
          SEASONALITY - TESTING * STABILITY OF COEFFICIENTS - REGRESSION * SEASONALITY
          - ESTIMATION , OLS
YA3673   WILDT A.R.
          "Multifirm analysis of competitive decision variables"   J, Mktg, Res,,
          vol.11, 1974, pp.50-62.
          MARKET SHARE - SECTOR : CONSUMER NON DURABLES * REGRESSION - SEEMINGLY
          UNRELATED * APPL - FIRM : CONSUMER NON DURABLES , FOOD * ADVERTISING -
          OPTIMALITY * ADVERTISING - DETERMINANTS
YA3674   WILDT A.R.
          "On evaluating market segmentation studies and the properties of R squared"
          Mgmt, Sci,, vol.22, 1976, pp.904-908.
          MARKET SEGMENTATION * DATA - AGGREGATION OVER TIME * REGRESSION - SUMMARY
          STATISTICS CONSUMER BEHAVIOUR - STOCHASTIC MODELS
YA3675   WILDT A.R., BRUNO A.V.
          "The prediction of preference for capital equipment using linear attitude
          models"   J, Mktg, Res,, vol.11, 1974, pp.203-205.
          BRAND CHOICE - INDICATORS * CONSUMER BEHAVIOUR - PSYCHOLOGICAL MODELS * APPL
          - SECTOR : PRODUCTION * CONSUMER BEHAVIOUR - PURCHASING , DETERMINANTS
YA3676   WILFORD D.S., WILFORD W.T.
          "On the monetary approach to the balance of payments"   J, Finance, vol.33,
          1978, pp.319-323.
          APPL - MACRO : MONEY , DEMAND * APPL - MACRO : INTERNATIONAL FINANCE ,
          FOREIGN RESERVES * APPL - MACRO , LATIN AMERICA
YA3677   WILKINSON M.
          "An econometric analysis of fertility in Sweden, 1870-1965"   Econometrica,
          vol.41, 1973, pp.633-642.
          POPULATION - FERTILITY * APPL - MACRO , SWEDEN
YA3678   WILKINSON R.K.
          "House prices and the measurement of externalities"   Econ, J,, vol, 83,
          1973, pp.72-86.
          APPL - SECTOR : CONSTRUCTION , RESIDENTIAL * PRICE - SECTOR : CONSTRUCTION ,
          RESIDENTIAL * FACTOR ANALYSIS - APPL * DATA - CROSS SECTION
YA3679   WILLASSEN Y.
          "An alternative econometric approach to the permanent income hypothesis, an
          international comparison: some comments"   Rev, Econ, Stats,, vol.57, 1975,
          pp.92-94.
          EVALUATION - PERMANENT INCOME * REGRESSION - ERRORS IN VARIABLES * DATA -
          INTERNATIONAL * APPL - MACRO : CONSUMPTION * INCOME - EFFECT OF , PERMANENT
YA3680   WILLIAMS D.
          "Estimating in levels or first differences: a defence of the method used for
          certain demand-for-money equations"   Econ, J,, vol.88, 1978, pp.564-568.
          APPL - MACRO : MONEY , DEMAND * STATIONARITY - TRANSFORMING TO * DISTRIBUTED
          LAG - RATIONAL POLYNOMIAL , IDENTIFICATION * DISTRIBUTED LAG - ERROR
          SPECIFICATION * REGRESSION - MODEL CHOICE
YA3681   WILLIAMS D., GOODHART C.A.E., GOWLAND D.H.
          "Money, income and causality: the UK experience"   Am, Econ, Rev,, vol.66,
          1976, pp.417-423.
          CAUSALITY - TEST * APPL - MACRO : MONEY * APPL - MACRO : GNP * TIME SERIES -
          ARIMA : APPL * APPL - MACRO , UK
YA3682   WILLIAMS R.A.
          "Demand for consumer durables: stock adjustment models and alternative
          specifications of stock depletion"   Rev, Econ, studies, vol.39, 1972,
          pp.281-295.
          ESTIMATION - NON LINEAR * APPL - SECTOR : CONSUMER DURABLES , CARS * APPL -
          SECTOR : CONSUMER DURABLES , APPLIANCES * DEPRECIATION * ERROR SPECIFICATION
          - MOVING AVERAGE * THEORY - STOCK ADJUSTMENT
YA3683   WILLIAMS R.A.
          "Growth in ownership of consumer durables in the UK"   Economica, vol.39,
          1972, pp.60-69.
          APPL - SECTOR : CONSUMER DURABLES , CARS * APPL - SECTOR : CONSUMER DURABLES
          , APPLIANCES , REFRIDGERATORS * ESTIMATION - MAXIMUM LIKELIHOOD * APPL -
          SECTOR : FINANCE , CONSUMER CREDIT
YA3684   WILLIAMS R.M.
          "Sources and uses of regional econometric data"   Bus, Econ,, vol.8:3,
          1973, pp.15-21.
          REGIONAL MODELS * REGIONAL MODELS - DATA

YA3685   WILLIAMS W.H., GOODMAN M.L.
          "A simple method for the construction of empirical confidence limits for
          economic forecasts"   J. Am. Statist. Ass., vol.66, 1971, pp.752-754.
          CONFIDENCE INTERVAL - EX ANTE * EVALUATION - CONFIDENCE INTERVAL * APPL -
          SECTOR : UTILITIES , TELEPHONE * EVALUATION - THEORY OF * TIME SERIES -
          POLYNOMIAL : APPL * PROBABILITY MODELS - GAMMA * LOSS FUNCTIONS -
          METHODOLOGY

YA3686   WILLIAMSON J.
          "International liquidity"   Econ. J., vol.83, 1973, pp.685-746.
          BIBLIOGRAPHY - INTERNATIONAL FINANCE * APPL - MACRO : INTERNATIONAL FINANCE
          , FOREIGN RESERVES

YA3687   WILLIAMSON J., WOOD G.E.,
          "The British inflation: indigenous or imported"   Am. Econ. Rev., vol.66,
          1976, pp.520-531.
          APPL - MACRO , UK * INFLATION - DETERMINANTS

YA3688   WILLIS R.E.
          "Fixed sum losses in functional forecasting"   Decis. Sci., vol.7, 1976,
          pp.425-431.
          LOSS FUNCTIONS - ASYMMETRICAL * LOSS FUNCTIONS - METHODOLOGY

YA3689   WILMOT P.D.
          "A comparison of the methods of technological forecasting"   Ind. Mktg.
          Mgmt., vol.1, 1971, pp.95-102.
          EVALUATION - TECHNOLOGICAL FORECASTING * BASIC

YA3690   WILSON H.G.
          "Least squares versus minimum absolute deviations estimation in linear
          models"   Decis. Sci., vol.9, 1978, pp.322-335.
          COMPARATIVE METHODS - ESTIMATION : OLS , MSAE * REGRESSION - OUTLIERS

YA3691   WILSON R.W.
          "The effect of technological environment and product rivalry on r & d effort
          and licensing of inventions"   Rev. Econ. Stats., vol.59, 1977, pp.171-178.
          APPL - FIRM : R & D

YA3692   WILSON T.F.
          "Responsiveness of bond yields to variations in short-term interest rates"
          Bus. Econ., vol.13:4, 1978, pp.28-31.
          APPL - SECTOR : FINANCE , BONDS * INTEREST RATE - DETERMINANTS * INTEREST
          RATE - EFFECT OF

YA3693   WILTON D.A.
          "An econometric model of the Canadian automotive manufacturing industry and
          the 1965 automotive agreement"   Can. J. Econ., vol.5, 1972, pp.157-181.
          APPL - SECTOR : INVESTMENT * COST - SECTOR : CONSUMER DURABLES * APPL -
          SECTOR : CONSUMER DURABLES , CARS * SIMULATION - APPL : SECTOR , CONSUMER
          DURABLES * POLICY EVALUATION - SECTOR : CONSUMER DURABLES * EX ANTE * PRICE
          - SECTOR : CONSUMER DURABLES * PRICE - EFFECT OF * APPL - SECTOR : EARNINGS

YA3694   WILTON D.A.
          "Structural shift with an interstructural transition function"   Can. J.
          Econ., vol.8, 1975, pp.423-432.
          APPL - SECTOR : CONSUMER DURABLES , CARS * REGRESSION - PIECEWISE * TARIFF -
          EFFECT OF * STABILITY OF COEFFICIENTS - REGRESSION * APPL - SECTOR :
          INTERNATIONAL TRADE , IMPORTS

YA3695   WIND Y.
          "Issues and advances in segmentation research"   J. Mktg. Res., vol.15,
          1978, pp.317-337.
          MARKET SEGMENTATION - REVIEW * BIBLIOGRAPHY - MARKET SEGMENTATION

YA3696   WINKLER R.L., SMITH W.S., KULKARNI R.B.
          "Adaptive forecasting models based on predictive distributions"   Mgmt.
          Sci., vol.24, 1978, pp.977-986.
          REGRESSION - PRIOR INFORMATION * JUDGEMENTAL FORECASTS - METHODOLOGY *
          JUDGEMENTAL FORECASTS - INCORPORATION * BAYESIAN - PRIOR INFORMATION

YA3697   WINSTON G.C.
          "Capital utilisation in economic development"   Econ. J., vol.81, 1971,
          pp.36-60.
          APPL - MACRO : CAPACITY UTILISATION * APPL - SECTOR : CAPACITY UTILISATION *
          APPL - MACRO , PAKISTAN

YA3698   WINTERS L.A.
          "UK exports and the pressure of demand: a note"   Econ. J., vol.84, 1974,
          pp.623-628.
          APPL - MACRO , UK * APPL - MACRO : INTERNATIONAL TRADE , EXPORTS

YA3699   WISE D.A.
          "Academic achievement and job performance"   Am. Econ. Rev., vol.65, 1975,
          pp.350-366.
          MANPOWER PLANNING - QUALIFIED MANPOWER * EDUCATION - EFFECT OF *
          BIBLIOGRAPHY - EDUCATION EFFECTIVENESS

YA3700   WISE D.A.
          "Personal attributes, job performance and probability of promotion"
          Econometrica, vol.43, 1975, pp.913-931.
          MANPOWER PLANNING - PROMOTION * REGRESSION - LIMITED DEPENDENT , LOGIT *
          APPL - SECTOR : SOCIAL , SUCCESS

YA3701　WISEMAN C.
"Windfalls and consumption under a consuming contraint　Rev. Econ. Stats.,
vol.57, 1975, pp.180-184.
DATA - CROSS SECTION * APPL - MACRO : CONSUMPTION * INCOME - EFFECT OF *
DATA - GROUPED

YA3702　WISEMAN F.
"A segmentation analysis on automobile buyers during the new model
transition period"　J. Mktg., vol.35, no.2, April 1971, pp.42-49.
MARKET SEGMENTATION * APPL - SECTOR : CONSUMER DURABLES , CARS *
DISCRIMINANT ANALYSIS - APPL * BASIC

YA3703　WISMER D.A.
"On the uses of industrial dynamic models"　Ops. Res., vol.15, 1967,
pp.752-767.
INDUSTRIAL DYNAMICS - APPL , FIRM * APPL - FIRM : PRODUCTION , CEMENT *
SIMULATION - APPL : FIRM

YA3704　WITHER G.A.
"Armed forces recruitment in GB"　Appl. Econ., vol.9, 1977, pp.289-306.
MANPOWER PLANNING - SECTOR : GOVERNMENT , MILITARY * APPL - SECTOR :
GOVERNMENT , DEFENCE * POLICY EVALUATION - MACRO : DEFENCE

YA3705　WITTE A.D., CLAGUE C.K.
"Alternative estimates of capital-labor substitution in manufacturing in
developing economies: comments"　Econometrica, vol.39, 1971, pp.1053-1056.
APPL - MACRO , LATIN AMERICA * PRODUCTION FUNCTIONS - METHODOLOGY *
PRODUCTION FUNCTIONS - SUBSTITUTION * PRODUCTION FUNCTIONS - SECTOR

YA3706　WITTE A.D., SCHMIDT P.
"An analysis of recidivism, using the truncated lognormal distribution
Appl. Stats., vol.26, 1977, pp.302-311.
REGRESSION - TRUNCATED * ERROR DISTRIBUTION - LOGNORMAL * APPL - SECTOR :
SOCIAL , CRIME

YA3707　WITTINK D.R.
"Advertising increases sensitivity to price"　J. Advtg. Res., vol.17:2,
1977, pp.39-42.
ADVERTISING - EFFECT OF * DATA - CROSS SECTION , TIME SERIES * APPL - FIRM :
CONSUMER NON DURABLES * MARKET SHARE - SECTOR : CONSUMER NON DURABLES *
REGRESSION - RANDOM COEFFICIENTS * PRICE - EFFECT OF * MARKET SHARE - EFFECT
OF

YA3708　WITTINK D.R.
"Exploring territorial differences in the relationship between marketing
variables"　J. Mktg. Res., vol.14, 1977, pp.145-155.
STABILITY OF COEFFICIENTS - REGRESSION * MARKET SHARE - SECTOR : CONSUMER
NON DURABLES * APPL - FIRM : CONSUMER NON DURABLES * ADVERTISING - EFFECT OF
* PRICE - EFFECT OF * COMPARATIVE METHODS - REGRESSION , RANDOM COEFFICIENTS
* COMPARATIVE METHODS - DATA : CROSS SECTION , TIME SERIES

YA3709　WOLD H.O.
"Econometrics as pioneering in non experimental model building"
Econometrica, vol.37, 1969, pp.369-381.
CAUSALITY - REVIEW * THEORY - MODELLING

YA3710　WOLF C.R.
"The demand for funds in the public and private corporate bond markets"
Rev. Econ. Stats., vol.56, 1974, pp.23-29.
APPL - SECTOR : FINANCE , BONDS * ERROR SPECIFICATION - AUTOCORRELATED *
SPECIFICATION ERROR - EFFECT OF , SIMULTANEOUS SYSTEM BIAS : APPL

YA3711　WOLPIN K.T.
"Capital punishment and homicide in England: a summary of results" with
discussion　Am. Econ. Ass. Proc., 1978, pp.422-427 & 435-436.
APPL - SECTOR : SOCIAL , CRIME * POLICY EVALUATION - SECTOR : SOCIAL

YA3712　WOOD J.T.
"An extension of the analysis of transformations of Box and Cox"　Appl.
Stats., vol.23, 1974, pp.278-283.
REGRESSION - NON LINEAR * REGRESSION - TRANSFORMATIONS , BOX COX * APPL -
SECTOR : NATURAL , PLANT POPULATIONS

YA3713　WOOD S.D., STEECE B.M.
"Forecasting the product of two time series with a linear asymmetric error
cost function"　Mgmt. Sci., vol.24, 1978, pp.690-701.
TIME SERIES - ARIMA : APPL * DATA - PRODUCT * LOSS FUNCTIONS - ASYMMETRICAL
* EX ANTE * LEAD TIME - EFFECT OF * COMPARATIVE METHODS - ARIMA ,
EXPONENTIAL SMOOTHING(ADAPTIVE)

YA3714　WOODLAND A.D.
"On testing weak separability"　J. Econometrics, vol.8, 1978, pp.383-398.
PRODUCTION FUNCTIONS - METHODOLOGY * DATA - DISAGGREGATION * SPECIFICATION
ERROR - TESTS , AGGREGATION BIAS

YA3715　WOODLAND A.D.
"Substitution of structures, equipment and labour in Canadian production"
Int. Econ. Rev., vol.16, 1975, pp.171-187.
COST - SECTOR * ERROR SPECIFICATION - AUTOCORRELATED * SUBSTITUTE FACTORS *
COST - SCALE ECONOMIES

YA3716   WOODRUFF R.S.
          "Use of a regression technique to produce area breakdowns of the monthly
          national estimates of retail trade"   J. Am. Statist. Ass., vol.61, 1966,
          pp.496-504.
          DATA - DISAGGREGATION , GEOGRAPHICAL * DATA - INTERPOLATION

YA3717   WRIGHT D.J.
          "The natural resource requirements of commodities"   Appl. Econ., vol.7,
          1975, pp.31-39.
          INPUT OUTPUT - MACRO : RAW MATERIALS * APPL - MACRO : RAW MATERIALS * APPL -
          SECTOR : ENERGY , SOURCES * INPUT OUTPUT - SECTOR : ENERGY

YA3718   WRIGHT R.D.
          "An industrial dynamics implementation: growth strategies for a trucking
          firm"   Sloan Mgmt. rev, vol.13, no.1, 1971, pp.71-86.
          INDUSTRIAL DYNAMICS - APPL , FIRM * APPL - FIRM : TRANSPORT , ROAD , FREIGHT
          * APPL - FIRM : GROWTH * USE - DISTRIBUTION * USER - FIRM : TRANSPORT *
          SIMULATION - APPL : FIRM * BASIC

YA3719   WRIGHT W.F.
          "Financial information processing models: an empirical study"   Acctg.
          Rev., vol.52, 1977, pp.676-689.
          JUDGEMENTAL FORECASTS - DETERMINANTS * EVALUATION - JUDGEMENTAL FORECASTS ,
          STOCK PRICES * APPL - FIRM : FINANCE , STOCK PRICES * BIBLIOGRAPHY -
          JUDGEMENTAL FORECASTS

YA3720   WU D.
          "Alternative tests of independence between stochastic regressors and
          disturbances"   Econometrica, vol.41, 1973, pp.733-750.
          SPECIFICATION ERROR - TESTS , INDEPENDENCE REGRESSORS , ERRORS * ADVANCED

YA3721   WU D.
          "Alternative tests of independence between stochastic regressors and
          disturbances: finite sample results"   Econometrica, vol.42, 1974,
          pp.529-546.
          SPECIFICATION ERROR - TESTS , INDEPENDENCE REGRESSORS , ERRORS

YA3722   WU R.Y.
          "On some aspects of linearly aggregated macro models"   Int. Econ. Rev.,
          vol.14, 1973, pp.785-788.
          DATA - AGGREGATION 'BIAS' * REGRESSION - AGGREGATION

YA3723   WYKOFF F.C.
          "A user cost approach to new automobile purchases"   Rev. Econ. Studies,
          vol.40, 1973, pp.377-390.
          APPL - SECTOR : CONSUMER DURABLES , CARS * INCOME - EFFECT OF * PRICE -
          EFFECT OF * REGRESSION - SPECIFICATION OF VARIABLES * EVALUATION - INCOME
          ELASTICITIES

YA3724   WYNNE A.J., HOFFER G.E.
          "Auto recalls: do they affect market share?"   Appl. Econ., vol.8, 1976,
          pp.157-163.
          APPL - FIRM : CONSUMER DURABLES , CARS * MARKET SHARE - SECTOR : CONSUMER
          DURABLES * QUALITY - EFFECT OF

YA3725   WYZGA R.E.
          "The effect of air pollution upon mortality: a consideration of distributed
          lag models" with discussion   J. Am. Statist. Ass., vol.73, 1978,
          pp.463-472.
          COMPARATIVE METHODS - DISTRIBUTED LAG * COMPARATIVE METHODS - DISTRIBUTED
          LAG , ERROR SPECIFICATION * HEALTH - DISEASE , INCIDENCE OF * ERROR
          SPECIFICATION - AUTOCORRELATED : APPL

YA3726   YADAV G.
          "A quarterly model of the Canadian demand for imports 1956-1972"   Can. J.
          Econ., vol.8, 1975, pp.410-422.
          APPL - MACRO : INTERNATIONAL TRADE , IMPORTS * INCOME - EFFECT OF * PRICE -
          EFFECT OF * DATA - AGGREGATION 'BIAS' * APPL - MACRO , CANADA

YA3727   YADAV G.
          "Discriminatory aspects of Canada's imports of manufactured foods from the
          less developed countries"   Can. J. Econ., vol.5, 1972, pp.70-83.
          DATA - LDC * TARIFF - EFFECT OF * APPL - SECTOR : INTERNATIONAL TRADE ,
          IMPORTS

YA3728   YADAV G.
          "Variable elasticities and non-price rationing in the import demand function
          of Canada, 1956:1-1973:4"   Can. J. Econ., vol.10, 1977, pp.702-712.
          APPL - SECTOR : INTERNATIONAL TRADE , IMPORTS * APPL - MACRO , CANADA * APPL
          - MACRO : INTERNATIONAL TRADE , IMPORTS

YA3729   YAMAMOTO T.
          "Asymptotic mean square prediction error for an autoregressive model with
          estimated coefficients"   Appl. Stats., vol.25, 1976, pp.123-127.
          TIME SERIES - ARIMA : FORECASTING * LEAD TIME - EFFECT OF * CONFIDENCE
          INTERVAL - PREDICTIONS : TIME SERIES * ADVANCED

YA3730   YAN C., CHUNG A.
          "The impact of pollution control on consumer income: a methodological study"
          Decis. Sci., vol.8, 1977, pp.121-133.
          POLLUTION - CONTROLS * INPUT OUTPUT - MACRO : POLLUTION * REGIONAL MODELS -
          POLLUTION

YA3731 YANCEY T.A., BOCK M.E., JUDGE G.G.
"Some finite sample results for Theil's mixed regression estimator" J.
Am. Statist. Ass., vol.67, 1972, pp.176-179.
PRIOR INFORMATION - EVALUATION * DATA - SIMULATION * REGRESSION - PRIOR
INFORMATION * ESTIMATION - THEIL GOLDBERGER * ESTIMATION - PRIOR INFORMATION
* ADVANCED

YA3732 YANCEY T.A., JUDGE G.G.
"A Monte Carlo comparison of traditional and Stein-rule estimators under
squared error loss" J. Econometrics, vol.4, 1976, pp.285-294.
DATA - SIMULATION * COMPARATIVE METHODS - ESTIMATION : REGRESSION *
ESTIMATION - STEIN * ESTIMATION - PRE TEST

YA3733 YANCEY T.A., JUDGE G.G., BOCK M.E.
"Wallace's weak mean square error criterion for testing linear restrictions
in regression: a tighter bound" Econometrica, vol.41, 1973, pp.1203-1206.
SPECIFICATION ERROR - TESTS , CONSTRAINTS * REGRESSION - HYPOTHESIS TESTS *
ADVANCED

YA3734 YARDENI E.E.
"A portfolio-balance model of corporate working capital" J. Finance,
vol.33, 1978, pp.535-552.
APPL - SECTOR : FINANCE , FINANCIAL STRUCTURE * INFLATION - EFFECT OF

YA3735 YEATS A.J.
"An alternative approach to the identification of leading indicators"
Bus. Econ., vol.7:4, 1972, pp.7-11.
BUSINESS INDICATORS - METHODOLOGY * BUSINESS CYCLE - PREDICTION

YA3736 YEATS A.J.
"An evaluation of predictions based on runs and magnitudes of change in
leading series" Bus. Econ., vol.10:3, 1975, pp.47-53.
BUSINESS INDICATORS - METHODOLOGY * EVALUATION - BUSINESS INDICATORS *
TURNING POINTS - FORECASTING * DATA - SMOOTHING

YA3737 YEATS A.J.
"An evaluation of the predictive ability of the FRB sensitive price index"
J. Am. Statist. Ass., vol.68, 1973, pp.782-787.
EVALUATION - BUSINESS INDICATORS * INFLATION - INDICATORS

YA3738 YEATS A.J., IRONS E.D., RHOADES S.A.
"An analysis of new bank growth" J. Business, vol.48, 1975, pp.199-203.
APPL - FIRM : FINANCE , BANK , LIABILITIES * APPL - FIRM : FINANCE , BANKS

YA3739 YELLE L.E.
"Estimating learning curves for potential products" Ind. Mktg. Mgmt.,
vol.5, 1976, pp.147-154.
COST - LEARNING CURVE * APPL - FIRM : PRODUCTION , ELECTRONICS * NEW
PRODUCTS - COST * COST - FIRM : PRODUCTION

YA3740 YETT D.E., ET AL.
"A microeconometric model of the health care system in the U.S." Anns.
Econ. Soc. Meas., vol.4, 1975, pp.407-433.
HEALTH - SERVICES * SIMULATION - APPL : SECTOR , HEALTH * HEALTH - HOSPITAL
* HEALTH - MANPOWER * MANPOWER PLANNING - SECTOR : HEALTH

YA3741 YING C.C.
"Stock market prices and volumes of sales" Econometrica, vol.34, 1966,
pp.676-685.
APPL - FIRM : FINANCE , STOCK PRICES * STOCK PRICES - TRADING VOLUME

YA3742 YOSHIHARA K.
"Demand functions: an application to the Japanese expenditure system"
Econometrica, vol.37, 1969, pp.257-274.
DEMAND EQUATIONS - SYSTEMS OF : METHODOLOGY , ESTIMATION * APPL - MACRO :
CONSUMER DEMAND * COMPARATIVE METHODS - ESTIMATION : DEMAND EQUATIONS *
CONSUMER BEHAVIOUR - ECONOMIC MODELS , THEORY * APPL - MACRO , JAPAN

YA3743 YOSHIHARA K., FURUYA K., SUZUKI T.
"The problem of accounting for productivity change in the construction price
index" J. Am. Statist. Ass., vol.66, 1971, pp.33-41.
APPL - SECTOR : CONSTRUCTION * PRICE - SECTOR : CONSTRUCTION * QUALITY -
PRICE * INDEX NUMBERS - SECTOR : CONSTRUCTION * APPL - SECTOR : PRODUCTIVITY
* INDEX NUMBERS - METHODOLOGY

YA3744 YOTOPOULOS P.A., LAU L.J.
"A test for relative economic efficiency: some further results" Am. Econ.
Rev., vol.63, 1973, pp.214-223.
PRODUCTION FUNCTIONS - THEORY * APPL - FIRM : AGRICULTURE , FARMING * APPL -
FIRM : EFFICIENCY * DATA - CROSS SECTION * PRODUCTION FUNCTIONS - FIRM *
APPL - FIRM : FINANCE , PROFITS * MANPOWER PLANNING - FIRM , SUPPLY * APPL -
FIRM : EMPLOYMENT

YA3745 YOU J.K.
"Embodied and disembodied technical progress in the US, 1929-1968" Rev.
Econ. Stats., vol.53, 1976, pp.123-127.
PRODUCTION FUNCTION - MACRO * TECHNOLOGY - EFFECT OF

YA3746 YOUNG A., VASSILIOU P.G.
"A non-linear model of the promotion of staff" R. Statist. Soc. (A)
vol.137, 1974, pp.584-595.
MANPOWER PLANNING - PROMOTION * EX ANTE * EVALUATION - MANPOWER PLANNING
MODELS

YA3747   YOUNG A.H.
          "Linear approximators to the census and BLS seasonal adjustment methods"
          J. Am. Statist. Ass., vol.63, 1968, pp.445-472.
          SEASONALITY - ESTIMATION , CENSUS * COMPARATIVE METHODS - SEASONALITY * TIME
          SERIES - DECOMPOSITION * SEASONALITY - ESTIMATION , OLS
YA3748   YOUNG G.
          "The choice of dependent variable for cross section studies of migration"
          Can. J. Econ., vol.8, 1975, pp.93-100.
          MANPOWER PLANNING - MIGRATION * DATA - SPECIFICATION OF VARIABLES *
          POPULATION - MIGRATION
YA3749   YOUNG H.T.
          "Can food prices be controlled?"   Can. J. Econ., vol.9, 1976, pp.689-702.
          APPL - SECTOR : AGRICULTURE * APPL - SECTOR : CONSUMER NON DURABLES , FOOD *
          PRICE - SECTOR : CONSUMER NON DURABLES * INPUT OUTPUT - SECTOR : AGRICULTURE
          * PRICE - CONTROLS
YA3750   YOUNG K.H.
          "A synthesis of time series and cross section analyses: demand for air
          transportation service"   J. Am. Statist. Ass., vol.67, 1972, pp.560-566.
          APPL - SECTOR : TRANSPORT , AIR * ESTIMATION - CROSS SECTION , TIME SERIES *
          ESTIMATION - PRIOR INFORMATION * ADVANCED
YA3751   YOUNG R.
          "An exploratory analysis of demand for the public library lending service"
          Appl. Econ., vol.5, 1973, pp.119-132.
          APPL - SECTOR : EDUCATION , LIBRARIES * DATA - CROSS SECTION
YA3752   YOUNG W.E.
          "Random walk of stock prices: a test of the variance-time function"
          Econometrica, vol.39,1971, pp.797-812.
          APPL - FIRM : FINANCE , STOCK PRICES * STOCK PRICES - RUNS * RANDOM WALK -
          TEST
YA3753   ZAREMBKA P., CHERNICOFF H.B.
          "Further results on the empirical relevance of the CES production function"
          Rev. Econ. Stats., vol.53, 1971, pp.106-110.
          PRODUCTION FUNCTIONS - SECTOR * PRODUCTION FUNCTIONS - SUBSTITUTION
YA3754   ZARNOWITZ V.
          "On the accuracy and properties of recent macroeconomic forecasts" with
          discussion   Am. Econ. Ass. Proc., 1978, pp.313-321.
          COMPARATIVE METHODS - AUTOREGRESSIVE , CAUSAL(SIMULTANEOUS SYSTEM) *
          COMPARATIVE METHODS - MACRO MODELS * EVALUATION - MACRO MODELS * COMPARATIVE
          METHODS - CAUSAL(SIMULTANEOUS SYSTEM) , JUDGEMENTAL * JUDGEMENTAL FORECASTS
          - ASA NBER SURVEY * MACRO MODEL - WHARTON * MACRO MODEL - MICHIGAN *
          COMPARATIVE METHODS - AUTOREGRESSIVE , JUDGEMENTAL * EX ANTE
YA3755   ZARNOWITZ V.
          "The new ASA-NBER survey of forecasts by economic statisticians"   Am.
          Stat'n., vol.23:1, 1969, pp.12-16.
          JUDGEMENTAL FORECASTS - ASA NBER SURVEY * EVALUATION - JUDGEMENTAL FORECASTS
          , MACRO
YA3756   ZAUMAS G.S., MEHRA Y.P.
          "The stability of the demand for money function: the evidence from quarterly
          data"   Rev. Econ. Stats., vol.53, 1976, pp.463-468.
          APPL - MACRO : MONEY , DEMAND * REGRESSION - STATE SPACE
YA3757   ZECHER R.
          "Monetary equilibrium and international reserve flows in Australia"   J.
          Finance, vol.29, 1974, pp.1523-1530
          APPL - MACRO : INTERNATIONAL FINANCE , FOREIGN RESERVES * INCOME - EFFECT OF
          , PERMANENT * APPL - MACRO , AUSTRALIA * INTEREST RATE - EFFECT OF
YA3758   ZECKHAUSER R., THOMPSON M.
          "Linear regression with non-normal error terms"   Rev. Econ. Stats.,
          vol.52, 1970, pp.280-286.
          ERROR DISTRIBUTION - NON NORMAL * COMPARATIVE METHODS - ERROR DISTRIBUTIONS
          * REGRESSION - ESTIMATION * ESTIMATION - ERROR DISTRIBUTION
YA3759   ZEISEL J.
          "Forecasting at the Federal Reserve"   Bus. Econ., vol.6:4, 1971, pp.14-17.
          USER - SECTOR : GOVERNMENT , CENTRAL * FORECASTING - PRACTICE
YA3760   ZELENITZ A.
          "Below-cost original equipment sales as a promotional means"   Rev. Econ.
          Stats., vol.59, 1977, pp.438-446.
          APPL - FIRM : CONSUMER DURABLES , CARS , SPARES * MARKET SHARE - SECTOR :
          CONSUMER DURABLES * APPL - FIRM : FINANCE , PROFITS * USE - PROMOTION
          EVALUATION
YA3761   ZELLNER A.
          "Bayesian analysis of regression error terms"   J. Am. Statist. Ass.,
          vol.70, 1975, pp.138-144.
          BAYESIAN - ESTIMATION : RESIDUALS * RESIDUALS - ESTIMATION , BAYESIAN *
          ADVANCED
YA3762   ZELLNER A.
          "Constraints often overlooked in analyses of simultaneous equation models"
          Econometrica, vol.40, 1972, pp.849-853.
          SIMULTANEOUS SYSTEM - CONSTRAINED * ADVANCED

YA3763   ZELLNER A., GEISEL M.S.
         "Analysis of distributed lag models with applications to consumption
         function estimation"   Econometrica, vol.38, 1970, pp.865-888.
         APPL - MACRO : CONSUMPTION * COMPARATIVE METHODS - ESTIMATION : DISTRIBUTED
         LAG * DISTRIBUTED LAG - IDENTIFICATION * THEORY - MODELLING * DISTRIBUTED
         LAG - ESTIMATION * BAYESIAN - MODEL SELECTION * DISTRIBUTED LAG - APPL ,
         INCOME * BAYESIAN - ESTIMATION : DISTRIBUTED LAG * COMPARATIVE METHODS -
         ESTIMATION : REGRESSION , ERROR SPECIFICATION * ADVANCED

YA3764   ZELLNER A., MONTMARQUETTE C.
         "A study of some aspects of temporal aggregation problems in econometric
         analysis"   Rev. Econ. Stats., vol.53, 1971, pp.335-342.
         DATA - AGGREGATION OVER TIME * APPL - MACRO : INCOME * APPL - MACRO : MONEY
         , SUPPLY * EX ANTE * COMPARATIVE METHODS - DATA : AGGREGATE , DISAGGREGATE *
         EVALUATION - EX POST MODELS * EVALUATION - SPECIFICATION OF VARIABLES *
         SPECIFICATION ERROR - EFFECT OF , VARIABLE INCLUSION * COMPARATIVE METHODS -
         ESTIMATION : OLS , GLS * COMPARATIVE METHODS - REGRESSION , ERROR
         SPECIFICATION

YA3765   ZELLNER A., PALM F.
         "Time series analysis and simultaneous equation econometric models"   J.
         Econometrics, vol.2, 1974 pp.17-54.
         TIME SERIES - ARIMA : INTERPRETATION * SIMULTANEOUS SYSTEM - ERROR
         SPECIFICATION * TIME SERIES - MULTIVARIATE * DIFFERENCE EQUATION *
         COMPARATIVE METHODS - ARIMA , CAUSAL * DISTRIBUTED LAG - MULTIVARIATE * APPL
         - MACRO : CONSUMPTION * APPL - MACRO : INVESTMENT * APPL - MACRO : GDP *
         DISTRIBUTED LAG - RATIONAL POLYNOMIAL * DISTRIBUTED LAG - ARIMA *
         DISTRIBUTED LAG - ERROR SPECIFICATION

YA3766   ZELLNER A., RICHARD J.F.
         "Use of prior information in the analysis and estimation of Cobb-Douglas
         production function models"   Int. Econ. Rev., vol.14, 1973, pp.107-119.
         BAYESIAN - PRIOR INFORMATION * BAYESIAN - ESTIMATION : REGRESSION , ERROR
         SPECIFICATION * COMPARATIVE METHODS - ESTIMATION : OLS , 2SLS * COMPARATIVE
         METHODS - ESTIMATION : OLS , BAYESIAN * COMPARATIVE METHODS - REGRESSION ,
         SIMULTANEOUS SYSTEM * COMPARATIVE METHODS - ESTIMATION : PRODUCTION
         FUNCTIONS * COMPARATIVE METHODS - ESTIMATION : REGRESSION , ERROR
         SPECIFICATION * COMPARATIVE METHODS - ESTIMATION : SIMULTANEOUS SYSTEM ,
         ERROR SPECIFICATION

YA3767   ZELLNER A., THORNBER H.
         "Computational accuracy and estimation of simultaneous equation econometric
         models"   Econometrica, vol.34, 1966, pp.727-729.
         MACRO MODEL - KLEIN * COMPARATIVE METHODS - ESTIMATION : SIMULTANEOUS SYSTEM
         : 2SLS , 3SLS * COMPUTERISATION - CALCULATION ERROR

YA3768   ZELLNER A., WILLIAMS A.D.
         "Bayesian analysis of the Federal Reserve-MIT-Penn model's Almon lag
         consumption function"   J. Econometrics, vol.1, 1973, pp.267-300.
         MACRO MODEL - FRB , MIT , PENN * BAYESIAN - PRIOR INFORMATION * EVALUATION -
         PRIOR INFORMATION * DISTRIBUTED LAG - APPL , INCOME * APPL - MACRO :
         CONSUMPTION * BAYESIAN - ESTIMATION : DISTRIBUTED LAG * CONSUMER BEHAVIOUR -
         ECONOMIC MODELS , THEORY

YA3769   ZERBST R.H., BRUEGGEMAN W.B.
         "FHA and VA mortgage discount points and housing prices"   J. Finance,
         vol.32, 1977, pp.1766-1733.
         APPL - SECTOR : FINANCE , MORTGAGES * DATA - CROSS SECTION * APPL - SECTOR :
         FINANCE , BUILDING SOCIETIES * PRICE - SECTOR : CONSTRUCTION , RESIDENTIAL

YA3770   ZIFF R.
         "Psychographic market segmentation"   J. Advtg. Res., vol.11:2, 1971,
         pp.3-9.
         CONSUMER BEHAVIOUR - PSYCHOLOGICAL MODELS * MARKET SEGMENTATION * APPL -
         FIRM : CONSUMER NON DURABLES , HEALTH AIDS * USE - MEDIA PLANNING

YA3771   ZIMMERMAN M.B.
         "Modeling depletion in a mineral industry: the case of coal"   Bell J.
         Econ., vol.8, 1977, pp.41-65.
         APPL - SECTOR : PRODUCTION , COAL * COST - SECTOR : PRODUCTION

YA3772   ZUFRYDEN F.S.
         "A methodology for minimising response to media effects"   Opl. Res. Q.,
         vol.26, 1975, pp.641-647.
         ADVERTISING - EFFECT OF * USE - MEDIA PLANNING * CONSUMER BEHAVIOUR -
         STOCHASTIC MODELS * BRAND CHOICE - APPL * DATA - SIMULATION * ESTIMATION -
         MINIMUM CHI - SQUARE

YA3773   ZUFRYDEN F.S.
         "An empirical evaluation of a composite heterogeneous model of brand choice
         and purchase timing behaviour"   Mgmt. Sci., vol.24, 1978, pp.761-773.
         MARKET SHARE - SECTOR : CONSUMER NON DURABLES * CONSUMER BEHAVIOUR -
         STOCHASTIC MODELS , ESTIMATION * EVALUATION - BRAND CHOICE MODELS *
         PROBABILITY MODELS - NBD * PROBABILITY MODELS - LINEAR LEARNING * BRAND
         CHOICE - METHODOLOGY * REPEAT BUYING * APPL - SECTOR : CONSUMER NON DURABLES
         , HEALTH AIDS

YA3774   ZUFRYDEN F.S.
         "Examining the pattern of response behaviour in a media model"   Mgmt.
         Sci., vol.22, 1976, pp.116-124.
         USE - MEDIA PLANNING * CONSUMER BEHAVIOUR - STOCHASTIC MODELS

YA3775   ZUFRYDEN F.S.
         "Patterns of TV program selection"   J. Advtg. Res., vol.16:6, 1976,
         pp.43-47.
         APPL - FIRM : SERVICES , MEDIA , TV * REPEAT BUYING * BRAND CHOICE -
         DETERMINANTS * PROBABILITY MODELS - LINEAR LEARNING

YA3776   ZWEIG M.E.
          "An investor expectations stock price predictive model using closed-end fund
          premiums"   J. Finance, vol.28, 1973, pp.67-78.
          THEORY - INVESTOR BEHAVIOUR * STOCK PRICES - RUNS * STOCK PRICES - TRADING
          RULES * APPL - SECTOR : FINANCE , STOCK PRICE INDEX * STOCK PRICES -
          DETERMINANTS

YB0000   AAKER D.A. (ED.)
"Multivariate analysis and marketing: theory and application"   Belmont,
California: Wadsworth, 1971.
DISCRIMINANT ANALYSIS - REVIEW * MARKET SEGMENTATION * NEW PRODUCTS -
IDENTIFYING * MULTIVARIATE METHODS - TEXT * REGRESSION - INTRODUCTION *
CANONICAL CORRELATION - INTRODUCTION * ADVERTISING - EXPERIMENTAL DESIGN *
FACTOR ANALYSIS - INTRODUCTION * MULTIDIMENSIONAL SCALING - INTRODUCTION *
CLUSTER ANALYSIS - INTRODUCTION

YB0001   ADAMS F.G., BEHRMAN J.R. (EDS.)
"Econometric modelling of world commodity policy"   Lexington, Mass:
Lexington Books, 1978.
APPL - SECTOR : COMMODITIES * POLICY EVALUATION - SECTOR : COMMODITIES *
BIBLIOGRAPHY - SECTOR : COMMODITIES

YB0002   ADAMS F.G., KLEIN S.A. (EDS.)
"Stabilising world commodity markets"   Lexington, Mass: Lexington Books,
1978.
POLICY EVALUATION - SECTOR : COMMODITIES * APPL - SECTOR : COMMODITIES

YB0003   ADVERTISING RESEARCH FOUNDATION
"Measuring payout: an annotated bibliography on the dollar effectiveness of
advertising"   New York: Advertising Research Foundation, 1973.
ADVERTISING - EFFECT OF * BIBLIOGRAPHY - ADVERTISING , EFFECTIVENESS

YB0004   AGARWALA R.
"An econometric model of India 1948-61"   London: Frank Cass, 1970.
MACRO MODEL - INDIA

YB0005   AHAMAD B., BLAUG M. (EDS.)
"The practice of manpower forecasting"   Amsterdam: Elsevier; San
Francisco: Jossey-Bass, 1973.
MANPOWER PLANNING - MACRO * MANPOWER PLANNING - QUALIFIED MANPOWER

YB0006   AITCHISON J., DUNSMORE I.R.
"Statistical prediction analsis"   Cambridge: Cambridge U.P., 1975.
TOLERANCE INTERVAL * BAYESIAN - ESTIMATION : PROBABILITY MODEL * PROBABILITY
MODELS - REVIEW

YB0007   ALBERT A.E., GARDNER L.A.
Stochastic approximation and nonlinear regression"   Cambridge, Mass: MIT
Press, 1967.   Research Monograph No. 42.
ESTIMATION - RECURSIVE * ESTIMATION - NON LINEAR * ESTIMATION - KALMAN
FILTER * ADVANCED

YB0008   ALLEN R.I.G., GOSSLING W.F. (EDS.)
"Estimating and projecting input output coefficients"   London:
Input-Output Publishing, 1975.
INPUT OUTPUT - PROJECTION OF STRUCTURE * INPUT OUTPUT - METHODOLOGY :
COEFFICIENT ESTIMATION

YB0009   ALMON C.
"The American economy to 1975 - an interindustry forecast"   New York:
Harper & Row, 1966.
INPUT OUTPUT - MACRO , US

YB0010   ALMON C., ET AL.
"1985: Interindustry forecasts of the American economy"   Lexington, Mass:
Lexington Books, 1974.
APPL - SECTOR : EMPLOYMENT * INPUT OUTPUT - MACRO , US * APPL - SECTOR :
INVESTMENT * APPL - SECTOR : CONSTRUCTION * APPL - SECTOR : GOVERNMENT *
INPUT OUTPUT - PROJECTION OF STRUCTURE

YB0011   ANDERSON O.D.
"Time series analysis and forecasting"   London: Butterworths, 1976.
TIME SERIES - ARIMA : TEXT

YB0012   ANDERSON T.W.
"The statistical analysis of time series"   New York: Wiley, 1971.
TIME SERIES - TEXT * SPECTRAL ANALYSIS - REVIEW * ADVANCED

YB0013   ARMSTRONG A.G.
"The demand for new cars: an econometric model for short term forecasting"
London: National Economic Development Office, 1974; Supplement, 1978.
APPL - SECTOR : CONSUMER DURABLES , CARS * BUSINESS CYCLE - EFFECT OF *
PRICE - EFFECT OF * INCOME - EFFECT OF * EXOGENOUS VARIABLES - PREDICTION OF
, EFFECT * EX ANTE * DEMAND - REPLACEMENT

YB0014   ARMSTRONG J.S.
"Long-range forecasting: from crystal ball to computer"   New York: Wiley,
1978.
EVALUATION - THEORY OF * DELPHI * FORECASTING - TEXT * AID - REVIEW *
ESTIMATION - PRIOR INFORMATION * COMPARATIVE METHODS - THEORY OF * PRIOR
INFORMATION * FORECASTING - VALUE OF * FORECASTING - COST OF * JUDGEMENTAL
FORECASTS - METHODOLOGY * LONG TERM FORECASTING - EVALUATION * REGRESSION ,
CONSTRAINED * COMPARATIVE METHODS - MACRO MODELS * COMPARATIVE METHODS -
REVIEW * BIBLIOGRAPHY - FORECASTING * (See also reference listed below)

YB0015   ARMSTRONG J.S.
"Long-range forecasting: from crystal ball to computer"
EVALUATION - JUDGEMENTAL FORECASTS , SPECIALIST * EVALUATION - JUDGEMENTAL
FORECASTS * COMPARATIVE METHODS - REGRESSION , MULTIVARIATE METHODS *
EVALUATION - MACRO MODELS * BOOTSTRAPPING - REVIEW * EVALUATION -
BOOTSTRAPPING * COMPARATIVE METHODS - CAUSAL , TREND CURVES * COMPARATIVE
METHODS - CAUSAL , JUDGEMENTAL * COMPARATIVE METHODS - JUDGEMENTAL , TREND
CURVES * (See also reference listed above)

YB0016   ASCHER H.
          "Forecasting: an appraisal for policy-makers and planners"   New York: John
          Hopkins, U.P., 1978.
          APPL - SECTOR : TRANSPORT * EVALUATION - TECHNOLOGICAL FORECASTING *
          EVALUATION - FORECASTING * FORECASTING - TEXT * LONG TERM FORECASTING *
          EVALUATION - ENERGY FORECASTS * EVALUATION - POPULATION FORECASTS *
          EVALUATION - TRANSPORTATION FORECASTS * EX ANTE * LEAD TIME - EFFECT OF *
          EVALUATION - MACRO FORECASTS
YB0017   ASKIN A.B., KRAFT J.
          "Econometric wage and price models"   Lexington, Mass: D.C. Heath, 1974.
          INFLATION - DETERMINANTS * MANPOWER PLANNING - MACRO , SUPPLY * INFLATION -
          GOVERNMENT CONTROLS * APPL - MACRO : EARNINGS * APPL - MACRO : EMPLOYMENT
YB0018   BALESTRA P.
          "The demand for natural gas in the US: a dynamic approach for the
          residential and commercial market"   Amsterdam: North Holland, 1967.
          APPL - SECTOR : UTILITIES , GAS
YB0019   BALL R.J. (ED.)
          "The international linkage of national economic models"   Amsterdam: North
          Holland; New York: American Elsevier, 1973.   Contributions to Economic
          Analysis, No. 78.
          APPL - MACRO : INTERNATIONAL LINKAGE * APPL - MACRO : INTERNATIONAL TRADE
YB0020   BALOPOULOS E.T.
          "Fiscal policy models of the British economy"   Amsterdam: North Holland,
          1967.
          MACRO MODEL - UK * POLICY EVALUATION - MACRO : FISCAL * CONSUMER BEHAVIOUR -
          ECONOMIC MODELS * APPL - MACRO : CONSUMER DEMAND
YB0021   BENTON W.K.
          "Forecasting for management"   Reading, Mass: Addison-Wesley, 1972.
          FORECASTING - TEXT * EXTREME VALUES * BASIC
YB0022   BERMAN P.I.
          "Inflation and the money supply in the US, 1956-1977"   Lexington, Mass:
          Lexington Books, 1978.
          INFLATION - DETERMINANTS * APPL - MACRO : MONEY , SUPPLY * POLICY EVALUATION
          - MACRO : MONETARY
YB0023   BEZDEK R.H.
          "Empirical tests of input-output forecasts: review and critique"
          Washington: US Dept. Commerce, 1974.   BEA Staff Paper No. 24.
          BIBLIOGRAPHY - INPUT OUTPUT * COMPARATIVE METHODS - INPUT OUTPUT *
          EVALUATION - INPUT OUTPUT
YB0024   BEZDEK R.H.
          "Long-range forecasting of manpower requirements: theory and applications"
          New York: I.E.E.E. Press, 1974.
          LONG TERM FORECASTING * MANPOWER PLANNING - TEXT
YB0025   BIBBY J., TOUTENBERG H.
          "Prediction and improved estimation in linear models"   Chichester, UK:
          Wiley; Berlin, GDR: Akademie-Verlag, 1977.
          ESTIMATION - TEXT * ESTIMATION - CONSTRAINED * ESTIMATION - MINIMAX *
          TOLERANCE INTERVALS * ADVANCED
YB0026   BLACKABY F.T. (ED.)
          "British economic policy, 1960-74"   London: Cambridge U.P., 1974.
          POLICY EVALUATION - MACRO * APPL - MACRO , UK
YB0027   BLAIR R.D., VOGEL R.J.
          "The cost of health insurance administration: an economic analysis"
          Lexington, Mass: Heath Lexington Books, 1975.
          COST - SECTOR : HEALTH * HEALTH - SERVICES * APPL - SECTOR : FINANCE ,
          INSURANCE COMPANIES
YB0028   BLOOM P.N.
          "Advertising, competition and public policy: a simulation study"
          Cambridge, Mass: Ballinger, 1976.
          SIMULATION - APPL : SECTOR , CONSUMER NON DURABLES * ADVERTISING - EFFECT OF
          * APPL - SECTOR : CONSUMER NON DURABLES , FOOD * MARKET SHARE - SECTOR :
          CONSUMER NON DURABLES * POLICY EVALUATION - MACRO : ADVERTISING * SIMULATION
          - APPL : ADVERTISING
YB0029   BLOOMFIELD P.
          "Fourier analysis of time series - an introduction"   New York: Wiley,
          1976.
          TIME SERIES - HARMONICS * SPECTRAL ANALYSIS - TEXT
YB0030   BOLT G.J.
          "Market and sales forecasting: a total approach"   London: Kogan Page,
          1971; New York: Halstead Press, 1972.
          FORECASTING - TEXT * LIFE CYCLE - PRODUCT * MIS * USE - FORECASTER
          EVALUATION * BASIC
YB0031   BOS G.G.J.
          "A logistic approach to the demand for private cars"   Tilburg: Tilburg
          U.P., 1970.
          APPL - SECTOR : CONSUMER DURABLES , CARS * LONG TERM FORECASTING * TREND
          CURVES - LOGISTIC : APPL

YB0032   BOWDEN R.J.
          "The econometrics of disequilibrium"   Amsterdam: North Holland, 1978,
          Studies in Mathematical and Managerial Economics, Vol. 28.
          ESTIMATION - NON LINEAR * APPL - SECTOR : CONSTRUCTION , RESIDENTIAL *
          SIMULTANEOUS SYSTEM - DISEQUILIBRIUM * APPL - SECTOR : CONSUMER DURABLES

YB0033   BOWERS J.
          "The anatomy of regional activity rates"   Cambridge: Cambridge U.P., 1970.
          In National Institute of Economics and Social Research, Regional Papers, 1.
          MANPOWER PLANNING - LABOUR PARTICIPATION , FEMALE * REGIONAL MODELS -
          MANPOWER PLANNING , LABOUR PARTICIPATION
          MODEL SELECTION * REGRESSION - ESTIMATION

YB0034   BOX G.E.P., JENKINS G.M.
          "Time series analysis: forecasting and control"   Revised ed.   San
          Francisco: Holden Day, 1976.
          TIME SERIES - ARIMA : TEXT * DISTRIBUTED LAG - ARIMA * DISTRIBUTED LAG -
          RATIONAL POLYNOMIAL * DISTRIBUTED LAG - ERROR SPECIFICATION * CONTROL THEORY
          - REVIEW

YB0035   BRADLEY A.A., KRAFT J. (EDS.)
          "Econometric dimensions of energy demand and supply"   Lexington, Mass:
          Heath Lexington Books, D.C. Heath, 1976.
          APPL - MACRO : ENERGY

YB0036   BRILLINGER D.R.
          "Time series - data analysis and theory"   New York: Holt, Rinehardt &
          Winston, 1975.
          TIME SERIES - TEXT * SPECTRAL ANALSYSI - REVIEW

YB0037   BRODY A., CARTER A.P. (EDS.)
          "Input output techniques"   Amsterdam: North Holland, 1972.   Conference
          Proceedings, Geneva, 1968.
          INPUT OUTPUT - MACRO : POLLUTION * INPUT OUTPUT - MACRO : INTERNATIONAL
          LINKAGE * APPL - MACRO : INTERNATIONAL LINKAGE * INPUT OUTPUT -
          INTERREGIONAL * INPUT OUTPUT - MACRO , AUSTRALIA * INPUT OUTPUT - THEORY *
          INPUT OUTPUT - TEXT

YB0038   BRONFENBRENNER M. (ED.)
          "Is the business cycle obsolete?"   New York: Wiley, 1969.
          BUSINESS CYCLE - REVIEW * MACRO MODEL - WHARTON EFU * MACRO MODEL -
          GOVERNMENT , NETHERLANDS * MACRO MODELS - REVIEW * DATA - INTERNATIONAL *
          POLICY EVALUATION - MACRO : STABILISATION

YB0039   BROWN F.E., OXENFELDT A.R.
          "Misperceptions of economic phenomena"   New York: Irvington, 1972.
          DATA ERRORS - TEXT

YB0040   BROWN R.G.
          "Decision rules for inventory management"   New York: Rinehart & Winston,
          1967.
          EXPONENTIAL SMOOTHING - TEXT * EXPONENTIAL SMOOTHING - THEORY * USE -
          PRODUCTION , CONTROL * USE - INVENTORY CONTROL * TRACKING SIGNAL - APPL

YB0041   BROWN R.G.
          "Smoothing, forecasting and prediction of discrete time series"   Englewood
          Cliffs, New Jersey: Prentice Hall, 1963.
          EXPONENTIAL SMOOTHING - TEXT * USE - INVENTORY CONTROL * EXPONENTIAL
          SMOOTHING - HIGHER ORDER * EXPONENTIAL SMOOTHING - COEFFICIENTS CHOICE *
          LEAD TIME - EFFECT OF

YB0042   BROWN R.G.
          "Statistical forecasting for inventory control"   New York: McGraw Hill,
          1959.
          TIME SERIES - TEXT * USE - INVENTORY CONTROL * EXPONENTIAL SMOOTHING - APPL

YB0043   BRUNNER K. (ED.)
          "Problems and issues in current econometric practice"   Columbus, Ohio:
          College of Administrative Science, Ohio State University, 1972.   Monograph
          No. AA-6.
          THEORY - MODELLING * EVALUATION - THEORY OF * MACRO MODEL - BROOKINGS *
          RECURSIVE MODELS * CAUSALITY - REVIEW * APPL - MACRO : INVESTMENT

YB0044   BRUNNER K., MELTZER A.H. (EDS.)
          "Economics of price and wage controls"   Amsterdam: North Holland; New
          York: American Elsevier, 1976.   Carnegie - Rochester Conference on Public
          Policy, Vol. 2.
          INFLATION - GOVERNMENT CONTROLS * PRICE - CONTROLS * INFLATION - PHILLIPS
          CURVE * APPL - MACRO , UK * APPL - MACRO : EARNINGS * EX ANTE

YB0045   BRY G., BOSCHAN C.
          "Cyclical analysis of time series: selected procedures and computer
          programs"   New York: National Bureau of Economic Research, 1971.
          BUSINESS CYCLE - IDENTIFICATION * BUSINESS INDICATORS - APPL *
          COMPUTERISATION - CYCLE , PROGRAMS * BUSINESS CYCLE - REVIEW

YB0046   BUNN D.W.
          "The synthesis of forecasting models in decision analysis"   Basel,
          Switzerland: Birkhauser Verlag, 1978.
          COMBINING FORECASTS - METHODOLOGY * COMBINING FORECASTS - TIME SERIES *
          COMBINING FORECASTS - CAUSAL , TIME SERIES * COMBINING FORECASTS - CAUSAL
          METHODS

YB0047   BUTLER W.F., KAVESH R.A., PLATT R.B. (EDS.)
         "Methods and techniques of business forecasting"   Englewood Cliffs, New
         Jersey: Prentice Hall, 1974.
         JUDGEMENTAL FORECASTS = ASA NBER SURVEY * EVALUATION = MACRO FORECASTS *
         EVALUATION = JUDGEMENTAL FORECASTS , MACRO = EX ANTE * LEAD TIME = EFFECT OF
         * FORECASTING = REVIEW * EVALUATION = THEORY OF * FORECASTING = PRACTICE *
         SURVEYS = REVIEW * APPL = MACRO * APPL = SECTOR * USER REQUIREMENTS
YB0048   CANTOR J.
         "Pragmatic forecasting"   New York: American Management Ass., 1971.
         USE = ORGANISATIONAL DESIGN * NEW PRODUCTS = EVALUATION * FORECASTING = TEXT
         * USE = INVENTORY CONTROL * USE = MARKETING POLICY * BASIC
YB0049   CARTER A.P., BRODY A. (EDS.)
         "Input output analysis" (2 vols.)   Amsterdam: North Holland, 1970.
         Conference proceedings, Geneva, 1968.
         INPUT OUTPUT = TEXT * INPUT OUTPUT = MACRO , EASTERN EUROPE * INPUT OUTPUT =
         MACRO , JAPAN * INPUT OUTPUT = PROJECTION OF STRUCTURE * STABILITY OF
         COEFFICIENTS = INPUT OUTPUT
YB0050   CHAMBERS E.J., ET AL.
         "National income analysis and forecasting"   Glenview, Ill: Scott, 1975.
         FORECASTING = TEXT
YB0051   CHAMBERS J.C., MULLICK S.K., SMITH D.D.
         "An executive's guide to forecasting"   New York: Wiley, 1974.
         FORECASTING = TEXT * LIFE CYCLE = PRODUCT * NEW PRODUCTS = EVALUATION * USE
         = FORECASTER EVALUATION * FORECASTING = COST OF * TURNING POINTS =
         FORECASTING
YB0052   CHATFIELD C.
         "The analysis of time series: theory and practice"   London: Chapman &
         Hall; New York: Halstead Press, 1975.
         TIME SERIES = TEXT * SPECTRAL ANALYSIS = TEXT
YB0053   CHATTERJEE S., PRICE B.
         "Regression analysis by example"   New York: Wiley, 1977.
         REGRESSION = TEXT * RESIDUALS = ANALYSIS OF , SPECIFICATION ERROR
YB0054   CHESHIRE P.C.
         "Regional unemployment differences in Great Britain"   Cambridge: Cambridge
         U.P., 1973.   In National Institue of Economic and Social Research,
         Regional Papers 2.
         APPL = MACRO , UK * REGIONAL MODELS = MANPOWER PLANNING , UNEMPLOYMENT *
         MANPOWER PLANNING = UNEMPLOYMENT
YB0055   CHISHOLM M., FREY A.E., HAGGET P. (EDS.)
         "Regional forecasting"   London: Butterworths, 1970.   Proceedings of
         22nd, symposium of the Colston Res. Soc., Bristol University, 1970.
         REGIONAL MODELS * REGIONAL MODELS = CITY * SPATIAL ANALYSIS * REGIONAL
         MODELS = SECTOR : AGRICULTURE * REGIONAL MODELS = LOCATION
YB0056   CHISHOLM R.K., WHITAKER G.R.
         "Forecasting metods"   Homewood, Ill: Irwin, 1971.
         FORECASTING = TEXT * REGRESSION = REVIEW * BUSINESS INDICATORS =
         INTRODUCTION * SURVEYS = REVIEW * BASIC
YB0057   CHOUDRY N.K., ET AL.
         "The TRACE econometric model of the Canadian economy"   Toronto: University
         of Toronto Press, 1972.
         MACRO MODEL = CANADA , TRACE * EX ANTE
YB0058   CHOW G.C.
         "Analysis and control of dynamic economic systems"   New York: Wiley, 1975.
         CONTROL THEORY = REVIEW * POLICY EVALUATION = METHODOLOGY * SIMULTANEOUS
         SYSTEM = CONTROL * SIMULTANEOUS SYSTEM = NONLINEAR * LOSS FUNCTION = MACRO *
         SPECTRAL ANALYSIS = REVIEW * SPECTRAL ANALYSIS = CROSS : REVIEW
YB0059   CHRIST C.F.
         "Economic models and methods"   New York: Wiley, 1966.
         ECONOMETRICS = TEXT * EVALUATION = THEORY OF * MACRO MODELS = TEXT
YB0060   CICCHETTI C.J.
         "Forecasting recreation in the US"   Lexington, Mass: Lexington Books, D.C.
         Heath, 1975.
         APPL = SECTOR : SERVICES , TOURISM * USE = TOURISM DEVELOPMENT
YB0061   CLAASSEN E., SALIN P.
         "Stabilization policies in interdependent economics"   Amsterdam: North
         Holland, 1972.
         INFLATION = DETERMINANTS * POLICY EVALUATION = MACRO : STABILISATION * APPL
         = MACRO : INTERNATIONAL LINKAGE
YB0062   CLARK J.A., ET AL.
         "Global simulation models: a comparative study"   London: Wiley, 1975.
         SIMULATION = APPL : WORLD * INDUSTRIAL DYNAMICS = APPL , WORLD * APPL =
         MACRO , WORLD
YB0063   CLARK J.J. (ED.)
         "The management of forecasting"   New York: St. Johns U.P., 1969.
         FORECASTING = PRACTICE * FORECASTING = TEXT * BUSINESS INDICATORS =
         INTRODUCTION * INPUT OUTPUT = INTRODUCTION * SURVEYS = CONSUMER , REVIEW *
         BIBLIOGRAPH) = SURVEYS , CONSUMER * USE = CORPORATE PLANNING * FORECASTING =
         VALUE OF

YB0064 CLARKE D.G. (ED.)
        "Cumulative advertising effects: sources and implications" Cambridge,
        Mass: Marketing Science Institute, 1977,
        ADVERTISING - EFFECT OF , REVIEW * DISTRIBUTED LAG - APPL , ADVERTISING
YB0065 CLIFF A.D., ORD J.K.
        "Spatial autocorrelation" London: Prior, 1973,
        SPATIAL ANALYSIS
YB0066 CLOUGH D.J., LEWIS C.G., OLIVER A.L. (EDS.)
        "Manpower planning models" London: English U.P.; New York: Crane, Russak,
        1974,
        HEALTH - HOSPITAL , NURSES * MANPOWER PLANNING - REVIEW * MARKOV MODELS -
        APPL : MANPOWER * MANPOWER PLANNING - SECTOR : GOVERNMENT , CENTRAL *
        MANPOWER PLANNING - SECTOR : HEALTH
YB0067 COLM G., WAGNER P.
        "Federal budget projections" Washington D.C.: The Brookings Institute,
        1966,
        EVALUATION - GOVERNMENT FORECASTS * APPL - SECTOR : GOVERNMENT , EXPENDITURE
YB0068 COLMAN D.
        "The United Kingdom cereal market: an econometric investigation into the
        effects of pricing policies" Manchester: Manchester U.P., 1972,
        APPL - SECTOR : AGRICULTURE , LIVESTOCK * APPL - SECTOR : AGRICULTURE ,
        GRAIN * POLICY EVALUATION - SECTOR : AGRICULTURE * APPL - SECTOR :
        INTERNATIONAL TRADE , IMPORTS
YB0069 COOPER J.P.
        "Development of the monetary sector, prediction and policy analysis in the
        FRB-MIT Penn model" Lexington, mass: D.C. Heath, 1974,
        MACRO MODEL - FRB , MIT , PENN * APPL - MACRO : FLOW OF FUNDS * INFLATION -
        DETERMINANTS * POLICY EVALUATION - MACRO * THEORY - MONETARY
YB0070 COOTNER P.
        "Random character of stock market prices" Cambridge, Mass: MIT Press,
        1967,
        APPL - SECTOR : FIRM , FINANCE , STOCK PRICES * STOCK PRICES - TEXT * RANDOM
        WALK - REVIEW * THEORY - EFFICIENT MARKETS
YB0071 COPULSKY W.
        "Practical sales forecasting" New York: American Management Ass., 1975,
        FORECASTING - TEXT * BASIC
YB0072 COUTIE G.A., ET AL.
        "Short-term forecasting" Edinburgh: Oliver & Boyd, 1964, ICI Monograph
        No. 2,
        EXPONENTIAL SMOOTHING - TEXT * CONTROL CHARTS - CUSUM
YB0073 COYLE R.G.
        "Management system dynamics" London: Wiley, 1977,
        SYSTEMS THEORY - REVIEW * INDUSTRIAL DYNAMICS - REVIEW * INDUSTRIAL DYNAMICS
        - APPL , FIRM
YB0074 CUMMINS J.D.
        "An econonometric model of the life insurance sector of the US economy"
        Lexington, Mass: Lexington Books, D.C. Heath, 1975,
        APPL - SECTOR : FINANCE , INSURANCE COMPANIES * SIMULATION - APPL : SECTOR ,
        FINANCE
YB0075 DANIELLS L.M.
        "Business forecasting for the 1970's" Cambridge, mass: Baker Library,
        Graduate School of Business Admistration, Harvard University, 1970,
        BIBLIOGRAPHY - FORECASTING
YB0076 DAUTEN C.A., VALENTINE L.M.
        "Business cycles and forecasting" 4th. ed. Cincinnati, Ohio: South
        Western Publishing Co., 1974,
        BUSINESS CYCLE - TEXT * BUSINESS INDICATORS - INTRODUCTION * APPL - MACRO :
        GNP * USER - FIRM
YB0077 DEANE R.S. (ED.)
        "A New Zealand model: structure, policy and some simulation results"
        Wellington, New Zealand: Reserve Bank of New Zealand, 1972,
        MACRO MODEL - NEW ZEALAND * SIMULATION - APPL : POLICY EVALUATION
YB0078 DEANE R.S., GILES D.E.
        "Consumption equations for New Zealand: tests of some alternative
        hypotheses" Wellington, New Zealand: Reserve Bank of New Zealand, 1972,
        APPL - MACRO , NEW ZEALAND * EVALUATION - CONSUMPTION MODELS * APPL - MACRO
        : CONSUMPTION
YB0079 DEANE R.S., LUMSDEN M.A.
        "A model of the New Zealand monetary sector" Wellington, New Zealand:
        Reserve Bank of New Zealand, 1971, Research Paper No. 2,
        APPL - MACRO , NEW ZEALAND * APPL - MACRO : FLOW OF FUNDS
YB0080 DEANE R.S., LUMSDEN M.A.
        "An econometric approach to forecasting New Zealand imports" Wellington,
        New Zealand: Reserve Bank of New Zealand, 1972, Research Paper No. 5,
        APPL - MACRO : INTERNATIONAL TRADE , IMPORTS * APPL - MACRO , NEW ZEALAND
YB0081 DEATON A.
        "Models and projections of demand in post war Britain" London: Chapman &
        Hall; New York: Wiley, 1975,
        BIBLIOGRAPHY - CONSUMER BEHAVIOUR , ECONOMIC MODELS * APPL - MACRO :
        CONSUMER DEMAND * PRICE - EFFECT OF * COMPARATIVE METHODS - DEMAND EQUATIONS
        * APPL - MACRO , UK

YB0082 DEDONNEA F.X.
"The determinants of transport mode choice in Dutch cities"   Rotterdam:
Rotterdam U.P., 1971.
APPL - SECTOR : TRANSPORT * REGIONAL MODELS - SECTOR : TRANSPORT * REGIONAL
MODELS - CITY * USE - TRANSPORT PLANNING

YB0083 DEMAKOPOULOS S.A.
"Methods and efficiency of long range industry forecasts; a case study of
the domestic air cargo industry"   New York: New York U., 1970.   Ph.D.
thesis.
APPL - SECTOR : TRANSPORT , AIR , FREIGHT * LONG TERM FORECASTING *
EVALUATION - LONG TERM FORECASTS

YB0084 DEUTSCH K.W., FRITSCH B.
"Problems of world modeling; political and social implications"
Cambridge, Mass: Lippincott, Ballinger, 1977.
SIMULATION - APPL : WORLD * APPL - MACRO , WORLD

YB0085 DHRYMES P.J.
"Distributed lags: problems of estimation and formulation"   San Francisco:
Holden Day, 1971.
DISTRIBUTED LAG - ESTIMATION * SPECTRAL ANALYSIS - APPL : DISTRIBUTED LAG *
DISTRIBUTED LAG - TEXT * DISTRIBUTED LAG - IDENTIFICATION * ADVANCED

YB0086 DODD T.F.
"Sales forecasting"   Farnborough, Hants: Gower Press, 1974.
FORECASTING - TEXT

YB0087 DOMENCICH T.A., McFADDEN D.
"Urban travel demand: a behavioural analysis"   New York: American
Elsevier; Amsterdam: North Holland, 1975.   Contributions to Economic
Analysis, No. 93.
REGIONAL MODELS - CITY * REGIONAL MODELS - SECTOR : TRANSPORT * CONSUMER
BEHAVIOUR - ECONOMIC MODELS , THEORY * REGRESSION - LIMITED DEPENDENT ,
LOGIT * APPL - SECTOR : TRANSPORT

YB0088 DRIEHUIS W.
"Fluctuations and growth in near full employment economy"   Rotterdam:
Rotterdam U.P., 1972.
MACRO MODEL - NETHERLANDS * SIMULATION - APPL : POLICY EVALUATION * EX ANTE

YB0089 DRIEHUIS W.
"Primary commodity prices; analysis and forecasting"   Rotterdam: Rotterdam
U.P., 1976.
SIMULTANEOUS SYSTEM - APPL * APPL - SECTOR : COMMODITIES * BIBLIOGRAPHY -
SECTOR : COMMODITIES * EX ANTE * APPL - SECTOR : PRODUCTION , STEEL *
EVALUATION - EXPECTATIONS , DATA * APPL - SECTOR : PRODUCTION , RUBBER

YB0090 DUESENBERRY J.S., ET AL.
"The Brookings model: some further results"   Chicago: Rand McNally, 1969.
MACRO MODEL - BROOKINGS

YB0091 DUESENBERRY J.S., ET AL.
"The Brookings quarterly econometric model of the United States"   Chicago:
Rand McNally; Amsterdam: North Holland, 1965.
MACRO MODEL - BROOKINGS

YB0092 DUPREZ C., KIRSCHEN E.S. (EDS.)
"MEGISTOS: a world union and trade model for 1975"   Amsterdam: North
Holland; New York: American Elsevier, 1970.
APPL - MACRO : INTERNATIONAL TRADE * APPL - MACRO , WORLD * LONG TERM
FORECASTING

YB0093 EASTERLIN R.A.
"Population, labor force and long swings in economic growth; the American
experience"   New York: National Bureau of Economic Research, distributed
by Columbia U.P., 1968.
BUSINESS CYCLE - LONG CYCLE * MANPOWER PLANNING - MACRO * POPULATION *
MANPOWER PLANNING - LABOUR PARTICIPATION

YB0094 EBY F.H., O'NEILL W.J.
"The management of sales forecasting"   Lexington, Mass: Lexington Books,
D.C. Heath, 1977.
FORECASTING - REVIEW

YB0095 EHRENBERG A.S.C.
"Repeat buying: theory and applications"   Amsterdam: North Holland; New
York: American Elsevier, 1972.
CONSUMER BEHAVIOUR - STOCHASTIC MODELS , REVIEW * BRAND CHOICE - REVIEW *
THEORY - MODELLING * REPEAT BUYING * PROBABILITY MODELS - NBD * APPL -
SECTOR : CONSUMER NON DURABLES

YB0096 EHRENBERG R.G.
"The demand for state and local government employees: An economic analysis"
Lexington, Mass: Lexington Books, D.C. Heath, 1972.
REGIONAL MODELS - SECTOR : GOVERNMENT , LOCAL * APPL - SECTOR : EARNINGS *
APPL - SECTOR : GOVERNMENT , LOCAL * POLICY EVALUATION - MACRO : EMPLOYMENT
* REGIONAL MODELS - MANPOWER PLANNING , EMPLOYMENT * DATA - CROSS SECTION ,
TIME SERIES

YB0097 EL-MOKADEM A.M.
"Econometric models of personal saving: the UK, 1948-1966"   London:
Butterworths, 1973.
APPL - MACRO : SAVINGS * APPL - MACRO : CONSUMER DEMAND , FINANCIAL ASSETS

YB0098   ELIASSON G. (ED.)
"A micro-to-macro model of the Swedish economy"   Stockholm: Industrial
Institute for Economic and Social Research, 1978.
MACRO MODEL - SWEDEN * MACRO MODELS - MICRO

YB0099   ENCEL S., MARSTRAND P.K., PAGE W. (EDS.)
"The art of anticipation: values and methods in forecasting"   London:
Martin Robertson; new York: Plia Press, 1978.
EVALUATION - THEORY OF * LONG TERM FORECASTING * TECHNOLOGICAL FORECASTING

YB0100   EVANS M.K.
"An econometric model of the French economy"   Paris: OECD, 1969.
MACRO MODEL - FRANCE

YB0101   EVANS M.K.
"Macroeconomic activity; theory, forecasting and control"   New York:
Harper & Row, 1969.
MACRO MODEL - WHARTON * BUSINESS CYCLE - DETERMINANTS * BUSINESS INDICATORS
- APPL * MULTIPLIERS - MACRO * ATTITUDINAL DATA * EXPECTATIONS - DATA *
COMPARATIVE METHODS - MACRO MODELS * EX ANTE

YB0102   EVANS R.G.
"Canadian inventory investment"   Ottawa: Bank of Canada, 1969.   Bank of
Canada Staff Research Studies.
APPL - MACRO : INVENTORIES * APPL - MACRO , CANADA

YB0103   EVANS R.G., HELLIWELL J.
"Quarterly business capital expenditure"   Ottawa: Bank of Canada, 1969.
APPL - MACRO : INVESTMENT * MACRO MODEL - CANADA , RDX1

YB0104   FAIR R.C.
"A model of macroeconomic activity" (in 2 vols.)   Cambridge, Mass:
Lippincott, Ballinger, 1974 & 1976.
MACRO MODEL - FAIR

YB0105   FAIR R.C.
"A short run forecasting model of the US economy"   Lexington, Mass: Heath
Lexington Books, 1971.
MACRO MODEL - FAIR * EVALUATION - MACRO MODELS * MACRO MODEL - OBE * MACRO
MODEL - WHARTON * EXOGENOUS VARIABLES - PREDICTION OF , EFFECT * MACRO
MODELS - METHODOLOGY , ADJUSTMENTS * EX ANTE * STABILITY OF COEFFICIENTS -
SIMULTANEOUS SYSTEM : APPL

YB0106   FAIR R.C.
"The short run demand for workers and hours"   Amsterdam: North Holland,
1969.
MANPOWER PLANNING - MACRO * APPL - MACRO : EMPLOYMENT * COMPARATIVE METHODS
- REGRESSION , ERROR SPECIFICATION * THEORY - EXPECTATIONS * ERROR
SPECIFICATION - AUTOCORRELATED

YB0107   FIENBERG S.E., ZELLNER A. (EDS.)
"Studies in Bayesian econometrics and statistics in honor of Leonard J.
Savage"   Amsterdam: North Holland; New York: American Elsevier, 1975.
Contributions to Economic Analysis, No. 86.
BAYESIAN - ESTIMATION : REGRESSION * BAYESIAN - ESTIMATION : SIMULTANEOUS
SYSTEM * BAYESIAN - CONTROL * BAYESIAN - PRIOR INFORMATION * BAYESIAN -
ESTIMATION : DISTRIBUTED LAG * CONTROL THEORY - ADAPTIVE * MACRO MODEL -
ST.LOUIS * CONTROL THEORY - STOCHASTIC , THEORY * CONTROL THEORY -
STOCHASTIC , APPL * ESTIMATION - STEIN

YB0108   FILDES R., WOOD D. (EDS.)
"Forecasting and planning"   Farnborough, Hants: Saxon House, 1978.
EVALUATION - MACRO FORECASTS * MACRO MODEL - UK , NIESR * MACRO MODEL - UK ,
LBS * MACRO MODEL - GOVERNMENT , UK * MACRO MODEL - UK , CAMBRIDGE * POLICY
EVALUATION - MACRO * LONG TERM FORECASTING * QUALITY - EFFECT OF * USER
REQUIREMENTS * SYSTEMS THEORY - REVIEW * APPL - MACRO : ENERGY * THEORY -
MODELLING * EVALUATION - THEORY OF * FORECASTING - REVIEW * STABILITY OF
COEFFICIENTS - REVIEW * (See also reference listed below)

YB0109   FILDES R., WOOD D. (EDS.)
"Forecasting and planning"
STYLE GOODS * DISTRIBUTED LAG - ARIMA * DISTRIBUTED LAG - RATIONAL
POLYNOMIAL * CAUSALITY - REVIEW * USE - MARKETING POLICY * EX ANTE *
EVALUATION - PRIOR INFORMATION * SIMULATION - APPL : FINANCIAL MODELLING *
USE - CORPORATE PLANNING * APPL - FIRM : FINANCE , PROFITS * MARKET SHARE -
EFFECT OF * BAYESIAN - FORECASTING * SEASONALITY - SINGLE SEASON * (See also
references listed above)

YB0110   FIRTH M.A.
"Forecasting methods in business and management"   London: Edward Arnold,
1977.
FORECASTING - TEXT * MIS * MODEL SELECTION

YB0111   FISHMAN G.S.
"Spectral methods in econometrics"   Cambridge, Mass: Harvard U.P.; Oxford:
Oxford U.P., 1969.
SPECTRAL ANALYSIS - TEXT * SPECTRAL ANALYSIS - METHODOLOGY * SPECTRAL
ANALYSIS - APPL : BUSINESS CYCLE , LONG CYCLE * SPECTRAL ANALYSIS - APPL :
DISTRIBUTED LAG * APPL - MACRO : CONSUMPTION

YB0112 FORRESTER N.B.
"The life cycle of economic development" Cambridge, Mass: Wright-Allen Press, 1973.
INDUSTRIAL DYNAMICS - APPL , MACRO * MACRO MODEL - US

YB0113 FRANK R.E., MASSY W.F.
"An econometric approach to a marketing decision model" Cambridge, Mass: MIT Press, 1971.
APPL - FIRM : CONSUMER NON DURABLES * PRICE - EFFECT OF * ADVERTISING - EFFECT OF * USE - PROMOTION EVALUATION * DATA - SIMULATION * APPL - SECTOR : RETAILING

YB0114 FREEMAN R.B.
"The market for college trained manpower" Cambridge, Mass: Harvard U.P., 1971.
MANPOWER PLANNING - EARNINGS * MANPOWER PLANNING - QUALIFIED MANPOWER , GRADUATES * EDUCATION - EFFECT OF

YB0115 FRIEDMAN B.M.
"Economic stabilization policy: methods in optimization" Amsterdam: North Holland; New York: American Elsevier, 1975. Studies in Mathematical & Managerial Economics, Vol. 15.
CONTROL THEORY - DETERMINISTIC * CONTROL THEORY - REVIEW * POLICY EVALUATION - MACRO : STABILISATION

YB0116 FROMM G.
"Forecasts of US long-run economic growth" Menlo Park, California: Centre for Economic Policy Research, Stanford Research Institute, 1976.
EVALUATION - MACRO MODELS * LONG TERM FORECASTING - APPL - MACRO : GROWTH

YB0117 FROMM G., KLEIN L.R. (EDS.)
"The Brookings model: perspective and recent developments" Amsterdam: North Holland; New York: American Elsevier, 1975.
APPL - MACRO : FLOW OF FUNDS * MACRO MODEL - BROOKINGS * APPL - MACRO : CONSUMPTION * EVALUATION - THEORY OF * INPUT OUTPUT - SECTOR

YB0118 FULLER W.A.
"Introduction to statistical time series" New York: Wiley, 1976.
TIME SERIES - TEXT * SPECTRAL ANALYSIS - REVIEW

YB0119 GERTLER L.O.
"Regional planning in Canada" Montreal: Harvest House, 1972.
REGIONAL MODELS

YB0120 GHOSH A.
"Experiments with input output models- an application to the economy of the UK, 1948-1955" Cambridge: Cambridge U.P., 1964.
INPUT OUTPUT - MACRO , UK * EVALUATION - INPUT OUTPUT * INPUT OUTPUT - METHODOLOGY : AGGREGATION * COMPARATIVE METHODS - MACRO MODELS * COMPARATIVE METHODS - CAUSAL , INPUT OUTPUT * MULTIPLIERS - INPUT OUTPUT

YB0121 GILCHRIST W.
"Statistical forecasting" London: Wiley, 1976.
FORECASTING - TEXT * MODEL SELECTION - INTRODUCTION * TIME SERIES - TEXT

YB0122 GLASS G.V., WILLSON V.L., GOTTMAN J.M.
"Design and analysis of time series experiments" Boulder, Colorado: Colorado Associated U.P., 1975.
TIME SERIES - ARIMA : INTERVENTION

YB0123 GOLDBERGER A.S., DUNCAN O.D. (EDS.)
"Structural equation models in the social sciences" New York: Seminar Press, 1973.
DATA - TRANSFORMED , DEFLATED * CAUSALITY - REVIEW * DATA - SAMPLE SIZE * SIMULTANEOUS SYSTEM - ERROR IN VARIABLES , UNOBSERVABLES * SIMULTANEOUS SYSTEM - TRANSFORMATIONS , RATIO * PATH ANALYSIS * EDUCATION - EFFECT OF * INCOME - EFFECT OF * APPL - SECTOR : SOCIAL , SUCCESS

YB0124 GOLDFELD S.M., QUANDT R.E.
"Non linear methods in econometrics" Amsterdam: North Holland, 1972.
Contributions to Economic Analysis, No. 77.
ESTIMATION - NON LINEAR , TEXT * ESTIMATION - MAXIMUM LIKELIHOOD * SIMULTANEOUS SYSTEM - ESTIMATION , ERROR SPECIFICATION * ERROR SPECIFICATION - MIXED

YB0125 GOLDFELD S.M., QUANDT R.E. (EDS.)
"Studies in nonlinear estimation" Cambridge, Mass: Lippincott, Ballinger, 1976.
REGRESSION - SWITCHING * DATA - SIMULATION * COMPARATIVE METHODS - ESTIMATION : SIMULTANEOUS SYSTEM , SWITCHING * SIMULTANEOUS SYSTEM - SWITCHING * PRODUCTION FUNCTIONS - ESTIMATION * DEMAND EQUATIONS - SYSTEMS OF : METHODOLOGY , ESTIMATION * ESTIMATION - NON LINEAR * DEMAND EQUATIONS - SYSTEMS OF : METHODOLOGY , ESTIMATION , ERROR SPECIFICATION * PRODUCTION FUNCTIONS - SECTOR * APPL - SECTOR : RETAILING

YB0126 GOLLNICK H.G.L.
"Dynamic structure of household expenditures in the Federal Republic of Germany" Amsterdam: North Holland, 1975.
APPL - SECTOR : INCOME - EFFECT OF * PRICE - EFFECT OF * DATA REVISIONS - EFFECT OF * CONSUMER BEHAVIOUR - ECONOMIC MODELS * DISTRIBUTED LAG - RATIONAL POLYNOMIAL , IDENTIFICATION * EVALUATION - DISTRIBUTED LAG , MODEL SPECIFICATION * APPL - MACRO : CONSUMPTION * EX ANTE * APPL - MACRO , GERMANY

YB0127   GOSSLING W.F. (ED.)
          "Capital coefficients and dynamic input-output models"   London:
          Input-Output Publishing, 1975.
          APPL - SECTOR : INVESTMENT * DEMAND - REPLACEMENT * INPUT OUTPUT - SECTOR :
          CAPITAL INVESTMENT * APPL - MACRO : INVESTMENT
YB0128   GRAFF P.
          "Die Wirtschaftsprognose"   Tubingen, West Germany: J.C.Mohr, 1977.
          TREND CURVES - REVIEW * EVALUATION - TREND CURVES * LONG TERM FORECASTING
YB0129   GRAMLICH E.M., JAFFEE D.M. (EDS.)
          "Savings deposits, mortgages and housing: studies for the FRB, MIT, PENN
          model"   Lexington, Mass: Lexington Books, D.C. Heath, 1972.
          APPL - SECTOR : CONSTRUCTION , RESIDENTIAL * MACRO MODEL - FRB , MIT , PENN
          * APPL - SECTOR : FINANCE , MORTGAGES
YB0130   GRANGER C.W.J., ANDERSEN A.P.
          "An introduction to the bilinear time series models"   Gottingen:
          Vanderbroeck & Ruprecht, 1978.
          TIME SERIES - NON LINEAR * ADVANCED
YB0131   GRANGER C.W.J., MORGENSTERN O.
          "Predictability of stock market prices"   Lexington, Mass: D.C. Heath,
          1970.
          SPECTRAL ANALYSIS - APPL : SECTOR , FINANCE * STOCK PRICES - TRADING RULES *
          APPL - FIRM : FINANCE , STOCK PRICES * STOCK PRICES - COVARIATION * STOCK
          PRICES - RUNS * STOCK PRICES - DETERMINANTS * RANDOM WALK - TEST * STOCK
          PRICES - TRADING VOLUME * RANDOM WALK - METHODOLOGY
YB0132   GRANGER C.W.J., NEWBOLD P.
          "Forecasting economic time series"   New York: Academic Press, 1977.
          TIME SERIES - NON STATIONARY * FORECASTING - TEXT * TIME SERIES - TEXT *
          SPECTRAL ANALYSIS - REVIEW * TIME SERIES - ARIMA : REVIEW * REGRESSION -
          SPURIOUS CORRELATION * CAUSALITY - REVIEW * DISTRIBUTED LAG - ERROR
          SPECIFICATION * COMBINING FORECASTS - METHODOLOGY * EVALUATION - MACRO
          FORECASTS
YB0133   GREEN D.W., HIGGINS C.I.
          "SOVMOD 1: a macroeconomic model of the Soviet Union"   New York: Crane,
          Russak, for the Strategic Centre of Stanford Research Institute, distributed
          by Harcourt Brace Jovanovich, 1977.
          MACRO MODEL - USSR
YB0134   GRILICHES Z. (ED.)
          "Price indexes and quality change"   Cambridge, Mass: Harvard U.P.; London:
          Oxford U.P., 1971.
          INDEX NUMBERS - TEXT
YB0135   GRONAU R.
          "The value of time in passenger transportation: the demand for air travel"
          New York: National Bureau of Economic Research, distributed by Columbia
          U.P., 1970.   Occasional Paper No. 109.
          APPL - SECTOR : TRANSPORT , AIR * TIME - VALUE OF
YB0136   GROSS C.W., PETERSON R.T.
          "Business forecasting"   Boston: Houghton Mifflin, 1976.
          FORECASTING - TEXT * JUDGEMENTAL FORECASTS - REVIEW * SURVEYS - REVIEW *
          CONSUMER BEHAVIOUR - STOCHASTIC MODELS , INTRODUCTION * BASIC
YB0137   GROSSMAN M.
          "The demand for health: a theoretical and empirical investigation"   New
          York: National Bureau of Economic Research, distributed by Columbia UP,
          1972.
          HEALTH - SERVICES
YB0138   GULBENKIAN FOUNDATION
          "Forecasting on a scientific basis"   Lisbon: Lisbon Centre de Economica e
          Finances for the Nato Science Committee and Gulbenkian Foundation, 1967.
          MACRO MODEL - MICHIGAN , SUITS * MACRO MODEL - GOVERNMENT , NETHERLANDS *
          POLICY EVALUATION - MACRO * COMPARATIVE METHODS - MACRO MODELS * COMPARATIVE
          METHODS - AUTOREGRESSIVE , CAUSAL * EVALUATION - MACRO MODELS * CAUSALITY -
          REVIEW
YB0139   GUPTA K.L.
          "Aggregation in economics"   Rotterdam: Rotterdam U.P., 1969.
          DATA - AGGREGATION , TEXT * DATA - AGGREGATION 'BIAS' * DATA - AGGREGATION
          OVER TIME * APPL - SECTOR : EARNINGS * APPL - MACRO : EARNINGS * REGRESSION
          - AGGREGATION
YB0140   HAITOVSKY Y.
          "Regression estimation from grouped observations"   London: Griffin, 1973.
          Monograph No. 33.
          REGRESSION - GROUPED OBSERVATIONS * DATA - GROUPED * ESTIMATION - GLS *
          ADVANCED
YB0141   HAITOVSKY Y., TREYZ G., SU V.
          "Forecasting with quarterly macroeconomic models"   New York: National
          Bureau of Economic Research, distributed by Columbia U.P., 1974.
          COMPARATIVE METHODS - AUTOREGRESSIVE , CAUSAL(SIMULTANEOUS SYSTEM) * MACRO
          MODEL - WHARTON * EVALUATION - MACRO MODELS * MACRO MODELS - METHODOLOGY ,
          ADJUSTMENTS * MACRO MODEL - OBE * COMPARITIVE METHODS - MACRO MODELS * EX
          ANTE

Y80142   HALVORSEN R.
         "Econometric models of US energy demand"   Lexington, Mass: Lexington
         Books, 1978.
         APPL - MACRO : ENERGY , SOURCES * APPL - SECTOR : UTILITIES , ELECTRICITY *
         APPL - SECTOR : UTILITIES , GAS * APPL - SECTOR : PRODUCTION , COAL * APPL -
         SECTOR : PRODUCTION , OIL * SUBSTITUTE FACTORS * PRICE - EFFECT OF
Y80143   HANNAN E.J.
         "Multiple time series"   New York: Wiley, 1971.
         TIME SERIES - TEXT * DISTRIBUTED LAG - REVIEW * ESTIMATION - HANNAN *
         SPECTRAL ANALYSIS - REVIEW * SPECTRAL ANALYSIS - THEORY * ADVANCED
Y80144   HARRIS B. (ED.)
         "Advanced seminar on spectral analysis of time series"   New York: Wiley,
         1967.
         TIME SERIES - ARIMA : ARIMA * SPECTRAL ANALYSIS - REVIEW * ADVANCED
Y80145   HARRIS C.C., HOPKINS F.E.
         "Locational Analysis - an inter-regional model of agriculture, mining,
         manufacturing and services"   Lexington, Mass: Lexington Books, 1973.
         REGIONAL MODELS - INTERREGIONAL * LP * APPL - SECTOR : LOCATION * REGIONAL
         MODELS - LOCATION
Y80146   HEESTERMAN A.R.G.
         "Forecasting models for national economic planning"   Dordrecht, Holland:
         D. Reidel, 1970.
         INPUT OUTPUT - REVIEW * MACRO MODELS - TEXT
Y80147   HELLIWELL J.F., ET AL.
         "Government sector equations for macroeconomic models"   Ottawa: Bank of
         Canada, 1969.
         APPL - SECTOR : GOVERNMENT , REVENUES * APPL - MACRO , CANADA * REGIONAL
         MODELS - TAX * MACRO MODEL - CANADA , RDX1 * APPL - SECTOR : GOVERNMENT ,
         EXPENDITURE
Y80148   HELLIWELL J.F., ET AL.
         "The structure of RDX2: parts 1 and 2"   Ottawa: Bank of Canada, 1971.
         Bank of Canada Research Studies, No. 7.
         MACRO MODEL - CANADA , RDX2
Y80149   HERZOG J.P., EARLEY J.S.
         "Home mortgage, delinquency and foreclosure"   New York: National Bureau of
         Economic Research, distributed by Columbia U.P., 1970.
         APPL - SECTOR : FINANCE , MORTGAGES * REGRESSION - LIMITED DEPENDENT * USE -
         CREDIT CONTROL , CONSUMER
Y80150   HICKMAN B.G. (ED.)
         "Econometric models of cyclical behaviour" vol. 1.   New York: National
         Bureau of Economic Research, distributed by Columbia U.P., 1972.   Studies
         in Income and Wealth No. 36.
         EVALUATION - TURNING POINT FORECASTS * MULTIPLIERS - MACRO * MACRO MODEL -
         FRB , MIT , PENN * MACRO MODEL - OBE * MACRO MODEL - BROOKINGS * BUSINESS
         CYCLE - DETERMINANTS * AUTOCORRELATION - EFFECT OF
Y80151   HICKMAN B.G. (ED.)
         "Econometric models of cyclical behaviour" vol. 2.   New York: National
         Bureau of Economic Research, distributed by Columbia U.P., 1972.   Studies
         in Income and Wealth No. 36.
         COMPARATIVE METHODS - DATA : AGGREGATE , DISAGGREGATE * MACRO MODEL -
         WHARTON * MACRO MODELS - METHODOLOGY * DATA - AGGREGATION OVER TIME * MACRO
         MODEL - LIU(MONTHLY) * COMPARATIVE METHODS - ESTIMATION : OLS , 2SLS *
         COMPARATIVE METHODS - SIMULTANEOUS SYSTEM , ERROR SPECIFICATION *
         MULTIPLIERS - MACRO * BUSINESS CYCLE - DETERMINANTS * BUSINESS INDICATORS -
         REVIEW * EVALUATION - THEORY OF * COMPARATIVE METHODS - MACRO MODELS * (See
         also reference listed below)
Y80152   HICKMAN B.G. (ED.)
         "Econometric models of cyclical behaviour" vol. 2.
         EVALUATION - MACRO MODELS * MACRO MODEL - FRIEND TAUBMAN * MACRO MODEL -
         KLEIN * EX ANTE * COMPARATIVE METHODS - AUTOREGRESSIVE , CAUSAL(SIMULTANEOUS
         SYSTEM) * (See also reference listed above)
Y80153   HICKMAN B.G., COEN R.M.
         "An annual growth model of the US economy"   Amsterdam: North Holland,
         1976.
         MACRO MODEL - US * MULTIPLIERS - MACRO * EX ANTE * LONG TERM FORECASTING
Y80154   HILTON K., HEATHFIELD D.F. (EDS.)
         "The economic study of the United Kingdom"   New Jersey: Augustus M.
         Kelley; London: Macmillan, 1970.
         MACRO MODEL - UK , NIESR * MACRO MODEL - UK , SOUTHAMPTON * APPL - MACRO :
         CONSUMPTION * APPL - MACRO : DIVIDENDS * APPL - MACRO : INVESTMENT * APPL -
         MACRO : FLOW OF FUNDS * POLICY EVALUATION - MACRO : FISCAL * REGRESSION -
         ESTIMATION , ERROR SPECIFICATION * BAYESIAN - ESTIMATION : REGRESSION ,
         ERROR SPECIFICATION
Y80155   HIRSCH A.A., LOVELL M.C.
         "Sales anticipations and inventory behaviour"   New York: Wiley, 1969.
         APPL - MACRO : OUTPUT * APPL - SECTOR : INVENTORY * APPL - SECTOR * APPL -
         MACRO : INVENTORY * DISTRIBUTED LAG - APPL , EXPECTATIONS HYPOTHESES * EX
         ANTE * EVALUATION - SALES FORECASTS * COMPARATIVE METHODS - AUTOREGRESSIVE ,
         JUDGEMENTAL * EXPECTATIONS - DETERMINANTS * EVALUATION - TURNING POINT
         FORECASTS * THEORY - EXPECTATIONS * EVALUATION - SURVEYS , BUSINESS *
         EVALUATION - EXPECTATIONS , DATA * EXPECTATIONS - ESTIMATING

YB0156   HIRSCH W.Z.
"Urban economic analysis"   Toronto: McGraw Hill, 1973.
REGIONAL MODELS - CITY

YB0157   HOLBROOK R.S.
"An approach to the choice of optimal policy using the large econometric
models"   Ottawa: Bank of Canada, 1973.   Bank of Canada Staff Research
Study, No. 8.
SIMULTANEOUS SYSTEM - NON LINEAR * CONTROL THEORY - DETERMINISTIC ,
METHODOLOGY * SIMULTANEOUS SYSTEM - CONTROL * MACRO MODEL - CANADA , RDX2 *
POLICY EVALUATION - MACRO : STABILISATION

YB0158   HOLT C.C., ET AL.
"Planning production, inventories and work force"   Englewood Cliffs, New
Jersey: Prentice Hall, 1960.
FORECASTING - VALUE OF * CONTROL THEORY - DETERMINISTIC , APPL * CONTROL
THEORY - DETERMINISTIC , THEORY * DECISION RULES - FIRM * USE - PRODUCTION ,
PLANNING * USE - INVENTORY CONTROL * USE - SCHEDULING , MANPOWER *
EXPONENTIAL SMOOTHING - APPL

YB0159   HOUTHAKKER H.S., TAYLOR L.D.
"Consumer demand in the United States: analysis and projections"   2nd ed.
Cambridge, Mass: Harvard U.P., 1970.
THEORY - STOCK ADJUSTMENT * APPL - MACRO : CONSUMER DEMAND * CONSUMER
BEHAVIOUR - ECONOMIC MODELS * DATA - INTERNATIONAL * CONSUMER BEHAVIOUR -
EXPENDITURE SURVEY * EX ANTE * COMPARATIVE METHODS - ESTIMATION : OLS , 3PLS

YB0160   HUGHES G.D.
"Demand analysis for marketing decisions"   Homewood, Ill: Irwin, 1973.
MARKET POTENTIAL - TEXT * CONSUMER BEHAVIOUR - PURCHASING , DETERMINANTS ,
REVIEW * CONSUMER BEHAVIOUR - PSYCHOLOGICAL MODELS , REVIEW * MARKET
SEGMENTATION - REVIEW * MARKETING RESEARCH - TEXT * BASIC

YB0161   HUNT L.H.
"Dynamics of forecasting financial cycles: theory,technique and implication"
Greenwich, Conn: JAI Press, 1976.   Contemporary Studies in Economic and
Financial Analysis, Vol.1.
APPL - MACRO : MONEY , SUPPLY * INTEREST RATE - DETERMINANTS * MULTIPLIERS -
MACRO * APPL - SECTOR : GOVERNMENT , LOCAL , FINANCE * APPL - SECTOR :
FINANCE , BONDS * APPL - SECTOR : FINANCE , MORTGAGES * APPL - SECTOR :
FINANCE , BANK , ASSETS * APPL - SECTOR : FINANCE , BANK , LIABILITIES *
APPL - SECTOR : GOVERNMENT , FINANCE * APPL - MACRO : FLOW OF FUNDS

YB0162   HURWOOD D.L., GROSSMAN E.S., BAILEY E.L.
"Sales forecasting"   New York: The Conference Board, 1978.
FORECASTING - TEXT * BASIC

YB0163   HUTTON J.P., MINFORD A.P.L.
"A model of UK manufacturing exports and export prices"   London: HMSO,
1975.   GES Occasional Papers, No, 11.
COMPARATIVE METHODS - REGRESSION , ERROR SPECIFICATION * APPL - MACRO :
INTERNATIONAL TRADE * APPL - MACRO : INTERNATIONAL TRADE , PRICE * APPL -
MACRO , UK

YB0164   IFAC/IFORS
"International conference on dynamic modelling and control of national
economies"   Hitchin, Herts: Inst, Elec, Engineers, 1973.
MACRO MODEL - UK * APPL - MACRO : FLOW OF FUNDS * CONTROL THEORY - REVIEW *
ADVERTISING - OPTIMALITY * BIBLIOGRAPHY - CONTROL THEORY * INDUSTRIAL
DYNAMICS - APPL , MACRO * EVALUATION - MACRO MODELS * APPL - MACRO , ITALY *
SIMULTANEOUS SYSTEM - STATE SPACE * REGIONAL MODELS - METHODOLOGY * BUSINESS
CYCLE - TURNING POINTS * DIFFERENTIAL EQUATIONS - ESTIMATION * APPL - MACRO
: INVENTORIES * APPL - MACRO : OUTPUT * APPL - MACRO : SALES

YB0165   INGRAM G.K., KAIN J.F., GINN J.R.
"The Detroit prototype of the NBER urban simulation model"   New York:
National Bureau of Economic Research, distributed by Columbia U.P., 1972.
REGIONAL MODELS - CITY * SIMULATION - APPL : REGIONAL MODELS

YB0166   INTRILIGATOR M.D. (ED.)
"Frontiers of quantitative economics"   London: North Holland, 1971.
Contributions to Economic Analysis, No, 71.
SIMULATION - APPL : POLICY EVALUATION * MACRO MODELS - METHODOLOGY * MACRO
MODELS - REVIEW * BAYESIAN - ESTIMATION : REVIEW * STOCK PRICES - REVIEW *
THEORY - EFFICIENT MARKETS * CONCENTRATION - EFFECT OF , REVIEW * APPL -
FIRM : FINANCE , PROFITS * APPL - FIRM : R & D * BIBLIOGRAPHY - INDUSTRIAL
ECONOMICS * BIBLIOGRAPHY - STOCK PRICES * BIBLIOGRAPHY - SIMULATION ,
EXPERIMENTS

YB0167   INTRILIGATOR M.D. (ED.)
"Frontiers of quantitative economics" vol. III (in 2 vols.)   Amsterdam:
North Holland, 1977.   Contributions to Economic Analysis, Nos, 105 & 106.
APPL - MACRO , INDIA * APPL - MACRO : ENERGY , SOURCES * APPL - SECTOR :
AGRICULTURE * EVALUATION - MACRO MODELS * MACRO MODEL - UK , LBS * MACRO
MODEL - UK , NIESR * EX ANTE * CAUSALITY - REVIEW * APPL - SECTOR : FINANCE
, BUILDING SOCIETIES * CONTROL THEORY - REVIEW * SIMULTANEOUS SYSTEM -
CONTROL * SIMULTANEOUS SYSTEM - NON LINEAR * REGRESSION - STATE SPACE

YB0168   INTRILIGATOR M.D., KENDRICK D.A. (EDS.)
          "Frontiers of quantitative economics" vol. II.   Amsterdam: North Holland;
          New York: American Elsevier, 1974.   Contributions to Economic Analysis,
          No. 87.
          SIMULTANEOUS SYSTEM = ESTIMATION,REVIEW * DISTRIBUTED LAG = REVIEW * HEALTH
          = SERVICES * EVALUATION = INVESTMENT MODELS * APPL = MACRO : INVESTMENT *
          PRODUCTION FUNCTIONS = SUBSTITUTION * EVALUATION = PRODUCTION FUNCTIONS *
          MANPOWER PLANNING = DISCRIMINATION
YB0169   IRONMONGER D.S.
          "New commodities and consumer behaviour"   Cambridge: Cambridge UP., 1972.
          NEW PRODUCTS = APPL * PRICE = EFFECT OF * CONSUMER BEHAVIOUR = ECONOMIC
          MODELS , THEORY * INCOME = EFFECT OF
YB0170   ISARD W., LANGFORD T.W.
          "Regional input output study: recollections reflections and diverse notes on
          the Philadelphia experience"   Cambridge, Mass: MIT Press, 1971.
          INPUT OUTPUT = REGIONAL * PUBLIC EXPENDITURE = EFFECT OF * APPL = SECTOR :
          GOVERNMENT , DEFENCE
YB0171   ISLAM N.
          "A short term model for Pakistan economy"   Lahore: Oxford U.P., Pakistan
          Branch; London: Oxford U.P., 1965.
          MACRO MODEL = PAKISTAN
YB0172   IVAKHNENKO A.G., LAPA V.G.
          "Cybernetics and forecasting techniques"   New York: American Elsevier,
          1967.   Modern Analytic and Computational Methods in Science & Maths, Vol.
          8.
          TIME SERIES = FILTER , NON LINEAR * TIME SERIES = FILTER , ADAPTIVE *
          PATTERN RECOGNITION * TIME SERIES = TEXT * ADVANCED
YB0173   JACOBSSON L.
          "An econometric model of Sweden"   Stockholm: Beckmans, 1972.
          MACRO MODEL = SWEDEN * COMPARATIVE METHODS = ESTIMATION : OLS , 2SLS
YB0174   JENKINS G.M., WATTS D.G.
          "Spectral analysis and its applications"   San Francisco: Holden Day, 1968.
          SPECTRAL ANALYSIS = TEXT * ADVANCED
YB0175   JILER H. (ED.)
          "Forecasting commodity prices; how the experts analyze the markets"   New
          York: Commodity Research Bureau, 1975.
          APPL = SECTOR : COMMODITIES
YB0176   JOHANSEN L.
          "Production functions"   Amsterdam: North Holland, 1972.
          APPL = MACRO : OUTPUT * PRODUCTION FUNCTIONS = SECTOR * PRODUCTION FUNCTIONS
          = REVIEW * APPL = SECTOR : TRANSPORT , SHIPPING * ADVANCED
YB0177   JONES H., TWISS B.C.
          "Forecasting technology for planning decisions"   London: Macmillan, 1978;
          New York: Petrocelli Books, 1979.
          FORECASTING = TEXT * USE = R&D * TECHNOLOGICAL FORECASTING
YB0178   JORGENSON D.W. (ED.)
          "Econometric studies of US energy policy"   Amsterdam: North Holland; New
          York; American Elsevier, 1976.   Data Resources Series, Vol, 1.
          APPL = SECTOR : RETAILING , GASOLINE * SUPPLY = SECTOR : PRODUCTION * INPUT
          OUTPUT = MACRO : ENERGY * TAX = EFFECT OF * APPL = MACRO : ENERGY , SOURCES
          * APPL = SECTOR : PRODUCTION , PETROLEUM * APPL = SECTOR : COMMODITIES , OIL
          * INCOME = EFFECT OF
YB0179   JUDGE G.G., BOCK M.E.
          "The statistical implications of pre-test and Stein-rule estimators in
          econometrics"   Amsterdam: North Holland, 1978.   Studies in Mathematics
          and Managerial Economics, Vol. 25.
          DATA = SIMULATION * ESTIMATION = PRE TEST * ESTIMATION = STEIN * REGRESSION
          = ESTIMATION * REGRESSION = ESTIMATION , ERROR SPECIFICATION * COMPARATIVE
          METHODS = ESTIMATION : REGRESSION * APPL = SECTOR : FINANCE , PROFITS *
          CONCENTRATION = EFFECT OF * INFLATION = PHILLIPS CURVE
YB0180   KEAY F.
          "Marketing and sales forecasting"   Oxford: Pergamon, 1971.
          FORECASTING = TEXT * MIS * USER REQUIREMENTS * BASIC
YB0181   KENDALL M.G.
          "Time series"   2nd. ed.   London: Griffin, 1976.
          TIME SERIES = TEXT * TIME SERIES = DECOMPOSITION * SPECTRAL ANALYSIS =
          REVIEW * EXPONENTIAL SMOOTHING = REVIEW * SEASONALITY = ESTIMATION , CENSUS
          * SEASONALITY = ESTIMATION , OLS
YB0182   KENEN P.B.
          "A model of the US balance of payments"   Lexington, Mass: Lexington Books,
          1978.
          APPL = MACRO : INTERNATIONAL TRADE * EXCHANGE RATE = EFFECT OF * POLICY
          EVALUATION = MACRO : INTERNATIONAL FINANCE , FOREIGN EXCHANGE * POLICY
          EVALUATION = MACRO : INTERNATIONAL TRADE * TAX = EFFECT OF
YB0183   KLEIJNEN J.P.C.
          "Statistical techniques in simulation" (in 2 vols.)   New York: Marcel
          Dekker, 1974.
          SIMULATION = METHODOLOGY , RANDOM DEVIATES * SIMULATION = EXPERIMENTAL
          DESIGN * SIMULATION = TEXT * ADVANCED

YB0184   KLEIN L.R.
         "A textbook of econometrics"   2nd ed.   Englewood Cliffs, New Jersey:
         Prentice Hall, 1973.
         ECONOMETRICS - TEXT * DATA - CROSS SECTION , TIME SERIES * DATA ERRORS -
         REVIEW * COMPARATIVE METHODS - ESTIMATION : OLS , 2SLS * COMPARATIVE METHODS
         - ESTIMATION : OLS , FIML * COMPARATIVE METHODS - ESTIMATION : SIMULTANEOUS
         SYSTEM , 2SLS , FIML * APPL - SECTOR : TRANSPORT , RAIL

YB0185   KLEIN L.R.
         "An essay on the theory of economic prediction"   Chicago: Markham
         Publishing, 1970; Helsinki: Yrjo Jahnsson Lectures, 1968.
         FORECASTING - REVIEW * EXOGENOUS VARIABLES - PREDICTION OF * DATA REVISIONS
         - ESTIMATION * ESTIMATION - PRINCIPAL COMPONENTS * EVALUATION - THEORY OF *
         LEAD TIME - EFFECT OF * CONFIDENCE INTERVAL - PREDICTIONS : SIMULTANEOUS
         SYSTEM * MULTIPLIERS - METHODOLOGY * EVALUATION - EXPECTATIONS , DATA *
         EVALUATION - ATTITUDINAL DATA * COMPARATIVE METHODS - ESTIMATION :
         SIMULTANEOUS SYSTEM * COMPARATIVE METHODS - ESTIMATION : OLS , FIML * MACRO
         MODELS - METHODOLOGY

YB0186   KLEIN L.R.
         "Essays in industrial econometrics" (in 3 vols.)   Philadelphia, Penn:
         Economics Research Unit, Department of Economics, Wharton School of Finance
         and Commerce, University of Pennsylvania, 1969 & 1971,   Studies in
         Quantitative Economics, Nos. 3-5.
         APPL - SECTOR : CONSUMER DURABLES , CARS * APPL - SECTOR : PRODUCTION ,
         PETROLEUM * APPL - SECTOR : PRODUCTION , STEEL * APPL - SECTOR : PRODUCTION
         , CHEMICALS * APPL - SECTOR : AGRICULTURE * EX ANTE * MARKET SHARE - SECTOR
         : CONSUMER DURABLES * APPL - SECTOR : CAPACITY UTILISATION * APPL - SECTOR :
         PRODUCTION , RUBBER * APPL - SECTOR : COMMODITIES , RUBBER

YB0187   KLEIN L.R., BURMEISTER E. (EDS.)
         "Econetric model performance: comparative simulation studies of the US
         economy"   Philadelphia: U. Penn. Press,, 1976.
         POLICY EVALUATION - MACRO * COMPARATIVE METHODS - ARIMA ,
         CAUSAL(SIMULTANEOUS SYSTEM) * LEAD TIME - EFFECT OF * MACRO MODEL - FAIR *
         MACRO MODEL - LIU(MONTHLY) * EVALUATION - EXPECTATIONS , THEORY * APPL -
         MACRO : INVESTMENT * MACRO MODEL - MIT , PENN , SSRC * MACRO MODEL - DATA
         RESOURCES * MACRO MODEL - BEA * MACRO MODEL - MICHIGAN * INPUT OUTPUT -
         MACRO , US * MULTIPLIERS - MACRO * LONG TERM FORECASTING * MACRO MODEL -
         ST.LOUIS * COMPARATIVE METHODS - MACRO MODELS

YB0188   KOOYMAN M.A.
         "Dummy variables in econometrics"   Tilburg, Netherlands: Tilburg U.P.,
         1976.   Tilburg Studies on Economics, Vol. 14.
         MACRO MODEL - NETHERLANDS * STABILITY OF COEFFICIENTS - REGRESSION *
         EVALUATION - TEST , STABILITY * REGRESSION - COVARIANCE MODEL

YB0189   KOSOBUD R., MINAMI R. (EDS.)
         "Econometric studies of Japan"   Urbana, Ill: U. Illinois Press, 1977.
         APPL - MACRO , JAPAN * APPL - MACRO : CONSUMER DEMAND * COMPARATIVE METHODS
         - DEMAND EQUATIONS * APPL - MACRO : MONEY , DEMAND * APPL - MACRO :
         INVESTMENT * PRODUCTION FUNCTIONS - SECTOR * PRODUCTION FUNCTIONS -
         SUBSTITUTION * APPL - MACRO : INTERNATIONAL TRADE * PRICE - EFFECT OF *
         MACRO MODEL - JAPAN * APPL - MACRO : GROWTH

YB0190   KUH E., SCHMALENSEE R.L.
         "An introduction to applied macroeconomics"   Amsterdam: North Holland; New
         York: American Elsevier, 1973.
         MACRO MODEL - US * POLICY EVALUATION - MACRO * DISTRIBUTED LAG - REVIEW *
         ECONOMETRICS - TEXT * MACRO MODELS - TEXT

YB0191   LABYS W.C. (ED.)
         "Quantitative models of commodity markets"   Cambridge, Mass: Lippincott,
         Ballinger, 1975.
         APPL - SECTOR : COMMODITIES , COPPER * APPL - SECTOR : COMMODITIES , COFFEE
         * APPL - SECTOR : COMMODITIES , COCOA * APPL - SECTOR : COMMODITIES , OIL *
         APPL - SECTOR : COMMODITIES , LIVESTOCK , HOGS * APPL - SECTOR : COMMODITIES
         , GRAIN * APPL - SECTOR : COMMODITIES * SUPPLY - SECTOR : PRODUCTION *
         CONTROL THEORY - STOCHASTIC , APPL * APPL - SECTOR : PRODUCTION

YB0192   LABYS W.C., GRANGER C.W.J.
         "Speculation, hedging and commodity price forecasts"   Lexington, Mass:
         Heath Lexington Books, 1970.
         COMPARATIVE METHODS - ARIMA , EXPONENTIAL SMOOTHING * APPL - SECTOR :
         COMMODITIES * RANDOM WALK - REVIEW * SPECTRAL ANALYSIS - APPL : SECTOR ,
         COMMODITIES * COMPARATIVE METHODS - ARIMA , CAUSAL * COMPARATIVE METHODS -
         ARIMA , AUTOREGRESSIVE * APPL - SECTOR : COMMODITIES , GRAIN * APPL - SECTOR
         : COMMODITIES , SOYBEAN * COMPARATIVE METHODS - AUTOREGRESSIVE , CAUSAL *
         COMPARATIVE METHODS - AUTOREGRESSIVE , EXPONENTIAL SMOOTHING * (See also
         reference listed below)

YB0193   LABYS W.C., GRANGER C.W.J.
         "Speculation, hedging and commodity price forecasts"
         COMPARATIVE METHODS - CAUSAL , EXPONENTIAL SMOOTHING * EX ANTE *
         BIBLIOGRAPHY - COMMODITIES * RANDOM WALK - METHODOLOGY * SPECTRAL ANALYSIS -
         CROSS : APPL * (See also reference listed above)

YB0194   LAMBIN J.J.
"Advertising, competition and market conduct in oligopoly over time: an econometric investigation in Western European countries"   Amsterdam: North Holland, 1976,   Contributions to Economic Analysis, No. 94.
ADVERTISING - DETERMINANTS * ADVERTISING - EFFECT OF * MARKET SHARE - EFFECT OF * PRICE - EFFECT OF * APPL - FIRM : CONSUMER NON DURABLES * APPL - FIRM : CONSUMER DURABLES * APPL - FIRM : FINANCE , BANKS

YB0195   LEAMER E.E.
"Specification searches"   New York: Wiley, 1978.
BAYESIAN - MODEL SELECTION * MODEL SELECTION - BAYESIAN - ESTIMATION : REGRESSION * REGRESSION - MODEL CHOICE * REGRESSION - VARIABLE INCLUSION * PROXY VARIABLES * EVALUATION - EX POST MODELS * THEORY - MODELLING * DATA - SPECIFICATION OF VARIABLES

YB0196   LEONTIEF W.
"Input output economics"   New York: Oxford U.P., 1966.
INPUT OUTPUT - TEXT * APPL - SECTOR : GOVERNMENT , DEFENCE * REGIONAL MODELS - INTERREGIONAL * INPUT OUTPUT - REGIONAL

YB0197   LEONTIEF W.W., ET AL.
"The future of the world economy: a United Nations study"   New York: Oxford U.P., 1978.
APPL - MACRO : INTERNATIONAL TRADE * INPUT OUTPUT - MACRO : WORLD * APPL - MACRO , WORLD * APPL - MACRO : INTERNATIONAL LINKAGE * APPL - SECTOR

YB0198   LEWIS C.D.
"Demand analysis and inventory control"   Farnborough, Hants: Saxon House: Lexington, Mass: Lexington Books, D.C. Heath, 1975.
USE - INVENTORY CONTROL * EXPONENTIAL SMOOTHING - TEXT * TIME SERIES - ADAPTIVE FILTERING , REVIEW * FORECAST - MONITORING

YB0199   LEWIS C.G.
"Manpower planning: a bibliography"   New York: American Elsevier, 1969.
MANPOWER PLANNING - REVIEW * BIBLIOGRAPHY - MANPOWER PLANNING

YB0200   LEWIS T.O., ODELL P.L.
"Estimation in linear models"   Englewood Cliffs, New Jersey: Prentice Hall, 1971.
ESTIMATION - REVIEW * ESTIMATION - CONSTRAINED * ESTIMATION - NON LINEAR * REGRESSION - ESTIMATION * ADVANCED

YB0201   LINNEMANN H.
"An econometric study of international trade flows"   Amsterdam: North Holland, 1966.
APPL - MACRO : INTERNATIONAL TRADE

YB0202   LINSTONE H.A., SAHAL D. (EDS.)
"Technological substitution: forecasting techniques and applications"   New York: Elsevier, 1976.
SUBSTITUTE FACTORS * TECHNOLOGICAL FORECASTING * INPUT OUTPUT - PROJECTION OF STRUCTURE * DIFFUSION MODEL

YB0203   LUND P.J., MELLISS C.L., HAMILTON J.
"Investment intentions, authorisations and expenditures"   London: HMSO, 1975.   GES Occasional Papers, No. 12.
EVALUATION - INVESTMENT MODELS * EVALUATION - SURVEYS , BUSINESS * APPL - SECTOR : INVESTMENT * EVALUATION - EXPECTATIONS , DATA * COMPARATIVE METHODS - ARIMA , RATIONAL POLYNOMIAL * COMPARATIVE METHODS - ARIMA , JUDGEMENTAL FORECASTS * COMPARATIVE METHODS - ARIMA , SURVEYS * EVALUATION - EX POST MODELS * COMPARATIVE METHODS - RATIONAL POLYNOMIAL

YB0204   LUND P.J., MINER D.A.
"An econometric study of the machine tool industry"   London: HMSO, 1973.
GES Occasional Papers, No. 4.
CAPACITY - EFFECT OF * REGRESSION - SPECIFICATION OF VARIABLES * COMPARATIVE METHODS - REGRESSION , ERROR SPECIFICATION * COMPARATIVE METHODS - DISTRIBUTED LAG * EX ANTE * APPL - SECTOR : PRODUCTION , MACHINE TOOLS

YB0205   LUNDSTEN L.L.
"Market share forecasting for banking offices"   New York: U. Microfilms, 1978.
USE - SITE SELECTION , RETAIL * APPL - FIRM : FINANCE , BANKS * MARKET SHARE - SECTOR : FINANCE * APPL - FIRM : RETAILING , BANKS

YB0206   MACAVOY P.W., PINDYCK R.S.
"The economics of the natural gas shortage (1960-1980)"   Amsterdam: North Holland; New York: American Elsevier, 1975.   Contributions to Economic Analysis, No. 92.
APPL - SECTOR : UTILITIES , GAS * USE - FINANCIAL , REGULATION * SUPPLY - SECTOR : PRODUCTION * APPL - SECTOR : PRODUCTION , GAS

YB0207   McCARTHY M.D.
"The Wharton quarterly econometric forecasting model Mark III"   Philadelphia: Wharton School of Finance and Commerce, University of Pennsylvania, 1972.   Studies in Quantitative Economics, No. 6.
MACRO MODEL - WHARTON * MACRO MODELS - METHODOLOGY , ADJUSTMENTS * ESTIMATION - 2SLS : APPL * EXOGENOUS VARIABLES - PREDICTION OF * EVALUATION - MACRO MODELS * EVALUATION - EXPECTATIONS , DATA

YB0208   McCRACKEN M.C.
          "An overview of CANDIDE model 1.0"   Ottawa: Economic Council of Canada for
          the Interdepartmental Committee on CANDIDE, 1973.   Project Paper No. 1.
          MACRO MODEL - GOVERNMENT , CANADA * MACRO MODEL - CANADA , CANDIDE 1

YB0209   McLAUGHLIN R.L., BOYLE J.J.
          "Short-term forecasting"   New York: American Marketing Association, 1968.
          Marketing Research Technique Series No. 13.
          BUSINESS INDICATORS - APPL * SEASONALITY - ESTIMATION , CENSUS * TIME SERIES
          - DECOMPOSITION

YB0210   McMAHON C.W.
          "OECD: techniques of economic forecasting. An account of the methods of
          short term economic forecasting used by the governments of Canada, France,
          Netherlands, Sweden, UK and US"   Paris: OECD, 1965.
          MACRO MODEL - GOVERNMENT , CANADA * MACRO MODEL - GOVERNMENT , FRANCE *
          MACRO MODEL - GOVERNMENT , NETHERLANDS * MACRO MODEL - GOVERNMENT , UK *
          MACRO MODEL - GOVERNMENT , US * EVALUATION - MACRO MODELS * EVALUATION -
          GOVERNMENT FORECASTS

YB0211   MADDALA G.S.
          "Econometrics"   New York: McGraw Hill, 1977.
          ECONOMETRICS - TEXT * BAYESIAN - ESTIMATION : REVIEW * DISTRIBUTED LAG -
          REVIEW

YB0212   MAKRIDAKIS S., WHEELWRIGHT S.C.
          "Forecasting: methods and applications"   Santa Barbara, California:
          Wiley/Hamilton, 1973.
          FORECASTING - USAGE * FORECASTING - TEXT * FORECASTING - PRACTICE * TIME
          SERIES - TEXT * BUSINESS CYCLE - PREDICTION * TECHNOLOGICAL FORECASTING *
          BIBLIOGRAPHY - FORECASTING * USE - CORPORATE PLANNING

YB0213   MAKRIDAKIS S., WHEELWRIGHT S.C.
          "Interactive forecasting" (in 2 vols.)   Palo Alto, California: Scientific
          Press, 1977.
          COMPUTERISATION - FORECASTING , PROGRAMS * COMPUTERISATION - ESTIMATION ,
          TIME SERIES , PROGRAMS * TIME SERIES - TEXT * TIME SERIES - ARIMA :
          INTRODUCTION

YB0214   MAKRIDAKIS S., WHEELWRIGHT S.C.
          "Interactive forecasting: univariate and multivariate methods"   2nd ed.
          San Francisco: Holden Day, 1978.
          FORECASTING - TEXT * COMPUTERISATION - FORECASTING , PROGRAMS * FORECASTING
          - COST OF * DISTRIBUTED LAG - RATIONAL POLYNOMIAL , INTRODUCTION

YB0215   MARZOUK M.S.
          "The predictability of predetermined variables in macro econometric models"
          Pennsylvania: U. Pennsylvania, 1969.   Ph.D. thesis.
          MACRO MODELS - METHODOLOGY * EXOGENOUS VARIABLES - PREDICTION OF

YB0216   MASS N.J.
          "Economic cycles: an analysis of underlying causes"   Cambridge, Mass:
          Wright-Allen Press, 1975.
          INDUSTRIAL DYNAMICS - APPL , MACRO * BUSINESS CYCLE - DETERMINANTS * APPL -
          MACRO : INVENTORY * APPL - MACRO : INVESTMENT * APPL - MACRO : EMPLOYMENT

YB0217   MASSY W.F., FRANK R.E., LODAHL T.M.
          "Purchasing behaviour and personal attributes"   Philadelphia: U.
          Pennsylvania Press, 1968.
          CONSUMER BEHAVIOUR - PSYCHOLOGICAL MODELS * FACTOR ANALYSIS - APPL * APPL -
          SECTOR : CONSUMER NON DURABLES , BEER * APPL - SECTOR : CONSUMER NON
          DURABLES , FOOD * CONSUMER BEHAVIOUR - PURCHASING , DETERMINANTS

YB0218   MASSY W.F., MONTGOMERY D.B., MORRISON D.G.
          "Stochastic models of buying behaviour"   Cambridge, Mass: MIT Press, 1970.
          CONSUMER BEHAVIOUR - STOCHASTIC MODELS , REVIEW * NEW PRODUCTS - APPL *
          PROBABILITY MODELS - BERNOUILLI , COMPOUND * MARKOV MODELS - APPL : BRAND
          CHOICE * PROBABILITY MODELS - LINEAR LEARNING * BRAND CHOICE - REVIEW *
          REPEAT BUYING - REVIEW

YB0219   MAYER T.
          "Permanent income, wealth and consumption: a critique of the permanent
          income theory, the life-cycle hypothesis, and related theory"   Berkeley,
          California: University of California Press, 1972.
          APPL - MACRO : CONSUMPTION * EVALUATION - PERMANENT INCOME * EVALUATION -
          CONSUMPTION MODELS * LIFE CYCLE - CONSUMER * EX ANTE * INCOME - EFFECT OF ,
          PERMANENT * WEALTH - EFFECT OF * CONSUMER BEHAVIOUR - ECONOMIC MODELS * DATA
          - INTERNATIONAL

YB0220   MEADOWS D.L., ET AL.
          "Dynamics of growth in a finite world"   Cambridge, Mass: Wright-Allen
          Press, 1974.
          INDUSTRIAL DYNAMICS - APPL , WORLD

YB0221   MENDEL J.M.
          "Discrete techniques of parameter estimation: the equation error
          formulation"   New York: Marcel Dekker, 1973.
          ESTIMATION - KALMAN FILTER * ESTIMATION - RECURSIVE * ESTIMATION - OLS *
          ESTIMATION - GLS * REGRESSION - ESTIMATION , TEXT

YB0222   MERKIES A.H.
      "Selection of models by forecasting intervals"   Dordrecht, Netherlands, &
      Boston: D. Reidel, 1972.
      MODEL SELECTION * REGRESSION - MODEL CHOICE * SIMULTANEOUS SYSTEM - MODEL
      CHOICE * CONFIDENCE INTERVAL - PREDICTIONS : REGRESSION * CONFIDENCE
      INTERVAL - PREDICTIONS : SIMULTANEOUS SYSTEM

YB0223   MEYER J.R., GLAUBER R.R.
      "Investment decisions, economic forecasting and public policy"   Boston:
      Graduate School of Business Administration, Harvard U., 1964.
      APPL - MACRO : INVESTMENT * THEORY - INVESTMENT BEHAVIOUR * EVALUATION -
      INVESTMENT MODELS * EX ANTE * COMPARATIVE METHODS - ESTIMATION : OLS , MSAE
      * LOSS FUNCTIONS - ASYMMETRICAL * ESTIMATION - MSAE * EVALUATION - LOSS
      FUNCTIONS

YB0224   MICHAEL R.T.
      "The effect of education on efficiency in consumption"   New York: National
      Bureau of Economic Research, distributed by Columbia U.P., 1972.
      Occasional paper No. 116.
      THEORY - CONSUMER DEMAND * CONSUMER BEHAVIOUR - ECONOMIC MODELS * CONSUMER
      BEHAVIOUR - PSYCHOLOGICAL MODELS * CONSUMER BEHAVIOUR - EXPENDITURE SURVEY *
      EDUCATION - EFFECT OF

YB0225   MIERNYK W.H., ET AL.
      "Simulating regional economic development: an interindustry analysis of the
      West Virginia economy"   Lexington, Mass: D.C. Heath, 1970.
      INPUT OUTPUT - REGIONAL * SIMULATION - APPL : REGIONAL MODELS

YB0226   MILLER R.L., WILLIAMS R.M.
      "Unemployment and inflation: the new economics of the wage price spiral"
      St. Paul, Minn: West Publishing, 1974.
      INFLATION - EXPECTATIONS * MANPOWER PLANNING - MACRO * APPL - MACRO :
      UNEMPLOYMENT * INFLATION - DETERMINANTS

YB0227   MILNE T.E.
      "Business forecasting: a managerial approach"   London: Longman, 1975.
      FORECASTING - TEXT * USER REQUIREMENTS * BASIC

YB0228   MINCER J. (ED.)
      "Economic forecasts and expectations: analysis of forecasting behaviour and
      performance"   New York: National Bureau of Economic Research, distributed
      by Columbia U.P., 1969.   Studies in Business Cycles No. 19.
      THEORY - EXPECTATIONS * DATA REVISIONS - EFFECT OF * DATA ERRORS - EFFECT OF
      * EX ANTE * EVALUATION - JUDGEMENTAL FORECASTS * EVALUATION - SURVEYS ,
      CONSUMER * INTEREST RATE - TERM STRUCTURE * COMPARATIVE METHODS - REGRESSION
      , MODEL SPECIFICATION * APPL - MACRO : CONSUMPTION * COMPARATIVE METHODS -
      AUTOREGRESSIVE , CAUSAL * EVALUATION - THEORY OF * INTEREST RATE -
      EXPECTATIONS * SURVEYS - CONSUMER , METHODOLOGY * EVALUATION - EXPECTATIONS
      , DATA * APPL - SECTOR : CONSUMER DURABLES , CARS

YB0229   MONTGOMERY D.C., JOHNSON L.A.
      "Forecasting and time series analysis"   New York: McGraw Hill, 1976.
      TIME SERIES - TEXT * EXPONENTIAL SMOOTHING - TEXT * EXPONENTIAL SMOOTHING -
      MONITORING * TRACKING SIGNAL - APPL * TIME SERIES - ARIMA : INTRODUCTION *
      FORECASTING - TEXT * DEMAND - CUMULATIVE

YB0230   MOORE G.H., SHISHKIN J.
      "Indicators of business expansions and contraction" New York: National
      Bureau of Economic Research, distributed by Columbia U.P., 1967.
      Occasional Paper No. 103.
      BUSINESS CYCLE - REVIEW * BUSINESS INDICATORS - REVIEW * EVALUATION -
      BUSINESS INDICATORS

YB0231   MORGENSTERN O.
      "On the accuracy of economic observations"   2nd ed..   Princeton, New
      Jersey: Princeton U.P., 1963.
      DATA ERRORS - EFFECT OF * DATA ERRORS - REVIEW

YB0232   MORGENSTERN O., KNORR K., HEISS K.P.
      "Long term projections of power: political, economic, and military
      forecasting"   Cambridge, Mass: Ballinger, 1973.
      APPL - MACRO : ENERGY * APPL - MACRO , WORLD * LONG TERM FORECASTING * APPL
      - SECTOR : GOVERNMENT , DEFENCE

YB0233   MORISHIMA M., ET AL.
      "The working of econometric models"   London: Cambridge U.P., 1972.
      INPUT OUTPUT - MACRO , UK * POLICY EVALUATION - MACRO : FISCAL * MACRO MODEL
      - JAPAN * MANPOWER PLANNING - MACRO * APPL - MACRO : UNEMPLOYMENT * INPUT
      OUTPUT - MACRO , JAPAN

YB0234   MORREL J. (ED.)
      "Management decisions and the role of forecasting"   Harmondsworth,
      Middlesex: Penguin, 1972.
      APPL - MACRO , UK * APPL - SECTOR : CONSTRUCTION * APPL - SECTOR :
      GOVERNMENT , EXPENDITURE * APPL - MACRO : INVESTMENT * APPL - SECTOR

YB0235   MOSBAEK E.J., WOLD H.O.
      "Interdependent systems: structure and estimation"   Amsterdam: North
      Holland; New York: American Elsevier, 1970.
      DEMAND EQUATIONS - SYSTEMS OF * SIMULTANEOUS SYSTEM - ESTIMATION *
      ESTIMATION - OLS * ESTIMATION - 2SLS * ESTIMATION - FIXED POINT *
      COMPARATIVE METHODS - ESTIMATION : SIMULTANEOUS SYSTEM * DATA - SIMULATION *
      COMPARATIVE METHODS - ESTIMATION : OLS , 2SLS * RECURSIVE SYSTEMS - REVIEW

YB0236 N.I.E.S.R.
"A listing of National Institute Model 3, May 1977 Review"   London:
National Institute for Economic and Social Research, 1977,   NIESR
Discussion Paper No. 7.
MACRO MODEL - UK , NIESR

YB0237 NAERT P.A., LEEFLANG P.S.H.
"Building implementable marketing models"   Leiden & Boston: Martinus
Nijhuff, 1978.
USER REQUIREMENTS * CONSUMER BEHAVIOUR - STOCHASTIC MODELS , REVIEW * USE -
MARKETING POLICY * EVALUATION - THEORY OF * PRIOR INFORMATION * MARKET SHARE
- SECTOR * BRAND CHOICE - APPL

YB0238 NAYLOR T.H.
"Computer simulation experiments with models of economic systems"   New
York: Wiley, 1971.
APPL - SECTOR : PRODUCTION , TEXTILES * SIMULATION - TEXT * SIMULATION -
APPL : FIRM * SIMULATION - APPL : SECTOR , PRODUCTION * APPL - SECTOR :
CONSUMER DURABLES , CLOTHING * SIMULATION - METHODOLOGY , STABILITY OF
SOLUTION * SIMULATION - EVALUATION OF RESULTS * SIMULATION - EXPERIMENTAL
DESIGN * SPECTRAL ANALYSIS - APPL : SIMULATION EVALUTION * SIMULATION -
METHODOLOGY , MONTE CARLO * SIMULATION - ANALYTICAL METHODS * (See also
references listed below)

YB0239 NAYLOR T.H.
"Computer simulation experiments with models of economic systems"
SIMULATION - SECTOR : AGRICULTURE * APPL - SECTOR : AGRICULTURE , TOBACCO
LEAF * USE - CORPORATE PLANNING * SIMULATION - APPL : SECTOR , CONSUMER
DURABLES * SIMULATION - METHODOLOGY , RANDOM DEVIATES * POLICY EVALUATION -
SECTOR : EDUCATION * (See also references listed above)

YB0240 NEELEMAN D.
"Multicollinearity in linear economic models"   Tilburg, Netherlands:
Tilburg U.P., 1973.   Tilburg Studies on Economics, Vol. 7,
MULTICOLLINEARITY - REVIEW

YB0241 NELSON C.R.
"Applied time series analysis for managerial forecasting"   San Francisco:
Holden Day, 1973.
FORECASTING - TEXT * TIME SERIES - ARIMA : TEXT * COMPARATIVE METHODS -
AUTOREGRESSIVE , CAUSAL(SIMULTANEOUS SYSTEM) * COMPARATIVE METHODS - ARIMA ,
CAUSAL(SIMULTANEOUS SYSTEM) * COMPARATIVE METHODS - MACRO MODELS *
EVALUATION - TURNING POINT FORECASTS * MACRO MODEL - FRB , MIT , PENN *
COMPARATIVE METHODS - ARIMA , AUTOREGRESSIVE

YB0242 NORD O.C.
"Growth of a new product"   Cambridge, Mass: MIT Press, 1963.
USE - CAPACITY EXPANSION * NEW PRODUCTS - APPL * INDUSTRIAL DYNAMICS - APPL
, FIRM * FORECASTER BEHAVIOUR - BIAS * BASIC

YB0243 O'DEA D.J.
"Cyclical indicators from the postwar British economy"   London: Cambridge
U.P., 1975.   NIESR Occasional Paper No. 28.
BUSINESS CYCLE - IDENTIFICATION * BUSINESS INDICATORS - APPL * APPL - MACRO
, UK

YB0244 OFFICER L.H.
"An econometric model of Canada under the fluctuating exchange rate"
Cambridge, Mass: Harvard U.P., 1968.
APPL - MACRO , CANADA * EXCHANGE RATE - EFFECT OF * MACRO MODEL - CANADA ,
OFFICER

YB0245 OFFICER L.H.
"Supply relationships in the Canadian economy"   East Lansing, Michigan:
Michigan State U.P., 1972.
APPL - SECTOR : FINANCE , PROFITS * SUPPLY - SECTOR * APPL - SECTOR :
EARNINGS * MANPOWER PLANNING - SECTOR * APPL - SECTOR : INVENTORIES * APPL -
MACRO , CANADA * SIMULATION - APPL : MACRO * MACRO MODEL - CANADA , OFFICER
* PRICE - EFFECT OF

YB0246 OSBORN D.R.
"An analysis of National Institute forecasting error in 1976"   London:
National Institute of Economic and Social Research, 1977.   NIESR
Discussion Paper No. 6.
MACRO MODEL - UK , NIESR * EVALUATION - MACRO MODELS

YB0247 OSBORN D.R.
"National Institute gross output forecasts: a comparision with US
performance"   London: National Institute for Economic and Social Research,
1977.   NIESR Discussion Paper No. 1.
MACRO MODEL - UK , NIESR * EVALUATION - MACRO MODELS

YB0248 OSBORN D.R., TEAL F.
"An analysis of National Institute forecasting erro in 1975"   London:
National Institure for Economic and Social Research, 1977,   NIESR
Discussion Paper No. 2.
MACRO MODEL - UK , NIESR * EVALUATION - MACRO MODELS

YB0249 OSTROM C.W.
"Time series analysis: regression techniques"   Beverley Hills, California:
Sage, 1978.   Quantitative Applications in the Social Sciences, Vol. 9.
REGRESSION - REVIEW * ERROR SPECIFICATION - AUTOCORRELATED

YB0250   OTNES R.K., ENOCHSON L.
"Digital time series analysis"   New York: Wiley Interscience, 1972.
TIME SERIES - TEXT * SPECTRAL ANALYSIS - TEXT * TIME SERIES - NONSTATIONARY
* ADVANCED

YB0251   PACKER A.H.
"Models of economic systems: a theory for their development and use"
Cambridge, Mass: MIT Press, 1972.
MACRO MODELS - METHODOLOGY * MACRO MODEL - US

YB0252   PALDA K.S.
"The measurement of cumulative advertising effects"   Englewood Cliffs, New
Jersey: Prentice Hall, 1964.   Ford Foundation Doctoral Dissertation Series
ADVERTISING - EFFECT OF * DISTRIBUTED LAG - APPL , ADVERTISING * APPL - FIRM
: CONSUMER NON DURABLES , HEALTH AIDS * COMPARATIVE METHODS - REGRESSION ,
MODEL SPECIFICATION

YB0253   PARSONS L.J., SCHULTZ R.L.
"Marketing models and econometric research"   Amsterdam: North Holland; New
York, American Elsevier, 1976.
USE - MARKETING POLICY * DISTRIBUTED LAG - APPL , ADVERTISING * ADVERTISING
- EFFECT OF , REVIEW * REGRESSION - SHIFTING COEFFICIENTS * LIFE CYCLE -
PRODUCT * MARKET SHARE - REVIEW * ECONOMETRICS - REVIEW * USER REQUIREMENTS

YB0254   PAVLOPOULOS P.
"A statistical model for the Greek economy: 1949-1959"   Amsterdam: North
Holland, 1966
MACRO MODEL - GREECE * EX ANTE * COMPARATIVE METHODS - ESTIMATION : OLS ,
2SLS * COMPARATIVE METHODS - AUTOREGRESSIVE , CAUSAL(SIMULTANEOUS SYSTEM) *
COMPARATIVE METHODS - MACRO MODELS

YB0255   PEARCE C.
"Prediction techniques for marketing planners"   London: Associated
Business Programmes, 1971; New York: Wiley, 1973.
FORECASTING - TEXT * USE - MARKETING POLICY * MIS * USE - CAPITAL INVESTMENT
* USE - ACQUISITION * BASIC

YB0256   PEARCE I.F., ET AL.
"A model of output, employment, wages and prices in the UK"   Cambridge:
Cambridge U.P., 1976.
MACRO MODEL - UK , SOUTHAMPTON * APPL - SECTOR : INTERNATIONAL TRADE ,
IMPORTS * APPL - SECTOR : EMPLOYMENT * INFLATION - DETERMINANTS

YB0257   PINDYCK R.S.
"Optimal planning for economic stabilisation: the application of control
theory to stabilisation policy"   Amsterdam: North Holland, 1973.
Contributions to Economic Analysis, No. 81.
MACRO MODEL - US * CONTROL THEORY - DETERMINISTIC , METHODOLOGY * POLICY
EVALUATION - MACRO : STABILISATION * SIMULTANEOUS SYSTEM - CONTROL

YB0258   PINDYCK R.S., RUBINFELD D.L.
"Econometric models and economic forecasts"   New York: McGraw Hill 1976.
ECONOMETRICS - TEXT * TIME SERIES - ARIMA : REVIEW * MACRO MODELS - TEXT *
APPL - SECTOR : UTILITIES , TELEPHONE * APPL - MACRO : INVENTORIES *
SIMULATION - APPL : SECTOR , CONSUMER NON DURABLES * SIMULATION - APPL :
FINANCIAL MODELLING * SIMULTANEOUS SYSTEM - DYNAMIC PROPERTIES * FORECASTING
- MULTISTAGE * FORECASTING - TEXT * MULTIPLIERS - METHODOLOGY

YB0259   POIRIER D.J.
"The econometrics of structural change"   Amsterdam: North Holland, 1976.
SPLINE FUNCTIONS * REGRESSION - PIECEWISE * PRODUCTION FUNCTIONS -
METHODOLOGY * DISTRIBUTED LAG - ALMON * STABILITY OF COEFFICIENTS -
REGRESSION

YB0260   POPKIN J. (ED.)
"Analysis of inflation: 1965-1974"   Cambridge, Mass: Ballinger, for the
National Bureau of Economic Research, 1977.   Proceedings of the Conference
on Price Behaviour, held in Bethesda, Maryland, 1974.
INFLATION - DETERMINANTS * INFLATION - GOVERNMENT CONTROLS * PRICE -
CONTROLS * MACRO MODEL - CANADA , CANDIDE * APPL - MACRO : INTERNATIONAL
LINKAGE * POLLUTION - EFFECT OF

YB0261   POWELL A.A.
"Empirical analysis of demand systems"   Lexington, Mass: Lexington Books,
D.C. Heath, 1974.
BIBLIOGRAPHY - DEMAND EQUATIONS * DEMAND EQUATIONS - SYSTEMS OF : REVIEW *
CONSUMER BEHAVIOUR - ECONOMIC MODELS , REVIEW * ADVANCED

YB0262   POWELL A.A., WILLIAMS R.A. (EDS.)
"Econometric studies of macro and monetary relations"   Amsterdam: North
Holland, 1973.
APPL - SECTOR : FINANCE * EVALUATION - MACRO MODELS * MACRO MODEL - OBE *
DATA - SAMPLE SIZE * MACRO MODEL - CANADA , RDX2 * MACRO MODEL - AUSTRALIA *
APPL - MACRO , NEW ZEALAND * MACRO MODEL - FRB , MIT , PENN * MACRO MODEL -
GOVERNMENT , AUSTRALIA * SIMULATION - METHODOLOGY * MONTE CARLO *
SIMULTANEOUS SYSTEM - NON LINEAR * APPL - MACRO : MONEY * APPL - MACRO , UK
* STOCK PRICES - EFFECT OF * APPL - SECTOR : FINANCE , COST OF CAPITAL

YB0263   PRESTON R.S.
"The Wharton annual and industry forecasting model"   Philadelphia: Wharton
School of Finance and Commerce, University of Pennsylvania, 1972.   Studies
in Quantitative Economics, No. 7.
MACRO MODEL - WHARTON * LONG TERM FORECASTING * MULTIPLIERS - MACRO *
COMPARATIVE METHODS - ESTIMATION : SIMULTANEOUS SYSTEM

YB0264 PYATT F.G.
        "Priority patterns and the demand for household durable goods"   Cambridge:
        Cambridge U.P., 1964.
        APPL - SECTOR : CONSUMER DURABLES * CONSUMER BEHAVIOUR - STOCHASTIC MODELS

YB0265 QUANDT R.E. (ED.)
        "The demand for travel: theory and measurement"   Lexington, Mass: D.C.
        Heath, 1970.
        APPL - SECTOR : TRANSPORT * CONSUMER BEHAVIOUR - ECONOMIC MODELS , THEORY *
        COMPARATIVE METHODS - REGRESSION , MODEL SPECIFICATION * REGRESSION - ERROR
        COMPONENTS * ERROR SPECIFICATION - CORRELATED * COMPARATIVE METHODS -
        ESTIMATION : OLS , GLS * COMPARATIVE METHODS - REGRESSION , ERROR COMPONENTS
        * TIME - VALUE OF

YB0266 RAMSEY J.B.
        "Economic forecasting: models or markets? an introduction to the role of
        econometrics in economic policy with a sceptical review of forecasting in
        Britain by Ralph Harris"   London: Institute of Economic Affairs, 1977.
        Hobart Paper No. 74.
        EVALUATION - MACRO MODELS * EVALUATION - MACRO FORECASTS * MACRO MODELS -
        METHODOLOGY * THEORY - MODELLING * BASIC

YB0267 RAO M., MILLER R.L.
        "Applied econometrics"   Belmont, California: Wadsworth, 1971.
        REGRESSION - TEXT * REGRESSION - SUMMARY STATISTICS * ECONOMETRICS - TEXT *
        RESIDUALS - ANALYSIS OF , SPECIFICATION ERROR

YB0268 RAO V.R., COX J.E.
        "Sales forecasting methods: a survey of recent developments"   Cambridge,
        Mass: Marketing Science Institute, 1978.
        FORECASTING - USAGE * BIBLIOGRAPHY - FORECASTING * FORECASTING - PRACTICE *
        FORECASTING - REVIEW * BASIC

YB0269 RENTON G.A. (ED.)
        "Modelling the economy"   London: Heinemann, for the SSRC; New York: Crane,
        Russak, 1975.
        MACRO MODEL - UK , LBS * MACRO MODEL - GOVERNMENT , UK * MACRO MODEL - UK ,
        NIESR * MACRO MODEL - UK , SOUTHAMPTON * MACRO MODEL - FRB , MIT , PEN *
        POLICY EVALUATION - MACRO * BUSINESS INDICATORS - APPL * INDEX NUMBERS -
        MACRO : EMPLOYMENT VACANCIES * APPL - SECTOR : CONSUMER DURABLES * APPL -
        MACRO : CONSUMER DEMAND , FINANCIAL ASSETS * TAX - EFFECT OF * (See also
        reference listed below)

YB0270 RENTON G.A. (ED.)
        "Modelling the economy"
        CONTROL THEORY - STOCHASTIC , APPL * APPL - MACRO : DIVIDENDS *
        SPECIFICATION ERROR - EFFECT OF , SIMULTANEOUS SYSTEM BIAS * CONTROL THEORY
        - STOCHASTIC , METHODOLOGY * APPL - SECTOR : FINANCE , BANKS * APPL - MACRO
        : INTERNATIONAL LINKAGE * COMPARATIVE METHODS - ESTIMATION : SIMULTANEOUS
        SYSTEM * AUTOCORRELATION - EFFECT OF * APPL - MACRO : INTERNATIONAL TRADE ,
        IMPORTS * COMPARATIVE METHODS - ARIMA , EXPONENTIAL SMOOTHING * EX ANTE *
        (See also reference listed above)

YB0271 RICHARDSON H.W.
        "Input output and regional economics"   London: Weidenfeld & Nicolson; New
        York: Wiley, 1972.
        INPUT OUTPUT - REGIONAL * BIBLIOGRAPHY - REGIONAL MODELS * REGIONAL MODELS

YB0272 RICHARDSON H.W.
        "Regional growth theory"   London: Macmillan, 1973.
        REGIONAL MODELS - GROWTH

YB0273 RICKS R.B. (ED.)
        "National housing models: applications of econometric techniques to problems
        of housing research"   Lexington, Mass: Lexington Books, D.C.Heath, 1973.
        Proceedings of a Conference sponsored by the Federal Home Loan Bank System.
        MACRO MODELS - MICRO MODELS * APPL - SECTOR : CONTRUCTION , RESIDENTIAL *
        PRICE - SECTOR : CONSTRUCTION , RESIDENTIAL * MACRO MODEL - FRB , MIT , PENN
        * EVALUATION - CONSTRUCTION MODELS * PRICE - EFFECT OF * INTEREST RATE -
        EFFECT OF * MACRO MODEL - FAIR

YB0274 ROBINSON E.A.
        "Multichannel time series analysis with digital computer programs"   San
        Fransisco: Holden Day, 1967.
        APPL - SECTOR : COMMODITIES , GRAIN * TIME SERIES - FILTER * TIME SERIES -
        MULTIVARIATE * SPECTRAL ANALYSIS - MULTIVARIATE * COMPUTERISATION - TIME
        SERIES , PROGRAMS * ADVANCED

YB0275 ROTHENBERG T.J.
        "Efficient estimation with a priori information"   New Haven: Yale U.P.,
        1973.   Cowles Foundation, Monograph No. 23.
        REGRESSION - PRIOR INFORMATION * BAYESIAN - ESTIMATION : SIMULTANEOUS SYSTEM
        * BAYESIAN - ESTIMATION : REGRESSION * BAYESIAN - PRIOR INFORMATION *
        SIMULTANEOUS SYSTEM - PRIOR INFORMATION

YB0276 ROWLEY J.C.R., TRIVEDI P.K.
        "Econometrics of investment"   London: Wiley, 1975.
        APPL - SECTOR : INVENTORIES * APPL - SECTOR : INVESTMENT * APPL - MACRO :
        INVENTORIES * EXPECTATIONS - ESTIMATING * APPL - MACRO : INVESTMENT * APPL -
        MACRO , UK

YB0277   SAVAGE D.
         "A comparision of accelerator models of manufacturing investment"   London:
         National Institute for Economic and Social Research, 1977,   NIESR
         Discussion Paper No. 9,
         EVALUATION - INVESTMENT MODELS * APPL - SECTOR : INVESTMENT

YB0278   SCHILDERINCK J.H.F.
         "Regression and factor analysis applied in econometrics"   Leiden,
         Netherlands: Nijhuff, 1977,   Tilburg Studies on Econometrics, Vol 1,
         FACTOR ANALYSIS - REVIEW * EVALUATION - CONSUMPTION MODELS * MACRO MODEL -
         NETHERLANDS * MULTICOLLINEARITY - REMOVAL OF * COMPARATIVE METHODS -
         ESTIMATION : OLS , 2SLS * COMPARATIVE METHODS - ESTIMATION : OLS , 3SLS *
         COMPARATIVE METHODS - ESTIMATION : SIMULTANEOUS SYSTEM , 2SLS , 3SLS *
         MULTICOLLINEARITY - TEST

YB0279   SCHMALENSEE R.
         "The economics of advertising"   Amsterdam: North Holland, 1972,
         APPL - SECTOR : CONSUMER NON DURABLES , CIGARETTES * APPL - MACRO :
         ADVERTISING * ADVERTISING - EFFECT OF , REVIEW * ADVERTISING - DETERMINANTS
         * MARKET SHARE - SECTOR : CONSUMER NON DURABLES * INDEX NUMBERS - MACRO :
         ADVERTISING

YB0280   SCHREIBER A.N. (ED,)
         "Corporate simulation models"   Seattle, Washington: University of
         Washington Graduate School of Business Admin,, 1970,
         APPL - SECTOR : AGRICULTURE * APPL - FIRM : FINANCE , INSURANCE COMPANIES *
         USER - FIRM * SIMULATION - REVIEW * USE - CAPACITY EXPANSION * SIMULATION -
         APPL : FIRM * SIMULATION - METHODOLOGY * APPL - FIRM : FINANCE , BANKS * USE
         - CORPORATE PLANNING * INDUSTRIAL DYNAMICS - APPL , FIRM * SIMULATION - APPL
         : ADVERTISING * COMPARATIVE METHODS - REGRESSION , SIMULTANEOUS SYSTEM

YB0281   SHEPHERD J.R,, EVANS H.P., RILEY C.J,
         "The Treasury short term forecasting model and simulations with the Treasury
         model"   London: HMSO, 1974,   GES Occasional Papers, No, 8,
         MACRO MODEL - GOVERNMENT , UK * SIMULATION - APPL : POLICY EVALUATION

YB0282   SMITH A.R. (ED,)
         "Models of manpower systems"   London: English U,P,, 1971,   Proceedings
         of conference, Oporto 1969, sponsored by NATO,
         MANPOWER PLANNING - FIRM * MANPOWER PLANNING - TEXT * MANPOWER PLANNING -
         MACRO , DEMAND * APPL - SECTOR : EDUCATION , UNIVERSITIES * MANPOWER
         PLANNING - SECTOR : GOVERNMENT , MILITARY * LP * MANPOWER PLANNING -
         PROMOTION

YB0283   SMITH B.T.
         "Focus forecasting: computer techniques for inventory control"   Boston:
         CBI Publishing, 1978,
         USE - INVENTORY CONTROL * BASIC

YB0284   SMITH L.B.
         "The postwar Canadian housing and residential mortgage markets, and the role
         of government"   Toronto: Univeristy of Toronto Press, 1974,
         APPL - SECTOR : CONSTRUCTION , RESIDENTIAL * APPL - SECTOR : FINANCE ,
         MORTGAGES * POLICY EVALUATION - SECTOR : CONSTRUCTION

YB0285   SMITH R.P.
         "Consumer demand for cars in the USA"   Cambridge: Cambridge U.P., 1975,
         APPL - SECTOR : CONSUMER DURABLES , CARS * EVALUATION - EXPECTATIONS , DATA

YB0286   SMITH V.K.
         "Monte Carlo methods: their role in econometrics"   Lexington, Mass:
         Lexington Books, D.C. Heath, 1973,
         MACRO MODEL - KLEIN * SIMULATION - METHODOLOGY , MONTE CARLO * COMPARATIVE
         METHODS - ESTIMATION : REGRESSION , REVIEW * COMPARATIVE METHODS -
         ESTIMATION : REGRESSION , LIMITED DEPENDENT * COMPARATIVE METHODS -
         ESTIMATION : SIMULTANEOUS SYSTEM , REVIEW * MACRO MODEL - KLEIN GOLDBERGER *
         COMPARATIVE METHODS - ESTIMATION : OLS , 2SLS

YB0287   SOLOW R.M.
         "Price expectations and the behaviour of the price level"   Manchester:
         Manchester U,P,, 1970,
         THEORY - EXPECTATIONS * APPL - MACRO , UK * CAPACITY - EFFECT OF * INFLATION
         - EXPECTATIONS * INFLATION - GOVERNMENT CONTROLS

YB0288   SOMERMEYER W,H,, BANNINK R.
         "A consumption-savings model and its application"   Amsterdam: North
         Holland; New York: American Elsevier, 1973,   Contributions to Economic
         Analysis, No. 79,
         APPL - MACRO : SAVINGS * CONSUMER BEHAVIOUR - ECONOMIC MODELS * APPL - MACRO
         , NETHERLANDS * ERROR SPECIFICATION - AUTOCORRELATED * COMPARATIVE METHODS -
         REGRESSION , ERROR SPECIFICATION * COMPARATIVE METHODS - ESTIMATION :
         REGRESSION , ERROR SPECIFICATION * INCOME - EFFECT OF * WEALTH - EFFECT OF

YB0289   STEELE J.L.
         "The use of econometric models by Federal regulatory agencies"   Lexington,
         Mass: D.C. Heath, 1971,
         USER - SECTOR : GOVERNMENT * USE - FINANCIAL , REGULATION * APPL - SECTOR :
         UTILITIES , GAS * SUPPLY - SECTOR : PRODUCTION * PRICE - EFFECT OF

YB0290 STEKLER H.O.
        "Economic forecasting"   New york: Praeger; London: Longman, 1970.
        MACRO MODELS - TEXT * EVALUATION - GOVERNMENT FORECASTS * EVALUATION = MACRO
        MODELS * EVALUATION - JUDGEMENTAL FORECASTS * APPL - MACRO : INVENTORIES *
        DATA REVISIONS - EFFECT OF * MACRO MODEL = MIT , FRB * COMPARATIVE METHODS =
        CAUSAL(SIMULTANEOUS SYSTEM) , JUDGEMENTAL * COMPARATIVE METHODS = MACRO
        MODELS

YB0291 STERN R.M., FRANCIS J., SCHUMACHER B.
        "Price elasticities in international trade: an annotated bibliography"
        London: Macmillan, for the Trade Policy Research Centre, 1976.
        BIBLIOGRAPHY - INTERNATIONAL TRADE * PRICE - EFFECT OF * APPL = MACRO :
        INTERNATIONAL TRADE * APPL - SECTOR : INTERNATIONAL TRADE

YB0292 STONE R.
        "Mathematical models of the economy and other essays"   London: Chapman &
        Hall, 1970.
        APPL - MACRO : CONSUMPTION * MACRO MODEL - UK , CAMBRIDGE GROWTH * MACRO
        MODEL - TEXT * POLICY EVALUATION - MACRO * INPUT OUTPUT = MACRO , UK * APPL
        - MACRO : CONSUMER DEMAND * WEALTH - EFFECT OF

YB0293 STRASZHEIM M.R.
        "An econometric analysis of the urban housing market"   New York: National
        Bureau of Economic Research, distributed by Columbia U.P., 1975.
        APPL - SECTOR : CONSTRUCTION , RESIDENTIAL * SIMULATION = APPL : REGIONAL
        MODELS * REGIONAL MODELS - CITY * REGIONAL MODELS = SECTOR : CONSTRUCTION ,
        RESIDENTIAL * POLICY EVALUATION - SECTOR : CONSTRUCTION , RESIDENTIAL

YB0294 STRUMPEL B., MORGAN J.N., ZAHN E. (EDS.)
        "Human behaviour in economic affairs; essays in honour of George Katona"
        Amsterdam: Elsevier; San Francisco: Jossey-Bass, 1972.
        APPL - MACRO : CONSUMER DEMAND , FINANCIAL ASSETS * CONSUMER BEHAVIOUR -
        ECONOMIC MODELS * EVALUATION - ATTITUDINAL DATA * INDEX NUMBERS = MACRO :
        CONSUMER SENTIMENT * SURVEYS - CONSUMER , DETERMINANTS * EX ANTE * APPL =
        SECTOR : CONSUMER DURABLES , CARS * MACRO MODEL - WHARTON * EVALUATION =
        EXPECTATIONS , DATA

YB0295 SUITS D.B.
        "An econometric model of the Greek economy"   Athens: Center of Economic
        Research, 1964.   Research Monograph 7.
        MACRO MODEL - GREECE

YB0296 SULLIVAN W.G., CLAYCOMBE W.W.
        "Fundamentals of forecasting"   Virginia: Reston, 1977.
        FORECASTING - TEXT * TECHNOLOGICAL FORECASTING * BASIC

YB0297 SURREY M.J.C.
        "The analysis and forecasting of the British economy"   London: Cambridge
        U.P., 1971.   NIESR Occasional Paper No. 25.
        MACRO MODEL - UK , NIESR

YB0298 SWAN N.M., WILTON D.A. (EDS.)
        "Inflation and the Canadian Experience"   Kingston, Canada: Queen's U.P.,
        1971.
        APPL - MACRO , CANADA * INFLATION - DETERMINANTS

YB0299 TEEKENS R.
        "Prediction methods in multiplicative models"   Rotterdam: Rotterdam U.P.,
        1972.
        REGRESSION - TRANSFORMATIONS , LOGARITHMIC * ERROR DISTRIBUTION = GAMMA *
        ESTIMATION - LOGARITHMIC MODEL

YB0300 TEIGEN L.D.
        "Costs, losses and forecasting errors: an evaluation of models for beef
        prices"   Michigan: Michigan State, 1973.   Ph.D. thesis
        APPL - SECTOR : AGRICULTURE , LIVESTOCK , BEEF * EVALUATION - LOSS FUNCTIONS
        * FORECASTING - VALUE OF

YB0301 THEIL H.
        "Principles of econometrics"   New York: Wiley, 1971.
        ECONOMETRICS - TEXT * MACRO MODEL - KLEIN GOLDBERGER

YB0302 THEIL H. (ED.)
        "Optimal decision rules for government and industry"   Amsterdam: North
        Holland, 1964.
        CONTROL THEORY - INTRODUCTION * LOSS FUNCTIONS - FIRM , PRODUCTION CONTROL *
        APPL - MACRO , NETHERLANDS * MACRO MODEL - KLEIN * MACRO MODEL = NETHERLANDS
        * LOSS FUNCTIONS - MACRO * DECISION RULES - SECTOR

YB0303 THEIL H., ET AL.
        "Applied economic forecasting"   Amsterdam: North Holland, 1966.
        APPL - MACRO , NETHERLANDS * COMPARATIVE METHODS - AUTOREGRESSIVE , CAUSAL *
        DATA ERRORS - EFFECT OF * EVALUATION - EXPECTATIONS , DATA * INPUT OUTPUT =
        MACRO , NETHERLANDS * APPL - SECTOR : PRODUCTION , MACHINE TOOLS * APPL =
        SECTOR : INVESTMENT * RANDOM WALK - TEST * EVALUATION - THEORY OF *
        FORECASTING - TEXT * LOSS FUNCTIONS - INFORMATION CRITERION * EVALUATION =
        MACRO MODELS , REVIEW * PROBABILITY MODELS - ENTROPY

YB0304 THONSTAD T.
        "Education and manpower, theoretical models and empirical applications"
        Edinburgh: Oliver & Boyd, 1969.
        MANPOWER PLANNING - QUALIFIED MANPOWER * MANPOWER PLANNING - SECTOR :
        EDUCATION * APPL - SECTOR : GOVERNMENT , EDUCATION * MARKOV MODELS = APPL :
        MANPOWER

YB0305   TURNER J.
"Forecasting practices in British Industry"   London: Surrey U.P., with
Intertext, 1974.
FORECASTING - PRACTICE * FORECASTING - USAGE * BASIC

YB0306   US NATIONAL SCIENCE FOUNDATION, AND ENERGY RESEARCH UNIT, QUEEN MARY COLLEGE,
LONDON
"Energy modelling"   Guildford, Surrey: IPC Business Press, 1974.
LP * APPL - MACRO : ENERGY * APPL - SECTOR : PRODUCTION , PETROLEUM * APPL -
SECTOR : COMMODITIES , OIL * APPL - SECTOR : UTILITIES , GAS * POLICY
EVALUATION - MACRO : ENERGY

YB0307   VAN DUIJN J.J.
"An interregional model of economic fluctuation"   Farnborough, Hants:
Saxon House, 1972.
BUSINESS CYCLE - REGIONAL * PUBLIC EXPENDITURE - EFFECT OF * POPULATION -
MIGRATION * REGIONAL MODELS - INTERREGIONAL * REGIONAL MODELS - AGGREGATION
* SIMULATION - APPL : REGIONAL MODELS

YB0308   VERNARDAKIS N.
"An econometric model for developing countries: a case study of Greece"
Farnborough, Hants: Saxon House, 1978.
MACRO MODEL - GREECE * SUPPLY - SECTOR * PUBLIC EXPENDITURE - EFFECT OF *
APPL - MACRO : INVESTMENT , INTERNATIONAL

YB0309   VISUWAKARMA K.P.
"Macroeconomic regulation"   Rotterdam: Rotterdam U.P., 1974.
ESTIMATION - KALMAN FILTER * CONTROL THEORY - STOCHASTIC , REVIEW * DATA
ERRORS - ESTIMATION OF * CONTROL THEORY - STOCHASTIC , METHODOLOGY * MACRO
MODELS - METHODOLOGY * MACRO MODEL - NETHERLANDS

YB0310   WABE J.S. (ED.)
"Problems in manpower forecasting"   Farnborough, Hants: Saxon House;
Lexington, Mass: Lexington Books, 1974.
APPL - SECTOR : PRODUCTION , ENGINEERING * MANPOWER PLANNING - SECTOR :
PRODUCTION * EX ANTE * MANPOWER PLANNING - QUALIFIED MANPOWER * MANPOWER
PLANNING - TEXT

YB0311   WAELBROECK J.L. (ED.)
"The models of Project LINK"   Amsterdam: North Holland, 1976.
Contributions to Economic Analysis, No. 102.
APPL - MACRO : INTERNATIONAL LINKAGE * MACRO MODEL - BELGIUM * MACRO MODEL -
AUSTRIA * MACRO MODEL - UK , LBS * MACRO MODEL - SWEDEN * MACRO MODEL -
NETHERLANDS * MACRO MODEL - WHARTON * MACRO MODEL - JAPAN * MACRO MODEL -
ITALY * MACRO MODEL - CANADA , TRACE * MACRO MODEL - FRANCE * MACRO MODEL -
FINLAND

YB0312   WALLIS K.F.
"Topics in applied econometrics"   London: Gray-Mills, 1973.
ECONOMETRICS - REVIEW * APPL - MACRO : CONSUMPTION * PRODUCTION FUNCTIONS -
REVIEW * APPL - MACRO : INVESTMENT

YB0313   WATERMAN A.M.C.
"Economic fluctuations in Australia: 1948 to 1964"   Canberra: Australian
National U.P., 1972.
APPL - MACRO , AUSTRALIA * BUSINESS CYCLE - IDENTIFICATION

YB0314   WEBB A.E.
"Unemployment, vacancies and the rate of change of earnings: a regional
analysis"   Cambridge: Cambridge U.P., 1974.   In National Institute of
Economic and Social Research, Regional Papers 2.
APPL - MACRO , UK * REGIONAL MODELS - MANPOWER PLANNING , UNEMPLOYMENT *
REGIONAL MODELS - MANPOWER PLANNING , EARNINGS * APPL - MACRO : UNEMPLOYMENT

YB0315   WEEDEN R.
"Interregional migration models and their application to Great Britain"
Cambridge: Cambridge UP., 1973.   In National Institute of Economics and
Social Research, Regional Papers 2.
REGIONAL MODELS - MIGRATION

YB0316   WHEELWRIGHT S.C., MAKIDAKIS S.
"Forecasting methods for managers"   2nd ed.   New York: Wiley, 1977.
FORECASTING - TEXT * USE - ORGANISATIONAL DESIGN * FORECASTING - PRACTICE *
JUDGEMENTAL FORECASTS - APPL * BASIC

YB0317   WHITEHEAD C.M.E.
"The UK housing market"   Farnborough, Hants: Saxon House; Lexington, Mass:
Lexington Books, 1974.
APPL - SECTOR : CONSTRUCTION , RESIDENTIAL * SUPPLY - SECTOR : CONSTRUCTION
, RESIDENTIAL

YB0318   WHITTINGTON G.
"The prediction of profitabilty"   Cambridge: Cambridge U.P., 1971.
APPL - SECTOR : FINANCE PROFITS * CONCENTRATION - EFFECT OF * APPL - SECTOR
: INVENTORIES * APPL - SECTOR : FINANCE , FINANCIAL STRUCTURE , LIQUID
ASSETS

YB0319   WHITTLE P.
"Prediction and regulation by linear least square methods"   London:
English U.P., 1963.
CONTROL THEORY - INTRODUCTION * TIME SERIES - TEXT * TIME SERIES -
CONTINUOUS * ADVANCED

YB0320 WIGLEY K., STONE R.
"The demand for fuel: 1948-1975"   London: Chapman & Hall, 1968.
INPUT OUTPUT - MACRO : ENERGY * APPL - MACRO : ENERGY * STABILILITY
OFCOEFFICIENTS - INPUT OUTPUT

YB0321 WILSON N.A.B. (ED.)
"Manpower research"   London: English U.P., 1969.
MANPOWER PLANNING - TEXT * PROBABILITY MODELS - RENEWAL THEORETIC * MANPOWER
PLANNING - SECTOR : GOVERNMENT , MILITARY * MANPOWER PLANNING - SECTOR :
PRODUCTION

YB0322 WITT S.F.
"Econometric forecasting for travel and tourism"   Bradford, England: MCB
Publications, 1978.   In Ashton D. (ed.), Management Bibliographies &
Reviews, Vol. 4.
TIME - VALUE OF * APPL - SECTOR : TRANSPORT * APPL - SECTOR : SERVICES ,
TOURISM * BIBLIOGRAPHY - SECTOR : TRANSPORT * BIBLIOGRAPHY - SECTOR :
SERVICES

YB0323 WOLD H., (ED.)
"Econometric model building: essays on the causal chain approach"
Amsterdam: North Holland, 1964.
APPL - SECTOR : AGRICULTURE * EVALUATION - ESTIMATION : OLS * REGRESSION -
ESTIMATION , ERROR SPECIFICATION * RECURSIVE SYSTEMS * EVALUATION - THEORY
OF * APPL - SECTOR : PRODUCTIVITY * STABILITY OF COEFFICIENTS - REGRESSION ,
TEST * TIME SERIES - FILTER * CAUSALITY - REVIEW

YB0324 WOOD D., FILDES R.
"Forecasting for business: methods and applications"   London: Longman,
1976.
FORECASTING - PRACTICE * REGRESSION - INTRODUCTION * TREND CURVES -
INTRODUCTION * MACRO MODELS - REVIEW * FORECASTING - VALUE OF * EXPONENTIAL
SMOOTHING - INTRODUCTION * TECHNOLOGICAL FORECASTING * DELPHI * FORECASTING
- TEXT * BASIC

YB0325 WOODWARD V.H.
"Regional social accounts for the United Kingdom"   Cambridge: Cambridge
U.P., 1970.   In National Institute of Economic and Social Research,
Regional Papers 1.
REGIONAL MODELS - SOCIAL ACCOUNTS * REGIONAL MODELS - DATA * DATA SOURCES ,
UK

YB0326 WORSWICK G.D.N., BLACKABY F.T. (EDS.)
"The medium term: models of the British economy'   London: Heinemann for
the SSRC and NIESR, 1974.
MACRO MODEL - UK , CAMBRIDGE * MACRO MODEL - GOVERNMENT , UK * INPUT OUTPUT
- MACRO : ENERGY * LONG TERM FORECASTING * INPUT OUTPUT - SECTOR :
PRODUCTION * APPL - SECTOR : PRODUCTION , TEXTILES

YB0327 ZAREMBKA P. (ED.)
"Frontiers in econometrics"   New York: Academic Press, 1974.
DEMAND EQUATIONS - SYSTEMS OF * SIMULTANEOUS SYSTEM - ESTIMATION *
ESTIMATION - INSTRUMENTAL VARIABLE * BAYESIAN - MODEL SELECTION *
SPECIFICATION ERROR - TESTS , REVIEW * PRIOR INFORMATION * REGRESSION -
TRANSFORMATIONS * REGRESSION - RANDOM COEFFICIENTS * APPL - MACRO : MONEY ,
DEMAND * REGRESSION - LIMITED DEPENDENT , LOGIT * ESTIMATION - MSAE * MODEL
SELECTION * REGRESSION - ERRORS IN VARIABLES , UNOBSERVABLES * (See also
reference listed below)

YB0328 ZAREMBKA P. (ED.)
"Frontiers in econometrics"
FACTOR ANALYSIS - APPL * SIMULTANEOUS SYSTEM - ERRORS IN VARIABLES ,
UNOBSERVABLES * APPL - SECTOR : TRANSPORT * USE - TRANSPORT PLANNING * APPL
- SECTOR : RETAILING * REGIONAL MODELS - SECTOR : RETAILING * (See also
reference listed above)

YB0329 ZARKOVICH S.S.
"Sampling methods and censuses: vol. II the quality of statistical data"
Rome: Food and Agriculture Organisation, 1967.
DATA ERRORS - REVIEW * DATA ERRORS - ESTIMATION OF

YB0330 ZARNOWITZ V.
"An appraisal of short term economic forecasts"   New York: National Bureau
of Economic Research, distributed by Columbia U.P., 1967.   Occasional
Papers No. 104.
EVALUATION - MACRO FORECASTS * COMPARATIVE METHODS - AUTOREGRESSIVE ,
JUDGEMENTAL

YB0331 ZARNOWITZ V.
"Orders, production and investment - a cyclical and structural analysis"
New York: National Bureau of Economic Research, distributed by Columbia
U.P., 1973.
BUSINESS CYCLE - IDENTIFICATION * APPL - SECTOR * DISTRIBUTED LAG - APPL ,
ORDERS * DISTRIBUTED LAG - VARIABLE LAG * COMPARATIVE METHODS - DISTRIBUTED
LAG * ERROR SPECIFICATION - AUTOCORRELATED * COMPARATIVE METHODS -
DISTRIBUTED LAG , ERROR SPECIFICATION * APPL - SECTOR : INVENTORIES * APPL -
SECTOR : INVESTMENT

YB0332   ZARNOWITZ V. (ED.)
          "Economic research: retrospect and prospect: vol.1: the business cycle
          today"   New York: National Bureau of Economic Research, distributed by
          Columbia U.P., 1972.
          BUSINESS CYCLE - IDENTIFICATION * EVALUATION - MACRO FORECASTS * POLICY
          EVALUATION - MACRO : FISCAL , MONETARY * MACRO MODEL - US
YB0333   ZELLNER A.
          "An introduction to Bayesian estimation in econometrics"   New York: Wiley,
          1971.
          BAYESIAN - ESTIMATION : TEXT * SIMULTANEOUS SYSTEM - ESTIMATION * BAYESIAN -